The Routledge Companion to Accounting History

The Routledge Companion to Accounting History reveals that the seemingly innocuous practice of accounting has pervaded human existence in fascinating ways at numerous times and places; from ancient civilisations to the modern day, and from the personal to the political.

Placing the history of accounting in context with other fields of study, the collection gives invaluable insights to subjects such as the rise of capitalism, the control of labour, gender and family relationships, racial exploitation, the functioning of the state and the pursuit of military conflict. An engaging as well as comprehensive overview which also examines geographical differences, the *Companion* is split into key sections which explore:

- changing technologies used to represent financial and other data
- historical development of accounting theory and practice
- accounting institutions and those who perform accounting
- accountancy and the economy
- accounting, society and culture
- the role of accounting in the government, protection and financing of states

Including chapters on the important role played by accountancy in religious organisations, a review of how accounting is portrayed in fine art and popular culture, and analysis of sharp practice and corporate scandals, *The Routledge Companion to Accounting History* has a breadth of coverage that is unmatched in this growing area of study. Bringing together the leading writers in the field, this is an essential reference work for any student of accounting, business and management, and history.

John Richard Edwards is a Professor of Accounting at Cardiff Business School, UK. He is a regular contributor to international refereed journals and the author of *A History of Financial Accounting* (Routledge, 1989).

Stephen P. Walker is a Professor of Accounting at Cardiff Business School, UK. He is a former editor of *Accounting Historians Journal* and President of the Academy of Accounting Historians. His publications are concerned with accounting histories of professionalisation, gender, social control and identity.

The Routledge Companion to Accounting History

Edited by
John Richard Edwards and
Stephen P. Walker

Routledge
Taylor & Francis Group

LONDON AND NEW YORK

First published 2009
by Routledge
2 Park Square, Milton Park, Abingdon, Oxon OX14 4RN

Simultaneously published in the USA and Canada
by Routledge
270 Madison Avenue, New York NY 10016

Routledge is an imprint of the Taylor and Francis Group, an informa business

Typeset in Bembo by Swales & Willis Ltd, Exeter, Devon
Printed and bound in Great Britain by
CPI Antony Rowe, Chippenham, Wiltshire

British Library Cataloguing in Publication Data
A catalogue record for this book is available from the British Library

Library of Congress Cataloging in Publication Data
A catalog record has been requested for this book

ISBN10: 0–415–41094–0 (hbk)

ISBN13: 978–0–415–41094–6 (hbk)

Contents

List of illustrations

Figures

Tables

Notes on contributors

Fiona Anderson-Gough is a Reader in Accounting at the University of Warwick. She has conducted empirical research on professional identity formation at the level of the individual and on accounting education within the UK context, and has written particularly on the power effects of socialisation.

Marcia Annisette is an Associate Professor of Accounting at the Schulich School of Business, York University, Canada. She has published research on the history of professional accountancy in Trinidad and Tobago. Her research interests include accounting and its interface with colonialism, imperialism and globalisation. She is currently conducting research on financial practices of Caribbean slave populations.

Salvador Carmona is Professor of Accounting and Management Control at IE Business School, Madrid. His research interests include accounting history, accounting and religion, and the design and functioning of cost accounting practices in non-competitive environments. He is currently the editor of *European Accounting Review* and is a past President of the Academy of Accounting Historians.

Frank L. Clarke is an Emeritus Professor at the University of Newcastle, Honorary Professor of Accounting at the University of Sydney, former editor of *Abacus*, and the author of books and articles addressing issues relating to financial reporting. Included among recent books with Graeme Dean is *Indecent Disclosure: Gilding the Corporate Lily* (2007).

Philip Colquhoun is a Senior Lecturer in the School of Accounting and Commercial Law at Victoria University of Wellington, New Zealand. His research interests include the history of accounting in the public sector. His PhD thesis was an analysis of the accounting and auditing requirements of local government in New Zealand from 1876 to 1988.

David J. Cooper is the CGA Chair in Accounting at the University of Alberta and Director of the Business School's PhD program. He has written seven books and over 70 articles. He is joint editor of *Critical Perspectives on Accounting*. He has published on the history of the accounting profession and currently studies performance measurement systems and the global regulation of accountants.

Graeme W. Dean is Professor of Accounting at the University of Sydney and since 1994 has been the sole editor of *Abacus*. He has published several books on the role of accounting in corporate failures and financial dilemmas including (with Frank Clarke and Kyle Oliver) *Corporate Collapse* (2003). He has also authored over 50 refereed articles.

Ignace de Beelde is Professor of Auditing at Ghent University. He has written on accounting and auditing, including the history of accounting and the development of the accounting profession in Belgium. His history publications include articles in *Accounting, Organizations and Society*; *Accounting, Business & Financial History*; *Accounting History* and *Accounting Historians Journal*.

Alisdair Dobie is a Lecturer in Accounting and Finance at the University of the West of Scotland. His specialism is medieval accounting, and his paper on financial management and control in monastic houses in later medieval England will be published in 2008. He is a member of the Newcastle University research group on Culture, Imperialism and Accounting Practices.

John Richard Edwards is a Professor at the Cardiff Business School. He has published articles on various aspects of accounting history in a range of leading international refereed journals. His books include *A History of Financial Accounting* (1989) and (jointly) *The Priesthood of Industry* (1998). He is joint editor of *Accounting, Business & Financial History*.

Mahmoud Ezzamel is Cardiff Professorial Fellow, Cardiff University. His research interests include accounting history, particularly in the ancient world, accounting and religion, the interface between accounting and social theory, accounting practices in the public sector, and corporate governance.

Richard Fleischman is Professor Emeritus from John Carroll University and Scholar in Residence at the University of South Florida. He has published extensively on British Industrial Revolution cost accounting, US standard costing, and slavery accounting. He has been honoured with the Hourglass Award from the Academy of Accounting Historians and named Ohio's Outstanding Accounting Educator.

Dale L. Flesher is the Arthur Andersen Alumni Professor of Accountancy and Associate Dean at the University of Mississippi. He is a past President of the Academy of Accounting Historians. He has authored 43 books (in 78 editions) and over 300 journal articles. He has specialised in railroad accounting, organisational histories, and biographies.

Warwick Funnell is Professor of Accounting at the University of Kent and the University of Wollongong. He is a member of the Cultures, Imperialism and Accounting Practices Group, Newcastle University. He has published widely on the history of public sector accounting. Recent books include *Accounting for War* (2006) and *In Government We Trust* (2008).

Sonja Gallhofer is Professor of Accounting and Management Control in the School of Accounting and Finance at the University of Dundee. She has published numerous critical analyses of accounting, focusing on feminist, historical, pedagogical and cultural subjects. She has worked previously at UMIST and the Universities of Essex, Waikato, Glasgow Caledonian and Aberdeen.

Susan Greer is a Lecturer in the Discipline of Accounting at the University of Sydney. In 2006, she was awarded the Emerald/EFMD Outstanding Doctoral Research Award for Inter-disciplinary Accounting Research for her history of accounting interventions in the government of the indigenous peoples of New South Wales.

Jim Haslam is Professor of Accountancy and Business Finance at the University of Dundee. He has published numerous articles which contribute to the critical, historical and social analysis of accounting. He was previously employed at Sheffield, Aston, Essex, Waikato and Heriot-Watt universities, the University College of North Wales and the London School of Economics.

Barbara E. Kemmerer retired in 2007 as an Associate Professor of Management at Eastern Illinois University. She has published on the gender of the accounting workforce, diversity in the workforce, job stress, and job complexity.

Rihab Khalifa is a Lecturer in the Accounting Group, Warwick Business School. Rihab holds a PhD in accounting from the University of Manchester. Her research interests and publications span the areas of audit firms, audit methodologies, gender issues in accounting, gender-responsive budgets, the sociology of professions, accounting and development, and corporate governance.

Eksa Kilfoyle is a chartered accountant and PhD student in accounting at the Schulich School of Business, York University, Canada. She has presented papers on the use of accounting in the development of postal systems. Her current research focuses on international management accounting standard setting and the interaction between national and international standard-setting organisations.

Linda M. Kirkham is Professor of Accounting at the Robert Gordon University, Aberdeen. She has written extensively on the accounting profession, gender and accounting history. Her publications include a number of key articles examining the interface of accounting history and gender processes.

Margaret Lamb is Director of the Individualized and Interdisciplinary Studies Program at the University of Connecticut. Previously she was a Reader in Accounting at Warwick Business School. She has published on the history of taxation and accounting, the public administration of taxation, interdisciplinary approaches to tax research and scholarship, and UK and international financial reporting.

Thomas A. Lee is Professor Emeritus of Accountancy at the University of Alabama and Honorary Professor of Accounting at the Universities of St Andrews and Newcastle-upon-Tyne. His research includes financial reporting as well as accounting history. Tom was President of the Academy of Accounting Historians (1999) and received a Life-time Achievement Award from the British Accounting Association (2005).

Josephine Maltby is Professor of Accounting and Finance at the York Management School, University of York. Her research interests are in accounting, finance and business history. She has published on corporate governance, financial reporting, corporate social reporting, and on women's activity as investors and wealth managers in the nineteenth and twentieth centuries.

Sam McKinstry is Professor of Accounting at the University of the West of Scotland. His publications on business and art history include: *Sure as the Sunrise: A History of Albion Motors*; *Twenty-Seven Queen Street: Home of Scottish Chartered Accountants 1891–2000*; *Rowand Anderson: The Premier Architect of Scotland*, and *'Greek' Thomson* (American Institute of Architects' Prize, 2000).

Christopher J. Napier is Professor of Accounting at Royal Holloway, University of London. After qualifying as a Chartered Accountant, he taught at the London School of Economics and the University of Southampton. He has served as a member of the Council of the Institute of Chartered Accountants in England and Wales.

Dean Neu is the Director of the Centre for Public Interest Accounting at the University of Calgary. He has published widely in the area of accounting history, including: *Accounting for Genocide: Canada's Bureaucratic Assault on Indigenous Peoples*, and *Truth or Profit? The Ethics and Business of Public Accounting*.

Ciarán Ó hÓgartaigh is Professor of Accountancy at University College Dublin. He has published widely on financial reporting and accounting history and is guest editor of a special issue of *Accounting, Business & Financial History* on Ireland (2008). He was a Fulbright Fellow at Northeastern University, Boston in 2000–1.

David Oldroyd is a member of the Cultures, Imperialism and Accounting Practices research group at Newcastle University. He has published on the Industrial Revolution and plantation economies of the British Caribbean and American South. He is particularly interested in the role played by landowners and their stewards in formative industrial enterprise in the eighteenth century.

Chris Poullaos is Associate Professor of Accounting at the University of Sydney. His work on the history of the accounting profession in Australia, Britain, Canada, South Africa and the Philippines has appeared in *Accounting, Organizations and Society*; *Abacus*; *Accounting, Auditing & Accountability Journal*; and *Critical Perspectives on Accounting*.

Gary J. Previts is Professor of Accountancy at Case Western Reserve University. His interests include the development of accounting thought, institutions, regulation and public policy. He has published in many academic and professional journals. He is co-author of *A History of Accountancy in the United States* (1998) and *The CPA Profession Opportunities, Responsibilities and Services* (2006).

Alan J. Richardson is a Professor at the Schulich School of Business, York University, Canada. He has published extensively on the regulation of practice rights and standard-setting processes. He is on the editorial board of eight journals including *Accounting, Organizations and Society*; *Contemporary Accounting Research*; *Accounting, Business & Financial History* and *Accounting Historians Journal*.

Keith Robson is Professor of Accounting at Cardiff University. Keith has published extensively on accounting practices, professional socialisation and regulation in journals such as *Accounting, Organizations and Society*; *Critical Perspectives on Accounting*; *Human Relations* and *Organization*. He is currently researching changing audit methodologies in multinational audit firms, and the development of audit institutions.

Janette Rutterford is Professor of Financial Management at the Open University. Her research interests are in corporate finance and the history of investment. She is currently researching women investors and is the author of *Introduction to Stock Exchange Investment*, now in its third edition.

Steven Toms is currently Professor of Accounting and Finance and Head of the York Management School. He is the joint editor of the journal *Business History*. His research has examined the financial aspects of business history, including the relationship between business organisation and the development of accounting.

Stephen P. Walker is Professor of Accounting at Cardiff University. He is a former editor of *Accounting Historians Journal*, a past President of the Academy of Accounting Historians and a recipient of the Academy's Hourglass Award. His research focuses on the history of the accounting profession and accounting histories of gender, social control and identity construction.

Charles W. Wootton is Professor of Accountancy at Eastern Illinois University. He has published on gender and the accounting workforce, the development of machine accounting, early financial reporting in the USA, and auditor concentration among large public accounting firms.

Acknowledgements

Thanks are due to Jacqueline Curthoys, formerly Business and Management Editor at Routledge, for planting the seed of this project. We appreciated the ongoing support of other Routledge staff during the various stages to publication of the *Routledge Companion*. The comments of academic referees helped refine our proposal and were much appreciated.

We owe a special debt of gratitude to our contributors for their enthusiastic participation in this challenging enterprise. Some authors were confronted with sparse, emergent literatures where the identification of themes and trends was difficult. Others committed themselves to remits of almost unmanageable proportions – topics which were not easily subjected to synthetic treatment, particularly when authoritarian editors imposed tight word limits. The extent to which the authors succeeded not only in providing syntheses but also writing stimulating and insightful chapters which identify opportunities for others is evidence of the committed scholarship which has firmly established history in the canon of accounting research. We hope that the authors have found this exercise personally rewarding, if not in the financial sense.

It seems appropriate that we pay tribute to the generations of accounting historians before us who made the case for the academic study of a subject invariably assumed to concern the present rather than the past. It is testament to their achievements that Chapter 1 of this book does not bear the legitimating title 'Why study accounting history?'

As ever, it is those closest to us, Liz and Sandie, who bear the heaviest burden of our marriage to accounting history as well as to them.

Introduction: synthesis and engagement

John Richard Edwards and Stephen P. Walker

If for many people history is boring and all about dead people, why produce a *Companion* to the history of a discipline that is widely perceived as a mind-numbing activity performed by the living dead – cold, colourless number crunchers? In this volume we hope to show that accounting history is much more than describing the content of crumbling ledgers, the scrutiny of faded balance sheets and charting impenetrable methods for recording transactions in the past. While we don't promise to excite readers with historical tales of lust, debauchery and murder, we do hope to reveal the manner in which the seemingly innocuous practice of accounting has pervaded human existence in numerous and fascinating ways.

As a process of information gathering, inscription, processing and dissemination, and as a basis for decision-making, accounting has impacted on lived experiences in the diverse arenas in which it has been practised throughout history. Sometimes its presence is conspicuous, as in large corporations, financial institutions and government organisations. In other places its operation is shrouded and its effects almost imperceptible. But present it invariably is – not only in the realms of capital markets, financial management and accountability structures but also in the pursuit of economic and social policy, the control of labour in organisations, the management of family relationships, the destruction of indigenous peoples, and the pursuit of military campaigns. It even features in religious belief systems, literature, art and architecture. Accounting has been implicated in key transitional events such as the emergence of capitalism and the Industrial Revolution. Further, those who practise accounting and the organisations that employ, regulate and represent them have amassed considerable power and significance in the modern age. It is the search for the presences, roles and impacts of accounting and accountants in manifold times and locations that excites those who research accounting history.

Why a *Companion to Accounting History*?

The aim of the *Routledge Companion* is to offer an introduction to the shifting arenas which attract the attention of accounting historians, relate the findings of their research and address the controversies that energise debate in the field. The *Routledge Companion* is not intended to offer a metahistory but a comprehensive overview of the current state of historical knowledge in accounting.

Accounting historians operate in an environment where the production of general histories of their subject is not encouraged. An emphasis by university funding bodies and promotion panels on publication through the medium of refereed academic journals tends toward the production of detailed investigations of specific and manageable subjects. Although specialist and particular histories are generally considered to require the most intellectual labour, they are also the histories which are read the least. Textbooks and popular histories attract larger audiences but tend to command less academic respect. Readers may be assured that we have no intention of excessively popularising a serious academic subject by preparing a book on 'awesome accountants', 'barmy bookkeepers', 'calamitous cash flows' or 'devilish depreciation'. However, we do perceive the need for a greater engagement with accounting history and recognise the potential of synthesis in achieving it. The production of a convenient vehicle for surveying and communicating the results of accounting history research to a wider audience and inspiring others to enter the field is desirable if the subject is to be dislodged from its status as a narrow specialism on the outer fringes of the history universe, a minor descendant on the economic and business branch of the history family tree. Catching the attention and engaging with a wider audience is also likely to prove beneficial to accounting historians who have recently been charged with exhibiting an unhealthy tendency to introversion (Walker 2005; Guthrie and Parker 2006).

This call for greater engagement has parallels with other maturing sub-disciplines of history. In the 1980s, labour historians discussed whether synthesis was necessary due to the 'truncated state of the field – rich in its findings, unclear as to larger meanings' (quoted in Schatz 1984). Diplomatic historians have discussed whether the greater infusion of theory in their subject would act as a palliative to its 'subdisciplinary fragmentation' (Leffler 1995). Some social historians have recently suggested that importations such as the 'cultural turn' have increased particularism and the consequent desirability of synthesis (Stearns 2003). Other social historians have critically explored whether grand and partial narratives are a fruitful way of integrating their splintering discipline given that its vitality rests largely on constantly extending the field (Linden 2003).

More broadly, there have also been demands for syntheses in American history with a view to making sense of the findings of the fragmented and increasingly remote 'new' (social and cultural) histories which have proliferated in recent times. This raised pedagogical issues such as how to address 'overspecialisation' without descending to superficiality (Curtin 1984). It was argued, controversially, that assimilation and crystallisation were necessary to restore history to its rightful place in the intellectual culture of the American nation and fulfil its role in informing political discourse. This was not only deemed to be conducive to raising the profile of the discipline and its practitioners, it was the historian's 'civic service' to interact with the wider public (Bender 1986, 1987). While we do not make such claims for accounting history, the need to showcase the enormous contribution to knowledge made by accounting historians as the discipline has blossomed in recent decades is apparent. It is true that the state of knowledge varies significantly across the subject areas featuring in this volume, but the advance of research in accounting history is such that the time appears ripe for ventures beyond particularity.

Indeed, attempts have already been made in this direction. In the 1990s, reference books appeared on accounting history. Most notably Chambers' *An Accounting Thesaurus: 500 Years of Accounting* was published in 1995, a work described by one reviewer as a 'filing cabinet full of apt and well-ordered quotations' on accounting (Baxter 1996). Chatfield and Vangermeersch produced *The History of Accounting: An International Encyclopedia* (1996). Also indicative of attempts to make sense of the field has been the appearance of multi-volume collections of some of the most significant academic articles published on accounting history (Edwards 2000; Fleischman 2006). Summary histories of core subjects such as financial accounting and management accounting have appeared as separate volumes (Edwards 1989) or within edited handbooks (Chapman *et al.* 2007). However, single-volume works of a synthetic character which address the numerous other themes in the widening field of accounting history research are not to be found.

There are other benefits of syntheses. While they may encourage excessive generalisation and 'open the way to erroneous and vacuous statements' (Monkkonen 1986), they can also be a route to the identification of emergent and overarching subjects, fresh interpretations, future possibilities, the posing of new research questions and the facilitation of theory development. The object of synthesis may be to attempt to survey a field, identify or reformulate essential themes. The *Routledge Companion* does not aspire to the latter lofty form of holism. It is not an attempt to present a grand or metanarrative from a particular philosophical perspective (Fulbrook 2002: 58–62). Rather, it begins the task of 'relating parts to a whole' (Bender 1987) by presenting in a single place segmented syntheses of extant work in 28 subject areas of accounting history. Collectively, the chapters provide a comprehensive and critical survey of the current scope of accounting history research. The contribution which we believe the *Routledge Companion* makes is encapsulated in the following statement about the virtues of syntheses:

> They give specialists a sense of what historians in other subfields are writing. Syntheses provide a quick overview of a discipline, note important starting points and useful bibliographies. Syntheses can make comprehensible the research agendas of narrow specializations. They can set narrowly focused work in appropriate contexts and can identify materials and issues critical to our understanding of the past. Syntheses may even acquaint a larger reading public with issues in historical research, although contributions of this type are rare.
>
> (Monkkonen 1986)

Like other aspects of the historical research process, synthesis involves questions of selection, interpretation and representation. Accordingly, synthesis is biased and, in various respects, its achievement is illusory (Painter 1987). Any attempt at universality and totalisation is problematical (Ryn 2000). The content of the *Routledge Companion* is inevitably partial in its reliance on history as performed and conveyed by accounting and other historians. Numerous untold histories of accounting remain silent, and will remain so until researched and articulated by historians. The *Routledge Companion* is also biased in that the editors' selection defines and privileges certain themes. The choice of authors conditions the emphases and standpoints which inform individual contributions. The *Routledge Companion* presents a series of narratives penned by 37 authors and joint authors, each offering their own interpretations of the extant histories produced in their specialist fields. There is no pretension that these are definitive or complete accounts. Indeed, if the experience of the past three decades is at all indicative of what may happen in the future, the contours of accounting history knowledge will be substantially different within a relatively short time frame. Fresh syntheses will be required as agendas shift and new controversies redirect the attention of accounting historians. For the purposes of the present exercise, the chosen authors were given an assignment aligned to our objective of engagement. They were requested to provide a balanced overview of current knowledge, identify issues, discuss relevant debates and reflect on research opportunities.

A review of the contents of previous single-volume edited works on accounting history in the English language illustrates the need to produce a work which reveals to a wider audience the broadening scope and contribution of accounting history. Richard Brown's landmark *A History of Accounting and Accountants* of 1905 comprised two parts. Chapters on the 'History of Accounting' were concerned with the technical, embracing Numeration, Ancient Systems of Accounting, Early Forms of Accounts, History of Auditing and two chapters on the History of Bookkeeping. There followed ten chapters on the 'History of Accountants' which explored the origins and progress of accounting practitioners in locations such as Italy, Scotland, England and Wales, the British colonies and the USA. Half a century later appeared Littleton and Yamey's (1956) *Studies in the History of Accounting*. This work had the history of double-entry bookkeeping at its heart. It offered a chronologically organised volume of chapters primarily on record keeping (before and after double entry), from classical antiquity to the nineteenth century.

By the end of the twentieth century the inclusion of sections on local government, cost and management accounting and accounting theory in Parker and Yamey's (1994) *Accounting History: Some British Contributions* revealed movement beyond the hitherto dominant focus of accounting history on bookkeeping and financial accounting. The inclusion of a final section on 'Accounting in Context' signalled the then recent extension of the subject beyond its traditional boundaries. When compared with these important works, the contents of the *Routledge Companion* indicate the new ground which accounting history has covered in a relatively short time. The inclusion of sections on institutions, economy, society and culture, polity, and discussion of the discipline itself, illustrate the transformational effects of greater interfacing with a range of knowledge fields. Moreover, readers of chapters in parts that resonate more strongly with traditional foci of accounting history – technologies, and theory and practice – will discern how new ways of conducting and interpreting the history of accounting as technique have emerged in recent years.

Design of the *Routledge Companion*

The design of a work intended to provide a synthesis of accounting history research could be approached in a number of ways. A chronological emphasis with chapters exploring developments from the earliest accountings in ancient civilisations through to the electronic accounting in the modern age would be an obvious way of organising a work on history. Another possibility would be to commission a set of accounting histories of individual nations organised by continent. This might also reveal sensitivity to calls for the greater inclusivity of histories and historical traditions beyond the Anglophone world which currently dominates the literature and institutions of the discipline. It might also satisfy an audience of academic accountants interested in the historical background to the complexities of achieving accounting harmonisation in the age of globalisation. However, the approach decided upon for the *Routledge Companion* is thematic, one that is sensitive to chronology and geographical coverage but also indicative of the established and emerging subjects of accounting history research.

This emphasis is in accord with our priority of engagement with those considering researching accounting history, with scholars of the past and present of accounting, and those hailing from the diverse other disciplines with which accounting is increasingly seen to interact. We particularly want to convey to the academic community, within and beyond accounting, the extent to which accounting history has advanced beyond a narrow concern with accounting as technique, a calculative method found predominantly in the realm of business. In an age when interdisciplinary engagement is high on the agenda, it is especially hoped that economic, social, cultural, literary, political and even military historians will discover points of connection between their own interests and the history of accounting through the themes explored in the *Routledge Companion*. In the past, many scholars operating in such disciplines have found accounting 'too devious and contrived a subject to be penetrated by the historian without special grounding in the art' (Stacey 1954: xv). The content of the *Routledge Companion* will hopefully illustrate that accounting is not so mysterious, particularly where it interfaces with numerous other fields of history.

Our emphasis on engagement also extended to the manner in which we suggested authors approached their chapters and formulated organising principles. While we indicated the importance of providing essential historical signposts and the inclusion of key literature for the guidance of those new to the subject, we also encouraged a focus on the discursive – a reflection on issues and debates, and consideration of research potentialities. Many of the contributors to the *Routledge Companion* took seriously our call to discuss their theme on as broad a geographical canvas as possible. That said, the emphasis in most chapters is on reviewing extant knowledge as conveyed in the language which has long dominated the accounting history literature – English.

The chapters reveal the various motivations behind accounting history research and the different perspectival paradigms employed in the literature and by the authors. Some scholars of accounting history have as their objective to understand symbols and calculations in their contemporary contexts or to uncover accounting relics in a search for the origins of a technique, concept or institution which features prominently in the accounting present. Other accounting historians seek to inform contemporary accounting policy-making by offering insights into the emergence of a modern-day issue, revealing how a similar problem was addressed in the past or merely to remind us that such issues endure or are incapable of resolution. Some use historical accounting data as the empirical basis for hypothesis testing or advancing a theory. Motivations for accounting history research also include the further exploration of issues and controversies raging in accounting history and evaluating an assertion about accounting made by a historian operating in another sub-field. Increasingly it is recognised that history may be deployed as part of the critical analysis of the accounting present or as a powerful way of exposing accounting in processes of oppression, exclusion or emancipation. As some of the chapters in the *Routledge Companion* illustrate, histories can be employed to draw into the accounting agenda groups hitherto largely invisible to it, such as the poor, women and ethnic minorities.

Structure of the *Routledge Companion*

Given that each chapter begins with a brief overview, it is not our intention here to detail the content of every contribution. But a few words about the structure of the *Routledge Companion* and some dominant themes are appropriate. The first four parts might be described as essentially *intra*disciplinary in character. In Part 1, 'The discipline', the various authors explain the growth of accounting history research, discuss the emergence and current state of disciplinary institutions, chart changes in the subjects studied, identify the practitioners of accounting history, the methods they employ and the outlets in which their work appears. Of particular importance to the development of the discipline has been a vibrant discourse on accounting historiography. This has had a significant impact on research in the subject areas which feature in later chapters.

Part 2 concerns 'Technologies'. Here the contributing authors provide contextualised insights to the varied and changing calculative techniques and devices employed for the measurement, representation and communication of financial (and other) data. They also discuss the mechanisms for holding persons accountable in diverse settings through ancient, classical, medieval and modern times. Accounting technologies are revealed as central to the functioning of governments, estates, traders, households and global corporations. At the chronological centre of this section lie enduring debates about the emergence of double-entry bookkeeping.

Part 3 explores the historical development of 'Theory and practice' in the core subjects of financial accounting, management accounting and auditing. The chapters therein discuss the frustrated search for a comprehensive theory of accounting, the relationship between accounting theory and practice, continuity and change in accounting practices, and consider the socio-economic motivations and impacts of those practices. It is in the history of managerial accounting that the search for motivations and impacts has been particularly intense. Controversy has been fuelled by the import of a range of theoretical perspectives, new methodologies and the investigation of a range of empirical sites. These controversies have been of significance beyond the pursuit of histories of management accounting. The concern with identifying motives for implementation has also encouraged polarised debate in the history of auditing, a practice increasingly understood as an almost omnipresent feature of modernity.

Part 4 on 'Institutions' focuses on those who perform accounting functions, the organisations in which they are employed and educated and by whom they are regulated. It is here that the sociologies of occupations, identity and socialisation meet accounting history. The chapters in this part reveal the complex histories of the professionalisation of accountants, their shifting work jurisdictions, the emergence and advancing power of accounting firms, the history of vocational preparation and pedagogical practice in accounting, and the development of the regulatory frameworks within which accounting is performed.

In Parts 5, 6 and 7, attention shifts to histories which explore the interfaces of accounting with the economy, society, culture, and politics. The sections are especially indicative of the *inter*disciplinary panorama and widening scope of accounting history research. The chapters in Part 5 discuss histories of accounting which relate to the 'Economy'. The Part commences with a chapter based on the essential observation that 'accounting is fundamentally implicated in all stages of the development of capitalism' and surfaces in the multiple structures of capitalist systems. The next chapter focuses on the visibility of accounting at the macroeconomic level – in the national accounting regimens of liberal democracies and totalitarian states. Accounting is closely associated with finance and financial institutions and histories of this interfacing field are examined in a separate chapter. Transport is another sector of the economy which is important in the history of accounting. The railroad companies, which raised and invested capital on an unprecedented scale, are much studied as a site of accounting innovation and the scene for debates over some long-standing accounting controversies. Accounting becomes most controversial and its economic effects most visible when it is implicated in scandal, when auditing fails or accountants are accused of sharp practice or resorting to outright criminality. A chapter which reviews histories of corporate reporting scandals closes Part 5.

'Society and culture' is the subject of Part 6. The opening chapters on gender, race and indigenous peoples contain two dominant features: first, the exclusion of women and ethnic groups from the accounting profession; and, second, the manner in which accounting and those who practise it are implicated in the construction and maintenance of unequal distributions of power and in the exploitation, discrimination and management of particular populations. The first three chapters of this part emphasise exclusion, repression and oppression. The fourth offers a corrective in its relating historical instances where accounting displayed a potential to mobilise and challenge when deployed in emancipatory projects. The subsequent chapters on religion and the creative arts examine some of the linkages between accounting and culture.

The application of accounting in religious organisations and its presence in religious texts are revealed as an emerging but important field, one which identifies new sites for exploring the development of accounting practices and the conceptual foundations of the craft. The breadth of accounting presences is also evident in the last chapter of Part 6 which reviews the significance of historical representations of accounting and accountants in architecture, literature, fine art, the graphic arts and film.

The final part of the *Routledge Companion* on 'Polity' contains chapters on the role of accounting in the government, protection and financing of states. The opening chapter shows how central and local governments and their agencies have been major locations for the institution of accountability relationships, debates over appropriate accounting techniques and the use of accounting for purposes of social control. The penultimate chapter illuminates the centrality of accounting to successful military interventions, legislative control of the military, and the importance of war to the development of core accounting practices such as costing. The concluding chapter emphasises the importance of taxation to the fabric and maintenance of political systems and explores some of the areas where the histories of accounting and taxation interrelate.

Through these themed chapters it is expected that readers will gain historical insights to the many places in which accounting has featured, the diverse reasons for its introduction, the identity of those who have performed it, the forms it has taken, the purposes to which it has been put, and the effects it has had on those subjected to it. The authors show how the study of many of these accounting phenomena has been illuminated by the application of theory. They also reveal the way in which accounting, like other forms of text, offers historical pathways into the economic, social, cultural and political realms.

Fifty years ago the eminent US accountant Sidney Davidson, when reviewing Littleton and Yamey's (1956) *Studies in the History of Accounting*, confessed:

> I began this volume with some reluctance, for essays on accounting history are frequently dull and uninspired. As I read on I felt that this volume had come closer than most to living up to its extravagant publisher's blurb that 'this book makes fascinating reading'.
>
> (Davidson 1957)

Our aim is that readers of the *Routledge Companion* will arrive at the same conclusion.

References

Baxter, W. T. (1996) Review of *An Accounting Thesaurus: 500 Years of Accounting, Accounting and Business Research*, 26 (4): 358.

Bender, T. (1986) Wholes and parts: the need for synthesis in American history, *Journal of American History*, 73 (1): 120–36.

Bender, T. (1987) Wholes and parts: continuing the conversation, *Journal of American History*, 74 (1): 123–30.

Brown, R. (ed.) (1905) *A History of Accounting and Accountants* (Edinburgh: T.C. and E.C. Jack).

Chambers, R. J. (1995) *An Accounting Thesaurus: 500 Years of Accounting* (Oxford: Pergamon Press).

Chapman, C. S., Hopwood, A. G. and Shields, M. D. (eds) (2007) *Handbook of Management Accounting Research* (Amsterdam: Elsevier).

Chatfield, M. and Vangermeersch, R. (1996) *The History of Accounting: An International Encyclopedia* (New York: Garland).

Curtin, P. D. (1984) Depth, span, and relevance, *American Historical Review*, 89 (1): 1–9.

Davidson, S. (1957) Review of *Studies in the History of Accounting, Economica*, 24 (94): 176–7.

Edwards, J. R. (1989) *A History of Financial Accounting* (London: Routledge).

Edwards, J. R. (ed.) (2000) *The History of Accounting: Critical Perspectives on Business and Management* (London: Routledge).

Fleischman, R. K. (ed.) (2006) *Accounting History* (London: Sage Publications).

Fulbrook, M. (2002) *Historical Theory* (London: Routledge).

Guthrie, J. and Parker, L. (2006) The coming out of accounting research specialisms, *Accounting, Auditing & Accountability Journal*, 19 (1): 5–16.

Leffler, M. P. (1995) New approaches, old interpretations, and prospective reconfigurations, *Diplomatic History*, 19 (2): 172–96.

Linden, M. van der (2003) Gaining ground, *Journal of Social History*, 37 (1): 69–75.

Littleton, A. C. and Yamey, B. S. (1956) Preface, in A. C. Littleton and B. S. Yamey (eds) *Studies in the History of Accounting*, pp. v–viii (London: Sweet & Maxwell Ltd).

Monkkonen, E. H. (1986) The dangers of synthesis, *American Historical Review*, 91 (5): 1146–57.

Painter, N. I. (1987) Bias and synthesis in history, *Journal of American History*, 74 (1): 109–12.

Parker, R. H. and Yamey, B. S. (eds) (1994) *Accounting History: Some British Contributions* (Oxford: Clarendon Press).

Ryn, C. G. (2000) History as synthesis, *Humanitas* 13 (1): 89–102.

Schatz, R. W. (1984) Labor historians, labor economics, and the question of synthesis, *Journal of American History*, 71 (1): 93–100.

Stacey, N. A. H. (1954) *English Accountancy: A Study in Social and Economic History* (London: Gee and Company).

Stearns, P. N. (2003) Social history present and future, *Journal of Social History*, 37 (1): 9–19.

Walker, S. P. (2005) Accounting in history, *Accounting Historians Journal*, 33 (2): 233–59.

Part 1

The discipline

1

Structures, territories and tribes

Stephen P. Walker

Overview

The aim of this chapter is to explore the development and current status of accounting history as a sub-discipline. The terrain of accounting history is mapped by surveying the institutions that characterise and legitimate its pursuit. In particular, the chapter examines the emergence of disciplinary organisations for accounting historians, the increasing numbers of conferences on the subject, the growth in accounting history publications and the pedagogical claims advanced by advocates of accounting history education. The principal intellectual currents which have run through these disciplinary structures are explored in Chapter 2 and the development of the subject areas of accounting research which they have helped to sustain are reviewed in Chapter 3.

In this chapter, it is shown that progress in some areas of disciplinary endeavour (such as establishing specialist journals and conferences) has been more marked than in others (such as creating enduring and inclusive organisations and integrating accounting history into the curriculum). The chapter begins by discussing the expansion of accounting history research, locating its disciplinary territory and exploring some of the features which define the 'academic tribe' of accounting historians (Becher and Trowler 2001: 23–4).

The growth of accounting history

According to Becher and Trowler:

> Disciplinary growth can be measured by the number and types of departments in universities, the change and increase in types of HE courses, the proliferation of disciplinary associations, the explosion in the number of journals and articles published and the multiplication of recognized research topics and research clusters.
>
> (2001: 14)

Similarly, Clark (1996) suggests that the growth of a discipline may be discerned by tracking the expansion of the institutions surrounding it. In particular, the growth of academic departments and units; degree programmes and courses; disciplinary associations; disciplinary journals; the existence of recognised research topics and related research clusters. While one would be hard pressed to identify university departments of accounting history and degree programmes in the subject, courses on various aspects of the history of accounting increasingly feature. Further, various organisations represent the practitioners of accounting history, several specialist journals exist and operate in traditional and web-based formats, and an increasing number of articles on accounting history are published in specialist and general accounting and business journals. There is also an increasing plurality of research themes and some research centres have been established (Walker 2006).

Although its advocates frequently relate the pedagogical and practical utility of knowledge of the subject, accounting history is not a field of study which grew in response to societal or professional calls for its inclusion in the curriculum. The growth of accounting history is more usefully interpreted as a response to various developments in higher education in recent decades. These include massification and the attendant expansion of academic knowledge, the increasing fragmentation of disciplines and the career-enhancing potential of academic special-isation in the context of 'the research imperative' (Blau 1973: 190–8; Metzger 1987; Clark 1987: 197–210; 1996; Henkel 2000: 29–145). A Marxist interpretation of this scene sees the prolifer-ation of accounting histories as a consequence of the commodification of history and historians under advanced capitalism. This interpretation perceives the expansion of histories as the production of self-referential signifiers in the interest of capital (Cooper and Puxty 1996).

More conventionally, the growth in accounting history research is explicable as both reactive and substantive. It is reactive in that the expansion of the sub-discipline represents a response to the increased demand for accounting labour and the consequential growth of vocationally relevant higher education in accounting and business. Educational expansion has been serviced by a rapid increase in the numbers of university staff teaching accounting. Those who instruct the student population are increasingly urged to comply with the institutional priority to pursue research and publication (Gray and Helliar 1994; Whittington 1995; Wallace 1997; Beattie and Goodacre 2004). Accounting history represents one research specialism which has attracted increasing numbers of accounting academics. However, the expansion of accounting history has also been substantive, or knowledge-led (Metzger 1987). Its growth illustrates the extension of the accounting research agenda beyond its technical core. This broadening in the scope of academic accounting has been attended by the dignification of a number of specialisms and the advancing status of the interdisciplinary study of the subject, including its history (Elzinga 1987).

Characterising the accounting history tribe and locating its territory

The fragmentation of academic disciplines into research sub-disciplines and specialisms is cer-tainly not unique to accounting. The discipline of history has not only witnessed the emer-gence of economic, social and cultural history but, in recent decades, the further splintering of each sub-discipline (Eley 1979; Marwick 1989: 72–141; Jordanova 2000: 34–46; Vincent 2001: 133–67). However, it would be wrong to perceive the growth of accounting history as a manifestation of subject dispersion and the emergence of new specialisms in the discipline of history. Accounting history arises from the broadening terrain of accounting. The pathways to academic careers in accounting history are diverse but are predominantly characterised by undergraduate, postgraduate and/or professional education in accounting rather than history, though, on occasion, both. Thus, from an early stage, disciplinary associations and various authors in accounting history have felt obliged to instruct entrants to the field on the historical research methodologies which are absent from an accounting education (Gaffikin 1981; Parker and Graves 1989; Fleischman *et al.* 2003).

The disciplinary habitation of accounting historians in accounting rather than history is also indicated by other institutional factors. The great majority of accounting historians reside in accounting and finance departments and business schools and everyday interaction tends to be with colleagues in these fields. Its practitioners tend to primarily identify themselves as operating in the discipline of accounting but belong to a research community that specialises in history. The instructional mission of accounting historians is grounded in accounting rather than history and the sustainability of the specialist courses they offer depends on attracting students following accounting rather than history programmes. In the absence of departments of accounting history, the institutional focus of its practitioners is the research conference, accounting history association and sometimes the research unit. Examples of the latter include the Accounting and Business History Research Unit at Cardiff University and the *Centro de Estudos de História da Contabilidade* (Accounting Research Centre) of the Portuguese Association of Accountants.

The institutional and disciplinary locus in accounting rather than history is confirmed by an examination of the research environment. In the UK Research Assessment Exercise, accounting history falls substantially within the remit of the sub-panel on Accounting and Finance and is also in the orbit of Business and Management Studies. While the principal historical focus of the latter – business history – is specifically identified as within the scope of the sub-panel on History, accounting history is not (RAE 2002, 2006). Moreover, the publication media favoured by accounting historians are conditioned by those that confer greatest esteem in accounting – articles in high-ranking journals tend to be the vehicle for the communication of new knowledge in accounting history rather than the monograph favoured by historians.

In addition to their career tracks being located in the disciplinary structures of accounting rather than history, accounting historians as a whole tend not to engage with the wider history community. Though there are notable exceptions, accounting historians have a limited presence in history journals and appear disinclined to embark on research collaborations with historians (Walker 2005). Despite its undoubted potential to do so, accounting history has not impacted on the historical mainstream in the way that, for example, women's history has. It does not feature in history textbooks, fire debates in the greater history literature or induce questions in the sister discipline about the nature and pursuit of history. That said, on a few occasions, relationships between accounting and near neighbours, such as business historians, have been explored (Johnson 1975; Boyns and Edwards 1990).

Given the general lack of interdisciplinary communication between accounting and other historians, it is not surprising that perceptions of the scope and character of accounting history appear to differ according to whether the stance is internal or external to the craft. For accounting historians, the potential scope of their subject is multidisciplinary and vast, and embraces research based on data which may be documentary or oral, qualitative or quantitative. For historians, accounting history is more likely perceived as a progeny of business history, a specialism which focuses on mysterious calculative techniques manifested in sources such as invoices, ledgers and balance sheets.

It would be wrong to suggest that the boundaries between accounting and other historians are closed. There are undoubtedly cross-disciplinary influences which suggest that accounting history is a 'hybrid field' (Dogan 1997). However, the communication is substantially unidirectional and involves more borrowing than lending. Accounting historians import methodologies and historiographical discourses from history and its sub-disciplines. Accounting history increasingly draws on standards in history when establishing and reinforcing the benchmarks of quality research in its own domain. These attributes are generally considered to emanate from comprehensive evidence gathering (accounting historians as auditors have an affinity with historians on this matter (Napier 2002; Walker 2004)), contextualisation, thorough literature review, analytical rather than descriptive writing, quality narrative and addressing the 'so what?' question. Whereas accounting historians have frequently been compelled to legitimise their research by illustrating its relevance to modern-day accounting issues and policy-making, as in history, accounting history is increasingly recognised as meritorious when it advances understandings and encourages debate about the past.

Accounting history is thus best understood as a sub-discipline of accounting which also draws inspiration from other disciplines. It embraces various specialisms based on configurations relating to: subject areas (such as management accounting, financial accounting, accounting institutions), theoretical approaches (such as Marxist, Foucauldian, economic rationalist), interdisciplinary influences (various sub-disciplines of history, and other disciplines such as economics, politics, sociology), methodologies and use of sources (oral, archival), and sectoral, spatial and/or temporal foci. Each of these arenas may contain sub-specialisms which represent compound delineations such as the history of cost accounting in the modern period, the sociological history of the accountancy profession, archival studies of financial accounting practice, or Marxist interpretations of the development of financial accounting. As the contents of this volume attest, the research field is potentially extraordinarily broad, offering scope for investigating historical phenomena across the corpus of accounting and accountability subjects.

The research themes that occupy accounting historians are sensitive to a range of influences. These are internal to the sub-discipline, as in the discourse generated by research findings and seeking answers to enduring questions. Influences are also external in the form of themes emerging in the contemporary academic discipline of accounting (such as international accounting, corporate social and sustainability reporting); the professional and institutional environment (regulation, organisations, ethics); and discourses and shifting themes in related disciplines such as history, management and sociology. Accounting history is a field where fresh methodological and theoretical approaches, new ways of seeing older debates, and the discovery of unexplored arenas for the operation of accounting in historical contexts are usually greeted with enthusiasm.

The practitioners of accounting history are predominantly male (Carnegie *et al.* 2003), operate in a range of national and cultural contexts and are socialised in various traditions of accounting and historical research. This range of situational contingencies together with the unbounded research field suggests that accounting historians operate in a divergent and potentially conflictual sub-discipline. Indeed, there have been heated contests over the merits of 'old' and 'new' accounting history, and cultural clashes over access to research journals and the perceived Anglo-American *Zeitgeist* in the institutions of the craft (Carmona 2004, see also Chapter 2). At the same time, accounting historians can display a capacity for commonality born of the unifying effects of challenges to the legitimacy of their discipline in the modern business school, exclusion of their work from certain high-ranking accounting journals, a common concern for the advance of the discipline and the quest for its greater recognition in the wider realm of history.

Accounting historians are an academic tribe whose identity and commonality are increasingly reinforced at numerous specialist conferences. They are a research community which canonises heroic figures who blaze trails in the past and present by conferring awards and producing league tables of influential contributors (Carmona 2006). In recent years some accounting historians have displayed an introverted concern with publication patterns. It is not entirely clear whether this represents an attempt to plot shifting disciplinary territories and explore the potential of new research themes or is symptomatic of intellectual exhaustion.

Accounting history is a sub-discipline in which identities are often constructed around the individual's approach to historical research (archival *v.* armchair theorising), writing history (description *v.* theorised analysis), and theoretical approaches employed. These distinctions are abstracted as identifiers such as the 'old' and 'new' accounting historian, a distinction based not on the age of the practitioner but her/his approach to historical research (Carnegie and Napier 1996). The potency of such labels has recently diminished amid calls for greater plurality, tolerance and a focus on what unites rather than what divides accounting historians (see Chapter 2).

Disciplinary associations

Given that accounting history is not institutionalised in academic departments, and research centres in the subject are few in number, organisations for practitioners beyond the university are of particular importance for sustaining communication and fostering collective identity. The development of disciplinary associations in accounting history is now considered.

The Academy of Accounting Historians

The foremost extant international disciplinary association in accounting history is the Academy of Accounting Historians, formed in 1973. The origins of the Academy are usually traced to 1968 when the American Accounting Association established a Committee on Accounting History chaired by Stephen Zeff of Tulane University. The remit of the Committee was

> [to] propose objectives for research in accounting history, develop guidelines for the teaching of accounting history in undergraduate and graduate courses, and provide a forum . . . through which those interested in the teaching or research of accounting history can hear papers and exchange ideas.
>
> (American Accounting Association 1970)

The Committee observed that the recent pursuit of accounting knowledge beyond the technical had encouraged increased interest in the history of accounting. However, the subject was not as advanced as the histories of other disciplines. The Committee stated forcibly that:

> [H]istorical research is a continuing and necessary element in the overall research effort of scholars in an academic discipline. Accounting is at once professional and academic, and its history is no less relevant than medical history is to medicine, legal history is to law, economic history is to economics, and architectural history is to architecture.
>
> (ibid.)

The Committee on Accounting History considered that the aims of accounting history research were to understand the development of accounting thought, practice and institutions and deemed that such knowledge would assist the formulation of solutions to modern-day accounting problems. The Committee was keen to encourage research in accounting history, particularly that which engaged business and economic historians. Further, recognising that identifying archival materials was a constraint, it provided a comprehensive review of sources for accounting history research. The Committee also noted the absence of an organisation for accounting historians and the need for a vehicle to communicate the results of research in the subject. It suggested that 'roundtables on accounting history' should be convened at gatherings of the American Accounting Association.

The fact that the American Accounting Association did not act on the report of the Committee on Accounting History inspired a small group of accounting professors to form an Academy of Accounting Historians (Coffman *et al.* 1989). The key meeting took place in Quebec on 15 August 1973. Gary J. Previts was elected President. The object of the new organisation was 'to encourage research, publication, teaching and personal interchanges in all phases of accounting history and its interrelation with business and economic history including the environment within which they developed' (*Accounting Historians Notebook*, Fall 1978).

Although the Academy was perceived as an organisation which would embrace researchers throughout the world, its founders and early office holders were American. The Academy was incorporated in Alabama, its research centres were established in Georgia and Mississippi, its journal editors were American and its meetings and conferences were focused in the USA. In the past two decades two thirds of the membership of the Academy has been US resident. The individual and institutional membership of the Academy reached a high point of 913 in 1995 but had declined to 709 by the end of 2006. The declining membership primarily reflects a number of threats to accounting history research in the USA (Fleischman and Radcliffe 2005). Hence, while in 1986 the ratio of US individual members to non-US individual members was 3.2:1, in 2006 it was 1.3:1. In response to the shifting composition of its membership, the Academy has recently sought to internationalise its activities and office bearers.

In accord with its original objectives the work of the Academy of Accounting Historians has centred on publication, research and education. The most important initiatives of the Academy have been in publication. It has performed valuable service as a vehicle for communication among accounting historians and the dissemination of their work. Most significantly it inaugurated *Accounting Historians Journal* (see below). It also commenced a working paper series in 1974 which published 80 articles until its discontinuance in 1991. An accounting history monograph series was introduced in 1976 as was the reproduction of key works in an Accounting History Classics series (until 1991).

The Academy has also encouraged research through its committee work on accounting history bibliography and the identification of archival sources. Given that limited awareness of relevant methodology has often been perceived as an impediment to the pursuit of historical research by accounting academics, the activities of the Accounting History Research Methodology Committee during the 1980s was particularly important (Parker and Graves 1989; Previts *et al.* 1990; Fleischman *et al.* 2003). The Academy has also sponsored research institutions such as the Accounting History Research Center opened in 1982 (and closed in 2005) and the Tax History Research Center in 1987. The Academy convenes an annual research conference in the USA and has co-sponsored World Congresses of Accounting Historians. A seminar series attempted to reveal the relevance of history to accounting practitioners and its significance to understanding contemporary issues. The Academy has also attempted to attract new researchers and encourage doctoral research by offering graduate stipends, grants, scholarships and manuscript awards (such as the Richard G. Vangermeersch Award since 1988 and the Schoenfeld Scholarship since 2008).

The third major area of Academy activity has been in accounting history education. From the early 1980s much attention was devoted to integrating accounting history into the university accounting curriculum (Coffman *et al.* 1989, 1998). This subject is discussed later in the chapter.

The International Committee of Accounting Historians

The formation of the Academy of Accounting Historians was not the earliest attempt to establish an international organisation for accounting historians. In October 1970, the First International Symposium of Accounting Historians was held in Brussels. The event was organized by the *Collège National des Experts Comptables de Belgique* (Coffman *et al.* 1989). The prime mover and Secretary-General of the Symposium was Ernest Stevelinck, a leading accounting historian and member of the Council of the *Collège National* (Dunlop 1970). The Symposium was attended by representatives of various national accounting organisations. Stevelinck argued that national committees on accounting history should be established and their activities co-ordinated by an international committee. He also suggested establishing a multilingual journal on accounting history as well as a number of bibliographical ventures.

A working party was formed during the First International Symposium. It was resolved that Stevelinck would chair a study group on accounting history under the auspices of the *Collège National* and the establishment of national accounting history committees would be encouraged. From this agenda emerged the International Committee of Accounting Historians, based at the *Collège National* with Stevelinck as Secretary-General. Its aim was to provide a means of communication between national accounting history groups, alerting members to the appearance of accounting history articles, encouraging the inclusion of accounting history in the curriculum, publishing a bulletin and inaugurating a programme of quinquennial international congresses on accounting history (*Accountant*, 8 April 1971: 451).

It was envisaged that the International Committee would embrace a broad range of interested researchers including academic and practitioner accountants, historians and archivists. However, little appears to have come of this organisation. Although references can be found to Stevelinck as President of the Belgium National Committee of Accounting Historians and Secretary of the International Committee of Accounting Historians during the 1980s (see *Accounting Historians Notebook* 1983, also 1987), neither organisation appears to have existed for long. The apparent failure of the International Committee resulted in the Academy of Accounting Historians assuming the mantle of the foremost organisation in the field, though its credentials as a representative international organisation were questionable given its US dominance.

Although an enduring and active International Committee of Accounting Historians did not materialise, the initiatives taken at the First International Symposium of Accounting Historians in 1970 did result in a programme of world congresses of accounting historians and the formation of a number of national accounting history committees.

National committees of accounting historians

In December 1970, on returning from the First International Symposium, Professor Robert H. Parker suggested to the Institute of Chartered Accountants of Scotland (ICAS) that an accounting history committee for Scotland be established. The Scottish Committee on Accounting History, comprising academics, practitioners and archivists, held its first meeting in December 1971. Its aim was 'to promote the study of accounting history and to establish and maintain contact with accounting historians and with other committees on accounting history throughout the world'. The Accounting History Committee of ICAS continued until 2002 when its functions were rolled into the Research Committee of the Institute. The Committee performed valuable work in bibliographical compilation, locating and preserving archives, managing the antiquarian book collection of its sponsoring institute, and supporting research projects and publications, primarily on Scottish subjects, including biographical and institutional studies on the history of the accountancy profession.

In 1971, the formation of a British Committee on Accounting History was also mooted. However, the early establishment of a separate committee for Scotland ensured that this venture was organised as the Accounting History Committee in England and Wales. The inaugural meeting of this committee took place in March 1972. Its aims were to promote the study of accounting history in England and Wales, encourage communication among those interested in the subject (especially with business and economic historians), hold conferences and deposit articles on accounting history in the Library of the Institute of Chartered Accountants in England and Wales (ICAEW). Much of the early work of the committee concerned the identification and preservation of business records, which it pursued with the Business Archives Council.

In 1974, the Accounting History Committee in England and Wales was re-constituted as the Accounting History Society. The aims of the society were as follows:

(a) to provide a forum for those interested in the subject;
(b) to improve facilities for research into accounting history;
(c) to encourage the publication of relevant material;
(d) to promote the preservation and recording of primary sources material; and
(e) to co-operate with others interested in the same or related fields of study.

(*Accounting History* 1976: 3)

The Accounting History Society was proactive in fostering links with its counterpart in Scotland, the Business Archives Council, the Academy of Accounting Historians and economic historians (*Accounting History* 1977, 2(2): 1). A major task was organising the Third International Congress of Accounting Historians in London, 1980, to coincide with the centenary of the formation of the ICAEW (Parker 1981). The society languished following the discontinuance of its journal, *Accounting History*, in 1986 and in 1994 it was described as extant 'but comatose' (Mumford 1994).

The Accounting History Special Interest Group of the Accounting and Finance Association of Australia and New Zealand also originated from the First International Symposium of Accounting Historians in Brussels in 1970. Louis Goldberg of the University of Melbourne had attended the Symposium and subsequently communicated with Ernest Stevelinck about the prospect of establishing a national committee for Australia (Goldberg 1987: 207). The Accounting History Committee was formed as a sub-group of the Accounting Association of Australia and New Zealand in 1973 (ibid.: 208). The aims of the committee were the promotion of accounting history research and teaching, communication with accounting historians overseas, the identification and archiving of records and the compilation of a bibliography of sources (*Accounting History Newsletter* 1980: 1). By 1980, there were over 50 members of the Committee and a newsletter was produced. In 1985, the committee became the Accounting History Section of the Accounting Association of Australia and New Zealand. Although the progress of the group has been frustrated by the geographical dispersal of its small membership (Goldberg 1987: 212–13), which currently numbers about 45, the accounting history community in Australasia is active and influential on the international scene both in terms of research and the institutions of the craft.

A number of other national accounting history committees have a less direct lineage to the First International Symposium of Accounting Historians in 1970.

In the early 1970s, the Japan Accounting Association had established a temporary study group on the History of Accounting Development in Japan to mark the centenary of the adoption of western bookkeeping there in 1873 (Nishikawa 1975). A more enduring organisation, the Accounting History Association, Japan, was formed in 1982 with 177 members. The aim of the Association is to promote research on accounting history through conferences and a journal. Membership has increased steadily and currently stands at 240. The Association is perceived as an important vehicle for new researchers in the field. Accounting history research in China has long been discouraged by political and cultural factors. However, economic reforms from the late 1970s created an environment more conducive to the formation of an accounting history research group of the Chinese Society of Accountants in 1988. During the mid-1990s the group was re-constituted as an Accounting History Committee (Lu and Aiken 2003).

In Italy, the *Società Italiana di Storia della Ragioneria* (SISR) (Italian Society of Accounting History), which has over 200 members, was formally constituted at the Fourth World Congress of Accounting Historians at Pisa in August 1984. Its objectives are to promote accounting history through research, publication and conferences. The Society emphasises the study of the history of accounting and business economics in private and public organisations as well as the history of the accounting profession.

In 1978, it was reported that an *Institut National des Historiens Comptables de France* (National Institute of Accounting Historians of France) had been established under the presidency of Yves Cleon. The Institute published a bi-annual bulletin from 1978 to 1982 but it subsequently disappeared. At the end of the 1980s a history of accounting study group was formed by *l'Ordre des Experts comptables* (Parker *et al.* 1997) and in 1990 an accounting history workshop was convened at the annual conference of the *Association Française de Comptabilité* (AFA).

In Spain, there exists a *Comisión de Historia de la Contabilidad* (Commission of Accounting History) of the *Asociación Española de Contabilidad y Auditoria* (AECA) (Spanish Association of Accounting and Management) (The Commission of Accounting History of AECA 2006). The Commission was formed in 1992 under the presidency of Esteban Hernández Esteve. Its aims are to encourage interest in accounting, business and management history, particularly in Spain, Portugal and Latin America; provide a medium of communication; promote publication in the subject; and seek the preservation of archival material (The Commission of Accounting History 2006). Since 1996, the Commission has presented an annual award for contributions to accounting history in an Iberian language. It also publishes works on Spanish accounting history and in 2004 commenced an on-line journal, *De Computis*. The Commission had 96 members at June 2006.

Disciplinary publication

Scale of publication

The 1990s have been described by some accounting historians as a glorious decade for their discipline (Carmona and Zan 2002; Fleischman and Radcliffe 2005). The increasing volume of publications on accounting history during this 'golden age' is the principal reason for this view.

The scale of publication in accounting history over the period 1995–2004 is apparent from Table 1.1 which is compiled from entries contained in annual bibliographies supplied by two of the specialist journals in the field. The bibliographies contained in *Accounting, Business &*

Table 1.1 Average annual and total publications on accounting history reported in bibliographies provided in specialist journals, 1995–2004

Year of publication	Accounting, Business & Financial History	Accounting History	
		Articles	Book Reviews
1995–9	154.0	55.8	24.4
2000–4	122.2	60.8	6.8
Total publications enumerated, 1995–2004	1,381	583	156

Financial History concern English language publications which fall in 'the general area of accounting history'. The lists appearing in *Accounting History* are not intended to be as wide-ranging but identify articles and book reviews written in English. It should be emphasised that the data from both journals exclude material not written in English, notably that appearing in journals in Italy, Japan and Spain. It should also be noted that for the purpose of consistency, books included in the lists appearing in *Accounting History*, 1995–97 have been excluded and the numbers of items appearing in *Accounting History* itself (which are not included in the annual lists) have been added to the data reported in Table 1.1.

The considerable publication output in accounting history during the decade 1995–2004 revealed in Table 1.1 compares with 626 items on the subject identified in bibliographies covering the years to 1980 (Parker 1980; Edwards 2004). Gaffikin (1981) enumerated 94 'historical' articles in six principal accounting journals, 1971–80. More recent studies of the content of non-specialist accounting journals also reveal a marked increase in accounting history papers published from the mid-1980s to the mid-1990s and, as also indicated in Table 1.1, stability thereafter. There is also a significant accounting history presence in general accounting journals. For example, 143 (14.2 per cent) of the articles appearing in *Accounting, Organizations and Society*, 1976–2005 have been identified as 'historical' (Napier 2006).

While Table 1.1 portrays a specialism with a healthy research output, some shifting patterns are discernible in relation to publication media. In the context of the contemporary research imperative, the practitioners of accounting history are now more inclined to produce outputs for academic journals. Hence, there has been a relative decline in the number of books on accounting history with a consequential impact on the number of book reviews. Short articles on accounting history produced for professional audiences also appear to have become less common of late. The decline of the latter two forms of output has implications for the broader dissemination of accounting history research and its popularisation (Edwards 2004 and Chapter 3). Conversely, the submission of research papers to refereed academic journals serves to increase the quality of accounting history outputs.

Specialist journals

Accounting historians publish their work in a variety of mainstream Anglophone accounting journals (most notably, *Abacus*; *Accounting, Auditing & Accountability Journal*; *Accounting and Business Research*; *Accounting, Organizations and Society*; and *Critical Perspectives on Accounting*), a number of which have produced special issues on the subject. A few authors have also ventured into business and economic history journals. There are also three specialist journals in accounting history. Analyses of their content suggest a degree of introspection – a predominance of authors operating from Anglo–American institutions, a focus on Anglo–American subjects in the modern period and limited engagement with other history literatures (Carnegie and Potter 2000; Anderson 2002; Carmona 2004; Walker 2005).

The specialist journal of longest standing is *Accounting Historians Journal* which traces its origins to 1974. In that year, the Academy of Accounting Historians produced a vehicle for short articles and news, *Accounting Historian*. This was superseded in 1977 by a research journal, *Accounting Historians Journal*, and (in 1978) by a newsletter, *Accounting Historians Notebook* in which short articles continue to appear. The policy of *Accounting Historians Journal* is to publish research on 'the development of accounting thought and practice, including but not limited to research that provides an historical perspective on contemporary accounting issues'. However, neither this statement nor the American location of the journal should be taken as an indicator of a narrow conceptual or spatial focus. Although the journal is produced by the Academy of Accounting Historians in the USA, its contributors and scope are international (Badua *et al.* 2003).

The launch of *Accounting History* (1976–86) was an attempt to provide impetus to the Accounting History Society (in England and Wales) referred to earlier. During its early existence this bi-annual refereed journal and newsletter (edited by J. Freer and temporarily by G.A. Lee and P. Boys) did attract interest and new members to the Society. However, the effect was short-lived. By 1980, a dearth of submissions was reported and in 1981 only one issue was produced. The last numbers of *Accounting History* appeared in December 1986 when the editor lamented that insufficient submissions prevented publication. Although its production was erratic, a number of the 37 articles which did appear in *Accounting History* were valuable contributions to the subject (Boys and Freer 1992).

Although the journal of the Accounting History Society folded in 1986, a new British-based medium, produced by a commercial publisher emerged in 1990: *Accounting, Business & Financial History (ABFH)*. *ABFH* aims to explore: 'the inter-relationship between accounting practices, financial markets and economic development, the influence of accounting on business decision-making and the environmental and social influences on the business and financial world'. The journal has a particular focus on histories which explain modern structures and practices and assist the search for solutions to modern–day accounting problems. The journal is especially famed for its special issues on the histories of accounting in countries such as France, Italy, Spain, Germany, the USA, China and Japan (Anderson 2002).

In 1980, an *Accounting History Newsletter* was established by the Accounting History Committee of the Accounting Association of Australia and New Zealand, to circulate items of interest among members. In 1989, the *Newsletter* was supplanted by a bi-annual journal, *Accounting History* edited by Robert W. Gibson. The journal title had been passed from the Accounting History Society (in England and Wales). In 1995, Garry Carnegie became editor of *Accounting History* (Carnegie and Wolnizer 1996) and in 1996 an international editorial board was appointed. *Accounting History* thereby became the third specialist journal in the field. The journal has produced special issues on a range of subjects. Its aims are:

> [to] publish high quality historical papers. These could be concerned with exploring the advent and development of accounting bodies, conventions, ideas, practices and rules. They should attempt to identify the individuals and also the local, time-specific environmental factors which affected accounting, and should endeavour to assess accounting's impact on organisational and social functioning.

There are also a number of journals which are not primarily orientated to English-speaking audiences. The Accounting History Association, Japan, has produced the *Yearbook of the*

Accounting History Association since its inception in 1982. The *Yearbook* is a medium for the publication of papers presented at the preceding annual conference of the Association. The journal primarily (but not exclusively) reports the results of research conducted by Japanese authors.

In 2001, appeared the first volume of the journal of the *Società Italiana di Storia Della Ragioneria* (SISR) (Italian Society of Accounting History), the biannual *Contabilità e Cultura Aziendale* (2006). The journal primarily contains the work of Italian authors. It encourages contributions on the history of accounting and the interface of accounting and economics, histories of firms and the accounting profession as well as reviews of literature on accounting history research themes, descriptive pieces on archival sources, interviews and book reviews.

In December 2004, the first issue of *De Computis: Revista Española de Historia de la Contabilidad* (Spanish Journal of Accounting History 2006) was published. This e-journal is produced by the Commission of Accounting History of AECA. It appears biannually, is free of charge and seeks to publish high quality, peer-reviewed, contributions in Spanish and other major languages. Abstracts of articles are provided in Spanish and English. In addition to research papers, the journal contains reports on conferences, abstracts of doctoral theses, book reviews, news on archives and other notices. The appearance of *De Computis* is explained by the Commission of Accounting History as a response to the need for a Spanish accounting history journal given the limited number of local publication outlets in a 'publish or perish' environment and the difficulties encountered by Spanish authors in securing publication in English language journals.

Other disciplinary publications

Important books and monographs on particular areas of accounting history will feature in later chapters. Early general histories of accounting in English and other languages are discussed in Chapter 2 (also Parker and Yamey 1994: 1–6). Here we need simply mention general works such as Brown's (1905) *A History of Accounting and Accountants*, Woolf's (1912) *A Short History of Accountants and Accountancy*, Green's (1930) *History and Survey of Accountancy*, Murray's (1930) *Chapters in the History of Bookkeeping, Accounting and Commercial Arithmetic* and Littleton's (1933) *Accounting Evolution to 1900*.

During the 1970s, other general histories were produced by O. Ten Have, *The History of Accountancy* (1976) and M. Chatfield, *A History of Accounting Thought* (1977). Such works have been less common in recent decades. While Chatfield and Vangermeersch attempted *The History of Accounting* in encyclopaedic format (1996), few present-day authors have displayed the bravado necessary to write general histories of accounting. This is not surprising given the rapid acceleration of research activity and knowledge creation since the 1980s.

While research in accounting history in recent decades has improved in scope and quality, it is also clear that considerable spatial and temporal territory remains unexplored. Debates on fundamental aspects of the history of accounting are ongoing. In this progressive context the publication of collections of papers indicative of the current state of knowledge is more common than metahistories of accounting. Indeed, there is an established tradition of such works. Early examples include Littleton and Yamey's *Studies in the History of Accounting* (1956) and Garner and Hughes' *Readings on Accounting Development* (1978). The state of more recent scholarship is apparent from the contents of edited volumes such as Parker and Yamey's *Accounting History: Some British Contributions* (1994), Edwards' *The History of Accounting: Critical Perspectives on Business and Management* (2000) and Fleischman's *Accounting History* (2006).

An important resource for accounting historians is the hundreds of books published from the mid-1970s first by Arno Press and later by Garland Publishing under the editorship of

Richard Brief. These series include reprints of major works and articles on accounting, reproductions of original documents, doctoral theses and new monographs on accounting history. The Arno Series commenced in 1976 with 29 volumes on 'The History of Accounting'. Other works were published under the series titles 'The Development of Contemporary Accounting Thought' (1978) and 'Dimensions of Accounting Theory and Practice' (1980). Garland subsequently published numerous books on the themes of 'Accountancy in Transition' (1982), 'Accounting History and the Development of the Profession' (1984), 'Accounting Thought and Practice through the Years' (1986), 'Foundations of Accounting' (1988), 'Accounting History and Thought' (1990), and 'New Works in Accounting History' (1991–2000). Although less voluminous than its predecessor series, important works have appeared since 2000 in the JAI: Elsevier series 'Studies in the Development of Accounting Thought' and since 2001 in the Routledge series 'New Works in Accounting History'.

Disciplinary conferences

The principal events in the accounting history calendar are the World Congresses of Accounting Historians, inaugurated by the First International Symposium of Accounting Historians in Brussels in 1970. Subsequent world congresses were held in Atlanta (1976), London (1980), Pisa (1984), Sydney (1988), Kyoto (1992), Kingston (1996), Madrid (2000), Melbourne (2002), St Louis and Oxford (2004), Nantes (2006) and Istanbul (2008). In addition, the Academy of Accounting Historians holds research conferences in the USA. An annual conference at Cardiff Business School, later aligned to *Accounting, Business & Financial History*, commenced in 1989. The Accounting History Association, Japan, has held annual conferences since its formation in 1982. An international biennial conference associated with *Accounting History* commenced in 1999 and has been convened in Melbourne, Osaka, Siena, Braga and Banff, Canada. A series of workshops on accounting and management in historical perspective has also been convened under the auspices of the European Institute for Advanced Studies in Management.

Also in Europe, the Italian Society of Accounting History has organised biennial national conferences since 1991, held a special international conference on Luca Pacioli in 1994 and from 1996 organised workshops for graduate researchers. Following an initiative by the President of the *Association Française de Comptabilité* a series of annual conferences on accounting and management history commenced in France in 1995 (Boyns and Nikitin 2001). The Commission on Accounting History in Spain arranged workshops and conferences in 1992, 1995, 1998, 2001, 2003 and 2005. These have engaged accounting, economic and business historians in discussions on topics ranging from accounting historiography to the history of accounting in banks and monasteries. Efforts to convene international accounting history conferences at Central and South American venues and in China are currently being explored. However, it is evident that several parts of the globe continue to remain outside such activity.

In addition to these specialist events, accounting history sessions also feature at national and international conferences on accounting, particularly those focusing on interdisciplinary and critical perspectives on accounting.

Education in the discipline

It was suggested earlier that although the growth of accounting history may be partly understood as a response to the expansion of accounting education, this was not attended by societal demands for the inclusion of the subject in the curriculum (Clark 1996). Accounting historians are primarily engaged in teaching modern-day accounting and have had to campaign hard for the introduction of research-led courses in their sub-discipline. Where it does feature, accounting history tends to be taught as a specialist module in the later stages of an undergraduate degree or as a component of graduate programmes.

In a period when research was a less dominant feature on the academic agenda, the first priority of many accounting historians and their disciplinary associations was to pursue the integration of the subject in the accounting curriculum. In 1970, the Committee on Accounting History of the American Accounting Association lamented the absence of historical instruction in accounting programmes and supported the development of graduate-level courses on the subject. Indeed, one of the Committee's leading members, Richard H. Homburger, had been a forceful advocate of the integration of history in the accounting curriculum as early as the 1950s (Homburger 1958).

During the 1970s, establishing a course in accounting history was perceived as a tangible manifestation of the 'arrival' of the subject in universities (Previts 1977). From 1984, the Accounting History Education Committee of the Academy of Accounting Historians sought to facilitate this by assembling and disseminating materials for integration in accounting courses (Coffman et al. 1989). The Academy's Syllabi Project of 1994 focused on encouraging accounting doctoral students to include a historical component in their dissertations, as well as collecting accounting history syllabi and materials for teaching. The Academy also supports an award for Innovation in Accounting History Education.

The integration of accounting history in the curriculum has proved a difficult objective given that the content of accounting programmes is heavily determined by the need for students to be instructed in the expanding technical and regulatory requirements of the craft, as enforced by professional accreditation, and where the value of historical study is often questioned in the modern business school. However, periodic calls from accounting organisations and professional firms, particularly in the USA, for more broadly educated accounting graduates have given cause for optimism even though the rhetoric has seldom become manifest in a requirement for instruction in accounting history (Coffman et al. 1993). In the UK, there is often scope in the latter stages of degree schemes for the inclusion of accounting history modules where there exists a resident accounting historian anxious to accommodate the demands of teaching quality agencies for research-led teaching. Here the emphasis has tended to be on instituting separate accounting history modules as opposed to integrating the subject into mainstream accounting courses. In Japan, accounting history is taught in some undergraduate and graduate programmes.

Accounting historians have tended to make the case for the inclusion of accounting history in teaching programmes by emphasising its capacity to enhance practical and theoretical understandings of accounting, increased awareness of the issues surrounding the rules and techniques applied in the modern day and its potential for contextualising student knowledge of accounting (Flegm 1991). Other commentators have emphasised that attempts to legitimate accounting history in the curriculum should be based not only on its capacity for knowledge enhancement but also on the intellectual and personal skills that the study of history develops (Walker 2002).

A number of American authors have related their experiences of teaching accounting history either as a separate module or integrated in mainstream accounting courses. These authors have also discussed the impediments to the inclusion of the subject in the curriculum, the use of historical materials in teaching, the stage of the programme at which the subject is best introduced, and the teaching methods most effectively deployed (Homburger 1958; Peragello 1974; Wichita State University 1978; Bloom and Collins 1988; Coffman et al. 1993; Armernic and

Elitzur 1992; Vruwink and Deines 2002; Williams and Schwartz 2002). Some commentators have explored the extent to which the subject is actually taught and the findings have been somewhat disappointing (Slocum and Sriram 2001; van Fleet and Wren 2006).

Conclusion

Becher and Trowler (2001: 41) suggest that the existence of an identifiable academic discipline is indicated by its separate organisational structures, particularly in the form of academic departments. While some of its practitioners have coalesced around university and cross-university research units, the primary affiliation of the majority of accounting historians is the department of accounting and finance and the business school. The emergence of departments of accounting history remains a distant prospect. Becher and Trowler also refer to the emergence of a 'free-standing international community' with its own associations and specialist journals. Judged by these criteria, accounting history has a more convincing claim to disciplinary status.

Accounting history is best understood as an expanding and maturing sub-discipline of accounting. It is a sub-discipline which embraces a number of specialisms and diverse research traditions. These features, together with the receptivity of its practitioners to fresh methodological and theoretical insights, ensure that the status of accounting history as a separate sub-discipline is seldom questioned, particularly when compared with the experience of its close neighbour, business history (Gourvish 1995). Indeed, accounting history displays increasing signs of 'free-standing' autonomy from the parent discipline of accounting. Guthrie and Parker (2006) assert that the advance and academic maturation of accounting history have been attended by diminishing engagement with the wider accounting community, a development contrary to the spirit of interdisciplinarity which encouraged the expansion of this and other sub-fields of accounting from the 1980s.

The fact that accounting historians increasingly congregate at their own specialist conferences and publish in journals devoted to their specialism are indeed signs of greater autonomy and introversion but they are also indicative of a confident sub-discipline whose practitioners have fought hard to legitimise their presence within a home discipline which emphasises its contemporaneity. Complaints about the increasing autonomy of sub-disciplines are not only levelled at accounting historians. In the discipline of history it is perceived that, while the 'fashionable breeze of specialization' (Gardiner 1988) has extended the scope of knowledge fragmentation, it has also tended towards disorientation. As noted in the Introduction to the *Routledge Companion*, calls have been made for specialists in various sub-disciplines of history to reconnect with each other, reveal the significance of their findings to empirical and epistemological debates of wider concern in the parent discipline, and revisit synthesis. The appearance of this *Routledge Companion* represents a partial response to this call by attempting to present insights into the current state of accounting history knowledge in a single volume.

The growing and increasingly autonomous sub-discipline of accounting history is not without its problems. There remain marked micro and macro spatial variations in the dignification of the craft. Expansion and rising esteem in many European sites contrast with the bleaker prospect for accounting history in the USA. The 'Anglo-American hegemony' in the disciplinary associations and publication media of accounting history remains a source of frustration among scholars operating in languages and cultures other than English. Concern has been expressed about a research agenda that focuses predominantly on the history of accounting in the industrial and post-industrial ages and on organizations that inhabit the economic sphere.

The research agenda is yet to embrace Central and South America, Africa and much of Asia and displays limited interdisciplinary engagement with the wider community of historians. The extent to which the results of accounting history scholarship have penetrated the accounting curriculum is a source of disappointment. But as the contributions in this volume show, accounting history is a sub-discipline where considerable advances in knowledge have been made in recent decades, advances which have enriched understandings of accounting, history and the increasing range of other disciplines from which it draws inspiration.

Acknowledgments

I am grateful to the following for their insights to the development of disciplinary associations in accounting history: Richard P. Brief, Garry Carnegie, John R. Edwards, Takehisa Hashimoto, Michael Mumford, Masayoshi Noguchi, Robert H. Parker and Gary Previts.

Key works

American Accounting Association (1970) Committee on Accounting History is something of a foundational document in accounting history. Its attempt to legitimate the discipline, identify research subject-matter and sources has enduring relevance.

Carmona (2004) offers an important exposition of the need to embrace a wider community of scholars in accounting history research.

Coffman et al. (1989) and **Coffman et al. (1998)** chart the history of the Academy of Accounting Historians, the principal disciplinary association in accounting history.

Fleischman and Radcliffe (2005) reviews the 'golden decade' of accounting history and is a potent expression of concerns about the future of the discipline in the USA.

References

The Accountant (1970–1).
Accounting Historians Notebook (various).
Accounting History (1976–86).
Accounting History Newsletter (1980).
American Accounting Association (1970) Committee on Accounting History, *Accounting Review*, 45 (Supplement): 53–64.
Anderson, M. (2002) An analysis of the first ten volumes of research in Accounting, Business and Financial History, *Accounting, Business & Financial History*, 12 (1): 1–24.
Armernic, J. and Elitzur, R. (1992) Using annual reports in teaching: letting the past benefit the present, *Accounting Historians Journal*, 19 (1): 29–50.
Badua, F. A., Previts, G. J. and Vasarhelyi, M. A. (2003) The Accounting Historians Journal index: employing the accounting research database to profile and support research, in R. K. Fleischman, V. S. Radcliffe, and P. A. Shoemaker (eds) *Doing Accounting History*, pp. 203–16 (Oxford: Elsevier).
Beattie, V. and Goodacre, A. (2004) Publishing patterns within the UK accounting and finance academic community, *British Accounting Review*, 36 (1): 7–44.
Becher, T. and Trowler, P. R. (2001) *Academic Tribes and Territories: Intellectual Enquiry and the Culture of Disciplines* (Buckingham: SRHE/Open University Press).

Blau, P. M. (1973) *The Organization of Academic Work* (New York: John Wiley & Sons).

Bloom, R. and Collins, M. (1988) Motivating students with an historical perspective in financial accounting courses, *Journal of Accounting Education*, 6 (1): 103–15.

Boyns, T. and Edwards, J.R. (1990) Editorial, *Accounting, Business & Financial History*, 1 (1): 1–4.

Boyns, T. and Nikitin, M. (2001) Introduction, *Accounting, Business & Financial History*, 11 (1): 1–6.

Boys, P. and Freer, J. (eds) (1992) *Accounting History 1976–1986* (London and New York: Garland).

Brown, R. (ed.) (1905) *A History of Accounting and Accountants* (Edinburgh: T. C. and E. C. Jack).

Carmona, S. (2004) Accounting history research and its diffusion in an international context, *Accounting History*, 9 (3): 7–23.

Carmona, S. (2006) Performance reviews, the impact of accounting research, and the role of publication forms, *Advances in Accounting*, 22: 241–67.

Carmona, S. and Zan, L. (2002) Mapping variety in the history of accounting and management practices, *European Accounting Review*, 11 (2): 291–304.

Carnegie, G. D. and Napier, C. J. (1996) Critical and interpretive histories: insights into accounting's present and future through its past, *Accounting, Auditing & Accountability Journal*, 9 (3): 7–39.

Carnegie, G. D. and Potter, B. N. (2000) Publishing patterns in specialist accounting history journals in the English language, 1996–1999, *Accounting Historians Journal*, 27 (2): 177–98.

Carnegie, G. D. and Wolnizer, P. W. (eds) (1996) *Accounting History Newsletter, 1980–1989 and Accounting History, 1989–1994: A Tribute to Robert William Gibson* (New York: Garland).

Carnegie, G. D., McWatters, C. S. and Potter, B. N. (2003) The development of the specialist accounting history literature in the English language. An analysis by gender, *Accounting, Auditing & Accountability Journal*, 16 (2): 186–207.

Chatfield, M. (1977) *A History of Accounting Thought* (Huntington, NY: R.E Krieger).

Chatfield, M. and Vangermeersch, R. (1996) *The History of Accounting: An International Encyclopedia* (New York: Garland).

Clark, B. R. (1987) *The Academic Life: Small Worlds, Different Worlds* (Princeton, NJ: The Carnegie Foundation for the Advancement of Teaching).

Clark, B. R. (1996) Substantive growth and innovative organization: new categories for higher education research, *Higher Education*, 32 (4): 417–30.

Coffman, E. N., Roberts, A. R. and Previts, G. J. (1989) A history of the Academy of Accounting Historians 1973–1988, *Accounting Historians Journal*, 16 (2): 155–206.

Coffman, E. N., Roberts, A. R. and Previts, G. J. (1998) A history of the Academy of Accounting Historians 1989–1998, *Accounting Historians Journal*, 25 (2): 167–210.

Coffman, E. N., Tondkar, R. H. and Previts, G. J. (1993) Integrating accounting history into financial accounting courses, *Issues in Accounting Education*, 8 (1): 18–39.

The Commission of Accounting History of AECA (2006) *De Computis*, No. 4: 183–96.

Contabilità e Cultura Aziendale. Available HTTP: <http://www.cca.unisi.it> (accessed 15 October 2006).

Cooper, C. and Puxty, A. (1996) On the proliferation of accounting (his)tories, *Critical Perspectives on Accounting*, 7 (3): 285–313.

De Computis. Revista Española de Historia de la Contabilidad. Available HTTP: <http://www.decomputis.org> (accessed 15 October 2006).

Dogan, M. (1997) The new social sciences: cracks in the disciplinary walls, *International Social Science Journal*, 49 (3): 429–43.

Dunlop, A. B. G. (1970) Accounting history: exhibition and first international symposium, *Accountant's Magazine*, 73 (November): 552–6.

Edwards, J. R. (ed.) (2000) *The History of Accounting: Critical Perspectives on Business and Management* (London: Routledge).

Edwards, J. R. (2004) Some problems and challenges in accounting history research. Paper presented at the 10th World Congress of Accounting Historians, St. Louis and Oxford, August.

Eley, G. (1979) Some recent tendencies in social histories, in G. G. Iggers and H. T. Parker (eds) *International Handbook of Historical Studies: Contemporary Research and Theory*, pp. 55–70 (Westport Conn: Greenwood Press).

Elzinga, A. (1987) Internal and external regulatives in research and higher education systems, in R. Premfors (ed.) *Disciplinary Perspectives on Higher Education and Research*, Report No. 37 (Stockholm: University of Stockholm Press).

Flegm, E. H. (1991) The relevance of history in accounting education: some observations, *Journal of Accounting Education*, 9 (2): 355–63.

Fleischman, R. K. (ed.) (2006), *Accounting History* (London: Sage).

Fleischman, R. K. and Radcliffe, V. S. (2005) The roaring nineties: accounting history comes of age, *Accounting Historians Journal*, 32 (1): 61–109.

Fleischman, R. K., Radcliffe, V. S. and Shoemaker, P. A. (2003) (eds) *Doing Accounting History* (Oxford: JAI Elsevier).

Gaffikin, M. J. R. (1981) Toward a taxonomy of historical research in accounting, *Accounting History*, 5 (1&2): 22–62.

Gardiner, J. (1988) Introduction, in J. Gardiner (ed.) *What is History Today?* pp. 1–3 (Basingstoke, Macmillan Education Ltd).

Garner, S. P and Hughes, M. (1978) *Readings in Accounting Development* (New York: Arno Press).

Goldberg, L. (1987) *Dynamics of an Entity: The History of the Accounting Association of Australia and New Zealand* (Accounting Association of Australia and New Zealand).

Gourvish, T. (1995) Business history: in defence of the empirical approach?, *Accounting, Business & Financial History*, 5 (1): 3–16.

Gray, R. and Helliar, C. (1994) UK accounting academics and publication: an exploration of observable variables associated with publication output, *British Accounting Review*, 26 (3): 235–54.

Green, W. L. (1930) *History and Survey of Accountancy* (New York: Standard Text).

Guthrie, J. and Parker, L. (2006) The coming out of accounting research specialisms, *Accounting, Auditing & Accountability Journal*, 19 (1): 5–16.

Have, O. Ten (1976) *The History of Accountancy* (Palo Alto, CA: Bay Books).

Henkel, M. (2000) *Academic Identities and Policy Change in Higher Education* (London: Jessica Kingsley).

Homburger, R. H. (1958) Study of history: gateway to perspective, *Accounting Review*, 33 (3): 501–3.

Johnson, H. T. (1975) The role of accounting history in the study of modern business enterprise, *Accounting Review*, 50 (3): 444–50.

Jordanova, L. (2000) *History in Practice* (London: Arnold).

Littleton, A. C. (1933) *Accounting Evolution to 1900* (New York: Institute Publishing Co).

Littleton, A. C. and Yamey, B. S. (eds) (1956) *Studies in the History of Accounting* (London: Sweet and Maxwell).

Lu, W. and Aiken, M. (2003) Accounting history: Chinese contributions and challenges, *Accounting, Business & Financial History*, 13 (1): 1–3.

Marwick, A. (1989) *The Nature of History* (Basingstoke: Macmillan).

Metzger, W. P. (1987) The academic profession in the United States, in B. R. Clark (ed.) *The Academic Profession. National, Disciplinary, and Institutional Settings*, pp. 123–208 (Berkeley: University of California Press).

Mumford, M. (1994) Book review of *Accounting History 1976–1986*, *Accounting, Business & Financial History*, 4 (3): 462–4.

Murray, D. (1930) *Chapters in the History of Bookkeeping, Accountancy and Commercial Arithmetic* (Glasgow: Jackson Wylie & Co).

Napier, C. J. (2002) The historian as auditor: facts, judgments as evidence, *Accounting Historians Journal*, 29 (2): 131–55.

Napier, C. J. (2006) Accounts of change: 30 years of historical accounting research, *Accounting, Organizations and Society*, 31 (4/5): 445–507.

Nishikawa, K. (1975), Historical studies in recent years in Japan, *Accounting Historian*, 2 (3): 1, 7.

Parker, L. D. and Graves, F. (eds) (1989), *Methodology and Method in History: A Bibliography* (New York: Garland).

Parker, R. H. (ed.) (1980) *Bibliographies for Accounting Historians* (New York: Arno Press).

Parker, R. H. (1981) The Third International Congress of Accounting Historians, *Journal of European Economic History*, 10 (3): 743–54.

Parker, R. H. and Yamey, B. S. (eds) (1994) *Accounting History: Some British Contributions* (Oxford: Clarendon Press).

Parker, R. H., Lemarchand, Y. and Boyns, T. (1997) Introduction, *Accounting, Business & Financial History*, 7 (3): 251–7.

Peragello, E. (1974) Challenges facing teachers of accounting history, *Accounting Historians Journal*, 1 (2): 1, 3.

Previts, G. J. (1977) Pawing over the past, *Accounting History*, 2 (1): 34–8.

Previts, G. J., Parker, L. D. and Coffman, E. N. (1990) Accounting history: definition and relevance, *Abacus*, 26 (1): 1–16.

RAE (2002) RAE 2001 – Overview reports from the panels. Available HTTP: <http://www.hero.ac.uk/rae/overview> (accessed 15 October 2006).

RAE (2006) RAE 2008 Panel criteria and working methods. Available HTTP: http://rae.ac.uk/pubs/2006/01 (accessed 15 October 2006).

Slocum, E. L. and Sriram, R. S. (2001) Accounting history: a survey of academic interest in the U.S., *Accounting Historians Journal*, 28 (1): 111–30.

van Fleet, D. D. and Wren, D. A. (2006) Accounting history in today's business schools, *Accounting Historians Notebook*, 29 (1): 10–20.

Vincent, J. (2001) *An Intelligent Person's Guide to History* (London: Duckbacks).

Vruwink, D. R and Deines, D. (2002) The case for teaching accounting history with accounting theory in the undergraduate curriculum, *Accounting Historians Notebook*, 24 (1): 15, 22–4.

Walker, S. P. (2002) Legitimating history in the accounting curriculum, *Accounting Historians Notebook*, 24 (1): 12–15.

Walker, S. P. (2004) The search for clues in accounting history, in C. Humphrey and B. Lee (eds), *Real-Life Guide to Accounting Research*, pp. 5–21 (Oxford: Elsevier).

Walker, S. P. (2005) Accounting in history, *Accounting Historians Journal*, 33 (2): 233–59.

Walker, S. P. (2006) Current trends in accounting history, *Irish Accounting Review*, 13 (1): 107–21.

Wallace, R. S. O. (1997) The development of accounting research in the UK, in T. E. Cooke and C. W. Nobes (eds) *The Development of Accounting in an International Context: A Festschrift in Honour of R.H. Parker*, pp. 218–54 (London: Routledge).

Whittington, G. (1995) Is accounting becoming too interesting? Sir Julian Hodge Accounting Lectures, University of Wales, Aberystwyth.

Wichita State University (1978) On the present and future importance of accounting history, *Accounting Historians Journal*, 5 (2): 63–5.

Williams, S. V. and Schwartz, B. N. (2002) Accounting history in undergraduate introductory financial accounting courses: an exploratory study, *Journal of Education for Business*, 77 (4): 198–203.

Woolf, A. H. (1912) *A Short History of Accountants and Accountancy* (London: Gee).

2

Historiography

Christopher J. Napier

Overview

Accounting historiography involves a study of how and why accounting has been written about as an object of historical study, how historical writings on accounting have developed, and the main topics and themes of accounting history. While Chapter 3 studies the main subject matter of historical accounting research in recent years, this chapter concentrates on the development of accounting history as a body of knowledge, and reviews issues relating to the historical craft, such as the nature of evidence, how the accounting historian draws conclusions from evidence, the role of theory in historical accounting research, and how accounting history is communicated – the centrality of narrative and the possibility of other modes of history-writing. Although historical accounting research has at times been antiquarian, with an interest in collecting examples of old accounting materials, much recent accounting history adopts an interpretive and critical attitude to understanding the past. Accounting historians may be classified in terms of their underlying theoretical perspective, with different historians advocating the relevance of a range of economic and social theories for the understanding of accounting's past, how accounting affects organisations and society, and change processes within accounting. Accounting historians continue to investigate both ideas and methods within accounting itself and the impact of accounting in broader contexts. The focus of enquiry includes both primary archival material and secondary sources.

Defining accounting history

Over the past 40 years, there have been several attempts to clarify the nature and purposes of accounting history, from the American Accounting Association's Committee on Accounting History (1970) to the survey of historical accounting research in the 1990s presented by Fleischman and Radcliffe (2005) and the present author's review of historical accounting research published in the leading journal *Accounting, Organizations and Society* (Napier 2006). Many of the central contributions were summarised by Oldroyd (1999), who noted the increasing tendency of those seeking to understand accounting history to develop categories into which different research approaches (and researchers) may be placed.

Traditional and new histories

The most significant of these categorisations is the divide between 'traditional' and 'new' accounting history, the latter being described as 'a loose assemblage of often quite disparate research questions and issues' (Miller *et al.* 1991: 396), but characterised by an intensive use of social theory to define research questions and provide a structure for understanding and interpreting the research results. Although the labelling of social theory-driven historical accounting research as 'new' was perhaps a sign of arrogance, it helped to expand interest in historical research beyond the relatively small group of specialists who had previously dominated accounting history. Despite the fears of 'traditional' researchers that the 'new' accounting history was downgrading careful archival research in favour of grand theorising (Fleischman and Tyson 1997), the general tendency of recent years has been for researchers from different 'streams' to appreciate the complementary contributions that their respective approaches may make to an understanding of accounting's past (Fleischman and Radcliffe 2003).

The debate between the 'traditional' and 'new' historians, even though it has resulted in a form of rapprochement, has emphasised historiographic issues. What is the role of theory in historical accounting research, and which theories are likely to prove most cogent? What counts as a significant research question, as evidence, as reasoning? Is narrative the main way in which histories are communicated, or is there space for a 'counter-narrative' (Funnell 1998a)? How does the historian cope with the absence of written or even oral evidence? If early accounting historians did not reflect on these issues, more recent historians have had to ask themselves questions such as these, even if their actual practice as historians remains close to 'tradition'.

An alternative categorisation

Instead of the 'traditional'/'new' dichotomy, it may be more helpful to separate historical accounting research into two other categories. The first of these may be called 'history of accounting'. Here, the researcher's objective is to understand accounting as a set of procedures or practices. Researching the 'history of accounting' is likely to involve the study of original accounting records, or secondary literature such as books and professional journals documenting how accounting was actually undertaken in the past. Researchers may seek to explain as well as describe the phenomena of past accounting: this may involve drawing on a theory to help pose and answer questions as to why accounting took the form that it did, why individuals and organisations adopted particular methods and rejected others, why accounting ideas emerged and changed at particular points in time. Theoretical explanations could be both economic (for example, that a particular accounting method provided reliable information at lowest cost) and social (for example, that an emerging accounting idea was influenced by new discourses within a specific society).

Much of the research within the 'history of accounting' category is likely to focus on technical matters such as the details of accounting practices and the form and content of accounting records, but such research is likely to go beyond simple description in order to develop understandings. For example, 'history of accounting' research could be motivated by a desire to understand how current accounting ideas and methods have developed. A concept that is often appealed to in this category of historical accounting research is 'evolution'

31

(American Accounting Association 1970). Although this may imply that the researcher sees modern-day accounting practices and ideas as the culmination of a process of progress, some researchers regard a study of accounting's past as providing a perspective from which today's practices may be viewed as contingent rather than necessary (Napier 2001).

The other category is 'socio-historical accounting research', where the researcher is primarily concerned with how accounting impacts on specific individuals and organisations, and more broadly on society. This category of historical accounting research shares characteristics with historical sociology (the study of past events using methods and theories drawn from sociology or social theory). Much of the 'new' accounting history emerging in the late 1980s and early 1990s showed the clear influence of theorists such as Marx, Weber, Foucault, Habermas, Derrida, Latour and Giddens, as well as sociological ideas such as institutional theory, feminist/gender theory and social constructivism. This category of historical accounting research often used an examination of key events (in some cases quite recent, in other cases several decades if not centuries in the past) as a means of gaining some insight into current situations. A common theme of such research is that accounting plays deep and complex roles in modern society that need to be excavated and revealed in order to gain an adequate understanding of how individuals are controlled, restricted and in some cases enabled through the use of records and calculations.

The two categories of historical accounting research are, or should be, mutually supportive, if we accept that accounting is shaped by its environment but also feeds back into shaping the world in which it operates. For example, the development of standard costing in the years around 1900 may be documented by reference to contemporary writings by accountants and engineers (Epstein and Epstein 1974), or explained as a specific case of the rational pursuit of profit by businesspeople (Johnson and Kaplan 1987: ch. 3). In these approaches, the researcher seeks to understand and explain the emergence and adoption of a specific accounting method as a consequence of external environmental factors. A 'new' accounting history of standard costing could also seek to explain the emergence of the method, but now by reference to emerging ideas of the administration of society centring on attempts to make individuals, in society and in specific organisations, 'visible' and 'calculable' (Miller and O'Leary 1987). In this explanation, standard costing is not just a form of measurement but actually acts on people in the organisation to affect and change their behaviours. It also presents a model that can inspire the use of similar types of calculation for controlling and modifying the behaviour of individuals in other social settings. The object of research is an understanding, not just of an accounting method, but more significantly of the impact of that method on broader social ideas and practices.

The development of accounting history

European beginnings

In his comprehensive international survey of nineteenth- and early twentieth-century accounting researchers, Mattessich (2003) provides a list of early contributors to the literature of accounting history, bringing out the extent to which Italian and, to a lesser degree, German scholars dominated the field until an English-language literature of accounting history began to emerge around 1900. Mattessich also indicates the continuing significance of a range of national traditions of historical accounting research, with important work in countries such as France, Belgium, the Netherlands and Spain within Europe and an emerging interest in accounting history in Japan. The 'Italian school' of accounting history has been explored in depth by Zan (1994), who documents the way in which scholarly writers on accounting theory and practice, from the nineteenth century, tended to support their current theoretical analyses by interpreting, or reinterpreting, the development of accounting ideas and methods. For example, Giovanni Cerboni, a leading member of the 'Tuscan school' of accounting theorists, and advocate of *logismografia* as a 'scientific' method for 'representing administrative facts' (Zan 1994: 281), underpinned his theoretical expositions (for example, Cerboni 1886) with a chronological survey of Italian writings on bookkeeping and accounting, and surviving Italian accounting records (Cerboni 1889). This trend was to continue into the twentieth century, with major Italian textbooks such as Besta's *La Ragioneria* (1922) containing chapters on such historical topics as early Italian double-entry treatises and records, and other accounting approaches such as the 'cameralist' system used by governmental bodies.

An early German contributor to the accounting history literature was Ernst Jäger, who was typical of early historians of accounting in concentrating on the historical development of double-entry bookkeeping (Jäger 1874), with much reference to early Italian and French sources. A greater focus on accounting's development in Germany itself was offered by Penndorf (1913), drawing on archival materials and early treatises. Early accounting historians were often bibliophiles, fascinated with reading, and in some cases collecting, early books on bookkeeping, accounting and commercial practices. An important collector was Karl Kheil, whose books were ultimately acquired by the Institute of Chartered Accountants in England and Wales (Yamey *et al.* 1963: v). Kheil had translated the first printed book on double-entry bookkeeping, Luca Pacioli's *Tractatus de Computis et Scripturis* (part of his *Summa de Arithmetica*) of 1494, into German (Kheil 1896); there had been an earlier German translation by Jäger (1876). Kheil's book was translated into Spanish (Kheil 1902) by Fernando López y López under the grand title *Historia de la Contabilidad* ('History of Accounting'), representing one of the earliest contributions to Spanish accounting historiography (González Ferrando, 2006). This interest in early writings on bookkeeping has been one of the more significant and persistent historiographic trends, and translations of books such as Pacioli's continue to emerge. The quincentenary of the publication of Pacioli's *Summa* stimulated renewed interest in this first and highly symbolic accounting textbook (see, for example, Hernández-Esteve 1994, for a discussion of translations, including his own). However, Pacioli's name has been regularly mobilised by accounting writers wanting to lend the authority of history to their work (Carnegie and Napier 1996: 9–11).

English-language contributions

The bibliographic theme is also shown in one of the earliest English-language histories, Benjamin Foster's *The Origin and Progress of Book-keeping* (1852). This is an annotated list of mainly British and American books on accounting published before 1850. Previts and Merino (1998: 80) describe this book as 'a unique and historical reference point', as it identifies a wide range of early English-language writings on accounting. Other early English-language histories demonstrate another important historiographic trend: an interest in accountants – the people involved in preparing and increasingly auditing accounts – as well as accounting as a practice. An early example of this type of history was Beresford Worthington's *Professional Accountants* (1895), and the most important was Richard Brown's *A History of Accounting and Accountants* (1905). This book, compiled by the Secretary of the Society of Accountants in Edinburgh to mark the 50th anniversary of the Society's Royal Charter, was at the same time a celebration of the professional status of chartered accountants in Scotland and propaganda for the idea that the accountancy profession should be regarded as equal in status to more established occupational groupings such as medicine and law, on the basis of accounting's deep historical roots. Hence the book emphasises the early origins of accountancy practice in ancient and classical periods as well as more current forms of accounting. Another early English-language general history was Woolf's *A Short History of Accountants and Accountancy* (1912).

Although accounting was established as a component of university business education in many European countries by the early years of the twentieth century (Zambon 1996), university-level accounting education was slower to emerge in the UK (Napier 1996) and the USA (Previts and Merino 1998: 150). One of the earliest full professors of accounting in the USA, Henry Rand Hatfield, appealed to accounting's early origins and long history as a justification for its inclusion on the university curriculum (Hatfield 1924; see also Zeff 2000), and his arguments were aided by an emerging interest among social and economic historians about the role of accounting in business development. The most significant contribution came from the German economic historian Werner Sombart, whose views were expressed in his compendious *Der moderne Kapitalismus* (1919 – see Chapter 15 for a discussion of the relationship between accounting and capitalism). The links between calculation and economic success drawn by Sombart had previously been expressed by other scholars, for example, Max Weber (Miller and Napier 1993: 635). Contemporary accounting historians, however, found that Sombart's emphasis on double-entry bookkeeping resonated with their own bibliographic interests in double-entry treatises stemming from Pacioli's initial work. In *Accounting Evolution to 1900*, undoubtedly the most influential English-language work on accounting history of the pre-war period, A. C. Littleton (1933) drew heavily on double-entry bookkeeping treatises to narrate a story of progress.

Littleton was aware that accounting could have an impact on the social and economic environment in which it operated, but put more stress on the external factors that stimulated accounting to change and develop. He suggested that there were various preconditions for the emergence of a systematic bookkeeping: writing, arithmetic, private property, money, credit, commerce and capital. These preconditions seem to fit double-entry particularly well, since it is a written, monetarised method of recording commercial transactions (frequently based on credit rather than cash exchange), and it emerges alongside modern capitalist economies. As Miller and Napier (1993) note, the tendency to equate systematic accounting with double-entry bookkeeping had historiographic significance, because it encouraged researchers to focus their attention on double-entry records (or, given the scarcity of surviving accounting documents, on double-entry treatises), at the expense of other forms of systematic record keeping and accounting (such as the charge and discharge system used on medieval manors and in a wide range of 'stewardship' contexts until comparatively recently (Baxter 1980)). Littleton's work also tended to induce a 'periodisation' in the thinking of accounting historians, with accounting appearing to emerge as a systematic activity with the Italian Renaissance and the coming of double entry, the Industrial Revolution creating a need for more sophisticated records of cost for manufacturers, and the emergence of the modern corporation stimulating a demand for professional accountants to act as auditors and business consultants (Carnegie and Napier 1996: 12).

By the 1930s and 1940s, accounting's past and historical development were attracting interest from economists and economic and social historians as well as accounting scholars. A key contributor to the more traditional accounting history literature over several decades has been the economist Basil Yamey, who was one of many accounting historians to be fascinated by old books (Yamey 1978). His critique of the 'Sombart Thesis' on the importance of double-entry bookkeeping to the rise of capitalism (Yamey 1949) was based on a study of early bookkeeping treatises in several languages. Yamey spent most of his career at the London

School of Economics (LSE), where early accounting scholars such as Ronald Edwards (1937) had shown an interest in accounting history. After the Second World War, when the LSE became one of the most important centres of accounting education and research in the UK, historical research continued to be of great interest to teachers such as Baxter (1956), Solomons (1952) and Edey (1956).

With Littleton, Yamey edited *Studies in the History of Accounting* (Littleton and Yamey 1956), a collection of both reprinted material and specially-commissioned articles covering a wide geographical and chronological spread. Chapters such as those by de Ste. Croix (1956) on Greek and Roman accounting, de Roover (1956) on bookkeeping in medieval Italy, Jackson (1956) on British bookkeeping treatises, Pollins (1956) on early railway accounting, Edey and Panitpakdi (1956) on the law relating to company accounting, and Nishikawa (1956) on early use of double entry in Japan, have remained classics of the literature. The collection, however, reflects preoccupations of many accounting historians of the time in being international until around 1600, largely Anglocentric thereafter, with a focus on double-entry bookkeeping and little attention given to costing and management accounting, or to the accountancy profession.

Developing a discipline

Similar biases may be observed in a range of general and more specific histories emerging in the 1950s and 1960s. The substantial accounting history offered by the Italian scholar Melis (1950) concentrates on the period before 1840, with emphasis being placed on accounting in the ancient world, a description of medieval and early Renaissance Italian records (mainly double-entry), a review of treatises after Pacioli with little reference to practice, and a hurried coverage of more modern developments. Melis did not neglect cost accounting, but exemplified it using double-entry accounts. A general history written in French by Vlaemminck (1956), a Belgian scholar, attempts to be comprehensive by beginning in the ancient world and finishing with modern management accounting (the final part of the book is entitled 'accounting in the age of the scientific organization'), though again with an emphasis on double-entry practice before 1500 and double-entry theory after that date. Outside Europe, a pioneering history of cost accounting by Garner (1954) described the emergence of ideas and methods relating to the measurement of production cost in the period up to 1925, with a particular emphasis on the writings of accountants and engineers. Again, descriptions in articles and textbooks of actual or potential accounting methods are allowed to stand in for reference to original business records.

In the mid-1960s, Parker (1965) was able to compile a bibliography of 231 items, ranging from book-length general histories (in a range of languages) to short papers and notes, covering a wide range of topics, and almost all written in English. By far the most prolific author in Parker's list was Yamey, with 19 entries (Raymond de Roover had seven entries, Littleton six, while most authors had one or at most two entries). Early Italian accounting features strongly, as does mercantile accounting from England and Scotland. On the other hand, few items reflect interest in accounting after about 1850, in particular themes such as costing, accounting by companies and auditing. With the growth in accounting as an academic discipline in many countries during the 1950s and 1960s, historical accounting research was to grow alongside other research approaches, and the establishment of new academic journals provided a wider range of outlets for scholars.

As well as experiencing a growth in publication opportunities, accounting history began to benefit from institutional interest (see Chapter 1). In 1968, the American Accounting Association set up a Committee on Accounting History. The committee defined accounting history as 'the study of the evolution in accounting thought, practices, and institutions in response to changes in the environment and societal needs', noting that accounting history 'also considers the effect that this evolution has worked on the environment' (American Accounting Association 1970: 53). An understanding of how accounting had changed in the past was seen as providing an appreciation of change processes in accounting.

Further institutional developments stimulated historical accounting research. In 1970, an International Congress of Accounting Historians took place in Brussels, organised by Ernest Stevelinck, a professional accountant and bibliophile who had been responsible for the first translation of Pacioli's *Tractatus* into French. In the USA, the Academy of Accounting Historians emerged in 1973 and began to publish a newsletter, which from 1977 became the *Accounting Historians Journal*. National accounting history societies were set up in a number of countries. Yet by the mid–1970s, historical accounting research was a fringe activity, with a small number of dedicated researchers and a rather larger group who combined an interest in accounting history with research addressing more contemporary issues, working in the context of a 'mainstream' of accounting researchers who had no interest in, and indeed strong theoretical and methodological objections to, historical accounting research.

Reaching maturity

By the 1970s, a desire to understand change processes in accounting had led various researchers to examine historical accounting research for insights. Goldberg, an Australian academic accountant with a strong interest in accounting history, provided both an intellectual and a methodological justification for studying accounting from a historical perspective, suggesting that this would:

> give us appreciation of how our current practices and problems came into being . . . [I]t should provide tools of thought for solving problems, not only by showing us how our predecessors solved or failed to solve some of their problems but also through its requirement for painstaking, meticulous accuracy in the examination of material.
>
> (Goldberg 1974: 410)

However, to the emerging generation of researchers imbued with a desire to understand accounting not just as a technical but also as a social phenomenon, this type of history was regarded as 'partial, uncritical, atheoretical and intellectually isolated' (Hopwood 1985: 366). A new, more theoretically grounded style of accounting history was called for.

One obvious theoretical foundation for accounting history was economics, and the emerging transaction cost economics that was also beginning to influence research into the choice of accounting policies and procedures in modern organisations began to appear in historical writing (Johnson 1981, 1983). Earlier historical researchers had tended to overlook the modern corporation as a site for accounting, but economists were identifying a central role for accounting in such organisations, to provide the co-ordination that in a market setting was achieved through the price mechanism. Accounting numbers could be seen as economically useful within a complex organisation for tracing costs to products, not only for control purposes (for example, helping to reveal waste) but also as a crucial input into the determination of prices for businesses that were no longer price takers in competitive economies but often price makers in situations of monopoly or oligopoly.

Further, economic theory provided uses for accounting information not just within the organisation but also externally in a world where corporate ownership was rapidly becoming divorced from control. Accounting could be used to monitor managers and both prevent them from acting against the interests of owners (and indeed other external stakeholders) and, more positively, provide the basis for performance-based incentive plans. Within such a conceptual framework for the modern corporation, accounting could be regarded as a technology of economic calculation, but certainly not a neutral technology. If some commentators (for example, Watts and Zimmerman 1983) tended to view conflicts over accounting policy choice and audit as unproblematic workings-out of economic processes, other researchers were beginning to regard such conflicts as amenable to understanding and analysis through a range of social and political theories that saw the conflicts as anything but unproblematic.

Marxist perspectives on accounting history

A particular example of theory based on social conflict is Marxism. Within the historical accounting literature, early advocates for a Marxist accounting history were Tinker and Neimark (1987, 1988). These writers argue that the transaction cost economics view of the role of accounting emphasises the concept of 'economic efficiency', so observed accounting practices are theorised as the least-cost solutions to technical problems of co-ordination and management. Tinker and Neimark criticise this view on three main grounds. First, they suggest that the basic concept of 'efficiency' is ideological rather than socially neutral; second, they identify a circularity of reasoning (by definition, only efficient methods survive, so the methods that survive must by definition be efficient); and, third, they note that transactions cost explanations tend to take the 'human' dimension out of the analysis (Tinker and Neimark 1988: 57). By contrast, it is suggested that the modern business organisation must be studied as a principal site of social conflict, not only between capital and labour, but also between different groups, including ethnic and gender groups. From this perspective, entities such as the state are not seen as neutral legislators and enforcers of contracts, but as allied with capital against labour, consumers and other sectors of society.

A Marxist influence may be identified in historical accounting research that makes use of the concept of the 'labour process' (for example, Armstrong 1985, 1987), where cost accounting and budgeting-based control systems are viewed as mechanisms for controlling labour, and financial reporting is theorised as a process for allocating surplus value among different 'fractions of capital'. The Marxist approach has been taken furthest by Bryer (2005), who has suggested that changing 'modes of production', most particularly the transition from feudalism through mercantilism to capitalism as exemplified by the Industrial Revolution in Britain, can be associated with changes in modes of accounting.

Marxist approaches to historical accounting research emphasise important factors that the more traditional histories of accounting had tended to downplay if not ignore: the ways in which accounting calculations in themselves promote particular kinds of social order and inhibit others, the roles of accounting in establishing relationships of control and in empowering some while disempowering others, and the central role of the state. These were all factors identified by Anthony Hopwood (1981) as crucial for a critical understanding of a rapidly changing accounting domain. Hopwood was editor of a relatively new journal, *Accounting, Organizations and Society* (first published in 1976), whose primary area of interest was the social and organisational impact of accounting. Hopwood himself was enthusiastic about history, and the journal was to become a central advocate of 'socio-historical accounting research'. Although the theoretical perspectives adopted by researchers ranged widely, there were two main inspirations: Marx and the French theorist Michel Foucault.

Foucault and historical accounting research

Foucault appealed to some accounting historians because he saw what appeared to be technical practices (such as accounting) as fundamentally based in 'discourse' – in language as practised at a social level. Accounting is not just about measuring phenomena such as 'income' or 'cost', or keeping track of resources, but accounting is used to construct categories or concepts, such as the 'standard cost' and the 'efficient worker', which themselves are mobilised in organisations and societies. Foucault stressed the intimate association between power and knowledge: those who have power are able to define what counts as knowledge (for example, what is measured, recorded and reported), while the knowledge thus produced can be used not just in a blatantly coercive way (as a Marxist would probably suggest) but in more subtle and personal ways, indeed, in some situations may even 'empower' individuals, enabling them to act in ways that would previously not have been conceivable. For example, the use of standard costs based on the time-and-motion studies encouraged by scientific management could be seen as a bid on the part of capital to extract greater productivity and hence more surplus value from workers, but could also be interpreted as making workers more aware of their repetitive actions and thus potentially reducing effort.

The Foucauldian programme in socio-historical accounting research has been one of the central aspects of the 'new accounting history'. It has concentrated on how accounting makes 'visible' various activities of human life and behaviour, using concepts such as the 'calculable man' (Foucault 1977: 193) to interpret accounting methods such as standard costing as helping to construct the worker as a 'governable person' (Miller and O'Leary 1987). This approach tends to view standard costing as part of a discourse of government emerging at the end of the nineteenth century, as the state (and organisations in general) seeks to achieve a more detailed form of administration over the lives of citizens. Foucauldian researchers have also made methodological claims about how historical research in accounting should be undertaken.

An early review of Foucauldian historical accounting research was provided by Napier (1989), as the main example of a research approach labelled 'contextualising accounting'. This paper was one of several contributions designed to influence the growing research literature in accounting history. This literature was encouraged by the creation of new academic accounting journals (see Chapter 1), some specialising in historical research and others, though more general in their scope, willing to publish historical work. At the same time, first, Arno Press and later Garland Publishing were reprinting many original accounting works and compilations of articles published in often hard-to-access sources. Expansion of the literature of accounting history tended to be coupled with greater theoretical and methodological rigour, something that most (though not all) contributors to a developing stream of historiographical writing within accounting history were keen to advocate.

Historiographies of accounting history

As already noted, Oldroyd (1999) has compiled a thorough survey of many of these historio-graphical contributions, so only the main writings are mentioned here. Previts *et al.* (1990) propose a range of broad subjects for research: biography, institutional history, development of accounting thought, general history of accounting, critical histories, databases (including biblio-graphies) and historiography itself. They advocate a typical social science research model, beginning with problem or hypothesis formulation, applying rigorous methods to clearly identified and evaluated data, and drawing conclusions in terms of the objective of the research.

Merino and Mayper (1993) see the key role of historical accounting research as being the provision of a critical commentary on 'archival/empirical' research using historical accounting data sets, to ensure that such research fully takes into account institutional and social factors that could be relevant in providing a more 'plausible story' of events being examined. Carnegie and Napier (1996) call for what they label 'critical and interpretive histories', and suggest a range of topics and approaches in which such critical and interpretive histories could be of interest. Some of these – examining surviving business records of firms, biography, institutional history, public sector accounting – are areas of research that have long been central to historical accounting research. Others, such as prosopography (the collective biography of a group of well-defined individuals, for example, the founders of a professional body), were less common within accounting history. Carnegie and Napier strongly supported the use of alternative research methods, in particular, oral history (see also Hammond and Sikka 1996), and called for comparative international accounting history (see also Carnegie and Napier 2002).

More recently, despite concerns expressed by Fleischman and Tyson (1997) that archival researchers in accounting history were an 'endangered species', there has been growing realisation that historical accounting research must at the same time be firmly grounded in archival evidence and have a clear theoretical perspective to provide a coherent philosophical basis and a rigorous structure. This does not imply that all historical research in accounting needs to use archival material directly – it is quite appropriate, for example, for researchers to make use of the labours of others in locating, extracting and transcribing primary materials (whether these are accounting records or original literature relevant to accounting), so long as they are conscious that 'examination of original accounting documents is crucial in giving our theories and generalizations some empirical content' (Napier 1989: 240). However, as a recent historiographical contribution calling for 'confluence' between the traditional and new streams of accounting history puts it: 'it is not enough, and it may be quite wasteful, for authors to simply present historical materials without a sense of how they illuminate broader developments of accountancy in the field' (Fleischman and Radcliffe 2003: 22).

At the beginning of the twenty-first century, historical accounting research has certainly reached a stage of maturity, with both the more traditional 'history of accounting' and the more recent 'socio-historical accounting research' streams constituting vibrant bodies of knowledge. Despite this, Fleischman and Radcliffe (2005) are pessimistic about the continued buoyancy of accounting history in the United States. They see threats from a dominant econometric orientation in accounting research, where statistical analysis of large data sets is carried out with little consciousness of the contexts within which the data emerged. Much historical accounting research is more like case study work, capable of generating insights but less easily generalised than statistical analysis of large samples. The challenge for historical accounting research is to continue to offer insights, firmly grounded in evidence and at the same time theoretically rich. Hence, in the next section, the broader philosophical and methodological issues of accounting history are considered.

Theories, methods and evidence

What counts as accounting

How does theory help the accounting historian? Are there specific issues relating to how the historian should go about the process of research? How can researchers convince themselves of the validity of their conclusions, and how can they go about convincing others? Despite their disagreements over which theory is likely to be most helpful in providing a foundation for understanding accounting's history, there has been wide agreement on methodological issues.

Methodological disputes have tended to focus on the scope of accounting history, and on the presentation of historical arguments. Miller and Napier (1993: 631) refused to offer a definition of accounting: 'There is no "essence" to accounting, and no invariant object to which the name "accounting" can be attached.' This reflected both the wide range of activities currently described as 'accounting' and/or undertaken by individuals and organisations describing themselves as 'accountants', and also the dramatic expansion in such activities since the 1960s. It also left open the scope of research into 'accounting' – Miller and Napier (1993) advocated a wider view that could potentially encompass any form of record keeping, rendering of account, or use of structured and systematic information in the context of personal and organisational management. More recently, Carmona *et al.* (2004: 34) have suggested that: 'Accounting is a constructor of economic value, and this "essence" is invariant across time and space.'

Although 'history of accounting' tends to limit its attention to records of transactions and activities expressed in monetary form, or used for purposes such as planning and controlling individual and organisational activities (for example, inventory records used to control against waste of physical resources), 'socio-historical accounting research' has cast its net much wider. Napier (2006) has suggested that two of the key characteristics of the new accounting history are 'broadening conceptions of accounting' and 'widening arenas for accounting'. Not only do researchers resist any limitation as to what counts as accounting, but also they see accounting operating in a wide range of contexts, going beyond an emphasis on business to encompass government, individuals, the household and estate, trade unions, the academy and other potential sites for research. The role of accounting has been explored in a wide range of contexts, from the oppression of native peoples (for example, Neu 2000) to the Holocaust (Funnell 1998b). Researchers show how particular types of accounting procedure and record, used in precise ways, not only facilitated but made possible particular actions within society. However, a danger of socio-historical accounting research is that practitioners do not probe deeply enough into the actual accounting that they claim is affecting organisations and society.

From this perspective, a clear theoretical position on the factors that affect accounting ideas and practices that are observed within the archive, and on how these ideas and practices can influence individual, social and organisational phenomena, is important, whether this position is derived from neo-classical economics, the ideas of Marx or Foucault, or some other source. Theory can help the researcher to clarify, even to identify, promising research questions, by suggesting influences, relationships and mechanisms. For example, a neo-classical economics perspective would prompt the researcher to consider the likely costs and benefits that would arise from the adoption of a particular accounting method in preference to an alternative method (for example, double-entry bookkeeping rather than charge/discharge accounting), and would consider on whom the respective costs and benefits might fall. A more interpretive theory might inspire the researcher to examine contemporary discourses in which particular accounting methods were promoted, in order to locate a specific accounting choice or change against a wider conceptual background (Napier 1998: 696).

Issues with evidence

In principle, theory can also inform attitudes to research method and to the validity of evidence. Among accounting historians, however, there is little sense of the sort of 'deconstructive' history that may be associated with contemporary historiographers such as Keith Jenkins (1991, 2003), although many accounting historians are sympathetic to views that multiple histories are possible and that evidential traces of the past are neither neutral nor objective (Napier 2002). Historians of accounting are well aware of the practical problems in accessing archival evidence

(Fleischman and Tyson 2003; Walker 2004), which include the need to identify documents of possible interest from often scanty catalogue references and the physical challenge of deciphering old handwriting. They are also conscious of the difficulties that come from interpreting items out of their original context, and are aware that the survival of particular records is the outcome of a combination of deliberate selection (and suppression) and pure chance.

It is certainly possible to debate the meaning and significance of particular surviving traces of the past, and there is a constant danger, on the one hand, of becoming fascinated by the source evidence while losing sight of the broader context, and, on the other, of reaching broad and possibly erroneous conclusions on the basis of inadequate evidence. Arnold and McCartney (2003) provide an interesting case study of how historians of nineteenth-century British railway accounting frequently either rely uncritically on earlier secondary literature or misinterpret primary sources, and they challenge both 'traditional' and 'new' accounting historians for poor use of evidence. Many of the historians that Arnold and McCartney cite were writing before the major debates over accounting historiography emerged, but the dangers of superficial use of evidence or reliance on a chain of secondary references still remain. A major source of revisionism in historical research more generally is the discovery of new sources of evidence, perhaps previously overlooked or not considered important, but revisionism can also come from new interpretations of existing evidence.

A current challenge to historical accounting research is how to research periods and places in respect of which written records have not survived. Sy and Tinker (2005: 63) have criticised what they perceive as a fetishism of archives by accounting historians: 'Under the shadow of Archivalism, too much history has been sidetracked into a cul-de-sac of sterile empiricism.' They note that accounting historians have largely ignored accounting in pre-colonial Africa, despite extensive evidence of sophisticated economic and social activity that could reasonably be expected to require some form of accounting. The difficulty is that much of this accounting was likely to be oral, hence no permanent writings or other artefacts could be expected to survive. Annisette (2006) explores the problems of researching accounting history in the absence of written records by examining the Yoruba *esusu*, a form of mutual finance not unlike a modern credit union. She notes that, in some contexts, this type of arrangement may have been chosen precisely because it was not permanently documented, and thus fell outside more formal social and economic relationships. The challenge for accounting historians in this type of situation is to be aware how far they can use whatever evidence of practices and procedures still survives as a basis for conclusions about accounting. The danger is that descriptions in secondary sources of behaviour that may appear to be accounting to an accounting historian may not be good proxies for any actual accounting activities.

Although there has been growing interest in the use of oral history methods as a way of enabling 'voices from below' (Napier 2006: 459) to be heard, the main sources of evidence for accounting historians remain surviving records and other documents. Combining different types of evidence can be fruitful. A good example of this is the recent history of auditing in the UK by Matthews (2006). This makes use of documentary sources, including the archives of professional associations, company reports, contemporary books and journals, and histories of accountancy firms, alongside a postal questionnaire designed to generate systematic data on the experiences of auditors working as long ago as the 1920s, and an extensive set of interviews. Matthews provides an explanation of changes in the prevalence of general audit approaches and specific audit techniques (such as statistical sampling) by referring to the internalisation of control that was not only economically feasible but operationally necessary for businesses as they became larger, and to the changing costs faced by auditors as junior audit staff became more expensive to employ while computers permitted mechanisation and automation of basic audit processes.

Methods for using evidence

Accounting historiographers are agreed that finding historical evidence of accounting is only part of the process of historical accounting research. If communication of the evidence is to go beyond simple transcription of archives, then the researcher needs to impose some structure on the material. Using the categories proposed by Munslow (2006), most accounting historians would see themselves as either 'reconstructionists' or 'constructionists'. That is, they believe that the past is real, and that the role of the historian is to uncover the facts – what actually happened – and then to communicate them. 'Reconstructionists' believe that the facts, including structures and relationships between events, are 'there' independently of historians' interpretations, while 'constructionists' suggest that interpretations of the facts are imposed by the historian. Interpretations may be more or less cogent and convincing, but no single interpretation is likely to be possible for all but the most simplistic historical facts. Also, interpretations are always conditional not only on the evidence available at any point in time, but also on ideas and concepts that are taken for granted by the researcher.

A particular issue in historical accounting research is whether causal relationships are independent of interpretations. It has been suggested (Keenan 1998: 662) that 'historical explanation is a necessary, constitutive feature of historical research', to such an extent that research into the past that either does not seek to explain or fails to explain is not worthy of being described as 'historical'. One type of explanation particularly common in historical research is causal, but causal explanations may operate at different levels of generality. At one extreme is the view that historical explanation involves showing that a specific event may be subsumed under some 'law-like generalization' (Hempel 1942). In practice, a historian may merely sketch out such a general explanation, but in principle, it ought to be possible to identify the general historical law that explains the event. Napier (2006: 452) suggests that accounting histories grounded in neo-classical economics come closest to providing such general historical explanations.

At the other extreme, specific events may be explained in terms of specific contingencies, with no implication that the events exhibit any sort of regularity. Although the events are not reduced to instances of some general historical mechanism, the research may gain significance from being seen as a case of some broader phenomenon. Higher-level concepts may be used to provide structure to individual episodes. For example, although the story of the development of the accountancy profession is different in each country, some common themes, such as the desire to 'close' the profession to outsiders (whether seen as a way of maintaining control over the quality of professional work or as a method of reducing competition), and the advancing of claims to uphold certain values, are frequently observed (see Chapter 11). The historian does not merely uncover relevant evidence, but shows how a particular case reflects features in common with other cases while presenting its own unique features, and explains why such similarities and differences have occurred.

Accounting historians working from a Foucauldian viewpoint are particularly loath to offer simple and broad explanations of historical events. The approach labelled 'genealogies of calculation' by Miller and Napier (1993) eschews the notion that different historical events have underlying common structures. Instead, researchers are encouraged to look for the 'accounting constellation', a 'very particular field of relations which existed between certain institutions, economic and administrative processes, bodies of knowledge, systems of norms and measurements, and classification techniques' (Burchell *et al.* 1985: 400). The idea of the accounting constellation suggests certain recurring aspects that may or may not help researchers to interpret a specific situation, and it locates accounting at the centre of a complex 'network of intersecting practices, processes and institutions' (Burchell *et al.* 1985: 400). In particular, researchers are directed to consider the meanings that actors (human and institutional) give to their calculations. Methodologically, researchers are encouraged to withhold their preconceptions about particular situations and events, rather than viewing them through a lens consisting of current concepts and values (Kearins and Hooper 2002). Although Foucauldian history is often described as a 'history of the present' in that it attempts to cast light on current concerns by tracing the emergence of contingencies and conditions that have made the present possible, it is also a 'history of the present' in that the historian tries to avoid judging the past with the benefit of hindsight – the past is treated as its own present.

Other historians using a Foucauldian approach have developed structures to help understand the events and episodes that they document. An influential approach, though one that the author denies should be regarded as a formal model of accounting change, was offered by Miller (1991). He noted that demands for change in methods of accounting and other economic calculations could arise because of the way in which particular issues were 'problematised'. That is, underlying difficulties could be expressed in certain ways rather than others, and this 'problematisation' allowed certain processes and procedures to appear as plausible solutions while others would not emerge. Miller also noted that specific methods of accounting and economic calculation could find themselves bound up with particular 'programmes', for example, a national quest for economic growth or a belief in scientific management. However, the relationship between a method and a programme is contingent. There is a need for 'translation', a process of reinterpretation of ideas and practices that makes the relationship begin to appear necessary rather than contingent. Finally, Miller made use of Latour's metaphor of 'action at a distance' to help understand how accounting and related calculations provide the ability to exercise power – they make visible what was previously not visible and allow different actors to 'capture' information in ways that allow them to achieve objectives that previously may have been literally inconceivable.

Narratives and explanations

Although accounting historians may offer explicit structural explanations and understandings of the events and phenomena that they have researched, more often the structure of any explanation is implicit in the way in which the historians present their histories. Historical studies in accounting usually convey some sense of the passing of time as the event under scrutiny unfolds. This conceptualisation of time as something that 'passes' (Quattrone 2005) is often associated with an assumption that history presents a 'story' that it is the responsibility of the historian to discern and narrate. 'Reconstructionist' accounting historians are thus aiming to reconstruct the 'story of accounting history'. Although 'constructionist' historians will deny that there is a unique story to find, they are increasingly aware of the central role of narrative in human life (Funnell 1998a; Llewellyn 1999). Napier (1989: 241) suggested that 'the sign of a good historian' is that they 'tell a good story'. A major feature of historiographical writing in accounting in recent years has been a growing self-consciousness about how accounting historians communicate their histories. The social science model advocated by Previts *et al.* (1990) often led to the writing of papers in which theory and narrative were not integrated, and accounting historians have been more likely to allow the theoretical contribution of their work to emerge subtly from a well-structured narrative.

Historical accounting researchers have referred to literary theory to understand different forms of narrative (see, for example, Napier 2001), and have suggested that many historical episodes can be narrated using a range of broad narrative structures. Funnell (1998a) has gone so

43

far as to suggest the use of 'counter-narrative' as an alternative way of telling accounting history, though it is not always clear how far this term refers simply to telling different stories as opposed to telling stories using different forms of communication. Parker (1999) has noted the rise in oral history, yet most historians 'read' such histories in printed form rather than 'hearing' them, with all the additional nuances that speech can communicate beyond bare words. Parker has also mentioned the possibility of visual histories of accounting (an initial attempt at such a history has been offered by Graves *et al.* 1996), and notes that even sound recordings of interviews that underpin oral history omit a visual dimension. If one of the methodological challenges facing accounting history is how to research accounting in cultures that have not left written records, another is how to narrate accounting's past in new and more sophisticated ways.

Conclusion

Historical accounting research has developed to address many new themes, going well beyond the traditional subject matter of the development of systematic record keeping of economic transactions by businesses. The strand identified in this chapter as 'history of accounting' has explored accounting ideas, practices and methods in broader settings, while the strand identified as 'socio-historical accounting research' has investigated how accounting (in a broad sense) affected society in the distant and recent past, helping us to understand how accounting changes and itself may act as an engine of social, economic and political change.

Carmona (2004) and Walker (2005) have pointed out that much recent historical research in accounting has focused on developments in predominantly English-speaking countries, and on events of the past 150 years (including the roles of accounting in the large industrial organisation, the growth of the accounting profession, and the contribution of financial reporting, auditing and governance to the modern corporation and its relationships with key stakeholders). Walker notes that important areas for historical accounting research exist outside the 'Anglo-Saxon' (or 'Anglo-Celtic') regions, not only in Continental Europe but in Asia, Africa and Latin America. Also, little is known about accounting in rural, pre-industrial settings (at least in comparison with our knowledge of industrial and corporate accounting). Walker points out that accounting historians are often unaware of research using accounting records within 'mainstream' historical research.

However, accounting history has made a salutary contribution to broadening the range and depth of accounting research, by providing an interdisciplinary perspective that has acted as an important counterbalance to a research discipline that has often been dominated by econometrics and behavioural psychology. If such approaches tend to dehumanise the basically human activity of giving an account, then historical research returns the human aspect of accounting firmly to the centre, not only in specifically human-oriented histories such as biographical studies but also through balanced consideration of the importance of human agency as well as structure in the development of accounting. The existence of accounting history has allowed for significant debates within the more interpretive and critical accounting research community to be mounted (for example, the discussion 'Accounting and Praxis: Marx after Foucault' in *Critical Perspectives on Accounting*, March 1994, and the debate over 'Critical Accounting History' in the same journal, December 1998).

The writing of accounting history has emerged from an interest in uncovering origins of accounting within the ancient world, a desire to document early records and treatises on double-entry bookkeeping to celebrate the role of Italy in presenting accounting to the modern world, and a fascination with old and curious books, to form a coherent and significant element of accounting's knowledge base. In doing so, costs have been incurred: accounting history has become specialised, and interested non-specialists (exemplified by individuals such as Ernest Stevelinck) are less prevalent among the ranks of accounting historians than they were 40 years ago. However, accounting historians have a more rigorous conception of historiographical issues, such as evidence, the role of theory, the nature of historical explanation, and the significance of narrative to the communication of history. The gaps in historical accounting research identified by commentators such as Walker (2005) may be celebrated as opportunities for encouraging new national and international traditions of historical accounting research to emerge, rather than as reasons for regret.

Key works

Carnegie and Napier (1996) advocates theoretically-based historical research in accounting and identifies a range of innovative research approaches.

Fleischman and Radcliffe (2003) argues that the 'traditional'/'new' distinctions in accounting history are no longer helpful, and calls for a synthesis in research methods and theoretical perspectives.

Miller et al. (1991) sets out the agenda for the 'new' accounting history, reflecting some of the main theoretical approaches adopted in that literature.

Napier (1989) is an early review of the then emerging 'socio-historical' accounting research in comparison with more traditional models of accounting history.

Napier (2006) reviews the development of accounting history since the 1970s and suggests possible future directions.

References

American Accounting Association (1970) Report of the Committee on Accounting History, *Accounting Review*, 45 (supplement): 53–64.

Annisette, M. (2006) People and periods untouched by accounting history: an ancient Yoruba practice, *Accounting History*, 11 (4): 399–417.

Armstrong, P. (1985) Changing management control strategies: the role of competition between accountancy and other organisational professions, *Accounting, Organizations and Society*, 10 (2): 129–48.

Armstrong, P. (1987) The rise of accounting controls in British capitalist enterprises, *Accounting, Organizations and Society*, 12 (5): 415–36.

Arnold, A. J. and McCartney, S. (2003) 'It may be earlier than you think': evidence, myths and informed debate in accounting history, *Critical Perspectives on Accounting*, 14 (3): 227–53.

Baxter, W. T. (1956), Accounting in colonial America, in A. C. Littleton and B. S. Yamey (eds) *Studies in the History of Accounting*, pp. 272–87 (London: Sweet & Maxwell).

Baxter, W. T. (1980) The account charge and discharge, *Accounting Historians Journal*, 7 (1): 69–71.

Besta, F. (1922) *La Ragioneria*, 2nd edn (Milan: Vallardi).

Brown, R. (ed.) (1905) *A History of Accounting and Accountants* (Edinburgh: T. C. and E. C. Jack).

Bryer, R. A. (2005) A Marxist accounting history of the British industrial revolution: a review of evidence and suggestions for research, *Accounting, Organizations and Society*, 30 (1): 25–65.

Burchell, S., Clubb, C. and Hopwood, A. (1985) Accounting in its social context: towards a history of value added in the United Kingdom, *Accounting, Organizations and Society*, 10 (4): 381–413.

Carmona, S. (2004) Accounting history research and its diffusion in an international context, *Accounting History*, 9 (3): 7–23.

Carmona, S., Ezzamel, M. and Gutiérrez, F. (2004) Accounting history research: traditional and new accounting history perspectives, *De Computis: Revista Española de Historia de la Contabilidad*, 1: 24–53.

Carnegie, G. D. and Napier, C. J. (1996) Critical and interpretive histories: understanding accounting's present and future through its past, *Accounting, Auditing & Accountability Journal*, 9 (3): 7–39.

Carnegie, G. D. and Napier, C. J. (2002) Exploring comparative international accounting history, *Accounting, Auditing & Accountability Journal*, 15 (5): 689–718.

Cerboni, G. (1886) *La Ragioneria Scientifica e le sue Relazioni con le Discipline Amministative e Sociali* (Rome: Loeschner).

Cerboni, G. (1889) *Elenco Cronologico delle Opere di Computisteria e Ragioneria Venute alla Luce in Italia dal 1202 al 1888* (Rome: Tipografia Nazionale).

de Roover, R. (1956) The development of accounting prior to Luca Pacioli according to the account-books of medieval merchants, in A. C. Littleton and B. S. Yamey (eds) *Studies in the History of Accounting*, pp. 114–74 (London: Sweet & Maxwell).

de Ste. Croix, G. E. M. (1956) Greek and Roman accounting, in A. C. Littleton and B. S. Yamey (eds) *Studies in the History of Accounting*, pp. 14–77 (London: Sweet & Maxwell).

Edey, H. C. (1956) Company accounting in the nineteenth and twentieth centuries, *Accountants Journal*, 48 (4): 95–6, (5) 127–9.

Edey, H. C. and Panitpakdi, P. (1956) British company accounting and the law 1844–1900, in A. C. Littleton and B. S. Yamey (eds) *Studies in the History of Accounting*, pp. 356–79 (London: Sweet & Maxwell).

Edwards, R. S. (1937) Some notes on the early literature and development of cost accounting in Great Britain, *Accountant* (7 August): 193–5; (14 August): 225–31; (21 August): 253–5; (28 August): 283–7; (4 September): 313–16; (11 September): 343–4.

Epstein, M. J. and Epstein, J. B. (1974) An annotated bibliography of scientific management and standard costing to 1920, *Abacus*, 10 (2): 165–74.

Fleischman, R. K. and Radcliffe, V. S. (2003) Divergent streams of accounting history: a review and call for confluence, in R. K. Fleischman, V. S. Radcliffe and P. A. Shoemaker (eds) *Doing Accounting History: Contributions to the Development of Accounting Thought*, pp. 1–29 (Kidlington, Oxford: Elsevier Science).

Fleischman, R. K. and Radcliffe, V. S. (2005) The roaring nineties: accounting history comes of age, *Accounting Historians Journal*, 32 (1): 61–109.

Fleischman. R. K. and Tyson, T. N. (1997) Archival researchers: an endangered species? *Accounting Historians Journal*, 24 (2): 91–109.

Fleischman, R. K. and Tyson, T. N. (2003) Archival research methodology, in R. K. Fleischman, V. S. Radcliffe and P. A. Shoemaker (eds) *Doing Accounting History: Contributions to the Development of Accounting Thought*, pp. 31–47 (Kidlington, Oxford: Elsevier Science).

Foster, B. F. (1852) *The Origin and Progress of Bookkeeping* (London: C. H. Law).

Foucault, M. (1977) *Discipline and Punish: The Birth of the Prison* (London: Allen Lane).

Funnell, W. (1998a) The narrative and its place in the new accounting history: the rise of the counter-narrative, *Accounting, Auditing & Accountability Journal*, 11 (2): 142–62.

Funnell, W. (1998b) Accounting in the service of the holocaust, *Critical Perspectives on Accounting*, 9 (4): 435–64.

Garner, S. P. (1954) *The Evolution of Cost Accounting to 1925* (Tuscaloosa, AL: University of Alabama Press).

Goldberg, L. (1974) The future of the past in accounting, *Accountant's Magazine*, 68 (820): 405–10.

González Ferrando, J. M. (2006) Balbuceos y primeros pasos de la historia de la contabilidad en España, *De Computis: Revista Española de Historia de la Contabilidad*, 5: 39–64.

Graves, O. F., Flesher, D. L. and Jordan, R. E. (1996) Pictures and the bottom line: the television epistemology of US annual reports, *Accounting, Organizations and Society*, 21 (1): 57–88.

Hammond, T. and Sikka, P. (1996) Radicalizing accounting history: the potential of oral history, *Accounting, Auditing & Accountability Journal*, 9 (3): 79–97.

Hatfield, H. R. (1924) An historical defense of bookkeeping, *Journal of Accountancy*, 37 (4): 241–53.

Hempel, C. G. (1942) The function of general laws in history, *Journal of Philosophy*, 39 (2): 35–48.

Hernández-Esteve, E. (1994) Comments on some obscure or ambiguous points of the treatise *De Computis et Scripturis* by Luca Pacioli, *Accounting Historians Journal*, 21 (1): 17–80.

Hopwood, A. G. (1981) Commentary on 'The study of accounting history' [by R. H. Parker], in M. Bromwich and A. G. Hopwood (eds) *Essays in British Accounting Research*, pp. 294–6 (London: Pitman).

Hopwood, A. G. (1985) The tale of a committee that never reported: disagreements on intertwining accounting with the social, *Accounting, Organizations and Society*, 10 (3): 361–77.

Jackson, J. G. C. (1956) The history of methods of exposition of double-entry book-keeping in England, in A. C. Littleton and B. S. Yamey (eds) *Studies in the History of Accounting*, pp. 288–312 (London: Sweet & Maxwell).

Jäger, E. L. (1874) *Beiträge zur Geschichte der Doppelbuchhaltung* (Stuttgart: Kröner).

Jäger, E. L. (1876) *Lucas Paccioli und Simon Stevin, nebst einigen jüngeren Schriftstellern über Buchhaltung. Skizzen zur Geschichte der kaufmännischen, staatlichen und landwirtschaftlichen Buchführung* (Stuttgart: Kröner).

Jenkins, K. (1991) *Re-thinking History* (London: Routledge).

Jenkins, K. (2003) *Refiguring History: New Thoughts on an Old Discipline* (London: Routledge).

Johnson, H. T. (1981) Toward a new understanding of nineteenth-century cost accounting, *Accounting Review*, 56 (3): 510–18.

Johnson, H. T. (1983) The search for gain in markets and firms: a review of the historical emergence of management accounting systems, *Accounting, Organizations and Society*, 8 (2/3): 139–46.

Johnson, H. T. and Kaplan, R. S. (1987) *Relevance Lost: The Rise and Fall of Management Accounting* (Boston: Harvard Business School Press).

Kearins, K. and Hooper, K. (2002) Genealogical method and analysis, *Accounting, Auditing & Accountability Journal*, 15 (5): 733–57.

Keenan, M. G. (1998) A defence of 'traditional' accounting history research methodology, *Critical Perspectives on Accounting*, 9 (6): 641–66.

Kheil, K. P. (1896) *Über einige ältere Bearbeitungen zur Geschichte des Buchhaltungs von Luca Pacioli – Ein Beitrage zur Geschichte der Buchhaltung* (Prague: Bursik & Kohout).

Kheil, K P. (1902) *Historia de la Contabilidad* (Alicante: Moscat y Oñate).

Littleton, A. C. (1933) *Accounting Evolution to 1900* (New York: American Institute Publishing Co.).

Littleton, A. C. and Yamey, B. S. (eds) (1956) *Studies in the History of Accounting* (London: Sweet & Maxwell).

Llewellyn, S. (1999) Narratives in accounting and management research, *Accounting, Auditing & Accountability Journal*, 12 (2): 220–36.

Mattessich, R. (2003) Accounting research and researchers of the nineteenth century and the beginning of the twentieth century: an international survey of authors, ideas and publications, *Accounting, Business & Financial History*, 13 (2): 125–70.

Matthews, D. (2006) *A History of Auditing: The Changing Audit Process in Britain from the Nineteenth Century to the Present Day* (London: Routledge).

Melis, F. (1950) *Storia della Ragioneria* (Bologna: Zuffi).

Merino, B. D. and Mayper, A. G. (1993) Accounting history and empirical research, *Accounting Historians Journal*, 20 (2): 237–67.

Miller, P. (1991) Accounting innovation beyond the enterprise: problematizing investment decisions and programming economic growth, *Accounting, Organizations and Society*, 16 (8): 733–62.

Miller, P. and Napier, C. (1993) Genealogies of calculation, *Accounting, Organizations and Society*, 18 (7/8): 631–47.

Miller, P. and O'Leary, T. (1987) Accounting and the construction of the governable person, *Accounting, Organizations and Society*, 12 (3): 235–65.

Miller, P., Hopper, T. and Laughlin, R. (1991) The new accounting history: an introduction, *Accounting, Organizations and Society*, 16 (5/6): 395–403.

Munslow, A. (2006) *Deconstructing History*, 2nd edn (London: Routledge).

Napier, C. J. (1989) Research directions in accounting history, *British Accounting Review*, 21 (3): 237–54.

Napier, C. J. (1996) Accounting and the absence of a business economics tradition in the United Kingdom, *European Accounting Review*, 5 (3): 449–81.

Napier, C. J. (1998) Giving an account of accounting history: a reply to Keenan, *Critical Perspectives on Accounting*, 9 (6): 685–700.

Napier, C. J. (2001) Accounting history and accounting progress, *Accounting History*, 6 (2): 7–31.

Napier, C. J. (2002) The historian as auditor: facts, judgments and evidence, *Accounting Historians Journal*, 29 (2): 131–55.

Napier, C. J. (2006) Accounts of change: 30 years of historical accounting research, *Accounting, Organizations and Society*, 31 (4/5): 445–507.

Neu, D. (2000) 'Presents' for the 'Indians': land, colonialism and accounting in Canada, *Accounting, Organizations and Society*, 25 (2): 162–84.

Nishikawa, K. (1956) The early history of double-entry book-keeping in Japan, in A. C. Littleton and B. S. Yamey (eds) *Studies in the History of Accounting*, pp. 380–7 (London: Sweet & Maxwell).

Oldroyd, D. (1999) Historiography, causality and positioning: an unsystematic view of accounting history, *Accounting Historians Journal*, 26 (1): 83–102.

Parker, L. D. (1999) Historiography for the new millennium: adventures in accounting and management, *Accounting History*, 4 (2): 11–42.

Parker, R. H. (1965) Accounting history: a select bibliography, *Abacus*, 1 (1): 62–84.

Penndorf, B. (1913) *Geschichte der Buchhaltung in Deutschland* (Leipzig: Gloeckner).

Pollins, H. (1956) Aspects of railway accounting before 1868, in A. C. Littleton and B. S. Yamey (eds) *Studies in the History of Accounting*, pp. 332–55 (London: Sweet & Maxwell).

Previts, G. J. and Merino, B. D. (1998) *A History of Accountancy in the United States: The Cultural Significance of Accounting* (Columbus, OH: Ohio State University Press).

Previts, G. J., Parker, L. D. and Coffman, E. N. (1990), An accounting historiography: subject matter and methodology, *Abacus*, 26 (2): 136–58.

Quattrone, P. (2005) Is time spent, passed or counted? The missing link between time and accounting history, *Accounting Historians Journal*, 32 (1): 185–218.

Solomons, D. (1952) The historical development of costing, in D. Solomons (ed.) *Studies in Costing*, pp. 1–52 (London: Sweet & Maxwell).

Sombart, W. (1919) *Der Moderne Kapitalismus* (Munich & Leipzig: Duncker & Humblot).

Sy, A. and Tinker, T. (2005) Archival research and the lost worlds of accounting, *Accounting History*, 10 (1): 47–69.

Tinker, T. and Neimark, M. (1987) The role of annual reports in gender and class contradictions at General Motors: 1917–1976, *Accounting, Organizations and Society*, 12 (1): 71–88.

Tinker, T. and Neimark, M. (1988) The struggle over meaning in accounting and corporate research: a comparative evaluation of conservative and critical historiography, *Accounting, Auditing & Accountability Journal*, 1 (1): 55–74.

Vlaemminck, J-H. (1956) *Histoire et Doctrines de la Comptabilité* (Brussels: Éditions du Treurenberg).

Walker, S. P. (2004) The search for clues in accounting history, in C. Humphrey and B. Lee (eds) *The Real Life Guide to Accounting Research: A Behind-the-Scenes View of Using Qualitative Research Methods*, pp. 3–21 (Kidlington, Oxford: Elsevier).

Walker, S. P. (2005) Accounting in history, *Accounting Historians Journal*, 32 (2): 233–59.

Watts, R. L. and Zimmerman, J. L. (1983) Agency problems, auditing and the theory of the firm: some evidence, *Journal of Law and Economics*, 26 (3): 613–33.

Woolf, A. H. (1912) *A Short History of Accountants and Accountancy* (London: Gee).

Worthington, B. (1895) *Professional Accountants: An Historical Sketch* (London: Gee).

Yamey, B. S. (1949) Scientific bookkeeping and the rise of capitalism, *Economic History Review*, Ser. II, 1 (2/3): 99–113.

Yamey, B. S. (1978) *Essays on the History of Accounting* (New York: Arno Press).

Yamey, B. S., Edey, H. C. and Thomson, H. W. (eds) (1963) *Accounting in England and Scotland: 1543–1800. Double Entry in Exposition and Practice* (London: Sweet & Maxwell).

Zambon, S. (1996) Accounting and business economics traditions: a missing European connection?, *European Accounting Review*, 5 (3): 401–11.

Zan, L. (1994) Toward a history of accounting histories: perspectives from the Italian tradition, *European Accounting Review*, 3 (2): 255–307.

Zeff, S. A. (2000) *Henry Rand Hatfield: Humanist, Scholar, and Accounting Educator* (Greenwich, CT: JAI Press).

3

Subjects, sources and dissemination

John Richard Edwards

Overview

This chapter starts by demonstrating the growing diversity of accounting history research. Significant changes in subject matter are identified and discussed. Ebb and flow in the presence of accounting history within generalist accounting journals is noted, and the encouragement provided by editors of critical journals for innovation in the application of methodologies capable of providing meaningful interpretations of accounting's past is acknowledged. The chapter profiles the content of specialist accounting history journals in terms of authorship, subject area studied, geographical and temporal coverage. Concerns about the restricted coverage of time and place in accounting history research are rehearsed, and the role of special issues in accounting history journals in addressing these deficiencies is considered. Sources of evidence in accounting history research are identified and the potential of written and oral sources is explored. The decision of the accounting history community to privilege articles over books and monographs is criticised, and use of the professional press to popularise findings and to connect with policy-makers is encouraged.

Subject matter

There exist a number of resources that enable researchers to discover what has previously been published in the field of accounting history. The first three of Parker's select bibliographies 'of secondary material on all aspects of accounting history' (1980: 'Introduction') cover publications to 1980.[1] Since their initial publication, *Accounting, Business & Financial History (ABFH)* (1989) and *Accounting History (AH)* (1996) have produced annual lists of publications, while the *Accounting Historians Journal (AHJ)* Index[2] contains details of all 'major research papers' (Badua *et al.* 2003: 205) published since 1974.

Parker's bibliographies contain a subject classification which was extended by Edwards (2004) to explore developments in the themes studied by accounting historians. Table 3.1 compares the subject areas of accounting history publications to 1980[3] with those for the

Table 3.1   Publishing patterns by subject area

Subject area	to 1980		1998–2002	
	Total	*%*	*Total*	*%*
Early accounting	286	45.7	28	6.0
Professional accountancy	56	9.0	58	12.4
Auditing	14	2.2	40	8.6
Cost and management accounting	72	11.5	80	17.1
Corporate accounting[a]	62	9.9	87	18.6
(Financial) Accounting theory	53	8.5	14	3.0
Mechanised accounting and computers	5	0.8	0	0.0
Executorship accounting	3	0.5	0	0.0
Education	12	1.9	13	2.8
Terminology	4	0.6	0	0.0
Bibliographies, biographies and chronologies	52	8.3	40	8.6
Bank accounting	7	1.1	0	0.0
Methodology			29	6.2
Public sector accounting[b]			27	5.8
Gender			9	1.9
Household/small business			3	0.6
Race, slavery and indigenous people			12	2.6
Taxation			27	5.8
	626	100.0	467	100.0

Source: Edwards (2004).

[a] This encapsulates a heterogeneous collection of papers covering such topics as the analysis of company reports, comparative international accounting, environmental reporting, ethical accounting, harmonisation, misleading and fraudulent accounts, price-level adjustments and regulation.
[b] A small number of publications on government accounting were classified by Parker under 'early accounting'.

period 1998–2002. The subject areas not included in Parker's taxonomy appear below the horizontal line in the table.

The spectacular difference between the two series is the decline in the number of publications on 'early accounting' (broadly speaking pre-industrial accounting). Prior to 1980, nearly one out of every two publications was in that area whereas, in the recent past, it was the subject of just 6 per cent of total outputs. The underlying philosophy of Hatfield's witty essay 'An historical defence of bookkeeping' (1924), that the study of bookkeeping is a respectable and interesting activity, seems not to have stood the test of time. The explanations for this decline are likely to include the possibility that relatively few of today's academics possess the skills required to interpret the content of early records, that articles offered for publication in this area tend to be descriptive rather than analytical, and that the study of early accounting has become unfashionable. However, 'early accounting' receives greater attention from non-Anglo-Saxon scholars. Spanish accounting historians, for example, are particularly active in researching accounting in pre-industrial contexts.

Given the dramatic fall in the proportion of papers devoted to 'early accounting', it is inevitably the case that virtually all other subject categories should report an increased share. Growth areas include methodology, taxation, public sector accounting, auditing and cost and management accounting.

There were no identifiable methodology papers pre-1980, and the emergence of this subject in accounting history is partly attributable to encouragement provided by the editors of critical journals (see below) for the application of a range of methodologies to help interpret the significance of historical data. Some of these papers arose from the debates between new and traditional historians that flourished during the 1990s (see Chapter 2). But many other methodological issues have also been the subject of study. For example: Napier (2002) explored new ways of understanding the nature of accounting history research through a comparison with the manner in which the auditor makes use of facts, judgement and evidence; Matthews (2002) considered the potential for using postal questionnaires in accounting history research.

There are some signs of taxation receiving more attention from accounting historians in recent years, though many of the articles included in Table 3.1 comprise fairly brief descriptive pieces published in *British Tax Review*. The growing attention to public sector accounting leaves much room for further development. Funnell (2007: 268–9) estimates that just 4.2 per cent of the 1,384 papers listed in annual surveys of accounting history publications, 1995–2004, focused on that subject. Confining attention to Britain for the period 1780–1880, Funnell (2007: 269–70) criticises such neglect but also points to the opportunities available for accounting historians because of the abundance of available source material.

The period 1998–2002 also saw a rise in the level of attention devoted to auditing, although some might consider it still to be the subject of relative neglect given its historical and contemporary importance to the work of the public accountant.

Cost and management accounting continues to be a thriving area of historical research (see Chapter 9) and the site for much of the debate concerning different ways of understanding accounting's past. It is a subject where provocative and scholarly papers enhanced interest in an established area of research. Three papers, all published in *Accounting, Organizations and Society* (*AOS*) stand out: Loft's (1986) investigation of cost accounting in Britain during and immediately after the First World War; Hopwood's call (1987) for studies of 'accounting in motion' within its organisational context; and Hoskin and Macve's research (1988) into the connection between West Point and the Springfield Armory. It was also, within this three-year period, that Johnson and Kaplan's *Relevance Lost* (1987) appeared and further stimulated debate. The significance of these publications can be inferred from Carmona's (2006) citation-based study that ranks all four within the top five 'most influential works' in accounting history.

Table 3.1 reveals another subject area that received increased attention between 1998 and 2002, and where the nature of research work also moved in a new direction – namely, professional accountancy. Here, the ideas of sociologists such as Max Weber and Magali Larson were applied by writers such as Macdonald (1984), Willmott (1986), Richardson (1997) and Walker (1995) to broaden our understanding of professional developments. Their work which demonstrated the application of sociological analysis to the professionalisation of accounting helps explain the prominent position occupied by that subject area in Table 3.1. The professionalisation of accounting is discussed in detail in Chapter 11.

As the chapters in this *Routledge Companion* demonstrate, by no means all the themes selected by the editors feature above (or even below) the line in Table 3.1. Confining attention to Parker's taxonomy, some of the *Routledge Companion*'s chapters, such as those on ancient accounting (Chapter 4), bookkeeping (Chapter 5) and accounting and capitalism (Chapter 15) are encapsulated within 'early accounting'. Some others, such as national accounting (Chapter 16) and railways (Chapter 18), were the subject of just one or two papers which Parker placed in a miscellaneous category. Reflecting the recent, widening dimensions of accounting historiography, the main themes that remain outside Parker's pre-1980 orbit appear in the final two sections of the *Routledge Companion* – 'society and culture' and 'polity'.

Studies of the history content of general accounting journals also point to shifts in the subject areas researched. Among the themes focused on by 'new' accounting historians, three have featured prominently in the columns of *AOS* (Napier 2006: 446). Publications on 'Accounting, power and knowledge' draw heavily on the work of Foucault in 'attempts to identify (or construct) networks of people, principles and practices ("accounting constellations") and to show how accounting can be "caught" in such networks' (Napier 2006: 462). Major contributions include Hoskin and Macve (1986, 1988), Loft (1986) and Miller and O'Leary (1987). The second theme identified by Napier was noted above, 'The accountant and the allure of professionalisation'. Here Willmott (1986) was 'one of the earliest writers to attempt to get beyond the official histories of professional accountancy bodies in the UK in order to apply ideas from the sociology of the professions' (Napier 2006: 464). The third theme provides new understandings of accounting's role in presenting the economic. Much of this work is Marxist-oriented with Rob Bryer its most active proponent.

The content of specialist accounting history journals – *AHJ, ABFH* and *AH* – have been the subject of scrutiny[4] that also suggest shifting research interests. Applying the classification devised by Carnegie and Napier (1996),[5] Williams and Wines (2006) found that research published in *AH* between 1996 and 2005 was dominated by 'institutional history' (21.2 per cent), 'using accounting records in business history' (19.2 per cent) and 'studies of surviving business records of firms' (14.4 per cent). Also receiving increasing attention was 'public sector accounting' (12.5 per cent). When the classification is applied to all three specialist accounting history journals for the period 1996–99, the areas of greatest interest were institutional history (particularly in *AHJ* and *AH*), business history (particularly *ABFH*) and the analysis of surviving business records (particularly *ABFH*). These foci accounted for 75.2 per cent of all publications between 1996 and 1999 (Carnegie and Potter 2000: 193).

The geographical scope of papers published in the three specialist journals was broadest in *ABFH*, 'with contributions on 16 countries or regions' (ibid.: 188) compared with eight for *AHJ* and five for *AH*. British accounting history (37.6 per cent) was comfortably the site most studied, followed by the US (21.7 per cent) (ibid.: 190). This did not leave a great deal of space for the rest of the world, but it must be remembered that this analysis is confined to histories contained in English-language journals.

Carnegie and Potter's (ibid.: 191) three-journal survey found that 72.9 per cent of published papers focused on the nineteenth and twentieth centuries, and both Williams and Wines (2006: 438) and Anderson (2002: 12) reveal similar temporal coverage of the papers they surveyed. Explanations for the neglect of earlier periods are not easy to find. Carnegie and Potter (2000: 191) attribute inattention to the eighteenth century (10 per cent) to 'lack of primary evidence during an era marked by revolutions across the globe, with implications for the contents of archives, then and now'.

Special issues on accounting history

We have noted significant changes in the direction of accounting history research over the last quarter century. Certain areas have flourished whereas others remain neglected or have become less fashionable. It is the case that 'accounting history research has ventured far beyond its technical core' as practitioners explore the operation of accounting in an increasing range of economic, social, cultural and political contexts (Walker 2008: 313). Special issues of journals devoted to accounting history have helped to raise the profile of the discipline generally and to widen coverage of subjects studied. Table 3.2 lists the 28 special issues and four substantial special sections within regular journal numbers that have appeared to date. Twenty-one of these

Table 3.2 Journal special issues on accounting history

Year	Journal/Volume		Title	Guest editor(s)
1980	*ABR*	10(37A)	Special history issue	
1991	*AOS*	16(5/6)	The new accounting history	
1992	*AOS*	★17(3/4)	Feminist perspectives on accounting research	
1993	*AOS*	★18(7/8)	Accounting, calculation and institutions: historical studies	
1993	*ABFH*	3(3)	Business history through accounting records	Trevor Boyns
1994	*ABFH*	4(1)	From clay tokens to *Fukushiki-Boki*: record keeping over ten millennia	John Richard Edwards and Basil S. Yamey
1995	*ABFH*	5(1)	Management accounting and empirical investigation	
1996	*ABFH*	6(3)	Further studies in accounting history: a *Festschrift* in honour of Basil S. Yamey	Robert H. Parker and John Richard Edwards
1996	*AAAJ*	9(3)	Accounting history into the twenty-first century	Christopher J. Napier and Garry D. Carnegie
1996	*CPA*	9(6)	Critical accounting history	
1997	*ABFH*	7(3)	Recent studies in French accounting history	Robert H. Parker, Yannick Lemarchand and Trevor Boyns
1998	*AH*	3(1)	Regulation	Christopher J. Napier
1999	*AAAJ*	12(3)	Organising the accounting profession in Asia	Chris Poullaos
1999	*ABFH*	9(1)	Histories of accounting professionalism	Stephen P. Walker
2000	*ABFH*	10(2)	US accounting history and historiography	Thomas N. Tyson and Richard K. Fleischman
2000	*AAAJ*	13(3)	Accounting and indigenous peoples	Sonja Gallhofer and Andrew Chow
2000	*AH*	5(2)	Accounting in crises	Stephen P. Walker
2001	*ABFH*	11(1)	Recent research in accounting, business and management history by French authors	Trevor Boyns and Marc Nikitin
2001	*ABFH*	11(3)	Studies in Japanese accounting history	Junichi Chiba and Terry Cooke
2002	*EAR*	★11(2)	Mapping variety in the history of accounting and management	Salvador Carmona and Luca Zan
2002	*ABFH*	12(2)	Recent research in Spanish accounting history: a *Festschrift* in honour of Esteban Hernández-Esteve	Trevor Boyns and Salvador Carmona
2002	*ABR*	32(2)	International accounting history special issue	Alan J. Richardson
2002	*AOS*	★27(4/5)	Studying accountancy's emergent occupational structures	
2003	*ABFH*	13(1)	Accounting history: Chinese contributions and challenges	Wei Lu and Max Aiken
2004	*ABFH*	14(3)	Mechanisation and computers in banking	Bernard Bàtiz-Lazo and Trevor Boyns

2005	*AH*	10(3)	Historical perspectives on accounting and audit Failure	Brendan O'Connell
2005	*ABFH*	15(3)	Accounting history in the German language arena	Lisa Evans
2006	*AH*	11(2)	Accounting and religion: a historical perspective	Salvador Carmona and Mahmoud Ezzamel
2006	*ABFH*	16(2)	Women, accounting and investment	Josephine Maltby and Janette Rutterford
2007	*AH*	12(3)	International perspectives on race and gender in accounting's past	Marcia Annisette
2007	*ABFH*	17(1)	Italian accounting history	Lino Cinquini and Alessandro Marelli
2008	*ABFH*	18(1)	Studies of Irish accounting history	Ciarán Ó hÓgartaigh

Note: *Special section.

are located in specialist accounting history journals (16 in *ABFH* and 5 in *AH*) and 11 in five generalist journals, with *AOS* and *Accounting, Auditing & Accountability Journal* (*AAAJ*) leading the way with four (including three special sections) and three respectively.

The first generalist journal to devote an issue to accounting history was *Accounting and Business Research* (*ABR*), in 1980, to mark the centenary of the Institute of Chartered Accountants in England and Wales (ICAEW). According to its editor: 'If this issue has a message it is that accounting history is a much wider subject than was generally realised. There is something of value here for everyone' (Parker 1980: ii).

The increasing historical content of *AOS* in the second half of the 1980s (Napier 2006: 447) received a further fillip from the 1991 special issue on 'The new accounting history' (Miller *et al.* 1991). In 1996, *AAAJ* published its first number devoted to historical studies, entitled 'Accounting history into the twenty-first century' and, in the same year, *Critical Perspectives on Accounting* (*CPA*) contributed to these initiatives through an issue appropriately labelled 'Critical accounting history'. Special issues have served a range of purposes. Those referred to in *AOS, CPA* and *AAAJ* have encouraged historiographical and methodological development. Other special issues have helped open up new research sites and raise the profile of areas judged to be neglected. For example, issues of *AAAJ* in 1999 and 2000 focused, respectively, on 'Organising the accounting profession in Asia' and 'Accounting and indigenous peoples'. The distinctive contribution of the special section of the *European Accounting Review* (*EAR*) in 2002 was to encourage accounting historians to broaden their coverage of time and space.

Extending the geographical coverage of accounting history research findings in English-language journals has also been a policy objective of the editors of *ABFH*, with special issues devoted to China, France, Germany, Ireland, Italy, Japan, Spain and the United States. *ABFH* has also looked to extend the domain of accounting history study through special issues on subjects such as 'Women, accounting and investment', while *AH*, also in 2006, published an important number on 'Accounting and religion'.

Limitations of time and space

Surveys of journal content not only reveal the increasing diversity of the subjects of accounting history research, they also suggest a temporal, disciplinary and spatial narrowness. Studies confirm Parker's (1993: 106) early observation that 'accounting history is increasingly dominated by writers in English discussing private sector accounting in English-speaking countries in the 19th and 20th centuries'.

Carmona (2004) has conducted a broad-based analytical study of the diffusion of accounting research in the international context. His review of the content of the three specialist accounting history journals and ten generalist accounting journals during the 1990s produced a database of 410 accounting history papers. Carmona's analysis revealed that scholars affiliated with Anglo-Saxon institutions accounted for a staggering 90.8 per cent of total output, with researchers from France and Spain second and third on 3.4 per cent and 1.8 per cent respectively. A ranking of the most prolific authors revealed just one non-Anglo-Saxon scholar (Esteban Hernández-Esteve) in the top twenty (Carmona 2004: 10). Turning to period covered, 72 per cent of the papers addressed events that happened after 1850 (ibid.: 12). Carmona also believes that the discipline cannot be properly regarded as international in scope because of the neglect of scholars operating in non-Anglo-Saxon settings who undertake work which is more diverse in time and space. Constructive proposals are put forward for addressing this concern (ibid.).

To help tackle the limited focus of much historical writing in accounting, Carmona and Zan have called for:

> mapping variety in the history of accounting and management practices by expanding the dimensions of time (i.e., history of the present but also of proto-industrial settings and ancient history) and space (i.e., Africa, Continental Europe, Islam, Latin-America, etc) that characterize present focus of accounting history research.
>
> (2002: 291)

In the same authors' estimation, a further part of the problem is differences in the nature of institutions available for historical study in various parts of the globe. Pointing out that considerable research effort has been devoted to the study of profit-seeking enterprises, they make the plea for more work on other types of organisation:

> Situations of stiff competition, though, are relatively modern phenomena that characterize a limited number of settings (i.e. Anglo-Saxon markets since the industrial revolution). In contrast, other countries and regions still fit well in the notion of emerging economies (i.e. Latin America) and economies in transition (i.e. Eastern Europe).
>
> (ibid.: 301)

They also argue that lack of direct association with the free market economy does not mean that 'the state, state-owned companies, firms, regulated markets, the church, the nobility' did not perform accounting which is worthy of examination (ibid.: 301).

Walker's (2005a) study of accounting history published outside accounting journals over the period 1954–2002 also points to a degree of introversion. In his attempt to locate promising avenues for interdisciplinary research with the wider community of historians, Walker noted a dominant focus on the age of modernity. However, his analysis of *Historical Abstracts* indicates the potential for accounting historians to study sites such as eastern and central Europe and central and South America. Akin to Carmona and Zan, Walker (ibid.: 233) argues that: 'Subjects particularly deserving of interdisciplinary research engaging accounting and other historians include accounting in agricultural economies, the institutions of pre-industrial rural societies and diverse systems of government.'

Attempts to extend the spatial scope of accounting history research have also found expression in the form of calls for comparative international studies. Quite apart from enhancing our knowledge of accounting's past, Carnegie and Napier (2002: 694–5; see also Carmona and Zan 2002: 301) consider such work to have considerable practical relevance by allowing us to improve 'our understanding of, and ability to critique, the roles, uses and impacts of accounting in today's global society, by providing a temporal dimension that may be lacking in studies focusing entirely on the contemporary state of accounting'. It was this conviction that motivated the editor of *ABR* to arrange a special issue on international accounting history in 2002.

Carnegie and Napier (2002: 695–6) identify three types of international comparison: 'synchronic' comparisons across countries based on a particular past moment in time; 'parallel' studies of accounting which take a given period and examine accounting phenomena of that period in different locations (for example, Boyns *et al.* 1997); and 'diffusion' studies examining the spread of accounting ideas, techniques, institutions and concepts, of which there are already a number of examples since that of Johnson Caygill (1971).

Sources

Having discussed the changing subjects which accounting historians investigate, we now turn to an overview of the sources they deploy.

Archival evidence

The historian (accounting or otherwise) aims to use evidence to craft a coherent and probable picture of what has happened in the past. Table 3.3 lists and classifies sources of historical evidence. According to its compilers (Fleischman *et al.* 1996: 61), 'most important for accounting history is communicative evidence, usually taken from written documents'.

The question of what counts as 'adequate' evidence is the subject of a wide-ranging study by Napier (2002). The process through which evidence is transformed into written history is set out in Figure 3.1.

Communicative evidence has long been considered the principal foundation for historical research, enabling investigators to make the discoveries from which their stories can be

Table 3.3   Evidences of history

Natural evidence	*Communicative evidence*
Past landscapes	*Written*
Natural objects	Chronicles, annals, biographies, genealogies
Human remains	Memoirs, diaries, letters, newspapers
Alterations of natural objects (tilled fields, cleared forests, etc.)	Literature, public documents, business records
	Inscriptions
Processive evidence	*Oral*
Language, customs, institutions	Ballads, anecdotes, tapes, sagas
Tools, other artefacts	Recordings (tapes, disks)
	Works of art
	Portraits, other paintings, sculpture, coins, medals
	Films, videotapes, music

Source: Fleischman *et al.* (1996: 61).

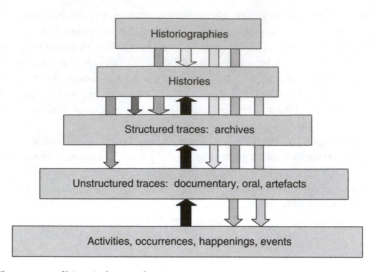

Figure 3.1 The process of historical research

Source: Napier (2002: 137)

constructed. The use of archival material is, of course, problematic. Quite apart from the question of what counts as evidence, only a fraction of evidence created continues to survive, that which does survive may not be in useable form (the material may be machine-readable but the required machinery may no longer exist or work), it may be non-representative of the past (for example, accounting archives often concentrate on large companies and exclude the small) and the meaning of what has been written down can be interpreted in different ways.

Critical historians have often criticised the traditional historians' use of archival evidence (for example, Miller and Napier 1993). Some are equally concerned with a lack of ambition on the part of traditional researchers and argue that they can do better:

> The traditional interpretive historian benefits from exposure to methodological choices which can facilitate greater rigour in the accessing and interpretation of primary sources and can lift the ensuing analysis above the level of naive antiquarian narrative.
>
> (Parker 1997: 131)

Under fire from critical historians, Fleischman and Tyson's (1997) concern that archival-oriented researchers might be 'an endangered species' possibly underestimates the latter's resilience. Also, their characterisation of archivists as the 'drones whose only job is to provide grist for the paradigmatic mills' caricatures historians of both persuasions. Fleischman and Tyson's generally thoughtful vindication of archival research elicits a number of inconsistencies in the criticisms levelled by critical historians at the traditional, which includes allegations that the former do not make the perceived mistake of searching for origins. Others agree. In Zan's estimation (2004: 182), the search by Hoskin and Macve (1994) for the 'Genesis of managerialism' is associated with the 'linear view of history' of which traditional historians are so often accused. Fleischman and Tyson (1997: 105) also raise the following interesting question: 'By what standard is it more acceptable to write an interpretive piece without doing archival research than it is to report the results of archival research without accompanying interpretation?' The answer that the former displays scholarship and intellect and the latter merely hard work has a degree of validity, but it is one that disregards the essential archaeological contribution of the archival researcher.

The limitations of archival records as representation of the past was one of the criticisms directed at traditional accounting historians by some critical writers (Fleischman and Tyson 1997: 97–100). But, of course, critical historians also use discoveries as the evidential basis for their own work. Perhaps this was not so evident in earlier times when practitioners of the new accounting history had a stock of prior discoveries to re-interpret (Willmott 1986; Hopwood 1987; Miller and O'Leary 1987; Bryer 1991; Hopper and Armstrong 1991). But some critical historians were immersed in archival research from the outset (for example, Hoskin and Macve 1986, 1988; Loft 1986), while others (such as Bryer 2006) have more recently turned to original records as the basis for theorising accounting's past.

Fleischman and Tyson (2003) staunchly defend the archival orientation of the so-called traditional researchers, but they also devote considerable space to rehearsing some of the pitfalls of doing archival research and in advising researchers how they might best prepare themselves for this labour (also Walker 2004). Johnson (2000) describes and analyses the hazards associated with archival research in her case study of the bookkeeping records of a company well-known in the accounting history literature – E. I. DuPont de Nemours & Co. Johnson (2000: 129) discovered that 'the process of understanding, interpreting, and validating the record keeping' of this company 'led to a number of misleading, confusing, and time-consuming issues which had to be resolved'. Her experience elicited the following warning to archival researchers who:

> must understand that they are able to rely on secondary sources, when they exist, only as long as they remain circumspect when depending on the secondary interpretation of primary sources, and that even the primary sources themselves may lead the researcher astray.
>
> (Johnson 2000: 129; see also Arnold and McCartney 2003)

Sy and Tinker (2005: 63) launch a scathing attack on accounting historians of all persuasions for their commitment to written, primary sources that encourages 'sterile empiricism'. They believe that, released from such constraint, the potential of historical research would be much enhanced. They demonstrate how it might be possible to escape from dead-end intellectualism 'by sketching a Post-Kuhnian panorama in terms of a Non-Eurocentric, social, gendered, environmental, public interest and labour orientation' (ibid.: 47). Hammond and Sikka (1996: abstract) also express concern that 'Much of the historical research in accounting continues to mimic idealized scientific methods in which written and official evidence is privileged.'

Oral history

Hammond (2003: 85) believes that enriched understandings of the past require 'examining new documentary sources, including "oral history" (talking to people about their experiences)'. More specifically, in collaboration with Sikka, she 'calls for the use of oral histories so that those marginalized and neglected by conventional history can be given a voice and problematize the narratives of "progress" dominating accounting history research' (Hammond and Sikka 1996: abstract). In a similar vein, Fleischman and Tyson (2003: 32) agree that archival materials (narrowly defined) suffer from 'failure to represent the suppressed voices of the past – the poor, the illiterate, women, the economically powerless for whom accounting records were not an available avenue of expression'. Returning to Hammond and Sikka (1996: 91): 'Without oral history, the role of accountancy practices and firms in colonizing organizations (Armstrong, 1987), influencing unemployment, divestment (Bryer and Brignall, 1986), crime (Mitchell *et al.*, 1996) and industrial disputes (Berry *et al.*, 1985), remains ill understood.'

Oral history is seen as 'giving greater insight into the "why" and "how" of events' (Burrows 1999: 100). The material collected may be about the interviewee or about people or events of which they are knowledgeable. Collins and Bloom (1991: 23) see the role of oral history as 'an historical methodology, [which] can be used as a research tool to supplement and clarify the written record or provide a record where no written record exists'. Or it might be undertaken to preserve evidence for future use. For example, a project funded by the Institute of Chartered Accountants of Scotland (ICAS) had as its purpose to record the life histories of influential figures in the Scottish accounting profession that might otherwise be lost (Walker 2005b: iii). Collins and Bloom (1991) provide guidance on the process of gathering oral testimony and, to illustrate its potential, explain how oral history could be used to study the evolution of accounting standards.

Initially, fears were expressed concerning the validity of oral history as an evidential base, and a literature developed to address allegations that it was 'too soft and subject to bias' (Hammond 2003: 85). Such reservations were put into context, though not resolved, by growing recognition of the fact that 'all histories are selective and biased' (ibid.: 85). In Hammond's estimation, traditional researchers rarely acknowledge this reality, and she welcomes a 'literature on the use of oral history [which] grapples with questions of validity and authority without contending that a purely scientific and unbiased approach is possible' (ibid.: 85). Indeed, proponents of oral history consider one of its strengths to be forthright recognition of its limitations: 'acknowledgement of the lack of objectivity is, in fact, key to the contribution of oral history' because, what the researcher strives to discover, 'must be based on the interviewees' own interpretation of their experiences' (ibid.: 86).

Teresa Hammond is also well placed to explain the potentials and pitfalls of the oral history methodology (see also, Hammond and Sikka 1996: 86–91; Matthews and Pirie 2001: ch. 1) based on her own extensive, pioneering research into the histories of African-American accountants and of women in accounting. In a witty and erudite essay, Louis Goldberg (1997) provided examples of the hazards of oral history. He cast doubt on the oral history contained in two studies of Australian accounting institutions (Burrows 1996; Linn 1996). Although favourably disposed towards historical research, Goldberg (1997: 113) was sufficiently aroused to conclude 'while both histories are well-written, how much of what they include about other people can I believe accords with perceived experiences of those people themselves?' Such a criticism is not exclusive to oral history, of course, but the importance of taking steps to ensure, as far as possible, the accuracy of the 'facts' reported is well made.

Some examples of oral history research

Although oral history has long been accepted as scholarly work, it was not until relatively recently that its use received much attention in accounting history (Collins and Bloom 1991). An early example of the use of this method occurred when Zeff was collecting material for *Forging Accounting Principles in Five Countries* (1972). While acknowledging the valuable role of committee minutes, internal reports, correspondence and other publicly available material, he observed that:

these documents will seldom yield useful insights into the *real factors* that influenced the course of standard-setting. It becomes necessary to conduct interviews with the principal policy makers and others who were close observers of the standard-setting process.

(Zeff 1980: 14, emphasis added)

Later in the 1970s, Mumford conducted a series of interviews of leading accountants, and 12 that took place between 1979 and 1984 formed the basis for a paper on 'Chartered accountants and business managers' (Mumford 1991). However, the practical problem of getting tapes transcribed slowed this project and it was not until recently that arrangements were made for the results to become publicly available thanks to a research grant from the ICAS (Mumford 2007).

Parker's (1994) study of Goldberg and Hammond and Streeter's (1994) research into early African-American certified public accountants are examples of the growing number of oral history based studies during the 1990s. Hammond nevertheless believes that there is a continued resistance to publishing such 'non-traditional work'. Editors of 'non-traditional journals' such as *CPA* and *AAAJ* are exempted from this allegation (Hammond 2003:94) but, unhelpfully, she fails to 'name and shame' the perceived transgressors.

The growing amount of oral history-based research being published is to be welcomed, even if much of it continues to contain stories of the great and the good rather than the marginalised voices from below. Matthews and Pirie (2001) explain how they tackled the thorny problem of who to interview when collecting material for their study of the British auditing profession. Their initial plan was to compile a random selection of interviewees from the ICAEW's list of members, but this was abandoned in favour of the 'purposeful' sample approved by Hammond and Sikka (1996: 88) so as to capture the 'key figures' (Matthews and Pirie 2001: 2) as well as ensuring adequate coverage of other voices.

Matthews and Pirie usefully discuss issues arising from conducting oral history projects. Several of the interviewees displayed misgivings over the publication of extracts from their interview, having seen the transcribed version. Most participants eventually acquiesced but seven, of 77, withdrew their permission. Four of these were retired partners from the then Big Six: 'One, an ex–Coopers and Lybrand partner, refused despite giving a charming and informative interview at the end of which he stated that he had no objection to almost all of what he said being ascribed to him' (ibid.: 9).

Dissemination

Fleischman and Radcliffe (2005: 61–2), in their celebration of the 'expansion and maturation' of accounting history research during the 'roaring nineties', consider its 'coming of age' to be signalled by the growth of publishing opportunities. The role of accounting journals in the dissemination of accounting history research is further considered in this section where attention is also drawn to other publication outlets which could be better exploited.

Generalist accounting journals and editorial policy

The growing diversity of accounting history is celebrated by Napier in a survey of 30 years of historical research published in *AOS* (2006: 445, see also Chapter 2):

The understanding of what counts as accounting has broadened, a greater awareness of how accounting is intertwined in the social has emerged, voices from below have been allowed to speak, while accounting has been seen to be implicated in wider arenas, with networks of practices, principles and people constituting varieties of 'accounting constellations'.

A number of generalist accounting journals have contributed significantly to this broadening of what counts as accounting history. However, not all can be said to have participated in the development of the subject. According to Fleischman and Radcliffe (2005: 62), 'certain flagship U.S. accounting journals were once willing to publish quality history articles' but this is no longer the case. In the 1960s and early 1970s, the *Journal of Accounting Research* published a number of historical works (for example, Carsberg 1966), but there was then a void until 1989 (when it published a three page comment by Scorgie), and nothing has appeared since.[6] Another elite journal, the *Accounting Review*, published one or two accounting history articles each year through the 1980s, but none since a paper by Fleischman and Parker in 1991.

The publication of historical material in generalist journals therefore depends on editorial policy, and it is for this reason that accounting history owes a debt to editors who opened the door to the discipline early on. Examples include Robert H. Parker at *Accounting and Business Research*, Stephen A. Zeff at the *Accounting Review* and Ray Chambers at *Abacus*. The publication culture which they helped develop has been important in making accounting history a respected area of investigation. *ABR* and *Abacus* remain receptive to historical work and have been joined by some of the more recently launched critical journals.

In the first issue of *Accounting, Organizations and Society*, Anthony Hopwood attacked the 'all too often' perception of accounting as 'a rather static and purely technical phenomenon' (Hopwood 1976: 1). Hopwood (1977), as Napier (2006: 446) points out, revealed 'an awareness that historical studies could be an important source of understanding of the roles of accounting in organizations and society'. Ten years later, Hopwood (1987) launched a withering attack on prior historical research. 'The archaeology of accounting systems' dismissed much previously published accounting history on the grounds that it adopted a rather technical perspective 'delineating the residues of accounting past rather than more actively probing the underlying processes and forces at work'. Hopwood advocated an examination of accounting over time through a consideration of the preconditions for change, the process of change and its organizational consequences. His critique of prior research naturally went down poorly with many traditional historians, but his support for what became labelled 'new accounting history' encouraged much greater diversity in historical methodology and an upsurge of interest in accounting history as a legitimate subject for study.

In their inaugural editorial, Guthrie and Parker (1988: 3) asserted that the *Accounting, Auditing & Accountability Journal* would 'offer a unique mix of research topics and traditions which have been marginalised by more traditional journals' including 'critical and historical perspectives of current issues and problems in accounting and auditing'. They also encouraged innovative theoretical approaches and the deployment of new methodologies. The columns of *AAAJ* have featured contributions to 'the great costing debate' (Tyson 1993; Hoskin and Macve 1994) and the history of accounting's professionalisation (Lee 1995; Carnegie *et al.* 2003a). *AAAJ* has also featured important papers that search for commonality (Funnell 1996) and plurality (Hammond and Sikka 1996) in accounting historiography, though Walker (2008) remains ambivalent about the extent that convergence and conciliation should be encouraged.

In a similar vein, the research areas within which *Critical Perspectives on Accounting* invites submissions include 'Studies of accounting's historical role, as a means of "remembering" the subject's social and conflictual character'. *CPA* too has been an important medium for the conduct of major debates in accounting history.

Authorship profile

As indicated in the earlier discussion on the subject matter of accounting history research, the contents of papers published in the three specialist accounting history journals have been the subject of scrutiny (Carnegie and Potter 2000; Anderson 2002; Williams and Wines 2006). These publications enable us to further profile various aspects of authorship.

Anderson (2002: 20) reveals that, in contrast to studies of the general accounting literature, which have found co-authorship to significantly outweigh sole authorship, the author profile for *ABFH* is consistent with Carnegie and Potter's finding (2000: 187) that collaboration, particularly international alliances, is less common in accounting history research. A similar pattern is evident in the case of *AH*, with Williams and Wines (2006: 425) reporting that 46 per cent of the papers published between 1996 and 2005 involved multiple authors and that less than one in five of these were contributed by authors from different regions. They also revealed that 78.5 per cent of individual-authored papers were by men (Williams and Wines 2006: 432). Carnegie *et al.* (2003b) found that only 12 per cent of papers published in the three specialist accounting history journals to 2000 were authored by women. Accounting history is clearly a male-dominated pursuit.

Carnegie and Potter's study (2000: 194) of the content of all three journals also suggests 'the existence of a relatively insular international accounting history community dominated by a small number of institutions and authors'. However, confining attention to *ABFH*, Anderson (2002: 20) found accounting history research to be less inward-looking. He reveals that the columns of *ABFH* featured contributions from authors in 16 different regions, with almost one-third of all articles written by scholars outside the Anglo-American world (ibid.: 20). Growing collaboration within the international community is, of course, facilitated by the rising number of international conferences (see Chapter 1) that provide a meeting place for researchers already working together on projects as well as a forum where new collaborative ventures can be developed.

Books and monographs

As the contents of Chapters 1 and 2 suggest, books on accounting history have also been of considerable importance in the development of the discipline. The results reported by Carmona (2006) confirm the significance of media beyond journals for the diffusion of accounting history knowledge. Empirical support for this contention is provided by measuring the frequency of citations in the accounting history literature during the 1990s. Whereas journal articles received 3,724 citations or 21 per cent of the total, other sources of accounting history literature, mainly books and research monographs, received 13,985 citations or 79 per cent of the total. Carmona (2006: 266) further reveals that 11 out of the 27 'most influential works' were published as books. He concluded that: 'books and research monographs constitute key venues for the dissemination of accounting knowledge' (ibid.: 265).

Despite their importance, Edwards' (2004) analysis of accounting history publications, 1998–2002, revealed that only 2.8 per cent of these were books. Indeed, eight of the eleven influential books identified by Carmona were published before 1980 and none of them after 1990. The operation of the Research Assessment Exercise[7] is certainly responsible for the emphasis on journal articles in the UK. While a wide range of eligible outputs are identified for submission to RAE panels and guidance notes suggest that output media is less significant than the quality of the research it contains, no one really believes it (Edwards 2004). For accountancy, the first type of output usually identified is 'refereed articles' and this is what university administrators encourage accounting faculty to publish.

This effective bias against books is at variance with the state of affairs in the sister discipline of history. Indeed, within university history departments in Britain, the book rather than the portfolio of articles is seen as the appropriate vehicle for communicating the results of sustained historical scholarship. A relevant book also becomes, as Carmona (2006) demonstrates, the source of initial reference for researchers working on a new area, and it is of course the purpose of the *Routledge Companion* to help fulfil this need. Parker (1999) also makes the case for book-length accounting history publications when calling for a 'return to the "grand tour" literary narrative' capable of 'offering a longer term, broader scope macro-scope view of the past' (ibid.: 24).[8]

Popularising research findings

Accounting history researchers publish their findings predominantly in academic rather than professional journals. This places limitations on their capacity to communicate with the wider accounting populace and influence policy-making. The importance of disseminating research findings to a non-academic readership is recognised by research funding institutions. The UK government-financed Economic and Social Research Council (ESRC), for example, attaches 'great importance to the communication of research findings both within and beyond the academic community'.

Accounting history research financed by an accounting organisation may result in a summary article in a sponsored professional journal or newsletter. Accounting historians may find their services in demand when professional organisations and accountancy firms seek to celebrate anniversaries, and when high profile corporate scandals and accounting failures excite searches for explanations and similar events in the past. But despite the importance of wider dissemination, the results of accounting history research seldom feature prominently in professional journals or the popular media. Beattie and Goodacre (2004: 25) observe a more general decline in publications by academics in the main professional accounting journals in Britain. This clearly has implications for the profile of accounting history beyond the academic community which practises it.

Conclusion

This chapter reveals a consensus among those who have observed the growth of accounting history as an academic pursuit. The subject areas studied are expanding, with the past 20 years witnessing diversity in the methods used to gather data and interpret the meaning of accounting's discovered past. The community of accounting historians is well served in terms of publication outlets; there are three specialist journals and many generalist journals that are open to their work. The editors of critical and interdisciplinary accounting journals have played a key role in expanding the methodological horizons of accounting historians. Three flourishing subject areas during the past decade or so have been historiography, cost and management accounting and the professionalisation of accountancy. It is possible that advance in these areas has crowded out work elsewhere. Subject areas such as record-keeping and central government accounting await papers and books to provide the impetus that, for example, Loft (1986),

Hopwood (1987), Johnson and Kaplan (1987) and Hoskin and Macve (1988) provided for the study of the history of management accounting.

There are concerns about the Anglo-Saxon dominance of the discipline. Most authors in English-language journals tend to focus on the accounting histories of their own countries post-1900. This is a highly restricted orientation in terms of authorship, time and place. There is no doubt that many of those whose first language is not English are at a significant disadvantage when targeting Australian, British and US-based journals as outlets for their work. Carmona (2004) puts forward interesting ideas concerning what might be done in the short and long term to support research 'outside the Anglo-Saxon box' (Carmona 2006: 12). Things are improving, however, with international conferences providing just one forum where ideas for transnational collaboration can emerge and develop. Also, special issues have been successfully employed by journal editors to help widen the scope of the subject and the geographical focus of historical studies.

Accounting historians have traditionally relied heavily on communicative evidences in the written form. There has been healthy discussion of the potential and pitfalls of archival sources for the work of both traditional and critical historians. Methodological debate has demonstrated how oral history can be employed not only 'to supplement and verify other forms of history' but also 'to problematize and contradict the traditional stories of accounting' and 'give sustained visibility to the lived experiences of the wide variety of communities affected by accounting' (Hammond and Sikka 1996: 80–1).

The existing subject matter of accounting history is enormous as revealed by numerous themes featuring in this *Routledge Companion*. Overall, the depth of coverage of these research areas varies; some are long-established, others are relatively new. Accounting history research is thriving, at least in some countries, but the scope for further development is great. The potential arenas for research are vast and the number of accounting historians meagre by comparison. Some topics receive less attention now than in the past, such as 'early accounting' and 'accounting theory'. Areas such as 'mechanised accounting and computers' and 'education' (per Table 3.1) have never been the focus of much historical research, and studies of new terrains such as 'gender studies' and 'accounting in the home and small businesses' have barely scratched the surface. Even areas that have proved highly popular would benefit from further methodological innovation (Walker 2008).

As the remaining chapters in this *Routledge Companion* reveal, there is reason for the accounting community to believe that progress has been made. But there is a lot more to do.

Key works

Carmona (2004) offers a broad-based study of the accounting history literature published during the 1990s. The authors and the coverage of their research are profiled and criticised.

Fleischman and Tyson (2003) offers a useful introduction to the pursuit of accounting history research based on archival sources. The chapter is a practical guide to locating primary materials.

Hammond and Sikka (1996) criticises written evidence on the grounds that it privileges major personalities and ignores ordinary people whose lives and experiences can be better captured and understood through oral history.

Previts *et al*. (1990b) represents an early attempt to identify the principal subject matter of accounting history which has informed subsequent classifications.

Walker (2006) examines the changing frontiers of accounting history and the challenges facing the discipline including limited interdisciplinary engagement and Anglo-Saxon dominance of research agendas.

Notes

1 These are reproduced in Parker (1980). Parker (1988) extends coverage to 1987.
2 It is available online as part of the *Accounting Research Database* at: http://rarc.rutgers.edu/publication/default.htm.
3 Parker's list has been amended to combine, as 'early accounting', his 'ancient accounting' and 'early accounting' in each of 10 different geographical locations. Parker's general and miscellaneous categories are omitted.
4 Anderson (2002) focuses on the first ten volumes of *Accounting, Business & Financial History*, 1990–2000; Williams and Wines (2006) on the initial ten issues of *Accounting History*, 1996–2005; and Carnegie and Potter (2000) on both of these journals together with the *Accounting Historians Journal* for the years 1996–9.
5 See Previts *et al.* (1990b) for another categorisation of the subjects of historical research.
6 Papers which use historical data, such as Basu's (2003) study of income smoothing in early nineteenth-century railroads, but make no attempt to place the discussion in the contemporary context or other relevant historical literature, would fall only within a very wide definition of accounting history.
7 The main purpose of the Research Assessment Exercise is to enable the higher education funding bodies to distribute public funds for research on the basis of quality.
8 Duke and Coffman (1993) offer helpful advice on writing accounting or business histories of this type.

References

Anderson, M. (2002) An analysis of the first ten volumes of research in *Accounting, Business & Financial History*, *Accounting, Business & Financial History*, 12 (1): 1–24.

Arnold, A. J. and McCartney, S. (2003) 'It may be earlier than you think': evidence, myths and informed debate in accounting history, *Critical Perspectives on Accounting*, 14 (3): 227–53.

Badua, F. A., Previts, G. J. and Vasarhelyi, M. A. (2003) The *Accounting Historians Journal* index: employing the *Accounting Research Database* to profile and support research, in R. K. Fleischman, V. S. Radcliffe and P. A. Shoemaker (eds) *Doing Accounting History: Contributions to the Development of Accounting Thought*, pp. 203–16 (Amsterdam: JAI).

Basu, S. (2003) Discussion of enforceable accounting rules and income measurement by early 20th-century railroads, *Journal of Accounting Research*, 41 (2): 433–44.

Beattie, V. and Goodacre, A. (2004) Publishing patterns within the UK accounting and finance academic community, *British Accounting Review*, 36 (1): 7–44.

Boyns, T., Edwards, J. R. and Nikitin, M. (1997) The development of industrial accounting in Britain and France before 1880: a comparative study of accounting literature and practice, *European Accounting Review*, 6 (3): 393–437.

Bryer, R. A. (1991) Accounting for the 'railway mania' of 1845: a great railway swindle?, *Accounting Organizations and Society*, 16 (5/6): 439–86.

Bryer, R. A. (2006) The genesis of the capitalist farmer: towards a Marxist accounting history of the origins of the English agricultural revolution, *Critical Perspectives on Accounting*, 17 (4): 367–97.

Burrows, G. H. (1996) *The Foundation: A History of the Australian Accounting Research Foundation 1966–1991* (Melbourne: Australian Accounting Research Foundation).

Burrows, G. H. (1999) A response to Lou Goldberg's concerns about oral history, *Accounting History*, 4 (1): 99–106.

Carmona, S. (2004) Accounting history research and its diffusion in an international context, *Accounting History*, 9 (3): 7–23.

Carmona, S. (2006) Performance reviews, the impact of accounting research, and the role of publication forms, *Advances in Accounting*, 22: 241–67.

Carmona, S. and Zan, L. (2002) Mapping variety in the history of accounting and management practices, *European Accounting Review*, 11 (2): 291–304.

Carnegie, G. D. and Napier, C. J. (1996) Critical and interpretive histories: understanding accounting's present and future through its past, *Accounting, Auditing & Accountability Journal*, 9 (3): 7–39.

Carnegie, G. D. and Napier, C. J. (2002) Exploring comparative international accounting history, *Accounting, Auditing & Accountability Journal*, 15 (5): 689–718.

Carnegie, G. D. and Potter, B. N. (2000) Publishing patterns in specialist accounting history journals in the English language, 1996–1999, *Accounting, Historians Journal*, 27 (2): 177–98.

Carnegie, G. D., Edwards, J. R. and West, B. (2003a) Understanding the dynamics of the Australian accounting profession: a prosopographical study of the founding members of the Incorporated Institute of Accountants, Victoria, 1886 to 1908, *Accounting, Auditing & Accountability Journal*, 16 (5): 790–820.

Carnegie, G. D., McWatters, C. S. and Potter, B. N. (2003b) The development of the specialist accounting history literature in the English language: an analysis by gender, *Accounting, Auditing & Accountability Journal*, 16 (2): 186–207.

Carsberg, B. K. (1966) The contribution of P. D. Leake to the theory of goodwill valuation, *Journal of Accounting Research*, 4 (1): 1–15.

Collins, M. and Bloom, R. (1991) The role of oral history in accounting, *Accounting, Auditing & Accountability Journal*, 4 (4): 23–31.

Duke, M. and Coffman, E. N. (1993) Writing an accounting or business history: notes toward a methodology, *Accounting Historians Journal*, 20 (2): 217–35.

Edwards, J. R. (2004) Some problems and challenges in accounting history research. Paper presented at Tenth World Congress of Accounting Historians, St. Louis, MO and Oxford, MS, 1–5 August.

Fleischman, R. K. and Parker, L. D. (1991) British entrepreneurs and preindustrial revolution evidence of cost management, *Accounting Review*, 66 (2): 361–75.

Fleischman, R. K. and Radcliffe, V. S. (2005) The roaring nineties: accounting history comes of age, *Accounting Historians Journal*, 32 (1): 61–109.

Fleischman, R. K. and Tyson, T. N. (1997) Archival researchers: an endangered species, *Accounting Historians Journal*, 24 (2): 91–109.

Fleischman, R. K. and Tyson, T. N. (2003) Archival research methodology, in R. K. Fleischman, V. S. Radcliffe and P. A. Shoemaker (eds) *Doing Accounting History: Contributions to the Development of Accounting Thought*, pp. 31–47 (Amsterdam: JAI).

Fleischman, R. K., Mills, P. A. and Tyson, T. N. (1996) A theoretical primer for evaluating and conducting historical research in accounting, *Accounting History*, 1 (1): 55–75.

Funnell, W. (1996) Preserving history in accounting: seeking common ground between old and new accounting history, *Accounting, Auditing & Accountability Journal*, 9 (4): 38–64.

Funnell, W. (2007) The reason why: the English constitution and the latent promise of liberty in the history of accounting, *Accounting, Business & Financial History*, 17 (2): 265–83.

Goldberg, L. (1997) Comment: send three and fourpence: some reflections on oral – and other – history, *Accounting History*, 2 (1): 107–14.

Guthrie, J. and Parker, L. D. (1988) Editorial, *Accounting, Auditing & Accountability Journal*, 1 (1): 3–5.

Hammond, T. D. (2003) Histories outside the mainstream: oral history and non-traditional approaches, in R. K. Fleischman, V. S. Radcliffe and P. A. Shoemaker (eds) *Doing Accounting History: Contributions to the Development of Accounting Thought*, pp. 81–96 (Amsterdam: JAI).

Hammond, T. and Sikka, P. (1996) Radicalizing accounting history: the potential of oral history, *Accounting, Auditing & Accountability Journal*, 9 (3): 79–97.

Hammond, T. and Streeter, D. W. (1994) Overcoming barriers: early African–American certified public accountants, *Accounting, Organizations and Society*, 19 (3): 271–88.

Hatfield, H. R. (1924) An historical defense of bookkeeping, *Journal of Accountancy*, 37 (4): 241–53.

Hopper, T. and Armstrong, P. (1991) Cost accounting, controlling labour and the rise of conglomerates, *Accounting, Organizations and Society*, 16 (5/6): 405–38.

Hopwood, A. G. (1976) Editorial: the path ahead, *Accounting, Organizations and Society*, 1 (1): 1–4.

Hopwood, A. G. (1977) Editorial, *Accounting, Organizations and Society*, 2 (4): 277–8.

Hopwood, A. G. (1987) The archaeology of accounting systems, *Accounting, Organizations and Society*, 12 (3): 207–34.

Hoskin, K. W. and Macve, R. H. (1986) Accounting and the examination: a genealogy of disciplinary power, *Accounting, Organizations & Society*, 11 (2): 105–36.

Hoskin, K. W. and Macve, R. H. (1988) The genesis of accountability: the West Point connections, *Accounting, Organizations and Society*, 13 (1): 37–73.

Hoskin, K. W. and Macve, R. H. (1994) Reappraising the genesis of managerialism: a re-examination of the role of accounting at Springfield Armory, 1815–1845, *Accounting, Auditing & Accountability Journal*, 7 (2): 4–29.

Johnson, H. T. and Kaplan, R. (1987) *Relevance Lost: The Rise and Fall of Management Accounting* (Boston: Harvard Business School Press).

Johnson, R. T. (2000) In search of E. I. duPont de Nemours & Company: the perils of archival research, *Accounting, Business & Financial History*, 10 (2): 129–68.

Johnson, T. J. and Caygill, M. (1971) The development of accountancy links in the Commonwealth, *Accounting and Business Research*, 1 (2): 155–73.

Lee, T. A. (1995) The professionalization of accountancy: a history of protecting the public interest in a self-interested way, *Accounting, Auditing & Accountability Journal*, 8 (4): 48–69.

Linn, R. (1996) *Power, Progress and Profit: A History of the Australian Accounting Profession* (Melbourne: Australian Society of Certified Practising Accountants).

Loft, A. (1986) Towards a critical understanding of accounting: the case of cost accounting in the UK, 1914–1925, *Accounting, Organizations and Society*, 11 (2): 137–69.

Macdonald, K. M. (1984) Professional formation: the case of the Scottish accountants, *British Journal of Sociology*, 35 (2): 174–89.

Matthews, D. (2002) The use of the postal questionnaire in accounting history research, *Accounting, Business & Financial History*, 12 (1): 113–29.

Matthews, D. and Pirie, J. (2001) *The Auditors Talk. An Oral History of a Profession from the 1920s to the Present Day* (New York: Garland).

Miller, P. and Napier, C. (1993) Genealogies of calculation, *Accounting, Organizations and Society*, 18 (7/8): 631–47.

Miller, P. and O'Leary, T. (1987) Accounting and the construction of the governable person, *Accounting, Organizations and Society* 12 (3): 235–65.

Miller, P., Hopper, T. and Laughlin, R. (1991) The new accounting history: an introduction, *Accounting, Organizations and Society*, 16 (5/6): 395–403.

Mumford, M. J. (1991) Chartered accountants as business managers: an oral history perspective, *Accounting, Business & Financial History*, 1 (2): 123–40.

Mumford, M. J. (2007) *Their Own Accounts. Views of Prominent 20th Century Accountants* (Edinburgh: Institute of Chartered Accountants of Scotland).

Napier, C. J. (2002) The historian as auditor: facts, judgments and evidence, *Accounting Historians Journal*, 29 (2): 131–55.

Napier, C. J. (2006) Accounts of change: 30 years of historical accounting research, *Accounting, Organizations and Society*, 31 (4/5): 445–507.

Parker, L. D. (1994) Impressions of a scholarly gentleman: Professor Louis Goldberg, *Accounting Historians Journal*, 21 (2): 1–40.

Parker, L. D. (1997) Informing historical research in accounting and management: traditions, philosophies and opportunities, *Accounting Historians Journal*, 24 (2): 111–49.

Parker, L. D. (1999) Historiography for the new millennium: adventures in accounting and management, *Accounting History*, 4 (2): 11–42.

Parker, R. H. (1980) Editorial, special accounting history issue, *Accounting and Business Research*, 10 (37A): ii.

Parker, R. H. (1988) Select bibliography of works on the history of accounting 1981–1987, *Accounting Historians Journal*, 15 (2): 1–81.

Parker, R. H. (1993) The scope of accounting history: a note, *Abacus*, 29 (1): 106–10.

Previts, G. J., Parker, L. D. and Coffman, E. N. (1990a) Accounting history: definition and relevance, *Abacus*, 26 (1): 1–16.

Previts, G. J., Parker, L. D. and Coffman, E. N. (1990b) An accounting historiography: subject matter and methodology, *Abacus*, 26 (2): 136–58.

Richardson, A. J. (1997) Social closure in dynamic markets: the incomplete professional project in accountancy, *Critical Perspectives on Accounting*, 8 (6): 635–53.

Scorgie, M. E. (1989) The role of negative numbers in the development of double entry bookkeeping: a comment, *Journal of Accounting Research*, 27 (2): 316–18.

Sy, A. and Tinker, T. (2005) Archival research and the lost worlds of accounting, *Accounting History*, 10 (1): 47–69.

Tyson, T. (1993) Keeping the record straight: Foucauldian revisionism and nineteenth century US cost accounting history, *Accounting, Auditing & Accountability Journal*, 6 (2): 4–16.

Walker, S. P. (1995) The genesis of professional organization in Scotland: a contextual analysis, *Accounting, Organizations and Society*, 20 (4): 285–310.

Walker, S. P. (2004) The search for clues in accounting history, in C. Humphrey and B. Lee (eds) *The Real Life Guide to Accounting Research: A Behind-the-Scenes View of Using Qualitative Research Methods*, pp. 3–21 (Kidlington, Oxford: Elsevier).

Walker, S. P. (2005a) Accounting in history, *Accounting Historians Journal*, 32 (2): 233–59.

Walker, S. P. (ed.) (2005b) *Giving an Account: Life Histories of Four CAs* (Edinburgh: Institute of Chartered Accountants of Scotland).

Walker, S. P. (2006) Current trends in accounting history, *Irish Accounting Review*, 13 (1): 107–21.

Walker, S. P. (2008) Innovation, convergence and argument without end in accounting history, *Accounting, Auditing & Accountability Journal*, 21 (2): 296–322.

Williams, B. and Wines, G. (2006) The first 10 years of *Accounting History* as an international refereed journal: 1996–2005, *Accounting History*, 11 (4): 419–45.

Willmott, H. (1986) Organising the profession: a theoretical and historical examination of the development of the major accountancy bodies in the UK, *Accounting, Organizations and Society*, 11 (6): 555–80.

Zan, L. (2004) Writing accounting and management history. Insights from unorthodox music historiography, *Accounting Historians Journal*, 31 (2): 171–92.

Zeff, S. A. (1972) *Forging Accounting Principles in Five Countries: A History and an Analysis of Trends* (Champaign, IL: Stipes Publishing).

Zeff, S. A. (1980) The promise of historical research in accounting: some personal experiences, in R. D. Nair and T. H. Williams (eds) *Perspectives on Research*, pp. 13–25 (Madison, WI: University of Wisconsin).

Part 2

Technologies

4

Ancient accounting

Salvador Carmona and Mahmoud Ezzamel

Overview

This chapter aims to provide an overview of prior research on ancient accounting derived from both the accounting and non-accounting disciplines. The intention is to address some of the remarkably rich insights drawn from a variety of ancient accounting practices, the contexts within which they emerged, and the applications to which they have been put. The review of the extant literature demonstrates that accounting played a key role in facilitating the functioning of ancient states and economies, helping to regulate and coordinate activities conducted at various levels in ancient societies. Further, the review points to the remarkable capacity of ancient accounting to intervene in the domain of state activities, religious institutions, private business and the household. Far from being a rudimentary and crude technology, the chapter shows just how these ancient accounting practices exhibited a quite complex and rich variety of valuing and recording techniques.

Providing a comprehensive review of the diverse literature on ancient accounting is beyond the scope of one chapter; hence the focus is on Mesopotamia and ancient Egypt. This excludes the important literature on other early civilisations (e.g., Greece: De Ste. Croix 1956; Costouros 1978; China: Fu 1971; India: Scorgie 1990; Rome: Oldroyd 1995; Persia: Vollmers 1996), some of which is covered in Chapter 5 of this volume. By restricting our attention to Mesopotamia and ancient Egypt, we examine ancient accounting in two civilisations that co-existed during similar historical eras, yet exhibited significantly different socio-political and economic contexts.

In the next section of the chapter are outlined some of the key challenges facing researchers in the field. Some of these challenges are specific to the nature of the accounting materials that the literature draws upon, whereas other challenges relate to the contexts of remote history. The chapter then summarises the main findings of the extant literature on the technical and social attributes of ancient accounting, and the domains covered by accounting; specifically, the state/royal domain, private business, and the household. A summary section pulls together the key arguments of the chapter.

Challenges

In undertaking research on ancient accounting, it is important to ask: what problems does one encounter, compared to, say, conducting research into other historical eras? What measures does one take to deal with these problems? The answer to these, and similar questions, is by no means easy. However, we believe it is important that we attempt to at least identify a number of particularly challenging problems that we have encountered as part of our own experience. Further, the significance of these challenges depends largely on the views of accounting that a researcher holds. If accounting is conceptualised as a set of neutral, technical tools that are virtually divorced of social, economic and historical contexts, then the challenges would be significantly reduced. However, a view of accounting as an assemblage of socially and historically embedded technologies of calculation and reporting would demand an appreciation of ancient socio-political and economic contexts, rendering the study of ancient accounting highly problematic (Miller 1998). Given that the authors' intellectual leanings are of the latter persuasion, the high significance we place on the challenges identified below should come as no surprise to the reader. The challenges we wish to emphasise here are by no means exhaustive (Vollmers 2003), but have particularly bedevilled our own research into the area; these are: what constitutes primary sources, material lacunae, translation, and theorising ancient accounting history.

Primary sources

For much accounting history research the archive represents the key primary data source, and the quality of the archive and the archivist are key determinants of the quality of published work. The archive is usually located in well-known spaces, such as a special building or a library. The question is: Is there an equivalent to the 'archive', as we have come to know it, in the case of ancient accounting history? In the case of remote civilisations, such as those of Mesopotamia and ancient Egypt, our concept of an 'archive', if we are to invoke one at all, has to be much broader; indeed, some may prefer instead to speak of historical material rather than an 'archive'. This is because ancient historical material is widely dispersed, maybe indeed all over the world.

If the material exists, an additional source of complexity comes from the varying surfaces on which the texts are inscribed. For example, in the case of ancient Egypt, historical material is inscribed upon the surfaces of stones (of walls of temples and monuments), ostraca (shreds of pottery), and papyri. Yet, there appears to be some sort of specialisation in the use of materials: literary, legal, and commercial matters are inscribed onto papyri and ostraca, whereas monumental and religious texts are mainly inscribed on stone. Any serious attempt to study the emergence and functioning of ancient accounting would require careful consultation of most of these sources. Consequently, we argue that the ancient 'archive' is rather complex, in many cases inaccessible except to experts in ancient history, and accounting researchers have little option but to be selective. The question of course is: how selective? This is an issue that we deal with later.

Lacunae

Any reader of ancient history material will not fail to notice the considerable gaps in the historical material that has survived to the present time. This creates an unwanted problem of discontinuity that bedevils any attempt to forge an account of ancient history. Many of the texts on seemingly 'permanent' and virtually indestructible writing surfaces, such as building stones have been lost forever because of acts of nature (e.g., floods), acts by the ancients themselves (reuse of stone in new buildings, revenge acts to erase the deeds of previous rulers) or acts by us (e.g. use of material for modern buildings, poor preservation, vandalism). This means that only a fraction, sometimes a very small one, of the original material has survived to the present time. Given this considerable loss, the answer to the question of *how selective* a researcher could be becomes simple: examine virtually everything you can lay your hands on!

The above statement concerning an all-inclusive consultation of original ancient historical material is not meant to be flippant; rather it is made in acknowledgement of the precious but sparse amount of original material that has reached us. This problem is made even more acute because much of the surviving material has been damaged, sometimes quite considerably, at times rendering a text almost meaningless. Indeed, the problem of data lacunae is so serious that, at times, the researcher has to make assumptions concerning missing material based on expected patterns of previous texts, sometimes reaching to other historical episodes because of the lack of comparable texts from the same era.

The choice is either that we attempt to forge accounts of such histories, no matter how incomplete, or do nothing. Finley (1992: 25) has lamented ancient historians who rely on anecdotes, calling for 'abandoning the anecdotal technique of dredging up an example or two as if that constituted proof'. While we would endorse Finley's suggestion when evidence is plentiful, we would disagree if all that is available as evidence is of an anecdotal nature. Historical researchers are aware that evidence is rarely well preserved and complete and is usually messy and deficient. Consequently, even small fragments of evidence can reveal much, and the careful researcher should highlight their source's limitations and any consequential implications for the findings from the study, but without shying away from using anecdotes.

Translation

A significant number, but by no means all, of the texts containing accounting entries from Mesopotamia and ancient Egypt have been transliterated and then translated into modern European languages. As to those texts that have not yet been translated into contemporary languages, the only way to access them is to learn how to read hieroglyphics in the case of ancient Egypt and cuneiform in the case of Mesopotamia (see Vollmers 2003). In addition to this, there is the daunting problem of translating a text from the remote past into the present, with all that this entails in terms of finding suitable equivalent contemporary terms to those the ancients have used. To what extent, for example, can we sensibly describe 'exchange of goods for a price' as being equivalent to 'market exchange'? How legitimate is it for us to speak of an ancient economy as a means of describing the creation, accumulation and distribution of ancient 'wealth'? Are we entitled to use terms such as 'tax' to represent levies imposed by the ancient state on its subjects? Can we speak of 'accounting' practices and techniques in the remote past? Indeed, given how controversial the use of the term 'government' is even today (Rose and Miller 1992), can we legitimately speak of government in the ancient world?

Even more importantly, there is the major concern with the constitutive power of language and its effect on forging a picture of the remote past; contemporary researchers may not be reproducing the past but, instead, creating it via the language they employ. Previts and Bricker (1994) use the notion of 'presentmindness' to refer to this concern; by intimating that the use of present-day notions to write about institutions and practices of the past brings about understandings that are afar from those held by our ancestors. For example, current understandings of accountability differ from those of ancient people (see Ezzamel and Hoskin 2002; Carmona and Ezzamel 2007). Consequently, an unproblematic use of such notion in writing on ancient accounting history would mistakenly suggest that contemporary practices of accountability and those of the ancient world are very similar. Although these concerns are well taken, we suggest that there is scope for accounting historians to carefully adapt notions such as the 'state', the 'economy', 'markets', 'monies of account' to the ancient world. We recognise that this is a controversial area and that there is considerable debate on the extent to which such terms can be extended beyond the specific contexts in which they were first developed. Much depends on how strict one wishes to be in delineating the conditions that have to be satisfied in order for the use of the term to be deemed acceptable. For example, the term 'state' can readily be applied to virtually all ancient societies as long as it is taken to imply only three conditions – a geographical area with a population and a visible authority – and this applies to country states as well as city states (for views on this debate, see Eisenstadt 1969; Ball 1995; Gills 1995; Warburton 1997).

On 'economy', Janssen (1975: 539) warns that 'the distance between ancient Egyptian and modern European economics is so wide that it is useful to stress and perhaps even overstress it in order to avoid a too modern conception of economic life in ancient Egypt'. Similarly, Finley argues at some length that the ancients did not have a concept similar to the notion of what we now understand as 'the economy':

> [The ancients] in fact lacked the concept of an 'economy', and *a fortiori*, they lacked the conceptual elements which together constitute what we call 'the economy'. Of course they farmed, traded, manufactured, mined, taxed, coined, deposited and loaned money, made profits or failed in their enterprises. And they discussed these activities in their talk and their writing. What they did not do, however, was to combine these particular activities conceptually into a unit, in Parsonian terms into 'a differentiated sub-system'.
>
> (Finley 1992: 21)

There is every reason to believe that the ancients did not develop a conceptual construct similar to that now called 'the economy', and care should be exercised when interpreting ancient practices so that they are not laboured by meanings the ancients would not have recognised. Reasonable apprehension, however, should not hamper efforts to study ancient economic and social practices, even though they may not correspond to conceptual categories that we now employ. There is also no reason why the word 'economy' and similar terms could not be used in an ancient context, as long as they are bracketed and their meanings are differentiated from those circulating in capitalist economies. Hence, we need to move away from such misplaced concern with what constitutes historical 'proof' (ibid.: 25) and acknowledge that there is no such a thing as a concrete history 'out there' to be captured in its reality, but rather accept that in writing history we 'construct history' (Ezzamel and Willmott 2004). In the context of our chapter, what we offer is our own account of these ancient histories via our own reconstruction of how previous researchers constructed these histories.

In a similar vein, we wish to address the extent to which 'markets' existed and functioned in the civilisations of the ancient Near East. Briefly, two schools of thought exist, one denying this possibility and the other affirming the existence (and indeed importance) of markets, even though proponents of the latter view would concede that such markets did not exhibit all the characteristics associated with the modern notion of market mechanism.

Polanyi (1957) is perhaps the most influential writer of the school denying the existence of markets in these societies. Commenting on trading in the time of Hammurabi, he stated, 'Babylonia, as a matter of fact, possessed neither market places nor a functioning market system of any description' (ibid.: 16). Other researchers attested to the existence of places for markets in Mesopotamia, but either insisted on the absence of a market economy (Oppenheim 1964), or spoke of a possible notion of a market price but then surmised that it might have been fixed by the government and not by trade in the market (Leemans 1960). For this school, even when places existed for markets, they were confined spaces where few items were exchanged and in a manner that did not contribute appreciably to the livelihood of producers and sellers (Dalton 1971).

Polanyi (1977: 125) refined his thoughts further by developing the notion of 'market elements' that seek to emphasise the institutional characteristics that constitute the market. These elements comprise:

> a site, physically present or available goods, a supply crowd, a demand crowd, custom or law, and, equivalencies . . . Whenever the market elements combine to form a supply–demand–price mechanism, we speak of price-making markets. Otherwise, the meeting of supply and demand crowds, carrying on exchange at fixed equivalencies, forms a non-price-making market. Short of this we should not speak of markets, but merely of the various combinations of the market elements the exchange situation happens to represent.

For Polanyi, ports of trade, and the provisioning at the gates of towns in what he terms 'redistributive oriental economies' exhibit market elements, but none of them are markets proper, because there is no supply–demand–price interaction. Given these refinements to Polanyi's thoughts, it can be stated that at the very least local markets existed in both ancient Egypt (Janssen 1975) and Mesopotamia (Renger 1984), although whether these local markets ever developed to become 'markets proper' by meeting Polanyi's criteria is unlikely.

It is within this understanding that we seek to approach our attempt to contextualise accounting practices analysed later in this chapter. Such contextualisation will enable us to embed the evidence in its wider environments and, hence, approach the meaning given by our ancestors to activities that present-day terminology can only describe superficially.

Theorising

There is considerable debate in the literature concerning how ancient accounting material can be theorised. For example, Silver (1985), Kemp (1989) and Warburton (1997) have each invoked rational economic ideas in interpreting ancient Egyptian records, in the belief that the ancient Egyptians displayed many of the rational attributes ascribed by modern economic theories to humans. In contrast, Polanyi (1977) and many of his followers (e.g. Dalton 1971) have provided the lead in suggesting that ancient civilisations should be studied using a lens different from that of modern economic analysis; in particular, they emphasise the desirability of using economic anthropology as the appropriate means of studying ancient peoples. To clarify, traditional economic thinking views humans, ancient and contemporary, as engaged in essentially economising behaviour. Such behaviour is based on the assumption that an efficient market allocation system exists and operates in a manner that motivates people to act accordingly. In contrast, economic anthropology starts from the position that humans' desire for material gain leads them to take actions aimed at achieving this aim, but such actions are constrained by the context of their specific culture. As we shall see below, allocation mechanisms different from market distribution and reciprocity play a significant role in ancient societies This alternative approach has found favour with a number of historians of the ancient world (e.g., for ancient Egypt, see Janssen 1975 and Bleiberg 1996).

It is clear from the above that debate on the forces that are assumed to underpin the behaviour of ancient peoples is far from resolved. The accounting literature we review below is suggestive of this theoretical diversity. Our own preference is for sensitive theorising of the ancient historical material within its specific socio-political, economic and cultural settings, rather than approaching the study of ancient accounting with a predetermined grand theoretical framing.

The technical attributes of ancient accounting: accounting, counting and duality

The bulk of the literature covering this theme relates to the work of Mattessich (1987, 1989, 1991, 1994, 2000) drawing on the path-breaking research of Schmandt-Besserat (1977, 1978, 1979, 1980, 1981a, 1981b, 1983, 1984, 1986a, 1986b, 1992, 1997) on counting and accounting in Mesopotamia. Schmandt-Besserat's work demonstrated that token accounting was invented before both abstract counting and writing. Motivated by Wittgenstein's search for symbolic representation, Mattessich (1987) forges a link between Mesopotamian token accounting and the correspondence theory of representation. Following the lead of Schmandt-Besserat (1992), he notes that an envelope of tokens (sealed clay envelops that contained the actual tokens inside and impressions of the same tokens on the outside surface) could have functioned as a personal account of a steward or debtor as well as an inventory list of his investments. Simple tokens were used for such items as grain and cattle (with tokens of different shapes being assigned to different commodity accounts), whereas more incised and perforated tokens recorded services and manufactured items. Mattessich stresses the dual significance of these tokens; being both a set of individual assets in their detail and a representation of equity in their totality. This early accounting was capable of monitoring obligations and levies from stewards and tax payers and recording the actual payments in kind by debtors. He then argues that not only does every piece of commercial reality (such as a jar of oil) correspond to a specific token, but also the relations (such as property rights) had proper correspondence through the location of certain tokens in a particular aggregate. Hence, input–output relations are exhibited not only in the actual transfer of commodities but also in their representations.

Accounting and modes of counting

One of Mattessich's key concerns has been to differentiate between types of counting and to revisit the argument that Mesopotamian accounting was based on the input–output principle. Mattessich (1991) distinguishes between three modes of counting:

1   Counting by one-to-one matching. This entails a one-to-one correspondence between a sign and the item or object being counted, via markings, pebbles, or sticks, where the sign is repeated for every additional unit of the item or object.
2   Concrete counting by tokens. Tokens used for specific counting were either simple or complex. Simple, plain clay tokens dating from 8000 BC were used for concrete counting of objects. From around 3250 BC these tokens were deposited inside hollow clay envelopes, or bulla, after the tokens were impressed on the surface of the bulla before they were sealed. Hence, it was possible at a glance to identify the token contents of the bulla by simply 'reading' the impressions made on the surface. This presents one of the earliest known accounting 'systems'. Each type of token signified only a particular object or number of items of the same object, so that every token sign is entwined exclusively

with a specific object. Complex tokens exhibit a greater range of shapes and markings, and are typically perforated for the purpose of being strung together. While counting in the abstract sense was not yet known, Schmandt-Besserat contends that the notion of cardinality was already implied in this concrete counting:

> The hypothesis that from the beginning of the token system groups of counters were no longer the mere representation of one unit ('and one more') but expressed a cardinal number is based on my argument that certain tokens stood for sets ($x = n$). I posit, for example, that tetrahedrons, which occur in two distinct sub-types 'small' and 'large' . . . represent two different units of the same commodity.
>
> (Schmandt-Besserat 1992: 189)

3   Abstract counting. Here the number becomes totally detached from the object, so that a given number (numeral) can be used to designate the *same quantity* of different objects; for example, the number '3' could be placed before the word for sheep and also before the word for apple to designate three sheep and three apples.

Mattessich (1989, 1991 1994), following Schmandt-Besserat, argues that every type of simple or complex token represented a specific type of account, whereas a sphere/bulla/envelope with tokens deposited inside it and a sealed string of tokens were equivalent to a personal account about stewards or debtors with accompanying lists of inventories. Thus, the total sum of tokens inside an envelope or on a string represented the equity that a creditor lent to a debtor. Mattessich argues that this is similar to a 'superaccount' or a balance sheet, and that the aggregation of the tokens had a dual meaning: in its details it revealed individual assets and in its totality it revealed an equity interest or part of it.

Duality and the input–output principle

Mattessich contends that, contrary to today's familiar understanding, the foundations of accounting were not based on double entry but on the logical form of a transaction. He considers economic events, such as sales, as the *empirical* manifestation of this logic and the journal entries as well as matrices, algebraic equations, or vectors, constituting the *conceptual* manifestation of this logic. Mattessich applies this understanding to the Mesopotamian account-ing evidence, arguing that 'Since the ancient people of the Middle East exploited the *transfer of clay tokens from one location to another* to represent various economic transactions, there can be little doubt that *an input–output structure dominated those early accounting systems*' (1991: 38, original emphases). Mattessich suggests that any attempt to treat the above point as trivial, since the transfer of objects from one place to another exhibits this duality, is misguided:

> this objection fails to grasp the essential point: the objection refers only to empirical structures and events and misses *the crucial idea of duplicating the input-output of actual commodities through the input–output of tokens by means of which conceptual representation of this duality becomes possible.*
>
> (ibid.: 38, original emphasis)

Mattessich then develops the notions of physical duality and social duality as applied to Mesopotamian accounting. For him, physical duality relates to the physical aspects of the 'output of a commodity from one place, and its input into another' (ibid.). Hence, physical duality expresses a one-to-one correspondence between a physical economic transaction as an empirical event and some representational scheme such as Mesopotamian token accounting. In contrast, social duality arises from the fact that every asset belongs to someone and hence it is simultaneously an equity or part of it. This social duality therefore relates to activities, such as owning, lending or borrowing which are economic transactions that become represented by accounting transactions through recording, with these activities sharing a social character. Mattessich (1991) distinguishes between two types of social duality on the basis of social and legal differences, debt claims (financial-legal relations between two persons) and ownership claims (legal or quasi-legal relations between a person and an object) which, in addition to the physical duality already mentioned, gives accounting three dualities. These two types of social duality, Mattessich (1991: 41) argues, were evident in Mesopotamian accounting: 'by 3250 B.C. – the time when the sealed clay envelopes and string systems emerged – accounting had already incorporated ownership claims as well as stewardship or debt relations'.

Mattessich (1991, 1994) was further interested in demonstrating the theoretical link between ancient Mesopotamian accounting and modern accounting via recourse to two sets of argument. First, he examined the underlying technical characteristics of both constructs, as evident in the input–output principle and the duality argument. This line of thinking was elaborated further by inserting terms such as 'credit' and 'debit' into Mattessich's (1994: 19) interpretations of the tokens, such that inputting tokens into an envelope was considered as equivalent to a debit entry, while output of a token from an envelope was treated as a credit entry. Similarly, impressing token shapes on the outside of envelopes was taken as equivalent to a credit entry in an equity account, whereas inserting tokens into the envelopes was treated as a debit entry in an asset account. He also identified what he saw as control features of these early accountings: empirical control and tautological control. He treated empirical control as tantamount to taking actual inventory (e.g. counting assets such as sheep) in a particular location and comparing it with tokens for the same object deposited in the appropriate envelope for that location to verify that the two are the same and, if not, identifying the discrepancy. Tautological control involved, according to Mattessich, counting the tokens inside an envelope and comparing that with the impressions on the outside surface of that same envelope.

The second approach Mattessich takes to enhance the similarity of Mesopotamian accounting to modern accounting emphasises the double-entry nature of both systems and proposes that the origin of modern accounting may indeed lie in the invention of the clay tokens. He contends that the use of tokens to record the transfer of physical objects from one location to another represents 'double' 'entry' and 'recording' (Mattessich 1994: 19–20), because it involves the simultaneous recording of the two aspects of input and output in different places in the system (structural characteristic); for example, the indentations of the tokens impressed on the outside surface of the envelope 'are the mirror pictures and true counter-entries (credit entries) on the equity side of this prehistoric record-keeping system' (Mattessich 1991: 44), and also because it combines both empirical control and tautological control (see above). This double-entry recording, however, should not be confused with 'double-entry *bookkeeping*' in the modern sense 'where a tautological control checks whether the *monetary* values were entered equally on both sides' (Mattessich 1994: 20, original emphasis). Nevertheless, Mattessich argues that the basic logical structure of this ancient double-entry recording is virtually identical to that of the modern double-entry system (Mattessich 1991: 43).

The social attributes of ancient accounting: accounting, writing and money

Ezzamel and Hoskin (2002) extend Mattessich's findings through the adoption of a wider, social perspective on ancient accounting. Drawing on a theoretical framing that integrates Foucault's work on practices and Derrida's ideas on the logic of the supplement, they analyse an extensive amount of evidence drawn from Mesopotamia and Ancient Egypt. Although Ezzamel and Hoskin argue that the technical aspects of ancient accounting were distinctly different from those featured by double-entry bookkeeping, they go on to show that such ancient accounting was sufficiently complex to yield important theoretical insights.

Ezzamel and Hoskin argue that writing emerged as a supplement to accounting, while money emerged as a double supplement to both accounting and writing. Yet, accounting itself became a supplement to prior ways of numbering and valuing, and so accounting was part of a play of supplements. In ancient history, accounting simultaneously named and counted objects as commodities, and in so doing it conferred a precise (denominated) value upon them: a value reproducing recontextualised actions, as items could, beyond the here and now, be called up, checked and demanded in precisely the amount denominated. Consequently, accounting, writing and money, as supplementary technologies, enact new power and knowledge relations which produce a transformation in the forms that power and knowledge can take.

After re-examining the role played by accounting in making possible the genesis of counting and writing, Ezzamel and Hoskin demonstrate the theoretical complexity of accounting's role as the supplement that produces further supplements. In this respect, they suggest that the invention of accounting, writing and money made it possible to enter a world of 'transactionality', which in turn represented a double break: (1) a break *from* a world in which equivalence and value reciprocity are meaningless because of the absence of money; (2) a break *into* a world where equivalence and value reciprocity are always enacted through supplementarity.

Accounting for what? On the domains of activities covered by accounting

In this section, we synthesise the literature that has examined the types of activities in which accounting intervened as a technology of measuring, 'valuing' and recording. These activities turned out to be quite varied. In order to embed the evidence in its wider environments, we organize our review around the broader contexts that witnessed the emergence of accounting practices in ancient societies, ranging from those that belong to the state to transactions involving barter or semi–barter exchange.

Accounting for the state or royal domain

Investigations addressing accounting for the royal domain come primarily from ancient Egypt and, to a lesser extent, from Mesopotamia. Prior research covers a number of important activities in ancient history, such as taxation, construction projects/workshops, bakeries, the royal palace, and the temples.

Taxation

In an economy as highly centralised as that of ancient Egypt, the importance of taxation looms large. While the genesis of levying and collecting tax goes back to pre-dynastic Egypt (5500–3100 BC; see Davies and Friedman 1998), work on ancient Egyptian taxation in the accounting literature has so far focused on the Middle Kingdom (2030–1640 BC) and beyond. Ezzamel (2002b) examined a tax-assessor's journal covering the end of the Twelfth (1991–1778 BC) and the beginning of the Thirteenth Dynasty (1778–1625 BC). The papyrus is badly damaged and as a result it contains no information on tax calculation, but it shows details of the steps taken by the scribe to assess tax. Initially, the land to be taxed was surveyed and the tax crop was measured. The tax scribe was accompanied by the following, each entrusted with a specific responsibility: the clerk of land (the custodian of the regulations of land registry); the envoy of the steward (who took internal measures of both land and crop on behalf of the steward); the stretcher of the cord, and the holder of the cords (who both took measures of the standing crop). The same paper reviews additional evidence pertaining to the levying and collection of tax from the Twelfth Dynasty, where specific individuals were charged with the responsibility for collecting given amounts of tax (wheat, corn, barley, bread, ducks and geese) levied as dues on the Pharaoh's subjects.

Further research on the functioning of taxation in ancient Egypt has examined the cycle of taxation 'which involves the definition of taxable entities, the estimation, final assessment, collection, transportation and storage of taxes' (Ezzamel 2002a: 17), with accounting procedures for each of these stages. Tax subjects were the temples, state officials (who were taxed only in exceptional circumstances), Khato-lands (lands earmarked to supply revenues to the Crown), and ordinary people. For example, in the case of Khato-lands, exact measures were determined for each plot assigned to a given individual, in addition to a precise assessment of tax due. Tax was assessed in capacity measures. The evidence suggests that harvest-tax assessment was a function of two variables: the area of land and its quality (fertility), with tax liability being the product of multiplying land area by the appropriate tax bracket for that type of land. The paper then proceeds to examine how the remaining parts of the cycle of taxation were carried out and discusses a case of tax defalcation that continued undetected for nine years.

In Mesopotamia, taxation played an important role in the economies of Sumerian city-states. The excise of tax was based on coercion and performed by the royal palace and the temple. As argued by several commentators (Schmandt-Besserat 1992), the royal palace relied on taxes to engage in public construction projects on a major scale (e.g., dams), invest in public buildings and strengthen state bureaucracy. On the other hand, the temples engaged in regular offerings to the gods and made their provision by designated individuals compulsory, leading some commentators to view these offerings as obligatory taxes (Beale 1978: 310).

In turn, the deployment of taxation exerted an important influence on accounting practices in Mesopotamian city-states (Rivero Menéndez 2000). According to Schmandt-Besserat (1994), the large number of bureaucrats employed by the state enabled increasing sophistication of accounting practices, which resulted in complex clay tablets, envelopes, bulla, and cylinders. The aim of these refined accounting instruments was twofold: (1) to make possible a precise tracking of transactions taking place in Sumerian cities, in particular, those affecting agricultural goods, food, textile, or perfumes; (2) to keep a record of unpaid taxes.

Royal construction projects/workshops

The most detailed evidence available from ancient Egypt comes from the late phase of the Middle Kingdom, and in particular from the reign of Senusret III (Twelfth Dynasty). This particular era witnessed a major expansion in administrative titles and practices, and also crucially in record keeping. Ezzamel (2004) examined some of this evidence within the context of ancient work organization. His analysis shows how detailed daily attendance lists were kept for royal projects, including names, titles, days spent by each workman on project work, days of absence, days in transit (between projects) and total days, payroll or provision allocations per day, tasks (work targets) allocated to workmen converted into equivalent man-days, work completed and work remaining. Workshop accounts included details of items delivered to be worked on converted in their diversity into a single common denominator as money of account (*deben*, a precise weight measure), amount of work completed and the remainder. Ezzamel argues that this evidence reveals a full system of ancient human accountability at work based on careful division of labour, allocation of predetermined work targets, and regular reporting on actual achievements and the remainder of work to be completed. The evidence also suggests that a finely tuned reward structure (in the form of fixed provisions) was used, which took careful account of the rank of every category of worker, hierarchical position, or responsibility. Ezzamel, however, notes:

> The notion of time emphasised in these practices was not 'timed labour', the concept associated with industrial capitalism, but rather was much closer to 'task orientation' . . . In this emphasis, concern was focused upon ensuring that a particular task was completed, rather than being obsessed with meeting time targets, such as those enshrined in modern time-and-motion studies.
>
> (ibid.: 530–1)

Bakeries

Ezzamel (1997) used pictorial evidence as well as a number of accounts to forge a preliminary depiction of accounting for the bakeries of ancient Egypt (with similar conclusions applying to breweries). He constructed a cycle of ancient accountability that began with input of grain transferred from the granaries to the bakery, as well as the detailed accounting for the baking process. Such process was scrutinised carefully by scribes to determine precise allowances for natural loss in baking, use of weight conversion rates to calculate number of loaves of a given weight/size expected of a given input of flour, use of a dilution (baking/cooking) ratio to control for the precise proportions of water and flour in making the dough, equivalent weight of baked bread transferred from the bakery to the storehouse, and a final comparison of output (numbers of breads of given weights and dilution actually produced) against expected output from the input of grain. The accounts also traced targets and actual output per individual baker every day. The system of accounting used entailed weighing, pure counting, a measure of quantity equivalence, a quality adjustment (the baking ratio), predetermined natural loss in baking, predetermined targets of output, measures of actual output, and calculation and reporting of variances between targets and actual achievements.

One may wonder why so much detailed accounting of the activities of a bakery. As in much of this work, the context is typically sparsely examined, because contextual evidence is usually lacking. However, some contextualising of the activities of the bakery examined by Ezzamel (1997) is now possible. For a start, bread in ancient Egypt had a great symbolic significance; it was endowed with life-giving and sustaining power; it was the very stuff of life (Wilkinson 1994). Moreover, the bakery examined by Ezzamel (1997) was an army bakery, dating to the reign of Seti I (1303–1290) who waged major military campaigns. In this respect, Ezzamel argues that the proliferation of the above detailed accounting practices for the bakery may have been underpinned by an incentive to ensure the careful monitoring of regular army supplies of bread.

The royal palace

Sparse evidence remains from records kept for the royal palaces throughout ancient history. The most complete and detailed evidence dates to the Middle Kingdom, ancient Egypt, in the form of summary accounts of a royal visit to Thebes from the Thirteenth Dynasty (Ezzamel 2002b). The royal entourage included the Pharaoh, his family, immediate dependants, the Vizier, high officials, and courtiers covering the treasury, the priesthood and the military. The papyri include: (1) statements of account covering the provisions, special deliveries, remainders, balances and surplus; (2) orders of provision earmarked for specific individuals; (3) expenditure of valuable commodities as lists of offerings; and (4) official reports and documents, detailing specific items received in the presence of witnesses.

The accounts reveal an intricate web of redistribution that co-ordinated the inflows and outflows of commodities. Ezzamel makes a number of observations. On a daily basis, the scribes kept a recurrent balance of bread as a safety-net in case supplies fell short of requirements; whereas for fresh and perishable goods, such as vegetables, supply exactly matched requirements without balances being kept. In a similar vein, the accounts were kept on a daily basis, with separate columns for each type of commodity. Finally, special requirements for a particular day were accounted for by the scribes via a new entry called 'due today' to trace this special requirement.

Ezzamel makes a number of remarks on the overall significance of these daily summary accounts. They established and reproduced social order by observing a particular sequence for the entries that reflected social status and power. Furthermore, the precisely determined rations of provisions reinforced dependency relations reflected in the social and political status of the recipient. Yet, they linked sources of revenues and provisions to specific institutions which reflected the dependency of the state on these institutions.

Accounting for the activities of the temples

Death is perhaps the most significant single event in the experience of any human society, and this is particularly true in ancient Egypt. It is not surprising therefore that, among surviving evidence, several fascinating papyri and inscriptions on stone relate to temple activities and the preservation of the cult of dead Pharaohs and important officials. Ezzamel (2005) examines a set of documents from the Old Kingdom relating to the temple of King Néferirkarê-Kakai (Fifth Dynasty).

Jobs were performed by phyles (gangs). The available papyri contain lists of attendance and allocation of work duties on a daily basis, along with daily and monthly accounts detailing collection of goods and their distribution, and inventory lists of equipment and various other items. In the case of inventory lists, a grid structure is used whereby items are grouped in specific categories that are organised under a hierarchy of three levels of classification. At the end of its period of work (usually two months), the departing phyle delivered the equipment to the stores and the scribe noted the exact state of each item of equipment and the repairs required. A mixture of red and black inks was used to differentiate the entries and the columns of the inventory list and to enhance visibility. Lines were drawn by the inspectors to indicate completion of their work. The departing phyle and the incoming phyle separately reported about the state of the equipment they were leaving behind or receiving. The temple income accounts again used a grid structure and black and red inks to record, on a daily basis, deliveries by name of porter and source, remainder, and the place to which they are sent as provisions.

In the case of inventory lists, recording items by using a combination of black and red inks in a tabular format (*organisational visibility*), and the enumeration of quantities of items and the classification taxonomy used (*technical visibility*), made it easy for the scribe to signal damaged items as well as the nature of the damage. Apart from legitimising the role of the scribes, this made it possible both to trace responsibility for damage to the appropriate (departing) phyle and to plan the repairs in time for the arrival of the new phyle. In the monthly income accounts of the temple, the scribes could trace a particular delivery to its exact amount and original source with such *dependency visibility* enshrined into accounting entries. Through the use of a grid system and the judicious combination of black and red inks the scribe could differentiate between amounts due as revenue, actual quantities delivered and balance remaining. Ezzamel argues that accounting played a key role in determining the precise allocations of provisions for every member of temple staff and in recording the delivery of these provisions.

Further evidence on accounting for the temple comes from the Middle Kingdom in the form of ten contracts intended to be executed after the death of a high-ranking official. In that study, Ezzamel (2002b) shows how accounting practices underpinned the contractual arrangements of the dead that were finalised in their lifetimes. The intervention of accounting was not simply restricted to the writing of a will; it also involved determining the precise amounts of offerings to be made of each type of commodity. Rather than being enforced by law, these contracts were sanctioned by social norms as well as incentives built into the contracts to motivate the priests entrusted with the execution of the contracts to ensure that the measured giving on behalf of the dead was observed.

Accounting for the private domain

In this section we examine the literature on accounting for the private domain in both Mesopotamia and ancient Egypt. Because Mesopotamia was a much less centralised economy compared to ancient Egypt, more material on accounting for the private domain in Mesopotamia is available.

Accounting for private business

Mattessich (1998a, 1998b) builds on the work of Niessen *et al.* (1993) to examine the role of Mesopotamian accounting in the private domain. Different types of cuneiform tablets emerged during the third millennium BC; three types seemingly performing auxiliary tasks, even though they include some numbers, and the fourth type, with columns and partitions, including entries identified by Niessen *et al.* as debits and credits, being the accounts of archaic bookkeeping. On these larger tablets, the reverse (credit/discharge) side typically contained the sum total of the numbers entered on the obverse (debit/charge) side. Mattessich (1998a: 5–6) argues that many of these later tablets still retained the kind of double-entry recording system identified in earlier token accounting. Unlike the token system, though, this was not a closed, or self-contained system, as not all of the discharges are matched to the charges and hence it has to be seen in conjunction with other recordings.

In commenting on the clay tablets of the fourth millennium, Niessen *et al.* (1993: 35) note how the level of detail varied according to the administrative level. Almost without exception, however, these tablets simply list numbers or quantities of items or commodities, without any reference to their purpose or context. These archaic tablets also 'document early types of information processing which led to "theoretical" amounts in the form of future calculations, debit postings, standardised obligation, and similar nonempirical accounting procedures' (ibid.). Such development of 'theoretical' amounts led Mattessich (1998a: 10–11) to invoke the modern term 'budgetary procedures' when discussing these developments.

Niessen *et al.* (1993) provide more detailed and intriguing accounting entries relating to a number of activities, including the administrative activities of Kushim, presumed to be an official responsible for a storage facility containing the basic ingredients (malt and cracked barley or barley groats) for the production of beer (Kushim could alternatively be an institution – the meaning rendered is not exact). The tablets recording these activities specified the amounts of the product, its quality, location, or connected responsibility for a given period of time. As barley left the granaries of Kushim for processing, the quantities were added up, with each entry quoting the title of the official, thereby locating responsibility for the allocated barley with that official, and both Kushim and the official signed the tablet. In these tablets, the amounts of barley were differentiated by type as to whether they were barley groats or malt. The individual quantities of each type were then aggregated into a total, before these two totals were combined into a grand total of barley groat and malt. Finally, the actual beer produced was recorded as were the names of the persons who received the beer, with a *possibility* that labour time required for beer production was also measured (ibid.: 46).

The accounting contents of the tablets became more meaningful with the evolution of writing, as language-related specifications began to be added to the entries to clarify the function of records and their relationships (ibid.: 47). Some tablets from the early dynastic III period (2500–2300 BC) detail bread baking while others included entries for bread and beer rations and the ingredients required to make them. Such tablets tended to begin by listing the names of individuals with the largest rations followed by those with smaller rations. At the end of the tablet, the amounts of bread and beer are totalled by type and the grand total for the flour and barley used was also recorded. These tablets were dated by day, and the scribes showed how the amount of flour corresponded exactly to the amount used in producing the bread, and the same applied to barley and beer. Niessen *et al.* (ibid.: 49) suggest that 'Perhaps the most important accounting operation introduced during the third millennium BC was the balancing of theoretical debits postings with real production.' The evidence suggests clearly that deficits in one year, arising from shortage of actual amounts compared to theoretical amounts, were carried forward to the following year and were liable to later reimbursement.

Niessen *et al.* (ibid.: 49) argue that, by 2100 BC (Ur III), accounting for theoretical (expected) and actual performance reached its most developed form. From then onwards, the entries record labour performance along with theoretical credits and duties. The balance of expected and actual labour performance was recorded at regular intervals for the foremen of the state-controlled labour force, using an accounting period of a 12-month year, with each month being 30 days long. Balances were carried forward to next periods; most frequently these balances were deficits (overdrawn) as expected performance seems to have been 'fixed as the maximum of what a foreman could reasonably demand of his workers' (ibid.: 49). Such balancing entries were underpinned by some measure of standardisation of performance and a value equivalence system:

> A precondition for the feasibility of such global balancing of all expected and real performances was the standardization and calculability of the expected performances, as well as a means of comparing all performances . . . Although we are often only able to trace the performance standards and value equivalences through calculation of account entries, there can be no doubt of the existence of explicitly formulated norms which were strictly adhered to. They can be reconstructed from conversions of labor performances and products into equivalent products specific to the respective centre of the economic organization.
>
> (ibid.: 49–51)

The organisation of the accounting texts of this era can be illustrated by reference to a more complete account of female labour (ibid.: 52–4). The top left-hand of the obverse side contains entries for the debit balance carried forward from the previous period and the expected (theoretical) performance for the current period, with the aggregate of these two items clearly written. The lower part of the left-hand and the whole right-hand of the obverse side have entries showing credits as amount of delivered flour, converted into female workdays, and other labour performance by the female labour force. The reverse side contains other credit entries, the aggregation of all performed labour as credit, and the final balance to be carried forward to the next period. In commenting on how these remaining balances were traced, Niessen *et al.* state:

> From other texts we know what drastic consequences such continuous control of deficits meant for the foreman and his household. Apparently the debts had to be settled at all costs. The death of a foreman in debt resulted in confiscation of his possessions as compensation for the state.
>
> (ibid.: 54)

Further evidence from the administration of fields attests to the use of length measures to calculate areas in order to determine the amount of grain required to sow a particular field. Figures on the obverse of a tablet typically represented the grain needed to sow the field area detailed on the reverse of the tablet, and these tended to be accompanied by entries of the name or title related to the activity/field, and it appears that grain seeds came from central granaries (ibid.: 55–9). Other field administrative texts dealing with domestic demands contain entries on field cultivation, expenditures, yield and current rights of disposition, amounts of grain required to plough and sow a given field, and fodder for the oxen used (ibid.: 64–8).

There is a significant amount of evidence concerning the distribution of rations and organisation of labour, especially as we move to the Old Sumerian era (2450 BC). The archaic evidence simply shows names of workmen and entries of rations, equivalent to 0.8 litre of grain per workman daily. This ration applied irrespective of the workman's particular employment; it approximated the minimum level of subsistence and remained virtually unchanged throughout the third millennium BC (ibid.: 70–4). Workmen were organised into gangs of 10 each plus a foreman (similar to ancient Egypt), and their rations were delivered to them through a chief supervisor.

It is not until the Old Sumerian period that we encounter evidence of calculation of expected work performance for each task, e.g. the amount of barley a labourer had to harvest. Levels of expected performance varied according to the sex and age of the labourer. Accounts of a grain processing workshop reveal detailed measures of control at work for 36 female labourers. Here, each day of the month, for several months, raw and finished products were recorded, with finished products converted into the standard value unit of barley. The entries also show in the total balance the labour time of the millers to an exactness of $\frac{1}{6}$th of a work-day. The balance showed the difference between raw materials and labour force expressed in labourer days at the end of an accounting period against actual data on production delivered and the work performed, and any deficits had to be cleared directly (ibid.: 83–4).

The final set of accounts discussed by Niessen *et al.* relate to animal husbandry during the archaic and Old Sumerian periods. Earlier than the twenty-fifth century BC, texts record compilation of flocks differentiated by type and sex, and amounts of 'dairy fat' (ibid.: 92–5). They comment: 'The modalities by which the processing of animal products was organized complied with the centralised structure of the administration of livestock herds itself' (ibid.: 93).

In the Old Sumerian period, cheese delivery quotas of herdsmen in charge are recorded, using jars with standardised liquid capacity as measures (these were the traditional measures used for grain), in contrast to archaic times when cheese was counted in discrete units (ibid.: 96–7). Cattle breeding were also accounted for, and the authors cite a document which calculated annual production of 'dairy fat' and cheese for four milk cows over ten years. This document does not appear to be a record of actual activities, but rather a theoretical calculation of expected reproduction of consecutive generations of cows. The text assumes a cow mortality rate of zero, calving at regular intervals and cows producing the same amount of milk irrespective of age. It assumes annual reproduction of cattle at the rate of one calf for every two adult cows, in addition to fixed amounts of 'dairy fat' and cheese per cow per year. The total amount of 'dairy fat' and cheese production over the ten-year period was calculated and converted into a value equivalence expressed in silver. An exchange rate of 10 sila of dairy fat or 150 sila of cheese for one shekel of silver was used. Reviewing this evidence, Niessen *et al.* suggest that the text represents a trial or model calculation concerning hypothetical herd growth.

In their examination of accounting practices in ancient Egypt, Ezzamel and Hoskin (2002) analysed transactions that involved a breakdown of the 'cost' of each of the various items that made a bigger item, say, the legs, head, and the body of a bed, along with the 'cost' of decorating each part. The evidence stops short of explaining what these breakdowns were used for. Perhaps it was the seller's way of justifying the full price of the complete item (bed in this case). Some other transactions revealed the payment for a share of an object (an ox): 'My share in the ox which he bought, makes 2½ *deben*. My share in the sheep . . . which he bought, makes 1 *deben*' (Janssen 1975: 532, cited in Ezzamel and Hoskin 2002: 356). The ability to make the ownership of an item divisible into smaller shares opened up the possibility, through the use of money of account, of sharing an expensive item among several owners.

Accounting for the household

Ezzamel (2002c) analysed a set of business letters and accounts belonging to a farmer from the Middle Kingdom – the only surviving evidence of household and farm accounts from the history of ancient Egypt. The household part of the letters and accounts deals with a new set of provisions for every member of the household, which had been reduced substantially following a drop in the level of the Nile. Not only did the rations ensure the careful matching of what the head of the family provided for consumption with the needs of every member of the family, they also reflected and reproduced the standing in which each member was held. The second part of the letters and accounts relates specifically to farm activities charged to a farmer's agent while he was absent from his farm, including cultivation of own land, renting and cultivating additional land, managing the herd and their fodder, a list of some agricultural produce, and private debt and its collection. As in evidence examined earlier, a variety of accounting measures were employed. Reasonably homogeneous items (for example, bundles of flax) were simply counted and recorded as identities, as the counted items in themselves carried implicit values through which equivalence within a given category of items could be observed. Where items were not homogenous, equivalence was secured via the specification of precise weights/volume or via the use of more direct monies of account, such as the *deben* (a precise weight measure) or the *khar* (a precise capacity measure). These monies of account exhibited a strong measure of internal consistency, as any of them could be easily inter-translated. Such accounting intervention made possible a process of accountability at a distance, helping the absent farmer not only to monitor the performance of his agent, but equally importantly to inform himself of what was going on in his household.

Accounting for exchange

In the fourth millennium BC, Mesopotamian scribes assigned tokens of different shapes to different commodity accounts. Simple tokens were used for such items as grain and cattle whereas more incised and perforated tokens recorded services and manufactured items. The tokens represented sheep and were signed by the shepherd Ziqarru; this form of accountability was vested in an enumeration of different types of sheep:

21 ewes that lamb
 6 female lambs
 8 rams
 4 male lambs
 6 she-goats that kid
 1 he-goat
 3 female kids

The entries kept in the tablets were recorded at the moment of the transaction. According to Rivero Menéndez (2000: 283), it was customary to call the scribe to the temple, palace, or private domain to record commercial transactions, irrespective of their volume. Written accounts of transactions were signed by the transacting parties, witnesses and the scribe (Keister 1963: 371; Chatfield 1977: 5), and such records were eventually used to resolve legal disputes (Basu and Waymire 2006). From the archaic period onwards, the name of the debtor was identified through his seal on the envelope (Schmandt-Besserat 1978). The following tablet, recording a lease of cattle, illustrates the level of detail when recording such transactions, stating dates, naming and counting items of cattle, stating the names of accountable individuals, and stipulating precise sanctions in cases of failure, and listing witnesses (Finkelstein 1968: 31):

92 ewes
20 rams
22 breeding lambs
24 [spring(?)] lambs
33 she-goats
 4 male goats
27 kids
Total: 158 sheep; total: 64 goats,

> Which Sinšamuh has entrusted to Dadā the shepherd.
>> He [i.e. Dadā] assumes liability [therefore] and will replace any lost [animals].
>> Should Nidnatum, his [i.e. Dadā's] shepherd boy, absent himself, he [i.e., Nidnatum] will bear responsibility for any [consequent] loss, [and] Dadā will measure out 5 *kōr* of barley.
>> Three witnesses; date; Samsuiluna year 1 (?), fourth month, 16th day.

Janssen (1975) collated the prices of a large number of commodities, covering a period of approximately 150 years, in the necropolis village of Deir El-Medina during the New Kingdom, but his main concern was with documenting and comparing prices rather than with account-ing transactions *per se*. Ezzamel and Hoskin (2002) departed from the price analysis performed by Janssen to examine the development of monies of account in ancient Egypt. Importantly, they explored how money and accounting were used by the ancient scribes to constitute value reciprocity. Two types of exchange were noted. The first type is simply a record of one person exchanging an item (say, a wooden stela) in return for receiving another item (say, a chest) from someone else; in this case, and in an economy where exchange typically ensures a strong element of economic reciprocity (see examples below), it may be reasonably assumed that the items exchanged were thought to be of the same value by both parties:

1. What draughtsman Neferehotep gave to Haremwia.
2. One wooden stela of Nofreteroy, may she live, which he gave to me.
3. One chest in exchange for it. (I) decorated two coffins for him.
4. On the riverbank (?) and he made one bed for me.

(Janssen 1975: 510, cited in Ezzamel and Hoskin 2002: 352)

The second, and most frequent, type of exchange involved valuation of items in terms of money of account. Entries for both types of transactions were made by the scribe who acted as a witness, stating the date of exchange, the names of parties to the exchange, and an enumeration and valuation of the items:

Year 5, third month of the summer season, day 20. Given to Hay by the chief policeman Nebsmen: I head of cattle, makes 120 *deben*. Given to him [i.e. Nebsmen]: 2 pots of fat, makes 60 *deben*; 5 mss–shirts of smooth fabric, makes 25 *deben*; 1 dress of Upper-Egyptian cloth, makes 20 *deben*; 1 hide, makes 15 *deben*.

(Černy 1954: 907, cited in Ezzamel and Hoskin 2002: 352)

In the above transaction, the debit side (the head of cattle received and valued at 120 *deben*) is equated to the credit side involving the giving of several items $(60 + 25 + 20 + 15) = 120$ *deben*. Although the entry does not add up the sums to demonstrate economic equivalence of the values of the goods exchanged to both parties to the transactions, this value equivalence was typically observed, and other entries emphasised such equality (Ezzamel and Hoskin 2002: 353).

Conclusion

Our survey has revealed a remarkably broad arena in which ancient accounting practices intervened. The arena ranging from the state and its various institutions, such as palaces, taxation, state workshops and the manufactories, through religious institutions, in particular, large temples which played a key role in ancient economies as well as in the spiritual domain, to private activities that included barter or semi–barter exchange, private businesses, and the household. In all these domains, the role of ancient accounting loomed large.

Concerning the role of accounting in state institutions, accounting functioned both as a means of ensuring that regular monitoring of progress on state projects could be carried out, appropriate provisions for the palace and its dependencies could be secured, tax levies could be assessed, collected and transferred to state coffers, and appropriate lines of accountability could be established. In all these activities, a measure of expectation by the state of individuals and institutions was inscribed through accounting–based targets. Equally important, our review suggests that a measure of the responsibility of the state towards its subjects was affirmed via the intervention of accounting, in the sense of determining precise rations or wages to be paid to individuals. Apparently, this arrangement was designed to secure the sustenance of individuals and their families, and a means of ensuring that these rations/wages were delivered on time and in the precise amounts stipulated. A measure of reciprocity, not entirely underpinned by some form of ancient economic reasoning, was at play here. For, in this game of reciprocity, it was not always a 'measure-for-measure' metric that was evidently in use. Payments for tasks performed for the state, as far as we can tell, were not determined on the basis of some modern notion of marginal productivity of human labour, or determined by the forces of supply of and demand for human effort in a kind of labour market. Rather, the state took as its responsibility the payment of what was deemed to be, at the lowest level of the hierarchy, sufficient rations that ensured the survival of the population, but also with clear recognition of rank with rations rising significantly for higher ranks.

The temples of the ancient world were not only spiritual institutions, but also significant economic institutions in their own right. Accounting for temple activities identified work targets, monitored work progress, and dealt with payment to appropriate individuals in the form of rations or wages. Moreover, accounting traced the inflow and outflow of goods and foodstuffs provided by other institutions to the temples for the upkeep of priests and other personnel working at temples. Readers are referred to Chapter 24 for additional evidence and analysis of accounting for this domain.

Concerning the private domain, ancient accounting could be seen to have played a major role in coordinating and facilitating many private activities, including accounting for private businesses, for the household, and for barter and semi-barter exchange. In these activities, surviving records traced accountability to the appropriate agents and reported on their performance, allowing for an ancient system of monitoring at a distance to function. In the case of exchange, a system of equivalence between the goods given and received from another party was established, by which economic reciprocity was observed in a more or less strict 'measure-for-measure' calculus underpinned by the use of monies of account and the recording of the transactions by vigilant scribes. In these transactions, as indeed in all the domains where accounting intervened, each accounting entry was assigned to a precise date of the week, month, season and year, as well as frequently providing an indication of the place where the activities recorded took place. This system, therefore, not only vested accountability in the relevant agents, but also qualified such accountability by time and location. There remains, however, much more historical evidence to be examined in these, and indeed novel, domains. Moreover, other researchers employing different theoretical lenses may emphasise other aspects of the roles of ancient accounting than has hitherto been revealed.

The literature has also attempted to tease out some of the technical attributes of ancient accounting systems, notably the work of Mattessich, by examining properties such as duality and input–output relations, and in the process arguing for some time-invariant attributes of accounting. Others, such as Ezzamel and Hoskin, have attempted to provide theoretical insights about accounting by exploring the role of accounting as a constructor of value, reciprocity and equivalence. In spite of their merits, these efforts represent an embryonic stage in the theorising of ancient accounting. Such theorising needs to be appraised, critiqued, and developed further by accounting historians.

Given the remoteness of the historical eras covered by the literature reviewed here, and the special challenges facing researchers working in that field, we have sought to make a number of points concerning these challenges in order to sensitise the reader to the nature of the evidence that the literature has drawn upon. We have sought to address this issue by prefacing the chapter with a discussion of specific challenges borne out of our own experience of working in the area. Other researchers are bound to emphasise other issues, but we have summarised the most salient of our concerns under the following headings: what counts as primary sources; how to deal with considerable lacunae in ancient records; the problems of interpreting translations of ancient texts into contemporary languages; and the difficulty of using contemporary theories to frame and theorise ancient accounting material. Although we acknowledge that these are very serious issues, we argue that a judicious approach that combines honesty in acknowledging the limitations of such research, coupled with great sensitivity and understanding of ancient contexts, and a very careful approach to gentle theorising, could go a long way towards confronting these constraints.

Our argument, thus far, is that the extant literature has provided some remarkable insights, but there is much more to do. The kinds of research challenges we have identified call for a more concerted research effort by skilled accounting historians to progress the field. Rather than being a cause for researchers to shy away from conducting research on ancient accounting, we believe the challenges provide an exciting prospect for an intellectually stimulating research agenda. With this in mind, we lament the lack of attention accorded by accounting historians to the study of ancient accounting, and contend that there is much to gain if mainstream accounting historians were to devote some of their time and expertise to a careful and systematic study of ancient times.

Key works

Carmona and Ezzamel (2007) traces the notion of accountability and provides an updated review of ancient accounting practices in Mesopotamia and ancient Egypt.

Ezzamel and Hoskin (2002), in contrast to the dominant, technical approach to ancient accounting, adopts a wider social perspective to illustrate the potentials of ancient accounting for advancing the theorisation of accounting.

Mattessich (2000) is a collection of articles previously published by the author in scholarly journals. It is an essential reference for those interested in the technical aspects of ancient accounting and its implications for accounting theory.

Niessen *et al.* (1993) is a must for those interested in examining ancient accounting practices in the Near East, either from a technical or social perspective.

Schmandt-Besserat (1992) constitutes an essential reference for those concerned to investigate the emergence of accounting and writing.

References

Ball, T. (1995) *Reappraising Political Theory: Revisionist Studies in the History of Political Thought* (Oxford: Oxford University Press).

Basu, S. and Waymire, G. B. (2006) Recordkeeping and human evolution, *Accounting Horizons*, 20 (3): 201–29.

Beale, T. W. (1978) Beveled rim bowls and their implications for change and economic organization in the later fourth millennium B.C., *Journal of Business Eastern Studies*, 37 (4): 289–313.

Bleiberg, E. (1996) *The Official Gift in Ancient Egypt* (Norman, OK: University of Oklahoma Press).

Carmona, S. and Ezzamel, M. (2007) Accounting and accountability in ancient civilizations: Mesopotamia and ancient Egypt, *Accounting, Auditing & Accountability Journal*, 20 (2): 177–209.

Černy, J. (1954) Prices and wages in Egypt in the Ramesside period, *Journal of World History*, 1: 903–21.

Chatfield, M. (1977) *A History of Accounting Thought* (New York: Krieger Publishing).

Costouros, G. J. (1978) Development of an accounting system in ancient Athens as a response to socio-economic changes, *Accounting Historians Journal*, 4 (1): 37–54.

Dalton G. (ed.) (1971) *Primitive Archaic and Modern Economies: Essays of Karl Polanyi* (Boston: Beacon Press).

Davies, V. and Friedman, R. (1998) *Egypt Uncovered* (New York: Stewart, Tabori & Chang).

de Ste. Croix, G. E. M. (1956) Greek and Roman accounting, in A. C. Littleton and B. S. Yamey (eds) *Studies in the History of Accounting*, pp. 14–74 (London: Sweet & Maxwell).

Eisenstadt, S. N. (1969) *The Political Systems of Empire: The Rise and Fall of the Historical Bureaucratic Societies* (New York: Free Press).

Ezzamel, M. (1997) Accounting, control and accountability: preliminary evidence from ancient Egypt, *Critical Perspectives on Accounting*, 8 (6): 563–601.

Ezzamel, M. (2002a) Accounting working for the state: tax assessment and collection during the New Kingdom, ancient Egypt, *Accounting and Business Research*, 32 (1): 17–39.

Ezzamel, M. (2002b) Accounting and redistribution: the palace and mortuary cult in the Middle Kingdom, ancient Egypt, *Accounting Historians Journal*, 29 (1): 61–103.

Ezzamel, M. (2002c) Accounting for private estates and the household in the twentieth century B.C. Middle Kingdom, ancient Egypt, *Abacus*, 38 (2): 235–62.

Ezzamel, M. (2004) Work organization in the Middle Kingdom: ancient Egypt, *Organization*, 11 (4): 497–537.

Ezzamel, M. (2005) Accounting for the practices of funerary temples: the intertwining of the sacred and the profane, *Accounting and Business Research*, 35 (1): 29–51.

Ezzamel, M. and Hoskin, K. (2002) Retheorizing accounting, writing and money with evidence from Mesopotamia and ancient Egypt, *Critical Perspectives on Accounting*, 13 (3): 333–67.

Ezzamel, M. and Willmott, H. (2004) Rethinking strategy: contemporary perspectives and debates, *European Management Review*, 1 (1): 43–8.

Finkelstein, J. J. (1968) An old Babylonian herding contract and Genesis 3l: 38f., *Journal of the American Oriental Society*, 88 (1): 30–6.

Finley, M. I. (1992) *The Ancient Economy* (London: Penguin Books).

Fu, P. (1971) Governmental accounting in China during the Chou dynasty (1122–256 BC), *Journal of Accounting Research*, 9 (1): 40–51.

Gills, B. K. (1995) Capital and power in the processes of world history, in S. Sanderson (ed.) *Civilizations and World Systems*, pp. 136–62 (Walnut Creek, CA.: Altamira Press).

Janssen, J. J. (1975) *Commodity Prices from the Ramessid Period* (Leiden: E. J. Brill).

Keister, O. R. (1963) Commercial record-keeping in ancient Mesopotamia, *Accounting Review*, 38 (2): 371–6.

Kemp, B. (1989) *Ancient Egypt: Anatomy of a Civilization* (London: Routledge).

Leemans, W. F. (1960) *Foreign Trade in the Old Babylonian Period* (Leiden: E. J. Brill).

Mattessich, R. (1987) Prehistoric accounting and the problem of representation: on recent archaeological evidence of the middle-east from 8000 B.C. to 3000 B.C., *Accounting Historians Journal*, 14 (2): 72–91.

Mattessich, R. (1989) Accounting and the input-output principle in the ancient and prehistoric world, *Abacus*, 25 (2): 74–84.

Mattessich, R. (1991) Counting, accounting, and the input-output principle: recent archaeological evidence revising our view on the evolution of early record keeping, in O. F. Graves (ed.) *The Costing Heritage: Studies in Honour of S. Paul Garner, Monograph No. 6*, pp. 25–49. (Harrisonburg, VA: Academy of Accounting Historians).

Mattessich, R. (1994) Archaeology of accounting and Schmandt-Besserat's contribution, *Accounting, Business & Financial History*, 4 (1): 5–28.

Mattessich, R. (1998a) Recent insights into Mesopotamian accounting of the 3rd millennium B.C. – successor to token accounting, *Accounting Historians Journal*, 25 (1): 1–27.

Mattessich, R. (1998b) Follow-up to: 'Recent insights into Mesopotamian accounting of the 3rd millennium B.C.': correction to table 1, *Accounting Historians Journal*, 25 (2): 147–9.

Mattessich, R. (2000) *The Beginnings of Accounting and Accounting Thought* (New York: Garland).

Miller, P. (1998) The margins of accounting, *European Accounting Review*, 7 (4): 605–21.

Niessen, H. J., Damerow, P. and Englund, R. K. (1993) *Archaic Bookkeeping*, trans. P. Larsen (Chicago: The University of Chicago Press).

Oldroyd, D. (1995) The role of accounting in public expenditure and monetary policy in the first century AD Roman empire, *Accounting Historians Journal*, 22 (2): 117–29.

Oppenheim, A. L. (1964) *Ancient Mesopotamia: Portrait of a Dead Civilization* (Chicago: The University of Chicago Press).

Polanyi, K. (1957) Trade and market, in K. Polanyi, C. M. Arsenberg and H. W. Pearson (eds) *Trade and Market in the Early Empires: Economies in History and Theory*, pp. 12–38 (New York: Free Press).

Polanyi, K. (1977) *The Livelihood of Man* (New York: Academic Press).

Previts, G. and Bricker, R (1994) Fact and theory in accounting history: present mindedness and capital market research, *Contemporary Accounting Research*, 10 (2): 625–41.

Renger, J. (1984) Patterns of non-institutional trade and non-commercial exchange in ancient Mesopotamia at the beginning of the second millennium B.C., in A. Archi (ed.) *Circulation of Goods in Non-Palatial Context in the Ancient Near East*, pp. 31–123 (Rome: Edizioni Dell'Ateneo).

Rivero Menéndez, M. R. (2000) *La Formación de los Registros Contables en Mesopotamia* (Madrid: Dimasoft).

Rose, N. and Miller, P. (1992) Political power beyond the state: problematics of government, *British Journal of Sociology*, 43 (2): 173–205.

Schmandt-Besserat, D. (1977) An archaic recording system and the origin of writing, *Syro-Mesopotamian Studies*, 1 (2): 1–32.

Schmandt-Besserat, D. (1978) The earliest precursor of writing, *Scientific American*, 238 (6): 50–8.

Schmandt-Besserat, D. (1979) Reckoning before writing, *Archaeology*, 32 (3): 23–31.

Schmandt-Besserat, D. (1980) The envelopes that bear the first writing, *Technology and Culture*, 21 (3): 357–85.

Schmandt-Besserat, D. (1981a) Tablets and tokens: a re-examination of the so-called 'Numerical Tablets', *Visible Language*, 15 (3): 321–44.

Schmandt-Besserat, D. (1981b) Decipherment of the earliest tablets, *Science*, 211 (4479): 283–5.

Schmandt-Besserat, D. (1983) Tokens and counting, *Biblical Archaeologist*, 46: 117–20.

Schmandt-Besserat, D. (1984) Before numerals, *Visible Language*, 15 (1): 48–59.

Schmandt-Besserat, D. (1986a) The origins of writing – an archaeologist's perspective, *Written Communication*, 3 (1): 31–45.

Schmandt-Besserat, D. (1986b) The precursor to numerals and writing, *Archaeology*, 39 (6): 32–8.

Schmandt-Besserat, D. (1992) *Before Writing*, Vol. I: *From Counting to Cuneiform* (Austin, TX: University of Texas Press).

Schmandt-Besserat, D. (1994) Forerunners of writing, in G. Harmut (ed.) *Schrift und Schriftlichkeit*, pp. 264–8 (Berlin: Walter de Gruyter).

Schmandt-Besserat, D. (1997) *The History of Counting* (New York: Morrow Junior Books).

Scorgie, M. (1990) Indian imitation of invention of cash-book and algebraic double-entry, *Abacus*, 26 (1): 63–70.

Silver, M. (1985) *Economic Structures of the Ancient Near East* (Totowa, NJ: Barnes and Noble).

Vollmers, G. (1996) The Persepolis fortification texts: accounting and control in ancient Persia from 509 to 494 BC, *Accounting Enquiries*, 6 (1): 1–43.

Vollmers, G. (2003) Accounting historiography using ancient sources: problems and rewards, in R. K. Fleischman, V. S. Radcliffe and P. A. Shoemaker, *Doing Accounting History*, pp. 49–62 (Oxford: Elsevier).

Warburton, D. A. (1997) *State and Economy in Ancient Egypt* (Fribourg: University Press Fribourg).

Wilkinson, R. D. (1994) *Symbol and Magic in Egyptian Art* (London: Thames & Hudson).

5

Bookkeeping

David Oldroyd and Alisdair Dobie

Overview

The chapter analyses key themes in the history of bookkeeping within a broadly chronological arrangement, starting with classical Greece and Rome and continuing with sections on the Roman legacy, manorial accounting, mercantile accounting, early industry and the Victorian expansion during the nineteenth century. The major aim of the chapter is to embed developments in bookkeeping practices within their social and economic contexts. Tracking rights and obligations, holding agents accountable, conveying information at a distance, dealing with complexity, and acting as a legal record are identified as the recurrent functions of bookkeeping throughout its history. Changes in practice were prompted by a diverse range of factors including economic opportunity, political and religious pressure, educational developments, and the influence of significant individuals. The history of bookkeeping is huge and, to give the chapter focus, the *modus operandi* is to concentrate mainly on Western Europe with particular reference to Italy and the British Isles. Italian practice is particularly significant because of the dual legacy of the classical world and the Renaissance. Britain too is important because of the links forged through trade and colonisation, and especially its close connections with North America. Key debates within the history of bookkeeping are explored, including the origins of double entry.

Introduction

The nature of the study of bookkeeping is a contentious area in accounting history. On the one hand, it is portrayed as simply the subject of antiquarian interest to 'the traditionalist' historians who 'decontextualise accounting' by fruitlessly focusing on its 'mechanical, procedural and technical aspects' (Johnson 1986: 67; Hopwood 1987: 207–9). On the other, there is an emerging consensus among accounting historians that technical practices such as bookkeeping can play a crucial role in shaping beliefs. Thus, Ezzamel and Hoskin (2002), approaching the origins of recording systems in antiquity (see Chapter 4 for further discussion) from a Foucauldian perspective, argued that the invention of token accounting in ancient Mesopotamia was significant not just because it facilitated economic exchanges, but because it encouraged people to see the world around them in terms of quantifiable outcomes. Miller and Napier (1993: 633) also portrayed accounting as part of the 'disparate and variable' assemblage of calculative practices that help create order in society. Such views are not confined to Foucauldians. As discussed in Chapter 15, Bryer (2000), an avowed Marxist, argues that the main significance of bookkeeping lies in its ability to bend the mentality of agents to the will of the principal by rendering them accountable for their actions.

Before embarking on a review of the historiography of 'bookkeeping', it is advisable to consider what is meant by the term. Certainly, it does not just encompass bound books of account. The recording of transactions has utilised a variety of other media, such as scrolls, indentures, tally sticks, potsherds, wax, wooden or clay tablets, inscriptions, and computers: essentially all media for the compilation and transcription of accounting data, which in the modern era constitute the basis of an organisation's internal management accounts and external reports to stakeholders.

To review writings on the history of 2,500 years of bookkeeping in a single chapter is a challenge. There is a danger that issues may become distorted through their juxtaposition in such a piece, and many historians prefer to analyse specific contexts. Taking a 'bird's eye view', however, was defended by Yamey (1981: 128), and followed by Baladouni (1989) and Lee (1990) as a means of developing a coherent theory of accounting history.

As described in Chapter 4, the invention of a form of bookkeeping using clay tokens in the early agricultural societies of the eastern Mediterranean and Iraq represented a huge cognitive leap for mankind. Bookkeeping has been described as a 'foundation stone of culture' (Mattessich 2000: 74), and this is perhaps as true of today as it is of its origins in antiquity. This chapter begins with classical Greece and Rome, a period when art, literature, history and philosophy flourished on an unprecedented scale, alongside trade, enterprise, record-keeping and accountability.

Classical Greece and Rome

This section follows de Ste. Croix's (1956) classic exposition of Greek and Roman accounting in discussing the two societies as a unity, although whether such an approach is entirely defensible is a moot point (Cohen 2002: 3). Greek and Roman civilisation was at its height for several hundred years and embraced many different races and cultures, but de Ste. Croix (1956: 33) observed remarkable consistency in bookkeeping practice over this period, with little in the way of 'important general advances'. The major difference relates to the status of accounts in law, which seem to have carried less sway as legal evidence in Athens in the fourth century BC compared to Rome in the first (ibid.: 28). The most noteworthy technical advance of Greek and Roman bookkeeping compared to earlier civilisations, such as that of the Egyptians, lay in the adoption of coinage, which *allowed* the Greeks and Romans to employ a monetary unit of measurement although 'they often failed to do so' (ibid.: 21–2). Typically, their books of account tracked receipts, payments, goods, debtors and creditors (ibid.: 42). However, according to de Ste. Croix (ibid.: 34–8), there was no distinction between capital and revenue expenditure, little conception of separating the costs of activities, and no evidence of double entry. In exceptional cases, transactions were recorded in columns in bilateral format.

Much of the discussion regarding the supposed lack of sophistication in Greek and Roman bookkeeping practice centres on the level of economic enterprise in society. Finley (1992), in particular, imputed a lack of interest in economic matters, which he believed was reflected in the rudimentary nature of their accounts (Macve 2002: 455). Economic enterprise was allegedly impeded by the structure of society, in particular, by the heavy reliance on slaves for economic activities, allied to a reluctance to exploit fellow citizens (ibid.: 454). Wealth was important in Graeco-Roman society because it reflected a citizen's status, but wealth was acquired first and foremost as a result of family and political connections, not through entrepreneurship (Macve 2002: 460). De Ste. Croix (1956: 15, 34) maintained that bookkeeping practices not only reflected a lack of economic endeavour in society, they actually prevented the Greeks and Romans from advancing economically. Hence, he argued that the confusion of capital and revenue in the books would have made profit calculations impossible and prevented the state from taxing income (ibid.: 38). While supporting de Ste. Croix's main theme – the rudimentary nature of the accounts – Macve (1994: 67; 2002: 460) disagreed that it impeded economic development. Instead, he proposed the hypothesis that the primitive nature of the bookkeeping reflected the 'limited [economic] opportunities and choices that were generally available in antiquity' (Macve 1994: 67).

However, Most's (1979: 10) observation that manufacturing industry and trade flourished on a large scale in the Roman Empire is supported by archaeological findings (Greene 1990: 169–71). Conquest played a major part in this, as it provided a valuable source of booty that directly impinged on the stocks of bullion in the Roman treasury (Howgego 1992: 4) and created new economic opportunities for merchants. Roman financiers, for instance, had a large stake in Julius Caesar's second expedition to Britain (54 BC), contributing ships to the invasion fleet in exchange for a share of the anticipated plunder and future trading opportunities (Grant 1969: 125). Trade ties between Britain and Rome increased significantly during the 90 years leading up to the Claudian invasion (AD 43) that brought 'a mass of fresh merchants, speculators and prospectors in the wake of the armies' (Frere 1974: 320).

The creation through conquest of a common market from the Danube to North Africa and from Spain to the Caspian Sea, supported by a uniform medium of exchange, produced unparalleled opportunities for trade. Indeed, the extent of the economic connections and the range of situations in which bookkeeping was deployed beg the question of whether the rather negative view of Greek and Roman bookkeeping presented by de Ste. Croix, Finley and Macve may have been overstated. Rathbone (1994) has certainly taken exception to the idea that the sole purpose of Roman accounts was 'to act as a check against carelessness or dishonesty on the part of subordinates' (ibid.: 17). His work on the Appianus estate in Roman Egypt in the third century AD revealed an interlocking and centrally controlled system of accounting over a dispersed range of activities that went far beyond tracking rights and obligations to encompass cost control and performance measurement, although he did concede that the Appianus estate may have been 'the exception which proves the rule' (ibid.: 55).

The existence of the Mediterranean Sea was vital to the development of classical society, including bookkeeping practice:

> It is in fact the major feature of the sea's destiny that it should be locked inside the largest group of landmasses on the globe, the 'gigantic linked continent' of Europe-Asia-Africa, a sort of planet in itself, where goods and people circulated from earliest times . . . This was where the crucial exchanges took place.
>
> (Braudel 2002: 25)

From a bookkeeping perspective, the continuous flow of goods throughout this natural waterway necessitated systems that were capable both of tracking the various exchanges taking place over wide distances and dealing with the complexities of the contractual arrangements. The simplest case in classical Rome was when the ship-owner and merchant were one and the same.

However, ships could be hired to third parties or owned in partnership, and sometimes carried multiple consignments for different merchants. On occasion, the management of the vessel was entrusted to agents; in other cases it was managed directly. The number of possible permutations bears witness to the flexibility of the bookkeeping procedures, with records kept 'at each step' of the voyage on behalf of the 'owners, shippers and their representatives on board' (Minaud 2006: 6).

Public accountability too was affected by the geography of the region. As well as economic goods, 'cultural goods' circulated throughout the Mediterranean, 'mingling ideas and beliefs' (Braudel 2002: 307). Rome was still in its infancy when the concept of the Greek city state (*polis*) was at its most developed, and the fledgling republic was inevitably influenced by the political institutions of its more mature neighbours. Despite the political differences between the various cities, the Greeks and Romans shared a common conception of the *polis* that went beyond the notion of a 'defined territory' or a particular form of government to embrace the idea of citizens 'acting in concert' (Finley 1975: 56). It was a society in which the elite members were expected to perform public service, and to apply large portions of their wealth for the benefit of the community for which they were accountable (Finley 1992: 150–3). This is particularly relevant to the development of bookkeeping, as many of the accounts that have survived or are referred to in the contemporary literature were of a public nature.

Indeed, the highly developed notion of public accountability in Greek and Roman society is evident from the physical form of the accounts, which were often inscribed on the walls of public buildings in order to endow them with a sense of permanence as well as high visibility. In most cases these accounts comprised simple lists of receipts and payments in chronological order. According to de Ste. Croix (1956: 26), their layout was 'clumsy and confusing'; usually the information was not tabulated, and expenditure was neither collated nor summarised. Instead it was shown in 'minute detail' (ibid.: 25). However, to criticise the bookkeeping for the lack of information in summary form would be unreasonable as the prime purpose of these documents was to render a full record of the financial accountability of officials' stewardship. What is most significant about these inscriptions, as far as the bookkeeping is concerned, is that they prove both that the information was recorded and that it could be retrieved, in some cases several years after the event, signifying the existence of public archives.

Bookkeeping was also deployed in the administration of the Roman Empire. Much public finance was conducted at a distance because of the dispersed locations of the provinces, and local officials were obliged to keep detailed records of tax revenues and expenditures. This was a requirement of law, and a necessary precaution by state officials against charges of corruption. Launching prosecutions in the law courts was an established method of gaining renown for young political aspirants in Athens and Rome (Grant 1969: 27; Finley 1992: 150–1). Cicero was involved in cases in which the level of detail in the accounting records was a major issue (de Ste. Croix 1956: 43–5), and the fact that bookkeeping could be used as a weapon in the courts illustrates its importance as legal evidence.

Tax assessments too required systematic information gathering procedures, a famous example being the census in Luke's Gospel (2, i–v). Provincial censuses of land, property and population formed the basis of direct taxation levies throughout the Roman Empire (Duncan-Jones 1990: 187–93). The provisioning of the army on campaign likewise required bookkeeping. The best example of the survival of written documents in the Empire, outside Egypt, comes from the fort of Vindolanda on Britain's northern frontier. These include a number of accounts prepared by clerks who were responsible 'for looking after the storage and issue of supplies and recording carefully what was taken in and what was dispensed' (Bowman and Thomas 1974: 30). Records, such as pay-sheets, were also kept to control payments to the troops (de Ste. Croix

1956: 39). Finally, bookkeeping was used to record the flows of bullion and obsolete coin into the Roman Treasury and, from there, to the Imperial Mint. As such, it was one of a range of control measures employed by the treasury to safeguard the stocks of precious metals (Oldroyd 1995: 121–2).

Returning to the accounts of private individuals, it was common practice for 'men of property at Rome' to update their permanent account-books from books of memoranda about once a month (de Ste. Croix 1956: 43). The distances over which goods were traded necessitated reliance on agents, who too would have recorded their transactions (Minaud 2006). The same was true of the management of landed estates. The practice of stewards rendering accounts to their masters for the discharge of their obligations is alluded to by Columella, a writer on agriculture in the first century AD, as well as mentioned in the Christian Gospels (Oldroyd 1997).

Therefore, the salient characteristic of Greek and Roman bookkeeping practice is its versatility in dealing with a wide range of situations, perhaps a reflection of its simplicity. It was deployed in tracking the rights and obligations of private property owners and the state, holding agents accountable, conveying information at a distance in relation to trade, landed estates and public administration, dealing with the complexity of contractual arrangements, and acting as a legal record enforceable in court.

Legacy of the Roman Empire in the West[1]

The four hundred years following the collapse of Roman authority in the West, in the fifth century AD, are commonly referred to as the 'Dark Ages' because of the lack of surviving documentary evidence, including accounts. However, it does not automatically follow that records never existed. Indeed, one of the most important documents to survive from this period relates to bookkeeping practice. The *Capitulare de Villis* comprises a series of written instructions for the management of estates, inspired by the Carolingian emperor Charlemagne towards the end of the eighth century.[2] Its existence reflects the importance of land both as a source of Crown revenue and a basis of political authority in the new post-Roman Europe (Latouche 1967: 180–1; Martindale 1983: 160, 165).

Essentially, two types of accounting can be distinguished in the document (see Loyn and Percival 1975: 68–73 for the full text). The first is a kind of charge and discharge accounting, whereby the steward was held accountable for the difference between the income of his district and his payments in goods or money (clauses 63, 20, 30–1, 44, 55). These accounts were subject to audit (clause 28). The second type, which is evident in the requirement for the steward to submit an account at Christmas-time of the estate's produce for the year, classified by type (clause 62), is more in the nature of a survey, known as a *polyptyque*, of possessions and revenues. The juxtaposition of estate survey and charge and discharge statements in the *Capitulare de Villis* indicates that both these forms of accounting went together: they shared a common aim of enabling the centre to exercise control at a distance over dispersed resources.

According to Latouche (1967: 179–80), these arrangements were initiated by Charlemagne as a control measure against 'sharp practices' that had crept into the administration of the royal estates. Hence, the emperor rebuked estate stewards for not having submitted proper returns in the past (clause 44). The inclusion of information concerning the gross product of the estate indicates that the records could also have been used for planning next year's output, as seems to have been the case at the abbey of Saint-Germain-des-Près (ibid.: 192).

It is difficult to tell the extent to which the *Capitulare de Villis* was an innovation as opposed to the formulation of established practice. The capitulary is pre-dated by a seventh-century

99

polyptyque from the abbey of St Martin of Tours (Wallace-Hadrill 1983: 125). The chance survival of this document – fragments of it were used to make a bookbinding – suggests that such returns were not necessarily retained on a permanent basis, and implies the existence of others which may not have survived.

The collapse of the Roman Empire in the West did not necessarily result in an end to Roman bookkeeping practice, and it is pertinent to question whether the *Capitulare de Villis* was influenced by Roman methods. After all, one of the main aims of Roman accounting seems to have been to expose any losses due to the dishonesty or negligence of officials (de Ste. Croix 1956: 38), which is consistent with the spirit of the *Capitulare de Villis*. It is possible that Roman estate practices never fully died out. There was continuity, for example, in late Roman field division, agricultural techniques and manorial organisation; and authors have commented on the ready integration of the incoming Germanic peoples into Gallo-Roman country life (Latouche 1967: 102; Boussard 1968: 10–12; Geary 1988: 96; James 1988: 189–91). The church too played a key role in preserving Roman ideas. According to Loyn (1991: 233, 283), 'there is much more than mere abstraction to the generalization that in the church appeared the true heir of Rome . . . In face of at times most savage difficulties the Gallic bishops kept alive the spirit of Roman administration.' The bishop took the place of the Roman official as the 'characteristic social leader' in the towns of Gaul in the fifth century, and tended to be drawn from the old aristocratic senatorial class (Geary 1988: 33–4).

Reference material too existed in the form of preserved classical texts. The Carolingian court, and the monasteries associated with it, made a concerted attempt from the late eighth century to preserve classical knowledge through the collection and copying of ancient material from Italy (Reynolds 1983: xxi–xxv; Bischoff 1994: 94–5). Columella's *On Agriculture* and Pliny the Elder's *Natural History* were copied at this time. Like the *Capitulare de Villis*, their writings described large estates that were dependent on stewards for their management, with Columella's text containing more information about accounting. A copy of Pliny existed in the court library at Aachen at around the time the *Capitulare de Villis* was compiled, and the same seems likely of Columella's treatise (Oldroyd 1997: 20–2).

While continuity between Roman and Carolingian bookkeeping practice is a possibility, subsequent links with English estates in the tenth and eleventh centuries are clearer. The Carolingian practice of surveying estates was preserved by the Church in the ninth century, and transmitted to England in the tenth via the Benedictine reform movement (Campbell 1986: 164). English monastic reform depended on European houses, which provided models for both spiritual living and the efficient estate management necessary to support new foundations. Corroboration that the European practice of surveying estates was disseminated to England at this time exists in the form of a number of surviving documents from the tenth and eleventh centuries, showing English monasteries surveying their estates and compiling lists of stocks, treasures and sources of income in the manner of the Carolingian *polyptyque* (Campbell 1986: 165–6, 173; Loyn 1986: 6).

The adoption of European estate practice in England in the tenth century raises the question of whether this included charge and discharge accounting as well as the estate surveys, as the two tended to go together under the Carolingians, and also later in England in the thirteenth and fourteenth centuries (Harvey 1984: 18–19). No examples of charge and discharge accounts relating to estates have survived in England prior to the thirteenth century, although this disparity may be a reflection of the vagaries of record survival which favoured the preservation of surveys over charge and discharge accounts. Specifically, estate surveys were intended for use on an ongoing basis, and thus tended to be copied into cartularies or registers more readily than other manorial records (ibid.: 15).

Manorial accounting[3]

The focus of this section is on medieval manorial accounting and agency relationships. Consequently, governmental accounts are not considered, although their form was similar, and it is likely that influences passed from one to the other as the great royal offices were filled by magnates who were concerned with the orderly running and exploitation of their own estates as well as the administration of the king's business.[4]

The form of a 'typical' medieval account has been described many times (Noke 1981: 141–5; Harvey 1984: 25–40; Bailey 2002: 97–116). Widely known as the charge and discharge account, its purpose was to enable a person entrusted with the management of the property of another to render an account of their stewardship. These written accounts were examined orally at the audit, and amendments made as necessary (Bailey 2002: 102–3).

Medieval landowners frequently owned estates scattered throughout the country, perhaps the result of deliberate royal policy (Stenton 1971: 627–8). For example, of the manors held by the Bishop of Winchester, although over half were concentrated within Hampshire, the remainder were spread throughout Berkshire, Buckinghamshire, Oxfordshire, Somerset, Surrey, and Wiltshire (Page 2002: 6). Even when a magnate was close at hand, other responsibilities and the sheer size of estates necessitated the delegation of managerial powers.

An individual manor or group of manors might be made the overall responsibility of an official known as a reeve, steward or bailiff (Denholm-Young 1963: 32–85). The manor would comprise land occupied and exploited by tenants in exchange for an agreed rent, and land known as 'demesne' managed directly for the benefit of the lord and worked either by tenants who owed labour dues or by paid labour. The reeve would be responsible for implementing decisions as to which crops should be grown, for the gathering of the harvest, and its safe storage for sale or consumption by the lord's household. Thus, the reeve would account to his lord for all rents and dues owed by those living on the estate, and for the income and expenses of managing the demesne (Poole 1970: 36–7, 56–7).

The account was perceived in terms of the personal responsibility of the reeve to the lord of the manor. It normally began with 'the charge': the income which was due to the lord. From this was deducted the 'discharge': all allowances and expenses which the reeve was entitled to claim or incur, which usually left a balance deliverable to the lord. On the dorse (reverse side) of the account might be found an inventory giving particulars of grain, livestock, or other goods and utensils (Kirk 1892: ix–x). A full account would normally be presented once a year after the gathering in of the harvest, with an interim view of the account being given part way through the year in order to discuss the income received to date and the expectations for the full year (Bailey 2002: 103).

Harvey (1984: 25–40; 1994) has analysed the forms of written manorial accounts and identified three broad phases in their development: an early phase (c.1200–70) with diverse formats; a second period (c.1270–1380) which shows great standardisation and great detail; and a final phase (c.1380–1530) in which the accounts are less detailed. The early phase is characterised by a great variety of formats and a lack of sub-headings, beyond those of receipts and expenditure. By the second phase the accounts have become much more detailed, the use of sub-headings and sub-totals for different categories of income and expense has expanded greatly, and there is much greater comparability between the accounts of different estates and institutions. In phase three, the accounts become more divergent in form and often much shorter (see Bailey 2002: 116–50 for examples).

Both Harvey (1984 and 1994) and Bailey (2002) explain these transitions in terms of the changing patterns of estate exploitation. Until the thirteenth century the bulk of income was received in the form of fixed rents, even the demesne being farmed out. In the thirteenth century, however, there occurred a movement towards the reclaiming of the demesne and its direct management, possibly a response to general economic growth. Commodity prices were rising whereas customary rents were fixed, and landlords perceived direct management as a means of increasing their income. In place of the fixed rent, landlords now received income from the sale of a variety of crops and livestock, and incurred a multiplicity of types of expense related to the direct exploitation of the land (Miller and Hatcher 1980: 198–239). Accounts in the second phase became more detailed to reflect these changes. Subsequently, this movement was reversed and land was returned from direct management to leasing. Phase three accounts are diverse as this process was spread over a long period and varied greatly from estate to estate: some estates still needing to account for the variety entailed by direct management; others having the much simpler accounts of rentiers (McKisack 1971: 341; Dobson 1973: 272; Duby 1976: 261).

Turning to the standardisation of accounts in the second phase, this may be seen as a reflection of the diffusion and adoption of improvements in business practice. For example, advances in accounting at the royal exchequer served as a model for others (Oschinsky 1971: 214). Royal methods appear to have been introduced and continued at a number of ecclesiastical estates when they were administered by a royal official during a vacancy (Hall 1903: xi–xii; Salter 1922: 80; Graham 1929: 253). The systems in use at the royal exchequer were documented in 1177–79 by Richard Fitz Nigel (1983), Bishop of London, in his *Dialogus de Scaccario*. This was soon followed from the mid-thirteenth century onwards by estate management manuals (such as Walter of Henley's) and accounting treatises which described procedures and gave examples of accounts (Oschinsky 1971: 235–57). From Beaulieu Abbey survives a formulary written in 1269–70, with an introduction giving rules for preparing accounts followed by a set of specimen accounts to be used as a guide for accounting and auditing in future years (Hockey 1975). Accounting was taught at universities, certainly from the second half of the fourteenth century onwards (Richardson 1941: 260). Additionally, pressure on ecclesiastical estates to prepare written accounts came from the papacy (Knowles 1956: 57–8; Dobie forthcoming), and on both ecclesiastical and lay estates from developments in legal practice which required well laid out accounts in order to be considered convincing evidence (Oschinsky 1971: 72; Bailey 2002: 19; Dobie forthcoming).

Thus far the manorial account has been considered in isolation, but a manor was likely to be one of many on a great estate which would also have other departments that would be required to prepare accounts. Thus, at Durham Cathedral Priory, in addition to manorial and livestock accounts, there survive accounts from a range of office bearers or obedientiaries such as the bursar and cellarer, the heads of dependent cells, and the proctors charged with administering more distant possessions in Scotland. Selections from these accounts have been published and it is possible to trace transactions from the discharge section of one account into the charge of another – an example of the dual nature of a transaction being reflected within a single-entry system of accounts (Fowler 1898–1900).

The accounts were of course the outcome of a whole series of underlying vouchers and records. Wooden tallies and written indentures were widely used to record and evidence the transfer of money from one agent to another, again reflecting the dual nature of financial transactions (Clanchy 1979: 95–6; Baxter 1994). Surveys summarised all the revenues due to a lord (Clanchy 1979: 72–3).[5] Other accounting records might include lists of rents due, debtors and creditors (Lomas and Piper 1989; Bailey 2002: 152–3).

Although the prime purpose of the accounts was to attest the stewardship of officials, the totals from individual accounts were on occasion summarised and combined with the totals from other accounts to yield a picture of overall financial position. Thus at Norwich Cathedral Priory, the *Status Obedientiariorum* (the earliest extant dates from 1345) combined the totals from the accounts of the individual obedientiaries to arrive at the total receipts, total expenditure and surplus or deficit for each year (Saunders 1930: 17). Stone (1962: 25) traces the development of a *proficium* (profit or gain) figure at Norwich Cathedral Priory from the second half of the thirteenth century. Expenditure on capital items such as the building of a new grange was excluded from the calculation, which was also adjusted for goods transferred elsewhere on the estates (Stone 1962: 28; Postles 1994: 118).

Bookkeeping on medieval estates therefore demonstrates a variety of forms, which emerged in response to changing economic conditions and opportunities. It attracted the attention of learned men who taught at the universities and wrote treatises laying out and explaining current best practice which aided the diffusion of more complex bookkeeping techniques and their standardisation. Such a movement was also encouraged by papal bulls demanding that accounts be prepared and audited for ecclesiastical offices, and by the increasing ability of creditors to enforce their claims in court, provided they could supply written accounting evidence.

Mercantile accounting – literature and practice

The factors which encouraged landlords to take land back into direct management – a growing population leading to both rising demand and rising prices for agricultural foodstuffs (Duby 1976: 260; Harvey 1984, 1994; Bailey 2002) – also underlie the expansion of trade which occurred throughout Europe as the Middle Ages progressed (Bernard 1972: 274–5; Russell 1972: 36; Jones 1997: 152–3). Two centuries of relative prosperity (*c.*1050–1250) were followed by a century and a half of disruption marked by the Black Death, financial crises, and political unrest (Trevor-Roper 1965: 161–75). The overall trend, however, was one of economic growth in which an urban class of merchants grew rich and influential. Families such as the Medici in Florence, whose fortune was founded in banking, became powerful rulers in their own right (de Roover 1966: 5; Bernard 1972: 289–302). The fifteenth and sixteenth centuries were an age of discovery of new worlds in the West, and a new seaborne trading route to the East, both of which had a profound impact on European trade and investment (Clough and Cole 1952: 108–33).

Producing goods for markets provided cash incomes for landlords which could be spent on imported luxury items. The inter-relatedness and interdependence of a large number of factors emerging in parallel is evident. A money economy surfaced against a background of sustained population growth, growth in towns and trade, a reduction in transaction costs, improvements in transport and distribution networks, supplies of silver for coinage, reliable coinage, increasing literacy and numeracy, systems of reckoning and recording, recognised weights and measures, and a legal process for the enforcement of credit over time (Bolton 2004: 7). These developments enabled and accompanied a revival in trade, while at the same time requiring more sophisticated accounting systems to track and provide evidence of increasingly complex networks of transactions.

Economic activity was at its most advanced in Italy between the twelfth and fifteenth centuries (Bernard 1972: 291); great banking houses, such as the Medici developed that were capable of transferring credit over the whole of Europe (de Roover 1966: 2–3). It is widely agreed today that double-entry bookkeeping emerged among the flourishing city states of Italy in the thirteenth and fourteenth centuries (Edwards 1989: 48–9; Mills 1994: 82). Most of the surviving examples of account-books exhibiting double entry elements are post 1290 (de Roover 1956; Edwards 1989: 49–50; Lee 1977, 1994). Fra Luca Pacioli's *Summa de Arithmetica, Geometrica, Proportioni et Proportionalita*, published in 1494, claims that the double-entry system he was describing (in the chapter entitled *De Computis et Scripturis*) had been used in Venice for more than 200 years (Galassi 1996). This would date its origin there as late-thirteenth century.

Born in 1445, Pacioli is often perceived as the father of double-entry bookkeeping and modern accounting (Hatfield 1968: 3). Certainly, *De Computis* was the first published work on double-entry bookkeeping. However, an earlier work written in 1458, but not published until 1573, by Benedetto Cotrugli (*Della Mercatura et del Mercante Perfecto*), also included an account of double-entry bookkeeping, and stated that a merchant should have three books: ledger, journal and memorial (a type of day book for collecting information prior to processing); and that the ledger should be closed off annually and a trial balance drawn up (Yamey 1994: 43–7; Kojima 1995: 69). It has since been suggested that the *Summa* is a combination of different works written at different times (Hernández-Esteve 1994a: 65–78; 1994b: 68). Pacioli stated that the objective of bookkeeping is 'to give the trader without delay information as to his assets and liabilities' (Brown 1968: 111–12). His work gave practical guidance to merchants, providing examples on how to open a new set of accounts, starting with an inventory of assets and liabilities and citing the initial double entry for opening the books still taught to students today: debit cash and credit capital (Geüsbeek 1974: 33–5, 43).

The main importance of Pacioli's work lies not so much in its originality as in its influence in disseminating knowledge of the double-entry method throughout Europe. It is significant that the work's publication coincided with the advent of the printing press, which made new ideas more accessible (Thompson, 1991; Mills 1994: 90–3). This was the heyday of the Italian Renaissance, when Italian influence in art, music, philosophy, science, technology and warfare was at its height. New learning spread northwards from Italy through France, Germany, the Low Countries and England. As a result, not only did Pacioli's *De Computis* attract considerable attention in his native Italy (Taylor 1956: 180–1), it was also widely reproduced elsewhere: 'All of the accounting books published during the sixteenth century in other European countries, particularly in Germany, the Netherlands, and England, presented descriptions of bookkeeping similar to that one by Pacioli' (Galassi 1996: 445). Authors borrowed freely from each other often without acknowledgement (Yamey 1979).

The first book in English on bookkeeping is Hugh Oldcastle's *A Profitable Treatyce* published in 1543, of which no copy is known to have survived (Coomber 1956: 206). It was used and acknowledged by John Mellis in his *A Briefe Instruction and Maner How to Keep Bookes of Accompts After the Order of Debitor and Creditor*, published in 1588. Both works were almost literal translations of Pacioli, notwithstanding the omission of certain sections of the earlier work (Yamey et al. 1963: 155–9; Chatfield 1977: 56). Jan Ympyn Christoffels' translation of his *Nieuwe Instructie* of 1543 into English in 1547, as *A Notable and Very Excellente Woorke*, moved beyond Pacioli by including a set of illustrative accounts and by incorporating a balance account into the ledger to record all of the closing balances prior to closing it off and opening up a new ledger (Yamey et al. 1963: 159–61; Chatfield 1996b: 616). James Peele's *The Maner and Fourme How to Kepe a Perfect Reconyng* followed in 1553. Important innovations included a general rule which could be applied to assist in the categorisation of transactions: 'To make the thinges Receivyd, or the receiver, Debter to the things delivered, or to the deliverer' (quoted in Chatfield 1996a: 455). Peele's second and larger work, *The Pathe-Waye to Perfectness* was published in 1569, and owed much to another English author, John Weddington, published two years earlier. The *Pathe-Way* took the form of a dialogue between teacher and student. In both his works, Peele supplied examples of journal entries to which a bookkeeper in doubt could refer (Yamey *et al.* 1963: 162–3; Chatfield 1996a: 455). As Jackson (1956: 288) notes, 'The history of the teaching of bookkeeping until almost the end of the nineteenth century consists . . . . of the evolution of methods of explaining how to find which accounts to debit and credit.'

These books of instruction contain a common core of recommendations. The accounting books to be maintained comprised as a minimum the ledger, journal and memorial, although the memorial was sometimes referred to as a 'waste book' (Yamey *et al.* 1963: 12; Mepham 1988: 176–98). From the memorial, which acted as a memory aid, transactions were formalised (and overseas currencies converted into a single currency) as debits and credits in the journal, from which postings were made to the ledger. Merchants might be engaged in an inherently complex trading environment involving credit sales and purchases, loans, interest, bills of exchange, and foreign currency losses/gains, and so examples of many types of transaction are provided in these texts and the use of references and cross-references described. Balancing off the ledger is also explained, although such an activity appears to have been conducted infrequently early on, mainly occurring when a partnership was concluded or a ledger full (Brown 1968: 106; Mepham 1988: 199).

There was instruction too about writing letters, which provided merchants with a means of controlling their operations at a distance, and were recognised by contemporary authors as part of the accounting process (Oldroyd 1998). Ympyn, Weddington and Peele all listed the copy letter-book among the merchant's account books (Yamey *et al.* 1963: 21, 25, 44), and a series of letter writing manuals such as *The Merchants' Avizo* of 1589 provided examples of business letters (Jeacle and Brown 2006: 30). Weddington in particular referred to the need for correspondence with factors, which would include abstracts of accounts and source data for the memorial in order to manage a merchant's affairs properly (Yamey *et al.* 1963: 48–9, 97). Finally, although the focus of these texts was on tracking exchanges and establishing accountability, there is some evidence of consideration given to the use of accounting for costing and decision-making purposes. For example, John Collins, in *The Perfect Method of Merchants Accompts Demonstrated* of 1697, detailed the application of double-entry bookkeeping to the internal transfers of raw materials from a stock account to a process account (Boyns *et al.* 1997; Boyns and Edwards 2007).

The steadily increasing number of books published on double-entry bookkeeping undoubtedly was a factor in the dissemination of knowledge of the technique. A 'small and intermittent trickle' became by the eighteenth century a 'steady and widening stream' (Yamey *et al.* 1963: vii). The popularity of such books can be seen by the number of editions published, although this could be more definitely assessed were details of the size of print-runs known. Webster's volume, first published in 1717, appeared in at least 13 editions. John Mair's *Bookkeeping Methodized* of 1736 was reissued in over 20 versions, with a further eight editions of his new 1773 title appearing in print by 1807 (Yamey *et al.* 1963: 213–14; Mepham 1988: 78–9).

The extent to which the publication of new textbooks contributed to the practical adoption of double entry is debatable (Yamey 1981: 128–32). Ramsey (1956: 186), for example, agreed with Ympyn that the extant accounts of sixteenth-century English merchants were generally 'grosly, obscurely and lewdely kept'. Single–entry accounting seems to have remained the norm in Britain even among large organisations until at least the nineteenth century (Hoskin and Macve 1986), as demonstrated by two references from the very end of the eighteenth century showing it to be still very much in use. Thus, Edward Thomas Jones, in his *English System of Book-keeping by Single or Double-Entry* of 1796 declared that single entry had an advantage over double entry in that the latter was more complex, and thus allowed greater secrecy and more scope for fraud (Yamey *et al.* 1963: 17);[6] and John Williamson Fulton, championing double entry in his text published four years later in 1800, acknowledged the enduring popularity of the single entry alternative (ibid.: 15–16). This situation was not unique to Britain. 'Many merchants' in Germany preferred single entry because of its simplicity. Charge and discharge accounting remained popular in France in the eighteenth century in certain industries (Lemarchand 1994). The Dutch East India Company too resisted the adoption of double entry, as did the Whitin Machine Company in the US until 1918 (Macve 1996: 29).

In answer to the question of why the rate of adoption of double-entry bookkeeping was so slow in Britain, Edwards (1989: 56–7) concluded that the absence of strong demand from business is the most likely explanation, rather than ignorance or lack of expertise on the part of the merchants. Merchants' accounts were intended primarily to eliminate errors, to prevent embezzlement, to establish the value of a business for probate or similar purposes (Pollard 1965: 212), to keep track of credit dealings, inventories, and partners' capital (Winjum 1972: 156; Chatfield 1977: 58), to serve as a memory aid (Lee 1990: 88), and to provide evidence in courts of law (Ramsey 1956: 187). Hence, the main purpose of account books was to safeguard a merchant's property rights. The enduring popularity of single-entry systems in Britain suggests that this end could be achieved without recourse to double entry.

Firms of merchants in England in the sixteenth and seventeenth centuries generally comprised loose associations of individuals who would band together for particular ventures, sharing the proceeds of the completed undertaking between them (Winchester 1955: 212–13). Because mercantile business was venture-based, the notion of periodic profit measurement as a means of calculating dividends did not apply. Similarly, there was no need to calculate profit for tax purposes, as income tax was not conceived in Britain until the end of the eighteenth century. In these circumstances it is unsurprising that the distinctions between capital and revenue items, and between business and personal expenditure were not sharply defined, and that the ability of double-entry bookkeeping to measure periodic profits on a routine basis was not exploited. Much diversity has been observed too in the treatment of fixed assets, stock valuation, and bad and doubtful debts, and there is also little evidence of the practical application of the accruals concept (Yamey 1962: 32–7; Yamey *et al.* 1963: 193–201).

Explaining the origins of double-entry bookkeeping

Pinpointing the origins of double-entry bookkeeping is particularly important given the alleged connections discussed in Chapter 15 between double entry and the rise of capitalism. Two key questions arise: why did double entry appear in Italy in the thirteenth century?; and why in the nineteenth century did its use apparently become widespread in the UK? The first of these questions is considered in this section and the second in the section entitled 'Victorian expansion'.

The emergence of double-entry systems in Italy from the thirteenth century onwards may have resulted from a process of 'trial and error' which eventually recognised that every transaction had two aspects. If a sale was made, either cash was received or the business had a debtor to monitor. Both features had to be written down for the books to show a correct record (Lee 1975: 7–8). It may be that a system of cross-checking was done, between the cash book and the debtors book: the accounting records of Giovanni Farolfi from 1299–1300 feature such cross-references (de Roover 1956: 119; Lee 1977). The duality of transactions was also evident from manorial accounts in which the discharge section of one account comprised the charge of another. Likewise, Chapter 4 has described how the notion of recording systems that were capable of representing the physical as well as the social realities of transactions may have existed as early as the Neolithic. Another possibility is that double entry evolved out of charge and discharge accounting. Although the systems of charge and discharge and double-entry book-keeping may be perceived as being distinct, numerous examples of hybrid systems containing elements of both charge and discharge and double-entry bookkeeping can be found, such as that used in 1759–60 on the Mackworth Estate (Neath) where the traditional accountability of charge and discharge statements was combined with the maintenance of a ledger based on double entry principles (Boyns and Edwards 2007).

However, double-entry bookkeeping goes much further in its classification of transactions into *nominal* (revenue and expenses), *personal* (debtors/creditors) or *real* (other assets/liabilities) accounts than any of its known antecedents (Galassi 1996). Indeed, its very distinctiveness allied to its sudden appearance in one part of Europe militates against an evolutionary explanation of its development, unless there are many sets of earlier records that have been lost. The earliest example containing double-entry elements identified so far relates to 1211, whereas by 1299 one is able to observe a fully developed system in operation in the branch accounts of the Florentine merchants, Giovanni Farolfi and Company. Lee (1977: 87), who described these books, subscribed to the idea 'of the gradual acceptance and application' by merchants of the underlying 'concepts' of double entry between 1211 and 1300. However, there is nothing gradual about such a radical departure occurring within the space of 90 years when viewed against the history of bookkeeping in Western Europe as a whole. Charge and discharge accounting is an example of a system that predominated on English estates from at least the thirteenth to the nineteenth centuries. The double-entry system employed by the Farolfi family in 1299–1300 was very similar to the one described by Pacioli two hundred years later, which in turn has remained largely unchanged through to the modern-day (Lee 1977; Galassi 1996: 447).

Given this tendency on the part of practitioners to follow existing methods, which helps explain why double entry did not sweep the board despite its apparent advantages,[7] one searches for a catalyst in the thirteenth century to account for the sudden change. Hoskin and Macve (1986; see also Macve 1996), approaching the issue from a Foucauldian perspective, grounded the origins of double entry in educational advances that occurred in medieval universities from the eleventh century, which affected the layout of written texts, among other matters.[8] Textual innovations in the Middle Ages included alphabetical ordering, subject indexing, subdividing material into sections, cross-referencing and commentary, all of which are relevant to a double-entry ledger. However, these developments were not confined to Italy or to the thirteenth century. Indeed, changes to the university curriculum, allied to religious pressure at the end of the fifteenth century 'to re emphasize a belief in order sanctified by God' (Thompson 1991: 584), possibly provide a more convincing explanation of why Pacioli, a professor of mathematics, was motivated to write his *Summa*, than why double entry was originally conceived.

Edwards (1989: 50–1) offers the increasing complexity of the business environment in Italy as another explanation for double entry, particularly the increase in credit transactions. However, as observed earlier, merchants seem to have been able to carry on their trade involving credit, loans, interest, negotiable instruments and foreign currencies through to the Victorian era without recourse to double entry, suggesting that a functionalist explanation of its origins will not alone suffice.

Hence, one seeks other external factors that would account for the emergence of double-entry bookkeeping in thirteenth century Italy, an obvious one being contact between Italian merchants and other cultures where proto-double-entry systems were already in use. Such an explanation is certainly possible. Extensive trade was conducted between Italy and the eastern Mediterranean during the medieval period, and perhaps new mercantile practices were observed and imitated or exchanged in both directions. There has, for instance, been debate between Zaid (2000, 2001) and Nobes (2001) over the possibility and extent of influences from the medieval Islamic world. The two protagonists are at least able to agree that 'several features of pre-double entry accounting were used in the Muslim world before they were used in the West' (ibid.: 212). The thirteenth century also witnessed the creation of the great Mongol Empire ruled by Genghis Khan and his descendants, which at its height stretched from China to the fringes of Western Europe, creating 'a huge free-trade area', and bringing 'Christendom, as never before, into touch with the great, old civilizations of the East' (Trevor-Roper 1965: 177, 180): 'The great, orderly, tolerant Mongol Empire crossed and re-crossed by continual caravans, provided one of the most effective means for the diffusion of culture and technology', the most famous examples being gunpowder and printing, which were transmitted from China to Europe around this time (ibid.: 178–9). The same could have applied to bookkeeping. The history of Chinese bookkeeping covers several thousand years (Lin 2003; Lu and Aiken 2003). This is also true of India, from whence, claims Lall Nigam (1986), although challenged by Nobes (1987) for lack of documentary evidence, double entry originated. Such claims remain unproven, and although the dissemination of bookkeeping practice from the East remains a possibility, double entry in its developed form appears 'unique' (Chatfield 1977: 34). Thus a number of factors, none of which individually explain the phenomenon satisfactorily, may have contributed to the origins of double entry.

Early industry

Some of the earliest examples of industrial accounting in Britain relate to landed estates. This is not surprising given that the landed estate was the largest, wealthiest and most clearly defined type of business organisation in existence at the dawn of the Industrial Revolution (Pollard 1965: 25, 29–30). Moreover, British landowners enjoyed a relative advantage over many of their continental counterparts, in that the law entitled them to the coal, ironstone, lead and other mineral deposits under their land, with no social disapprobation attaching to the economic exploitation of their properties (Habakkuk 1953: 96, 99). Indeed, the early development of industry on estates, together with the major part played by landowners as investors in other enterprises, such as canal and railway companies, favours the notion of the dissemination of estate management practice to other sectors of the British economy (Napier 1997).

As far as bookkeeping was concerned, charge and discharge accounts prepared by individual stewards persisted as the dominant form of accounting on estates throughout the eighteenth and nineteenth centuries (Napier 1991, 1997), and were used to record industrial activities on estates (James 1955: xliv; Hatcher 1993: 303). According to Hatcher (ibid.), charge and discharge persisted as the only form of bookkeeping in many collieries until the 1670s. Generally, however, the system proved incapable of dealing with the full complexities of the trading operations, and a range of other types of report containing a common 'core of vital data on costs, output, and sales' was needed to address the shortfall (ibid.: 304). For example, 'coalpit' and 'sinking books' were used to analyse output, sales and production costs, on the Willoughbys' estate, at Wollaton in the sixteenth century, as supplements to the traditional charge and discharge statements (Lee 1991: 70).

Diversification in the types of records kept was a prominent feature of eighteenth-century estates in the north-east of England where a range of different reports was prepared in addition to the charge and discharge statements. For example, schedules of output were used to verify payments to and from subcontractors and lessees; stocks of goods and materials were listed and quantified; payments to workmen were dealt with through pay-bills which priced their daily output at the agreed rates; and the profitability of particular activities was calculated. The number of parties that were involved in the operations is quite striking, and included stewards, lessees, partners, shareholders, labourers, agents, and tenants, in addition to a host of different kinds of subcontractor. The method used to regulate these relationships was legally enforceable contracts supported by accounting to monitor compliance and, if necessary, seek redress in court. Bookkeeping was thus used throughout the estate operations to quantify and track the various exchanges taking place, and without it the various participants would have been unable to trade (Oldroyd 2007: 81, 102).

The main method of bookkeeping employed by these estates was the bilateral recording of cash receipts and payments, with adjustments for opening and closing debtors, creditors and stocks if the intention was to calculate profit. Bilateral cash accounting seems to have been commonplace on eighteenth century landed estates. For example, it was the method recommended in Charles Snell's *Accompts for Landed-Men* (1711), and Edward Laurence's *The Duty and Office of a Land Steward* (1731). Other guides such as Thomas Richards' *The Gentlemans Auditor* (1707) and Roger North's *The Gentleman Accomptant* (1714) advocated the use of double entry. However, the relative advantage of the bilateral method over double entry lay in its simplicity, which allowed it to be applied to all of the trading situations described, without requiring specialist bookkeeping knowledge (ibid.: 46, 60).

If the need to protect property rights was the prime motivator of the bookkeeping arrangements on estates, detailed costing records were maintained as well to help plan the operations and inform investment decisions (ibid.: 107). This was true also of other early industrial enterprises where, in certain instances, the financial and management record-keeping systems were kept separately, and in others they were integrated. A review of 25 British firms between 1760 and 1850 revealed that 'costing activities were rarely reported in financial accounting records' (Fleischman and Parker 1991). By way of contrast, 'an integrated system of financial/management accounting' was uncovered in the iron-making industry in Sheffield *c.*1690 (Edwards and Boyns, 1992).

Management accounting practice is considered in Chapter 9. However, it is worth stressing in the context of a chapter on bookkeeping that the distinction which exists today between 'financial' and 'management' accounting procedures was rarely relevant prior to the mid-nineteenth century. In the first place, the boundaries over who was responsible for collating and reporting different types of information were more fluid in the absence of defined engineering and accountancy professions. In the second, the division between external and internal reporting did not apply to most industrial enterprises, which were privately owned either by individuals or limited numbers of partners.

Returning to estates, the business interests of landowners were often varied and dispersed. The Earl of Balcarres, for example, owned coal and cannel mines in Scotland in addition to plantations in Jamaica (Oldroyd 2007: 105). No matter how conscientious proprietors were in visiting their properties, they would need a management system that was capable of controlling the operations at a distance and, in this respect, chief stewards played a vital role. These were highly remunerated full-time officials who operated through a central estate office normally situated in the landowner's main residence. It was through this office that accounting returns from all the various activities were channelled (Mingay 1967: 18–19).

Although the chief stewards were responsible for determining the bookkeeping arrangements, they were not primarily bookkeepers. According to Spring (1963: 100), stewards tended to be the sons of tenant farmers, yeomen, land agents, builders, surveyors and mining engineers: 'In a word they were the sons of practical men, often familiar from youth with the varied business of land management.' Pollard (1965: 29) maintained that stewards, in the north of England especially, were renowned for their industrial, commercial and financial acumen. Thus, John Hardy, a chief steward in the West Riding of Yorkshire, advised his master on a variety of matters, including taxation, investment in canal and iron companies, as well as mineral exploitation and textile production on the estate (Beckett 1986: 143). In the north-east of England, where the main business of many estates was coalmining, it was commonplace to employ *viewers* (mining engineers) as stewards. Chief stewards were highly remunerated. Hardy, whose tenure stretched for 30 years (1773–1803), received £80 a year in addition to a favourable lease of Barnby Hall with extensive farmlands. Personal wealth was desirable in the case of a steward as it conferred the social status needed to command the respect of tenants (Mingay 1967: 7–12; Martin 1979: 17).

Although stewards were not specialist bookkeepers, they needed to acquire a knowledge of bookkeeping. Various sources of guidance were available to them in addition to the printed handbooks mentioned previously. For example, Charles Snell described himself in his text as a 'teacher of writing and accompts at the free writing-school in Foster Lane with whom young gentlemen may board', which indicates the availability of external tuition. In most cases, however, the knowledge would have been acquired internally, with stewards either replicating the practice of their predecessors, or following exemplars. Boyns and Edwards (1996) highlighted the role of proprietors and their agents in the 'dissemination of accounting techniques' in Welsh industry in the eighteenth and nineteenth centuries (see also Boyns and Edwards 2007). Bookkeeping exemplars have survived on the Bowes estates in County Durham relating to the lead and salt operations. Family dynasties of stewards were common on these estates, and the marked similarity in the layout and presentation of the account-books over several generations of stewards confirms that they learnt from each other (Oldroyd 2007: 60–1).

Victorian expansion

The nineteenth century is, for the UK, the century when double-entry bookkeeping allegedly assumed the hegemony which it continues to claim today (Yamey 1956: 11; Hoskin and Macve 1986). Two factors supported this change: first, the widening gulf between investors and managers in a period of increasing industrialisation, which necessitated a transformation in business financial reporting practices; second, the increasing professionalisation of accountancy, which resulted in the adoption and diffusion through training and teaching of uniform accounting methods. This section will focus on the first of these developments as the effects of professionalisation are considered in Chapter 11.

At the outset, however, it should be acknowledged that the archives which have survived, and on which the research findings reported in this section have been based, tend to be from larger companies. In contrast, most businesses in existence in the mid-1800s were small (More 1997: 105–6; Boyce and Ville 2002: 148): 'most industrial labour continued to be carried out in homes and small workshops until the late Victorian period' (Morgan 1999: 48). Many of the individuals keeping the books probably would have been family members, and household accounting 'featured prominently in the everyday life and culture of the middle class family' (Walker 1998: 485). Household management books extolled the virtues of maintaining household accounts to ensure that insolvency, waste and fraud were avoided. It is unlikely that these accounts would have comprised a full set of double-entry records, but instead might have included a cash book listing receipts and expenditure, lists of credit transactions and their subsequent settlement, and inventories of goods (ibid.: 493), representing little development in the techniques employed.

Company accounts, however, tell a different story. In the nineteenth century, the Industrial Revolution, expansion of transport networks and growing markets created an increasing demand for capital. This demand was matched by an increase in the number of companies aiming to attract funds from debt and equity investors who were concerned to protect and monitor their investments.[9] Shareholder and creditor concern was further strengthened by the high profile frauds and bankruptcies which occurred frequently during the nineteenth century. George Hudson, the 'Railway King', was in 1855 obliged to move abroad to escape lawsuits arising from alleged frauds, including doctoring the books, amounting to a total of £598,785 (Glynn 1994: 331). In 1878, the City of Glasgow Bank collapsed. Its insolvency had been concealed and dividends continued to be paid by a deliberate policy of overvaluing assets (about £7 million of bad debts were treated as though they were good debts), and by falsifying figures submitted in government returns (French 1985: 10, 15). Such instances increased the demand for credible financial statements based on reliable accounting records.

Government was not necessarily keen to intervene, however, and a conflict can be seen between the forces of *laissez-faire* and those attempting to regulate and control. On the one hand, the nature of the accounting systems and information published by companies was regarded as a matter to be negotiated between the shareholders and the directors. Thus, Poulett Thomson, a minister at the Board of Trade, could say in 1837: 'It is by the Government not meddling with capital that this country has been able to obtain a superiority over every other country' (Hansard 1837: xxxvi, 1161–2; Glynn 1994: 330). On the other hand, the power of individual shareholders to influence such matters was seen as limited because of the widening gap between directors and shareholders (Littleton 1933: 206).

Consequently, some limited intervention did take place, although it was not until the Companies Act of 1928 that, for the generality of companies, any attempt was made to prescribe the form and content of the balance sheet (Edey 1968: 141–2). The Joint Stock Companies Act of 1844 had made accounting compulsory: companies were to keep books of account and to present 'full and fair' balance sheets to members at general meetings, which balance sheets were to be reported on by appointed auditors. However, little detail was given, the books of account were not described, and the contents and the format of the balance sheet were not laid down. Even these limited conditions were removed in the Joint Stock Companies Act of 1856, although the non-mandatory model articles of association specified the use of double entry; a provision dropped from the model articles attached to the consolidating act of 1862 (Edey and Panitpakdi 1956). As Edey (1968: 137) has stated, the entire period between 1855 and 1900 is 'marked by a complete absence of statutory regulation in matters relating to accounting and audit for companies incorporated under the general company law, the only exceptions being those carrying on a few special classes of business'.

Although the government was hesitant to intervene in the affairs of companies in general, it did intercede in the affairs of public bodies and of specific industries such as the railways, banks, life assurance and gas on the grounds of public interest (Parker 1990). The 1835 Municipal Corporation Act was a watershed in extending the accountability of local authorities (Edwards 1992), and in 1867 all parishes were obliged to adopt double entry as the old method of receipts and expenditure statements ignored outstanding liabilities (Jones 1994: 400). Local government had on occasion moved in advance of this: in 1785 the City of Bristol adopted a double-entry system (Jones 1994: 399) but, even as late as 1907, it could only be said that double-entry bookkeeping was employed by 'almost all local authorities' (Coombs and Edwards 1993: 41; 1994: 176).

A major factor prompting the adoption of double-entry systems by companies was the need to calculate dividends. Lenders required assurance that the security of their capital would be maintained, and so companies needed to be able to identify clearly the profits available for distribution. The Companies Acts of 1855–56 included a provision within the model articles that no dividend should be paid except out of profits (Edey and Panitpakdi 1956: 362) – accounts were therefore needed that were capable of enabling capital to be maintained. Double-entry bookkeeping, with its distinction between nominal, real and capital accounts, was ideal for that purpose.

Thus, the need to produce financial statements to protect the interests of lenders and investors necessitated the maintenance of appropriate records which recognised expenses fully and distinguished between capital and revenue items. The increasing emphasis during the nineteenth century on regular year-end reporting was significant in elevating the status of financial statements. At the start of the period, financial statements were very much a residual product of the bookkeeping system, whereas by 1900 and, increasingly thereafter, it was the form and requirements of the annual financial statements which informed and drove the bookkeeping system and led to the increasing adoption of double-entry methods.

Conclusion

Although this account of bookkeeping practice spans some 2,500 years, a number of common threads emerge. The most important one is the role bookkeeping has played in safeguarding property entitlements throughout the whole of this period, without which trade would have been impossible. Funnell (2001) considers the association between accounting, justice and property, arguing that the protection of property rights, for which accounting is vital, lies at the heart of capitalist law-codes as the ultimate end of justice. What he is essentially referring to, therefore, is bookkeeping, for it is this which tracks the rights and obligations attaching to property, and provides the necessary legal evidence for claims to be enforced in court. The chapter has observed bookkeeping fulfilling these functions from classical times onwards, showing that the triangular relationship subsisting between accounting, justice and property rights is not confined to capitalist societies.

The second theme is the role that distance from events has played in creating agency relationships, which in turn necessitated bookkeeping systems that were capable of holding agents accountable. This was as true on medieval estates as on those of the nineteenth century, or in the operations of sixteenth-century merchants, or those of Victorian joint-stock companies where the desire to protect the interests of shareholders provided an impetus for better record keeping. Thus, the chapter has observed bookkeeping continually adapting to a variety of modes of organisational control in order to fulfil these two related functions of protecting property rights and holding agents accountable at a distance. This leads to the final theme, which is the relationship between bookkeeping and complexity.

Throughout its history, bookkeeping has been effectively deployed in a range of contractual situations, modes of operation or business environments. However, here there is a paradox, as the adaptability displayed by bookkeeping seems to have stemmed from its simplicity throughout most of its history. The range of situations in which bookkeeping was utilised in Roman society is a case in point. For most of the 2,500 years reviewed in this chapter, cash accounting supported by supplementary schedules of assets and liabilities has sufficed. Indeed, the success of single-entry recording systems long after the invention of double entry raises a question mark over the inevitability of the latter. As Jack (1966) pointed out in her historical defence of single-entry bookkeeping, a system that was fit for purpose should not be dismissed as inferior simply because more sophisticated systems existed.

In terms of future research directions and challenges, the foregoing analysis suggests certain possibilities. For instance, how extensive were the gaps between bookkeeping instruction and practice? A lack of archival research means that accounting historians have only begun to answer this question (Yamey 1981: 128). There is still not a satisfactory explanation for the emergence of double-entry bookkeeping in Italy in the thirteenth century. What were the effects of interaction between merchants trading within and outside Europe? A worthwhile site for comparison would be the records of the merchant communities of different nationalities living side-by-side in great trading centres such as Antwerp or London. Given the intercontinental scale of trade from the classical period onwards, there is a relative dearth of comparative studies. Sadly, lack of space has prevented consideration of the rich bookkeeping traditions of the many non-European cultures involved in this global trade. Did double entry really become commonplace in nineteenth-century Britain as is usually assumed? And what about other countries? What were the effects of changes in bookkeeping practice in terms of economic and social development and the ways in which people viewed the world around them? Aside from the accounting records themselves, the articles of association might provide an additional source of evidence for joint-stock companies, although these would not help with the more numerous unincorporated organisations. The legal documents pertaining to bankruptcy proceedings might provide clues here. These are but a few suggestions for study which may interest future researchers.

Key works

Chatfield (1977) is a comprehensive general history of accounting, with the first seven chapters focusing on 'the development of basic accounting methods'.

Edwards and Yamey (1994) celebrates the 500th anniversary of the publication of Pacioli's *Summa*. It contains articles on the history of bookkeeping from ancient times through to the nineteenth century.

Littleton and Yamey (1956) remains one of the best collections of articles on bookkeeping, covering the period from classical times to the nineteenth century.

Parker and Yamey (1994) starts with ten articles dealing with the ancient world through to the development of double-entry bookkeeping.

Yamey *et al.* (1963) brings together commentary, analysis and extracts from original treatises on bookkeeping.

Notes

1 The information in this section is drawn mainly from Oldroyd (1997: 18–22).
2 The Carolingian dynasty dominated Western Europe c.750–987.
3 The information in this section is drawn mainly from Dobie (forthcoming).
4 A wealth of accounting material survives from medieval England: from ecclesiastical institutions (Kitchin 1892; Fowler 1898–1900; Saunders, 1930; Smith, 1943; Greatrex 1984; Page 1996, 1999; Harvey 2002), from manorial and lay household accounts (Clanchy 1979: 72; Woolgar 1992–3: 6), and from government records (Hunter 1844: Foreword).

5   On a macro level, the Domesday Book (1085–86), which contains a detailed survey of all the manors of England with the exception of the northern counties, has been claimed to be a working accounting document used in the raising of revenue (Godfrey and Hooper 1996; Oldroyd 1997; McDonald 2005).

6   Jones was to change his opinion by 1820, proclaiming instead the advantages of double entry (Edwards 1989: 70).

7   The advantages of double entry over single entry are elucidated by Yamey (1956: 7–8).

8   Hoskin and Macve (1986) also advance educational changes as the catalyst for double entry's growing acceptance in the nineteenth century.

9   The advantages of double-entry bookkeeping in reducing the scope for errors and omissions and the difficulties of ensuring a complete representation of all assets and liabilities with single-entry methods were realised before the nineteenth century. In 1784, when the Forth and Clyde Navigation appointed a new accountant, Richard Smellie, it was specifically to post up the books of account using the principles of double entry, with the aim of giving the proprietors a clear and distinct view of the application of the money (Forrester 1994: 302–3). Smellie's new approach uncovered numerous errors and inaccuracies which resulted in £1,223 being reclaimed from his predecessor.

References

Bailey, M. (2002) *The English Manor c. 1200–1500* (Manchester: Manchester University Press).

Baladouni, V. (1989) A paradigm for the analysis of accounting history, in R. H. Tondkar and E. N. Coffman (eds) *Working Paper 66, Working Paper Series 4*, pp. 95–109 (Alabama: Academy of Accounting Historians).

Baxter, W. T. (1994) Early accounting: the tally and the checker-board, in R. H. Parker and B. S. Yamey (eds) *Accounting History: Some British Contributions*, pp. 197–235 (Oxford: Clarendon Press).

Beckett, J. V. (1986) *The Aristocracy in England 1660–1914* (Oxford: Basil Blackwell).

Bernard, J. (1972) Trade and finance in the Middle Ages 900–500, in C. M. Cipolla (ed.) *The Fontana Economic History of Europe: The Middle Ages*, pp. 274–338 (Glasgow: Collins).

Bischoff, B. (1994) *Manuscripts and Libraries in the Age of Charlemagne* (Cambridge: Cambridge University Press).

Bolton, J. (2004) What is money? What is a money economy? When did a money economy emerge in medieval England?, in D. Wood (ed.) *Medieval Money Matters*, pp. 1–15 (Oxford: Oxbow Books).

Boussard, J. (1968) *The Civilisation of Charlemagne* (London: Weidenfeld and Nicolson).

Bowman, A. K. and Thomas, J. D. (1974) *The Vindolanda Writing Tablets* (Newcastle upon Tyne: Frank Graham).

Boyce, G. and Ville, S. (2002) *The Development of Modern Business* (Basingstoke: Palgrave).

Boyns, T. and Edwards, J. R. (1996) Change agents and the dissemination of accounting technology: Wales' basic industries, c.1750–1870, *Accounting History*, 1 (1): 11–34.

Boyns, T. and Edwards, J. R. (2007) The development of cost and management accounting in Britain, in C. S. Chapman, A. G. Hopwood and M. D. Shields (eds) *Handbook of Management Accounting Research, Vol. 2*, pp. 969–1,034 (London: Elsevier).

Boyns, T., Edwards, J. R. and Nikitin, M. (1997) The development of industrial accounting in Britain and France before 1880: a comparative study of accounting literature and practice, *European Accounting Review*, 6 (3): 393–437.

Braudel, F. (2002) *The Mediterranean in the Ancient World* (Harmondsworth: Penguin).

Brown, R. (1968) *A History of Accounting and Accountants* (London: Frank Cass).

Bryer, R. A. (2000) The history of accounting and the transition to capitalism in England. Part one: theory, *Accounting, Organizations and Society*, 25 (2): 131–62.

Campbell, J. (1986) *Essays in Anglo-Saxon History* (London: Hambledon Press).

Chatfield, M. (1977) *A History of Accounting Thought* (New York: Robert E. Krieger).

Chatfield, M. (1996a) Peele, James, in M. Chatfield and R. Vangermeersch (eds) *The History of Accounting: an International Encyclopedia*, pp. 455–6 (New York: Garland).

Chatfield, M. (1996b) Ympyn, Jan, in M. Chatfield and R. Vangermeersch (eds) *The History of Accounting: an International Encyclopedia*, p. 616 (New York: Garland).

Clanchy, M. T. (1979) *From Memory to Written Record: England 1066–1307* (London: Edward Arnold).

Clough, S. B. and Cole, C. W. (1952) *Economic History of Europe* (Boston: D. C. Heath).

Cohen, E. E. (2002) Introduction, in P. Cartledge, E. E. Cohen and L. Foxhall (eds) *Money, Labour and Land: Approaches to the Economics of Ancient Greece*, pp. 1–7 (London: Routledge).

Coomber, R. R. (1956) Hugh Oldcastle and John Mellis, in A. C. Littleton and B. S. Yamey (eds) *Studies in the History of Accounting*, pp. 206–14 (London: Sweet and Maxwell).

Coombs, H. M. and Edwards, J. R. (1993) The accountability of municipal corporations, *Abacus*, 29 (1): 26–52.

Coombs, H. M. and Edwards, J. R. (1994) Record keeping in municipal corporations: a triumph for double entry bookkeeping, *Accounting, Business & Financial History*, 4 (1): 163–80.

de Roover, R. (1956) The development of accounting prior to Luca Pacioli according to the account books of medieval merchants, in A. C. Littleton and B. S. Yamey (eds) *Studies in the History of Accounting*, pp. 114–74 (London: Sweet & Maxwell).

de Roover, R. (1966) *The Rise and Decline of the Medici Bank* (New York: Norton Library).

de Ste. Croix, G. E. M. (1956) Greek and Roman accounting, in A. C. Littleton and B. S. Yamey (eds) *Studies in the History of Accounting*, pp. 15–74 (London: Sweet & Maxwell).

Denholm-Young, N. (1963) *Seignorial Administration in England* (London: Frank Cass).

Dobie, A. (forthcoming) The development of financial management and control in monastic houses and estates in England c.1200–1540, *Accounting, Business & Financial History*.

Dobson, R. B. (1973) *Durham Priory 1400–1450* (Cambridge: Cambridge University Press).

Duby, G. (1976) *Rural Economy and Country Life in the Medieval West* (Columbia: University of South Carolina Press).

Duncan-Jones, R. (1990) *Structure and Scale in the Roman Economy* (Cambridge: Cambridge University Press).

Edey, H. C. (1968) Company accounting in the nineteenth and twentieth centuries, in M. Chatfield (ed.) *Contemporary Studies in the Evolution of Accounting Thought*, pp. 135–43 (Belmont, CA: Dickinson).

Edey, H. C. and Panitpakdi, P. (1956) British company and the law 1844–1900, in A. C. Littleton and B. S. Yamey (eds) *Studies in the History of Accounting*, pp. 356–79 (London: Sweet and Maxwell).

Edwards, J. R. (1989) *A History of Financial Accounting* (London: Routledge).

Edwards, J. R. (1992) Companies, corporations and accounting change, 1835–1933, *Accounting and Business Research*, 23 (89): 59–73.

Edwards, J. R. and Boyns, T. (1992) Industrial organization and accounting innovation: charcoal ironmaking in England 1690–1783, *Management Accounting Research*, 3 (2): 151–69.

Edwards, J. R. and Yamey, B. S. (eds) (1994) From clay tokens to *Fukushiki-Boki*: record keeping over ten millennia, special issue of *Accounting, Business & Financial History*, 4 (1).

Ezzamel, M. and Hoskin, K. (2002) Retheorizing accounting, writing and money with evidence from Mesopotamia and Ancient Egypt, *Critical Perspectives on Accounting*, 13 (3): 333–67.

Finley, M. I. (1975) *The Ancient Greeks* (Harmondsworth: Penguin).

Finley, M. I. (1992) *The Ancient Economy* (Harmondsworth: Penguin).

Fitz Nigel, R. (1983) *Dialogus de Scaccario* (Oxford: Clarendon Press).

Fleischman, R. K. and Parker, L. D. (1991) British entrepreneurs and pre-industrial revolution evidence of cost management, *Accounting Review*, 66 (2): 361–75.

Forrester, D. A. R. (1994) Early canal company accounts: financial and accounting aspects of the Forth and Clyde Navigation, 1768–1816, in R. H. Parker and B. S. Yamey (eds) *Accounting History: Some British Contributions*, pp. 297–326 (Oxford: Clarendon Press).

Fowler, J. T. (ed.) (1898–1900) *Extracts from the Account-Rolls of the Abbey of Durham, from the original MSS*, 3 vols (Durham: Surtees Society, 99, 100, 103).

French, E. A. (1985) *Unlimited Liability: The Case of the City of Glasgow Bank* (London: Certified Accountant Publications).

Frere, S. (1974) *Britannia: A History of Roman Britain* (London: Cardinal).

115

Funnell, W. (2001) Accounting for justice: entitlement, want and the Irish famine of 1845–7, *Accounting Historians Journal*, 28 (2): 187–206.

Galassi, G. (1996) Pacioli, Luca, in M. Chatfield and R. Vangermeersch (eds) *The History of Accounting: An International Encyclopedia*, pp. 445–7 (New York: Garland).

Geary, P. J. (1988) *Before France and Germany* (New York: Oxford University Press).

Geüsbeek, J. B. (1974) *Ancient Double-Entry Bookkeeping* (Houston, TX: Scholars Book).

Glynn, J. J. (1994) The development of British railway accounting 1800–1911, in R. H. Parker and B. S. Yamey (eds) *Accounting History: Some British Contributions*, pp. 327–42 (Oxford: Clarendon Press).

Godfrey, A. and Hooper, K. (1996) Accountability and decision-making in feudal England: Domesday Book revisited, *Accounting History*, 1 (1): 35–54.

Graham, R. (1929) *English Ecclesiastical Studies* (London: SPCK).

Grant, M. (1969) *Julius Caesar* (London: Weidenfeld & Nicolson).

Greatrex, J. (ed.) (1984) *Account Rolls of the Obedientiaries of Peterborough* (Wellingborough: Northampton-shire Record Society, 33).

Greene, K. (1990) *The Archaeology of the Roman Economy* (Berkeley, CA: University of California Press).

Habakkuk, J. (1953) Economic functions of English landowners in the seventeenth and eighteenth centuries, *Explorations in Entrepreneurial History*, 6: 92–102.

Hall, H. (ed.) (1903) *The Pipe Roll of the Bishopric of Winchester for the Fourth Year of the Pontificate of Peter des Roches, 1208–1209* (London: King & Son).

Harvey, B. (2002) *The Obedientiaries of Westminster Abbey and their Financial Records* (Woodbridge: Boydell Press).

Harvey, P. D. A. (1984) *Manorial Records* (British Record Association, Archives and the User, No. 5, Gloucester: Alan Sutton).

Harvey, P. D. A. (1994) Manorial accounts, in R. H. Parker and B. S. Yamey (eds) *Accounting History: Some British Contributions*, pp. 91–115 (Oxford: Clarendon Press).

Hatcher, J. (1993) *The History of the British Coal Industry*, Vol. 1: *Before 1700* (Oxford: Clarendon Press).

Hatfield, H. R. (1968) An historical defense of bookkeeping, in M. Chatfield (ed.) *Contemporary Studies in the Evolution of Accounting Thought*, pp. 1–11 (Belmont, CA: Dickinson).

Hernández-Esteve, E. (1994a) Comments on some obscure or ambiguous points of the treatise *De Computis et Scripturis* by Luca Pacioli, *Accounting Historians Journal*, 21 (1): 17–80.

Hernández-Esteve, E. (1994b) Luca Pacioli's treatise *De Computis et Scripturis*: a composite or a unified work?, *Accounting, Business & Financial History*, 4 (1): 67–82.

Hockey, S. F. (ed.) (1975) *The Account-Book of Beaulieu Abbey* (London: Royal Historical Society).

Hopwood, A. G. (1987) The archaeology of accounting systems, *Accounting, Organizations and Society*, 12 (3): 207–34.

Hoskin, K. W. and Macve, R. H. (1986) Accounting and the examination: a genealogy of disciplinary power, *Accounting, Organizations and Society*, 11 (2): 105–36.

Howgego, C. (1992) The supply and use of money in the Roman world 200 B. C. to A. D. 300, *Journal of Roman Studies*, 82: 1–31.

Hunter, J. (ed.) (1844), *The Great Rolls of the Pipe for the Second, Third, and Fourth Years of the Reign of King Henry the Second, A. D. 1155, 1156, 1157, 1158* (London: Spottiswoode).

Jack, S. M. (1966) An historical defence of single entry book-keeping, *Abacus*, 2 (2): 137–58.

Jackson, J. G. C. (1956) The history of methods of exposition of double-entry book-keeping in England, in A. C. Littleton and B. S. Yamey (eds) *Studies in the History of Accounting*, pp. 206–14 (London: Sweet & Maxwell).

James, E. (1988) *The Franks* (Oxford: Basil Blackwell).

James, M. E. (1955) *Estate Accounts of the Earls of Northumberland 1562–1637* (Durham: Surtees Society, 163).

Jeacle, I. and Brown, T. (2006) The construction of the credible: epistolary transformations and the origins of the business letter, *Accounting, Business & Financial History*, 16 (1): 27–43.

Johnson, H. T. (1986) The organizational awakening in management accounting history, in M. Bromwich and A. G. Hopwood (eds) *Research and Current Issues in Management Accounting*, pp. 67–77 (London: Pitman).

Jones, P. (1997) *The Italian City-State: From Commune to Signoria* (Oxford: Clarendon Press).

Jones, R. H. (1994) Accounting in English local government from the Middle Ages to c.1835, in R. H. Parker and B. S. Yamey (eds) *Accounting History: Some British Contributions*, pp. 377–406 (Oxford: Clarendon Press).

Kirk, R. E. G. (ed.) (1892) *Accounts of the Obedientars of Abingdon Abbey* (Camden, New Series, 51).

Kitchin G. W. (ed.) (1892) *Compotus Rolls of the Obedientiaries of St. Swithun's Priory, Winchester* (London: Simpkin).

Knowles, D. (1956) *The Religious Orders in England:* Vol. I (Cambridge: Cambridge University Press).

Kojima, O. (1995) *Accounting History* (Osaka: Offset).

Lall Nigam, B. M. (1986) Bahi-Khata: the pre-Pacioli Indian double-entry system of Bookkeeping, *Abacus*, 22 (2): 148–61.

Latouche, R. (1967) *The Birth of Western Economy: Economic Aspects of the Dark Ages* (London: Methuen).

Lee, G. A. (1975) *Modern Financial Accounting* (London: Nelson).

Lee, G. A. (1977) The coming of age of double entry: the Giovanni Farolfi ledger of 1299–1300, *Accounting Historians Journal*, 4 (2): 79–95.

Lee, G. A. (1991) Colliery accounting in sixteenth-century England: the Willoughbys of Wollaton, Nottinghamshire, in O. F. Graves (ed.) *The Costing Heritage: Studies in Honor of S. Paul Garner*, pp. 50–73 (Harrisonburg, VA: The Academy of Accounting Historians).

Lee, G. A. (1994) The oldest European account book: a Florentine bank ledger of 1211, in R. H. Parker and B. S. Yamey (eds) *Accounting History: Some British Contributions*, pp. 116–38 (Oxford: Clarendon Press).

Lee, T. A. (1990) A systematic view of the history of the world of accounting, *Accounting, Business & Financial History*, 1 (1): 73–107.

Lemarchand, Y. (1994) Double entry versus charge and discharge accounting in eighteenth-century France, *Accounting, Business & Financial History*, 4 (1): 119–45.

Lin, Z. J. (2003) Chinese bookkeeping systems: a study of accounting adaptation and change, *Accounting, Business & Financial History*, 13 (1): 83–98.

Littleton, A. C. (1933) *Accounting Evolution to 1900* (New York: American Institute Publishing).

Littleton, A. C. and Yamey, B. S. (eds) (1956) *Studies in the History of Accounting* (London: Sweet and Maxwell).

Lomas, R. A. and Piper, A J. (eds) (1989) *Durham Cathedral Priory Rentals* (Durham: Surtees Society, 197).

Loyn, H. R. (1986) Progress in Anglo-Saxon monetary history, in M. A. S. Blackburn (ed.) *Anglo-Saxon Monetary History, Essays in Memory of Michael Dolley*, pp. 1–10 (Leicester: Leicester University Press).

Loyn, H. R. (1991) *Anglo-Saxon England and the Norman Conquest* (London: Longman).

Loyn, H. R. and Percival, J. (1975) *The Reign of Charlemagne: Documents on Carolingian Government and Administration* (London: Edward Arnold).

Lu, W. and Aiken, M. (2003) Accounting history: Chinese contributions and challenges, *Accounting, Business & Financial History*, 13 (1): 1–3.

McDonald, J. (2005) Using William the Conqueror's accounting record to assess manorial efficiency, *Accounting History*, 10 (2): 125–45.

McKisack, M. (1971) *The Fourteenth Century* (Oxford: Clarendon Press).

Macve, R. H. (1994) Some glosses on Greek and Roman accounting, in R. H. Parker and B. S. Yamey (eds) *Accounting History: Some British Contributions*, pp. 57–87 (Oxford: Clarendon Press).

Macve, R. H. (1996) Pacioli's legacy, in T. A. Lee, R. Bishop and R. H. Parker (eds) *Accounting History from the Renaissance to the Present*, pp. 3–30 (New York: Garland).

Macve, R. H. (2002) Insights to be gained from the study of ancient accounting history: some reflections on the new edition of Finley's *The Ancient Economy, European Accounting Review*, 11 (2): 453–71.

Martin, J. (1979) Estate stewards and their work in Glamorgan, 1660–1760: a regional study of estate management, *Morgannwg*: 9–28.

Martindale, J. (1983) The kingdom of Acquitaine and the dissolution of the Carolingian fisc, *Francia*, 11: 131–91.

Mattessich, R. (2000) *The Beginnings of Accounting and Accounting Thought: Accounting Practice in the Middle East (8000BC to 2000BC) and Accounting Thought in India (300BC and the Middle Ages)* (London: Routledge).

Mepham, M. J. (1988) *Accounting in Eighteenth Century Scotland* (New York: Garland).

Miller, E. and Hatcher, J. (1980) *Medieval England: Rural Society and Economic Change 1086–1348* (London: Longman).

Miller, P. and Napier, C. (1993) Genealogies of calculation, *Accounting, Organizations and Society*, 18 (7/8): 631–47.

Mills, G. T. (1994) Early accounting in northern Italy: the role of commercial development and the printing press in the expansion of double-entry from Genoa, Florence and Venice, *Accounting Historians Journal*, 21 (1): 81–96.

Minaud, G. (2006) Accounting and maritime trade in ancient Rome, *Proceedings of the Eleventh World Congress of Accounting Historians*, Nantes.

Mingay, G. E. (1967) The eighteenth century land steward, in E. L. Jones and G. E. Mingay (eds) *Land, Labour and Population in the Industrial Revolution: Essays Presented to J. D. Chambers*, pp. 6–12 (London: Edward Arnold).

More, C. (1997) *The Industrial Age: Economy and Society in Britain 1750–1995* (Harlow: Pearson).

Morgan, K. (1999) *The Birth of Industrial Britain: Economic Change 1750–1850* (Harlow: Addison Wesley Longman).

Most, K. (1979) The accounts of ancient Rome, in E. N. Coffman (ed.), *Working Paper 3, Working Paper Series 1*, pp. 22–31 (Alabama: The Academy of Accounting Historians).

Napier, C. J. (1991) Aristocratic accounting: the Bute estate in Glamorgan 1814–1880, *Accounting and Business Research*, 21 (82): 163–74.

Napier, C. J. (1997) The British aristocracy, capital and income, and nineteenth century company accounting, *Proceedings of the Fifth Interdisciplinary Perspectives on Accounting Conference*, Manchester.

Nobes, C. W. (1987) The pre-Pacioli Indian double-entry system of bookkeeping: a comment, *Abacus*, 23 (2): 182–4.

Nobes, C. W. (2001) Were Islamic records precursors to accounting books based on the Italian Method? A comment, *Accounting Historians Journal*, 28 (2): 207–14.

Noke, C. (1981) Accounting for bailiffship in thirteenth century England, *Accounting and Business Research*, 11 (42): 137–51.

Oldroyd, D. (1995) The role of accounting in public expenditure and monetary policy in the first century AD Roman Empire, *Accounting Historians Journal*, 22 (2): 117–29.

Oldroyd, D. (1997) Accounting in Anglo-Saxon England: context and evidence, *Accounting History*, 2 (1): 7–23.

Oldroyd, D. (1998) John Johnson's letters: the accounting role of Tudor merchants' correspondence, *Accounting Historians Journal*, 25 (1): 57–72.

Oldroyd, D. (2007) *Estates, Enterprise and Investment at the Dawn of the Industrial Revolution: Estate Management and Accounting in the North-East of England c. 1700–1780* (Aldershot: Ashgate).

Oschinsky, D. (1971) *Walter of Henley and Other Treatises on Estate Management and Accounting* (Oxford: Clarendon Press).

Page, M. (ed.) (1996) *The Pipe Roll of the Bishopric of Winchester 1301–2* (Winchester: Hampshire County Council).

Page, M. (ed.) (1999) *The Pipe Roll of the Bishopric of Winchester 1409–10* (Winchester: Hampshire County Council).

Page, M. (2002) *The Medieval Bishops of Winchester: Estate, Archive and Administration* (Hampshire Record Office, Hampshire Papers 24).

Parker, R. H. (1990) Regulating British corporate financial reporting in the late nineteenth century, *Accounting, Business & Financial History*, 1 (1): 51–71.

Parker, R. H. and Yamey, B. S. (eds) (1994) *Accounting History, Some British Contributions* (Oxford: Clarendon Press).

Pollard, S. (1965) *The Genesis of Modern Management* (London: Edward Arnold).

Poole, A. L. (1970) *From Domesday Book to Magna Carta* (Oxford: Clarendon Press).

Postles, D. (1994) The perception of profit before the leasing of demesnes, in R. H. Parker and B. S. Yamey (eds) *Accounting History: Some British Contributions*, pp. 116–38 (Oxford: Clarendon Press).

Ramsey, G. D. (1956) Some Tudor merchant accounts, in A. C. Littleton and B. S. Yamey (eds) *Studies in the History of Accounting*, pp. 185–201 (London: Sweet and Maxwell).

Rathbone, D. (1994) Accounting on a large estate in Roman Egypt, in R. H. Parker and B. S. Yamey (eds) *Accounting History: Some British Contributions*, pp. 13–56 (Oxford: Clarendon Press).

Reynolds, L. D. (ed.) (1983) *Texts and Transmission: A Survey of the Latin Classics* (Oxford: Clarendon Press).

Richardson, H. G. (1941) Business Training in Medieval Oxford, *American Historical Review*, 46 (2): 259–80.

Russell, J. C. (1972) Population in Europe 500–1500, in C. M. Cipolla (ed.) *The Fontana Economic History of Europe: The Middle Ages*, pp. 25–70 (Glasgow: Collins).

Salter, H. (1922) The death of Henry of Blois, Bishop of Winchester, *English Historical Review*, 37: 79–80.

Saunders, H. W. (1930) *An Introduction to the Obedientiary and Manor Rolls of Norwich Cathedral Priory* (Norwich: Jarrold).

Smith, R. A. L. (1943) *Canterbury Cathedral Priory: A Study in Monastic Administration* (Cambridge: Cambridge University Press).

Spring, D. (1963) *The English Landed Estate in the Nineteenth Century: Its Administration* (Baltimore, MD: Johns Hopkins Press).

Stenton, F. (1971) *Anglo-Saxon England* (Oxford: Oxford University Press).

Stone, E. (1962) Profit-and-loss accountancy at Norwich Cathedral Priory, *Transactions of the Royal Historical Society*, Fifth Series, 12: 25–48.

Taylor, R. E. (1956) Luca Pacioli, in A. C. Littleton and B. S. Yamey (eds) *Studies in the History of Accounting*, pp. 175–84 (London: Sweet & Maxwell).

Thompson, G. (1991) Is accounting rhetorical? Methodology, Luca Pacioli and printing, *Accounting, Organizations and Society*, 16 (5/6): 572–99.

Trevor-Roper, H. (1965) *The Rise of Christian Europe* (London: Thames & Hudson).

Walker, S. P. (1998) How to secure your husband's esteem: accounting and private patriarchy in the British middle class household during the nineteenth century, *Accounting, Organizations and Society*, 23 (5/6): 485–514.

Wallace-Hadrill, J. M. (1983) *The Frankish Church* (Oxford: Clarendon Press).

Winchester, B. (1955) *Tudor Family Portrait* (London: Jonathan Cape).

Winjum, J. O. (1972) *The Role of Accounting in the Economic Development of England: 1500–1750* (Urbana, IL: Center for International Education and Research in Accounting).

Woolgar, C. M. (ed.) (1992–93) *Household Accounts from Medieval England* (British Academy: Records of Social and Economic History, New Series 17–18).

Yamey, B. S. (1956) Introduction, in A. C. Littleton and B. S. Yamey (eds) *Studies in the History of Accounting*, pp. 1–13 (London: Sweet & Maxwell).

Yamey, B. S. (1962) Some topics in the history of financial accounting in England 1500–1900, in W. T. Baxter and S. Davidson (eds) *Studies in Accounting Theory*, pp. 11–34 (London: Sweet & Maxwell).

Yamey, B. S. (1979) Oldcastle, Peele and Mellis: a case of plagiarism in the sixteenth century, *Accounting and Business Research*, 9 (35): 209–16.

Yamey, B. S. (1981) Some reflections on the writing of a general history of accounting, *Accounting and Business Research*, 11 (42): 127–35.

Yamey, B. S. (1994) Benedetto Cotrugli on bookkeeping (1458), *Accounting, Business & Financial History*, 4 (1): 43–50.

Yamey, B. S., Edey, H. C. and Thomson, H. W. (1963) *Accounting in England and Scotland: 1543–1800, Double Entry in Exposition and Practice* (London: Sweet & Maxwell).

Zaid O. A. (2000) Were Islamic records precursors to accounting books based on the Italian method?, *Accounting Historians Journal*, 27 (1): 73–90.

Zaid O. A. (2001) Were Islamic records precursors to accounting books based on the Italian method? A response, *Accounting Historians Journal*, 28 (2): 215–18.

6

Mechanisation and computerisation

Charles W. Wootton and Barbara E. Kemmerer

Overview

This chapter examines the effects of technical innovations in record keeping upon accounting. The type and time frame of these innovations can be separated into two eras. The first era, mechanisation, began around 1870, and by 1930 mechanical accounting was widely used throughout the world. Major innovations introduced in this period included typewriters, calculators, bookkeeping machines, loose leaf accounting systems and tabulators. For the next twenty or thirty years, few innovations occurred in the processing of accounting information. Although machines became faster, the manner in which data was processed essentially did not change. Then, in the early 1950s, the second era (computerisation) began. However, it would be the mid-1960s before the computer found a substantive role in information processing. Twenty years later, with the introduction of the personal computer and innovative software, computers became an essential element of the accounting process. More recently, the emergence of fibre optical cables, e-mail, and the Internet has created instantaneous exchange of information over great distances.

Mechanisation and then computerisation transformed accounting and the accounting workforce. Mechanisation, through the lowering of processing costs, was a major contributory factor to the increased availability of information required for the expansion and control of large corporations. However, mechanisation also hastened the separation of the bookkeeping function from the reporting function. This in turn resulted in the deskilling of bookkeeping and contributed to the regenderisation of the bookkeeping workforce. Although mechanisation and especially computerisation expanded the services that accounting firms could offer, the computer also became a nemesis for the auditor. With few physical records to examine, accounting firms had to revise and rethink the audit process. However, computerisation also played an important role in allowing accounting firms to expand and adapt to the globalisation of businesses.

Introduction

Starting in the late nineteenth century, a series of innovations occurred that dramatically changed the way accounting tasks were performed, the information provided and, indeed, the accounting occupation itself. In the early coverage of mechanisation and computerisation in this chapter, special attention is devoted to developments in the USA. Although inventions, such as the calculator and computer, had their origin outside of the USA, initial business applications of these and other innovations often occurred in the USA. However, over the study period, technical advances in various countries are discussed.

The background to mechanical accounting

Until the late nineteenth century, accounting was basically a manual process. Transactions were entered by hand into large bound journals which were posted by hand to large bound ledgers. As only one person could work on a journal at a time, entries could not be made in the journal while postings were taking place. To counter this, some companies maintained more than one set of journals (Betz 1944: 515). In an article in *The Accountant*, Price (1902: 259) wrote that one company employed 200 day books and 15 ledgers to record its daily transactions. Thus, the closing process required a time-consuming search through numerous vast bound ledgers for individual accounts. Trial balances required the listing of account balances on paper and the manual computation of the totals. As a result, some businesses did not close accounts and the preparation of financial statements often was avoided. For most of the nineteenth century, as Yates (1985: 144) points out, this failure normally did not create problems because owners usually were involved in their companies' day-to-day operations and thus had direct knowledge of their financial conditions.

As companies increased in size and the need for capital increased, management became separated from ownership. With increased complexity, new layers of management appeared. Although railroads had always required vast amounts of information (see Chapter 18), with the emergence of new, large and geographically diverse corporations, the demand for information accelerated. In his classic book, *The Invisible Hand*, Alfred Chandler (1977: 19) noted that for these large companies to succeed, there had to be an increased flow of information to both managers and owners. As demand increased, the first major innovations in information processing also occurred. Noting the interrelationship and interdependence between the two, Yates (1991: 120) writes: 'This increased demand for internal information might have been curtailed by its high cost, except for some changes [innovations] on the supply side of the equation.'

The first mechanical devices

De Wit *et al.* (2002: 69–70) point out that machines are often introduced with one purpose in mind, but their functions normally expand. This was the case with the typewriter. Introduced with the purpose of aiding authors, reporters and lawyers in the writing process, the typewriter became the predecessor of the bookkeeping machine. Although dozens of 'writing' machines had been patented, it was not until the introduction of E. Remington & Sons' 'type-writer', in 1873, that the appliance found commercial success (Bliven 1954: 42–56).

Although first used for letters, businesses found the typewriter especially useful in preparing invoices and reports. Invoices could be prepared in a few minutes, especially if a business used pre-printed forms, containing standard information such as a company's name and address (Yates 1991: 122). To companies like Sears, Roebuck & Co. this was important for, on some days, Sears had to fill 100,000 orders from a single plant (Chandler 1990: 61). However, report forms could only be used if departments reported financial information in the same manner. Thus, businesses were forced to standardise reporting practices and, with this greater uniformity, the analysis of information became easier (Yates 1994: 32). With typewriters, prepared forms, carbon paper, and standardised reporting, the cost of information processing noticeably dropped (Page 1906: 7682).

In 1891, the first major modification of the typewriter occurred with the introduction of the book-typewriter. As journals and ledgers were traditionally bound, pages could not be removed and placed around the typewriter's platen for processing. Thus, the traditional typewriter had to be modified so that it could type downward on a flat surface. With the 'book-typewriter', an accountant could enter a transaction directly in a bound journal or ledger. Another advantage was its capacity to create multiple-copies (manifolder) of invoices. Due to the strength of the downward stroke and the use of carbon paper, the book-typewriter could make a dozen copies of an invoice (Moore 1932: 57).

During this same period, the first commercially successful calculator in the US was launched. Although the abacus achieved widespread application in Asia early on, and a basic calculator (often defined as a machine having adding and subtracting capabilities) had been used in Europe for more than fifty years, neither device had proved popular in the USA. This is ironic since, in Europe, the Thomas Arithmometer, developed by Charles Xavier Thomas de Colmar in France around 1820, had proved itself and was widely accepted by businesses. So successful, in fact, that the Arithmometer, along with other European designed machines (Odhner, Brunsviga), continued to be used (with improvements) for nearly a century (Cortada 1993: 27–8). However in the USA, the Thomas Arithmometer was little adopted, and most computations continued to be performed manually.

In the late 1880s, Dorr Eugene Felt developed a key-driven calculating machine called the 'Comptometer' (Turck 1921: 75). The Comptometer could add, subtract, multiply and divide. It was especially proficient with addition and subtraction as computations took place directly as the numbers were entered. During the same period, William S. Burroughs introduced a recording adding machine that provided a permanent record of transactions. These machines had an immediate effect on accounting. Previously, account balances had to be listed on paper and manually added and then re-added as a check. Addition was such a major part of accounting that George Seward (1904: 607), in *Engineering Magazine*, estimated that 95 per cent of accounting work in a factory could be attributed to performance of that task. Given the increased speed and accuracy with which accounts could be totalled, preparation of trial balances became more common. With the advent of the Comptometer, the determination of unit costs, and data analysis generally, also became a simpler process. Whereas, previously, many companies did not analyse financial/managerial data because of the time involved, this drawback no longer applied (Galloway 1919: 83).

The introduction of the Comptometer had another consequence; it relegated many office practices to routine operations. Up to the late nineteenth century, office clerks often were considered as the 'predecessors of modern middle management' (Cooper and Taylor 2000: 561). The collection and computation functions related to financial data were handled by an accountant/bookkeeper, as they were considered skilled tasks. However, as the processing of information became more routine, more repetitive and more mechanised, the tasks and the people performing the task became 'deskilled', and with deskilling came much lower wages

(Cooper and Taylor 2000: 556–8). With the greater productivity of the Comptometer, and a lower wage paid to the person performing the task, the cost of processing information fell dramatically. With lower costs, the demand for information increased. As the demand for processors of information (typists, stenographers, clerks) rose, there developed a shortage of white, middle-class, educated men to perform these tasks. Companies were forced to hire women, which procured a further advantage for the firm; women were paid substantially less than the men they replaced. Starting in the early twentieth century, the entry of women first into clerical and then into bookkeeping positions would hasten the separation of bookkeeping from accounting in the USA, Britain, and probably a number of other countries.

More innovations in information processing

From bound volumes to loose leaf

Although the typewriter had gained acceptance and the value of the calculator was recognised at larger companies, by the end of the nineteenth century, the efficiencies of both innovations were limited by the continued use of bound volumes to record transactions. Although the deficiencies of a bound system had long been recognised, it continued to be used because of its perceived integrity and security – in a bound system, an entry could only be removed by tearing a page from the volume. To retain this security as companies became bigger, personnel had to work with ledgers sometimes weighing fifty pounds and numbering a thousand pages (Wootton and Wolk 2000: 82). Companies had to forego the possibility of more than one person at a time processing transactions which were the subject of individual volumes, and this significantly lengthened the time required for recording and closing accounts. Moreover, a company could not insert journal or ledger pages directly into a typewriter but, as noted above, had to rely upon a book-typewriter, which was slow and difficult to use, to record transactions in the bound volumes.

As the size of companies increased and transactions multiplied, the deficiencies and unworkability of a bound system became more apparent. Thus, at the end of the nineteenth century, there emerged a rather simple but an amazingly effective innovation for processing data – the loose leaf accounting system. The forerunner of the loose leaf was the card system used primarily by libraries to record their book collection, and by a few factories to maintain inventory records. After several modifications and improvements, the Baker-Vawter Company began sales of a loose leaf system – two flat boards connected by two steel posts – in the USA in 1896. In Sweden, at about the same time, a system developed by Andreas Tengwall, similar in design to today's three-ring binder, was manufactured and sold by the Krag Manufacturing Company (Wootton and Wolk 2000: 87–9).

Soon, companies throughout the world were introducing similar systems. However, the initial reaction to this innovation was underwhelming. In some countries, bound volumes were required by regulation (see Chapter 5). Even where there were no legal considerations, businesses often were reluctant to adopt loose leaf systems as they were perceived to have questionable security. In publications such as *The Accountant*, hundreds of articles and letters were published on the merits and weaknesses of the system. The common criticism was that since pages could be easily removed from the volume, it would encourage dishonesty which in turn would be harder to detect. Those in favour cited the system's greater flexibility and efficiency (Dicksee 1911: 652–7). This debate, and how to overcome the system's weaknesses (Aspray 1917: 311–13), continued into the early 1920s. One feature of the system that received considerable attention in *The Accountant* was the use of slips for postings (Price 1902: 9–18). Under

123

the slip system, instead of posting the ledger from the journal, the preparation of the slip (sales invoice, bank deposit slip) served as the original entry from which the ledger was posted ('Slip' or 'card' bookkeeping 1902: 1069–72).

To overcome the reluctance to accept loose leaf accounting, manufacturers began an extensive advertising campaign citing its greater efficiency and even its security features. One major selling point was the fact that loose leaf forms could be inserted directly into bookkeeping machines. Over time, the system's advantages began to be recognised; however, such recognition often was slow. For example, the Post Office Savings Bank in Britain evaluated the loose system in 1908–10, but rejected it because of security concerns. Not until 1925 did it finally adopted a card-based ledger (Campbell-Kelly 1998: 23–9).

Tabulating, billing and duplex adding machines

During the early twentieth century, another major mechanical innovation gained ground – the tabulating machine. Actually, the tabulator was only the computation part of a three-part tabulating system – the others being the card punch machine and the card sorter. The initial incentive for the development of the tabulator was a concern to address the seven and a half years required to complete the administration of the 1880 US Census. Employed at the Census Office at this time, Herman Hollerith began work on the development of a machine that could process vast amounts of data. In 1889, Hollerith's tabulator was selected to process the 1890 Census, which it completed in less than two months (Harmon 1975: 106–7). Sensing the commercial possibilities, Hollerith started his own company which ultimately became IBM. The principal competitor for Hollerith was the Powers Accounting Machine Company (later acquired by Remington Rand) which, in 1915, became the first to market a printing tabulator.

In companies where vast amounts of data were processed, the tabulator quickly found acceptance. Railroads recognised its utility for freight accounting – using a Hollerith tabulator, the New York Central processed more than four million waybills in 1897 (Norberg 1990: 762). Railroads also discovered that they could replace an expensive accountant with a clerk or bookkeeper to handle data entry. Insurance companies also became major users. With hundreds of thousands of policyholders and tens of thousands of claims, insurance companies found the card system ideal for their needs. After the policyholder's information was punched onto a card, the cards could be sorted at the rate of 300 per minute. With this capability, insurance companies could quickly analyse the costs of their policies and claims. Recognising the economic value of tabulators to their users, manufacturers normally refused to sell the machines but would instead lease them, guaranteeing continuous cash inflow.

One further useful innovation was the billing machine. Often utilising loose leaf forms, the billing machine combined the typewriter with the adding machine. Using a billing machine, a bookkeeping clerk could prepare an invoice and post the transaction to the ledger at the same time. Although the cost of the widely used Elliott-Fischer billing machine was $325 ('A billing and adding machine combined', 1906), its purchase usually was cost effective, for a clerk with a billing machine often could replace two accountants.

Another aid to the accounting process was the 'duplex' adder. The duplex had two adding wheels and could transfer amounts between the wheels, allowing it to perform two operations at once. With a duplex, a company could record both cost and retail price at the same time. Probably, the duplex was most useful in the payroll area. With the duplex, a company could keep track of the payroll of individual departments while determining the total payroll. The Burroughs Company even offered a duplex that could record employees' earnings on individual payroll envelopes while it recorded the payroll sheet (Lewis 1914: 179–88).

Growing acceptance of mechanical accounting

The 1920s would see efforts by US companies, for example, to more efficiently employ the mechanical devices that had emerged over the previous forty years. Early on, use of the tabulator had been restricted to a few large insurance companies and railroads. By 1920, the market for tabulating machines was international and tabulator users had expanded to large manufacturers and retail firms. Companies such as Marshall Field and Eastman-Kodak found the tabulator valuable in cost and sales analysis and in inventory control (Strom 1992: 181–2). The textile industry became a leader in expanding the uses of the tabulator to areas such as payroll, stock control, dispatching, and standard costing (Norberg 1990: 772–3).

In Europe, the tabulator also found widespread application. In the Netherlands in 1920, Rotterdamsche Bankvereeniging (Robaver Bank) installed a Hollerith system to help handle its expanding giro department (de Wit and van den Ende 2000: 97). In 1915, the Prudential Assurance Company (UK) began to install the Powers Tabulating System in its offices, and by 1923 the Prudential had in operation 35 tabulators, 24 sorters, and 100 card punches (Campbell-Kelly 1992: 131). Prudential even acquired the British rights to the Powers machine and established a company (Powers-Samas) to manufacture and distribute the machine throughout the British Empire. At one time, its punch card machine held nearly 50 per cent of the British market (ibid.: 130–1).

As the capabilities of bookkeeping machines rose, and their use gained growing acceptance in Europe as well as in the USA, they were increasingly imported by the former from the latter. In the early 1920s, the large French bank Société Générale, set out two major goals; cost reduction and mechanisation, with the latter expected to contribute to the former. To begin the process, Société Générale installed Ellis calculating machines in all branch offices and ordered 207 Underwood bookkeeping machines, usually considered superior for the preparation of financial reports. At the Banque Générale du Nord, the introduction of typing and calculating machines, at a cost of 900,000 francs, was claimed to eliminate the need for 70 to 80 jobs – reducing annual operating costs by 500,000 francs (Bonin 2004: 266–7). The mechanisation of bank accounting had another consequence – increased centralisation. To gain even greater efficiencies, bookkeeping machines often were located at a single office. As a result, banks increasingly transferred the accounting function from the various branches to a central location (ibid.: 269).

The cost of business machines continued to fall, allowing smaller firms to purchase them. In 1921, the Victor Adding Machine Company introduced a machine costing $100, which was approximately one-half of the price of a comparable machine purchased elsewhere (Darby 1968: 29). Several companies began to market electric calculators in competition with the widely used Comptometer. Monroe Calculating Machine Company offered (1921) its Model K electric calculators with prices from $200 to $400 (Martin 1925: 250–1). With lower costs, most large businesses and many small ones employed some form of mechanical accounting to record information and to reduce the manual aspects of accounting by 1930.

As noted previously, over time, mechanisation changed the nature of the tasks required of a bookkeeper, which came to be perceived as more repetitive and menial. While bookkeeping was relegated to the status of a technical trade, accounting had evolved into a profession. As bookkeeping's perception as a repetitive, non-managerial trade grew, the feminisation of the workforce increased. This transition was encouraged by a company's ability to pay women lower wages and was also attributable to a shortage of white middle-class males. From comprising only 1 per cent of the bookkeeping workforce in the USA in 1870, women were 63 per cent of the bookkeeping workforce by 1930. At the same time, the emergence of accounting as a profession closed off for a time the opportunities for women (see Chapter 20 for a discussion of gender and professionalisation); the established professions, at this time, remained male dominated (Perks 1993: 11). In contrast to bookkeeping, in 1930, only 9 per cent of accountants were women, and this percentage did not notably change until the early 1960s (Wootton and Kemmerer 2000: 172).

The general acceptance of mechanical accounting that had occurred by the Second World War was not without controversy. In 1949, a report (*Mechanised Accounting and the Auditor*) was issued by the Mechanised Accounting Sub-Committee of the Taxation and Financial Relations Committee of the Institute of Chartered Accountants in England and Wales. In its report, the Sub-Committee (Mechanised Accounting 1949: 14) set forth the concept of mechanical accounting, identified the problems associated with it, and issued a warning: 'it must not, however, be assumed that mechanisation is always justified or always desirable'. The Report stated that, while mechanised accounting seemed to be nothing more than a change in the way information was processed, in reality, mechanisation sometimes resulted in the loss of documentation without a 'compensating' increase in the information required for an audit. The Report suggested actions for the company and the auditor to take. The principal emphasis was that the company and the auditor should work together at all stages of mechanisation – from the selection of machines to the determination of records to be mechanised. The Report also set forth steps that a company might take to make the examination of mechanised records easier, and it reminded the auditor to exploit the potential of mechanisation as an aid to the audit process itself. It is interesting to note that this report was issued on the threshold of the second major innovation in information processing – computerisation. Instead of helping guide technological innovations, it seems the accounting profession sometimes simply reacts to the effect of these changes, and even then often rather late.

The first computers

For nearly thirty years following general acceptance of mechanical accounting, few innovations occurred in processing accounting information. Although machines became faster, the manner in which data was processed essentially did not change. This altered with the onset of the Second World War, which was a time of innovation – especially in regard to the processing of information. To encode their messages, the German military used ENIGMA machines, and for the most secret messages, Geheimschreiber machines. To decode these messages, the British Intelligence developed the COLOSSUS, a huge 1,800 vacuum tubes, paper-tape-driven, 'mainframe' computer which came into operation in December 1943 (Shurkin 1984: 140–3). In the USA, there also was a push to develop a machine that could process vast amounts of mathematical information. This resulted in the creation of a giant electronic computer called ENIAC. The computer was 100 feet long, 10 feet high, weighed 30 tons and contained more than 17,000 vacuum tubes (ibid.: 166).

At the outset, computerisation was not expected to have a major impact on business. In 1950, both business executives and computer manufacturers expressed the belief that around ten large computers would satisfy business needs (Sanders 1968: 28). There were two major factors in this prediction. First, only the largest companies generated the amount of data that would require a computer to process. Second, only very large corporations could afford the high initial cost of acquiring a computer and the substantial daily operating costs. In sharp contrast to this prediction, accounting soon became a major factor in the expansion of the computer's use. For the next two decades, the need to more efficiently process financial information was a catalyst for the further development of the computer. As late as the mid-1960s, studies found that nearly 50 per cent of a computer's time was used to process accounting-related information (Li 1968: 12).

Early years of computerisation

In 1951, the first Remington Rand's UNIVAC Computer was placed in operation at the US Bureau of the Census, and three years later General Electric purchased a UNIVAC Computer to process business information at its Appliance Division in Louisville, Kentucky (Li 1968: 5). Arthur Andersen & Co. had recommended the UNIVAC to GE as a part of an accounting system that it was installing (Spacek 1989: 176–7). Thus, in the first years of the computer age, an accounting firm had established itself as a provider of computer expertise. Leonard Spacek, chief executive of Arthur Andersen & Co., stated that the firm's installation of the UNIVAC was one of the key elements in the development of the Administrative Services practice at Arthur Andersen & Co. (Spacek 1989: 197). But at this time the computer's future did not seem particularly bright – Spacek recalled a meeting with Vince Learson (head of sales at IBM), shortly after the GE installation, where Learson stated that 'there was no future in the accounting field for computers' (ibid.: 136–7).

In 1953, a significant breakthrough occurred when IBM introduced its 650 Magnetic Drum Data Processing Machine. Included in the accounting functions were payroll processing, actuarial computations, customer billing, and branch store accounting ('650 applications', n.d.). It was predicted that only 50 IBM 650 computers would be sold, whereas nearly 2,000 were retailed by 1962 (IBM 650, n.d.). The first IBM 650 was installed in the controller's department of the John Hancock Life Insurance Company in Boston ('650 chronology', n.d.). Another earlier user was the Gulf Oil Corporation which purchased the IBM 650 to handle payroll and crude oil accounting ('650 applications', n.d.). It was not long before the IBM 650 found use in Europe; in 1957, the Dutch Land Cultivation Company purchased one to computerise its administrative operations (de Wit *et al.* 2002: 65).

In 1956, IBM announced its 305 RAMAC and 650 RAMAC, both of which utilised a random access memory (RAM). In its announcement, IBM stated that its RAMAC computers would revolutionise office procedures, for accounting could now be a 'continuous' process with data being entered and retrieved nearly instantaneously. With the RAMAC remote feature, accountants in other offices could check sales figures and determine the level of current inventories (650 RAMAC announcement, n.d.).

In the UK, in the 1950s, there was an interesting chapter in computer development, and it involved J. Lyons & Co., an old British Company well known for its teas, cakes and teashops. In the late 1940s, J. Lyons (especially through John Simmons) recognised the potential of electronic machines to process business data. To learn more about computers, Raymond Thompson and Oliver Standingford travelled to the USA, where they learned that many of the most exciting developments were actually occurring in the UK, especially at Cambridge. Shortly thereafter, J. Lyons and a team from Cambridge began work on developing a computer that could handle accounting tasks, with J. Lyons providing major financial support for the development (Ferry 2003: 34–70). On Christmas Eve 1953, the computer, called LEO, was finished and put into use. Its first task was to process the payroll of Cadby Hall bakeries and soon LEO was processing payrolls for other companies such as the Ford Motor Company (ibid.: 111, 149). Two years later LEO became 'the heart of [Lyon's] ordering and distribution system' (ibid.: 129). The computer was so successful that J. Lyons set up a separate company (Leo

Computers Ltd) to provide computers and services. LEO was followed by LEO II, LEO II½, and LEO III, and all were recognised as 'groundbreaking' machines (ibid.: 166). However, the development of a computer and its marketing require vast amounts of capital, and J. Lyons was faced with these costs at the time its previously successful teashops were in decline. In 1963, Leo Computers merged with English Electric. Although LEO III was comparable (maybe superior) to the IBM System 360, the introduction of the 360 and IBM's vast resources hastened the demise of LEO. In 1967, regular production of LEO ceased (ibid.: 184–95), and in 1978 J. Lyons & Co. was purchased by Allied Breweries.

The end of mechanical accounting

In 1962, Bank of America implemented its ERMA (Electronic Recording Machine Accounting) system. This was an historic attempt to change the ways cheques were processed, recorded, and chequing accounts updated. Instead of the customer's name, as had been used for a century, the system used a magnetic character recognition account number to sort and process checks. By 1962, ERMA was handling more than 2.3 million of the Bank of America's cheque accounts, resulting in the elimination of 2,332 jobs for proof and transit operators and book-keepers (McKenney *et al.* 1997: 332–5).

In 1962, IBM introduced the 6400 Magnetic Ledger Accounting Machine, which through magnetic tape or cards could handle billings, inventory, accounts receivables, payroll, and general accounting ('New: the IBM alpha-numeric magnetic ledger card', 1963: 5). But IBM was not the only company that offered a computer capable of performing these functions. Both Frident's 6010 ('Frident 6010 electronic computer', 1963: 14) and General Electric's GE-225 ('Computer progress at General Electric', 1963: 26) computers had similar features. However, the cost was significant; the rental for the 200 Series Computers ranged from $4,000 to $10,000 per month ('Announcing the GE-215', 1963: 10–11).

In Germany, computers were also finding greater use in accounting. Heinz Nixdorf, while a physics student, concluded that large computer manufacturers were ignoring the demand of small- and medium-sized companies for a smaller, inexpensive computer to process their data. As a result, he founded the Heinz Nixdorf Company and, by the mid-1960s, the company had sold 5,000 small computers specially designed to perform daily accounting functions. The company's success in Germany encouraged the Victor Comptometer Corporation to sign a marketing agreement which allowed it to sell (under the Victor name) the computer in the USA and Canada. With prices between $8,500 and $80,000, Victor's computers were priced significantly lower than the larger IBM computers (Darby 1968: 217–19).

The computer comes of age

By the early 1970s, the computer was an essential tool for many larger corporations. Moreover, the cost of a computer had dropped significantly. An IBM System/3 minicomputer could be rented for around $1,000 a month (Ceruzzi 1998: 158). Although the computer created problems for auditors, it achieved widespread acceptance at major accounting firms, proving helpful in reducing the time required for tabulation and verification. For some tasks, computerisation reduced the completion time from weeks to hours (Allen and McDermott 1993: 124). Through the use of tax packages, tax preparation became less of a manual process and more of a planning exercise. Accounting firms could even 'outsource' their tax work, as one company offered to 'computer process your client's income tax returns' for $5 per client ('For $5 PTS will computer process your client's income tax return!', 1969: 9). In addition, the speed of processing was significantly increased. One firm, for example, processed more than 95,000 tax returns in one week ('The Computax system', 1972: 15).

The advent of the computer age also provided accounting firms with the opportunity to find an important new source of revenue. By 1970, all major accounting firms had established management consultancy departments, and these departments' growth and profit margins provided the impetus for the continued rapid expansion of firms that had by this time achieved a monopoly of large audit clients. For instance, at Price Waterhouse in the UK, the Management Consultancy Services department's billings expanded at the rate of 15 to 20 per cent per year 'throughout the mid- to late seventies' (Jones 1995: 295). The emergence of management consultancy departments also had an effect on the hiring practices of accounting firms. Traditionally, in the USA, for example, firms hired accounting majors and expected them to become CPAs. However, in the management consultancy area, where a key requirement was that personnel possessed a strong computer background, firms began to hire non-accountants and in many firms management consultancy departments became nominated by non-CPAs (Allen and McDermott 1993: 132–3).

Auditing the computer

With the growing reliance on computers for accounting information, companies and accounting firms were faced with a problem – incompatibility with the traditional audit function. At Touche Ross's 1956 annual meeting, its Management Committee reported that clients were committed to installing large computers and, with their installation, the way an audit was conducted would have to 'radically' change (Collard 1983: 123). This was a recognition that the computerisation of accounting would have a much greater effect on the audit process than had mechanisation. Although mechanical accounting had changed the audit process, the use of mechanical machines still resulted in the creation of hard documents that could be inspected. With a computer, visual inspections of records were often not possible. Transactions were now entered directly into the computer or recorded on magnetic tapes or cards. The important question became how to audit a computer-based accounting system. Some people advocated auditing 'through the computer' while others favoured auditing 'around the computer' (Monteverde 1966: 92–7). Despite the differences of opinion regarding the appropriate method of auditing computer systems, there was a consensus that major changes had to occur in the audit process itself. With this in mind, accounting firms, accounting educators and companies devoted thousands of hours and millions of dollars on developing new programmes, concepts, and methods for auditing a computer-based accounting system.

Regardless of the individual procedures developed to handle such an audit, there were common characteristics among them. People involved with the audit had to be knowledgeable of the computer (Davis et al. 1983: 305–6), which required hiring individuals with appropriate skill sets or providing accountants with additional computer training. The auditor had to become more flexible in thinking, for each company, each accounting system, and each computer was different. In order to plan an audit, auditors had to access management's attitudes toward controls and 'obtain a sufficient understanding of a client's internal control system' (Konrath 1999: 208, 236). Moreover, firms had to recognise that the audit was a continuous process. The risk involved in each area of the audit had to be identified and properly incorporated into the audit plan (ibid.: 332–40). It was also important for an audit firm 'to make the machines work for you' (Monteverde 1966: 95–7), that is, to use the computer's vast speed and efficiency in the audit process itself. Audit tests that were impossible through manual or mechanical means could be performed in minutes or seconds with the computer.

Smaller computers, lower costs and new software

In 1975, IBM introduced its first 'portable' computer: portable, not in the sense of the later laptop computer, but portable (moveable) when compared to the mainframe computers of the period. Moreover, in contrast to previous computers, the IBM 5100 Portable Computer was a lower cost, more flexible computer aimed at individual users. Weighing around 50 pounds, the computer and its peripheral components could be placed in individual offices and relocated as required ('IBM 5100 Portable Computer', n.d.). This computer was to be followed by the IBM 5110 Computer that was more aimed at business and accounting areas. The first IBM 5110 was sold to Punxsutawney Electric Repair Company, which used it for billing, inventory control, accounts receivables, and sales analysis ('IBM 5110', n.d.). In 1980, IBM introduced its lowest priced computer up to that time, the IBM 5120 Model costing from $9,340 to $23,990 ('IBM 5120', n.d.). Along with the 5120, IBM introduced six application programmes to perform most accounting functions: payroll, accounts payable, accounts receivable and general ledger accounting ('IBM 5120 applications', n.d.).

In 1979, a radical change occurred in the way financial information could be examined. The first major spreadsheet package (VisiCalc) was introduced for use on the Apple II Computer. The software was an immediate success with more than 100,000 copies sold in the first year. Three years later, the more powerful and faster spreadsheet, Lotus 1–2–3, package was introduced. Moreover, this software could run on the more commonly used IBM computers. Costing just $495, more than 800,000 copies of Lotus 1–2–3 were sold in eighteen months (Campbell-Kelly and Aspray 2004: 134). The availability of a spreadsheet package also made the emerging personal computer more attractive to users. For several years, Lotus dominated the spreadsheet market; however, ultimately, Microsoft's Excel would take control of that market (Campbell-Kelly 2001: 131).

By the late 1980s, the computer had secured its place in processing accounting information, and the major reasons were reductions in its price and size. In 1981, IBM introduced a personal computer with a price of around $1,600, making the computer attractive to smaller businesses ('The IBM PC's debut', n.d.). In 1983, IBM introduced the System/36, a minicomputer, also aimed at small businesses, and in three years 100,000 units were sold ('IBM System/36', n.d.). For many, the 'mini' computer became an ideal replacement for the much larger and expensive mainframe computer. Through remote terminals or personal computers, information could be directly entered and updated. Sales could be recorded as they were made, receivables updated, and inventories reduced. At many companies, through deskilling these operations, the accountant and also even the bookkeeper were removed from the recording process. It was the sales or office clerk who made the original entry, and the computer that posted it.

Specialised accounting software packages (for mainframe, mini, and personal computers) had become common for both the corporation and the accounting firm. For the company, software was available to handle the payroll, accounts payable, fixed assets, personnel and capital project analysis. For accounting firms, software packages were available for depreciation schedules, tax preparation, records management, not-for-profit organisations, work scheduling, management reports, and client billings ('All we provide is the best accounting software', 1982: 23). With a portable computer and specialised software, the field audit became easier. Audit software packages were available for accounting firms that had not developed their own EDP audit programmes. Combining the personal computer and dial-ups, accounting firms could access vast tax and accounting research service centres.

Globalisation and communications

There remained a critical factor that limited the efficiency and the use of the computer. Although dial ups were available, they were slow. Thus, over great distances, the rapid and efficient exchange of information was limited and sometimes impossible. Globalisation created internal and external problems for companies. Internally, each location had to be able to communicate with worldwide offices and factories, and the exchange had to be instantaneous. Externally, producers had to communicate effectively with worldwide suppliers and customers, and accounting firms had to exchange information with clients operating different accounting and information systems.

The future of globalisation and the success of international companies depended upon the development of a much better worldwide communication system. This occurred in the 1990s. With the installation of fibre-optic cables and satellite systems, the arrival of e-mail, and the creation of what became known as the Internet, communications over great distances became routine. From being accessible to only a few hundred computers in the early 1980s, by the mid-1990s around 25 million computers could use it, and by 2000 more than 100 million computers had access to the Internet. Although available in a limited form since the early 1980s, therefore, by the mid-1990s e-mail had become a common form of communications for most businesses. Thus, accounting firms now had access to countless research sources and the capacity for instantaneous communications with clients and potential clients. Document exchanges between offices became routine and field reports could be filed as they were created. Accounting software packages proliferated. Whether it was studying for accounting certification or establishing an accounting system for a small business, there was a software package available. Moreover, each major accounting firm now had a web site providing information on its history, locations, services offered, employment opportunities, and commentaries on the rapidly changing accounting profession.

Mechanisation and computerisation – review and prospect

Mechanical and then computer accounting transformed the functions of accounting and the accounting workforce. With the onset of mechanical accounting, the initial recording of accounting information became routine and repetitive. A bookkeeper or clerk could process, at lower cost, the information that an accountant once had recorded. The accountant became a manager – a person who decided what information should be collected, how the information should be presented, and the one responsible for its analysis. With its perception as a manual and repetitive task, bookkeeping became an occupation for women while accounting with its management and analytical concepts remained largely male. This dominance continued for nearly half a century. In the USA, the employment of women in accounting began to change, in the 1960s, with the passage of Title VII of the Civil Rights Act and the decision of women to major in accounting. By 1986, more women were receiving accounting degrees in the USA than men (Wootton and Kemmerer 2000: 176–8). Today, at most US accounting firms, the majority of new hires are women. However, the percentage of women partners remains relatively low. In the United Kingdom, approximately 10 per cent of the partners in the top fifty accounting firms are women ('Top 50: failing to be diverse', 2007). Among the Big Four International Accounting Firms, Deloitte Touche Tohmatsu is the leading firm with women constituting nearly 20 per cent of its partners, principals and directors.

With the increased demand for financial information and accountants, the accounting area grew more complex with new layers of management. Within the accounting function, changes had to occur to accommodate mechanisation for machines could only process uniformly presented data. Thus, standardisation of accounts and reporting became necessary for the efficient processing and analysis of information. With mechanisation also came administrative centralisation as the bookkeeping function increasingly was located in one office.

Mechanisation and especially computerisation greatly expanded the services that accounting firms offered. Although often involved with clients' selection of bookkeeping machines, accountants were somewhat slow in realising the importance of computers to their clients, allowing computer manufacturers or Management Information System providers to gain an initial advantage in their selection, installation, and programming. However, once they realised the market significance of computers, and especially computer services, accounting firms established separate departments to provide these services.

In turn, accounting firms were able themselves to exploit the computer and computer software to process and analyse data, whether it was word processing, tax preparation, or audit. But although the computer was a valuable tool in the audit process, it also proved a nemesis for the auditor. With few physical records to examine, accounting firms had to revise their audit procedures. They had to rely upon strong accounting systems and internal controls within the company as the basis for their assertions. Moreover, accountants had to be involved in all aspects of internal controls; from their creation, to their implementation, to their review.

Although the computer's importance had been established, computerisation also created problems for the accounting profession. With increased concern about security and privacy rights, accounting firms were forced to rethink their policies toward maintaining records, exchanging data, and creating more secure computer-based accounting systems. It is securing these systems that will drive many of the future actions of the accounting profession. Because one malicious act can disable or compromise an entire system for hours or days, the first goal must be to prevent such an act from occurring. However, as this cannot always be achieved, the second goal must be the implementation of procedures that will ensure a quick response to, and recovery from, attack.

Mechanisation, computerisation and globalisation have greatly changed accounting and those working in the profession. Accounting is no longer a regional or even a nationwide profession, it is a global profession. Regardless of how small a firm or company is, today aspects of its operation are affected by globalisation. A small accounting firm in Chicago may outsource a part of its tax preparation work to a firm in India. A local firm in Stockholm may ask a company in Poland to create its accounting software. A manufacturer in Japan may acquire a company in Ireland and have to merge different computers and accounting systems.

For the next couple of years, the four major accounting firms each expect to hire thousands of accountants annually. Some of the highest demands for accountants will be in countries such as China or Russia. Already, firms are offsetting accountant shortages in one country by 'importing' accountants from other countries to fill temporary needs; however, language problems can sometimes be overwhelming for the firms. At the same time, some firms report that they are facing changing attitudes from their new hires, who seem less willing to work the long hours often required of accountants, are less willing to travel, and place greater value on their free time. Moreover, people want to spend more time with their families or leave to have children. In the latter case, they sometimes choose not to return to the firm.

Thus, accounting is faced with three problems: the globalisation of accounting, a potential shortage of accountants, and an accounting workforce possibly less flexible and more demanding. However, technological innovations and firms' willingness to adapt can help address these difficulties. With instantaneous, worldwide access to information, there is little reason why more work cannot be done at home, allowing individuals to spend more time with their families or allowing them to work part-time. With worldwide access, there is little reason that a tax write-up has to occur in London when it can be handled in Hong Kong or Prague. With time differences and worldwide offices, accounting work should be able to be shifted from Sydney to Paris to Los Angeles as the day progresses. Through high speed networks, more clients' records should be accessed, processed, and returned electronically. Accounting firms must think of themselves, not as local firms, or national firms, but as worldwide firms with worldwide resources on which to draw. Finally, accountants must become worldwide managers and employees. Through the internet, software packages, and on-line courses, workers should be encouraged to learn new languages and to become acquainted with different cultures.

The preceding concepts and their implications are areas for future investigation. There are a number of important research questions. How much of an accounting firm's work can be done in the home, and what are the best ways of accomplishing this? Are additional information processing innovations necessary for this to prove successful? Do certain countries have advantages (technology, language, time zone) in becoming major accounting processing centres? Can a shortage of accountants in one country be offset by the electronic transfer of work to another country?

Key works

Bonin (2004) contains an examination of how French banks used emerging technology to reduce their costs in processing financial information.

Campbell-Kelly (1992) is an interesting account of how a large British insurance company reacted to and finally accepted mechanical accounting.

Cortada (1993) examines all the major contributors (e.g. tabulators, calculators) to the mechanisation of accounting.

McKenney et al. (1997) discusses the development of an electronic accounting system that dramatically changed the way cheques were processed and recorded, and the bank's failure to maintain its lead as a technological innovator.

Wootton and Kemmerer (2007) examines the development and acceptance of business machines in the USA.

References

A billing and adding machine combined. The Elliott-Fisher (1906) *System*, 10 (July): n. p.
All we provide is the best accounting software (1982) *Journal of Accountancy*, 153 (6): 23.

Allen, D. G. and McDermott, K. (1993) *Accounting for Success A History of Price Waterhouse in America 1890–1990* (Boston: Harvard Business School Press).

Announcing the GE-215 (1963) *Journal of Accountancy*, 115 (4): 10–11.

Aspray, N. (1917) Loose-leaf books, *Accountant*, 57 (2237): 311–13.

Betz, W. L. (1944) The evolution of business records since 1900, *New York Certified Public Accountant*, 14 (11): 514–520.

Bliven Jr., B. (1954) *The Wonderful Writing Machine* (New York: Random House).

Bonin, H. (2004) The development of accounting machines in French banks from the 1920s to the 1960s, *Accounting, Business & Financial History*, 14 (3): 257–76.

Campbell-Kelly, M. (1992) Large-scale data processing in the Prudential, 1850–1930, *Accounting, Business & Financial History*, 2 (2): 117–39.

Campbell-Kelly, M. (1998) Data processing and technological change: the Post Office Savings Bank, 1861–1930, *Technology and Culture*, 39 (1): 1–32.

Campbell-Kelly, M. (2001) Not only Microsoft: the maturing of the personal computer software industry, 1982–1995, *Business History Review*, 75 (1): 103–45.

Campbell-Kelly, M. and Aspray, W. (2004) *Computer: A History of the Information Machine* (Boulder, CO: Westview Press).

Ceruzzi, P. E. (1998) *A History of Modern Computing* (Cambridge, MA: MIT Press).

Chandler Jr., A. D. (1977) *The Visible Hand: The Managerial Revolution in American Business* (Cambridge, MA: Harvard University Press).

Chandler Jr., A. D. (1990) *Scale and Scope: The Dynamics of Industrial Capitalism* (Cambridge, MA: Harvard University Press).

Collard, E. A. (1983) *Stories About 125 Years at Touche Ross* (Canada: Touche Ross).

Computer progress at General Electric (1963) *Journal of Accountancy*, 115 (2): 26.

Cooper, C. and Taylor, P. (2000) From Taylorism to Ms Taylor: the transformation of the accounting craft, *Accounting, Organizations and Society*, 25 (6): 555–78.

Cortada, J. W. (1993) *Before the Computer* (Princeton, NJ: Princeton University Press).

Darby, E. (1968) *It All Adds Up: the Growth of Victor Comptometer Corporation* (Chicago, IL: Victor Comptometer Corporation).

Davis, G. B., Adams, D. L. and Schaller, C. A. (1983) *Auditing & EDP*, 2nd edn, (New York: American Institute of Certified Public Accountants).

de Wit, O. and van den Ende, J. (2000) The emergence of a new regime: business management and office mechanisation in the Dutch financial sector in the 1920s, *Business History*, 42 (2): 87–118.

de Wit, O., van den Ende, J., Schot, J. and van Oost, E. (2002) Office technologies in the Netherlands, 1880–1980, *Technology and Culture*, 43 (1): 50–72.

Dicksee, L. R. (1911) Loose-leaf systems, *Accountant*, 44 (1927): 652–7.

Ferry, G. (2003) *A Computer Called LEO* (London: Fourth Estate).

For $5 PTS will computer process your client's income tax return! (1969) *Journal of Accountancy*, 128 (10): 9.

Frident 6010 electronic computer (1963) *Journal of Accountancy*, 116 (11): 14.

Galloway, L. (1919) *Office Management its Principles and Practice* (New York: Ronald Press).

Harmon, M. (1975) *Stretching Man's Mind: A History of Data Processing* (New York: Mason/Charter Publishers).

IBM 5100 Portable Computer. Available HTTP: <http://www-03.ibm.com/ibm/history/exhibits/pc/pc_2.html> (accessed 3 September 2006).

IBM 5110. Available HTTP: <http://www-03.ibm.com/ibm/history/exhibits/pc/pc_4.html> (accessed 3 September 2006).

IBM 5120. Available HTTP: <http://www-03.ibm.com/ibm/history/exhibits/pc/pc_6.html> (accessed 3 September 2006).

IBM 5120 applications. Available HTTP: <http://www-03.ibm.com/ibm/history/exhibits/pc/pc_7.html> (accessed 3 September 2006).

IBM 650. Available HTTP: <http://www-03.ibm.com/ibm/history/exhibits/650/650_intro.html> (accessed 3 September 2006).

IBM System/36. Available HTTP: <http://www-03.ibm.com/ibm/history/exhibits/rochester/rochester_4018.html> (accessed 3 September 2006).

Jones, E. (1995) *True and Fair A History of Price Waterhouse* (London: Hamish Hamilton).

Konrath, L. F. (1999) *Auditing Concepts and Applications: A Risk Analysis Approach* (Cincinnati, OH: South-Western College Publishing).

Lewis, E. S. (1914) *Efficient Cost Keeping* (Detroit: Burroughs Adding Machine Company).

Li, D. H. (1968) *Accounting Computers Management Information Systems* (New York: McGraw-Hill).

McKenney, J. L., Mason, R. O. and Copeland, D. G. (1997) Bank of America: the crest and trough of technological leadership, *MIS Quarterly*, 21 (3): 321–53.

Martin, E. (1925) *The Calculating Machines: Their History and Development*, trans. P. A. Kidwell and M. R. Williams (Germany: Johannes Meyer).

Mechanised Accounting Sub-Committee of the Taxation and Financial Relations Committee – Institute of Chartered Accountants in England and Wales (1949) *Mechanised Accounting and the Auditor* (London: Institute of Chartered Accountants in England and Wales).

Monteverde, R. J. (1966) Audits of electronically produced records, in J. M. Palen (ed.) *Encyclopedia of Auditing Techniques*, Vol. 1, pp. 75–116 (Englewood Cliffs, NJ: Prentice-Hall).

Moore, P. (1932) *Business Machines* (London: Longmans, Green).

New: the IBM alpha-numeric magnetic ledger card (1963) *Journal of Accountancy*, 116 (12): 5.

Norberg, A. L. (1990) High-technology calculation in the early 20th century: punched card machinery in business and government, *Technology and Culture*, 31 (4): 753–79.

Page, E. D. (1906) The new science of business: making an office efficient, *World's Work*, 12 (June): 7682–4.

Perks, R. W. (1993) *Accounting and Society* (London: Chapman & Hall).

Price, E. E. (1902) Ledger posting on the slip system, *Accountant*, 28 (1422): 256–66.

Sanders, D. H. (1968) *Computers in Business* (New York: McGraw-Hill).

Seward, G. H. (1904) Mechanical aids in factory-office economy, *Engineering Magazine*, 27 (July): 605–25.

Shurkin, J. (1984) *Engines of the Mind* (New York: W. W. Norton).

650 applications. Available HTTP: <http://www-03.ibm.com/ibm/history/exhibits/650/650_ap1.html> (accessed 3 September 2006).

650 chronology. Available HTTP: <http://www-03.ibm.com/ibm/history/exhibits/650/650_ch1.html> (accessed 3 September 2006).

650 RAMAC announcement. Available HTTP: <http://www-03.ibm.com/ibm/history/exhibits/650/650_pr2.html> (accessed 3 September 2006).

'Slip' or 'card' bookkeeping. –1 (1902) *Accountant*, 28 (1455): 1069–72.

Spacek, L. (1989) *The Growth of Arthur Andersen & Co. 1928–1973: An Oral History* (New York: Garland Publishing).

Strom, S. H. (1992) *Beyond the Typewriter: Gender, Class, and the Origins of Modern American Office Work* (Urbana, IL: University of Illinois Press).

The Computax system (1972) *Journal of Accountancy*, 133 (9): 15.

The IBM PC's debut. Available HTTP: <http://www-03.ibm.com/ibm/history/exhibits/pc25/pc25_intro.html> (accessed 3 September 2006).

Top 50: failing to be diverse (2007) *Accountancy Age*, June. Available HTTP: <http://www.accountancyage.com/articles/print/2191537/top-50-failing-diverse> (accessed 22 August 2007).

Turck, J. A. V. (1921) *Origin of Modern Calculating Machines* (Chicago: Western Society of Engineers).

Wootton, C. W. and Kemmerer, B. E. (2000) The changing genderization of the accounting workforce in the US, 1930–90, *Accounting, Business & Financial History*, 10 (2): 169–90.

Wootton, C. W. and Kemmerer, B. E. (2007) The emergence of mechanical accounting in the U.S., 1880–1930, *Accounting Historians Journal*, 34 (1): 91–124.

Wootton, C. W. and Wolk, C. M. (2000) The evolution and acceptance of the loose-leaf accounting system, 1885–1935, *Technology and Culture*, 41 (1): 80–98.

Yates, J. (1985) Internal communication systems in American business structures: a framework to aid appraisal, *American Archivist*, 48 (2): 141–58.

Yates, J. (1991) Investing in information: supply and demand forces in the use of information in American firms, 1850–1920, in P. Temin (ed.) *Inside the Business Enterprise*, pp. 117–59 (Chicago: The University of Chicago Press).

Yates, J. (1994) Evolving information use in firms, 1850–1920, in L. Bud-Frierman (ed.) *Information Acumen*, pp. 26–50 (London: Routledge).

Part 3

Theory and practice

7

Financial accounting theory

Thomas A. Lee

Overview

This chapter provides a history of financial accounting theory (FAT) in the English-speaking world. Its two principal objectives are to identify the most significant contributions in the development of FAT and assess its success in changing accounting practice. The narrative is written in the context of corporate business, accounting practice, public accountancy, and academic research. The chapter begins with a statement on the meaning of theory and its connection to financial accounting practice. The initial history of FAT extends from the late nineteenth century (with theories of double-entry bookkeeping) to the middle of the twentieth century (with individual theories on specific accounting practice problems). The continuing history, which then extends from mid-twentieth century to the present day, considers government regulation of corporate business affairs and individual and institutional attempts to produce a general statement of FAT in response. The impact of voluntary and mandatory accounting standards is considered in the context of conceptual framework projects, as are theoretical contributions by contemporary academics in the name of science. The chapter concludes with an assessment of the history of FAT and its impact on practice. The overall conclusion is that the long-standing search for a universal FAT has been a failure, although individual theoretical contributions have from time to time produced practice changes and, more generally, served a political role for public accountants and academic researchers seeking professional legitimacy. The question for the future is whether there is merit in continuing to search for a universal FAT to rationalise, explain, and predict financial accounting practice.

Definitions and restrictions

It is necessary to contain this review within manageable proportions by means of definitions and topic boundaries. These are pragmatic and subjective restrictions that map the chapter and recognise it is not a complete review of the history of FAT. For example, there have been various histories of specific aspects of FAT and these are not covered in this review (e.g. Wells 1976, on changing accounting thought, Tweedie and Whittington 1984, on price changes, Mattessich 1996, on accounting research, and Storey and Storey 1998, on conceptual frameworks). In effect, there are two main restrictions to chapter content. The first concerns the meaning of theory, i.e. what is regarded as a theoretical statement about financial accounting. The second restriction deals with the meaning of financial accounting, i.e. what is regarded as financial accounting for purposes of this history.

In this chapter, the term theory means any linguistic statement of belief about the function of financial accounting, expressed in logical argument, and intended to rationalise, explain, or predict financial accounting practice. Theoretical statements can be deductive (i.e. starting from a normative and general position about practice and arguing to a specific theoretical conclusion that can be tested by empirical observation) or inductive (i.e. starting from specific empirical observations of practice and arguing to a generalised theoretical conclusion or explanation). All theoretical statements in this chapter are perceived as arguing to conclusions that assist in understanding the nature, role, and impact of financial accounting information. Such definitions are made to permit this history of FAT to be as broad as possible and allow different approaches to theorising over time.

The term financial accounting in this chapter connotes the accounting information (and processes of producing such information) communicated in corporate financial reports. Most statements of FAT implicitly or explicitly acknowledge this restriction and, as later sections of the chapter demonstrate, anomalies and problems in corporate financial reporting are typically triggers for theoretical contributions to the financial accounting literature. With respect to the latter, the FAT in this chapter is that of the English-speaking world and, more specifically, of the UK and the USA. Justification for this restriction is grounded in the argument that the UK and the USA have dominated thinking about global accounting standards – particularly those of the International Accounting Standards Board (IASB) whose standards are expected to be consistent with those of the US Financial Accounting Standards Board (FASB 2002a) and have been adopted by most countries.

An additional caveat concerns the specific contributions to FAT cited in this review. Because of space limitations and the size of the literature, it has been possible only to select those writings that appear to have been important influences in the history of FAT. Most of these writings have been cited or debated in the literature as seminal works.

Preview

Inanga and Schneider (2005: 245) argue accounting research has been irrelevant to the needs of accounting practitioners and users because there has been no universal FAT with which to test and evaluate practice. They believe this failure is connected to a separation of researchers and practitioners as evidenced by lack of research content in classroom instruction and practice standards. If true, Inanga and Schneider's claim is an indictment of accounting research generally and FAT specifically because each function has a long history and considerable economic resources have been devoted to them. This chapter examines the conclusions of Inanga and Schneider from the perspective of a review of the history of FAT and its impact on practice.

The historical analyses relating to FAT in the following sections cover a period from the end of the nineteenth century to the present day. They examine individual and institutional contributions to FAT and reveal an evolutionary pattern. Initial contributions came from accounting practitioners largely concerned with resolving practical issues. Gradually, however, academic researchers joined practitioners in an expanded effort to confront practice problems by reference to theory. Despite this co-operative effort, there remained a lack of resolution of practice problems. This led to accountancy institutions becoming involved with FAT as they attempted to exercise control over accounting and reporting practice, deflate public criticism, and avoid government regulation. In turn, individual and institutional applications of a theoretical approach to financial accounting issues expanded into comprehensive statements of FAT. These theories were typically normative and focused on the decision usefulness model of satisfying information needs of investors and others. Further developments led to institutional theories presented as conceptual frameworks apparently structured by accounting standard setters to justify specific financial accounting principles and practices. Despite this attention to FAT, however, established practice problems continued to remain unresolved and new problems to emerge. The normative focus was eventually proscribed as unscientific by academics and replaced by empirical observations of financial accounting practices. Perhaps unsurprisingly, because these scientific studies offered no resolution of practice issues, the problems of practice persisted. The consequence of this was that attempts to produce theories to resolve practical problems disappeared from the accounting research literature. Today, all that remains of FAT in the active literature are conceptual frameworks intended to support principles-based standards. In addition, doubts have emerged in the academic literature about the validity and worth of scientific observations of accounting practices. The conclusions of Inanga and Schneider therefore do not appear unreasonable and the following sections attempt to provide a detailed history to validate their position.

The historical analysis is divided into three approximate time periods. The first from 1881 to 1940 includes the first individual attempts to theorise about financial accounting problems. The second period from 1941 to 1970 includes a classical or golden age of normative accounting theory. The third period from 1971 to the present day is one in which public accountancy institutions responded to practice deficiencies with conceptual frameworks, and academic researchers abandoned the normative approach to FAT in favour of apparently more scientific research.

Initial attempts at theory: 1881 to 1940

The expansion of trading and monetary systems of the European Renaissance (Crosby 1997) evolved into complex and continuous commercial activity in the seventeenth, eighteenth, and nineteenth centuries (Edwards 1989: *passim*). Technological changes in manufacturing created by innovations of the industrial revolution, the introduction and expansion of capital markets, and the evolution of capital-intensive enterprises, contributed to accounting-related functions such as financial reporting and auditing that, in turn, became part of corporate regulation and legislation. Unsurprisingly, public accountants from the mid-nineteenth century onwards organised to create institutions to defend their economic and social interests in such matters. However, reporting scandals and accounting frauds were frequent (see Chapter 19 for a full discussion of such issues) and much was left initially to lawyers in court cases to determine appropriate accounting practice (e.g. profits available for dividends). Public accountancy institutions appeared reluctant to interfere in these matters although, from time to time, leading practitioners communicated their concern about financial accounting practices. Practitioner articles began to appear in a fledgling accounting literature (e.g. *The Accountant* from 1874).

Initial UK contributions

The process in which public accountants began to articulate what now is described as FAT started in the nineteenth century when double-entry bookkeeping was adopted by them as their core body of knowledge (Macve 1996: 23). This was particularly the case in the UK where public accountancy developed earlier than elsewhere in the English-speaking world and where, for example, Pixley (1881: 78) concluded that knowledge and experience of bookkeeping was one of the most important qualifications for an auditor.

Other writers elaborated on this theme. George Lisle (1900) began his *Accounting in Theory and Practice* with a theoretical section on double-entry bookkeeping to facilitate a permanent record of business transactions and their impact on the wealth of the business owner – thus implicitly emphasising the proprietary theory of accounting. Lisle followed his theoretical exposition with a section on practical bookkeeping that explained the use of specific account-ing records. But he also addressed individual accounting topics from a theoretical perspective. For example, he defined profit in terms of economic theory allowing for the replacement of capital (ibid.: 48). Lisle also explored accounting concepts more specifically in a later article on foreign exchange conversion in which he enunciated the need to represent assets and liabilities at market rates quoted on the balance sheet date (ibid.: 1903). He also examined average conversion rates and his theoretical exposition is comparable to contemporary statements of principle in this area (e.g. IASB 2004).

Somewhat earlier than Lisle, Edwin Guthrie, identified by Kitchen and Parker (1980: 22) as a pioneer of accounting thought, looked beyond double-entry bookkeeping to the production of financial statements such as the balance sheet and the need for consistency of accounting treatment and disclosure over time and between entities (Guthrie 1882). His arguments are similar to those of individuals involved with contemporary conceptual frameworks of account-ing standard setters (e.g. Schipper 2003: 62–3).

Other British writers in the late nineteenth century began to explore theoretical accounting issues. For example, Lawrence R. Dicksee, described by Brief (1980: 1) as 'the father of modern accounting', wrote articles in the early 1890s in which he applied 'logical imagination' and 'first principles' to emerging issues (Brief 1980: 2). For example, in 1893, Dicksee examined the form and content of financial statements and addressed issues that continue to be of theoretical and practical significance today – e.g. charging interest on capital to profit and defining assets for accounting purposes (Dicksee 1893). In 1895, in a series of public lectures, Dicksee (1895) tackled a subject that was introduced earlier by Ernest Cooper (1888), a leading public account-ant of his time, and remains central to FAT, i.e. the nature and purpose of periodic profit. He asked the question 'What is profit of a company?' (Dicksee 1895: 40) and addressed issues such as unrealised operating and non-operating profits, undisclosed liabilities, and depreciation of fixed assets. In 1903, Dicksee (1903a) reviewed the purpose of financial statements and emphasised that, despite their subjective nature, they needed to be reliable for effective use. Dicksee was one of the earliest proponents of FAT – although he never used the term in his writings. In his emphasis on income, he appears to have been an early if inadvertent advocate of a theoretical focus on entity income.

Other leading British public accountancy practitioners of this period with contributions to FAT include Richard Brown in the UK and Arthur L. Dickinson in the USA and the UK. Brown did much to develop the early Scottish public accountancy profession. In 1904, in *The Accountant's Magazine*, the journal he founded and edited from 1897, he wrote about financial statements based on the modern theoretical accounting notion of economic substance being of greater importance than legal form and of the 'theory of accounts' (Brown 1904: 146). Brown explained how financial statements could be restated in percentage form in order to assist users to compare periods and entities – an early example of the statement user approach to FAT.

Dickinson was a partner in Price, Waterhouse & Company in the US and the UK who did much to develop American institutionalised public accountancy. He was the audit engagement partner for the United States Steel Corporation from 1902 when it started to publish consolidated financial statements. Dickinson was credited with this development and Price Waterhouse with its origins in the early 1890s (DeMond 1951: 60). Although there may be doubts concerning these claims, there is no doubt that Dickinson worked with the Corporation's comptroller and wrote about consolidated accounting in 1906 when it was in its infancy as a reporting technique (Dickinson 1906). His work can be argued as an early contribution to entity theory in financial accounting – in this respect, concerned with identifying the income and financial position of a group of companies regarded as one economic entity.

The previously mentioned contributions to FAT have certain characteristics. For example, they are the writings of practitioners and teachers dealing with practice problems. Each writing has a theoretical component although they were not written as theoretical pieces. In particular, they reflect a focus away from double-entry bookkeeping to growing problems associated with financial statements for public disclosure. They contain ideas that remain central to modern FAT. And they all reflect an inductive approach to theorising, i.e. a practitioner drawing on practical observations and experience to theorise.

Ad hoc contributions such as those above began to develop in a number of ways in the early 1900s. First, and occasionally, practitioner writers extended their thoughts into book-length treatises. For example, Dicksee published books on accounting issues with a theoretical content, i.e. depreciation (Dicksee 1903b) and goodwill (Dicksee and Tillyard 1906). Second, practitioner contributions became part of long-standing and continuous debates in the literature, e.g. accounting for the depreciation of fixed assets in relation to determining profit for dividends (Brief 1976). Such debates began to inform thinking about income and capital in accounting beyond the existing contributions of lawyers and, in turn, extended into a wider discussion in the early decades of the twentieth century on the nature of income, capital, and capital maintenance (Lee 1983). These later contributions to FAT included topics such as income realisation, financial and physical capital maintenance, operating and holding gains, and price and price-level changes – all matters theorised about in the era of normative accounting thought (e.g. in Chambers 1966). Third, inputs to these debates began to include academics and practitioners and, consequently, the arguments became more explicitly theoretical. This was a period that started in the early 1900s and continued into the 1940s. Much of the writing was American in origin although there were occasional contributions from the UK.

Initial US contributions

One of the earliest American contributions to FAT was *The Philosophy of Accounts* by Charles E. Sprague (Sprague 1907). The book adopted the earlier focus of George Lisle and is an explanation of the theory and practice of double-entry bookkeeping with an added emphasis on the balance sheet, assets and liabilities and, particularly, income as a change in capital. Sprague's focus was on the distinction between entity and proprietary theory (i.e. whether financial accounting is about the business entity or the owner's capital in it). He rejected the entity theory in favour of the proprietary alternative as he did not regard owner's capital as a liability. His bookkeeping framework therefore focused on profit as a change to proprietorship rather than a measure of entity performance.

Sprague's contribution to FAT was followed in 1909 by Henry R. Hatfield and *Modern*

Accounting (Hatfield 1909). This book was revised several years later as *Accounting* (Hatfield 1927) and the latter is used in this and later sections. *Accounting* was arguably the first comprehensive attempt to explain financial accounting from a theoretical perspective. It used an inductive process of observing practice and contains real-world illustrations. Each chapter ended with an annotated bibliography of other writings. Hatfield (ibid.: 6) advocated a proprietary approach to accounting and started with the balance sheet before moving on to assets and valuations, intangible assets, depreciation, capital, and liabilities. He then examined the nature of profit and related this to matters such as dividends and capital losses. Surpluses, reserves, and sinking funds were analysed. As a proprietary theorist, Hatfield regarded liabilities as negative assets. His approach was analytical and critical as well as explanatory, and he asked and discussed basic theoretical questions that remain unresolved today. For example, 'Does the balance sheet record costs or exhibit values?' (ibid.: 25) and 'When are profits realized?' (ibid.: 251). He was particularly critical of the inability of lawyers in early cases to understand the nature of accounting capital (ibid.: 274).

Hatfield was an explicit proponent of historical cost accounting (HCA). This was not the case with William A. Paton, who can be regarded as the father of modern FAT. Educated as an economist, Paton revolutionised FAT in his *Accounting Theory: With Special Reference to the Corporate Enterprise* (1922). He rejected the proprietary accounting model of Sprague and Hatfield, and stated theory by focusing on accounting for a specific economic unit, the corporate business enterprise. This was an entity theory of accounting that recognised shareholders separately from creditors, and was contrary to existing economic theories of property rights. The principal accounting focus ceased to be double-entry bookkeeping and, instead, became accounting information as a guide to effective entity management of capital. Paton addressed the issue of current valuation in accounting and his model for financial accounting was based on the value information needs of corporate managers rather than proprietors. He argued at length about the limitations of HCA and the need for replacement costs and price-level adjustments to permit corporate management to maintain physical capital without having to raise additional financial capital. This was a theory that recognised total income as a combination of operating, holding, and financial gains and losses – an all-inclusive concept.

Accounting Theory used practice only to illustrate theory. It ended with a chapter familiar to modern readers of normative theory, i.e. the postulates or basic premises of accounting. Accounting issues of the twenty-first century such as revenue recognition, capital maintenance and the monetary unit, and goodwill were discussed by Paton and he linked the idea of judging managerial efficiency with reported income. *Accounting Theory* could have been written in the 1960s and 1970s yet its impact at the time of writing was negligible and it was several decades before accounting standard-setters began to reflect Paton's ideas in their prescriptions (Chambers 1963). The accounting model propounded by Sprague and Hatfield had more impact presumably because it reflected existing and therefore familiar practice. That of Paton did not and he appears to have succumbed to the practical dominance of the HCA model by the end of the 1930s in his co-authorship of Paton and Littleton (1940).

Paton's arguments about income, capital, and the monetary unit were developed in greater detail by Henry W. Sweeney. Sweeney was a professor of accounting and law before practising as a public accountant. He adapted his doctoral dissertation to produce *Stabilized Accounting* in 1927 with publication in 1936 (Sweeney 1936; see also Clarke 1976). *Stabilized Accounting* brought together theoretical ideas from accounting and economics in order to reveal the problems in financial accounting practice caused by a monetary unit that fluctuates in value over time. Sweeney was influenced by German and Dutch thinkers and his work provided a theoretical basis for later institutional attempts to mandate price-level accounting using a monetary unit of constant purchasing power (e.g. Jones 1956). Sweeney criticised the use in practice of different monetary units in a single set of financial statements, and advocated a uniform unit for accounting. More specifically, in order to maintain proprietary capital in real purchasing power terms, he argued for the application of replacement costs to non-monetary assets and purchasing power adjustments to monetary assets and liabilities – thus introducing to FAT the ideas of realised and unrealised holding gains and losses, coupled with realised and unrealised monetary gains and losses that were to become part of current cost accounting in the 1970s and 1980s (Tweedie and Whittington 1984: 60–189).

US contributions post Paton and Sweeney

If Paton and Sweeney provided the first comprehensive statements of FAT built on economic and accounting concepts, Canning (1929) produced a framework of economic theory with which to explain and discuss financial accounting. John B. Canning was a professor of economics with a responsibility for accounting education and wrote *The Economics of Accountancy* as a means of educating economists about accounting practice by focusing on valuation and income. The book had little immediate impact on accountants but gradually influenced later accounting theorists concerned with integrating economic concepts into FAT. Canning's importance was in drawing attention to deficiencies in financial accounting. This was particularly true with respect to accounting for income, the central theme of *The Economics of Accountancy*.

As proprietary theorists, leading writers of the time such as Hatfield emphasised the balance sheet as the core of accounting thought and Canning, perhaps unsurprisingly, perceived such accountants as lacking a philosophy of income. He believed accounting income reported at the time to be no more than a residue of various accounting procedures applied to the production of the balance sheet under the proprietary theory. In contrast, financial position according to Canning should be a statement of prospect and future cash flows, and he advocated an entity approach to such accounting. The value of capital in an ideal world was, for him, discounted net future cash flow. He decried accountants' lack of a concept of value and what he termed the 'mongrel origins' of accounting numbers in balance sheets (a mix of various bases) (Canning 1929: 319). Canning defined assets in terms of 'future service in money' (ibid.: 187) and advocated direct valuation on this basis where possible and indirect valuation where reasonable forecasting was not possible. In this respect, Canning's single greatest influence was his contemporary, the American economist Irving Fisher (1906). The importance of Canning's theory was its identification of economic notions inherent in accounting practices such as the calculation of income and capital – particularly the idea of future benefits or services as the basis for valuing assets and therefore determining income. He was, however, somewhat ambiguous in his support of valuation bases other than historical cost.

The contributions of Paton and Canning were published in times of increasing criticism of corporate financial reporting quality – particularly in the USA (Carey 1969). This eventually led to institutional action involving regulators and public accountants (e.g. the Securities Act, 1933). However, there was no attempt by public accountancy institutions to produce a coherent FAT. In 1929, for example, despite the American Society of Certified Public Accountants' criticism of the inadequacies of professional bodies in relation to FAT, the American Institute of Accountants (AIA) in 1931 limited its efforts to a definitional statement on *Accounting Terminology* (AIA 1931). Unsurprisingly, Greer (1932) called for a council of accounting research to improve institutional efforts.

Theories by individuals, however, continued to appear. D.R. Scott wrote *The Cultural Significance of Accounts* (Scott 1931) not so much as a new theory of accounting but more as a historical review of the evolution of financial accounting as a cultural and social practice. Scott's work was based on a study of economic organisation and control through time. It was therefore the first major study of accounting in a social context and can be related to the institutional, organisational, and social literature of accounting today (as in journals such as *Accounting, Organizations and Society* and *Accounting, Auditing & Accountability Journal*). Using a historical lens, Scott examined the rise and fall of market control in economic activity, blaming its disintegration on market factors such as size, complexity, instability, technological change, regulation, and law. He criticised traditional economic value theory and studied changes in corporate management and accountability. Scott concluded that the decline of control in economic markets required re-assessment of the growing importance and role of accounting information in economic activity. He argued that better use of accounting information permitted business enterprises to adapt to changing economic circumstances. Accounting was a means of mediating conflicts of interest in business and providing 'justice' (Scott 1931: 202). Scott concluded that, if accounting information was to supplant the market as the principal tool of economic organization, then FAT was needed to supplant market theory as the means of understanding economic theory. In other words, despite its debatable analyses of economic theory and practice, Scott's FAT as a primary cultural influence was the precursor to later critical theories about accounting's influence in society (e.g. as in Hopwood 1983).

Unlike the above, Kenneth MacNeal was not an academic. He worked as a public accountancy practitioner and used his practice experience to write *Truth in Accounting* in 1939 as a repost to what he perceived as the neglect by public accountants of unrealised gains in calculating periodic income. MacNeal (1939: vii) argued that the majority of audited financial statements were untrue and misleading due to unsound accounting principles. His analysis started with three fables on the misleading nature of reported accounting information before explaining the deception in terms of lack of market values and unrealised gains, inclusion of unrealised losses, and exclusion of non-recurrent realised gains and losses from periodic income. MacNeal (ibid.: 82–3) was criticising accounting principles designed for a past proprietary age instead of an era of corporate businesses often marked by a divorce between shareholders and managers. The remainder of his book dealt with a theoretical argument for using net realisable values as the basis for financial accounting practice. MacNeal concluded his book by linking the existing system of HCA with a decline in the reputation of public accountancy, and the need for public accountants to admit the irrelevance of the system (ibid.: 323–4). MacNeal was an early example of a writer associating failure in FAT with professional reputation and status. His text was the beginning of a long line of critical research about professionalism in public accountancy (see Lee 2006a). It was also the precursor for a later persistent stream of theoretical argument for the use of net realisable values in financial accounting (e.g. Chambers 1966; Sterling 1970).

Stephen Gilman was a public accountancy practitioner and educator who published *Accounting Concepts of Profit* in 1939 (Gilman 1939). This was not a book of original FAT. Instead, Gilman emphasised the then prevailing trend in financial accounting away from the balance sheet to the income statement (i.e. from proprietary to entity theory). He concentrated on the flexibility associated with the calculation of income (particularly through topics such as inventory adjustment), a matter of increasing criticism in practice over the previous two decades that eventually led to the introduction of mandatory accounting standards.

US institutional theories

Institutional involvement with FAT began to emerge at the end of the 1930s as a result of public criticism of financial accounting. First, the American Accounting Association (AAA) stated twenty basic accounting propositions dealing with costs and values, income, and capital and surplus (AAA 1936). This was not a complete FAT, rather a theoretical review of certain financial accounting practices using a deductive approach. The statement reinforced the accounting convention of conservatism and the historical cost principle, and advocated an all-inclusive concept of income (differentiating between operating and non-operating gains and losses). The 1936 AAA statement was explicitly expanded into a larger work (Paton and Littleton 1940). This can be argued as the first institutional attempt at producing a fully integrated FAT and is certainly the first conceptual framework for accounting standards (ibid.: ix). The monograph uses an inductive approach to FAT and provides a conceptual explanation of HCA based on notions such as business entity, going concern, historical cost, and matching. These ideas were expanded by Paton and Littleton into chapters explaining cost, revenue, income, and surplus. The principal objective of financial accounting was seen as periodically reporting on managerial performance in terms of its 'effort' (costs) and 'accomplishment' (revenue) (ibid.: 14–15). Although practitioners and academics were not convinced by the entity approach of Paton and Littleton, the importance of their study is demonstrated by the fact that many of its basic ideas remain in conceptual frameworks and accounting standards today.

The 1936 statement of the AAA also evoked a practitioner response from the AIA because of its recommendation of all-inclusive income. Funded by a leading public accountancy firm, three academics (including Hatfield) were asked to review accounting practice. They wrote *A Statement of Accounting Principles* (Sanders *et al.* 1938). The *Statement* was published by the AIA and drew criticism from academics because it accepted existing practice. It also emphasised the subjectivity of accounting because of the need for personal judgment. Many of the basic ideas in the *Statement* are also to be found in Paton and Littleton (1940) (e.g. the information needs of management, historical cost, and going concern). However, it introduced to the accounting literature the notion of generally accepted accounting principles – not as matters of law but from consensus in practice, speech, and writing (Sanders *et al.* 1938: 5). In combination, the 1936 and 1940 statements of the AAA and the 1938 statement of the AIA can be argued as the origins of later institutional statements. In particular, Paton and Littleton (1940) brought legitimacy and authority to HCA theory in the USA and elsewhere, and it remains an active publication of the AAA. By 1939, the AIA had created a research function within its accounting standards activities.

In the UK, there were few significant developments in the 1930s with respect to FAT. However, two attempts to bring together academics and practitioners to discuss theory and practice are noteworthy (Edwards 1989: 240–1). In 1935, the Society of Incorporated Accountants and Auditors created the first British research committee whose most significant achievement was the launch, in 1948, of the first British journal devoted to FAT and related practice issues (*Accounting Research*). In 1936, academics at the London School of Economics created the Accounting Research Association to influence practice change. Neither development appears to have had long-term impact in terms of FAT but reflect concern about the need for co-operation between researchers and practitioners.

Classical financial accounting theory: 1941–70

The Second World War affected activity associated with FAT in different ways. In the UK in 1942, for example, the Institute of Chartered Accountants in England and Wales (ICAEW) created a research committee to publish guidance on financial accounting practice. However, it would be several decades before it and other UK bodies published statements on FAT. In the USA, on the other hand, the war postponed until 1947 an AIA initiative to study business income (Study Group 1952). The inflationary effects of the war resurrected the initiative and papers were written by economists and debated by the Study Group (Alexander *et al.* 1950). Alexander and his fellow authors revealed a spectrum of economic ideas applicable to accounting for business income (i.e. real and monetary, operating and holding, and realised and accrued gains and losses; and general and specific price-level changes). The Study Group examined the meaning of income from economic, legal, and accounting standpoints before reviewing several accepted accounting assumptions or principles seen in previous theoretical studies (e.g. monetary unit, realisation, going concern, matching, and historical cost). Specific accounting income issues were discussed including the stability of the monetary unit and the all-inclusive concept of income. The Study Group (1952: 107) came to the conclusion there was a need for greater uniformity in financial accounting practice but that no single system could meet all the needs of financial statement users.

The 1952 Study Group report reflects the primacy of entity income in FAT at this time and a growing debate about the conservatism of accounting thought and practice in periods of dynamic economics. In particular, the debate concerned the questionable relevance of the historical cost and realisation conventions that dominated practice. The exclusion of unrealised gains and monetary gains and losses from reported business income was to become the central issue addressed by writers of the classical or golden age of theorising from 1941 to 1970 (Nelson 1973: 4). Even professional accountancy bodies became involved. For example, in 1949, the ICAEW published a guidance statement on general price-level accounting and in the USA in 1956 the AAA produced a similar study (Jones 1956).

Individual academic contributions on both sides of the debate began to multiply after the Second World War. For example, in the USA, William J. Vatter published his *Fund Theory of Accounting* (Vatter 1947). Vatter explicitly recognised the speculative nature of his theory, in which he argued for a series of statements based on a balance sheet decomposed into funds or business activities (i.e. operating, investing, financing, and capital). These statements were intended to describe periodic movements in these funds. Conventional notions such as periodic income would not be reported although the statement user could construct such a number from reported flows. Vatter based his arguments on what he regarded as the inadequacies of the proprietary and entity theories of accounting, and the attempts of theorists to meet the needs of specific user groups such as investors. Although it was not well received or followed up because of its arbitrary classifications and user unfriendliness, Vatter's fund theory can be seen as a precursor to later financial accounting theories based on fund and cash flows, and as innovative in seeking to satisfy multiple user needs.

Ananias C. Littleton was a considerable influence on American accountancy for several decades and published books and articles on FAT. Littleton believed theory and practice to be a single subject of financial accounting and it is unsurprising to find that in *Structure of Accounting Theory* (Littleton 1953) he sought to defend HCA by means of the inductive approach to theory, i.e. observing practices and drawing concepts and principles from the observations. 'Experience, let it be noted, is not the same as experiment' (ibid.: 185). He argued that the best way to advance financial accounting was to allow practitioners to develop and evolve practices and then, by observation of these practical experiences, derive the principles on which they are based. 'Good experience becomes accepted practice' (ibid.: 186). Littleton argued that reported accounting numbers require to be based on objective evidence thereby validating the continued use of historical costs. Income was the 'centre of gravity' of accounting (ibid.: 18). Financial statements should assist users to evaluate managerial performance. They were therefore not valuation statements because values were transient and subjective. As Littleton (1953: 34) concluded, the purpose of accounting was to permit 'calculated judgment' of enterprise success.

Structure of Accounting Theory provided many legacies. It emphasised a general purpose approach to financial reporting with a stewardship objective. It used the inductive approach to theorising and presented FAT within a framework of objectives, concepts, and principles. It gave considerable comfort to practitioners wedded to the historical cost, income-orientated system of financial reporting. In fact, it could be used today to justify contemporary practice. However, Littleton's work can be viewed in a different way. It is consistent with the philosophy of a later theoretical approach, positive accounting theory (PAT), in that it perceives the role of the theorist as observing, explaining, and predicting actual practices rather than prescribing alternative practices (Watts and Zimmerman 1986: 2).

Laying down classical theory

As the previous sections indicate, there were many attempts to articulate FAT prior to the mid-1950s. Their origins lay in practitioner explanations of bookkeeping theory that evolved into commentaries about financial statements and their basic elements. Practitioners were joined by academics and the theorising became more formal although the subject matter tended to be specific problems from practice rather than overall systems of reporting. The preference of early theorists was for inductive studies based on observations of practice, and for proprietary rather than entity theory. Gradually, however, FAT was influenced by economic thinking and, because of the importance of income concepts in economic theory, the focus in FAT became periodic income and problems associated with it (e.g. values and prices). The meaning of numbers based on historical costs was challenged and defended, and seminal works on FAT published and recognised as such (e.g. Sprague 1907; Hatfield 1909; Paton 1922; Sweeney 1936; Canning 1929; Gilman 1939; MacNeal 1939; Paton and Littleton 1940; Littleton 1953). Professional accountancy bodies in the USA began to examine theoretical aspects of financial accounting practice.

Hatfield, Paton, Canning, Littleton, and MacNeal became the intellectual basis for study by a community of financial accounting theorists in the 1950s and 1960s. Their work was frequently cited predominantly by academics intent on changing practice. More specifically, the studies of Paton and Littleton (1940) and Littleton (1953) provided a model with which to construct a theory. The new theorists appeared to be more aware of the nature, role, and structure of FAT. This was particularly true of Raymond J. Chambers, an Australian professor.

Chambers advocated continuously contemporary accounting, a reporting system based on net realisable values in which financial position is central and income a derivative as in the proprietary approach to FAT. The development of his theory was influenced by practical experience of price regulation, teaching management, concern about inductive reasoning from practice by previous theorists, lack of methodology in prior theories, and increasing evidence of the unreliability of reported numbers. Chambers developed a deductive theory of financial accounting using ideas from disciplines such as communication, economics, management, mathematics, measurement, organisational behaviour, and philosophy. His initial thesis appeared in Chambers (1955) with four fundamentals, i.e. entities, rational management, monetary statements, and accounting as a service function. He developed these ideas in various papers by normative thinking using a deductive approach. For example, in Chambers (1962), theory was explained in terms of actors, decisions, and actions in a market economy (including exchange, money, credit, and price), the need for and qualities of information for decisions and actions (including relevance, neutrality, correspondence, consistency, and objectivity), and the business entity and its financial position (monetary and non-monetary based on net realisable values) and changes therein (realised and unrealised). The full theory appeared as *Accounting, Evaluation, and Economic Behaviour* (Chambers 1966).

The importance of Chambers in the history of FAT is not so much the specifics of his theory (e.g. the relevance of net realisable values). It has more to do with the methodology of theorising (e.g. the context, structure, and relationships of a theory and its application to practice). The deductive work of Chambers was a direct challenge to the inductive approach and pragmatism of Paton and Littleton. His legacy is seen in later FAT (including conceptual frameworks), and in practice as embodied in the increasing attention to financial position and the use of net realisable value to operationalise fair value accounting (e.g. Wyatt 1991).

Building on classical theory tradition

Other classical contributions to FAT in the 1960s were predominantly American and include Edwards and Bell (1961), Moonitz (1961), Sprouse and Moonitz (1962), Mattessich (1964), Grady (1965), AAA (1966), Ijiri (1967), and Sterling (1970). They each reveal a formal theoretical structure and follow a deductive approach and normative prescription.

Edwards and Bell (1961) was written by Edgar O. Edwards and Philip W. Bell, both professors of economics. Based on the economic theory of the firm under conditions of uncertainty, Edwards and Bell developed a concept of business income argued to be useful to internal management, investors, creditors, and others, and also for taxation purposes. They related measurement of business activity to current value and to general price changes, and advocated calculating income on short-term assets on a net realisable value basis and long-term assets using replacement costs. Edwards and Bell applied their recommendations to inventory and depreciable fixed assets, distinguishing between operating and holding gains and losses, and real and fictitious gains and losses due to general price-level adjustments. In order to maintain capital, holding gains were not regarded as distributable or taxable. Edwards and Bell (1961) was a normative proprietary theory of income using multiple current valuation bases and lacked the theoretical superstructure of studies such as Chambers (1966). However, it influenced the current cost accounting debate of the 1970s in its argument for mixed values and the separation of operating and holding income (Tweedie and Whittington 1984: *passim*). The study failed to explore FAT in relation to financial position and ignored the problem of aggregation of different values.

The American Institute of Certified Public Accountants (AICPA) in the late 1950s decided to explore the basic foundations of financial accounting in order to determine the broad principles upon which practice was based at that time and from which practice improvements could be made. It did so in two studies. Moonitz (1961) was a study of the foundations (or postulates) of accounting and Sprouse and Moonitz (1962) a study of accounting principles (the broad guidelines to help formulate specific practice rules). The studies fall within the definition of FAT and both evoked a critical reaction from practitioners and academics. However, Moonitz's postulates were unremarkable and most could be found in previous studies, e.g. exchange, entity, periodicity, unit of account, continuity, and consistency. They could be argued to frame financial accounting in relatively uncontroversial truths. The most serious criticism was in relation to Sprouse and Moonitz (1962) and the focus on financial position before income, and the use of a mixture of historical costs, values, and price-level adjustments. The recommended move from HCA to an all-inclusive income-orientated reporting based on mixed valuations was apparently seen as too radical.

The postulates and principles studies were shelved by the AICPA, although some features re-emerged in later conceptual frameworks and specific accounting standards of the Financial Accounting Standards Board (FASB). In addition, effectively as an antidote, the AICPA produced *Inventory of Generally Accepted Accounting Principles for Business Enterprises* (Grady 1965). This was a deliberate attempt to encapsulate conventional practice within a theoretical framework of basic concepts needed to support HCA. Grady (1965) placed considerable emphasis on notions: of government 'reserving the economic area primarily for development by the people' (ibid.: 25), that 'diversity in accounting among independent business entities is a basic fact of life' (ibid.: 33), that 'conservatism is an essential quality in the performance of the auditing function' (ibid.: 35), of disclosure as material if it 'would be likely to influence or 'make a difference' in 'the judgment and conduct of a reasonable person' (ibid.: 40). These were not concepts addressed in Moonitz (1961) and Sprouse and Moonitz (1962). Indeed, Grady (1965: 43–4) identified those postulates from Moonitz (1961) that had been ignored when constructing his own framework. All those omitted supported principles associated with the use of current values. FAT, at least from an institutional public accountancy perspective in the USA in the 1960s, was therefore to be one supporting HCA.

While the AICPA was attempting to formulate a statement of FAT, academics continued to produce individual theories, reflecting the multi-disciplinary approach seen in the work of Chambers (1966). Richard V. Mattessich, for example, is an Austrian accountant who worked in Canada. He was also an engineer and economist and this background is reflected in *Accounting and Analytical Methods* (Mattessich 1964) which is a quantitative-analytical explanation of financial accounting from an ex post and ex ante position. Mattessich brought ideas from logic, economics, sociology, decision theory, and measurement to his analysis of income and capital. He advocated a mixed system of current values. In particular, he emphasised the idea of accounting for 'real and financial objects' (ibid.: 36), i.e. distinguishing between physical and social realities, a subject he developed in the 1990s as part of a debate on accounting for economic reality (Mattessich 1991; see also Lee 2006b).

Yuji Ijiri is a Japanese scholar who has pursued his academic career in the USA. He brought a mathematical rigour to his research as in *The Foundations of Accounting Measurements* (Ijiri 1967). This was FAT based on three mathematical axioms of control, value, and exchange. Ijiri argued for accounting based on historical costs and for using double-entry bookkeeping as the only logical means of providing reliable and objective information. He argued against the use of current values as these do not comply with his axioms. His arguments reflected the information needs of management and external users of financial statements. As with Mattessich, Ijiri made use of measurement and decision theories. Also, as with Mattessich, Ijiri covered ideas that were part of a continuing debate concerning improvements in financial accounting. He focused on accounting as a function concerned with phenomena or 'principals' represented by phenomena or 'surrogates' in a linguistic form and therefore with issues of representation, language, and measurement (Ijiri 1967: 3–28). Ijiri (1981) extended his case for HCA in less complex terms than his 1967 work.

Sterling (1970) initially appeared as a doctoral dissertation in 1962. Robert R. Sterling is an economist and philosopher of science. He brought this background to his study of accounting in the 1960s and his career has been devoted to criticising the meaninglessness of HCA and advocating a system based on net realisable values. Sterling (1970) gathered together his initial ideas on FAT, and did so by examining income from the perspective of four competing models: economic (evolving from Irving Fisher), accounting (historical cost-realisation), market value, and Kenneth Boulding's constant (adopting a constant value to avoid arbitrary choice). He examined each of these alternatives in terms of two principal characteristics: verity (representational faithfulness or reliability) and relevance (to decisions). Sterling's arguments were made within the context of a simple business model of a wheat trader under conditions of certainty and uncertainty. He concluded that current market price alone 'relates all the extant alternatives' (Sterling 1970: 339). Sterling later developed his theory in a number of studies, most notably in Sterling (1979) in which he argued decision relevance as the primary criterion of financial accounting (ibid.: 85) and identified a flaw of most previous and later FAT, i.e. they describe decision-makers rather than decisions and therefore lack sufficient detail to determine what accounting numbers are relevant to these decisions.

End of classical theorising

By the late 1960s, FAT had a chaotic flavour. Theorists such as Littleton, Grady, and Ijiri argued for HCA. Chambers advocated net realisable values. Edwards and Bell were primarily concerned with mixed values. Sprouse and Moonitz and Mattessich wanted a range of current values in financial reports. A further study by the AAA (1966) gave another theoretical alternative – HCA supplemented by current cost accounting (defined in terms of replacement costs, realisable values, and price indices). AAA (1966) was a report arguing for general-purpose financial statements to satisfy the decision needs of a variety of user groups. Stewardship was also recognised as a reporting aim and four basic standards were recommended. The latter were to become the cornerstones of contemporary conceptual frameworks of accounting standard setters – i.e. decision relevance, verifiability, freedom from bias, and quantifiability (AAA 1966: 7).

The incoherence of this situation was reviewed by an AAA committee in 1977, a decade after its *Statement of Basic Accounting Theory* (AAA 1977). The review was US-centric based on the work of Paton (1922), Hatfield (1909 in its 1927 reissue), Canning (1929), Sweeney (1936), Gilman (1939), MacNeal (1939), Paton and Littleton (1940), Alexander *et al.* (1950), Littleton (1953), Edwards and Bell (1961), Moonitz (1961), Sprouse and Moonitz (1962), and Ijiri (1975). The review therefore focused primarily on theories relating to historical costs, replacement costs, and mixed current values. With the exception of MacNeal, the net realisable value argument was ignored. The committee believed the lack of a generally accepted FAT was due to the difficulty of relating theories to practice, coping with arbitrary accounting allocations, the subjectivity of normative argument, interpreting user behaviour, cost-benefit considerations, and information overload (AAA 1977: 31–9). Events of the next three decades did little to change this perception.

Conceptual frameworks and scientific theory: 1971–2006

There have been four developments in FAT over the past three or so decades. First, with the exception of a handful of academic researchers, classical normative theory has disappeared from the literature generally and from financial accounting instruction specifically. Second, the cause of this decline can be attributed to the emergence of empirical finance-based accounting research generally, and PAT research particularly. Third, despite the disappearance of normative theory in research and teaching, it appears in the literature of accounting standard setters in their conceptual frameworks. Fourth, a succession of financial reporting scandals contributed to accounting standard setters committing to use conceptual frameworks to produce principles-based standards. Each of these developments is explained below.

Fall of normative research

For those theorists willing to continue to argue normatively, the 1970s and 1980s witnessed a diminishing contribution in the public domain. For example, Chambers advocated continuously contemporary accounting theory into the 1980s (see Chambers and Dean 1986), and Sterling argued for net realisable value accounting into the 1990s (see Lee and Wolnizer 1997). The reason for the decline was reaction by empirical researchers to normative theorising. Normative theorists such as Chambers and Sterling found leading research journals became closed to classical FAT in favour of a new 'science' of accounting empiricism (largely connected to PAT).

There were, of course, exceptions to this general trend. For example, in the 1970s as a result of high rates of inflation and government concern, accounting researchers debated practical alternatives to HCA, e.g. current purchasing power accounting and current cost accounting (Tweedie and Whittington 1984: 60–258). There were many individual contributions to this debate. For example, Baxter (1975) advanced an income theory based on an insurance concept of value to the owner, the maximum loss from permanent deprivation of an asset. The theory used a mixture of replacement cost, economic value, net realisable value, and indexed historical costs, and produced operating and holding gains and losses as well as monetary gains and losses. The argument for such a system had been made a decade before by Solomons (1966). Variants of value to the owner were adopted by accounting standard setters in the UK and the USA for a short period in the early 1980s as a mandatory supplement to HCA (e.g. FASB 1979; Accounting Standards Committee 1980). The change in practice, however, was brief – in part because inflation decreased and the additional numbers created confusion to users, and also because there was no formal theoretical framework in place with which to judge the relevance of a system of mixed values (Tweedie and Whittington 1984: 329–31).

A further exception to the decline of normative theorising was the development of cash flow accounting (CFA) and reporting theory from the early 1970s – particularly in the UK. CFA arguments eventually led to mandatory standards in the USA in 1987 and the UK in 1991. The main motivation for suggesting a change from an accrual and allocation-based system of financial accounting to a cash-based one was a debate in the UK in the late 1960s about the lack of uniformity, incompleteness, and meaninglessness of HCA. Thomas A. Lee is a British academic who argues for a theory of CFA in two steps, i.e. as an articulating system, first, of statements of actual and forecast cash flows and, second, of statements of realised and unrealised flows, and financial position based on net realisable values as potential cash flows (Lee 1986). Lee's arguments are entity-based and use characteristics such as decision relevance and informational reliability. Gerald H. Lawson is also a British academic who advocates the reporting of actual and forecast cash flows but in combination with the market value of enterprise capital in order to assist internal management and investors in assessing enterprise performance (Lawson 1997). Lawson's arguments take FAT into the macro-economic areas of dividend policy, inflation, and taxation.

Rise of scientific theory

Arguably the single most damaging influence on classical FAT has been the emergence in the late 1960s of empirical financial accounting research. This research stream started with studies such as Ball and Brown (1968) and is based on economic theories such as efficient markets, capital asset pricing, agency, and regulation. The various strands of research were merged into a single PAT by Watts and Zimmerman (1986). PAT explains and predicts accounting practice in specific circumstances, and is an off-shoot of positive economics based on free capital markets and minimal government regulation. PAT is intended to assist accountants, auditors, and standard setters to assess the consequences of their accounting choices. In particular, it observes the behaviour of accountants, auditors, and users with respect to specific disclosures and practices. PAT is claimed to be scientific because of the apparent statistical objectivity of the empirical observations. It is also stated not to be aimed at changing practice. Its impact can be seen in terms of the increase of empirical studies and decrease of normative studies in leading journals. Indeed, PAT theorists condemn normative theory as lacking empirical validity (Watts and Zimmerman 1986: 4–5) and fulfilling a political role of providing excuses for practice failures or prescriptions (ibid.: 344–5).

Sterling (1990: 129–30) concludes that PAT is not FAT. It does not examine accounting practice or financial statements. Instead, it examines the behaviour of those individuals associated with such practice and statements. Mouck (1992: 54) categorises PAT as rhetoric to disseminate the political ideology of *laissez-faire*. Even proponents of PAT in the form of capital market research admit to its inability to explain anomalies in the empirical results about market efficiency (Beaver 2002: 456–7), its use of 'contextual accounting arguments' instead of a general theory (ibid.: 462), the need for a better understanding of accounting users (ibid.: 465), and the lack of understanding of the nature of earnings management (ibid.: 468). However, despite its limitations as a theory, PAT in its various forms has proved highly influential in driving classical normative research from leading research journals.

A recent research stream relating to capital markets can be associated with the search for a generally acceptable FAT. James A. Ohlson (e.g. 1995, 2006), an American researcher, described FAT based on HCA and attempted to minimise the problems of allocation and valuation. The theory used an accounting income number that included all gains and losses associated with changes in the book value of capital (i.e. the clean surplus). Ohlson defined the price of equity as the sum of an entity's reported book value and the present value of its expected abnormal income stream. The latter was defined as the difference between total income on a modified cash basis and the required rate of return on the beginning-of-period book value of capital. Modified cash income was defined as the periodic change in cash-related net assets at book value plus the net dividend (i.e. dividend payments minus capital issued). Ohlson's model attempts to provide a theoretical prescription of accounting numbers based on a conventional practice that can be used to input a variant of the capital asset pricing model. The theory is controversial as it remains rooted in a proprietary approach related to income calculation and depended on historical costs.

Rise of conceptual frameworks

At a time when financial accounting researchers were turning away from normative theory and promoting empirical economic studies, the public accountancy profession in the USA and the UK perversely became involved in normative theorising in the form of conceptual frameworks designed to provide an intellectual basis for accounting standards. This was first seen in two conceptual studies in the USA by the AICPA (1970, 1971). It gathered momentum when the AICPA's Wheat Committee recommended the creation of the FASB in 1972 to produce accounting standards independent of public accountancy bodies. From then on, a series of studies associated with conceptual frameworks can be observed. Each emphasised a conceptual approach that related to the use of financial statements.

The Trueblood Committee was created in 1972 by the AICPA and reported a year later (AICPA 1973). Although explicitly focusing on the objectives of financial reporting, Trueblood provided a blueprint for later conceptual frameworks. Its focus was the provision of information useful for economic decisions, service to users relying on financial statements, and earning power, accountability, and prediction. The study also examined the elements and characteristics of financial statements.

The theoretical framework for standards pioneered by Trueblood was centred on reporting objectives, statement elements, and information qualities or characteristics. These issues were also addressed in the UK Accounting Standards Steering Committee's (1975) *The Corporate Report* which reviewed the objectives and concepts of financial reporting in the context of making business enterprises more publicly accountable. It advocated a user approach and recommended the calculational basis as price–level adjusted historical cost. In the same year, the Sandilands Committee (Inflation Accounting Committee 1975) set up by the UK government in 1974 to consider whether and how corporate financial statements should account for changing prices, also argued for a user approach and looked at various reporting characteristics previously examined in individual works of FAT. It advocated a value to the business approach using current values.

In the USA, the FASB (1976) began a long-term project to produce a conceptual framework. It published a statement on reporting objectives in 1978 (FASB 1978) followed by supporting statements to guide practice between 1980 and 2000 (i.e. qualitative characteristics, elements of financial statements, and recognition and measurement). In combination, these statements provided the foundation for the current American conceptual framework. All were based on a decision usefulness approach, the entity approach to income derived from a statement of assets and liabilities, normative and deductive reasoning, and previous studies of FAT. The user approach was emphasised in an AICPA review by the Jenkins Committee (AICPA 1999). A similar project in the UK was begun in 1991 (see Arnold *et al.* 1991) and culminated in a conceptual framework produced by the Accounting Standards Board (1999). The Accounting Standards Board's framework did not appear to have been influenced greatly by an Institute of Chartered Accountants of Scotland study which specifically argued for the reporting of cash flows and net realisable values as a means of portraying economic reality in terms of substance not form (McMonnies 1988).

Scandal and principle

The most recent position with respect to FAT relates to financial scandals such as Cendant, Enron, and WorldCom in the USA, and BCCI and Maxwell Communications in the UK. In 2002, the FASB (2002b) announced its intention to use its conceptual framework to produce principles-based accounting standards, i.e. to explicitly associate standards with theoretical notions such as decision relevance and reliability. This approach was endorsed by the Securities Exchange Commission (SEC 2003) and effectively became a global project when the FASB and the IASB agreed in 2002 to harmonise their standard setting (FASB 2002a). Bullen and Crook (2006) reviewed the FASB-IASB initiative and suggested it would not unduly change existing ideas, emphases, and approaches in existing frameworks. For example, the proprietary approach to the calculation of income would be retained (ibid.: 9).

Whether ideas prescribed in conceptual frameworks which have been drawn from previous individual and institutional studies of FAT will result in significant change to accounting practice is therefore doubtful. One of the leading standard setters in the USA revealed that the decision usefulness approach would be practised in terms of comparability and consistency (Schipper 2003: 62). In other words, despite more than a century of searching for FAT, the fundamental reporting framework remained an income statement and balance sheet based predominantly on accrued historical costs. Schipper suggested that this system is improved by consistency of that practice over time in order to achieve comparable numbers. It is therefore not unreasonable to support the conclusion argued by Hines (1991) and others that the role of the conceptual framework is not to provide a theoretical basis to examine and improve financial accounting practice. Instead, its mission lies in its use as a tool of public accountants in their goal to achieve professional legitimacy as an occupational grouping. Conceptual frameworks or theories can therefore be seen as the means by which professional institutions of public accountants demonstrate the professionalism of their members by revealing the existence of an intellectual body of knowledge that appears to support their reporting practices. In a curious way, this supports the market-for-excuses thesis of Watts and Zimmerman (1986).

Conclusion and the future

FAT has a history of about one hundred and twenty-five years in the English-speaking world. It began with practitioners expressing concern about emerging issues in practice and continued with practitioners attempting to address practical problems by reference to theoretical notions. For example, Guthrie (1882) argued for consistency and Schipper (2003) declared consistency a primary reporting objective. At the end of the nineteenth century and beginning of the twentieth century, practitioners shaped FAT before giving way to ideas and arguments from academics. By mid-twentieth century, the latter were producing competing FAT. Inductive reasoning was overtaken by deduction. Purely accounting notions were supplemented and then driven by ideas from related disciplines.

In the early years of FAT, the inductive approach meant that practical applications became the subject of later theoretical definition and explanation. Occasionally in recent times, deductive arguments contributed to changes in practice, e.g. current cost accounting in the early 1980s and CFA since the 1980s. Only CFA, however, established a permanent position in practice. Thus, if FAT exists to improve practice, it does not appear to have done much after more than a century of individual and institutional effort. Despite a massive increase in detailed disclosure, the primary overall emphasis of the late nineteenth century remains that of 2008, i.e. accounting numbers representing income and financial position, and based on historical costs supplemented by market values. The relative emphasis has changed from a proprietary perspective concentrating on the financial position of owners to an entity perspective focusing on income or earnings. The most explicit theoretical switch has been to the user of financial statements, i.e. a consumer-orientated FAT highlighting information needs in decision situations. But the practical means of satisfying these needs has not changed in general terms over the years and the theory of satisfying user needs remains a relatively empty one when little or nothing is known about these needs in practice. Declaring decision usefulness as the primary reporting objective is a hollow gesture in such circumstances.

So what can be concluded from this review of the history of FAT? First, it has been a continuous, sustained, and long-term effort to improve the quality of financial reporting. Second, the search has involved practitioners and academics using inductive then deductive reasoning, and then back to inductive reasoning. Third, no theory has won out over others and, during the golden age of theory, theorists effectively competed with one another rather than changed practice. Fourth, despite their lack of influence on practice, individual theorists gained considerable reputations and their theories became so-called classics. Fifth, standard setters introduced FAT through their conceptual frameworks and standards and therefore, indirectly, to practice. No FAT has resulted in the formulation of general laws of practice. However, FAT has influenced the introduction of cash flows and fair values in reports. Finally, despite considerable cost and effort, individual theories have not been used by practitioners to do what theories should do, i.e. predict practice, produce testable hypotheses, and guide problem-solving.

This last point is a concern. Accountants appear to use FAT to demonstrate professional status to a wider world of users and regulators. FAT appears in the classroom but only as a separate topic from practice and typically at the end of a degree course before employment. Future practitioners do not learn about FAT as a basis to practice. It is therefore doubtful if problems in practice can be thought through from theoretical principles. In other words, the FAT contributions of writers such as Hatfield, Paton, Chambers, and Sterling can be argued to have had marginal impact on the general state of practice and education. This is not a healthy position to be in after more than a century of continuous effort with FAT.

What of the future of FAT? The history described here suggests there have been two types of theories and theorists. The first relates to individual attempts to rationalise, explain, and predict practice. These developed from inductive studies of practice to normative prescriptions that became competitive and were eventually proscribed as unscientific and replaced by empirical observations of practice. The result has been an overall lack of success in challenging problems associated with conventional practice. A question for the future is whether further normative or empirical studies will result in significant change to conventional practice. This review suggests a negative answer – unless there is a fundamental commitment by practitioners, managers, and regulators to such change. The second type of theory and theorist relates to institutional conceptual frameworks that appear to support and therefore perpetuate conventional practice. Again a question for the future is whether more tinkering with frameworks is likely to significantly change conventional practice. And, again, the answer appears to be negative unless there is a commitment to change. All of this suggests that FAT as the basis for improving practice may not be a viable project. Rather, FAT appears to be a will-o-the-wisp that attracts and seduces accountants from their primary task of finding accounting numbers that users can trust. The principal challenge for accountants, therefore, is deciding whether or not financial accounting is a practical function that can have a credible basis in theory. If it does not, then spending considerable cost and effort merely to enhance the reputation and social status of academics and practitioners seems to be a very dubious custom.

Key works

Cushing (1989) uses Kuhn's model of the evolution of scientific thought to explore the development of financial accounting paradigms, theories, and practice. Cushing argues that the dominant financial accounting paradigm is double-entry bookkeeping which is incapable of dealing with the challenges inherent in the search for FAT.

Gaffikin and Aitken (1982) reviews various attempts at FAT from 1907 to 1978. Each theory is examined through a contemporary book review and a biography of the author or authors. Gaffikin and Aitken argue the importance of the intellectual history of theories and their effectiveness in resolving problems.

Hines (1989) reviews several attempts at constructing FAT in the form of a conceptual framework. She examines the history of FAT to demonstrate how the need for it emerged from criticisms about practice. She further argues that conceptual frameworks should be interpreted as political claims to knowledge and therefore as part of the professional project of public accountants.

157

Lee (2006a) reviews the lack of achievement by accountants historically in improving the quality of corporate reports. In particular, he identifies the self-interest of key participants in the reporting function and the need for public accountants to be better educated in matters such as FAT.

Mouck (1992) examines the history of PAT and questions its success. He concludes it is a creation of its times and reflects dominant political and economic ideologies. This paper takes PAT and demonstrates its use historically as a resource in the argument for and support of a particular economic system.

References

AAA (1936) *A Tentative Statement of Accounting Principles Underlying Corporate Financial Statements* (New York: AAA).

AAA (1966) *A Statement of Basic Accounting Theory* (Evanston, IL: AAA).

AAA (1977) *Statement on Accounting Theory and Theory Acceptance* (Evanston, IL: AAA).

Accounting Standards Board (1999) *Statement of Principles for Financial Reporting* (London: Accounting Standards Board).

Accounting Standards Committee (1980) Current cost accounting, *Statement of Standard Accounting Practice 16* (London: Accounting Standards Committee).

Accounting Standards Steering Committee (1975) *The Corporate Report* (London: Institute of Chartered Accountants in England and Wales).

AIA (1931) *Accounting Terminology* (New York: AAA).

AICPA (1970) Basic concepts and accounting principles underlying financial statements of business enterprises, *Statement of Accounting Principles Board 4* (New York: AICPA).

AICPA (1971) *Establishing Financial Accounting Standards* (New York: AICPA).

AICPA (1973) *Objectives of Financial Statements* (New York: AICPA).

AICPA (1999) *Report of the Special Committee on Financial Reporting* (New York: AICPA).

Alexander, S. S., Bronfenbrenner, M., Fabricant, S. and Warburton, C. (1950) *Five Monographs on Business Income* (New York: AIA).

American Society of Certified Public Accountants (1929) Report of Committee on Technical Affairs, *Certified Public Accountant*, September: 293.

Arnold, J., Boyle, P., Carey, A., Cooper, M. and Wild, K. (1991) *The Future Shape of Financial Reports* (London: Institutes of Chartered Accountants in England and Wales and of Scotland).

Ball, R. and Brown, P. (1968) An empirical evaluation of accounting income numbers, *Journal of Accounting Research*, 6 (2): 159–78.

Baxter, W. T. (1975) *Accounting Values and Inflation* (New York: McGraw Hill).

Beaver, W. H. (2002) Perspectives on recent capital market research, *Accounting Review*, 77 (2): 453–74.

Brief, R. P. (1976) *The Late Nineteenth Century Debate over Depreciation, Capital, and Income* (New York: Arno Press).

Brief, R. P. (1980) *Dicksee's Contribution to Accounting Theory and Practice* (New York: Arno Press).

Brown, R. (1904) The form of revenue accounts and balance sheets, and the use of percentages in connection therewith, *Accountant's Magazine*, 8 (73): 145–64.

Bullen, H. G. and Crook, K. (2006) *A New Conceptual Framework Project* (Norwalk: CT: FASB).

Canning, J. B. (1929) *Economics of Accountancy: a Critical Analysis of Accounting Theory* (New York: Ronald Press).

Carey, J. (1969) The origins of modern financial accounting, *Journal of Accountancy*, 128 (3): 35–48.

Chambers, R. J. (1955) Blueprint for a theory of accounting, *Accounting Research*, 6 (1): 17–25.

Chambers, R. J. (1962) Towards a general theory of accounting, *Australian Society of Accountants Annual Lecture* (Adelaide: University of Adelaide Press).

Chambers, R. J. (1963) Book review, *Accounting Review*, 38 (4): 448–9.

Chambers, R. J. (1966) *Accounting, Evaluation, and Economic Behaviour* (Englewood Cliffs, NJ: Prentice Hall).

Chambers, R. J. and Dean, G. W. (1986) *Chambers on Accounting* (New York: Garland).

Clarke, F. L. (1976) A closer look at Sweeney's stabilized accounting proposals, *Accounting and Business Research*, 6 (24): 264–75.

Cooper, E. (1888) What is profit of a company? *Accountant*, 14 (727): 740–6.

Crosby, A. W. (1997) *The Measure of Reality: Quantification and Western Society, 1250–1600* (Cambridge: Cambridge University Press).

Cushing, B. E. (1989) A Kuhnian interpretation of the historical evolution of accounting, *Accounting Historians Journal*, 16 (2): 1–41.

DeMond, C. W. (1951) *Price, Waterhouse & Co in America: a History of a Public Accounting Firm* (New York: Comet Press for Price, Waterhouse).

Dickinson, A. L. (1906) Notes on some problems relating to the accounts of holding companies, *Journal of Accountancy*, 1 (6): 487–91.

Dicksee, L. R. (1893) Form of accounts and balance sheets, *Accountant*, 19 (988–9): 954–9, 973–81.

Dicksee, L. R. (1895) Profits available for dividends, in L. R. Dicksee *Four Lectures Delivered to the Institute of Chartered Accountants in England and Wales during the Years 1894 and 1895*, pp. 33–59 (London: Gee).

Dicksee, L. R. (1903a) The nature and limitations of accounts, *Accountant*, 29 (1478): 469–74.

Dicksee, L. R. (1903b) *Depreciation, Reserves, and Reserve Funds* (London: Gee).

Dicksee, L. R. and Tillyard, F. (1906) *Goodwill and its Treatment in Accounts* (London: Gee).

Edwards, E. O. and Bell, P. W. (1961) *The Theory and Measurement of Business Income* (Berkeley, CA: University of California Press).

Edwards, J. R. (1989) *A History of Financial Accounting* (London: Routledge).

FASB (1976) *Scope and Limitations of Conceptual Framework Project* (Stamford, CT: FASB).

FASB (1978) Objectives of financial reporting of business enterprises, *Statement of Financial Accounting Concepts 1* (Stamford, CT: FASB).

FASB (1979) Financial reporting and changing prices, *Statement of Financial Accounting Standards 33* (Stamford, CT: FASB).

FASB (2002a) *The Norwalk Agreement* (Norwalk, CT: FASB).

FASB (2002b) *Proposal for a Principles-Based Approach to US Standard Setting* (Norwalk, CT: FASB).

Fisher, I. (1906) *The Nature of Capital and Income* (New York: Macmillan).

Gaffikin, M. J. R. and Aitken, M. J. (1982) *The Development of Accounting Theory: Significant Contributors to Accounting Thought in the 20th Century* (New York: Garland Publishing).

Gilman, S. (1939) *Accounting Concepts of Profit* (New York: Ronald Press).

Grady, P. (1965) Inventory of generally accepted accounting principles for business enterprises, *Accounting Research Study 7* (New York: AICPA).

Greer, H. C. (1932) A council on accounting research, *Accounting Review*, 7 (3): 176–81.

Guthrie, E. (1882) The want of uniformity in accounts, *Accountant*, 8 (412): 8–13.

Hatfield, H. R. ([1909] 1927) *Modern Accounting: Its Principles and Some of Its Problems* (New York: D. Appleton).

Hines, R. D. (1989) Financial accounting knowledge, conceptual framework projects, and the social construction of the accounting profession, *Accounting, Auditing & Accountability Journal*, 2 (2): 72–92.

Hines, R. D. (1991) The FASB's conceptual framework, financial accounting and the maintenance of the social world, *Accounting, Organizations and Society*, 16 (4): 313–31.

Hopwood, A. G. (1983) On trying to study accounting in the contexts in which it operates, *Accounting, Organizations and Society*, 8 (2/3): 287–305.

IASB (2004) The effects of changes in foreign exchange rates, *International Accounting Standard 21* (London: IASB).

Ijiri, Y. (1967) *The Foundations of Accounting Measurement* (Englewood Cliffs, NJ: Prentice-Hall).

Ijiri, Y. (1975) Theory of accounting measurement, *Studies in Accounting Research 10* (Sarasota, FL: AAA).

Ijiri, Y. (1981) Historical cost accounting and its rationality, *Research Monograph 1* (Vancouver, BC: Canadian Certified General Accountants' Research Foundation).

Inanga, E. L. and Schneider, W. B. (2005) The failure of accounting research to improve accounting practice: a problem of theory and lack of communication, *Critical Perspectives on Accounting*, 16 (3): 227–48.

Inflation Accounting Committee (1975) *Inflation Accounting* (London: HMSO).

Jones, R. (1956) *Effects of Price Level Changes on Business Income, Capital, and Taxes* (Columbus, OH: AAA).

Kitchen, J. and Parker, R. H. (1980) *Accounting Thought and Education: Six English Pioneers* (London: Institute of Chartered Accountants in England and Wales).

Lawson, G. H. (1997) *Aspects of the Economic Implications of Accounting* (New York: Garland).

Lee, T. A. (1983) The early debate on financial and physical capital, *Accounting Historians Journal*, 10 (1): 25–50.

Lee, T. A. (1986) *Towards a Theory and Practice of Cash Flow Accounting* (New York: Garland Publishing).

Lee, T. A. (2006a) The war of the sidewardly mobile corporate financial report, *Critical Perspectives on Accounting*, 17 (4): 419–55.

Lee, T. A. (2006b) FASB and accounting for economic reality, *Accounting in the Public Interest*, 6: 1–21.

Lee, T. A. and Wolnizer, P. W. (1997) *The Quest for a Science of Accounting: an Anthology of the Research of Robert R Sterling* (New York: Garland).

Lisle, G. (1900) *Accounting in Theory and Practice* (Edinburgh: William Green).

Lisle, G. (1903) Foreign currencies and their treatment in home accounts, in G. Lisle (ed.) *Encyclopaedia of Accounting*, Vol. 3, pp. 88–96 (Edinburgh: William Green).

Littleton, A. C. (1953) *Structure of Accounting Theory* (Sarasota, FL: AAA).

McMonnies, P. (1988) *Making Corporate Reports Valuable* (Edinburgh: Institute of Chartered Accountants of Scotland).

MacNeal, K. F. (1939) *Truth in Accounting* (Philadelphia, PA: University of Philadelphia Press).

Macve, R. H. (1996) Pacioli's legacy, in T. A. Lee, A. G. Bishop and R. H. Parker (eds) *Accounting History from the Renaissance to the Present: A Remembrance of Luca Pacioli*, pp. 3–30 (New York: Garland Publishing).

Mattessich, R. V. (1964) *Accounting and Analytical Methods* (Homewood, IL: Richard D. Irwin).

Mattessich, R. V. (1991) Social reality and the measurement of its phenomena, *Advances in Accounting*, 8: 3–17.

Moonitz, M. (1961) The basic postulates of accounting, *Accounting Research Study 1* (New York: AICPA).

Mouck, T. (1992) The rhetoric of science and the rhetoric of revolt in the 'story' of positive accounting theory, *Accounting, Auditing & Accountability Journal*, 5 (4): 35–56.

Nelson, C. L. (1973) A priori research in accounting, in N. Dopuch and L. Revsine (eds) *Accounting Research 1960–1970: a Critical Evaluation*, pp. 3–19 (Urbana-Champagne, IL: University of Illinois).

Ohlson, J. A. (1995) Earnings, book values, and dividends in security valuation, *Contemporary Research in Accounting*, 11 (2): 661–87.

Ohlson, J. A. (2006) A practical model of earnings measurement, *Accounting Review*, 81 (1): 271–79.

Paton, W. A. (1922) *Accounting Theory, with Special Reference to the Corporate Enterprise* (New York: Ronald Press).

Paton, W. A. and Littleton, A. C. (1940) *An Introduction to Corporate Accounting Standards* (Evanston, IL: AAA).

Pixley, F. W. (1881) *Auditors: Their Duties and Responsibilities* (London: Effingham Wilson).

Sanders, T. H., Hatfield, H. R. and Moore, U. (1938) *A Statement of Accounting Principles* (New York: AIA).

Schipper, K. (2003) Principles-based accounting standards, *Accounting Horizons*, 17 (1): 61–72.

Scott, D.R. (1931) *The Cultural Significance of Accounts* (New York: Henry Holt).

Securities Exchange Commission (SEC) (2003) *Study Pursuant to Section 108 (d) of the Sarbanes–Oxley Act of 2002 on the Adoption of the United States Reporting System of a Principles-Based Accounting System* (Washington, DC: Securities Exchange Commission).

Solomons, D. (1966) Economic and accounting concepts of cost and value, in M. Backer (ed.) *Modern Accounting Theory*, pp. 117–40 (Englewood Cliffs, NJ: Prentice Hall).

Sprague, C. E. (1907) *The Philosophy of Accounts* (New York: Ronald Press).

Sprouse, R. T. and Moonitz, M. (1962) A tentative set of broad accounting principles for business enterprises, *Accounting Research Study 3* (New York: AICPA).

Sterling, R. R. (1970) *Theory of the Measurement of Enterprise Income* (Kansas, MO: University of Kansas Press).

Sterling, R. R. (1979) *Toward a Science of Accounting* (Houston, TX: Scholars Book Company).

Sterling, R. R. (1990) Positive accounting: an assessment, *Abacus*, 26 (2): 97–135.

Storey, R. K. and Storey, S. (1998) *The Framework of Financial Accounting Concepts and Standards* (Stamford, CT: FASB).

Study Group on Business Income (1952) *Changing Concepts of Business Income* (New York: AIA).

Sweeney, H. W. (1936) *Stabilized Accounting* (New York: Harper).

Tweedie, D. P. and Whittington, G. (1984) *The Debate on Inflation Accounting* (Cambridge: Cambridge University Press).

Vatter, W. (1947) *The Fund Theory of Accounting and its Implications for Financial Reports* (Chicago, IL: University of Chicago Press).

Watts, R. L. and Zimmerman, J. L. (1986) *Positive Accounting Theory* (Englewood Cliffs, NJ: Prentice-Hall).

Wells, M. C. (1976) A revolution in accounting thought? *Accounting Review*, 51 (3): 471–82.

Wyatt, A. (1991) The SEC says mark to market, *Accounting Horizons*, 5 (1): 80–4.

8

Financial accounting practice

Ciarán Ó hÓgartaigh

Overview

Hopwood remarks that:

> [T]he institutional and social aspects of financial accounting are still relatively unexplored. Compared with our insights into the economic theory of income calculation and the economic determinants and consequences of modes of corporate financial reporting, our knowledge of how forms of financial accounting emerge from, sustain and modify wider institutional and social structures is modest.
>
> (2000: 763)

This view of the history of accounting – and of accounting practice in particular – is increasingly prevalent (e.g. Burchell *et al.* 1980; Cooper and Sherer 1984; Tinker 1985): 'the technical practices of accounting must be understood, not as the expression of some transcendental rationality, but as reflection and reinforcement of social, political, and economic relationships' (Bryer 1993: 649).

Recognising that accounting is 'constitutive as well as reflective' (Napier 2006: 455), this chapter focuses specifically on the main issues and changes in financial accounting practice, as distinct from – but shaped by – financial accounting theory (Chapter 7) and financial accounting regulation (Chapter 14). On that basis, the chapter will set out the context and the content (and historical discontents) of financial accounting practice. The chapter will conclude with brief observations on continuity and change in financial statements since the mid-nineteenth century.[1]

The context of financial accounting practice

Agency theory and financial accounting practice

Defined conventionally, financial accounting has been widely characterised as an instrument of agency, a means of providing information to (primarily) external users. Within the accounting history literature, the existence and expansion of financial accounting have often been attributed to agency problems (e.g. de Roover 1938; Yamey 1960; Watts and Zimmerman 1983), through providing a mechanism for monitoring the actions of the agent (e.g. management) by the principal (e.g. shareholders and other users). This chapter employs agency theory as a useful lens through which to observe the contours of change in financial accounting practice. First, it limits the landscape by delineating the boundaries of several centuries of practice. Given that Chapter 5 deals in detail with bookkeeping, this chapter will begin by briefly exploring the relevant literature on the origins of final accounts and the preparation of certain forms of balance sheet, particularly in the late eighteenth and early nineteenth centuries. Second, an appropriately nuanced perspective of the landscape shaped by agency problems recognises that the essence of the principal–agent relationship is not constant but is one whose contours shift with changes in the relative importance of stakeholders and in the structures of capital markets.[2] Previts and Bricker (1994) and Bricker and Chandar (1998; 2000), for example, caution that conventional characterisations of historical principal–agent relationships are sometimes overly embedded in today's context. As reporting entities are financed in different ways and as societal expectations change, the composition of principals shifts, as does the motivation of agents.

Hence, while 'in the typical pre-industrial organization profit measurement . . . was rarely a priority' (Edwards 1989: 77), the increasing capital-intensiveness of commercial enterprise during and after the Industrial Revolution arguably (Sombart 1924; Yamey 1964; Bryer 2000a, 2000b; Napier 2006) nurtured the need for – and was facilitated by – improved accounting procedures. The demand for capital led to the expansion of new forms of industrial organisation, including partnerships and the joint stock and limited liability company, and a consequent need to measure and record profits to be divided between the partners and/or the investors. The emergence of the industrial organisation – and the corporate *persona* – also marked a transition from a proprietorship view of the firm to the entity view. This led to a significant shift in the practice of profit calculation, from a valuation approach to a matching approach manifest in the widespread adoption of depreciated historical cost (Hendriksen 1977; Edwards 1989). Later, the increasing complexity of forms of organisation and finance prompted the emergence of the concept of 'substance over form', manifest in accounting practices such as consolidated accounting.

New forms of business organisation extended the distance between principal and agent, rendering more acute the need for increased statutory protection of shareholders and other providers of finance (Storrar and Pratt 2000). Financial accounting, and periodic reporting, were employed as one of the mechanisms for monitoring management. In the UK, legislation from 1844 onwards initially required and subsequently shaped periodic reporting to shareholders (and others) through financial statements (e.g. Edwards 1981, 1986a, 1986b; Gilmore and Willmott 1992; Arnold and Matthews 2002). The impact and implications of these nineteenth and twentieth century legislative changes for financial accounting practice will be examined in this chapter.

While macro- and micro-economic failures gave an impetus to legislative change, company law was perceived as increasingly inadequate in responding to, and reflecting, the complexity faced by the modern corporation. As a consequence in the UK, the Accounting Standards Steering Committee (later renamed the Accounting Standards Committee – ASC) was formed in 1969 and, in the USA, the Financial Accounting Standards Board (FASB) in 1973. These issued accounting standards which increasingly codified, in particular, the meaning of the 'true and fair view' and 'generally accepted accounting principles' (GAAP). Towards the end of the twentieth century, the globalisation of capital markets had their most significant impact in accounting terms with the formation of the International Accounting Standards

Board (IASB) and the drive to develop a set of global accounting standards which would be acceptable internationally, particularly in the US (Cooke and Nobes 1997; Zeff 2002; see also Chapter 14).

Financial accounting practice prior to the Industrial Revolution

Early forms of financial accounting, which may be seen as serving a management accounting purpose (see Chapter 9), migrated into (external) financial reporting on the formation of the limited liability company and the obligation on directors to 'inform outside financial supporters of the states of the financial affairs of their companies from time to time' (Chambers 1987: 98). These tendencies in calculation revealed the basic financial information needs of owner-managers – position and performance – which were, through financial reporting, transmitted to external stakeholders and, through regulation and other influences, transfigured over time.

While, in the fifteenth and sixteenth centuries, most overseas trade was undertaken by 'merchants operating entirely on their own account, or with one or two partners, who were often related to them by blood or marriage' (Clay 1984: 191), the joint stock company emerged as a means of financing overseas exploration and trade in the mid-sixteenth century. The capital base of such trade was extended, representing a transfer of capital from the land to trade: it also extended the distance between those managing and financing those activities. While this did not yet give rise to a pervasive practice of financial accounting, it rendered necessary an increased accountability (Winjum 1971).

A case in point is the East India Company (EIC), a chartered company whose accounting practices are studied in some detail by Bryer (2000b) and others (for example, Baladouni 1981; Keay 1991). As it evolved, the EIC was increasingly financed by the merchant 'élite' and the 'generality' of investors. The EIC represented an opportunity for the élite to acquire commodities cheap to sell dear on their own account. For the generality, the EIC was simply a form of investment (Keay 1991). Baladouni (1981: 69) suggests that the accounting of the EIC does not constitute evidence of a widespread 'practice'. However, Bryer (2000b: 345) claims that it is indicative of a 'calculative mentality' and a function of an 'escalating conflict of interest between the generality and the merchant élite'. As a 'case study' of the development of accounting in the EIC from 1600 to 1657, Bryer describes two sets of accounts arising from the establishment of the *Lawes or Standing Orders of the East India Company* in 1621. These comprised the *Accompts Proper*, providing a summary of the Company's capital, and the *Accompts Currant*, detailing the movements on capital during the year. The EIC also produced 'financial statements' which were headed 'The Success of the Second Joynt Stock Briefly Valued'; the first surviving example was produced around 1640.

While Baladouni (1986: 28) suggests that the 'financial statements' of the EIC are not balance sheets and seem 'to be a product of an uncertain conceptual framework', the second surviving financial statement of the EIC, headed 'The Ballance of Estate of the 3d Joint Stock taken to the fine of April 1641 continued and encluding the Crispiana', comprises debit[or] and creditor balances. Yamey (1970: 73–4) describes the underlying technology of these accounts as precursors to 'what today we would call a balance sheet, a statement of the sources and uses of an entity's capital'. Early accounting reports such as those of the EIC may arguably be viewed as part of the lineage of more contemporary financial accounting practice even though the gait and guise of its accounting ancestors is markedly different. In particular, we can here trace the outline if not touch the flesh of modern financial accounting practice through the realisation of a need for the disclosure of a statement of position and financial flows.

The joint stock company became a vessel for financing endeavours such as overseas trade (e.g. the EIC), mining (e.g. Mines Royal and the Mineral and Battery Works) and public utilities (e.g. the New River Company). This form of incorporation led to the emergence of several corporate characteristics which are precursors of contemporary structures. For example, by 1630, the investors in the EIC began to invest on a time basis rather than in particular ventures: 'this marks the transition from adventurers jointly financing a stock of goods to investors holding shares in a company' (Edwards 1989: 94). By 1657, this concept was extended to the 'non-terminable stock'.

The Industrial Revolution and beyond

The late eighteenth and early nineteenth centuries saw increasing competition for capital among joint stock companies, fed by and feeding the Industrial Revolution (Davies 1952). A 'search for industrial accounting records' by Jones (1985: 8) reveals examples of the emergence of financial accounting by industrial companies in the context of 'Welsh industrial development, decay and redevelopment' between 1700 and 1830. While material on the early industrial context is relatively underexplored, Jones provides some detailed discussion on the development of accountability and reporting practices by Welsh industrial companies during this period.

In the USA, railroads gave an impetus to the development of financial markets. Railroads crisscross the course and discourse of financial accounting practice reflecting the extent to which they laid the sleepers of that practice particularly in areas such as fixed assets and accruals. They are generally viewed as pioneers in the development of US financial accounting practices (see Chapter 18). Previts and Merino (1998) attribute this to the different geographic as well as financial stretch of railroads *vis-à-vis*, for example, textiles (which constituted an important element of the Industrial Revolution). In the UK, in response to regulations, railway companies published standardised or uniform financial statements from 1868, a requirement which extended, for example, to life assurance companies (1870), gas companies (1871) and electric lighting companies (1882) with the objective of improving investor protection through increased comparability (Edwards 1989).

The development of the limited liability company and accompanying legislation, which initially required a balance sheet but not an income statement, privileged the balance sheet as 'the primary financial statement'. While the income statement became a matter of public record, with the growth of the railways in the nineteenth century (ibid.) and the need for the railways to report their performance to the providers of finance, in a world where firms operating in most industrial sectors were externally financed largely through bank lending, ability to pay as represented in the balance sheet remained a primary focus (Edey and Panitpakdi 1956).

The origins of the balance sheet – as information for creditors and an indication of ability to pay – shaped the valuation practices stitched into its fabric: 'essentially, asset valuation and income determination were based on an incomplete application of the going concern convention tempered by conservatism' (Storey 1959: 272). Early balance sheets were representations of the investment of the owner (Winjum 1970; Hendriksen 1977), being essentially at historical cost.

Accrual accounting became a cornerstone of accounting practice as 'operating continuity' (Chatfield 1996c: 24), going concern and income measurement gained in importance in the nineteenth century. Matching of revenues and expenses is at the heart of accrual accounting and this became increasingly significant with the advent of the limited liability company, the need for 'periodic reckonings as a prelude to dividend payments' and investors' eyes on the bottom line (Chatfield 1996c). Edwards (1989: 165) finds evidence of the use of 'partial accruals accounting' by railway companies in the mid-nineteenth century and comments that, elsewhere, accrual accounting was in widespread use at the time. While noting considerable variation in practice, he also identifies (ibid.: 171–2) 'stages' of accounting development whereby, between 1840 and the early 1900s, first, the railways and then public utilities more generally made a transition towards 'full' accruals accounting. Coombs and Edwards (1996: 53–9) find similar trends in the accounting practices of UK municipal corporations in the latter half of the nineteenth century. In the USA, accounting objections to cash-based tax laws in favour of the use of accrual accounting for tax purposes (Previts and Merino 1998: 181) suggests a widespread use of the latter by the beginning of the twentieth century. This in turn 'facilitated accounting obtaining an institutional status in society' (Takatera and Sawabe 2000: 790).

While the 'constitutive', 'disciplinary' influences of cost and management accounting have been actively explored throughout this and later periods (e.g. Hoskin and Macve 1986; Miller and O'Leary 1987), less critical attention has been paid to the manner in which financial accounting practices shaped managerial and societal behaviour. Nonetheless, the late nineteenth century marked the 'birth' of modern financial accounting, 'founded on the principles of cost-based accrual accounting and independent professional audits' (Bryer 1993: 649–50). Developments in the corporate form had profound implications for financial accounting practice. Echoing Yamey's (1970) invocation of agency problems as an impetus for accounting change in the late nineteenth century, Chandler (1977: 10) describes the emergence of the modern corporation in the USA thus: 'Ownership became widely scattered. The stockholders did not have the influence, knowledge, experience, or commitment to take part in the high command'. Bryer (1993: 650) challenges this unnuanced agency explanation of the development of 'modern financial reporting', arguing that 'an alternative explanation is suggested by Marx's view that the age of individual capitalists was rapidly closing, and the age of collective capitalism dawning'.

This period was marked by a *laissez-faire*[3] approach to accounting regulation. Several authors (e.g. Brief 1966; Chatfield 1977; Yamey 1977; Previts and Bricker 1994; Previts and Merino 1998) as a consequence suggest as Edwards concludes:

> [I]n these circumstances, management was free to choose, and in fact chose, the set of accounting principles and practices that had the highest utility, given the goals the organization was trying to achieve and the non-regulatory constraints under which it operated. One of these constraints was the requirement for shareholders and creditors to believe the content of published financial statements . . . The fact is that assets and profits were probably both under- and overstated at different times and in different places. This was a result of both error and systematic bias . . . The main causes of error and bias were the failure systematically (a) to distinguish between capital and revenue expenditure and (b) to allocate the original cost of fixed assets to expense.
>
> (1989: 109–10)

Although the reporting of a profit and loss account was not legally required in the UK until 1928, there is evidence that business entities, at least those which were large-scale, calculated profits (Edwards and Baber 1979; Edwards and Boyns 1992; Edwards *et al.* 1995) or produced a profit and loss account for shareholders prior to the late nineteenth century (Edey and Panikpandi 1956; Yamey 1960). Chatfield (1996b: 63) argues that, from the 1920s onwards in the USA, 'when stock [share] sales became the chief external source of funds, and stockholders became the primary readers of financial statements, the income statement became the more meaningful report'.

These trends have been traced to changes in the nature and context of the reporting entity over this period. First, the 'transition from venture to going concern' (Chatfield 1977: 98) marked the corresponding shift from the proprietorship view of the firm – which saw assets as the personal possessions of the owner – to the entity basis – which sees assets and liabilities as an integral part of the body corporate (Yamey 1964; Edwards 1989). The entity, and its assets and liabilities, had the potential to exist beyond the current owners and the assets and liabilities were not intended to be realised separately from the entity itself. The extension of the life of the corporation beyond the single venture and, more significantly, beyond the single reporting period gave rise to the problem of allocating the effects of transactions between consecutive accounting periods: Littleton (1933) and Thomas (1969, 1974) correctly characterise this 'allocation problem', arising from the need for 'periodic reporting', as the enduring challenge of financial accounting.

Second, the emergence of a 'corporate personality' separate and distinct from the owners (or indeed the managers) of the firm established its existence in space as well as in time: owners could (and would) come and go and the firm would continue in existence. Agency issues were, therefore, exacerbated as the involvement and interest of owners became increasingly distant and short-term. While management accounting was generally *of* management *for* management, financial accounting developed as information *of* management *for* others, bringing with it the need for monitoring through market, contractual and/or regulatory means.

Third, in practical terms, managers were motivated by the link between dividend distributions and realised profits. There was less motivation for asset revaluation in profit terms as unrealised profits were in practice not distributable: while it was not yet a legal requirement that dividends not be paid out of capital or unrealised profits, it was an increasing characteristic of articles of association (Weiner 1928; Yamey 1962). Finally, cost based valuation and its increased 'reliability' *vis-à-vis* non-transaction based valuations was also appealing to the newly professionalised accounting cadre of the late nineteenth century (Cowan 1965; Edwards 1989; Richard 2004).

The twentieth-century context

Focusing on the USA, Hendriksen comments that:

> the historical development of the corporation during the latter part of the 19th century and the early 20th century gave rise to new institutions and new relationships which were in turn to influence the development of accounting thought. Of these new developments, the more important include the development of the holding company as a common form of organisation, the formation of the New York Stock Exchange (NYSE), and the investment in American corporations by foreign investors and American investment abroad.
>
> (1977: 52)

Also in Britain, these characteristics suffused the accounting context of the twentieth century which was marked by increased levels of regulation and globalisation, accompanied by a growing emphasis on disclosure and on statements which reported the financial affairs of the economic – as well as the legal – entity. Further, an increase in mandatory forms of financial reporting was consistent with an ebb and flow of obligatory and voluntary disclosure, marked at the end of the twentieth century by a high tide of regulation. In particular, in the early 1970s, a new era of accounting standard-setting was introduced which is reflected in the structure of the discussion in this section.

The increased complexity of the organisational form meant that methods of group accounting (increasingly framed as consolidated financial statements), which were published voluntarily early on, became a more substantive part of the fabric of financial reporting as the century progressed. New forms of financial statements also emerged, such as the funds flow statement (which came and went), the cash flow statement, the statement of changes in equity and the value added statement. In the latter decades of the century, new largely unregulated-for forms of accounting – such as social and environmental accounting – reflected a broader conceptualisation of accountability and stewardship. Underlying all these changes were – and are – the prevalence and persistence of the balance sheet and income statement as the primary forms of financial reporting.

The presentation of a profit and loss account to shareholders was not legally required in Britain until the Companies Act, 1928 but 'was by no means unknown prior to that date' (Edwards 1989: 129). Similarly, in the USA, 'while income statements had long been included in the annual reports of railroads, the industrial trusts of the late 1800s and the very early 1900s rarely included income statements' (Vangermeersch 1996a: 317), but, in a context of increased equity financing, were thereafter increasingly evident in practice. In the USA, publication of the income statement was required by the Securities and Exchange Commission (SEC) from 1935, having been recommended in 1917 in *Uniform Accounting* (Vangermeersch 1996a).

Earnings and trends in earnings – as represented in the income statement – were 'of cardinal importance to investors' in their assessment of the reporting entity (American Institute of Accountants 1931: 3). Indeed, Vangermeersch (1979: 64) comments that the disclosure of earnings per share (EPS) was 'apparently a common practice in annual reports' between 1923 and 1959 (cf. Hendriksen 1977: 537). Previts and Merino (1998: 81) trace the beginnings of the disclosure of numbers such as EPS to the development of geographically dispersed sources of finance, and its subsequent importance reflects the increasing hegemony of capital markets in the twentieth century. Buckmaster (1992), invoking agency theory, traces the beginnings of earnings manipulation to the same circumstances.

The increased globalisation of financial structures and the growing dominion of equity markets gave weight to a shifting emphasis from the balance sheet (and ability to pay) to the income statement (and earnings capacity). The shift in focus from the balance sheet (and stewardship) to the income statement (and decision-making) was also reflected in preparer behaviour and a consequent movement in regulatory focus from 'secret reserves' in the early part of the century to 'earnings management' in the latter decades.

Twentieth-century practice prior to 1970

At the beginning of the twentieth century, the NYSE in particular mediated requirements with regard to the publication and presentation of financial statements in the USA. In 1900, it was agreed that all companies listed on the exchange would make statements of their 'financial condition and operating results' available to their stockholders; a requirement expanded to 'an annual financial report' in 1926 (Greidinger 1950). The principle of 'full disclosure' was also at the heart of the financial reporting reforms introduced by the SEC in the 1930s (May 1932; Moyer 1955; Previts and Merino 1998).

In the UK, 1900 marked, 'after a long period of "non-interference" in accounting matters, a decisive step towards the detailed regulation with which we are now familiar' (Edey and Panitpakdi 1956: 356).[4] The Companies Act, 1900 (re)introduced the requirement for an external audit for registered companies. Although it did not contain an explicit requirement for companies to prepare and make public a balance sheet, that requirement was implicitly contained in section 23 which placed a duty on auditors to report to shareholders on every balance sheet laid before the company. The Companies Act, 1907 added the requirement to prepare and publish a balance sheet − but not a profit and loss account − and also introduced the 'minimum disclosure' principle (a tendency extended in 1928, 1948, 1967 and 1976) requiring a minimum level of disclosure which the directors 'are at liberty to exceed' (Edwards 1981: 3). From the beginning of the twentieth century, stock exchange requirements stipulated that quoted companies make their financial statements available to shareholders.

The holding company, the economic entity and consolidated financial statements

The development of the holding company gave rise to the need in practice for group accounts, presenting the performance and position of the group as a whole as well as that of the holding company, further reflecting the trend towards supplementary disclosure (Edwards and Webb 1984). Peloubet (1955) traces the first US consolidated accounts to 1886, although he comments that they were not in 'common usage' until the first decade of the twentieth century. Greidinger (1950) and Hendriksen (1977) credit the more widespread promulgation of consolidated financial statements to the initiative of the US Steel Corporation in 1901: 'it has also been hailed as the first really modern type of annual report which attempted to provide adequate financial information to stockholders' (Hendriksen 1977: 53).

Bircher (1988: 5) finds a 'relatively low' rate of adoption of consolidated accounting in the UK prior to the Companies Act 1948. Edwards and Webb (1984) find evidence for the use of consolidated accounts in the UK before the First World War, although the most publicised early application of the technique was by ICI (then Nobel Industries) in the early 1920s and Dunlop in the early 1930s (Kitchen 1972; Parker 1977). Commenting that the 'preparation of an aggregate statement of assets and liabilities for the group' was 'apparently the [group] reporting method favoured by British accountants in the early 1920s', Edwards and Webb (1984: 47) conclude that 'experimentation' with the introduction of consolidated accounts in the UK began in 1910 'but that the pace of adoption was slow' and certainly slower than in the USA. They posit several reasons for this, including the fact that 'during this period secret reserves, as a means of fostering financial stability, were highly regarded' (ibid.: 44).

From 'secret reserves' to 'earnings manipulation'

Clare (1945), Hawkins (1963) and Previts and Bricker (1994) also associate the early twentieth century with a culture of secrecy in the USA and a characterisation of corporate publicity as conducting business with 'glass pockets' (Chandler and Tedlow 1985). In the first decade of the twentieth century, much of the financing for corporate growth was provided through 'money trusts' which were the subject of several public hearings, including the Pujo Committee 'Money Trust' Hearings. The money trusts were closely associated with a series of mergers between 1898 and 1903, termed by Sobel (1965) the 'Morganisation of America'. One consequence of this trend, according to Previts and Merino (1998: 222), was that 'financial capitalists, not accountants, led the drive for consolidated statements'. Another was the prevalence of 'secret reserves' (Joplin 1914; Marriner 1980; Lister 1981; Edwards and Boyns 1994). The development of these practices provoked much debate in the USA (e.g. Montgomery 1912; Paton and Stevenson 1918) even prior to the publication in 1917 of *Uniform Accounting. Uniform*

Accounting was a symptom of an increasing propensity to view uniformity – or consistency – as a cure-all for the ills of accounting practice (Merino and Coe 1978; Chatfield 1996a).

The Stock Market Crash of 1929, the subsequent passing of the Securities Acts, 1933 and 1934 and the consequent establishment of the SEC, changed the face of accounting practice in the USA. By the end of the 1930s, the income statement had become the 'focal point' of US accounting practice, based on the widely held view that investors were interested in 'future income' as well as an acceptance of the 'entity concept' of the firm (Previts and Merino 1998: 278, 283; Husband 1938). This development also reflected the growing primacy of equity markets – and of shareholders – as providers of finance, which Chatfield (1996b) partly attributes to the retreat from commercial lending in the USA as a result of the collapse of inventory prices in 1920–21 and 'mass marketing of stock issues' in the 1920s.

Once again, however, the history of financial accounting practice was marked by an exogenous change prompted by accounting failures (see Chapter 19). In the USA, the McKesson-Robbins case reflected 'certain fundamental weaknesses in the preparation of financial statements by large corporations' (Bennett 1939: 14). Similarly, in the UK, *Rex v. Kyslant* – the Royal Mail case – of 1931 (Davies and Bourn 1972) prompted a voluntary 'general raising of financial reporting standards during the 1930s' (Edwards 1989: 155). In both the UK and the USA, several companies appeared to take a lead in pushing forward the boundaries of disclosure, including for example, Unilever (Camfferman and Zeff 2003) and US Steel (Greidinger 1950; Hendriksen 1977).

Levels of inflation in the real economy during the Second World War saw certain firms mount challenges to conventional practices. US Steel attempted unsuccessfully to value its plant at depreciated replacement cost (Previts and Merino 1998). In the same period, Chrysler adopted accelerated depreciation which, it argued, approximated replacement cost (May 1949). However, this did not shake the resolve of the SEC or the Committee on Accounting Procedure that income be presented as 'an accurate historical record' (SEC 1945). An increasing level of debate regarding income measurement and the development of normative theories of accounting contributed to criticism of the Committee on Accounting Procedure, particularly on the grounds that its accounting standards drew inordinately on existing practice (Spacek 1956; Briloff 1964; Chambers 1973).

In the UK, while a series of 29 non-mandatory Recommendations issued by the ICAEW between 1942 and 1969 are thought to have significantly improved financial reporting practices (Zeff 1972), they were effectively *laissez-faire* and proved acceptable to preparers largely because of their flexibility; a position reflected in the debate in 1968 on the ills of financial accounting practice between Professor Edward Stamp and Sir Ronald Leach, then President of the ICAEW (Stamp and Marley 1970; Leach 1981; Singleton-Green 1990). This debate in part represented a discourse between theoretically grounded accounting principles and the pragmatism of the profession. In both jurisdictions, the interplays of theory and practice signified the hegemony of accounting practice and served as a signal to contemporary and future standard setters of the wisdom of an evolutionary development of financial reporting (see Accounting Standards Board (ASB) 1990: para 7). As a consequence, accounting practice did not change radically in this period and, to the extent that change did occur, it was again largely though not exclusively as a necessity arising from accounting and corporate failure.

The 1960s was a decade of considerable economic growth globally. The failure in the USA to narrow the options permitted by accounting standards and, therefore, to limit earnings manipulation and diverse accounting practices, was exposed particularly in the context of accounting for mergers and consolidations (Kripke 1970; Briloff and Engler 1979). Lenders also voiced concerns that the balance sheet – with its emphasis on conservative valuations – did not give a basis for the estimation of future cash flows and that financial statements in general – with the flexibility embedded in permissible accounting practice – did not allow for comparability (Laeri 1966).

Similarly, in the UK, the GEC–AEI takeover battle of 1968 revealed another symptom of the ills of flexibility in accounting practice, as more conservative valuations of AEI assets after the takeover transformed a forecast profit of £10 million into a reported loss of £4.5 million, with much of the discrepancy attributable to differing applications of GAAP. Further evidence of the imprecision of UK GAAP followed in 1969 with revelations surrounding Rolls-Royce and the Leasco-Pergamon affair (Tweedie and Whittington 1984; Whittington 1989; Napier and Noke 1992). As in the USA, public concern was fuelled by press comment (see Stamp and Marley 1970; Stamp 1984) and, in both jurisdictions, concerns led to the establishment of new accounting standard-setting infrastructures which shaped accounting practice from the 1970s onwards.

Financial accounting practice in the 'new era' of standard setting post-1970

After a period of 'complacency' concerning accounting practice (Napier and Noke 1992) and precipitated by public pressure (Edwards 1989), the ASC was formed in the UK in 1969[5] and the FASB in the USA in 1973. There followed a 'new era' in accounting standard setting which saw an increased emphasis on the provision of accounting information for decision-making (Leach 1981; Olson 1982; Street 1996). A period of codification also followed which once again extended the scope of disclosure without radically altering the fundamental shape of financial statements (Power 1990).

Other forms of financial statements

One of the extensions to disclosure related to segment reporting. The preparation of consolidated financial statements resulted in the aggregation in financial statements of elements of financial performance and position which had differing risk profiles. Given that mergers and acquisition were often motivated by a desire for diversification, consolidated financial statements masked that diversity by reporting a single consolidated balance sheet and income statement. As a consequence, the need for better analysis of these conglomerations led to a desire for disaggregated data and the reporting of segment information (see, for example, Mautz 1967a, 1967b, 1967c; Sommer 1967; Schachner 1968). These disclosures had existed in Sweden since the Swedish Stock Incorporation Act of 1944 and were first required in the UK by the Companies Act, 1967 (Walker 1968). The requirement for segmental reporting in registration statements in the US was first promulgated by the SEC in 1969 and extended to all annual reports filed with the SEC in 1974 (Hendriksen 1977).

Likewise, the statement of sources and applications of funds (or 'funds flow statement') came into common use in the USA (Käfer and Zimmerman 1967; Roberts and Gabhart 1972), Germany (Haller and Jakoby 1995), Japan (Nissan et al. 1995) and elsewhere, before being required by regulation, for example, in the USA in 1969 and in the UK in 1976, and being introduced as an option in France in 1982 (Boussard and Colasse 1992). Käfer and Zimmerman (1967: 89), reviewing the early development of funds flow statements, describe the statement as a 'supplement to the two traditional financial statements', representing a link between the opening and closing balance sheets and, in particular, identifying working capital as a key flow in the business. However, the failure of the funds flow statement to alert readers to large financial failures such as Penn Central (1969), WT Grant (1976) and, later, Coloroll (1990) highlighted the statement's limitations (Smith 1992) and, on the basis that cash is a better representation of financial health, led to the development of the cash flow statement as a 'primary financial statement' (ASB 1991) framed by the ASB as a 'radical change in financial reporting' (ASB 1996a: para. 4).

Asset valuation practices and the fragile persistence of historical cost

The boundaries of accounting practice – and the choices between revolutionary and evolutionary change – were also tested in the discussions regarding inflation accounting which were played out again when general price changes had significant single-period economic effects in the 1970s. In 1979 when inflation in the USA reached 13 per cent, the FASB issued FASB Statement (FAS 33) requiring supplemental price-level adjusted and current cost disclosures (replacing its earlier replacement cost approach) until it was rescinded in 1986 as inflation rates declined. Inflation rates in the UK resulted in efforts to introduce inflation-adjusted accounting, through Provisional Statement on Standard Accounting Practice 7, and, subsequently, current cost accounting through Statement on Standard Accounting Practice (SSAP) 16 (Sandilands 1975; Stamp and Mason 1977). Hanson (1989) provides *inter alia* a useful survey of the number of UK companies producing 'price-level statements' between 1977 and 1988: the percentage of such firms peaked at 95 per cent in 1981, falling to 3 per cent in 1987 as inflation abated. Pong and Whittington conclude:

> the dramatic collapse in support for CCA [Current Cost Accounting] demonstrates that, however compelling the theoretical case for a particular accounting practice or reform, it will not be followed, in the absence of legal compulsion, if preparers of accounts do not regard it as being in their economic interests.
>
> (1996: 51)

The limited life of these accounting practices, as well as their supplemental nature, did not therefore mark a substantive change in financial reporting practice, but did further reflect a trend towards the extension of disclosures as a means of mitigating the limitations of prevailing recognition and measurement practices.

Globalisation and accounting practice

The increased globalisation of the world economy – and of capital markets in particular – from the 1960s onwards shaped developments in financial accounting practice. This initially manifested itself in the desire by the European Union (EU) to facilitate free movement of capital within the EU and led to early efforts at international harmonisation of accounting practices by way of European Directives (Defliese 1981). In an attempt to enhance international comparability, a particular legacy of the Fourth EC Directive was standardisation of the format of financial statements of member states, introduced in the UK for example by the Companies Act, 1981. This was the culmination of a debate on a standardised presentation that ebbed and flowed since the formation of the limited liability company in the UK and whose trackbed had been laid by the railway companies over a century earlier (Edwards 1989).

The Fourth Directive was a product of compromise, particularly as it allowed options in asset valuation and as the interpretation of 'the true and fair view' enshrined in the Directive varied across jurisdictions. This facilitated the consensus which gave it life in the short-term but also sowed the seeds of its failure (Freedman and Power 1992). However, the diversity of European accounting traditions signified in the Directive broadened the canvass of European accounting practices (Mueller *et al.* 1997; Nobes and Parker 2006).

Historically, European countries placed contrasting emphases on different 'users' of financial statements – in agency terms, different 'principals' – for example, the state sector in France, financial institutions in Germany and the public good in Scandinavia. This generated a variety of accounting practices including, for example, the *plan comptable* in France, differing valuation and reserve accounting practices in Germany and the more sophisticated accounting technologies of Scandinavian companies such as Skandia and Nokia (Walton 2006). While there is archival evidence of corporate social reporting in the financial statements of, for example, US Steel (Hogner 1982) and the UK steel company Hadfields (Maltby 2004), globalising entities such as Skandia and Nokia brought with them local reporting traditions which reflected a wider set of value choices than those of capital markets, and validated a wider set of users of financial statements than shareholders. The history and implications of these reporting practices are considered in, for example, Hogner (1982), Lewis *et al.* (1984), Guthrie and Parker (1989, 1990), Carroll (1999) and Maltby (2004).

Throughout the twentieth century, in particular in the USA and in the UK, capital markets played an increasingly important role in providing finance. More frequent (quarterly) periodic reporting placed increased demands on financial accounting and provided further impetus for earnings management (e.g. Healy and Wahlen 1999; Dechow and Skinner 2000), creative accounting (Griffiths 1986; Smith 1992) and 'exceptional innovation' in financial reporting in the UK and elsewhere (Tweedie and Whittington 1990: 87). These demands were fed in the late twentieth century by the 'irrational exuberance' (Greenspan 1996; Shiller 2000) associated with technology stocks, accompanied by increasingly aggressive incidences of revenue recognition. Other practices peculiar to particular sectors also emerged within, for example, financial services and exploration. Many of these sectoral practices may be traced through historical seams (see in banking, e.g. Capie and Billings 2001; and in exploration and mining, e.g. Edwards and Boyns 1994). Moreover, many of the accounting practices developed historically in these sectors – such as mark-to-market accounting in banking – spilled over into other sectors – such as energy trading – with differing and sometimes detrimental consequences (Baker and Hayes 2004; Eichenwald 2005; Stewart 2006).

Earnings management and the 'relevance' of financial accounting

Healy and Wahlen (1999), in a review of the earnings management literature, conclude that while such financial accounting practices were (and are) motivated by capital market, contractual and regulatory considerations, the extant research provides little evidence of the extent and scope of earnings management in the latter half of the twentieth century. The chronicle of financial accounting suggests that such practices are not new: Edwards (1989: 143) contends that 'Accounting history is littered with examples of financial information used a means of deception'. Dicksee (1927) discusses 'window dressing' and Samson *et al.* (2003) provide specific, firm-level historical examples of creative accounting (see also Chapter 19).

The turn of the millennium also saw discussion regarding the relevance of financial accounting practice to ordinary shareholders (Lev and Zarowin 1999; Levitt and Dwyer 2002) with arguments supporting the decision-usefulness of financial accounting information (e.g. Francis *et al.* 2002) drawing sustenance from the extended disclosures in financial statements, consistent with historical trends.

Whereas the income statement – and the presentation of financial performance – were perceived as a vital element of financial accounting throughout the twentieth century, income measurement – linked to valuation – was and is one of the intractable problems in financial accounting theory and practice (Sweeney 1936; Solomons 1961; Hendriksen 1977). While the

173

completed cycles of early trading ventures rendered the calculation of profit relatively easy, if unsophisticated, the need to allocate revenues and expenses between accounting periods and to value assets and liabilities at the end of an accounting period raised problems – Thomas's (1969) 'allocation problem' – which continue to the present day (Lee 1979; Tweedie and Whittington 1990).

The implications of these controversies and 'discontents' for the recognition and measurement of the elements of financial statements – assets and liabilities in particular – are explored in the next section.

The contents and historical discontents of financial accounting practice

Property, plant and equipment

Issues in practice regarding the treatment of property, plant and equipment extend from, in the railway age, the recognition/capitalisation of repairs, renewals and maintenance costs (Pollins 1956; Edwards 1986c; Glynn 1984) to the capitalisation of borrowing costs (discussed in the context of the nineteenth century by Ladelle 1890; Brief 1969). However, the 'pervasive' problem in the practice of accounting for property, plant and equipment is the question of valuation (Tweedie and Whittington 1990). Brief (1966: 3) asserts that 'Historically, permanent enterprise [such as railroads and utilities] practiced some form of cash accounting and determined profit by matching receipts and disbursements', and that

> [the] shortcomings [of this approach] became apparent at an early date and some railroads began periodically to record depreciation in the accounts. However, the attempt to record regular provisions for depreciation did not persist over time, and most railroads began to practice replacement cost accounting, which is a modification of strict cash accounting.
>
> (Brief 1966: 4)

Capital investment by the railroad companies and other capital-intensive enterprises exposed the soft underbelly of unadjusted historical cost accounting (Pollins 1956; Brief 1966; Kitchen 1979; Glynn 1984). Dicksee was critical of the absence of a depreciation charge: assets should be valued 'as a going concern' (1902: 180–1), meaning 'at such value as they would stand in the books if proper depreciation had been provided for' (see also Kitchen 1980; Brief 1966). The perpetual life of the corporate entity also ruled out the use of exit values as fixed assets were to be used in the business and not sold at a profit: 'there being no intention to sell such assets, fluctuations in their market prices could not be considered gains or losses. Long-term assets should be valued at acquisition cost less depreciation' (Chatfield 1996c: 256). Edwards (1989: 122–4) characterises this period as 'the coming of age' of depreciation. While depreciation was not statutorily required, in the face of increasing criticism regarding inflated profits and inadequate retentions against future acquisitions of fixed assets, 'the practice of charging depreciation gained in popularity' in the early twentieth century (Edwards 1989: 124).

While a consistent cause of debate, historical cost has proved, in practice, an unshakeable foundation for financial reporting in the USA (Walker 1992), whereas in the UK, inflation levels in the 1950s and 1960s encouraged British companies to 'experiment' with a 'variety of *ad hoc* adjustments designed to take account of changing prices' (Edwards 1989: 252; see also Noguchi and Edwards 2004). More recently, on the issue of FRS 15 entitled *Tangible Fixed*

Assets, the ASB noted that 'in the past, companies have taken advantage of the alternative accounting rules in the Companies Act, 1985 to revalue selected tangible fixed assets (usually properties) as and when it has suited them to do so' (ASB 1999). In a further, contemporary indication of the hegemony of practice over theory, FRS 15 does not require the recognition of fixed assets at a revalued amount (unless there is impairment) but, where a policy of remeasurement is adopted, carrying values should be kept up to date.

Financial fixed assets

In the case of financial fixed assets, Edwards (1989: 135–6) comments that iron and steel was one of the first industries in the UK where companies invested in the shares of other companies and that, in the early decades of the twentieth century, 'trade investments' were reported 'at cost', 'at cost less amount written off', 'at under cost' and 'at cost less depreciation'. The separate disclosure of shares in and amounts due to and from subsidiaries was first required by the Companies Act, 1928. Vangermeersch, in his survey of US reporting practices since 1861, finds (1979: 8 and 72) that 'there have been many valuation bases for marketable securities', including cost, 'cost or less', market value, lower of cost or market value, estimated realisable value and 'market value or less'. A logical extension of the valuation of assets on a 'going concern' basis was that financial fixed assets – intended for realisation – be valued at realisable values. The history of the use of current values in accounting – particularly with respect to marketable financial instruments but also in times of inflation accounting – is explored in, for example, Boer (1966) and Tweedie and Whittington (1984). More recently, fair value 'has entered certain accounting standards [e.g. FAS 115 and 133 in the USA and IAS 39 in international standards] as a response to needs, on a standard-by-standard basis rather than as a result of a formal amendment to conceptual frameworks' (van Zijl and Whittington 2006: 122).

Intangible assets

Yang (1927: 19) argues that, when balance sheets were primarily used by financial institutions to assess ability to pay and collateral, intangible assets were 'ordinarily looked upon with considerable disfavour, particularly by bankers, because they have been subject to manipulations of value to such a degree that they have become more or less a nuisance'. While there is evidence of capitalisation and amortisation of patents in the early twentieth century (Montgomery 1912; Yang 1927; Vangermeersch 1979), the capitalisation of research and development costs remained a matter of contention (Bierman and Dukes 1975; Hope and Gray 1982; Gray 1986). Following the introduction of regulations, in the USA (FASB Statement No. 2, 1974) such expenditures were written off as incurred while, in the UK (through SSAP 13 *Accounting for Research and Development*, 1977), development costs could be capitalised if they met specified criteria.

Problems regarding the elusive and inexclusive nature of intangibles materialised early on, particularly in the case of goodwill where, in the fifteenth and sixteenth centuries, 'the sale of goodwill ran afoul of then-existing "restraint of trade" doctrines' (Hughes 1996: 281). However, in partnerships, the transferability of goodwill on the death or retirement of a partner led to nineteenth-century discussion regarding its valuation (Veblen 1908; Hughes 1996). The increasingly corporate focus of accounting – and rising number of mergers and acquisitions – drew attention away from goodwill in partnerships and towards the recognition and measurement of purchased goodwill in corporate financial statements.

In the USA, different accounting treatments of goodwill 'proliferated' prior to 1929 and 'its financial-statement presentation was also a matter of some flexibility' (Hughes 1996: 282).

Following the Stock Market Crash of 1929, conservatism intervened, and all treatments other than the recording of goodwill at cost disappeared and immediate write-off was viewed as good practice (Hughes 1996). In 1944, Accounting Research Bulletin (ARB) No. 24 *Accounting for Intangible Assets* drew two distinctions: one between purchased intangibles (which could be capitalised) and non-purchased intangibles (where the related expenditures were to be written off), the other between purchased intangible assets with a limited life and those with a permanent life. ARB 24 gave equal weight to permanent retention and systematic write-off of purchased goodwill and discouraged discretionary write-offs (Committee on Accounting Procedure 1944). ARB No. 43 – issued in 1953 – indicated a preference for systematic amortisation. By 1970, this requirement was further refined by the Accounting Principles Board (APB) in APB No. 17 *Intangible Assets*, which required the amortisation of purchased goodwill over a period not exceeding 40 years.

Around the same time in the UK, Lee (1971, 1973, 1974) reviewed the accounting treatment of goodwill by 66 companies. Characterising accounting for goodwill as 'will o' the wisp accounting' (1971), he found a wide variety of accounting practices including capitalisation with and without amortisation and write-off to reserves. This dichotomy in accounting treatments – capitalisation or write-off to reserves – continued into the 1980s in the UK, and was preserved by the ASC's first standard on the subject, SSAP 22 *Accounting for Goodwill*. Write-off to reserves was permitted probably because it was favoured business practice at the time (Tonkin and Skerratt 1991) – writing off goodwill in this manner by-passed the income statement and left reported earnings and EPS unaffected. The permitted flexibility reflected the ASC's declining authority following, for example, its failure to devise a system of price-level accounting that garnered sufficient support from government, professional accountants, and the business community (Pong and Whittington 1996). More recently, the capitalisation of purchased goodwill has been the trend in international accounting standards with annual impairment reviews replacing amortisation (international accounting standards on intangible assets, 1998, 2004), a treatment proposed by Montgomery (1912) at the beginning of the twentieth century.

Current assets

It has been argued that, prior to the emergence of the corporate entity and the consequent development of the need for periodic reporting, inventories were measured in quantity not value (Vangermeersch 1996b) or, indeed, were not measured at all given that their measurement remained irrelevant to the merchant who monitored profit or loss on a venture-by-venture basis (de Roover 1956). However, there is growing evidence that inventory was often the subject of financial measurement though methods of recognition varied considerably before, during and after the Industrial Revolution (Fleischman and Parker 1990).

The adoption of the practice of valuing inventories at the lower of cost or market value, as enunciated by Montgomery (1912), is attributed to a variety of factors (which are not mutually exclusive). Storey (1959: 235) suggests that, while the valuation of fixed assets was set down by legislation, 'the law [in the US] apparently made no stipulation as to the valuation of current floating assets'. He believes that the valuation of inventories at the 'lower of cost or market' was the logical extension of the going concern concept. Parker (1965) suggests that the adoption of the lower of cost or market in the UK was the product of an accounting profession which expanded, during the nineteenth century, on the back of liquidation and bankruptcy work at a time of falling prices. By the second decade of the twentieth century, the practice of valuing inventories at the lower of cost and market value appears to have been widely accepted (Gilman 1939; Littleton 1941), although Edwards (1989: 137) remarks that it was 'not uncommon' before the First World War to value inventories 'well below cost' to create secret reserves and, one might imagine, help smooth reported profit. This treatment 'came under attack' by the issuance of Inland Revenue guidance in 1919 that inventory be valued at the lower of cost or market price.

Methods of calculating cost varied and were undoubtedly influenced by developments in cost accounting. 'Base stock', whereby the reporting entity would specify a portion of its inventory as the minimum required for the business to continue in operation, 'apparently originated in Britain during the nineteenth century . . . mainly in the metals trades and the textile industry' but was phased out by taxation and legal pronouncements in the UK (1919) and the USA (1919 and 1930) (Chatfield 1996d: 68). The last-in first-out (LIFO) method emerged in the USA in the 1930s, largely for tax reasons; its use was sanctioned by the 1938 Revenue Act (Davis and Strawser 1996) and continued to be used on a 'widespread' basis (Davis 1982; Lee and Hsieh 1985). In contrast, the tax authorities in the UK disallowed the use of LIFO accounting and FIFO or average cost became the normal practice and was institutionalised by the ASC in SSAP 9 *Stocks and Long-term Contracts*.

The practice of accounting for receivables and the recognition of provisions for bad debts sometimes also followed conservative principles. While there is some evidence of accounting for bad debts in early accounts:

> After 1850, pressures for consistency in bad debt accounting came from three sources: the companies acts, the courts and the accounting profession. The Companies Act of 1855–6 contained a model balance sheet, which included a space for 'debts considered doubtful and bad'. This suggests that the preferred practice, if not the common practice, favoured making provision for doubtful accounts.
>
> (Chatfield 1996e: 58–9)

The judgement at the heart of doubtful debt calculations left considerable scope for variety in practice. The recognition of write-offs for taxation purposes, in the early twentieth century, 'did most to standardise the accounting treatment of bad debts' (ibid.: 59).

Liabilities

With the increasing complexity of business transactions and the changing nature of business financing, the recognition and measurement of liabilities in financial statements posed commensurate challenges in practice. The overstatement of liabilities through the creation of secret reserves (Edwards 1981, 1989; Arnold 1996), and over-enthusiastic applications of conservatism to asset valuation (Sterling 1967; Hendriksen 1977) was subtly mitigated by regulatory change throughout the twentieth century. In the USA, consistent with the notion that the conservative recognition of provisions was a cushion against uncertainty, a practice emerged during the Second World War of recognising special contingency reserves (ARB No. 13). ARB No. 28 (1948), which outlawed the utilisation of such reserves in determining net income, marked the beginning of a series of accounting regulations reining in the overzealous recognition of contingencies (US: ARB No. 50, Statement of Financial Accounting Standards (SFAS) No. 5, SFAS No. 105 – UK: SSAP 18, FRS 12). Turning to the UK, when issuing FRS 12, the ASB (1996b, Appendix VII, para. 3) noted that:

> in the absence of an accounting standard on provisions the practice has grown up of aggregating liabilities with expected liabilities of future years, and sometimes even with

expected expenditures related to ongoing operations, in one large provision, often reported as an exceptional item.[6]

Over time, accruals, liabilities and other obligations became the unsecure territory in which contrasting conceptualisations of income and the balance sheet were pragmatically played out in practice. Hendriksen (1977: 446) comments disapprovingly that 'traditionally . . . the recording of liabilities has been closely interrelated to the matching of expenses and related revenue' (the income approach) as opposed to recognition and measurement which would 'permit economic and financial interpretation' (the balance sheet or 'liability' approach). The matching concept shaped recognition practices with respect to provisions generally as well as in specific instances, before a renewed focus on the balance sheet shifted the emphasis towards a 'liability' approach.

For example, while Vangermeersch (1979: 63, 97) finds some evidence that deferred taxation was recognised in the USA from the early 1960s, with a majority of the companies in his sample employing the deferred method, Johnson (1996) argues that the preferred accounting for deferred taxation varied depending on the balance of emphases placed by the regulators on the income statement compared with the balance sheet. Between 1967 and 1987, APB No. 11 – emphasising the income statement and the matching concept – required 'the deferred method of comprehensive interperiod tax allocation . . . resulting in virtual permanent deferrals of reversing differences' (ibid.: 190). A revision in 1987 (further revised in 1992) of this accounting treatment required the use of the liability method, with an asset and liability orientation for the financial reporting of income taxes in 1987 and 1992 (FASB Statement Nos 96 and 102). A similar approach, described as 'pragmatic' by Edwards (1989: 249), was adopted in the UK. The short-lived SSAP 11 allowed for the use of either the deferral or liability methods before SSAP 15 required the liability method with partial provision, amended to full provision by the ASB in FRS 19, reflecting trends towards international harmonisation.

The accounting treatment of pensions is also a site for conflict between recognising pension obligations in the balance sheet and matching (smoothing) pension costs in the income statement (Hendriksen 1977: 478–9). Baker (1964: 52) writes that, in the USA, 'by and large the very early industrial plans recognised pension costs on a pay-as-you-go basis or cash disbursement basis', as 'continuing pension payments were predicated upon the financial ability of the company to maintain such payments'. However, in the early 1920s, 'using actuarial procedures some companies made financial provisions through balance sheet reserves, some made financial provisions through the facilities of an insurance company, still others used the pension trust to reduce the financial outlay of growing pension requirements'. These variations in practice were reflected in ARB No 47 (Baker 1964) and, to a certain extent, shaped the development of SFAS 87 on accounting for pensions. Street (1996: 88) concludes that SFAS 87 clearly reveals the impact of compromise resulting from special interest intervention and resulted in 'earlier but gradual recognition of significant liabilities . . . Other compromises (e.g. smoothing rules) further softened the impact.'

Likewise in the UK, the ASC (1988: para. 16), while noting that 'many companies have, until now, simply charged the contributions payable to the pension scheme as the pension cost in each accounting period', required recognition of 'the cost of providing pensions on a systematic and rational basis over the period which benefits from the employees' services'. This was based on the matching concept and, with some exceptions, smoothed variations in pension costs over the average expected service lives of employees. More recent amendments by the ASB and the International Accounting Standards Board reflect the shifting emphasis between the income statement and the balance sheet approaches by controversially requiring the recognition of pension assets and liabilities; an approach which moved away from income smoothing and introduced more volatility to both the balance sheet and the income statement (Federation des Experts Comptables Européens 2001). In that regard, the recognition of pension liabilities is an example of the accrued history between the 'liability' and 'matching' approaches, between principle and practice, between the regulator and the regulated: an enduring discontent made new by its context.

Conclusion

The content of financial accounting practice was shaped by, and in turn shaped, its context. From an agency perspective, the development of the corporate form and the need for finance to sustain the reporting entity led to the representation of financial position as a primary focus of mid-nineteenth century financial statements. In turn, the emergence and importance of equity markets as a form of business finance in the late nineteenth and early twentieth centuries led to an increasing focus on the income statement whose publication was required by regulation in the UK and the USA from the third decade of the twentieth century.

A number of authors have mapped the changes in financial statements (e.g. Edwards 1981; Lee 1994; Arnold and Matthews 2002) and in annual reports more generally (e.g. Clagett and Hirasuna 1988; McKinstry 1996; Graves *et al.* 1996). Change is evident in these representations of the reporting entity throughout the twentieth century. The reasons for such changes are manifold, although they often result from efforts by financial accounting practice to respond to or compensate for accounting and business failure either voluntarily (for example, after the Royal Mail case) or through legislation. The hegemony of practice at times constrained regulatory change, at times provided an impetus for innovation. Conversely, changes in practice, while often codified or constrained by statute, were not limited to legislation but were also influenced by economic and political events. For example, value added reporting in the UK is attributed by Burchell *et al.* (1985: 400) to an 'accounting constellation', a 'very particular' variety of factors which existed at the time. It has been argued that changes in reporting practices are, hence, also signifiers of change in society, whether through the development of social and environmental reporting or the design–intensification of annual reports (McKinstry 1996; Graves *et al.* 1996). These frontiers and frontlines of financial accounting practice, these contested territories, these times of transition, represent opportunities for further research into the appearances and 'disappearances' (Pong and Mitchell 2005) of financial accounting practice.

Consistent with Edwards' characterisation of financial accounting practice as a chronicle of 'continuity and change' (1996: 31), the extent to which practices that existed prior to the Industrial Revolution represent a *mappa mundi* of contemporary financial statements – the balance sheet and income statement – is worthy of further exploration. The balance sheet and income statement formed the basic edifice of financial statements. The increasing complexity of business relationships and structures did not alter this basic shape but did stretch and ultimately extend the boundaries of financial reporting through additional disclosures, voluntary and involuntary.

The income statement supplemented and then, to a certain extent, supplanted the balance sheet. Statements such as the funds flow statement and the value added statement appeared and then disappeared (Burchell *et al.* 1985; Pong and Mitchell 2005). The appearance of the cash flow statement was a response to the perceived limitations of the balance sheet and income statement (Lee 1981). The steady extension of disclosures of information regarding, for example, business segments, the nature of earnings, financial instruments and risk reflected the increasing complexity of business and businesses. They extended the financial accounting house but left its frame intact. Throughout this period, there is evidence at times of an entrenched continuity, evidence of financial accounting practice struggling to represent an increasingly complex world while clinging to principles such as prudence and historical cost.

Consequently, financial accounting practice has, through its history, struggled to accommodate uncertainty between its (balance) sheets. Furthermore, in agency terms, the asymmetrical contest in both information and intention between the providers of finance and managers continued to test the reliability of financial statements in the form of 'secret reserves', 'earnings management' and 'creative accounting'. Many of the challenges posed by the growing complexity of business have been without resolution and without revolution: the accounting revolution has been, in Lee's words (1979: 299), 'as if on a spinning wheel'.

Hence, financial accounting practice, as a setting for iterative change, is a creature of its past. Coming full circle once more, in the special issue of *Accounting, Organizations and Society* cited at the beginning of this chapter (Hopwood 2000), McSweeney (2000: 784–5) argues that periodic reporting means that 'financial reports are not mere records, not the equivalent of pointing. They are descriptions of the past made before all that is essential for such accounts has happened . . . the end of a financial accounting story is in the future.' As with financial statements themselves, the story of financial accounting practice – rooted in the past – remains to be played out in the future.

Acknowledgements

I am grateful to Rachel Baskerville, Peter Clarke, Nora Munhuu, Brendan O'Dwyer, Philip O'Regan, Keith Warnock, Geoff Whittington and, in particular, Margaret Ó hÓgartaigh for their contributions to the development of this chapter.

Key Works

Edwards (1989) provides an accessible, mainstream history of financial accounting from earliest times, giving particular attention to corporate accounting developments in the UK since the Industrial Revolution.

Hopwood (2000) argues for the importance of research that can provide more adequate insights into the wider institutional and social positioning of financial accounting.

Napier (2006) reviews financial reporting themes in the 'new accounting history' and their contribution to understanding the processes of change within accounting.

Previts and Merino (1998) is a comprehensive and highly readable discussion of the history of accountancy in the USA from colonial times onwards. This book has a wide-ranging disciplinary and contextual focus, with a particular emphasis on political and professional influences on accounting.

Notes

1   Given the broad canvass represented by financial accounting practice, the chapter will focus in particular on its contrasting history in the USA and the UK. The undoubtedly significant and rich histories of

financial accounting in other contexts, for example, Continental Europe and Japan, can be found in Walton (2006) and Cooke and Kikuya (1992) respectively.

2   The invocation of agency theory as an explanation of the motivations of the various actors in financial accounting is not without its critics. Mills (1993: 802) argues that agency theory is 'flawed' by 'granting economic activities a privileged position over other forms of human behaviour'. Other critics, such as Barzun and Graff (1977: 43), express concern regarding 'the habit of reading into the past our own modern ideas and intentions'. These admonitions are less a call to disregard agency theory but more evocative of different and multi-faceted characterisations of agency: see, for example, discussions of the 'rhetorical agency' (Carruthers and Espeland 1991), the 'surveillant agency' of accounts (Hopper and Macintosh 1993) and the discussions in new accounting history which brings 'into its exposition new actors' (Napier 2006: 456).

3   Reid (1987: 29) challenges this view by reviewing a number of legal cases involving 'judicial intervention in accounting behaviour' which saw 'the birth of many ideas which are basic to accounting today'. Her conclusion, drawing on Littleton (1933: 221), that the courts were not 'formulating new principles' but rather that 'it is more probable that principles which it was customary for auditors to apply in their professional engagements were being given public and legal sanction' suggests an institutionalisation rather than a rebuttal of *laissez-faire*.

4   Edey and Panitpakdi's conclusions relate to the general regulatory context. Parker (1990) finds that financial accounting practices of companies in major British industrial sectors, such as railways, public utilities and financial institutions, were in fact regulated prior to 1900 and argues (ibid.: 51) that the reason for such regulation 'was not primarily to protect investors but in order to control monopoly, privilege and safety'.

5   Hanson (1989) provides a wide-ranging summary of developments in financial reporting between 1969 (the formation of the ASC) and 1989 (the advent of the ASB), based on Tonkin and Skerratt's surveys of UK Reporting Practices.

6   Empirical evidence of 'big bath' accounting in the 1980s can be found in, for example, Elliott and Shaw (1988), Griffiths (1986) and Smith (1992).

References

American Institute of Accountants (1931) *Resumé of Special Report of the Accounting Procedures Committee of the American Institute of Accountants* (New York: AICPA).

Arnold, A. J. (1996) Should historians trust late nineteenth century financial statements?, *Business History*, 38 (2): 40–54.

Arnold, A. J. and Matthews, D. R. (2002) Corporate financial disclosures in the UK, 1920–1950: the effects of legislative change and managerial discretion, *Accounting and Business Research*, 32 (1): 3–16.

ASB (1990) *Statement of Aims* (London: ASB).

ASB (1991) *FRS 1 Cash Flow Statements* (London: ASB).

ASB (1996a) *FRS 1 Cash Flow Statements (revised)* (London: ASB).

ASB (1996b) *FRS 12 Provisions, Contingent Liabilities and Contingent Assets* (London: ASB).

ASB (1999) *Press Notice: Tangible Fixed Assets – New Accounting Standard Published*, ASB PN 132, 18 February (London: ASB).

ASC (1988) *SSAP 24 Accounting for Pension Costs* (London: ASC).

Baker, C. R. and Hayes, R. (2004) Reflecting form over substance: the case of Enron Corp., *Critical Perspectives on Accounting*, 15 (6/7): 767–85.

Baker, R. E. (1964) The pension cost problem, *Accounting Review*, 39 (1): 52–62.

Baladouni, V. (1981) The accounting records of the East India Company, *Accounting Historians Journal*, 8 (1): 67–9.

Baladouni, V. (1986) Financial reporting in the early years of the East India Company, *Accounting Historians Journal*, 13 (1): 19–30.

Barzun, J. and Graff, H. F. (1977) *The Modern Researcher* (Boston: Houghton Mifflin).

Bennett, J. (1939) *Transcript of Conference with John Bennett, Attorney-General of New York State, the American Institute of Certified Public Accountants and the New York Society of CPAs, January 6* (New York: AICPA).

Bierman, H. and Dukes, R. E. (1975) Accounting for research and development costs, *Journal of Accountancy*, 139 (4): 48–56.

Bircher, P. (1988) The adoption of consolidated accounting in Great Britain, *Accounting and Business Research*, 19 (73): 3–13.

Boer, G. (1966) Replacement cost: a historical look, *Accounting Review*, 41 (1): 92–7.

Boussard, D. and Colasse, B. (1992) Funds-flow accounting and cash-flow accounting in France, *European Accounting Review*, 1 (2): 229–54.

Bricker, R. and Chandar, N. (1998) On applying agency theory in historical accounting research, *Business and Economic History*, 27 (2): 486–500.

Bricker, R. and Chandar, N. (2000) Where Berle and Means went wrong: a reassessment of capital market agency and financial reporting, *Accounting, Organizations and Society*, 25 (6): 529–54.

Brief, R. P. (1966) The origin and evolution of eighteenth century asset accounting, *Business History Review*, 40 (1): 1–23.

Brief, R. P. (1969) A late nineteenth century contribution to the theory of depreciation, *Journal of Accounting Research*, 5 (1): 27–38.

Briloff, A. J. (1964) Needed: a revolution in the determination and application of accounting principles, *Accounting Review*, 39 (1): 12–14.

Briloff, A. J. and Engler, C. (1979) Accountancy and the merger movement: a symbiotic relationship, *Journal of Corporation Law*, 5 (1): 81–104.

Bryer, R. A. (1993) The late nineteenth century revolution in financial reporting: accounting for the rise of investor or managerial capitalism, *Accounting, Organizations and Society*, 18 (7/8): 649–90.

Bryer, R. A. (2000a) The history of accounting and the transition to capitalism in England. Part one: theory, *Accounting, Organizations and Society*, 25 (2): 131–62.

Bryer, R. A. (2000b) The history of accounting and the transition to capitalism in England. Part two: evidence, *Accounting, Organizations and Society*, 25 (4/5): 327–81.

Buckmaster, D. A. (1992) Income smoothing in accounting and business literature prior to 1954, *Accounting Historians Journal*, 19 (4): 147–73.

Burchell, S., Clubb, C. and Hopwood, A. G. (1985) Accounting in its social context: towards a history of value added in the United Kingdom, *Accounting, Organizations and Society*, 10 (4): 381–413.

Burchell, S., Clubb, C., Hopwood, A. G. and Hughes, J. (1980) The roles of accounting in organizations and society, *Accounting, Organizations and Society*, 5 (1): 5–27.

Camfferman, K. and Zeff, S. A. (2003) The apotheosis of company accounting: Unilever's financial reporting innovations from the 1920s to the 1940s, *Accounting, Business & Financial History*, 13 (2): 171–206.

Capie, F. and Billings, M. (2001) Accounting issues and the measurement of profits – English banks 1920–68, *Accounting, Business & Financial History*, 11 (2): 225–51.

Carroll, A. B. (1999) Corporate social responsibility, *Business & Society*, 38 (3): 268–96.

Carruthers, B. G. and Espeland, W. N. (1991) Accounting for rationality: double-entry bookkeeping and the rhetoric of economic rationality, *American Journal of Sociology*, 97 (1): 31–70.

Chambers, R. J. (1973) Accounting principles or accounting politics, *Journal of Accountancy*, 135 (5): 48–52.

Chambers, R. J. (1987) Accounting education for the twenty-first century, *Abacus*, 23 (2): 97–106.

Chandler, A. D. (1977) *The Visible Hand: The Managerial Revolution in American Business* (Cambridge, MA: Harvard University Press).

Chandler, A. D. and Tedlow, R. (1985) *The Coming of Managerial Capitalism: A Casebook* (Homewood, IL: Richard D. Irwin).

Chatfield, M. (1996a) Comparability, in M. Chatfield and R. Vangermeersch (eds) *The History of Accounting: An International Encyclopaedia*, pp. 139–44 (New York: Garland).

Chatfield, M. (1996b) Balance sheet, in M. Chatfield and R. Vangermeersch (eds) *The History of Accounting: An International Encyclopaedia*, pp. 60–4 (New York: Garland).

Chatfield, M. (1996c) Accrual accounting, in M. Chatfield and R. Vangermeersch (eds) *The History of Accounting: An International Encyclopaedia*, pp. 23–4 (New York: Garland).

Chatfield, M. (1996d) Base stock method, in M. Chatfield and R. Vangermeersch (eds) *The History of Accounting: An International Encyclopaedia*, p. 68 (New York: Garland).

Chatfield, M. (1996e) Bad debts, in M. Chatfield and R. Vangermeersch (eds) *The History of Accounting: An International Encyclopaedia*, pp. 58–9 (New York: Garland).

Chatfield, R. H. (1977) *A History of Accounting Thought* (Huntington, NY: Robert E. Krieger).

Clagett, L. and Hirasuna, D. (1988) *A Historical Review of Annual Report Design* (New York: Cooper-Hewitt Museum, The Smithsonian Institution's National Museum of Design).

Clare, R. S. (1945) Evolution of corporate reports, *Journal of Accountancy*, 79 (1): 39–51.

Clay, C. G. A. (1984) *Economic Expansion and Social Change: England 1500–1700* (Cambridge: Cambridge University Press).

Committee on Accounting Procedure (1944) *Accounting Research Bulletin No. 24: Accounting for Intangible Assets* (New York: AICPA).

Cooke, T. E. and Kikuya, M. (1992) *Japanese Reporting in its Environmental Context* (London: ICAEW).

Cooke, T. E. and Nobes, C. W. (1997) *The Development of Accounting in an International Context: A Festschrift in Honour of R. H. Parker* (London: Routledge).

Coombs, H. M. and Edwards, J. R. (1996) *Accounting Innovation – Municipal Corporations 1835–1935* (New York: Garland).

Cooper, D. J. and Sherer, M. J. (1984) The value of corporate accounting: argument for a political economy of accounting, *Accounting, Organizations and Society*, 9 (3): 207–32.

Cowan, T. K. (1965) A resources theory of accounting, *Accounting Review*, 40 (1): 12–21.

Davies, K. G. (1952) Joint stock investment in the later seventeenth century, *Economic History Review*, 4 (3): 283–301.

Davies, P. M. and Bourn, A. M. (1972) Lord Kyslant and the Royal Mail, *Business History*, 14 (2): 102–23.

Davis, H. Z. (1982) History of LIFO, *Accounting Historians Journal*, 9 (1): 1–23.

Davis, H. Z. and Strawser, J. A. (1996) Last-in, first-out, in M. Chatfield and R. Vangermeersch (eds) *The History of Accounting: An International Encyclopaedia*, pp. 367–9 (New York: Garland).

Dechow, P. M. and Skinner, D. J. (2000) Earnings management: reconciling the views of accounting academics, practitioners, and regulators, *Accounting Horizons*, 14 (2): 235–50.

Defliese, P. L. (1981) British accounting standards in a world setting, in R. Leach and E. Stamp (eds) *British Accounting Standards: The First Ten Years*, pp. 105–18 (Cambridge: Woodhead-Faulkner).

De Roover, R. (1938) Characteristics of bookkeeping before Paciolo, *Accounting Review*, 13 (2): 144–50.

De Roover, R. (1956) The development of accounting prior to Luca Pacioli according to the account-books of medieval merchants, in A. C. Littleton and B. S. Yamey (eds) *Studies in the History of Accounting*, pp. 114–74 (London: Sweet & Maxwell).

Dicksee, L. R. (1902) *Auditing*, 5th edn (London: Gee).

Dicksee, L. R. (1927) *Published Balance Sheets and Window Dressing* (London: Gee).

Dye, R. A. (2001) An evaluation of 'essays on disclosure' and the disclosure literature in accounting, *Journal of Accounting & Economics*, 32 (1/3): 181–235.

Edey H. C. and Panitpakdi, P. (1956) British Company Accounting and the Law 1844–1900, in A. C. Littleton and B. S. Yamey (eds) *Studies in the History of Accounting*, pp. 356–79 (London: Sweet & Maxwell).

Edwards, J. R. (1981) *Company Legislation and Changing Patterns of Disclosure in British Company Accounts 1900–1940* (London: ICAEW).

Edwards, J. R. (1986a) *Reporting Fixed Assets in Nineteenth-Century Company Accounts* (New York: Garland).

Edwards, J. R. (1986b) *Legal Regulation of British Company Accounts 1836–1900*, Vol. I: *Statutory Companies* (New York: Garland).

Edwards, J. R. (1986c) Depreciation and fixed asset valuation in British railway company accounts to 1911, *Accounting and Business Research*, 16 (63): 251–63.

Edwards, J. R. (1989) *A History of Financial Accounting* (London: Routledge).

Edwards, J. R. (1996) Financial accounting practice: 1600–1970: continuity and change, in T. A. Lee, A. Bishop and R. H. Parker (eds) *Accounting History from the Renaissance to the Present – A Remembrance of Luca Pacioli*, pp. 31–70 (New York: Garland).

Edwards, J. R. and Baber, C. (1979) Dowlais Iron Company: accounting policies and procedures for profit measurement and reporting purposes, *Accounting and Business Research*, 9 (34): 139–51.

Edwards, J. R. and Boyns, T. (1992) Industrial organization and accounting innovation: Charcoal iron-making in England 1690–1783, *Management Accounting Research*, 3 (2): 151–69.

Edwards, J. R. and Boyns, T. (1994) Accounting practice and business finance, case studies from the iron and coal industry 1865–1914, *Journal of Business Finance & Accounting*, 21 (4): 1151–78.

Edwards, J. R. and Webb, K. M. (1984) The development of group accounting in the United Kingdom to 1933, *Accounting Historians Journal*, 11 (1): 31–61.

Edwards, J. R., Boyns, T. and Anderson, M. (1995) British cost accounting development: continuity and change, *Accounting Historians Journal*, 22 (2): 1–41.

Eichenwald, K. (2005) *A Conspiracy of Fools* (New York: Random House).

Elliott, J. A. and Shaw, W. H. (1988) Write offs as accounting procedures to manage perceptions, *Journal of Accounting Research*, 26 (Supplement): 91–117.

Federation des Experts Comptables Européens (2001) *How European Companies Are Applying IAS 19 (revised) in the First Year of Application* (Brussells: FEE).

Fleischman, R. K. and Parker, L. D. (1990) Managerial accounting early in the British industrial revolution: the Carron Company, a case study, *Accounting & Business Research*, 20 (79): 211–21.

Francis, J., Schipper, K. and Vincent, L. (2002) Earnings announcements and competing information, *Journal of Accounting & Economics*, 33 (3): 313–44.

Freedman, J. and Power, M. (1992) Law and accounting: transition and transformation, in J. Freedman and M. Power (eds) *Law and Accountancy: Conflict and Cooperation in the 1990s*, pp. 1–23 (London: Paul Chapman).

Gilman, S. (1939) *The Accounting Concept of Profit* (New York: Ronald Press Co.).

Gilmore, C. and Willmott, H. (1992) Company law and financial reporting: a sociological history of the UK experience, in M. Bromwich and A. Hopwood (eds) *Accounting and the Law*, pp. 159–90 (London: Prentice Hall).

Glynn, J. J. (1984) The development of British railway accounting: 1800–1911, *Accounting Historians Journal*, 11 (1): 103–18.

Graves, O. F., Flesher, D. L. and Jordan, R. E. (1996) Pictures and the bottom line: the television epistemology of U.S. annual reports, *Accounting, Organizations and Society*, 21 (1): 57–88.

Gray, R. H. (1986) *Accounting for R&D: A Review of Experiences with SSAP 13* (London: ICAEW).

Greenspan, A. (1996) The challenge of central banking in a democratic society, remarks by Chairman Alan Greenspan at the annual dinner and Francis Boyer lecture of the American Enterprise Institute for Public Policy Research, Washington, D.C., 5 December.

Greidinger, B. B. (1950) *Preparation and Certification of Financial Statements* (New York: Ronald Press Co.).

Griffiths, I. (1986) *Creative Accounting: How to Make Your Profits What You Want Them to Be* (London: Unwin).

Guthrie, J. and Parker, L. D. (1989) Corporate social reporting: a rebuttal of legitimacy theory, *Accounting and Business Research*, 19 (76): 343–52.

Guthrie, J. and Parker, L. D. (1990) Comparative social disclosure practice: a comparative international analysis, *Advances in Public Interest Accounting*, 3: 159–75.

Haller, A. and Jakoby, S. (1995) Funds flow reporting in Germany: a conceptual and empirical state of the art, *European Accounting Review*, 4 (3): 515–34.

Hanson, J. D. (1989) Developments in financial reporting practice over the last twenty years, in D. J. Tonkin and L. C. L. Skerratt (eds) *Financial Reporting 1988–89: A Survey of UK Reporting Practice*, pp. 3–66 (London: ICAEW).

Hawkins, D. F. (1963) The development of modern financial reporting practices among American manufacturing corporations, *Business History Review*, 37 (3): 135–68.

Healy, P. and Wahlen, J. (1999) A review of the earnings management literature and its implications for standard setting, *Accounting Horizons*, 13 (4): 365–84.

Hendriksen, E. S. (1977) *Accounting Theory* (Homewood, IL: Richard D. Unwin).

Hogner, R. H. (1982) Corporate social reporting: eight decades of development in US Steel, *Research in Corporate Performance and Policy*, 4: 243–50.

Hope, T. and Gray, R. H. (1982) Power and policy making: the development of an R&D standard, *Journal of Business Finance & Accounting*, 9 (4): 531–58.

Hopper, T. and Macintosh, N. (1993) Management accounting as disciplinary practice: the case of ITT under Harold Geneen, *Management Accounting Research*, 4 (2): 181–216.

Hopwood, A. G. (2000) Understanding financial accounting practice, *Accounting, Organizations and Society*, 25 (8): 763–6.

Hoskin, K. and Macve, R. H. (1986) Accounting and the examination: a genealogy of disciplinary power, *Accounting, Organizations and Society*, 11 (2): 105–36.

Hughes, H. P. (1996) Goodwill, in M. Chatfield and R. Vangermeersch (eds) *The History of Accounting: An International Encyclopaedia*, pp. 281–3 (New York: Garland).

Husband, G. R. (1938) The corporate entity fiction and accounting theory, *Accounting Review*, 13 (3): 241–53.

Johnson, R. T. (1996) Deferred income tax accounting, in M. Chatfield and R. Vangermeersch (eds) *The History of Accounting: An International Encyclopaedia*, pp. 190–3 (New York: Garland).

Jones, H. (1985) *Accounting, Costing and Cost Estimation* (Cardiff: University of Wales Press).

Joplin, J. P. (1914) Secret reserves, *Journal of Accountancy*, 18 (6): 407–17.

Käfer, K. and Zimmerman, V. K. (1967) Notes on the evolution of the statement of sources and applications of funds, *International Journal of Accounting*, 2 (2): 89–121.

Keay, J. (1991) *The Honourable Company: A History of the English East India Company* (London: HarperCollins).

Kitchen, J. (1972) The accounts of British holding company groups: development and attitudes to disclosure in the early years, *Accounting and Business Research*, 2 (6): 114–36.

Kitchen, J. (1979) Fixed asset values: ideas on depreciation 1892–1914, *Accounting and Business Research*, 9 (36): 281–91.

Kitchen, J. (1980) Lawrence Dicksee, depreciation and the double account system, in H. Edey and B. S. Yamey (eds) *Debits, Credits, Finance and Profits*, pp. 109–30 (London: Sweet & Maxwell).

Kripke, H. (1970) Conglomerates and the moment of truth in accounting, *St. John's Law Review*, 44 (Special Issue): 791–7.

Ladelle, O. G. (1890) The calculation of depreciation, *Accountant*, 16 (834): 659–60.

Laeri, J. H. (1966) Statement in quotes, *Journal of Accountancy*, 121 (3): 57–8.

Leach, R. G. (1981) The birth of British accounting standards, in R. G. Leach and E. Stamp (eds) *British Accounting Standards in the First 10 Years*, pp. 3–11 (Cambridge: Woodhead-Faulkner).

Lee, C-W. J. and Hsieh, D. A. (1985) Choice of inventory accounting methods: comparative analyses of alternative hypotheses, *Journal of Accounting Research*, 23 (2): 468–85.

Lee, T. A. (1971) Goodwill. An example of will o' the wisp accounting', *Accounting and Business Research*, 11 (43): 318–28.

Lee, T. A. (1973) Accounting for goodwill, *Accounting and Business Research*, 13 (50): 175–96.

Lee, T. A. (1974) Accounting for and disclosure of business combinations, *Journal of Business Finance & Accounting*, 1 (1): 1–33.

Lee, T. A. (1979) The evolution and revolution of financial accounting practice; a review article, *Accounting and Business Research*, 19 (75): 292–9.

Lee, T. A. (1981) Cash flow accounting and corporate financial reporting, in M. Bromwich and A. G. Hopwood (eds) *Essays in British Accounting Research*, pp. 63–78 (London: Pitman).

Lee, T. A. (1994) The changing form of the corporate annual report, *Accounting Historians Journal*, 21 (1): 215–34.

Lev, A. and Zarowin, P. (1999) The boundaries of financial reporting and how to extend them, *Journal of Accounting Research*, 37 (2): 353–85.

Levitt, A. and Dwyer, P. (2002) *Take on the Street: What Wall Street and Corporate America Don't Want You to Know. What You Can Do To Fight Back* (New York: Pantheon).

Lewis, N., Parker, L. and Sutcliffe, P. (1984) Financial reporting to employees: the pattern of development 1919 to 1979, *Accounting, Organizations and Society*, 9 (3/4): 275–89.

Lister, R. (1981) Company financial statements as source material for business historians: observations on the underlying conceptual framework, *Business History*, 23 (2): 223–39.

Littleton, A. C. (1933) *Accounting Evolution to 1900* (New York: American Institute Publishing Company).

Littleton, A. C. (1941) A genealogy of cost and market, *Accounting Review*, 16 (2): 141–66.

McKinstry, S. (1996) Designing the annual reports of Burton plc from 1930 to 1994, *Accounting, Organizations and Society*, 21 (1): 89–111.

McSweeney, B. (2000) Looking forward to the past, *Accounting, Organizations and Society*, 25 (8): 767–86.

Maltby, J. (2004) Hadfields Ltd: its annual general meetings 1903–1939 and their relevance for contemporary corporate social reporting, *British Accounting Review*, 36 (4): 415–38.

Marriner, S. (1980) Company financial statements as source material for business historians, *Business History*, 22 (2): 203–35.

Mautz, R. K. (1967a) Identification of the conglomerate company, *Financial Executive*, 4 (7): 18–26.

Mautz, R. K. (1967b) Conglomerate reporting and data reliability, *Financial Executive*, 4 (9): 25–35.

Mautz, R. K. (1967c) Bases for more detailed reporting by diversified companies, *Financial Executive*, 4 (11): 52–60.

May, G. O. (1932) Influence of the depression on the practice of accountancy, *Journal of Accountancy*, 52 (5): 336–50.

May, G. O. (1949) *Business Income and Price Levels: An Accounting Study* (New York: AICPA).

Merino, B. D. and Coe, T. (1978) Uniformity in accounting: a historical perspective, *Journal of Accountancy*, 146 (2): 62–9.

Miller, P. and O'Leary, T. (1987) Accounting and the construction of the governable person, *Accounting, Organizations and Society*, 12 (3): 235–65.

Mills, P. A. (1993) Accounting history as social science: a cautionary note, *Accounting, Organizations and Society*, 18 (7/8): 801–3.

Montgomery, R. H. (1912) *Auditing: Theory and Practice* (New York: Ronald Press).

Moyer, C. A. (1955) Trends in presentation of financial statement and reports, in M. Backer (ed.) *Handbook of Modern Accounting Theory*, pp. 425–52 (New York: Prentice-Hall).

Mueller, G. H., Gernon, H. and Meek, G. K. (1997) *Accounting: An International Perspective*, 4th edn (Chicago, IL: Richard D. Irwin).

Napier, C. J. (2006) Accounts of change: 30 years of historical accounting research, *Accounting, Organizations and Society*, 31 (4/5): 445–507.

Napier, C. J. and C. Noke (1992) Accounting and the law: an historical overview of an uneasy relationship, in M. Bromwich and A. G. Hopwood (eds) *Accounting and the Law*, pp. 30–54 (Hemel Hempstead: Prentice-Hall).

Nissan, S., Kamata, N. and Okata, R. (1995) Cash reporting in Japan, *International Journal of Accounting*, 30 (2): 168–80.

Nobes, C. (1992) A political history of goodwill in the UK: an illustration of cyclical standard setting, *Abacus*, 28 (2): 142–67.

Nobes, C. and Parker, R. H. (2006) *Comparative International Accounting*, 9th edn (London: Pearson).

Noguchi, M. and Edwards, J. R. (2004) Accounting principles, internal conflict and the state: the case of the ICAEW, 1948–1966, *Abacus*, 40 (3): 280–320.

Olson, W. E. (1982) *The Accounting Profession: Years of Trial: 1969–1980* (New York: AICPA).

Parker, R. H. (1965) Lower of cost and market in Britain and the United States: an historical survey, *Abacus*, 1 (2): 156–72.

Parker, R. H. (1977) Explaining national differences in consolidated accounts, *Accounting and Business Research*, 6 (22): 203–7.

Parker, R. H. (1990) Regulating British corporate financial reporting in the late nineteenth century, *Accounting, Business & Financial History*, 1 (1): 51–71.

Paton, W. A. and Stevenson, R. (1918) *Principles of Accounting*, 3rd edn (New York: Macmillan).

Peloubet, M. E. (1955) The historical background of accounting, in M. Backer (ed.) *Handbook of Modern Accounting Theory*, pp. 5–39 (New York: Prentice-Hall).

Pollins, H. (1956) Aspects of railway accounting before 1868, in A. C. Littleton and B. S. Yamey (eds) *Studies in the History of Accounting*, pp. 332–55 (London: Sweet & Maxwell).

Pong, C. M. and Mitchell, F. (2005) Accounting for a disappearance: a contribution to the history of the value added statement in the UK, *Accounting Historians Journal*, 32 (2): 173–99.

Pong, C. M. and Whittington, G. (1996) The withdrawal of Current Cost Accounting in the United Kingdom: a study of the Accounting Standards Committee, *Abacus*, 32 (1): 30–53.

Power, M. (1990) The horizons of financial reporting, in M. Power (ed.) *Brand and Goodwill Strategies*, pp. 1–8 (Cambridge: Woodhead Faulkner).

Previts, G. J. and Bricker, R. (1994) Fact and theory in accounting history: presentmindedness and capital markets research, *Contemporary Accounting Research*, 10 (2): 625–41.

Previts, G. J. and Merino, B. D. (1998) *A History of Accountancy in the United States: The Cultural Significance of Accounting* (Columbus, OH: Ohio State University Press).

Reid, J. R. (1987) Judicial intervention in accounting behavior: a reevaluation of the nineteenth century experience, *Journal of Accounting and Public Policy*, 6 (1): 19–34.

Richard, J. (2004) The secret past of fair value: lessons from history applied to the French case, *Accounting in Europe*, 1: 95–107.

Roberts, A. C. and Gabhart, D. R. L. (1972) Statement of funds: a glimpse of the future?, *Journal of Accountancy*, 133 (4): 54–9.

Samson, W. D., Flesher, D. L. and Previts, G. J. (2003) Quality of earnings: the case of the Mobile and Ohio Railroad in the 19th century, *Issues in Accounting Education*, 18 (4): 335–57.

Sandilands, F. E. P. [Chairman] (1975) *Inflation Accounting: Report of the Inflation Accounting Committee* (London: HMSO).

Schachner, L. (1968) Accountability under industrial diversification, *Accounting Review*, 43 (2): 304–26.

SEC (1945) *Accounting Series Release No. 53*, November 16.

Shiller, R. E. (2000) *Irrational Exuberance* (Princeton, NJ: Princeton University Press).

Singleton-Green, B. (1990) The rise and fall of the ASC, *Accountancy*, 122 (1164): 84–5.

Smith, T. E. (1992) *Accounting for Growth: Stripping the Camouflage from Company Accounts* (London: Century Business).

Sobel, R. (1965) *The Big Board: A History of the New York Stock Market* (New York: The Free Press).

Solomons, D. (1961) Economic and accounting concepts of income, *Accounting Review*, 39 (2): 374–83.

Sombart, W. (1924) *Der moderne Kapitalismus* (Munich: Duncker & Humblot).

Sommer, A. A. (1967) Conglomerate disclosure: friend or foe?, *Journal of Accountancy*, 123 (5): 61–7.

Spacek, L. (1956) *Are Industrial Common Stocks Selling at Fictitious Earnings? Address before Financial Analysts of Philadelphia* (Chicago: Arthur Andersen Library).

Stamp, E. (1984) *Selected Papers on Accounting, Auditing and Professional Problems* (New York: Garland Publishing).

Stamp, E. and Marley, C. (1970) *Accounting Principles and the City Code: The Case for Reform* (London: Butterworths).

Stamp, E. and Mason, A. K. (1977) Current cost accounting: British panacea or quagmire, *Journal of Accountancy*, 143 (4): 66–73.

Sterling, R. R. (1967) Conservatism: the fundamental principle of valuation in traditional accounting, *Abacus*, 3 (4): 109–32.

Stewart, B. (2006) The real reasons Enron failed, *Journal of Applied Corporate Finance*, 18 (20): 116–99.

Storey, R. K. (1959) Revenue realization, going concern and the measurement of income, *Accounting Review*, 34 (2): 232–9.

Storrar, A. C. and Pratt, K. C. (2000) Accountability vs Privacy, 1944–1907: the coming of the private company, *Accounting, Business & Financial History*, 10 (3): 259–91.

Street, D. L. (1996) A recent history of financial reporting in the UK and US, in T. A. Lee, A. Bishop and R. H. Parker (eds) *Accounting History from the Renaissance to the Present: A Remembrance of Luca Pacioli*, pp. 71–118 (New York: Garland).

Sweeney, H. W. (1936) *Stabilized Accounting* (New York: Harper & Row).

Takatera, S. and Sawabe, N. (2000) Time and space in income accounting, *Accounting Organizations and Society*, 25 (8): 787–98.

Thomas, A. L. (1969) *The Allocation Problem in Financial Accounting Theory*, Study in Accounting Research No. 3 (Sarasota, FL: American Accounting Association).

Thomas, A. L. (1974) *The Allocation Problem: Part 2*, Study in Accounting Research No. 3 (Sarasota, FL: American Accounting Association).

Tinker, A. M. (1985) *Paper Prophets: a Social Critique of Accounting* (Eastbourne: Holt, Rinehart & Winston).

Tonkin, D. J. and Skerratt, L. C. L. (1991) *Financial Reporting: A Survey of UK Reporting Practice* (London: ICAEW).

Tweedie, D. P. and Whittington, G. (1984) *The Debate on Inflation Accounting* (Cambridge: Cambridge University Press).

Tweedie, D. P. and Whittington, G. (1990) Financial reporting: current problems and their implications for systematic reform, *Accounting and Business Research*, 21 (81): 87–102.

Vangermeersch, R. (1979) *Financial Reporting Techniques in 20 Industrial Companies since 1861* (Gainesville: University Presses of Florida).

Vangermeersch, R. (1996a) Income statement/income account, in M. Chatfield and R. Vangermeersch (eds) *The History of Accounting: An International Encyclopaedia*, pp. 315–18 (New York: Garland).

Vangermeersch, R. (1996b) Inventory valuation, in M. Chatfield and R. Vangermeersch (eds) *The History of Accounting: An International Encyclopaedia*, pp. 346–7 (New York: Garland).

van Zijl, T. and Whittington, G. (2006) Deprival value and fair value: a reinterpretation and a reconciliation, *Accounting and Business Research*, 36 (2): 121–30.

Veblen, T. (1908) On the nature of capital: investment, intangible assets, and the pecuniary magnate, *Quarterly Journal of Economics*, 23 (1): 104–36.

Walker, R. G. (1968) Disclosure by diversified companies, *Abacus*, 4 (1): 27–38.

Walker, R. G. (1992) The SEC'S ban on upward asset revaluations and the disclosure of current values, *Abacus*, 28 (1): 3–35.

Walton, P. (2006) *Accounting in Europe* (London: Taylor & Francis).

Watts, R. L. and Zimmerman, J. L. (1983) Agency problems, auditing, and the theory of the firm: some evidence, *Journal of Law and Economics*, 26 (4): 613–34.

Weiner, J. L. (1928) Theory of Anglo-American dividend law: the English cases, *Columbia Law Review*, 28 (8): 1046–60.

Whittington, G. (1989) Accounting standard setting in the UK after 20 years: a critique of the Dearing and Solomons Reports, *Accounting and Business Research*, 19 (75): 195–205.

Winjum, J. O. (1970) Accounting in its age of stagnation, *Accounting Review*, 45 (4): 743–61.

Winjum, J. O. (1971) Accounting and the rise of capitalism: an accountant's view, *Journal of Accounting Research*, 9 (2): 333–50.

Yamey, B. S. (1960) The development of company accounting conventions, *Three Banks Review*, 47: 3–18.

Yamey, B. S. (1962) The case law relating to company dividends, in W. T. Baxter and S. Davidson (eds) *Studies in Accounting History*, pp. 428–42 (Homewood, IL: Irwin).

Yamey, B. S. (1964) Accounting and the rise of capitalism: further notes on a theme by Sombart, *Journal of Accounting Research*, 2 (2): 117–36.

Yamey, B. S. (1970) Closing the ledger, Simon Stevin, and the balance sheet, *Accounting and Business Research*, 1 (1): 71–7.

Yamey, B. S. (1977) Some topics in the history of financial accounting in England, 1500–1900, in W. T. Baxter and S. Davidson (eds) *Studies in Accounting*, pp. 11–34 (London: ICAEW).

Yang, J. M. (1927) *Goodwill and Other Intangibles: Their Significance and Treatment in Accounts* (New York: Ronald Press).

Zeff, S. A. (1972) *Forging Accounting Principles in Four Countries: A History and an Analysis of Trends* (Springfield, IL: Stipes Publishing).

Zeff, S. A. (2002) 'Political' lobbying on proposed standards: a challenge to the IASB, *Accounting Horizons*, 16 (1): 43–54.

9

Management accounting

Theory and practice

Richard Fleischman

Overview

When Johnson and Kaplan's (J&K) *Relevance Lost* appeared in 1987, Ezzamel *et al.* (1990: 157), though disputing many of the historical interpretations advanced in the book, did concede that it had 'moved accounting's *history* centre-stage'. J&K's message was that everything significant in US managerial accounting was known by 1925 and, thus, with the passage of six decades, had lost its relevance. America appeared to be in imminent danger of being dispossessed of its global economic hegemony because of its failure to embrace the modern productive technologies of its international competitors.

Is it conceivable that there is a grain of truth in this indictment? Only the recourse to history can inform our attempts to answer this question. The investigation is necessarily broader than a study of US managerial accounting theory and practice in the years 1925–87. It is imperative to examine events on a global stage as well as ages predating 1925 to appreciate the origins and evolution of the methodologies that J&K claim were not significantly altered during the twentieth century.

Not only did J&K lay down the gauntlet to management accountancy to re-examine its past, but it was during the late 1980s that accounting history was broadened quantitatively and qualitatively with paradigmatic debates about the significance of past events. The reader is referred to Chapter 2 for a full discussion of these developments (see also, Fleischman *et al.* 1996; Fleischman and Radcliffe 2003, 2005).

The chapter is structured as follows. The next section is an examination of the costing antecedents of contemporary practice with a particular focus on the search for what has been called 'the genesis of modern management' (Pollard 1965). Following thereon, we will examine some of the debates that have figured prominently in managerial accounting historiography. These discourses include the theory/practice 'schism', the impact of scientific management, and the furore over direct and absorption costing. Attention will then turn to a number of prominent themes that accounting historians have studied in depth, including the integration of costing and financial records, the impact of war on cost/managerial accounting, the rise of the mega–corporation, and the professionalisation of cost accountancy. The conclusion will provide some thoughts for future research directions and a response to the J&K indictment mentioned above. However, before turning to these topics, a word about the scope and limitations of this study is appropriate.

Scope and limitations

In recent years, there has been an explosion of investigations into archives written in languages other than English, which has become, rightfully or wrongfully, the *lingua franca* of accounting history publications. European scholars, notably Carmona and Zan, have vociferously but justifiably protested the Anglo-Saxon domination of mainstream journals in the field (Carmona and Zan 2002; Carmona 2004; Zan 2004b). A clarion call to action has been answered by a cadre of young academicians, primarily from France, Italy, Portugal, and Spain, but with other parts of the globe well represented. Some of these emerging researchers have chosen to present their findings in English-language journals. More often than not, however, managerial accounting historians have chosen to publish in their native tongues, resulting in a substantial knowledge loss to the traditional mainstream. Particularly noteworthy in this regard is a singular lack of knowledge about management accounting theory and practice in the German-speaking countries and in Japan. Notwithstanding the prominence and significance of these new directions, I feel the need to play to my strengths in principally featuring herein theory and practice as it evolved in the USA and the UK.

Since Garner's (1954) seminal book, *The Evolution of Cost Accounting to 1925*, the few studies that have attempted a general, broad-brush approach to managerial accounting history, have either followed a chronological narrative (e.g., Johnson and Kaplan 1987; Fleischman 1996; Boyns and Edwards 2007; Fleischman and Tyson 2007) or adopted a paradigmatic presentation (e.g., Loft 1995). Here the organisation is going to parallel Garner's topical approach (see also, Fleischman and Funnell 2007). Given the vast amount of archival research that has been done since Garner's time, such an approach in a single chapter would not have been feasible had it not been for the recent publication of the *Handbook of Management Accounting Research* (Chapman *et al.* 2007) which includes individual chapters on management accounting history for France, Italy, Portugal, and Spain (Carmona); China (Chow *et al.*); the UK (Boyns and Edwards); German-speaking countries (Ewert and Wagenhofer); the USA (Fleischman and Tyson); the Nordic countries (Näsi and Rohde); and Japan (Okano and Suzuki).

Costing antecedents

It is clearly the case that costing antecedents are broadly disbursed geographically. Ancient and classical accounting, covered in Chapters 4 and 5 of this *Routledge Companion*, have been extensively studied by scholars. This research has typically revealed governmental bureaucrats performing accounting functions with frequent attention to aspects of costing. Sometimes the accounting had profound theocratic overtones (e.g., Egyptian and biblical accounting). Scholars fascinated by the antiquities have performed yeoman service in bringing accounting's long history to light of day (e.g., Ezzamel, Mattessich), even when required to fashion bricks out of straw (see Vollmers 2003, for a discussion of the methodologies for ancient history research).

Cost accounting had its genesis also in China, inaugurated there as a function of government rather than private-sector enterprise. Fu (1971) and Guo (1988) described budgeting processes in evidence during the Zhou (Chou) Dynasty (1122–256 BC) that featured expenditure control and accountability through periodic auditing. Subsequent Chinese rulers apparently did not perpetuate these techniques. Absent this leadership, accounting developed slowly in China because of the lack of private rights, poor commercial networks, and perhaps Confucian value systems (Lin 1992). However, independent double-entry bookkeeping (DEB), similar in some ways but inferior to the Italian method, was developed at approximately the same point in time (Lin 1992, 2003). Guo (1988: 8) concluded that 'Chinese accounting deserved to be called a bright pearl in the history of the development of the Eastern accounting.'

This international dispersion of costing antecedents continued as Europe entered its medieval and Renaissance periods. Evidence of industrial accounting predated the takeoffs in Spain and in Britain during its Industrial Revolution, to be discussed subsequently. Some even appeared before Pacioli's *Summa* published in 1494. De Roover (1941) analysed the archives of the cloth manufacturing operations of the Medicis, the Florentine ruling family, and Elder (1937) the accounts of Christopher Plantin, a Flemish printer. These records, mostly sixteenth-century documents, reflect evidence of attention to 'cost finding' and, in the case of Plantin, the movement of costs through multiple inventory accounts. Plantin apparently achieved a separation of direct costs from other expenses in an effort to calculate a '*prix de revient*', a modified French equivalent of cost of goods sold (Holzer and Rogers 1990). Other Italian textile operations have been studied with particular reference to production cost control – the Dantinis in Prato (Brun 1930), the Bracci in Arezzo (Melis 1950), and Francisco del Bene & Co. (Sapori 1932). Some of these records date from the early fourteenth century.

Other European antecedents appeared somewhat later and were not of an Italian vintage. Scheuermann (1929) describes the accounting for the Fugger mining and smelting operations in Germany in 1548–1655. Llopis *et al.* (2002) relate how, at the Spanish Monastery of Guadalupe, an accounting system was devised to aid managerial decision making. A study of the archive of the Newmills Cloth Manufactory, Haddington, Scotland uncovered the use of costing procedures for process evaluation, product-line decisions, raw material control, and 'rational planning' in the late seventeenth century (Marshall 1980). Managers at the Crowley iron enterprise on Tyneside, dating from the early eighteenth century, used cost accounting methods to prepare ten-week production plans and to achieve conformity to waste standards (Flinn 1957, 1962; Fleischman and Parker 1992). James Dodson (1759), an early textbook writer, reported the system of accounts employed by Hugh Crispin, an English shoemaker, that later commentators have called an early example of batch costing (Edwards 1937; Solomons 1952). Other antecedents of the British Industrial Revolution are to be found in Edwards *et al.* (1990) and Edwards and Boyns (1992). This latter study focuses on two charcoal iron-making firms, the DN Works and the Staveley Group, in the vicinity of Sheffield in the late seventeenth and early eighteenth centuries. There was found an integration of the cost and financial records and the use of market-based transfer pricing to measure the profitability of individual departments.

The search for origins

American events

Some accounting historians tend to be obsessed with origins, particularly when studying methods that have direct linkages to contemporary practice. Management accounting historiography is no exception as scholars scour the past searching for what has come to be called 'the genesis of modern management'. Fifty-odd years ago there was consensus as to when managerial accounting methodology advanced to a stage where it could be called sophisticated, purposeful, and/or an aid to managerial decision-making. The early studies of costing history

(Littleton 1933; Edwards 1937; Yamey 1949; Solomons 1952; Garner 1954) all focused on the age of Taylor and scientific management.

Since then, historians, both economic and accounting, have succeeded in turning back the chronological clock. Chandler (1977), the noted economic historian, has made a strong case for the US transcontinental railroads of the mid-nineteenth century as the first corporations of a modern type. It was only then that a separation occurred between ownership and management, a development central to the advent of the modern corporation in Chandler's way of thinking. Also, Chandler felt that railroad accounting signalled the emergence of accounting from bookkeeping.

Prime movers in railroad accounting were Latrobe of the Baltimore & Ohio, Thomson and Haupt of the Pennsylvania, and Fink of the Louisville & Nashville (see also Chapter 18). Early US railroading has been extensively studied by Heier (e.g., 2000); Flesher, Previts, and the late Bill Samson (e.g., Flesher *et al.* 2003; Samson *et al.* 2006); and Hoskin and Macve (H&M) (2007); while for UK railroads, Arnold and McCartney (e.g., 2002, 2004) have written prolifically.

H&M (1988, 1994, 2000) date the genesis of modern management from events that transpired at the Springfield Armory (SA) during the 1830s and 1840s. According to H&M, post-1840 productivity improvements were attributable to the 'invention' of managerialism, which they defined as managers' ability to enforce accounting norms and exert discipline over labour (H&M 1996). They contend that modern accounting emerged from the confluence of two critical events at Springfield: (1) Daniel Tyler's formal inspection and revised piece rates in 1832, and (2) the establishment of military superintendence in 1841 which brought West Point discipline and examination procedures to the manufactory.

Tyson's (1990) examination of the SA archives revealed that a comprehensive piece-rate regime was in evidence as early as 1815. He concluded that economic factors (falling prices, skilled-labour surpluses, technological improvements, etc.) better explain management's desire and ability to reduce piece rates and significantly increased productivity after 1841. Tyson also disagreed with H&M with respect to the piece-rate system Tyler established. H&M claimed that the rates reflected norms of output that good workers should achieve and that those who failed were disciplined. Tyson argued that an average-to-good operative could aspire to the articulated productivity levels and could earn thereby a living wage. He saw no evidence in the archives of calculations of cost variances from the norms, or of discipline meted out to those who failed to achieve them. H&M's interpretation, explicitly based on Foucauldian principles of panopticism, functional disciplinarity, and discontinuity, therefore, was refuted by Tyson (1990, 1993, 2000) and reaffirmed by H&M (1994, 1996, 2000) in a series of point/counter-point articles and conference debates. This discourse was carried over into the next contender for honours as the birthplace of sophisticated cost accounting – the New England textile industry.

A short but seminal study of the Lyman Mills at the mid-nineteenth century by Johnson (1972) awakened an interest in the closer investigation of the accounting features of the New England textile industry. Johnson advanced the theory that the accounting innovations in evidence there, albeit significant, were designed for internal control issues alone, and that developments related to external competition awaited the age of scientific management.

Cost accounting information, broadly interpreted, was first used in the USA in a managerial fashion in the New England textile industry of the early nineteenth century (Tyson 1992, 1998; Fleischman and Tyson 1998, 2007). Prior to that time, most businesses were small and entrepreneurial, and owners were hands-on managers. Large-scale textile manufacturing in New England reflected the transition from mercantile to industrial accounting. The New England mills were fully integrated and employed hundreds of full-time, residential workers and professional managers. Each mill was supervised by a factory agent chosen for his managerial skills and executive ability. A variety of cost accounting information included comparative costing between different mills, time periods, and product lines. Comparative cost data were used in a number of managerial ways – deciding whether to make or subcontract particular products, identifying which mills were relatively more or less efficient than others, and determining if the prices charged for cloth fully covered costs of production.

These and other traditional interpretations of early nineteenth-century New England mill costing were countered by H&M (1996), who argued that the cost reports were based on arbitrary allocations and were clearly suboptimal, thus lacking managerial utility. Only at SA, they countered, could managers discipline workers, hold them accountable to empirically based standards, and improve labour productivity. Tyson (1998) acknowledged that the formal ledger-based cost reports did result from simple averaging and allocations and that labour norms were never established in the New England mills. Notwithstanding, mill owners and managers clearly made do with suboptimal information to make important and ongoing business decisions.

The British Industrial Revolution (BIR)

The first venue investigated extensively as the potential point of origin of purposeful cost accounting is Britain during the Industrial Revolution. The leading naysayer is Pollard (1965) who, having undertaken substantial archival research, attributed a shortfall of British costing to a 'cavalier attitude' occasioned by his perception of substantial profit margins for BIR enterprises; a position supported by Edwards (1937), Hudson (1977), and Parker (1986). It has also been suggested that the orientation of entrepreneurs toward technological innovation distracted them from the more commercial side of their firms (Urwick and Brech 1964; Parker 1986). The absence of important elements of an accounting infrastructure reinforced these views. Existing commerce curricula did not include industrial accounting topics (Stacey 1954); few accountants in public practice serviced industrial clients (Parker 1986); there were no organised professional societies and no accepted accounting conventions (Yamey 1960). Influential historians of accounting (Solomons 1952; J&K 1987) argued that the British should have been pioneers in the evolution of managerial accounting practices in light of the level of economic activity achieved during the BIR, but that this leadership role never materialised.

Fleischman and Parker (1991; see also Edwards 1989), by contrast, hypothesised that given the entrepreneurial savvy of the new industrialists who harnessed technological innovation, engineered capital accumulation, and developed marketing and distribution structures, it is inconceivable that they would fail to appreciate the value of cost accounting to their nascent enterprises. This optimism was furthered by early studies of BIR enterprises in which both economic and accounting historians found evidence of a lengthy list of cost accounting innovations.

Fleischman et al. (1996; Fleischman and Radcliffe 2003) called for moderation in the paradigmatic posturing among accounting historians researching the origins of managerial accounting during the early stages of US and UK industrialisation. They suggested alternatively that the insights furnished by researchers representing rival worldviews could contribute additively and synergistically to our understanding of vital historical events such as the BIR. Two such studies were undertaken. Fleischman et al. (1995; cf. Bryer 2005) analysed the accounting at Boulton & Watt, the famed steam engine enterprise, with a particular focus on the material standards derived for costing engine components, and the labour standards reflected in piece rates for internal subcontractors. It was concluded that the accounting generally and the material standards specifically mirrored high levels of cost accounting expertise, but that the severe rounding and infrequent amending of the labour standards suggested that a modern managerial regime that rendered the labour force visible and calculable was not in evidence there. A like conclusion was reached in Fleischman and Macve's (2002) study of Tyneside coal mining. Here again, the accounting found was far in advance of anything the cost accounting historians of the mid-twentieth century expected to exist, but the effectiveness of attempts at labour control was insufficient to achieve 'systems that quietly order us about' (Foucault, quoted in Megill 1979: 493).

These joint projects did not include a Marxist perspective, although the authors were sensitive to that shortcoming. Bryer *et al.* (2007) is a tripartite investigation of the Carron Company archive by historians representing the three paradigms that have been most prominently featured in cost accounting historiography over the past two decades. While there were many more disagreements than meetings of the mind, each author remaining fairly true to his paradigmatic grounding, there was consensus that the accounting methodology at Carron was impressive for its time, early in the BIR. It is clear that Carron achieved DEB and the integration of the financial and costing records at a time when such accomplishments were rare. Bryer (2006) found that Carron's accounting methodology aided in the establishment of a managerial regime that reflected a modern 'capitalist mentality' (i.e., the subsumption of labour; control of the valorisation process; capitalist extortion of surplus value).

Macve, while not finding the labour control mechanisms sufficient to satisfy a Foucauldian that a new age had dawned, was impressed by the volume of *ex post* accounting documents. However, he contended that they were most likely so hopelessly inaccurate that they could not possibly have aided in managerial decision-making. This pessimism with respect to accounting accuracy was an old chestnut, previously raised by Ezzamel *et al.* (1990) in a critique of J&K's (1987) belief that 'managing by the numbers' could permit US industry to regain its relevance. Fleischman found that the accounting processes in evidence at Carron supported economically rational actions on the part of management whether directed towards the exploitation of labour, the establishment of accountability, or whatever it took to achieve profit maximisation. He felt the accounting numbers, although not reflecting the accuracy Bryer believed necessary to achieve maximum exploitation, were usually sufficient to guide management toward correct business decisions. Ultimately, the Carron project failed as the team split its findings into separate statements (Bryer 2006; Fleischman and Macve 2007).

French cost accounting theory

While the BIR featured a significant volume of costing activity over a wide range of industries and firms in the absence of a theoretical literature, corresponding developments in France were quite the opposite (Boyns *et al.* 1997). Focused mainly in the 1820s, there was a spate of French theory at a time when French industrial enterprises were relatively small and family-owned. Hence, adoptions of the innovations suggested were correspondingly few.

Payen (1817) related accounting systems at a carriage manufactory and a glue factory that resembled job-order and process-costing methods respectively, though he did not label them as such (Garner 1954). Payen is also credited with insights into the areas of transfer pricing, the allocation of production costs to products, waste cost management, and the integration of cost and financial records (Garner 1954; Holzer and Rogers 1990). De Cazaux (1824), although he dealt primarily with agricultural accounting, had a better sense than Payen of input factors in costing individual transformation processes (Holzer and Rogers 1990) and was an early theorist on budgeting (Solomons 1952). Godard, who embodied both theory and practice, was the owner/manager of the Baccarat Crystalworks and the author of a managerial accounting classic, *Traité Générale et Sommaire de la Comptabilité Commerciale* (1827). Some of the advances at Baccarat, noted by Nikitin (1996), were rigorous quality control procedures, sensitivity analyses, the allocation of acquisition and installation costs over multiple periods, and a general awareness of the differences between fixed and variable costs. Simon (1830) anticipated J&K's argument that there should be no period costs; that expenses such as rent, administrative salaries, and taxes should be allocated as overhead to productive processes (Garner 1954; Holzer and Rogers 1990).

Nikitin (1990) has studied a number of other French industrial firms operating at approximately the same time as the theoretical outpouring. Saint-Gobain, a glassworks, had implemented DEB by 1820, and by 1880 had developed a full-costing system that included transfer pricing, depreciation, and the allocation of overhead cost to activity centres. The Decazeville ironworks were founded in the 1820s. Here the big story was the disciplinary regime established to control labour. It was sufficiently impressive to cause H&M to link developments at Decazeville to the SA. Boyns *et al.* (1997) also found evidence that, by the late 1830s, managers of French enterprises were analysing the causes of cost variations.

Iberian roots

Within the past decade, a rich literature has appeared in which is detailed costing developments in a number of Spanish royal factories, some predating the BIR. Much of the early work was written in the authors' native tongue, but in recent years acclaimed studies have appeared in English-language journals.

The Royal Soap Factory of Seville received a governmental monopoly in the late fourteenth century. The main focus of accounting there, in the sixteenth and seventeenth centuries, was the intricate calculation of production costs in order to determine a 'just price' for soap. Performance standards for raw materials and labour went into its determination. Outside experts were called in to observe testing procedures for these standards. Factory costs, including capacity considerations and opportunity costs, were also factored in (Carmona and Donoso 2004; Carmona 2007).

Carmona and Gómez (2002) studied the Royal Textile Mill of Guadalajara, 1714–44, and found cost accounting technology used to control raw material usage and waste as well as labour and management productivity. In contrast to the findings of Fleischman *et al.* (1995), that material standards typically predate labour standards, evidence at the textile mill suggested the reverse. One interesting feature was the utilisation of standards to compare the efficiency of native Spanish workers with that of imported Dutch labour.

Núñez (2002) wrote of the accounting associated with the gunpowder monopoly plied in the Spanish colony of Mexico (New Spain) during the seventeenth century. Accounting was necessary to track a very sensitive commodity through various stages of production. The system not only regulated the flow but provided for rewards and punishments to operatives and managers based on their relative efficiencies.

The showcase for eighteenth-century Spanish industrial accounting was the Royal Tobacco Factory of Seville. Gutiérrez (1993) was the first to investigate the archive and narrate its costing practices. Carmona *et al.* (1997, 1998) wrote of the raw material and labour controls in evidence there. Specified amounts of tobacco were delivered to the cigar makers who received piece rates plus bonuses for production in excess of standards but were fired in the event of production shortfalls. Alvarez *et al.* (2002) averred that these production standards at the individual operative level guaranteed the quality of the product.

Gutiérrez *et al.* (2005) expanded the study of Spanish industrialisation to encompass 13 large- and medium-sized firms for the period 1760–1800. The authors confirmed that the findings of Fleischman and Parker (1991, 1997) in the UK paralleled those in Spain. The authors did point out that cost accounting methods varied among the studied enterprises as a function of product and ownership structure. It has also been demonstrated that the factories run by the Spanish government in monopolistic environments tended to be more successful than those operating under certain market conditions (Carmona 2007). By contrast, in later history, Macías (2002a, 2000b) has shown that privatisation had the opposite effect as far as managerial accounting is concerned. For example, when the tobacco monopoly was leased to the Bank of Spain in 1887, the use of cost data for decision-making and the monitoring of managerial performance markedly increased. In the final analysis, the 'imposing presence of the Spanish state in all spheres of life kept privately owned firms relatively small and unsophisticated, so there are few surviving records of cost management systems' (Carmona 2007: 933).

A recent study of the Silk Factory Company in Portugal has seconded the claim made by Spanish scholars that purposeful cost accounting on the Iberian Peninsula predated the BIR and escalated the pace of innovation and the expansion of enterprises in which change took place. Matos Carvalho *et al.* (2007: 83) point out that in the period 1745–47, while the Silk Factory Company was still under private ownership, albeit enjoying a governmental monopoly, not only was DEB and the integration of its costing and financial accounts present, but a job-order costing system was operational that 'allocated overhead costs to products, allowed for direct materials shrinkage, . . . [and evinced] elements of a rudimentary standard raw material costing system'.

There are interesting parallels and distinctions to be made between the Iberian and British experiences. Clearly the cost accounting advances in evidence at the royal factories rivalled BIR innovations in sophistication. However, many more UK archives have been examined and found worthy in terms of their cost accounting. It remains to be seen if Spanish innovations were widely extended to enterprises where the government did not play a major role. In point of fact, it has been observed that the factories that operated entirely under governmental control or enjoyed a royal monopoly were more profitable than those that faced competition in a market environment (Carmona 2007).

Debates in accounting history

The theory/practice schism

One complexity in relating the history of management accounting is what has come to be called 'the schism'. Management accounting theory and practice often move in tandem, but at certain key junctures in their history, there have been notable departures which induced historians to commit manifest error. The schism in management accountancy's past has featured a dichotomy between the volume and erudition of a period's managerial accounting literature, on the one hand, and the prevalence of advocated methodologies within industrial enterprises on the other. There were at least two formative epochs which have been misevaluated by historians who have drawn conclusions about management accounting in practice from the theoretical literature. The first of these concerns the BIR, where the consensus of learned opinion, until *c.*1990, was that cost accounting was in a nascent state during the BIR. This impression was generated as a natural outgrowth of the virtual absence of a British industrial accounting literature. There were several pre-1980 studies of individual BIR firms that inspired later researchers to look more deeply into the period. Most significant were Roll's book (1930) on Boulton & Watt, McKendrick's article (1970) on Wedgwood, and Stone's investigation (1973) of the Chorlton cotton mills in Manchester. The large-scale rehabilitation of BIR costing was initially undertaken by Edwards, Boyns and Newell (Edwards 1989; Edwards and Newell 1991; Boyns and Edwards 1996a, 1996b, 1997) and, working independently, Fleischman and Parker (1990, 1991, 1992, 1997). Subsequently, other researchers joined the project putting paid to Pollard's (1965: 248) oft-quoted claim that 'the practice of using accounts as direct aids to management was not one of the achievements of the British industrial revolution'.

A second theory/practice schism involves the scientific management era of pre-First World War America. By virtue of the vast outpouring of theoretical literature authored by such luminaries as Garcke and Fells (1887), Norton (1889), Church (1901), Taylor (1903, 1911, 1912), Emerson (1914), Gantt (1916), and Harrison (1918–19, 1930), to mention a few of the most noteworthy, many accounting historians still consider this epoch the dawning of modern managerial accounting. However, the query suggested by the schism is, to what degree was this theoretical bonanza reflected in actual practice? Fleischman (2000) has compiled a list of US businesses identified in the Taylor archives as firms that embraced scientific management based upon research done by Hoxie (1920), Nelson (1974), and Epstein (1978). Instead of numbering in the hundreds as one might expect, the result was a rather meagre 80.

So why is it that accounting historians have been misguided? The venerated cost accounting historians of a half-century ago, rather than undertaking archival research into BIR records, took it for granted that since nobody was writing about industrial costing, there was nothing to write about. Even Pollard (1965), who did a substantial amount of archival investigation, tended to ignore the best evidence, examining letter books rather than production reports. It was much the same for the scientific management era but in reverse. Since so much was being written about time-and-motion studies, standard costing, and variance analysis, it was easy to assume that these innovations were embraced into practice. Great names representing each of the prevailing paradigms in managerial accounting history – J&K (1987) for economic rationalism, Miller and O'Leary (1987) for Foucauldianism, and Hopper and Armstrong (1991) for Marxism – assumed prevalent standard costing in the USA although subsequent researchers failed to find wide-spread evidence of its utilisation until after the Second World War. These scholars, like those who wrote the early BIR histories, had bigger fish to fry in their broad surveys than to concentrate upon a single component.

Sharing information

It has been suggested by early cost accounting historians that the dictates of competitive advantage militated against the dissemination of costing innovations during the BIR (Edwards 1937; Garner 1954; Urwick and Brech 1964; Wells 1977, 1978). Secrecy was offered as an explanation for the absence of a theoretical literature. Since any public disclosure of costing and pricing could lead to competitive disadvantage, cost accounting methodology could only have been passed by word of mouth (Garner 1954; Chatfield 1977). The discussion continues today as evidenced by the differing views of the co-authors in Bryer et al.'s (2007) study of Carron.

Boyns and Edwards (2007) pointed out that the movement of individuals around the country was a catalyst for the dissemination of ideas. Two examples offered as proof were the activities of Smeaton, perhaps the second most famous BIR engineer behind Watt and its most prominent consultant, who seemed to pop up everywhere (Fleischman and Parker 1997), and the coal-mining 'viewers' who went from mine to mine performing a number of managerial functions including cost accounting (Oldroyd 1996; Fleischman and Macve 2002).

Twentieth-century developments support the contention that the sharing of technology and methodology is the way of business. Vent and Milne (1997) uncovered similar developments in their study of Australian gold mining. In the late nineteenth century, people moved and ideas spread from country to country and from company to company. Vent and Milne (1997: 77) claimed that 'cost accounting practices continued to evolve from and improve upon methods previously developed in Britain'. Vent (1991) also examined the activities of Bewick, Moreing & Co., a British firm of professional mine managers and consulting engineers, who operated in like fashion to the viewers in Britain a century before.

The most compelling example revealing that secrecy was not a high priority was the dissemination of the various costing and measurement techniques that comprise scientific management. In 1910, John Jensen, on behalf of the Australian Defence Department, visited a number of leading American and Canadian manufacturers (e.g., Underwood, Colt, Remington, and a number of armouries including Springfield). Foreman (2001: 31) observed that he brought back Taylorite practices that became 'significantly modified' to conform to the control requirements and environment of the Australian government's munitions factories.

Antonelli et al. (forthcoming) report that the Italian firm Ansaldo sent directors to the USA and Germany in the 1910s to study cutting-edge techniques. Destinations included such business giants as Ford, Bethlehem Steel, and Krupp. Again, in the 1920s, an Ansaldo engineer, Agostino Rocca, was sent to various European and American venues to learn about scientific management. In 1935, as general manager, he established an office, the ONI, which unsuccessfully promoted studies and programmes based on Taylorite methods.

In the aftermath of the Second World War (1948), the Anglo-American Council on Productivity was established under the auspices of the Marshall Plan. American experts visited Britain as consultants and British missions to the USA were undertaken to learn first-hand about American scientific management techniques. However, no great explosion of scientific management techniques eventuated for a variety of economic, cultural, and political reasons, but also because the methods touted by the Americans were already well known in Britain (Boyns and Edwards 2007; Fleischman et al. 2007).

In 1954, Palle Hansen, the founder of the Copenhagen Business School, was chosen by the Danish Ministry of Trade's Productivity Committee to lead a delegation on a six-week tour of the USA (Näsi and Rohde 2007). The next year, the recently founded Japanese Productivity Center organized a similar study tour. Perhaps the most significant story line here was the participation of Taiichi Ohno, years later the architect of Toyota's meteoric rise to greatness.

Scientific management

It was not until the late nineteenth century that a costing literature appeared in significant volume. In particular, it was the engineering profession and its journal literature on the development of scientific management launched cost accounting into the modern era. Sowell (1973: 524) wrote how 'the industrial engineer, rather than the cost accountant, recognised the need for a revolution in the industrial order and initiated ideas that grew into predetermined cost techniques'. The contribution of the engineering profession and a host of individual commentators to the development of scientific management theory in the USA is well documented (Garner 1954; Sowell 1973; Epstein 1978; Wells 1978; Fleischman 1996, 2000).

In the discussion that follows, there will appear frequent mention of standard costing as the *sine qua non* of scientific management. However, the term 'standard' is often bandied about to describe a wide range of different approaches to costing. Fleischman and Parker (1991), for example, use the term for BIR enterprises that based standards on historical experience, sometimes only the preceding year's results, and then compared those 'standards' to the current period's actuals. Labour standards at Boulton & Watt were based on time-and-motion study, but were badly rounded and infrequently amended (Fleischman *et al.* 1995). The standard costing theory of the scientific management movement described here was at a much higher level of sophistication and science, with engineers determining optimal work routines and standards of efficiency. What was most innovative at this point in time was the advent of variance analysis techniques.

Early UK theorists (Garcke and Fells 1887; Norton 1889) also had significant insights on the subject. Garcke and Fells' classic *Factory Accounts, Their Principles and Practice* (1887) is often regarded as the first truly authoritative contribution to cost accounting literature although a case can be made for BIR theorists Hamilton (1777) for his insights on return-on-investment (ROI) and Babbage (1835) for his differentiation between fixed and variable costs. Garcke and Fells suggested the value of establishing norms of cost wherein the person best acquainted with a particular process should estimate a probable cost in terms of wages and materials. They, as well as Mann (1903a, 1903b), argued for the allocation of overhead based on direct labour hours or dollars, and this became typical practice for decades. Nicholson (1909), meanwhile, made the case for machine hours. Church (1901), although critical of Taylor, did not substantively differ in his discussion of engineered standards and their utilisation in predetermining costs and comparing estimates with actual results (Sowell 1973). He argued that product and period costs (shop and establishment) could be applied to products using a variety of allocation bases, thereby presaging ABC. He urged the establishment of production centres to facilitate these applications (J&K 1987; Fleischman 1996). Norton (1889) and Dicksee (1911) spoke to the idea of having each processing department operate as a separate profit centre, with the development of transfer pricing to allow for the flow of costs throughout an enterprise. Solomons (1952) credited Whitmore (1908) with detailing a standard cost system based on the ideas of Taylor and Church, though he made original contributions in his own right in handling idle time and material use variations (Parker 1969; Sowell 1973). Emerson (1914) distinguished a new method of ascertaining costs contemporarily coming into vogue in large plants wherein costs were determined in advance of manufacturing.

Continental European theorists were likewise heard during the Age of Taylor, although not on the subject of scientific management. Holzer and Rogers (1990) caution us not to ignore French contributions that were concerned with integrating cost accounting within DEB. Léautey and Guilbault (1889) emphasised the accuracy of the *prix de revient* and its overhead component. Croizé and Croizé (1907) made important distinctions between period and product costs (Holzer and Rogers 1990). In Germany, meanwhile, Ballewski (1877) considered cost behaviours at different output levels, and Tolkmitt (1894) analysed the role of costing in management decision making (Coenenberg and Schoenfeld 1990). Schmalenbach (1899), early in his illustrious career, wrote of the dichotomy between fixed and variable costs and the appropriate exclusion of the former for purposes of cost estimation and pricing policy (Schweitzer 1992).

Yet it was Frederick Taylor, as the premier populariser and consultant on scientific management in its early years, who stamped the age with his imprimatur. A concentration on his ideas is not intended in any way to marginalise the systematising efforts of his collaborators or competitors, such as Barth, Emerson, Gantt, Gilbreth, and Thompson, all of whom shared many of the same ideas with nuances of difference. Taylor (1911) generalised scientific management to mean:

1   the deployment of science in management to replace rules of thumb;
2   harmony in industrial relations rather than discord;

3   cooperation in the productive process rather than individualism;
4   maximisation of output rather than restriction ('soldiering');
5   the development of each worker to maximum efficiency and, hence, economic well-being.

Taylor's industrial philosophy broadly extended to such issues as machine layout and design, tool standardisation and tool-room reorganisation, standard purchasing and stores methodology, and functional foremanship (a proliferation of supervisors each with a specialised expertise). However, the two features that were most central to the emerging theory of scientific management were stopwatch-based time study and incentive wage schemes.

Taylor (1903: 58, 65) himself called time study the 'foundation' of his system. Taylor wrote, 'the whole system rests upon an accurate and scientific study of unit time, which is by far the most important element in scientific management'. Although Taylor (1912) was forced to admit before a Congressional hearing that time study had resulted only in 'unscientific approximations', ostensibly because of worker resistance, his emphasis upon it as a mechanism to popularise the movement fixated attention on scientific management as a labour control mechanism.

Taylor's approach to time study was more scientific than merely repeated observations, stopwatch in hand. Taylor was convinced that managers could improve productivity by identifying the most efficient way to perform each task physically and psychologically and by then communicating those directions to individual workers. This was the procedure used in the famous episode featuring Schmidt, the pig-iron handler at Bethlehem Steel (Taylor 1911). Labour standards and incentive wage schemes went hand-in-glove with time study. Indeed, the primary purposes of time study were to identify 'first-class' workers in particular functions through measurement against standards, to enhance productivity by linking workers to tasks for which they appeared to be naturally selected, and to improve their living standards through the payment of bonuses and differential piece-rate schemes covering a wide variety of parameters. Taylor believed that the determination of incentive wages, based upon scientific time study and motivational considerations, could provide solutions to many, if not all, labour problems (Nelson 1975).

A number of other industrial philosophies were germinated that deserve mention as components of the scientific management movement. Fordism, celebrating Henry Ford, featured mass production techniques and the payment of high wages to labour. Fordism has been linked to Keynesian economics for its objective of promoting national demand via a prosperous consumer class. It was a keynote of Ford's approach that his workers should be able to afford the product they produced. Fordism was embraced in post-Revolution Russia, favoured by Lenin and inculcated into the early five-year plans. Bedaux, born in France but an early émigré to the USA, functioned as an industrial consultant in the 1920s and 1930s, primarily, although his worldwide enterprise was founded before the First World War. He had studied Taylorism extensively and disagreed with Taylor's approach to time study. The Bedaux system was founded upon a scientific investigation of the relationship between a prescribed amount of work, the fatigue that it produced, and the time required for recovery. Based on these factors, an optimum rate of work and a standard time for any activity (expressed in Bedaux points) would be established. Bedaux's system was immensely popular with businessmen and a British study concluded that a 50 per cent increase in productivity could be achieved by companies embracing the method. However, the hatred aroused among labour, which saw it as an ultimate 'speeding' device, led to numerous violent strikes in Britain and the USA. Consequently, Bedauxism suffered an ignominious death (Levant and Nikitin 2006).

Parker and Lewis (1995) have brought to light the career of Fayol, the managing director of a French mining company, whom the authors identify, along with Taylor, as embodiments of the 'classical management model'. Both embraced an authority-based model of control to achieve efficiency and effective management. The difference between their philosophies lay in the focal point of their control mechanisms. Taylorism was directed toward improving the performance of the shop-floor operative while Fayol's emphasis was on the operations of managers.

Budgeting

Scientific management and business budgeting are closely related, each born, theoretically at least, in the era of the First World War. However, the venues in which they were conceived were quite different. Scientific management, as we have seen, grew out of industrial engineering, with cost accountants jumping on the bandwagon at a rather late point in its evolution. In point of fact, the *Journal of Accountancy* featured a fascinating series of articles during the 1910s in which the engineers and cost accountants battled for dominance (Fleischman and Tyson 2000). By contrast, budgeting as applied to business enterprises, at least in America, evolved from the governmental sector, particularly at the municipal government level.

There is ample evidence to suggest that budgeting was a lesson conveyed from government to business during the 1920s in the USA. At the 1922 conference of the National Association of Cost Accountants (NACA), Gilman (1922: 263) claimed that 'the modern business budget is an inheritance from the municipal and governmental budget'. J. O. McKinsey, a Chicago certified public accountant (CPA), deserves most credit for sounding a clarion call to which businesses in the USA responded. During 1921, he published a series of nine articles in *Administration* which provided a cogent rationale for business budgeting, followed by an in-depth development of a master budget. He also described the importance of the budget committee and internal lines of authority and responsibility for effective budgetary control (McKinsey 1922; Marquette and Fleischman 1992). By the early 1930s, production budgeting had become well established. Rudimentary flexible budgets were introduced into the management literature by Maynard (1928) and Drucker (1929). Like government, business had learned that 'there can be no effective control of . . . costs unless there is a proper classification of accounts' (Rogers 1932: 196), with costs recorded by line item linked to the department that incurred them. Financial institutions contributed to the evolutionary process by according superior credit ratings to businesses that had instituted budgeting (Theiss 1937). From these beginnings, budgeting theorists began a decades-long process of formulating the psychological parameters of effective budgeting and the processes by which budgets could be most effectively constructed within business enterprises.

Standard costing and budgeting around the world

Despite these differences in origin, the authors of the histories of individual nations and regions featured in Chapman *et al.* (2007) tend to link the two because of the closeness of the time frames in which each developed. Notable differences might be observed in the degree to which scientific management in general and standard costing/budgeting in particular were adopted in countries other than the USA. The dissemination of scientific management was significantly aided by an international movement to spread the gospel. The First International Congress in Scientific Management was held in Prague in 1924. This event led to the establishment of national associations in several European nations to popularise and disseminate the new methodologies.

Fleischman *et al.* (2007) found that standard costing followed an evolutionary progression in Britain from the First World War through the 1950s and 1960s and, as such, was not as much in arrears of US developments as has been popularly believed (Boyns 1998). This pattern differs from findings in the USA where standard costing developed slowly until the end of the Second World War and then underwent a substantial boom at least in quantitative, if not qualitative, terms. As in America, the literature suggests that knowledge of scientific methods came to Britain earlier than their widespread introduction into practice. Garry wrote a precursor to full standard costing as early as 1902, and Preen spoke to the value of budgeting in 1907 (Garner 1954). Standard costing was frequently mentioned in the 1920s in *The Cost Accountant*. Boyns (1998, 2003) has studied the archives of the Manchester firm Hans Renold Ltd. and found that standard costing emerged there in the 1910s following a consulting engagement by Church. Likewise, budgetary control was in evidence there as well as at Austin Motors in the 1920s.

The pattern in France more closely resembled the American experience. Standard costing was known in the 1920s, albeit not seen much in practice until the late 1950s or early 1960s (Carmona 2007). This may have been due in part to the fact that Fayol was as influential as Taylor in France (Antonelli *et al.* forthcoming). Again, a few French firms were in the vanguard at much earlier points in time. The most prominent was car manufacturer Renault which adopted '*la méthode Taylor*' (Bhimani 1993, 1994). Budgeting had an earlier genesis in France and has been extensively studied by Berland (1998, 2001; Berland and Boyns 2002).

Antonelli *et al.* (2006) found that, in the 1880s, the Italian pottery giant Manifattura Ginori was comparing actual output to pre-determined standards as a basis for bonuses and punishments. Of course, these standards were probably of an earlier genre than the scientifically engineered variety of the age of Taylor. Fiat had embraced scientific management preceding the First World War and was using fatigue-and-motion study to establish maximally efficient work routines (Antonelli *et al.* forthcoming). An Italian organisation identified by the acronym ENIOS was established in the 1920s to popularise and diffuse scientific management principles. However, the take-up was minimal due to specifics in the industrial environment there – small firms, small markets, little technological innovation, and managerial hostility. A preliminary study (Antonelli *et al.* forthcoming) of the diversified Genoese firm Ansaldo has revealed the use of some budgeting in the 1910s. Although Ansaldo executives were exposed to Taylorism, temporary installation of a Bedaux system occurred and appears to have been the scientific management system of choice.

Scientific management apparently received considerable play in the Nordic countries as reported by Näsi and Rohde (2007). Taylorism arrived early in the twentieth century and gained a 'foothold' there. Hansen visited the USA in 1954 and transported back an appreciation for standard and direct costing and budgetary control. In terms of the theory of budgeting, Kari Lukka has made a substantial contribution to the exploration of its behavioural aspects (Näsi and Rhode 2007).

Japan presents an interesting case. Okano and Suzuki (2007) identified Mitsubishi Electric, Toyobo, and Fukusuke as early developers of scientific management but as a version that was adapted to Japan's cultural environment. Taylorism made substantial inroads during the 1930s as its emphasis on efficiency was viewed as a means to promote recovery from the Great Depression. Standard costing was also promoted during the 1930s among governmental suppliers of war materiel as the militarists anticipated the road to war. Okano and Suzuki also report that standard costing during the 1930s did not work well because of volatile price fluctuations and the nation's tax laws that did not accept standard costing for inventory valuation.

It should be noted in conclusion that there was virtually no mention in Chapman *et al.* (2007) of standard costing or budgeting in the national histories of China, Spain, or the

German-speaking countries. In the case of Australia, we have seen an example of the very early introduction of scientific management as a result of Jensen's efforts. However, progress was only made in governmentally run factories so far as we know. Presumably private industry was too small to consider Taylorite innovations worthwhile. This pattern of adoption might also explain the situation in Spain where clear antecedents of scientific management were evident in the royal factories of an earlier time but had passed from the scene by the twentieth century. More perplexing was the absence of discussion of scientific management in Ewert and Wagenhofer (2007). Of course, the Germanic industrial scene in the 1930s was totally directed by the Hitlerian regime which did not see standard costing as relevant to its war preparations. Given the meteoric recovery of German industrial capacity following the war, however, it might be expected that standard costing played a role.

Direct vs. absorption costing

The 1950s and 1960s witnessed a theoretical battle royal between traditionalists defending absorption or full costing and 'progressives' advancing the cause of direct (variable, marginal) costing. The literature is replete with references to 'fierce warfare', 'vitriolic confrontation', and 'ferocious, ongoing debate'. Direct costing first appeared in popular parlance in a *N.A.C.A. Bulletin* article by Harris (1965), but it was not until the aftermath of the Second World War that numerous articles began to appear there and in its British counterpart, *The Cost Accountant*, in which the pros and cons of direct costing were argued. The American literature on this topic, which continued for several decades, has been collected in Marple (1965b); the British is reviewed by Dugdale and Jones (2003, 2005) and Baxter (2005).

Defenders of the orthodoxy argued that absorption costing was even more necessary as fixed factory overhead became an increasingly substantial component of product cost. Eliminating those costs from inventory would badly understate inventory asset values, a particularly critical shortcoming to those academics who favour balance sheet as opposed to income statement accuracy. Also, it was argued, direct costing would lead to perilously low pricing. It was felt that absorption costing would provide better information for stockholders and the public at large. Supporters also urged that the separation of costs into fixed and variable is not realistic since costs are not 'unalterably fixed or undeviatingly variable under all possible manufacturing conditions' (Greer 1965: 151; Ludwig 1965).

Dugdale and Jones identify support from non-academic sources for absorption costing in Great Britain. The Inland Revenue opposed direct costing because it felt that it would result in the loss of short-term tax revenues. This position came to a head in the noted Duple Motor Bodies case (1961), when the Inland Revenue was told it could not force a taxpayer to use absorption costing. Although denied, the Inland Revenue continued to press its case strongly. The accounting profession, through Recommendation 10 issued by the Institute of Chartered Accountants in England and Wales, meanwhile favoured absorption costing for external reporting purposes for the sake of consistency with past practice and was unwilling to offer a choice of costing methods in the interest of harmonisation. Finally, trade associations, such as the printers, trying to effectuate uniform accounting among their memberships (Walker and Mitchell 1997), perceived absorption costing as the path of least resistance.

Direct costing advocacy was particularly strong among academicians. Virtually every cost accounting textbook avers direct costing's superiority for managerial decision-making given that variable costs are more controllable than fixed. The same textbooks bespeak the arbitrary nature of overhead allocation techniques and their failure to apportion these costs to individual product lines with any precision whatsoever (Luenstroth 1965). Moreover, absorption costing is judged to be 'misguided' for long-term pricing and planning policy decisions since, as J&K argue, all costs tend to be variable in the long term (Dugdale and Jones 2005; National Association of Accountants 1957). On a more positive note, direct costing is perceived as better suited than absorption costing for such control tools as flexible budgeting, standard costing, cost-volume-profit calculations, and breakeven analysis.

Dugdale and Jones (2003), in evaluating the outcome of the absorption/direct costing contretemps, declared there could be no winner. One or the other of the approaches is more appropriate for different enterprises under different circumstances. In the contemporary world, the debate has been rendered moot by the advent of computer technology which permits companies to readily maintain both systems. Back in the 1950s and 1960s, however, the cost accounting professional organisations in the UK and the USA respectively took opposite positions. The ICWA officially supported direct costing while the National Association of Accountants (1957), successor to the NACA, in its Research Series No. 23, after identifying the advantages and disadvantages of direct costing, concluded that its shortcomings could be more easily overcome and opted for absorption costing. Standard-setting bodies on both sides of the Atlantic (the US Committee on Accounting Procedure and the UK Accounting Standards Steering Committee) in due course made absorption costing mandatory for financial reporting.

Direct costing came in a highly altered form to the Germanic countries. Ewert and Wagenhofer (2007: 1065) write of *Grenzplankostenrechnung* (GPK) as a 'widely used cost accounting system for cost planning and control purposes', similar to direct costing that was developed independently in Germany by Plaut, a management consultant, and Kilger, an academic, in the mid-1950s and early 1960s. The major feature was the separation of variable ('relevant') costs from fixed costs for decision-making purposes. GPK utilises a variety of cost drivers and hundreds of cost centres in attempting to track relevant costs through the production process. In many ways, GPK may be conceived as a forerunner of ABC and leads Ewert and Wagenhofer to claim that German cost accounting systems and theory were more advanced than in the rest of the world. The one disadvantage of GPK that they identify is the insufficient attention accorded to fixed costs as it was believed theoretically that there was no justifiable basis upon which they could be allocated. In this regard, GPK theory anticipated J&K, but it is not at all clear that failing to allocate fixed costs is truly a disadvantage.

As with so many other cost accounting innovations, the Nordic countries seem to have followed in the footsteps of Germany, although Näsi and Rohde (2007) trace the originating spark of variable costing to the influence to the London School of Economics. As US costing literature began to supplant German as the most influential in the mid-1950s, a full-blown debate between full and variable costing emerged. Näsi and Rohde provide figures reflecting a vastly greater acceptance of variable costing in Norway than anything that occurred in the USA or the UK. Apparently, all Norwegian companies used full costing in 1948, but by 1963 45 per cent had adopted variable costing. By 1975, two-thirds of all companies in the country were using the method.

Time-honoured themes

The integration of costing records

A time-honoured theme has been the timing of the integration of the costing and financial records within the context of DEB. Examples of DEB implementation were pretty universal by the eighteenth century with the possible exception of Japan where Kimizuka (1992) and

Okano and Suzuki (2007) claim it was not in evidence until the 1870s, following the Meiji Restoration. The larger question is, when did the integration of the costing and financial records occur? Iberia is an interesting case. Carmona (2007) felt that the integration came late to Spain while Matos Carvalho *et al.* (2007), in a most welcome study of Portuguese cost accounting, found integration at the Silk Factory Company in the eighteenth century. Integration in France appeared in the immediate post-Napoleonic period, particularly evidenced at Godard's Baccarat Chrystalworks. However, early factories operating under royal patent were not as successful in achieving cost accounting innovation in France as they were in Spain. After the Napoleonic era, French cost accounting markedly improved, helped in large part by integration (Boyns *et al.* 1997; Nikitin 1990, 1996). Manifattura Ginari, the Italian pottery concern, had DEB in place by the early 1900s (Antonelli *et al.* 2006) but, although there are surviving costing records, the authors are unable to state definitively whether they were integrated with the financial accounts.

Integration has been an important focus in the BIR rehabilitation project. Edwards (1989) drew inspiration from the extensive survey of Welsh industrial accounting undertaken by Jones (1985) when he reported the integration of the costing records at the huge Cyfarthfa iron enterprise in the 1780s. Bryer (2006) and Fleischman and Macve (2007) found evidence of integration at Carron from its foundation in 1760, overlooked by Campbell (1961) and Fleischman and Parker (1990) in earlier investigations.

Cost accountancy and war

The impact of war on the development of cost accounting has been mixed (see also Chapter 27). The preparation for war has had a positive effect on methodology as measured at governmental installations which manufacture the wherewithal for war. Serious attention has been accorded to two arsenals separated by thousands of miles of distance and two centuries of time – the Venice Arsenal and the Springfield Armory (SA).

Zan (2004a) and Zambon and Zan (2007) have recently explored the Venice Arsenal archives for the period 1580–1679. In evidence there was the productive potential to build a warship in a matter of hours. Carmona (2007) summarised the cost accounting advances found in this research. One innovative aspect was a form of budgeting for planning and control purposes. Accountants and supervisors met regularly for forecasting and target planning. The participation of gang bosses in the budgeting process reflects modern notions of establishing accountability by involving production floor personnel. Other features of accounting at the Arsenal were the control of waste and the articulation of a system of rewards and punishments for operatives and foremen ostensibly based on expected performance. However, as Zan and Carmona both caution, the events at the Venice Arsenal, as well as at other governmental installations of this type, should be evaluated in the context of an organisation committed to the public welfare rather than a profit-seeking motive.

The SA story has been partially told already in this chapter as it is featured in the H&M/Tyson debate over the origins of purposeful managerial accounting. At this juncture, it is important to investigate more closely the costing innovations introduced there by the cadre of West Point graduates who H&M claim introduced at Springfield a management regime of the modern type.

Chandler (1977: 4), while perceiving the SA as something of a one-off, was impressed with the management there and described the accounting controls as 'the most sophisticated used in any American industrial establishment before the 1840s'. There can be no question that some very impressive accounting innovations were taking place. A piece-rate system was instituted based on a series of time-and-motion studies that exposed both slack and waste. Accountability was established at the level of the individual operative via objectively derived, norm-based measures of performance. Substantial productivity gains were the end result. The historiographic debate focuses on issues other than whether or not substantive advances were made. H&M feel that West Point systems of examination and grading were instilled into a management structure of the modern type which created a disciplined environment in which these productivity gains could be accomplished. Tyson, by contrast, argues that the adoption of new technology, the introduction of control mechanisms already present in the private sector (e.g., textiles), and periodic economic downturns are more explanatory of the piece-rate system introduced. Disagreements in the discourse also surround the timing of significant events and interpretations of the evidence.

If the events at Springfield augur cost accounting advance at military facilities, a counterindication was the attempt of the US government to install Taylorite systems, particularly time-and-motion studies, at arsenals and other locations in the immediate pre-First World War era. Prominent among labour disruptions in response to these efforts were those at the Naval Shipyard at Mare Island and the Watertown Arsenal. The strike at Watertown in 1911 was so severe that the US Congress passed legislation prohibiting time study in governmental shipyards and arsenals; a prohibition that lasted from 1915 to 1949 (Fleischman and Marquette 2003).

There has been conflicting evidence with respect to the impact of war on cost accounting practice. The most famous study is that of Loft (1986) who wrote of significant advances in Britain during the First World War. The improvement was magnified in Loft's estimation by her perception that Britain's costing expertise was effectively at ground zero in the pre-war milieu. Loft concurred with Chandler's (1984) view that the prevalence of family firms, coupled with the power of British trade unions, forestalled interest in innovative management techniques, such as cost accounting systems. However, neither Loft's perception of the bankruptcy of British costing before the war (cf. Boyns 1993; Boyns and Edwards 2007) nor the salubrious developments she felt occurred during the war are agreed upon universally (cf. Marriner 1980; Boyns and Edwards 2007).

In any event, the infamous shell shortage at Gallipoli and other logistical nightmares inspired the Ministry of Munitions (MM) to adopt new contracting arrangements with its suppliers. In this effort, the MM had to overcome a serious shortfall of accountants (especially cost accountants), the absence of market mechanisms for price fixing (competitive tendering was traditional), and the non-existence of standards that could aid in determining productive expectations from a given amount of raw material (Marriner 1980). The MM ascertained costs upon which to base contract prices in two distinct processes. First, investigatory teams were dispatched to private-sector providers to determine costs that could serve as standards for the industry. Second, the MM was responsible for some 200 nationalised factories where cost records were maintained in minute detail and, thus, became the basis for comparison throughout the public and private sectors (Loft 1986). At the national shell factories, every process was costed in terms of materials, labour, and establishment costs, so that managers could determine the impact of material waste and poor workmanship.

Obviously, the quantity of cost accounting functions being undertaken, if not so obviously the quality, mandated a tremendous growth in the number of practitioners. The participation of noted chartered accountants such as Peat and Whinney gave the costing side of the profession a boost and justified Loft's image of cost accountancy 'coming into the light'. In terms of the sophistication and the permanency of the innovations, however, there is considerable debate (Fleischman and Tyson 2000). Loft reacted favourably to what might have been MM puffery in evaluating its influence in inspiring the nation to a more broadly based costing awareness. Marriner (1980) was more sceptical in her response to the claim of the MM that its efforts had widely expanded 'best practice' cost accounting to large segments of British industry. Marriner found that most cost records mandated by the MM were worthless because of the absence of standardised procedures. Also, costing before and after the war suffered mutually from poor allocation techniques for incorporating capital costs into pricing. The Balfour Committee, which investigated the state of industrial accounting in the mid-1920s, found a lack of consistency across industries and the absence of scientific practice. Marriner concluded that if the MM's wartime directives had widespread influence, it soon dissipated. Boyns and Edwards (2007 1008–11), having carefully weighed the conflicting evidence, came down in support of Marriner's position.

A similar lack of consistency during the First World War period is reflected in the work of McWatters and Foreman (2005) in their comparative study of two meat-packing concerns in Australia and Canada during the war. Here, and in earlier work (Foreman and Tyson 1998; Foreman 2001), the war decade in Australia saw the advent of scientific management in governmental factories, the only industrial enterprises of significant size. Meanwhile, in Canada, the verdict was that the effect of the war on accounting was minimal. Likewise, Fleischman and Tyson (2000) found no discernible costing innovations in the US as a result of the First World War, and there is general agreement among all observers that the Second World War negatively influenced standard costing. Stempf (1943: 500) observed in the *Journal of Accountancy* that 'prewar standards have become relatively meaningless, and, in general, industry has been forced to fall back on actual costs'. It is easy to understand why standard costing was not appropriate in the industrial environment of the Second World War, quite apart from the government's preference for dealing with actual costs. Factors included inexperienced workers, high labour turnover, unfamiliar products, lack of time-study engineers, material shortages, uncontrollable prices, small-lot emergency purchases, frequent specification changes, new inspection requirements and numerous artificial controls (Caminez 1944; Hoyt 1943). Kohler and Cooper (1945: 306) concluded their 41-page survey of Second World War accounting in the *Accounting Review* by observing that 'accounting practice suffered perceptibly and even degenerated as the result of the war'.

Fleischman and Marquette (2003), in a micro-level investigation of the Sperry Corporation, found that even world-class industrial enterprises that supplied military weaponry suffered declines in their use of scientific management during the war. Time-study-based routines and evaluation techniques that had been developed and honed during the interwar period became dead letters. This retreat came at a time when Sperry made a number of management accounting advances that appear to be more contemporary than what was lost (e.g., the development of subcontracting agreements that established control over suppliers; the focus on time rather than cost management; the elevation in importance of design and product launch measures; the utilisation of learning curves).

Uniform cost accounting

One discernible impact that government has had historically is seen in those instances when government takes uniform accounting initiatives. The success rate of these efforts has been dismal. An early movement in the USA featured the efforts of Harvey Chase to inspire uniform municipal accounting. This platform was carried forward in the municipal research bureau movement and its journal, *National Municipal Review*, but without much in the way of concrete results. A multitude of trade associations, established during the 1920s, tried to effect industry-wide costing uniformity. During the Great Depression, the US government attempted standardisation across virtually every industry in the hope of minimising unfair competition that might impair recovery efforts. Despite the weightiness of these efforts, absolutely nothing was achieved.

A bit more success was evident in the UK in the private sector with uniform costing efforts in the printing industry chronicled by Walker and Mitchell (1996, 1997, 1998). Edwards *et al.* (2003: 25) studied uniform costing initiatives in the British steel industry, a cooperative venture between the British Iron and Steel Federation and various governmental regulatory agencies, commencing in 1935 and lasting for some 35 years. It was found to be a difficult arrangement as the companies on occasion refused 'to supply neutral accounting numbers to help the government reach decisions'. With the post-Second World War nationalisation of industries such as coal, railways, and electricity, uniform accounting was demanded by the regulatory agencies.

Likewise, in countries where the government closely controlled the economy, standardised cost accounting methodology was imposed. On the road to war in Japan, the adoption of *Cost Accounting Standards* was demanded by the government for all munitions suppliers. The Chinese government in 1986 established uniform accounting rules for 'state-owned enterprises'. Governmental efforts to impose cost accounting uniformity is not conducive to methodological improvement since the government promotes approaches that are easy to administer rather than those that are the more efficient.

The rise of the mega-corporation and ROI

A series of events of profound importance coexisted chronologically with the evolution of scientific management in America. These produced the rise of the decentralised mega-corporation. The two firms that have received extensive study from Chandler (1962, 1977; Chandler and Salisbury 1971) and J&K (Johnson 1980a, 1980b; Kaplan 1983; J&K 1987) are DuPont and General Motors (GM). Certainly, there were huge enterprises that predated these two, such as Carnegie Steel, Standard Oil, and the American Tobacco Company, but what differentiated DuPont and GM was the appearance of a managerial hierarchy that made a multidivisional structure feasible. Earlier industrial giants tended to be highly centralised, depending on an omnipotent CEO of the calibre of Carnegie, Rockefeller, or Duke. Drawing upon Williamson (1970), J&K (1987: 98) explained:

> Multidivisional organizations arose to supplant these markets [labour and capital] by internalizing the multi-activity operations of several integrated firms to earn higher asset returns than the market could elicit from the same firms if they operated independently.

Nowhere in the immense scrutiny of DuPont and GM was there mention of standard costing, time-and-motion studies, or the scientific development of work routines, although Pierre DuPont was impressed by the raw material and labour cost controls important in the Taylorite system (Johnson 1980a). Furthermore, Alfred Sloan (1964), long-time chief executive of GM and architect of its managerial structure, made no mention in his autobiography of scientific management being practised there.

The story of the DuPont Powder Company, founded in 1903, tells of the transition from a single to a multi-activity firm. As the organisation became increasingly diversified during the First World War and beyond, it became necessary to devise a management accounting system to control the value chain and to harmonise departmental performance with ownership interests. DuPont was the first major industrial firm in the USA to be decentralised, although it continued to manifest certain centralised features that characterised nineteenth-century enterprises. A number of innovative managerial accounting methods were devised to control the organisation. The most ingenious and famous was the adoption of an elaborate return-on-investment (ROI) measure developed by Donaldson Brown. ROI was primarily used to make decisions about alternative uses of capital rather than its more familiar role as a mechanism to evaluate managerial performance (Flesher and Previts 2007). This focus on capital investment decisions was a new development that came with diversification. Chandler pointed out that Brown's ROI formula was also used for more routine analyses of each mill's performance, the locating of inefficiencies, and the adjustment of plans and processes when appropriate. DuPont was also heavily involved in business forecasting for inventory control and central purchasing. In this regard, it stands as an early example of a demand-pull manufacturing environment, a forerunner of the just-in-time approach.

By 1918, Pierre DuPont had taken control of GM and brought Brown in to implement DuPont's accounting and financial control structures. Brown's ROI formula was used prominently, but more traditionally to evaluate divisional and managerial performance than at DuPont where the focus was on capital decisions. The art of forecasting was well developed at GM. Chandler said of Brown that he moved the organisation forward from decision-making based on past and present performance to anticipated conditions in the future. GM was a pathfinder in introducing a number of accounting and managerial methods common in today's world, including flexible budgeting, market-based transfer pricing, and divisional autonomy.

The costing/financial reporting interface

A major component of J&K's (1987) indictment of US managerial accounting was its domination by financial reporting. An important element is the requirement that inventory be reported using absorption costing despite the greater value of direct costing for managerial decision-making.

Managerial accountants in the USA have been relegated to second-class citizenship within the accountancy profession. New Deal legislation of the Depression era, designed to rescue the economy from the downturn and forestall possible recurrence, included enactments directly relevant to accountants. The Securities Acts of 1933 and 1934 mandated audited financial statements for all publicly traded firms, guaranteeing a high-profile role for public accountants. The attempt in 1933 to establish industrial codes for most US industries to guarantee fair labour practices, to eliminate unfair and destructive competition, and to maintain consumer purchasing power, caused cost accountants and the NACA's leadership to envision a golden age, since a more scientific approach to costing would be required and uniform costing systems needed. Cost accountants would be vital in governmental service to collect data according to prescribed formats and to ensure that rules were followed. These dreams were soon dashed (Fleischman and Tyson 1999).

The impact of the Securities and Exchange Commission on the US accounting profession has been incalculable. For one, the Securities Acts formalised the audit process, limited its practice to CPAs, and glamorised that side of the profession. Clearly, the highest prestige has been enjoyed by accountants who work for the international firms. In essence, Securities and Exchange Commission audit regulations helped enforce a CPA-based career path for ambitious accountants. While it is impossible to prove that the best and the brightest minds are drawn to public accountancy, the CPA designation certainly had a 50-year head start over other competing professional certifications. Corporate accountants and other observers often lament the portrayal of cost accountants and bookkeepers as second-class accounting citizens. For example,

Young (1953: 644) entitled his brief article, 'Wanted: added lustre for cost accounting', noting that 'The student may come to associate cost accounting with the green eye shade, the high bookkeeper's stool and an endless diet of dry mathematical computations. Something must be done.'

The American experience has been replicated over time in France, China, and the UK, as recently reported. Carmona (2007) referenced Zimnovitch (1997) who observed the delay of standard costing's advent in France until the 1950s and 1960s because French accountants, struggling to attain professional status, stonewalled its implementation as it was perceived to be a non-accounting method. In China, meanwhile, Chow *et al.* (2007) have labelled the management research and education there as introductory, lacking in theorisation, and viewed as supplemental to financial accounting (Wang and Zhang 2000). The story of UK struggles has been detailed by Boyns and Edwards (2007: 980–4).

In many parts of the world, cultural and historical developments have combined to forestall the intertwining of the two branches of the profession. This is best reflected in the role of the controller. Okano and Suzuki (2007) write that, in Japan, greater effort is given to the improvement of managerial accounting rather than financial reporting. In Japanese industrial enterprises generally, controllers are responsible only for the financial statements while more relevant tasks related to planning and control are relegated to lower organisational levels and personnel where greater expertise might well reside.

By contrast, in the Germanic countries, and probably among the Nordic nations, there has been a conscious effort historically to avoid integration. 'A characteristic feature of German management accounting is the divorce of cost accounting from financial accounting' (Ewert and Wagenhofer 2007: 1056). Ewert and Wagenhofer explained the case in Germany against the harmonisation of the costing and financial reporting systems: (1) the two systems served different purposes; (2) the dominance of financial accounting standards and their revision undermines consistency; and (3) the impact of basing management accountants' incentives on financial numbers is dysfunctional.

In Germany, the educational system is rigidly dichotomised into financial reporting and what is called 'controlling'. German students have the option to major in 'control' as distinct from accounting. The functions of the controller differ markedly from what is typical in the USA. Stoeffel (1995) did a comparison between German and American controllers and found that the majority of US controllers were responsible for financial accounting, cost accounting, financial planning, financial reporting, and tax planning. Meanwhile, German controllers are more engaged in operative planning, strategic planning, and capital budgeting. Ewert and Wagenhofer (2007) conclude that historically a characteristic function of German management accounting has been to divorce itself from financial accounting, but that in the contemporary world the two branches are becoming increasingly reconciled.

Cost accountancy's professionalisation

While there has been a substantial volume of work done on the professionalisation of public accountancy (see Chapter 11), there has been comparatively less done on similar processes for cost/managerial accountants. Professional organisations of cost accountants whose origins have been studied were all twentieth century and mainly Anglo phenomena. The most famous story is that of the formation of the Institute of Cost and Works Accountants (ICWA) in the UK in 1919 (Loft 1990). The stage was set in one of the most-cited articles in accounting historiography (Loft 1986), in which she studied how British cost accountants were elevated in status by virtue of service to the state during the First World War.

The NACA, the American equivalent of the ICWA, was established in the same year. Here, however, the foundation of the organisation arose out of controversy with the American Institute of Accountants (AIA), then the professional society of CPAs. In 1919, at a council meeting of the AIA, a cost accounting section was proposed. The suggestion was rejected on the grounds that the primary purpose of the AIA was to serve practising public accountants. Immediately subsequent to this stinging rebuff, the NACA (today the Institute of Management Accountants) was formed (Carey 1969).

Notwithstanding the need to form a separate group, early membership statistics indicate that American CPAs did not stand aloof from the fledgling professional organisation. A list of 95 'Charter Members of the Association' include the names of some of the most distinguished CPAs in the country – Andersen, Castenholz, Gilman, Lybrand, Montgomery, Niven, Scovill, Wellington, and Wildman. All of the officers of the NACA in its first year were CPAs. Its second president in 1920 was no less a luminary than William Lybrand. The membership numbers confirm the thought that, despite the unpleasantness of the formation process, the NACA had the firm backing of public accountancy. While American CPAs may have wished to maintain control over the fledgling organisation, this degree of support contrasted markedly with the experience of the ICWA in Britain.

Anderson (1996) tells the story of the early history of the Australian Institute of Cost Accountants, founded in 1921. This professional body grew out of the events of the First World War and was modelled after the US and UK organisations founded two years before. Anderson points out that the Australian Institute did not grow its membership because of the absence of a journal (the *Australian Accountant* did not commence publication until 1936) and because the adoption of costing techniques came haltingly and was not widespread.

It was not until 1931 that the German accountants formed a professional society. Within two years, however, Hitler had risen to power and perverted the organisation to his purposes. Cost accountancy was forced to serve the public interest as interpreted by the Third Reich. That meant that practitioners were instructed to undertake such heinous assignments as costing slave labour in the concentration camps and determining the cost-efficient way to gas Jewish prisoners. The story of these activities is told in Funnell (1998) and Lippman and Wilson (2007). On 11 November 1937, the German government mandated the *Uniform Chart of Accounts*, the Goering Plan, which identified the purpose of accounting as pricing and unit valuation. When the Association of German Manufacturers replaced the Nazi regime, the common chart of accounts became voluntary, although practically all German firms continued to adhere to it. A distinctive feature of the German approach is its orientation toward current costing as the market price of factor inputs rather than acquisition costs (Coenenberg and Schoenfeld 1990).

Recent costing developments in Asia

The survey of Chinese management accounting by Chow *et al.* (2007) is almost entirely centred on post-1949 events following the establishment of the People's Republic of China. Accounting, both financial and managerial, is seen as a tool for central planning by the Communist regime. The industrial economy is comprised almost entirely of state-owned enterprises which operate under totally uniform accounting systems. The word '*shanbufeng*' connotes the lack of separation between government and the firm. As a system, there is little incentive to adopt any management techniques that would improve efficiency. Profit is not a major concern, and with prices dictated by the government rather than market mechanisms, there are no incentives for managers. Chow *et al.*'s (2007) survey does highlight the fact that certain practices reflect cultural differences from the West. Budgeting starts from handed-down targets rather than forecasting. Responsibility accounting is imposed at the group rather than the individual level. '*Guanxi*' refers to interpersonal relationships as the key factor in business and team-building as opposed to individual-based performance evaluation. From the government's perspective, cost/managerial accounting is clearly secondary to financial reporting.

The story of Japanese management accounting is a fascinating one since the dichotomy between myth and reality is extraordinarily broad. Here the significant development came in peacetime, after a devastating war. When one hears all the buzzwords that have become associated with Japanese managerial expertise, words and phrases such as '*kanban*' (just-in-time), '*kaizen*' (continuous improvement) budgeting and costing, target costing, value engineering, one thinks of ultimate managerial innovation and sophistication. Yet, Okano and Suzuki (2007) dispel much of this expertise as mythical. Of course, it is well known that following the Second World War western management gurus went to Japan to participate in the nation's reconstruction. Most famous was W. Edwards Deming and his 14 points related to business leadership and continuous improvement. Also involved were Juran and Feigenbaum; the latter introducing the concepts associated with total quality control later refined by Motorola into Six Sigma. If one were to read the survey of leading industrial giants compiled in the book *When Lean Enterprises Collide* (Cooper 1995), one could only feel the exhilaration of competition as experienced by globally competitive Japanese firms. Notwithstanding, Okano and Suzuki question which, if any, of these innovations are particularly Japanese. For example, there is nothing ethnically Japanese about target costing although the attribution is invariably made. They point out that westerners hear only about a few of the giants, most obviously Toyota. This assertion is borne out in Scarbrough *et al.* (1991) who surveyed a large number of Japanese firms and found that most used traditional cost accounting methods, such as single cost systems, payback and accounting rate of return for analysing investment opportunities, ROI and residual income for evaluating managers, and standard costing. Target costing and total quality control were found to be prominent in Japan, but just-in-time production control, that for which Japan is probably most noted, was found to be used in only 20 per cent of the firms surveyed.

Conclusion

Management accounting historians have been very active in recent decades, but there has been a concentration of effort on relatively few countries and epochs. We know little about developments in South and Central America, Africa, and many parts of Asia. The work of scholars whose first language is not English must become known to the English-speaking world. Foreign language archives must be accessed. The accomplishment of these goals will allow more international comparisons of managerial accounting developments through history. Likewise, more work needs to be done in historical epochs before and after the coming of Industrial Revolution. The concentration on the origins of purposeful cost accounting and the genesis of modern managerialism has given short shrift to centuries of antecedents and even to developments of the mid- and late twentieth century. There is also opportunity for new methodological approaches within the discipline. My urging for paradigmatic joint venturing has fallen mainly on deaf ears. Another exciting approach has come to be called 'action' research, longitudinal case studies of business enterprises, pioneered by Sten Jönsson, wherein academic researchers engage with managers in collaborative efforts to solve problems.

J&K (1987: 125), perhaps overly impressed by the accounting developments at DuPont and General Motors in the 1920s, observed that 'by 1925, American industrial firms had developed every management accounting procedure known today'. I feel it imperative to conclude this chapter by arguing how misguided this comment is. J&K were misinformed as to the volume of standard costing and variance analysis actually in practice in 1925. Perhaps they should have taken their clue from the fact that standard costing was not a feature of the innovations implemented by Brown at either DuPont or GM. We have considered here the direct/absorption costing debate of the 1950s and 1960s. Marple (1965a), in an introduction to his collection of articles, observed that the advent of direct costing was the culmination of a series of developments. Steps included the use of overhead rates to eliminate fixed costs associated with idle capacity, the development of breakeven analysis, the detailed separation of fixed and variable costs for flexible budgeting, and the recognition of volume's impact on developing cost data for decision making. US pioneers, Harris, Harrison, and Kohl wrote in the 1930s, but the bulk of the theory was developed in the UK during the 1940s, featured in articles on marginal costing in *The Cost Accountant* by Reece, Impey, and Smallpeice (reproduced in Boyns *et al.* 1996). The first textbook on the subject was Lawrence and Humphrey's *Marginal Costing* which appeared in the UK in 1947. Marple was of the opinion that theory flourished more in the UK because of the positive emphasis there on the value of marginal costing for planning and control, while US articles tended to take the more negative stance of opposition to absorption costing. Schweitzer (1992) described how marginal costing developments in the German-speaking world paralleled these events and led to contribution costing, mostly as a result of Schmalenbach's influence.

In addition, since 1925, there has been a widening of the theory and practice for a variety of overhead allocation bases apart from traditional direct labour and machine hours. Hathaway was urging as early as the 1920s and 1930s an expansion of horizons to include not only production but non-production apportionment bases (Seay and Schoenfeld 1989). Schnutenhaus (1948) identified certain fixed costs (e.g., research and development) that should not be allocated at all. Guru Peter Drucker (1963) warned the management accounting world of the dangers inherent in using traditional, labour-based product cost data in making product line and other marketing decisions. Many of the basic concepts of ABC were articulated by academics Staubus and Shillinglaw in the early 1960s and put into practice in limited fashion at GE (Johnson 1992).

After the Second World War, accounting data came to be seen as increasingly relevant for managerial decision-making, planning, and managerial (as distinct from cost) control activities. A most important contribution to this transition was the classic study of Simon *et al.* (1954: 4). Based on field studies, three functions of the controller's service were identified. Score-card (How well am I doing?) and attention-direction (What problems should I look into?) had traditionally been the focus of the controller's operation. Now problem-solving (decision-making) uses of accounting information were perceived to be 'a more promising direction of progress'.

The transition to direct costing for internal decision-making reflected this new direction. Schmalenbach (1948) articulated a theory of management based on decision-oriented transfer pricing dependent upon linear programming (simultaneous optimisation models) developed in the USA during the war to generate marginal-utility rates (Schweitzer 1992). Responsibility accounting matured in the late 1950s and 1960s as various mathematical techniques evolved to identify more accurately those costs controllable by managers (Scapens 1991). Variance analysis became more directly linked to decision-making, incorporating theoretical techniques espoused in Dopuch *et al.* (1967) and Demski (1967). Early editions of popular managerial textbooks embraced a greater decision-making orientation by the early 1960s (Parker 1969). Parker made the point that it was not until accounting theorists began to take serious cognisance of economic theory (e.g., Clark 1923) that widespread improvements were forthcoming in dis-counted cash flows, CVP analysis, and identification of costs relevant to decision-making.

The J&K indictment of US managerial accounting was quickly seconded by a chorus of well-known theorists (Berliner and Brimson 1988; Bromwich and Bhimani 1989; Cooper and Kaplan 1988; Sakuri 1989; Shank and Govindajaran 1989) who argued that labour-based standard costing should be replaced by cost management procedures more attuned to strategic issues and more aligned with the cost structures of automated manufacturing. Traditional standard costing, however, had been developed in an era that prioritised cost control rather than cost reduction. Achieving currently attainable standards would no longer suffice in the globally competitive world of the 1970s and beyond. From an organisational perspective, the post-1970 era is marked by continual change and innovation, multi-task flexibility, customer-focus creativity, and the need for continual cost reduction. Traditional, labour-based standard cost systems assumed a clearly defined responsibility and accountability framework. They were simply not designed to handle an environment of constant change, flexible relationships, and continuous innovation (Fleischman and Tyson 2007).

There can be little doubt that contemporary management accounting is probably more discontinuous from its past than at any other time in its long history. Computer technology has made many things possible in our discipline that were inconceivable even three and a half decades ago. At a blue-ribbon conference of academicians in 1970, Robert Anthony of Harvard was accorded the honour of concluding the proceedings by expressing his vision of the future of management accounting. Most of his prognostications were spot-on with respect to the three groupings of growth areas he identified – information content, analytical tools, control systems (Anthony 1973; Fleischman and Tyson 2007). However, Anthony (1970: 470) in his principles of managerial accounting textbook made one *faux pas* which for us with 20/20 historical hindsight appears monumental:

> Although most companies will use computers, it is by no means clear that most companies will have their own computers. Because of the great advantage that large computers have over small computers in terms of cost per calculation, it is quite possible that all but the large companies will use time on computers owned by someone else.

Where Anthony missed the boat was his failure to anticipate the impact of the computer, the agency that has made all things possible and was to change the face of management accounting for all time.

Key works

Chapman *et al.* (2007) contains a collection of contemporary and historical chapters on many aspects of management accounting.

Edwards (ed.) (2000), volume III, reprints 17 of the most cited articles on cost and management accounting in accounting historiography.

Fleischman (ed.) (2006) contains a number of highly regarded articles on cost and management account-ing, especially in volume 1, part 2 (the great debates) and volume 2, part 3 (US scientific management).

Johnson and Kaplan (1987) is the all-time, best-selling book about the history of managerial accounting that moved the discipline of accounting history centre-stage.

References

Alvarez, M. J., Gutiérrez, F. and Romero, D. (2002) Accounting and quality control in the Royal Tobacco Factory of Seville, 1744–1790: an historical perspective, *Accounting Business & Financial History*, 12 (2): 253–74.

Anderson, R. H. (1996) A history of the Australian Institute of Cost Accountants: a progress report 1921–1939, in G. D. Carnegie and P. W. Wolnizer (eds) *Accounting History Newsletter 1980–1989 and Accounting History 1989–1994*, pp. 169–86 (New York: Garland).

Anthony, R. N. (1970) *Management Accounting Principles* (Homewood, IL: Irwin).

Anthony, R. N. (1973) Some fruitful directions for research in management accounting, in N. Dopuch and L. Revsine (eds) *Accounting Research 1960–1970: A Critical Examination*, pp. 37–68 (Champaigne, IL: Center for International Education and Research in Accounting).

Antonelli, V., Boyns, T. and Cerbioni, F. (2006) Multiple origins of accounting? An early Italian example of the development of accounting for managerial purposes, *European Accounting Review*, 15 (3): 367–401.

Antonelli, V., Boyns, T. and Cerbioni, F. (forthcoming) The development of management accounting in Italy: Ansaldo in the early decades of the twentieth century, *Accounting Historians Journal*.

Arnold, A. J. and McCartney, S. (2002) The beginnings of accounting for capital consumption: disclosure practices in the British railway industry, 1830–55, *Accounting and Business Research*, 32 (4): 195–208.

Arnold, A. J. and McCartney, S. (2004) Were they ever 'productive to the capitalist'? Rates of return on Britain's railways, 1830–55, *Journal of European Economic History*, 33 (2): 383–410.

Babbage, C. (1835) *On the Economy of Machinery and Manufactures*, 4th edn (London: Charles Knight).

Ballewski, D. (1877) *Die Calculation von Maschinenfabriken* (Magdeburg).

Baxter, W. T. (2005) Direct versus absorption costing: a comment, *Accounting, Business & Financial History*, 15 (1): 89–91.

Berland, N. (1998) The availability of information and the accumulation of experience as motors for the diffusion of budgetary control: the French experience from the 1920s to the1960s, *Accounting, Business & Financial History*, 8 (3): 303–29.

Berland, N. (2001) Environmental turbulence and the functions of budgetary control, *Accounting, Business & Financial History*, 11 (1): 59–77.

Berland, N. and Boyns, T. (2002) The development of budgetary control in France and Britain from the 1920s to the 1960s: a comparison, *European Accounting Review*, 11 (2): 329–56.

Berliner, C. and Brimson, J. A. (eds) (1988) *Cost Management in Today's Advanced Manufacturing: The CAM-1 Conceptual Design* (Boston: Harvard Business School Press).

Bhimani, A. (1993) Indeterminacy and the specificity of accounting change: Renault 1898–1938, *Accounting, Organizations and Society*, 18 (1): 1–39.

Bhimani, A. (1994) Accounting and the emergence of the 'economic man', *Accounting, Organizations and Society*, 19 (8): 637–74.

Boyns, T. (1993) Cost accounting in the south Wales coal industry, c.1870–1913, *Accounting, Business & Financial History*, 9 (3): 327–52.

Boyns, T. (1998) Budgets and budgetary control in British businesses to c.1945, *Accounting, Business & Financial History*, 8 (3): 261–301.

Boyns, T. (2003) In memoriam: Alexander Hamilton Church's system of 'scientific machine rates' at Hans Renold Ltd., c.1901–c.1920, *Accounting Historians Journal*, 30 (1): 3–44.

Boyns, T. and Edwards, J. R. (1996a) Change agents and the dissemination of accounting technology: Wales' basic industries, c.1750–c.1870, *Accounting History*, 1 (1): 9–34.

Boyns, T. and Edwards, J. R. (1996b) The development of accounting in mid-nineteenth century Britain: a non-disciplinary view, *Accounting, Auditing & Accountability Journal*, 9 (3): 40–60.

Boyns, T. and Edwards, J. R. (1997) Cost and management accounting in early Victorian Britain: a Chandleresque analysis?, *Management Accounting Research*, 8 (1): 19–46.

Boyns, T. and Edwards, J. R. (2007) The development of cost and management accounting in Britain, in C. S. Chapman, A. G. Hopwood and M. D. Shields (eds) *Handbook of Management Accounting Research*, pp. 987–1052 (Oxford: Elsevier).

Boyns, T., Anderson, M. and Edwards, J. R. (eds) (1996) *British Cost Accounting 1887–1952* (New York: Garland).

Boyns, T., Edwards, J. R. and Nikitin, M. (1997) *The Birth of Industrial Accounting in France and Britain* (New York: Garland).

Bromwich, M. and Bhimani, A. (1989) *Management Accounting: Evolution Not Revolution* (London: Chartered Institute of Management Accountants).

Brun, R. (1930) A fourteenth-century merchant in Italy, *Journal of Economic and Business History*, 2 (3): 451–66.

Bryer, R. A. (2005) A Marxist accounting history of the British industrial revolution: a review of the evidence and suggestions for research, *Accounting, Organizations and Society*, 30 (1): 25–65.

Bryer, R. A. (2006) Capitalist accountability and the British industrial revolution: the Carron Company, 1759–circa 1850, *Accounting, Organizations and Society*, 31 (8): 687–734.

Bryer, R. A., Fleischman, R. K. and Macve, R. H. (2007) Smith, Marx, or Foucault in understanding the early British industrial revolution? Paper presented at Seventeenth Accounting, Business & Financial History Conference, Cardiff Business School, 14–15 September.

Caminez, D. B. (1944) Controlling costs with physical unit budgets, *NACA Year Book*, 25: 143–69.

Campbell, R. H. (1961) *Carron Company* (Edinburgh and London: Oliver & Boyd).

Carey, J. L. (1969) *The Rise of the Accounting Profession* (New York: AICPA).

Carmona, S. (2004) Accounting history research and its diffusion in an international context, *Accounting History*, 9 (3): 7–23.

Carmona, S. (2007) The history of management accounting in France, Italy, Portugal, and Spain, in C. S. Chapman, A. G. Hopwood and M. D. Shields (eds) *Handbook of Management Accounting Research*, pp. 923–40 (Oxford: Elsevier).

Carmona S. and Donoso, R. (2004) Cost accounting in early regulated markets: the case of the Royal Soap Factory of Seville (1525–1692), *Journal of Accounting and Public Policy*, 23 (2): 129–57.

Carmona, S. and Gómez, D. (2002) Early cost management practices, state ownership and market competition: the case of the Royal Textile Mill of Guadalajara, 1714–1744, *Accounting, Business & Financial History*, 12 (3): 231–51.

Carmona, S. and Zan, L. (2002) Mapping variety in the history of accounting and management practices, *European Accounting Review*, 11 (2): 291–304.

Carmona, S., Ezzamel, M. and Gutiérrez, F. (1997) Control and cost accounting practices in the Spanish Royal Tobacco Factory, *Accounting, Organizations and Society*, 22 (5): 411–66.

Carmona, S., Ezzamel, M. and Gutiérrez, F. (1998) Towards an institutional analysis of accounting change in the Royal Tobacco factory of Seville, *Accounting Historians Journal*, 25 (1): 115–47.

Chandler, A. D. (1962) *Strategy and Structure* (Cambridge, MA: MIT Press).

Chandler, A. D. (1977) *The Visible Hand: The Managerial Revolution in American Business* (Cambridge, MA: Harvard University Press).

Chandler, A. D. (1984) The emergence of managerial capitalism, *Business History Review*, 58 (4): 473–503.

Chandler, A. D. and Salisbury, S. (1971) *Pierre DuPont and the Making of the Modern Corporation* (New York: Harper & Row).

Chapman, C. S., Hopwood, A. G. and Shields, M. D. (eds) (2007) *Handbook of Management Accounting Research* (Oxford: Elsevier).

Chatfield, M. (1977) *A History of Accounting Thought* (Huntington, NY: Krieger).

Chow, C. W., Duh, R. -R. and Xiao, J. Z. (2007) Management accounting practices in the People's Republic of China, in S. C. Chapman, A. G. Hopwood and M. D. Shields (eds) *Handbook of Management Accounting Research*, pp. 941–86 (Oxford: Elsevier).

Church, A. H. (1901) The proper distribution of establishment charges, *Engineering Magazine*, 21: 508–17, 725–34, 904–12; 22: 31–40, 231–40, 367–76.

Clark, J. M. (1923) *Studies in the Economics of Overhead Costs* (Chicago: University of Chicago Press).

Coenenberg, A. G. and Schoenfeld, H. M. W. (1990) The development of managerial accounting in Germany: a historical analysis, *Accounting Historians Journal*, 17 (2): 95–112.

Cooper, R. (1995) *When Lean Enterprises Collide* (Boston: Harvard Business School Press).

Cooper, R. and Kaplan, R. S. (1988) Measure costs right: make the right decisions, *Harvard Business Review*, 88 (5): 96–103.

Croizé, A. and Croizé, H. (1907) *De l'Inventaire Commercial* (Paris: Librairie Comptable Pigier).

De Cazaux, L. F. G. (1824) *De la Comptabilité dans une Enterprise Industrielle et Spécialement dans une Exploitation Rurale* (Toulouse: J. M. Douladoure).

Demski, J. S. (1967) An accounting system structured on a linear programming model, *Accounting Review*, 42 (4): 701–12.

De Roover, R. (1941) A Florentine firm of cloth manufacturers, *Speculum*, 16 (1): 3–33.

Dicksee, L. R. (1911) *Advanced Accounting* (London: Gee).

Dodson, J. (1759) *The Accountant or the Method of Book-keeping* (London: J. Norse).

Dopuch, N., Birnberg, J. G. and Demski, J. S. (1967) An analysis of standard cost variance analysis, *Accounting Review*, 42 (3): 526–36.

Drucker, A. P. R. (1929) Budgeting and the sales quota, *Accounting Review*, 4 (1): 75–80.

Drucker, P. F. (1963) The five deadly business sins, *Wall Street Journal*, 21 October: A18.

Dugdale, D. and Jones, T. C. (2003) Battles in the costing war: UK debates, 1950–75, *Accounting, Business & Financial History*, 13 (3): 305–38.

Dugdale, D. and Jones, T. C. (2005) Direct versus absorption costing: a reply, *Accounting, Business & Financial History*, 15 (1): 93–5.

Edwards, J. R. (1989) Industrial cost accounting development in Britain to 1830: a review article, *Accounting and Business Research*, 19 (76): 305–17.

Edwards, J. R. (ed.) (2000) *The History of Accounting. Critical Perspectives on Business and Management* (London & New York: Routledge).

Edwards, J. R. and Boyns, T. (1992) Industrial organization and accounting innovation: charcoal iron-making in England 1690–1783, *Management Accounting Research*, 3 (2): 51–69.

Edwards, J. R. and Newell, E. (1991) The development of industrial cost and management accounting before 1850: a survey of the evidence, *Business History*, 33 (1): 35–57.

Edwards, J. R., Boyns, T. and Matthews, M. (2003) Cost, pricing and politics in the British steel industry, 1918–1967, *Management Accounting Research*, 14 (2): 25–49.

Edwards, J. R., Hammersley, G. and Newell, E. (1990) Cost accounting at Keswick, England, c.1598–1615: the German connection, *Accounting Historians Journal*, 17 (1): 61–80.

Edwards, R. S. (1937) Some notes on the early literature and development of cost accounting in Great Britain, *Accountant*, 97: 193–5, 225–31, 253–5, 283–7.

Elder, F. (1937) Cost accounting in the sixteenth century, *Accounting Review*, 12 (3): 226–37.

Emerson, H. (1914) *Efficiencies as a Basis for Operation and Wages*, 4th edn (New York: Engineering Magazine Co.).

Epstein, M. J. (1978) *The Effect of Scientific Management on the Development of Standard Costing* (New York: Arno Press).

Ewert, R. and Wagenhofer, A. (2007) Management accounting theory and practice in German-speaking countries, in C. S. Chapman, A. G. Hopwood and M. D. Shields (eds) *Handbook of Management Accounting Research*, pp. 1053–87 (Oxford: Elsevier).

Ezzamel, M., Hoskin, K. and Macve, R. (1990) Managing it all by numbers: a review of Johnson and Kaplan's *Relevance Lost, Accounting and Business Research*, 20 (78): 153–66.

Fleischman, R. K. (1996) A history of management accounting through the 1960s, in T. A. Lee, A. Bishop and R. H. Parker (eds) *Accounting History from the Renaissance to the Present*, pp. 119–42 (New York: Garland).

Fleischman, R. K. (2000) Completing the triangle: Taylorism and the paradigms, *Accounting, Auditing & Accountability Journal*, 13 (5): 597–623.

Fleischman, R. K. (ed.) (2006) *Accounting History* (London: Sage).

Fleischman, R. K. and Funnell, W. N. (2007) The relevance of the past, in T. Hopper, D. Northcott and R. Scapens (eds) *Issues in Management Accounting*, 3rd edn, pp. 377–97 (London: Prentice Hall).

217

Fleischman, R. K. and Macve, R. H. (2002) Coals from Newcastle: alternative histories of cost and management accounting in the northeast coal mining during the British industrial revolution, *Accounting and Business Research*, 32 (3): 133–52.

Fleischman, R. K. and Macve, R. H. (2007) Carron Company, non-Marxist perspectives: responses to Bryer. Paper presented at Fifth Accounting History Conference, Banff, 9–11 August.

Fleischman, R. K. and Marquette, R. P. (2003) The impact of World War II on cost accounting at the Sperry Corporation, *Accounting Historians Journal*, 30 (2): 67–104.

Fleischman, R. K. and Parker, L. D. (1990) Management accounting early in the British industrial revolution: the Carron Company, a case study, *Accounting and Business Research*, 20 (79): 211–21.

Fleischman, R. K. and Parker, L. D. (1991) British entrepreneurs and pre-industrial revolution evidence of cost management, *Accounting Review*, 66 (2): 361–75.

Fleischman, R. K. and Parker, L. D. (1992) The cost accounting environment in the British industrial revolution iron industry, *Accounting, Business & Financial History*, 2 (2): 141–60.

Fleischman, R. K. and Parker, L. D. (1997) *What is Past is Prologue: Cost Accounting in the British Industrial Revolution, 1760–1850* (New York: Garland).

Fleischman, R. K. and Radcliffe, V. S. (2003) Divergent streams of accounting history: a review and call for confluence, in R. K. Fleischman, V. S. Radcliffe and P. A. Shoemaker (eds) *Doing Accounting History*, pp. 1–29 (Amsterdam: JAI).

Fleischman, R. K. and Radcliffe, V. S. (2005) The roaring nineties: accounting history comes of age, *Accounting Historians Journal*, 32 (1): 61–109.

Fleischman, R. K. and Tyson, T. N. (1998) The evolution of standard costing in the UK and US: from decision making to control, *Abacus*, 34 (1): 92–119.

Fleischman, R. K. and Tyson, T. N. (1999) Opportunity lost? Chances for cost accountants' professionalization under the National Recovery Act of 1933, *Accounting, Business & Financial History*, 9 (1): 51–75.

Fleischman, R. K. and Tyson, T. N. (2000) Parallels between US and UK cost accountancy in the World War I era, *Accounting, Business & Financial History*, 10 (2): 191–212.

Fleischman, R. K. and Tyson, T. N. (2007) The history of management accounting in the U.S., in C. S. Chapman, A. G. Hopwood and M. D. Shields (eds) *Handbook of Management Accounting Research*, pp. 1089–107 (Oxford: Elsevier).

Fleischman, R. K., Boyns, T. and Tyson, T. N. (2007) The search for standard costing in the United States and Britain, working paper.

Fleischman, R. K., Hoskin, K. W. and Macve, R. H. (1995) The Boulton & Watt case: the crux of alternative approaches to accounting history?, *Accounting and Business Research*, 25 (99): 162–76.

Fleischman, R. K., Kalbers, L. P. and Parker, L. D. (1996) Expanding the dialogue: industrial revolution costing historiography, *Critical Perspectives on Accounting*, 7 (3): 315–37.

Flesher, D. L. and Previts, G. J. (2007) Donaldson Brown (1885–1965): twentieth-century financial management innovator. Paper presented at Business History Conference, Cleveland, 31 May-2 June.

Flesher, D. L., Samson, W. D. and Previts, G. J. (2003) Accounting, economic development, and financial reporting: the case of three pre-Civil War US railroads, *Accounting History*, 8 (2): 61–77.

Flinn, M. W. (1962) *Men of Iron: The Crowleys in the Early Iron Industry* (Edinburgh: Edinburgh University Press).

Flinn, M. W. (ed.) (1957) *The Law Book of the Crowley Ironworks* (Durham: Andrews).

Foreman, P. (2001) The transfer of accounting technology: a study of the Commonwealth of Australia government factories, 1910–1916, *Accounting History*, 6 (1): 31–59.

Foreman, P. and Tyson, T. N. (1998) Accounting, accountability and cost efficiency at the Commonwealth of Australia clothing factory, 1911–1918, *Accounting History*, 3 (2): 7–36.

Fu, P. Y. (1971) Government accounting in China during the Chou dynasty, *Journal of Accounting Research*, 9 (1): 40–51.

Funnell, W. N. (1998) Accounting in the service of the Holocaust, *Critical Perspectives on Accounting*, 9 (4): 435–64.

Gantt, H. L. (1916) Production and sales, *Engineering Magazine*, 50: 593–600.

Garcke, F. and Fells, J. M. (1887) *Factory Accounts, their Principles and Practice* (London: Crosby, Lockwood).

Garner, S. P. (1954) *The Evolution of Cost Accounting to 1925* (University, AL: University of Alabama Press).

Gilman, S. (1922) Discussion, *NACA Year Book*, 3: 263–6.

Godard, M. (1827) *Traité Général et Sommaire de la Comptabilité Commerciale* (Paris).

Greer, H. C. (1965) Alternatives to direct costing, in R. P. Marple (ed.) *National Association of Accountants on Direct Costing*, pp. 147–58 (New York: Ronald Press).

Guo, D. (1988) The historical contribution of Chinese accounting, in A. T. Craswell (ed.) *Collected Papers of the Fifth World Congress of Accounting Historians*, pp. 1–8 (Sydney: University of Sydney).

Gutiérrez, F. (1993) 'Distribución Espacial y Cambio Contable: El Caso de la Real Fábrica de Tabacos de Sevilla en el Siglo XVIII', unpublished thesis, University of Seville.

Gutiérrez, F., Larrinaga, C. and Núñez, M. (2005) Pre-industrial revolution evidence of cost and management accounting in Spain, *Accounting Historians Journal*, 32 (1) 111–48.

Hamilton, R. (1777) *An Introduction to Merchandise* (Edinburgh: privately printed).

Harris, J. N. (1965) What did we earn last month?, in R. P. Marple (ed.) *National Association of Accountants on Direct Costing*, pp. 17–40 (New York: Ronald Press).

Harrison, G. C. (1918–19) Cost accounting to aid production, *Industrial Management*, 56 (4): 273–82, (5): 391–8, (6): 456–63; 57 (1): 49–55, (2): 131–8, (3): 218–24, (4): 314–17, (5): 400–3, (6): 483–7.

Harrison, G. C. (1930) Standard costs: installation, operation and use (New York: Ronald Press).

Heier, J. R. (2000) The foundation of modern cost management: the life and work of Albert Fink, *Accounting, Business & Financial History*, 10 (2): 213–43.

Holzer, H. P. and Rogers, W. (1990) The origins and developments of French costing systems, *Accounting Historians Journal*, 17 (2): 57–71.

Hopper T. M. and Armstrong, P. (1991) Cost accounting, controlling labour and the rise of conglomerates, *Accounting, Organizations and Society*, 16 (5/6): 405–38.

Hoskin, K. W. and Macve, R. H. (1988) The genesis of accountability: the West Point connections, *Accounting, Organizations and Society*, 13 (1): 37–73.

Hoskin, K. W. and Macve, R. H. (1994) Reappraising the genesis of managerialism: a re-examination of the role of accounting at the Springfield Armory 1815–1845, *Accounting, Auditing & Accountability Journal*, 7 (2): 4–29.

Hoskin, K. W. and Macve, R. H. (1996) The Lawrence Manufacturing Company: a note on early cost accounting in US textile mills, *Accounting, Business & Financial History*, 6 (3): 337–61.

Hoskin, K. W. and Macve, R. H. (2000) Knowing more as knowing less? Alternative histories of cost and management accounting in the U.S. and the U.K., *Accounting Historians Journal*, 27 (1): 91–149.

Hoskin, K. W. and Macve, R. H. (2007) The Pennsylvania Railroad, 1849 and the invention of modern management, working paper.

Hoxie, R. F. (1920) *Scientific Management and Labor* (New York: D. Appleton).

Hoyt, F. F. (1943) Cost control in wartime, *NACA Year Book*, 24: 81–97.

Hudson, P. (1977) Some aspects of nineteenth-century accounting development in the West Riding textile industry, *Accounting History*, 2 (2): 4–22.

Johnson, H. T. (1972) Early cost accounting for internal management control: Lyman Mills in the 1850s, *Business History Review*, 46 (4): 466–74.

Johnson, H. T. (1980a) Management accounting in an early integrated industrial: E. I. DuPont de Nemours Powder Co., 1903–1912, in H. T. Johnson (ed.) *System and Profits*, pp. 184–204 (New York: Arno Press).

Johnson, H. T. (1980b) Management accounting in an early multidivisional organization: General Motors in the 1920s, in H. T. Johnson (ed.) *System and Profits*, pp. 490–517 (New York: Arno Press).

Johnson, H. T. (1992) *Relevance Regained: From Top-down Control to Bottom-up Empowerment* (New York: Free Press).

Johnson, H. T. and Kaplan, R. S. (1987) *Relevance Lost: The Rise and Fall of Management Accounting* (Boston: Harvard Business School Press).

Jones, H. (1985) *Accounting, Costing and Cost Estimation, Welsh Industry: 1700–1830* (Cardiff: University of Wales Press).

Kaplan, R. S. (1983) Measuring manufacturing performance: a new challenge for managerial accounting research, *Accounting Review*, 58 (4): 686–705.

Kimizuka, Y. (1992) Cost accounting in the Meiji era (1868–1912), *Sakushin Business Review*, 1: 13–42.

Kohler, E. L. and Cooper, W. W. (1945) Costs, prices and profits: accounting in the war program, *Accounting Review*, 20 (3): 267–308.

Lawrence, F. C. and Humphrey, E. N. (1947) *Marginal Costing* (London: Macdonald & Evans).

Léautey, E. and Guilbault, A. (1889) *La Science des Comptes Mise à la Portée de tous* (Paris: Librairie Comptable et Administrative).

Levant, Y. and Nikitin, M. (2006) Should Charles Eugène Bedaux be revisited?? Paper presented at Eighteenth Accounting, Business & Financial History Conference, Cardiff Business School, 14–15 September.

Lin, Z. J. (1992) Chinese double-entry bookkeeping before the nineteenth century, *Accounting Historians Journal*, 19 (2): 103–22.

Lin, Z. J. (2003) Chinese bookkeeping systems: a study of accounting adaptation an change, *Accounting, Business & Financial History*, 13 (1): 83–98.

Lippman, E. J. and Wilson, P. A. (2007) The culpability of accounting in perpetuating the Holocaust, *Accounting History*, 12 (3): 283–303.

Littleton, A. C. (1933) *Accounting Evolution to 1900* (New York: American Institute Publishing Co.).

Llopis, E., Fidalgo, E. and Méndez, T. (2002) The 'Hojas de Ganado' of the Monastery of Guadalupe, 1597–1784: an accounting instrument for fundamental economic decisions, *Accounting, Business & Financial History*, 12 (2): 203–29.

Loft, A. (1986) Towards a critical understanding of accounting: the case of accounting in the UK, 1914–1925, *Accounting, Organizations and Society*, 11 (2): 137–69.

Loft, A. (1990) *Coming into the Light* (New York: Chartered Institute of Management Accountants).

Loft, A. (1995) The history of management accounting: relevance found, in D. Ashton, T. Hopper, and R. W. Scapens (eds) *Issues in Management Accounting*, pp. 17–38 (London & New York: Prentice Hall).

Ludwig, J. W. (1965) Inaccuracies of direct costing, in R. P. Marple (ed.) *National Association of Accountants on Direct Costing*, pp. 167–79 (New York: Ronald Press).

Luenstroth, H. W. (1965) The case for direct costing, in R. P. Marple (ed.) *National Association of Accountants on Direct Costing*, pp. 95–112 (New York: Ronald Press).

McKendrick, N. (1970) Josiah Wedgwood and cost accounting in the industrial revolution, *Economic History Review*, 23 (1): 45–67.

McKinsey, J. O. (1922) *Budgetary Control* (New York: Ronald Press).

McWatters, C. S. and Foreman, P. (2005) Reaction to World War I constraints to normal trade: the meat-packing industry in Canada and Australia, *Accounting History*, 10 (2): 67–102.

Macias, M. (2002a) Ownership structure and accountability: the case of the privatization of the Spanish tobacco monopoly, 1887–96, *Accounting, Business & Financial History*, 12 (2): 317–45.

Macias, M., (2002b) Privatization and management accounting systems change: the case of the 19th century Spanish tobacco monopoly, *Accounting Historians Journal*, 29 (2): 31–57.

Mann, J. (1903a) Cost records or factory accounts, *Encyclopaedia of Accounting* (London: William Green).

Mann, J. (1903b) Oncosts, *Encyclopaedia of Accounting* (London: William Green).

Marple, R. P. (1965a) Historical background, in R. P. Marple (ed.) *National Association of Accountants on Direct Costing*, pp. 3–14 (New York: Ronald Press).

Marple, R. P. (ed.) (1965b) *National Association of Accountants on Direct Costing* (New York: Ronald Press)

Marquette, R. P. and Fleischman, R. K. (1992) Government/business synergy: early American innovation in budgeting and cost accounting, *Accounting Historians Journal*, 19 (2): 123–45.

Marriner, S. (1980) The Ministry of Munitions 1915–1919 and government accounting procedures, *Accounting and Business Research*, 10 (37A): 130–42.

Marshall, G. (1980) *Presbyteries and Profits* (Oxford: Clarendon Press).

Matos Carvalho, J., Lima Rodrigues, L. and Craig, R. (2007) Early cost accounting practices and private ownership: the Silk Factory Company of Portugal, 1745–1747, *Accounting Historians Journal*, 34 (1): 57–89.

Maynard, H. W. (1928) What the standard costs and the flexible budget are doing for the reduction of costs in the manufacturing department, *NACA Year Book*, 9: 300–8.

Megill, A. (1979) Foucault, structuralism and the ends of history, *Journal of Modern History*, 51 (3): 451–503.

Melis, F. (1950) *Storia della Ragioneria* (Bologna: Dott, Cesare Zuffi).

Miller, P. and O'Leary, T. (1987) Accounting and the construction of the governable person, *Accounting, Organizations and Society*, 12 (3): 235–65.

Näsi, S. and Rohde, C. (2007) Development of cost and management accounting ideas in the Nordic countries, in C. S. Chapman, A. G. Hopwood and M. D. Shields (eds) *Handbook of Management Accounting Research*, pp. 1109–37 (Oxford: Elsevier).

National Association of Accountants (1957) *NAA Research Series no. 23: Direct Costing* (New York: National Association of Accountants).

Nelson, D. (1974) Scientific management, systematic management, and labor, 1880–1915, *Business History Review*, 48 (4): 479–500.

Nelson, D. (1975) *Frederick W. Taylor and the Rise of Scientific Management* (Madison, WI: University of Wisconsin Press).

Nicholson, J. L. (1909) *Factory Organisation and Costs* (New York: Kohl Technical Publishing Co.).

Nikitin, M. (1990) Setting up an industrial accounting system at Saint-Gobain (1820–1880), *Accounting Historians Journal*, 17 (2): 73–93.

Nikitin, M. (1996) The birth of industrial accounting in France: the role of Pierre-Antoine Godard-Desmarest (1767–1850) as strategist, industrialist, and accountant at the Baccarat Crystalworks, *Accounting, Business & Financial History*, 6 (1): 93–110.

Norton, G. P. (1889) *Textile Manufacturers' Bookkeeping for the Counting House, Mill and Warehouse* (London: Simpkin, Marshall, Hamilton & Kent).

Núñez, T. M. (2002) Organizational change and accounting: the gunpowder monopoly in New Spain, 1757–87, *Accounting, Business & Financial History*, 12 (2): 275–315.

Okano, H. and Suzuki, T. (2007) A history of Japanese management accounting, in C. S. Chapman, A. G. Hopwood and M. D. Shields (eds) *Handbook of Management Accounting Research*, pp. 1139–57 (Oxford: Elsevier).

Oldroyd, D. (1996) The costing records of George Bowes and the grand allies in the north–east coal trade in the eighteenth century: their type and significance, *Accounting, Business & Financial History*, 9 (2): 175–201.

Parker, L. D. and Lewis, N. R. (1995) Classical management control in contemporary management and accounting: the persistence of Taylor and Fayol's world, *Accounting, Business & Financial History*, 5 (2): 211–35.

Parker, R. H. (1969) *Management Accounting: An Historical Perspective* (New York: Augustus Kelley).

Parker, R. H. (1986) *The Development of the Accountancy Profession in Britain in the Early Twentieth Century* (San Antonio, TX: Academy of Accounting Historians).

Payen, A. (1817) *Essai sur la Tenue des Livres d'un Manufactureur* (Paris: Chez A. Johanneau).

Pollard, S. (1965) *The Genesis of Modern Management* (Cambridge, MA: Harvard University Press).

Rogers, D. M. (1932) Development of the modern business budget, *Journal of Accountancy*, 53 (3): 186–205.

Roll, E. (1930) *An Early Experiment in Industrial Organization* (New York: Augustus Kelley).

Sakuri, M. (1989) Target costing and how to use it, *Journal of Cost Management*, 3 (2): 39–50.

Samson, W. D., Flesher, D. L. and Previts, G. D. (2006) Corporate governance and external and internal controls: the case of the Baltimore and Ohio Railroad, circa 1831, *Issues in Accounting Education*, 21 (1): 45–62.

Sapori, A. (1932) *Una Compagnia di Calimala ai Primi del Trecento* (Florence: Olschki).

Scapens, R. W. (1991) *Management Accounting: A Review of Recent Developments* (London: Macmillan).

Scarbrough, P., Nanni, A. J. and Sakurai, M. (1991) Japanese management accounting practices and the effects of assembly and process automation, *Management Accounting Research*, 2 (1): 27–46.

Scheuermann, L. (1929) *Die Fugger als Montanindustrielle in Tirol und Karnten* (Munich: Duncker & Humbolt).

Schmalenbach, E. (1899) Buchführung und Kalkulation in Fabrikgeschäft, *Deutsche Metallindustriezeitung*, 15.

Schmalenbach, E. (1948) *Pretiale Wirschaftslenkung* (Bremen-Horn: W. Dorn).

Schnutenhaus, O. R. (1948) *Neue Grundlagen der 'Feste' Kostenrechnung. Die Betriebstrukturkostenrechnung* (Berlin: Deutscher Betriebswirte-Verlag).

Schweitzer, M. (1992) Eugèn Schmalenbach as the founder of cost accounting in the German-speaking world, in A. Tsuji (ed.) *Collected Papers of the Sixth World Congress of Accounting Historians*, Vol. II, pp. 393–418 (Japan: Accounting History Association).

Seay, R. A. and Schoenfeldt, R. C. (1989) H. K. Hathaway on product costing: relevant issues of contemporary concern, *Accounting Historians Journal*, 16 (1): 111–24.

Shank, J. K. and Govindarajan, V. (1989) *Strategic Cost Analysis: The Evolution from Managerial to Strategic Accounting* (Homewood, IL: Irwin).

Simon, F. N. (1830) *Méthode Complète de Tenue des Livres* (Châtillon sur Seine: Cornillac).

Simon, H. A., Guetzkow, H., Kozmetsky, G. and Tyndall, G. (1954) *Centralization vs. Decentralization in Organizing the Controller's Department* (New York: Controllership Foundation).

Sloan, A. P. (1964) *My Years at General Motors* (Garden City, NY: Doubleday).

Solomons, D. (1952) *Studies in Costing* (London: Sweet & Maxwell).

Sowell, E. M. (1973) *The Evolution of the Theories and Techniques of Standard Costs* (Tuscaloosa, AL: University of Alabama Press).

Stacey, N. A. H. (1954) *English Accountancy 1800–1954* (London: Gee).

Stempf, V. H. (1943) War contracts, costs, and profits, *Journal of Accountancy*, 75 (6): 496–509.

Stoeffel, K. (1995) *Controllership im Internationalen Vergleich* (Wiesbaden: Gabler).

Stone, W. E. (1973) An early English cotton mill cost accounting system: Charlton Mills, 1810–1889, *Accounting and Business Research*, 4 (17): 71–8.

Taylor, F. W. (1903) *Shop Management* (New York: Harper & Brothers).

Taylor, F. W. (1911) *The Principles of Scientific Management* (New York: Harper).

Taylor, F. W. (1912) *Scientific Management* (New York: Harper).

Theiss, E. L. (1937) The beginnings of business budgeting, *Accounting Review*, 12 (1): 43–55.

Tolkmitt, H. (1894) *Grundriss der Fabrik-Geschäftsführung* (Leipzig: Verlag von G. A. Gloeckner).

Tyson, T. N. (1990) Accounting for labor in the early nineteenth century: the U.S. arms making experience, *Accounting Historians Journal*, 17 (1): 47–59.

Tyson, T. N. (1992) The nature and environment of cost management among early 19th century U.S. textile manufacturers, *Accounting Historians Journal*, 19 (1): 1–24.

Tyson, T. N. (1993) Keeping the record straight: Foucauldian revisionism and 19th century cost accounting history, *Accounting, Auditing & Accountability Journal*, 6 (2): 4–16.

Tyson, T. N. (1998) Mercantilism, management accounting or managerialism? Cost accounting in early 19th century US textile mill, *Accounting, Business & Financial History*, 8 (2): 211–29.

Tyson, T. N. (2000) Accounting history and the emperor's new clothes: a response to 'knowing more or knowing less'?, *Accounting Historians Journal*, 27 (1): 159–71.

Urwick, L. and Brech E. F. L. (1964) *The Making of Scientific Management* (London: Sir Isaac Pitman).

Vent, G. A. (1991) The standardization of the Bewick, Moreing & Co. cost accounts, *Accounting History*, 2 (2): 65–79.

Vent, G. A. and Milne R. A. (1997) Cost accounting practices at precious metal mines: a comparative study, 1869–1905, *Accounting History*, 2 (2): 77–104.

Vollmers, G. L. (2003) Accounting historiography using ancient sources: problems and rewards, in R. K. Fleischman, V. S. Radcliffe and P. A. Shoemaker (eds) *Doing Accounting History*, pp. 49–62 (Amsterdam: JAI).

Walker, S. P. and Mitchell, F. (1996) Propaganda, attitude change and uniform costing in the British printing industry, 1913–1939, *Accounting, Auditing & Accountability Journal*, 9 (3): 98–126.

Walker, S. P. and Mitchell, F. (eds) (1997) *Trade Associations and Uniform Costing in the British Printing Industry, 1900–1963* (New York & London: Garland).

Walker, S. P. and Mitchell, F. (1998) Labor and costing: the employees' dilemma, *Accounting Historians Journal*, 25 (2): 35–62.

Wang, L. Y. and Zhang, R. (2000) The management value of accounting information – past, present and future of management accounting, *Finance and Accounting*, 2: 20–3.

Wells, M. C. (1977) Some influences on the development of cost accounting, *Accounting Historians Journal*, 4 (2): 47–61.

Wells, M. C. (1978) *Accounting for Common Costs* (Urbana, IL: Center for International Education and Research in Accounting).

Whitmore, J. (1908) Shoe factory cost accounts, *Journal of Accountancy*, 4 (1): 12–25.

Williamson, O. E. (1970) *Corporate Control and Business Behavior: an Inquiry into the Effects of Organization Form on Enterprise Behavior* (Englewood Cliffs, NJ: Prentice-Hall).

Yamey, B. S. (1949) Scientific bookkeeping and the rise of capitalism, *Economic History Review*, 1 (2/3): 99–113.

Yamey, B. S. (1960) The development of company accounting conventions, *Three Banks Review*, 47 (September): 3–18.

Young, K. G. (1953) Wanted: added lustre for cost accounting, *NACA Bulletin*, 34: 644.

Zambon, S. and Zan, L. (2007) Controlling expenditure, or the slow emergence of costing at the Venice Arsenal, 1586–1633, *Accounting, Business & Financial History*, 17 (1): 105–28.

Zan, L. (2004a) Accounting and management discourse in proto-industrial settings: the Venice Arsenal in the turn of the 16th century, *Accounting and Business Research*, 34 (2): 145–75.

Zan, L. (2004b) Writing accounting and management history: insights from unorthodox music historiography, *Accounting Historians Journal*, 31 (2): 171–92.

Zimnovitch, H. (1997) Les calculs du prix de revient dans la seconde industrialisation en France, unpublished dissertation, Poitiers University.

10

Auditing

Josephine Maltby

Overview

There is a continuing debate about the reasons for which firms undergo audit. In an influential paper, Watts and Zimmerman (1983: 614) characterise audit as 'part of the efficient technology for organising firms', enabling managers to add credibility to their position as stewards or confirming the reliability of information issued to investors. Their opponents argue that audit is not market-driven: firms undergo audit when it suits their needs – for instance, as a means of avoiding stringent regulation of their financial reports or in order to obtain professional advice. Historical evidence provides an opportunity to study the adoption of audit in a variety of different legal and economic environments.

Closely linked to this is the question of the role of audit within corporate governance. Is the auditor's primary responsibility that of defender of the shareholders' interests or as advisor to the directors; are the two roles complementary or competing? This has implications for audit objectives – should the audit be primarily directed at statement verification, or fraud detection, or at preventing error and misstatement? It also has an impact on audit technique – the importance of substantive and of systems testing, the use of sampling and the emphasis on risk in planning audit work. These are issues which began to be debated during the nineteenth century as investors took an increasing interest in the audit report; they continue to be controversial.

In the late twentieth century, audit of public sector bodies, including local and national government, education and the health service, was centralised and intensified with the aim of economising on resources and promoting efficiency and effectiveness. Commentators suggested that there was an inherent tension between a public-sector ethic of delivering services and an audit approach derived from private enterprise. The history of public sector audit is potentially useful as an insight into the extent of the changes wrought in the 1980s.

Auditing practices, it is claimed, are converging worldwide because of the demands of globalised markets. This, combined with the economic changes in Eastern Europe and in China, has led to the development of accounting professions which are heavily influenced by UK/US models. Growing research interest in international audit – the extent to which national practices have developed independently or from the diffusion of Anglo-Saxon influence – offers a critical perspective on the forces underlying change and the prospects for its success.

Introduction

A recurring theme in academic accounting journals of the late twentieth/early twenty-first centuries is that of a major expansion in writing about accounting history.[1] Work on the history of audit was part of that expansion, as is evident from the dates of the majority of the pieces cited in what follows. This chapter will attempt to identify the major themes and controversies that have emerged in writing about the history of audit during this busy period, and suggest future directions that research might take, with an indication of the topics that have not yet attracted attention. The view given here is inevitably a partial one; what follows is intended as an invitation to further discussion and debate.

The chapter does not offer a detailed chronological study of audit – although key events are briefly outlined below – nor does it attempt to be comprehensive in its coverage of relevant themes. It begins by reviewing writing about the reasons for the growth of audit – the account offered by Watts and Zimmerman and some of the challenges to it – and, in particular, the links between audit and the development of corporate governance. Connected with this is the involvement of audit in the growth of the accounting profession. The chapter gives an overview of writing about the history of audit objectives and audit techniques, with particular attention to the continuing argument about the auditor's responsibility for the detection of fraud. Much of the above (like most historical writing about audit) has dealt with the private sector and the UK. The concluding sections of the chapter address the history of public and non-profit sector audit and some of the emerging research on international audit. The chapter does not attempt a complete geographical coverage – it does not, for instance, touch on the development of audit within the British Empire/Commonwealth, nor on the wide variety of European practices and issues. It is intended to point out a number of key issues that deserve further exploration – in particular, the dissemination of audit practice, and the extent to which new techniques and regimes worldwide can be reconciled with existing legal and professional frameworks.

Before 'The Roaring Nineties' (Fleischman and Radcliffe 2005), when accounting history was a field that attracted less academic attention, a number of publications nevertheless appeared on topics in audit history.[2] Examples include Moyer (1951), Brown (1962), Jones (1981), Watts and Zimmerman (1983). Moyer is concerned with the diffusion of audit techniques, Brown with changes in audit objectives and practices, Jones with the role of audit in the growth of the accounting profession, Watts and Zimmerman with audit as evidence for the validity of agency theory. What they have in common, it will be suggested in this chapter, is that they are inspired by what Moyer (1951: 8) calls 'auditing as we have come to know it' – that is, professional audit of limited companies and the associated arguments about what shareholders, managers and a variety of other stakeholders expect the auditor to do. These are all themes which subsequently recur in various forms in writing about audit – indeed, they are among the most popular topics in subsequent historical writing, as discussed later in this chapter.

Miller and Napier (1993: 631), writing about the 'genealogies of calculation', warn against the 'a priori limiting of the field of study to accounting as it currently exists'. In some of the early papers cited above, the a priori temptation is strongly apparent – that of framing audit as having always been, or always having tried to be, the activity of that name in the late twentieth/early twenty-first centuries. Moyer and Brown's papers, for instance, are both about the development of audit, and both are written from the perspective that history is valuable because it enables modern practitioners to chart the course of future events from what has happened in the past. Moyer (1951: 3) hopes that a study of early developments 'may lead to a better understanding of what is happening in the present and offer clues to what future trends may be'. Brown (1962: 703). is more confident in regarding auditing as following a predictable trajectory: 'In most professions it is rather difficult to predict the future, but there are some significant trends revealed by the history of auditing which should carry forward into succeeding years.'

When Humphrey *et al.* entitled their 1992 paper 'The audit expectations gap – plus ca change, plus c'est la meme chose?' and Chandler and Edwards in 1996 called theirs 'Recurring issues in auditing: back to the future?' they were arguably taking the same perspective as Brown and Moyer, with the difference that they saw unsatisfactory stasis whereas the earlier writers had looked towards a future of improvement. This is not to deny that there are points of comparison between audit practice in the nineteenth, twentieth and twenty-first centuries – but it is to suggest that historians should be prepared to recognise differences as well as similarities. It can be argued that there is a need to see audit in the nineteenth century as other than the twenty-first, and attend to 'the different meanings that have been attached to practices at different moments in time' (Miller and Napier 1993: 632). It also carries with it the possibility that historians will have a better understanding of accounting and auditing change if they stop looking for what Miller and Napier call 'immobile forms that appear to move without difficulty across time and space' and attend to 'the piecemeal fashion in which . . . technologies have been invented and assembled' (ibid.). The history of audit in times and places other than the UK and the end of the nineteenth century deserves exploration in pursuit of that possibility.

Audit chronology

There is evidence for auditing, in the sense of a review of accounts rendered, from Babylonian times onwards (Edwards 1989: 23–31). In England, manorial and government accounts were the subject of a highly developed system of public audits (see below), and audit was rapidly introduced to joint stock companies (as discussed below for the East India Company in the seventeenth century). The late eighteenth and nineteenth centuries saw the growth of the joint stock company – most importantly at first the formation of canal, utility and railway companies. The Acts of Parliament instituting these often called for shareholder audits (Matthews *et al.* 1998: 35) but, as discussed below, there was a steady transition to professional audit. Mid-nineteenth-century legislation first made audit of joint stock companies compulsory (Joint Stock Companies Act, 1844) then, after the introduction of limited liability, put both reporting and audit on a voluntary basis (Joint Stock Companies Act, 1856) (Edwards 1989: 190–2). It was not until the 1900 Companies Act that audit was again mandatory for the generality of joint stock companies, and only with the 1947 Act that companies were required to appoint a professionally qualified accountant as auditor. Despite this apparently slow growth in regulatory requirements, audit became a crucial factor in the growth of the accounting profession in Great Britain (see below).

Reasons why firms undergo audit

One of the most frequently cited pieces of work on the origins of audit, by Watts and Zimmerman (1983), puts forward the thesis that audit arose as a solution to the problem created by the separation of ownership and control. They cite Jensen and Meckling's identification of audit as 'one type of monitoring activity that increases the value of the firm' (Watts and Zimmerman 1983: 613), that will therefore be welcomed by the two main parties to the firm – principals and agents, here owners and managers. Owners want the audit because it confirms the reliability of information being provided to them; managers because it confirms their trustworthiness as stewards. In support of their argument, Watts and Zimmerman (ibid.: 614) point to the existence of audit as 'part of the efficient technology for organising firms' which existed from the fourteenth century onwards, as firms' legal status altered from merchant guilds to joint stock to limited liability companies (ibid.: 618–26). It is an explanation which suggests that legal and regulatory interventions are unnecessary because market demand will elicit a supply of suitably independent auditors at a suitable price.

As an explanation for audit, this has substantial advantages. It explains the persistence of the activity over a long period – auditors' faculty of being 'invulnerable to their own failure' (Power 1994a: 7; see also Chapter 19): whatever the shortcomings of the individual audit, the provision of the service remains desirable because it reduces the risks inherent in agency relationships. It also argues against the need for 'government fiat' (Watts and Zimmerman 1983: 613) in the form of legislation, or for professional regulation. Audit services, Watts and Zimmerman argue, alter in response to market conditions. They cite the transition from shareholder to professional auditors in the mid-nineteenth century as an example of the work of market forces, ascribing it to an expansion either in the demand for audit (because of the increase in the number of limited companies) or in the supply of auditors (because accounting firms had grown in response to a new demand for insolvency services). Audit anticipated legislative provisions; it did not follow them. The agency model therefore enjoys considerable popularity – see, for instance, Lee (1993: 23), Nikkinen and Petri (2004) on audit fees and agency theory, or the Institute of Chartered Accountants in England and Wales (2005: 8) *Audit Quality: Agency Theory and the Role of Audit*, which summarises audit history by stating that 'the modern audit function has evolved over centuries, apparently in response to agency issues'.

A number of objections have been raised to the agency theorists' explanation for the rise of audit, which suggest that the motives for audit are more complex than Watts and Zimmerman believe, and that audit needs to be understood as an activity changing within, and shaping, a changing environment, rather than as 'static and purely technocratic' (Hopwood 1977: 277).

One major objection relates to the terms of the contracts under which agency relations operate. Watts and Zimmerman argue (1983: *passim*) that the need to maintain a reputation for acting independently was and remains a crucial asset for auditors who wish to maintain their credibility and thus their value in the market. Armstrong (1991: 1), in his 'attempt to re-think the theory of agency', points out that the agency theoretical explanation of audit 'immediately raises the question of how the independence of third party monitors is to be guaranteed, particularly when these are normally engaged by agents rather than principals' (ibid.: 12). In Armstrong's words (ibid.: 13) 'monitors are agents too'. Auditors' agency duties concern oversight and review rather than control of resources, but their function for owners is as much a delegated one as that of managers. If 'both managers and monitors are agents . . . the analysis of how independence in monitors might be secured leads to an infinite regress within the present paradigm of agency theory' (ibid.). Although the auditing profession is likely to benefit from being viewed as independent, it may, he points out, be in the interests of individual auditors *not* to act independently, and it is possible for the auditor to decouple reputation from behaviour (ibid.). If there is no foundation to Watts and Zimmerman's assumption that individual auditors will see themselves as contractually obliged to act independently, agency theory is in trouble. Armstrong proposes instead a 'radical agency theory' which bases relationships between agents and principals not on contract but on 'seeking and allocating trust' (ibid.: 20) – and hence on the mechanisms for creating and identifying a *reputation* for trustworthiness. Armstrong's account touches on a number of issues in audit history which will be discussed later in this chapter: the role of the auditor within corporate governance, the continuing debate about auditor independence, and the increasing importance of audit as a management tool within organisations.

The paradox of Watts and Zimmerman's paper is that, in offering a *history* of audit, it ignores the possibility of historical change. They trace the recurrence of audit from the fourteenth century to the beginning of the twentieth, in what they describe as 'early English business corporations' (Watts and Zimmerman 1983: 615) and subsequently in joint stock and limited companies. Underlying their history is the assumption that the owners and the managers of guilds, merchant adventurers and railway companies all had the same expectations and incentives, and thus that both the agency relationship and the audit passed fundamentally unchanged from the Middle Ages to the end of Queen Victoria's reign. Napier (2006: 449) is criticising this kind of approach when he refers to accounting research that treats the subject as 'a phenomenon of the present' and the textbooks that

> discuss different aspects of the . . . discipline . . . in terms of the recognized rules and practices of the day, with little or no suggestion that these might have been different at some earlier time (and therefore by implication might be different again in the future).

Mennicken, writing about the introduction of Anglo-American auditing techniques to post-Soviet Russia, describes the import of auditing textbooks which treat audit as an 'a-contextual, universal and homogeneous activity' (Mennicken 2006: 22) that can fit seamlessly into any setting. This description could equally be applied to Watts and Zimmerman's conception of audit.

It is a stance that has exposed them to challenge by a variety of writers, who look from different perspectives on the context in which audit took place and the possibility of understanding it as a product of political, legal and social as well as economic factors. Some of this work is discussed in the following sections of the chapter, looking first at audit and corporate governance.

The audit and corporate governance

Fundamental to the debates about the demand for audit and its objectives is the assumption that audit plays an important role within systems of corporate governance. An important reason for the different conclusions reached, concerning the role of the audit within corporate governance, is the variety of understandings of the way in which the auditor relates to the framework of company law, to managers and to shareholders. Histories of audit play an important part in arriving at these understandings.

An analysis of the role of audit in corporate governance needs to assign the auditor a role within the governance structure: is the audit conducted primarily for the benefit of shareholders or that of managers, or can the auditor hold the ring between the two? Agency theory suggests that the latter is the case – the manager gains assured reputation and the shareholder has the value of information confirmed. But historical studies have suggested that audit can be understood as a service principally to *one* of these groups, and that the demand for audit comes from this understanding among contemporaries.

An early instance of this is given in Bryer's study (2000) of the East India Company at the beginning of the seventeenth century. He charts the dissatisfaction of the 'generality' of investors with the small elite mercantile group of governors. The resulting 'revolution' in the Company 'abolished its feudal directorate and replaced them by modern managers, specialised wage workers accountable to a social capital' (ibid.: 328). As the number of investors increased, 'the generality' demanded more frequent and accurate information about the performance of their capital.

On 2 July 1619 the Court minutes note a 'disturbance':

> attributed to 'gentlemen who, having been taken into the company by courtesy, do aim to get all the government into their hands' which is a business proper only for merchants . . . *Desire of the generality to have auditors chosen from among themselves; resolved to offer four or six, as they please, 'as a means to take away all exceptions, and to dash and quell all other plots, because nothing is done by the company but will justify itself'* . . . (Sainsbury, 1964b, p. 282).
>
> (Bryer 2000: 347, emphasis added)

Part of Bryer's history of a further three decades of arguments between the governors and the generality is the regular recourse to audit. In 1642, for instance, the governor 'acquaints [i.e. reminds] the generality that they may appoint three or four among themselves to examine the said accounts and valuation, with liberty to see any of the Company's books, letters, or accounts'.

By the middle of the century, the generality had effectively 'abolished its feudal directorate and replaced them by modern managers . . . accountable to a social capital' (Bryer 2000). The audit was part of this seizure of power by the investors, because it was part of their campaign to be given more frequent and reliable information than they believed the Company was prepared to volunteer to them.

The Lancashire cotton mills, the 'Oldham Limiteds' of the late nineteenth century, operating on the principle of one shareholder, one vote, had widely dispersed share ownerships, amateur shareholder auditors and intense investor involvement in their governance. Quarterly cash accounts with detailed information about performance were discussed at general meetings and reported in local newspapers. Toms (2002) treats this as part of the continuing process of socialisation of capital which Bryer discerns in the East India Company – except that in the mill companies, socialisation is conducted via co-operation rather than capitalism. Toms (2002: 81) describes the amateur audit, together with cash-based accounting, as 'imposed' by shareholders as a means of carrying out socialisation. 'Socialized capital . . . demanded accurate accounting information (and got it) . . . through cash based accounting and amateur audit.' After the cotton slump, at the end of the century, financial cliques bought out the local shareholders, building up large blocks of investment. It was at this stage that amateurs were replaced by professional auditors. For Toms, the change of ownership marks a turning-point in the use of audit in these companies. The new owners represented concentrated blocks of shares, and accordingly amended the companies' articles to match voting powers to the numbers of shares held, giving themselves block votes, and to exclude mill managers from boards of directors. These owners could monitor performance via financial controls such as the review of bank balances and the authorisation of expenditure; unlike the former dispersed owners, they placed 'little reliance . . . on the publication or auditing of financial statements' (ibid.: 77).

A number of historians contribute, like Toms, to a view of nineteenth-century audit as a weak discipline on directors. Jones (1995) looks at the recommendations by witnesses to various committees on company law between the 1830s and the 1890s in Great Britain to establish how much support was given for mandatory auditing. His conclusion is that witnesses seem in general to have favoured mandatory audit over compulsory financial reporting as a means of control. Jones (ibid.: 181) suggests that this preference existed despite the fact that the scope of audit was 'quite restricted' and 'there was little sense of the auditor as an independent third party'. Audit was preferable to a requirement for financial reports because the latter entailed the disclosure of information to competitors; thus there was a 'trade-off' between audit and report-ing (ibid.: 182).[3] A similar point is made by Collier (1996) about the more recent phenomenon of the audit committee. He links its rise in the USA with the McKesson & Robbins fraud of the late 1930s, and suggests that both there and later in the UK, audit committees became popular less because of their effectiveness than as 'an attempt to avoid legislative solutions to deficiencies in corporate governance' (ibid.: 135).

The development of audit is inextricably linked with the development of the accounting — and the auditing — profession.[4] Self-promotion as skilled, reliable and independent auditors was crucial to the profession in establishing its jurisdiction over an area that was contested between accountants, lawyers, and amateur shareholder auditors.[5] Matthews *et al.* (1998: 35) stress the importance of auditing in Britain — 'the basis of the accountancy profession's future growth' from the early nineteenth century onwards. They emphasise that, although insolvency was a major activity in the early years of firm formation, it was audit that took firms into the 'upper echelons' (ibid.: 36). Audit was remarkably effective at giving some firms a leading position that they maintained for more than a century. The table of 'top auditors 1891–1995' contained in Matthews *et al.* (1998: 46–7) shows that four of the five top audit firms in 1995 (Coopers & Lybrand, KPMG, Price Waterhouse, Ernst & Young) had predecessors in the top ten in 1891.

Maltby (1999) explores the extent to which the nineteenth-century auditing profession depicted itself as the ally of directors and large shareholders, *against* small (and feckless) specu-lators. This promoted the profession's strategy for establishing its area of jurisdiction, as did the view of informative financial reports as unnecessary and possibly damaging — the directors knew what was going on, and would tell shareholders all that it was in the company's and their own interests to disclose. The profession could portray itself as a 'guide, philosopher and friend' as *The Accountant* of 1898 put it (quoted in Maltby 1999: 43), providing expert knowledge for directors, rather than as the representative of the interests of the mass of shareholders. This is supported by Popp's study (2000) of an auditor–director relationship in the audit reports sent to Mintons Ltd between 1876 and 1900. They 'did focus on the veracity of . . . the financial statements' but 'very frequently far exceeded this brief and contained detailed discussion of and recommendations concerning production strategy' (ibid.: 357), apparently with the aim of improving the company's profitability in a period of severe financial difficulties. He concludes that the reports 'were used as a vehicle for expanding the role to be played by auditors' (ibid.).

Napier (1998: 117) draws on the changing role of the auditor when discussing the arguments for and against limiting auditor liability. He traces a movement in the nineteenth century from a view of company as 'a collectivity model of the interests of shareholders, with directors and auditors being elected from the mass of shareholders' (ibid.: 117) to a 'business company' where 'the auditor "intermediates" between shareholders and directors *whose interests are not necessarily aligned with those of the shareholders*' (ibid.: emphasis added). This traces a similar path to that outlined above — from Bryer's and Toms' auditors as representatives of socialised capital to the auditors as allies and advisors of the directors, and it makes up a strand in the 'running debate' about the objectives of the audit, discussed below, which drew in the accounting and legal professions as well as shareholders.

The collectivity model places auditors on a par with directors and hence confines their liability to that of directors. In cases such as Kingston Cotton Mills (1896), brought by defrauded shareholders, 'judges were reluctant to impose on auditors a duty of care more onerous than that imposed on (non-executive) directors' (Napier 1998: 125). Judges were, arguably, slower than accountants to move to the business company model, in which the auditor would not necessarily stand as a representative of shareholder interests. Napier, writing before the Companies Act 2006 enabled accountants to set a contractual limit on their liability, warned that auditors' attempts to move in that direction reflected 'a trend away from regarding auditing as a profession' (ibid.: 126).

The argument about limitation of liability continues. Opponents of extended liability claim that it is a necessary part of professional judgement for auditors to 'sail close to the wind'. They argue that a system that imposed more detailed regulation (i.e. extension of auditors' liabilities to third parties) would reduce their scope for applying professional judgement and would also open them up to 'opportunistic' behaviour by dissatisfied investors who could treat them as a form of insurance (Grout et al. 1994: 343). The Grout argument is of interest as evidence of the extent to which auditors have, by some commentators, been decoupled from shareholders. In the same vein, O'Sullivan (1993: 417) warns that increased auditor liability would encourage investors to place too much reliance on the audit report. On the other hand, Cousins et al. (1999) argue that auditors are neglecting their duty to shareholders, as does Sikka (1998):

> The social bargain of 'external audit' has been understood to be based upon a 'duty of care' to individual stakeholders and risk sharing arrangements. Statutory concessions, case law and further demands of the industry have significantly altered the terms of such a bargain.

The argument about auditors' liability that went on through the nineteenth and twentieth centuries and beyond was a continuation of the argument about the place of the auditor within corporate governance that had begun in the Victorian era. It linked with new situations and expectations – a change in the composition of the shareholder population, more detailed financial reporting regulation, the move of accounting firms to limited liability partnerships, for instance – but in Napier's words (1998: 126), it took shape 'against the shadows and residues of the past'.

Audit objectives and audit technique

The early development of audit objectives

Jones (2006: 1) argues that medieval administrative and accounting systems – both Treasury and manorial – drew on a battery of internal control mechanisms, including accountability, supervision and audit. Oschinsky's (1971) collection of texts on medieval estate management and accounting includes reference to internal controls including the division of duties (see also Chapter 5). The *Seneschausy*, an accounting text of *c*.1275, details the responsibilities of estate workers, who reported to the reeve. Responsibility was passed on from the reeve to the bailiff and then to the steward (Jones 2006: 8), and 'the steward ought not act as auditor for things which concern his own office' (Oschinsky 1971: 267).

There are frequent references in the medieval accounting literature of the thirteenth and fourteenth centuries to the manorial audit. It was an oral examination, a structured process designed to challenge the fairness of the accounts rendered and arrive at an agreed value. Harvey (1994: 101) describes an audit of the mid-thirteenth century as 'virtually a dialogue, a debate between local official and auditors'. The auditors frequently annotated and amended the accounts presented to them, adding to the cash liability of the local official if expenses were disallowed or output was below fixed minimum returns (ibid.: 104).

Harvey's description is supported by texts such as the *Husbandry* of 1300, which includes a manual of audit procedures. The audit is to begin with an oath by the accountant 'that he will render true accounts' (Oschinsky 1971: c1, 419). The auditor should proceed by investigating the corn account (ibid.: c2, 419) working out the desirable yield (ibid.: c3–c9) so that any shortages could be charged against the accountant, then the stock account, including cattle, sheep, poultry, pigs, the output from the dairy, and cash income including rents in cash and in kind, and finally proceeds from sales of wood, stock, dairy products and wool. The auditor is then told:

> After the account has been heard compare how the figures differ from the particulars, and if they show any deficiencies in cash, corn or stock, or any other items commute all of them into cash: to charge the accountant with these deficiencies must be your first duty before you can total the account.
>
> (ibid.: c40, 435)

As a result, accounts of this period show:

> what happened at the audit: we see what the local official claimed, what was queried or disallowed by the auditors, and very often why, for revealing notes and comments may be added to explain the alterations made on the account – 'in future so much will not be allowed' . . . 'this has been sworn to at the audit'.
>
> (Harvey 1994: 101)

The audit appears to have been not merely an examination but an integral part of estate management: the auditors were engaged in making sure that the official rendering account was not merely telling the truth but was thereby producing an acceptable yield.[6] Hoskin and Macve (1986: 122) describe manorial accounting as 'rudimentary indeed' – but the audit was part of a managerial system structured to convert measures of agricultural production into cash values that could be recovered from officials.

The medieval case is of particular interest because there is substantial documentary evidence of the techniques employed by manorial auditors of the period, both in the various treatises on audit which have survived (see Oschinsky 1971, for a collection of short texts) and in manuscript accounts with auditors' amendments (as discussed by Harvey 1994: *supra*). But the early modern period, and indeed the nineteenth century until the accession of the professional auditor, have not been studied for evidence of audit objectives and audit techniques. Bryer, as discussed above, refers to the importance of the East India Company auditors as investor representatives, but the nature of the work they carried out is not part of his analysis. Forrester (1994) notes the recurring concern among shareholders and managers of the Forth and Clyde Navigation that the accounts should be audited, but does not quote evidence of the type of work involved.

The auditor and fraud in the nineteenth century

Brown (1962: 696), in an early contribution to the history of audit techniques, identified possible audit objectives as detection of fraud and/or of clerical error, and 'determination of fairness of reported financial position'. According to his summary, audit verification in pursuit of these objectives could be either 'detailed' or 'testing', and the importance of internal controls, 'not recognized' from ancient times until 1905, progressively attracted 'slight recognition . . . awakening of interest . . . substantial emphasis' in the course of the twentieth century (ibid.). Brown matched the move to the audit of internal control with a change in audit emphasis from detecting fraud to identifying misstatement; he was confident that this process would continue as 'the modern audit . . . has shifted from a review of past operations to a review of the system of internal control' (ibid.: 703, quoting Nielsen 1960).

Brown sees audit technique as following an orderly progression, with a clear development based on a shared professional understanding of objectives. He links advances in audit with a development in client systems that began with the emergence of internal control – an 'order and method' – in the mid-nineteenth century (ibid.: 697). But subsequent research has suggested that audit objectives changed in a much less orderly fashion, and that their relationship with techniques and with client internal controls was less direct and consequential.

In 1849, a Select Committee set up by the House of Lords 'with a view of providing for a more effectual audit of [railway] accounts' (the Monteagle Committee) stated, in its third report (Select Committee 1849: xvii), that an independent public audit would be 'indispensable' in ensuring the reliability of financial accounts. The committee further stated that the auditor's duties should be limited to 'verification [of the accounts], to the comparison of the entries with the vouchers, and to the investigation of the authorities under which payments are made, and their legality' (ibid.: xv). But he must not 'acquire any power whatever to interfere in the internal administration of the company as a commercial enterprise' (ibid.). It is not clear from the evidence whether the Committee was setting out its requirements on the basis of existing practice or was designing a programme of work to eliminate existing shortcomings.[7]

There was a running debate throughout the latter part of the nineteenth century, contemporaneously with the growth of professional audit, about the extent to which the auditor could be held responsible for the detection of fraud. Chandler *et al.* (1993) describe it as a 'continuing and fluctuating theme', with a shift in emphasis between responsibility for statement verification and fraud detection, rather than the steady progress which Brown identified from fraud in the mid-nineteenth century to fairness by the early twentieth century. The disagreement about audit responsibility was a major part of the audit expectations gap, which Teo and Cobbin (2005) recognise within the accounting profession, as well as between auditors and users of accounts. They quote Dicksee's (1892) *Auditing*, which remarked that some auditors:

> claim an auditor's duty is confined to a comparison of the Balance Sheet with the books, while others assert that it is the auditor's duty to trace every transaction back to its source. Between those two extremes every shade of opinion may be found and among others the opinion of most practical men.
>
> (Teo and Cobbin 2005: 42)

The recurrent nineteenth-century argument about the auditor and fraud has attracted considerable research attention (e.g. Humphrey *et al.* 1992; Chandler 1997; Chandler and Fry 2005). The moral drawn tends to resemble that of Chandler and Edwards (1996: 5–6) that 'the essential problems which troubled the auditing profession at its birth remain unresolved and recur through its maturity'. Teo and Cobbin describe (2005: 53, 54) the situation within the profession at the end of the nineteenth century as 'precarious' with an 'abject lack of guidance' about responsibility. But the profession has survived this continuing crisis without decisive clarification of its responsibility. Research has concentrated on the judicial battles of the late nineteenth century and the discussion within the profession (e.g. in journals, as reviewed by Teo and Cobbin 2005: *passim*); it has paid less attention to what the profession had to gain from downplaying its responsibility for fraud.

Relevant here is the work of Power (1992: 58) on a subsequent episode in the history of audit techniques which has attracted less research attention – the emergence in the 1930s of what he describes as 'a discourse of sampling'. He argues that the *use* of selective audit testing preceded by some thirty or so years its *discussion* in professional texts such as those of Montgomery or Dicksee, and consequently that the installation in textbooks of scientific sampling was intended 'to rationalise practices that had been in place for some years and to invest auditing with a new scientific authority' (ibid.: 37). Power's paper is of interest for a number of reasons. He is directing research attention to the development of audit in the early twentieth century, which has attracted far less concern than in the late nineteenth, and he is making the important point that historical writing needs to avoid assuming 'a historically neutral concept of auditing' (ibid.: 38). The 'neutral' characterisation of audit is liable to view it as a process whose objectives are given, so that changes in technique are evolutionary stages leading to a more perfect exercise of the craft. Power challenges this stance by suggesting that the discourse of sampling was intended to justify and rationalise techniques which had already proved to be cost-saving, and to reinforce the image of accountants as part of a scientific profession.

This idea offers another perspective on the argument about the auditor's responsibility for fraud detection – that the recurrent debate did not represent a failure by the profession in the nineteenth century to come to an agreement with the users of accounts. Rather, it needs to be understood in its context, as the outcome of the professional orientation towards the interests of social capital – the mission of the accountant to be seen as the 'guide, philosopher and friend' of management and large insider investors (Maltby 1999). The development of the professional auditor's role in the late nineteenth century can be understood as a social process rather than a project aimed at aligning nineteenth-century audit with a timeless 'best practice'. McMillan (1997: 13) quotes an article from *The Accountant* of 1883 which is particularly telling in this context:

> A true audit . . . goes far beyond the checking of vouchers, items and balances. It means going beyond the scenes, searching out the causes by which the effects have been created, the discovery of managerial errors, and the suggestion of remedies.
>
> A true auditor is in the confidence of his client. The latter almost invariably consults him on matters far removed from the simple question of the balance sheet and profit and loss.

It is instructive to compare this mission statement with the Monteagle Committee's 1849 recommendations for the duties of the auditor, quoted above, which focused his work on verification and vouchers, and stipulated that he should not 'interfere' in the running of the company. The late nineteenth-century orientation of the audit away from fraud detection reflected the developing idea of the auditor as an ally of management (the singular 'client' in the extract above) rather than of small outsider investors. Robson *et al.* (2007) develop the idea of the continuing process of professional legitimation – the extension of the field of professional jurisdiction. They perceive it at work in the continuing development of business-risk based methods of auditing, which reduce audit time (and hence costs) and can be presented as resulting in the generation of business advice rather than merely in audit testing:

> [N]ew business risk audit techniques, and their associated discourses and rationales, can be seen as being intertwined with the status accountants and auditors perceive of themselves and their craft, and with their identity as auditors or, rather, as 'business advisers'.
>
> (ibid.: 431)

They conclude that business risk audit:

> offered to the audit industry and the profession a new form of rationality and legitimacy for the audit task. It occluded the distinction between audit and business (or value-adding) services in a seeming harmony of interest between auditor and corporate management.

> (ibid.: 430)

Their analysis is consonant with the interpretation offered by Maltby (1999) and Power (1992) of audit techniques being developed in line with the interests of the audit profession rather than in the service of a timeless notion of best audit practice. From this viewpoint, the argument within the profession about fraud detection may be attributed to divided views about the way forward for the profession. Was the audit client the shareholder, who was served by fraud detection, or the corporate manager who would pay for business advice? The comments by Robson *et al.* suggest that this dichotomy persists, and is a major contributor to the audit expectation gap.

Audit techniques – the process of auditing

Power (1992) derives his understanding of the 'discourse of sampling' from professional journals and key texts such as Dicksee, rather than by an examination of evidence of the work actually carried out by auditors. He admits that the latter would be desirable – but that 'such evidence is almost impossible to obtain' and that in any case 'we might still be concerned as to whether such documents "truly" reflected practice' (ibid.: 39). This is a point of difference between Matthews (2006) and Power. In his *History of Auditing*, Matthews makes substantial use of texts and journals, but also of interviews with 77 chartered accountants, including 'the oldest accountants we could find' who had trained and qualified in the 1920s. There, he maps out a movement away from the 'bookkeeping audit' – in which auditors prepared as well as audited financial statements – and an increase in the use of audit programmes and of sampling, and the audit of internal control systems. The main focus of the audit became less with the profit and loss account transactions and more with the balance sheet, using direct tests to confirm balances. Specially devised audit programmes began to be adopted, and in the latter part of the twentieth century, risk assessment and computer audit became increasingly important.

Matthews concludes (2006: 163) that the twentieth-century developments were 'determined by structural economic change occurring among the auditor's clients'. He identifies as crucial factors: pressure on cost reduction and the growing importance of electronic data processing. For Matthews, 'the autonomous and unproblematic development of the technical' (Hopwood 1985: 366) is not the sole driver of change as was implied by Brown in his 1962 account of audit change, nor is the profession in charge of its destiny by its ability to deploy rationalising and justifying discourses. He views audit techniques as a product of economic pressures – transmitted by the client to the auditor – as well as of professional strategies.

Audit in the public sector

In one of her 2002 Reith Lectures, part of a series entitled 'A Question of Trust', O'Neill (2002) attacked the extent to which audit in the public sector had subverted previous relations of trust:

The idea of audit has been exported from its original financial context to cover ever more detailed scrutiny of non-financial processes and systems . . . This audit explosion, as Michael Power has so aptly called it, has often displaced or marginalised older systems of accountability.

O'Neill is voicing here a widely held view that public-sector audit was a product of the 1980s, part of a 'proliferation' (Power 1994a) which also included the arrival of environmental audit, value for money audit and many others. Power's prolific writing on audit (Power 1994a, 1994b, 1997, 2000a, 2000b, 2003) has been influential in promoting the idea of public-sector audit as colonisation of 'older systems' by private-sector practices. According to Power, the explosion of audit has introduced alien values into the public sector, promoted by a 'rhetoric of account-ability' which has imposed a model of financial accountability on a disparate collection of activities and outcomes. The mere fact of undergoing audit, under this new dispensation, confers legitimacy, replacing trustworthiness with submission to inspection. The intrusion of audit, according to Power, leads to a preoccupation with 'making things auditable' by pro-ducing quantifiable results, however inappropriate these are to the organisations or activities under inspection.

There is, however, scope for this view to be challenged on the basis of the historical devel-opment of public sector audit. The fundamental question is how far it is valid to regard audit as a new activity which is necessarily inimical to the objectives of the public sector. Jones and Pendlebury (2000: 233) claim that government audit is 'the oldest aspect of the auditing profession'. Public-sector audit has not been the subject of as much historical research as corporate audit, but there are a number of relevant studies of various periods and in various contexts: in central government, in local government, and in voluntary charitable institutions.

Descriptions of early government audit do not suggest that it was introduced as a reflection of commercial audit practices. Hoskin and Macve (1986: 114) note that accounting and audit-ing change took place in 'the administrative arena before . . . the merchant world'. The *Dialogus de Scaccario* (1177–79) provides an overview of the internal control and audit methods of the royal treasury, giving evidence of concern with systems and of confrontational dialogues between the accountant and the auditor.[8] Exchequer audit was a powerful practice, part of what Hoskin and Macve term an 'examinatorial discourse'. Jones (2006: 11) emphasises not only the importance of the audit as a model for that of other institutions, but also the existence in the Exchequer of other forms of internal control which were more widely used in manorial systems – seals, personal supervision, sampling and division of duties (ibid.: 14, 15).

The history of public-sector audit between the Middle Ages and the nineteenth century, even more than that of corporate audit, has been neglected by accounting historians: the early modern period has not so far attracted attention. Studies by Funnell (1994, 2004) deal with the resurgence of governmental audit in the early Victorian period. Funnell points to the import-ance of government audit as part of the reforms undertaken by Gladstone's government, and to their continuing significance:

> The purpose of writing this paper is to identify the origins of economy as a concern of modern central government auditors by recognising the irresistible influence . . . of the belief that Gladstone, Graham and Trevelyan had in the virtue of economy.
>
> (Funnell 2004: 28)

Funnell (ibid.: 27) suggests that public-sector audit's 'arid technicalities' ensured its neglect by government reformers until crisis made it a matter for urgent attention: it may be that the same has been true of historical research in the area.

Work by Coombs and Edwards (1990 and 2004) has studied the growth of local authority audit, again a relatively neglected area despite its long history. They focus on the nineteenth-century development of audit, when there was an urgent need to adapt and reform practices in response to the pressures of very rapid urban growth. Audit grew in response, in a piecemeal fashion and with various clashes between new and existing structures. The auditor regularly challenged expenditure on the grounds of value for money as well as compliance with regulations.[9] A further complication was the continuing tussle for audit work in municipal corporations between three groups – the elected ratepayer auditors, government-appointed district auditors, and professional accountants. Arguments about democratic representation, efficiency and technical expertise suffused a 'strenuously contested power struggle between vested interests' (Coombs and Edwards 2004: 80) that continued from the early nineteenth century to the 1930s. When the municipal corporations were dissolved in 1974, 202 had moved to professional audit, 119 to district audit and 21 still had elected auditors (ibid.: 82).

Baker and Collins (2005) describe another instance of internal control and audit outside the commercial sector, in an endowed charitable trust from the early eighteenth to the mid-nineteenth century. The trust, as they point out, was part of a group of charitable organisations that fulfilled an important social role, offering education, health care and benefits in cash or kind. They examine the Lady Hastings Trust, a Yorkshire foundation, which ran schools and almshouses and gave money to the poor and needy. The Trust was governed by an elaborate control structure (ibid.: 119) involving a group of trustees, a board of local clergy, a bailiff and the Chancellor of the diocese. The clergy examined the accounts annually: there was also a quinquennial audit performed by the Chancellor. The Chancellor's reports on occasion included detailed criticism of the board's conduct. This included poor management of cash, poor oversight, and bad investment decisions: in 1827, the Chancellor commented on expenditure 'which would not have been warranted by any principle of managing the trust estates to the best extent' (ibid.: 125). Baker and Collins suggest that there is further scope for examining the audit and control structure of charitable trusts in order to understand the management of what were substantial holders of assets.

Nothing has yet been written that offers an overview of the growth of public-sector audit, of the changes it underwent, and of its relationship with the private sector. The studies above are all of episodes in public-sector audit. They suggest that the relationship between the public and the private sector are older and more closely interwoven than has recently been claimed, and that the incursion of auditors into issues of value for money as well as authorisation can be traced back at least to the beginning of the twentieth century (Coombs and Edwards 1990: 168). The evidence available so far suggests that the rhetoric of the 'audit explosion' may deserve to be challenged by historical research.

International audit

The widely accepted model in writing about audit outside Great Britain is that practices which originated in Great Britain were gradually transmitted overseas, first, to the USA, and subsequently the Empire/Commonwealth, to Europe and finally to the developing world and to the former Communist countries of Eastern Europe and Asia.

Moyer (1951: 3) states that, 'The first audits in America were of course patterned after the British general model' because of the influence of British auditors retained by British investors. The pattern of US and British work diverged at the end of the nineteenth century, according to Moyer, because 'bookkeeper audits' on the British model, with 'endless checking of posting' were too expensive for the USA. Moyer (1951: 7) ascribes the growth of sampling and systems in the USA to the profession's need to demonstrate value for money. Flesher *et al.* (2005) contest Moyer's premise that US practice derived from UK corporate audit. They suggest that audit activity had begun in the seventeenth century with the companies financing settlers, and continued through the colonial period, with a government auditor appointed by Congress in 1789 (ibid.: 22–6). In the nineteenth century, the growth of the road, canal and railway companies produced a demand for accounting and audit which generated 'a pool of talent' (ibid.: 36) for the new profession.

The two papers – Moyer (1951) and Flesher *et al.* (2005) – typify two views which recur in research about international changes in audit. Moyer's view is that the USA was a *tabula rasa* which could be inscribed with British accounting practices: Flesher *et al.* point to the pre-existence of auditing activity, so that British practices were absorbed by accountants who were already familiar with audit in various contexts. The most interesting research about the development of audit internationally recognises some of the issues that arise when new practices are introduced to existing structures and norms, and some of the varied instances of this are discussed below.

Evans (2003) and Quick (2005) both trace the history of the German auditing profession, and point to significant differences between the Anglo-American and German regimes; the long-established limited liability partnerships in Germany, the specialisation of audit firms and the low level of auditor liability. They stress the extent to which these features are embedded in the history of corporate governance in Germany – the key role played by banks as both shareholders and investors thereby reducing the separation of ownership from control. Evans (2003: 56) quotes a German lawyer who commented in 1930 that 'the "auditors" of the English law have to fulfil a large part of the functions of the German supervisory board'. Gietzmann and Quick (1998: 81), in their discussion of proposed changes in auditor liability in the EU, make the point that audit is embedded in a 'model of corporate governance' and that one feature of audit cannot sensibly be changed without a view to the corporate governance system as a whole. This is an issue that recurs in other studies of international change in a variety of contexts.

Ramirez (2007) deals with the development of the accounting profession in France from the 1970s onwards. He points to the extent to which the Big Four Anglo/American audit firms displaced existing French practitioners from the market for the audit of large corporations. This, he argues, was not simply the result of 'global forces' resulting in the inevitable expansion of market economies: 'large professional firms have first and foremost played an essential part in the development and internationalisation of those market economies' (ibid.: 65). The Big Four needed to adapt to a market in which the sole practitioner had up till then prevailed: they needed State patronage, as part of a modernising movement, and they needed to wait until a French alternative had failed (ibid.: 65–6).

Studies of the development of audit in China and in Eastern Europe again bring to the foreground the extent to which audit needs to adapt itself, or adapt the economy into which it is moving. The simultaneous arrival of corporate audit and of new corporate structures creates problems of adjustment. Tang *et al.* (1999), for instance, describe the difficulties in China of introducing audit to the newly privatised state-owned enterprises during the 1980s and 1990s. They point to a shortage of audit staff, a mismatch between the commercial state-owned enterprises and the government auditors, and the change in the role of audit, from monitoring compliance with rules to verification of statements. Changes in regulation are found to be ineffectual without addressing the network of structures and expectations that already exist.

Sucher and Zelenka (1998) outline the problems caused in the Czech Republic by the very rapid transition to a market economy. Audit prior to 'marketisation' had taken the form of internal managerial 'revision' or of state control, in either case aimed at ensuring compliance with regulations. The adjustment to an audit based on systems review and an opinion on truth and fairness was problematical, partly because of the shortage of staff with relevant training, and partly because of clients' expectations of audit. They quote an auditor's comment that '[Czech companies] see the objective of the audit as the tax return' (ibid.: 739), and note that audit continues to be associated with regulatory inspection rather than with advice (ibid.: 740).

Similar issues are raised in papers by Bychkova (1996), Samsonova and Turley (2006) and Mennicken (2006) about the development of audit in Russia after the collapse of the Soviet Union. Here again, audit is based on a tradition of state inspection and control (Bychkova 1996: 78–83). The arrival of an audit regime based on international standards demands the development of a new profession and client understanding of, and demand for, a new mode of audit. But here, problems have again arisen. Samsonova and Turley (2006: n.p.), like Sucher and Zelenka (1998), highlight the effect of the 'revision tradition', carrying with it the idea of audit as a routine compliance activity, helping clients to fill in forms or solve problems in accounts. They describe the development of an audit profession as segmented. It includes an 'elite' group of audit firms involved in modernisation of practice and in regulation, but also a large group of smaller firms of 'pseudo auditors' who see their function as providing services to the client, ' "serving" the client's business' and not paying much attention to professional ethics/standards. In between is a group of auditors doing their best to comply with international standards despite low fees and lack of legal guidance. Samsonova and Turley (2006: n.p.) conclude that institutional influences alone do not determine auditor behaviour – it is also determined by 'their internal motivations and degrees of responsiveness' to those pressures.

Mennicken (2006: 1) suggests that new audit regulations have not necessarily arisen in response to investor demand, but rather as part of a drive towards modernisation and globalisation; a means of 'integrating the Russian economy into the international marketplace'. The absence of stable regulatory institutions means that there is no framework within which audit activity can be anchored.[10] She concludes that, 'the Russian auditing profession has emerged on the basis of highly rationalised and idealised imaginations of market-oriented development that are not tailored to the context of Russia's transitional economy' (ibid.: 27).

Conclusion and directions for further research

This chapter, in a necessarily brief and selective survey of historical work on auditing, has attempted to do two things. One is to draw attention to the main elements of historical writing to date, and the other to suggest routes that might usefully be taken in future. The annotated bibliography at the end of this chapter accordingly identifies pieces of work for one of two reasons. Some have played a major role in discussion so far. Watts and Zimmerman (1983), in their application of agency theory to the origins of audit, have produced an explanation that figures repeatedly in subsequent discussions. Power's paper, one of a number on this topic, has been important in encouraging debate about the extent and impact of public sector audit during the 1980s and subsequently. Chandler and Edwards (1996) represent the intensive study of corporate audit during the late nineteenth century and the identification of problem areas which appear to have been carried on into the twentieth century and beyond.

The other two papers identified below touch on areas that have attracted less attention.

Napier's (1998) piece on auditor liability is important because of its suggestion that the role of the auditor is not a fixed one, but has altered in response to different models of corporate governance. He demonstrates the value of attempting to understand audit by considering the differences, as well as the similarities, between the auditor/director/shareholder relationship with the passage of time. Mennicken's (2006) paper is of particular interest because it explores the contradictions and difficulties of imposing Anglo-American audit standards on an economy with a massively different history, and also because it highlights the ideological significance of audit as a symbol of internationalisation rather than as a set of achievable practices.

Napier's and Mennicken's papers suggest two areas that deserve further research – but there are numerous others. One of the major gaps in knowledge is the development of audit before and after what Lee (1993: 59) calls the 'formal inception in the mid-1800s' of corporate audit. We know very little about the shareholder audits of joint stock and limited companies, and hence little about the expectations that were brought to bear on the first professional corporate auditors. Curiously, there is very little research into audit from the early twentieth century onwards. The end of the century, the era of the major corporate scandals such as BCCI and Enron, has attracted terrific interest (see, for instance, O'Connell 2004; Carnegie and Napier 2006). But auditing in the period which included major changes in company law and regulation – the Companies Acts of 1929 and 1947, the institution of accounting and auditing standards – has so far been the subject of little research.[11]

The development of audit and the legal and professional controversies of the mid- to late nineteenth century, as they appeared in the press and in textbooks, have been thoroughly researched. Little is known about the nature of the work undertaken, as distinct from the debate about it. Plainly this is difficult, but Popp's use of archival audit reports (2000) and Matthews' use of oral history (2006) have made important contributions to understanding. There is a strong case for attempting further archival research to enrich our understanding.

Another major area that deserves further investigation is that of public-sector audit. Power's writing on the subject (e.g. Power 1994a) is part of a large literature about its potentially disruptive arrival at the end of the twentieth century. Little work has been done about its earlier presence and impact, although existing studies (e.g. Coombs and Edwards 1990) suggest that it played an important though contested part in government from a much earlier date.

Auditing is an activity that appears capable of resisting severe challenges – most recently the 2001 collapse of Enron and the complicity of its auditors in misleading the public, which were claimed to have had a catastrophic effect on the reputation of both auditors and audit (O'Connell 2004; Carnegie and Napier 2006, *passim*). But in 2006 a *Guardian* headline announced that 'UK accounting firms enjoy £1bn bonanza in wake of Enron' (Inman 2006) with a 14 per cent overall increase in fee income, much of it attributed to the increased demand for corporate governance advice following the Sarbanes–Oxley legislation in the USA. At the end of the year, in a playlet in *Accountancy* (2006: 27), an accountant made an unsuccessful attempt to bemoan the long-term effects of Enron:

> All right, but apart from the extra jobs, higher profits, record fees, higher standards, cool image, greater visibility, more shareholder protection, better behaviour, enhanced ethical codes, us being taken seriously, and gripping drama, what has Enron done for us?

One of the abiding challenges for historians, in whatever context, is to understand why auditing displays such extraordinary resilience.

Key works

Chandler and Edwards (1996) is a useful introduction to the growing literature on late Victorian audit. It reviews the existence, from the late nineteenth century onwards, of controversies about problems of audit independence, the expectations gap, reporting and regulation.

Mennicken (2006) studies the significance of the introduction of international audit practice as part of a wider economic and social change being attempted within Russia. The paper is particularly interesting as a basis for discussing initiatives for globalising audit practices.

Napier (1998) discusses the close relationships between audit and law and between audit and corporate governance, and the need to understand the auditor's role within changing systems of corporate governance.

Watts and Zimmerman (1983) introduced the widely-cited argument that audit has arisen as a voluntary response to agency problems in firms rather than because of legislative requirements.

Notes

1 See for instance Fleischman and Radcliffe (2005) and Chapters 1–3 of the *Routledge Companion*.
2 See Lee (1989) for an overview of the prior, sparse writing on the history of audit.
3 Jones' discussion does not examine the witnesses' occupations. These may have had an impact on their support for audit, to the extent that the advocates of audit were suppliers, rather than users, of information.
4 See also Chapter 12 on the importance of audit for the development of the accounting profession.
5 See Edwards *et al.* (2007) on the 'jurisdictional battle' waged by the professional against, for instance, the shareholder auditor in the mid-nineteenth century, and Sikka and Willmott (1995) on the relationship between professional jurisdiction and independence.
6 See Harvey (1994: 101–5) for a detailed exposition of the managerial function of the audit.
7 Bryer points out (1991: 459) that railway audits were described during the mania of 1845 as 'the greatest farce possible . . . arithmetical rather than judicial' and 'a mere child's play'.
8 See Baxter (1994: esp. 223–8) for a description of the highly ritualised process of the audit.
9 See, for instance, Coombs and Edwards (1990: 161, 168) on clashes between district auditors and first Poor Law unions and later town councils on this matter.
10 Cf. Samsonova and Turley's (2006) description of the mismatch between international standards and Russian practice.
11 One rare study is that by Matthews (2005) of the audit failures that preceded the collapse of London and County Securities Bank in 1973.

References

Accountancy (2006) What Enron did for us, 138 (1360): 27.
Armstrong, P. (1991) Contradiction and social dynamics in the capitalist agency relationship, *Accounting, Organizations and Society*, 16 (1): 1–25.
Baker, M. and Collins, M. (2005) Audit and control in the not-for-profit sector: an endowed charity case 1739–1853, *Accounting and Business Research*, 33 (2): 111–28.
Baxter, W. T. (1994) Early accounting: the tally and the checker-board, in R. H. Parker and B. S. Yamey (eds) *Accounting History: Some British Contributions*, pp. 197–235 (Oxford: Clarendon Press).
Brown, R. G. (1962) Changing audit objectives and techniques, *Accounting Review*, 37 (4): 696–703.
Bryer, R. A. (1991) Accounting for the 'railway mania' of 1845 – a great railway swindle?, *Accounting, Organizations and Society*, 16 (5/6): 439–86.

Bryer, R. A (2000) The history of accounting and the transition to capitalism in England. Part two: evidence, *Accounting, Organizations and Society*, 25 (4/5): 327–81.

Bychkova, S. (1996) The development and status of auditing in Russia, *European Accounting Review*, 5 (1): 77–90.

Carnegie, G. D. and Napier, C. J. (2006) The portrayal of accounting and accountants following the Enron collapse. Paper presented at Eighth Interdisciplinary Perspectives on Accounting Conference, Cardiff University, 10–12 July.

Chandler, R. A. (1997) Judicial views on auditing from the nineteenth century, *Accounting History*, 2 (1): 61–80.

Chandler, R. A. and Edwards, J. R. (1996) Recurring issues in auditing: back to the future?, *Accounting, Auditing & Accountability Journal*, 9 (2): 4–29.

Chandler, R. and Fry, N. (2005) Audit failure, litigation, and insurance in early twentieth century Britain, *Accounting History*, 10 (3): 13–38.

Chandler, R. A., Edwards, J. R. and Anderson, M. (1993) Changing perceptions of the role of the company auditor, 1840–1940, *Accounting and Business Research*, 23 (92): 443–59.

Collier, P. (1996) The rise of the audit committee in UK companies: a curious phenomenon?, *Accounting, Business & Financial History*, 6 (2): 121–140.

Coombs, H. M. and Edwards, J. R. (1990) The evolution of the district audit, *Financial Accountability and Management*, 6 (3): 153–76.

Coombs, H. M. and Edwards, J. R. (2004) The audit of municipal corporations: a quest for professional dominance, *Managerial Auditing Journal*, 19 (1): 68–83.

Cousins, J., Mitchell, A. and Sikka, P. (1999) Auditor liability: the other side of the debate, *Critical Perspectives on Accounting*, 10 (3): 283–312.

Edwards, J. R. (1989) *A History of Financial Accounting* (London: Routledge).

Edwards, J. R., Anderson, M. and Chandler, R. (2007) Claiming a jurisdiction for the 'public accountant' in England prior to organisational fusion, *Accounting, Organizations and Society*, 32 (1/2): 61–100.

Evans, L. (2003) Auditing and audit firms in Germany before 1931, *Accounting Historians Journal*, 30 (1): 28–65.

Fleischman, R. K. and Radcliffe, V. S. (2005) The roaring nineties: accounting history comes of age, *Accounting Historians Journal*, 32 (1): 61–110.

Flesher, D. L., Previts, G. J. and Samson, W. D. (2005) Auditing in the United States: a historical perspective, *Abacus*, 41 (1): 21–39.

Forrester, D. A. R. (1994) Early canal company accounts: financial and accounting aspects of the Forth and Clyde Navigation, in R. H. Parker and B. S. Yamey (eds) *Accounting History. Some British Contributions*, pp. 297–326 (Oxford: Clarendon Press).

Funnell, W. (1994) Independence and the state auditor in Britain: a constitutional keystone or a case of reified imagery?, *Abacus*, 30 (2): 175–95.

Funnell, W. (2004) Victorian parsimony and the early champions of modern public sector audit, *Accounting History*, 9 (1): 25–60.

Gietzmann, M. B. and Quick, R. (1998) Capping auditor liability: the German experience, *Accounting, Organizations and Society*, 23 (1): 81–103.

Grout, P., Jewitt, I., Pong, C. and Whittington, G. (1994) 'Auditor professional judgement': implications for regulation and the law, *Economic Policy*, 9 (2): 308–51.

Harvey, P. D. A. (1994) Manorial accounts, in R. H. Parker and B. S. Yamey (eds) *Accounting History: Some British Contributions*, pp. 91–115 (Oxford: Clarendon Press).

Hopwood, A. G. (1977) Editorial, *Accounting, Organizations and Society*, 2 (4): 277–8.

Hopwood, A. G. (1985) The tale of a committee that never reported: disagreements on intertwining accounting with the social, *Accounting, Organizations and Society*, 10 (3): 361–77.

Hoskin, K. W. and Macve, R. H. (1986) Accounting and the examination; a genealogy of disciplinary power, *Accounting, Organizations and Society*, 11 (1): 105–36.

Humphrey, C., Moizer, P. and Turley, S. (1992) The audit expectations gap – plus ca change, plus c'est la meme chose?, *Critical Perspectives on Accounting*, 3 (2): 137–61.

Inman, P. (2006) UK accounting firms enjoy £1bn bonanza in wake of Enron, *Guardian*, 28 June. Available HTTP: <http://business.guardian.co.uk/story/0,,1807374,00. html> (accessed 15 October 2007).

Institute of Chartered Accountants in England and Wales (2005) *Audit Quality: Agency Theory and the Role of Audit* (London: ICAEW).

Jones, E. (1981) *Accountancy and the British Economy 1840–1980: The Evolution of Ernst & Whinney* (London: Batsford).

Jones, M. J. (2006) Medieval modes of accounting, control and accountability. Paper presented at Eighteenth Accounting, Business and Financial History Conference, Cardiff University, 14–15 September.

Jones, R. and Pendlebury, M. (2000) *Public Sector Accounting*, 5th edn (Harlow: Pearson).

Jones, S. (1995) A cross-sectional analysis of recommendations for company financial disclosure and auditing by nineteenth-century parliamentary witnesses, *Accounting, Business & Financial History*, 5 (2): 159–86.

Lee, T. A. (1989) *The Evolution of Audit Thought and Practice* (London: Taylor & Francis).

Lee, T. A. (1993) *Corporate Audit Theory* (London: Chapman & Hall).

McMillan, K. P. (1997) The audit-auditor ideal: a positive image for British accountants 1875–1890. Paper presented at European Accounting Association Conference, Graz, 23–25 April.

Maltby, J. (1999) 'A sort of guide, philosopher and friend': the rise of the professional auditor in Britain, *Accounting, Business & Financial History*, 9 (1): 29–50.

Matthews, D. (2005) London and County Securities: a case study in audit and regulatory failure, *Accounting, Auditing & Accountability Journal* 18 (4): 518–36.

Matthews, D. (2006) *A History of Auditing: the Changing Audit Process in Britain from the Nineteenth Century to the Present Day* (London: Routledge).

Matthews, D., Anderson, M., and Edwards, J. R. (1998) *The Priesthood of Industry: The Rise of the Professional Accountant in British Management* (Oxford: Oxford University Press).

Mennicken, A. (2006) Changing rationalities of government: the rise of audit professionalism in post-Soviet Russia. Paper presented at Eighth Interdisciplinary Perspectives on Accounting Conference, Cardiff, 10–12 July.

Miller P. and Napier, C. J. (1993) Genealogies of calculation, *Accounting, Organizations and Society*, 18 (7/8): 631–47.

Moyer, C. A. (1951) Early developments in American auditing, *Accounting Review*, 26 (1): 3–8.

Napier, C. J. (1998) Intersections of law and accountancy: unlimited auditor liability in the United Kingdom, *Accounting, Organizations and Society*, 23 (1): 105–28.

Napier, C. J. (2006) Accounts of change: 30 years of historical accounting research, *Accounting, Organizations and Society*, 31 (4/5): 445–507.

Nielsen, O. (1960) New challenges in accounting, *Accounting Review*, 35 (4): 583–9.

Nikkinen, J. and Petri, S. (2004) Does agency theory provide a general framework for audit pricing?, *International Journal of Auditing*, 8 (3): 253–62.

O'Connell, B. T. (2004) Enron. Con. 'He that filches from me my good name . . . makes me poor indeed', *Critical Perspectives on Accounting*, 15 (6/7): 733–49.

O'Neill, O. (2002) A question of trust, Reith lectures. Available HTTP <http://www. bbc.co. uk/radio4/reith2002> (accessed 15 October 2007).

Oschinsky, D. (ed.) (1971) *Walter of Henley and Other Treatises on Estate Management and Accountancy* (Oxford: Clarendon Press).

O'Sullivan, N. (1993) Auditors' liability: its role in the corporate governance debate, *Accounting and Business Research*, 23 (91A): 412–20.

Popp, A. (2000) Specialty production, personal capitalism and auditors' reports: Mintons Ltd, c.1870–1900, *Accounting, Business & Financial History*, 10 (3): 347–69.

Power, M. K. (1992) From common sense to expertise: reflections on the prehistory of audit sampling, *Accounting, Organizations and Society*, 17 (1): 37–62.

Power, M. (1994a) *The Audit Explosion* (London: Demos).

Power, M. (1994b) The audit society, in A. G. Hopwood and P. Miller (eds) *Accounting as Social and Institutional Practice*, pp. 299–316 (Cambridge: Cambridge University Press).

Power, M. (1997) *The Audit Society: Rituals of Verification* (Oxford: Oxford University Press).

Power, M. (2000a) Editorial – exploring the audit society, *International Journal of Auditing*, 4 (1): 1.

Power, M. (2000b) The audit society: second thoughts, *International Journal of Auditing* 4 (1): 111–19.

Power, M. (2003) Evaluating the audit explosion, *Law & Policy*, 25 (3): 185–202.

Quick, R. (2005) The formation and early development of German audit firms, *Accounting, Business & Financial History*, 15 (3): 317–43.

Ramirez, C. (2007) Exporting professional models: the expansion of the multinational audit firm and the transformation of the French accountancy profession since 1970. Available HTTP <http://www.hec.fr/hec/fr/professeurs_recherche/upload/cahiers/cr864Ramirez> (accessed 7 November 2007).

Robson, K., Humphrey, C., Khalifa, R. and Jones, J. (2007) Transforming audit technologies: business risk audit methodologies and the audit field, *Accounting, Organizations and Society*, 32 (4/5): 409–38.

Samsonova, A. and Turley, S. (2006) A critical review of the transformation of audit practices in Russia: an institutional theory perspective. Paper presented at Eighth Interdisciplinary Perspectives on Accounting Conference, Cardiff, 10–12 July. Available HTTP <http://www.cardiff.ac.uk/carbs/news_events/events/past/conferences/ipa/ipa_papers/00189.pdf> (accessed 14 November 2007).

Select Committee on the Amending of Railways Acts as to the Audit of Accounts (1849), House of Lords, Third report, BPP 1849, x, 469.

Sikka, P. (1998) Memorandum submitted to the Select Committee on Trade and Industry. Available HTTP: <http://www.publications.parliament.uk/pa/cm199899/cmselect/cmtrdind/59/81201a01.htm> (accessed 7 November 2007).

Sikka, P. and Willmott, H. (1995) The power of 'independence': defending and extending the jurisdiction of accounting in the United Kingdom, *Accounting, Organizations and Society*, 20 (6): 547–81.

Sucher, P. and Zelenka, I. (1998) The development of the role of the audit in the Czech Republic, *European Accounting Review*, 7 (4): 723–51.

Tang, Q., Chow, C. W. and Lau, A. (1999) Auditing of state-owned enterprises in China: historic development, current practice and emerging issues, *International Journal of Accounting*, 34 (2): 173–87.

Teo, E. and Cobbin, P. (2005) A revisitation of the 'audit expectations gap': judicial and practitioner views on the role of the auditor in late-Victorian England, *Accounting History*, 10 (2): 35–66.

Toms, J. S. (2002) The rise of modern accounting and the fall of the public company: the Lancashire cotton mills 1870–1914, *Accounting, Organizations and Society*, 27 (1/2): 61–84.

Watts, R. L. and Zimmerman, J. L. (1983) Agency problems, auditing, and the theory of the firm: some evidence, *Journal of Law and Economics*, 26 (4): 613–34.

Part 4

Institutions

11

Professionalisation

Chris Poullaos

Overview

In Chapter 3, professionalisation was identified as an important research area in accounting history. The aim of this chapter is to examine its contribution by highlighting the major themes and findings of the academic research published in the past two decades. The chapter tracks the geographical spread of professional organisation via the relays of empire and international capital in the late nineteenth and early twentieth centuries and processes of regional integration and globalisation in the late twentieth and early twenty-first centuries. It shows not only that professionalisation processes are diverse but also that the construction of professional identity in accountancy is intimately connected to relations both internal and external to the occupation, and to the wealth, social status and power of accountants. The chapter shows, furthermore, that the forms and outcomes of professionalisation endeavours are also intimately connected with the broader social context within which they occur. In this respect, histories of professionalisation falls squarely within the 'new' accounting history and the tradition of socio-historical accounting research discussed in Chapter 2. Suggestions for further research are also offered.

Introduction

From the second half of the nineteenth century onwards strenuous efforts were made in the Anglo-American world to organise the occupation of accountancy as a profession and thereby sharing, to a greater or lesser degree, the enhanced wealth, social status and power of doctors and lawyers as opposed to, say, plumbers or clerks. From this perspective, professionalisation refers to actions and processes undertaken to achieve the status of professional and to subsequently maintain and enhance that status through professionalism. These processes take time and they change over time. That is, they are historical. This chapter provides an overview of the motivations, elements and the outcomes of professionalisation at various times and places; and the key institutions (within the occupation and outside it) initiating, supporting, opposing and otherwise shaping professionalisation processes; and the resources at their disposal.

It will touch upon:

- the meaning and significance of 'profession', 'professionalisation' and the importance of organisation;
- explanations for the 'success' or 'failure' of particular professionalisation endeavours;
- competition within the occupation and rivalry with other occupations;
- the role of symbols, credentials, designations;
- relationships between the profession and the institutions of state and market;
- professionalisation and social structure;
- imperialism, globalisation and professionalisation.

The first modern professional accountants emerged in Scotland, their formal organisations becoming visible in the 1850s. Within 30 years, accountants in England, Wales and Ireland had started to organise along similar lines, taking advantage of opportunities arising under industrial capitalism. By the end of the twentieth century a British accountancy arena had emerged. By then, Britain was the major imperial power and self-governing settler communities had become established in Canada, Australia and elsewhere. As well as being a significant industrial and trading nation, Britain was also a major supplier of international finance. British accountants followed British capital throughout the British Empire and beyond. Some settled where capital led and became important contributors to local accountancy professions which, although modelled on British exemplars, developed their own momentum and history. By around 1910, an imperial accountancy arena was starting to emerge. Also by this time an American accountancy profession had become established with its own trajectory. Sections devoted to these developments appear below.

Britain's empire was not restricted to white, settler, self-governing colonies. Trinidad and Tobago, Jamaica, Kenya and Nigeria (for example) did not experience local professional organisation until after independence in the latter half of the twentieth century. Historians of professionalisation in former colonies, in continental Europe, and beyond have been at pains to highlight the perils of generalisations based on Anglo-American experiences. Some of this work has captured the rise of neo-liberalism in the late twentieth century, coupled with the demise of the Soviet bloc and the expansion of the European Union project. The dynamics of professionalisation in these sites are also surveyed.

It is also important to note the intellectual heritage of accounting history research discussed below. Over the past century or so, the sociology of the professions has built on the ideas of Marx, Durkheim, Weber and their followers. A critical version of this literature, drawing mostly on aspects of Weber's thought but incorporating Marxian elements as well, has dominated analysis of accountancy professionalisation over the past two decades. The publication of Willmott (1986) may be taken as a marker for the introduction of sociological insights to the study of professions in the accounting literature. This contribution was part of the studying-accounting-in-its-social-context movement (Burchell *et al.* 1980; also Parker 1980). Analyses of accounting professionalisation produced since then have, in contrast to 'official' histories commissioned by professional organisations (such as Brown 1905; Garrett 1961; Collard 1980) and others sympathetic to accountants' endeavours (such as Stacey 1954), tended to be sceptical of claims of altruistic service and functional contribution which emanated from within the accountancy profession.

Some preliminary questions arise: what does it mean to study accounting as a 'profession'? What are the limitations of the approach taken in the chapter?

Studying the history of accountancy as a profession

While concerted attempts were made by sociologists to define 'profession' as an analytical term in the 1950s and 1960s, the resultant definitions have since largely fallen by the wayside – plagued as they were by the special pleading of status-seeking occupations, the diversity of activities and occupations to which the term had already been socially attached and the political struggles involved in professionalisation (Habenstein 1963; Millerson 1964; Rueschemeyer 1964, 1983; Johnson 1972; Roth 1974; Klegon 1978; Saks 1983; Macdonald 1995). These latter works capture the decline of both: (a) the view that there is a common path or set of steps to professional status; and (b) functionalism as the favoured mode of explaining the social role and outcome of professionalising activity; notwithstanding that accountants themselves have represented their social contribution in functionalist terms.

While the definitional issue has continued to trouble sociologists, accounting historians operating since the 1980s have had the luxury of focusing (mostly) on one occupation whose social acceptance as a 'profession' has been established for some time. They have thus been able to analyse particular efforts by accountants to achieve market control or other goals of a 'professional project'[1] without being constrained or enabled by an overarching definition of 'profession' or a fixed endpoint of professionalisation (see Freidson 1983; Collins 1990; Walker 2004a). This is not to suggest that the meaning of 'profession' is a trivial matter. Rather, it is to say that it is the understandings of the term deployed by historical actors that count and to remind us that it is not necessarily the case that historical actors are perpetually and centrally focused on the meaning of 'profession'.

The functional contribution of accountants – what they do, for whom, and how well they do it – is also far from trivial. How could accountants gain a privileged position without some contribution to significant others or some minimal level of competence or honesty? What has been questioned in accounting history is whether the forms and outcomes of professionalisation processes are a simple by-product of accountants' work. In the Anglo-American world at least, important aspects of an accountancy community's activities and rewards have been affected by efforts to construct a collective occupational identity and to then 'keep up a continual effort to maintain and if possible enhance the position of the group' (Macdonald 1995: 188). The 'continual effort' – the *accountancy professional project* – is what researchers of accounting professionalisation are interrogating, with process being given as much attention as outcome.

Some general cautions are advisable at this point. The coverage of accountancy professional projects in the next section is necessarily selective. Readers seeking further detail of theory or empirics are urged to explore the original works referred to in the main text. Additional histories of professionalisation, particularly in countries not explicitly discussed in the chapter are cited in an appendix. Reflecting the literature, this chapter concentrates largely on activities and events in which professional associations have participated. Nevertheless activities at the individual and firm levels of practice are clearly relevant to the standing of the occupation before as well as during the emergence of formal organisation. There will be no market control, for example, if practitioners cannot perform to the level demanded by market and state. In addition, the major firms have often provided the office bearers and other resources vital to the activities of professional associations. In the limit the latter may be a 'front' for the firms. In short, the focus on the association limits the analysis of professional projects. On the other hand, it is dangerous to read off the state of a professional project from the activities of firms alone.

Further analysis of firms and areas of work that accountants have moved in and out of may be found in Chapter 12. Exclusionary processes operating on the bases of race and gender have implications both for those excluded and the exclusionary professional projects themselves. These are given separate treatment in Chapters 20 and 21. Forms of occupational preparation and knowledge are important to professional claims and these are touched on in Chapter 13. Similarly, professionalism, the organisation of an occupation along professional lines, is itself a form of regulation so Chapter 14 is relevant as well.

The review of histories of the professionalisation of accountancy is arranged on a broadly geographical and chronological basis. The discussion begins with Britain, where professionalisation began and proceeds to examine professionalisation in British settler colonies, the USA, post-colonial settings, and continental Europe and beyond.

Britain and some settler colonies

Scotland (to 1914)

The incorporation by royal charter of the Society of Accountants in Edinburgh (SAE) in 1854, the Institute of Accountants and Actuaries in Glasgow (IAAG) in 1855 and the Society of Accountants in Aberdeen (SAA) in 1867 provide convenient markers of professional organisation. What has been learnt about the pioneering efforts of the Scots?[2] The move to formal organisation was prompted by a 'massive . . . threat to the *whole insolvency practice* of Scottish accountants' (Walker 1995: 292, original emphasis) emanating from English merchants. The founders of the Scottish bodies were elite accountants with close links to the legal profession and the higher strata of Scottish society. Formal organisation was crucial as a means of mobilising allies and other resources, building group identity and putting arguments in relevant fora, public and private. Also involved was a more general desire to dominate lucrative markets. The interplay of economic class and social status, collective mobility and market control, and social closure and professional closure, are all evident.

Other features of Scottish professionalisation and its dynamics were replicated elsewhere in Britain and abroad. One was the delineation of the range of 'professional' work to more closely align with the values of societal elites. Another was the establishment of demanding examinations and tests of 'character'. These helped – possibly crucially – to establish both market (and social) reputation, and were implicated in efforts to control the numbers entering accountancy. An associated development was the realisation that reputation could be impounded in designations like 'chartered accountant' and 'CA'. Consequently, exclusive access to such symbolic capital was defended vigorously against the efforts of other determined (and often excluded) accountants and their newly-formed professional bodies who could organise examinations easily enough, but found the other advantages of the chartered bodies harder to replicate or overcome.

Fragmentation of the occupation has been widely remarked upon both in the Scottish case and elsewhere in the Anglo-American world. In both the defence of bankruptcy work in the 1850s and the protracted defence of 'CA' up to 1914, the Scottish chartered bodies drew upon prevailing professional and broader societal ideologies. Major targets of the accountants' discursive barrages were various arms of the state, the legal profession, the business community and members of other social elites. The Scots were also pioneers in 'equating public practice with *professional* accountancy' (Walker 1995: 286), a strategy imported into England and then exported abroad, creating even further fragmentation of the accountancy community. Co-operation among the chartered bodies to deal with external threats went hand in hand with disputes between and within them.

The relationship between professionalisation and social mobility has also been explored. Lee

(2004: 27) argues that the SAE, IAAG and SAA 'coped with the economics of a growing market for their services by increasingly recruiting men from lower middle class and working class backgrounds while maintaining social respectability with leaderships almost exclusively of upper class and upper middle class origins'. Analysis of recruitment to the SAE to 1914 shows how complex the relationship could be. The relative newness of (organised) accountancy and other contextual factors enhanced its potential to be a vehicle for upward social mobility. Limiting it, however, was: the indenture fees payable to the master and entry fees payable to the SAE; the amount and circulation of vocational advice; increasingly demanding training systems; the difficulties of gaining advantageous connections if one was not already connected; and the extensive social pressures on well-to-do Edinburghers to prepare their sons for the learned professions regardless of the availability of places (Walker 1988: 264–8; 194–9). Consequently, a significant proportion of Edinburgh chartered accountants left town, a form of mobility they did not necessarily desire (ibid.: 40–51, 64–6; Lee, 2002a, 2002b, 2004).

By the time of the SAE's fiftieth anniversary, the Scottish chartered bodies had not only 'developed expanding, high standing professional organizations, they had also gained domination of the practice of their vocation, secured judgements which provided legal protection for the source of that dominance and, witnessed the demoralization and ineffectiveness of their competitors' (Walker 1991: 281). The following 100 years have not been studied by academics in the same detail. Analyses of the Scots' professionalising endeavours after 1914 see them as a player in the British professional arena.

England

The professionalisation dynamics behind the formation of the predecessors of the Institute of Chartered Accountants in England and Wales (ICAEW), namely, the Incorporated Society of Liverpool Accountants (1870), the Institute of Accountants in London (1870), the Manchester Institute of Accountants (1871) and the Institute of Accountants in Sheffield (1877) are discussed in Walker (2004a).[3] Again the key event involved changes to insolvency administration. Ironically, the Scottish model of bankruptcy was imported into England setting in motion competition between accountants and lawyers and efforts to create shelters *from* the market (Freidson 1994) and to protect professional elites. As Walker notes (2004a: 127), in Liverpool:

> the organisation of accountants . . . was instigated by lawyers anxious to establish a medium for negotiating the boundaries of bankruptcy work with local accountants. In London, Manchester and Sheffield (and partly in Liverpool) organisation concerned the protection of established accountants from interlopers and was actualised by erecting market shelters and the imposition of exclusionary closure.

Formal organisation facilitated all these processes in a context where there were no legal barriers to entry. Contrary to Abbott (1988), disturbances and work on the one hand and structures and organisation on the other could not meaningfully be untangled or prioritised. Nor could the drive to capture jurisdiction be unpicked from 'status protection, exclusion and differentiation' (Walker 2004a: 152) in the face of intense *intra*-professional rivalry. Furthermore, the accountants seeking a market shelter were protecting their elite status rather than conspiring to achieve collective upward mobility *per se*.

The bedding in of organisation can be awkward, as shown in Anderson *et al.*'s (2005) analysis of the ICAEW from its incorporation by royal charter in 1880 to the turn of the century. Its leadership went down the exclusionary closure/credentialism path by constructing the 'well-qualified' chartered accountant, in image if not always in actual outcome. Constructive elements included, among others, tough exams, an extended period of articles involving payment of a premium to a master and tests of financial probity. These may have helped to establish the ICAEW's reputation – but they also prompted criticisms from entry applicants and members. For example: the examinations were too hard, the difficulty or assessment of examinations varied over time and some masters were more interested in cheap labour than imparting training. The exam requirement became particularly problematic when a new non-examination route was introduced in 1893 to attract eminent non-member practitioners with sizable audit clients. It is not entirely clear how these tensions were managed,[4] but the resulting fracas illustrates the difficulties of jointly managing internal and external relations in the early days of a professional project.

Noguchi and Edwards (2004) have tackled a quite different aspect of the ICAEW's professional project, namely, the promulgation of Recommendations on Accounting Principles (RoAPs) on alternatives to historical cost accounting in a different period (1948–66). What distinguishes this from a 'standard-setting' paper or a 'normative' accounting paper is consideration of professionalisation dynamics, namely: state-profession relations; a desire to maintain professional authority over work (audit and financial reporting); and management of relations between different categories of membership (practising v. industrial). The differences between practising and industrial members threatened other aspects of the ICAEW's professional project. With the former group being dominant, the issue was temporarily resolved by RoAPs being 'irregularly' drafted (my usage) at levels at which the views of the latter group were under-represented.

The above analysis captures the ICAEW: (a) at a more mature stage in its professional project, with its training systems, symbolic capital and credibility with the state and business sector solidly established; (b) dealing with a new issue, viz, a potentially dramatic transformation to its members' intellectual base; and (c) developing a response to (b) conditioned by (a). By the 1940s the ICAEW had long since been functioning in a British accountancy arena, aspects of which are explored in the next section.

Britain/the United Kingdom

A significant body of research into professionalisation has used 'Britain' or 'the UK' or 'the British Isles' as its geographic unit of analysis. Macdonald (1985), for example, seeks to explain the failure of British and Irish accountants (up to 1954) to achieve registration – a means of achieving a legal monopoly 'at the upper end of a range of exclusionary devices' (ibid.: 543). The analysis offers a range of explanatory factors:

- tension between liberalism and closure;
- endemic quarrelling between large numbers of professional bodies as to relative status and access to work within varying locales;
- variations in accounting knowledge needed to service different types of clients;
- the perception by elite accountants that their position in the accountancy hierarchy would be threatened by a common register;
- the difficulty of proving that registration was in 'the public interest' – that there was societal demand for registration or that non-registration would result in societal damage;
- the evolution of 'adequate' closure for the accountancy elite, e.g., via investment in designations or other means.

The conclusion (ibid.: 554) offers a synoptic view of three time/path dependent strategies of market control, namely: the careful building up of professional organisations with reputations for competence, probity and respectability; the amalgamation of those organisations while maintaining reputability; and the piecemeal achievement of control by obtaining the statutory restriction of accountancy functions to members of the senior professional bodies for an increasing number and range of organisations. Willmott's analysis (1986) of the same period identifies factors behind the merger of the ICAEW and the Society of Incorporated Accountants and Auditors (SIAA) in 1957. These include the breakdown in previous efforts to unify the profession, the avoidance of disputation over post-war competition for accounting labour, and the problem of dealing with partnerships between their respective members.

Walker and Shackleton's (1995) examination of a smaller time span (1930–57) highlights the dramatic expansion of the state's planning and central coordination role, in which accountants were acknowledged to have played a significant part. One result was the emergence of a corporatist state in which accountants could potentially move from 'mere' pressure group status to becoming part of the governing apparatus – if they could become unified. But they could not. At one stage their response was to propose something that looked like registration, thereby alienating business and key state actors. The Scots, the Irish and some second tier accountants were suspicious of the ICAEW on the basis of past engagements. The cost and works accountants and municipal treasurers resented being excluded on the grounds that they weren't public accountants. The accountants couldn't even agree (in 1946) on what a 'public accountant' was. Nevertheless the arduous negotiations between segments of the occupation and the state did encourage the Scots to merge in 1951 (into the Institute of Chartered Accountants of Scotland). They also contributed to the merger between the ICAEW and the SIAA in 1957. Walker and Shackleton detect a slowly emerging momentum towards amalgamation, supported by the Board of Trade, the objective being to reduce the problems arising from the multiplicity of accountants' voices.

The profession's leaders were again disappointed during the 1960s when they tried to erect a 'ring fence' around existing associations via legislation to: 'restrict the right to practice accountancy to members of the unified profession; restrict audit and certain tax work to chartered public accountants, and to prohibit the formation of further organisations of public accountants' (Walker and Shackleton 1998: 44). This involved achieving consensus as between the leaders of first, second and third tier accounting bodies, gaining the support of their members and convincing the Board of Trade and politicians. Although the first condition was met, the others were not, in a context where corporatism and the public sector were being wound back and a long-held suspicion of 'monopolisation' re-emerged. Overall, closing-off the British profession through political/legal means has proved to be a mountain too big to climb.

The Institute of Cost and Works Accountants (ICWA, formed in 1919) and Corporate Treasurers and Accountants' Institute (CTAI, 1885) were not originally formed to provide their members with access to public practice. To date, the ICWA and the CTAI have received limited scholarly attention compared to bodies with historical roots in public accountancy. The major examination of the ICWA's formation is Loft (1986). What was the objective of the ICWA's professional project? Achieving a status equal to that of the chartered accountants, apparently, but to what end? Applicants from 'the industrial community' felt 'the need of a body which would cater for an entirely works outlook upon costing instead of the hitherto professional auditors view' (ibid.: 155). Presumably they did not want their field to be constructed by chartered accountants. But what was the danger in that? Some interviewees in Loft's study reported that they got a sense of *identity* from joining. But, is this an outcome or an objective? Possibly the ICWA wanted its members to have 'the same status and monetary awards as the

253

chartered accountants' (ibid.: 157). But it is not evident that a payment mechanism along these lines existed. The question about the ICWA's objective remains open and there is limited knowledge of the process through which its project evolved to the point that it 'had' to be included inside the ring fence by 1966.

It may be too soon to examine in historical perspective shifts in British professional project(s) over the decades characterised by the rise of neo-liberalism internationally. Nevertheless, a steady stream of papers analysing 'current' or 'very recent' events at the time of writing, by authors aware of professionalisation dynamics are suggestive. For example, the state–profession relationship has been, and is still, undergoing dramatic change. Cooper *et al.* (1996) highlight the role of British state agents, conscious of the contribution of accountancy as an industry to national interests, in promoting the British professional project *into the rest of Europe*. Yet, the government was reluctant to give the accountancy associations legal authority over auditors (ibid.: 602; see also Robson *et al.* 1994; Sikka and Willmott 1995a).

On a different note, accountancy's long-established professional status encouraged the Thatcher Government to use accountants to keep an eye on company directors (Halliday and Carruthers 1996). In another twist, accountancy bodies were authorised under the Financial Services Act, 1986 to arrange inspection of their members' practices on behalf of government (Radcliffe *et al.* 1994; Robson *et al.* 1994). In an era of hyper-liberalism accountants became both the watchers and watched. At the same time their dealings with clients were 'commercialised', a process involving the loosening of 'professional' constraints (Hanlon 1994, 1996, 1997; Willmott and Sikka 1997). In short the British accountancy project has been undergoing major, contradictory changes since the 1980s. Future historians of late twentieth-century accountancy professional projects will have a field day.

Canada

The early history of Canadian professional projects has not been researched in the same depth as the British. More could be done to illuminate:

- the acquisition/creation of 'CA' as a by-product of incorporation by statute (Institutes of CAs had been established in Quebec, Ontario, Manitoba, Nova Scotia, British Columbia, Alberta and Saskatchewan by 1908.);
- the spread of professional accountancy from the east to the west of the country as part of the 'settling' or 'development' of a large territory in a series of separate but connected provincial professional projects;
- the complications arising from a federal political structure;
- the arduous construction of a national accountancy arena;
- ethnic division – the French factor;
- tensions between British and Canadian accountants;
- the supplanting of British by American influence; the travails and opportunities of having a major, then super then hyper-power as a neighbour.

While all these matters have received some attention,[5] they have not been examined systematically utilising available archival sources (see also Richardson 1993: 553).

Nevertheless, Richardson's (1987) analysis of the 1879–1979 period, based on secondary sources, goes directly to the themes of this chapter:

[The] ability of associations to publicly differentiate themselves, and the lack of mechanisms by which the elite segments could enforce their preferences, encouraged competition for professional status and access to professional roles among associations. This competition occurred within a poorly specified but widely shared ideological conviction that accounting was a profession. [There were two effects.] First, associations continually escalated their commitment to professional standards and symbolism in order to establish their superiority to other associations on a range of professional criteria . . .

Second, . . . the competition among associations . . . was not simply pushing associations along a scale of predetermined steps toward professionalism. Each response to competitive pressures was defining what professionalism would mean to this field.

(ibid.: 610)

Richardson's overall judgement seems broadly compatible with the British experience. Nevertheless, breaking down such a large period into sub-periods and using original sources may add greatly to our understanding of Canadian professional projects.

The analyses by Richardson (1989a) and MacDonald and Richardson (2004) of occupational licensing in Ontario (beginning with the formation of a Public Accountants' Council (PAC) – a state agency – in 1950) move in this direction. The formation of the PAC required suspicion about the CAs excluding non-CAs from public practice to be overcome. This was a corporatist period *at the provincial level* suggesting a 'need' for an accountants' organisation to be available for integration into the provincial governing apparatus, while amalgamations and negotiations within the accountancy community helped to defuse internal tensions within the occupation. Unlike their British counterparts, the Ontario accountants got their ring fence. The PAC was empowered to grant or refuse licences to engage in public practice, speak for the profession, exercise disciplinary powers and prosecute offenders. The ICAO (Institute of Chartered Accountants of Ontario) appointed eight of the PAC's fifteen council members, its public practice rival the Certified Public Accountants Association of Ontario (CPAA) five, while the remaining two were elected by licensees other than members of the ICAO and CPAA.

The PAC slowly worked towards a situation of having to deal with only one body (the ICAO), establishing it as the sole or main port of entry to public practice while gradually raising entry standards, thereby achieving what the ICAO's founders could only have dreamed of: a body with both exclusive access to 'CA' *and* a more or less exclusive occupational licence, enforceable by law. Unfortunately, for present purposes, the more detailed analysis of MacDonald and Richardson (2004) seems to be more concerned with the PAC's handling of the situation as a *regulatory* project than with the PAC's relations with the ICAO. The paper ends with the CGA using the rise of neo-liberalism to fight its exclusion into the twenty-first century.

In Britain, tests of 'character' – the personal attributes of the accountant – were used as ascriptive barriers to entry and to align the social status of members with those of their clients and other social elites. Richardson's (1989b) analysis suggests that a variant of these tendencies applied to Canada in the period 1880–1930. Accountancy was not open to all social groups, did not represent the diversity of social interests in the population and was 'significantly linked with other sectoral elites' (ibid.: 18).

Neu and Saleem (1996) have used ICAO published ethical codes to analyse the ICAO's handling of 'character issues' from its incorporation in 1883 to 1993. At first, 'character' was an admission criterion and there was no published code. By 1961, however, 40 behavioural injunctions were in print. More generally, published codes effaced both internal divisions between members and contradictions between self-interest and public interest; while locating ICAO's members among other high-status professions – at least discursively. The 1973 revision constructed a mythical past for the ICAO and its members as *having always* been responsible to the public, even as the publication of detailed ethical codes marked a loss of faith on the part of ICAO leaders in the 'character' of its own members. Similarly from the 1980s onwards, in the wake of corporate scandals, escalating litigation and the overt commercialisation of practitioner–client relations, 'independence' and 'objectivity' became – again discursively – the cornerstone of the Canadian profession *from its very beginnings* even though the terms were rarely used before the 1920s (Everett *et al.* 2005). The authors also note the replacement of the religion-based character discourse by a secular scientific discourse favouring independence and objectivity, a point also made about the USA (Preston *et al.* 1995), Australia and New Zealand (Velayutham 2003).

Simmons and Neu (1997) examine the use of the editorials of the *Canadian Chartered Accountant* (1936–50) both to interpret the changing world to members in a manner consistent with the views of social and professional elites and to articulate modes of professionalism aligned with those views. The authors concede the difficulty of establishing how the ICAO's members responded to the editorials (ibid.: 821). Neu *et al.* (2003) return to the editorials, demonstrating further that projected images of professional identity and behaviour varied according to shifts in the broader material and ideological context. The 1980–99 period, for example, finds the ideal CA in a neo-liberal world of winners and losers, dealing with overt commercialisation, increasing complexity and the decline of moral standards in society. However, even if the CA maintains *inner* integrity and independence, the disenchanted world outside will not believe – thus the tragic schism between the appearance and substance of independence. Ineluctably, we must have character, regrettably, we must have ethical rules as well. As Neu *et al.* concede (ibid.: 100), they have provided a reading of the editorials rather than an analysis of either the motives of the editorialists or the response of the readers. Overall, the Canadian papers alluded to here provide a potentially fruitful counterpoint to further analyses using other sources and examining other dimensions of Canadian profession projects.

On a different tack, Richardson (2002) has explored relations between Canadian financial and management accountants from 1926 to 1986. The two groupings are seen as competing for jurisdiction over the firm's accounting processes and the uses to which their outputs are put. As in Britain, the financial accountants were the established professional elite and the management accountants' search for legitimacy was severely hampered by the former's professional dominance. To give just one example: the former's insistence that the cost accounts reconcile with the general ledger restricted the latter's capacity to innovate (with marginal costing, for example) and resulted in the production of information that the latter believed to be inappropriate for managerial decision-making. If the timing and context are comparable, Richardson's analysis provides considerable insight into the need, noted by Loft (1986), felt by ICWA members for a body that catered 'for an entirely works outlook' rather than the 'professional auditors view'.

Australia

Both the *idea* of professional accountancy and British accountancy *qualifications per se* were exported from Britain to Australia (Parker 1989). But neither British-trained *accountants* nor British accounting *associations* were dominant players in Australian accountancy from the mid-1880s to 1914 (Carnegie and Parker 1999). By 1910, there were at least 18 accountancy bodies around Australia, some focusing on cities, some on regions within states, some on states, while others organised nationally (ibid.: 99; see also Carnegie 1993).

Carnegie and Edwards (2001) have examined the occupation prior to the formation of the

Incorporated Institute of Accountants in Victoria (IIAV) in 1886, the first accounting association formed in the state of Victoria. Of the IIAV's 45 founders 41 were immigrants, but 10 at
most were 'accountants' at the time of arrival and only two were members of British accountancy bodies. By 1886, all 45 founders were offering a range of services to the public and for the
most part they were not sons of a pre-existing accountancy elite. The key event prompting the
establishment of a professional body in Melbourne was the attempt by an SIAA[6] member to
start a local branch. At least some of the IIAV's founders were approached to join, but they
formed a local association instead. Possibly nationalism and the logistics of running a professional project in conjunction with the SIAA in London played a part. There were, furthermore,
a growing number of public accountants in Melbourne who might join and many more clerks
that they might want to distinguish themselves from (ibid.: see also Carnegie *et al.* 2003).

Thereafter the IIAV and other Australian bodies played out local variations of factors and
patterns evident in Britain and Canada. One was a registration attempt led by the IIAV in
Victoria in the late 1890s during an economic crisis, when significant amounts of British capital
was lost and the prospect of competition from British accountants was in the air. The IIAV's
professional project was new and although its examinations were respected, the capacity of its
members to undertake credible audits was not. In its early days, with the economy booming, the
IIAV leadership had adopted an inclusive entry policy thereby gaining more financial resources,
more links with market and state – and a defence against the charge of exclusivism – a common
enough position in Britain but having a sharper edge in a more egalitarian Australian polity. It
was also a time when *laissez-faire* doctrine, in the sense of freedom of the individual *from an
oppressive sovereign*, could resonate with more radical philosophies. When boom turned to bust
in the 1890s, there seemed to be an opportunity to switch from openness to closure. The IIAV
put up a registration proposal that was broadly similar to the British and Ontario ring-fence
proposals of the mid-twentieth century. But with the economy recovering somewhat, the social
anxieties about exclusiveness and suspicions about the IIAV's motives again reared their heads
in political circles and the IIAV's proposal faded away.

The narrative above, being a simplified version of the one in Chua and Poullaos (1998),
makes the point that to posit that closure is always preferred to openness as an entry strategy is
problematic. Also, rather than focus on a presumed endless struggle between dominant and
subordinate accountants it suggests that third-party hostility to 'monopolisation' established
clear bounds on what was achievable even though the major accountancy bodies had agreed on
a registration scheme.

With the registration attempt out of the way, there followed a sustained campaign by various
combinations of elite Australian accountants to obtain a royal charter from the Privy Council in
London in the first three decades of the twentieth century. They succeeded at the third attempt
in 1928 (Chua and Poullaos 1993; Poullaos 1994). Broadly speaking, their efforts reflected their
desire to be able to compete successfully with British CAs in Australia, to construct a national
accountancy arena that distinguished unequivocally between practising ('public') and non-
practising accountants and to establish the former as the elite occupational grouping. The
reasons for the failure of the first two charter attempts and the success of the third (1922–28) are
discussed in detail in the cited sources (Poullaos 1994: Chap 9 provides an overview).

Of interest here is the complex interplay of Australian and British state agencies and professional bodies involved in a decidedly cross-border, state–profession formation process. To
achieve success, those seeking a royal charter were required by the Colonial Office (and later
the Dominions Office (DO)) to attain the support of each of five state governments as well as
the federal government. The state governments pressured accountants to settle their differences.
Victoria (while W. A. Watt was premier or treasurer) would not, nor support a charter attempt

as it effectively represented CO interference in Australian affairs. The successful charter attempt only took place after Watt departed from Victorian politics. The Australian promoters also had had to negotiate conditions with both the ICAEW and the SIAA, managing the status rivalry between them in the process. In the third attempt, with all other conditions being satisfied, the promoters were fortunate that an Anglophile Prime Minister (S. M. Bruce) was in London for the 1926 Imperial Conference. In the heat of the moment Bruce ignored a long-standing 'neutrality' position and sent a telegram of support. No wonder it took decades to get 'British CA' from outside Britain and no wonder few others have tried to get it, let alone succeeded!

Parker's (1987) survey of the ethical pronouncements of Australian accountancy bodies from their formation to the time of writing suggests that they are more concerned with protecting the profession than protecting society. Advertising restrictions are a case in point. But how did they protect the profession given that, first, advertising by competitors not subject to such restrictions seems to have been instrumental in the professional bodies' relaxing bans on advertising from the 1970s on; and second, that Australian accountants had faced such competition from day one? Relevant factors can be identified. Professionalisation was a collective strategy. Banning advertising reduced competition within the group and promoted group cohesion. Also, if other professions that accountants wanted to emulate did not advertise, then organised accountants ran the risk of falling outside the professional club. Being seen to prohibit advertising was an advertisement of professional aspiration, if not status. It seems that in the late nineteenth and early twentieth centuries organised elite accountants could not afford to advertise but by the late twentieth century they could not afford not to advertise. What happened in between to turn things around? The Canadian ethics papers and Preston *et al.* (1995) contain some clues and professional archives may provide insights into the internal battles. On the whole, our knowledge of Australian accountancy projects from 1930 to the current period of dominance of the market over the social has more holes in it than their Canadian and especially British counterparts.[7]

South Africa and the Imperial accountancy arena

Around 1900, the ICAEW suddenly realised that the Canadians had been organising 'CA' bodies and started a long campaign, through the Colonial Office, to stop them. Negotiations were in train with promoters of an Australian royal charter application. In South Africa, the SIAA, more successful there than in Australia, was heavily involved in setting up a society in the Transvaal (in 1904) under an ordinance which gave the Transvaal Society of Accountants (TSA) considerable authority over the organisation of public accountants. Resident CAs were accommodated, on the whole, but there was a lot of politicking involved in coming to an understanding about British CAs who spent only part of their time in the Transvaal. Also controversial was their tendency to practise under the names of London accountants not actually resident in the Transvaal. The TSA could not persuade local politicians to stamp the practice out. Not only 'CA' but also '*individual accountants' names* had become symbolic capital by the early years of the twentieth century' (Chua and Poullaos 2002: 426). News about the Transvaal Ordinance spread throughout the British Empire as fast as steamship and telegraph would allow. By 1907, the ICAEW was improvising responses to registration attempts in Natal, the Cape Colony (in South Africa), New Zealand, New South Wales (in Australia) and various provinces in Canada. It appointed solicitors to represent it in all those places plus India, Ceylon and Hong Kong and came under pressure from the Canadians and Australians to deal in reciprocity.

The state–profession dynamics alluded to here are far more extensive than any discussed so far. Each locale had some serious bargaining power and there was no central authority to adjudicate claims authoritatively. A web of negotiations, spun around the relays of empire, had been set up and it was not likely to end soon. It could be called an imperial accountancy arena. The professional projects alluded to above were (and are) ongoing and extended beyond the imperial stage. Further analysis may provide insights into the accountancy politics of modern-day globalisation (see Arnold 2005).

Parker (2005) has mapped the spread of 'CA' and 'CPA' through the British Empire/Commonwealth from 1853 to 2003 by seeking patterns in the names given to accounting associations. While there is a limit to how much of a professionalisation dynamic can be read from the choice of a name, a range of future research sites has been identified. Briston and Kedslie (1997) have sketched the rise of the British-based Chartered Association of Certified Accountants (ACCA) as an examining body throughout the British Empire/Commonwealth and beyond to places where professional projects barely existed, local training did not suit the requirements of global capital, or the locals preferred an 'international' credential to a local one. Further historical analysis of how the ACCA has found a way to profitably create accountants at a distance by producing them where they live is to be welcomed.

The United States of America

The major elements of accountancy professionalisation projects in the USA to 1940 have been identified in the research literature, albeit in less detail than for Britain. Between 1874 and 1889, 13 societies were formed 'with identities related to accounting activities' (Previts and Merino 1998: 136). The Institute of Accountants and Book-keepers of New York (hereafter 'NYIA', formed 1882) offered an examination-based accountancy credential to both public and salaried accountants more than a decade before any state-recognised credential had been established (ibid.: 135–7). For present purposes, the NYIA is of interest as the vehicle through which American accountants, such as Charles Waldo Haskins and Charles E. Sprague, expressed views at odds with those emanating from the American Association of Public Accountants (AAPA – formed in 1886, incorporated in 1887), a body influenced by resident British CAs.

The most sustained analysis of the American accountancy community to 1940 is by Miranti (1990; see also Miranti 1986, 1988). The remarks below will be based on his work and restricted to the period from 1800–1906, the aim being to *illustrate* differences between American accountancy projects and those discussed previously. An obvious preliminary point is that by 1880 the USA had long since asserted its independence from Britain. Although America was a destination for both British capital and accountants (Lee, 1997, 2001, 2002a, 2002b, 2004), there was much less leverage to be had over American affairs from Britain *via* diplomatic channels than was the case in the 'self-governing' Canada and Australia.

The AAPA was formed ostensibly as a national body for public accountants. It had the potential to be part of a network of practitioners capable of serving clients with interests across the nation – a role for formal organisation not previously highlighted. The AAPA also appealed to American accountants whose clients 'had developed strong connections with British business interests' (Miranti 1990: 34) and to those in accountancy and business circles concerned about the wave of non-British immigrants to the USA. This point was not highlighted elsewhere as a reason for preferring one professionalisation model over another. But there was little in the way of national accountancy regulation and most accountants lacked clients with national reach. Consequently, instead of attracting recruits from across the country, the AAPA found itself struggling with the NYIA.

One issue dividing the AAPA and the NYIA was quasi-epistemological. Was accounting an art or a science? American–born accountants felt that accountancy should be developed along 'scientific' lines in contrast to their British counterparts who stressed the necessity of 'the virtue, experience, and steady judgment of the seasoned accountant' (ibid.: 39; McMillan 1999; Kimball 1992). These would be learnt in a long apprenticeship, taking us to the second area of difference: vocational preparation. In spite of the scepticism of some British CAs, the institutionalisation of college/university instruction as an essential part of professional training came about much earlier in the USA than in Britain or Australia. One implication was that the NYIA and AAPA fought for recognition from the bodies regulating the granting of degrees.

The third area of conflict revolved around the challenges to American identity created by mass immigration. Charles Waldo Haskins responded with a strident form of anti-British patriotism while Charles E. Sprague and others allegedly harboured lingering resentment of British support for the Confederates in the Civil War. Sprague and Hopkins had served in the Union army. Haskins, furthermore, had married into the Havermeyer family which was probably well aware of English/German imperial rivalry and was anti-imperialist in any case. It did not help that American and British imperial rivalries were manifesting in Latin America and the Pacific during the 1890s. Further, leading figures in the NYIA were of Irish descent. For them, 'the great famine of 1842 and the suppression of the revolutionary Fenian Brotherhood' (ibid.: 45) were within living memory.

The mood of such people was not helped by the market success of chartered accountants. 'CA' was recognised as a significant contributing factor taking us to the fourth point: competition over designations. The NYIA stiffened its examinations, developed its own designation and tried (unsuccessfully) to claim for itself 'CA' – 'certified accountant'. A subsequent bitter public controversy made division within the occupation highly visible, damaging the prospects of profession-led accountancy regulation. One result was that the New York licensing law of 1896 – the outcome of a process where the NYIA and AAPA put up competing bills – 'merely provided legal protection to a special title of professional competency' (ibid.: 47) rather than legal exclusion of competitors. The title was 'CPA' – 'certified *public* accountant'.

As the New York law became the model for other states, tensions between British and American accountants spilled over state borders (ibid.: 48–60). State CPA associations were formed to organise those who had passed state CPA examinations. One of these, the New York State Society of CPAs (NYSSCPA) became a new vehicle for the opposition of Haskins, Sprague and others to the AAPA.

In the late 1890s, the merger boom created a new crop of national business entities, creating potential for the parallel formation of national accountancy practices and state accounting associations seeking local licensing legislation. The national accountancy firms were, however, vulnerable to the efforts of local accountants to keep them out by tapping into intense local preferences for local autonomy. In this context, competition between the AAPA, the NYSSCPA (and CPAs in other states) made the process of forming national practice and regulatory networks a tortuous one (ibid.: 59–68). Events external to the profession resulted in a compromise whereby the AAPA became, for the time being, the national body to which the state CPA societies became affiliated, with the NYSSCPA claiming New York as its preserve.

Preston *et al.*'s (1995) study of the American profession's ethical codes of 1917 and 1988 illustrates how historical analysis can illuminate the present by contrasting it to the past. Informing the 1917 code was a not entirely coherent blend of ideologies resulting in an individualistic orientation tempered by belief in the value of cooperation and common purpose. CPAs were ideally men of character and integrity joining together to serve the public interest. The CPA, although responsible for his own conduct, would be guided by divine law, subject himself to ongoing scrutiny by his brethren to whom he owed duties of 'loyalty, devotion and above all, preserving the good name of the profession' (ibid.: 522). He did not need detailed rules.

This had turned around by 1988, with the profession facing severe threats to its autonomy in the face of perceived breakdowns of practitioner independence, adequacy of accounting standards and the quality of audit in the 1970s and 1980s. What counted now were the individual's utility-maximising choices, rights, self-chosen morality and personality. Paradoxically, legally defensible competence in following rules replaced character; regulation replaced inspirational guidance. Expertise in following ethical rules was subsumed within a process of quality review by peers which, in turn, was part of a strategy of creating 'a *demonstrable* quality of service' (ibid.: 533, original emphasis, but see Fogarty 1996; Fogarty *et al.* 1997). In short, the 1988 ethical code became part of the public relations package intended to change external perceptions of quality without necessarily stiffening disciplinary processes. The visibility of detailed rules, however, highlighted the profession's restrictions on members' actions in the market-place. Their subsequent watering down has allowed the profession to intensify its contribution to neo-liberalism.

Growing resistance to professional 'monopoly' also found expression in American courts (Mills and Young 1999). From the 1920s to the 1990s a series of cases have held that state CPA laws could not be used to exclude non-CPAs from public accountancy, that CPAs did not have the exclusive right to the use of the label 'accountant' and (in 1994) that it was not unlawful for a CPA to use that designation when employed outside public practice. The returns on accountants' symbolic capital can now, apparently, be appropriated by non-accountants competing with CPA firms! Mills and Young's analysis joins those of Preston *et al.* (1995), Zeff (2003a, 2003b) and others in providing insights into how the stolid professionalism of the early twentieth century has since eroded.

Further investigation of the American experience is also relevant in light of the global importance of American capital since 1945 and its role as the hegemonic power in the rampant neo-liberalism of the past several decades. We know much less about American overseas influence than we do about the British. Dyball *et al.*'s (2007) analysis of the sudden passing in 1923 of American-style CPA public accountancy legislation in the American-ruled Philippines illustrates the potential of this suggestion. The legislation is seen as an attempt by the Filipino elite, faced with a difficult American governor-general, to capture the CPA role for its own familial networks. In arriving at this suggestion Dyball *et al.* note that the disparate interactions analysed in previous research have involved some combination of a proactive accountancy community, a (more or less) competitive market for public accountancy services and a self-directed, modernist state. The authors cannot find evidence or rationale for the existence of these factors in the Philippines prior to 1923. The problematic grafting of American accountancy institutions overseas is also noted in Sakagami *et al.*'s (1999) analysis of Japanese accountancy subsequent to the creation of Japanese CPAs during the American-led occupation after the Second World War. While the Japanese Institute of CPAs was able to establish its members' social status through difficult examinations and legal monopoly over external audit, their functional contribution has been challenged in the wake of corporate scandals. CPAs have not been able to sufficiently extricate themselves from the domination of the Ministry of Finance with strong links to the *Zaibatsu*. 'It is certain that individual auditors must change their consciousness about independence. But it might also be true that we really need the reform of social relationships based on interdependence' (ibid.: 353).

Post-colonial professionalisation

This section discusses briefly the contrasting, rather different professional projects that have emerged in some 'former' British colonies hard upon the heels of formal decolonisation.

Trinidad and Tobago (T&T) – formal independence 1962

Neither practitioners nor state agencies had much use for a professionalisation project prior to 1962 (Annisette 1999). After independence the nationalist government led by Dr Eric Williams actively sought to replace expatriates with Trinidadians and stressed financial propriety as part of a programme of 'public sector reform and wider public accountability' (ibid.: 114). The government played a major role in developing the economy, becoming a major employer of accountants in the process. Accountancy rapidly emerging as a high-status occupation. In 1964, a CA social club formed prior to 1962 merged with the local branch of the ACCA (dominated by Trinidadians working in the public sector) to form the T&T Association of Chartered Accountants and Certified Accountants (TTACACA). The former were seeking protection from an aggressive government while the latter were seeking 'support for a state-endorsed plan to develop an indigenous system of professional accountancy training' (Annisette 2000: 643). Again, inclusion rather than exclusion was the order of the day, and the distinction between public and salaried accountants was a non-issue. By 1965, arrangements had been made for the University of the West Indies (UWI) to feed accounting graduates into the final examination of the ACCA and then into articles with public accountants. The non-activity of the ICAEW outside Britain had left the examining field in T&T to the ACCA. University-trained Trinidadians could, theoretically, receive an ACCA qualification and be trained by a British-trained chartered accountant – a most unlikely outcome in Britain. Furthermore, a plan to integrate the profession in Britain was afoot under which the ACCA would cease to offer examinations in T&T. It was in this context that the Institute of Chartered Accountants of T&T (ICATT) was incorporated by legislation.

But things did not go according to plan. The Williams Government remained dependent on British and then American capital as T&T became increasingly integrated into an American-dominated world economy. Informal domination replaced formal empire, local accounting firms became integrated into international accountancy networks and the internationalisation of accounting standards was brewing. The British accountancy integration plan did not proceed and the ACCA examinations remained in place to emerge. The University's accountancy programme was marginalised by the local accountancy elite with its eye on international developments and metropolitan recognition. The ICATT effectively became the ACCA's 'local agents' (Annisette 2000: 647).

Jamaica – formal independence 1962

The formation of the Institute of Chartered Accountants of Jamaica (ICAJ) in 1965 represented a similar drive by a new government and a section of the local accountancy community to open accountancy to Jamaicans. The ICAJ would 'replace all forms of colonial bodies operating on the island' (Bakre 2005: 996). These objectives were to be enacted by a national accountancy law 'which would guarantee the conduct of local examinations and also protect the interest of the Jamaican accountants against any external encroachments' (ibid.). The ICAJ, however, contained an influential ACCA-trained grouping with internationalist leanings which leveraged the local power of global capital to defeat these objectives and managed to procure a clause allowing the ICAJ to seek external examination and credentials, notwithstanding the support among some local capitalists for Jamaican accountancy independence. Thus, the ACCA moved from being the 'caretaker' of the profession prior to independence to being the 'landlord' afterwards (ibid.). Variations in this dynamic continued into the 1980s with similar results (Bakre 2006). The ACCA's London headquarters ended up adjudicating on the quality of the accounting courses of its competitor, the UWI, in conveniently negative terms. Bakre's analyses, along with those of Annisette (2000) and Briston and Kedslie (1997), provide strong motivation for close examination of the ACCA's offshore activities.

Kenya – formal independence 1963

As analysed by Sian (2006), the new Kenyatta Government sought to transfer control of high-level accountancy work from expatriates to Kenyans as part of its Africanisation policy. Although a form of 'revolutionary usurpation' on the part of African Kenyans was involved, implementation was characterised by extensive openness. Not only were British CAs included on the register of company auditors, but also British cost and municipal accountants, Indian and Canadian CAs, American CPAs and successful candidates in examinations run by the local examination board. Furthermore, when pressures arose from 'unqualified' accountants and bookkeepers to protect their interests, they were generously accommodated as well. So aware were the project's leaders of occupational segmentation in Britain, that 'CPA' was preferred to 'CA'. This is Britain as anti-model.

Nigeria – formal independence 1960

In Nigeria it seemed that pre-independence UK-style status differentials within the account-ancy community would bequeath an already divided occupation to the newly independent nation (Wallace 1992). However, the nationalist objective of setting up a local infrastructure for the production of an indigenous accountancy workforce and breaking down the dominance of expatriates came to the fore immediately after independence (ibid.: 37–40), continuing the pattern noted in T&T, Jamaica and Kenya. The newly formed (in 1965) Institute of Chartered Accountants of Nigeria (ICAN) was handed 'the monopoly of regulating the accounting profession' (Uche 2002: 480).

Uche tracks the challenges to ICAN's subsequent domination. Nigeria is unusual in having experienced since 1965 a succession of military governments interspersed with the occasional civilian government, making 'the State unstable and less accountable' (ibid.: 477). Uche also analyses attempts from the 1970s to the 1990s by promoters of other bodies, the Association of National Accountants of Nigeria (ANAN) particularly, to break ICAN's monopoly. ANAN hammered away using its best argument (ICAN wasn't producing enough qualified account-ants) while ICAN continually stressed the need to maintain quality. ANAN was eventually formally recognised by decree of General Babangida in 1993 the day before he stepped down as President. The possibility of corruption is implied (ibid.: 489). Nevertheless, the outcomes of the attacks on ICAN's hegemony, namely, recognition of a second accountancy body, the creation of a class of registered accountants to do basic work for small businesses and traders, the eventual inclusion of ICWA and IMTA members on the register of auditors, and the establishment by ICAN of an accelerated training scheme, may be said to constitute a Nigerian version of the movement against 'monopoly'. The further issue of how Nigerian accountants have coped with business practices affected by respect for elders, loyalty to family and tribe has troubled Wallace (1992) and Okike (2004) and merits further investigation by accounting historians.[8]

Continental Europe and beyond

Greece

The purposeful organisation of Greek auditors began as a post-war project by the state. In 1955, the Greek Parliament founded a body of auditors (its Greek name yields the initials SOL) to help collect tax revenues from privately owned companies. SOL was both 'a professional association [and] a practicing firm of auditors' (Ballas 1998: 716). Caramanis (1999, 2002, 2005) and Ballas (1998, 1999) have analysed in detail the long struggle during the 1990s to break down SOL's monopoly over statutory audit, establish a form of audit familiar to global capital and create space for international audit firms in an era of aggressive neo-liberalism in Greek political economy and culture. The application of political and economic pressure by the USA and the European Union was a major factor in SOL's eventual defeat as at 2001. Caramanis (2002: 401) pessimistically concludes, that for minor nations at least, 'inward-looking ideologies and discourses rooted in national distinctiveness and cultural uniqueness . . . are increasingly the politics of losers'.

France

Ramirez' (2001) analysis of the accountancy profession in France from 1880 to 1939 reveals significant difference from the Anglo-Saxon experience. The more established professions such as engineering and law were firmly entrenched in relation to both the state and the elite academic institutions. Accounting (as discipline) and accountancy (as occupational grouping) were not. The design of cost accounting systems was dominated by engineers and financial accounting codes were designed by civil servants and economists. Accountants were generally lacking in social, cultural and economic capital compared to elite state and business actors. The latter, furthermore, were not reliant upon audited financial statements to attract funds from capital markets. The position and status of the 'accounting' field had not yet been established. It took the support of the Vichy Government during the German occupation to bring some meaningful *ordre* to French accountancy.

Belgium, Spain, Portugal

De Beelde's (2002) analysis of the Belgian audit profession in the 1940s and 1950s also highlights variation from the Anglophone model of professionalism. Belgium follows a continental tradition where the state initiates the organisation of civil servants in public administration – an approach potentially applicable to professional organisation. Also striking is the debate in Belgium about the role of audit. Was it to verify financial data for works councils or to verify annual financial statements for shareholders? Parliament eventually agreed to a combination of roles. Belgian politicians also drew a clear line between *experts-comptables* (offering unregulated accounting and advisory services) and *revisers* (auditors). They also protected the preferential path into the profession for university graduates, reflecting the ongoing influence of the civil service model, in sharp contrast to T&T and Jamaica.

Bougen's (1997) analysis of the Spanish Audit Law, 1988 introduced by a post-Franco socialist government entering the European Community, sees it as a way of realigning professional expertise to a state in transition. At the time of writing, the Spanish auditor was 'becoming' professional. Rodrigues *et al.* (2003) have laid the groundwork for future detailed studies of accountancy professional projects in Portugal by mapping shifts in state ideology and accountancy regulation from 1755 to 2003. Clearly there are other parts of continental Europe for historians of accountancy professionalisation to examine. Such endeavours would be timely in light of the European integration project presently in train.

Former planned economies

Seal *et al.* (1996) analysed the early years of radical transformation of Czech political economy since the Velvet Revolution of 1989. Czech accountants had, seemingly, a golden opportunity to advance their collective mobility project given the rising pay and status of accountants and 'the renewed emphasis on monetary calculation' (ibid.: 486). At the time of writing, however, the organisational vehicles for advancing such a project were still in an experimental phase in light of the wariness of regulation among local state actors. Czech accountants also face major challenges to revise their knowledge base, establish new functional categories and sort out relations between local associations. Such a situation is tailor-made for the Big Six (as they were then) as 'multinational firms with reputations built up over decades in mature capitalist societies to invade the potential domain of Czech auditing and accounting professionals' (ibid.: 485).

A contrast is provided by the Chinese government's more gradual move, since 1978, from a planned to a 'socialist market economy' (Hao 1999: 291) absorbing substantial amounts of foreign capital. This has led to the *re-emergence* of a practitioner community (Xu and Xu, 2003), albeit one still constrained at the time of writing by government scrutiny and direction. As Hao (1999: 301) observes, time will tell whether the gradualist path to an autonomous profession is preferable to the sudden-shock alternative – yet another issue for historians to examine.

It seems that state–profession relations have been of even greater import outside the Anglo-American world than within it. Studies capture historically constituted institutional and cultural differences that resist generalisation about the purpose, nature and outcomes of professionalisation projects.

Conclusion

The accountancy professionalisation literature – a form of socio-historical accounting research – now includes a substantial number of historical, context-sensitive case studies of professional projects in train across the world at various times. Examination of how the professional associations have negotiated the conditions under which their members perform their socially and economically significant work has starkly highlighted the 'political' roots of professional 'neutrality' and the sustained efforts they have made to achieve 'higher remuneration and prestige for their labour' (Willmott 1986: 559).

The literature reveals patterns but they only go so far. Within the Anglo-American world Larson's notions of market-dominance and collective social mobility have aided understanding of efforts made to achieve more concrete goals. However, they need to be tempered against the extensive resistance to 'monopoly' by the state, market and communal actors observed across the full spectrum of cases. Indeed, openness features in the early days of a number of professional projects. The rise of the market over the past few decades has further highlighted the difficulties of positing closure or market dominance as the major problematic in professionalisation research. Even within the Anglo-American world, variations in tactics, allies, opponents and institutions faced by leaders of professional projects have been noted, although the state–profession dynamic has been a persistent theme.

The role of the state in initiating or directing professional projects is now widely remarked upon and the engagement of numerous parts of the accountancy world with each other under 'globalisation' has put a premium on understanding historically constructed and distinctive state–profession dynamics. Researchers have certainly noted this point just as they are beginning to grapple with the recent global dominance of market capitalism, and financial capitalism in particular. It is an argument for both looking more closely at non-Anglophone experiences and for addressing the large gaps in the temporal mid-range between the historical emergence and the present state of accountancy projects.

A corollary of the last point is that we know relatively little about the different stages of professional projects. There is, for example, a huge literature on standard-setting but there has been little in-depth examination of how the emergence of regulatory space has changed the course of professional projects and vice versa. We also know little about the impact of other areas of occupational interest (such as taxation) outside of the trilogy of external reporting, management accounting and audit/assurance. We also know surprisingly little about how professional projects have been driven (or not) by accounting firms, the 'Big N' in particular. This is a major issue now if 'the brand names of these firms have become better known than [those of the] accountancy bodies' (Parker 2005: 39). Particularly so as national accountancy associations face big problems operating across borders. They stand in each other's way. Nor do they have a cross-border sovereign to settle disputes.

Geopolitics is a substantively different dynamic from national regulation. A state–market–community–geopolitics model might be a useful way of thinking about shifts in the increasingly tenuous nature of professional dominance. In the meantime, the Big N appear to extend their influence much more easily (Arnold 2005; Cooper and Robson 2006). Analysis of changes in relations between associations and firms would be particularly helpful here. It might aid contemporary analysis of questions like: do the firms need the associations any longer? Do they even need professional status or collective action any longer? Who better to address post-professionalism, if we are there or nearing there, than students of professionalisation?

Key works

The main text identifies major papers on specific episodes of professionalisation. The following are important reviews and general works.

Cooper and Robson (2006) provides a useful review linking professionalisation with regulation and also suggests new research foci (see also Chapter 12 of this volume).

Habgood (1994) is an important resource for students intending to research professionalisation in England and Wales.

Richardson (1993) contains a chronology of selected events 'from the history of [Canadian] accounting associations' from 1879 to 1979 and also identifies secondary sources on the history of the Canadian profession.

West (1996) provides an alternative review of the professionalisation literature to that provided in this chapter.

Zeff (1988) provides a helpful collection of essays on a formative period in the history of the profession in the USA.

Notes

1   A term emphasising 'the coherence and consistency' of a particular course of action, even though 'the goals and strategies pursued by a given group are not entirely clear or deliberate for all members' (Larson 1977: 6 cited in Macdonald 1995: 10).
2   The discussion below is based on Macdonald (1984, 1985, 1987), Briston and Kedslie (1986), Kedslie (1990a, 1990b), Walker (1988, 1991, 1995, 1996), Shackleton (1995) and Lee (1996a, 1996b, 2000, 2006).
3   On the period prior to the formation of these bodies, see Edwards *et al.* (2007). On their unification *via* the formation of the ICAEW, see Walker (2004b).
4   The numbers entering under the 1893 examination route declined quickly from 1900. By 1886, chartered accountants were dominating the audit market (Anderson *et al.* 1996).
5   Creighton (1984), Richardson (1987) and Chua and Poullaos (2002) touch lightly on these various points. Richardson (1989a) and MacDonald and Richardson (2004) show that federation is still a factor in Canadian professional projects. American influence is noted in Neu and Saleem (1996) and Everett *et al.* (2005). Richardson (1997) provides an update to Macdonald (1985) applied to Canadian data.
6   The SIAA added 'Incorporated' to its name in 1908. I have used the abbreviation 'SIAA' throughout.
7   In a pioneering effort, Allen (1991) sought to assess the extent of the Australian professional dominance in the 1953–85 period. In my view, her evidential base is too limited to support her conclusions. Velayutham and Rahman (2000) take seriously Greenwood's problematic (1957) view of the stages of professionalisation. Nevertheless, both papers identify events and factors that historians might examine more closely in the future.
8   These cultural patterns resonate with the loyalty to 'family' noted in analyses of the Philippines (Dyball and Valcarcel 1999; Dyball *et al.* 2006, 2007).

References

Abbott, A. (1988) *The System of Professions: An Essay on the Expert Division of Labor* (Chicago: The University of Chicago Press).

Allen, K. (1991) In pursuit of professional dominance: Australian accounting 1953–1985, *Accounting, Auditing & Accountability Journal*, 4 (1): 51–67.

Anderson, M., Edwards, J. R. and Chandler, R. A. (2005) Constructing the 'well qualified' chartered accountant in England and Wales, *Accounting Historians Journal*, 32 (2): 5–54.

Anderson, M., Edwards, J. R. and Matthews, D. (1996) A study of the quoted company audit market in 1886, *Accounting, Business & Financial History*, 6 (3): 363–87.

Annisette, M. (1999) Importing accounting: the case of Trinidad and Tobago, *Accounting, Business & Financial History*, 9 (1): 103–33.

Annisette, M. (2000) Imperialism and the professions: the education and certification of accountants in Trinidad and Tobago, *Accounting, Organizations and Society*, 25 (7): 631–59.

Arnold, P. J. (2005) Disciplining domestic regulation: the World Trade Organization and the market for professional services, *Accounting, Organizations and Society*, 30 (4): 299–330.

Bailey, D. (1992) The attempt to establish the Russian accounting profession 1875–1931, *Accounting, Business & Financial History*, 2 (1): 1–23.

Bakre, O. M. (2005) First attempt at localising imperial accountancy: the case of the Institute of Chartered Accountants of Jamaica (ICAJ) (1950s–1970s), *Critical Perspectives on Accounting*, 16 (8): 995–1018.

Bakre, O. M. (2006) Second attempt at localising imperial accountancy: the case of the Institute of Chartered Accountants of Jamaica (ICAJ) (1970s–1980s), *Critical Perspectives on Accounting*, 17 (1): 1–28.

Ballas, A. A. (1998) The creation of the auditing profession in Greece, *Accounting, Organizations and Society*, 23 (8): 715–36.

Ballas, A. A. (1999) Privatising the statutory auditing services in Greece, *Accounting, Business & Financial History*, 9 (3): 349–73.

Baskerville, R. F. (2006) Professional closure by proxy: the impact of changing educational requirements on class mobility for a cohort of Big 8 partners, *Accounting History*, 11 (3): 289–317.

Bocqueraz, C. (2001) The development of professional associations: the experience of French accountants from the 1880s to the 1940s, *Accounting, Business & Financial History*, 11 (1): 7–27.

Bougen, P. D. (1997) Spain, July, 1988: some observations on becoming professional, *Accounting, Organizations and Society*, 22 (8): 757–77.

Briston, R. J. and Kedslie, M. J. M. (1986) Professional formation: the case of Scottish accountants-some corrections and further thoughts, *British Journal of Sociology*, 37 (1): 122–30.

Briston, R. J. and Kedslie, M. J. M. (1997) The internationalization of British professional accounting: the role of the examination exporting bodies, *Accounting, Business & Financial History*, 7 (2): 175–94.

Brown, R. (ed.) (1905) *A History of Accounting and Accountants* (Edinburgh: T. C. and E. C. Jack).

Burchell, S., Clubb, C., Hopwood, A, Hughes, J. and Nahapiet, J. (1980) The role of accounting in organizations and society, *Accounting, Organizations and Society*, 5 (1): 5–27.

Caramanis, C. V. (1999) International accounting firms versus indigenous auditors: intra-professional competition in the Greek auditing profession, 1990–1993, *Critical Perspectives on Accounting*, 10 (2): 153–96.

Caramanis, C. V. (2002) The interplay between professional groups, the state and supranational agents: Pax Americana in the age of 'globalisation', *Accounting, Organizations and Society*, 27 (4): 379–409.

Caramanis, C. V. (2005) Rationalism, charisma and accounting professionalism, *Accounting, Organizations and Society*, 30 (2): 195–222.

Carnegie, G. D. (1993) The Australian Institute of Incorporate Accountants (1892–1938), *Accounting, Business & Financial History*, 3 (1): 61–80.

Carnegie, G. D. and Edwards, J. R. (2001) The construction of the professional accountant: the case of the Incorporated Institute of Accountants, Victoria (1886), *Accounting, Organizations and Society*, 26 (4/5): 301–25.

Carnegie, G. D. and Parker, R. H. (1999) Accountants and empire: the case of co-membership of Australian and UK accountancy bodies, 1885 to 1914, *Accounting, Business & Financial History*, 9 (1): 77–102.

Carnegie, G. D., Edwards, J. R. and West, B. P. (2003) Understanding the dynamics of the Australian accounting profession: a prosopographical study of the founding members of the Incorporated Institute of Accountants, Victoria, 1886 to 1908, *Accounting, Auditing & Accountability Journal*, 16 (5): 790–820.

Chua, W-F. and Poullaos, C. (1993) Rethinking the profession-state dynamic: the case of the Victorian charter attempt, 1885–1906, *Accounting, Organizations and Society*, 18 (7/8): 691–728.

Chua, W-F. and Poullaos, C. (1998) The dynamics of closure amidst the construction of market, profession, empire and nationhood: an historical analysis of an Australian accounting association, 1886–1903, *Accounting, Organizations and Society*, 23 (2): 155–88.

Chua, W-F. and Poullaos, C. (2002) The Empire strikes back? An exploration of centre-periphery interaction between the ICAEW and accounting associations in the self-governing colonies of Australia, Canada and South Africa, 1880–1907, *Accounting, Organizations and Society*, 27 (4/5): 409–45.

Collard, E. A. (1980) *First in North America* (Montréal: Ordre des Comptables Agreés du Québec).

Collins, R. (1990) Changing conceptions in the sociology of the professions, in R. Torstendahl and M. Burrage (eds.) *The Formation of Professions: Knowledge, State and Strategy*, pp. 11–23 (London: Sage).

Cooper, D., Puxty, T., Robson, K. and Willmott, H. (1996) Changes in the international regulation of auditors: (In)stalling the eighth directive in the UK, *Critical Perspectives on Accounting*, 7 (6): 589–613.

Cooper, D. J. and Robson, K. (2006) Accounting, professions and regulation: locating the sites of professionalisation, *Accounting, Organizations and Society*, 31 (4/5): 415–44.

Creighton, P. (1984) *A Sum of Yesterdays* (Toronto: ICAO).

Cross, J. N. (1998) The first Wisconsin accountancy bill: an historical perspective, *Accounting Historians Journal*, 25 (2): 113–28.

De Beelde, I. (2002) Creating a profession 'out of nothing'? The case of the Belgian auditing profession, *Accounting, Organizations and Society*, 27 (4/5): 447–70.

Dedoulis, E. and Caramanis, C. (2007) Imperialism of influence and the state-profession relationship: the formation of the Greek auditing profession in the post-WWII era, *Critical Perspectives on Accounting*, 18 (4): 393–412.

Dyball, M. C. and Valcarcel, L. J. (1999) The 'rational' and 'traditional': the regulation of accounting in the Philippines, *Accounting, Auditing & Accountability Journal*, 12 (3): 303–27.

Dyball, M., Chua, W-F. and Poullaos, C. (2006) Mediating between colonizer and colonized in the American empire: accounting for government monies in the Philippines, *Accounting, Auditing & Accountability Journal*, 19 (1): 47–81.

Dyball, M., Poullaos, C. and Chua, W- F. (2007) Accounting and empire: professionalization as resistance – the case of the Philippines, *Critical Perspectives on Accounting*, 18 (4): 415–49.

Edwards, J. R., Anderson, M. and Chandler, R. A. (2007) Claiming a jurisdiction for the 'Public Accountant' in England prior to organisational fusion, *Accounting, Organizations and Society*, 32 (1/2): 61–100.

Everett, J., Green, D. and Neu, D. (2005) Independence, objectivity and the Canadian CA profession, *Critical Perspectives on Accounting*, 16 (4): 415–40.

Fogarty, T. J. (1996) The imagery and reality of peer review in the U.S.: insights from institutional theory, *Accounting, Organizations and Society*, 21 (2/3): 243–67.

Fogarty, T. J., Zucca, L. J., Meonske, N. and Kirch, D. P. (1997) Proactive practice review: a critical case study of accounting regulation that never was, *Critical Perspectives on Accounting*, 8 (3): 167–87.

Freidson, E. (1983) The theory of the professions: the state of the art, in R. Dingwall and P. Lewis (eds) *The Sociology of the Professions: Lawyers Doctors and Others*, pp. 19–37 (London: Macmillan).

Freidson, E. (1994) *Professionalism Reborn: Theory, Prophecy, and Policy* (Cambridge: Polity Press).

Garrett, A. A. (1961) *History of the Society of Incorporated Accountants 1885–1957* (Oxford: Oxford University Press).

Gavens, J. J. and Gibson, R. W. (1992) An Australian attempt to internationalize accounting professional organizations, *Accounting Historians Journal*, 19 (2): 79–102.

Greenwood, E. (1957) Attributes of a profession, *Social Work*, 2 (1): 45–55.

Habenstein, R. (1963) Critique of 'profession' as a sociological category, *Sociological Quarterly*, 4 (4): 291–300.

Habgood, W. (ed.) (1994) *Chartered Accountants in England and Wales: a Guide to Historical Records* (Manchester: Manchester University Press).

Halliday, T. C. and Carruthers, B. G. (1996) The moral regulation of markets: professions, privatization and the English Insolvency Act 1986, *Accounting, Organizations and Society*, 21 (4): 371–413.

Hanlon, G. (1994) *The Commercialisation of Accountancy* (London: Macmillan).

Hanlon, G. (1996) 'Casino capitalism' and the rise of the commercialized service class – an examination of the accountant, *Critical Perspectives on Accounting*, 7 (3): 339–63.

Hanlon, G. (1997) Commercialising the service class and economic restructuring – a response to my critics, *Accounting, Organizations and Society*, 22 (8): 843–55.

Hao, Z. P. (1999) Regulation and organization of accountants in China, *Accounting, Auditing & Accountability Journal*, 12 (3): 286–302.

Harston, M. E. and Welch, S. T. (1997) Evolution of professional enforcement in Texas: an examination of violations and sanctions, *Accounting Historians Journal*, 24 (1): 25–73.

Johnson, T. J. (1972) *Professions and Power* (London: Macmillan).

Kedslie, M. J. (1990a) Mutual self-interest – a unifying force: the dominance of societal closure over social background in the early professional accounting bodies, *Accounting Historians Journal*, 17 (2): 1–9.

Kedslie, M. J. (1990b) *Firm Foundations: The Development of Professional Accounting in Scotland* (Hull: Hull University Press).

Keenan, M. G. (2000) Between anarchy and authority: The New Zealand Society of Accountants' management of crisis, 1989–1993, *Accounting History* 5 (2): 95–118.

Kimball, B. A. (1992) *The True Professional Ideal in America: A History* (Cambridge MA: Blackwell).

Klegon, D. (1978) The sociology of the professions: an emerging perspective, *Sociology of Work and Occupations*, 5 (3): 259–83.

Larson, M. S. (1977) *The Rise of Professionalism: A Sociological Analysis* (Berkeley, CA: University of California).

Larsson, B. (2005) Auditor regulation and economic crime policy in Sweden, 1965–2000, *Accounting, Organizations and Society*, 30 (2): 127–44.

269

Lee, T. (1996a) Identifying the founding fathers of public accountancy: the formation of the Society of Accountants in Edinburgh, *Accounting, Business & Financial History*, 6 (3): 315–35.

Lee, T. (1996b) *Shaping the Accountancy Profession: The Story of Three Scottish Pioneers* (New York: Garland).

Lee, T. A. (1997) The influence of Scottish accountants in the United States: the early case of the Society of Accountants in Edinburgh, *Accounting Historians Journal*, 24 (1): 117–41.

Lee, T. A. (2000) A social network analysis of the founders of institutionalized public accountancy, *Accounting Historians Journal*, 27 (2): 1–48.

Lee, T. A. (2001) US public accountancy firms and the recruitment of UK immigrants: 1850–1914, *Accounting, Auditing & Accountability Journal*, 14 (5): 537–64.

Lee, T. A. (2002a) UK immigrants and the foundation of the US public accountancy profession, *Accounting, Business & Financial History*, 12 (1): 73–94.

Lee, T. A. (2002b) US public accountancy firms and the recruitment of UK immigrants: 1850–1914, *Accounting, Auditing & Accountability Journal*, 14 (5): 537–64.

Lee, T. A. (2004) Economic class, social status and early Scottish chartered accountants, *Accounting Historians Journal*, 31 (2): 27–51.

Lee, T. A. (2006) Going where no accounting historian has gone before: a counterfactual history of the early institutionalization of modern public accountancy, *Accounting, Auditing & Accountability Journal*, 19 (6): 918–44.

Loeb, S. E. and Miranti, P. J. (2004) *The Institute of Accounts: Nineteenth Century Origins of Accounting Professionalism in the United States* (London & New York: Routledge).

Loft, A. (1986) Towards a critical understanding of the accounting: the case of cost accounting in the U.K., 1914–1925, *Accounting, Organizations and Society*, 11 (2): 137–69.

McClelland, P. and Stanton, P. (2004) 'An ignorant set of men': an episode in the clash of the legal and accounting professions over jurisdiction, *Accounting History*, 9 (2): 107–26.

Macdonald, K. M. (1984) Professional formation: the case of Scottish chartered accountants, *British Journal of Sociology*, 35 (2): 174–89.

Macdonald, K. M. (1985) Social closure and occupational registration, *Sociology*, 19 (4): 541–56.

Macdonald, K. M. (1987) Professional formation: a reply to Briston and Kedslie, *British Journal of Sociology*, 38 (1): 106–11.

Macdonald, K. M. (1995) *The Sociology of the Professions* (London: Sage).

MacDonald, L. D. and Richardson, A. J. (2004) Identity, appropriateness and the construction of regulatory space: the formation of the Public Accountant's Council of Ontario, *Accounting, Organizations and Society*, 29 (5/6): 489–524.

McMillan, K. P. (1999) The Institute of Accounts: a community of the competent, *Accounting, Business & Financial History*, 9 (1): 7–28.

Markus, H. B. (1997) *The History of the German Public Accounting Profession* (New York: Garland Publishing).

Martens, S. C. and McEnroe, J. E. (1991) Interprofessional struggles over definition: lawyers, accountants and illegal acts, *Critical Perspectives on Accounting*, 2 (4): 375–84.

Martens, S. C. and McEnroe, J. E. (1998) Interprofessional conflict, accommodation, and the flow of capital: the ASB vs the securities industry and its lawyers, *Accounting, Organizations and Society*, 23 (4): 361–76.

Millerson, G. (1964) *The Qualifying Associations: A Study in Professionalisation* (London: Routledge & Kegan Paul).

Mills, P. A. and Young, J. J. (1999) From contract to speech: the courts and CPA licensing laws 1921–1996, *Accounting, Organizations and Society*, 24 (3): 243–62.

Miranti, P. J. (1986) Associationalism, statism, and professionalisation regulation: public accountants and the reform of the financial markets, 1896–1940, *Business History Review*, 60 (3): 438–69.

Miranti, P. J. (1988) Professionalism and nativism: the competition in securing public accountancy legislation in New York during the 1890s, *Social Science Quarterly*, 60 (2): 361–82.

Miranti, P. J. (1990) *Accountancy Comes of Age: The Rise of an American Profession, 1886–1940* (Chapel Hill, NC: University of North Carolina Press).

Neu, D. and Saleem, L. (1996) The Institute of Chartered Accountants of Ontario (ICAO) and the emergence of ethical codes, *Accounting Historians Journal*, 23 (2): 35–68.

Neu, D., Friesen, C. and Everett, J. (2003) The changing internal market for ethical discourses in the Canadian CA profession, *Accounting, Auditing & Accountability Journal*, 16 (1): 70–103.

Noguchi, M. and Edwards, J. R. (2004) Accounting principles, internal conflict and the state: the case of the ICAEW, 1948–1966, *Abacus*, 40 (3): 280–320.

Okike, E. (2004) Management of crisis: the response of the auditing profession in Nigeria to the challenge to its legitimacy, *Accounting, Auditing & Accountability Journal*, 17 (5): 705–30.

Parker, L. D. (1987) An historical analysis of ethical pronouncements and debate in the Australian accounting profession, *Abacus*, 23 (2): 122–40.

Parker, R. H. (1980) *The Study of Accounting History* (Exeter: Exeter University Research Group #8).

Parker, R. H. (1989) Importing and exporting accounting: the British experience, in Hopwood, A. (ed.) *International Pressures for Accounting Change*, pp. 7–29 (Hertfordshire: Prentice-Hall International & ICAEW).

Parker, R. H. (2004) Accountancy on the periphery: the profession in Exeter to 1939, *Accounting, Business & Financial History*, 14 (1): 53–89.

Parker, R. H. (2005) Naming and branding: accountants and accountancy bodies in the British Empire and Commonwealth, 1853–2003, *Accounting History*, 10 (1): 7–46.

Pong, C. K. M. (1999) Jurisdictional contests between accountants and lawyers: the case of off-balance sheet finance 1985–1990, *Accounting History*, 4 (1): 7–29.

Poullaos, C. (1994) *Making the Australian Chartered Accountant* (New York: Garland).

Preston, A. M., Cooper, D. J., Scarbrough, D. P. and Chilton, R. C. (1995) Changes in the code of ethics of the U.S. accounting profession, 1917 and 1988: the continual quest for legitimation, *Accounting, Organizations and Society*, 20 (6): 507–46.

Previts, G. J. and Merino, B. D. (1998) *A History of Accountancy in the United States: The Cultural Significance of Accounting*, 2nd edn (Columbus, OH: Ohio State University Press).

Radcliffe, V., Cooper, D. J. and Robson, K. (1994) The management of professional enterprises and regulatory change: British accountancy and the Financial Services Act, 1986, *Accounting, Organizations and Society*, 19 (7): 601–28.

Ramirez, C. (2001) Understanding social closure in its cultural context: accounting practitioners in France (1920–1939), *Accounting, Organizations and Society*, 26 (4/5): 391–418.

Richardson, A. J. (1987) Professionalization and intraprofessional competition in the Canadian accounting profession, *Work and Occupations*, 14 (4): 591–615.

Richardson, A. J. (1989a) Corporatism and intraprofessional hegemony: a study of regulation and internal social order, *Accounting, Organizations and Society*, 14 (5/6): 415–31.

Richardson, A. J. (1989b) Canada's accounting elite: 1880–1930, *Accounting Historians Journal*, 16 (1): 1–20.

Richardson, A. J. (1993) An interpretative chronology of the development of accounting associations in Canada: 1879–1979, in G. J. Murphy (ed.) *A History of Canadian Accounting Thought and Practice*, pp. 551–627 (New York: Garland).

Richardson, A. J. (1997) Social closure in dynamic markets: the incomplete professional project in accountancy, *Critical Perspectives on Accounting*, 8 (6): 635–53.

Richardson, A. J. (2002) Professional dominance: the relationship between financial accounting and management accounting, 1926–1986, *Accounting Historians Journal*, 29 (2): 91–122.

Robson, K., Willmott, H., Cooper, D. and Puxty, T. (1994) The ideology of professional regulation and the markets for accounting labour: three episodes in the recent history of the UK accountancy profession, *Accounting, Organizations and Society*, 19 (6): 527–53.

Rodrigues, L. L., Gomes, D. and Craig, R. (2003) Corporatism, liberalism and the accounting profession in Portugal since 1755, *Accounting Historians Journal*, 30 (1): 95–127.

Romeo, G. C. and Kyj, L. S. (1998) The forgotten accounting association: The Institute of Accounts, *Accounting Historians Journal*, 25 (1): 29–55.

Romeo, G. C. and Leauby, B. A. (2004) The Bookkeepers' Beneficial Association of Philadelphia: an early signal in the United States for a professional organization, *Accounting History*, 9 (2): 7–33.

Roth, J. (1974) Professionalism: The sociologist's decoy, *Sociology of Work and Occupations*, 1 (1): 6–23.

Rueschemeyer, D. (1964) Doctors and lawyers: a commentary on the theory of the professions, *Canadian Review of Sociology and Anthropology*, 1 (1): 17–30.

Rueschemeyer, D. (1983) Professional autonomy and the social control of expertise, in Dingwall, R. and Lewis, P. (eds) *The Sociology of the Professions: Lawyers, Doctors and Others* (London: Macmillan) pp. 38–58.

Sakagami, M., Yoshimi, H. and Okano, H. (1999) Japanese accounting profession in transition, *Accounting, Auditing & Accountability Journal*, 12 (3): 340–57.

Saks, M. (1983) Removing the blinkers? A critique of recent contributions to the sociology of the professions, *Sociological Review*, 31 (1): 1–21.

Seal, W., Sucher, P. and Zelenka, I. (1996) Post-socialist transition and the development of an accountancy profession in the Czech Republic, *Critical Perspectives on Accounting*, 7 (4): 485–508.

Shackleton, K. (1995) Scottish chartered accountants: internal and external political relationships, 1853–1916, *Accounting, Auditing & Accountability Journal*, 8 (2): 18–46.

Sian, S. (2006) Inclusion, exclusion and control: the case of the Kenyan accounting professionalisation project, *Accounting, Organizations and Society*, 31 (3): 295–322.

Sikka, P. and Willmott, H. (1995) Illuminating the state-profession relationship: accountants acting as Department of Trade and Industry investigators, *Critical Perspectives on Accounting*, 6 (4): 341–69.

Simmons, C. and Neu, D. (1997) Re-presenting the external: editorials and the Canadian CAs (1936–1950), *Accounting, Organizations and Society*, 22 (8): 799–824.

Sriram, R. S. and Vollmers, G. (1997) A re-examination of the development of the accounting profession – critical events from 1912–1940, *Accounting Historians Journal*, 24 (2): 65–90.

Stacey, N. A. H. (1954) *English Accountancy 1800–1954: A Study in Social and Economic History* (London: Gee & Co.).

Susela, S. D. (1999) 'Interests' and accounting standard setting in Malaysia, *Accounting, Auditing & Accountability Journal*, 12 (3): 358–87.

Uche, C. U. (2002) Professional accounting development in Nigeria: threats from the inside and outside, *Accounting, Organizations and Society*, 27 (4/5): 471–96.

Velayutham, S. (2003) The accounting profession's code of ethics: is it a code of ethics or a code of quality assurance?, *Critical Perspectives on Accounting*, 14 (4): 483–503.

Velayutham, S. and Perera, H. (1996) Recent developments in the accounting profession in New Zealand: a case of deprofessionalization?, *International Journal of Accounting*, 31 (4): 445–62.

Velayutham, S. and Rahman, A. (2000) Towards market differentiation in the accounting profession: the case of Australia and New Zealand, *Critical Perspectives on Accounting*, 11 (6): 691–711.

Verma, S. and Gray, S. J. (2006) The creation of the institute of Chartered Accountants of India: the first steps in the development of an indigenous accounting profession post-independence, *Accounting Historians Journal*, 33 (2): 131–56.

Walker, S. P. (1988) *The Society of Accountants in Edinburgh 1854–1914: A Study of Recruitment to a New Profession* (New York: Garland).

Walker, S. P. (1991) The defence of professional monopoly: Scottish chartered accountants and 'satellites in the accountancy firmament', *Accounting, Organizations and Society*, 16 (3): 257–83.

Walker, S. P. (1995) The genesis of professional organization in Scotland: a contextual analysis, *Accounting, Organizations and Society*, 20 (4): 285–310.

Walker, S. P. (1996) The criminal upperworld and the emergence of a disciplinary code in the early chartered accountancy profession, *Accounting History*, 1 (2): 7–36.

Walker, S. P. (2004a) The genesis of professional organisation in English accountancy, *Accounting, Organizations and Society*, 29 (2): 127–56.

Walker, S. P. (2004b) *Towards the 'Great Desideratum': The Unification of the Accountancy Bodies in England, 1870–1880* (Edinburgh: ICAS).

Walker, S. P. (2004c) Conflict, collaboration, fuzzy jurisdictions and partial settlements. Accountants, lawyers and insolvency practice during the late nineteenth century, *Accounting and Business Research*, 34 (3): 247–65.

Walker, S. P. and Shackleton, K. (1995) Corporatism and structural change in the British accountancy profession, 1930–1957, *Accounting, Organizations and Society*, 20 (6): 467–503.

Walker, S. P. and Shackleton, K. (1998) A ring fence for the profession: advancing the closure of British accountancy 1957–1970, *Accounting, Auditing & Accountability Journal*, 11 (1): 34–71.

Wallace, R. S. O. (1992) Growing pains of an indigenous accountancy profession: the Nigerian experience, *Accounting, Business & Financial History*, 2 (1): 25–53.

West, B. P. (1996) The professionalisation of accounting: a review of recent historical research and its implications, *Accounting History*, 1 (1): 77–102.

Willmott, H. (1986) Organising the profession: a theoretical and historical examination of the development of the major accountancy bodies in the U.K., *Accounting, Organizations and Society*, 11 (6): 555–80.

Willmott, H., and Sikka, P. (1997) On the commercialization of accountancy thesis: a review essay, *Accounting, Organizations and Society*, 22 (8): 831–42.

Xu, X. and Xu, X. (2003) Becoming professional: Chinese accountants in early 20th century China, *Accounting Historians Journal*, 30 (1): 129–53.

Yapa, P. W. S. (1999) Professional accounting environment in Brunei Darussalam, *Accounting, Auditing & Accountability Journal*, 12 (3): 328–39.

Yapa, P. W. S. (2006) Cross-border competition and the professionalisation of accounting: the case of Sri Lanka, *Accounting History*, 11 (4): 447–73.

Zeff, S. A. (ed.) (1988) *The U.S. Accounting Profession in the 1890s and Early 1900s* (New York & London: Garland).

Zeff, S. A. (2003a) How the U.S. profession got where it is today: part I, *Accounting Horizons*, 17 (3): 189–205.

Zeff, S. A. (2003b) How the U.S. profession got where it is today: part II, *Accounting Horizons*, 17 (4): 267–86.

Appendix: Additional references to works on professionalisation in particular countries

Australia: Gavens and Gibson (1992)

Brunei Darussalam: Yapa (1999)

France: Bocqueraz (2001)

Germany: Markus (1997)

Greece: Dedoulis and Caramanis (2007)

India: Verma and Gray (2006)

Malaysia: Susela (1999)

New Zealand: Baskerville (2006), Keenan (2000), Velayutham and Perera (1996), Velayutham and Rahman (2000)

Russia: Bailey (1992)

Sri Lanka: Yapa (2006)

Sweden: Larsson (2005)

UK: McClelland and Stanton (2004), Parker (2004), Pong (1999), Walker (2004c)

USA: Cross (1998), Harston and Welch (1997), Loeb and Miranti (2004), Martens and McEnroe (1991, 1998), Romeo and Kyj (1998), Romeo and Leauby (2004), Sriram and Vollmers (1997)

12

Practitioners, work and firms

David J. Cooper and Keith Robson

Overview

In this chapter the focus is on one crucial site of accounting practice: the multinational professional service firms (the Big Four), and the historical studies that have examined their emergence and development. Six characteristic contributions of these histories are identified and their strengths and limitations are pointed out. First, most histories serve as celebrations of individual firms, practitioners and the service of the audit function. Second, clients are presented as the motor force in the growth and characteristics of the multinational firms. The third theme is the contribution of elite practitioners to the development of the accounting profession. Fourth, histories recount the spread of practitioners and accounting knowledges across geographical space. The fifth theme is the account of the nature of the practice of accounting firms – from bankruptcy, to audit, to management consultancy. Finally, the histories account for the formal organisational structures of the firms. Later in the chapter suggestions are offered for further research on firm histories: histories as managed organisations, the experience and practices of work, and the firms' role as cultural and political actors.

Introduction

Accounting practices affect not just how resources are produced and distributed in an economy, but also what is deemed socially rational and valuable, and what is deemed to be irrelevant. Burchell *et al.* (1980) highlighted the importance of the institutionalisation of accounting practices, that what are regarded as legitimate reports and descriptions of organisational behaviour are affected not just by developments in accounting thought. They are also the product of developments in institutional fields, comprised of professional associations, universities, regulators and professional firms (as well as institutions typically seen as external to accounting, such as statistical bureaux, the state, other professions and corporations). Drawing on an analysis of the histories of accounting firms, this chapter takes Burchell *et al.*'s argument further by examining the role of professional firms in both the development of the accounting profession and professional identity, as well as the development of practices that are now deemed to be part of accounting. The nature of accounting practitioners, the work they do and the firms in which they trained, learned and practiced their craft are important factors that have influenced accounting and society.

As we have argued elsewhere (Cooper and Robson 2006), accounting research has tended to neglect the role of firms, particularly the larger organisations, and has instead concentrated on prominent accountants (both leaders of the professional bodies and innovators in accounting thought) and their professional associations. Much accounting research has assumed that these factors explain how and why accounting and accountants have become a powerful social and economic force in society.

In this chapter we focus on one crucial site of accounting practice: the multinational business ('professional') service firms (currently known as the Big Four), and the historical studies that have examined their emergence and development. From their origins in accountancy partnerships dating, in some cases, as far back as the mid-nineteenth century, mergers between founding accountancy partnerships and revenue growth have since established the multinational accountancy firms as major global organizations.[1] Table 12.1 indicates the current size and scope of these firms. It is perhaps unsurprising that these firms audit almost all the publicly quoted companies in the major stock exchanges of the world, and are typically the preferred advisors to governments concerning economic and social reforms (from health care and education to tax policy and the management of governments themselves). Accounting firms (even if the Big Four no longer call themselves such) are everywhere, even advising regimes that present themselves as suspicious of capitalism (Catchpowle and Cooper 1999).

Who are these Big Four firms and what are their antecedents? Since the mid-1980s, Price Waterhouse and Coopers and Lybrand have combined to form PricewaterhouseCoopers; KPMG was the product of a merger between Peat Marwick and Kleinveld Main Goerdeler; Ernst and Whinney merged with Arthur Young to form Ernst and Young; Deloitte Haskins and Sells combined with Touche Ross; and Arthur Andersen would implode after the scandals of Enron, WorldCom and others. These firms would be included in the largest 500 firms in the world, although they rarely appear on such lists because they are not required to publish audited statements of their own activities. Tracing their histories provides important insights into how

Table 12.1 Growth in scale of Big Eight (Five): 1980 to 2000

1980 Big Eight			1999 Big Five		
Firm	Global Revenue ($US millions)	Number of Employees	Firm	Global Revenue ($US millions)	Number of Employees
Arthur Andersen	645	15,500	Pricewaterhouse Coopers	17.3	155,000
Coopers & Lybrand	595	12,000	Arthur Andersen	16.21	135,000
Peat Marwick & Mitchell	586	14,000	Ernst & Young	12.58	97,800
Ernst & Whinney	500	14,000	KPMG	10.86	102,000
Deloitte Haskins & Sells	450	10,000	Deloitte & Touche	10.6	90,000
Arthur Young	400	15,000			
Touche Ross					
Price Waterhouse					

Source: *Fortune*, (1980) and *Public Accounting Report*, (1981, 2000).

accounting and accounting firms have been transformed in the past 150 years from a minor actor to a central figure on the world stage.

We acknowledge that the majority of professionally qualified accountants no longer work in 'public practice', and certainly not in multinational accounting firms. But these firms are important locations where accounting and auditing practices emerge, become standardised and regulated, where accounting rules and standards are translated into practice, and where professional identities are mediated, formed and transformed. The alumni of such firms play a major role in the corporate accounting and finance function in many countries (Armstrong 1987; Iyer 1998). And while there are historical studies of local accounting firms in earlier eras (such as Walker 1993; Habgood 1994), few studies exist of accountants and the work of smaller and regional firms in the current day (notable exceptions include Ramirez 2001, 2003). So, for reasons both of practicality and due to their importance in the development of accounting work and ideas, this chapter focuses on the histories of what have emerged as global accounting firms.

The sources that we draw upon in this chapter are diverse: historical overviews of firms have been produced or sponsored by the firms themselves (De Mond 1980; Wise 1982; Cooper Brothers & Co. 1986; Falkus 1993; White 2003) many were commissioned (Richards 1950; Pollard 1975; Richards 1981; Marshall 1982; Coopers and Lybrand 1984; Jones 1981, 1995; Allen and McDermott 1993) or were the work ('memoirs') of former partners (Kettle 1957; Spacek 1985; Benson 1989). Other studies follow biographical traditions of business research: the study of professional elites (Howitt 1966), firm mergers (Boys 1989; Cypert 1991), or key individuals and their contributions to firm and professional development (Jones 1988). Some studies pursue journalistic themes or express insider accounts, perhaps written in response to event-specific crises or scandal (Toffler 2003; Squires et al. 2003; Stevens 1981). Other studies are not presented as accounting history but comment on the professional firms and their practices in a historical context and in the light of other theoretical engagements (Loft 1986; Hanlon 1994; Dirsmith et al. 1997).

This chapter has a distinctly Anglo-American orientation, which reflects much of the research literature, but begs the question whether the concept of a profession is understood in the same way outside the Anglo-American world (Evans 2003; Gietzmann and Quick 1998), and whether these firms either did, or now do, operate in the way presented in these histories (Sluyterman 1998; Post et al. 1998). With this caveat in mind, our main purpose is, first, to attend to the dominant themes within histories of accounting firms and, second, to set out research issues and themes that we consider have not been sufficiently addressed. Our review suggests that much of the literature on the major accounting firms has taken as its subject the lives and work of elite practitioners – those who founded the firms or succeeded to the position of senior partner. Indeed, many firm histories seem to be indistinguishable from biographies of the ruling senior members (e.g. White 2003). Their efforts in establishing and extending their firms have been complemented by accounts of the contributions of these figures to the growth of major professional associations.

The contributions of firm histories

In this section we identify six features of firm histories. First, most histories serve as celebrations of individual firms, practitioners and the service of the audit function. Second, clients, sometimes explicitly, and often more vaguely, are presented as the motor force in the growth and characteristics of the multinational firms and their predecessors. The third feature highlights the contribution of elite practitioners ('leaders' of the various firms) in the development of the accounting profession. Fourth, histories provide considerable detail about the spread of practitioners and accounting knowledges across geographical space, albeit largely with a UK focus. The fifth feature is the changing service offerings of accounting firms. Finally, the histories offer an account of the formal structures of the firms themselves.

Celebratory histories

For almost as long as there has been a tradition of accounting research, there has been a series of studies on the history of accounting firms. Given this tradition, it might be expected that there is a great deal to be learned from these histories. They might be expected to have mirrored mainstream economic and social histories of industrial and commercial firms (Chandler 1962; Pollard 1965), histories that have explored topics such as evolving conceptions of markets, industries, management practice, the spatial dimensions of economic activity, shifting production technologies, and the impact of firms on economic and social activity (Perrow 2002). Histories of railroads (Chandler 1965; Dobbin and Dowd 2000), textile companies (McGouldrick 1968), financial institutions (Chernow 1990) and so on have illuminated important aspects of the changing nature of the economy, the relationship between commercial and political life, industrial relations, and much else. Histories of accounting firms offer the potential to understand the development of accounting and audit work, changes in understandings of professionalism, and the relation between accounting, other professions, the economy and society.

Yet, with few exceptions, accounting firm histories could be characterised as public relations documents that have been written for the firms themselves. Most firm histories extol the virtues of the firm, celebrate its contributions and offer a functionalist analysis of its activities (Robson and Cooper 1990). These histories are often expressed in chronological and dynastic terms, where one leader gives way to another in a parade of great men.

The prefaces of many firm histories stress the celebratory nature of these histories, which are often commissioned by the firms themselves to commemorate an anniversary or significant moment in the firm's development. Indeed, the same motives can be seen in many histories of commercial organisations. The histories are often limited in terms of the access to internal information about the operations and strategies of the firms, and many histories are quite explicit about confidentiality agreements with their firm subject.

In one sense, then, it would be churlish and redundant to complain about this uncritical and triumphant attribute, and there is no doubt that researching accounting firms has special challenges, given the lack of public data and accessibility to firm data. Further, many of these histories may be seen as important elements in the formation of the identities and self-understanding of firms and the accountants associated with them, and this indeed may be reason enough to study these texts.

The celebratory nature of firm histories comes at a significant cost to the accounting researcher. Absent from them is an analysis of employment and work practices of accountants or auditors, or a careful examination of relations with clients, the state and the economy. To learn about the sort of issues studied by modern economic and management historians, the accounting researcher has to infer a great deal and re-read these works in ways unanticipated by the authors. The life and achievements of the founding partners of the big firms may be interesting, but there is room for greater focus on the work of the professional firms, their development as organisations, and their development of knowledge and expertise. So, this chapter is forced to make inferences from what has been written, it frequently neglects the celebration of the achievements of the firms and senior partners. Instead it considers issues that arise from reading between the lines of these texts.

Histories in the name of the client

Certain rhetorical themes are repeated throughout the firm histories, and these themes offer insight both into the implicit perspectives of their authors, as well as the belief systems that permeate the firms. The most prominent rhetorical theme is the 'in the name of the client', used to justify changes in organisation and activities. For example, conformity in dress is justified by the assumption that clients have a view of what an accountant should look like (Stevens 1981: 24).

Anderson-Gough *et al.* (2000) have drawn attention to how this theme endures in the current practices of accounting firms in the UK, as a form of internal discipline. Hammond (2002) indicates that assumptions about client expectations were a major reason offered by accounting firms in the USA to exclude African-Americans for much of the twentieth century. In firm histories, 'the client' is used to justify the expansion of the firms; client pressures and needs are said to explain why individual partnerships have grown to be huge multinational enterprises. While large clients may often prefer large firms, this pressure does not seem to have operated for other professional service firms (e.g. in law). We wonder why accounting firms studiously claim that they did not seek growth for its own sake (Previts and Merino 1998: 132). Haskins and Sells reportedly realised the value of overseas operations when Barnum and Bailey's Circus ran into financial troubles while touring Europe, and thus merged with a London firm (Wootton *et al.* 2003). Price Waterhouse (PW) only opened their first office in the USA in 1890 to investigate American breweries for British investors (Allen and McDermott 1993: xiii.). PW opened their Pittsburgh office in 1902 to cater to their new client, US Steel (Jones 1995: 93). PW expanded to Liverpool in 1904 because of their work for shipping lines. Arthur Andersen apparently began to open overseas offices when they were appalled at the class-ridden treatment to clients offered by their London correspondence firm (Arthur Andersen, n.d.). Jones reports that even in 1973, an influential paper presented to the PW partnership meeting declared 'excellence rather than size for its own sake should be our goal' but it went on to argue that:

> nevertheless, it is agreed that a certain size is inescapable to enable us to have a large enough base to provide a full range of external and internal services and in order to be able to attract the cream of the young men coming into the profession. In practice this means that we must aim to be broadly comparable in terms of size with our major competitors.
>
> (Jones 1995: 258)

Embedded in this quote is another motive for expansion – to provide partnership opportunities necessary for recruiting, which are themselves couched in terms of what is best for the client. Throughout Jones' (1995) history of PW, there is a tendency to underplay commercial motivations for firm activities, such as concerns with staff recruiting, retention and promotion, and to interpret firm actions as client driven. In Jones' account, the development of PW is driven by clients and the marketplace, and in this sense, the history is not only functionalist, but also determinist, curiously out of keeping with the otherwise individualist ethos of many histories. The history of PW is presented as great leaders responding to clients. There is little consideration that accounting firms may help to construct the market for their services and the 'needs' of clients, as shown, for example, in accounts of the creation of 'needs' in cost accounting (Loft 1986), auditing (Power 1997) and public sector accounting (Gendron *et al.* 2007).

Similarly, the history of Ernst & Whinney (EW), a constituent of Big Four firm Ernst & Young, portrays British accountancy in general as responding to the needs of clients (Jones

1981). An illustrative example is the claim that Whinney Murray began operating in continental Europe and the Middle East in the inter-war period as British and American investment expanded there (ibid.: 174–6). The brief history of Cooper Brothers (1986), prepared for the firm in 1954, is also written in terms of client needs:

> The policy originally laid down by the four Cooper brothers was that the business should be conducted only from the office in London. They felt that unless they could give personal supervision to the work of the firm they would not be able to maintain the standards that they felt to be important . . . Gradually, however, the necessity of providing services for clients with interests in other parts of the country and overseas and the improvement of communications caused this policy to be reversed.
>
> (Cooper Brothers & Co 1986: 37)

In another house history, Duane Kullberg, head of Arthur Andersen in 1980, stated 'we are not seduced by size' but that growth was necessary to secure the firm's leadership in its field (Arthur Andersen n.d: 171). In the same vein, Kullberg claims:

> We establish offices for one of two reasons – primarily to serve our existing or new clients as they expand geographically and secondarily to enter attractive new markets. Either way, we have always been committed to staffing our offices to meet client needs.
>
> (Arthur Andersen n.d: 177)

This rationalising of growth for the purpose of benefiting the client barely considers alternative motives, such as the desire to secure increased fee income and profit for the partners. Allen and McDermott (1993) repeatedly stress that PW best serves its clients by protecting its own reputation, for example, saying that PW's best reference were clients who fired them for being too scrupulous (ibid.: 144). A client-centred rhetoric seems like a boilerplate justification for almost any policy. Yet as Pastra (2004) shows, the increasing internal leverage (where more and more employed accountants report to an individual partner) is an important explanation for the dramatic growth of the firms, particularly in the past 20 years. Others (such as Burrows and Black 1998) have shown that the internal profit sharing and the promotion structures within accounting firms are important explanations for their growth. Such issues remain profoundly undeveloped in the firm history literature.

The firm as contributor to the profession

A dominant theme in many accounts of the history of Anglo–American-based firms has been the role of the senior partners in the governance and development of professional associations. As noted earlier, most histories provide some insight into the social and cultural capital of the senior men (almost always men, except during war years – see Cooper Brothers 1986: 27; Jones 1995: 114–15) involved in the development of the firms and the profession. And to be clear, the social, political, economic and cultural allegiances of early pioneers were very important in professional formation and legitimation (Fielding and Portwood 1980). However, many histories provide no direct analysis, treating them as of little importance in understanding the history of accounting practice and work. Jones (1981) is to some degree an exception, devoting considerable space to the role of senior partners in Ernst & Whinney in establishing professional bodies. Turquand (of Turquand, Barton, Mayhew, later merged into Whinneys) was the first ICAEW President, and the third was Frederick Whinney. Similarly, Cooper Brothers (1986)

279

starts with a quote from Ernest Cooper, an early partner, describing the status of accountants in 1864, 'We could hardly, South of the Tweed, claim to be a profession . . . Our social position was not enviable' (1986: 4). The text goes on to indicate that 'the concerted efforts of these two brothers (Ernest and Arthur Cooper) played a not inconsiderable part in the formation of the Institute' (ibid.: 6), each going on to be presidents of the English Institute. The narrative continues, 'Ever since the Institute was formed, one or more of the partners of the firm have been a member of the Council' (ibid.: 6). The first 20 presidents also included William Deloitte, Edwin Waterhouse and William Peat, as well as partners of several firms later absorbed into the modern-day Big Four.

Jones' history of Ernst & Whinney (1981) examines the role and prominence of accountants in Scotland. Professional associations were created in Edinburgh (1853), Glasgow (1853) and Aberdeen (1866). Many Scottish accountants were also associated with the law, and indeed Sir Walter Scott in 1820 referred to accountancy as a branch of law, which aided its status. There have been several studies of Scottish pioneers (e.g. Walker 1988, 1993; Lee 1997) which tend to stress the connection to law. Jones concludes by quoting a study of Glasgow chartered accountants:

> Almost the majority are the children of a tiny fraction of business and professional people. As in other professions, wealth and influence are as important in shaping the opportunities and interests of children as the ability with which they are endowed.
>
> (Cairncross 1937: 374, cited in Jones 1981: 91)

This characterisation would seem to apply to British accountants generally, and is unsurprising given that most firms required a 'premium' for those articled in the firm (£500 in 1945, according to Cooper Brothers, 1986), and often didn't pay a salary until qualification.

While histories of US firms say less about the role of senior partners in professional development, Allen and McDermott's (1993) history of PW devotes considerable space to the importance of George O. May in the American Institute of Certified Public Accountants and in negotiations surrounding the creation of the Securities and Exchange Commission. Biographies of senior partners emphasise their role in professional developments. Benson (1989) is perhaps the most explicit, offering an account of a senior partner of Coopers who was highly influential in both the development of accounting standard setting in the UK and the setting up of the International Accounting Standards Committee.

More generally, however, such histories have little to say about the tensions that have arisen in the professional associations' oversight and regulation of the professional coalition. Although conflicts between the demands of larger firms and the interests of the small and medium practices (and between those in public practice and those in industry) have been a central component of professional heterogeneity since the 1970s (Robson et al. 1994), firm histories have little to say about the role of firms in the management of the professional associations, although it seems likely they are as central now as they were in the founding of the associations.

Geographical spread of firms and accounting practices

The expansion of partnerships is a recurring theme in firm histories. Many discuss the internationalisation of the firm and the migration of accountants from one national jurisdiction to another. The case of PW's emergence in the USA is an example. Jones (1995: Chap. 4) shifts briskly from an account of the formation of regional offices of PW in England to the development of American, European and Australian offices. In contrast to the motive stressed in the firm histories of 'responding to clients', Cooper *et al.* (1998) discuss different motivations for geographic spread, including perceptions of the potential profitability of regional and overseas markets, the geographical preferences of influential partners, a colonising spirit of bringing accounting to regions and nations that had not experienced its benefits, and the pressures from international lending agencies for financial oversight by 'legitimate' audit firms.

The shift from a single office, often controlled by one or two patriarchs, is a recurrent theme in all the histories. For example, William Cooper, son of a founder of a major British bank, left a small accounting firm to set up on his own in 1854, and he was soon joined by three of his brothers. Daniels *et al.* (1989) offer a helpful analysis of the international expansion of accounting firms, indicating that such expansion is often associated with shifts in the relation between the home firm and the overseas units. They discuss a range of associations between offices (from corresponding firms, to associations and federations (sometimes using an international name), to more or less integrated national firms to the 'world firms' of the Big four) and track the patterns of expansion both geographically and historically. Their empirical analysis is now dated, reflecting the firms that existed in 1985 and is focused on UK-based firms. Moreover, their historical analysis seems largely based on the firm histories discussed in this chapter, categorising the period between 1890 and 1945 as 'guided by requirements of individual clients' (1989: 86), and the period since 1945 as 'heavily influenced by mergers at the international level' (ibid.), even when firms operated more or less independently under the same name. However, Daniels *et al.* (1989) go on to examine the location of firm offices for 20 UK firms between 1975 and 1985, showing that the major growth actually was in medium-sized accounting firms.

Table 12.2 shows the global expansion of the major multinational firms. Some now have over 1,000 offices. While the story of global expansion may leave an impression of the diffusion of offices worldwide, it is important to appreciate that more than 50 per cent of worldwide fee revenue for the multinational accounting firms arises in North America, and that partners are concentrated in major financial centres, especially London and New York. Daniels *et al.* (1989) suggest that research on the spatial division of labour of accounting firms is in its infancy, and that we know little about the local socio-economic effects of their location patterns.

We obtain some insight into these socio-economic effects by examining the detailed firm histories. The history of Cooper Brothers, for example, discusses 'associated firms overseas' (1986: 37). It appears that the firm initially opened offices in Brussels (1921), New York (1926), Paris (1930), Johannesburg (1931) and Durban (1933), but no information is provided in the histories about the process of setting up and funding remote offices, the arrangements for referral and control of work, and any profit sharing. Evidence about the difficulties of establishing overseas operations is found in the case of an office in Moscow in the early 1990s in Cooper *et al.* (1998). In this case national stereotyping made the process of investing in an overseas office difficult. Yet in the official history of Coopers, there is no hint of the micro politics of organising an accounting firm, or any reference to disagreements about strategies for producing and distributing profits.

Almost a quarter of the history of Cooper Brothers (1986) describes the location and chronology of setting up overseas offices. What is noticeable, however is the extensive coverage of offices located in the British Empire (as it then was) and the dearth of information about European and US offices. From other, confidential, sources, we suspect that this emphasis on the British Empire reflects those offices where the UK firm had a direct ownership interest. The focus on British firms perhaps reflects the firms which have an interest in accounting history, and in itself says something about the role of tradition and colonisation in these firms. Indeed, Jones (1981) explicitly thanks the 'history committee' of Ernst & Whinney.

Table 12.2   Global expansion of Big Eight (Five): 1982 to 1995: twelve-year change in total number of offices and partners

A. Number of offices worldwide

Firm	1982	1988	1991	1992	1995	% growth
Arthur Andersen	155	217	289	392	454	109
Coopers & Lybrand	424	565	737	805	814	44
Deloitte Touche	697	986	722	757	781	−20
Ernst & Young	530	796	777	812	803	1
KPMG	673	641	864	1,056	1,066	66
Price Waterhouse	326	424	496	548	536	26

B. Number of partners worldwide

Firm	1982	1988	1991	1992	1995	% growth
Arthur Andersen	1,438	2,133	2,478	2,507	4,294	101
Coopers & Lybrand	2,282	3,341	5,152	5,373	5,528	65
Deloitte Touche	3,831	5,137	4,823	4,625	4,709	−8
Ernst & Young	3,439	5,283	5,700	6,059	6,452	22
KPMG	5,424	5,161	6,530	6,190	6,036	17
Price Waterhouse	1,677	2,570	3,113	3,245	3,211	25

Source: Centre for International Financial and Accounting Research (1994: 283) (Princeton, NJ: CIFAR Publishing), and Suddaby *et al.* (2007).

Hanlon (1994) provides further insight to accounting firms and the international division of labour. His analysis of the migration patterns and aspirations of Irish accountants within the global firms offers a valuable glimpse into the extent and effects of such movements and the crucial importance of global financial centres in affecting the offices in the semi-periphery. Published sources (e.g. White 2003) say little about geographic spread for KPMG (which might be expected to have spread in a different manner given its combined Dutch, UK and US antecedents) and some of the multinational firms where the US firm was more dominant. So, while we know quite a lot about the patterns of overseas expansion for UK firms, the firm histories provide little insight to the conditions that shaped overseas expansion of the major accounting firms, and the impact on firm management and practices.

Nature and scope of work in accounting firms

The histories provide some insight into the work of early accountants. Cooper Brothers (1986: 4) summarises the nature of the UK business in the nineteenth century. Insolvency work was stimulated by the Bankruptcy Act, 1869 but declined after the 1883 Act, and audit work increased after the Companies Acts of 1862, 1879 (which required the audit of banks) and 1900 (requiring audits of all companies). Cooper Brothers (1986: 25) also briefly outlines hours of work, dress codes and food offered to clerks who had to work overtime. Jones (1995) offers some detail on the early links to law and the importance of the railways in the early accounting work of PW.

That said, most firm histories focus on audit with only occasional reference to tax, bankruptcy and consulting work. White (2003: 113) justifies feebly this lack of attention by insisting that KPMG is distinctive in avoiding over-investment in non-audit activities. Jones (1995) offers six pages (out of 337) on the development of professional work and stresses the expansion into business services as a market-led phenomenon. He repeats the standard firm explanation: 'By the seventies . . . the ability of accountancy practices to add value to their clients through audit services became more difficult.' The stress is on the client and his or her 'value', not the motives that might require firm members to add value to themselves. Jones usefully summarises the split in the occupation of professional staff in 1973, but offers no contemporary data.

An important (but often unacknowledged) background to the firm histories is the long-standing controversy about the scope of services provided by accounting firms. In particular, concern has been expressed over the provision of 'other services' and whether such services compromise the independence of the audit. Tables 12.3 and 12.4 indicate the scope of work of the multinational accounting firms before their consulting work was restricted by legislation after Enron and the collapse of Arthur Andersen. The marked rise in income from tax work,

Table 12.3   Revenue split (%) for individual US Big Six (Five) firms: 1975 to 1999

	Audit %	Tax %	Consulting %
Arthur Andersen			
1975	66	18	16
1986	47	21	32
1994	33	18	49
1999	18	12	70
KPMG			
1975	70	20	10
1986	56	22	22
1994	49	21	30
1999	34	23	43
Deloitte Touche			
1975	68	17	5
1986	64	23	13
1994	52	22	25
1999	31	19	41
Ernst & Young			
1975	68	21	11
1986	56	26	18
1994	45	19	36
1999	38	25	37
Coopers & Lybrand			
1975	69	19	12
1986	60	21	19
1994	58	1	24
1999	34	19	34
Price Waterhouse			
1975	76	16	8
1986	58	24	18
1994	43	25	32
1999	34	19	34

Source: Suddaby *et al.* (2007).

Table 12.4 Proportional US revenue sources for Big Eight (Five) firms: 1975, 1990 and 1999

	Year		
	1975 %	1990 %	1999 %
Audit	71	49	30
Tax	17	25	21
Consulting	12	26	49

Sources: Public Accounting Report, various years and Fortune and Suddaby *et al.* (2007).

and even more so, from management consulting occurs in all the firms (see also Zeff 2003a, 2003b). While management consulting accounted for 12 per cent of aggregate fees among the Big Eight in 1979, this proportion had risen to 49 per cent in 1999.

The histories of accounting firms shed some light on the historical evolution of the services provided by accounting firms, and indeed, what is regarded as proper work for accountants. One of the most interesting features of Jones' (1981) history of Ernst & Whinney is the careful attempt to trace the shifting work conducted within accounting firms. He analyses the fees for a series of predecessor firms from 1848, showing that 93 per cent of fee income in 1858 was derived from bankruptcy work. He demonstrates that the fees of firms in the Victorian era were closely related to the state of the economy and various banking and other financial crises: 'accountants did particularly well in times of financial disaster and depression . . . they were the rich undertakers of the economic world' (ibid.: 45). Although the dominance of accountants in insolvency work declined after the 1883 Bankruptcy Act, corporate audit was a small proportion of work till the late nineteenth century, when it began to predominate. But auditing in the late Victorian era seems to have included general accounting work, including the compilation of financial statements and the detection of fraud.

Jones' analysis suggests that the work of accounting firms varied quite significantly over time, and was largely affected by changing legislation and the state of the economy. Auditing was the major source of fees throughout the first half of the twentieth century, with insolvency work declining more or less consistently so that by 1935 the latter had become insignificant. Tax work only became significant after 1945, but was rarely above 10 per cent of total fees up to 1960. As might be expected from an economic history commissioned and 'overseen' by the subject firm, Jones' (1981) history of Ernst & Whinney focuses on how the firm contributes to the economy. There is little to nothing about activities that may not be 'productive' – their possible involvement in scandals, frauds, money laundering, tax avoidance schemes, short-termism and so on, that are part of the less celebrated history of the accounting industry. Jones' (1995) PW history, however, provides an extensive discussion of the Royal Mail case, refers to Hary and Kreuger and the 1929 stock market crash, and the more recent Guinness and BCCI scandals. There is some mention of the firm's reluctance until the twentieth century to be associated with manufacturing, and its close allegiance to financial interests in the City of London, but no commentary on whether these were 'contributions' to the British economy.

The firm histories reveal that increased regulation and the use of computers led to decreased differentiation in how different firms produced audits (Arthur Andersen n.d: 172; Jones 1981: 249, 1995: 288; Allen and McDermott 1993: 196–8, 213, 222). The need for personnel with specialised skills was resisted by older partners. For example, at PW America, it was only when the number of partners expanded, and as young recruits came to favour specialisation (it gave them a clearer sense of their role and a route for career progression), that resistance faded (Allen and McDermott 1993: 230–2). By the same token, Arthur Andersen cite a demand by consulting partners for a larger share of the profits as the motivation for creating a distinct consulting organisation in 1987. Management advisory service specialists at Andersen felt that they were being held back by the outmoded attitudes of auditors, and thus sought greater organisational freedom (Stevens, 1991: 116–19), eventually leading to the consultants separating to form Accenture in 1997 (Whitford 1997). Thus, it can be seen that the broadening of services resulted in substantial tensions within the firms in ways not fully discussed in firm histories.

The structure and organisation of firms

The expansion in the number of partners necessitated structural changes in the firms, which were a reflection of changes in what it meant to be a partner. All of the firms began as essentially personal partnerships, where decisions could be made jointly and face-to-face. However, even in their earliest days, it was common for different partners to specialise in different activities, often with one partner performing most of the actual accounting work in the home office, while the other sought primarily to build up the client list (Jones 1981: 95). Structures based on personal relationships lasted surprisingly long – into the 1960s in the cases of both PW and Whinney Smith & Whinney in the UK – but eventually the increase in the number of partners beyond a dozen or two, and the related increasing importance of non-auditing services, made these management structures unworkable. In large firms, partnerships had expanded until 'partners' came to be complete strangers from one another (Stevens 1981: 15, 1991: 102).

We learn comparatively little about the organisation and management of the firms from their histories. Consistent with the dynastic approach that most exhibit, what can be gleaned are some of the power struggles over leadership (Cypert 1991; Stevens 1991; Squires *et al.* 2003; Toffler 2003). These are typically expressed from the viewpoint of the victors. Histories may indicate organisation charts, which depict formal structures but say little about the operation and management of the firms, especially given their tendency to use informal mentoring (Dirsmith and Covaleski 1985) and committees to manage work and relationships (Greenwood *et al.* 1990, 1999).

The general pattern was to have the partners choose an 'inner circle', often referred to as the executive committee, to lead the firm (Jones 1981: 214, 1995: 255). The level of democracy in these elections was time- and firm-dependent – for example, in the UK practice of PW during the 1970s, partners voted whether or not to accept the single nomination of a selection committee (Jones 1995: 252). However, even hand-picked choices could be rejected, as evidenced by the 'Battle of Boca Raton', wherein Peats partners rejected the reformist candidate selected by the previous leadership (Stevens 1981: 5). Cypert's book on the merger that created KPMG (1991) similarly illustrates at great length the need to get support from a worldwide partnership with diverse priorities and national objectives.

Within an executive committee, there were divisions of responsibility, which only slowly became more formalised. The firm histories also suggest that efforts were made to ensure a regional balance in senior management (Allen and McDermott 1993: 157; Jones 1981: 214), although Anglo-Americans still dominated. Most notably, the work of the executive committee tended to evolve into policy-making and strategic guidance, while another committee was made responsible for day-to-day oversight (Allen and McDermott 1993: 151).

Leadership tensions within are also suggested by the eventual creation (in the case of

Whinney Murray, in 1973) of a 'national office' to handle the firm's coordination, instead of simply having a particular office (i.e. London or New York) as a first among equals (Allen and McDermott 1993: 96–8; Jones 1981: 233). As mentioned above, Arthur Andersen went further than the other firms in restructuring their partnership as they expanded, by giving Andersen Consulting a distinct status loosely within the larger firm in 1987 (Squires *et al.* 2003; Toffler 2003). In general, however, extant histories say little about strategic, HR, marketing or co-ordination practices within the firms.

Firm histories: towards an expanded research agenda

In this section we set out an agenda for future work in order that firm histories contribute not simply to a better understanding of these major organisations and their impact, but also to permit theoretical understandings related to organisational and management practices, professionalisation and regulation. Accordingly, we suggest a history agenda that includes explorations of the changing nature of firm work; the everyday practices and experiences of employees across time; the changing organisational control structures and forms of the firms; their contributions to new forms of business knowledge, technique and expertise; and the emergence of the role of the large firms as social and political actors in regulatory fields.

Histories of firms as managed organisations

Historians of firms have taken the partnership model of ownership and control as the archetype for firm histories. Partners are the only actors that are deemed to 'count'. Significant developments within firms are associated with the actions of senior partners. Since the founding of accounting firms involves specific individuals, then of course the narrative of the firm is intimately related to their actions in establishing or merging their partnerships. However, this focus results in a neglect of firms as managed and contested organisations.

Information about firms' internal structures is often lacking and the concepts and practices of management control have little place in most firm histories. Jones (1981, 1995) considers the problems of geographical expansion and firm organisation, but even his discussion is invariably connected to the attitudes of senior partners, particularly towards expanding the number of partners. Certainly, Jones and others usefully emphasise the metropolitan bias of senior partners, as demonstrated by the reluctance for many years to sanction the appointment of partners in the provincial offices.

Later analyses of the firms are less specific as to the changes in organisational structures that firms have adopted. The (typically partnership) legal form adopted is one of the more visible aspects of firm organisation. Yet, we know relatively little about the organisational and ownership structures across national jurisdictions, or how these partnerships actually operate. For example, what are the decision rights related to being a partner, what are the actual practices of inclusion and exclusion, and how do these vary? In some countries, audit firms have been subsidiaries of other financial service corporations such as banks. Others adopted a limited liability form in the late 1990s but we do not know how such changes have affected controls and behaviour within the firm.

The legal form of firms is a visible aspect of their organisation, but firm histories tell us little even about the organisational and ownership structures across national jurisdictions. What are their practices of co-ordination and control within the context of their claims about global reach? It is now taken for granted that Arthur Andersen tried to operate with a global, 'one-firm' philosophy, whereas KPMG, for example, seemed to prefer operating a looser coalition of heterogeneous partnerships (Greenwood *et al.* 1999; White 2003: 113), but the histories are silent on the degree to which these organisational rhetorics were matched by practical differences in organisation and control.

The partnership model would suggest that compensation for equity partners would reflect a profit-sharing arrangement (although firms historically have appointed some partners to salaried positions). Firm histories have little to say about governance, performance and compensation mechanisms. In studies where the economic motive of firms is often taken as the explanation for actions, it is disappointing that little attention has been given to the firms' management control practices and the implications of these mechanisms for behaviour. The work of Covaleski, Dirsmith and their associates (Dirsmith and Covaleski 1985; Dirsmith *et al.* 1997; Covaleski *et al.* 1998) in the USA, and Anderson-Gough *et al.* (1998, 2002, 2005, 2006; Grey 1998) in the UK have tried to address the career progression process within firms and their implications for the construction of professional identities within firms, but much more from a historical viewpoint could be done. One recent announcement by the 'CEOs of the international audit networks' suggested that in response to past 'errors' the firms 'have changed, putting much greater emphasis on audit quality in all of our work and in our compensation systems' (2006: 7). This statement suggests that, at least in part, they accept that the audit failures of the early twenty-first century are connected to the consequences of compensation and management methods within the firms. It is also clear that the split of Andersen Consulting (now Accenture) from Arthur Andersen was tied to conflicts over compensation mechanisms (Squires *et al.* 2003). Yet there exists little systematic historical study of firms' organisational controls, governance and compensation practices.

Other aspects of the firms as managed entities would include their role as sites of identity formation – both organisational and professional. While the majority of firm histories extol the virtues of professionalism, debates about the commercialisation of accounting (and shifting historical and jurisdictional conceptions of professional and commercial) are an important discursive background to firm histories. Mitchell and Sikka (2004), Zeff (2003a, 2003b) and Wyatt (2004) claim that the commercialisation of the Big Four went too far and emphasise the importance of not relying on the claims of professional associations and firm leaders. Researchers would also be well advised to go beyond the dualistic debates about commercialisation and professionalism, and examine what it means for the practices of accountants to talk in terms of commercialisation, being businesslike, enterprising and modern (Hanlon 1996; Sikka and Willmott 1997). For example, it would be useful to examine whether claims to 'gentlemanly' and professional values might be a historically contingent strategy to be commercial. Appeals to such forms of social and cultural capital can be an effective strategy for accountants in developing their business and being profitable. Rather than reproducing a conception that commercialisation may be antithetical to professionalisation, studies of accounting and audit practices will benefit from examining the work practices and client relations of professional organisations (firms and associations).

Histories of the practice and experience of work

Firm histories indicate that in their founding years during the nineteenth century the principal concerns were insolvency practice and the struggle to establish legitimacy and professional status within the (British) establishment. They then tend to explore the growth of audit functions in terms of client demands and regulatory changes. Little of the scope of the modern audit firm has been analysed by such narratives, except for the more recent insider reports of the demise of

Arthur Andersen (Squires *et al.* 2003; Toffler 2003). These insider accounts emphasise the growth of non-audit services within Arthur Andersen during the 1990s and pressures on the firm's profit-sharing arrangements due to the comparative profitability of consulting. Some research has tried to explore the different experiences of professional training in different areas of work (Khalifa 2004), but such research is preliminary and has little historical dimension. One has to turn to novels (for example, W. Somerset Maugham (2002)) and a few sociological studies (Hanlon 1994; Montagna 1968, 1974) to obtain historical insight into the work practices of accounting firms.

In various studies, Hanlon (1994) discusses the implications of professionalisation for an analysis of power and the division of work in society. He suggests that many accountants are part of the service class, often occupied in marginalised activities which are threatened by automation and low wage competition. Furthermore, he argues that the accounting profession is segmented into a small elite, who act as the agents of capital and obtain very great rewards for their efforts, and the mass, comprising junior accountants, bookkeepers and others at the periphery (often women or new immigrants). The latter experience poor working conditions, for example, low pay, oppressive control systems, threats of automation and increasing part-time work (see also Cooper and Taylor 2000; Tinker and Koutsaumadi 1997). Hanlon's studies of human resource and work practices suggest that the internal dynamic of multinational accounting firms explains how the elitist values of accountants (gentlemanly, aristocratic and paternalistic) are transformed into the commercial values of the large professional firm, in which profitability and contribution to the growth of capital are dominant. The mass of junior accountants consent to their position to the extent that they aspire to join the partnership elite through internal promotion.

With one or two exceptions, the experience of work and the transformation in audit and other technologies are largely absent from historical studies of accounting firms. Matthews and Pirie's (2001) oral history of audit offer a valuable insight in this respect. The work of Dirsmith and associates (Carpenter and Dirsmith 1993; Dirsmith *et al.* 1997) has begun to consider the audit technologies and markets that firms develop as related to their activities as organisations and the contexts in which they are embedded. Other studies have begun to unpack the development of new audit techniques in ways that connect to the management of front line audit staff, as efforts to control audit costs and mediate the impact of regulatory requirements (Power 1992, 2000, 2003). Barrett *et al.* (2005) have analysed problems of co-ordination and how the interpretation of standards, regulations and work manuals vary within the same, but geographically dispersed, firm. More recently, Knechel (2007), Curtis and Turley (2007) and Robson *et al.* (2007) have begun to explore the development of business risk audit methodologies, and show that they reflect internal tensions in the development of 'professional service firms'. They do not merely serve or satisfy existing markets, but accounting firms attempt through their techniques to construct new markets, re-order regulatory space and control the work of juniors.

The development of audit techniques is thus intimately related to the management, organisation and expansion of the large firms. Further historical work might address in a focused way how and why firms develop particular techniques at particular points in time, rather than treating all technical innovations as technological inventions with no social and organizational implications. Power (1992) offers such a history of audit sampling, but much more can be done on other domains of accounting work, including the nature and focus of tax and management consulting.

Histories of firms as political and cultural actors

While it is clear that the better histories of firms do address the impact of regulations and the involvement of key individuals in advising on new regulation (Jones 1995: 102–4, 143–56), little has been written on the role of firms as political actors on the stage of accounting and auditing regulation. Of course, there is a literature that looks at the development and work of regulatory agencies, both governmental and non-governmental organisations (e.g. Zeff and Camfferman 2007; Chapter 14 of this volume), but our point is that the relays and linkages between the work of these bodies and the large audit firms are relatively unexplored as an aspect of the history of the Big Eight/Six/Four.

It is now scarcely possible to discuss seriously accounting regulations without considering the complex of alliances, agreements and accords that now exists between the big firms and agencies (such as the International Accounting Standards Board, the International Federation of Accountants, the Accounting Standards Board, the Financial Accounting Standards Board, the International Organization of Securities Commissions or the European Union) on various accounting and auditing matters, and how these agreements and alliances affect implementation in specific jurisdictions (Graham and Neu 2003; Robson *et al.* 2005). While the importance of accounting regulations in the internationalisation of markets and policy regimes is now almost a cliché, many studies at the international level tend to focus on one particular 'international' institution or standard. Much less attention is given to the polycentric, network or co-ordinated character of 'regulation work' and the complex of relations between accounting firms and national agencies (Caramanis 1999, 2002).

The Big Four firms are important in the establishment of policy, the staffing of these agencies and the enactment and enforcement of international regulations, yet little research has examined whether the relationships of the Big Firms to non-governmental organisations and government networks continue to be mediated through the national professional associations, or whether these bodies are now effectively by-passed by the Big Four (Suddaby *et al.* 2007). The work of accounting firms and associations, as well as 'non-accounting' institutions (such as the Organisation for Economic Co-operation and Development, the World Trade Organization, the World Bank, and the International Monetary Fund) in the cultural normalisation and transmission of accounting and auditing practices needs to be examined. Further, accounting historians can provide important insight into the changing roles that the large firms have played in staffing these bodies, lobbying and advising on company regulation, and informing judgements on free trade and the regulation of professional services. Graham and Neu (2003) show how accounting and accounting firms are central in World Bank attempts to reform educational systems in Central America. Arnold (2005) examines the World Trade Organization and negotiations over regulations on practice rights of accountants across national jurisdictions and indicates the influence that accounting firms have as political actors.

Studies of the relationships between, for example, big firm partners, former partners, regulators' professional firm backgrounds and professional association administrators would help to examine the 'social' or informal backdrop to relationships between firms and regulatory agencies (Anderson-Gough *et al.* 2005). Social network analyses (Burt 1992; Richardson 2006) or prosopographical approaches (Carnegie and Napier 1996) might help to further explore these interrelationships in the historical development of the firms and their burgeoning influence.

Aside from the direct political influences and effects of big firm activities, we know little about the influences of accounting firms on culture. For example, modern ways of thinking about the accountability and governance of all kinds of organisations (corporations, public sector, charities) are imbued with the accounting concepts and notions of audit that professional firms articulate and embed in social, political and cultural life. The very idea of organisational 'transparency' is seemingly inseparable from the production of financial statements. As Power notes (1997), the term audit has colonised all kinds of inspection and accountability practices that, although separate from traditional financial audit, are linked to the cultural influence and commercial activities of accounting firms. We are now accustomed to hearing of medical audit, efficiency audit, effectiveness audit, value-for-money audit, environmental audit, to name but a few, and it would be useful to understand the development of accounting firm service offerings in these areas. Although the character, methods, rationales and claims of these offerings may vary, financial audit is the model that has inspired the form of these administrative procedures and reforms (Pentland 2000). Many of the large accounting firms have been in the vanguard of consulting on these new audit technologies, and in so doing, important cognitive categories of everyday life (about accountability, transparency, responsibility, performance and management) have been shaped and transformed by them.

Moreover, the efforts of large firms to manage their environment and work may be subject to 'turf wars'. We know that the work domain of accountants *vis-à-vis* other occupations (such as lawyers, engineers, information analysts, actuaries and statisticians) varies according to national jurisdictions, yet the occupational and jurisdictional boundaries are never fixed. Dezalay and Garth show (2004) the big firms have engaged in disputes concerning accounting and legal activities, the role of the multi-disciplinary practice and the future organisation of and inter-relations between the legal and accounting professions. Such issues have also been touched upon in the work of Cooper *et al.* (1996, 2000), Greenwood *et al.* (2002), Suddaby and Greenwood (2006), Morgan *et al.* (2001), Morgan and Quack (2006) and Brock *et al.* (2007). Many of these issues remain relevant to contemporary activities of the large firms. Firm histor-ies have yet to address this very significant theme; the role of firms in defining their tasks, structure and regulatory environment in relation to other occupations. Further, the challenges of managing multi-disciplinary practices – of coordinating the work of professionals with quite different orientations, values and presuppositions have yet to be addressed, but doing so would add insight to a range of theories relating to, for example, occupational competition and identity. The activities and practices of the large firms as political and cultural actors could usefully gather much more attention from historians.

Conclusion

In this chapter we reviewed the histories of accounting firms and the key themes that emerge from them. Clearly some firms (Price Waterhouse, Ernst & Young), are better covered than others, and some have been served well by the scholarly celebrations offered by business historians. However, we find most firm histories somewhat 'Whiggish' in their perspectives and orientations. Much of the historical work on firms focuses on professional elites – those who founded or led the firms through important periods of expansion – and what they enabled. Events are constructed as the accomplishment of key individuals leading their organisations in response to the demands of clients and the market; firms are presented as serving both their clients and professional ideals.

Much of the 'work' of accounting firms seems to be confined to the expansion of audit activities and the regulation that it has supported. The array of services that firms offer seems to have merited little attention. Yet at the same time studies seem to have little to say about the everyday experience of work, confining their attention to the actions of the senior partners of the firm. The practices and technologies of work are relatively uncharted.

It is also worth stressing that most histories focus upon single firms, as if the story of each were independent and unique, despite the similarities of the underlying narratives. Few histories have attempted to address the organisational field of institutional activities in which firms practice or the common connections that exist in the audit field (Lounsbury 2008; Robson *et al.* 2007; Staubus 1996). Yet as the recent business risk audit phenomenon has shown, the adoption of similar technologies at the same time suggests that accounting firms are addressing a shared set of economic and institutional conditions.

Finally, we suggest that firm histories give more attention to the role of firms as actors in their field. Audit practices now extend beyond the accounting firms and their corporate clients (Power 1997), and the firms have actively sponsored developments in governments and the private sector (McSweeney 1994). They have been active in promoting new technologies of organisation, management and governance in the corporation, often through their consulting arms, and often in association with academics (Armstrong 2002; Jones and Dugdale 2002; Roberts and Bobek 2004; Roberts *et al.* 2003). The firms are significant cultural, economic and political actors, promoting and disseminating technologies of corporate and governmental performance across the globe. Accounting and accounting firms are seemingly everywhere. As we have argued, research will probably require access to firms' archives and their willingness to co-operate in studies that may question their own sense of identity. Yet it is time for historical research to catch up with the practice and influence of firms in ways that extend beyond individualist accounts of elite practitioners. Firm histories have the potential to address important theoretical issues of professionalisation, regulation and organisational management, and we encourage new studies that embrace multiple theoretical orientations.

Acknowledgements

Thanks to Stephen Walker, Chris Napier and Dick Edwards for their help and guidance, and to David Dolf for his excellent research assistance. David Cooper acknowledges the financial support of the Certified General Accountants of Alberta and the Social Science and Humanities Research Council.

Key works

Covaleski et al. (1998) is a seminal examination of management control and performance appraisal in large public accounting firms.

Jones (1995) is the pre-eminent firm history of its type: a business historian's study of the origins and growth of Price Waterhouse.

Sluyterman (1998) considers the dynamics of the internationalisation of audit firms.

Stevens (1991) is a journalistic study of the power and politics of the Big Six firms. Offers a type of analysis not found in official histories.

Walker (1993) provides an historical analysis of the emergence and development of a CA practice in Edinburgh.

Note

1   For example, one of the antecedent firms of PricewaterhouseCoopers, Price Waterhouse dates from Stanley Price's London firm founded 1849; Edwin Waterhouse and William Holyland joined in 1865. The other main component, Coopers & Lybrand, dates from William Cooper's London firm of 1854, and the firm of William Lybrand, Adam & Edward Ross, & Robert Montgomery, founded in 1898 in Philadelphia. William Deloitte founded his London firm in 1854 and the firm of Haskins & Sells dates from New York firm of Haskins founded in 1898. Ernst & Young dates from 1849 when Frederick Whinney joined the London firm of Harding & Pullein, later Whinney, Smith & Whinney after Whinney became a partner in 1857, and the Cleveland firm of Ernst & Ernst founded in Cleveland in 1903. Arthur Young's firm was established in Chicago in 1898. KPMG's antecedents include William Peat, who joined the London firm of Robert Fletcher (founded 1867) in 1870 and was made a partner in 1877, and James Marwick's Glasgow firm, established in 1887.

References

Allen, D. G. and McDermott, K. (1993) *Accounting for Success: A History of Price Waterhouse in America, 1890–1990* (Boston: Harvard Business School Press).

Anderson-Gough, F., Grey, C. and Robson, K. (1998) *Making Up Accountants: The Organizational and Professional Socialization of Trainee Chartered Accountants* (Aldershot: Ashgate Publishing).

Anderson-Gough, F., Grey, C. and Robson, K. (2000) In the name of the client: the service ethic in two professional services firms, *Human Relations*, 53 (9): 1151–74.

Anderson-Gough, F., Grey, C. and Robson, K. (2002) Accounting professionals and the accounting profession: linking conduct and context, *Accounting and Business Research*, 32 (1): 41–56.

Anderson-Gough, F., Grey, C. and Robson, K. (2005) 'Helping them to Forget . . .': the organizational embedding of gender relations in two large audit firms, *Accounting, Organizations and Society*, 30 (5): 468–90.

Anderson-Gough, F., Grey, C. and Robson, K. (2006) The networked professional, in R. Greenwood, and R. Suddaby (eds) *Professional Service Firms: Research in the Sociology of Organizations, 24*, pp. 403–31 (Oxford: Elsevier JAI).

Armstrong, P. (1987) The rise of accounting controls in British capitalist enterprises, *Accounting, Organizations and Society*, 12 (5): 415–36.

Armstrong, P. (2002) The cost of activity based costing, *Accounting, Organizations and Society*, 27 (1/2): 99–120.

Arnold, P. J. (2005) Disciplining domestic regulation: the World Trade Organization and the market for professional services, *Accounting, Organizations and Society*, 30 (4): 299–330.

Arthur Andersen (n.d.) *Responding to New Challenges* (Chicago: Arthur Andersen).

Barrett, M., Cooper, D. J. and Jamal, K. (2005) Globalization and the coordinating of work in multinational audits, *Accounting, Organizations and Society*, 30 (1): 1–24.

Benson, H. (1989) *Accounting for Life* (London: Kogan Page).

Boys, P. (1989) What's in a name – Firms' simplified family trees, *Accountancy*, 103–104 (various numbers).

Brock, D. M., Powell, M. J. and Hinings, C. R. (2007) Archetypal change and the professional service firm, in W. A. Passmore and R. W. Woodman (eds) *Research in Organizational Change and Development, 16*, pp. 221–51 (Oxford: Elsevier JAI).

Burchell, S., Clubb, C., Hopwood, A. G., Hughes, J. and Nahapiet, J. (1980) The roles of accounting in organizations and society, *Accounting, Organizations and Society*, 5 (1): 5–27.

Burrows, G. and Black, C. (1998) Profit sharing in Australian Big Six accounting firms: an exploratory study, *Accounting, Organizations and Society*, 23 (5/6): 517–30.

Burt, R. (1992) *Structural Holes* (Cambridge, MA: Harvard University Press).

Cairncross, A. (1937) The social origins of accountants, *Accountant*, 3276 (18 September).

Caramanis, C. V. (1999) International accounting firms versus indigenous auditors: intra- professional conflict in the Greek auditing profession 1990–1993, *Critical Perspectives on Accounting*, 10 (2): 153–96.

Caramanis, C. V. (2002) The interplay between professional groups, the state and supranational agents: Pax Americana in the age of 'globalisation', *Accounting, Organizations and Society*, 27 (4): 379–409.

Carnegie, G. and Napier, C. (1996) Critical and interpretive histories: insights into accounting's present and future through its past, *Accounting, Auditing & Accountability Journal*, 9 (3): 7–39.

Carpenter, B. and Dirsmith, M. (1993) Sampling and the abstraction of knowledge in the auditing profession: an extended institutional theory perspective, *Accounting, Organizations and Society*, 18 (1): 41–63.

Catchpowle, L. and Cooper, C. (1999) No escaping the financial: the economic referent in South Africa, *Critical Perspectives on Accounting*, 10 (6): 711–46.

CEOs of the International Audit Networks (2006) *Global Capital Markets and the Global Economy: A Vision from the CEOs of the International Audit Networks*, Global Public Policy Symposium III, Paris, 7–8 November.

Chandler, A. (1962) *Strategy and Structure: Chapters in the History of the Industrial Enterprise* (Cambridge, MA: MIT Press).

Chandler, A. (1965) *The Railroads: The Nation's First Big Business* (New York: Harcourt Brace and World).

Chernow, R. (1990) *The House of Morgan: An American Banking Dynasty and the Rise of Modern Finance* (New York: Simon and Schuster).

Cooper Brothers and Co (1986) *A History of Cooper Brothers and Co., 1854 to 1954* (New York: Garland Press).

Cooper, C. and Taylor, P. (2000) From Taylorism to Ms Taylor: the transformation of the accounting craft, *Accounting, Organizations and Society*, 25 (6): 555–78.

Cooper, D. J. and Robson, K. (2006) Accounting, professions and regulation: locating the sites of professionalization, *Accounting, Organizations and Society*, 31 (4/5): 415–44.

Cooper, D. J., Rose, T., Greeenwood, R. and Hinings, B. (2000) History and contingency in international accounting firms, in Y. Aharoni and L. Nachum (eds) *Globalization of Services: Some Implications for Theory and Practice*, pp. 93–125 (London: Routledge).

Cooper, D. J., Greenwood, R., Hinings, B. and Brown, J. L. (1998) Globalisation and nationalism in a multinational accounting firm: the case of opening new markets in Eastern Europe, *Accounting, Organizations and Society*, 23 (5/6): 531–48.

Cooper, D. J., Hinings, B., Greenwood, R. and Brown, J. L (1996) Sedimentation and transformation in organizational change: the case of Canadian law firms, *Organization Studies*, 17 (4): 623–47.

Coopers & Lybrand (1984) *The Early History of Coopers & Lybrand* (New York: Garland Publishing).

Covaleski, M. A., Dirsmith, M. W. and Rittenberg, L. (2003) Jurisdictional disputes over professional work: the institutionalization of the global knowledge expert, *Accounting, Organizations and Society*, 28 (4): 323–56.

Covaleski, M. A., Dirsmith, M. W., Heian, J. B. and Samuel, S. (1998) The calculated and the avowed: techniques of discipline and struggles over identity in Big Six public accounting firms, *Administrative Science Quarterly*, 43 (2): 293–327.

Curtis, E. and Turley S. (2007) The business risk audit: a longitudinal case study of an audit engagement, *Accounting, Organizations and Society*, 32 (4/5): 439–61.

Cypert, S. A. (1991) *Following the Money: The Inside Story of Accounting's First Mega-Merger* (New York: Amacom).

Daniels, P. W., Thrift, N. J. and Leyshon, A. (1989) Internationalization of professional producer services: accountancy conglomerates, in P. Enderwick (ed.) *Multi-national Services Firms*, pp. 79–106 (London: Routledge).

De Mond, C. W. (1980) *Price, Waterhouse & Company in America* (New York: Arno Press).

Dezalay, Y. and Garth, B. G. (2004) The confrontation between the Big Five and Big Law: turf battles and ethical debates as contests for professional credibility, *Law & Social Inquiry*, 29 (3): 615–38.

Dirsmith, M. W. and Covaleski, M. A. (1985) Informal communication, nonformal communications and mentoring in public accounting firms, *Accounting, Organizations and Society*, 10 (2): 149–69.

Dirsmith, M. W., Heian, J. B. and Covaleski, M. A. (1997) Structure and agency in an institutionalized setting: the application and social transformation of control in the Big Six, *Accounting, Organizations and Society*, 22 (1): 1–27.

293

Dobbin, F. and Dowd, T. J. (2000) The market that antitrust built: public policy, private coercion and railroad acquisitions, 1825 to 1922, *American Sociological Review*, 65 (5): 631–57.

Evans, L. (2003) Auditing and audit firms in Germany before 1931, *Accounting Historians Journal*, 30 (2): 29–65.

Falkus, M. (1993) *Called to Account. A History of Coopers and Lybrand in Australia* (St. Leonards, NSW: Allen & Unwin).

Fielding, A. and Portwood, D. (1980) Professions and the state: towards a typology of bureaucratic professions, *Sociological Review*, 28 (1): 23–53.

Gendron Y., Cooper, D. J. and Townley, B. (2007) The construction of auditing expertise in measuring government performance, *Accounting, Organizations and Society*, 32 (1/2): 101–29.

Gietzmann M. and Quick R. (1998) Capping auditor liability: the German experience, *Accounting, Organizations and Society*, 23 (1): 81–104.

Graham, C. and Neu, D. (2003) Accounting for globalization, *Accounting Forum*, 27 (4): 449–71.

Greenwood, R., Hinings, C. R. and Brown, J. (1990) P²-form of strategic management: corporate practices in professional partnerships, *Academy of Management Journal*, 33 (4): 725–55.

Greenwood, R., Suddaby, R. and Hinings, C.R. (2002) Theorizing change: the role of professional associations in the transformation of institutionalized fields, *Academy of Management Journal*, 45 (1): 58–80.

Greenwood, R., Rose, T., Hinings, C. R. and Cooper, D. J. (1999) The global management of professional services: the example of accounting, in S. R. Clegg, E. Ibarra-Colado and L. Bueno-Rodriguez (eds) *Global Management: Universal Theories and Local Realities*, pp. 265–96 (London: Sage Publications).

Grey, C. (1998) On being a professional in a 'big six' firm, *Accounting, Organizations and Society*, 23 (5/6): 569–87.

Habgood, W. (ed.) (1994) *Chartered Accountants in England and Wales: A Guide to Historical Records* (Manchester: Manchester University Press).

Hammond, T. (2002) *A White-Collar Profession: African American Certified Public Accountants since 1921* (Chapel Hill, NC: University of North Carolina Press).

Hanlon, G. (1994) *The Commercialization of Accountancy: Flexible Accumulation and the Transformation of the Service Class* (New York: St Martins Press).

Hanlon, G. (1996) 'Casino capitalism' and the rise of the 'commercialised' service class-an examination of the accountant, *Critical Perspectives on* Accounting, 7 (3): 339–63.

Howitt, H. (1966) *The History of The Institute of Chartered Accountants in England and Wales 1880–1965 and its Founder Bodies 1870–1880* (London: Heinemann).

Iyer, V. M. (1998) Characteristics of accounting firm alumni who benefit their former firm, *Accounting Horizons*, 12 (1): 18–30.

Jones, C. and Dugdale, D. (2002) The ABC bandwagon and the juggernaut of modernity, *Accounting, Organizations and Society*, 27 (1/2): 121–64.

Jones, E. (1981) *Accountancy and the British Economy, 1840–1980: The Evolution of Ernst & Whinney* (London: B. T. Batsford Ltd).

Jones, E. (1988) *The Memoirs of Edwin Waterhouse* (London: B. T. Batsford).

Jones, E. (1995) *True and Fair: A History of Price Waterhouse* (London: Hamish Hamilton).

Kettle, Sir R. (1957) *Deloitte and Co. 1845–1956* (Oxford: Oxford University Press).

Khalifa, R. (2004) 'Gendered divisions of expert labour: Professional specialisms in UK accountancy', unpublished PhD thesis, University of Manchester.

Knechel, W. R. (2007) The business risk audit: origins, obstacles and opportunities, *Accounting, Organizations and Society*, 32 (4/5): 383–408.

Lee, T.A. (ed.) (1997) *Shaping the Accountancy Profession: The Story of Three Scottish Pioneers* (New York: Garland).

Loft, A. (1986) Towards a critical understanding of accounting: the case of cost accounting in the UK, 1914–1925, *Accounting, Organizations and Society*, 11 (2): 137–60.

Lounsbury, M. (2008) Institutional rationality and practice variation: new directions in the institutional analysis of practice, *Accounting, Organizations and Society*, 33 (4/5): 349–61.

McGouldrick, P. (1968) *New England Textiles in the 19th Century: Profits and Investments* (Cambridge, MA: Harvard University Press).

McSweeney, B. (1994) Management by accounting, in A. G. Hopwood and P. Miller (eds) *Accounting as Social and Institutional Practice*, pp. 237–69 (Cambridge: Cambridge University Press).

Marshall, N. J. (1982) *Accounting for a Century: A History of the Antecedent Firms of Touche Ross & Co., Australia 1882–1982* (Australia: Touche Ross & Co).

Matthews D. and Pirie J. (2001) *The Auditors Talk: An Oral History of the Profession from the 1920's to the Present Day* (London: Routledge).

Maughan, W. S. (2002) *Of Human Bondage* (London: Vintage Classics).

Mitchell, A. and Sikka, P. (2004) Accountability of the accountancy bodies: the peculiarities of a British accountancy body, *British Accounting Review*, 36 (4): 395–414.

Montagna, P. (1968) Professionalization and bureaucratization in large professional organizations, *American Journal of Sociology*, 74 (2): 138–45.

Montagna, P. (1974) *Certified Public Accounting: A Sociological Analysis of a Profession in Change* (Houston, TX: Scholars Book Co).

Morgan, G. and Quack, S. (2006) The internationalization of professional service firms, in R. Greenwood, and R. Suddaby (eds) *Professional Service Firms: Research in the Sociology of Organizations, 24*, pp. 403–31 (Oxford: Elsevier JAI).

Morgan, G., Kristensen, P. H. and Whitley, R. (eds) (2001) *The Multinational Firm* (Oxford: Oxford University Press).

Pastra, Y. (2004) A descriptive theory of the big accounting firms, unpublished PhD thesis, Strathclyde University.

Pentland, B. (2000) Will auditors take over the world? Program, technique and the verification of everything, *Accounting, Organizations and Society*, 25 (3): 307–12.

Perrow, C. (2002) *Organizing America: Wealth, Power and the Origins of Corporate Capitalism* (Princeton, NJ: Princeton University Press).

Pollard, G. B. (1975) *A History of Price Waterhouse in Europe 1914–1969* (London: Price Waterhouse).

Pollard, S. (1965) *The Genesis of Modern Management* (Cambridge: Cambridge University Press).

Post, H., Wilderon, C. and Douma, S. (1998) Internationalization of Dutch accounting firms, *European Accounting Review*, 7 (4): 697–707.

Power, M. (1992) From common sense to expertise: the pre-history of audit sampling, *Accounting, Organizations and Society*, 17 (1): 37–62.

Power, M. (1997) *The Audit Society* (Oxford: Oxford University Press).

Power, M. (2000) *The Audit Implosion: Regulating Risk from the Inside* (London: ICAEW).

Power, M. (2003) Auditing and the production of legitimacy, *Accounting, Organizations and Society*, 28 (4): 379–94.

Previts, G. J. and Merino, B. D. (1998) *A History of Accountancy in the United States: The Cultural Significance of Accounting*, 2nd edn (Columbus, OH: Ohio State University Press).

Ramirez, C. (2001) Understanding social closure in its cultural context: accounting practitioners in France (1920–1939), *Accounting, Organizations and Society*, 26 (4/5): 391–418.

Ramirez, C. (2003) Constructing the governable small practitioner: the changing nature of professional bodies and the management of professional accountants' identities in the UK, Cahier de Recherche du Groupe HEC, Paris, no. 782/2003.

Richards, A. B. (1981) *Touche Ross & Co. 1899–1981* (London: Touche Ross).

Richards, G. E. (1950) *History of the Firm: The First Fifty Years, 1850–1900* (Price Waterhouse & Co: unpublished).

Richardson, A. (2006) Regulatory networks for accounting standards: a social network analysis of Canadian accounting standard-setting. Paper presented at the 8th Interdisciplinary Perspectives on Accounting Conference, Cardiff, 10–12 July.

Roberts, R. W. and Bobek, D. D. (2004) The politics of tax accounting in the United States: evidence from the Taxpayer Relief Act of 1997, *Accounting, Organizations and Society*, 29 (5/6): 565–90.

Roberts, R. W., Dwyer, P. D. and Sweeney, J. T. (2003) Political strategies used by the US public account-ing profession during auditor liability reform: the case of the Private Securities Litigation Reform, *Journal of Accounting and Public Policy*, 22 (5): 433–57.

Robson, K. and Cooper, D. J. (1990) Understanding the development of the accountancy profession in the UK, in D. J. Cooper and T. Hopper (eds) *Critical Accounts*, pp. 366–90 (London: Macmillan).

Robson, K., Humphrey, C., Khalifa, R. and Jones, J. (2007) Transforming audit technologies: business risk audit methodologies and the audit field, *Accounting, Organizations and Society*, 30 (1/2): 163–70.

Robson, K., Humphrey, C. and Loft, A. (2005) Globalizing technologies of performance: from national jurisdictional competition to co-ordinated network governance. Paper presented at the Governance without Government Conference, Cardiff, 11–13 May.

Robson, K., Willmott, H., Cooper, D. J. and Puxty, A. G. (1994) The ideology of professional regulation and the markets for accounting labour: three episodes in the recent history of the UK accountancy profession, *Accounting, Organizations and Society*, 19 (6): 527–53.

Sikka, P. and Willmott, H. (1997) On the commercialization of accountancy thesis, *Accounting, Organiza-tions and Society*, 22 (8): 831–42.

Sluyterman, K. A. (1998) The internationalisation of Dutch accounting firms, *Business History*, 40 (2): 1–21.

Spacek, L. (1985) *The Growth of Arthur Andersen and Company* (Chicago: Arthur Andersen and Company).

Squires, S. E., Smith, C. J., McDougall, L. and Yeack, W. R. (2003) *Inside Arthur Andersen: Shifting Values, Unexpected Consequences* (Upper Saddle River, NJ: Pearson Education/Financial Times Prentice Hall).

Staubus, G. J. (1996) *Economic Influences on the Development of Accounting Firms* (New York: Garland).

Stevens, M. (1981) *The Big Eight* (New York: Mcmillan Publishing Co).

Stevens, M. (1991) *The Big Six: The Selling Out of America's Top Accounting Firms* (Toronto: Simon and Schuster).

Suddaby, R. and Greenwood, R. (2006) Introduction, in R. Greenwood, and R. Suddaby (eds) *Professional Service Firms: Research in the Sociology of Organizations, 24*, pp. 1–16 (Oxford: Elsevier JAI).

Suddaby, R., Cooper, D. J. and Greenwood, R. (2007) Transnational regulation of professional services: governance dynamics of field level organizational change, *Accounting, Organizations and Society*, 32 (4/5): 333–62.

Tinker, T. and Koutsaumadi, A. (1997) A mind is a wonderful thing to waste: 'think like a commodity', become a CPA, *Accounting, Auditing & Accountability Journal*, 10 (3): 454–67.

Toffler, B. L. (with Reingold, J.) (2003) *Final Accounting: Ambition, Greed and the Fall of Arthur Andersen* (New York: Broadway Books).

Walker, S. P. (1988) *The Society of Accountants in Edinburgh 1854–1914: A Study of Recruitment to a New Profession* (New York: Garland).

Walker, S. P. (1993) Anatomy of a Scottish CA practice: Lindsay, Jamieson & Haldane 1818–1918, *Account-ing, Business & Financial History*, 3 (2), 127–54.

White, R. (2003) *Peats to KPMG: Gracious Family to Global Firm* (Wickford: Bradell Ltd).

Whitford, D. (1997) Arthur, Arthur . . ., *Fortune*, 10 November: 169–78.

Wise, T. A. (1982) *Peat, Marwick, Mitchell and Co. 85 Years* (New York: Peat, Marwick, Mitchell & Co).

Wootton, C. W., Wolk, C. M. and Normand, C. (2003) An historical perspective on mergers and acquisi-tions by major US accounting firms, *Accounting History*, 8 (1): 25–60.

Wyatt, A. (2004) Accounting professionalism: they just don't get it!, *Accounting Horizons*, 18 (1): 45–53.

Zeff, S. A. (2003a) How the U.S. accounting profession got where it is today: part 1, *Accounting Horizons*, 17 (3): 189–205.

Zeff, S. A. (2003b) How the U.S. accounting profession got where it is today: part II, *Accounting Horizons*, 17 (4): 267–86.

Zeff, S. A. and Camfferman, K. (2007) *Financial Reporting and Global Capital Markets: A History of the International Accounting Standards Committee, 1973–2000* (Oxford: Oxford University Press).

13

Education

Fiona Anderson-Gough

Overview

This chapter explores the history of education in relation to accounting, from medieval to recent times. The geographical context of England and Scotland provides the focal point of the review, but themes relevant to those researching the subject across the globe are identified. The chapter begins by exploring key themes and pedagogic practices during the pre–modern era of formal education. There the formative practices of licence and qualification, and open–ended knowledge systems are discerned, as are the spaces for alleged dichotomies between theory and practice, usefulness and subtlety, and academic and practitioner, which remain with us today. The discussion proceeds to consider works on the accounting profession in the modern age and the changes that ensue once accounting education *per se* has to find an institutional base, the pressures for an academic treatment of the subject gather momentum and accounting becomes increasingly widespread as a practice. The themes of examination form, content, location of study and relevance are used to review the relevant literature on the fragmented UK profession. Consideration is also given to what a more comprehensive history of accounting education might look like.

The boundaries of a history of accounting education

> [E]ducation, far from being subordinate, is superordinate; and . . . an understanding of education and *its* power is the only way to understand the genesis of disciplinarity and the subsequent apparently inexorable growth of disciplinarity's power.
>
> (Hoskin 1993: 272)

Histories of accounting education *per se* appear to be relatively few and far between. There is no paucity of historical information about accounting education but it is scattered across histories of education, societies, professional bodies and firms, and the literature on the professionalisation of accounting. The preparation of a comprehensive and comparative review of historical work on accounting and education, and accounting education more specifically is a challenging task. Important questions relate to what such a review should contain and why histories of accounting education are still uncommon.

It could be argued that this chapter cannot easily position itself as a full literature review of the history of accounting education *per se* because of the power–knowledge relations of accounting and education as knowledge disciplines. As implied in the quotation which introduces this section, education is often regarded as a secondary knowledge base and this in turn colours perceptions of the nature and purpose of accounting education. Education experienced a critical self-reflexivity through the lenses of Marxist, Foucauldian and gender theory critiques in the 1970s and beyond, demonstrating that it is itself a powerful knowledge base. Accounting too underwent a similarly reflexive turn in the late 1970s and 1980s drawing on similar theoretical insights. However, on the whole, accounting education has retained a secondary or subordinate position in relation to accounting. It seems that accounting education is often seen as simply following accounting, something which supports technicist and professional (academic and practitioner) agendas. It is rarely presented as a formative power shaping the conditions of possibility of accounting (Hoskin and Macve 1986) and the individual and collective professional subjectivities of accountants (Anderson-Gough 2002).

If it is accepted that modern accounting and education are powerful knowledge bases and disciplinary practices, then accounting education can be understood as a set of disciplinary practices. This means that a review of the history of accounting education is a foray into the intricacies of accounting and its power–knowledge relations, in other words, the intricacies of accounting and education in their broader social contexts.

Such an approach to a history of accounting education requires a starting point well before the nineteenth century when education emerges as an issue for the new accounting profession. Modern accounting and its education did not simply appear when professional organisation commenced during the 1850s. There are formative traces in wider educational practices long before in which accounting education is embroiled and which informed consideration of recruitment and qualification requirements of the emerging professional bodies. These educational issues need to be explored in order to understand the shaping of accounting education. Further, given that accounting work has been undertaken through the ages, recognition of the learning context of those learning calculative functions over time is required.

A variety of theoretical foci exists for those interested in education, especially professional education, in historical and modern-day contexts. Indeed, knowledge/education has been at the centre of work on the professions since sociologists began to explore the phenomenon. Trait theorists identify an abstract body of knowledge, formal education and the testing of competence as key characteristics of a true professional status. Critical theorists of professions examine the role of education and qualifications, and education as ideology, in the pursuit of social closure and occupational dominance (see also Chapter 11). Symbolic interactionists look at the behaviours required to survive socialisation experiences. These diverse approaches ensure that future comprehensive histories of accounting education must draw on a broad literature.

The theoretical focus in this chapter is informed by the work of Hoskin (1981, 1986, 1993) and Hoskin and Macve (1986, 1988). Their superordinate view of education recognises the importance of understanding the formative aspects of the learning context and experience from which, and within which, expertise in calculative functions has developed over time. Hence, the first part of the chapter on early accounting education utilises a number of works from the history of education more generally. The second part on modern accounting education draws on the findings of research on the professionalisation of accounting and histories of accounting education. Many of these works draw on standard histories of the profession such as Stacey (1954) and Howitt (1966) which are not reviewed in detail here. This chapter focuses on developments in England and Scotland but it is hoped that the broader thematic perspective will be of interest to those working within and across other geographical contexts. For the reasons above, the chapter does not claim to offer a comprehensive review of the history of accounting education. Given the current state of historical knowledge, it is more appropriate to perceive this chapter as a review of work-in-progress.

Early accounting education

Long before the modern professions were created, the activity of keeping accounts was performed by those educated and trained within the institutions of religion, monarchy and empire in order to carry out the administrative duties of those institutions. In early medieval England, the Church was the source of literary education and educational practices. Ensuring there were sufficient clerics schooled in Latin to perform the everyday administrative and ecclesiastical work of the Church was central to its success and survival. Consequently administrative expertise was shaped through the learning experiences of those who attended cathedral schools (such as Canterbury, Rochester, London, York and Winchester) which were established in the late sixth and early seventh centuries (Curtis 1963: 685). At this time there was no vernacular literary language and so, in Western Europe, writing was in Latin (except where it was in Greek). Thus, although local fee-paying boys were taught Latin, the experience of the written, calculative and oral techniques that contemporary administration required was limited to a relatively exclusive body of men.

The practice of licensing, whereby laymen were allowed to teach when licensed by the Church, enabled the development of grammar schools across England. This growth in schooling, and engagement with methods of writing and calculation, is seen as fundamental to sustaining the 'sophisticated machinery of royal administration' which was 'dependent on the use of written documents' (Lawson and Silver 1973: 25). The rise of the university offered a further strengthening of the administrative elite. Famous schools, as in Paris and Bologna became permanent self-governing communities (universities) after 1150 (ibid.: 19). Oxford effectively gained its first charter in 1214 and Cambridge became a university shortly after. The *magistri* (university graduates) were much sought after and dominated the ecclesiastical hierarchy until the early sixteenth century. Both ecclesiastical and secular administration was 'largely in the hands of an intellectual and managerial elite of graduate clerics, rigorously trained in arts and often in law or theology' (ibid.: 30–1).

Early university education directs Hoskin's early work, particularly his thesis which proposes a theory of professionalisation 'as something produced out of examination around 1200' (1986: 2). A formal practice of examination, involving at first a new reading and writing of texts, developed in the elite schools of France and Italy during the twelfth century. There was a new critical reading of such texts, known as *lectio* or *inquisitio* and the formal posing and answering of questions by students in these schools, namely a *quaestio* or *disputatio*, which was derived from ancient rhetorical educational practices. From these new practices formal bodies of esoteric knowledge were developed (particularly in the arts of grammar, logic and rhetoric and in fields such as theology and law). These bodies became known as *disciplinae* (Evans 1981, quoted in Hoskin 1986), and the sense of discipline extended to the practice of making students learn *and* demonstrate the degree to which they had successfully learned that body of knowledge. That practice also became formally known as examination, and the idea emerged that passing a rigorous form of examination was the test by which a student may take the step up in degree (*gradus*) from apprentice learner to 'master'.

Such educational practices were carried down to professional education and training systems in the modern age. For Hoskin:

> Professionalism, even today, in fields as different as law, medicine, teaching, accounting and engineering, follows the parameters of the medieval *disciplina*: it requires ideally (i) the critical reading and knowing of a whole defined corpus of received texts – the *lectio* process, (ii) the posing of proper questions on the basis of this knowledge, plus the ability to answer them – *quaestio/disputatio* and (iii) the ability to pronounce in speaking and/or writing the authoritative word in the style thus learned.
>
> (1986: 4)

The commitment to studying an abstract field of knowledge as part of one's training and the incentive of the credential for those who pass required examinations were also inherited from this period. An early manifestation of the 'service ideal' was also apparent in contemporary debates over whether graduates of the new institutions who wished to teach could/should charge fees for imparting 'God's knowledge' (ibid.: 2). Hoskin also traces the modern professional entitlement to practice on the basis of qualification *and* licence (which permits a professional or disciplinary rather than narrowly geographical right to practice) to developments in the thirteenth century. The shifting of licensing power to learned/expert bodies (rather then religious bodies *per se*) came to include professions such as accountancy in later years. Hence, pedagogical elements were crucial in establishing the modern forms of profession, particularly once engagement with knowledge itself shifted to an open-ended system of disciplinary knowledge from the late eighteenth century (Hoskin 1993).

Also important to a comprehension of later developments in accounting education was the manner in which the content of education increasingly became contested. The grammar schools, which became feeder schools for the universities, and the universities themselves, based their education on the notion of the seven liberal arts. Education was seen as consisting of the *Trivium* which comprised grammar, logic, and rhetoric, and, for students going beyond this, arithmetic, astronomy, geometry and music. During this early period, tensions between what we would understand today as vocational education and classical education did not arise. In fact the liberal arts were understood to relate to the world of work in that:

> the early universities did not aim to provide general academic culture for a social elite; they were centres of professional training – equipping men for careers as teachers, preachers, civil and canon lawyers, officials and administrators. Nor did they exist to pursue knowledge for its own sake or to prosecute research in any modern sense.
>
> (Lawson and Silver 1973: 31)

However, tensions around the notion of utility did arise. Those teaching the *ars dictaminis*,[1] the art of prose composition, claimed the superiority of their subject because of its practical applications (Clanchy 1975: 686). Indeed, the contest between the use and truth of 'ancients' *versus* the 'moderns' featured in the twelfth century (Clanchy 1975: 679). Even though largely artificial, the central distinction between expertises was identified as one of *subtilitas* or *utilitas* (subtlety or usefulness). As Clanchy (ibid.: 679) points out 'Subtle men, trained to think ingeniously in the schools, could prove useful in worldly affairs.' Indeed, this point could be well heeded in any study of education such that the complex and unpredictable value of formal teaching and learning is not falsely understood through simplistic models of knowledge transfer.

The difficulty of learning the alphanumeric techniques of administrative and organisational practice helped impart an elite status on such work during the medieval age. Hoskin (1981: 20), discussing Murray (1978), states in relation to changes in medieval mathematics 'We move from a pre-Arabic world where mathematical pioneers like Richer, Abbo of Fleury, Bernelius and Gerbert of Aurillac speak of the "sweat", "tears" and "almost impossible" toil of mathematical reckoning.' By the middle of the thirteenth century, the *ars dictaminis* was central to teaching in law schools (Clanchy 1975: 686) and there is circumstantial evidence that a law and business school, based on a modified Bologna model, was in place at Oxford by the time of King John's reign (see ibid.: 686). By the mid-thirteenth century, facilitated by, among other things, the growth of the *ars dictaminis*, the practices of writing, re-writing and ordering were spreading, making double-entry bookkeeping a popular practice in Italy (see Chapter 5).

The value of a basic education subsequently gained wider popularity and methods for learning developed which permitted the engagement of more students of differing levels of ability. During the sixteenth and seventeenth centuries, instruction in accounting was considered of value for those intending to pursue an apprenticeship (rather than university), particularly in commercial occupations and for the less wealthy classes (Curtis 1963: 91; Hunt, 1996). There is evidence which indicates that bookkeeping/casting accounts was taught in English schools.

In relation to St Olave's School in 1561, Curtis (1963: 103) quotes the churchwardens as saying:

> We have a great number of poor people in our parish who are not able to keep their children at grammar. But we are desirous to have them taught the principles of Christian religion and to write, read and cast accounts and so to put them forth to prentice.

In fact, Curtis notes a number of other instances of the teaching of accounts:

> Bungay, Suffolk, 1592. The schoolmaster and scholars to keep school every Saturday and every half-holiday until 3pm 'for writing and casting accounts with the pen and counters according to their capacities'.
>
> Stainmore, Westmorland, 1594. Instruction of children in reading, writing and accounts.
>
> Wellingborough, Northampton, 1596. Master and usher to teach Latin, and also reading, writing and accounts.
>
> Aldenham, Herts, 1599. The usher to teach English, writing, ciphering, and accounts.
>
> (ibid.: 91–2)

Rather than being exclusive to the training of the administrative elite, accounting is here linked to elementary reading and writing. While accounting was a useful addition to the education of 'noblemen and gentlemen' (James Boevey in 1670, cited in Lawson and Silver 1973: 173), this positioning locates accounting learning and knowledge in schools, apprenticeships, businesses and families. Indeed, the multilateral and technical private academies which developed from the end of the seventeenth century covered commercially relevant subjects, and the Soho Academy (*c.* 1690) appears to be the earliest multilateral academy to include merchant's accounts in its curriculum (Hans 1951: 69).

The teaching of accounting was also potentially encouraged by increasing dissatisfaction with the content of the grammar school and university curriculum from the late seventeenth century, particularly among the mercantile classes. Whereas early university education was vocational in that it developed out of a demand for those fluent in Latin, it offered less vocational relevance as the use of accounting knowledge extended beyond the administrative and governmental arenas to the commercial. The neglect of mathematics, science and technology in the classical teaching programme was deemed detrimental to the economic and technological progress of England (Lawson and Silver 1973: 195) and this became an issue of much importance during industrialism. The growth of printed media and instructional works on accounting also facilitated learning practice in institutions and beyond (see Chapter 5; Hunt 1996). Connor (2004: 28–9) has observed that 40 didactic texts on accounting appeared from 1630 to 1649 as did 80 from 1730 to 1749. Moreover, 'by 1700 people from all points of the social scale were accounting with facility' (also Yamey *et al.* 1963). Indeed, printing enabled data-based scientific activity which generated new understandings of accuracy and truth (e.g. Eisenstein 1979) which were to shape possibilities for accounting itself.

The perceived irrelevance of the content of the university curriculum, the institutionalisation of accounting teaching in schools, instruction through apprenticeships and the opportunities for private study thus opened the possibility of various sites of learning, some deemed more vocationally relevant and successful than others.[2] This provides a backdrop to the later emergence of issues about the site of 'real learning' for the professional accountant.

The educational context of the emergent accounting profession

So, by the nineteenth century there exists a set of educational practices and possibilities within which the emergent professional bodies in accounting must work. Accounting may have once been associated with elite administration but now had a socially dubious association with trade and therefore did not attract those with elite educational experiences. The university, once viewed as a site of expertise in producing experts generally, now offered learning of limited vocational relevance. There were other pedagogical developments from the mid-eighteenth century which were to be significant to education including accounting education. The human will to detail, which is at the heart of a new disciplinarity, emerges through new forms of grading and examining (in its broadest sense) and in this way the disciplinary system was opened up, allowing space for new knowledge bases to develop and gain expertise status (Hoskin 1993).

Scotland and England were sites of contestation over the best way to teach, learn and be an expert. The elite universities in England were dominated by a model of student matriculation followed by immediate specialisation, in Classics, for example. Scotland was embroiled in a battle over 'educational anglicisation' which went right to the heart of battles for democracy and national identity (Davie 1961). The traditional reliance in Scottish universities on oral methods of examination for judging ability were in direct competition with new quantitative methods of examining (through writing and grading) which were increasingly (through their detail and 'objectivity') postulated as superior methods. However, the relation between written and oral examination within 'the class' suggests there is no easy resistance to disciplinarity here (Hoskin 1993).

The practice of undertaking vocational learning outside the school and university was becoming established with the growth of scientific and voluntary associations and institutes devoted to learning about contemporary knowledge. This trend continued into the nineteenth and early twentieth centuries (Morris 1993). The apprenticeship model also sited vocationally relevant learning beyond the classroom. Mass education was also extended during the nineteenth century. In England, a national compulsory schooling system was established during the 1870s (earlier in Scotland) and a variety of school examining bodies established public examinations in elementary bookkeeping in the years following this. It was in the midst of all these disciplinary developments that the early accountancy profession was created. Issues concerning the form of education and qualification, sites of learning, and the value of theory *v.* practice (relevance of curriculum) confronted the accountancy bodies which emerged in the mid and late nineteenth century and, remain key issues today.

Modern accounting education – professionalisation and the growth of accounting knowledge

Accountants (or similar occupational descriptions) appear in trade directories from the late eighteenth century (Matthews *et al.* 1998). The numbers occupied in the areas of bookkeeping, insolvency, and audit and accounts preparation expanded greatly during the nineteenth century. It is difficult to generalise about the education and training of new entrants to accounting work prior to the formation of the professional organisations as the term 'accountant' was used to describe those performing a wide variety of functions (Walker 2002; Edwards and Walker 2007). Likewise, a concise review of the history of issues relating to professional accounting education from 1850 is made difficult by the fragmented organisation of the profession in Britain. Consequently the discussion presented here is illustrative rather than comprehensive.

Works on the early accounting profession reveal *inter alia* interest in the establishment of the first examinations and the form of the examinations; the content of examinations; links to higher education; and the perceived relevance of examinations to practice. This section is organised around these themes.

The first organisations of professional accountants in Britain were formed in educationally tumultuous Scotland. The predecessor organisations of the Institute of Chartered Accountants of Scotland (ICAS) were established in Edinburgh and Glasgow in 1853 and in Aberdeen in 1866. Historical insights to Scottish accounting education have been rigorously analysed within broader contextualised studies of professionalisation (Walker 1988; Kedslie 1990). Walker (1988) presents a detailed exposition of professional education and training requirements as part of his systematic analysis of the first 60 years of the Society of Accountants in Edinburgh (SAE) and the process of recruitment to that body. He stresses that Edinburgh accountants were different to other fledgling professional accountants due to their close association with local lawyers. Drawing on Davie (1961), we can see that this association linked Edinburgh accountants to the pedagogic practices of the legal profession who were embroiled in disputes about the nature of Scottish education and issues such as matriculation, specialisation and the study of philosophy as the founding and connective base of other subject studies.

Form and content of professional bodies' examinations

Walker (1988: 21) argues that formal examining was not initially a key concern of the SAE. The original members of this body tended to be from professional families, would have had a good secondary schooling and were instructed in the expert practices (the teaching, learning and working practices) of the esteemed profession of law. Some 53 per cent of them also attended university classes (mainly in law), and the notion of learning through an apprenticeship was well established (*A History of the Chartered Accountants of Scotland* 1954: Chap. 7). Walker points out, however, that the lawyers (with their background in examination) quickly criticised the lack of any formal test of knowledge in the constitution of the SAE in 1853. This criticism was addressed in 1855 by the introduction of an oral examination at the end of the period of indenture and this emulated the practices of the lawyers at the time. While we can characterise these accounting professionals as 'pre-industrial' in one sense (Walker 1988: 13), we can also understand how these learning and examining practices were of a changing time and characteristic of, and formative to, how these men understood the nature of expertise and sought to signal it.

The shift to written examinations for Scottish accountants came (not surprisingly perhaps given the prevailing educational turmoil) later in the century. In the 1890s, the local organisations of professional accountants in Scotland unified their examination arrangements (Shackleton 1995) and final examinations came to consist of written papers with no formal oral component. In 1873, the SAE had adopted the increasingly popular three-stage examination consisting of a preliminary, intermediate and final examination (standing at odds to some degrees with the national fight against models of matriculation). The Aberdeen society also moved to a more formal system of examination in 1889 (Kedslie 1990: 211). Walker (1988) suggests that the decision to adopt preliminary tests centred around relative reputation *vis-à-vis* other developing professions, and middle-class parental pressure for high status career destinations for the increasing number of middle-class boys schooled for the professions but unable to gain places in the overstocked older professions. While the SAE may have been initially prodded into considering the role of written examinations by the fact that other new (lower status) professions were doing so (Walker 1988: 139), a wider disciplinary analysis points to the need to also understand why these other bodies themselves were considering the use of written examinations and how this contest over pedagogic practice entwined the professional bodies (in terms of acceptance and resistance). A broader focus on educational history and its power–knowledge practices may indeed assist such endeavours.

In England and Wales, the adoption of the written examination was a clear feature of professionalisation strategy. The predecessor organisations of the Institute of Chartered Accountants in England and Wales (ICAEW), which were formed in the 1870s, merged and acquired a Royal Charter in 1880. The ICAEW immediately perceived the institution of a comprehensive system of education and training as central to its efforts to distinguish the chartered from the non-chartered accountant and it set its first written exams in 1882 (Anderson *et al.* 2005). These too followed the three-stage form adopted by the Scottish profession and from then on passing the examinations and completing a five-year (or three-year for graduates) period of apprenticeship or articles became the norm for the education and training of the chartered accountant.

The Association of Chartered Certified Accountants (ACCA) differed somewhat in its use of examinations. This body was formed in 1938 on the merger of the Corporation of Accountants (formed in 1891) and the London Association of Accountants (LAA) (formed in 1904). The ACCA ostensibly used the written examination in a manner aligned with its open access policy. Stafford (2002) offers a history of the educational practices of the ACCA. Her detailed focus on education and discipline, with due recognition of the broader educational context, facilitates a connected analysis of educational practice through four eras of strategic development. Stafford concludes that the ACCA's education strategy was key to its professionalisation project and the identity construction of its members. The predecessor bodies of the ACCA were fundamentally concerned with providing the benefits of professional status to those denied access to the older elite institutes. Those individuals who were unable to afford the premium required for articles were given an opportunity to study for a professional qualification otherwise denied them. The provision of this opportunity was eagerly taken up in the context of the spread of mass education and the growing number of individuals who had studied commercial subjects. The LAA established written examinations in 1906 but these were not compulsory until 1920. In this way, the LAA was less exclusionary in its mode of assessment and changed its position when the written form of assessment had become commonplace in Britain.

Content

Summaries of the syllabi of professional bodies in Britain can be found in a number of sources already referred to (Banyard 1985; Walker 1988; Kedslie 1990; Geddes 1995; Stafford 2002; Anderson *et al.* 2005). These also act as useful references to the professional and governmental reviews which contributed to the shaping of educational provision, and to the various crises surrounding pass rates which accompanied the shift towards increasing reliance on examinations within the qualification process.

Most writers allude to the changing ways in which specialisation has been assessed. When the older accountancy bodies moved to three-stage examinations, the preliminary exam was a test of general competence. Specialist occupational knowledge was tested later in the examination stream. Jurisdictional shifts (see Abbott 1988) and the emergence of new specialisms were variously reflected in curricula over time. There was a shift away from an early heavy presence of law in the syllabi to the inclusion of tax and costing. This move occurred within the ICAEW after a review of the syllabus in 1944 (Howitt 1966: 105). However, at the ACCA, the desire to appeal to a broad range of recruits and the pursuit of educational innovation ensured that these subjects were included from 1917. The ACCA monitored its appeal for 'business relevance' systematically from the 1960s and the ICAEW was to follow this in later years. Syllabi also changed from the 1970s onwards to include subjects such as economics, systems and data processing and financial decision-making. These changes reflected technological advance, the changing nature of accounting work and shifts in academic accounting.

Sector-relevant qualifications were always at the heart of the two main professional bodies in Britain yet to be mentioned here. The Chartered Institute of Public Finance and Accountancy (founded as the Corporate Treasurers and Accountants Institute in 1885), and the Chartered Institute of Management Accountants (CIMA) (founded as the Institute of Cost and Works Accountants in 1919). These organisations were formed during the same era as the other professional bodies and were obliged to play by the same power–knowledge, or disciplinary rules.

They were identified with more specific work jurisdictions than the chartered institutes and the ACCA. Their same capture by, and capture of, examination did not, however, always lead to a clear-cut relation between education and work jurisdiction in the years to follow. Armstrong and Jones (1992) provide a study of the changing qualification requirements of CIMA within a framework which reminds us that the syllabus and examination are tools of professional identity and professionalisation as opposed to simple functionalist attributes. Just as the ICAEW and ACCA used entry requirements and syllabus content to shape reputation and to close down and open up work jurisdictions, CIMA has altered its syllabus in response to issues concerning relative status and perceived career opportunities.

In its earliest (three-tier) examinations, which were developed between 1920 and 1924, CIMA's predecessor body required examinations to be passed in two different disciplines (Banyard 1985: 8) namely: (1) costing – accounting and (2) 'workshop knowledge' and 'general business methods'. Knowledge of the latter would have been deemed appropriate for engineers. As Armstrong and Jones (1992: 65) observe, the importance of process knowledge for costing and management accounting remained central for many years. Its presence was salient in the practical experience requirements of the institute until the mid-1980s. However, its presence in the examinations by this time was being eroded by an emphasis on long-range planning and financial management. These subjects, representing aspects of senior-level management work, were perceived as key indicators to potential members and clients, of the lucrative career paths and competence in advanced work which the Institute offered (Armstrong and Jones 1992).

Thus, the form and content of professional examinations (and study) have been shaped by the practices of other educational institutions and professions. It should also be noted that the need to comprehend the relevant educational and socio-economic contexts and strategic considerations are also important to understanding the history of examination structures in other countries. For those professional organisations operating within a colonial relationship, such as the British Empire, the models adopted in the metropolitan centre assume importance to developments in peripheral states, particularly where professional bodies seek to expand their international jurisdictions (Briston and Kedslie 1997; Annisette 2000).

Location of formal study

The precise role of examination and studying, and where it should take place, have a contested existence. In the USA, the fledgling profession turned to the universities for assistance in the learning and qualification aspect of professional expertise (see Van Wyhe 1994 for a concise review of accounting education in the USA). The value and acceptability of commercial education within the higher education sector were established in the USA by the 1880s. This was not the case in England. In Scotland, the universities were identified as useful suppliers of some of the relevant knowledge necessary for professional expertise. In 1866, the SAE required that all apprentices attend law classes at the University of Edinburgh. In 1926, attendance at university classes in accountancy became compulsory and in 1960–61 the 'academic year' was introduced (Solomons 1974: 17; Walker 1994).

Using Abbott's (1988) model of jurisdictional competition between professions, Geddes (1995) offers a comprehensive review of the ICAEW's education and training. She explains how provision came to be dominated by private tutor firms, and consequently how control of professional education was retained by practitioners. The ICAEW always regarded itself as an examining and not a teaching body (Howitt 1966: 201). Consequently, the manner in which its students acquired the examinable knowledge was left open. Unlike the tradition in Scotland where the professional bodies stipulated university classes and provided lectures at its own premises, the ICAEW provided no such tuition (at least not systematically). Articled clerks in England and Wales therefore had to rely on private sector tutors who offered correspondence courses. According to Geddes, the first company to be established for this purpose was H. Foulks Lynch and Co in 1884. Student pressure for taught sessions later grew and in 1949 Ronnie Anderson began pre-examination residential courses at Caer Rhun Hall in North Wales. Tutor firms were, and continue to be, staffed by practitioners and the focus of classes is to get students through their professional examinations.

The 'location' of the education shapes pedagogic practices, assumptions about knowledge and expertise and the profession's relation to its knowledge base (Power 1991; Anderson-Gough 2002). The structure of educational provision and the style of delivery shape the form of intellectual engagement with accounting. This varies according to the national context and the power relations within such structures. For example, the ICAEW has long had the controlling hand over the form and content of its examinations, and pedagogues from the tutor firms (and the universities) have traditionally had little say in this. Even within membership ranks, battles ensue over how the educational experience should be structured, with intra-professional differences such as 'large firm' and 'small firm' setting the battle lines.

As they expanded, accounting firms developed their own formal in-house training pro-grammes. In his history of Ernst & Young, Jones (1981: 241) notes that Whinney, Smith & Whinney began to offer these courses in 1960 and Whinney Murray appointed a full-time training manager in 1967. The courses provided by firms were generally designed to provide instruction in their own methodologies and update the technical knowledge of employees.

In considering how the learning of accounting has been located, the case of the ACCA is also worthy of note (Kedslie 1990; Stafford 2002). As mentioned above, in making membership possible for those unable to afford apprenticeship, the forerunners of the ACCA deemed it acceptable to receive training outside a practising accountancy firm. Likewise those taking examinations overseas were not required to sign to a British principal. In future years, the ACCA developed relationships with colleges and training firms and the possibility of periods of full-time study was also created (Stafford 2002: 229). Thus the ACCA took the separation of formal study and workplace learning even further than the other institutes. The global export of the ACCA qualification to the nationals of numerous British colonies, protectorates and mandated territories, effectively drew numerous groups into the British disciplinary field (Briston and Kedslie 1997; Annisette 2000).

It should also be recalled that accounting education also took place beyond the realm of the professional bodies. Bookkeeping examinations were offered by local examinations boards by the early twentieth century and accounting and bookkeeping classes were also provided in numerous other institutes and colleges, some of which later attained university status. In the late nineteenth century Liberal Feminists argued that bookkeeping was a suitable vocation for single women and bookkeeping classes were established at various schools and colleges, especially in London (Kirkham and Loft 1993; Walker 2003).

Relevance of the examination/curriculum/form of study

A key aspect of the process of becoming an expert, of becoming qualified, and being seen to be such, is the gaining of 'experience'. Hence apprenticeship became an essential component of the training of accountants. The combination of practical training and theoretical instruction has periodically aroused concerns about the relative roles of training office, classroom and examination. The question of whether a general or a specialist education should be provided also has a long lineage. For example, Walker (1988) and Kedslie (1990) cite articles in the professional press in the early 1890s which question the value and/or efficiency of contempor-ary examinations. The perceived difference between the role of 'education' and 'training' were played out over time and continue today as a source of the power–knowledge dynamic affect-ing decisions about course content and delivery, location of study, and the identity/background of examiners.

As examinations were increasingly seen as tests of the skills necessary to practise professional accounting, debates arose as to the best way to test those skills. Geddes' (1995) concise review of ICAEW educational policy provides some illustration of this. For example, she notes that the ICAEW council's policy statement on education and training in 1972 marked a shift from questions 'involving the ability to reproduce memorized facts' to those 'designed to test the ability to analyse, appraise and comment intelligently and clearly' (ibid.: 152). This policy statement also recognised the impossibility of achieving an easy relationship between examin-ation content and what accountants do on a daily basis because 'practical experience . . . varies widely' (ibid.: 154).

All professional bodies have faced similar dilemmas not only because work changes but because the relation of performance to competence is itself problematic (Anderson-Gough *et al.* forthcoming). Simplistic notions of transfer from one site of learning to another hinder pedagogical practice which looks to foster expert subjectivity across fields of learning. The accounting profession is not alone in struggling to grapple with understanding the formative possibilities of formal learning (Anderson–Gough 2002). There is perhaps though a particular irony in the case of this set of experts not recognising this formative potential. Accounting history research provides one of the most cogent descriptions of this formative element of formal education in the work of Hoskin and Macve (1986, 1988; see also Chapters 9 and 27 of this volume). The West Point graduates discussed in their work become a new type of expert, doubly-disciplined[3] and able to tackle the massive organisational problems of pioneering America because of the (unpredicted or unplanned) absorption of the doubly-disciplinary ways of being an expert. However this theoretical insight tends to be overlooked in interpretations and critiques of Hoskin and Macve's work, and the significance of formal education as formative in ways far beyond that captured by any simplistic model of knowledge transfer is seldom recognised (Anderson–Gough 2002). In this way, accounting history can be of great value in understanding the narrowness of assumptions about subordinate education.

The universities

National contexts set the conditions for the development of accounting in universities. As noted above, universities in Britain were slow to offer expertise in commercial subjects. The accountancy profession in the UK was not initially a 'graduate profession'. Indeed, Geddes (1995) notes that graduates accounted for less than 10 per cent of the annual intake of the profession before the Second World War. However, Matthews *et al.* (1998) argue that in the absence of commercial education in British universities, professional accountancy proved to be the best available qualification for senior positions in industry.

The education and training of qualified accountants follow the pattern of examining, credentialling and licensing practices that Hoskin (1986) identifies as central to the creation of the conditions of possibility for the modern profession. That is, we may observe the practices that originated in the early universities moving beyond that setting and into widespread use in organisations such as the accounting bodies who thereby established themselves as sites of 'learned' expertise (McMillan 1999). The development and widespread uptake of educational performance/behaviour evaluation technologies and norms enabled the creation of professional organisations with membership based on examined levels of ability. That this education did not take place in a university did not prevent accountants creating a professional identity and a market for their services. For the clients of these individuals and their firms, the credentialling and status of the accountancy bodies conferred the status of 'expert'. While the power–knowledge practice of credentialing and licensing was successfully employed in accountancy in England, its location outside of the universities has had a significant impact on: the nature of accounting education in universities, the character of the accounting profession, and the relation of practitioners to knowledge and their knowledge identity (Geddes 1995; Anderson–Gough 2002).

The presence of accounting as a subject in British universities can be traced to the turn of the twentieth century. However, accounting was taught in Italian and American universities before this. The teaching of modern accounting in Italian universities appears to have begun during the first half of the nineteenth century. In 1839, chairs in public accounting were established at Pavia and Padua (Zan 1994: 278). Accounting's place within Italian academia is quite different to that of the Anglo-Saxon tradition. Here accounting is one of a number of strands of the multidisciplinary and 'holistic' *Economia Aziendale* (ibid.: 288). Accounting education in American universities commenced in the 1880s and full professors of accounting were appointed at New York University in 1900 (Zeff 1997). Here, as later in Britain, accounting eventually became a university specialism in its own right (a specialism which advocates of the *Economia Aziendale* often regard as fragmented and insular).

The introduction of accounting to British universities is often associated with demands from the late nineteenth century for the provision of commercial education in order to address concerns about loss of industrial leadership and the fear that the country was falling behind in terms of the production of experts in science and technology. The lack of vocationally oriented education within the universities was seen as part of the problem. In England, the University of Birmingham established a Chair in Accounting in 1902, as did the London School of Economics in 1919 (Solomons 1974; Craner and Jones, 1995: 39). In Ireland, a full-time chair was established at the University of Galway in 1914 (Zeff 1997). In Scotland, a Chair of Accounting and Business Method was instituted at Edinburgh University in 1919 (Walker 1994).[4] These early accounting academics tended to retain close links with their practitioner backgrounds. Much of their teaching was on accounting components of commerce degrees.[5] Keeble (1984) suggests that these commerce degrees should be understood as precursors to business studies and the MBA in England rather than accounting degrees *per se*. However, as Geddes (1995) notes, the problems that bedevilled the commerce degrees can be usefully explored as they were to characterise the context of academic accounting too. Indeed, commerce failed to establish a jurisdictional base within English universities at this time[6]:

> Three major reasons can be identified as having contributed to the failure of the commerce degrees:
>
> i.   the strength of traditional patterns of education in England;
> ii. the attitude of the universities (particularly of Oxford and Cambridge) to commerce as an academic subject; and.
> iii. the attitude of employers and industry to graduate education in general and commerce in particular.
>
> (ibid.: 195)

Similarly, where chairs of accounting were established, their holders often encountered a degree of 'academic disdain' from the practitioners of more established disciplines including economics (Napier 1996; Walker 1994). The early practitioner academics in accounting were credentialled and licensed outside of the university, they were qualified in their field but their expertise was not that of the universities. Thus, the growth of university accounting education can be seen as the continuing story of the dynamic of the credentialling and licensing practice. The initial exporting of the practice of credentialling and licensing (as in accounting) beyond the university was one thing. People recognised the universities as the experts in expertise in general and were willing to see the qualification in general as a sign of expertise. However, trying to use this new knowledge identity to establish a different set of rules about the nature of expertise (one dominated by technique, by teaching not research) within the university was quite a different matter.

There was no easy 'home' for the subject and accounting was often subsumed within economics departments. Indeed, the disciplinary background of many of the early academic accountants was in economics and the authors on accounting conventions and accounting theory (especially in the USA) shaped the discussions of value and income that still resound today. This relationship with economics is important to understanding the character of accounting education, and to understanding accounting itself through educational practices. However, accounting itself was to become increasingly distanced from a very theoretical mathematically oriented economics (Sanderson 1972: 202). Solomons (1974) identifies the McNair Report (which instigated the Universities Scheme) as the source of a problematic relationship with economics. In Solomons' view, this scheme maintained accounting in a subordinate position within universities.

Another separation between expert groups – of the profession and the universities – persisted in the immediate post-war period. This was despite projects such as the Universities Scheme from 1945, which attracted a relatively small number of graduates (Geddes, 1995: 199). However, the Solomons Report (1974) marked a shift in this relationship. David Solomons was a key voice in accounting education at the time. In his inaugural lecture as Professor of Accounting at Bristol University in 1955, Solomons criticised attitudes towards education in the profession (Parker 1995). He later considered the recommendations contained in the report of the ICAEW's Parker Committee (1961) as disastrous and backward-looking. In 1972, Solomons was requested to undertake a comprehensive review of accounting education and training. The resultant report (Solomons 1974) is a useful source on the history of accounting education and for insights to contemporary pedagogical concerns. Solomons' main recommendation, for basic accounting-relevant education to be provided in universities or polytechnics (leading to a Diploma or degree), was, however, not taken up.

Following the Robbins Report on Higher Education of 1963, there was a considerable expansion of the university sector in Britain. This period was also to witness the growth of business schools and management departments in universities. Accounting education in the universities grew likewise. With the development of mass higher education an increasing proportion of recruits to the profession were graduates. In 2007, more than 40 per cent of current students of CIMA are graduates, as are more than 50 per cent of students of ACCA and CIPFA. In the chartered profession more than 80 per cent of the students of the ICAEW are graduates as are more than 90 per cent of ICAS and ICAI students. A significant proportion of these recruits have degrees in accounting and related 'relevant' subjects.

During the 1960s, the teaching of accounting in universities continued to be provided by a mix of accounting practitioners and specialist academics. Instruction continued to be orientated towards techniques and practice. As the 1970s and 1980s progressed, the development of a quite different approach to academic accounting developed. The labour shortage that accompanied the increased demand for accounting teaching (Nobes 1983: 78) resulted in more staff being recruited on the basis of a wider range of academic as opposed to purely accounting qualifications. This shaped the nature of accounting teaching and research in the UK and a more disciplinary diverse academic community was created. Research looking to challenge the image of accounting as simply a neutral and technical exercise developed apace. The impact of philosophical, sociological and psychological insights featured in accounting, and these characteristics have been suggested as akin to European accounting (Panozzo 1997). With an increasingly diverse mix of experts populating accounting academia, tensions and fragmenting tendencies surfaced, over issues such as theory *v.* practice and technical *v.* critical approaches.

While understandings of accounting were changing, and the mix of experts and expertise were changing, it is not so clear that accounting teaching was changing. The requirement to teach in technically segregated compartments which match areas of practitioner work (financial accounting and reporting, management accounting, auditing, cost management systems, taxation, etc.) has persisted. In consequence, earlier tensions between academic and practitioner relevance endure. The issue of connection and relevance across sites of learning is not automatically solved by simply increasing the influence of academics within the production of experts and expertise. This can be seen in the USA where accounting degrees are compulsory for membership of the profession but where problems of relevance and ethical competence still continue (Albrecht and Sack 2000).

Clearly the need for practical relevance and nurturing understandings within the world of the practitioner is a requirement of any university accounting syllabus. Subject segmentations which reflect areas of practice may be seen as the most obvious answer to this. However, such accommodation is attended by a concern that the syllabus would be tightly defined by accounting practitioners rather than academics. This has been a periodic source of resistance to increased collaboration between the accounting profession and academe over time and is manifested in a number of ways including shifting debates over professional accreditation requirements. Such resistance was less apparent, however, in the polytechnics. Established in 1968, this sector had a specific focus on commercial and vocational education. The polytechnics recruited large numbers of accounting staff and offered accounting courses tailored to the needs of the profession (Geddes 1995: 234). The ACCA was certainly keen to develop its relationship with the polytechnics for this reason. This sector became increasingly established as 'good' providers of technical education in accounting. The reputation of the ACCA, as linked to this higher education sector, was correspondingly enhanced (Stafford 2002). The association allowed the ACCA to more clearly distinguish itself from lesser accounting bodies and achieve a standing closer to the elite chartered institutes. The ICAEW stood aloof from developing relationships with the polytechnics. It wanted to emphasise its relation to the universities from which its recruits were increasingly drawn and demanded more exclusive content and timing arrangements which the polytechnics were not willing/able to meet (Geddes 1995: 234).

Despite the relatively late development of accounting in UK universities, it had clearly attained disciplinary status by the end of the twentieth century. This is particularly the case if we assume that: 'Disciplinarity is about the coherence of a set of otherwise disparate elements: objects of study, methods of analysis, scholars, students, journals, and grants' (Messer-Davidow *et al.* 1993: 3). Indeed, accounting education itself is now considered as a sub-discipline of accounting. A significant number of accounting academics in the UK and beyond identify accounting education as a research interest.[7] Three journals devoted to accounting education were established in the 1980s and 1990s.[8] In 1991, a special interest group in accounting education was established by the British Accounting Association. There is an international society with this focus and accounting education conferences take place. As Neimark wrote in 1996, accounting education, with all its problems and opportunities, 'just won't go away':

> In 1979, I attended the American Accounting Association's doctoral consortium in Honolulu, Hawaii and, at one of the roundtable meetings with a distinguished accounting faculty member, I had the temerity to ask a question about teaching. After the laughter subsided, the distinguished faculty member explained that what mattered for tenure and promotion was publication; he had nothing further to say about teaching . . . Since then, the subject of accounting education just won't go away. There have been committees and commissions, new accreditation standards, [and] a new journal from the AAA . . .
>
> (Neimark 1996: 1)

This quotation indicates a still commonplace reaction to expressions of interest in teaching among accounting academe operating in the context of the 'research imperative'. Such responses run the risk of alienating and suppressing those interested in this important aspect of the discipline. If we understand accounting as a knowledge discipline, with all that entails, it becomes apparent that teaching practices are part of the set of knowledge practices that are consequently brought to bear in research and accounting practice (Anderson-Gough 2002; Anderson-Gough and Hoskin forthcoming). To try to write out education from accounting's powerful status is at best misguided and at worst irresponsible.

Conclusion

Tracing the history of accounting reveals enduring contestations about the nature of the discipline, accounting expertise, and the specifics of 'relevance', the right to be called 'expert' and jurisdictional claims based thereon. Disputes over the value, and nature of accounting, and the emergence of dichotomies of abstraction v. specificity, theory v. practice, doing v. being and academic v. practitioner are commonalities through the history of accounting and accounting education, particularly in the modern age. These issues in turn are fuelled by the specific experiences, beliefs and practices of the periods in which they are rehearsed. Such contestations and the impact they have on the changing nature of accounting are shaped by accounting education just as accounting education is itself shaped by those contests. How accounting and accounting education looks, what it covers, who does it, where they do it and what status it has, have never been fixed. The field of accounting as a knowledge base has been dynamically shaped by academics, practitioners, clients, students, citizens, governments, regulatory bodies, economic institutions and the media.

Future research on the history of accounting education might usefully explore a number of themes. For those interested in the professionalisation process and education's role within that, better understandings of the nature of expertise in different times could be gleaned from (comparative) studies of the form, content and location of learning. Understanding how 'competence' was shaped and presented through learning and teaching within and across changing technical specialisations, interdisciplinary curricula and underpinning notions of ethical competence would add to developing understandings of how accounting education shapes expertise. Relatedly, while presentations of indeterminacy, mystique or judgement versus mundane ability have already been explored in some studies (Kirkham and Loft 1993), this would still appear to offer a fruitful line of inquiry for those interested in the jurisdictional competitions that accounting has faced and the role of education within the profession's responses. Similarly, a detailed review of presentations of 'theory' versus 'practice' over time and space would further reveal the dynamics of expertise and professional identity.

At the level of educational policy there is a danger that we might lose the benefits of a historical knowledge of past accounting education initiatives (Van Wyhe 1994: xi). A more detailed knowledge of how the content and techniques of accounting education have changed and been reviewed is likely to be of value both at the functional and the theoretical levels.

How one researches the history of accounting education will of course be shaped by one's understanding of education. Investigations into accounting education may be bounded by an understanding that the study of education should only contain the details of what occurs within the site of education. Or, as this chapter has suggested, one may understand education primarily as a powerful site of formative learning which shapes individual and collective expertise and identity in a myriad of ways: some predictable, others less so (if at all).

In order to understand the different ways that accounting education has, through the ages, been a site of complex formative effects upon people and practice, a connective approach to accounting education history may be particularly fruitful. A connective framing may look to map the total field of formative expert experience in order to understand the role education has played for different organisations during different eras. Seeking the effects of the combined forces of education site, training site and work experience on the nature of expertise is, however, a challenging task. Yet such connective research exploring the locations of learning and teaching might also generate greater insight to the ways education shapes technical management and accounting innovations (Hoskin and Macve 1986; Quattrone 2004).

Given the dearth of histories of accounting education *per se*, it seems fair to assert that, whether one's understanding is of education as subordinate or superordinate, much more historical investigation of education in accounting in various times and places would be welcome. It appears that older disciplines are much more comfortable at reflecting on their education histories than is the case in accounting and doing so in ways which incorporate such matters in contemporary education practice. The more we know about how accounting and accountants were made in the past through education and other social processes the more we also understand current contingencies and possibilities.

Acknowledgements

Thanks to Stephen Walker, Keith Hoskin and Dick Edwards for their comments and suggestions.

Key works

Armstrong and Jones (1992) offers a relatively brief review of the core disciplinary shifts in management accounting and an exploration of the relationship between education and jurisdictional knowledge.

Geddes (1995) is a comprehensive study of accounting education and training in England analysed (using Abbott's framework of jurisdictional competition) from the nineteenth century to the 1980s.

Hoskin and Macve (1986) is a comprehensive and theoretically informed review of medieval education practices and their relation to accounting.

Stafford (2002) presents a theorised study of the educational policies and practices of the ACCA from 1891 to 1998.

Van Wyhe (1994) provides a history of accounting education in the USA which focuses on the development of key pedagogic themes and tensions.

Notes

1 The *ars dictaminis* was a branch of rhetoric. As Clanchy (1993: 126) explains, 'Writing was distinguished from composition because putting a pen to parchment was an art in itself.'
2 See O'Day (2000) for the emergence of apprenticeship systems in the education of professionals.
3 'Doubly-disciplined' (Hoskin 1981, 1993) refers to the fact that individuals have gained knowledge of disciplinary subject areas (they know about the disciplines) *and* at the same time are themselves objects known through the practices of disciplinary teaching.
4 The number of professors did not increase substantially until the 1980s by which time most accounting departments had a chair (Groves and Perks, 1984). The first *full-time* chairs of accounting in Britain were appointed (at LSE and Birmingham) in 1947 (Parker 1995: 311). In Australia, the first chair of accounting was established at the University of Melbourne in 1954 (Carnegie and Williams 2001).

5 Birmingham introduced a commerce degree in 1900, Manchester, Liverpool and London did so in 1906 and Edinburgh in 1919 (Geddes 1995).
6 This also set the UK apart from the USA where, as Jones (1981: 119) notes, 'over 100 universities offered options in accountancy to over 3,500 students annually as early as 1914'.
7 Just over 10 per cent of UK accounting academics in the British Accounting Review's *Research Register* (2000) state accounting education as a research interest. Thanks to Dr Rhoda Brown for providing access to this data (Brown *et al.* 2007).
8 *Journal of Accounting Education* (1983), *Issues in Accounting Education* (1986) and *Accounting Education* (1992).

References

A History of the Chartered Accountants of Scotland: From the Earliest Times to 1954 (Edinburgh: ICAS).

Abbott, A. (1988) *The System of Professions: An Essay on the Division of Expert Labor* (Chicago: The University of Chicago Press).

Albrecht, W. S. and Sack, R. J. (2000) *Accounting Education, Charting the Course through a Perilous Future* (Sarasota, FL: American Accounting Association).

Anderson, M., Edwards J. R. and Chandler, R. A. (2005) Constructing the 'well qualified' chartered accountant in England and Wales, *Accounting Historians Journal*, 32 (2): 5–54.

Anderson-Gough, F. (2002) On becoming the new accounting expert: Between formal and informal learning, unpublished PhD thesis, University of Leeds.

Anderson-Gough, F. and Hoskin, K. (forthcoming) *'Specialisation Plus': The Key to Tomorrow's Profession Today?* (London: ICAEW).

Anderson-Gough, F., Hoskin, K. and Lucas, U. (forthcoming) *Between Workplace and Qualification: Engineering Integrative Learning* (London: ICAEW).

Annisette, M. (2000) Imperialism and the professions: the education and certification of accountants in Trinidad and Tobago, *Accounting, Organizations and Society*, 25 (7): 631–59.

Armstrong, P. and Jones, C. (1992) The decline of operational expertise in the knowledge-base of management accounting: an examination of some post-war trends in the qualifying requirements of the Chartered Institute of Management Accountants, *Management Accounting Research*, 3: 53–75.

Banyard, C. W. (1985) *The Institute of Cost and Management Accountants: A History* (London: Institute of Cost and Management Accountants).

Briston, R. J. and Kedslie, M. J. M. (1997) The internationalization of British professional accounting: the role of the examination reporting bodies, *Accounting, Business & Financial History*, 7 (2): 175–94.

Brown, R., Jones, M. and Steele, T. (2007) Still flickering at the margins of existence? Publishing patterns and themes in accounting and finance research over the last two decades, *British Accounting Review*, 39 (2): 125–51.

Carnegie, G. and Williams, B .G. (2001) The first professors of aaccounting in Australia, *Accounting History*, 6 (1): 103–15.

Clanchy, M. T. (1975) Moderni in education and government in England, *Speculum*, 50 (4): 671–88.

Clanchy, M. T. (1993) *From Memory to Written Record*, 2nd edn (Oxford: Blackwell).

Connor, R. (2004) *Women, Accounting and Narrative. Keeping Accounts in Eighteenth-Century England* (London: Routledge).

Craner, J. and Jones, R. (1995) *The First Fifty Years of the Professor of Accounting at the University of Birmingham* (Birmingham: The University of Birmingham).

Curtis, S. J. (1963) *History of Education in Great Britain* (London: University Tutorial Press Ltd).

Davie, G. (1961) *The Democratic Intellect: Scotland and her Universities in the Nineteenth Century* (Edinburgh: Edinburgh University Press).

Edwards, J. R. and Walker, S. P. (2007) Accountants in late nineteenth century Britain: a spatial, demographic and occupational profile, *Accounting and Business Research*, 37 (1): 63–89.

Eisenstein, E. (1979) *The Printing Press as an Agent of Change: Communications and Cultural transformations in Early-Modern Europe* (Cambridge: Cambridge University Press).

Evans, G. (1981) *Old Arts and New Theology* (Oxford: Clarendon Press).

Geddes, S. B. (1995) The development of accountancy education, training and research in England: A study of the relationships between professional education and training, academic education and research, and professional practice in English chartered accountancy, unpublished PhD thesis, University of Manchester.

Groves, R. E. V. and Perks, R. W. (1984) The teaching and researching of accounting in UK universities: a survey, *British Accounting Review*, 16 (4): 10–20.

Hans, N. (1951) *New Trends in Education in the Eighteenth Century* (London: Routledge & Kegan Paul).

Hoskin, K. (1981) The history of education and the history of writing, unpublished review, University of Warwick.

Hoskin, K. (1986) The professional in educational history, in J. Wilkes (ed.) *The Professional Teacher: Proceedings of the 1985 Annual Conference of the History of Education Society of Great Britain*, pp. 1–17 (London: History of Education Society).

Hoskin, K. (1993) Education and the genesis of disciplinarity: the unexpected reversal, in E. Messer-Davidow, D. R. Shumway and D. J. Sylvan (eds) *Knowledges: Historical and Critical Studies in Disciplinarity*, pp. 271–304 (Charlottesville, VA: The University Press of Virginia).

Hoskin, K. W. and Macve, R. H. (1986) Accounting and the examination: a genealogy of disciplinary power, *Accounting, Organizations and Society*, 11 (2): 105–36.

Hoskin, K. W. and Macve, R. H. (1988) The genesis of accountability: the West Point connections, *Accounting, Organizations and Society*, 13 (1): 37–73.

Howitt, H. (1966) *The History of the Institute of Chartered Accountants in England and Wales* (London: Heinemann).

Hunt, M. R. (1996) *The Middling Sort: Commerce, Gender, and the Family in England, 1680–1780* (Berkeley, CA: University of California Press).

Jones, E. (1981) *Accountancy and the British Economy 1840–1980: The Evolution of Ernst & Whinney* (London: B.T. Batsford Ltd).

Kedslie, M. J. M. (1990) *Firm Foundations: The Development of Professional Accounting in Scotland 1850–1900* (Hull: Hull University Press).

Keeble, S.P. (1984) University education and business management from the 1890s to the 1950s: A reluctant relationship, unpublished PhD thesis, London School of Economics and Political Science.

Kirkham, L. M. and Loft, A. (1993) Gender and the construction of the professional accountant, *Accounting, Organizations and Society*, 18 (6): 507–58.

Lawson, J. and Silver, H. (1973) *A Social History of Education in England* (London: Methuen & Co.).

McMillan, K. P. (1999) The Institute of Accounts: a community of the competent, *Accounting, Business & Financial History*, 9 (1): 7–28.

Matthews, D., Anderson, M. and Edwards, J. R. (1998) *The Priesthood of Industry: The Rise of the Professional Accountant in British Management* (Oxford: Oxford University Press).

Messer-Davidow, E., Shumway, D. R. and Sylvan, D. J. (1993) Disciplinary ways of knowing, in E. Messer-Davidow, D. R. Shumway and D. J. Sylvan (eds) *Knowledges: Historical and Critical Studies in Disciplinarity*, pp. 1–21 (Charlottesville, VA: The University Press of Virginia).

Morris, R. J. (1993) Clubs, societies and associations, in F. M. L. Thompson (ed.) *The Cambridge Social History of Britain 1750–1950*, vol. 3, pp. 395–443 (Cambridge: Cambridge University Press).

Murray, A. (1978) *Reason and Society in the Middle Ages* (Oxford: Oxford University Press).

Napier, C. J. (1996), Academic disdain? Economists and accounting in Britain, 1850–1950, *Accounting, Business & Financial History*, 6 (3): 427–50.

Neimark, M. (1996) Caught in the squeeze: an essay on higher education in accounting, *Critical Perspectives on Accounting*, 7 (1): 1–11.

Nobes, C. W. (1983) *Becoming an Accountant* (Harlow: Longman).

O'Day, R. (2000) *The Professions in Early Modern England, 1450–1800* (Harlow: Pearson Education).

Panozzo, F. (1997) The making of the good academic accountant, *Accounting, Organizations and Society*, 22 (5): 447–80.

Parker, R. H. (1995) David Solomons and British accounting, *Accounting and Business Research*, 25 (100): 311–14.

Power, M. K. (1991) Educating accountants: towards a critical ethnography, *Accounting, Organizations and Society*, 16 (4): 333–53.

Quattrone, P. (2004) Accounting for God: accounting and accountability practices in the Society of Jesus (Italy, XV–XVII Centuries), *Accounting, Organizations and Society*, 29 (7): 647–83.

Sanderson, M. (1972) *The Universities and British Industry 1850–1970* (London: Routledge and Kegan Paul).

Shackleton, K. (1995) Scottish chartered accountants: internal and external political relationships, *Accounting, Auditing & Accountability Journal*, 8 (2): 18–46.

Solomons, D. (1974) *Prospectus for a Profession: The Report of the Long Range Enquiry into Education and Training for the Accountancy Profession* (London: Gee & Co).

Stacey, N. A. H. (1954) *English Accountancy. A Study in Social and Economic History, 1800–1954* (London: Gee & Co).

Stafford, A. P. (2002) Capitalising education: exploring the development of professional identity in certified accountants through the role of education and training, unpublished PhD thesis, University of Warwick.

Van Wyhe, G. (1994) *The Struggle for Status: A History of Accounting Education* (New York: Garland Publishing Inc).

Walker, S. P. (1988) *The Society of Accountants in Edinburgh 1854–1914: A Study of Recruitment to a New Profession* (New York: Garland).

Walker, S. P. (1994) *Accountancy at the University of Edinburgh 1919–1994. The Emergence of a 'Viable Academic Department'* (Edinburgh: ICAS).

Walker, S. P. (2002) 'Men of Small Standing'? Locating accountants in English society during the mid-nineteenth century, *European Accounting Review*, 11 (2): 377–99.

Walker, S. P. (2003) Identifying the woman behind the 'railed-in desk': the proto-feminisation of bookkeeping in Britain, *Accounting, Auditing & Accountability Journal*, 16 (4): 606–38.

Yamey, B. S., Edey, H. C. and Thomson, H. W. (1963) *Accounting in England and Scotland: 1543–1800, Double Entry in Exposition and Practice* (London: Sweet & Maxwell).

Zan, L. (1994) Toward a history of accounting histories: perspectives from the Italian tradition, *European Accounting Review*, 3 (2): 255–307.

Zeff, S. A. (1997) The early years of the Association of University Teachers of Accounting: 1947–1959, *British Accounting Review*, 29 (1/2, supplement): 3–39.

14

Regulation

Alan J. Richardson and Eksa Kilfoyle

Overview

This chapter examines the interplay between general theories of regulation and histories of accounting regulation. It defines regulation as the set of institutions, or 'rules of the game,' that constrain and enable the practice of accounting. It identifies five theoretical frames (public interest theory, regulatory capture theory, corporatist theory, negotiated order theories and cultural theories) and explores the way that these theories inform interpretations of the introduction, consequences, persistence and disappearance of regulatory institutions in accounting. These theories include teleological, evolutionary and naturalistic perspectives.

The chapter begins by examining the contested interpretation of the motivation for the US Securities Acts, 1933/34 and their impact on financial disclosure; a topic that has dominated the historical literature on accounting regulation. Then it considers the impact on the history of accounting regulation of the common law, social norms, and private regulatory initiatives by stock exchanges and investment banks. This literature expands the concept of regulation beyond the intended action of the state on market actors to a more general concern with the rules, principles and social contexts of financial disclosure. This literature also provides insights into the situated emergence of regulation without assuming teleology. Finally, it concludes by identifying areas in which our understanding of accounting regulation can be advanced by a historical perspective.

Introduction

Accounting is both a technology of regulation in society and a highly regulated professional activity. The history of regulation in accounting is thus concerned with a three-way interaction between social processes (typically mediated by the state), regulatory bodies and those affected by regulation. Broadly speaking, we can identify three bodies of research in this area: (1) the regulation of professional practice rights; (2) the regulation of accounting and auditing technologies particularly through formal standard-setting processes; and (3) the use of accounting in the regulation of the economy.

Regulation is a common theme through this volume. The specific work of standard-setting agencies in relation to financial accounting theory and practice has been referred to in Chapters 7 and 8. The regulation of auditing was considered in Chapter 10 while the regulation of the profession featured in Chapter 11. Accounting scandals emerging from regulatory failure, and the manner in which accounting in the public sector and the military have been regulated, are discussed in later chapters. Our main concern here is to illustrate the interplay between histories of accounting regulation and theories of regulation. We focus on the regulation of financial reporting and the use of accounting to regulate publicly traded companies. In fact, the disclosure of information has become a key method of regulation in developed economies since Justice Brandeis (1914) extolled: 'Publicity is justly commended as a remedy for social and industrial disease. Sunlight is said to be the best disinfectant and electric light the most efficient policeman.' The rationale is that by releasing information, those with an interest in an issue will take action (Graham 2002; see also Chapter 23 on Bentham and publicity). The problem is to determine if disclosure must be regulated and to specify what information should be released to whom and in what form.

We limit our review of histories of regulation by distinguishing between inductive (or descriptive) histories of regulation and deductive (or theory informed) histories of regulation. We do not review descriptive histories of accounting regulation or regulatory bodies. These histories include insider accounts by regulators (Beresford 1998; Leach and Stamp 1981), commissioned histories of regulatory bodies (Auditing Practices Board 1986; Dearing 1988; Camferrman and Zeff 2007), and general histories of regulatory processes (Zeff 1972; Walton 1995).

There has been an active debate about the many forms of historical scholarship in accounting – this has typically been framed as a distinction between traditional and 'new' history (Miller *et al.* 1991; Funnell 1996). For the most part, 'new accounting history' has reinterpreted events through macro-social lenses; for example, trying to understand the role of accounting in gender relations (see Chapter 20), race relations (Chapter 21), and imperialism (Chapter 22). Our approach is more of a 'mid-range' history of accounting regulation (inspired by Merton (1968: 39–73) but more in line with Laughlin's (1995), use of the term). We use theories of regulation as a starting point for the interrogation of the histories of regulation and seek, modestly, to address the descriptive completeness of alternative theories of regulation. We review in particular works that have attempted to answer such basic questions as why are regulations developed, who benefits from them, how do they develop and emerge from social practices, and why do they persist?

Defining regulation

The term 'regulation' typically connotes the intervention of the state in human affairs. But the state is neither the only nor necessarily the most effective source of regulation in society. Human affairs are structured by 'institutions', which Douglas North (1990) has defined as 'the rules of the game', that may arise from within civil society or from political processes at sub-national, national and transnational levels. There has been a resurgence of interest in institutions in both economics and politics. This has been occasioned by two developments: one academic and one practical. On the practical side, there have been a series of remarkable global experiments in *laissez-faire* policies that have resulted in, at best, mixed results (Jordana and Levi-Faur 2004). The transition from planned to market economies and the liberalisation of capital markets have both provided vivid examples of how the success of economic markets is affected by the institutional framework within which transactions occur.

On the academic side, there has been growing recognition of the contributions of institutional theorists such as Ronald Coase and Douglas North (awarded the Nobel Prize in Economics 1991 and 1993 respectively) who drew attention to the relationship between institutions and economic outcomes and the work of political institutionalists such as March and Olsen (1989) who emphasised institutional design as a political choice. These developments have fostered the development of a new institutionalism differentiated from prior research that tended to emphasise description over theory-building and idiosyncratic differences over patterns of similarity and difference. The new institutionalism is based on three contestable assumptions: (1) institutions affect economic outcomes; (2) we can choose the institutions that frame our conduct (that is, institutions are endogenous rather than exogenous variables); and (3) the evolution of institutions is related to individual self-interest-seeking behaviour. The form that the 'rules of the game' take in any historical period will vary and hence the emergence, persistence, and change (or disappearance) of a set of rules, are phenomena that need to be explained.

These literatures have supported the repositioning of studies of regulation as part of a more general concern with 'governance', which 'comprises the traditions, institutions and processes that determine how power is exercised, how citizens are given a voice, and how decisions are made on issues of public concern' (PHAC 2007). By recasting regulation as a form of governance, neo–institutional theory recognises regulation as historically contingent achievements that reflect ongoing adjustments among actors within a framework of power and rights.

Theoretical frames

The explanations of the emergence, persistence and change of the institutions affecting market transactions can be clustered under five headings:

1 Public interest theory
2 Regulatory capture theory
3 Corporatist theory
4 Negotiated order theories
5 Cultural theories.

We briefly review each of these theories below and refer to these approaches as we review histories of accounting regulation.

Public interest theory

There are two variants of public interest theory. The classic version holds that markets are the most efficient mechanism for allocating resources but markets fail due to factors such as information asymmetries or monopoly power. Regulation is the means by which the state intervenes to overcome market failures. The work of Ronald Coase has enriched this perspective by demonstrating that where property rights are complete and transaction costs are zero, actors can negotiate efficient outcomes regardless of rules. This has refocused attention on market failures as incomplete property rights specifications and/or high transaction costs to the rearrangement of property rights rather than as an immutable characteristic of any situation. Williamson (1985) extends this insight to suggest that transactions are 'assigned' to alternative governance mechanisms – including the market and the state – in order to minimise costs.

Bozeman (2002) offered a variant on the market failure approach. He argued that regulation is used when public values are not realised by other means. This framework is particularly relevant when state intervention is unrelated to the efficiency of markets (e.g. social versus economic regulation). For example, if the mechanisms for identifying and aggregating social preferences fail or if efficient markets result in a short-term focus at the expense of long-run social goals, authoritative intervention may be used to ensure that public values are realised. This concern reflects the fact that, while in a Coasian world economic efficiency can be achieved, the distribution of wealth is greatly affected by the definition of property rights. Bozeman's concern is primarily with the distributional consequences of market outcomes.

Regulatory capture theory

Regulatory capture theory was developed in the work of Stigler (1971) and Peltzman (1976). The basic premise is that regulation is an economic good subject to the forces of supply and demand. The demand for regulation arises because regulation can result in wealth transfers. Those who will benefit from regulation will lobby the state to enact a favourable law. Regulation is assumed to be granted by elected legislators who gain utility from holding these positions. Their decision to grant regulation is based on the likelihood that the votes gained from the lobbying group will be greater than the votes lost from the group harmed by the regulation. This is most likely when the benefits of regulation are concentrated and the costs are diffused across a large population. Peltzman (1976) generalised this result to allow for the effect of different elasticities of demand for the regulated product.

Corporatism

The concept of corporatism draws attention to the private sector bodies that implement state policy (Schmitter and Lehmbruch 1979; Richardson 1989). The theory suggests that the state enters into a bargain with private sector bodies providing them with access to state power and resources in return for their control of the regulated population. An important part of the corporatist bargain is that social conflicts are contained within functionally defined bodies (such as professional associations and regulatory bodies) rather than acting to disrupt broader social processes.

Negotiated order theory

The three approaches described above assume that regulation is embedded in a rational social order characterised by a search for social benefit or a game-theoretic search for equilibrium among competing interests. Several approaches to regulation eschew this model of social order and focus instead on the practical production of order in the face of uncertainty. In an uncertain environment the possibility of rational calculation disappears because the alternatives cannot be fully enumerated, costs and benefits are not known, or preferences are unstable or unformed. In spite of these impediments to rational action, coordination among actors is still required. In these circumstances, a negotiated order may arise that allows successful interaction to occur. Negotiated order theories tend to be more focused on process than on the teleology of regulation, that is, the question becomes *how* regulation is created and implemented rather than *why* regulation is created.

Cultural theories

Cultural theories of regulation are concerned with the interplay between institutions rather than focusing on a single institution at a time. Social groups develop core values and/or generic social mechanisms that are reflected across many institutions. These values are highly resistant to change because they are pre-cognitive from the perspective of participants, that is, they represent deeply socialised and taken-for-granted assumptions, and/or the mutual interdependence of institutions based on these values makes piecemeal adjustment of any single institution within a society virtually impossible. These theories initially used the nation-state as a proxy for culture. More recent work has moved to mid-range levels such as the nature of the legal system (code law versus common law).

Empirical frames

The historical study of accounting regulation has typically followed one of five empirical strategies. The first strategy is a simple cross-sectional description of regulation. The remaining four represent alternative 'periodization strategies' (Lieberman 2001) that use longitudinal analysis to explore possible causes and consequences of regulatory events. First, historians may explore the factors surrounding regulatory emergence (Merino and Mayper 2001). This requires a demarcation of pre- and post-regulatory periods. Second, historians identify 'exogenous shocks' and look for the impact of those events on continuing regulations and regulatory processes (for example, the impact on Japanese accounting institutions of the American occupation (Harrison and McKinnon 1986)). Third, historians look for regulatory changes and examine the motives and implications of the change (for example, the effect of changes in US financial accounting standard-setting process on the value relevance of accounting information (Ely and Waymire 1999)). Finally, historians compare cases (typically jurisdictions) or periods with variation in specific factors ('rival causes') thought to affect accounting regulation (Puxty *et al.* 1987).

The study of regulatory history has largely focused on the United States although this is changing. Many European countries look at the Securities and Exchange Commission (SEC) as a model for the regulation of securities markets and financial disclosure (Meier-Schatz 1986). The position of the USA in the forefront of regulatory innovation emerged during the inter-war depression. The New Deal policies of F. D. Roosevelt were implemented through administrative agencies designed as 'rational' administrative structures characterised by professional management, evidence-based decision-making and due process to control both the influence of special interests and the discretionary powers of administrators. The US Securities Acts, 1933/34 and the creation of the SEC, in particular, are seen as innovations in the use of disclosure regulation to control corporate behaviour administered through an independent agency (Benston 1973; Vogel 1986).

The US Securities Acts, 1933/34: a natural experiment

One of the longest-running debates in the history of accounting regulation is whether or not the regulation of financial reporting is necessary. This debate involves two dimensions: first, what is the purpose of regulation; and second, did regulation achieve that purpose? The debate has been protracted largely because of disagreements over the purpose of regulation which establishes the criterion used to judge success.

For many researchers, the introduction of financial disclosure requirements in the Securities Act of 1933 and Securities Exchange Act of 1934 in the midst of the Great Depression provides a naturally occurring experiment in which to explore the rationale for and effectiveness of regulation. The adoption process was relatively short and the change from the status quo was significant. The circumstances surrounding the creation of the Acts have been explored to understand the motivations for regulation while the performance of the US stock market (particularly the New York Stock Exchange) before and after the legislation has been used to evaluate the effectiveness of regulation.

The debate has focused on the work of Benston (1969a, 1969b, 1973, 1975, 1982) who begins with the premise, building on Stigler (1964) that the only rationale for regulation of financial disclosure is to correct market failures. From his perspective, if there is no evidence of informational failures prior to regulation and there is no difference in the performance of the stock markets before and after regulation, then there is no justification for regulation. This is a straightforward application of classical public interest theory to the regulation of financial reporting. Benston's work has been relied on by others and occasioned a response by the SEC (1977) that disputed his claim that regulation of financial disclosure is unnecessary.

Benston (1969a) argues that the common justification for the 1933/34 Acts – that financial disclosure prior to the Great Depression was often fraudulent – cannot be supported by the evidence. He bases this claim on a review of legislative records and secondary sources. These records show very few criminal convictions for securities fraud during this period. Okcabol and Tinker (1993) have noted that this is a very narrow definition of the possible concerns of investors; it is limited to acts of commission (fraud) to the exclusion of acts of omission (non-disclosure). Seligman (1983), moreover, provides evidence that the latter type of misrepresentation was more common and Edwards (1989) presents evidence that the quality of financial statement disclosure declined during the 1920s.

Benston (1973) claims that the level of voluntary disclosure prior to regulation was sufficient to support informed trading and stewardship. Further, he holds that the change in the information regime brought about by the Acts was not consistent with the needs of informationally efficient markets: information was released too late and was based on conservative accounting principles that were inconsistent with investment decision–making. The empirical results show no stock market reaction to the new information. Hence, Benston concludes that the information was not needed by investors. Finally, he argues that there are effective and efficient alternatives to monitor management including the capital and labour markets.

Contrary to this interpretation, Merino and Neimark (1982) question whether the disclosure of accounting numbers without the simultaneous disclosure of management assumptions and the basis for measurement would support investment decision–making either *before* or after the introduction of the Acts. They also document that the Federal Trade Commission hearings (1928–32) investigating the financial disclosures of companies leading up to the stock market crash had difficulty in gaining cooperation indicating that companies were either unwilling or unable to provide disclosure even under subpoena. They report contemporary commentary to support a general concern with the quality of financial reporting but neither Benston nor Merino and Neimark are able to provide any firm baseline for the level of financial misstatements during this period.

Davis (1999) examines Benston's claim that voluntary agreements between the stock exchanges and listing firms provided sufficient information to safeguard investors. He begins by noting that Benston's approach to data collection was unsound – he simply wrote to the exchanges and asked them whether disclosure requirements were in place. Davis (1999) examines the 'listing standards' of 34 US stock exchanges during the 1920s. He found that the listing agreements were highly varied, did not specify accounting standards where disclosure was required, and suffered from exemptions and lax enforcement. He further discovered that while these standards had evolved over time, the changes were due to government investigation of the exchanges rather than being initiated by firms or exchanges to achieve a comparative advantage in information transparency. The role of government in the emergence of stock exchange disclosure regulations raises doubts about the 'voluntary' nature of such rules, i.e., the potential for government intervention may be considered an effective and low cost form of regulation.

Focusing on econometric issues, Friend and Westerfield (1975) raise concerns that Benston (1973) focused on the impact of a single change in disclosure on the market while the Acts had multiple effects. The sample used by Benston is criticised for including only firms that differed on one disclosure (sales) even though more extreme differences in the level of disclosure between firms existed before the Acts. They also raise concern that Benston found statistically significant results but discounted them in his conclusion as not being economically meaningful – hence allowing him to say that the disclosure requirements had no effect. Friend and Westerfield (1975) also question whether or not Benston correctly identified the right 'event' on which to base his comparison. They suggest that while he focused on the 1934 Act, it was actually the 1933 Act that had the greatest impact on financial disclosure. They also point out that the tests used by Benston relate to market efficiency but not to distributional issues even though Benston uses the term 'market fairness' in reference to his tests. Benston (1975) provides a detailed response to these issues.

Benston's work is often based on the reinterpretation of common historical knowledge rather than being designed to specifically test his hypotheses (see Okcabol and Tinker (1993) for critiques of Benston's data and methods). His basic model however has been examined by others such as Simon (1989) and in a series of studies by Waymire and colleagues. Ely and Waymire (1999), for example, examined the earnings relevance of financial disclosures on the New York Stock Exchange (NYSE) between 1927 and 1993. This study includes the pre-SEC period as well as regulation under the Committee on Accounting Procedure (1939–59), the Accounting Principles Board (1973–93) and the Financial Accounting Standards Board (1973–93). They do not find significant evidence of improved correlation between earnings and stock prices over these periods. Ely and Waymire infer that regulation has not improved the information environment for investors but recognise that the correlation may also be affected by changes in the economy and technology. They, of course, cannot compare their results to a counterfactual control where no regulation exists. This continues to be an active area of research.

Gjerde *et al.* (2005) conducted a similar study to Ely and Waymire (1999) although they do not cite this work, examining the value relevance of Norwegian financial statements from 1964 to 2003 after Norway changed their standards from a tax/creditor orientation to a market/investor orientation. Importantly Norway's standards emphasise the income statement rather than the balance sheet (so earnings relevance is more likely than under US and international accounting standards). They find a significant increase in earnings relevance over time but only when controls are included for market risk, industry composition and the proportion of companies reporting losses. Their study may indicate that regulation has a positive effect on the information environment depending on the nature of the regulation and the context in which it is introduced.

A common approach to demonstrating that regulation was not necessary is to show that firms were voluntarily using audits and disclosing the same financial information that was required by regulation (Benston 1973). In the absence of regulation, these voluntary decisions are suggested to reflect a balancing of costs and benefits by management/shareholders. Regulation, it is suggested, requires an economically unsound use of resources to disclose information that is not required by the markets. Merino *et al.* (1994) correctly point out that to support this interpretation, alternative explanations must be eliminated and/or that the mechanism linking economic incentives to audit/disclosure decisions must be demonstrated. For example, the need for a monitoring/bonding mechanism does not imply which of many alternative mechanisms would be chosen or which would have been the most efficient in the circumstances.

Chow (1983) also examined the period of the Securities Acts to determine if the regulations resulted in wealth transfers between shareholders and bondholders. His approach has elements of a regulatory capture model where the key premise is that the Acts had distributional effects among groups. His work, however, has been challenged by Merino *et al.* (1987) who identify problems in the definition of the event window, the separation of control and treatment samples, and biases in the interpretation of the consequences of the legislation for different stakeholders.

From 'market failure' to 'public value failure' and 'regulatory capture'

The tests of the value relevance of accounting information coincident with changes in regulation presume that this was the intended purpose of the regulation. The work by Benston and Waymire may be characterised as cliometrics (quantitative history based largely on neo-classical models). This approach, however, is limited by the models used and the lack of attention to the broader context in which the events occurred (see North 1997). As Crafts (1987) concluded, following a review of the contributions of cliometrics to economic history, 'econometric methods need to be supplemented in historical work by other forms of evidence to obtain persuasive answers to historical questions'. This challenge was taken up by Merino and others who examined the debates leading up to the Securities Acts and the broader social context in which the legislation emerged.

Merino and Neimark (1982) argued that the Acts were intended to maintain the US ideology of individualism and competition during a period of increased economic concentration. The US Constitution was designed as a series of checks-and-balances against the concentration of political power. The rise of trusts and cartels in the late nineteenth and early twentieth centuries, however, raised the spectre of a weak political structure facing a focused economic bloc. The contemporary debates in Congress and the press suggest that increased disclosure and widespread stock ownership were seen as a means of democratising the economy and maintaining accountability over managers. The debates, however, did not assume that disclosures would be used directly by investors but rather by bankers, government agencies and a market for corporate control (takeovers to replace inept managements). The structure of the market envisioned was thus a 'two-tier market structure' and 'moral regulation' by knowledgeable elites. Merino and Neimark thus challenge both the purpose of the Acts and the 'users' of the increased information.

Edwards and Chandler (2001) examine the introduction of accounting regulation on UK friendly societies (non-profit, mutual benefit organisations). This is an unusual setting where fraud or other crises were not the catalyst for regulation. Friendly societies were created by the UK working class and often associated with particular groups (such as Masons). These organisations were seen as reducing the demand on the state to alleviate the conditions of the working class but were also posed a risk as bases for working-class collaboration and radicalisation. State regulation of these organisations tended to precede the regulation of limited liability companies. Edwards and Chandler (2001) attribute this to the UK government's perception of these groups as less educated and less able to guard their own interests hence a 'paternalistic' approach to regulation was adopted. This is similar to Merino and Mayper's view of US regulation.

Merino and Mayper (2001) continue the analysis of the symbolic role of regulation drawing on Edelman (1964). Their study is based on private correspondence among 'New Dealers' and with key members of the accounting profession. The analysis is consistent with the regulatory capture model which assumes that regulation will benefit small groups for whom the benefits of regulation are concentrated as opposed to larger groups over whom the costs of regulation are diffused. In the case of the Securities Acts, 1933/34, Merino and Mayper see the laws as placating the public's demand for protection from systemic market failures without fundamentally changing business operating conditions. This was, in fact, Roosevelt's explicit intention: 'The purpose of the legislation I suggest is to protect the public with the least possible interference with honest business' (Woolley and Peters 2007).

Others have suggested that the emergence and content of financial disclosure regulation were more closely associated with the interests of specific groups in society rather than a more general public interest. Mahoney (2001), examining the details of the Securities Exchange Acts, notes that the disclosures required of companies were selective and favoured investment bankers over other groups. Mezias and Chung (2006) focusing on standard-setting between 1973 and 1989, show that private interests affected the content of 'non-substantive' rules but found that 'substantive' rules were independent of such interests where 'substantive' rules represent fundamental changes in requirements while 'non-substantive' rules represent clarifications, implementation guidelines or applications to particular industries. Similar histories have been written about other jurisdictions. Maltby (1998), for example, argues that in the UK the changing disclosure provisions of the early companies acts were more consistent with the interests of large investors than small investors. Walker (1987) raised concerns about the capture of the Australian Accounting Standards Board by auditors and their clients. Overall, the evidence suggests that the economic consequences of financial disclosure regulation attract considerable lobbying pressure and may reflect the interests of a sub-set of society.

The impression that emerges from the studies above is one of a degree of consensus on facts but significant disagreement on interpretation. The consensus is that, in general, the regulation of financial disclosure in the USA during the twentieth century has been relatively ineffective in generating information that is more useful to investors than voluntary disclosures. It may have reduced the riskiness of stocks (Simon 1989) but has not generated information with greater relevance to stock valuation. Benston and others have concluded that this is a failed experiment and regulation, with its attendant costs, could be reduced without ill-effect. Merino and others, by contrast, argue that disclosure regulation plays a symbolic role in maintaining the confidence of small investors and reducing the political pressure for more intensive regulation of business. The purpose of the legislation was to protect private ownership and individual participation in the stock markets while reducing the opportunities for insider exploitation of uninformed traders. This suggests that the reduction of regulation is unlikely but that it could be used to more effectively monitor businesses independent of the market.

Searching for regulation

The periodisation used by Benston and others to judge the effect of the Securities Acts, 1933/34 on the US capital markets relies on the correct specification of the timing of a switch from an unregulated to a regulated environment. One criticism of Benston's characterisation of the pre-1933 period as unregulated is that the stock exchanges during that period provided an authoritative standard of financial disclosure through their listing agreements. While this implies that some regulation existed during the 'unregulated' period, Davis (1999: 53) notes: 'Although the stock exchanges were the clear leaders in setting national financial disclosure standards, the level of corporate disclosures through the stock exchanges prior to 1934 was inadequate.' This does not imply, however, that the level of regulation is determined solely by either the stock exchanges on which a firm is listed or the state regulations affecting that group of companies.

Walker and Mack (1998), in a reanalysis of the work of Whittred (1986) on the history of consolidated financial statements in Australia, shows that practice was influenced by regulations in other jurisdictions to which a company was exposed. For example, while the focus was on companies listed on the Sydney Stock Exchange, if the company had a subsidiary incorporated in a jurisdiction requiring consolidated statements, then that company was more likely to file consolidated statements in Australia voluntarily. Walker and Mack also demonstrate that the likelihood of issuing consolidated statements increases as the authority of the standard increases. For example, a standard 'recommending' consolidation had less effect than a standard 'requiring' consolidation; a standard issued by government had more effect on behaviour than a standard issued by a professional association.

In addition to the effect of stock exchanges on financial disclosure there were also common law requirements. Mills (1993, see also 1990, 1994) provides a summary of the case law affecting accounting practices prior to the introduction of regulated financial disclosure. Her motivation is two-fold: to examine the claim that the only role of government/courts prior to regulation is to enforce contracts, and to examine conflicting accounts of the role of the courts with regard to accounting for depreciation and goodwill. She reports that, particularly in the UK, the courts played an active role in defining appropriate accounting – even overturning accounting methods specified in contracts. This approach in common law represents a change from the reliance of the courts on social norms and precedents to a focus on expressed agreements between consenting parties. The latter logic supported and fostered commercial interests. The evidence, however, shows a reluctance of US judges compared with UK judges to overturn contractual terms in favour of common meanings of accounting abstractions (Mills 1993). Mills' work thus shows that even in an 'unregulated' environment authoritative forces affected the development of financial measurement and disclosure, and that this unregulated environment, in spite of great similarities of institutions, varied across cultures.

It is also possible that the accounting firms may have been a source of financial disclosure norms. Cooper and Robson (2006) suggest that the source of current practice standards is large firms rather than formal regulatory bodies. Although during the pre-1933 era the audit firms had not achieved their current level of market dominance, there is evidence that a small group of firms had established their presence and may have been able to exert influence on financial disclosure (see Richardson 2006). Bricker and Chandar (1998) identify investment bankers as another source of influence. These sources of regulation blur the boundaries between the market and regulatory bodies.

Negotiated order, regulatory 'progress' and cycles

The administrative agencies created by the New Deal were provided with unusual discretionary powers to restore the US economy after the Great Depression. This resulted in concern about these agencies acting simultaneously in executive, legislative and judicial roles (Shepard 1996). The legislative role played by these agencies arose because the Acts creating them were incomplete and the agency (such as the SEC) was expected to create regulations (such as accounting standards) to implement the intent of the legislation. This, in turn, often resulted in regulations that allowed considerable flexibility of behaviour of the regulated. In other words, the creation of regulation provided a context in which the precise form would be negotiated but did not provide 'black letter' law. A persistent issue in US regulation has thus been the negotiation of the role of the regulatory body and the flexibility allowed under regulations.

The negotiation of the details of accounting regulation is reflected in the literature on lobbying standard-setting bodies (see Taylor and Turley 1986; Zeff 2006; Rutherford 2007) and on the form that regulations take. The literature on lobbying is related to theories of regulatory capture but, while regulatory capture refers to the control of the entire regulatory process, lobbying studies focus on events specific to one issue. There is little historical work on lobbying of regulatory bodies in accounting. This probably reflects the lack of records concerning such activities (with the exception of letters on exposure drafts and other formal due process opportunities more recently). There is literature on lobbying for early UK regulation since hearings on the Companies Acts (in which financial disclosure regulation was embedded) occurred in public and lobbyists/witnesses comments are on record (e.g. Jones 1995; Jones and Aiken 1995; Walker 1996; Maltby 1998). The literature on lobbying regulators is also limited by a tendency to focus on individual issues in such studies (such as cross-sectional rather than longitudinal research). Saemann (1999) is an exception to this trend. She examines lobbying by four industry representative bodies across 20 controversial standards of the Financial Accounting Standards Board and identifies consistencies in their lobbying patterns.

There is significantly more historical research on the form that accounting regulation takes. The contemporary debate on the form of regulation/standards in accounting is framed in terms of 'rules versus principles'. This has appeared in various guises in the literature such as concern with the degree of 'uniformity' in reporting practice (Mueller 1965). There is also a large literature on uniform cost systems. Jucius (1943), for example, traced the history of uniform accounting from 1875 to 1940. He attributes the rise of uniform accounting systems to the activities of trade associations who sought to provide members with a system to determine costs and thereby to end cut-throat price competition.

Merino and Coe (1978) discuss the history of 'uniformity' in accounting in the USA, beginning with the Interstate Commerce Commission in 1887. The government demand for uniformity arises from the desire to have information to support policy analysis and rate regulation in certain industries (notably transportation). These systems were industry-specific and allowed for variations among companies to reflect technological and scale differences. The demand for uniformity was generalised from these specific circumstances to corporate reporting. In general, Merino and Coe report a consistent reluctance of professional accounting associations to support uniformity of financial reporting. This arises from the recognition that accounting numbers (accruals) require judgments that cannot be reduced to simple rules.

The essence of the debate between rules versus principles is also reflected in the concept of 'true and fair' presentation (Alexander and Jermakowicz 2006). Under a rules-based system an auditor can give a 'clean' opinion if financial statements have been prepared according to Generally Accepted Accounting Principles (GAAP). GAAP may be further defined under law to refer to a specific set of documents or to the standards that are produced by a particular organisation/standard setting body. Under a principles-based system, there is an additional requirement that the financial statements reflect a true and fair view of the financial position of the company even if the financial statements have been prepared according to GAAP. This additional requirement reflects a concern with the substance over the form of financial statements.

Chambers and Wolnizer (1991) provide a history of the concept of true and fair based on legislative records and the charters of partnerships and companies that specified the quality of financial reports prior to formal regulations. They find that common usage of the term prior to its incorporation into British companies legislation in 1844 connoted two things: (1) that the financial statements contained no falsehoods; and (2) that assets should be valued at selling prices rather than cost. The charters that referred to the quality of financial information typically intended financial statements to have probative value in the event of the dissolution of the company or partnership. Maltby (2000) provides a related history of prudent accounting.

Jones *et al.* (2000) compare the development of 'truth in advertising' and the rejection of true and fair in US accounting/auditing standards during the Progressive era. They note the professional success of accountants who rejected 'truth' as a criterion for financial statements compared with the professional failure of marketers who succeeded in institutionalising 'truth in advertising'. The marketers' campaign resulted in legislation and criminal penalties based on the findings of the courts, while accountants were able to retain control over the definition of GAAP and hence with the standards that would be used to evaluate the adequacy of financial disclosures.

Hopwood (1987) raised concerns about the teleology of much accounting history. History was interpreted as the inexorable movement towards 'better' accounting and auditing practice (see Napier (2001) on the concept of progress in accounting history). In many cases, however, historical work has shown that 'progress', regardless of how this is defined, is elusive. The debates surrounding 'rules versus principles', 'uniformity versus flexibility', and 'GAAP versus true and fair' have not achieved closure. Instead, the complex interplay of factors in the regulatory environment encourages symbolic changes without real change in the behaviour of firms, or a recycling of issues without resolution.

One approach to reconciling this is to suggest that accounting regulation is subject to countervailing pressures that change in force over time resulting in an oscillation between alternatives. Nobes (1991, 1992) for example, proposed a cyclical model of regulatory history to account for the dramatic swings in proposed standards over time. This model has been used by some (Gordon and Morris 1996; Cooper and Deo 2005) but challenged by others (Skerratt and Whittington 1992).

The basic premise behind the cyclical model is that there are two opposing forces in the economy: for example, a force towards standardisation originating in the profession and various governmental agencies, and a force opposed to standardisation originating in corporate management (Moran and Previts 1984); or changes in stakeholder concerns linked to the business cycle with standardisation following business downturns and benign neglect of regulatory standards during business booms (Clarke 2004). The trigger for a change in the form of regulation may be a crisis or scandal in a particular industry or company that implicates the flexibility of accounting regulation in the problem (Walker 2000; Chapter 19 of this volume) or the enactment of an accounting standard in another country that is used as a benchmark. The form of regulation develops in a particular direction until countervailing forces reverse the process.

A similar account is provided by Byington and Sutton (1991) and Gaa (1991) who suggest that accounting standard-setting activity is correlated with government challenges to self-regulating the profession. Gaa suggests that the relationship between the state and the profession can be modelled as a sequential game in which the state initiates a challenge to self-regulation, usually emerging out of crisis and the profession responds to demonstrate that the crisis can be managed while maintaining self-regulation intact. Gaa suggests that this reflects a 'social contract' between the profession and the state (this may also be interpreted as a corporatist bargain).

Byington and Sutton (1991) identify four events that they argue challenged self-regulation in the USA: the 1938 issuance of an accounting standard by the SEC, the 1971 Act on accounting for tax credits; the Moss and Metcalfe hearings on the 'accounting establishment'; and, the Dingell hearings on the 'expectations gap' in 1985. They find that the introduction of accounting and auditing standards in the USA increases during each of these episodes compared with other periods. They see regulation emerging out of a force to maintain self-regulation by the profession versus a desire by government to intervene directly during times of crisis.

The cyclical model sketched above highlights the negotiation process from which accounting standards emerge. One interpretation of the standard-setting process, in fact, is that it is designed to create an 'arena' in which interests are defined and interact. This view of standard-setting is reflected in several contributions to the literature.

Miranti (1989) traced the development of accounting by the Interstate Commerce Commission (ICC) as a by-product of their statistical department's attempt to define a model to allow them to monitor the railroad industry. The Commission was concerned to regulate rates to prevent abuse of monopoly power (overcharging consumers who had no options and undercharging to bankrupt competitive transportation modes). It was also concerned about watered stock and the potential bankruptcy of railroads. The accounting requirements grew out of the ICC's attempt to provide a context in which interests, including farmers, miners, individual state regulatory bodies, and railroad associations, could negotiate; the accounting system reflected the information needs on which those relationships would be based.

Work by Robson (1991, 1992) developed the idea of 'constellations' to explain the development of reporting standards. This concept recognises that any proposed standard will affect various segments of society and become a site for negotiations of interests. The constellation of forces that is activated will depend upon the particular standard and hence is not a regular and predictable feature of standard-setting processes. Sivakumar and Waymire (2003) look at this issue in a more limited way in their exploration of the effect of accounting choice by managers facing both product market regulation and financial disclosure regulation.

King and Waymire (1994) provide a theoretical analysis of the evolution of US standard-setting processes within a transaction cost framework. Their basic insight is that accounting standards are used in 'incomplete contracts', that is, contracts where, because of uncertainty or complexity, all future information needs cannot be specified. The parties to the agreement, however, agree to be bound to a set of standards emerging from a predefined process. They suggest that a successful standard-setter must: (1) respond quickly to emerging issues (e.g. new transactions for which there is no apparent authoritative accounting treatment); (2) be perceived as independent of the major interests affected by the contracts; (3) be capable of penalising deviations from the standards; and (4) allow ex-post recontracting to deal with adverse effects from the standards that are set. The standard-setting process within this model is regarded as a super-structure that arises from negotiations among interests and reflects the *a priori* agreement of parties to reduce *ex post* conflicts.

Culture and accounting regulation

The US experience of regulating financial disclosure should not be over-generalised. The creation of the SEC and mandatory financial disclosures arose during a stock market crash and a deep depression. The form that regulation took reflected an interaction between those conditions, the set of institutions upon which legislators could draw as models, and the culture in which regulation would be embedded. The histories of other countries show the influence of these variables on regulatory structures and the variety of possible reactions (Walton 1995).

Merino and Neimark (1982) and Merino and Mayper (2001) emphasise that the concept of 'regulatory capitalism' in the USA grew out of the New Deal era and an attempt by reformers to enact the American Dream – a combination of communitarian ideals (equality of opportunity) and meritocracy. The initial shape of regulatory institutions was premised on the protection of private property rights subject to constraints on the 'unfair' accumulation of wealth (such as through trusts and the exercise of monopoly power). Within four years of the passage of the Securities Acts, however, the 'radical' version of the New Deal had given way to a philosophy that reaffirmed the role of the market over direct state intervention. The disclosure of financial information about corporate activities was seen as preserving individual investor opportunity (to make investment decisions, to evaluate management) without curtailing the same rights of management. Standardised disclosures provide a powerful image of equality within this rhetorical context.

The pattern identified by Merino and Mayper (2001) after the shock of the stock market crash of 1929 parallels the pattern observed by Harrison and McKinnon (1986) in Japan after the US occupation. Initially the reform of Japanese institutions followed the US model but over time the operation of those institutions returned to the patterns embedded in Japanese culture. In both cases the interaction of the institutions of financial disclosure regulation with other segments of society, including the courts and capital markets, resulted in a realignment of regulatory reforms to the broader social order in which these changes were embedded.

Baylin *et al.* (1996) trace the evolution of Canadian standard-setting structures over a hundred year period. They show the influence of colonial heritage (see Walton 1986 for further examples) and changing trading patterns on the models referenced by standard-setters and the demands for harmonisation. They also emphasise the interplay between technical developments and the need to maintain the political legitimacy of the process. In spite of the close connection between the USA and Canada, and the similarity of experience with the Great Depression, Canada did not follow the USA in changing their approach to financial disclosure; instead Canada retained the UK tradition of specifying financial disclosure requirements through the companies acts.

The US experience with accounting regulation has been contrasted with that of Europe. May (1939) observed that US intervention in financial markets has been concentrated around periods of economic downturn while in the UK, France, Germany and the Netherlands, regulation appears more measured; reflecting political philosophies rather than market dynamics. The form of regulation has also differed with the USA establishing a formal administrative body (the SEC) that has no direct parallel in European systems of regulation. May (1939) and Benston (1975) suggest that regulation in the USA has been 'explicit' while regulation in the UK has been 'implicit'. Explicit regulation was built into law and formal standard-setting bodies with enforcement. Implicit regulation occurs through social norms monitored and enforced informally by market participants. In the UK, the operation of informal regulation is facilitated by the physical concentration of financing activities in the City of London. May (1939) also notes in Europe a greater reliance on criminal law to prosecute financial crimes rather than relying on the Companies Act or related regulations. This means that the bar for formal intervention by the state, i.e. criminal guilt, is higher than in countries using administrative mechanisms of enforcement.

Parker (1990) reviews the extent of regulation of UK financial reporting after the Companies Act, 1856, during a period regarded as typifying an 'unregulated economy'. He recognises that a large part of the UK economy was regulated under legislation specific to those industries (such as railroads, public utilities and banks). These industries are typically excluded from discussions of private economic activity because of their rather unusual technologies (natural monopolies and public safety issues) and long-term capital requirements. Initially each company had specific reporting requirements included in their acts of incorporation. Contrary to US tradition, British disclosure requirements typically opened the account books to inspection rather than just requiring disclosure of financial statements. In the mid-nineteenth century, however, common clauses were consolidated (e.g. Companies Clauses Consolidation Act, 1845) so that they could be incorporated into new legislation by reference. This approach encouraged the development of uniform financial reporting among companies within the same industries.

Bryer (1993) provides a more general perspective on this period arguing that financial disclosure requirements emerged out of shifts in the nature of capitalism from a focus on the individual investor to capitalism as a system. He emphasises the systematic departures of accounting measurements from neo-classic economic theory focusing on depreciation as a key concept. Richard (2005) provides a similar analysis tracing the development of measurement bases (historic cost versus fair value) in European accounting practice as an outcome of conflicts between segments of the capitalist economy (such as bankers and the state versus entrepreneurs).

The next wave of regulation: networked governance

The conception of regulation as a constraint imposed on the markets by the state tended to limit histories of regulation to events within national boundaries. As we argued at the beginning of this chapter, regulation theory has moved beyond this to consider the interconnections between regulators in multiple nations and at the transnational. This reconceptualisation of regulation highlights the need for accounting historians to examine the international (between nations), transnational (above nations) and global (beyond nations) process by which accounting and auditing are regulated (Botzem and Quack 2006).

There is, of course, a considerable literature on international differences in accounting regulation between countries and on the harmonisation of regulation among countries. Schoenfeld (1981), for example, provided an early but brief history of the development of international accounting. He emphasised the information needs of multinational enterprises (MNEs) and the state regulatory bodies that tried to tax and control them. The material since his seminal survey is adequately captured in standard international accounting textbooks such as Nobes and Parker (2002).

Where more effort is needed is to develop theoretically informed histories of the key international bodies that now collectively set the direction for accounting regulation. This would include both formal bodies such as the World Bank (Arnold 2005), the International Federation of Accountants (Loft et al. 2006), the International Accounting Standards Committee (Martinez-Diaz 2005; Camfferman and Zeff 2007), as well as informal bodies such as the G4+1 (Street and Shaughnessy 1998), and the relationships between them (Richardson 2006). More generally, there has been increasing emphasis among students of regulation on the networks of regulators that coordinate actions in establishing accounting standards. These bodies have been increasingly intertwined with the 'international financial architecture', a term that gained currency during the financial crises of the late 1980s to refer to the World Bank and the International Monetary Fund (among others) that regulated currency flows and credit among sovereign nations. While there have been a small number of studies of particular aspects of this architecture, there needs to be better histories of the integration of accountants into this network (see Richardson and MacDonald 2002).

Conclusion: the three 'moments' of regulatory history

Histories of accounting regulation have struggled with three 'moments'[1] of regulation. The first moment concerns the existence of regulation; why did regulations arise? The second moment concerns what effects regulation has on those subject to it. This moment also concerns the inherent ambiguities of implementation and the negotiation that occurs as a regulatory body establishes its place within an institutional order. The third moment concerns the persistence of regulations. As circumstances change, the original rationale for regulation may disappear but the existence of regulation creates its own incentives and costs that activate interests. One of the fundamental problems facing this literature is that the logic of these moments may not be reducible to a single set of factors.

The reason for the introduction of financial disclosure regulation in the USA is still subject to debate. There have been two approaches to this question. The first is to identify a reason based on theory and test the implications of that theory. Benston's work and that of others who followed has taken this approach. Curiously, however, when the data is inconsistent with theory, the suggestion made is that the creation of financial disclosure regulation was a mistake rather than to search for alternative explanations. The second approach has been to work with the archival record around the origins of statutes and to identify a plausible historical explanation. This approach, however, is susceptible to criticism for inferential weaknesses – there are undoubtedly alternative explanations consistent with the historical record and the data may be biased and incomplete.

Our understanding of this 'first moment' in regulatory history has been advanced by international comparative studies that demonstrate that the US experience was conditioned by the institutional environment at that time. Other nations experiencing similar shocks to their economic systems relied more on 'implicit' regulation, that is, the functioning of social norms within a more closely knit community of financiers and companies. The literature has also broadened our conception of 'regulation' to include the influence of stock exchanges, common law, and cross-jurisdiction influences. One of the lacunae in the current regulatory literature is an understanding of the epistemic community of early regulators of financial disclosure. This type of analysis is implicit in Merino and Mayper's analysis of correspondence among key actors around the introduction of the Securities Acts but needs to be extended to understand, for example, the interplay between state and federal regulators in the USA[2] and between the USA and other key trading partners at the time.

There is evidence that regulatory initiatives arise in times of crisis in the USA and may have substantial symbolic roles in managing public reactions to systemic issues. The political context of the creation of regulation opens the phenomenon to a range of interest group phenomenon and ties regulation into the problems of social order within the nation state. Once regulation is established, however, the actors affected and able to play a role in the regulatory process changes. This new context allows for implementation to drift from the trajectory established during the creation phase. In particular, the precise form that regulations take and the way they are implemented emerge from a complex negotiation among a 'constellation' of actors.

One perspective conspicuously absent from the histories of regulation has been the reaction of those subject to regulation. In part, this is reflected in work concerned with lobbying but, in addition, we need to understand the practical accommodations made to the changing regulatory regimes as they are implemented. The success of regulation ultimately requires the 'consent of the governed' (McCraw 1982) or the cost of enforcement will eradicate any possible benefit. But consent is never absolute and corporate archives may provide some insight into the impact of legislation on corporate behaviours.

The 'third moment' of regulatory history, the persistence and rare disappearance of accounting regulation, opens up additional questions and perspectives. The SEC in the USA, for example, is one of the few New Deal agencies that has survived relatively unchanged since the 1930s. Its persistence may reflect its economic value-added, its capture by interests who continue to benefit from it, its integration within a network of other domestic and international standard-setters, or other reasons. The continued existence of such a body, however, is not guaranteed and there are recurrent suggestions to modify the agency and the means by which it regulates financial disclosure (the key alternatives being to rely on private contracting or to allow competing standard-setting bodies).

The persistence of regulation (that is, explaining the lack of variation or isomorphism, rather than variation in a phenomenon) is the realm of institutional theory. The study of the effect of culture on regulation reflects some of these concerns. As the pressure for institutional isomorphism in regulation increases through the impact of international standard-setting bodies, the requirements of the World Trade Organization, and the entry criteria of regional trading blocs, it is important to illustrate and explicate how these processes unfold. These studies must be sensitive to the dual role of accounting as a subject of regulation and a technology of regulation.

The history of regulation is also in need of more genealogical work that examines the emergence, transformation, dispersion and disappearance of regulatory concepts. The concept of 'true and fair' has attracted some attention so that it is possible to understand the connection of this term to specific times and practices, its variations as it was disembedded and re-embedded in particular contexts, and the symbolic power that it attained within particular institutional and economic settings. Other concepts, for example, 'moral regulation' and 'prudence', have fallen into disuse but the history of such changes has not been written. The sets of regulatory concepts that currently receive widespread discussion are derived from neo-classical economic theory and may be enriched by developing our understanding of other regulatory concepts that have been used and abandoned.

Finally, the history of regulation should contribute to our understanding of the continued de-centring of the nation-state (Richardson and MacDonald 2002). The regulation of accounting is becoming increasingly intertwined with the 'global financial architecture'. It has been identified as a key mechanism of international financial stability both through its ability to provide data for aggregate regulatory surveillance and to ensure that local decision-making reflects the risks of specific transactions. The way in which this regulatory network has emerged is still being written and must be carefully traced to avoid a view of the process limited to commissioned histories and the records of the organisations that survived the tumultuous emergence of global regulation.

Key works

Benston (1973) argues that there is no evidence that the Securities Exchange Act of 1934 was needed or desirable and that there are no measurable positive effects of the Act on prices of securities traded on the NYSE.

Ely and Waymire (1999) offers a time series analysis which provides weak support for an increase in earnings relevance following the introduction of US standard-setting bodies.

Merino and Neimark (1982) interprets Securities Acts as an attempt to maintain the social and economic status quo while reconciling the contradictions between an individualistic market-based philosophy and the corporate dominance due to economic concentration.

Young (1994) comprises three studies which illustrate how accounting policy issues need to be constructed as a problem and assessed using the 'logic of appropriateness' to become an issue addressed by the standard setters within the regulatory space.

Notes

1   We use the term 'moment' in its mathematical sense as different dimensions of a distribution rather than a temporal sense of a moment in time.
2   F. D. Roosevelt explicitly refers to state regulators in some of his announcements on the Securities Acts.

References

Alexander, D. and Jermakowicz, E. (2006) A true and fair view of the principles/rules debate, *Abacus*, 42 (2): 132–64.

Arnold, P. A. (2005) Disciplining domestic regulation: the World Trade Organization and the market for professional services, *Accounting, Organizations and Society*, 30 (4): 299–330.

Auditing Practices Board (1986) *APC: The First Ten Years* (London: APC).

Baylin, G., MacDonald, L. and Richardson, A. J. (1996) Accounting standard-setting in Canada 1864–1992: a theoretical analysis of structural evolution, *Journal of International Accounting and Taxation*, 5 (1): 113–32.

Benston, G. J. (1969a) The effectiveness and effects of the SEC's accounting disclosure requirements, in H. G. Manne (ed.) *Economic Policy and the Regulation of Corporate Securities*, pp. 23–79 (Washington, DC: The American Enterprise Institute).

Benston, G. J. (1969b) The value of the SEC's accounting disclosure requirements, *Accounting Review*, 44 (3): 515–32.

Benston, G. J. (1973) Required disclosure and the stock markets: an evaluation of the Securities Exchange Act of 1934, *American Economic Review*, 63 (1): 132–55.

Benston, G. J. (1975) Accounting standards in the United States and the United Kingdom: their nature, causes and consequences, *Vanderbilt Law Review*, 28 (1): 235–68.

Benston, G. J. (1982) An analysis of the role of accounting standards for enhancing corporate governance and social responsibility, *Journal of Accounting and Public Policy*, 1 (1): 5–17.

Beresford, D. R. (1998) FASB's accomplishments to date: one participant's views, *Accounting Historians Journal*, 25 (2): 151–66.

Botzem, S. and Quack, S. (2006) Contested rules and shifting boundaries: international standard setting in accounting, in M.-L. Djelic and K. Sahlin-Andersson (eds) *Transnational Governance: Institutional Dynamics of Regulation*, pp. 266–86 (Cambridge: Cambridge University Press).

Bozeman, B. (2002) Public-value failure: when efficient markets may not do, *Public Administration Review*, 62 (2): 134–51.

Brandeis, L. (1914) *Others People's Money – and How the Bankers Use It* (New York: Stokes).

Bricker, R. and Chandar, N. (1998) On applying agency theory in historical accounting research, *Business and Economic History*, 27 (2): 486–99.

Bryer, R.A. (1993) The late nineteenth–century revolution in financial reporting: accounting for the rise of investor or managerial capitalism? *Accounting, Organizations and Society*, 18 (7/8): 649–90.

Byington, R. and Sutton, S. (1991) The self-regulating profession: an analysis of the political monopoly tendencies of the audit profession, *Critical Perspectives on Accounting*, 2 (4): 315–30.

Camfferman, K. and Zeff, S. A. (2007) *Financial Reporting and Global Capital Markets: A History of the International Accounting Standards Committee, 1973–2000* (Oxford: Oxford University Press).

Chambers, R. J. and Wolnizer, P. W. (1991) A true and fair view of position and results: the historical background, *Accounting, Business & Financial History*, 1 (2): 197–213.

Chow, C. W. (1983) The impacts of accounting regulation on bondholder and shareholder wealth: the case of the Securities Acts, *Accounting Review*, 58 (3): 485–520.

Clarke, T. (2004) Cycles of crisis and regulation: the enduring agency and stewardship problems of corporate governance, *Corporate Governance: An International Review* 12 (2): 153–61.

Cooper, D. J. and Robson, K. (2006) Accounting, professions and regulation: locating the sites of professionalization, *Accounting, Organizations and Society*, 31 (4/5): 415–44.

Cooper, K. and Deo, H. (2005) Recurring cycle of Australian corporate reforms: a never ending story, *Journal of American Academy of Business*, 7 (2): 156–63.

Crafts, N. F. R. (1987) Cliometrics, 1971–1986: a survey, *Journal of Applied Econometrics*, 2 (3): 171–92.

Davis J. E. (1999) Corporate disclosure through stock exchanges, working paper, Harvard Law. Available HTTP: <http://cyber.law.harvard.edu/rfi/papers/disclose.pdf> (accessed February 2007).

Dearing, Sir R. (1988) *The Making of Accounting Standards* (London: ICAEW).

Edelman, M. (1964) *The Symbolic Uses of Politics* (London: University of Illinois Press).

Edwards, J. R. (1989) *A History of Financial Accounting* (London: Routledge).

Edwards, J. R. and Chandler, R. (2001) Contextualizing the process of accounting regulation: a study of nineteenth-century British friendly societies, *Abacus*, 37 (2): 188–216.

Ely, K. and Waymire, G. (1999) Accounting standard-setting organizations and earnings relevance: longitudinal evidence from NYSE common stocks, 1927–93, *Journal of Accounting Research*, 37 (2): 293–317.

Friend, I. and Westerfield, R. (1975) Required disclosure and the stock market: comment, *American Economic Review*, 65 (3): 467–72.

Funnell, W. (1996) Preserving history in accounting: seeking common ground between 'new' and 'old' accounting history, *Accounting, Auditing & Accountability Journal*, 9 (4): 38–64.

Gaa, J. C. (1991) The expectations game: regulation of auditors by government and the profession, *Critical Perspectives on Accounting*, 2 (1): 83–107.

Gjerde, Ø., Knivsflå, K. and Sættem, F. (2005) The value relevance of financial reporting on the Oslo Stock Exchange over the period 1964–2003. Discussion papers 2005/23, Department of Finance and Management Science, Norwegian School of Economics and Business Administration.

Gordon, I. and Morris, R. D. (1996) The equity accounting saga in Australia: cyclical standard setting, *Abacus* 32 (2): 153–77.

Graham, M. (2002) *Democracy by Disclosure: The Rise of Technopopulism* (Washington, DC: Brookings/ Governance Institute).

Harrison, G. L. and McKinnon, J. L. (1986) Culture and accounting change: a new perspective on corporate reporting regulation and accounting policy formulation, *Accounting, Organizations and Society*, 11 (3): 233–52.

Hopwood, A. G. (1987) The archaeology of accounting systems, *Accounting, Organizations and Society*, 12 (3): 207–34.

Jones, D. G. B., Richardson, A. J. and Shearer, T. (2000) Truth and the evolution of the professions: a comparative study of 'Truth in Advertising' and 'True-and-Fair' financial statements during the Progressive Era in North America, *Journal of Macromarketing*, 20 (6): 23–35.

Jones, S. (1995) A cross-sectional analysis of recommendations for company financial disclosure and auditing by nineteenth-century parliamentary witnesses, *Accounting, Business & Financial History*, 5 (2): 159–86.

Jones, S. and Aiken, M. (1995) British companies legislation and social and political evolution during the nineteenth century, *British Accounting Review*, 27 (1): 61–82.

Jordana, J. and Levi-Faur, D. (2004) The politics of regulation in the age of governance, in J. Jordana and D. Levi-Faur (eds) *The Politics of Regulation: Institutions and Regulatory Reforms for the Age of Governance*, pp. 1–27 (London: Edward Elgar Publishing).

Jucius, M. J. (1943) Historical development of uniform accounting, *Journal of Business of the University of Chicago*, 16 (4): 219–29.

King, R. and Waymire, G. (1994) Accounting standard-setting institutions and the governance of incomplete contracts, *Journal of Accounting, Auditing and Finance*, 9 (3): 579–605.

Laughlin, R. (1995) Empirical research in accounting: alternative approaches and a case for 'middle-range' thinking, *Accounting, Auditing & Accountability Journal*, 8 (1): 63–87.

Leach, S. R. and Stamp, E. (eds) (1981) *British Accounting Standards: The First 10 Years* (Cambridge: Woodhead-Faulkner).

Lieberman, E. S. (2001) Causal inference in historical institutional analysis: a specification of periodization strategies, *Comparative Political Studies*, 34 (9): 1011–35.

Loft, A., Humphrey, C. and Turley, S. (2006) In pursuit of global regulation changing governance and accountability structures at the International Federation of Accountants (IFAC), *Accounting, Auditing & Accountability Journal*, 19 (3): 428–51.

McCraw, T. K. (1982) With consent of the governed: SEC's formative years, *Journal of Policy Analysis and Management*, 1 (3): 346–70.

Mahoney, P. G. (2001) The political economy of the Securities Act of 1933, *Journal of Legal Studies*, 30 (1): 1–31.

Maltby, J. (1998) UK joint stock companies legislation 1844–1900: accounting publicity and 'mercantile caution', *Accounting History*, 3 (1): 9–32.

Maltby, J. (2000) The origins of prudence in accounting, *Critical Perspectives on Accounting*, 11 (1): 51–70.

March, J. G. and Olsen, J. P. (1989) *Rediscovering Institutions: The Organizational Basis of Politics* (New York: The Free Press).

Martinez-Diaz, L. (2005) Strategic experts and improvising regulators: explaining the IASC's rise to global influence, 1973–2001, *Business and Politics*, 7 (3): article 3. Available HTTP: <http://www.bepress.com/bap/vol7/iss3/art3>.

May A. W. (1939) Financial regulation abroad: the contrasts with American technique, *Journal of Political Economy*, 47 (4): 457–96.

Meier-Schatz, C. J. (1986) Disclosure rules in the U. S., Germany and Switzerland, *American Journal of Comparative Law*, 34 (2): 271–94.

Merino, B. D. and Coe, L. T. (1978) Uniformity in accounting: a historical perspective, *Journal of Accountancy*, 146 (2): 62–9.

Merino, B. D. and Mayper, A. G. (2001) Securities legislation and the accounting profession in the 1930s: the rhetoric and reality of the American dream, *Critical Perspectives on Accounting*, 12 (4): 501–25.

Merino, B. D. and Neimark, M. D. (1982) Disclosure regulation and public policy: a socio-historical reappraisal, *Journal of Accounting and Public Policy*, 1 (1): 33–57.

Merino, B. D., Koch, B. S. and MacRitchie, K. L. (1987) Historical analysis – A diagnostic tool for 'Events' studies: The impact of the Securities Act of 1933, *Accounting Review*, 62 (4): 748–62.

Merino, B. D., Mayper, A. G. and Sriram R. S. (1994) Voluntary audits in New York markets in 1927: a case study, *Journal of Business Finance & Accounting*, 21 (5): 619–42.

Merton, R. (1968) *Social Theory and Social Structure*, Enlarged edn (New York: The Free Press).

Mezias, S. J. and Chung, S. (2006) Regulatory capture, interest group theory, and institutional mediation: the regulatory politics of financial reporting rules, 1973–1987. Paper presented at the First Annual Conference on Institutional Mechanisms for Industry Self-Regulation, Hanover, 24–25 February.

Miller, P., Hopper, T. and Laughlin, R. (1991) The new accounting history: an introduction, *Accounting, Organizations and Society*, 16 (5/6) 395–403.

Mills, P. A. (1990) Agency, auditing and the unregulated environment: some further historical evidence, *Accounting, Auditing & Accountability Journal*, 3 (1): 54–66.

Mills, P. A. (1993) The courts, accounting evolution and freedom of contract: a comment on the case law research, *Accounting, Organizations and Society*, 18 (7/8): 765–81.

Mills, P. A. (1994) The adjudication of accounting-based compensation contracts in the pre-1934 period, *Accounting, Business & Financial History*, 4 (3): 385–402.

Miranti, P. J. (1989) The mind's eye of reform: the ICC's Bureau of Statistics and Accounts and a vision of regulation, 1887–1940, *Business History Review*, 63 (3): 469–509.

Moran, M. and Previts, G. J. (1984) The SEC and the profession, 1934–84: the realities of self-regulation, *Journal of Accountancy*, 158 (1): 68–80.

Mueller, G. G. (1965) International experience with uniform accounting, *Law and Contemporary Problems*, 30 (4): 850–73.

Napier, C. (2001) Accounting history and accounting progress, *Accounting History*, 6 (2): 7–31.

Nobes, C. W. (1991) Cycles in UK standard setting, *Accounting and Business Research*, 21 (83): 265–74.

Nobes, C. W. (1992) A political history of goodwill in the U.K.: an illustration of cyclical standard setting, *Abacus*, 28 (2): 142–67.

Nobes, C. W. and Parker, R. (2002) *Comparative International Accounting*, 7th edn (Harlow: Pearson Education).

North, D. C. (1990) *Institutions, Institutional Change, and Economic Performance*, (Cambridge: Cambridge University Press).

North, D. C. (1997) Cliometrics-40 years later, *American Economic Review*, 87 (2): 412–14.

Okcabol, F. and Tinker, T. (1993) Dismantling financial disclosure regulations: testing the Stigler–Benston Hypothesis, *Accounting, Auditing & Accountability Journal*, 6 (1): 10–36.

Parker, R. H. (1990) Regulating British corporate financial reporting in the late nineteenth century, *Accounting, Business & Financial History*, 1 (1): 51–71.

Peltzman, S. (1976) Toward a more general theory of regulation, *Journal of Law and Economics*, 19 (2): 211–40.

PHAC (2007) Glossary of terms. Available HTTP: http://www.phac-aspc.gc.ca/vs-sb/glossary_e.html#_G_-_L (accessed 2 November 2007).

Puxty, A. G., Willmott, H., Cooper, D. and Lowe, T. (1987) Modes of regulation in advanced capitalism: locating accountancy in four countries, *Accounting, Organizations and Society*, 12 (3): 273–92.

Richard, J. (2005) The concept of fair value in French and German accounting regulations from 1673 to 1914 and its consequences for the interpretation of the stages of development of capitalist accounting, *Critical Perspectives on Accounting*, 16 (6): 825–50.

Richardson, A. J. (1989) Corporatism and intraprofessional hegemony: a study of regulation and internal social order, *Accounting, Organizations and Society*, 14 (5/6): 415–31.

Richardson, A. J. (2006) Regulatory networks for accounting standards: a social network analysis of Canadian accounting standard-setting. Paper presented at Interdisciplinary Perspectives on Accounting Conference, Cardiff, July.

Richardson, A. J. and MacDonald, L. D. (2002) Linking international business theory to accounting history: implications of the international evolution of the state and firm for accounting history research, *Accounting and Business Research*, 32 (2): 67–78.

Robson, K. (1991) On the arenas of accounting change: the process of translation, *Accounting, Organizations and Society*, 16 (5/6): 547–70.

Robson, K. (1992) Accounting numbers as inscription: action at a distance and the development of accounting, *Accounting, Organizations and Society*, 17 (7): 685–708.

Rutherford, B. A. (2007) *Financial Reporting in UK: A History of the Accounting Standards Committee, 1969–1990* (London: Routledge).

Saemann, G. (1999) An examination of comment letters filed in the U.S. financial accounting standard-setting process by institutional interest groups, *Abacus*, 35 (1): 1–28.

Schmitter, P. C. and Lehmbruch, G. (eds) (1979) *Trends toward Corporatist Intermediation* (London: Sage).

Schoenfeld, H-M. W. (1981) International accounting: development, issues, and future directions, *Journal of International Business Studies*, 12 (2): 83–100.

SEC (Securities and Exchange Commission) (1977) *Report of the Advisory Committee on Corporate Disclosure to the Securities and Exchange Commission*, Committee Print 95–29, House Committee on Interstate and Foreign Commerce, 95th Cong., 1st sess., 3 November.

Seligman, J. (1983) The historical need for a mandatory corporate disclosure system, *Journal of Corporate Law*, 9 (1): 10–34.

Shepard, G. B. (1996) Fierce compromise: the Administrative Procedure Act emerges from New Deal politics, *Northwestern University Law Review*, 90 (4): 1557–683.

Simon, C. J. (1989) The effect of the 1933 Securities Act on investor information and the performance of new issues, *American Economic Review*, 79 (3): 295–318.

Sivakumar, K. and Waymire, G. (2003) Enforceable accounting rules and income measurement by early 20th century railroads, *Journal of Accounting Research*, 41 (2): 397–432.

Skerratt, L. and Whittington, G. (1992) Does the Nobes Cycle exist, and if so, what does it signify?, *Accounting and Business Research*, 22 (86): 173–7.

Stigler, G. J. (1964) Public regulation of the securities markets, *Journal of Business*, 37 (2): 117–42.

Stigler, G. J. (1971) Theory of economic regulation, *Bell Journal of Economics and Management Science*, 2 (1): 3–21.

Street D. L. and Shaughnessy, K. A. (1998) The evolution of the G4 + 1 and its impact on international harmonization of accounting standards, *Journal of International Accounting, Auditing and Taxation*, 7 (2): 131–61.

Taylor, P. and Turley, S. (1986) *The Regulation of Accounting* (London: Blackwell).

Vogel, D. (1986) *National Styles of Regulation* (Ithaca, NY: Cornell University Press).

Walker, R. G. (1987) Australia's ASRB. A case study of political activity and regulatory 'capture', *Accounting and Business Research* 17 (67): 269–86.

Walker, R. G. and Mack, J. (1998) The influence of regulation on the publication of consolidated statements, *Abacus*, 34 (1): 48–74.

Walker, S. P. (1996) Laissez faire, collectivism and companies legislation in nineteenth-century Britain, *British Accounting Review*, 28 (4): 305–24.

Walker, S. P. (2000) Editorial, *Accounting History*, 5 (2): 5–12.

Walton, P. J. (1986) The export of British accounting legislation to Commonwealth countries, *Accounting and Business Research*, 16 (64): 353–7.

Walton, P. J. (1995) *European Financial Reporting: A History* (London: Academic Press).

Whittred, G. (1986) The evolution of consolidated financial reporting in Australia, *Abacus*, 22 (2): 103–20.

Williamson, O. E. (1985) *The Economic Institutions of Capitalism* (New York: The Free Press).

Woolley, J. T. and Peters, G. (2007) *The American Presidency Project*. Available HTTP http://www.presidency.ucsb.edu/ws/?pid=14602 (accessed 2 November 2007).

Young, J. (1994) Outlining regulatory space: agenda issues and the FASB, *Accounting, Organizations and Society*, 19 (1): 83–109.

Zeff, S. A. (1972) *Forging Accounting Principles in Five Countries: A History and an Analysis of Trends* (Champaign, IL: Stipes Publishing Company).

Zeff, S. A. (2006) Political lobbying on accounting standards – national and international experience, in C. W. Nobes and R. Parker (eds), *Comparative International Accounting*, 9th edn, pp. 189–220 (London: Prentice Hall).

Part 5

Economy

15

Capitalism

Steven Toms

Overview

It is difficult to imagine capitalist economic organisation without the techniques of double-entry bookkeeping. At the same time, capitalism is a system that constantly transforms economic organisation. It would be expected therefore that economic and social change contribute fundamentally to accounting change. Moreover, accounting itself may be an agent of such change. In short, accounting is fundamentally implicated in all stages of the development of capitalism, in its different forms and its geographical variations.

Accounting is also thereby implicated in transformations in ownership, with war and social upheaval, and is also vital to our understanding of the more stable phases of capitalist development. Accounting enjoys a symbiotic relationship with social change, so that analysing social processes is necessary to our understanding of accounting, while accounting itself is a useful tool for historians and others for understanding those processes.

In this chapter, these relationships will be analysed using a critical framework, so that approaches from several research traditions can be acknowledged. Within this framework, the links between relevant literatures from various disciplines, particularly history, economics and politics, and commonly appreciated aspects of accounting theory and practice will be explained.

Having introduced this theoretical framework, the chapter is then structured with reference to important periods of history in chronological order using examples of empirical research drawn from the main theoretical perspectives. It begins with a review of the major contributions to each of the theoretical perspectives. These are then illustrated in the next section which examines a series of historical contexts following in chronological order. These are, first, the transition from feudalism to capitalism, and how accounting was implicated in the transition, which has been the subject of debate for nearly a hundred years. Second, the role of accounting in the upheavals of the Industrial Revolution is examined. Third, the rise of managerial capitalism and the associated development of accounting techniques are considered. Recent developments are then examined, with a focus on the Enron scandal. A concluding section sets out some future directions and challenges.

Some theoretical contrasts

A common focus of accounting historians is the relative power of social groups, especially managers and shareholders. Even so, there are a larger number of interpretations of the relationships implied by differential power and the consequences for accounting. For example, accounting might be located in the social relations of production (Tinker 1980), or alternatively it may be incorporated into a legitimacy theory perspective (Gray *et al.* 1995). The former view implies a Marxist interpretation in which the accounting historian analyses how capital is created, accumulated and distributed. Because of the exploitation that underlies theses processes, the corporation, and capitalist accounting itself, are seen as illegitimate. In the alternative view, the corporation's activities can ultimately be legitimised. To the extent that it is engaging in illegitimate activity, for example, environmental degradation, accounting becomes a device to be used by managers to enable the firm to be rehabilitated in the public imagination, thereby justifying and continuing its activities. The legitimacy issue clearly separates these views. A further distinction is that, in the latter case, management uses accounting proactively, whereas in the former, managers and by implication accountants can make no difference to the systematic outcome, since power resides with the owners of capital. A method is needed to disentangle some of the competing approaches in a fashion helpful to the accounting historian.

Table 15.1 suggests a grouping with two dimensions. The first is the attitude of the researcher towards capitalism, which might be characterised as mainstream or radical.

> To be 'mainstream' is almost by definition to believe in, or at least to be open to, the legitimacy of the capitalist firm and the economic system in which it is embedded, while to be radical seems to require some display of hostility toward them.
>
> (Putterman 1986: 25)

The second dimension is the researchers' ontological perspective, which might be characterised as objective or subjective. Burrell and Morgan (1989) use a similar approach when considering research generally in the social sciences. The subjective view implies knowledge is grounded in individual experience and free will, the objective view implies a concrete reality where knowledge can be gained through observation. In accounting history research, the distinction has an important impact on the research focus as well as the method. A subjectivist accounting historian will focus on individuals and interpret their contribution using archival investigation. An objectivist accounting historian will more typically focus on institutions and markets and may for example compile numerical datasets to test hypotheses. In Table 15.1, the subjective-objective axis is shown horizontally and the mainstream-radical axis is shown vertically.[1] As a result there are four possible approaches in accounting history, managerialist and positivist are the mainstream approaches and structuralist and post-modernist are the radical approaches.[2] Each is now discussed in turn, citing examples from the accounting history literature.

Table 15.1 Theoretical contrasts

		View of subject matter	
		Subjective	*Objective*
View of society	*Radical change*	Post-modernist	Structuralist
	Mainstream	Managerialist	Positivist

Mainstream approaches: managerialist accounting history

The managerialist approach gives primacy to the role of managers as independent and usually rational decision-makers. There is little explicit reliance on theory. Emphasis is placed on the empirical relationship between the emergence of managerial capitalism (Chandler 1977) and the development of modern accounting (Chatfield 1977; Edwards 1989).[3] For example, it has been argued that the *laissez-faire* environment of the late nineteenth century implied a high degree of managerial choice, which became an important determinant of the financial reporting mechanism (Edwards 1989: 125; Baldwin 1994). Furthermore, excess directors' power, reinforced by lack of rules on disclosure, prevented the emergence of an efficient capital market (Kennedy 1987: 126). Even so, for this school of thought, managerial action is both rational and legitimate. An obvious criticism of the managerialist approach is that in separating the manager as an independent rational decision-maker, the governance issue, which lies at the centre of the positivist approach, is ignored. Accountability structures imposed by governance arrangements can significantly constrain managerial freedom of action.

Mainstream approaches: positivist accounting history

Unlike the empirical and atheoretical approach adopted by the managerialists, positive accounting has developed from two strands of theory in economics: transaction cost and principal agent theory. Transaction cost theory explains organisational forms in terms of governance costs and their minimisation, along with production costs, in conditions of managerial opportunism and asymmetric information (Coase 1937; Williamson 1975, 1981). For an example of the application of this approach to management accounting, see Johnson and Kaplan (1987). Similarly, principal agent theory explains the consequences of asymmetric information in terms of monitoring costs incurred by principals to ensure managerial compliance with shareholder objectives (Jensen and Meckling 1976). Accounting information and processes are important in both theories for mitigating information asymmetry. For example, positivism suggests that management have an incentive to voluntarily submit to audit as a quality signal (Jensen and Meckling 1976; Watts and Zimmerman 1983; Edwards *et al.* 1997). An extension of the positivist methodology is the use of the event study, which in certain limited cases has been applied to historical data (Chow 1983; Sivakumar and Waymire 1993; Toms 2001). In the world of positivism, managerial attitudes are predetermined as rational and are therefore irrelevant. Because they respond rationally to market forces in the presence of information asymmetry and transaction cost, it is pointless for the historian or anyone else to consider their attitudes any further.

The positivist approach is problematic for several related reasons. First, it is often unsupported by historical analysis (Merino *et al.* 1987). Second, there is little empirical evidence on market efficiency in the periods analysed (Sivakumar and Waymire 1993: 88; Toms 2001). Third, from Ball and Brown (1968) onwards, studies of accounting earnings and share price relationship have taken informational market efficiency as descriptive (Watts and Zimmerman 1986: 37), notwithstanding the logical impossibility of market efficiency where transaction costs exist (Grossman and Stiglitz 1980). Consequently, empirical studies exclude from samples those companies whose stocks are likely to demonstrate attributes of inefficiency such as thin trading (for example, Sivakumar and Waymire 1993: 68).[4]

Radical approaches: post-modern accounting history

The post-modernist perspective stresses the role of accounting, especially management accounting, in the control of labour. Ezzamel *et al.* (1990) attribute the rise of managerialism identified by Chandler (1977) to a genealogy of the disciplinary use of accounting controls traced to military training at West Point in the early nineteenth century. According to Hoskin and Macve (2000), in the coal, iron and other industries, the accounting management used went beyond 'economic rationalism' and 'labour control' so that Foucault's 'disciplinary' power, exercised through continuous surveillance, forms the basis of human accountability essential to Chandler's (1977) 'visible hand' of administrative co-ordination. It has been this approach, characterised as the 'new accounting history' that has sought to increase accounting history's impact through broadening its methodologies so that it stands more centrally within the social sciences. Although this view implies attention to transformations in accounting knowledge, there is post-modernist inspired scepticism towards the notions of progress and evolution (Miller *et al.* 1991).

Critics of the post-modernist interpretation in general and Hoskin and Macve in particular, have suggested that accounting cannot function as part of a continuous surveillance mechanism. Accounting by definition implies intermittent measurement. Boyns and Edwards (2000) argue that the process of gathering archival evidence has scarcely begun and therefore it is dangerous to locate the origins of techniques so specifically and so definitively. Moreover, as Tyson suggests (2000), over-reliance on theory can lead to denial of subsequent evidence where inconvenient.

Radical approaches: structuralist accounting history

The radical structuralist method is best exemplified by political economy approaches. The usual focus of political economy of accounting (PEA) is the relative power of social groups (Cooper and Sherer 1984: 218), especially managers and shareholders.[5] The radical structuralist approach, like the positivist, accordingly stresses the rise of the capital market, and underpins an alternative hypothesis of powerful shareholders and investor groups as the social instigators of modern accounting. Collective interests of capital dominate managers who assume the role of mere 'functionaries', as capital becomes 'socialised' (Bryer 1993a, 2000a). Consequently, modern accounting materialises as a response to the interests of collective capital. In these conditions, management is 'the eclectic pursuit of surplus value' (Bryer 2006). At the same time empirical progress towards global capital market efficiency is evidence of the unexpended progressive tendencies of capitalism (Desai 2002). Even so, PEA advocates rarely extol the virtues of markets, arguing that they are a poor description of the reality of scandal and corruption in resource allocation and distribution between labour and capital (Tinker *et al.* 1982: 171–2). Other variants of Marxism and radical structuralism tend to reify and even 'hypostatise' giant corporations, describing a form of capitalism without capitalists (Zeitlin 1989).

The main problem with the radical structuralist perspectives is their tendency to over-determine the evidence. In contrast to the post-modernists, they require everything to fit a grand narrative and unlike the mainstream approaches, they tend to look for single over-arching causes. Strands of radical structuralism are also fundamental incompatible with one another. Are managers in large corporations powerful or not, for example? Or does power reside anonymously with 'capital'?

Contexts and debates

Each of the four perspectives introduced in the previous section surfaces to some extent in the major debates in accounting history that concern the relationship between accounting and capitalism. These are now dealt with chronologically, with examples of each of the four perspectives highlighted.

Accounting and the rise of capitalism

The debate on accounting and the rise of capitalism begins with Sombart (1916). The 'Sombart thesis' is based on six pages of *Der moderne Kapitalismus*, in which he suggests that it is impossible to envisage accounting without capitalism and impossible to envisage capitalism without accounting. For Sombart, double-entry bookkeeping (DEB) is a sufficient condition for capitalism to exist, and he locates the origins of capitalism with DEB in medieval and Renaissance Catholic Italy. As DEB replaced narrative accounts, it brought order to the affairs of merchants. Specifically it facilitated the process of valuing and accumulating capital, set out capital as a concept and allowed the business entity concept, or the separation of the business from its owner(s), to develop. Needless to say, the Sombart assertion has since enervated accounting history as an empirical project, as scholars have conducted extensive searches in the archives for falsifying examples.

As the Sombart hypothesis has been examined against the evidence, it has also been subject to refinement. Max Weber (1927) makes a far more specific claim. He makes no mention of the contribution of DEB to the birth and development of capitalism, but more precisely equates the universal condition of capitalism with the development of the capital account. He attributes the original advocacy of the capital account to the Dutch Calvinist Simon Stevin in 1698, which all would acknowledge post-dates Pacioli and DEB by two hundred years. In other words, for Weber at least, DEB is a necessary but not sufficient condition for capitalism.

Bryer, as an illustration of the structuralist perspective, refines Sombart and Weber by a further stage, suggesting that the ability to calculate the rate of return on capital is the defining feature of capitalism. Such a calculation is impossible without Weber's capital account. However, Bryer's perspective differs in a fundamental respect, which is important for the accounting historian to recognise. His suggestion is that the historian should look for evidence of the calculations performed, not simply the existence of accounts of a certain type. These calculations are the 'accounting signatures' which encapsulate certain 'calculative mentalities'. Examples include the calculation of 'consumable surplus' by feudal landowners and profit calculations by capitalist farmers (Bryer 2004, 2006b), rate of return calculations by Italian merchants from the late fourteenth century (Bryer 1993b) and the calculation of return on capital employed by investing capitalists holding 'socialised' (i.e. collectively owned) capital (Bryer 2000a, 2000b).

Chiapello (2007) demonstrates that the idea or notion of accounting as important to the birth of the notion of capitalism. A similar refinement, suggested by Carruthers and Espeland (1991), is that accounting should be evaluated according to its rhetorical significance. Accounting is, for Weber and others, a set of rational techniques which produce apparently objective and neutral results. These results provide symbolic legitimacy to the forms of business organization adopting them. In other words, Carruthers and Espeland, like Bryer, are interested in how the objective content of accounts is subjectively determined. Unlike Bryer, they are concerned with a legitimation process at societal level and might therefore be classed as promoting a managerialist perspective, so that the advantages of DEB from the point of view of the merchant can be appreciated.

In contrast to those scholars whose project is to refine the Sombart thesis, others have been more concerned with refuting it altogether. The most prominent of these is Yamey (1964, 2005). For Yamey, it is entirely possible to calculate the capital of a business without using DEB, for example, by valuing individual assets and adding the result. Accounts compiled using DEB and rates of return calculations were, in any case, he suggested, not very useful for decision-making purposes. He also challenges Sombart's argument that the separation of the business from its owners is only made possible by DEB, by suggesting that partnership businesses predate DEB. Lemarchand (1994) is sceptical about Sombart for similar reasons and finds evidence in French businesses of relatively late evolution of DEB, notwithstanding the earlier emergence of capitalistic organisations. Although coming to different conclusions, like Carruthers and Espeland, these interpretations are essentially managerialist as they are concerned with evaluating the utility of DEB to managerial decision-makers. Empirically, they expect to find DEB where it has useful context.

A final and recent contribution worth noting comes from Aho (2005), who broadly agrees with Sombart but challenges the aspects of Weber that link the rise of capitalism to Protestantism.[6] In contrast to Weber, Aho locates the origins of DEB in the rhetoric and practice of the Roman Catholic Church. Medieval merchants used the rhetoric of DEB to justify their behaviour in an age when business activity was likely to offend moral sensibilities. Aho therefore takes issue with Weber and, like Sombart, believes medieval Catholicism encouraged the pursuit of wealth and created the conditions for DEB and the emergence of capitalism. The extent to which these general social forces and religious ideology determined capitalism and therefore the development of DEB is a matter for debate within the structuralist school of thought.

To summarise all the debates, the Sombart thesis remains useful to the accounting historian for two reasons. First, it provides a framework for evaluating empirical research. The evidence from France alone suggests some very uneven patterns in the adoption of specific aspects of DEB. So the more the Sombart thesis is refined, the more focused the empirical project becomes. In turn, this may encourage further refinement of the thesis. Second, therefore, through further historical accounting research, a good deal more can be discovered by accounting historians about the process of transition from feudalism to capitalism.

The Industrial Revolution and nineteenth-century Britain

It is commonly accepted that Britain experienced an 'industrial revolution' between around 1760 to 1850 (Landes 1969). The Industrial Revolution and its associated developments in accounting methods have generated more interest for accounting historians than the Sombart thesis. A likely reason is that the operations of industrial companies provide a more obvious starting point for the discovery of early examples of the use of 'modern' accounting techniques. Ironically, one of the first major studies, carried out by Pollard (1965), found that accounting did nothing to aid entrepreneurial decision-making (ibid.: 248). Since then, revisionist, typically managerialist, historians have set out to discover evidence of good practice and in some cases have found it. For example, Edwards and Newell (1991) reject Pollard's pessimistic conclusions and Fleischman and Parker (1991) conclude that accounting historians have by and large refuted Pollard's view of inadequate costing methods, but tend to agree with him on the inadequacy of financial accounting.

While the managerialists have found plenty of examples of the evolution of managerial accounting techniques in the nineteenth century, positivists have advanced regulatory interpretations of nineteenth-century accounting developments. The effect has been to concentrate studies in particular industries to the exclusion of others. On the basis of such limited evidence, accounting change might be seen as a response to the demand for self-interested accounting choices. For example, the development of depreciation accounting as a response to changes in taxation law (Watts and Zimmerman 1979: 293–5). For Parker (1990), accounting change in the late Victorian period was a response to increasing regulation, particularly in the banking sector (Parker 1990; Walker 1996) and railways and utilities (Edwards 1992). So when applied in a historical context, these authors suggest larger British firms tended to adopt professional auditors voluntarily. Therefore they concluded, the unregulated free market was sufficient for adequate accountability (Edwards *et al.* 1997: 22), and that the emergence of a large capital market, and associated reductions in unit audit costs was the prime determinant of the development of modern auditing (Watts and Zimmerman 1983: 630).

From a structuralist perspective, Bryer (2005) examines the accounting histories of the New Mills (Haddingtonshire, formed in 1681), the New Lanark Cotton Factory (1800 to 1812), and the Carron Company (formed in 1759), arguing that these cases show that the primary cause of variations in modern accounts were variations in the 'social relations of production'. He concludes that the published accounting evidence supports the theory that the Industrial Revolution was the victory of the capitalist mentality. Later, as the railways developed, the collective interests of capital dominate managers who assume the role of mere 'functionaries' as capital ownership became increasingly 'socialised' (Bryer 1993).

The post-modern perspective offers interesting new insights from an accounting history and social science perspective. These can be summarised as the necessity of context (Hopwood 1983), through the use of the Foucauldian notions of *archaeology*, or the emergence of forms of discourse and how they are configured in their non-discursive domains (for example, economic and institutional). *Genealogy*, on the other hand looks at ruptures, or transitions leading to the adoption of new practices which as a result achieve new significance in the revised context (Hopwood 1983: 230). Using the example of Josiah Wedgwood's pottery business, Hopwood explains how a financial crisis caused Wedgwood to set up an accounting system for the first time in order to investigate the situation. As a result, the system was permanently adopted and adapted to form a crucial part of the strategy and decision-making process. As Hopwood (1987: 213) suggests, organisational accounts are not merely a technical reflection of pre-given economic imperatives but are actively constructed to create economic visibility, as a powerful means for positively enabling the governance and economic control of the organization. Notwithstanding these useful insights, there has been relatively little empirical work on the Industrial Revolution from this perspective.

As can be seen from this very brief review, the debates on the Industrial Revolution have concentrated on empirical sources, primarily with a view to finding evidence of managers using accounts to make rational decisions. In terms of debates, the Industrial Revolution, excepting some marginal contribution from the positivists, is primarily about structuralist and managerialist interpretations. Both have found plenty of evidence of 'rational decisions' and 'capitalist signatures'. Unfortunately it is easy to infer either conclusion from the same body of evidence and the attitude of the reader will have a strong influence on which view is believed. Meanwhile the new accounting history offers the possibility of further studies and new interpretations.

The rise of the managerial capitalism

Managerial capitalism is associated with the work of Chandler and his extensive research which documents the rise of the large business organisation in the United States from the late nineteenth century onwards. Accounting and managerial accounting techniques were important components of managerial capitalism. In contrast to the USA, where managerialism flourished, Britain, in the Chandlerian view, remained wedded to an increasingly out-of-date and uncompetitive system of personal capitalism. If the Chandler thesis is correct, it is to the large US industrial firm that the accounting historian should direct attention. It might be expected therefore that this section is dominated by mainstream managerialism, but the other perspectives also offer important insights into the role of accounting in big business.

An influential application of transaction cost theory to management accounting history is Johnson and Kaplan's (1987) *Relevance Lost*. They examine the transition from a market environment where entrepreneurial instinct and centralised ownership prevailed to decentralised business enterprises guided by accounting techniques that assisted in the reduction of transaction cost. Through this process, the vast majority of management accounting techniques in use today were developed by the 1920s and a period of stagnation ensued. According to their thesis, the stagnation was the result of the privileging of financial accounting by accountants and the failure of academics to go beyond simplified abstract questions.

If Johnson and Kaplan's approach can be characterised as positivist, there has been implicit or explicit criticism from all three alternative schools of thought in Table 15.1. From the mainstream managerialist perspective, Chandler (1981, 1990) stresses the role of vertical integration and managerial co-ordination as the determinant of organisational efficiency rather than transaction cost. Hopper and Armstrong (1991), taking a radical structuralist perspective assign similar importance to market power, which the transaction cost approach neglects, showing how budgeting was used to facilitate monopoly pricing at DuPont. Labour management and control of the labour process are also offered as important explanations for the development of twentieth century budgeting techniques ignored by both Johnson and Kaplan's transaction cost and Chandler's managerialist perspectives. Using examples from the Boston district textile industry and US metals and arms manufacturers, Hopper and Armstrong show that techniques were adopted for the purposes of surveillance, workshop control and profit appropriation, even if such control was achieved at the expense of short-term efficiency. Surveillance also lies at the centre of post-modernist explanations of the genesis of accounting techniques. Hoskin and Macve's (2000) critique of Johnson and Kaplan suggested that 'managing it all by numbers' was a futile exercise from this point of view and, in any case, accounting numbers could not capture economic magnitudes properly.

In summary, Johnson and Kaplan's work has been influential in the development of accounting history in part from the strength of its original thesis and also as a result of the robustness of the responses. Table 15.1 provides a useful mechanism for triangulating and contrasting these interpretations.

'Financialisation' and the 'Enron' stage

Since the 1980s, there has been evidence that the rise of managerial capitalism has been reversed in Britain and the USA (Toms and Wright 2002, 2005). Layered structures of management have been removed through downsizing and the scope of business activity has been reduced through refocusing. While these issues have dominated the agenda of management research, the implications for accounting history have been sparsely investigated. Indeed, mainstream accounting historians have had little to say about these admittedly quite recent developments.

Berle and Means (1932) claimed that the wide dispersion of stock ownership allowed management to control corporate finances, including the distribution of earnings. Central to management's power was its ability to engage in accounting manipulation, and these manipulations have formed an important part of the research agenda for accounting historians up to and including events surrounding Enron. Unsurprisingly this agenda lends itself to radical perspectives, but post-modernists denial of objectivity makes even the substantiation of creative accounting difficult, since creativity is but one of many possible 'truths'.

Where post-modern approaches have been applied, they have therefore investigated the role of accounting within organizations. A leading example is the notion of the 'governable person' controlled through the language of 'economic citizenship' exemplified by the Caterpillar case (Miller and O'Leary 1987, 1994). In this account, the scientific management of the managerial capitalism era is replaced by management rhetoric and teamwork. Miller (1986, 1991) also suggests that in the course of historical change, there are temporary and often fragile stabilities, or 'accounting complexes', which can be used to explain the adoption of accounting techniques, for example, value-added accounting, in the context of national economic objectives and political priorities. It is Caterpillar in particular that has attracted considerable criticism from other historians, particularly because of the way management rhetoric has been used as evidence, notwithstanding the difficulty of proving that the will of management altered actual events and practices on the shop-floor (Armstrong 2006).

In addition to their critique of the post-modernists, the radical structuralists add perspectives of their own to these and other developments. The period since 1945 has witnessed the rise of accountancy and finance specialists. Their dominance of the British boardroom was manifested in the solution of monitoring problems associated with diversification through the use of financial controls (Armstrong 1987: 415). Therefore, as Armstrong (1985: 137) suggests, the role of accountancy within the global function of capital has created a horizontal fission within the profession, whereby the activities of an elite have routinised, fragmented and de-skilled the work of their nominal professional colleagues. These tendencies were, if anything, more pronounced for accounting workers outside of the accounting profession (Cooper and Taylor 2000).

Armstrong (1991) has called for a re-theorisation of and empirical investigation of the history of the agency relationship. Toms (2005: 648–9) attempts this through a dialectic of financial capital socialisation (efficient and globalised capital markets being the fullest expression of socialised or pooled capital), on the one hand, and the centralisation of physical capital, on the other. Historical variations along a continuum of socialisation and physical concentration jointly explain the relative power of managerial and ownership groups, which determine in turn the character of financial and management accounting. Such a synthesis combines the positivists' view of agency as contract with the radical view of agency as control. The management of large corporations appears to be a self-perpetuating oligarchy (Zeitlin 1989: 64), but only during some phases of history. In other phases, for example, following the liberalisation of international capital markets, managerial dominance has been reversed in Britain if not in the USA; a tendency reinforced by differential development of rules on corporate governance, accounting disclosure and accounting standards (Toms and Wright 2005).

Conclusion

Accounting history has made a move towards the centre stage of social sciences in the past 20 years. In doing so, it has focused on the question of 'accounting and capitalism', by placing accounting history in the appropriate context of the economic and political system in which it operates. Accordingly, accounting history has become a dynamic and polemical discipline which has also begun to address debates among accounting researchers and future directions for accounting research as a whole.

This chapter has presented a conceptual framework and analysed the theoretical contributions on the relationship between accounting and capitalism into four principal schools of thought. None of these can be said to be truly dominant. Accounting history, where dominated by empiricism, almost by definition has little to say about the more fundamental aspects of the accounting and capitalism symbiosis discussed earlier, leaving the mainstream boxes in the grid relatively sparsely populated. On the radical side, the dominant events have been the rise of post-modern relativism and the decline of orthodox Marxism. These trends can be traced back to the 1940s and the rise of the Frankfurt School, but have been accentuated by political events in the past two decades. Even so, although post-modernism has emerged in the debates on accounting and the relationship with capitalism, and has influenced their direction, it has yet to become a dominant tendency. Meanwhile, the radical structuralists have had some of their perspectives confirmed by the Enron scandal.

How these debates evolve will depend very much on what happens to capitalism itself. Whatever the outcome in that respect, the relationship between accounting and capitalism will remain important and, as this chapter has demonstrated, provide valuable theoretical perspective and social context to the study of accounting history.

Key works

Bryer (2005) contains a comprehensive analysis of the relationship between the development of capitalism and the development of accounting from a radical perspective.

Chiapello (2007) provides an intelligent overview of accounting and the rise of capitalism and useful summaries of the debates.

Toms (2005) analyses the linkages between capitalist organisation, the development of accounting techniques and the methods of accounting control.

Notes

1   The grid in Table 15.1 is adapted from Hopper and Powell (1995) who use a similar approach to define critical accounting. See also Bryer (1998) and Rowlinson et al. (2006).
2   A fifth category can be envisioned which avoids ideology and concentrates merely on the discovery of facts. For the purposes of this chapter, such approaches are labelled 'antiquarian' and are not considered further.
3   For more detail on Chandler's influential perspective, see Chapter 9.
4   For further critique of this approach and example studies, see Chapter 17, section entitled 'Positive approach'.
5   Political economy is the interplay of power, the goals of power wielders and the productive exchange system (Zald 1970), and is concerned with the origins and distribution of power in society (Jackson 1982).
6   For a more detailed discussion, see Chapter 24.

References

Aho, J. (2005) *Confession and Bookkeeping: The Religious, Moral and Rhetorical Roots of Accounting* (Albany, NY: State University of New York Press).

Armstrong, P. (1985) Changing management control strategies: the role of competition between accountancy and other organisational professions, *Accounting, Organizations and Society*, 10 (2): 129–48.

Armstrong, P. (1987) The rise of accounting controls in British capitalist enterprises, *Accounting, Organizations and Society*, 12 (5): 415–36.

Armstrong, P. (1991) Contradiction and social dynamics in the capitalist agency relationship, *Accounting, Organizations and Society*, 16 (1): 1–25.

Armstrong, P. (2006) Ideology and the grammar of idealism: the Caterpillar controversy revisited, *Critical Perspectives on Accounting*, 17 (5): 529–48.

Baldwin, T. J. (1994) Management aspiration and audit opinion: fixed asset accounting at the Staveley Coal and Iron Company, 1863–1883, *Accounting and Business Research*, 25 (97): 3–12.

Ball, R. and Brown, P. (1968) An empirical evaluation of accounting income numbers, *Journal of Accounting Research*, 6 (2): 159–78.

Berle, A. A. and Means, G. C. (1932) *The Modern Corporation and Private Property* (Chicago: Commerce Clearing House).

Boyns, T. and Edwards, J. R. (2000) Pluralistic approaches to knowing more: a comment on Hoskin and Macve, *Accounting Historian's Journal*, 27 (1): 151–8.

Bryer, R. (1993a) The late nineteenth century revolution in financial reporting: accounting for the rise of investor or managerial capitalism, *Accounting Organizations and Society*, 18 (7/8): 649–90.

Bryer, R. (1993b) Double-entry bookkeeping and the birth of capitalism: accounting for the commercial revolution in medieval northern Italy, *Critical Perspectives on Accounting*, 4 (2): 113–40.

Bryer, R. (1998) The struggle to maturity in writing the history of accounting, and the promise – some reflections on Keenan's defence of 'traditional methodology', *Critical Perspectives on Accounting*, 9 (6): 669–81.

Bryer, R. (2000a) The history of accounting and the transition to capitalism in England. Part one: theory, *Accounting, Organizations and Society*, 25 (2): 131–62.

Bryer, R. (2000b) The history of accounting and the transition to capitalism in England. Part two: evidence, *Accounting, Organizations and Society*, 25 (4/5): 327–81.

Bryer, R. (2004) The roots of modern capitalism: a Marxist accounting history of the origins and consequences of capitalist landlords in England, *Accounting Historians Journal*, 31 (1): 1–56.

Bryer, R. (2005) A Marxist accounting history of the British industrial revolution: a review of the evidence and suggestions for research, *Accounting, Organizations and Society*, 30 (1): 25–65.

Bryer, R. (2006a) Accounting and control of the labour process, *Critical Perspectives on Accounting*, 17 (5): 551–98.

Bryer, R. (2006b) The genesis of the capitalist farmer: towards a Marxist accounting history of the English agricultural revolution, *Critical Perspectives on Accounting*, 17 (4): 367–97.

Burrell, G. and Morgan, G. (1989) *Sociological Paradigms and Organizational Analysis: Elements of the Sociology of Corporate Life* (London: Heinemann).

Carruthers, B. G. and Espeland, W. N. (1991) Accounting for rationality: double-entry bookkeeping and the rhetoric of economic rationality, *American Journal of Sociology*, 97 (1): 31–69.

Chandler, A. D. (1977) *The Visible Hand: The Managerial Revolution in American Business* (Cambridge MA: Belknap Press).

Chandler, A. D. (1981) Historical determinants of managerial hierarchies: a response to Perrow, in A. Van de Ven and W. F Joyce (eds) *Perspectives on Organisational Design and Behaviour*, pp. 391–402 (New York: Wiley).

Chandler, A. D. (1990) *Scale and Scope* (London: Belknap).

Chatfield, M. (1977) *A History of Accounting Thought* (New York: Robert Krieger).

Chiapello, E. (2007) Accounting and the birth of the notion of capitalism, *Critical Perspectives on Accounting*, 18 (6): 263–96.

Chow, C. W. (1983) The impact of accounting regulation on bondholder and shareholder wealth: the case of the Securities Acts, *Accounting Review*: 485–520.

Coase, R. (1937) The nature of the firm, *Economica*, 4 (16): 386–405.

Cooper, C. and Taylor, P. (2000) From Taylorism to Ms Taylor: the transformation of the accounting craft, *Accounting, Organizations and Society*, 25 (6): 555–78.

Cooper, D. and Sherer, M. (1984) The value of accounting reports: arguments for a political economy of accounting, *Accounting Organizations and Society*, 9 (3/4): 207–32.

Desai, M. (2002) *Marx's Revenge: The Resurgence of Capitalism and the Death of Statist Socialism* (London: Verso).

Edwards, J. R. (1989) *A History of Financial Accounting* (London: Routledge).

Edwards, J. R. (1992) Companies, corporations and accounting change, 1835–1933: a comparative study, *Accounting and Business Research*, 22 (89): 59–73.

Edwards, J. R. and Newell, E. (1991) The development of industrial cost and management accounting before 1850: a survey of the evidence, *Business History*, 33 (1): 35–57.

Edwards, J. R., Anderson, M. and Matthews, D. (1997) Accountability in a free-market economy: the British company audit, 1886, *Abacus*, 33 (1): 1–25.

Ezzamel, M., Hoskin, K. and Macve, R. (1990) Managing it all by numbers: A review of Johnson and Kaplan's *Relevance Lost*, *Accounting and Business Research*, 20 (78): 153–66.

Fleischman, R. K. and Parker, L. D. (1991) British entrepreneurs and pre-industrial revolution evidence of cost management, *Accounting Review*, 66 (8): 361–75.

Gray, R., Kouhy, R. and Lavers, S. (1995) Corporate social and environmental reporting: a review of the literature and a longitudinal study of UK disclosure, *Accounting, Auditing & Accountability Journal*, 8 (2): 47–77.

Grossman, S. and Stiglitz, J. (1980) On the impossibility of informationally efficient markets, *American Economic Review*, 70 (3): 393–408.

Hopper, T. and Armstrong, P. (1991) Cost accounting, controlling labour and the rise of conglomerates, *Accounting Organizations and Society*, 16 (5/6): 405–38.

Hopper, T. and Powell, A. (1995) Making sense of research into the organizational and social aspects of management accounting: a review of its underlying assumptions, *Journal of Management Studies*, 22 (5): 429–65.

Hopwood, A. G. (1983) On trying to study accounting in the contexts in which it operates, *Accounting Organizations and Society*, 8 (2/3): 287–305.

Hopwood, A. G. (1987) The archaeology of accounting systems, *Accounting, Organizations and Society*, 12 (3): 207–34.

Hoskin, K. and Macve, R. (2000) Knowing more as knowing less? Alternative histories of cost and management accounting in the US and the UK, *Accounting Historians Journal*, 27 (1): 91–150.

Jackson, B. (1982) *The Political Economy of Bureaucracy* (Oxford: Oxford University Press).

Jensen, M. and Meckling, W. (1976) Theory of the firm: managerial behaviour, agency costs and ownership structure, *Journal of Financial Economics*, 3 (4): 305–60.

Johnson, H. T. and Kaplan, R. (1987) *Relevance Lost* (Boston: Harvard University Press).

Kennedy, W. (1987) *Industrial Structure, Capital Markets and the Origin of British Economic Decline* (Cambridge: Cambridge University Press).

Landes, D. (1969) *The Unbound Prometheus* (Cambridge: Cambridge University Press).

Lemarchand, Y. (1994) Double entry versus charge and discharge in eighteenth century France, *Accounting, Business & Financial History*, 4 (1): 119–45.

Merino, B. D., Koch, B. S. and MacRitchie, K. L. (1987) Historical analysis – a diagnostic tool for event studies: the impact of the Securities Acts, 1933, *Accounting Review*, 62 (4): 748–62.

Miller, P. (1986) Accounting in progress – national accounting and planning in France: a review essay, *Accounting, Organizations and Society*, 11 (1): 83–104.

Miller, P. (1991) Accounting innovation beyond the enterprise: problematizing investment decisions and programming economic growth in the UK in the 1960s, *Accounting, Organizations and Society*, 16 (8): 733–62.

Miller, P. and O'Leary, T. (1987) Accounting and the construction of the governable person, *Accounting, Organizations and Society*, 12 (3): 235–66.

Miller, P. and O'Leary, T. (1994) Accounting, 'economic citizenship' and the spatial reordering of manufacture, *Accounting, Organizations and Society*, 19 (1): 15–43.

Miller, P., Hopper, T. and Laughlin, R. (1991) The new accounting history, *Accounting, Organizations and Society*, 18 (7/8): 631–47.

Parker, R. H. (1990) Regulating British corporate financial reporting in the late nineteenth century, *Accounting, Business & Financial History*, 1 (1): 51–71.

Pollard, S. (1965) *The Genesis of Modern Management: A Study of the Industrial Revolution in Great Britain* (London: Edward Arnold).

Putterman, L. (1986) The economic nature of the firm: overview, in L. Putterman (ed.) *The Economic Nature of the Firm*, pp. 1–29 (Cambridge: Cambridge University Press).

Rowlinson, M., Toms, S. and Wilson, J. F. (2006) Legitimacy and the capitalist corporation: cross-cutting perspectives on ownership and control, *Critical Perspectives on Accounting*, 17 (5): 681–702.

Sivakumar, K. and Waymire, G. (1993) The information content of earnings in a discretionary reporting environment: evidence from NYSE industrials, 1905–1910, *Journal of Accounting Research*, 31 (1): 62–91.

Sombart, W. (1916) *Der moderne Kapitalismus* (Leipzig: Duncker & Humblot).

Tinker. T. (1980) Towards a political economy of accounting: an empirical illustration of the Cambridge controversies, *Accounting, Organizations and Society*, 5 (1): 147–60.

Tinker, T. (1985) *Paper Prophets: A Social Critique of Accounting* (London: Holt, Rinehart & Winston).

Tinker T., Merino, B. and Neimark, M. (1982) The normative origins of positive theories: ideology and accounting thought, *Accounting, Organizations and Society*, 7 (2): 167–200.

Toms, J. S. (2001) Information content of earnings announcements in an unregulated market: the co-operative Cotton Mills of Lancashire, 1880–1900, *Accounting and Business Research*, 31 (3): 175–90.

Toms, J. S. (2005) Financial control, managerial control and accountability: evidence from the British cotton industry, 1700–2000, *Accounting, Organizations and Society*, 30 (7/8): 627–53.

Toms, J. S. and Wright, D. M. (2002) Corporate governance, strategy and structure in British business history, 1950–2000, *Business History*, 44 (3): 91–124.

Toms, J. S. and Wright, D. M. (2005) Corporate governance, strategy and refocusing: US and British comparatives, 1950–2000, *Business History*, 47 (2): 267–295.

Tyson, T. (2000) Accounting history and the emperor's new clothes: a response to knowing more as knowing less, *Accounting Historian's Journal*, 27 (1): 159–72.

Walker, S. P. (1996) Laissez-faire, collectivism and companies legislation in nineteenth century Britain, *British Accounting Review*, 28 (4): 305–24.

Watts, R. and Zimmerman, J. (1979) The demand and supply of accounting theories: the market for excuses, *Accounting Review*, 54 (2): 273–305.

Watts, R. and Zimmerman, J. (1983) Agency problems, auditing, and the theory of the firm: some evidence, *Journal of Law and Economics*, 26 (3): 613–34.

Watts, R. and Zimmerman, J. (1986) *Positive Accounting Theory* (New Jersey: Prentice Hall).

Weber, M. (1927) *General Economic History*, trans. by F. H. Knight (London: Allen & Unwin).

Williamson, O. E. (1975) *Markets and Hierarchies* (London: Free Press).

Williamson, O. E. (1981) The modern corporation: origins, evolution and attributes, *Journal of Economic Literature*, 19 (4): 1537–68.

Yamey, B. S. (1964) Accounting and the rise of capitalism: further notes of a theme by Sombart, *Journal of Accounting Research*, 2 (2): 117–36.

Yamey, B. S. (2005) The historical significance of double entry bookkeeping: some non-Sombartian claims, *Accounting, Business & Financial History*, 15 (1): 77–88.

Zald, M. (1970) Political economy: a framework for comparative analysis, in M. Zald (ed.) *Power in Organisations*, pp. 221–261 (Nashville, TN: Vanderbilt University Press).

Zeitlin, M. (1989) *The Large Corporation and Contemporary Classes* (Cambridge: Polity Press).

16

National accounting

Ignace de Beelde

Overview

This chapter first defines national accounting and, next, briefly discusses early developments in estimating national income and the transition to national accounting. Systems of national accounts developed mainly after the Second World War. International harmonisation became stronger in the 1990s.

As national accounting provides macroeconomic information, it could be expected that there would be an interaction between economists and accountants. However, this interaction was limited, and only in the 1940s are initiatives identified that brought together both professions. The current situation is characterised by an almost complete separation between these groups.

National accounting developed in different ways across different countries. To a large extent, this variation can be linked to the political aspects of national accounting and different opinions on the economic role of governments. Governments that directly control economic life have a considerable impact on the broad area of accounting, but also favour systems that directly link micro-level and macro-level accounting. This leads us to explore the relation between both levels. Accounting traditions that favour the use of standardised charts of accounts make integration easier. However, differences in concepts and valuation frameworks continue to make this a difficult task. The chapter concludes with a number of suggestions for future research.

National accounting defined

National accounting is a key arena where economics and accounting meet. Attempts to account for the national economy have existed for a long time but, until the first half of the twentieth century, these remained isolated initiatives. Only around the period of the Second World War did the measurement of national income become more systematic. Over time, terminology has changed and the subject of this chapter has been variously designated as national accounting, national income accounting, national economic accounting and social accounting. All refer to the same concept: measuring and reporting the effects of the activities of the economic actors within a nation. National accounting is not, therefore, the same as government budgeting. Both measure financial wealth but they have different conceptual frameworks and are implemented by different government institutions (Jones 2000a). National accounting – the label used in this chapter – also has a clear political aspect. As a specific type of 'governing by numbers' (Rose 1991: 673), it can be linked with the concept of democracy and the relation between the state and individual economic entities.

Following the Second World War, the use of accounting in an economic context was apparently unproblematic, especially from the accountants' point of view. At the end of the 1940s, Everett Hagen described the analysis of national accounts in *The Accounting Review* as 'the application of accounting principles to an entire economic system' and stated that 'national income measurement is best thought of as double-entry bookkeeping, involving the consolidation of the operating accounts of all productive enterprises in the economic system, including government' (Hagen 1949: 248). Mattessich (1959: 86) thought that the term 'national accounting' could be understood as a 'recognition that this area of economics actually is a kind of accounting' and argued that 'social accounting is distinct from business and other micro-accounting systems only by a higher degree of aggregation and a somewhat different technique in collecting and processing data'. Moonitz and Nelson (1960) considered the rapid development in national accounting theory and systems in the 1950s to be one of the major developments in accounting theory.

However, during the second half of the twentieth century things changed and the terminology itself has become controversial. Gradually, economists started speaking of 'national accounts' rather than 'national accounting', and even that term has now largely disappeared. For example, the *Journal of Economic Literature* no longer lists national accounts as a separate topic and most US universities no longer include it in the curriculum (Ruggles and Ruggles 1995; Jones 2000a).

This chapter highlights some key steps in the development of national accounting. The first section deals with the development of the national accounting frameworks under different social and economic systems, culminating in the United Nations' (UN) System of National Accounts, 1993. A second section focuses on the role of Keynes and the interactions between accountants and economists in the 1940s. Literature dealing with developments in specific countries is referred to in the third section. As differences between ideologies with respect to state intervention have an impact on national accounting, some examples are discussed in the fourth section. The next section deals with the links between micro-accounting and the macro level through charts of accounts. The chapter ends by identifying issues for further research.

Before proceeding further, we need to acknowledge the difficulty of delineating what to include and what to exclude from this chapter, with a particular problem being the fact that national accounting lies at the crossroads of accounting and macro-economics. The number of articles concerning national accounting from the macro-economic perspective is huge. Some of them are included, but this chapter is not about how national accounts should optimally measure and represent the economy of a country. Consequently, most of the macro-economic literature is omitted.[1] Napier (2006) observes that there have been few studies of the relation between accounting and national income calculations (see also Suzuki 2003a). The number of research articles on the history of national accounting written from an accounting perspective is also extremely limited: the annual listings of accounting history publications in *Accounting, Business & Financial History* and *Accounting History* reveal only a few relevant articles published since 1991.

Developing national accounting frameworks

A starting point, but not the subject of this section, is the long history of the development of national income estimates, which has been discussed in Studenski (1958) and Vanoli (2005). Generally the origin of national income estimates is attributed to William Petty in England in the 1660s. With the exception of the work of Gregory King on the social accounts of England between 1688 and 1695, no links were made in the literature between estimates of national income and accounting for over 250 years (Vanoli 2006).

The main concerns of those preparing early national income estimates related to taxes and the assessment of the economic strength of a country (Vanoli 2005). Until the early nineteenth century, interest in preparing such estimations remained limited to a few countries and, even there, long periods without any notable work can be observed. The methods used to collect data were quite diverse, significantly reducing comparability between countries.

The idea of looking at the national economy from an accounting perspective became more widespread during the 1930s. It was present in the works of Irving Fisher, Morris E. Copeland and Robert F. Martin in the USA, André Vincent in France and Ed van Cleeff in The Netherlands (Vanoli 2005). After the stock market crisis of 1929 and the Great Depression, interest further increased and more estimates were made, not only of income but also of expenditure. However, significant conceptual differences between these estimations persisted at that time (Jones 2000a).

The publication of Keynes' *General Theory* in 1936 was important as it provided a theoretical basis for the measurement of income, consumption, investment and saving. During the Second World War, in Britain, national accounting rose higher on the agenda of a government which needed measures to help coordinate the economy and in order to be able to assess better the financial implications of policy decisions (Tomlinson 1994). An example of this increased interest occurred in 1941 with the official publication, *An Analysis of the Sources of War Finance and Estimate of the National Income and Expenditure in 1938 and 1940* (Vanoli 2005: 20). Similar developments were observed in the USA, and accounting and calculation came to be seen as an essential prerequisite for governing a democratic society in the national interest (Rose 1991).

In June 1941, James Meade and Richard Stone published their accounting framework reporting net national income, net national output and net national expenditure (Meade and Stone 1941). Their tables were a systematic representation of macroeconomic aggregates showing the links between them. Stone also focused strongly on the quality of measurement and the development of adjusting techniques by constructing variance matrices of measurement errors (Comim 2001).

At the end of the war, attempts to bring about the international harmonisation of national accounting became more prominent. In December 1945, a statistical subcommittee at the League of Nations adopted a number of recommendations based on a memorandum prepared by Stone in the same year. The system that Stone proposed was more elaborate than the one presented in 1941, and it recommended the aggregation of individual entities within five main sectors: productive enterprises, financial intermediaries, insurance and social security agencies, final consumers, and the rest of the world (Vanoli 2005: 24). There were different accounts for operations, appropriation, revenue, capital and reserves. However, the recommendations were never officially endorsed by the League of Nations.

Following the war, international harmonisation was slow to develop. The USA introduced its National Income and Product Accounts in 1947. In 1952, the UK had its National Income and Expenditure Accounts. Both bear a close resemblance to the first Standardised System of National Accounts introduced by the Organization for European Economic Co-operation in

1952. The Standardised System consisted of six national accounts and ten more detailed standard tables. The six national accounts were:

- a consolidated product and expenditure account, showing national income at factor cost, the other components of gross national product at market prices and the main types of expenditure;
- a breakdown of national income;
- an appropriation account for government;
- an appropriation account for households and private institutions;
- a consolidated capital transactions account;
- a consolidated account for the rest of the world.

Countries with centrally planned economies did not adopt this framework. Instead, they relied on the material product system (MPS), primarily because it was only the production of goods that was considered to create value. This resulted in a '[s]ystem of balances of the national economy' with essential contributions by P. Popov in 1926, T. Ryabushkin in 1950 and V. Sobol in 1960 (Vanoli 2005: 100–1). Although there are links to be made between the Soviet accounting system and German business economics traditions (see below), the national accounting systems of countries within the Soviet Union's sphere of influence in general developed separately from those in the West. Consequently, the introduction of the Standardised System should, in theory, have resulted in the existence of two main systems: the Anglo-Saxon and the Soviet models. However, within the Western world many differences continued to exist between individual countries as the 1952 Standardised System was not universally accepted. The French, for example, considered it to be both too aggregated and too confused. Consequently, they developed their own distinctive system (see Vanoli 2005, for a full discussion).

The Organization for European Economic Co-operation's 1952 Standardised System was adopted in 1953 by the UN as a System of National Accounts (abbreviated to SNA). The harmonisation of accounting frameworks throughout much of the Western world was considered important because of its links with the operation of the Marshall Plan (ibid.). In the 1960s, there was growing pressure on the UN standard setters to change the 1953 SNA. In 1964, Vanoli proposed a national accounting framework that would harmonise reporting in Europe, and Stone suggested a model rather closer to the French tradition and including the Social Accounting Matrix developed at Cambridge.[2] The negotiations that followed eventually led to a revision of the framework, published as the 1968 SNA by the UN and the 1970 European System of Integrated Economic Accounts (ESA) by the European Community. Stone's influence on the 1968 SNA was quite obvious (Ward 2004). The new framework included input–output tables, sector accounts and financial tables. Its general structure adopted a matrix format with one column and one row for each account.

The 1968 SNA and 1970 ESA frameworks had considerable impact, although many countries failed to comply fully with their provisions (for a critical evaluation, see Vanoli 1969). The major exception to the implementation of the new frameworks was the USA, which continued to apply the National Income and Product Accounts that it had developed (Carson 1975). The sophistication of the 1968 SNA made its application to the affairs of many developing countries difficult, although adoption of the accompanying Social Accounting Matrices proved feasible in countries such as Indonesia, Sri Lanka, Malaysia and Botswana. To a large extent, the problems in applying the 1968 SNA were a consequence of the economic importance in developing countries of a non-productive non-market sector and the existence of inefficient state enterprises (Ward 2004). The lack of relevant data is another factor that reduced the reliability of national accounts in many developing countries.[3]

The SNA 1968 was eventually revised in 1993 (Jones 2000b). The main reasons for this revision were the increasing complexity of economic and financial systems and rapid technological changes such as electronic transfer mechanisms, intellectual capital, financial services and other intangible activities (Ward 2004). Originally, the revision was intended to be of a limited character, but it turned out to be both revolutionary and fundamental. The new framework was supported by the UN, the European Economic Community, the International Monetary Fund, the World Bank and the Organization for Economic Co-operation and Development. The European involvement resulted in a high level of comparability between the 1993 SNA and the 1995 ESA, the successor of the 1970 ESA. This collaboration of leading international institutions significantly increased its impact and its potential to lead to far-reaching harmonisation. The new framework was more prescriptive and presented a complete accounting sequence, including current accounts, accumulation accounts and balance sheets. It introduced an integrated 'stock-flow' framework that allowed relating all transactions that took place within an accounting period to comprehensive opening and closing balance sheets (Ward 2004; Jones 2000a).

Following the collapse of the Soviet Union, countries that previously adopted the MPS replaced their systems with the SNA in the early 1990s. Hungary was a forerunner in this process as it had had experience of both MPS and SNA since 1968 (Ward 2006).[4] The compilation of long-term series of Gross Domestic Product (GDP) proved a complex process in many former MPS countries, as it required the retrospective construction of the SNA accounts. One method has been to use conversion keys to calculate GDP from the MPS. This is a difficult process because there are not only incidental differences between both systems, but also differences in the fundamental underlying concepts and definitions (Ivanov 2006). Finally, the USA also, at last, seems to be moving towards the SNA and, when it happens, will result in worldwide harmonisation of national accounting (Vanoli 2005: 125).

The role of Keynes and the relation between economists and accountants

There have always been strong links between national accounting and economic theory,[5] and many key persons in the development of national accounting were also important for the development of economic theory. Examples include Gregory King, William Petty, John Hicks, Richard Stone and John Maynard Keynes in England; Simon Kuznets and Wassily Leontief in the USA; and Ragnar Frisch in Norway (Bos 1997). Keynes played a key role in the development of macroeconomics and consequently also had a great impact on national accounting. An early example of the work of Keynes in this field is the landmark pamphlet *How to Pay for the War*, written in the winter of 1939–40 in collaboration with Erwin Rothbarth. This pamphlet is important because it was the first to develop a system of double-entry-based national accounts for the UK. Although quite rudimentary, it predates the work of Meade and Stone and could be considered a 'first attempt' (Cuyvers 1983).

Suzuki (2003b) also discusses early examples of attempts to present national accounts for the UK. The main interest of his paper is that it provides a detailed discussion of the relation between the development of UK national accounting and macroeconomics, highlighting the role of Keynes, Stone, Meade and Frank Sewell Bray. The growth of national economic management (a macroeconomic issue) can be linked to the rise of a concern with productivity, which was itself linked to attempts to regulate companies in the endeavour to increase output and efficiency (a microeconomic problem) (Tomlinson 1994). In the debates of the 1940s, issues that needed to be resolved included questions such as whether monetary units were suitable measurements for representing the affairs of a national economy, what was an appropriate accounting period, and how to define entities and sectors. Moreover, the relative importance of stock versus flow variables was discussed, as was the way the government sector should be included in the accounts. A further important issue was how to balance the accounts in the case of missing data: for instance, the practice of residual calculation was not accepted by all.

In the 1940s, accountants began to share the interest of economists in national accounting. In 1945–46, Richard Stone and the accountant Frank Sewell Bray organised meetings between accountants and economists to discuss how company accounts could become more useful for macroeconomic management (Comim 2001; Suzuki 2003b; Vanoli 2006). Because the accountants and their professional bodies believed that the outcome of these discussions neglected the conventions of business accounting, the direct output was confined to an analysis of common terms and concepts, published as a report by the Institute of Chartered Accountants in England and Wales and the National Institute of Economic and Social Research, in February 1948, under the title 'Terms and concepts in common use' (Suzuki 2003b: 499).

The attempted collaboration between accountants and economists thus proved difficult. Moonitz and Nelson (1960), for example, thought that the developments of national accounting in the 1950s would bring accountants and economists together, leading to a theory of accounting that would not only cover the enterprise but also embrace the national level, and result in financial statements that could be used more readily as inputs for the creation of national accounts. However, this did not happen. In the UK, for example, accountants often know little about economics and economists are perceived to be dismissive of accountants (Napier 1996a, 1996b). To an extent, the national income debate in the 1940s was an exception, in that accountants such as Bray worked with economists. In the following years co-operation between 'the uncongenial twins' (Boulding 1977) evaporated. Bray continued to develop proposals to present statistical data in an accounting format (e.g. Bray 1951) but, after Bray, there is little evidence of the active involvement of accountants in the development of national accounting – the 1993 SNA/1995 ESA were prepared by expert groups or officials that did not include accountants (Jones 2000b).

Accounting and the interventionist state

Ideological positions had a significant impact on debates with respect to national accounting. In Western countries, ideas on national income calculation tended to be the subject of suspicion during an era when the ideology of *laissez-faire* and non-intervention remained dominant. The opposite can be expected in countries with political regimes that actively intervene in economic life. The latter countries comprise two categories. The first is where new states are being created; the other where governments adopt an ideology of coordinating economic activity. Several papers have addressed the role of accounting in such circumstances.

During German unification in the 1870s, economic policy was a central theme in political debate (Gallhofer and Haslam 1991). Accounting practice in companies became strictly regulated by the state and linked with taxation. At the same time, intriguingly, accounting regulation accepted the practice of creating secret reserves. The widespread acceptance of accounting regulation was fostered by the economic success of state-led industrial policy. It came under pressure during the First World War, however, because of the tax regime relating to war profits and different views on the utility of secret reserves. The reporting of war profits gave accounting a conflict-enhancing role in German society during and after the First World War. Although secret reserve accounting continued to be an acceptable practice (Spoerer 1998), criticism appears to have been a stimulus to the development of uniform accounting as later adopted by the Nazis (see next section). Markus (1997) demonstrates how the accounting profession in Germany became increasingly integrated in the party and state under Nazism and how accounting was an important instrument in operating the state-controlled industries.

Cinquini (2007) studied the relationships between business studies and accounting and the construction of the corporative economy in Italy together with its fascist ideology. He observed points of convergence between fascist ideology and accounting discourse in the 1930s. Economic sectors were to be organised within fascist corporations conceived as government instruments to regulate economic activities without the need to abolish the private sector. In fascist ideology, the objectives of firms became subordinate to 'national interests'. A number of authors proposed changes in accounting statements and valuations to make accounting data useful for the construction of 'enterprise statistical and accounting indexes'. These in turn were used for the fascist corporations' purposes of coordination (ibid.). Within each industry, uniform accounting methods were used. Although individual firms were subordinated to national interests, the general position was that the internal management within the firm remained independent and autonomous.

These arrangements contrasted with those put in place by the Soviet Union. Although there was the continuing influence of German accountants (such as Schmalenbach) on accounting ideas in the Soviet Union (Richard 1995a), the basic function of accounting was different. Whereas the continental European tradition considered the individual enterprise as the focus of accounting, this was not the case within Soviet accounting. There, the accounting system was used by the central authorities to maintain control over the activities of the state enterprises (Bailey 1988). Bailey (1990) discusses the debate in the 1930s between 'bourgeois accountants' and 'Soviet accountants' and links it with the debates under Stalin on Marxism. Accounting had to be modernised to fit with the needs of an industrial society, as was the case in other countries. At the same time, business activities within the Soviet Union became focused on the enterprise's corporate plan which was a component of the national economic plan. Accounting gradually changed into data keeping and the performance of enterprises was measured using physical and monetary (mainly cost) indicators. The accounting systems of individual enterprises were simplified and combined into a comprehensive scheme. In this way, the national economy became the accounting entity and enterprise accounting became more macro-oriented. At the same time, accounting procedures were standardised. Within enterprises, centralised accounting offices were oriented towards state control and the accountant became a state controller. A centralised perspective also existed in countries that were under Soviet influence. Arvay reports on Hungary as follows:

the reliability of national accounting is favourable in Hungary, as they are based mostly (92 percent) on the bookkeeping data of enterprises, cooperatives and institutions. The bookkeeping system is uniform in all economic organizations, in conformity with central regulations, and it takes into account the demand of computations for national accounting.

(Arvay 1974: 55)

Linking the macro and micro perspectives: the use of charts of accounts

The previous section has demonstrated the linking of micro-level data to national aggregates. In many continental European countries (and countries in other parts of the world historically under their influence), standardised charts of accounts were considered to help connect the macro and micro perspectives. However, a standardised chart of accounts does not solve the conceptual issues.

Although terminology is sometimes similar for national and business accounting, concepts and ways of operation are not always directly comparable. In the 1940s, both systems used a different concept of double-entry bookkeeping (Jones 2000a; Suzuki 2003b). In business accounting, each transaction is recorded twice because it affects both assets or liabilities and income, or different types of balance sheet items. In national accounting, the double-entry aspect is that a transaction affects different entities in the economy. From the 1993 SNA onwards, national accounts have been based on the principle of quadruple entry, each transaction typically involving two accounting entities and being recorded twice within each entity.[6]

There also exist significant differences between business accounting and national accounting in valuation principles.[7] Both systems now generally follow accrual accounting principles, which has created more difficulties for national accounting because government accounts were (and still are in a number of countries) prepared essentially on a cash basis. Bray and Stone considered the change towards accrual accounting one of the major steps in the reform of governmental accounting (Bray and Stone 1948). However, national accounting never used the historical cost models that were (and still are) dominant in business accounting (Jones 2000b). Adoption of the fair-value perspective was easier to implement than the introduction of fair value at the individual company transaction level, due to the availability of price indices for national accounting aggregates.

In both systems, we have balance sheets and accumulation accounts or cash flow statements. Apart from disparities in valuation systems, the differences are quite limited. However, the differences are more important between income statements for businesses and current accounts in national accounting. Some items are not recorded in national accounts, but have an impact on business income (e.g., bad debt provisions). More importantly, in national accounting, the emphasis is more on value added and output than on sales and profit (Vanoli 2006). The distance between both systems is especially significant if business income statements are prepared by function: income statements by nature of expense, as traditionally prepared by most companies in continental Europe, are much easier to link with national accounting.

On a global level, value added represents the value created by an economic system. At the level of an individual entity, such as a company, it shows the value created by that company exclusive of its consumption of items created by other economic entities. The issue is not widely discussed in the accounting literature in continental countries, probably because it is considered non-problematic. In the Anglo-Saxon literature, there has been some debate on this issue which, for the UK, Hopwood *et al.* (1994) locates essentially in the late 1970s. Disclosure of value added could be linked with payment for labour and profit sharing, but also with performance evaluation in British industry. The widespread debate on value added in the UK during the 1970s was related to, among other factors, incomes policies through value-added incentive payment schemes.

The difference in concepts between business and national accounting raises the question of how to link them. The relation between business accounting and national accounts is not always clear in Keynes' work. However, the system proposed by Stone in 1945 included the idea of aggregating national accounts from the accounts of individual entities (Vanoli 2006). This idea did not develop further in the UK, but the French example illustrates a country where data taken from business accounts were rearranged and served as inputs in national accounts through intermediate accounts (Vanoli 2005). The French model was adopted in a UN (2000) *Handbook on National Accounting*. However, not many countries have succeeded in using business accounts directly for the compilation of national accounts. Vanoli (2006) mentions two major difficulties in this respect: availability of company accounts and the lack of standardisation of company accounts. Postner (1986) reports two cases where micro-accounting data are used in modelling: a micro-to-macro model of the Swedish economy, and an econometric model of the UK economy developed at Cambridge. However, statistical inconsistencies remain an issue.[8]

As discussed above, the continental European tradition of standardised charts of accounts often prefers income statements classified by nature of expense. This tradition predates the national accounting debate of the twentieth century. In the nineteenth century, the development of company law resulted in the introduction of codified regulations of accounting and auditing in many continental countries.[9] The models that were used to regulate accounting can be traced from France to other countries such as Germany (Gallhofer and Haslam 1991). Although the level of regulation was not very detailed compared to current accounting and auditing standards, continental European countries often prescribed at least the minimum contents of financial statements.

In principle, countries that introduced standardised charts of accounts could more easily transfer business data into national accounts.[10] Most of these countries were part of continental Europe, which might explain why the (dominantly Anglo-Saxon) research literature has given little attention to this subject until recently. A first series of studies was published in the *European Accounting Review* in 1995. As well as a discussion of the development of accounting charts in different countries in the nineteenth and twentieth centuries (Richard 1995a), the special issue includes analyses of charts of accounts and their implementation in Spain (Chauveau 1995), Germany (Bechtel 1995), Russia and Romania (Richard 1995b). Studies of other countries followed: Slovakia (Daniel *et al.* 2001), Poland (Jaruga and Szychta 1997) and Belgium (De Beelde 2003). There were important differences between the structure of these charts in different countries: Richard (1995a) distinguished between monistic and dualistic charts (depending on whether there is one or more than one type of valuation and a unity or distinction between financial and managerial accounting) and between charts that focus on the balance sheet and charts that follow the logic of an economic circuit.

There are two exceptions to the limited attention generally accorded by researchers, until recently, to charts of accounts: these involves the French *Plan comptable général* and (to a lesser extent) corresponding developments in Germany. The developments in Germany were strongly influenced by the growing impact of Taylorism and a German business economics tradition that focused on economic circuits, including Rathenau and Schmalenbach (Richard 1995a). Discussion in Germany has focused to a large extent on the impact of Schmalenbach on the development of accounting charts that could be used to control an economy in its preparation for war (Forrester 1977). Schmalenbach wanted charts of accounts: (1) to be sufficiently flexible to allow decentralised decision making; and (2) to include detailed cost accounts so as to facilitate the improvement of German industrial performance by allowing cost comparisons.

There is obviously a line from the German chart, introduced in 1937, to the first French *Plan comptable*, developed under German occupation in 1942 (Standish 1990). Following the Second

362

World War, there was a greater acceptance in France of a significant state role in economic coordination, and the idea of a general chart of accounts was reintroduced in 1947. The *Plan comptable* has been studied extensively, with its development rooted within the context of post-war economic reconstruction and political modernisation (Miller 1986). The 1947 chart of accounts had different objectives: creating a control instrument for tax authorities and creditors, serving as legal evidence, but above all providing information for economic statistics and national accounting (Hoarau 2003). It was an instrument to create a *Comptabilité nationale* with industrial input–output charts similar to those that Leontief developed for the USA and the UK (Colasse and Durand 1994). As a consequence of European unification, the plan itself became gradually less central to French regulation.

The French state supervised all accounting regulation; on a micro level via the *Conseil National de Comptabilité* (National Accounting Board) and on a macro level through the *Institut National de la Statistique et les Etudes Economiques* (National Institute of Statistics and Economic Surveys). The Institut National is also present in micro-level accounting standard setting. Its impact is significant in the presentation of income statements that are organised by nature of expense and consequently show value-added or gross operating surplus; data that can be conveniently used in the compilation of national accounts. However, there still is no automatic reconciliation of French micro-accounting and national accounting. Adjustments have to be made in the aggregation process due to differences in valuation, recognition dates and classification (Lande 2000).

In Eastern European countries, charts of accounts were part of the centralised organisation of bookkeeping under Soviet influence. After the political changes of the 1990s, many countries maintained their chart-based systems. Examples include Poland, Hungary and the Czech Republic (King *et al.* 2001). In Russia, the structure of the new charts was strongly influenced by those used in the Soviet period, and it still adopts the 'circuit' principle that goes back to Schmalenbach (Richard 1995b). In Ukraine, on the contrary, the new charts were more influenced by French models (Golov 2006).

Issues for further research

National accounting is an area of accounting history that is largely unresearched. Historically, this can partly be attributed to a lack of data. However, databases of national accounts or aggregates, such as those kept by the UN Statistics Division, as well as more detailed data in individual countries, are now more easily available.[11] Another obvious explanation for the absence of national accounting from scholarly journals is the lack of collaboration between accountants and economists demonstrated earlier. It leads Suzuki (2003b: 505) to conclude that key questions – such as 'how did accounting affect the perception of the public sphere of the economy, the approach to economic problems and the policies adopted, and the consequences that may be desirable or undesirable in relation to the socio-economic welfare?' – remain almost entirely unexplored.

Consequently, identifying future research possibilities is not difficult. The historic relation between macroeconomics and accounting is one such possibility. Much of what is available deals with the UK. There is a need for an expansion of this focus to other countries such as the USA, France, the Netherlands, Italy and Germany. Some of these countries used to have specific business economics traditions (e.g. the *economia aziendale* in Italy and the work of Limperg in the Netherlands), and one can expect that this interaction between economics and accounting was perceived differently compared with the UK. Such a study could include an analysis of the writings of leading theorists and scholars. Following the same line of thought, research into joint initiatives and working parties, such as those organised by Stone and Bray in the 1940s in the UK, could expand our understanding of the relationship between accounting and economics in other countries.

The absence of work by the professional accounting bodies is also striking. At a time when these organised bodies commented on a wide range of issues, they apparently did not address, for example, the development of the SNA 1993. Further work on the evolution of the position of the organised accounting profession with respect to the developments in national accounting would be welcome. Again, it would be interesting to study a wider range of countries to see whether this lack of involvement in national accounting was universal.

Business accounting has been struggling with fair value concepts for many years. However, in macro-accounts, fair value has been applied for a long time. It might be insightful to find out how these concepts were historically introduced, how fair values were measured and why these concepts apparently were not easily transferred to business accounting. Such work would also be of contemporary relevance in the current International Financial Reporting Standards (IFRS) context.

There are also a number of wider issues that are challenging for the future but that at the same time can be studied from a historical perspective. Very often they relate to what should be included in the national accounts (see Ward 2006). A typical example is the limited presence of households in national accounts and the related absence of unpaid household production (Froud et al. 2000; Walker and Llewellyn 2000). Many other issues have been discussed since the early twentieth century which are also examined in the context of business accounting. Examples include accounting for human capital and reporting the social performance of companies. A number of countries (e.g. Belgium 1996) have introduced requirements for companies to prepare social balance sheets disclosing details of salaries, social expenses and training. It can be debated to what extent such financial statements actually measure human capital. It is also unclear how they could be linked with national accounts. Another example relates to environmental issues. Sustainability reports and 'green accounting' are strongly debated issues in micro-accounting. However, there is also a growing literature on natural resource accounting, green national accounting and a green national product (e.g. Aaheim and Nyborg 1995; Harris and Fraser 2002; Asheim 2004). Are there links between these debates at the micro and macro levels? Should national accounts report welfare and, if so, how should this be measured? Are only items that can be expressed in money terms relevant? Again, how do you link this with business accounting, knowing that an optimal solution at a micro level is not always optimal at the macro level? Understanding how these questions were considered in the past might also be revealing for the future.

Key works

de Vries et al. (1993) comprises a collection of essays on 50 years of national accounting in The Netherlands, not only discussing Dutch developments but also broader methodological issues.

Gilbert and Stone (1954) summarises the status of national accounting during a key period in its development – the 1930s to 1950s.

Studenski (1958) is an impressive study of the history and contemporary practice of national income calculation. It covers developments in a wide range of countries from the seventeenth century to the twentieth century and discusses the methodology of estimating national income.

Suzuki (2003b), focusing on the Keynesian revolution from an accounting point of view, examines an important period in the development of national accounting.

Vanoli (2005), written by a former director of the French Central Statistical Office (INSEE), looks from the inside at the development of national accounting and supplies extensive discussion of historical events, concepts and issues.

Notes

1 For those interested in the evolution of technical and methodological issues in national accounting, the *Review of Income and Wealth* is the premier source. A historical analysis of developments in national accounting in the USA is Perlman and Marietta (2005); their article also includes some discussion on Germany and the UK.
2 According to Ward (2004), the Social Accounting Matrices were pioneered by Thorbecke, Pyatt and Keuning in the Netherlands.
3 For a general discussion, see Barkay (1975); for individual cases, see Hardman (1986) on Papua New Guinea, Barkay (1982) on Nepal, van der Eng (1999, 2005) on Indonesia, and Sourrouille (1976) on Argentina.
4 Arvay (1969) analysed the differences between the two systems.
5 On the relation between accounting and economics, see Suzuki (2003a).
6 There had been attempts in some countries to introduce double-entry bookkeeping in government agencies quite early. Edwards and Greener (2003) report on such initiatives in the UK between 1828 and 1844.
7 This does not mean that the concepts of value and income in national accounting are the same as those in economic theory. They are descriptive concepts that should be understood in their specific accounting framework (Bos 1997).
8 Postner (1988) gives a number of examples and refers at the same time to the French 'intermediate accounts' approach supported by the French *Plan comptable générale* as a solution.
9 Standardised accounts were not only found in continental Europe. In the UK and the USA, however, standardisation did not take place on an overall level but rather at an industry level (see Chapter 9 and, for railways, Chapter 18). In the late nineteenth century, standardised accounts were introduced for certain industries in Britain starting with the railways in 1868 (Edwards 1989: Chapter 17). In the 1930s, many UK and US industries used uniform systems of accounts and forms of financial statements (Lengyel 1949). Contrary to continental Europe, this standardisation was not based on a general chart and often related to cost accounts.
10 Post-Second World War Japan is an interesting case where, in the context of macroeconomic data construction, 'the need for standardised corporate accounting and regulation came to be recognized as a micro-foundation of macro-data' (Suzuki 2007: 275).
11 An example of the increasing interest in national accounting data among economic historians is the Historical National Accounting Group hosted at Trinity College Dublin, Ireland.

References

Aaheim, A. and Nyborg, K. (1995) On the interpretation and applicability of a 'green national product', *Review of Income and Wealth*, 41 (1): 57–71.
Arvay, J. (1969) Development of the national accounting system in Hungary, *Review of Income and Wealth*, 15 (2): 185–95.
Arvay, J. (1974) Problems of determining and measuring the reliability of the national accounts: Hungary's experiences, *Review of Income and Wealth*, 20 (1): 55–69.
Asheim, G. B. (2004) Green national accounting with a changing population, *Economic Theory*, 23 (3): 601–19.
Bailey, D. (1988) *Accounting in Socialist Countries* (London: Routledge).

Bailey, D. (1990) Accounting in the shadow of Stalinism, *Accounting, Organizations and Society*, 15 (6): 513–25.

Barkay, R. M. (1975) National accounting as planning tool in less developed countries: lessons of experience, *Review of Income and Wealth*, 21 (4): 349–69.

Barkay, R. M. (1982) National accounting with limited data: lessons from Nepal, *Review of Income and Wealth*, 28 (3): 305–23.

Bechtel, W. (1995) Charts of accounts in Germany, *European Accounting Review*, 4 (2): 283–304.

Bos, F. (1997) Value and income in the national accounts and economic theory, *Review of Income and Wealth*, 43 (2): 173–90.

Bos, F. (2006) The development of the Dutch national accounts as a tool for analysis and policy, *Statistica Neerlandica*, 60 (2): 225–58.

Boulding, K. E. (1977) Economics and accounting: the uncongenial twins, in W. T. Baxter and S. Davidson (eds) *Studies in Accounting Theory*, pp. 86–95 (London: ICAEW).

Bray, F. S. (1951) A national balance sheet, *Accounting Research*, 2 (3): 279–300.

Bray, F. S. and Stone, R. (1948) The presentation of the central government accounts, *Accounting Research*, 1 (1): 1–12.

Carson, C. S. (1975) The history of the United States national income and product accounts, *Review of Income and Wealth*, 21 (2): 153–81.

Chauveau, B. (1995) The Spanish Plan General de Contabilidad: agent of development and innovation?, *European Accounting Review*, 4 (1): 125–40.

Cinquini, L. (2007) Fascist corporative economy and accounting in Italy during the thirties: exploring the relation between a totalitarian ideology and business studies, *Accounting, Business & Financial History*, 17 (2): 209–40.

Colasse, B. and Durand, R. (1994) French accounting theorists of the twentieth century, in J. R. Edwards (ed.) *Twentieth-Century Accounting Thinkers*, pp. 41–59 (London: Routledge).

Comim, F. (2001) Richard Stone and measurement criteria for national accounts, *History of Political Economy*, 23 (annual supplement): 213–34.

Cuyvers, L. (1983) Keynes' collaboration with Erwin Rothbarth, *Economic Journal*, 93 (371): 629–36.

Daniel, P., Suranova, Z. and de Beelde, I. (2001) The development of accounting in Slovakia, *European Accounting Review*, 10 (2): 343–59.

de Beelde, I. (2003) The development of a Belgian accounting code during the first half of the 20th century, *Accounting Historians Journal*, 30 (2): 1–28.

de Vries, W., den Bakker, G., Gircour, M., Keuning, S. and Lenson, A. (1993) *The Value Added of National Accounting* (Amsterdam: Netherlands Central Bureau of Statistics).

Edwards, J. R. (1989) *A History of Financial Accounting* (London: Routledge).

Edwards, J. R. and Greener, H. T. (2003) Introducing 'mercantile' bookkeeping into British central government 1858–1844, *Accounting and Business Research*, 33 (1): 51–64.

Forrester, D. (1977) *Schmalenbach and After: A Study in the Evolution of German Business Economics* (Strathclyde: Strathclyde Convergencies).

Froud, J., Haslam, C., Johal, S. and Williams, K. (2000) Representing the household: in and after national income accounting, *Accounting, Auditing & Accountability Journal*, 13 (4): 535–60.

Gallhofer S. and Haslam, J. (1991) The aura of accounting in the context of a crisis: Germany and the First World War, *Accounting, Organizations and Society*, 16 (5/6): 487–520.

Gilbert, M. and Stone, R. (1954) Recent developments in national income and social accounting, *Accounting Research*, 5 (1): 1–31.

Golov, S. (2006) Development of chart of accounts in Ukraine and Russia since 1991. Paper presented at Annual Congress of the European Accounting Association, Dublin, 22–24 March.

Hagen, E. (1949) National accounting systems and the European recovery program, *Accounting Review*, 24 (3): 248–54.

Hardman, D. J. (1986) Paradigms of public financial administration in the evolution of Papua New Guinea, *Public Administration and Development*, 6 (2): 151–61.

Harris, M. and Fraser, I. (2002) Natural resource accounting in theory and practice: a critical assessment, *Australian Journal of Agricultural and Resource Economics*, 46 (2): 139–92.

Hoarau, C. (2003) Place et rôle de la normalisation comptable en France, *Revue Française de Gestion*, 29 (147): 33–47.

Hopwood, A. G., Burchell, S. and Clubb, C. (1994) Value-added accounting and national economic policy, in A. G. Hopwood and P. Miller (eds) *Accounting as Social and Institutional Practice*, pp. 211–36 (Cambridge: Cambridge University Press).

Ivanov, Y. N. (2006) On compilation of long term series of GDP for the former USSR Republics, *Hitotsubashi University Discussion Paper Series*, 173: 1–13.

Jaruga, A. and Szychta, A. (1997) The origin and evolution of charts of accounts in Poland, *European Accounting Review*, 6 (3): 509–26.

Jones, R. (2000a) National accounting, government budgeting and the accounting discipline, *Financial Accountability and Management*, 16 (2): 101–16.

Jones, R. (2000b) Public versus private: the empty definitions of national accounting, *Financial Accountability and Management*, 16 (2): 167–78.

Keynes, J. M. (1936) *The General Theory of Employment, Interest and Money* (London: Macmillan).

Keynes, J. M. (1940) *How to Pay for the War: A Radical Plan for the Chancellor of the Exchequer* (New York: Harcourt, Brace).

King, N., Beattie, A., Cristescu, A. M. and Weetman, P. (2001), Developing accounting and audit in a transition economy: the Romanian experience, *European Accounting Review*, 10 (1): 149–71.

Lande, E. (2000) Macro-accounting and micro-accounting relationships in France, *Financial Accountability & Management*, 16 (2): 151–65.

Lengyel, S. J. (1949) Standardised accountancy considered internationally, *Accounting Research*, 1(2): 133–41.

Markus, H. B. (1997) *The History of the German Public Accounting Profession* (New York: Garland Publishing).

Mattessich, R. (1959) Accounting reconsidered, *California Management Review*, 2 (1): 85–91.

Meade, J. E. and Stone, R. (1941) The construction of tables of national income, expenditure, savings and investment, *Economic Journal*, 51 (206/7): 216–33.

Miller, P. (1986) Accounting for progress – national accounting and planning in France: a review essay, *Accounting, Organizations and Society*, 11 (1): 83–104.

Moonitz, M. and. Nelson, C. M. (1960) Recent developments in accounting theory, *Accounting Review*, 35 (2): 206–17.

Napier, C. J. (1996a) Accounting and the absence of a business economics tradition in the United Kingdom, *European Accounting Review*, 5 (3): 449–82.

Napier, C. J. (1996b) Academic disdain? Economists and accounting in Britain, 1850–1950, *Accounting, Business & Financial History*, 6 (3): 427–50.

Napier, C. J. (2006) Accounts of change: 30 years of historical accounting research, *Accounting, Organizations and Society*, 30 (4/5): 445–507.

Perlman, M. and Marietta, M. (2005) The politics of social accounting: public goals and the evolution of the national accounts in Germany, the United Kingdom and the United States, *Review of Political Economy*, 17 (2): 211–30.

Postner, H. H. (1986) Microbusiness accounting and macroeconomic accounting: the limits to consistency, *Review of Income and Wealth*, 32 (3): 217–44.

Postner, H. H. (1988) Linkages between macro and micro business accounts: implications for economic measurement, *Review of Income and Wealth*, 34 (3): 313–35.

Richard, J. (1995a) The evolution of accounting chart models in Europe from 1900 to 1945: some historical elements, *European Accounting Review*, 4 (1): 87–124.

Richard, J. (1995b) The evolution of the Romanian and Russian accounting charts after the collapse of the communist system, *European Accounting Review*, 5 (2): 305–24.

Rose, N. (1991) Governing by numbers: figuring out democracy, *Accounting, Organizations and Society*, 16 (7): 673–92.

Ruggles, R. and Ruggles, P. (1995) The value added of national accounting, *Review of Income and Wealth*, 41 (3): 367–71.

Sourrouille, J. V. (1976) The development of national accounts in Argentina, *Review of Income and Wealth*, 22 (4): 353–75.

Spoerer, M. (1998) Window-dressing in German inter-war balance sheets, *Accounting, Business & Financial History*, 8 (3): 351–69.

Standish, P. (1990) Origins of the Plan Comptable Général: a study in cultural intrusion and reaction, *Accounting and Business Research*, 20 (80): 337–51.

Studenski, P. (1958) *The Income of Nations. Theory, Measurement and Analysis: Past and Present* (New York: New York University Press).

Suzuki, T. (2003a) The accounting figuration of business statistics as a foundation for the spread of economic ideas, *Accounting, Organizations and Society*, 28 (1): 65–95.

Suzuki, T. (2003b) The epistemology of macroeconomic reality: the Keynesian Revolution from an accounting point of view, *Accounting, Organizations and Society*, 28 (5): 471–517.

Suzuki, T. (2007) Accountics: impacts of internationally standardized accounting on the Japanese socio-economy, *Accounting, Organizations and Society*, 32 (3): 263–301.

Tomlinson, J. (1994) The politics of economic measurement: the rise of the 'productivity problem' in the 1940s, in A. G. Hopwood and P. Miller (eds) *Accounting as Social and Institutional Practice*, pp. 168–89 (Cambridge: Cambridge University Press).

United Nations (2000) *Studies in Methods: Handbook of National Accounting. Series F, n° 76, Links Between Business Accounting and National Accounting* (New York: United Nations).

Van der Eng, P. (1999) Some obscurities in Indonesia's new national accounts, *Bulletin of Indonesian Economic Studies*, 35 (2): 91–106.

Van der Eng, P. (2005) Indonesia's new national accounts, *Bulletin of Indonesian Economic Studies*, 41 (2): 243–52.

Vanoli, A. (1969) Le système actuel de comptabilité nationale et la planification, *Review of Income and Wealth*, 15 (2): 171–84.

Vanoli, A. (2005) *A History of National Accounting* (Amsterdam: IOS Press).

Vanoli, A. (2006) Is national accounting accounting? National accounting between accounting, statistics and economics. Paper presented at Eleventh World Congress of Accounting Historians, Nantes, 19–22 July.

Walker, S. P. and Llewellyn, S. (2000) Accounting at home: some interdisciplinary perspectives, *Accounting, Auditing & Accountability Journal*, 13 (4): 425–49.

Ward, M. P. (2004) Some reflections on the 1968–93 SNA Revision, *Review of Income and Wealth*, 50 (2): 299–313.

Ward, M. P. (2006) An intellectual history of national accounting, *Review of Income and Wealth*, 52 (2): 327–40.

Williams, D. W. (2003) Measuring government in the early twentieth century, *Public Administration Review*, 63 (6): 643–59.

17

Finance and financial institutions

Janette Rutterford

Overview

This chapter examines prior research into the history of finance and financial institutions, ranging across academic disciplines such as economic history, business history, accounting history, banking history, tax and legal history, social history, geography and gender studies.

The chapter is divided into two parts and starts with the history of the major institutions in the financial landscape. The size, age and importance of British financial institutions have allowed many the luxury of retaining important archival material which, together with some sponsorship, has made possible a significant business and banking history literature, with many financial institutions and most financial industries having at least one published history from inception to the present day. In addition to these narratives, researchers have questioned why the British financial sector (in particular 'the City') has proved such a success, whereas key elements of British industry failed to make the transition from the heady days of world trade domination in the mid-nineteenth century to the managerial capitalism of the twentieth century. Much research has been devoted to the thorny question of whether British financial institutions were to blame, with the finger pointing both at the banks – for not lending long term – and at the stock market – for preferring to finance overseas investments rather than the home-grown variety.

The second thread in this chapter is the history of finance itself – in particular, corporate finance – and of investment. This research area has been given much less attention, in part because contemporary research in finance and investment is highly quantitative, requiring large amounts of high quality historical data. In many cases such data is simply not available until the 1960s when computers allowed its large-scale collection and analysis. However, researchers are now beginning to turn their attention to both corporate and investor behaviour over time, looking at path dependence to explain current institutional and corporate financial decision-making.

The chapter concludes with an analysis of where the major omissions in research to date (and there are many) and, hence, where opportunities for future research lie.

Histories of financial institutions

The first London private banks were already operating in Stuart times; the Bank of England was founded in 1694, and a number of insurance companies between 1695 and 1720. Indeed, many insurance companies today exploit their longevity as a marketing tool to convince potential policyholders and investors that they are reliable long-term propositions. The substantial literature on British financial institutions is helped by the fact that many have well-funded and well-catalogued archives. For example, there is a tradition of successful financial institutions commissioning the writing of their histories, often for publication at landmark dates such as the Halifax Building Society's 'jubilee memorial' (Anon. 1903). A guide to bank archives is provided by Orbell and Turton (2001) and to insurance archives by Cockerell and Green (1994). It is useful to review research on the history of financial institutions by considering four categories: banks, insurance companies, investing institutions, and savings banks.

Banks

In the banking sector, we have the Bank of England, the private banks and the joint stock banks. The first bankers were goldsmiths, and their activities developed during the Stuart period, especially after the appearance of cheques and notes in the 1650s and the availability of government debt after 1688. Most of these banks were based in London; there were few country banks until the second half of the eighteenth century. Numbers rose from 12 in 1750 to more than 300 in 1800 (Foxwell 1927: 412; Cottrell 1980: 14). These private banks operated as partnerships, limited to a maximum of six partners by the charter of the Bank of England which enjoyed a monopoly of joint stock banking. In 1826, larger co-partnerships were allowed to operate outside a 65-mile radius of London, with non-issuing joint stock banks also permitted to function outside London from 1833. Stringent banking rules were introduced in 1844, reducing new entrants and thereby allowing existing joint stock banks to improve their profitability. Following further legislation in 1857 to 1862, more joint stock banks were formed to take advantage of high returns and the protection of limited liability. Thus began competition between private and joint stock banks, which led to a massive concentration of the industry in pursuit of economies of scale or sheer size, with merger activity, mostly between joint stock and private banks, peaking in 1891 (Capie and Rodrik-Bali 1982: 280–1). Altogether, 370 banks disappeared between 1870 and 1921. After the First World War, the 'Big Five' banks dominated the banking landscape. However, there were also the so-called 'merchant banks', based in London and trading in international bills of exchange, which were powerful in new issues, particularly of overseas securities. Related firms, such as stockbrokers, jobbers and discount houses, also operated within what was known as 'the City' or 'the Square Mile'.

There are numerous histories of the banking industry – from early work by Joslin (1954, 1960) and Pressnell (1960) on private bankers, to work on deposit banking in London by Melton (1986), to studies of Scottish banking (Checkland 1975) and provincial banking – Liverpool by Andersen and Cottrell (1975) and Birmingham by Moss (1982). Individual bank histories have flourished since the first comprehensive history of one of the major clearing banks, Barclays, by Matthews and Tuke (1926). There is no major bank without its own business history text; a recent classic being a new history of Barclays from 1690 to 1996 by Ackrill and Hannah (2001). Goodhart (1986) and others have looked at the financial structure of banks, their asset and liability configurations, and the business of banking, as well as the regulatory aspects of central banking and commercial banking.

There are studies of international banking by, for example, Battilossi (2000). Jones (1986) has looked at a British bank operating overseas (the British Bank of the Middle East) and has also written on British multinational banking more generally (Jones 1992). International banking comparisons are relatively few but include, for example, Batiz-Lazo and del Angel's (2003) study of Mexican and British banks between 1945 and 1975 based on interviews with bankers from both countries. Batiz-Lazo and Boyns (2004) have also helped to open up a relatively new field of research, into the mechanisation and technical change of banks in the twentieth century, by editing a special issue of *Accounting, Business & Financial History* which also includes international comparisons. There is insufficient room in this chapter to elaborate on the comparable US, French, German and Japanese literature on banking history.

Insurance companies

Insurance companies grew to maturity on a global scale during the nineteenth century. Raynes, himself an actuary, wrote a history of the British insurance industry in 1948. Examples of individual insurance company histories include: Dickson (1960) on The Sun Insurance Office; Drew (1949) on London Assurance; Supple (1970) on Royal Exchange; Street and Glen (1980) on National Mutual; Ryan (1983) on Norwich Union; and Trebilcock (1998) on Phoenix Assurance. Robin Pearson has written extensively on the insurance sector (1990, 1992, 1993, 1997a). In recent work (1997b, 2002) he has looked at innovation and globalisation in the insurance industry, following the path recommended by Baskin and Miranti (1997). Kenely (2001, 2004) has studied the Australian life insurance industry.

Investing institutions

Pension funds have received relatively little attention. Hannah (1986, 1988) traces the history of pensions and pension fund managers in Britain and abroad. Thane (2005) has taken the social historian's perspective when looking at individual retirement issues, rather than studying the financial intermediaries themselves. Unit trust history has been chronicled by Gleeson (1981) and the investment industry as a whole has been explored by Cassis (1990b), with a history of the earliest English investment trust, Foreign & Colonial, by McKendrick and Newlands (1999). Rutterford (2006c) compares British and US mutual fund industries since their inception, suggesting that the relative success of British investment trusts compared to their US counterparts, the closed end mutual funds, can be explained by management conservatism in accounting for financial assets and by investment strategy.

Savings institutions

Building societies also have their business histories: for example, Coventry by Davis (1985) and the Halifax by Hobson (1953). Industry-wide coverage is provided by Ashworth (1980) and the life (and death) of the Australian permanent building societies by Thomson and Abbott (1998). Smaller financial institutions have been described in the context of a particular savings sector: for example, the Glasgow penny banks by Ross (2002); the trustees savings banks by Fishlow (1961), Moss and Slaven (1992) and Moss and Russell (1994); friendly societies by Gorsky (1998); and a single credit union by Burness (1991). As yet, there is no complete history of the post office savings banks.

History of capital markets

In this section, we turn to the history of capital markets, considering, in particular, stock exchanges. The most international of stock markets, the London Stock Exchange was also the largest until overtaken by New York in the aftermath of the forced sales of foreign investments during the First World War (Michie 2006: 164) – British investors had remained responsible for 40 per cent of cross-border investment in 1913 (Pollard 1985). Today, the London Stock Exchange remains the third largest in the world; far more prominent than Britain's relative economic importance might imply. Indeed, it was capitalised at 225 per cent of GDP in 1999 compared to 109 per cent in 1913 (Michie 2006: 7). Its early success in the seventeenth and eighteenth centuries has been explored by writers such as Neal (2000) and Neal and Quinn (2001), who focus on the role of trade, and Ferguson (2001) who has argued that government debt, which played a vital role in funding government military expenditure, helped develop London's financial markets. Michie (1987, 2006) has compared the progress of the London Stock Exchange with its counterpart in New York, and has argued that the lack of regulation assisted the former's rapid growth pre-First World War. Davis (1966) also provided an institutional explanation of the different development paths of the British and American capital markets.

The London Stock Exchange and related capital raising institutions have an historical literature of their own: a classic text is Michie's *The London Stock Exchange: A History* (1999). Kynaston's (1994, 1995, 1999, 2001) comprehensive four-volume history of the City of London covers all major institutions and players from 1815 to 2000. Less work has been done on the provincial stock exchanges, but notable works include Killick and Thomas (1970) and Thomas (1973). There are business histories of the major merchant banks, for example, Ziegler (1988) on Barings, Burk (1989) on Morgan Grenfell, Roberts (1992) on Schroders and Ferguson (1998) on N. M. Rothschild & Sons Ltd. There are also histories of stockbrokers, such as that of Foster & Braithwaite by Reader (1979), of James Capel by Reed (1975), of Cazenove & Co. by Kynaston (1991) and of stock jobbers in general by Attard (2000). Cassis has specialised in studying the role of banking families (Cassis 1984, 1987).

A fascinating aspect of the history of stock markets is that, prior to the First World War – before the regulation of new issue prospectuses, the introduction of stringent accounting standards and audit requirements, and the development of sophisticated portfolio management tools – there were 106 stock exchanges around the world, including 55 in Europe alone (Michie 2006: 136). Hannah (2007b) compares their size and importance as at 1900. There are far fewer stock exchanges today, with the top four (New York, Nasdaq, Tokyo and London) accounting for over 80 per cent of equity turnover (Michie 2006: 7). Geisst (1999) has written a comprehensive study of the New York Stock Exchange. Cassis (2006) has attempted to compare the major financial centres, to explain their relative success and failure through the prism of competitive strengths and weaknesses and historical events. Michie (2006) has looked more at the processes that have led to the development of a single, global securities market.

Rajan and Zingales (2003), in a much-cited paper in the 'law and finance' literature, have attempted to explain the relative success over time of the North American and London stock exchanges and the relative failure of their Belgian, French and German counterparts. They argue that, since there is an increasing body of evidence that the development of a country's financial markets facilitates its economic growth, it is important to understand why some countries do not have successful stock markets. They demonstrate reversal in stock market development in, for example, the French and German stock markets, compared to their pre-First World War positions, and show that cross-border openness is an explanatory factor in financial market development. They also blame relative failure on institutions in individual countries, such as the banks in Japan and the labour movements in France, as well as concluding that common law (as in Britain and the USA) is more investor-friendly than the civil law applied in continental European countries (as, also, do La Porta *et al.* 1998). This latter point is contested by Franks *et al.* (2003), who argue that the new issue market was active in the UK before the First World War, and particularly before investor-friendly legislation such as the protection of minority investors, was introduced.

The key research area in the history of British financial institutions and capital markets, which has preoccupied economic historians since the First World War through to recent years, has been the issue of whether British financial institutions or markets in some way failed British industry.

Did British financial institutions fail British industry?

There is a substantial research literature questioning whether financial institutions failed to provide adequate financial support to British industry, and thus were complicit in the failure of key British industrial sectors to compete with their German and American counterparts in the twentieth century. Supple (1994) describes the preoccupation of economic historians with the failure of the British economy to keep up with its rivals. Kennedy (1990: 23) cites the failure of Victorian Britain to sustain early technological advances, which 'culminated in an actual productivity decline in the period 1899–1913 – an unprecedented event in an advanced industrial economy during peacetime'. The following sub-sections consider, in turn, the role of the banks, 'the City' and overseas investment bias and 'gentlemanly capitalism' in explaining relative economic decline before turning to the issue of the restructuring of British industry.

The role of the banks

The criticism of banks' lending policies has a long and venerable history stretching back before the First World War. It has been argued that, up to the late nineteenth century, local banks were happy to lend to their industrial customers and not just for purposes of short-term liquidity. Jefferys (1938: 15) attributes the failure of about 100 banks, both private and joint stock, between 1846 and 1857 to being 'too closely linked to one firm or local industry'. Cottrell (1980: 194–257) describes the lending policies of a number of banks from the 1840s to the 1890s. Newton (2003) analyses the network of relationships between Sheffield industrialists and Sheffield bankers in the third quarter, and Wale (1994) looks at bank lending in the Midlands in the last quarter of the nineteenth century. Cottrell, Newton and Wale are agreed that banks did try to accommodate their industrial clients by rolling over overdrafts, for example, but all also point to the banks' emphasis on short-term lending for working capital purposes, usually to the exclusion of medium- or long-term lending for fixed investment. More recent work by Collins and Baker (2003), building on that of Capie and Collins (1992), examines 3,010 accounts of industrial firms at 268 separate provincial branches of 20 different banks between 1880 and 1914. They reveal that over 95 per cent of loans were for under 12 months and less than 15 per cent of loans were for expenditure on fixed capital, plant or premises (Collins and Baker 2003: 186). Also, although banks were often prepared to lend without collateral, the proportion of unsecured loans fell from just under a half between 1880–4 to under 18 per cent between 1910–14 (ibid.: 187).

Cassis (1990a) attributes increased aversion to industrial lending to the rapid concentration of the banking sector in the late nineteenth and early twentieth centuries. Just 41 banks were left in England and Wales by 1913, and a dozen London-headquartered banks controlled about two-thirds of all deposits. As lending decisions became formalised and centralised, and as the international nature of the London money markets made the London-based banks risk-averse (Ingham 1984: 149–50), so the relationships between bankers and their corporate clients broke down. Reflecting these concerns, the Macmillan Committee was set up to investigate whether the banks were failing small and medium-sized companies by only providing short-term or even 'temporary' funds – it reported in 1931 and found them guilty as charged: the so-called 'Macmillan gap'. Although Ross (1990; see also Higgins and Toms 2000) argues, discussing the inter-war period, that banks did not discriminate against their customers when formulating lending policies, and that there is some evidence that they helped industries such as cotton during that period, British banks are adversely compared with their German counterparts which, it was concluded, not only lent long-term but also invested in the equity of their clients. Other research argues that the role of the German banks in funding German industry has been overstated (Cassis 1990a; Watson 1996).

The role of 'the City' and overseas investment bias

The London Stock Exchange, and the capital markets over which it presides, are also believed to have 'failed' British industry not, as in the case of the banks, because of excess caution, but because of a cultural divide between 'the City' and industry, and because of a preference for encouraging overseas rather than domestic investment. The preference for overseas investment gained pace in the 1820s with the financing of American states, and grew to encompass investments in government bonds, utilities, mining, agriculture, and foreign railways, which represented a massive 40 per cent of British investment overseas between 1870 and 1914 (Pollard 1985). This was helped by the fact that, from 1821, the major currencies were on the gold standard, thus removing exchange risk from overseas investing. Moreover, the guarantees offered on empire stocks, such as Indian railways, together with their higher yields compared with domestic equivalents, made such investments even more attractive. At the turn of the twentieth century, with declining yields at home and the broadening of the definition of trustee stocks to include certain overseas securities, both institutional and private investors are believed to have preferred to invest overseas to achieve their desired risk-return profile (Rutterford 2006a: Goetzmann and Ukhov 2005). Figure 17.1 shows an example of an international portfolio recommended in 1909 for a British investor seeking an overall return of 5½ per cent.

Edelstein (1974, 1982), on the other hand, has argued that yields available overseas were no higher than those for industrial shares at home, and that the relative attractions of domestic and overseas securities varied according to the economic conditions in Britain. But, if this is the case, why would British investors have preferred to invest in, say, Argentine securities, despite political risk, when compared with buying shares in 'new' British industries such as motor cars or electrical engineering? Kennedy (e.g. 1974, 1990) laid the blame on segmented capital markets, with the London stock market concentrating on large enterprises such as Guinness or Cunard and leaving the small- to medium-sized and newer industries to company promoters, regional stock exchanges or non-member brokers. Evidence of the important role of company promoters is provided by authors such as Armstrong (1990). Poor accounting practices and deficient marketing made it difficult for non-local investors to gain sufficient information on new and risky companies, leading them to prefer overseas investments (Paish 1951). Lazonick (1991) blamed institutional market rigidities; a view supported by Davis and Huttenback's

5½% INVESTMENT SCHEME.

Price Movement copied from Geographical Division Charts. (chart years 1893–1908)

Geographical Division	Name and Quantity of Stock	Dealing Number	Table showing Annual Values at average prices of year.										Table showing Annual Income.									
			1899	1900	1901	1902	1903	1904	1905	1906	1907	1908	1899	1900	1901	1902	1903	1904	1905	1906	1907	1908
BRITISH.	50 Shares Alliance and Dublin Consumers' Gas	1	1112	987	967	965	962	960	1075	1062	1025	981	$52\frac{1}{2}$	$52\frac{1}{2}$	$52\frac{1}{2}$	$52\frac{1}{4}$	$52\frac{1}{2}$	$52\frac{1}{2}$	$52\frac{1}{2}$	$52\frac{1}{2}$	$51\frac{1}{4}$	50
BRITISH COLONIES	£1,300 Toronto Mortgage Company Common Stock	2	975	1007	1111	1199	1176	1248	1355	1436	1324	1371	50	50	50	50	50	60	60	60	60	60
EUROPE, NORTH.	12 Shares Hamburg Electric Supply Ordinary	3	984	870	879	882	873	870	954	960	909	906	54	48	42	42	45	45	48	48	48	48
EUROPE, SOUTH.	50 Shares Vienna Bank Verein	4	1040	1080	1000	920	984	1040	1136	1096	1072	1100	64	60	52	56	56	60	60	60	60	60
ASIA.	£1,000 Nagasaki Harbour Improvement Loan 6% Bonds	5	900	880	840	870	900	870	900	980	940	930	60	60	60	60	60	60	60	60	60	60
AFRICA.	£1,000 Upper Congo Belgian Trading Company 6% Preference Stock	6	1060	1050	1040	1040	1060	980	1080	1060	1050	1050	60	60	60	60	60	60	60	60	60	60
NORTH AMERICA.	£1,000 Laclede Gas Light 5% Cumulative Preferred Stock	7	930	980	1030	1010	990	975	1030	950	900	900	50	50	50	50	50	50	50	50	50	50
CENTRAL AMERICA.	£1,000 New Trinidad Lake Asphalts 6% Debentures	8	980	985	1000	980	950	960	1020	1030	1000	1020	60	60	60	60	60	60	60	60	60	60
SOUTH AMERICA.	£1,500 Brazil Great Southern Railway 6% 1st Debentures	9	1095	1065	1200	1305	1440	1485	1530	1545	1470	1485	90	90	90	90	90	90	90	90	90	90
INTER-NATIONAL	£1,500 Anglo-American Telegraph Ordinary Stock	10	975	892	787	735	727	787	900	945	900	870	$55\frac{5}{8}$	$46\frac{7}{8}$	$45\frac{3}{4}$	$45\frac{5}{8}$	$45\frac{1}{4}$	$41\frac{1}{4}$	$48\frac{3}{4}$	$58\frac{1}{8}$	$52\frac{1}{2}$	$52\frac{1}{2}$
Totals of Annual Values and Annual Income		£	10051	9796	9854	9906	10062	10175	10880	11064	10590	10613	$596\frac{5}{8}$	$577\frac{3}{8}$	$562\frac{1}{4}$	$565\frac{5}{8}$	$569\frac{1}{4}$	$578\frac{3}{4}$	$589\frac{1}{4}$	$598\frac{5}{8}$	$591\frac{3}{4}$	$590\frac{1}{2}$

~ Estimated

Figure 17.1 5½ per cent investment portfolio

Source: Financial Review of Reviews, 1909.

(1986) survey of 260 share registers of companies officially listed on the London Stock Exchange between 1883 and 1907.

There is some discussion as to absolute amounts invested overseas, but Davis and Huttenback (1986) estimate that, on average, only one-third of finance went to British-based companies or home government stocks between 1865 and 1914, being as low as one-fifth between 1909 and 1913. Of the 5,000 stocks listed on the London Stock Exchange in 1910, only 600 were industrial and commercial (Cassis 1987: 48) and only 6 per cent of funds raised on the exchange between 1865 and 1914 went to British manufacturing enterprises (Cain and Hopkins 1993: 191). And yet, by 1914, Britain was the largest overseas lender by far, with a total of £20,000 million invested overseas, representing 44 per cent of total overseas investment worldwide. Its nearest rival was France, with 19.9 per cent of the total, and the USA had a mere 7.8 per cent (Pollard 1985). Despite the repatriation of much overseas investment during the First World War, and restrictions on non-empire new issues, the London Stock Exchange was still not viewed as a major provider of long-term funding for British industry by the time the Macmillan Committee reported. Significantly, the London Stock Exchange was not even summoned as witness to help shed light on this situation!

'Gentlemanly capitalism'

Davis and Huttenback (1986) found that financiers preferred foreign stocks, peers and gentlemen (the elite investors) empire stocks, and businessmen domestic stocks. Davis and Huttenback's concept of elite investors is consistent with the 'gentlemanly capitalism' argument put forward by Cain and Hopkins (1987, 1993) who argue that, by the nineteenth century, the traditional aristocratic landed elite were being replaced by gentlemen capitalists drawn from the new financial service sector and not from the industrialist class. Although the thrust of Cain and Hopkins' argument is that the British imperialist development was driven by the preferences of the elite rather than of industrialists, the implication is that there was a divide between industry and finance in Britain (Collins and Baker 2003: 4–5). The financial sector grew faster than the industrial sector from the 1860s onwards, and Rubinstein (1993, 2006) has shown that the new financial elite, with fortunes of over half a million pounds, were drawn primarily from the landed gentry and the City and not from the ranks of industrialists.

There was also a geographical bias in wealth, with the richest based in the south rather than the manufacturing north. It is notable how bankers frequently became peers. Cassis (1984, 1987) has chronicled how the top merchant-banking families of the City intermarried with the aristocracy and were made directors of a wide variety of financial institutions, including the Bank of England. Compare Lord Revelstoke of Barings, who famously remarked in 1911: 'I confess that personally I have a horror of all industrial companies and that I should not think of placing my hard-earned gains into such a venture' with Arnold Hills. Hills worked among the London East End poor for five years, single-handedly kept his shipbuilding and engineering firm, Thames Iron, afloat for 20 years, of which he spent nine in a wheelchair, founded the first English vegetarian restaurant, and provided for his staff through savings clubs, educational and sports clubs. He died in 1923 without official recognition (Rutterford 2006b: 48–9).

Thus Rubinstein supports Kennedy in blaming the City for distancing itself from, and failing to finance, British industry, leading to underinvestment. Ingham (1984) argues that city institutions failed to finance British industry, not because of their distance from industry, but rather because they found it more profitable to raise money for large international governments and companies than small British firms. They chose to establish close links with the Treasury and the Bank of England and, with them, promoted both the maintenance of sterling on the gold standard and free trade; policies not necessarily in the best interests of British industrialists.

Restructuring of industry

A number of researchers have chosen to study particular industries to determine whether the stock market could have played a more significant role in financing British industry with risk capital. Harrison (1981) found that the new bicycle companies of the late nineteenth and early twentieth centuries were too small to warrant interest from brokers and tended to organise their own share issues, some of which failed to raise sufficient finance in this way. Watson (1995) found that brewers were so well served by the stock market that they made limited demands on their bankers. It can be argued that the brewing industry is a special case, however, being able to issue fixed interest loans secured on fixed assets. Much use was made of debentures to finance brewing firms; ordinary shares were kept under family control with only 49 per cent of breweries' new share capital issued to the public between 1895 and 1899 (Hannah 2007b: 416). Higgins and Toms (1997), in their study of the cotton industry post-First World War, do not blame its decline on the failure to raise capital on the stock market – indeed, there was a stock market new issue boom in 1919–20 – and attribute only part of the blame to the impact of calls on unpaid capital and pressure for maintenance of high dividends. Michie (e.g. 1987, 1999) is a firm supporter of the role of stock markets, arguing: that the London Stock Exchange was not averse to risk (he gives the example of risky mining shares listed at the end of the nineteenth century); that critics ignore the role of the provincial exchanges; and that, in any case, much of the required finance was provided locally by banks, friends and fellow business-men. However, Kynaston (1994, 1995, 1999, 2001) has argued that deals were struck based on trust not technical know-how. This had the advantage of allowing deals to go through 'on the nod' but meant that the stock market was not an efficient mechanism for the placing of risk capital.

One possible reason why British industry suffered sharp relative economic decline post 1870 was because it failed to restructure. British companies were small and geographically dispersed compared to the giant trusts of the USA. Pressure to create these large enterprises in the USA in the late nineteenth and early twentieth centuries came from a number of sources. One was the Sherman anti-trust legislation (1890) which forbade collusion between firms and thus encour-aged mergers to create monopolies such as United States Steel. Another was the fragmented nature of the US banking system, which did not allow inter-state branch networks and thus allowed financiers such as J. P. Morgan the opportunity to create monopolies for which he arranged funding in their stead (Davis 1966). A third factor was the different policies towards industrial company financing between the New York Stock Exchange and the London Stock Exchange. The former, which had refused access to industrial companies until the late nineteenth century (Davis 1966: 262), then had a minimum size requirement for listing which was five times the London equivalent. It also required that the company seeking a listing on the New York Stock Exchange already be quoted elsewhere and have a ready market in its shares. As a result, by 1905, the top 50 firms listed on the New York Stock Exchange averaged $79.5m capitalisation compared with £4.4m ($21.4m) for the top 50 British listed firms (Michie 1986: 185–6).

Both banks and city institutions could have played a role in restructuring British industry along the lines of Morgan's restructuring of the steel industry and Harriman's of the railroads in the USA (DeLong 1991; Hannah 2007a). There is some evidence of attempts at restructuring in Britain. For example, Lloyd Jones and Lewis (2000) document evidence that Raleigh Bicycle Company's bankers were actively involved in management and took a seat on the board. In addition, there were attempts by the British government to help industries in trouble in the inter-war years. For example, Matthews *et al.* (1998: 155) refer to the setting up of the Bankers' Industrial Development Company in 1929, one of whose creations was the Lancashire Cotton Corporation which took over more than 100 companies. Wilson (1998) provides similar evidence of bank involvement with the management of Ferranti and Matthews *et al.* also refer to accountants being called in to suggest how to restructure failing industries, for example, Scottish steel-making in 1923 (ibid.: 156). However, major industry restructuring did not take place.

Best and Humphries (1986) are the strongest critics of the banks' failure to act, although Collins and Baker (2003) counter that there is no evidence that it would have had a beneficial effect and that comparisons with Germany tell us nothing about what would have happened in Britain. Such criticisms have also been levelled at City institutions. Rutterford (2006b), examining the role of Hambro (the merchant bank) in structuring a new issue for Thames Iron, in 1899, notes that it failed to visit the company, took no account of risk issues when devising a capital structure and was not involved in subsequent financings. However, Franks *et al.* (2003) note that there were three merger booms in the 1900s, the 1920s and the 1930s and that many acquirers were able to use their own shares as consideration. Thus, industry to some extent carried out its own restructurings unaided by banks and the stock market. Counter-factual history might try to answer the 'what if' question, but there is no way of knowing whether a finance-led restructuring, such as is taking place today, would have made British companies perform better than they did.

The next two sections of the chapter are devoted, respectively, to the history of finance and of investment decision making.

History of finance

Accounting history, as described by Napier (2006), emerged from the study of accounting change and, although there are differences between the 'new' and 'traditional' approaches, accounting history has been accepted and integrated into accounting research in general. The study of the history of finance has not had such a smooth path.

In this section, the more traditional approach to the history of finance is first considered, then the more modern, positive approach.

Traditional approach

Traditional histories of industrial or corporate finance include Evans's (1936) *British Corporation Finance* which deals with the period 1775 to 1880, Cottrell's (1980) *Industrial Finance* which covers British finance from 1830 to 1914, and Thomas's (1978) *The Finance of British Industry*, which takes up the story from 1918 to 1976. Wright and Sylla's six-volume *History of Corporate Finance* (2003) contains primary source materials illustrating the development of Anglo-American securities markets as well as their financial practices, theories and laws. Jefferys' (1938) PhD thesis sheds light on changes in corporate financing strategies from before limited liability became generally available to companies in 1855 through to the First World War.

It was not until the late twentieth century – Baskin (1988) and Baskin and Miranti (1997) – that a serious attempt was made to integrate the modern finance models into historical analysis.

In *A History of Corporate Finance*, Baskin and Miranti explore concepts such as agency theory (Jensen and Meckling 1976) and information asymmetry (Myers and Majluf 1984) when studying US and UK corporate financing methods from the pre-industrial world to the end of the twentieth century. They argue that more recognition of path dependence and historical evolution will allow modern finance researchers to explore previously unidentified explanatory variables. They also consider that it is vitally important to study the evolution and path dependence of financial innovation.

Following on from this approach, the law and finance literature spawned by La Porta *et al.* (1998), has used the path dependence approach to argue that the survival of the US and UK stock markets, in comparison to the relative decline of the continental European stock markets between 1913 and 2000, is due to the greater flexibility of those countries' common law. This explanation has been the subject of much recent criticism. Authors such as Kynaston (1999, 2001), Franks *et al.* (2003), and Hannah (2007b) have argued that the British stock market was efficient *before* the introduction of regulation to protect investors' interests and, therefore, legal differences between countries cannot be used to explain the relative success or failure of their stock markets. They argue that trust was a vital element in the efficiency of the market, allowing transactions to take place despite the presence of information asymmetry, contrasting with Kynaston's negative view of the impact of trust on efficient pricing of deals.

Positive approach

Finance research began to emerge in its more modern form in the 1930s in the USA, when there was a perceived need for rigour and formality in the valuation of share prices and in the management of financial institutions following the 1929 stock market crash. Money was provided via such institutions such as the Cowles Commission, the Ford Foundation and the Carnegie Foundation for research into finance and investment, in particular using share price and economic databases. This coincided with improvements in data processing capability and in statistical and econometric techniques. The study of finance was framed on a positive basis, with *a priori* assumptions formalised and tested empirically, assuming rational behaviour. Finance questions such as 'What is a firm's optimal capital structure?' and 'What is a firm's optimal dividend policy?' were answered – subject to assuming that investors were rational, that markets were efficient and that managers always acted to maximise shareholder value. A chasm therefore opened up between quantitative modern finance research and more descriptive, traditional studies of the financial past.

Recently, however, corporate finance researchers have begun to adopt a more structured or quantitative approach towards historical corporate finance issues. A constraint on this type of research, of course, is the lack of historical data for the purpose of analysis, particularly for time periods prior to the last few decades of the twentieth century. However, cliometrics – the study of economic history using quantitative analysis and economic theory – is now well established, particularly in the USA, with journals such as *Explorations in Economic History* publishing articles using this approach.

An example of such research using long-run stock market returns is that of Wilson and Jones (1987) in their study of US share returns between 1871 and 1985. However, the returns calculated were affected by the major change in the composition of their sample over time. Barsky and DeLong (1992), aware of the changes in type and importance of sectors between the nineteenth and twentieth centuries, chose to focus only on share prices in the latter period. Shiller (2005), in his work on stock market efficiency, has put together what he argues is a valid US share price index going back to 1870, and has used it to show excess price volatility.

More recently, Goetzmann and Ibbotson (2005) have employed a painstakingly constructed price series to look at the historical performance of share prices on the New York Stock Exchange as far back as 1792. Dimson *et al.* (2002) conducted a comprehensive comparative analysis of bond, bill and share returns for the major stock markets for the period 1900 to 2000, taking specific note of both sector and survivor bias, which they argued had produced misleading return figures in earlier analyses of the UK market. They found much lower real rates of return before 1955 than did previous estimates. Critics of the quantitative approach, such as Rutterford (2004) and Bank (2007), argue that the use of total returns in long-run analyses may not be appropriate, with dividend yield being a much-used measure of return until the 1960s, at least in the UK. Rutterford argues, therefore, that looking at share returns over the long term, ignoring dividend yield, gives misleading results. Baskin and Miranti (1997) also document changing investor attitudes to equity investment, with Jefferys (1938) noting that, as companies geared up with debentures and preference shares in the early twentieth century, commentators advised against investing in shares at all: 'the fluctuating character of equity being anathema to these instructors on investment' (quoted in Jefferys 1938: 356).

Turning to new issues, Wright (2002) argues that today's Initial Public Offering in the USA under-price new issues, whereas issues in the period 1781 to 1861 were fairly priced through direct contact with investors that avoided intermediaries such as investment banks. By contrast, researchers into British new issues have argued that such markets have always been inefficient. Barnes and Firman (2001), looking at case studies of the issue of new companies during the mid-1860s, argue that poor quality accounting information hindered the efficiency of the process. Jefferys refers to the increasing use of over-optimistic prospectuses for marketing purposes, with one of the purposes of the 1907 Companies Act being to stop 'word painting' (1938: 351), though Rutterford (2007) has pointed out that it was not until 1929 that directors were actually fined for making untrue statements in prospectuses. The Macmillan Committee (1931) asserted that the inclusion of banks' names in prospectuses during the stock market boom of 1928 and 1929 had caused the inexperienced investor to believe that the bank in some way 'vouched' for the issue (Willcock 1929: 22). Quantitative work by Chambers (2006) on post-Second World War new issues on the London Stock Exchange has suggested that under-pricing was a severe problem, and this finding has been interpreted as evidence of the continued failure of the financial sector to help British industry. Chambers attributes this failure to information asymmetry as well as to lack of competition in the UK investment-banking sector.

History of investment

In the final survey section of this chapter, attention is devoted to the history of investment, arguably the most under-researched feature of the history of finance and financial institutions. History of investment is interpreted as both the study of different types of investors and of their investment behaviour. This section starts with the most researched topic – that of stock-market bubbles, which have fascinated observers from the South Sea Bubble of 1720 to the internet dot.com boom of the late twentieth century. Attention then turns to investors themselves and investment strategies.

Stock market bubbles

The South Sea Bubble has attracted interest from family historians studying the written correspondence of women trading in the South Sea company's shares (Laurence 2006). It has also engaged economic historians, such as Carlos and Neal (2006), who have analysed the profits and losses of investors in Bank of England stock in the fateful year, 1720, and Harrison (2001) who has considered how investors valued shares at that time. A complete history of this first stock market crash has been written by Dale (2004).

Other spectacular collapses of individual financial institutions, which impacted severely on the stock market are that of Overend & Gurney in 1866 and of the City of Glasgow Bank in 1878, respectively recounted by Elliott (2006) and French (1985). The speculative railway boom of the 1840s has been covered by Kellett (1979) and Robb (1992), and the 1890s mining mania by Van Helten (1990). In fact, an entire issue of *Victorian Studies* (45 (1)) has been devoted to the Victorian fascination with speculation, which was reflected in the pages of numerous novels written at the time. Both Anthony Trollope's *The Way We Live Now* and Emile Zola's *L'Argent* are stories based on investor speculation: for Trollope, the market boom of the early 1870s and for Zola, the Union Générale collapse of 1881–82. The economist Irving Fisher, who famously failed to foresee the Wall Street Crash in 1929 (Dimand 2007: 153–5), wrote immediately after the event to explain the market's fall (Fisher 1930).

More recently, the kind of positive approach preferred by financial economists has been applied to long-run historical share price data and, in particular, boom and bust. Shiller (1989, 2005) believes that stock markets were overvalued in the heady last years of the twentieth century, suggesting that markets were, indeed, irrational. It is during stock market highs and lows that financial economists who seek to prove that markets and investors are rational have the most difficulty. It is not surprising to find, after the collapse of the dot.com boom in 2000, an increase in so-called 'behavioral finance' research, which allows for market efficiency but considers that investors can and do behave irrationally (Ritter 2006).

Investors

Traditional research into the characteristics of investors concentrated on their occupation and their location. For example, Cottrell (1980) devotes a chapter to shares and shareholders of early limited companies and provides data on their geographical location – in terms of distance from the London registered offices of a sample of companies in 1860 and 1865 – as well as a breakdown by profession. Davis and Huttenback (1986) report the occupations of shareholders in domestic, empire and foreign companies, all listed on the London Stock Exchange, over the period 1883–1907. Surveys of shareholders in particular sectors or locations – Anderson and Cottrell (1975) of banking and bank investors on Merseyside, Van Helten (1990) of investors in mining shares in the late nineteenth-century boom, Newton (2003) on shareholders in Sheffield companies in the third quarter of the nineteenth century – have also provided useful information on the prevalence of local investors and the preference of different social classes for different types of investment.

In recent years, there has been an upsurge of interest in the role of women investors and this has led to a number of papers which re-examine previously studied share registers or sample new ones to ascertain their importance. Women are revealed to have accounted for 40 per cent of investors by number in government consols as early as 1840 (Green and Owens, 2003), long before the Married Women's Property Acts of 1870 and 1882 allowed married women to hold financial assets in their own name. Researchers (Maltby and Rutterford 2006a; Rutterford and

Maltby 2006) have identified three types of women investor in company securities – speculator, income-seeker and family member, and also note that women appear to invest more heavily in lower-risk securities. Carlos *et al.* (2006) and Laurence (2006) report on female investment activity in the eighteenth-century stock market boom; Freeman *et al.* (2006) on women investors in insurance companies; Hudson (2001) on women investors in canal and railway companies; Newton and Cottrell (2006) on women owning early joint stock bank shares; and Acheson and Turner (2006) on Irish banking shares in the late nineteenth and early twentieth centuries. Much work remains to be done to ascertain the extent of women's involvement in stock market securities at particular points in time, given that, overall, their financial interest went from 3 per cent of share capital in 1860 (Cottrell, 1980: 96) to almost 50 per cent by 1948 (Maltby and Rutterford 2006b: 137).

Investment strategies

Investing institutions have also been researched in terms of changes in investment strategy over time, in terms of their approach to portfolio diversification and to choice of assets to include in their portfolios. May (1912) refers to the incremental strategy of insurance companies in the nineteenth and early twentieth centuries, adding investments one by one without considering the impact of each separate investment on the structure of the portfolio In contrast to this so-called 'bottom up' approach to building a portfolio, there is also evidence that a 'top down' approach to diversification was well advanced among some investors early on (Rutterford 2006a; Goetzmann and Ukhov 2005). For example, pre-First World War investment advisers advised clients to divide the world into ten geographic regions and to invest in one security in each region (see Figure 17.1). Goetzmann and Ukhov show that such top-down strategies would indeed have improved the risk-return ratio, decades before the efficient portfolio model of Markowitz (1952) was developed.

In terms of asset allocation, Rutterford *et al.* (2007) have shown that institutions were significant, in value terms, as investors in equities only from the 1930s. Private investors were the dominant type of investor. British institutions such as insurance companies and investment trusts preferred fixed income securities to equities, achieving higher yields on equity by investing overseas (Rutterford 2006c). It was not until 1937 that Raynes, a British actuary, wrote a paper showing that a diversified portfolio of equities outperformed a diversified portfolio of fixed income securities; a relationship which had been demonstrated in a US context for individual investors by Smith in 1925. Scott (2002), Baker and Collins (2003) and Rutterford (2006c) show how British insurance companies and unit trusts took until the 1930s to make a major switch to equities, with investment trusts not making the change until after the Second World War. Kenely (2006) shows how the switch to equities occurred even later for Australian life companies.

Conclusion and future directions

In this summary of a voluminous literature, a few aspects of the research undertaken so far stand out. There has been a concentration on the nineteenth and early twentieth centuries, the heyday of British finance and financial institutions. In particular, this period has intrigued economic historians who have devoted numerous papers and books to the single question of whether the financial sector is in some way to blame for the relatively poor record of British industry, post 1870, compared to that of its rivals in Germany and the USA. It has to be remembered that much of this analysis was carried out in the 1960s to 1980s, when Britain's economic performance looked poor in comparison to that achieved pre-First World War. Indeed, Hannah (2007a: 34) notes dryly that 'Many historians of Britain – the recent critics of "declinism" have plausibly alleged – are programmed to discern the causes of decline in everything.' In recent years, he and other researchers, such as Michie (1999, 2006), perhaps reflecting Britain's improved economic performance since the 1980s, have recounted a more positive British financial history.

The second feature of the works surveyed is the divide between the descriptive or narrative business histories and the more quantitative approach adopted by economists and finance academics reaching back into the past. Economic historians are applying econometric techniques to their work and, interestingly, finance academics, such as those writing the 'law and finance' literature, are beginning to take account of qualitative as well as quantitative aspects of their data when attempting to explain the past. For example, Franks *et al.* (2003) and Kynaston (1999, 2001) have both referred to the role of trust in enabling relatively efficient markets to exist pre-regulation. At the same time, more accurate historical data bases are now being established stretching back to 1870 (Shiller 2005), and even earlier, on total returns, share prices, and dividends, for a number of markets, taking account of survivor and sector biases, and thus allowing long-term time series analysis to be carried out.

There is still plenty of room for improvement. First, there is potential for more cross-disciplinary research, combining aspects of, say, accounting, finance, social, political, and literary history, as well as geography, to create a much richer understanding of the financial past. It is important not just to describe events or to analyse numbers, revealing the 'what', but also to understand the 'why'. As Pollard has remarked: 'the psychology of the individual has received less than its due attention' (1985: 512). Second, there is surprisingly little international comparative work undertaken, apart from a few UK/US comparisons and the recent law and finance literature which compares countries in terms of their different legal systems, in particular, variations with respect to investors' rights.

The final major research gap is for the post-First World War period. This is not true for banking and other financial institution histories which cover inception to the present day – for example, Michie's 1999 history of the London Stock Exchange and Kynaston's four-volume history of the City. However, these histories tend to be narratives of institutional evolution through time. There is ample scope for more historical analysis of traditional finance and investment issues, such as debt and dividend policy, new and secondary issues, takeovers and mergers, and corporate governance, to follow the path initially proposed by Baskin (1988) and Baskin and Miranti (1997).

Key works

Ackrill and Hannah (2001) is a classic banking history text.

Baskin and Miranti (1997) is a detailed history of US and UK corporate finance from the eighteenth century to the present day which attempts to apply modern approaches, such as agency theory, to explain past corporate financial behaviour.

Collins and Baker (2003) is an empirical study of British commercial banks' lending behaviour that includes a comprehensive overview of the literature on whether or not British banks 'failed' British industry up to the First World War.

Dimson et al. (2002) is the definitive empirical study of global share and bond returns over the past 100 years, making due allowance for historical differences in dividend yields, liquidity, and real prices.

Rajan and Zingales (2003) is a key article in the 'law and finance' literature which, focusing on legal infrastructure differences, attempts to explain the relative success of the UK and US stock markets compared with their continental European counterparts since before the First World War.

References

Acheson, G. G. and Turner, J. D. (2006) The impact of limited liability on ownership and control: Irish banking, 1877–1914, *Economic History Review*, 59 (2): 320–46.

Ackrill, M. and Hannah, L. (2001) *Barclays: The Business of Banking 1690–1996* (Cambridge: Cambridge University Press).

Andersen, B. L. and Cottrell, P. L. (1975) Another Victorian capital market: a study of banking and bank investors on Merseyside, *Economic History Review*, 28 (4): 598–616.

Anon. (1903) *The History of the Halifax Permanent Benefit Building Society* (London: Reed).

Armstrong, J. (1990) The rise and the fall of the company promoter and the financing of British industry, in J. J. Van Helten and Y. Cassis (eds) *Capitalism in a Mature Economy*, pp. 115–38 (Aldershot: Edward Elgar).

Ashworth, H. (1980) *The Building Society Story* (London: Franey).

Attard, B. (2000) Making a market: the jobbers of the London Stock Exchange, 1800–1986, *Financial History Review*, 7 (1): 5–24.

Baker, M. and Collins, M. (2003) The asset portfolio composition of British life insurance firms, 1900–1965, *Financial History Review*, 10 (2): 137–64.

Bank, S. A. (2007) Dividends and tax policy in the long run, *University of Illinois Law Review*, 2: 533–74.

Barnes, P. and Firman, R. J. (2001) Difficulties in establishing a limited liability company in Great Britain during the 1860 and the role of financial information: a case history, *Financial History Review*, 8 (2): 143–62.

Barsky, R. and DeLong, J. B. (1992) Why does the stock market fluctuate?, working paper no. 3995, National Bureau of Economic Research.

Baskin, J. B. (1988) The development of corporate financial markets in Britain and the United States, 1600–1914: overcoming asymmetric information, *Business History Review*, 62 (2): 199–237.

Baskin, J. B. and Miranti, P. J. (1997) *A History of Corporate Finance* (Cambridge: Cambridge University Press).

Batiz-Lazo, B. and Boyns, T. (2004) The business and financial history of mechanisation and technological change in twentieth-century banking, *Accounting, Business & Financial History*, 14 (3): 225–32.

Batiz-Lazo, B. and Del Angel, G. (2003) Competitive collaboration and market contestability: cases in Mexican and UK banking, 1945–75, *Accounting, Business & Financial History*, 13 (3): 339–68.

Battilossi, S. (2000) Financial innovation and the golden ages of international banking, 1890–1931 and 1958–81, *Financial History Review*, 7 (2): 141–76.

Best, M. H. and Humphries, J. (1986) The City and industrial decline, in B. Elbaum and W. Lazonick (eds) *The Decline of the British Economy*, pp. 223–39 (Oxford: Oxford University Press).

Burk, K. (1989) *Morgan Grenfell 1838–1988: The Biography of a Merchant Bank* (Oxford: Oxford University Press).

Burness, C. (1991) *The People's Bank: Drumchapel Community Credit Union Ltd* (Glasgow: The Union).

Cain, P. J. and Hopkins, A. G. (1987) Gentlemanly capitalism and British expansion overseas II: new imperialism, 1850–1945, *Economic History Review*, 40 (1): 1–26.

Cain, P. J. and Hopkins, A. G. (1993) *British Imperialism: Innovation and Expansion 1688–1914* (London: Longman).

Capie, F. and Collins, M. (1992) *Have the Banks Failed British Industry?* (London: Institute of Economic Affairs).

Capie, F. and Rodrik-Bali, G. (1982) Concentration in British banking, 1870–1920, *Business History*, 24 (3): 280–7.

Carlos, A. and Neal, L. (2006) The micro-foundations of the early London capital market: Bank of England shareholders before and after the South Sea Bubble, 1720–1725, *Economic History Review*, 59 (3): 498–538.

Carlos, A., MacGuire, K. and Neal, L. (2006) Financial acumen, women speculators, and the Royal African Company during the South Sea Bubble, *Accounting, Business & Financial History*, 16 (2): 219–44.

Cassis, Y. (1984) *City Bankers, 1890–1914* (Cambridge: Cambridge University Press).

Cassis, Y. (1987) *La City de Londres* (Paris: Librairie Belin).

Cassis, Y. (1990a) British finance: success and controversy, in J. J. Van Helten and Y. Cassis (eds) *Capitalism in a Mature Economy*, pp. 1–22 (Aldershot: Edward Elgar).

Cassis, Y. (1990b) The emergence of a new financial institution: investment trusts in Britain, 1870–1939, in J. J. Van Helten and Y. Cassis (eds) *Capitalism in a Mature Economy*, pp. 139–58 (Aldershot: Edward Elgar).

Cassis, Y. (2006) *Capitals of Capital: A History of International Financial Centres, 1780–2005* (Cambridge: Cambridge University Press).

Chambers, D. (2006) The missed opportunity of IPOs by tender: a case study in British capital market failure, discussion paper series, Department of Economics, University of Oxford.

Checkland, S. G. (1975) *Scottish Banking: A History 1695–1973* (London: Collins).

Cockerell, H. A. L. and Green, E. (1994) *The British Insurance Business: A Guide to its Business and Records* (Sheffield: Sheffield University Press).

Collins, M. and Baker, M. (2003) *Commercial Banks and Industrial Finance in England and Wales, 1860–1913* (Oxford: Oxford University Press).

Cottrell, P. L. (1980) *Industrial Finance 1830–1914* (London: Methuen).

Dale, R. (2004) *The First Crash: Lessons from the South Sea Bubble* (Princeton, NJ: Princeton University Press).

Davis, L. (1966) The capital markets and industrial concentration: the U.S. and U.K. a comparative study, *Economic History Review*, 19 (2): 255–72.

Davis, L. E. and Huttenback, R. A. (1986) *Mammon and the Pursuit of Empire: The Political Economy of British Imperialism, 1860–1912* (Cambridge: Cambridge University Press).

Davis, M. (1985) *Every Man his Own Landlord: A History of the Coventry Building Society* (Coventry: Coventry Building Society).

DeLong, J. B. (1991) Did J. P. Morgan's men add value? in P. Temin, (ed.) *Inside the Business Enterprise*, pp. 205–36 (Chicago: The University of Chicago Press).

Dickson, P. G. M. (1960) *The Sun Insurance Office 1710–1960* (London: Oxford University Press).

Dimand, R. W. (2007) Irving Fisher and financial economics: the equity premium puzzle, the predictability of stock prices, and inter-temporal allocation under risk, *Journal of the History of Economic Thought*, 29 (2): 153–66.

Dimson, E., Marsh, P. and Staunton. M. (2002) *Triumph of the Optimists: 101 Years of Global Investment Returns* (Princeton, NJ: Princeton University Press).

Drew, B. (1949) *The London Assurance: A Second Chronicle* (Plaistow: Curwen Press).

Edelstein, M. (1974) The determinants of U.K. investment abroad, 1870–1913: the U.S. case, *Journal of Economic History*, 34 (4): 980–1007.

Edelstein, M. (1982) *Overseas Investment in the Age of High Imperialism: The United Kingdom, 1850–1914* (London: Methuen).

Elliott, G. (2006) *The Mystery of Overend & Gurney: Adventures in the Victorian Financial Underworld* (London: Methuen).

Evans, G. H. (1936) *British Corporation Finance 1775–1850: A Study of Preference Shares* (Baltimore, MD: Johns Hopkins University Press).

Ferguson, N. (1998) *The House of Rothschild: The World's Banker* (London: Weidenfeld & Nicolson).

Ferguson, N. (2001) *The Cash Nexus* (London: Allen Lane).

Fisher, I. (1930) *The Stock Market Crash and After* (New York: Macmillan).

Fishlow, A. (1961) The trustee savings banks, *Journal of Economic History*, 21 (1): 26–40.

Foxwell, H. S. (1927) A history of Barclays Bank, *Economic Journal*, 37 (147): 411–17.

Franks, J., Mayer, C. and Rossi, S. (2003) Ownership: evolution and regulation, working paper, ECGI, University of Oxford.

Freeman, M., Pearson, R. and Taylor, J. (2006) 'A doe in the city': women shareholders in early nineteenth-century Britain, *Accounting, Business & Financial History*, 16 (2): 265–91.

French, E. A. (1985) *Unlimited Liability: The Case of the City of Glasgow Bank* (London: Certified Accountant Publications).

Geisst, C. R. (1999) *Wall Street* (New York: Oxford University Press).

Gleeson, A. (1981) *People and their Money: 50 Years of Private Investment* (London: M&G Group).

Goetzmann, W. N. and Ibbotson, R. G. (2005) History and the equity risk premium, working paper, International Center for Finance, Yale School of Management.

Goetzmann, W. N. and Ukhov, A. (2005) British investment overseas 1870–1913: a modern portfolio theory approach, working paper, International Center for Finance, Yale School of Management.

Goodhart, C. A. E. (1986) *The Business of Banking, 1891–1914* (Aldershot: Gower).

Gorsky, M. (1998) The growth and distribution of English friendly societies in the early nineteenth century, *Economic History Review*, 51 (3): 489–511.

Green, D. R. and Owens, A. (2003) Gentlewomanly capitalism: widows and wealth-holding in England and Wales c.1800–1860, *Economic History Review*, 56 (3): 510–36.

Hannah, L. (1986) *Inventing Retirement: The Development of Occupational Pensions in Britain* (Cambridge: Cambridge University Press).

Hannah, L. (1988) *Pension Asset Management: An International Perspective* (Homewood, IL: Irwin).

Hannah, L. (2007a) What did Morgan's men really do? Paper presented at Business History Conference, Cleveland, Ohio, 31 May–2 June.

Hannah, L. (2007b) The 'divorce' of ownership from control from 1900 onwards: re-calibrating imagined global historical trends, *Business History*, 49 (4): 404–38.

Harrison, A. E. (1981) Joint-stock company flotation in the cycle, motor-vehicle and related industries, 1882–1914, *Business History*, 23 (2): 165–90.

Harrison, P. (2001) Rational equity valuation at the time of the South Sea Bubble, *Journal of Political Economy*, 33 (2): 269–81.

Higgins, D. and Toms, S. (1997) Firm structure and financial performance: the Lancashire textile industry c.1884 to 1960, *Accounting, Business & Financial History*, 7 (2): 195–232.

Higgins, D. and Toms, S. (2000) Public subsidy and private divestment: the Lancashire cotton textile industry, c.1950–c.1965, *Business History*, 42 (1): 59–84.

Hobson, O. R. (1953) *A Hundred Years of the Halifax: A History of the Halifax Building Society, 1853–1953* (London: Batsford).

Hudson, S. (2001) Attitudes to investment risk among West Midland canal and railway company investors, 1760–1850, unpublished PhD thesis, University of Warwick.

Ingham, G. (1984) *Capitalism Divided? The City and Industry in British Social Development* (Basingstoke: Macmillan).

Jefferys, J. B. (1938) Trends in business organisation in Great Britain since 1856, unpublished PhD thesis, University of London.

Jensen, M. C. and Meckling, W. H. (1976) Theory of the firm: managerial behavior, agency costs and ownership structure, *Journal of Financial Economics*, 3 (4): 305–60.

Jones, G. (1986) *Banking and Empire in Iran: The History of the British Bank of the Middle East* (Cambridge: Cambridge University Press).

Jones, G. (1992) *British Multinational Banking 1830–1990* (Oxford: Clarendon Press).

Joslin, D. M. (1954) London private bankers: 1720–1785, *Economic History Review*, 7 (2): 167–86.

Joslin, D. M. (1960) London bankers in wartime, 1739–84, in L. S. Presnell (ed.) *Studies in the Industrial Revolution*, pp. 156–77 (London: Athlone Press).

Kellett, J. R. (1979) *Railways and Victorian Cities* (London: Routledge & Kegan Paul).

Kenely, M. (2001) The evolution of the Australian life insurance industry, *Accounting, Business & Financial History*, 11 (2): 145–70.

Kenely, M. (2004) Adaptation and change in the Australian life insurance industry: an historical perspective, *Accounting, Business & Financial History*, 14 (1): 91–109.

Kenely, M. (2006) Mortgages and bonds: the asset management practices of Australian life insurers to 1960, *Accounting, Business & Financial History*, 16 (1): 99–119.

Kennedy, W. P. (1974) Foreign investment, trade and growth in the United Kingdom, 1870–1913, *Explorations in Economic History*, 11 (4): 415–44.

Kennedy, W. P. (1990) Capital markets and industrial structure in the Victorian economy, in J. J. Van Helten and Y. Cassis (eds) *Capitalism in a Mature Economy*, pp. 23–51 (Aldershot: Edward Elgar).

Killick, J. R. and Thomas, W. A. (1970) The provincial stock exchanges, 1830–1870, *Economic History Review*, 23 (1): 96–111.

Kynaston, D. (1991) *Cazenove & Co.: A History* (London: Batsford).

Kynaston, D. (1994) *The City of London: A World of its Own: 1815–90* (London: Chatto & Windus).

Kynaston, D. (1995) *The City of London: Golden Years, 1890–1914* (London: Chatto & Windus).

Kynaston, D. (1999) *The City of London: Illusions of Gold, 1914–45* (London: Chatto & Windus).

Kynaston, D. (2001) *The City of London: A Club No More, 1945–2000* (London: Chatto & Windus).

La Porta, R., Lopez-de-Silanes, F., Shleifer, A. and Vishny, R. W. (1998) Law and finance, *Journal of Political Economy*, 106 (6): 1113–55.

Laurence, A. E. (2006) Women investors, 'That nasty South Sea affair' and the rage to speculate in early eighteenth-century England, *Accounting, Business & Financial History*, 16 (2): 245–64.

Lazonick, W. (1991) *Business Organization and the Myth of the Market Economy* (Cambridge: Cambridge University Press).

Lloyd-Jones, R. and Lewis, P. J. (2001) *Raleigh and the British Bicycle Industry: An Economic and Business History, 1870–1960* (Burlington, Vt.: Ashgate Publishing).

Lloyd-Jones, R., Lewis, M. J., Matthews, M. D. and Maltby, J. (2004) Personal capitalism, governance, and the development of organisational hierarchies: Hadfield's 1919–45. Paper presented at Accounting, Business & Financial History Conference, Cardiff University, 16–17 September.

McKendrick, N. and Newlands, J. (1999) *'F&C': a History of Foreign & Colonial Investment Trust* (London: Foreign & Colonial Investment Trust).

Maltby, J. and Rutterford, J. (2006a) 'She possessed her own fortune': women investors from the late nineteenth century to the early twentieth century, *Business History*, 48 (2): 220–53.

Maltby, J. and Rutterford, J. (2006b) Editorial: women, accounting and investment, *Accounting, Business & Financial History*, 16 (2): 133–42.

Markowitz, H. (1952) Portfolio selection, *Journal of Finance*, 7 (1): 77–91.

Matthews, D., Anderson, M. and Edwards, J. R. (1998) *The Priesthood of Industry: The Rise of the Professional Accountant in British Management* (Oxford: Oxford University Press).

Matthews, P. W. and Tuke, A. W. (1926) *History of Barclays Bank Limited: Including the Many Private and Joint Stock Banks Amalgamated and Affiliated with it* (London: Blade, East & Blades).

May, G. E. (1912) The investment of life assurance funds, *Journal of the Institute of Actuaries*, 46: 134–68.

Melton, F. T. (1986) Deposit banking in London, 1700–90, *Business History*, 28 (3): 40–50.

Michie, R. C. (1986) The London and New York Stock Exchanges, 1850–1914, *Journal of Economic History*, 46 (1): 171–87.

Michie, R. C. (1987) *The London and New York Stock Exchanges, 1850–1914* (London: Allen & Unwin).

Michie, R. C. (1999) *The London Stock Exchange: A History* (Oxford: Oxford University Press).

Michie, R. C. (2006) *The Global Securities Market: A History* (Oxford: Oxford University Press).

Moss, M. (1982) The private banks of Birmingham, 1800–1827, *Business History*, 24 (1): 79–94.

Moss, M. and Russell, I. (1994) *An Invaluable Treasure: A History of the TSB* (London: Weidenfeld & Nicolson).

Moss, M. and Slaven, A. (1992) *From Ledger Book to Laser Beam: A History of the TSB in Scotland from 1810 to 1990* (Glasgow: TSB Bank).

Myers, S. and Majluf, N. (1984) Corporate financing and investment decisions when firms have information that investors do not have, *Journal of Financial Economics*, 13 (2): 187–221.

Napier, C. J. (2006) Accounts of change: 30 years of historical accounting research, *Accounting, Organizations and Society*, 31 (4/5): 445–508.

Neal, L. (2000) How it all began: the monetary and financial architecture of Europe during the first global capital markets, 1648–1815, *Financial History Review*, 7 (2): 117–40.

Neal, L. and Quinn, S. (2001) Networks of information, markets, and institutions in the rise of London as a financial centre, 1660–1720, *Financial History Review*, 8 (1): 7–26.

Newton, L. (2003) Capital networks in the Sheffield Region, 1850–1885, in J. F. Wilson and A. Popp (eds) *Industrial Clusters and Regional Business Networks in England, 1750–1970*, pp. 130–54 (Aldershot: Ashgate).

Newton, L. and Cottrell, P. L. (2006) Female investors in the first English and Welsh commercial joint-stock banks, *Accounting, Business & Financial History*, 16 (2): 315–40.

Orbell, J. and Turton, A. (2001) *British Banking: A Guide to Historical Records* (Aldershot: Ashgate).

Paish, F. W. (1951) The London new issue market, *Economica*, 18 (69): 1–17.

Pearson, R. (1990) Thrift or dissipation? The business of life assurance in the early nineteenth century, *Economic History Review*, 43 (2): 236–54.

Pearson, R. (1992) Fire insurance and the British textile industries during the industrial revolution, *Business History*, 34 (4): 1–19.

Pearson, R. (1993) Taking risks and containing competition: diversification and oligopoly in the fire insurance markets of the north of England in the early 19th century, *Economic History Review*, 46 (1): 39–64.

Pearson, R. (1997a) Towards an historical model of financial services innovation: the case of the insurance industry 1700–1914, *Economic History Review*, 50 (2): 235–56.

Pearson, R. (1997b) British and European insurance enterprise in American markets, 1850–1914, *Business and Economic History*, 26 (2): 438–51.

Pearson, R. (2002) Growth, crisis and change in the insurance industry: a retrospective, *Accounting, Business & Financial History*, 12 (3): 487–504.

Pollard, S. (1985) Capital exports, 1870–1914: harmful or beneficial?, *Economic History Review*, 38 (4): 489–514.

Pressnell, L. S. (1960) Family bankers, *Business History*, 2 (2): 91–6.

Rajan, R. G. and Zingales, L. (2003) The great reversals: the politics of financial development in the 20th century, *Journal of Financial Economics*, 69 (1): 5–50.

Raynes, H. E. (1937) Equities and fixed interest stocks during twenty-five years, *Journal of the Institute of Actuaries*, 68: 483–507.

Raynes, H. E. (1948) *A History of British Insurance* (London: Pitman).

Reader, W. J. (1979) *A House in the City: A Study of the City and of the Stock Exchange Based on the Records of Foster & Braithwaite, 1825–1975* (London: Batsford).

Reed, M. C. (1975) *A History of James Capel & Co.* (London: Longman).

Ritter, J. R. (2006) Behavioral finance, in J. Rutterford, M. Upton and D. Kodwani (eds) *Financial Strategy*, pp. 42–52 (Chichester: John Wiley).

Robb, G. (1992) *White-Collar Crime in Modern England: Financial Fraud and Business Morality* (Cambridge: Cambridge University Press).

Roberts, R. (1992) *Schroders: Merchants and Bankers* (Basingstoke: Macmillan).

Ross, D. M. (1990) The clearing banks and industry – new perspectives on the inter-war years, in J. J. Van Helten and Y. Cassis (eds) *Capitalism in a Mature Economy*, pp. 52–70 (Aldershot: Edward Elgar).

Ross, D. M. (2002) 'Penny banks' in Glasgow, 1850–1914, *Financial History Review*, 9 (9): 11–39.

Rubinstein, W. D. (1993) *Capitalism, Culture and Decline in Britain 1750–1990* (London: Routledge).

Rubinstein, W. D. (2006) *Men of Property: The Very Wealthy in Britain since the Industrial Revolution* (London: Social Affairs Unit).

Rutterford, J. (2004) From dividend yield to discounted cash flow: a history of US and UK equity valuation techniques, *Accounting, Business & Financial History*, 14 (2): 115–49.

Rutterford, J. (2006a) The world was their oyster: international diversification pre-World War I, in J. Rutterford, M. Upton and D. Kodwani (eds) *Financial Strategy*, pp. 5–24 (Chichester: John Wiley).

Rutterford, J. (2006b) The merchant banker, the broker and the company chairman: a new issue case study, *Accounting, Business & Financial History*. 16 (1): 45–68.

Rutterford, J. (2006c) Learning from one's mistakes? Managing risk in the mutual fund industry. Paper presented at International Conference on Long-term Perspectives on Institutions, Business and Finance, What Have We Learned from the Past?, University of Antwerp, 19–20 October.

Rutterford, J. (2007) The company prospectus: marketing shares on the London Stock Exchange, 1850 to 1940. Paper presented at ABH and Chord Conference, University of Wolverhampton, 29–30 June.

Rutterford, J. and Maltby, J. (2006) The widow, the clergyman and the reckless: women investors in England, 1830–1914, *Feminist Economics*, 12 (1/2): 111–38.

Rutterford, J., Maltby, J., Green, D. and Owens, A. (2007) The sleeping partners?: Women investors in England and Wales, 1870 to 1935. Paper presented at Eleventh Annual Conference of the European Business History Association, University of Geneva, 13–15 September.

Ryan, R. (1983) *A History of the Norwich Union Fire and Life Insurance Societies from 1797 to 1914* (Norwich: University of East Anglia).

Scott, P. (2002) Towards the 'cult of the equity'? Insurance companies and the interwar capital market, *Economic History Review*, 55 (1): 78–104.

Shiller, R. (1989) *Market Volatility* (Cambridge, MA: MIT Press).

Shiller, R. (2005) *Irrational Exuberance* (Princeton, NJ.: Princeton University Press).

Shiller, R. J. (2002) Bubbles, human judgment, and expert opinion, *Financial Analysts Journal*, 58 (3): 18–26.

Street, E. and Glenn, R. (1980) *The History of National Mutual Life Assurance Society 1830–1980* (London: National Mutual Life Assurance Society).

Supple, B. E. (1970) *The Royal Exchange Assurance* (Cambridge: Cambridge University Press).

Supple, B. E. (1994) Fear of failing: economic history and the decline of Britain, *Economic History Review*, 47 (3): 441–58.

Thane, P. (2005) *The Long History of Old Age* (London: Thames & Hudson).

Thomas, W. A. (1973) *The Provincial Stock Exchanges* (London: Frank Cass).

Thomas, W. A. (1978) *The Finance of British Industry 1918–1976* (London: Methuen).

Thomson, D. and Abbott, M. (1998) The life and death of the Australian Permanent Building Societies, *Accounting, Business & Financial* History, 8 (1): 73–103.

Trebilcock, C. (1998) *Phoenix Assurance and the Development of British Insurance, II: The Era of the Insurance Giants, 1870–1984* (Cambridge: Cambridge University Press).

Van Helten, J. J. (1990) Mining, share manias and speculation: British investment in overseas mining. 1880–1913, in J. J. Van Helten and Y. Cassis (eds) *Capitalism in a Mature Economy*, pp. 159–85 (Aldershot: Edward Elgar).

Wale, J. (1994) What help have the banks given British Industry? Some evidence on bank lending in the Midlands in the late nineteenth century, *Accounting, Business & Financial History*, 4 (2): 321–42.

Watson, K. (1995) The new issue market as a source of finance for the UK brewing and iron and steel industries, 1870–1913, in Y. Cassis, G. D. Feldman and U. Olsson, (eds) *The Evolution of Financial Institutions and Markets in Twentieth-Century Europe*, pp. 209–48 (Aldershot: Scholar Press).

Watson, K. (1996) Banks and industrial finance: the experience of brewers, 1880–1913, *Economic History Review*, 4 (1): 58–81.

Willcock, P. D. (1929) Limited companies III, *Banker*, 12 (47): 315–18.

Wilson, J. F. (1998) Ferranti and the accountant, 1896–1975: the struggle between priorities and reality, *Accounting, Business & Financial History*, 8 (1): 53–72.

Wilson, J. W. and Jones, C. P. (1987) A comparison of annual common stock returns: 1871–1925 with 1926–1985, *Journal of Business*, 60 (2): 239–58.

Wright, R. E. (2002) Reforming the US IPO market: lessons from history and theory, *Accounting, Business & Financial History*, 12 (3): 419–37.

Wright, R. E. and Sylla, R. (eds) (2003) *The History of Corporate Finance* (London: Pickering & Chatto).

Ziegler, P. (1988) *The Sixth Great Power, Barings, 1762–1929* (London: Collins).

18

Railroads

Dale L. Flesher and Gary J. Previts[*]

Overview

Railroads played a major role in the development of the nineteenth-century American and British economies, and their contribution to the development of accounting and auditing has attracted considerable scholarly attention.[1] The first important aspect of railroad accounting is related to the way they were founded – as joint stock companies, a type of business organisation that created agency problems and the need for governance. Because railroads accomplished many objectives, they grew, and with growth came the need for accounting and auditing. Since corporate financial reporting (see Chapter 8) and corporate auditing (see Chapter 10) were not well developed in the mid-nineteenth century, the railroads had to devise effective practices to operate their businesses. The procedures that they developed were later adopted by industrial corporations. As a result, the railroad industry can be looked to for an explanation of the formulation of many accounting techniques.

Railroads utilised several innovative reporting practices: early use of cash flow statements, the identification of 'net earnings', extensive socioeconomic reporting, and the development of the double account system. In the USA, the Baltimore and Ohio Railroad Company was an innovator with respect to governance and auditing, while the Mobile and Ohio Railroad Company pioneered the use of accounting for the better determination of earnings power. At the same time, railroad companies in both the USA (including the Mobile and Ohio) and Britain published accounts that were the subject of 'nineteenth century accounting error' (Brief 1965) – inaccuracy due to the omission of depreciation and other non-cash expenses and the failure to classify transactions accurately as capital or revenue. Nineteenth-century account-ing error may be simply that – an error; alternatively, as we will see, it may constitute 'bias' (ibid.: 12) reflecting management optimism, window dressing or even fraudulent behaviour when constructing published financial reports.

The principal focus of this chapter is the nineteenth century, because it was then that issues of accounting, auditing and accountability came to the fore, were addressed and to some extent resolved. Given space constraints, this chapter is confined to the USA and, to a more limited extent, Britain. The presentational approach adopted is to augment a review of the relevant literature with some detailed case studies from US railroad history.

Introduction

As Chandler established in *The Visible Hand* (1977), the railroads were America's first modern businesses. The Baltimore and Ohio Railroad Company (B&O), formed in 1827, and based on a British concept, was the first major US railroad (Cleveland and Powell 1909: 61). In Britain, it was the success of the Stockton and Darlington Railway (1825) and the Liverpool and Manchester Railway (1830) that encouraged the start-up of many similar operations (McCartney and Arnold 2000: 294). Although scores of other railroads were developed in the following decades throughout the USA, Britain and continental Europe, it was the B&O that was reputed to be the 'university' of railroad accounting and operations. For a quarter of a century, the B&O was a source of substantial technical, accounting, and management innovation in railroading. Then, in the early 1850s, a new railroading environment in the USA led to the Illinois Central Railroad and the Mobile and Ohio Railroad becoming important leaders. An analysis of the accounting innovations of these three lines essentially covers many important aspects of the first half century of railroading, although the chief financial officer of the Louisville and Nashville Railroad, Albert Fink, an alumnus of the B&O, is recognised as having made important contributions near the end of the period.

The history of railways in Britain is in many respects similar to that of the USA, but the environment was different. In the USA, most early railroads were developmental enterprises whose profits were dependent on future geographic expansion. There were few opportunities for quick profits. In Britain railways had more in common with other business opportunities in that they were built to exploit existing trade channels. On both sides of the Atlantic, the need for vast capital outlays was the same, but an investment in a US railroad was a less economic-rational business decision than in Britain. As a result, US governmental entities assisted private investors by providing subsidies either in the form of direct investment or grants of various types, including land which could be sold to provide money to help build the railroads. These subsidies introduced accounting questions that did not exist in Britain.

The first half century of railroad operations was essentially a growth phase and was followed by what has been called a regulatory phase. The detailed regulatory phase began with state-based regulatory regimes such as the Massachusetts Railroad law of 1846 (Neidert 1950: 34–6), was followed by the Regulation of Railways Act, 1868, in Britain and the creation of the federal Interstate Commerce Commission in the USA in 1887. The last of these government initiatives signalled a period of controversy as railroads both responded to 'Sunshine' regulation – i.e. requests for information that cast light on the financial and operating aspects of the roads – and also attempted to capture the regulatory mechanisms to achieve economic benefits of cartelisation (Kolko 1965).

This chapter is based on the work of many scholars who have studied railroad accounting over the years. The first important railway accounting researcher in the UK was Harold Pollins, who dealt primarily with the period prior to 1868 (Pollins 1952, 1954, 1956), although some might argue that Dionysius Lardner's treatise was essentially a history and analysis to its 1850 publication date. Others in the UK have followed Pollins, particularly in the past two decades, including some who have attempted to clarify Pollins' work (such as Richards 1972). Edwards (1986, 1989) and the team of McCartney and Arnold (2000, 2002, 2003) have also made important contributions. In the USA, there are hundreds of original publications from the 1800s,[2] but the first real synthesis was undertaken by Neidert in 1950, although his work is strongest for the post-1887 period. Recently, the work of Flesher, Previts and Samson (Flesher *et al.* 2000, 2003a, 2003b, 2006; Previts and Samson 2000; Samson and Previts 1999; Samson *et al.* 2003) has explored in detail the earlier period in the USA. However, it should be noted that Brief (1965, 1976) made important contributions with respect to capital consumption allowances.

The economics and environment of the railroad industry

An attribute that established large railroads as modern businesses was the capital requirements of these natural monopoly enterprises, which far exceeded those of other contemporary businesses and in turn created barriers to competitive entry. Large capital requirements meant that external financing and public markets were needed to initiate or expand a railroad line. While most other contemporary businesses were owner-operated ventures, requiring local bank loans at most for seasonal financing, railroads, by contrast, with the long-term capital needed to construct a line, required more capital than one person could risk; so many individuals, including both debt and equity investors external to the railroad operations, were needed to provide capital. This created new issues of how to communicate with external investors regarding the performance of the railroad and how to monitor the managers who were deemed to be stewards of the company's assets. These so-called 'agency' problems are still being addressed today, wherein the separation of the providers of capital from the management is fundamental to the control and communication structure, and to corporate governance.

The B&O Railroad was formed (1827) as merchants of Baltimore, Maryland, sought to preserve their city's commercial advantage as a seaport link with the American interior. These merchants met and quickly seized on the railed-road idea (Dilts 1993: 38). The passage of similar incorporation acts in neighbouring Virginia and Pennsylvania soon followed. Thirty thousand shares of $100 stock were swiftly subscribed, as virtually every citizen of Baltimore supported the enterprise (Jacobs 1995: 13). City of Baltimore and State of Maryland funds were also invested; indeed, these entities received half the shares, making the B&O a quasi-public entity. The incorporation Act specified that the Maryland legislature would set freight and passenger rates, but that no taxes would be paid by the B&O. An annual report (Statement of Affairs) issued by the corporation to its shareholders was required by the B&O corporate charter, though the contents of the annual report remained unspecified (Previts and Samson 2000: 5).

The growth of the B&O from the time of the initial public offering was staggering. The previously constructed Erie Canal was a fully-state-funded enterprise, and the cost of $8.8 million established a record for a US business project at the time of completion in 1825. The B&O started as a $3 million business and grew to a $30 million enterprise by the time it reached the Ohio River 25 years later. Railroads attracted large numbers of individual investors, outside the business and outside the region, who needed communication from management as the basis for exercising an element of control from a distance. The railroad management quickly evolved into a separate professional class, possessing only a small ownership interest but providing the expertise to run the operations. This early evolution would lead to agency relationships significant in the development of accounting, auditing, finance and business.

In accounting, the corporate annual report would evolve, becoming an essential financial communication device with management describing the company's performance and its role as stewards of shareholder assets. Their financial statements developed into an income statement, balance sheet, and early cash flow report (Previts and Samson 2000: 18–30). Significantly, the compilation of financial statements became the prime object of accounting whereas, previously, record-keeping had been its main goal (Chatfield 1974: 222). For external investors, the financial statements were the basis for assessing the earnings-power of the enterprise as well as evaluating solvency and liquidity. Hence decision-making, as well as control, became the end-use of accounting. Ratios to assess railroad performance from period to period and from division to division and to compare the B&O versus other railroads were utilised early on (Previts and Samson 2000: 33–4).

Path-breaking annual reports

The B&O published annual reports from its earliest years, primarily for the benefit of its existing investors, but it was the Illinois Central (IC) Railroad that took forward the concept of the annual report. From as early as the 1850s, the first years of its existence, the IC Railroad published annual reports that were aimed at both the general American public and the European capital markets, with the latter providing the majority of investors. The IC Railroad, because of its financing arrangements, was a unique type of corporation that had a greater responsibility to the general public than did most for-profit corporations. Its reporting practices provide a textbook example of duality reporting as the corporation's annual report appears to have satisfied the needs of both audiences.

At a time when patterns and expectations concerning the content of published annual reports were not well established, the IC Railroad's management took increasingly seriously its accounting obligations. In retrospect, it is probably fair to say that the European investors should have been able to obtain a reasonable understanding of the company's operations from its published reports. The stockholder report series began with a three-page document which covered activities from the founding of the company on 10 February 1851 through to 1 November 1852. A rudimentary receipts and expenditures statement and a budget statement are all that accompany the single-page letter from President Schuyler. This first report provided few clues about the capital formation and construction issues that would become highly important in the years that followed. The statements provided two years later, in the 1854 report, are identified with the capital letters A, B, C, and D, with (A) comprising a type of balance sheet, (B) a form of expenditures statement, (C) a unique Interest Fund statement, and (D) a budget (Ways and Means) reporting the status of bonded indebtedness. The latter two statements were published to comply with the terms of the mortgage bond indenture agreement, of 23 June 1852, between the IC Railroad and the trustees for the bonds that had been issued.

The alphabetic designation of reports was also a common practice in the B&O statements, beginning shortly after it was established in 1827 (Previts and Samson 2000). However, the B&O statements are different in content, so it does not appear that the IC Railroad was simply following an established pattern. More likely, management was responding to the information needs of the European creditors who were concerned about the integrity of their interest payments and the related principal. Although there was no external auditor, the statements for years after 1854 were examined and approved by a three-man audit committee of the board of directors. By the end of 1855, the first full year of operations, the IC Railroad's published report had expanded to over 50 pages of fine print.

Reporting regional economic development

Beginning in 1854, the tenor of the IC Railroad's annual reports began to change as they began to incorporate information about the role and impact of the road on economic development. Page 1 of the 1854 report refers to the growth of new towns along the line and the financing by bankers of coalfields in the vicinity of the railroad. Economic development was occurring, and was following the path of the railroad.

When train operations began, management presented financial information in great detail, including revenues and costs, by month, for each depot along the line. Revenues, by depot, were also listed by the nature of the item shipped; the 1855 report included a statement with 32 columns for transportation of different types of commodities, including wheat, rye, hogs, whiskey, apples, butter, cheese, and coal. Such detail, in ever-declining print size, continued throughout the pre-Civil War era; by 1860, the statement had 42 columns. The IC Railroad's management also provided extensive commentary on the economic environment within which the company operated. For instance, a table listed every station along the line, with columns for the population in 1850 and 1855, the number of houses in 1850 and 1855, and the number of churches, schools, stores, hotels, mills, factories, and physicians.

In another section of the 1855 annual report, containing the Report of the Land Commissioner, there were indications that the accounts might have some public relations or marketing objectives – a factor not atypical of modern annual reports (Graves *et al.* 1996). The Land Commissioner noted that some of the company's land 'is rolling, undulating like the waves of the ocean under the influence of a gentle breeze' (IC Railroad's annual report 1855: 42). Other paragraphs note the fertility of the soil, the extensive deposits of coal and other minerals, and the fact that the lands were well watered. Their report concluded with an indication of the impact on economic development:

> In no other instance, probably, have such abundant benefits flowed from like causes. To the Government, the lands were comparatively valueless; to the State, they were in no way profitable; to the farmers, their productiveness was of no avail, while the quarries of stone and marble, and mines of coal with which the lands abound, were wholly undeveloped . . . This Company took these lands thus comparatively valueless . . . and by the expenditure of about twenty millions of dollars, imparted vitality to the whole matter by the construction and equipment of this road.
>
> (IC Railroad's annual report 1855: 43–4)

A full balance sheet appears for the first time for 1856. Each line of the balance sheet is keyed to supplementary abstracts (identified A through H) printed immediately below the balance sheet that provided details of the capital stock, the construction bonds, the free land bonds, and the other keyed lines on the balance sheet, for example, short-term debt ('scrip') and floating ('working capital') liabilities. The statement set concludes with a novel determination of net earnings that is then reconciled with the Interest Fund to assure adequacy of that account. This latter statement was unique in that earnings were closed out to bondholders' equity, rather than to the traditional stockholders' equity. Statements for the next year end (1857) follow this pattern of reporting, and a resumé of cash transactions (a cash flow statement, in full particulars) is added. With minor exceptions, through to the year ended 1861, the form and content of the IC Railroad's financial statements remain substantially unchanged. A balance sheet focusing on the assets committed to the Interest Fund is the principal statement. Comparative columns are added in some instances detailing, for example, expenditures, so that trends between years, starting in 1852, can be studied. In fact, the reports are ideal benchmarking documents with many examples of five-year trends reported. They also contain numerous analyses of managerial decisions; for instance, the IC Railroad's annual report for 1859 (p. 6) includes a study of the advantage of burning coal over wood.

Did these accounts provide the information that investors needed? Certainly management thought so. The IC Railroad's 1857 annual report contains an opening statement which seemingly recognises it as an extensive database for investors:

> The Directors submit herewith the Reports and Statements of the Officers of the Company in charge of the several Departments of its business, to which the careful examination of the Shareholders is invited, as affording sufficient data to enable each proprietor to form his own judgment as to the value of his investment and the details of its administration.

During the 1850s, the IC Railroad was more than a railroad; it was the change agent in a major social experiment – an attempt by government to foster economic development by using raw fertile land to motivate not only corporate management, but also to attract a population. This experiment, as detailed in the narrative of the annual report to shareholders, proved successful; at least that is the conclusion reached based on the information provided by IC Railroad's management.

Why such informative financial reports?

The IC Railroad's annual corporate reports contained not only a financial report for the benefit of European capitalists who invested in the railroad, but also a longitudinal view of the results of the company's impact on the development of Illinois and the markets thereto related. As an indication of the appreciation investors had for such reporting, an 1857 article in the *American Railroad Journal* stated that 'No other company enjoyed the unlimited confidence of money lenders of England and America to the same extent' (Sunderland 1955: 31). Further, the farmers and merchants, who were to be the principal customers and beneficiaries of the IC Railroad's services, were also interested in the information provided in the increasingly complex annual reports. The IC Railroad's annual reports of the 1850s were detailed and information laden. Why did the IC's management publish the type and amount of information found in the 1851–61 annual reports? Such reports were not mandatory, nor were they common. Other railroads, including the Pennsylvania, which began in 1847, and the B&O produced quite different reports in terms of style, content, and form. It appears that both the reporting obligations arising from the bond indenture entered into with European investors, who needed reassurance of the control that management had over the company's operations, and the desire to promote the sale of land granted to them by the government were addressed by the evolving form and content of the annual reports.

Ultimately, the IC Railroad was the source of many precedents. Later land-grant railroads adopted its classification and appraisal system and its contract and credit systems. In addition, the IC Railroad's colonisation and advertising techniques were later used by other land-grant railroads (Decker 1964: 101). The IC Railroad utilised several reporting practices that had not heretofore been acknowledged. Examples are the early use of cash flow statements, the identification of 'Net earnings', and extensive socioeconomic reporting. These are not to be construed as 'firsts'. However, these early uses support an *a priori* belief that the corporate form of business, and the need to satisfy requirements of accountability to distant European investors, served to justify and cause such reporting practices to emerge.

The double account system[3]

Although there were earlier important innovations among canal companies, the development of the distinctive financial reporting model, called the double account system, came to fruition among British railway companies. In essence, the system divides the conventional balance sheet into two sections: the capital account which sets out capital raised and expended and the general balance sheet which lists the remaining assets and liabilities of the enterprise, as well as the balance of undistributed revenue and any under-spend or over-spend on the capital account. It appears that the capital account was designed to fulfil a legal-stewardship function by providing a history of the application of money raised under statutory authority. In the early days, with accounts often wholly or substantially cash based, no general balance sheet was published – this emerged as receivables, payables, inventory, etc. were given recognition as railroad managers began to embrace accruals accounting. The move towards accruals account-ing was designed to achieve a higher level of accountability and to help counter defective practices. For example, the British accountant George Bott, writing in the *Railway Times* in 1843, demonstrated numerically how 'a railway in almost bankrupt condition, may represent itself as a fair remunerative concern' by following the then popular practice of preparing accounts mainly on the cash basis (quoted in Edwards 1985: 26).

The earliest known example of the double account system was published by the London & Birmingham Railway for the half-year ending 31 December 1838. Then, and in the 1840s, most railroads continued to publish only a capital account, and their continued failure to publish a general balance sheet was the subject of criticism by a government committee on the audit of railway accounts which reported in 1849. The importance of the general balance sheet was also stressed in a letter to *Herepath's Journal* by a shareholder in the London, Brighton & South Coast Railway. In his view:

> [Its value] to the shareholders cannot be sufficiently appreciated, unless shareholders are aware of the borrowing and lending, the advances to forward other schemes, and the abuses which may be made of a trusteeship which gives no account of its assets and debts.
>
> (quoted in Edwards 1985: 31)

The number of companies preparing balance sheets in accordance with the double account system gradually increased due to shareholder demand for better information, the leadership provided by the London & North Western Railway company (formed from the amalgamation of the London & Birmingham and the Grand Junction Railway companies), the threat of legislation (*c.*1850) and the actions of public accountants. Adoption of the double account system became a statutory requirement for all railway companies in 1868, and for certain categories of public utility in the years that followed. It was also adopted voluntarily in other sectors of the economy where the pattern of expenditure possessed similar characteristics, i.e. where a large initial investment was required to establish the infrastructure of the concern, followed by the need to finance only current operations, e.g. dock companies and companies working wasting assets such as mines and quarries. The companies required by law to use the double account system in the UK disappeared in the spate of nationalisation that followed the Second World War.

A nineteenth-century accounting error

Within the accounting history literature, it is the issue of 'error or bias' (Brief 1965: 12) in the published financial reports of nineteenth-century railroads that has perhaps been the subject of most attention and debate. For the period up to 1868, Pollins (1956: 354) has drawn attention to the fact that 'The basis for the allocation of certain important items between capital and revenue accounts was not the same in all companies, and that the allocation was not carried out in a consistent manner by any major company.' Edwards (1986) has demonstrated significant variation in methods of accounting for fixed assets both between railroad companies and over time during much of the nineteenth century, with Brief (1965: 30) concluding that 'capital consumption charges were neglected or at least delayed by the accounting methods employed'. Whether or not such inconsistency, variation and neglect were intentional is a moot point. Pollins thinks that lack of experience may have been a factor early on, but later: 'It is more realistic to recognise that in practice the calculation of profits was often influenced by changing financial circumstances and the dictates of management policy' (1956: 353).

In the remainder of this section, we turn to the USA and consider the actions of the Mobile and Ohio Railroad (M&O), in the mid-1860s, as an illustration of how financial reports might be manipulated to communicate a particular message to stakeholders, and the kinds of issues that arose among railroad companies, in both the USA and Britain, concerning how to account for the fixed assets of these atypically capital-intensive nineteenth-century entities.

Mobile and Ohio Railroad – an exemplification

In April 1865, the M&O lay ravaged by the Civil War, and the burning question was how the company could overcome the many obstacles it faced, survive and eventually thrive. The 1866 annual report of the M&O is a 'case book' of how the accounting methods of the day were used to portray the capacity of the M&O to provide earnings, and thus attract capital, even as it faced a bleak situation. Looked at differently, these same financial statements contain prime examples of what has been called 'nineteenth century accounting error' (Brief 1965).

As M&O's annual report for 1866 recounts, during the Civil War, the Confederate Government took control of the railroad to transport men and supplies. The M&O was paid in Confederate notes and bonds with about $5 million owed to the company by the end of hostilities. These receivables proved worthless as the Confederacy fell in April 1865. The loss was further magnified by the State of Alabama declaring its bonds (the company held $125,000 of these), issued for the purposes of war, to be void. Also, fifty slaves owned by the M&O were freed, causing another loss – $120,000, the cost of the slaves. Further, as described in the 1866 annual report, half of the railroad line had been destroyed by the Union troops as General Sherman swept across the Deep South on the way to Atlanta. Locomotives and cars had been seized by the Union such that only one-fourth of the rolling stock remained with the M&O at the year's end, and the remaining equipment was in such poor condition that the railroad could not operate on the portion of the track that remained open. The total estimated loss due to war was more than $7 million.

During post-war reconstruction, and with the federal troops occupying the South, the M&O was allowed to re-commence operations with the reservation that the federal government might still confiscate railroad assets at some future point in time. With this power unlikely to be exercised, however, it proved possible for the M&O to borrow money in order to get restarted.

The interesting aspects of the 1865 M&O annual report (published 17 April 1866) were not the recounting of the aforementioned current financial and operational problems; the railroad's condition was indeed bleak. The interesting issue is why such a bleak description of its financial position was presented. Perhaps it wished to be as forthright with investors as possible – to enhance trust that the management and directors were not attempting to paint a distorted picture of the railroad's condition. By painting such a realistic portrait of the railway's operating condition, investors, particularly British investors, may have been persuaded to entrust the railroad management with new financing.

The second interesting feature of the 1865 M&O annual report was the detailing of both the 1864 and the 1865 operating results – because of the Civil War, the 1864 annual report had not been published. In addition, the year 1865 was broken into two periods: 1 January through 30 April and 1 May to 31 December. The 1 May breakpoint was used as the 'currency adjustment' point (i.e. the fall of the Confederacy). What is interesting is that on one dimension the 1864 and early 1865 periods of earnings were moot given that the Confederacy failed and the revenues were unpaid by the Confederacy prior to its demise. Yet, as Table 18.1 shows, the income numbers were presented in bold fashion.

Captured by these otherwise meaningless income statement numbers (meaningless because they were denominated, in the main, in immeasurable and irrelevant Confederate dollars) is the essence that management was conveying to investors and potential investors: the earnings power of the railroad made its recovery viable and this earnings power would repay investors for their risk and patience.

The annual report goes on to state that M&O debt held by the State of Alabama, $300,000, and the State of Mississippi, $220,949, had been repaid as had $319,000 of income bonds that were due in 1862 and $168,000 of the income bonds due in 1865 and $103,000 of the second mortgage bonds. Thus, in this difficult period, the M&O still had found a way to repay well over $1,000,000 of company debt. This, again, communicated to investors that the company should be able to do likewise on future loans.

At the M&O, the above disclosures set the stage for raising new capital. Because the 1864 and early 1865 data were denominated in valueless Confederate dollars, they had an 'as if' quality that required investors to gauge whether the M&O was a viable operating entity. Given the land holdings and, it seems, the demonstrated potential for 'earnings', capital providers were attracted. By the early 1870s, investors were rewarded as the company earnings were annually

Table 18.1 Income statements for war years

1864	
'Earnings' (i.e. Revenues)	$3,674,498.99
Expense*	2,281,596.38
Net 'revenue'	$1,392,902.61
1865 (1 January–30 April)	
'Earnings'	$1,183,220.42
Expense*	906,663.84
Net 'revenue'	$276,556.58
1865 (1 May–31 December)	
'Earnings' (Revenues)	$1,524,675.81
Expenses	699,898.14
Net 'revenue'§	$824,777.67

Notes:
* 'The expenses during the periods referred to were greatly increased by the extraordinary repairs made necessary from injuries inflicted by the contending armies'. (Annual accounts: 11)
§ 'This last statement is not a fair specimen of the *earnings power* of the road in times of peace, as we did not have the rolling stock necessary to meet the wants of the country' (Annual accounts: 11, emphasis added).

again at the one million dollar level, which the 'pro forma' income numbers suggested. Also, after the war, 8 per cent M&O bonds that had matured were exchanged for Sterling bonds. The unpaid interest on bonds was paid in kind by the issuances of '8 per cent interest bonds' in exchange for the coupons on outstanding debt. Since the accounting records were maintained on a modified cash basis, the interest expense was not recorded when the interest notes were issued. Consequently, the above financial statements showed an overstated income.

Accounting for fixed assets [4]

With the accounts prepared mainly on the cash basis, the reported earnings of the M&O were also overstated in the sense that no provision was made for the depreciation of its rails or rolling stock. This was not an uncommon practice, as pointed out by Brief who concluded: 'reported profits and dividends were higher than they would have been if modern accounting practices prevailed. Thus, business investment, which is a function of reported profits, was overstimulated' (Brief 1965: 3). Arnold and McCartney (2002) noted, however, that the failure to record depreciation by British railroads was a later phenomenon; some of the earliest railways did record depreciation in the 1830s and early 1840s. Edwards (1986: 253) reports that the London and Birmingham Railway transferred £5,500 to 'a reserve Fund for the Depreciation of Stock' as soon as part of the line was opened in 1838. Others, including the Midland, followed (ibid.: 255–6). The practice in Britain was encouraged by the Companies Clauses Consolidation Act of 1845, which stated that the directors may, 'if they think fit, set aside . . . such Sum as they may think proper to meet contingencies, or for enlarging, repairing, or improving the Works connected with the Undertaking, or any part thereof' (Pollins 1956: 343).

The early practice of charging depreciation by British railway companies was abandoned for a range of reasons which include, according to Edwards (1986: 257), the desire to pay dividends when profits were low. Management's argument, on the other hand, was that depreciation charges were unnecessary. By the 1850s, the railroads had a concept in place that served in lieu of depreciation accounting, namely replacement accounting, which involved the charging of current expenditures on renewals and maintenance against revenue (Arnold and McCartney 2002: 206; Edwards, 1986). Some recording of depreciation also occurred in the USA in the late 1840s, perhaps because of British influence, but the US experiment was also short-lived. Again, as in Britain, it was believed that railway equipment kept in good repair would last forever.

Investors continued to provide funding based on replacement or betterment accounting models that deemed assets to have indefinite lives. But as long-lived assets expired, such models proved deficient and, over time, appeared to overstate earnings and thereby exaggerate earnings power and income as a percentage of the investment. Also, balance sheets were inflated because equipment was reported at cost without an offsetting provision for obsolescence or wear and tear. The limitations of financial statements were recognised by some who spoke out strongly. For instance, an 1879 article in the *North American Review* noted that even the venerable New York Central Railroad issued statements 'based, apparently, on improper book-keeping' (The mysteries 1879: 147). Lack of effective governance was blamed for the accounting problems of the 1870s:

> With rare exceptions, either in this country or in England, have directors been found, no matter how important their titles or their families, who could or would safely and honestly administer the business of great corporations, unchecked and uncontrolled, by complete and absolute publicity both in general and in detail. Absolute knowledge and unlimited publicity can alone prevent such disasters as have recently, in England, been so

great as to paralyze private credit and to beggar whole classes of people, who trusted everything to the respectable names of those controlling their property. Once given all the facts, the press will soon discover the weak spots in the balance-sheet, the errors of administration, or the frauds of managers. Figures cannot lie. But, that this truism may be made effective, all the figures and all the facts must be given.

(The mysteries 1879: 147)

Frauds

According to Edwards (1989: 143) 'Accounting history is littered with examples of financial information used as a means of deception', with the events of Enron and WorldCom simply recent manifestations of managerial behaviour that is examined in detail in Chapter 19. In Britain, the period of intense speculation in railway shares – the 'railway mania', which reached its zenith in 1846 played a major role in the general financial crisis of 1847, and was followed by investigations that showed railway company accounts to be deficient in important respects. As Wang (quoted in Edwards, 1985: 26) put it: 'Railway shareholders were so bewildered and mystified by cooked accounts, manipulated figures, partial statements, and delusive representations of railway property that they actually regarded the payment of dividend out of capital as a legitimate practice.' The accountants Quilter, Ball & Co., for example, were called in to examine the affairs of the Eastern Counties Railway – run by George Hudson known as the Railway King – which was revealed to have overstated income by £438,050 through debiting expenditure to capital rather than revenue, failing to record payables outstanding or write off bad debts, wrongly crediting significant amounts to revenue and charging interest to capital instead of the income account (Edwards 1989: 167).

At the general level, Lee argued that laxity in classification between capital and revenue expenditures during railway companies' early years led to wilful manipulation in the boom years of the 1840s to justify inflated dividends (Lee 1975: 21–2). McCartney and Arnold (2003) believe that the boom and slump of 1845–47 was the most important of the nineteenth-century railroad manias in terms of its effect on the economy as a whole. Although originally viewed as 'market irrationality', Bryer claims the mania was the result of deliberate and collusive actions by wealthy investors, aided by the central government, to 'swindle' middle-class investors. Accounting processes and distortions were critical to the success of this class-based fraud (Bryer 1991). Regardless of the reason for the mania, Edwards (1986) observed that, following revelations of deficient financial reporting practice, there was an increase in the quantity of accounting information provided to investors and a move towards accrual-based reporting at large railway companies such as the London and North Western. McCartney and Arnold confirm this observation with respect to the quantity of information provided, but were sceptical concerning its quality (McCartney and Arnold 2002: 412). In a later publication, McCartney and Arnold (2003) also challenged Bryer's assertion that a fraud had been knowingly perpetrated. In their view, it was debatable whether the fact that wealthy investors ended up owning the railroads was indicative of a collusive fraud. They expressed doubts primarily because of their further observation that the railroads remained unprofitable in subsequent years. Thus, the middle class who had given up their ownership were actually better off for having sold when they did (McCartney and Arnold 2003: 843). If a swindle, it certainly was not a successful one.

In the US context, early frauds were committed at the IC Railroad (1854–5) and the M&O (1856), but the most prominent railroad fraud involved the financing of the transcontinental railroad. Credit Mobilier was formed by Thomas Durant of the Union Pacific Railroad to construct the transcontinental railroad, primarily because creation of a separate entity allowed Durant to 'line his pockets' without oversight from either Union Pacific or Congress. President Abraham Lincoln was an avid supporter of the transcontinental project but, following his assassination in April 1865, before any tracks had yet been laid, Durant, and his successor, Oakes Ames, were worried that Congress would vote to cut its losses and abandon the government contracts. The solution was to obtain support from Congressional leaders by selling them stock in the company at bargain prices.

An article in the influential *New York Sun* on 4 September 1872 accused US Vice President Schuyler Colfax and other noted politicians of accepting stock in Credit Mobilier in exchange for the favourable exercise of their influence in Congress. Credit Mobilier was the construction company that built the transcontinental railroad on behalf of the Union Pacific Railroad. The objective of the bribes was to ensure that there would be no interference from Congress that would delay federal money from being funnelled into railroad construction. To make the matters worse, it is thought that one of the functions of Credit Mobilier, besides building the railroad, was to defraud the government by overcharging for construction of the tracks. Insiders at the Union Pacific Railroad had, therefore, created the construction company to enable them to pay themselves millions of dollars to build the railroad. Thus, Credit Mobilier was a scandal of unprecedented proportions (Ambrose 2000: 373–6).

The fraud investigation disclosed that Colfax had received 20 shares of stock in Credit Mobilier and dividends from that investment of $1,200. Colfax asserted that he had never owned any stock other than that which he had purchased. Similarly, he claimed never to have received the supposed $1,200 of dividends. However, the House Judiciary Committee investigation determined that Colfax had indeed deposited $1,200 into his bank account just two days after the supposed dividend payment. After two weeks, Colfax explained that the deposit had been a campaign contribution from a friend who had since died. Even his strongest supporters doubted this story.

The impact of politics and regulation

In Britain, railways were built by statutory companies with rights (e.g. powers of compulsory purchase) conferred by Parliament. The authorising statutes normally did not refer to matters of accounting, early on, although there were exceptions; for instance, the Great Western Railway Act of 1835 required the company to prepare accounts twice a year and to make them available at meetings of shareholders and pay dividends out of 'clear Profits' (Lee 1975: 20). General Acts were passed in 1844 (Railway Regulation Act) and 1845 (Companies Clauses Consolidation Act) that affected railroad accounting (Pollins 1956: 336–9). The 1845 Act, which contained model clauses for statutory companies to adopt, included provisions for a bookkeeper to be appointed and the preparation of 'an exact balance sheet' giving 'a distinct view of the profit and loss' (Pollard 1956: 338). Auditors, who were required to hold at least one share in the company, were to be appointed. The Regulation of Railways Act, 1868, helped stabilise railway accounting in the United Kingdom (Pollins 1956: 355). As was later to be true in the USA, the Act of 1868 not only stabilised railway accounting, it also reduced innovation. That Act laid out a standard format for each of the 14 separate statements that railway companies were required to publish (Simmons and Biddle 1997: 6). Unfortunately, the Act did not address the way in which capital and revenue expenditures were to be defined. In 1911, the Railway Companies (Accounts and Returns) Act increased the amount of detail that companies had to provide in their accounts. The entire railway network was brought under government control during the First World War, and the Railways Act, 1921 gave the new Ministry of Transport licence to specify the form of railway accounts (Simmons and Biddle 1997: 6). Whereas the industry had long been an innovator in the development of accounting principles and practices, that was to decline with the advent of government scrutiny.

The nature of the transportation service was also acknowledged as making standardisation desirable in the USA. Because freight and passengers were often transferred from one company to the next, the problems of interline accounting became acute. The need for uniformity was first recognised at the state level with New England's Massachusetts Railroad Commission making appropriate provision as early as 1876 (Neidert 1950: 309–10). The move towards national provision began when the National Convention of Railroad Commissioners met in Saratoga, New York, in June 1879 (Cullen 1926: 798). There, the main topic was uniformity of accounts prepared by railroads for the purpose of reporting to state regulators. The theme of this conference is unsurprising, given that the leading Massachusetts state regulator was Charles Francis Adams Jr. who had long worked to encourage standardised financial reporting in order to hold the railroad management accountable to the public. The presentations at the Convention were reported in *Railroad Gazette* and *Railway Age*, and this meeting of state railroad commissioners caused the Association of American Railway Accounting Officers – the voluntary organisation of railroad accountants that formed to deal with inter-railroad billing practices – to take up the issue (Cullen 1926).

The early Massachusetts initiative served as a model for the so-called 'Sunshine' disclosure requirements when federal involvement, as noted above, followed with the passage of legislation (1887) that established the Interstate Commerce Commission (ICC). Miranti's (1990) research in this area has assisted in providing an understanding of the features of the system initiated by Henry Carter Adams, the younger brother of Charles Frances Adams, Jr., which included Henry's preference for 'rigidly uniform reporting formats and methods' (Miranti 1990: 183). About 20 years later, the Hepburn Act (1906) gave the ICC the power to set maximum rates. More importantly, the ICC could view the railroads' financial records, which had to be prepared using a standardised accounting system. Along with the Elkins Act of 1903, the Hepburn Act fulfilled one of President Theodore Roosevelt's major goals – improving railroad regulation. The requirement for uniform accounting methods was not, for the most part, oppressive to railroads; the need for such practices had long been recognised by the railroads themselves.

Managerial accounting innovations

Albert Fink, famous for his design of iron bridges, began his distinctive railroad career at the B&O in December 1849. Galambos and Pratt (1986: 48) consider Fink to be worthy of the title, 'The father of cost accounting'.[5] Much of the innovation for which Fink received credit, however, was in fact being utilised by the B&O prior to his arrival. The B&O and other railroads were quick to integrate the data from bookkeeping sources into a system of information that managers employed to operate and measure business operations. The B&O's 'University' employees and 'alumni', including Fink, led the way in internal managerial reporting as they did with external financial reporting (Flesher *et. al.* 2000: 115; Heier 2000).[6]

The early B&O annual reports reflect the existence of types of analysis that were also to provide efficient managerial information; performance statistics included not only physical measures, but also per-dollar cost calculations including 'cost per mile' and 'cost per cubic yard'. With the coming of steam locomotives (early trains were pulled by horses), some costs began being measured in terms of 'cost per train', 'cost per round trip', and 'cost per train per day'. The next evolvement was to 'cost per ton of freight' and 'cost per passenger'. Given that most trains carried both freight and passengers, the breakdown by type of customer indicates that a rationale existed for joint cost allocation. A further refinement was to calculate 'cost per passenger mile' and 'cost per ton mile'. By 1833, the calculations were being adjusted for differences in grade and curvature of tracks. Although first introduced at the B&O, these statistics were quickly adopted by other railroads and became standard for the industry (Knight and Latrobe 1838: 1–42). Such comparative displays were useful in demonstrating to legislators that the railroads were efficient, low-cost providers of rail services. Such data also supported the case for rate increases to meet patterns of enhanced cost experienced at efficient levels of operation. Comparative data also included ratio analysis, whose use was evident in the B&O annual report from as early as 1831 (Flesher *et al.* 2000). Benchmarking occurred in the late 1840s, with the B&O's accounts containing comparisons with other 'leading' railroads.

Cost-volume-profit analysis was used early in the history of railroads. Solomons (1952) suggests that Fink may have learned to group cost accounts, based on behaviour, through reading Dionysius Lardner's 1850 treatise entitled *Railway Economy*. However, analysis of the B&O's records again reveals that cost behaviour was understood by Fink's predecessors, including Benjamin Latrobe and W. Woodville. Indeed, Fink was Latrobe's understudy at the B&O. Woodville noted, in the 1831 B&O annual report, that some expenses increased as revenues increased, while others remained the same regardless of the level of revenue. By 1833, expenses in the annual report were being grouped as either fixed or proportional. Albert Fink moved from the B&O to the Louisville and Nashville Railroad in 1857 and in 1875 wrote a treatise on cost behaviour (Fink 1875: 48). In summary, transaction accounting numbers were developed to manage the railroad comparatively and in unit operating measures. Costs were reported by activity centre and by object. Comparison of costs helped managers monitor performance. Cost behaviour and the relationship with revenue were understood early on and afforded better planning of both construction and operations. Whether Fink was the source is less relevant than the fact that little further innovation occurred after his contributions had been made. A book published in 1900 noted: 'The late Mr. Albert Fink, as far back as 1873, laid the lines upon which practically all scientific railroad thought has since proceeded' (Woodlock 1900: 60).

Conclusion

The first important aspect of railroad accounting arose from the way railroad companies were founded – as joint stock companies; an organisational arrangement that created agency problems (see Chapter 8) and the need for governance. Thus, from the beginning, accounting and accountability were centre-stage. In Britain, railways were built as modes of transportation to service a recognised market. In the USA, railroads were initially built not principally as modes of transportation but as change agents. The B&O was intended to maintain Baltimore's position as a major seaport. The investors, many of them merchants of Baltimore, were less concerned with making money on the railroad and more concerned with achieving a return on their investment in local businesses. A generation later, the investors in the IC Railroad and M&O did expect a return on their investments, but they were able to convince the federal government that the railroads could be used for economic development. Thus, the government, with its land grants, was the majority investor, albeit these investments were never recorded in any financial statements. Perhaps Mitchell (1964: 333; see also May 1936) summed it up best when he explained that the railroads led to industrialisation in the US, but Britain was already industrialised when the railways appeared. What was the same on both sides of the Atlantic was the impact on capital markets: 'the major influence of the coming of the railway was on the development of the capital market and on the level of savings' (Mitchell 1964: 333).

Because the railroads accomplished so many objectives, they grew, and with growth came the need for regular accounting and auditing. Because corporate financial reporting and auditing were undeveloped in the mid-nineteenth century, at the professional level, the railroads themselves had to formulate the practices needed to effectively operate their businesses. The principles of accounting and auditing that they formulated were later adopted by industrial corporations. Railroads in the USA utilised several innovative reporting practices such as cash flow statements, the identification of 'Net earnings', and extensive socioeconomic reporting; in Britain, there was developed the double account system. In the USA, the B&O was an innovator with respect to governance and auditing, while the M&O pioneered the use of accounting for determination of earnings power. At the same time, the accounts of many railroad companies, including America's M&O and Britain's Eastern Counties Railway, contained early examples of what came to be known as 'nineteenth-century accounting error' – the inaccuracy of financial statements due to the omission of depreciation and other non-cash expenses and the failure to classify transactions accurately as capital or revenue.

Even the adverse features of railroad accounting, it could be argued, had a favourable influence. The system of government oversight that arose when questionable accounting practices were revealed in Britain, in the mid-1860s, led to the passage of the widely acclaimed 1868 regulatory Act. Similarly, in the USA, the bankruptcies of the 1890s gave rise to a model for regulating natural monopolies in that country. That system relied on prescribed uniform accounting methods to inform investors and rate regulators. The ICC uniformity rules differed markedly from the approaches followed by the SEC beginning in the 1930s. Not charged with the responsibility of regulating market competition, the SEC delegated the responsibility for the financial reporting process to professional groups who standardised accounting information on the basis of generally accepted principles rather than uniform methods. Nevertheless, the regulatory system of prescribed accounting methods for the railroads lasted for over a century and was forsaken only with the passage of the Staggers Transportation Act of 1978.

Future research needs in this area should be guided by a careful assessment of what has been outlined above, as to accounting and reporting, and further by the general developments in railroading history, using, for example, the review essay recently prepared by Churella (2006) on the variety of recent approaches to railroad history in the USA. Also, as mentioned early in this chapter, there is great opportunity for research into the accounting contributions of other forms of transport, including canals (Russ et al. 2006; Forrester 1994), steamboats (Flesher and Soroosh 1987), trucking, and horse tramways (Pollins 1991). Finally, study of railway accounting in the twentieth century has hardly begun.

Key works

Brief (1965) is the first major study of the impact of the failure to record depreciation in a capital-intensive industry.

Edwards (1986) discusses the depreciation accounting practices of early British railway companies and the impact of the 1868 Regulation of Railways Act.

Pollins (1956) is the pioneer study of railroad accounting history and contains a good early overview of the subject.

Samson *et al.* **(2003)** present and analyse important examples of 'nineteenth century accounting error' at a leading US railroad.

Notes

* In spirit, if not in person, our departed colleague and co-author William D. Samson and his scholarship are reflected in this work.
1 There is also a limited literature on other early forms of transport such as canal companies (Edwards, 1985; Forrester 1994; Kistler 1980; Russ *et al.* 2006).
2 The Railway Accounting Officers Association published a 150-page bibliography on railway accounting in 1926–27 (Cullen 1926).
3 The material in this section is taken from Edwards (1985, 1989).
4 The more general literature is examined in Chapter 8, particularly in the section on 'The contents and historical discontents of financial accounting practice'.
5 A full review of managerial accounting historiography is contained in Chapter 9.
6 See also Hoskin and Macve (1988) for comment on the contribution of railroads to the early developments in the control of multi-unit enterprises identified by Chandler.

References

Ambrose, S. E. (2000) *Nothing Like It in the World* (New York: Simon & Schuster).

Arnold, A. J. and McCartney, S. (2002) The beginnings of accounting for capital consumption: disclosure practices in the British railway industry, 1830–55, *Accounting and Business Research*, 32 (4): 195–208.

Baltimore and Ohio Railroad Company, annual reports, 1828–40 (available at the Bruno Library at the University of Alabama, at the B&O Library and Museum in Baltimore, and on-line at Proquest Historical Annual Report Service).

Brief, R. P. (1965) Nineteenth century accounting error, *Journal of Accounting Research*, 3 (1): 12–31.

Brief, R. P. (1976) *Nineteenth Century Capital Accounting and Business Investment* (New York: Arno Press).

Bryer, R. A. (1991) Accounting for the 'railway mania' of 1845 – a great railway swindle?, *Accounting, Organizations and Society*, 16 (5/6): 439–86.

Chandler, A. D. (1977) *The Visible Hand: The Managerial Revolution in American Business* (Cambridge, MA: Belknap Press).

Chatfield, M. (1974) *A History of Accounting Thought* (Fort Worth, TX: Dryden Press).

Churella, A. (2006) Company, state, and region: three approaches to railroad history, *Enterprise & Society*, 7 (3): 581–91.

Cleveland, F. A. and Powell, W. F. (1909) *Railroad Promotion and Capitalization in the United States* (New York: Longmans, Green).

Cullen, E. (1926) *American Railway Accounting: A Bibliography* (Washington, DC: Railway Accounting Officers Association).

Decker, L. E. (1964) *Railroads, Lands, and Politics: The Taxation of the Railroad Land Grants, 1864–1897* (Providence, RI: Brown University Press).

Dilts, J. D. (1993) *The Great Road: The Building of the Baltimore & Ohio, the Nation's First Railroad, 1828–1853* (Stanford, CA: Stanford University Press).

Edwards, J. R. (1985) The origins and evolution of the double account system: an example of accounting innovation, *Abacus*, 21 (1): 19–43.

Edwards, J. R. (1986) Depreciation and fixed asset valuation in railway company accounts to 1911, *Accounting and Business Research*, 16 (63): 251–63.

Edwards, J. R. (1989) *A History of Financial Accounting* (London: Routledge).

Fink, A. (1875) *Cost of Railroad Transportation* (Louisville, KY: J. P. Morton).

Flesher, D. L. and Soroosh, J. (1987) Riverboat accounting and profitability: the Betsey Ann, *Journal of Mississippi History*, 49: 23–33.

Flesher, D. L., Previts, G. J. and Samson, W. D. (2000) Using accounting to manage: a case of railroad managerial accounting in the 1850s, in *Accounting and History. A Selection of Papers Presented at the 8th World Congress of Accounting Historians*, pp. 91–126 (Madrid: Asociación Española de Compatabilided v Administración de Empresas).

Flesher, D. L., Previts, G. J. and Samson, W. D. (2003a) The origins of value for money auditing: the Baltimore & Ohio Railroad 1827–1830, *Managerial Auditing Journal*, 18 (5): 374–86.

Flesher, D. L., Previts, G. J. and Samson, W. D. (2003b) Accounting, economic development and financial reporting: the case of three pre Civil War US railroads, *Accounting History*, 8 (2): 61–78.

Flesher, D. L., Previts, G. J. and Samson, W. D. (2006) Early American corporate reporting and European capital markets: the case of the Illinois Central Railroad, 1851–1861, *Accounting Historians Journal*, 33 (1): 3–24.

Forrester, D. A. R. (1994) Early canal company accounts: financial and accounting aspects of the Forth and Clyde Navigation, 1768–1816, in R. H. Parker and B. S. Yamey (eds), *Accounting History: Some British Contributions*, pp. 297–326 (Oxford: Clarendon Press).

Galambos, L. and Pratt, J. (1986) *The Rise of the Corporate Commonwealth* (New York: Basic Books).

Graves, O. F., Flesher, D. L. and Jordan, R. (1996) Pictures and the bottom line: the television epistemology of U.S. annual reports, *Accounting, Organizations and Society*, 21 (1): 57–88.

Heier, J. (2000) The foundations of modern cost management: the life and work of Albert Fink, *Accounting, Business & Financial History*, 10 (2): 213–43.

Hoskin, K. and Macve, R. (1988) The genesis of accountability: the West Point connections, *Accounting, Organizations and Society*, 13 (1): 37–73.

Illinois Central Railroad Company, annual reports 1851–63 (available at the National Library of the Accounting Profession at the University of Mississippi, the Newberry Library in Chicago, and on-line at Proquest Historical Annual Report Service).

Jacobs, T. (ed.) (1995) *The B&O: America's First Railroad* (New York: Smithmark).

Kistler, L. (1980) Middlesex Canal – an analysis of its accounting and management, *Accounting Historians Journal*, 7 (1): 43–57.

Knight, J. and Latrobe, B. H. (1838) *Report upon the Locomotive Engines and the Policy and Management of Several Principal Railroads in the Northern and Middle States* (Baltimore, MD: Lucas & Deaver).

Kolko, G. (1965) *Railroads and Regulation, 1877–1916* (New York: W. W. Norton).

Lardner, D. (1850) *Railway Economy* (New York: Harper & Brothers).

Lee, G. A. (1975) The concept of profit in British accounting, 1760–1900, *Business History Review*, 49 (1): 6–36.

McCartney, S. and Arnold, A. J. (2000) George Hudson's financial reporting practices: putting the Eastern Counties Railway in context, *Accounting, Business & Financial History*, 10 (3): 293–316.

McCartney, S. and Arnold, A. J. (2002) Financial reporting in the context of crisis: reconsidering the impact of the 'mania' on early railway accounting, *European Accounting Review*, 11 (2): 401–17.

McCartney, S. and Arnold, A. J. (2003) The railway mania of 1845–1847: market irrationality or collusive swindle based on accounting distortions, *Accounting, Auditing & Accountability Journal*, 16 (5): 821–52.

May, G. O. (1936) The influence of accounting on the development of an economy, *Journal of Accountancy*, 61 (3): 171–84.

Miranti, P. J. (1990) Measurement and organizational effectiveness: the ICC's Bureau of Statistics and Accounts and railroad regulation, 1887–1940, *Business & Economic History*, 19: 183–92.

Mitchell, B. R. (1964) The coming of the railway and United Kingdom economic growth, *Journal of Economic History*, 24 (3): 315–36.

Mobile and Ohio Railroad Company, annual reports, 1850–76 (available at the University of South Alabama Library, and on-line at Proquest Historical Annual Report Service).

Neidert, K. (1950) The development of railroad accounting as it relates to the general ledger and the financial statements, unpublished dissertation, Washington University.

Pollins, H. (1952) The finances of the Liverpool and Manchester Railway, *Economic History Review*, 5 (1): 90–7.

Pollins, H. (1954) Marketing of the railway shares in the first half of the nineteenth century, *Economic History Review*, 7 (2): 230–9.

Pollins, H. (1956) Aspects of railway accounting before 1868, in A. C. Littleton and B. S. Yamey (eds) *Studies in the History of Accounting*, pp. 332–55 (London: Sweet & Maxwell).

Pollins, H. (1991) British horse tramway company accounting practices, 1870–1914, *Accounting, Business & Financial History*, 1 (3): 279–302.

Previts, G. J. and Samson, W. D. (2000) Exploring the contents of the Baltimore and Ohio Railroad annual reports: 1827–1856, *Accounting Historians Journal*, 27 (1) 1–42.

Richards, E. S. (1972) The finances of the Liverpool and Manchester Railway again, *Economic History Review*, 25 (2): 284–92.

Russ, R. W., Coffman, E. N. and Previts, G. J. (2006) The stockholder review committee of the Chesapeake and Ohio Canal Company (1828–1857): evidence of changes in financial reporting and corporate governance, *Accounting Historians Journal*, 33 (1): 125–44.

Samson, W. D. and Previts, G. J. (1999) Reporting for success: the Baltimore and Ohio Railroad and management information, 1827–1856, *Business and Economic History Journal*, 28 (2): 235–54.

Samson, W. D., Flesher, D. L. and Previts, G. J. (2003) Quality of earnings: the case of the Mobile and Ohio Railroad in the 19th century, *Issues in Accounting Education*, 18 (4): 335–57.

Simmons, J. and Biddle, G. (1997) *The Oxford Companion to British Railway History: from 1603 to the 1990s* (Oxford: Oxford University Press).

Solomons, D. (1952) The historical development of costing, in D. Solomons (ed.) *Studies in Costing*, pp. 1–52 (London: Sweet & Maxwell).

Sunderland, E. S. S. (1955) *Abraham Lincoln and the Illinois Central Railroad* (New York: Pandick Press).

The mysteries of American railway accounting (1879) *North American Review*, 129 (267): 135–47.

Woodlock, T. F. (1900) *The Anatomy of a Railroad Report and Ton-Mile Cost* (New York: S. A. Nelson).

19

Scandals

Thomas A. Lee, Frank L. Clarke and Graeme W. Dean

Overview

This chapter examines accounting scandals in the history of corporate financial reporting that threaten its credibility as a viable means of protecting stakeholders from corrupt senior managers. The first section addresses the effectiveness of accounting as a system of governance instrumentation. Corporate failures provide impetus for successive revisions of accounting standards intended to remove perceived malpractices. Paradoxically, however, they appear to have had the opposite effect. Instead of increasing the extent to which financial statements reveal wealth and financial progress, they have spawned greater problems, institutionalising tensions in the social function of accounting. The second section examines recurring issues, evaluating the effectiveness of auditing in detecting material fraud by senior corporate managers. It analyses the responses of the state and the public accountancy profession to accounting scandals over many decades and in several jurisdictions, examining the credibility of audit as a means of protecting stakeholders from corrupt senior managers. Through instances of fraudulent reporting, it reveals auditors denying or limiting their responsibility to detect material accounting misstatement by dominant senior managers upon whose honesty they rely.

Accounting as governance instrumentation

Autopsies of corporate failures have led to the questioning of the usefulness of audited accounting data as effective instrumentation – whether it is a credible basis for regular and ongoing financial assessments and evaluations of a company's wealth and progress.[1] But that questioning has evoked little effective action to improve the instrumentation. For well over a century and a half, misleading financial statements have involved massaging expense and revenue data and the exploitation of complex business group structures. It is what is now described euphemistically as 'aggressive' accounting. Repeatedly, corporate managers have argued that they are best able to assess their appropriateness in the circumstances. Incongruously, to the likes of R. J. Chambers, corporate managers remain the scorekeepers. Despite intermittent governmental intervention, expectations that auditors will uncover accounting malpractices have been no better met in recent years than in the more distant past.

Several episodes during the past one hundred years aptly illustrate the ineffectiveness of the responses by governmental and the public accountancy profession to corporate failure when reported financial numbers reasonably evoked opposite expectations. The first major episode culminated in reforms on two continents – a new Companies Act (in 1929) in the UK and Roosevelt's New Deal in the USA that created the Securities and Exchange Commission (SEC). Both occurred around the time of the stock market crash of 1929 that exposed many corporate financial statements 'full of water'. The second episode involved a wave of failures and alleged accounting and auditing irregularities. It commenced in the early 1990s with the crashes of the Maxwell and Polly Peck empires in the UK and intensified in the USA with the Enron and WorldCom affairs and numerous accounting restatement scandals a decade later. The spectre of corporate malpractice was fuelled by Eliot Spitzer's enquiries into the analyst–merchant banker nexus, hedge funds' timing of trades, and reinsurance frauds. There were also Australian cases, such as Ansett, Harris Scarfe, HIH, and One.Tel, which spawned legislative reforms. The Sarbanes–Oxley Act, 2002 in the USA and *CLERP 9* (Commonwealth of Australia 2004/05) in Australia typified governmental responses.

Material accounting misstatement (MAM) by companies with complex group structures, frequently controlled by dominant senior managers (DSM), characterised each scandal. The backgrounds of the most recent scandals provide a template for a later comparison with earlier events, auditing issues, and responses to them by the state and the public accountancy profession.

Post-Enron knee-jerk

Immediately preceding Jeffrey Skilling's 24-year sentence in the Enron case, and following Kenneth Lay's sudden death, other notorious corporate managers were imprisoned in the USA. Chief executive officer (CEO) Bernie Ebbers of WorldCom received a 25-year custodial sentence and Tyco's CEO Dennis Kozlowski a minimum eight-year gaol term. These were prestigious 'heads–on–poles' for regulators, but they did not answer questions about the need for fundamental and systemic reform of corporate financial reporting.

Dotcom collapses and related major failures were also potentially a watershed in corporate affairs – a catalyst for the Bush administration to push through its Sarbanes–Oxley legislation to 'clean up corporate America'. In retrospect and arguably, Enron's alleged devious accounting was possibly little more so than that of many of its contemporary recalcitrants – e.g. Sunbeam, Cendant, Waste Management, Tyco, Adelphia, Qwest, WorldCom, Alhold, Fannie Mae, Freddie Mac, and Vivendi – with their imposed downwards restatements of earlier quarterly earnings predictions. But Enron appears to have been the straw that broke the corporate camel's back. It was possibly too big and allegedly too well connected with Capitol Hill and the Bush administration to ignore. Significantly, despite the prominence of alleged MAM in these corporate collapses and failures, governmental reaction focused on other matters, e.g. alleged audit failure and poor internal governance. Inevitably, an inference to be drawn is that, despite repeated MAM, regulators considered accounting was in good shape. The *problem* was not that there was anything wrong with accounting, but that the fraudulent manipulation of it by DSM was being accepted by auditors lacking independence.

Although an explicit connection was typically not made, the focus on the influence of DSM on accounting practice and auditing implied a commonsense, causal link of managers behaving badly by manipulating otherwise sound accounting rules. Unsurprisingly in this climate, public comment on Enron usually implied that its accounting was grossly deviant due to managerial manipulation. Few commentators seemed to notice that a large part of Enron's accounting had been approved by the SEC and the Financial Accounting Standards Board (FASB). Although there was significant accounting malpractice at Enron, the oft-mentioned 'mark-to-model' techniques underpinning its 'front-end loading' of profits scheduled to be earned on its natural gas trading contracts had been approved by the SEC in 1992. Similarly, loading debt into its special-purpose entities (SPE) was using them as leverage instruments exactly as they had been designed. And, whereas dubious practices appear to have improperly nullified the SPE control and 3 per cent equity criteria (i.e. effectively placing the vehicles outside SPE status), had they satisfied the criteria, the financial statements of Enron would have been no less misleading and its debt no less masked in its consolidated statements.

Given the US response to corporate accounting malpractice, it is unsurprising that the Australian government pursued the issues of executive remuneration and, in particular, auditor independence when Australia's largest insurer HIH and high-flying telecommunications company One.Tel collapsed in 2001. Mimicking the US approach, the Australian federal government commissioned an inquiry that produced the Ramsay Report (*Independence of Australian Company Auditors: Review of Current Australian Requirements and Proposals for Reform*) in 2001. However, somewhat different from that of the USA was Australia's commitment to the 2005 Australian version of international financial reporting standards (IFRS). In Australia, capitulation to the IFRS push was already *fait accompli*. By implication, whenever IFRS differed from the national status quo, the Australian public accountancy profession had already declared the previous accounting standards delinquent – what had been compliant and thus true and fair was, in fact, no longer so. Consistent with the US strategy, corrupt managers and allegedly insufficiently independent auditors were targeted as the major villains. Accounting *per se* was let off the hook.

Convictions and sentences related to HIH's Ray Williams and Rodney Adler (on charges not directly linked to HIH's collapse) were relatively minor compared to those in the USA. They provide a background to the Australian corporate regulator's action to recover $92 million from One.Tel's Jodee Rich and Mark Silberman for overseeing alleged trading when it was insolvent. Revelations in court illustrate how accounting potentially can mask corporate insolvency. A judgment is not expected until the middle of 2008. Meanwhile, public insights into the behaviour of non-executive directors are to be gleaned in that case from the revelations of witnesses Lachlan Murdoch and James Packer. Each of these non-executive directors was able to recall little of their involvement with One.Tel on many issues, other than being profoundly misled by disclosures to them of the company's financial performance and position leading up to its collapse. The One.Tel collapse cost the companies with which they were connected reportedly in the order of $900 million. Yet there has been little suggestion publicly that One.Tel's accounting was other than basically compliant with existing Australian accounting standards.

At about the same time, Italian courts and regulators were busy untangling the Parmalat failure (Hamilton and Micklethwait 2006). The well-placed Tanzi family emerged as corporate malefactors. Their alleged deeds rivalled those in Italy a quarter of a century earlier perpetrated by 'God's bankers' (Michele Sindona and Roberto Calvi) in relation to the Vatican Bank (Raw 1992). And in the USA three-quarters of a century earlier, Ivar Krueger and Samuel Insull (and many others labelled financial rogues in decades in between) were household names (Clarke *et al.* 2003). The alleged acts of deception are similar. Significantly, neither time and the different legal framework underpinning (say) Parmalat's incorporation, and the different board structures it promotes, nor rules relating to auditor appointments of the kind under the

Sarbanes–Oxley regime, negate that stark similarity. Indeed, they are similar to descriptions of malpractice in the USA made in Ferdinand Pecora's 1930s Commission into the practices of financial intermediaries and investment trusts in the years preceding the Great Depression.

Clarke and Dean (2007: 6) note the complexity entailed in the contested alleged insurance accounting irregularities by some executives at Berkshire Hathaway's General Re Corporation and American International Group. They also discuss (Clarke and Dean 2007: Chapter 5) the exposure of undisclosed (to the auditor) *side-letters* (secret agreements between certain corporate parties) which had reduced the financial impact of HIH's re-insurance contracts to that of loans. The general public's expectation that auditors should have uncovered the HIH fraud is mitigated by such practices. Evidence in the HIH and other cases suggest the practice of side-letters may be far from unique in the industry (Anonymous 2006a, 2006b).

It is worth contemplating whether an expectation that the introduction of IFRS will rectify accounting's failing to 'show it how it is', where such complexity is endemic, will be fulfilled. With respect to the insurance industry, for example, the signs are less than encouraging, even when side-letters do not exist. Two-thirds of respondents to a KPMG survey of Australian insurance companies perceived that the 'adoption of IFRS had actually increased the risk of inaccuracy in financial reporting' (Johnston 2006). Some suggest that directors should report to shareholders in myriad ways, resulting in the 'annual report being less relevant' (Kitney and Buffini 2006). Others are concerned about the volatility in earnings associated with applying IFRS (AIA 2006) or, more generally, with the empirical impact of the IRFS (see Clarke *et al.* 2003; *Abacus* 2006; Walker 2007).

Whereas the noting of accounting defaults and anomalies, featuring in post-2000 reports, might be taken as indicative of the *new* corporate governance mechanisms exposing corporate wrongdoing, arguably these episodes are little more than repeats of responses to embarrassing revelations concerning corporate behaviour that have occurred on numerous occasions over the past one hundred and sixty years. Current regimes contain 'more of the same' rules prevailing over that long period. There is little reason to expect that the latest IFRS would have prevented or disclosed the matters currently under judicial review. In a curious way, the plight of the victims of many unexpected corporate collapses in different jurisdictions in recent times has made it clear – possibly the clearest in one hundred and sixty years – that the corporate structure (especially when group relationships are prevalent) is not sacred. At the end of the day, if company structure no longer serves commerce in the way the 1841 UK Gladstone Committee intended when pressing the British Parliament to enact the first Companies Act of 1844, it can and ought to be changed.

'Truth in securities' and earlier knee-jerk responses?

Following the 1929 world-wide crash, a debate raged over corporate malpractices similar to that of the recent past. In the UK, Lord Kylsant's imprisonment following prosecution under the 1861 Larceny Act for his part in publication of the Royal Mail's misleading prospectus no doubt shocked the establishment. General criticism was levelled at the way in which corporate financial statements significantly misled and failed to depict the drifts in companies' financial affairs over time. In the USA, there was the jiggery-pokery with group structures of the kind that Samuel Insull and Ivar Kreuger employed. Moreover, following prescribed rules or everyday accounting conventions, even with the best of intentions, generally proved inadequate for the purpose of revealing a company's wealth and progress. Then, as now, the intention to mislead was an unnecessary condition for the creation of misleading financial statements.

Roosevelt's introduction of the 1933 Securities and 1934 Securities and Exchange Acts was promoted as injecting 'truth in securities' replacing the trust lost in corporate disclosures in the Great Crash fallout.[2] Compliance with accounting rules was tightened. This set the nation on the accounting rule-making path reflected today in FASB standards. Cleaning up accounting was to be achieved by more clearly articulating fundamental ideas both in the 1930s and, more recently, by a search for the principles underpinning accounting practices, financial reporting disclosure, and monitoring mechanisms. In each ensuing decade, the drive appeared to be to protect an essentially co-regulatory mechanism, with the public accountancy profession's significant influence retained.

Ferdinand Percora as chair of the Senate's Banking and Currency Committee launched a scathing attack on accounting. But professional oratory by Price Waterhouse & Company partner George Oliver May cut the public accountancy profession in for its share of Roosevelt's New Deal measures designed to put 'truth in securities' – the ultimate corporate governance sentiment. The profession's self-regulatory status and its importance in the emerging co-regulatory regime (see Zeff 1971; Chatov 1975) were the beneficiaries. Nonetheless threat of government regulation, were the profession to fail to inject financial statements with Roosevelt's 'truth', nurtured attempts to articulate the main principles underpinning accounting practice. The American Accounting Association's (AAA) *Accounting Principles Underlying Corporate Financial Statements* in 1936 and Sanders, Hatfield and Moore's *A Tentative Statement of Accounting Principles* in 1938 are indicative of the *thinkers* in the accounting discipline in the USA being as much concerned as its practitioners.

In more recent times, the impact of faulty accounting has fuelled attempts to purge corporate activity of its present ills. In this setting, what the principles ought to be, and any possible distinction compared with what are stated as rules, appear as uncertain now as it was in the 1930s (see Chambers 1964; Staunton 2006; Walker 2007). As in the past, the profession's resolve to define the underpinnings of conventional practice, to search for *principles*,[3] diminishes once threats of unwelcome external intervention in its business have dissipated (Chatov 1975; Clarke *et al.* 2003: particularly Chapters 2, 3, 6 and 10).

Juxtaposition of events post-1930 and those post-2000 places Samuel Insull as the corporate poster bad-boy, similar to Kenneth Lay, Jeffrey Skilling, and the Arthur Andersen firm of more recent years. For, in a curious twist, just as Enron's fall instigated Andersen's collapse, Roosevelt's New Deal edged Andersen into the auditing super-league: Roosevelt's appointment of the fledgling Andersen to unravel the wreckage of the Insull empire established it as the 'paragon of virtue' of the public accountancy firms (which may have been justified at that time).

Insull's corporate life was distinguished. Having previously headed up the Chicago-based Edison Company, he went it alone, establishing Insull Utility Investments in the 1920s to compete with Edison. Just as Lay and Skilling used the separate status claimed for Enron's SPEs as the way to shuffle assets through the group undetected and unaccounted for, Insull shuffled assets through the group's subsidiaries at ever-increasing amounts to pyramid their booked values. Group structures prevailed as an effective accounting manipulation *modus operandi*. Consolidation accounting's elimination of double-accounting Insull-like and debt-washing of the Enron-SPEs variety (Walker 1976), does not ensure serviceable asset values are disclosed. Consolidation would have had little impact on either Insull's or Enron's exploitation of group structures. Misrepresenting that it does improve accountability effectively makes consolidation a potential accounting hazard. Like others since, Insull 'gilded the corporate lily'. When stocks generally fell in the 1929 Great Crash, his companies were found to be 'full of water', with grossly misleading accounting values ascribed to assets. Insolvent, brought to trial for suspected fraud in 1932, Insull was ultimately acquitted on all counts (see Clarke and Dean 2007).[4]

The Insull affair (like the contiguous Royal Mail affair described below) demonstrated the frequent conflict between outcomes from applying the accounting rules of the day and the financial commonsense that non-accountants might draw upon in their reading of corporate financial statements. A considerable part of Insull's defence rested on the appeal of his financial commonsense rationale for his accounting practices and, by implication, the financial nonsense peddled in the conventional accounting wisdom. The contemporary rules prohibited treating stock dividends as income. The prosecution was unable to deny that the matter was controversial or that reputable accountants were divided on the issue. Similar to charges against WorldCom post-2000, the capitalisation of 'organisation expenditure' was allegedly improper – certainly contrary to the conventional wisdom. And questions as to the appropriate forms of infrastructure valuation and depreciation – contentious accounting areas where Insull again debunked conventional accounting wisdom – remain hotly debated nearly three-quarters of a century later (see Walker *et al.* 2000). Significantly, some of what Insull did is now the accepted wisdom.

In the early 1930s, the general approach taken in the USA was to specify accounting rules and pass them off as principles. The 'tick-the-box' mentality to accounting practice compliance has been pursued for the best part of 70 years. Comparability is claimed when each company consistently uses the same rules (Schipper 2003: 62–3). But variations between the outputs in financial statements prepared under the same input and processing rules demonstrate that the comparability expected by statement users is not guaranteed. The expectations gap remains.

Current concern over the serviceability of data reported in financial statements for determining the wealth, progress, and solvency differs little in its essential features from its counterparts of the best part of a century ago. Few commentators seem to recall that, in the 1920s in the UK, Royal Mail's undisclosed drawing upon past profits to pay current dividends accorded with the rules of the day (conservatism was a virtue – as was secrecy).[5] The holding company's legal entity-based balance sheet was the Royal Mail's sole statutory financial disclosure document for an extremely complex group (see Clarke *et al.* 2003 which drew on Brooks 1933 and Greene and Moss 1982). In that setting, the company had maintained dividends of between 4 and 6 per cent during the period 1921 to 1927 by drawing upon secret reserves containing the top-up refunds of Excess Profits Duty compensating for ships lost on First World War service. A vague omnibus description masked the dividend source, inviting misleading inferences that the payments signified current profits were being earned. To the contrary, the Royal Mail incurred trading losses over the period (see Brooks 1933: Appendix). Drawing from so-called secret reserves was a common practice, but Lord Plender, former President of the Institute of Chartered Accountants in England and Wales agreed to Sir Patrick Hastings' suggestion that 'there might come a time' (Hastings 1949: 224) when disclosure was required for such material items – the forerunner of today's materiality concept. Sir William Jowitt, the Attorney-General, aptly noted that false impressions given though complying with the rules meant that 'the accountants' profession has failed to carry out its primary and obvious duty . . . to ensure . . . a true and accurate account' (as cited in Brooks 1933: 210).

Returning to recent events, Enron's use of SPEs to hide debt was facilitated by a professionally prescribed ownership rule. Its 'mark-to-model' valuations bringing prospective profits into account had regulatory approval. WorldCom's expense capitalisation was arguably the product of the conventional accrual system (with a questionable twist) and differs little from the Australian case of Reid Murray and Stanley Korman capitalisations of development expenditures in the 1960s (see Clarke *et al.* 2003). Arguably, the devil is in the conventional view of capitalising expenditures *per se*.

WorldCom's expenditure capitalisation practice raises issues similar to those experienced in the fall of UK's Rolls-Royce in the 1970s – in particular, the capitalisation of development costs for its innovative RB-211 engine. Waste Management's alleged depreciation manipulation is associated as much with the accountants' claim that depreciation is an allocation of cost rather than a decrease in price as with any deviation from a reliable practice. US airline companies in the 1950s were embroiled in similar issues. 'Following the rules' therefore has emerged consistently to be a well-intentioned, though inherently deceitful, means of producing accounting numbers – a simulacrum of a quality mechanism.

Principles-based accounting standards

Rules of the kind known to have failed in the past are reinforced despite their dismal histories. Lack of transparency, misleading disclosure, arguably 'indecent disclosure', characterised the traumatic failures of companies such as Enron, WorldCom, Parmalat, HIH, and One.Tel. Statements of financial performance and financial position have failed consistently to present reasonably reliable portrayals of companies' dated wealth and periodic progress. They are neither 'transparent' nor 'truthful'. 'Truth in securities' has failed miserably.

Rules-based or principles-based accounting has become a major conundrum (AAA 2003; Schipper 2003). Regulators claim that rules are followed frequently, but that the intention underpinning them is not. Accounting rules are said to encourage financial engineering (FASB 2002: 2). But that is not supported by compelling argument about the soundness of the rules or by evidence of any principles underlying them. In contrast, those promoting principles-based accounting standards argue for adherence to a complete and internally consistent conceptual framework (FASB 2002: 6) rather than attempting to identify any undergirding primary principles drawn from commercial affairs. Indeed, Schipper (2003: 62–3), when advocating principles-based accounting standards, explicitly supports the conventional rules. Consistency in their application is her primary objective – to achieve numerical comparability. The consequences of fully following through on principles-based accounting standards have been exposed by Lee (2006b). Yet, principles do not seem to be on the regulators' radar whereas buttressing the conventional system is! Accounting's beauty therefore seems to be in the eye of the beholder.

That accounting ought to be principles-based rather than rules-based appears to be generally conceded by regulators. IFRS are being presented as principles-based and some suggest those of the FASB are too (see *Abacus* 2006). Clearly the appeal of 'principles' is strong. In virtually every domain outside accounting, the primary quality criterion of 'serviceability' or 'fitness for use' is embraced. Goods and services are universally recognised to be serviceable, meeting society's demands, when they can be employed to produce the desired outcomes in the uses ordinarily made of them. No good reasons to the contrary have emerged over the past one hundred and sixty years to suggest that accounting data should be seen any differently. To that end, the 2005 PN119 statement by the UK Financial Reporting Council, that the true and fair criterion remains the 'cornerstone' of British accounting, might be taken as the necessary underlying primary principle. Few would disagree that corporate financial statements are true and fair when, overall, they show their wealth and financial progress, and are serviceable for deriving those companies' salient financial characteristics, i.e. rate of return, debt to equity, solvency, asset backing, and the like. But the history of corporate financial reporting reveals that accounting has not developed in that fashion. The question is, why?

Lee (2006a) identifies four contributing groups that have somehow engineered the state of reporting to be 'sidewardly mobile' over the last one hundred and sixty years. Reporting quality has been static over time, despite criticism and regulatory attention and action, rather than improving or being upwardly mobile. These groups are financial statement preparers (predominantly senior corporate executives), auditors (the public accountancy profession), regulators (including bodies such as FASB), and academic accountants (the so-called conscience of the profession). Within this nexus of relationships, protecting the public interest by producing high quality financial statements has not characterised the annals of finance. Radically changing either accounting as business instrumentation or business structures has not been a primary objective. Instead, self-interest appears to have driven each group. Senior corporate executives have no incentive to change the conventional accounting model. It permits them to remain the scorekeepers. Their often short-term remuneration is dependent on accounting's poverty of principle. Nor do auditors have an incentive for change. Verifying bad accounting while pretending to seek better ways of instrumentation remains profitable. Were there no problems with corporate business structures and accounting, there would be no need for regulators. Academic accountants earn their reputations by observing and reporting participants' behaviour in the accounting 'game'. Without a refocusing to public interest protection, without a public awareness and censorship of the over-arching power of self-interest among the participants in corporate financial reporting, it is hard to see how the present state will change. The unwanted paradox will remain. Bad accounting will provoke responses that evoke further bad accounting.

Auditing as detection

A parallel and equally unwanted paradox in auditing reinforces the parlous state of corporate financial reports. It reflects the same sequence of financial scandal followed by regulatory response evidenced in accounting. It concerns the repeated failure by auditors to detect MAM perpetrated by DSM. Through audit standards and other sources, public accountants articulate at best a limited responsibility for the detection of MAM by DSM. An over-riding instruction of dependence on managerial honesty prevails.

In these circumstances, auditing education and training appear to concentrate on the wrong target. Public accountants have emphasised reliance on internal control systems (frequently over-ridden by DSM) and compliance with prescribed accounting rules (that can be manipulated by DSM). This approach has been to the fore, rather than one that ensures auditors can identify and cope with DSM. Reviewing the history of governmental and professional responses to unexpected corporate auditing failures illustrates the paradox. Over many decades, several jurisdictions have maintained a persistent expectations gap between what audit beneficiaries desire and what audit practitioners provide by way of protection.[6] The paradox threatens the credibility of the current audit as a means of protecting stakeholders from corrupt senior managers. The historical analysis draws upon a selection of significant legal cases of fraudulent reporting and subsequent public accountancy response, some of which have been examined in relation to accounting instrumentation. It reveals the persistent presence of MAM by DSM and equally persistent denial or limitation of responsibility of public accountants for detecting it.

Accounting misstatement and dominant managers

MAM by DSM is often found to be evident irrespective of the size of company, audit regulations or the skills of the auditor. Reflecting the willingness and capacity of senior managers to practise deceitful behaviour is closely associated with corporate failure and scandal. Despite the expectation of a reasonably careful, skilful, and cautious auditor at work, it has created a model of excuses by public accountants that denies or limits their responsibility. History reveals public accountants not getting involved in setting audit standards until a more evolved stage, and of appearing then to assume responsibility when, in effect, accepting very little. The consequence has been a permanent expectations gap between audit providers and preparers with respect to the detection of MAM by DSM. Paradoxically, as we reveal below, courts and the public accountancy profession have continually promoted the notion of auditors trusting the honesty of senior managers in relation to corporate financial reporting. Auditors can be trained to identify MAM. But this is irrelevant if they are not also trained to identify DSM. Unsurprisingly, the history of corporate reporting reveals numerous audit failures associated with MAM, DSM, and unexpected corporate collapse.

The following analysis assumes that MAM occurs because of DSM and that the two are characteristic of a general condition in corporate financial reporting. MAM cannot exist without DSM. But the existence of DSM does not automatically signal MAM. The DSM motivation for MAM is irrelevant. Ultimately, its potential to damage any company and its stakeholders is the significance of the historical paradox.

Model for excuses

From 1844 to 1900 in Britain, the current limited audit responsibility for detecting MAM by DSM was forged from a model of excuses created not by public accountants but by lawyers. Accounting and auditing regulations emerged within a scenario of considerable state intervention in the regulation of corporate behaviour, and of numerous court cases addressing corrupt and deceitful practices by corporate managers. This regulatory basis underpinned professional accountants gradually becoming engaged in accounting and auditing services as they reduced their earlier focus on the provision of court-related services. The public accountancy profession was newly institutionalised and primarily focused on securing and maintaining its legitimacy (Walker 1991).

Various Companies Acts from 1844 onwards in the UK introduced regulations involving incorporation, limited liability, balance sheet reports, and compulsory (then voluntary and again compulsory) audit (Hein 1978). At first, auditors were shareholders (the amateur auditor) but, later, public accountants began to recognise a lucrative service market (Maltby 1999). However, public accountancy institutions did not attempt to influence or comment on these arrangements. By default, the field was left to lawyers without accounting education or training. Also at this time, partly due to the lack of adequate auditing, a number of corporate *causes célèbres* revealed the dangers associated with MAM by DSM. For example, in 1849, there was George Hudson, the 'Railway King' and CEO of the Eastern Counties Railway Company. A DSM, he falsified reported profits using insider information to manipulate the company's share price, and sold land the company did not own (Arnold and McCartney 2004). His case and another in 1866 led to legislation, in 1867 and 1868, as a governmental response to MAM by DSM in the railway industry. These Acts required railway companies to publish an audited balance sheet conforming to a standardised format. In 1878, despite years of reported profitability, the City of Glasgow Bank collapsed, with a large deficit revealed (Couper 1879; French 1985). The entire board of directors was implicated and imprisoned because of falsification of several balance sheets involving fictitious accounting entries, manipulated valuations, and coercion of employees. The Companies Act, 1879, was the British government's response and required banks to publish audited balance sheets. Despite these interventions, by 1900 there was no overall regulation of companies in the UK and no consistent provision for financial statements audited by professionally qualified accountants. Nor had there been substantial comment by public accountancy institutions on reporting and auditing failures. Legal comment from a succession of court decisions in the late nineteenth century filled the vacuum.

In the late nineteenth century, a number of court decisions addressed the auditor's responsibility for detecting MAM: *Leeds Estate, Building and Investment Company* (1887), *London and General Bank* (1895) and *Kingston Cotton Mill* (1896).[7] These cases and individual public accountants' responses to criticism, created a model of excuses that persists to current times, i.e. a structure of credible excuses permitting public accountants to deny a primary responsibility for detecting MAM by DSM.[8] They ring-fenced accounting records and the balance sheet as the audit focus, and distanced auditors from senior managers – even where (as in *Leeds Estate, Building and Investment Company* and *Kingston Cotton Mill*) DSM was identified as facilitating MAM.

The ring-fence embraced several connected arguments. The auditor's duty was said to be checking the accounting records, not to question the honesty of senior managers. It was not the auditor's responsibility to tell senior managers how to manage the company. The auditor had to have his suspicions aroused, which depended on the circumstances, and was expected to audit with reasonable care, skill, caution, and diligence. Taken together, these excuses ensured that the general standard by which auditors could be judged was to be decided on a case-by-case basis, creating flexibility with respect to responsibility for MAM detection. Consistent with the dictum in *London and General Bank*, they effectively signalled to the public that detecting MAM by DSM was not a matter reducible to the auditor following prescribed rules – the auditor was not an insurer against MAM.

The court cases relating to MAM in the late nineteenth century gave rise to regular criticism of the corporate auditor. In response, public accountants supplied excuses for their failure to detect MAM. These took various forms but captured judicial statements of the time. Most popular were complaints that audit fees were too small to provide for effective auditing, and that there was insufficient time to permit the detection of complex MAM – although some observed that the audit should not be restricted merely because the fee was inadequate. The comments about fees reinforced similar comments in court cases. They are also consistent with the 'low-balling' competitive nature arguments of current times. Indeed, up until recently, public accountants have protested their inability to assume detection of MAM as a primary audit objective because of cost and time factors (DeAngelo 1981).

The British professional publication, *The Accountant*, in the late nineteenth century also contained explicit excuses to limit the auditor's responsibilities. These related primarily to the relationship of auditors with senior corporate managers. Today, these are enshrined in legislative provision, e.g. management is responsible for accounting systems and therefore for preventing and detecting fraudulent activity through internal control systems. Practitioners also reflected on matters that appear just as apposite today, e.g. the difficulty of detecting management fraud because of senior managers' position of influence, the board of directors' influence over the audit appointment, the need to assume senior managers' honesty when relying on their representations, and avoiding audit functions that could be construed critical of management (see evidence in Chandler and Edwards 1994a). These excuses effectively created a long-standing paradox in corporate auditing, i.e. auditors denying or limiting responsibility for detection MAM by DSM.

The principal driver in the construction by lawyers of a model of excuses for corporate auditors was the Court of Appeal, with *London and General Bank* and *Kingston Cotton Mill* as the major cases legitimising it (Teo and Cobbin 2005). *London and General Bank* contains many of the previously mentioned arguments; *Kingston Cotton Mill* reinforces them. The language of the two cases characterises the public accountancy profession's official position of limited responsibility. They contained common features – each had aspects that facilitated the MAM – a DSM who took advantage of complex corporate structures, boom economic conditions, and related financing. In *London and General Bank*, its CEO, Jabez Balfour was a leading businessman controlling a group including the bank. He orchestrated inter-company transfers to facilitate payment of dividends out of non-existent profits (Valance 1955). On appeal, the bank's auditor was found guilty of a breach of duty to the shareholders when not reporting the illegality of dividends. The profession's reaction emphasised the constraints to the audit function mentioned above rather than addressing the problem of a DSM who could override internal controls and employees to facilitate MAM within a complex corporate structure. Interestingly, in later company law reform inquiries (e.g. Davey Report 1895 and Greene Report 1926), there were consistent references to corporate businesses being managed in general by honest men. This view entrenched a tradition of auditors' reliance on assumed managerial honesty, obviously misplaced when there is MAM by DSM.

The 1896 *Kingston Cotton Mill* case involved overstating the value of assets for several years and dividends were declared on inflated profits. Inventory data were manipulated by the general manager and director William Jackson without deference to his fellow directors – 'to benefit the company, and bolster up its credit' (Chandler and Edwards 1994a: 152). On appeal, the auditor was found not guilty of negligence. The judgment used the same criteria about the boundaries of auditing as enunciated in *London and General Bank*, expanding on them in the context of the auditor as a 'watchdog rather than a bloodhound' (Teo and Cobbin 2005: 49). The case particularly emphasised the acceptability of relying on the honesty of senior managers but, as before, ignored the need of a solution to auditing in the presence of a DSM who facilitate MAM.

The *London and General Bank* and *Kingston Cotton Mill* cases popularised the audit mantra of 'reasonable care and skill in the circumstances' as the foundation for the model of excuses by corporate auditors regarding MAM detection. It was to be a further half century before public accountants formally included it in their guidance to auditors.

Mandated audits and co-regulation

The Companies Act, 1900, required publication of an audited balance sheet. It did not require professionally qualified auditors, although it is clear that professional audits were common by this time (Maltby 1999; see also Anderson *et al.* 1996: 363–88). The difficulty of detecting MAM continued to be discussed in the literature. Practitioners demanded and supplied excuses to support denials or limitations of responsibility (e.g. Wardhaugh 1908 and Jenkinson 1913 in the UK, and Montgomery 1912 in the USA). Attention was turning to the burgeoning audit market in the USA where, by the mid to late 1920s, there were out-of-control money markets, investment trusts, and myriad corporate combinations.

As noted above, two of the most notorious robber barons of the period were CEO Samuel Insull (of Insull Utility Investments) and Ivar Kreuger (of Kreuger & Toll), both of whom were well-known globally and found the doors of presidents, kings, and high officials seemingly always open to them. McDonald (1962) provides an account of Insull's corporate empire of utility monopolies organised in a labyrinth of hundreds of holding and subsidiary companies across the USA. Funding and controls by several trusts sitting at the apex of the Insull Utility Investments' 'top heavy pyramid' obscured understanding of its operations (Valance 1955: 167–79). Issues of corporate governance relating to this corporate structure, asset valuation and other accounting practices emerged after Insull's death in 1938. Flesher and Flesher's (1986: 421–34) account of Kreuger's 'giant pyramid scheme' suggests the timing and scale of the fraud 'contributed significantly to the passage of the Securities Acts' in the early 1930s. Kreuger & Toll became one of the largest conglomerates and multinationals imaginable. However, when Kreuger died in 1932, the façade was revealed as a vehicle for deceiving millions of investors who received false financial statements over many years. Kreuger & Toll had the 'most widely-held securities in America (and also in the world) during the 1920s' (Flesher and Flesher 1986: 421). As later, with the likes of Enron and WorldCom, the market was shocked by revelations at Kreuger & Toll. Stoneman (1962: 936) attributes the Kreuger & Toll affair to a combination of Kreuger's managerial dominance and the company's complex structure. His dominance was acknowledged by the investigating accountants Price Waterhouse (May 1936: 110), who were unable to determine the exact magnitude of the fraud due to Kreuger & Toll's organisational complexity.

The events at Insull Utility Investments and Kreuger & Toll demanded a strong regulatory response. It came in the form of the SEC in 1933 and legislation such as the 1935 Public Utility Holding Company Act. Despite these responses, it soon became evident that the existing model of professional self-regulation (then co-regulation) would continue to be promoted (Chatov 1975). Limitations of audit responsibility characterised the post-Insull Utility Investments and Kreuger & Toll debate. When the American Institute of Accountants (AIA) published an audit guidance statement (AIA 1936) as a revision of earlier statements, scope limitation was repeated with respect to the detection of defalcation, understatement, and manipulation. Company directors were stated to be assuming greater responsibility for accounting, detection of irregularities was deemed to require a special investigation, and reliance on internal controls and management representations became the foundations of the modern audit. Thus American public accountants formally stated the model of excuses in 1936. The paradox for the auditor of MAM facilitated by trusted DSM became institutionalised.

The US position on audit responsibility was disrupted by the 1939 McKesson & Robbins case (Baxter 1999) involving a wholesale drug company which was, by 1937, one of the largest in the USA. Its CEO Donald Coster had founded the business in 1923. However, much of the reported profitability and asset structure was false due to fictitious transactions in a fictional subsidiary. Price Waterhouse failed to discover the deception. The SEC investigated and its report criticised the inadequacies of the audit, particularly the lack of scepticism of DSM representations. While these strictures were generally accepted at the time, within months the AIA issued standards on asset verification and reporting to counter criticisms. Nonetheless, AIA standards continued to limit auditor responsibility on the following grounds: the auditor is not an insurer or guarantor; the need for 'reasonable care and skill in the circumstances'; management is responsible for accounting and safeguarding assets; the discovery of defalcations is not a primary objective of auditing; and reliance on internal control and the integrity of management acceptable in the absence of suspicions to the contrary.

In 1947, the AIA's (1947) *Tentative Statement of Auditing Standards: Their Generally Accepted Significance and Scope* clarified auditor responsibilities in the USA. It gave guidance on general, field work, and reporting standards, and emphasised competence, independence, and due care – a re-badging of the English legal concept of 'reasonable care and skill in the circumstances'. The discovery of errors and irregularities was mentioned only indirectly. MAM was mentioned only briefly. Thus, in 1947, the US limitation of responsibility to detect MAM remained. Indeed, four years later, the American Institute of Certified Public Accountants (AICPA) in its *Codification of Statements on Auditing Procedure* (AICPA 1951) reiterated the 1939 denial of a primary responsibility for detecting defalcations and other irregularities. In 1960, however, the AICPA's (1960) *Statement of Auditing Procedure 30* appeared to modify the 1951 position, arguing responsibility where there was non-compliance with generally accepted auditing standards. Nevertheless, it restated the mantra of the auditor as neither an insurer nor guarantor and the expectation to act with due professional care and skill.

At approximately the same time, the Institute of Chartered Accountants in England and Wales (1961) adopted a similar position in *General Principles of Auditing*. The statement was expressed in terms of the 1896 dictum of the *Kingston Cotton Mill* case, i.e. reasonable care, skill, and caution in particular circumstances, adopting a position and using the AICPA (1960) statement terminology. Denial of primary responsibility by major professional bodies thus continued. Detection of MAM was regarded as an additional service to the client. The approaches in the UK and USA clearly drew on late nineteenth-century British judicial pronouncements.

1960s to present day

The 1960s saw little change to the position in the UK and USA. MAM by DSM continued and the growing Australian commercial environment mirrored British and American character-istics. For example, in 1963, the case of Reid Murray Holdings attracted considerable interest (Clarke *et al.* 2003: 55–65). One of Australia's largest retailers in the early 1960s, Reid Murray Holdings entered receivership in 1963. CEO Oswald O'Grady was a charismatic but dominant manager with a favourable reputation in the wider community. MAM included overstatement and misclassification of assets over several years. A government investigation found O'Grady not guilty of fraud. However, according to the inspectors, he was an 'inept manager' – an 'artless victim of his own incompetence'. As DSM, O'Grady had swept public investors along in his enthusiasm for property development.

In the USA, in 1973, public scrutiny of the auditor's role intensified with respect to MAM (Seidler *et al.* 1977). Equity Funding Corporation of America specialised in innovative financial products combining life insurance with mutual fund investment. Its profits came from commis-sion from mutual fund share sales and life insurance policies sold to re-insurance companies. With Stanley Goldblum as chairman in 1969, the company became one of the largest life insurance companies in the USA. Goldblum appointed Fred Levin as vice-president of life insurance operations. Both were central to the fraud. Equity Funding Corporation collapsed when a whistleblower revealed a fraud of more than $60 million of inflated mutual fund assets and $80 million of other fictitious or inflated assets. Some $2 billion of life insurance policies were bogus due to Goldblum and Levin generating computerised documents, circumventing internal controls, pressuring employees, and deceiving the auditors. Goldblum and Levin, and the audit engagement partner and two audit managers, were convicted of fraud and two audit firms paid a large out-of-court settlement.

The AICPA created a special committee to examine whether current audit standards were sufficient to cope with a situation such as Equity Funding Corporation (AICPA 1975). Also, other large corporate collapses of the time (including Penn Central, Stirling Homex, and National Student Marketing) presaged establishment of the 1974 Cohen Commission on Auditors' Responsibilities to examine the role of the auditor and the adequacy of generally accepted auditing standards. The Commission reported that users were entitled to assume that corporate financial statements were reliable because the auditor gave reasonable assurance they were free of MAM (AICPA 1978). *Statement on Auditing Standards 16* (AICPA 1977) repeated the approach of limited acceptance of responsibility as enunciated in the 1960 AICPA state-ment, i.e. the auditor was neither an insurer nor guarantor, and that he should exercise due care in the application of generally accepted auditing standards. Little of substance changed in the 1970s in the USA. MAM by DSM was not addressed.

The UK position was equally static. Humphrey *et al.* (1993) report on institutional activities in the 1980s concerning the detection of MAM. These culminated in an audit guideline from the Auditing Practices Committee (1990) maintaining a limited role for the auditor. Meantime, leading public accountancy firms offered fraud investigation as a separate service. The background to the 1990 statement was relatively clear. Research revealed perceptions of the auditor being responsible for the detection of fraud generally, and the guidance statement suggested auditors should plan to have a reasonable expectation of detecting MAM. However, following financial scandals in the 1980s (e.g. Johnson Matthey Bank) and UK government pressure for auditors to assume greater responsibility, the British professional bodies initiated two investigations. On fraud reporting, the recommendation was that auditors should communicate directly with relevant supervisory bodies rather than shareholders because of client confidentiality. With respect to fraud, both investigations supported the *status quo* of limited responsibility in the guidance statement. Humphrey *et al.* (1993) perceived little change in the British profession's lack of acceptance of responsibility for detecting MAM in the 1980s. British auditors appeared to claim an ability to detect MAM if this was a separate engagement involving a less litigious environment than the audit. Humphries *et al.* particularly question in these circumstances what the audit was capable of detecting in relation to MAM by senior management.

Then along came Robert Maxwell. Maxwell had an unusual career for a British businessman, having been a Member of Parliament and the subject of a 1973 Department of Trade and Industry report that stated he was not to be relied on to exercise proper stewardship of a public company. He had used false information in his attempt in 1969 to sell his company, Pergamon Press.[9] In 1974, Maxwell regained control of Pergamon Press and, by 1981, had also obtained control of the British Printing Corporation (renamed Maxwell Communications Corporation) in 1986. Two years earlier, a private company owned by Maxwell purchased Mirror Group Newspapers, which became a public company in 1991 following other media and publishing acquisitions. A catastrophic financial collapse of Maxwell Communications then occurred. Maxwell died in mysterious circumstances the same year and his companies filed for bankruptcy in 1992. Three years later, a Department of Trade and Industry report (Thomas and Turner 2001) stated that the primary responsibility for a massive fraud lay with Maxwell. Misappropriation of funds coupled with MAM were achieved through a complex private ownership of more than four hundred Maxwell companies intertwined in a public group (Clarke *et al.* 2003). The Mirror Group Newspapers' cash flow funded his other businesses, and its pension funds were raided to repay debt elsewhere in the group. In effect, all parts of Maxwell Communications, including its pension funds, were treated by Maxwell as one entity. Eventually, there was no cash available to meet due debts. By 1991, missing pension fund assets totalled £458 million.

In 1991, Bank of Credit and Commerce International (BCCI) closed with the discovery by its auditors Price Waterhouse of a fraud involving billions of dollars of lost or fictitious assets. Because of a multiplicity of ongoing legal actions and several national governments not releasing documents, it is hard to determine the exact size of the fraud. It is estimated there were $13 billion of missing assets and claims of creditors totalling $16 billion. In 1998, Price Waterhouse paid a large out-of-court settlement without admitting liability. The most comprehensive account of the fraud is the US Senate report on BCCI in 1992 and what follows is a brief summary from that source (Kerry and Brown 1992).

Agha Hasan Abedi founded BCCI in 1972 and had worked in Indian and Pakistani banks. BCCI was based in Luxembourg and its activities from 1973 to 1991 became global. BCCI entered the US banking system through acquisition and became banker for governmental funds of many nations. It was alleged to be involved in money laundering, drug and arms dealing and trafficking, fraud, extortion, bribery involving fictitious loans and other transactions, imprudent lending and investment, stolen deposits and investments, and unrecorded deposits. Price Waterhouse became the overall BCCI auditors in 1987, having previously shared the audit with Ernst & Young. The pre-1987 arrangement of dual auditors was likely a key factor in the ability of BCCI senior managers to hide their fraud. The US Senate report accused Price Waterhouse of failing to protect BCCI depositors and creditors when it had been aware of its accounting practices. The full story of BCCI may never be told but it focuses on the existence of DSM in a multinational corporate structure of such complexity and depth that no individual jurisdiction was fully aware of what BCCI was doing.

Returning to the USA, in 2001, Enron Corporation announced a large third-quarter loss and an even larger write-down of impaired assets connected to SPEs controlled by its chief financial officer Andrew Fastow (Sridharan *et al.* 2002). An SEC investigation into perceived conflicts of interest resulting from SPEs caused a downward restatement of its published earnings from 1997 to 2001 and it entered bankruptcy protection. A criminal investigation took place and Enron's auditors Andersen, and its engagement partner, were found guilty of obstruction of justice at the initial judgement. Andersen admitted shredding Enron audit working papers and was liquidated in 2003.

Enron was a global energy trading company and Andersen was not the auditor of the SPEs associated with it. Enron began to trade in energy units in 1994 following deregulation of the industry. Its chairman and CEO from 1986 was Kenneth Lay and its chief operating officer was Jeffrey Skilling from 2001. Shortly after the Enron collapse in 2001, Skilling resigned and Lay replaced him as chief operating officer. An Enron vice-president Sharon Watkins testified to the House Energy & Commerce Committee, suggesting that Lay had not understood Enron's trading and accounting practices and that Skilling and Fastow managed in an intimidating style. To date, there have been several court decisions and settlements. Andrew Fastow was found guilty of fraud and entered a plea bargain.

Enron shocked the global financial community with the scale of MAM in the presence of DSM and auditors. However, as the facts of the Enron scandal emerged, another became headline news (Clarke *et al.* 2003). WorldCom was one of the largest US corporations in 2002 when it collapsed with an apparent $11 billion of MAM. WorldCom handled one-half of the world's e-mail traffic and it was the second largest US long-distance phone carrier. The company entered bankruptcy protection in 2002 with $41 billion of debt. It was later renamed MCI and, by 2003, had returned to profitability. While investigations are ongoing, two reports have been lodged with the Bankruptcy Court. These relate to investigations by a former Chief of Enforcement at the SEC (on behalf of WorldCom) and a former US Attorney General (on behalf of the Bankruptcy Court). Their findings are that the fraud was associated with DSM (including CEO Bernie Ebbers and chief financial officer Scott Sullivan), and there were two sets of accounting records, lax internal controls, and poor oversight by the board of directors. The alleged MAM included inflated revenues, treating maintenance costs as capital expenditure, and failure to write off bad debts. The company's auditor was again Andersen. Sullivan pleaded guilty to securities fraud, conspiracy, and reporting false information to the SEC and was sentenced to gaol. He and Ebbers had unfettered control in the company. Other WorldCom accounting executives pled guilty to fraud charges.

Clarke *et al.* (2003) observe several largely unexpected failures in the 1980s and 1990s also in Australia. For example, Bond Corporation, one of Australia's leading companies in the 1980s, with over six hundred subsidiaries, suffered financial problems *circa* the 1987 stock market crash and was placed in provisional liquidation in the early 1990s. Founder Alan Bond was found guilty of Australia's largest corporate fraud, the so-called Bond Corporation/Bell Resources 'cash cow transaction'. Intermediaries were used to facilitate upstream transfers of more than $1 billion of cash funds from Bell Resources to other Bond Corporation subsidiaries and related parties. Both Bond Corporation and Bell Resources were listed holding companies and under the control of Alan Bond through direct holdings and by virtue of holdings through related parties. Because of the dominance of Alan Bond and other top-level Bond Corporation executives, information about Bond Corporation was released to shareholders and lower-level operational managers on a need-to-know basis. Mr Justice Sir Nicholas Browne noted regarding Alan Bond's 1980s failed attempt to take over Lonrho: 'It is a very remarkable phenomenon when you think that you have a company that had by that stage invested £360 million – odd that not a single piece of paper is available supporting that fact' (Haigh 1989: 41).

Then HIH, reportedly the second largest insurance company in Australia, suddenly became one of the country's largest corporate collapses with an estimated deficiency of more than $5 billion (Clarke *et al.* 2003). Interestingly, the HIH Royal Commission Report (HIHRC 2003: I, xiii) concluded that:

> despite (myriad governance) mechanisms the corporate officers, auditors and regulators of HIH failed to see, remedy or report . . . [the] obvious. This was a situation not assisted by the dominance of HIH CEO and founder Ray Williams. Williams might be considered the epitome of the DSM genre.

At all times Ray Williams played a dominant role at HIH (HIHRC 2003), with its board proving to be an ineffective monitor of his activities. The HIHRC report (ibid.: III, para.273–7) further details how two major and ultimately fatal transactions were allegedly actioned by Williams – the FAI acquisition by HIH and Allianz's purchase of a major part of HIH's cash flow base just before its ultimate collapse. Williams, with the absolute trust and confidence of his board, or too much strength for them to contain, was able to ensnare HIH in the FAI takeover without presenting an appropriate due diligence report. According to the HIHRC report (ibid.: III, para.273) 'Decisions . . . were often made by the Board on short notice with insufficient information and without adequate analysis . . . [The board accepted] views of management uncritically.' For the most part, the HIH board, and contestably perhaps the auditor, accepted virtually everything Williams put to them. His dominance overrode his sensitivity to the commercial reality of HIH's circumstances. However, whereas Andersen was subjected to some criticism in respect of its audit of HIH (primarily for what it did not detect), no charges were laid against the firm.

Institutional responses of public accountants

Enron and WorldCom precipitated responses by the AICPA to the problem of the audit detection of MAM. First, the Private Securities Litigation Reform Act, 1995 enshrined the dictum of auditors providing reasonable assurance that they would detect illegal acts having a material effect on financial statements. It therefore legitimated a credible legal excuse to limit responsibility. 'Reasonable assurance' has not been defined and is circumstantial in nature (Cullinan and Sutton 2002). Nevertheless, the AICPA continued to use it in *Statement on Auditing Standards 82* (AICPA 1997); auditors being responsible for providing reasonable assurance that financial statements were free of MAM. Misstatement was defined in terms of errors and fraud. The Statement also limited responsibility by recourse to excuses used in the past – i.e. managerial concealment and collusion, and the difficulty of judging risk factors. *Statement*

82 had two specific requirements for the auditor – assessing and judging the risk of MAM when designing the audit and documenting these assessments and judgments.

Statement 82 did not change the previous limited responsibility policy of American auditors, but it did make more explicit the need for auditors to think carefully about the risk of MAM in relation to audit procedure. *Statement 82* also provided an appendix containing examples of risk factors relating to MAM. These were categorised as incentives and pressures on management (e.g. economic threats, market expectations, and compensation packages), opportunities (e.g. the nature of the business, monitoring of management, complex organisational structures, and internal control systems), and attitudes and rationalisations of management. The need for auditors to emphasise even a limited responsibility for detecting MAM was made with more clarity in a report completed for the AICPA in 2001 (Beasley *et al.* 2001).

Statement on Auditing Standards 99 (AICPA 2002) is the most recent American statement on responsibility for the audit detection of MAM. It does not alter the previous acceptance of limited responsibility based on reasonable assurance. And it continues the tradition of excuses to emphasise this limitation.

Peroration on inconvenient outcomes

The previous sections identify two paradoxes from the history of corporate financial reporting generally and accounting scandals particularly. Both result from unexpected outcomes. Both are inconvenient and unwanted. Both threaten the credibility of the reporting system.

Paradox of false expectations – accounting as a governance instrument

Whereas the expectation that corporate financial statements will inform the public periodically about corporate wealth and progress appears eminently reasonable, they habitually fail to do so. This is highlighted when companies collapse unexpectedly. Those collapses that closely follow clean audit reports serve to increase tensions between the public and accountants. That tension is manifest in complaints and criticism levelled at the profession as it stumbles time after time to deliver a product reasonably meeting the corporate information needs and expectations of investors and other interested parties.

Complaint has spawned the push for further means by which accountants can demonstrate their compliance with standards of the day. However, despite express and implied defence of past accounting practices, contemporary moves in the EU, Australia, Canada, and elsewhere to introduce IFRS effectively refute the alleged technical propriety of these practices. Regulatory actions implying MAM is the product of deviating from accounting standards has been shown to be wrong. By implication, compliance with previous standards was a means of producing misleading disclosure, albeit with the best of intentions in some cases.

Corporate collapses have possibly influenced IFRS adoption though, curiously, not in the USA. Enron has become the exemplar for corporations behaving badly, however, and its collapse, followed by that of WorldCom, almost certainly was the catalyst for the corporate governance push post-2000 in the USA. Spread of the corporate governance contagion was fuelled by similar events elsewhere. In Australia, for example, the push gathered momentum following the failures or financial dilemmas of HIH, Harris Scarfe and One.Tel.

President Bush's post-Enron resolve to clean up corporate America bears a remarkable similarity to President Roosevelt's 'truth in securities' vow following the Great Crash of 1929. Likewise, the market impact of the enactment of the Sarbanes–Oxley Act, 2002 bears a similarity to that of the passing of the 1932 Securities Act and the Securities and Exchange Act, 1933.

Despite strong talk, legislation and litigation, little of substance appears to have been learned over the years. IFRS are as likely to produce misleading financial information as not. There is no good reason to expect that FASB compliant data will any better disclose the wealth and progress of compliant companies in the future than in the past. Paradoxically, the push and the discussion may have allayed disquiet regarding the serviceability of accounting as instrumentation to the point of increasing false expectations of accounting's potential to disclose corporate wealth and progress.

Paradox of false expectations – auditing as fraud detector

Detection by corporate auditors of MAM by DSM is frustrated by a limited responsibility couched in ambiguous terms such as due care, proper scepticism, reasonable assurance, and reliance on management. The reflective combination of court judgments and professional pronouncements portray corporate auditors as reasonably careful, skilful, and cautious individuals responsible for an attest function with boundaries. More specifically, the current audit is paradoxical insofar as the auditor is expected to presume the honesty of senior managers when relying on their representations while concurrently recognising that DSM can use its position and authority to override internal controls, coerce junior managers and employees, and induce compliant external service providers in order to create the necessary conditions for MAM. Much is therefore left to the auditor's assessment of individual circumstances and, in that respect, the economic cost of MAM detection plays an important part in limiting the extent of audit procedures. Public expectations about corporate auditor responsibility, on the other hand, assume an unequivocal public duty to detect MAM by DSM irrespective of cost.

The history of this complex and potentially damaging situation has its genesis in mid to late nineteenth-century court cases of fraudulent reporting in the UK. At this time, the institutions of public accountancy failed to set viable parameters for corporate audit responsibility and much was left to lawyers. Ambiguous and undefined legal terminology such as reasonable care and skill in the circumstances were invoked by public accountants later to create the reasonably careful, skilful, and cautious image.

The historical evidence suggests that DSM is a sign of potential reporting difficulty. Whether always, is a matter of conjecture and research. The problem for the auditor is that, frequently, DSM feature in successful companies. Perhaps the argument should be that, DSM makes a bad situation worse and corporate governance mechanisms less effective than they should be. More specifically, DSM coupled with any of a number of contributing factors such as boom economic conditions, lax internal controls, generous executive compensation packages, and complex organisational and financial structures, may exacerbate the risk of MAM. Individual public accountants and their institutions over many decades have focused on symptoms of a disease (e.g. poor internal controls or manipulation of accounting standards) rather than the disease itself (i.e. DSM utilising complex organisational structures and financial engineering, tolerating weak controls, and pressuring employees). Public accountants have consistently placed the major responsibility for detecting and preventing MAM on senior managers – the very individuals whose honesty they are expected to rely on.

The events reviewed here have had previous exposure in the literature. Professional responses have been fully debated and the expectations gap is a familiar topic. Ambiguity about the auditor's responsibility for detecting MAM is a subject of continuous professional reference and public concern. Bringing these matters together, by connecting the pieces of the jigsaw, the historian 'bears witness' to decades of writing, comment, and debate (Jordanova 2000: 204). It reveals an issue of public anxiety. Though perhaps circumstance- and time-specific – the events used in this study *may* be unique, they have been such high profile affairs in their time as to be, arguably, the publicly visible tip of a much larger invisible iceberg. Identifying icebergs is a reasonable way of bearing witness for the accounting and auditing historian.

This enquiry indicates the need for further research into the DSM phenomenon and how audit firms react to it. Of particular interest might be in-detail enquiry into whether DSM is tolerated more or less according to the size of the audit firm – whether there is evidence of differences between the reactions to DSM by the Big Four, middle-tier firms and the remainder. Likewise, whether reactions differ according to the frequency of fee hikes and client size are obvious potential foci of enquiry with a view to better understanding how DSM phenomena continue to prevail. The task for researchers in this area is to redirect attention to those icebergs, thereby providing further evidence showing regulators that the current governance paths being followed will not prevent more unexpected failures, like Enron, Kreuger, Maxwell and HIH, again leading to criticisms of accounting and audit practices.

Key works

Chambers (1965) explains and illustrates the multiplicity of accounting numbers that can be generated when applying the conventional accounting standards of the 1960s. It illustrates the technical defect of claims that uniformity of method produces uniformity of outcomes that facilitate the making of valid inter-firm comparisons.

Clarke and Dean (2007) pursues the theme that misleading financial disclosures arise more by virtue of compliance with the approved accounting standards than by dint of deviation from them with the intent to deceive. MAM of the kind discussed in this chapter are shown to be endemic of a seriously flawed (but approved) system of corporate group activity conducive to the relatively uncontrolled behaviour of DSM.

Edwards (1976) discusses disclosure issues generally over the period 1925–35, including those related to the Royal Mail affair. It notes that 'a consensus in favour of disclosure evolved gradually' over the half a century to 1976, 'prior to which secrecy in financial reporting met with very little opposition' (ibid.: 289).

Lee (2006b) examines recent attempts by the FASB to use a principles-based approach to accounting standards. In particular, it argues that the FASB and similar bodies are paying lip-service to the notion of representing socially constructed realities and, instead, are more concerned with traditional accounting conventions such as consistency and comparability.

Notes

1   This type of analysis has a long history and is well captured in Chambers (1965).
2   This section is a modification of Clarke and Dean (2003) which was based on Chapter 14 of Clarke *et al.* (2003). What follows here is limited to examining accounting and auditing reforms primarily.
3   Walker (2007) questions whether what were referred to in the 1920s and 1930s were really principles – as have many others including Chambers (1964), Sterling (1970), Staunton (2006) and Clarke and Dean (2007).
4   For accounts of the main disclosure and auditing issues and professional responses in the 1920s and 1930s, refer, *inter alia*, to Edwards (1976), Manley (1973) and Walker (1977).
5   Green and Moss (1982: 141–2) support this claim, noting that the defence case made much of the auditor's use of the phrase 'after adjustment of taxations reserves' to describe the fortification of the

1926 and 1927 accounts. They were also able to plead successfully that, rightly or wrongly, the secret transfer of inner reserves was a fact of life in large conglomerate companies.

6 This section is derived mainly from a more extensive study of the phenomenon in Lee *et al.* (forthcoming).

7 These and other cases are discussed in several papers in Stamp *et al.* (1980).

8 This commentary is based on anthologies of court cases and contemporary contributions in *The Accountant* noted in Chandler and Edwards (1994a, 1994b) relating to the auditor and MAM and judicial parameters of responsibility set in the absence of public accountancy guidance or legislative mandate.

9 Stamp (1969) and Stamp and Marley (1970) describe the events at Pergamon and contiguous concerns related to myriad takeovers that led to the development of accounting standards in the UK (see Rutherford 1996).

References

AAA Financial Accounting Standards Committee (2003) Evaluating concept-based vs rules-based approaches to standard setting, *Accounting Horizons*, 17 (1): 73–89.

Abacus (2006) Special issue, 42 (3), 42 (4).

AIA (1936) *Examination of Financial Statements by Independent Public Accountants* (New York: AIA).

AIA (1947) *Tentative Statement of Auditing Standards: Their Generally Accepted Significance and Scope* (New York: AIA).

AIA *Accountancy E-News* (2006) 27 October.

AICPA (1951) *Codification of Statements on Auditing Procedure* (New York: AICPA).

AICPA (1960) Responsibilities and functions of the independent auditor in the examination of financial statements, *Statement of Auditing Procedure 30* (New York: AICPA).

AICPA (1975) The adequacy of auditing standards and procedures currently applied in the examination of financial statements, *Report of the Special Committee on Equity Funding* (New York: AICPA).

AICPA (1977) The independent auditor's responsibility for the detection of errors and irregularities, *Statement on Auditing Standards 16* (New York: AICPA).

AICPA (1978) *The Commission on Auditors' Responsibilities: Report, Conclusions, and Recommendations* (New York: AICPA).

AICPA (1997) Consideration of fraud in a financial statement audit, *Statement on Auditing Standards 82* (New York: AICPA).

AICPA (2002) Consideration of fraud in a financial statement audit, *Statement on Auditing Standards 99* (New York: AICPA).

Anderson, M., Edwards J. R. and Matthews, D. (1996) A study of the quoted company audit market in 1886, *Accounting, Business & Financial History*, 6 (3): 363–88.

Anonymous (2006a) The advocate, *Connecticut News*, 20 September.

Anonymous (2006b) US grand jury indicts former General Re executive, *Reuters News*, 21 September.

Arnold, A. J. and McCartney, S. (2004) *George Hudson: The Rise and Fall of the Railway King* (London: Hambledon).

Auditing Practices Committee (1990) *Auditor's Responsibility in Relation to Fraud, Other Irregularities, and Errors* (London: Auditing Practices Committee).

Baxter, W. T. (1999) McKesson & Robbins: a milestone in auditing, *Accounting, Business & Financial History*, 9 (2): 157–74.

Beasley, M. S., Carcello, J. V. and Hermanson, D. R. (2001) Top ten audit deficiencies, *Journal of Accountancy*, 177 (4): 63–6.

Brooks, C. (1933) *The Royal Mail Case* (London: Butterworth).

Chambers, R. J. (1964) Conventions, doctrines and commonsense, *Accountants' Journal*, July: 182–7.

Chambers, R. J. (1965) Financial information and the securities market, *Abacus*, 1 (2): 3–30.

Chandler, R. A. and Edwards J. R. (1994a) *British Audit Practice 1884–1900: A Case Law Perspective* (New York: Garland).

Chandler, R. A. and Edwards J. R. (1994b) *Recurring Issues in Auditing: Professional Debate 1875–1900* (New York: Garland).

Chatov, R. (1975) *Corporate Financial Reporting* (New York: Free Press).

Clarke, F. L. and Dean, G. W. (2003) An evolving conceptual framework? *Abacus*, 39 (3): 279–97.

Clarke, F. L. and Dean, G. W. (2007) *Indecent Disclosure: Gilding the Corporate Lily* (Cambridge: Cambridge University Press).

Clarke, F. L., Dean, G. W. and Oliver, K. (2003) *Corporate Collapse: Accounting, Regulatory, and Ethical Failure* (Cambridge: Cambridge University Press).

Commonwealth of Australia (2004/05) Corporate Law and Economic Reform Program (Audit Reform and Disclosure) Act (Canberra: AGPA).

Couper, C. T. (1879) *Report of the Trial of the City of Glasgow Bank Directors* (Edinburgh: Edinburgh Publishing).

Cullinan, C. P. and Sutton, S. G. (2002) Defrauding the public interest: a critical examination of reengineered audit processes and the likelihood of detecting fraud, *Critical Perspectives on Accounting*, 13 (3): 297–310.

DeAngelo, L. E. (1981) Auditor independence, 'low balling', and disclosure regulation, *Journal of Accounting and Economics*, 3 (2): 113–27.

Edwards, J. R. (1976) The accounting profession and disclosure in published reports, 1925–1935, *Accounting and Business Research*, 6 (24): 289–303.

FASB (2002) *Principles-Based Approach to US Standard Setting* (Stamford, CT: FASB).

Flesher, D. and Flesher, T. (1986) Ivar Kreuger's contribution to US financial reporting, *Accounting Review*, 61 (3): 421–34.

French, E. A. (1985) *Unlimited Liability: The Case of the City of Glasgow Bank* (London: Certified Accountant Publications).

Green, E. and Moss, M. (1982) *A Business of National Importance: The Royal Mail Shipping Group, 1902–1937* (London & New York: Methuen).

Haigh, G. (1989) UK judge chides Bond over lack of Bell records, *Sydney Morning Herald*, 22 July: 41.

Hamilton, S. and Micklethwait, A. (2006) *Greed and Corporate Failure: The Lessons from Recent Failures* (London: Palgrave Macmillan).

Hastings, P. (1949) *Cases in Court* (London: Heinemann).

Hein, L. W. (1978) *The British Companies Acts and the Practice of Accountancy, 1844–1962* (New York: Arno Press).

HIH Royal Commission Report (HIHRC) (2003) *The Failure of the HIH Insurance – Vol. III: Reasons, Circumstances and Responsibilities* (Canberra: Commonwealth of Australia).

Humphrey, C., Turley, S. and Moizer, P. (1993) Protecting against detection: the case of auditors and fraud, *Accounting, Auditing & Accountability Journal*, 6 (1): 39–62.

Institute of Chartered Accountants in England and Wales (1961) *General Principles of Auditing* (London: Institute of Chartered Accountants in England and Wales).

Jenkinson, M. W. (1913) The audit of a public limited company, *Glasgow CA Students' Society Transactions*, pp. 113–26 (Glasgow: Institute of Accountants and Actuaries of Glasgow).

Johnston, E. (2006) Disclosure proves toughest challenge for insurers, *Australian Financial Review*, 31 July: 53.

Jordanova, L. (2000) *History in Practice* (London: Arnold).

Kerry, J. and Brown, H. (1992) *The BCCI Affair* (Washington, DC: Committee on Foreign Relations of the United States Senate).

Kitney, D. and Buffini, F. (2006) ASIC offers reprieve on tough reporting rules, *Australian Financial Review*, 7 August: 1, 11.

Lee, T. A. (2006a) The war of the sidewardly mobile corporate financial report, *Critical Perspectives on Accounting*, 17 (4): 419–55.

Lee, T. A. (2006b) The FASB and accounting for economic reality, *Accounting in the Public Interest*, 6: 1–21.

Lee, T. A., Clarke, F. L. and Dean, G. W. (forthcoming) The dominant corporate manager and the reasonably careful, skillful, and cautious auditor, *Critical Perspectives on Accounting*.

McDonald, F. (1962) *Insull* (Chicago: The University of Chicago Press).

Maltby, J. A. (1999) A sort of guide, philosopher and friend: the rise of the professional auditor in Britain, *Accounting, Business & Financial History*, 9 (1): 29–50.

Manley, P. S. (1973) Gerard Lee Bevan and the City Equitable Companies, *Abacus*, 9 (2): 107–15.

May, G. O. (1936) *Twenty-Five Years of Accounting Responsibility: 1911–1936* (New York: Price, Waterhouse).

Montgomery, R. (1912) *Audit Theory and Practice* (New York: Ronald Press).

Raw, C. (1992) *The Money Changers: How the Vatican Bank Enabled Roberto Calvi to Steal $250 million for the Heads of the P2 Masonic Lodge* (London: Harvill).

Rutherford, B. A. (1996) The AEI–GEC gap revisited, *Accounting, Business & Financial History*, 6 (2): 141–61.

Schipper, K. (2003) Principles-based accounting standards, *Accounting Horizons*, 17 (1): 61–72.

Seidler, L. J., Andrews, F. and Epstein, M. J. (1977) *The Equity Funding Papers: The Anatomy of a Fraud* (Santa Barbara, CA: Wiley).

Sridharan, U. V., Caines, W. R., McMillan, J. and Summers, S. (2002) Financial statement transparency and auditor responsibility: Enron and Andersen, *International Journal of Auditing*, 6 (2): 277–86.

Stamp, E. (1969) The public accountant and the public interest, *Journal of Business Finance*, 1 (1): 32–42.

Stamp, E. and Marley, C. (1970) *Accounting Principles and the City Code: The Case for Reform* (London: Butterworths).

Stamp, E., Dean, G. W. and Wolnizer, P. W. (eds) (1980) *Notable Financial Causes Célèbres* (New York: Arno Press).

Staunton, J. (2006) Existing intellectual grooves in the reporting of liabilities: an analysis of the reporting of liabilities under Chambers' continuously contemporary accounting, unpublished PhD thesis, University of Sydney.

Sterling, R. R. (1970) *Theory of the Measurement of Enterprise Income* (Lawrence, KS: University Press of Kansas).

Stoneman, W. H. (1962) The matchless career of Ivar Kreuger – the match king, in *World of Business*, pp. 934–38 (New York: Simon & Schuster).

Teo, E. and Cobbin, P. E. (2005) A revisitation of the 'audit expectations gap': judicial and practitioner views on the role of the auditor in late-Victorian England, *Accounting History*, 10 (2): 35–66.

Thomas, R. J. L. and Turner, R. T. (2001) *Mirror Group Newspapers plc: Investigations under Sections 432 (2) and 442 of the Companies Act 1985* (London: Department of Trade and Industry).

Valance, A. (1955) *Very Private Enterprise* (London: Thames & Hudson).

Walker, R. G. (1976) *Consolidated Statements: A History and Analysis* (New York: Arno Press).

Walker, R. G. (1977) The Hatry affair, *Abacus*, 13 (1): 78–82.

Walker, R. G. (2007) Reporting entity concept: a case study of the failure of principles-based regulation, *Abacus*, 43 (1): 49–75.

Walker, R. G., Clarke, F. L. and Dean, G. W. (2000) Infrastructure reporting options, *Abacus*, 36 (2): 123–59.

Walker, S. P. (1991) The defence of professional monopoly: Scottish Chartered Accountants and 'satellites in the accountancy firmament', 1854–1914, *Accounting, Organizations and Society*, 20 (4): 257–83.

Wardhaugh, J. B. (1908) The legal limitations of an auditor's duties and responsibilities, *Transactions of the Chartered Accountants Students' Societies*, pp. 173–98 (Edinburgh: Chartered Accountants Students' Society of Edinburgh).

Zeff, S. (1971) *Forging Accounting Principles in Five Countries* (Champaign, IL: Stipes).

Part 6

Society and culture

20

Gender

Rihab Khalifa and Linda M. Kirkham

Overview

There is very little, if anything, in our past that can claim to be unaffected by gender processes and gendered understandings of the roles and identities of people, occupations, activities and institutions (Hines 1992). And yet, academic interest in gender and accounting history only really emerged in the 1980s and did not become established until the 1990s.

The early focus of this literature was on examining the discriminatory and exclusionary practices that surrounded the accounting profession in the Anglo-American context (Lehman 1992). More recently, however, some writers have broadened the focus both temporally and spatially, to include 'private' domains, non-professional occupational groups, non-Anglo-American contexts and earlier historical periods. Although still in its infancy, the literature on gender and accounting history has opened up important new areas of research and provided new insights to accounting's past.

This chapter reviews the literature on gender and accounting history following three themes. First, the literature on gender and the accounting profession. Then gendered understandings of who counts as an accountant are examined to reveal how male-centric notions of who constituted an accountant have served to restrict and distort our understanding of accounting's past. In the third section it is highlighted how a gendered concept of accounting and its history has served to restrict where and when accounting historians have looked for evidence of accounting in the past. In the final section, focus shifts from the past accomplishments and disappointments of gender research in accounting history towards a vision for the future.

Gender and accounting history: making the link

Since occupations and activities have gendered identities which are not dependent upon, though they may be related to, the physical persons who practise them (Kirkham and Loft 1993), examining gender in accounting history involves more than an examination of the role and participation of women. Inspired by feminist writers who argue that male and female roles are both socially and historically constructed, not biologically determined, researchers have begun to question the adequacy of our historical understanding of what counts as an accountant and an accounting task and to challenge where we might look for evidence of accounting practices in the past.

Writers have begun to examine how gendered discourses and practices have contributed to our understanding of what constitutes expert knowledge in accounting and the boundaries and legitimacy of accounting practices in historical settings. In particular, gender processes have been shown to be critical for the trajectory and success of the accounting profession in the USA and UK and have contributed to a reassessment of the factors which contributed to the profession's ascendancy (Lehman 1992; Kirkham and Loft 1993).

Other work has identified the limitations of male-centric notions of what constitutes accounting in the past and what is and is not important to our appreciation of accounting history. For example, there have been explorations of the gendered nature of accounting tasks, particularly bookkeeping, in the private and in the public domains (Walker 1998; Cooper and Taylor 2000). A further major contribution in this area has emerged from the focus that writers such as Walker (1998, 2003a, 2003b) have given to alternative, marginalised locations for the performance of accounting such as the home or small family business.

Accounting history was arguably alerted to the potential importance of gender with the publication of a special section of *Accounting, Organizations and Society* in 1992. This contained a number of formative histories of the accountancy profession (Lehman 1992; Thane 1992) and a number of contributions which explored the possibilities and imperatives of a gendered analysis of accounting history (Loft 1992; Kirkham 1992). Subsequently, the focus of the gender and accounting history literature continued to centre on the professional accountant. In consequence, writers have invariably focused on the nineteenth and twentieth centuries and the Anglo-American contexts of professionalism in particular. While the focus of enquiry has recently begun to widen both temporally (Kirkham and Loft 2001; Oldroyd 2003, 2004; Walker and Carnegie 2007) and spatially (Komori and Humphrey 2000; McNicholas *et al.* 2004; Carmona and Gutiérrez 2005; Carrera *et al.* 2001), explorations of these wider dimensions remain in their infancy.

A common theme in the literature covered here is the argument that gender should not be marginalised within accounting history research since, without an appreciation of the processes and influences of gender, accounting history is at best incomplete, and at worst, misleading (Kirkham and Loft 1993). By beginning the process of identifying the gendered nature of accounting knowledge, practices and institutions, these writers have challenged accounting historians to integrate a gender analysis into the mainstream questions of the discipline.

In the rest of this chapter we aim to highlight some of the main gender themes, insights and arguments which have featured in the accounting history literature over the past few decades. However, while some writers claim that '[a] substantial body of recent historical accounting literature emphasizes gender as an important explanatory factor' (Napier 2006: 459), our review might suggest otherwise. Thus, when gender is understood to signify more than biological sex and is viewed as the social construction of what it means to be male or female, masculine or feminine, accounting histories which encompass a gender perspective are disappointingly thin on the ground. When we extract the literature which simply accounts for women in accounting's past as a separate biological group and does not question the underlying distribution of power relationships or the sex-defined roles and identities assumed for them (Scott 1986), a much smaller but nevertheless significant body of literature remains. It is to this literature which we now turn our attention.

Gender and the accounting profession

Gender can be viewed as part of the 'new' accounting history which 'attempts to give voice to individuals and groups that traditional histories have tended to ignore' (Napier 2006: 459). Such an approach seeks to create new understandings by probing and challenging the taken-for-granted understandings of what we know of accounting as a historical subject (Chua 1998; Merino 1998; Miller *et al.* 1991).

Despite the potential range of issues which might be examined from a gender perspective, the majority of the gender literature in accounting history has been concerned with women's entry to, and their progression through, the accountancy profession (Cooper 2001). This literature has followed a number of strands ranging from studies of some of the pioneer women in the profession (Buckner and Slocum 1985; Reid *et al.* 1987) to studies which have adopted a historical framework to examine the ways in which the division of labour in accounting has been mediated and constituted by male-dominated structures and unequal gender processes (Lehman 1992). In this section we give a brief overview of this literature and attempt to highlight its contribution to understanding accounting history.

Pioneer women in accounting's history

Since the 1980s, the focus on women's history has elicited a number of biographical studies of notable individuals in various branches of accounting and bookkeeping. Most of these studies have examined the lives and contributions of pioneer women in the USA (Buckner and Slocum 1985; Reid *et al.* 1987; Slocum 1994; Slocum and Vangermeersch 1996; Spruill and Wootton 1995, 1996). Although some recent studies have broadened the focus to pioneer women outside the USA (McKeen and Richardson 1998) and outside the profession of accounting (Walker 2006), most of the studies of pioneers have concerned the 'heroic' struggle of North American women to gain entry to the professional bodies.

Kirkham and Loft (1993) note how the work of some pioneer women accountants in the UK, such as Ethel Ayres Purdy, was associated with their political activism, particularly in the suffrage movement. For other pioneer women, their success as accountants was facilitated by social connections and/or educational advantages. In England and Wales in 1931, 12 years after women had been permitted by law to enter the profession, the census recorded just 119 women accountants. As the following observation in *The Accountant* illustrates, these pioneers were not representative of women in general or even of educated women of the period:

> It is interesting to note that some of these new women Chartered Accountants bear names well known in the accountancy profession . . . Miss Christine Mosley represents the third generation of Chartered Accountants in her family . . . Miss M.C.B. Aston is the daughter of Mr. Hugh Aston head of the firm Aston, Wilde & Co, of Birmingham and is the second woman Chartered Accountant in that city.
>
> (*The Accountant*, 23 August 1930, quoted in Kirkham and Loft 1993: 547)

Biographies have helped make pioneer women and their achievements visible in accounting history. While such studies have examined the struggles and contributions of the individuals concerned, they have made a limited contribution to our understanding of the development of the division of labour within accounting more generally. Accounts of pioneer women are important in the overall story of the profession, but critics have argued that an overemphasis on this narrow group risks obscuring and detracting from the majority of women who have acted

435

as accounting functionaries through history. Pioneer women were by their very nature 'special', frequently privileged and by definition successful in their struggles. As such, their lives reveal little about the mass of women denied entry to, and progression within, the profession and the structures of male domination and oppression which denied and prevented their access. It is to the literature which attempts to shed light on these structures and processes that we now turn.

Pre 1990 – gender and the profession remain hidden from view

By the 1980s the critical accounting history literature had begun to explore different aspects of professionalisation (for a summary, see Napier 2006: 464–66 and Chapter 11 of this volume) but failed to link such histories to gender processes in any significant way. In the mid-1980s a number of studies appeared which examined the participation (or otherwise) of women in the public accounting profession during the twentieth century. They examined the contribution of individual women and/or the overall participation of women in the USA (Buckner and Slocum 1985; Reid *et al.* 1987; Pillsbury *et al.* 1989), the UK (Silverstone and Williams 1979; Ciancanelli *et al.* 1990) and Australia (Dando and Watson 1986). These studies served to highlight the presence of women in the accounting craft and emphasised their unequal and unfair treatment in the past.

However, these early studies of women in the profession rarely went beyond a celebration of the achievements of notable women or simply gave a brief overview of the multitude of factors which may have contributed to women's limited aspirations, inclusion and progression (Pillsbury *et al.* 1989). While differences between men and women were identified in such studies, gender as an analytical tool was invariably reduced to biological sex. Although barriers to the advancement of women and modes of discrimination were identified, the sources and means of their production and reproduction were left unexplored. Such studies thus failed to trace the origins of the gendered divisions of accounting labour and contributed little to our understanding of the historical organisation of the profession more generally. They leave unexplored the lives of the masses of women who continued to be excluded from the profession even though they were undertaking accounting work or had aspirations to do so. By failing to engage with the broader gendered structures and processes which have mediated and helped determine the division of labour within accounting, extant histories of the professionalisation process remained unchallenged.

The studies dealing with women's lives or gender issues in the 1980s rarely employed a feminist perspective and, where one could be discerned, they invariably adopted a liberal feminist framework. One exception was the study by Tinker and Neimark (1987) which explored gender and class relations between 1917 and 1976 through a longitudinal study of General Motors' accounts and company archives. Adopting a largely socialist feminist framework, the authors suggested that the position of women altered with changes in the wider capitalist system. Focusing on the context of accounting work, they showed how in times of over-production and under-consumption, capitalism invented a consumerist role for women to help solve the crisis of surplus value.

In summary, very few pre-1990 gender studies shed light on the accounting history of women. Although the potential importance of adopting gender as an analytical category was highlighted in the 1980s and the possible roles that gender might play in the emergence and development of the accounting profession was acknowledged (Hopwood 1987), detailed historical analyses had yet to emerge. This was to change in the 1990s.

Post 1990 – gender on the agenda: professionalisation, feminisation and accounting history

To some extent, the literature on gender and accounting history can take its reference point from a group of papers which appeared in a special edition of *Accounting, Organizations and Society* in 1992 (Kirkham 1992; Lehman 1992; Loft 1992; Roberts and Coutts 1992; Thane 1992). Although 1992 also saw a special edition of *Accounting, Auditing & Accountability Journal* devoted to gender issues, the papers published therein ventured little into accounting history, being more focused on critiques of accounting theory and the implications of feminist approaches for accounting practice.

Through a focus on the historical division of labour, the papers in *Accounting, Organizations and Society* sought to begin the process of revealing how accounting history may be (re)evaluated from a gender perspective. Lehman (1992) adopted a historical framework to examine gender issues in the accounting profession in an Anglo-American context. Lehman examined the 'first eighty years' of women in the accounting profession and attempted to document some of the ways in which the accounting profession has been implicated in the discrimination and oppression of women to the 1980s. She highlighted three levels of discrimination against women to which the accounting profession contributed in varying degrees: economic deprivation, socio-economic hierarchies and ideology. Lehman concluded that practices detrimental to women are periodically re-established and continue, albeit in altered forms. Thane (1992) explored the gendered division of labour in accountancy in Britain from pre-industrial times and reflected on the discriminatory processes that accompanied the development of the profession and restricted the access of women. By 1992, as these studies reveal, linkages between feminisation and the professionalisation of accounting were being more firmly established, especially in the Anglo-American context (Roberts and Coutts 1992).

In commenting on Lehman's article, Kirkham (1992) asserted a more comprehensive role for gender analysis in accounting history. She argued that simply 'adding' women to accounting history could be misleading. The challenge for accounting historians was to move towards a more integrated approach which placed gender at the centre of analyses of the accounting profession. Kirkham (ibid.: 295) asserted that any attempt to understand how the profession emerged and developed without an appreciation of the fundamentally gendered structures and processes which engulfed and facilitated change, may 'at best give us partial unsatisfactory understandings' and 'at worst, may result in misleading explanations which serve to perpetuate inequality and oppression'.

Following the theme of exploring the role of gender in understanding accounting history through a wider lens, Loft (1992) highlighted the importance of broadening the focus of enquiry beyond the profession and alerted researchers to the need to examine the role and development of other accounting functionaries, notably clerks and bookkeepers. Such an approach was manifest in the detailed historical study by Kirkham and Loft (1993) which established a crucial link between the rise of the professional male accountant and the fall of the increasingly female bookkeeper/clerk in the occupational hierarchy.

In England and Wales, accountancy became an established profession in the period 1870–1930, in part, by elevating itself from related occupational groups like bookkeepers and clerks which were increasingly dominated by women (Kirkham and Loft 1993). Kirkham and Loft (ibid.: 552) argued that the success of the professionalisation project 'was not simply a matter of establishing accountancy as a profession but involved creating and maintaining a masculine identity for the "professional accountant" '. By viewing the professionalisation process as fundamentally gendered, the authors revealed the important part played by developments in clerical work and a gendered discourse of professionalism in the 'construction of the professional accountant'. By establishing the role of gender in the creation of the professional accountant, they also revealed how extant histories could be considered as incomplete or even flawed.

Following these studies, which critically examined the formative years of the development of the profession, a number of writers returned to the preoccupations of earlier studies and focused on women's progression within the profession in the twentieth century. The employment of women in the offices of accountants in the UK became an issue during the First World War as male accountants left to fight or work for the government (Loft 1986). These new opportunities for women to work in accounting disappeared as soon as the war ended and men went back to their jobs, despite the fact that women became eligible in theory at least for entry to the professional bodies. In 1919, the Sex Disqualification (Removal) Act was passed making it illegal to exclude women on the basis of their biological sex (Lehman 1992).

For some writers this early period marked the start of the progressive, although token, entry of women to the profession (Shackleton 1999). Others have noted how, once the war ended, women's contribution within accountants' offices was once again limited and trivialised (Kirkham and Loft 1993) and how women's progress and participation in the profession continued to be severely hampered until the 1970s (Ciancanelli *et al.* 1990). This lack of advance was despite women having re-entered accountants' offices as substitute labour during the Second World War in the USA (Wootton and Spruill 1994), the UK (Cooper 2001), and Australia and New Zealand (Linn 1996; Emery *et al.* 2002).

The increasing presence of women in the profession since the 1970s has been identified by some as evidence of improvements in the gender balance of the profession (French and Meredith 1994). However, researchers have also cautioned against measuring women's progress by looking only at their numerical representation, rather than their location within the profession (Khalifa 2004). Other studies have emphasised the importance of discursive and material mechanisms which produce and reproduce inequalities in the recruitment and progression of women, especially the phenomenon commonly known as the 'glass ceiling' (Ciancanelli *et al.* 1990; Barker and Monks 1998; McKeen and Richardson 1998; Shackleton 1999; Emery *et al.* 2002; Khalifa 2004). Emery *et al.* (2002) examined the development of the New Zealand accounting profession and revealed how it was male-dominated despite the lack of any formal barriers to women's entry. These studies utilised archival and oral testimony to illustrate how discrimination and patriarchy are complex and not overcome by simple number balancing.

In summary, in the 1990s, accounting historians were more alert to the potential and actuality of incorporating a gender analysis in examinations of the emergence and development of the profession. A few detailed studies appeared which demonstrated the centrality of patriarchal structures, discriminatory processes and practices, and gendered discourses to the professionalisation process in accountancy. While such insights added new understandings to extant histories, they also established the need for accounting history to re-evaluate and reconsider existing explanations and the completeness and validity of the historical evidence on which they were based.

Gendered understandings of what counts as accounting: bookkeepers and other accounting functionaries

As mentioned earlier, since the early 1990s, there has been greater recognition of the need to study gender in accounting history by examining the accounting function as a whole and not simply the professional accountant (Loft 1992). Nearly a decade later, Cooper and Taylor (2000) noted the paucity of accounting literature on the 'non-qualified' clerical workers who undertake routinised accounting tasks. This lack of attention raises questions about taken-for-granted assumptions such as what is understood and accepted as an accounting task, and why such understandings emerge. While such questions remain on the agenda, a few studies have begun to examine developments in bookkeeping and clerical work to better understand the relationship of these activities to professional accounting as well the links between feminisation, professionalisation and deskilling (Kirkham and Loft 1993; Emery *et al.* 2002; Cooper and Taylor 2000; Walker 2003a).

In their 1993 study, Kirkham and Loft demonstrated how the gendering of accounting tasks served to create the identities of those who practised them. During the late nineteenth century, clerks and accountants in England and Wales were predominantly men. By 1931, however, women constituted 42.1 per cent of clerical labour and only 1 per cent of accountants (Kirkham and Loft 1993: 510). The authors show how the progressive feminisation and downgrading of bookkeeping were closely linked to the professionalisation and elevation of the accountant. Their gender analyses go beyond a history of women in or on the margins of accounting and reveal how gendered discourses of professionalism served to separate and differentiate types of accounting work and classes of people. In this way, accounting tasks undertaken by men as well as women clerks came to be reconstituted as both 'menial' and 'women's work' (ibid.: 549).

Similar processes were observed in New Zealand as women were slotted into routinised office and bookkeeping work under the title of clerk, thus 'reinforcing the male closure of the accounting profession' (Emery *et al.* 2002: 2). In the USA, the separation of the 'trade' of bookkeeping from 'professional' accounting and its feminisation is argued to have taken place between 1870 and 1930 (Wootton and Kemmerer 1996, 2000). Other studies have identified a range of (related) factors involved in the feminisation of bookkeeping in the USA, including the growth of cost accounting, the deskilling effects of increasing mechanisation and the scientific management movement (Hedstrom 1988; Strom 1992).

Utilising a labour process framework, Cooper and Taylor (2000) attempted to provide a 'history of bookkeepers' in Britain from the mid-nineteenth century to the 1990s, focusing on the transformation of clerical labour during this period. The transformation is attributed in part to the impacts of mechanisation and computerisation which resulted in the de-skilling and dehumanisation of bookkeeping. Using secondary sources, Cooper and Taylor note the gendered transformation which accompanied these processes and contend that during the late nineteenth and early twentieth centuries, bookkeeping clerks tended to be men. However, by the 1990s women comprised nearly 80 per cent of the occupation (ibid.: 576).

While overall the evidence suggests that the majority of clerks in the latter part of the nineteenth century were men, the evidence pertaining to the gendered distribution of bookkeeping is less established. The feminisation of clerical work has invariably been conflated with the feminisation of bookkeeping temporally. However, Walker (2003b) provides evidence that woman were a significant presence in bookkeeping in certain industries and geographical areas during the late nineteenth century. These women bookkeepers have remained hidden from view because historians have traditionally attempted to trace the employment of women in 'large, bureaucratised organisations such as banks, insurance companies, railways and the postal and telegraph services' (ibid.: 630). Walker uses data from the electronic version of the transcribed census enumerators' books and documentary sources to bring these women bookkeepers into view. His study is revealing and suggestive of the need to trace the involvement of women as bookkeepers in smaller-scale enterprises and craft or retailing sectors.

It has been assumed that bookkeeping was a male preserve until the early twentieth century. However, this conclusion has been based on published census data which conflates bookkeepers with clerks (Strom 1987; 1992; Walker 2003b). Walker (2003b: 631) reveals how, by the late nineteenth century, long before the introduction of office mechanisation during the inter-war years, the majority of bookkeepers in the south of England were women. Other studies have emerged which reveal women as bookkeepers and accounting functionaries in a variety of temporal and spatial settings where they were hitherto invisible – in state organisations during the First World War (Black 2006), not-for-profit organisations in the nineteenth century (Walker 2006), genteel households in the eighteenth century (Kirkham and Loft 2001) and in their own businesses during the eighteenth and nineteenth centuries (Hunt 1996; Walker 2003b).

Gender and the location of historical enquiry – focus and neglect

> Sociological studies focus on the public, official, visible, and/or dramatic role players and definitions of situations; yet unofficial, supportive, less dramatic, private, and invisible spheres of social life and organisations may be equally important.
>
> (Harding 1987: 32)

Since the early 1990s, an increasing number of writers have argued for a 'new accounting history' which questions notions of natural progression in the development of accounting (Miller *et al.* 1991) and calls for the celebration of difference in the telling of historical stories (Chua 1998). Such an approach seeks a broadening of the 'conception of what counts as accounting and what counts as evidence' (Miller and Napier 1993: 645). This appeal reflects and reinforces the broader emergence of 'new history' (Gaffikin 1998) which encourages views from 'below' rather than views from 'above' (Burke 1991).

Despite seeking views from 'below' and arguing for difference to be recognised and celebrated, accounting histories have tended to focus on the dramatic players; the large organisation, the successful entrepreneur and the public arena. More recently, Walker (1998) has drawn attention to the paucity of research which has sought to explore the home, household or small family business as a location of accounting history enquiry. The emphasis given to the accounting practices of the 'male' merchant, 'male' manager of large households or male 'entrepreneur' have been questioned by Kirkham and Loft (2001) since the genteel household could be larger than a small business and more women ran businesses than has been commonly thought (Hunt 1996). The household, family and small business, provide potential arenas for examining accounting and gender in everyday life and culture (Hopwood 1994) which, though still relatively neglected, have begun to attract the attention of some accounting historians.

Gender and history in marginal spaces: the example of accounting in the home

The limited emphasis on the home and household as a focus of accounting history has been attributed to their conceptualisation as the secluded private domain in contrast to the public world of work. This conceptualisation has embodied gendered notions of separate spheres which have dominated social and women's history (Davidoff and Hall 1987) and have served to influence what is and what is not considered important in accounting history research (Walker 1998; Llewellyn and Walker 2000a, 2000b; Walker and Llewellyn 2000; Kirkham and Loft 2001).

Walker and Llewellyn (2000) suggest that the home has been construed as a trivial arena in accounting research and unworthy of academic study. Academic accountants are argued to have sought to establish their legitimacy through a focus on the 'public' nature of professional accounting and its importance to the workings of the modern economy. This has involved emphasising professional accountants in 'public' practice and their engagement with the 'owners and managers of large scale "visible" organizations' (ibid.: 443). Additionally, the authors argue that the home has been marginalised due to its representation as a site of consumption rather than production (Llewellyn and Walker 2000a). Such a representation has been questioned both in terms of its applicability to all historical periods (Kirkham and Loft 2001) and the underlying assumptions of productive labour which it embodies (Walker and Llewellyn 2000).

The identification of the home as a potential site for the exercise of male power has inspired a number of historical studies which have explored the potentialities and actualities of household accounting as a technique of male domination (Walker and Llewellyn 2000). Walker's (1998) was the first major study which explored accounting history in the home. Through an analysis of instructional texts aimed predominantly at bourgeois families in Victorian England, Walker demonstrated how accounting served to assist in the promotion and maintenance of patriarchy. While accounting provided women with responsibilities and opportunities for decision-making, these were confined to a narrow domestic sphere which constrained their horizons and limited their aspirations. Domestic accounting systems were seen to discipline and subjugate middle-class women in Victorian England and contributed to the maintenance of male-dominated structures in society. Accounting in middle-class homes in the nineteenth century was understood to be both repressive and disabling.

In a later study, Walker (2003a) found further evidence of the repressive properties of household accounting. His study revealed how, during the early part of the twentieth century, in the wake of suffragism and scientific management, household accounting in the USA and Britain served to divert the aspirations of women from notions of career-building outside the home and reinforced their role as consumers.

The potentially repressive nature of household accounting has been observed in other contexts, notably Australia. Ideological discourses and instructional texts on household accounting in Australia from the early nineteenth century to the mid-twentieth century may have acted as instruments for restraining female consumption by attempting to contain female extravagance in matters of dress and fashion (Walker and Carnegie 2007). The budgetary earmarking ideology which was promoted served as a social process which was reflexive of gendered asymmetries of power in the home (ibid.).

Most of the extant research on accounting in the home has demonstrated how household accounting was associated with patriarchal practices and the preservation of inequality. However, studies of the accounting practices of genteel households in the eighteenth century suggest that accounting had the potential to empower and enable women in the management and control of their households (Kirkham and Loft 2001). Genteel household management during this period was shown to involve a more diverse set of tasks and responsibilities which were recognised and prized by the male members of the household (Vickery 1998). In various aspects 'the household functioned like most eighteenth century commercial enterprises' (ibid.: 141) and genteel women were more akin to master or gentleman farmers than the ladies of leisure commonly portrayed in the literature. Such insights serve to problematise the meaning of private and public and to question the analytical frame of separate spheres during this period.

The gendered nature of concepts such as work and home, private and public and separate spheres has been shown to be both historically and contextually constituted. While the literature has begun to explore the relationship and meaning of these concepts through accounting in the home in post-industrial contexts, there have been very few studies of pre-industrial times, although the potential for such work has been noted (Walker and Llewellyn 2000). Oldroyd (2003, 2004) has begun this endeavour by examining the perform- ance and functioning of prehistoric calculation and counting in relation to gendered structures and relationships. Although the evidence is inconclusive, analysis suggests that calculation and counting functions were performed by women and sustained a matriarchal structure in early societies (Oldroyd 2003).

The potentially enabling qualities of household accounting have been examined for other cultures, notably Japan (Komori and Humphrey 2000; Komori 2006). By viewing accounting practices through a non-Western lens, the authors claim that Japanese household accounting over the past half decade, exhibited a number of positive and emancipatory qualities which allowed women to improve their lives. In contrast to the revelations of other authors, Japanese accounting is claimed to be detailed, inclusive and co-operative. Nevertheless the authors acknowledge that at times accounting systems 'generally did not really challenge the essential underpinnings of the Japanese family system and its commitment to corporate Japan . . . but rather acted to accommodate or eliminate tensions' (Komori and Humphrey 2000: 467). From the late nineteenth century onwards, Japanese women's household accounting role was strongly linked to state savings drives designed to provide funds for corporate investment and to construct the social foundations necessary to achieve national goals (Komori 2006). Thus, in common with the observations in Anglo-Saxon countries during this period (Walker 1998; Walker and Carnegie 2007), accounting discourse and practice have served to contain Japanese women at home and limit their economic participation.

To summarise, the home or household has increasingly been revealed as an important site for the study of accounting and gender in pre-industrial and industrial societies. The few studies which have emerged in accounting history have demonstrated how accounting and accountabilities at home are implicated in gender relations, the ideology of the home and the separation between the public world of work and the private realm of the home (Llewellyn and Walker 2002a).

Revealing accounting beyond and outside the male business enterprise

Accounting historians have predominantly focused on the accounting practices of the male merchant, male entrepreneur (see various chapters in Parker and Yamey 1994) or the male manager of aristocratic estates (Napier 1991) as opposed to the woman trader or woman household manager. Conceptualising accounting beyond professional practice has revealed women account keepers in a variety of domestic, business and financial settings (Hopwood 1994). Family trading or farming concerns constitute arenas where the boundary between public and private is more obscure and where it was accepted that business accounting might be performed by women (Cooper and Taylor 2000; Walker 2003b). Despite this recognition, there have been few detailed studies of women's involvement with the accounting practices in such organisations.

As noted previously, the accounting history literature has begun to acknowledge and inte- grate women and gender perspectives into some of its central concerns, albeit in a limited way. Much of this literature concerns the period from the nineteenth century. For earlier periods the accounting history literature presents a story of the development and practice of accounting which for the most part excludes women. Before the nineteenth century, accounting was regarded as an essential skill for a merchant and was a recommended skill for the nobility and gentry on landed estates (Hunt 1996). However it was also one expected and acquired by some women during this period and historians have provided evidence of women's role as account keepers in a variety of trades and organizations (Vickery 1993, 1998; Hunt 1996; Dingwall 1999).

Historians have shown how women in seventeenth- and eighteenth-century Britain were prominent among rentiers, moneylenders and investors (Hunt 1996; Dingwall 1999). Wiskin (2006) conducted case studies of three English businesswomen in the eighteenth century. Her study suggested that both men and women maintained records and conducted business dealings on credit in similar ways, despite earlier studies suggesting that women's credit transactions were gendered 'feminine' and therefore different to those conducted by men during this period.

Women also participated in various investment activities in the UK and Australia during the eighteenth and nineteenth centuries (Carlos *et al.* 2006; Freeman *et al.* 2006; Johns 2006; Laurence 2006; Newton and Cottrell 2006). The papers published in a special issue of *Accounting, Business & Financial History* in 2006, reveal how women did not always behave in ways suggested by the separate spheres thesis. However, although the distinction between the private world of home and the public world of work may have been blurred, structural impediments prevented the full participation of women as investors in the governance of joint stock companies (Freeman *et al.* 2006; Johns 2006). In the early nineteenth century, 31 per cent of shareholders in Australia's first bank were women but they were prevented from exercising their power as shareholders by being denied the right to vote directly or exercise proxy votes (Johns 2006). Such insights raise questions about how such gendered inequalities have influenced the role of governance and development of large corporations.

Prior to the eighteenth century, women were often able to contribute actively or independently as merchants and traders (Dingwall 1999). A recurrent role adopted by these women, with or without their husband's participation, was that of bookkeeping and handling money. Researchers have found evidence of women's participation in numerous industries and activities. For example, women in the brewing industry in Scotland during the sixteenth century were involved in the selling of ale, handling income and performing bookkeeping tasks while their husbands managed the practical side of the business (Mayhew 1995). Marshall (1983) suggests that such insights are not untypical and points to an abundance of printed and manuscript materials which provide evidence of women's active role in business and financial matters in Scotland over the past 150 years. She points to the existence of census reports, newspapers, government records, business archives and minute books of societies and organisations which reveal women's presence, not as pioneers or exceptions but as hitherto unrecognised participants in several aspects of everyday life in Scotland.

Walker (2006) draws attention to another previously 'hidden' group of women accountants in the nineteenth century whose philanthropic work involved them in a variety of accounting practices. Through a biographical study of Octavia Hill, a housing reformer, he explores the relationship between Hill's accounting, prevailing notions of domesticity and gendered spheres and he illustrates the importance of accounting to her philanthropic endeavour. Few other studies have even alluded to this group of women or the relationship of their work and activities to accounting.

In summary, a small but growing body of research has recognised the need for accounting historians to incorporate and assimilate accounts of accounting performed outside public practice; in the office, in the home or in the small business or craft organization (Loft 1992; Walker and Llewellyn 2000; Cooper and Taylor 2000; Walker 2003a, 2003b; Walker and Carnegie 2007). Explorations of these hitherto marginalised domains have revealed new understandings of the development and functioning of the accounting craft and suggest the need for further research which questions taken-for-granted assumptions concerning where, how and why accounting was practised in the past.

Future research: challenge and change

Our review has suggested that the literature on gender and accounting history has experienced a slow development. It has also highlighted how gendered analyses have opened up new and important areas of research and provided fresh insights into accountings past. Gender processes have been shown to be central to understanding the trajectory of accounting professionalisation in the USA, the UK and elsewhere and have contributed to a reassessment of the factors which contributed to the profession's ascendancy (Lehman 1992; Shackleton 1999; Kirkham and Loft 2001).

In the remainder of the chapter we shift the focus from the past accomplishments and disappointments of gender research in accounting towards a vision for the future. In particular, we suggest some ways in which gender might be accorded a larger role in accounting history. We highlight the potential for deploying a feminist methodology which involves listening to the 'female voice' and argue for a general reassessment of the questions asked in the field of accounting history. Thus we seek to reinforce and strengthen the voices of those who have already questioned the locations and boundaries of historical enquiry and argue for a broader, gendered appreciation of the practices and people who were involved in accounting's past.

Including the female voice: 'The gender of history' [1]

> It does make a difference who says what and when. When people speak from the opposite sides of power relations, the perspective from the lives of the less powerful can provide a more objective view than the perspective from the lives of the more powerful.
>
> (Harding 1986: 26)

Presently, most research in accounting history is told by men of men (Carnegie *et al.* 2003). Researchers who adopt 'feminist standpoint' theory challenge the taken-for-granted assumptions about neutrality and objectivity that underlie the sciences and their (his)tory (Harding 1991). Hammond and Oakes trace the origins of this theoretical approach through the work of Hegel, arguing that 'the slave has a privileged perspective compared to that of the master. The slave can see social relations more clearly because he or she does not have an interest in distorting reality' (Hammond and Oakes 1992: 60). Standpoint theories have demonstrated the usefulness of moving away from 'adding others' experiences to research, to 'starting from' those experiences to come up with research questions, develop theories, collect data and interpret research findings (Haraway 1988; Harding 1991).

Writers have argued that research in accounting history could benefit from avoiding the 'add and stir' approach by adopting a more integrative approach (Hammond and Oakes 1992; Kirkham 1992). Harding suggests that history has been added to gender, and gender has been added to history without developing genuine insights into the 'other' gender's historical experience (Harding 1991). Women's subordination and accounting history are not independent of each other and simply adding women to accounting history could be misleading (Kirkham 1992; Kirkham and Loft 1993). Professional exclusionary and marginalising practices, which adversely affected women, some men (e.g. working-class clerks) and minority groups, were essential to the definition of expert knowledge in accounting and the development of professional legitimacy.

Simply 'adding' women to accounting history is to construct women's experiences as 'supplementary' to accounting history and risks foreclosing the option of alternative histories, leaving extant accounts unchallenged and unchanged. A feminist approach invites historians and researchers to look at and question the assumed and taken-for-granted 'truths' about accounting and to unpick the gendered identities of institutions, activities and occupations. In this way, it is argued, previously marginalised and hidden knowledge might be revealed and other forms of knowledge may emerge and perhaps change our understanding of what constitutes accounting history. Gender, as an analytical category and a fresh perspective, can also help challenge historical accounts of the profession of accountancy by probing more into the process of knowledge and history production, as we ask questions about the process of selecting research questions, gathering evidence and interpreting data.

Another area of feminist historiography is linked to methodological aspects of data gathering and interpretation. It urges historians to ask questions about the choice of substantive areas of historical inquiry, the delineation of the historical record that is deemed suitable for research, and the methods for interpreting data. It is suggested that male-centric notions of 'data' and 'evidence' have produced biased histories because the concerns of women and other oppressed groups are less likely to be represented in official, public records. Their concerns were more likely to be expressed orally than in writing or within domestic and personal records. Assumptions about the definition and legitimacy of the 'public' domain militated against the inclusion of women in the written record. Only recently have historians begun to accept methods such as oral history as legitimate ways to gather evidence (Carnegie and Napier 1996). Through the adoption of such approaches in accounting history, women and other marginalised actors can emerge as new agents of knowledge.

Re-thinking who and what constitutes an accountant

Professional identities as generally represented in accounting history and in professionalisation studies are invariably masculine, incorporating prevailing gendered notions of what it means to be a man or a woman (Kirkham and Loft 1993). In turn, such masculine representations serve to perpetuate and reinforce the discriminatory practices and unequal power relations that they embed. By adopting a narrow conception of what it means to be a professional or an accountant, accounting historians have ignored important aspects of professional identity such as gender, race, sexuality and class.

While a less male-centric notion of an accountant has been incorporated in some recent studies which explore aspects of race (Hammond and Streeter 1994; Hammond 2002; McNichols et al. 2004) as well as gender (Walker 1998, 2003b), the masculine identity continues to dominate accounting histories, old and new. By explicitly questioning the gender of the accountant, accounting practices and institutions researchers will challenge existing interpretations and reveal new understandings of who practised accounting in the past, and where and why it was practised.

Our review has highlighted how accounting historians have chosen to define accountants predominantly within the narrow confines of organised professions and large organisations and have left the underlying gendered structures of male domination and gendered processes of inequality largely unexamined. Such narrow accounts risk obscuring and distorting our understanding of 'the underlying processes and forces at work' (Hopwood 1987: 207). Histories which focus on the 'public' identity of the male accountant have neglected to incorporate the contribution, not only of the myriad women who were performing accounting tasks outside the 'public' but also the contribution of men who were also deemed 'outside' public accounting. By questioning, rather than accepting, gendered notions of expertise, skill, knowledge and practice, accounting historians will not only extend the focus of enquiry to include new locations and hidden contributions but they will also reveal altered understandings of accounting's past.

Conclusion

While historians in general have produced a substantial body of literature over the past 30 years which has deployed feminist perspectives and explored women's lives in detail, this development has only been partly evident in accounting history. Although a small body of literature has emerged which concerns accounting performed outside public practice – in the office, the home or the small business or craft organisation – the majority of accounting history continues to focus on the male accountant and the masculine location.

Despite the potential range of issues which might be examined from a gender perspective, until recently, the majority of the gender literature in accounting history has been concerned with women's entry into, and their progression through, the profession. Although new areas of research in gender and accounting history have recently begun to emerge, revealing new insights into accounting's past, our review would suggest claims that a 'substantial body of recent historical accounting literature emphasizes gender as an important explanatory factor' (Napier 2006: 459) are premature. What is now required is for *all* accounting historians to accept that existing histories that fail to incorporate any consideration of gender are likely to be misleading or incomplete. Only when gender is accepted as integral to the subject itself, will future research begin to cast light on *all* the people and practices involved in accounting's past.

Key works

Kirkham and Loft (1993) is a major paper which offered a re-evaluation of the formative years of the accounting profession in England and Wales from a gender perspective.

Lehman (1992) provides a useful introduction to feminist perspectives on history as applied to the early years of the accounting profession. Usefully read in conjunction with the article by Kirkham in the same issue.

Scott (1986) is not accounting-specific but is very useful in highlighting research possibilities for accounting history from a gender perspective. The paper calls for new ways to study history and ask old questions in new ways.

Walker (1998) is an excellent historical study of the gender implications of household accounting in Victorian Britain.

Note

1   The subtitle 'the gender of history' is borrowed from Smith (1998).

References

Barker, P. C. and Monks, K. (1998) Irish women accountants and career progression: a research note, *Accounting, Organizations and Society*, 23 (8): 813–23.

Black, J. (2006) War, women and accounting: female staff in the UK Army Pay Department offices, 1914–1920, *Accounting, Business & Financial History*, 16 (2): 195–218.

Buckner, K. C. and Slocum, E. L. (1985) Women CPAs – pioneers in the first quarter of this century, *The Woman CPA*, 47 (October): 20–4.

Burke, P. (1991) History of events and the revival of narrative, in P. Burke (ed.) *New Perspectives on Historical Writing*, pp. 233–48 (Cambridge: Polity Press).

Carlos, A., Maguire, K. and Neal, L. (2006) Financial acumen, women speculators, and the Royal African Company during the South Sea Bubble, *Accounting, Business & Financial History*, 16 (2): 219–43.

Carmona, S. and Gutiérrez, F. (2005) Outsourcing as compassion? The case of cigarette manufacturing by poor Catholic nuns (1817–1819), *Critical Perspectives on Accounting*, 16 (7): 875–903.

Carnegie, G. D. and Napier, C. J. (1996) Critical and interpretive histories: insights into accounting's present and future through its past, *Accounting, Auditing & Accountability Journal*, 9 (3): 7–39.

Carnegie, G. D., McWatters, C. S. and Potter, B. N. (2003) The development of the specialist accounting history literature in the English language. An analysis by gender, *Accounting, Auditing & Accountability Journal*, 16 (2): 186–207.

Carrera, N., Gutiérrez, I. and Carmona, S. (2001) Gender, the state and the audit profession: evidence from Spain (1942–88), *European Accounting Review*, 10 (4): 803–15.

Chua, W. F. (1998) Historical allegories: let us have diversity, *Critical Perspectives on Accounting*, 9 (6): 617–30.

Ciancanelli, P., Gallhofer, S., Humphrey, C. and Kirkham, L. (1990) Gender and accountancy: some evidence from the UK, *Critical Perspectives on Accounting*, 1 (2): 117–44.

Cooper, C. (2001) From women's liberation to feminism: reflections in accounting academia, *Accounting Forum*, 25 (3): 214–45.

Cooper, C. and Taylor, P. (2000) From Taylorism to Ms Taylor: the transformation of the accounting craft, *Accounting, Organizations and Society*, 25 (6): 555–78.

Dando, C. and Watson, R. (1986) Women in accounting, *Australian Accountant*, 56: 12–19.

Davidoff, L. and Hall, C. (1987) *Family Fortunes: Men and Women of the English Middle Class, 1780–1850* (Chicago: The University of Chicago Press).

Dingwall, H. (1999) The power behind the merchant? Women and the economy in the late 17th century, in E. Ewan and M. M. Meikle (eds) *Women in Scotland c. 1100–c. 1750* (Edinburgh: Tuckwell Press).

Emery, M., Hooks, J. and Stewart, R. (2002) Born at the wrong time? An oral history of women professional accountants in New Zealand, *Accounting History*, 7 (2): 9–34.

Freeman, M., Pearson, R. and Taylor, J. (2006) 'A doe in the city': women shareholders in eighteenth and early nineteenth-century Britain, *Accounting, Business & Financial History*, 16 (2): 265–91.

French, S. and Meredith, V. (1994) Women in public accounting: growth and advancement, *Critical Perspectives on Accounting*, 5 (3): 227–41.

Gaffikin, M. (1998) History is dead, long live history, *Critical Perspectives on Accounting*, 9 (6): 631–40.

Hammond, T. (2002) *A White-Collar Profession: African-American Certified Public Accountants since 1921* (Chapel Hill, NC: University of North Carolina Press).

Hammond, T. and Oakes, L. S. (1992) Some feminisms and their implications for accounting practice, *Accounting, Auditing & Accountability Journal*, 5 (3): 52–70.

Hammond, T. and Streeter, D. W. (1994) Overcoming barriers: early African-American Certified Public Accountants, *Accounting, Organizations and Society*, 19 (3): 271–88.

Haraway, D. (1988) Situated knowledge: the science question in feminism as a site of discourse on the privilege of partial perspective, *Feminist Studies*, 14 (3): 575–99.

Harding, S. (1986) *The Science Question in Feminism* (Ithaca, NY: Cornell University Press).

Harding, S. (ed.) (1987) *Feminism and Methodology: Social Science Issues* (Bloomington, IN: Indiana University Press).

Harding, S. (1991) *Whose Science? Whose Knowledge? Thinking from Women's Lives*, (Ithaca, NY: Cornell University Press).

Hedstrom, M. L. (1988) Beyond feminisation: clerical workers in the United States from the 1920s through the 1960s, in G. Anderson (ed.), *The White-blouse Revolution*, pp. 143–69 (Manchester: Manchester University Press).

Hines, R. D. (1992) Accounting: filling the negative space, *Accounting, Organizations and Society*, 17 (3/4): 313–41.

Hopwood, A. (1987) Accounting and gender: an introduction, *Accounting, Organizations and Society*, 12 (1): 65–9.

Hopwood, A. (1994) Accounting and everyday life: an introduction, *Accounting, Organizations and Society*, 19 (3): 299–301.

Hunt, M. R. (1996) *The Middling Sort: Commerce, Gender, and the Family in England 1680–1780* (Berkeley, CA: University of California Press).

Johns, L. (2006) The first female shareholders of the bank of New South Wales: examination of shareholdings in Australia's first bank, 1817–1824, *Accounting, Business & Financial History*, 16 (2): 293–314.

Khalifa, R. (2004) Gendered divisions of expert labour: Professional specialisms in UK accountancy, unpublished PhD thesis, University of Manchester.

Kirkham, L. M. (1992) Integrating *her*story and *his*tory in accountancy, *Accounting, Organizations and Society*, 17 (3/4): 287–97.

Kirkham, L. M. and Loft, A. (1993) Gender and the construction of the professional accountant, *Accounting, Organizations and Society*, 18 (6): 507–58.

Kirkham, L. M and Loft, A. (2001) The lady and the accounts: missing from accounting history, *Accounting Historians Journal*, 28 (1): 76–90.

Komori, N. (2006) Choosing to be Kyapi Yuapi or Gati Gati: the real life experiences of women in the accounting profession in Japan. Paper presented at the 8th Interdisciplinary Perspectives on Accounting Conference, Cardiff, July.

Komori, N. and Humphrey, C. (2000) From an envelope to a dream note and a computer: the award-winning experiences of post-war Japanese household accounting practices, *Accounting, Auditing & Accountability Journal*, 13 (4): 450–74.

Laurence, A. (2006) Women investors, 'that nasty South Sea affair' and the rage to speculate in early eighteenth-century England, *Accounting, Business & Financial History*, 16 (2): 245–64.

Lehman, C. R. (1992) Herstory in accounting: the first eighty years, *Accounting, Organizations and Society*, 17 (3/4): 261–85.

Linn, R. (1996) *Power, Progress & Profit: A History of the Australian Accounting Profession* (Blackwood: Historical Consultants Pty Ltd).

Llewellyn, S. and Walker, S. P. (2000a) Household accounting as an interface activity: the home, the economy and gender, *Critical Perspectives on Accounting*, 11 (4): 447–78.

Llewellyn, S. and Walker, S. P. (2000b) Accounting in the most basic of social and economic institutions – the home, *Accounting, Auditing & Accountability Journal*, 13 (4): 418–24.

Loft, A. (1986) Understanding accounting in its social and historical context: the case of cost accounting in the UK 1914–1925, *Accounting, Organizations and Society*, 11 (2): 137–69.

Loft, A. (1992) Accountancy and the gendered division of labour: a review essay, *Accounting, Organizations and Society*, 17 (3/4): 367–78.

McKeen, C. A. and Richardson, A. J. (1998) Education, employment and certification: an oral history of the entry of women into the Canadian accounting profession, *Business and Economic History*, 27 (2): 500–21.

McNicholas, P., Humphries, M. and Gallhofer, S. (2004) Maintaining the empire: Maori women's experiences in the accountancy profession, *Critical Perspectives on Accounting*, 15 (1): 57–93.

Marshall, R. K. (1983) *Virgins and Viragos: A History of Women in Scotland from 1080–1980* (Chicago: Academy of Chicago Ltd).

Mayhew, N. (1995) The status of women and the brewing of ale in medieval Aberdeen, *Review of Scottish Culture*, 10: 16–22.

Merino, B. (1998) Critical theory and accounting history: challenges and opportunities, *Critical Perspectives on Accounting*, 9 (6): 603–16.

Miller, P. and Napier, C. (1993) Genealogies of calculation, *Accounting, Organizations and Society*, 18 (7/8): 631–48.

Miller, P., Hopper, T. and Laughlin, R. (1991) The new accounting history: an introduction, *Accounting, Organizations and Society*, 16 (5/6): 395–403.

Napier, C. J. (1991) Aristocratic accounting: the Bute estate in Glamorgan, 1814–1880, *Accounting and Business Research*, 21 (82): 163–74.

Napier, C. J. (2006) Accounts of change: 30 years of historical accounting research, *Accounting, Organizations and Society*, 31 (4/5): 445–507.

Newton, L. and Cottrell, P. (2006) Female investors in the first English and Welsh commercial joint-stock banks, *Accounting, Business & Financial History*, 16 (2): 315–40.

Oldroyd, D. (2003) Feminine context of prehistoric notation systems, *Accounting Historians Notebook*, 26 (2): 23–8.

Oldroyd, D. (2004) 'Feminising' prehistory, *Accounting Historians Notebook*, 27 (2): 27–30.

Parker, R. H. and Yamey, B. S. (eds) (1994) *Accounting History: Some British Contributions* (Oxford: Clarendon Press).

Pillsbury, C. M., Capozzoli, L. and Ciampa, A. (1989) A synthesis of research studies regarding the upward mobility of women in public accounting, *Accounting Horizons*, 3 (1): 63–70.

Reid, G. E., Acken, B. T. and Jancura, E. G. (1987) An historical perspective on women in accounting, *Journal of Accountancy*, 163 (5): 338–55.

Ritchie, D. A. (2003) *Doing Oral History: A Practical Guide* (Oxford: Oxford University Press).

Roberts, J. and Coutts, J. A. (1992) Feminisation and professionalisation: a review of an emerging literature on the development of accounting in the United Kingdom, *Accounting, Organizations and Society*, 17 (3/4): 379–95.

Scott, J. W. (1986) Gender: a useful category of historical analysis, *American Historical Review*, 91 (5): 1053–75.

Shackleton, K. (1999) Gender segregation in Scottish chartered accountancy: the deployment of male concerns about the admission of women, 1900–25, *Accounting, Business & Financial History*, 9 (1): 135–56.

Silverstone, R. and Williams, A. (1979) Recruitment, training, employment and careers of women chartered accountants in England and Wales, *Accounting and Business Research*, 9 (34): 105–21.

Slocum, E. (1994) Women in accountancy: a reminder of a century past, *Accounting Historians Notebook*, 17 (2): 18–22.

Slocum, E. L. and Vangermeersch, R. G. (1996) A search for Lena E. Mendelsohn, *Accounting Historians Notebook*, 19 (1): 10–11, 22–7.

Smith, B. G. (1998) *The Gender of History: Men, Women and Historical Practice* (Cambridge, MA, Harvard University Press).

Spruill, W. G. and Wootton, C. W. (1995) The struggle of women in accounting: the case of Jennie Palen, pioneer, accountant, historian and poet, *Critical Perspectives on Accounting*, 6 (4): 371–89.

Spruill, W. G. and Wootton, C. W. (1996) Jennie M. Palen, *CPA Journal*, 66 (6): 74–5.

Strom, S. H. (1987) Machines instead of clerks: technology and the feminization of bookkeeping, 1910–1950, in H. I. Hartmannn (ed.), *Computer Chips and Paper Clips: Technology and Women's Employment*, pp. 63–97 (Washington, DC: National Academy Press).

Strom, S. H. (1992) *Beyond the Typewriter: Gender, Class and the Origins of Modern American Office Work 1900–1930* (Urbana, IL: University of Illinois Press).

Thane, P. (1992) The history of the gender division of labour in Britain: reflections on 'herstory' in accounting: the first eighty years, *Accounting, Organizations and Society*, 17 (3/4): 299–312.

Tinker, T. and Neimark, M. (1987) The role of annual reports in gender and class contradictions at General Motors, 1917–1976, *Accounting, Organizations and Society*, 12 (1): 71–88.

Vickery, A. (1993) Golden age to separate spheres? A review of the categories and chronology of English women's history, *Historical Journal*, 36 (2): 383–414.

Vickery, A. (1998) *The Gentleman's Daughter: Women's Lives in Georgian England* (London: Yale University Press).

Walker, S. P. (1998) How to secure your husband's esteem: accounting and private patriarchy in the British middle class household during the nineteenth century, *Accounting, Organizations and Society*, 23 (5/6): 485–514.

Walker, S. P. (2003a) Professionalisation or incarceration? Household engineering, accounting and the domestic ideal, *Accounting, Organizations and Society*, 28 (8): 743–72.

Walker, S. P. (2003b) Identifying the woman behind the 'railed-in desk': the proto-feminisation of bookkeeping in Britain, *Accounting, Auditing & Accountability Journal*, 16 (4): 606–39.

Walker, S. P. (2006) Philanthropic women and accounting: Octavia Hill and the exercise of 'quiet power and sympathy', *Accounting, Business & Financial History*, 16 (2): 163–94.

Walker, S. P. and Carnegie, G. D. (2007) Budgetary earmarking and the control of the extravagant woman in Australia 1850–1920, *Critical Perspectives on Accounting*, 18 (2): 233–61.

Walker, S. P. and Llewellyn, S. (2000) Accounting at home: some interdisciplinary perspectives, *Accounting, Auditing & Accountability Journal*, 13 (4): 425–49.

Wiskin, C. (2006) Businesswomen and financial management: three eighteenth-century case studies, *Accounting, Business & Financial History*, 16 (2): 143–61.

Wootton, C. W. and Kemmerer, B. E. (1996) The changing genderization of bookkeeping in the United States, 1870–1930, *Business History Review*, 70 (4): 541–86.

Wootton, C. W. and Kemmerer, B. E. (2000) The changing genderization of the accounting workforce in the US, 1930–90, *Accounting, Business & Financial History*, 10 (2): 169–90.

Wootton, C. W. and Spruill, W. G. (1994) The role of women in major public accounting firms in the United States during World War II, *Business and Economic History*, 23 (1): 241–52.

21

Race and ethnicity

Marcia Annisette

Overview

The chapter gives a synopsis of the ways in which accounting historians have studied the complex interplay between accounting, race and ethnicity. The major aim of the chapter will be to critically assess accounting history's progress in the area, giving particular emphasis to assessing its overall contribution to the socio-scientific study of racial and ethnic phenomena. Motivated by the overall objective of identifying directions for future accounting history research, the chapter will also sketch the broad contours of racial and ethnic studies, highlighting the growing importance of historical research to the field. The chapter will be organised as follows. Its introductory section argues that the increasing salience of racial and ethnic phenomena throughout our contemporary world calls for greater scholarly attention to the manner in which race and ethnicity have been historically constituted, thereby reinforcing the critical and contemporary significance of historical studies in general and historical studies of racial and ethnic identity construction in particular. Also discussed here is the conceptual distinctiveness between race and ethnicity – two concepts that still are confusingly and interchangeably used by accounting historians. In the second section, a review of the small universe of historical research in accounting that takes on race as its central theme is undertaken. The literature is structured around four themes and some of the underdeveloped lines of inquiry within each of these areas are identified. The third and final section addresses the narrowness of the field of inquiry of race and ethnicity in accounting and points to three shifts of focus which might yield fruitful research outcomes and so enhance accounting history's contribution to the wider study of race and ethnicity.

Introduction

Race and its conceptual twin ethnicity have without doubt emerged as the most potent of social forces of our times. The Rwandan Genocide of 1994, the 'ethnic cleansing' atrocities that plagued the Balkans during the 1990s, the violent 'Rodney King riots' in Los Angeles in April 1992, and, more recently, the riots in the *banlieues* of France in November 2005, are vivid reminders of the mobilising power of race and ethnic identity and their unquestionable salience as fundamental organising principles in the contemporary world. Indeed, it is hardly an over-statement to assert that 'almost every aspect of contemporary social and political relations is deeply inflected with a racial or ethnic dimension' (Bulmer and Solomons 1998: 823).

The increased salience of identity politics in modern social life has contributed to a meteoric rise in the prominence of race and ethnic issues in many branches of the academy. Initially confined to the disciplines of sociology, anthropology and history, current interest in race and ethnicity has extended to social geography, political science, political economy, social psychology, language studies, cultural studies, philosophy and archaeology (ibid.: 820). This heightened academic interest in race and ethnic phenomena is not, however, reflected in historical research in accounting. To date, few accounting historians have broached these topics and so far, the range of inquiry has remained quite limited. As a consequence, accounting history has contributed little to our contemporary understanding of race and ethnicity. More critically, as explained later, given the very narrow focus of the subject to date, accounting history runs the risk of unintentionally propagating fixed, essentialist notions of race – notions long discredited by social and biological scientists.

The present-day dynamics of race and ethnicity are inextricably linked with historical forces. Sociologists of race and ethnicity point out that the forces associated with modernity and post-modernity – rationalisation, industrialisation, urbanisation, immigration and migration, and globalisation – have shaped the context in which contemporary ethnic and racial identities are constructed and reconstructed (Bulmer and Solomons 1998: 824; Cornell and Hartmann 1998: xvii). Thus it is firmly recognised that historical insight is *essential* to a sociological understanding of the racial and ethnic dramas of our times. To this end, accounting historians have a vital role to play in illuminating accounting's involvement in the ongoing projects of race and ethnic identity construction.

The idea that race and ethnicity are socially fabricated identities whose construction involve dynamic, ongoing and unfinished projects has now taken root in the social scientific literature (Frankenberg 1993; Nagel 1994; Omi and Winant 1994; Bulmer and Solomons 1998; Cornell and Hartmann 1998; Kibria 1998) and has placed historical work centre stage of inquiry into race and ethnic phenomena. But this has not always been the case. History has not always been seen as central to such understandings. Indeed, it can be argued that for all of the nineteenth century and the early part of the twentieth, the prevailing Social Darwinist concept of race (which, at the time, was not analytically separate from ethnicity) rendered history quite irrelevant to the subject. By the 1920s, however, in what might be characterised as a 'cultural turn', ethnicity emerged as a theoretical construct distinct from race and replaced race as the explanation of human difference (Frankenberg 1993; Omi and Winant 1994). These new understandings stressed that it was culture and not some inherent genetic attribute that was the source of the widespread political and economic disparities between population groups. With its biological basis discredited, race was re-conceptualised as a social category, subsumed under ethnicity; and it was ethnicity which drew scholarly attention and elaboration.

Based as it was on common heritage and descent, comprehending ethnicity required a measure of historical engagement. But history's role in shedding light on a sociological understanding of ethnicity remained somewhat limited, for dominating the early social scientific study of ethnicity were adherents to the US assimilation school of sociology whose primary focus was to explain why European immigrant groups (deemed ethnic) had a better assimilation experience in the USA than other population groups (deemed racial). Arguing that the non-assimilation of the native African, Asian and Latin American population was a consequence of these groups' respective cultures, the assimilation school nonetheless predicted their eventual integration into mainstream US society and the gradual melting away of their distinct racial and ethnic identities. The demise of the assimilation school in the 1960s, the failure of the American melting pot to materialise, as well as the emergence of newly independent post-colonial states with their own brand of post-colonial identity politics, all gave rise to a frenzied search for explanations for the resilience of race and ethnic identity (Nagel 1994; Omi and Winant 1994; Cornell and Hartmann 1998). This search led ultimately to the widespread recognition that history offered a reservoir of insight and understanding of present-day race and ethnic phenomena. There is now little disagreement with the view that answers to critical questions about the construction, maintenance and transformation of racial and ethnic boundaries and meanings cannot be comprehensively addressed without resort to history.

Accompanying the appreciation of history's indispensability to understanding race and ethnic phenomena has been greater conceptual clarity about the nature of race and ethnicity, and their analytical distinctiveness. Few now debate the ontological status of race. Race is variously described as a 'social', 'historical' or 'ideological' construct – a human creation – and not a biological fact. Race refers to a group of people socially defined on the basis of physical characteristics. Race is 'made' through a socially creative process since 'Determining which characteristics constitute the race – the selection of markers and therefore the constructions of racial categories itself is a choice human beings make. Neither markers nor categories are predetermined by any biological factors' (Cornell and Hartmann 1998: 24).

But race would be meaningless were it merely a human creative act. Race derives its social significance because it represents the fault line along which power, prestige and respect are distributed (Dalton 2005: 16). Race, therefore, is tightly fused with hierarchy and power, and, as Cornell and Hartman (1998: 27) remind us, it has been 'first and foremost a way of describing "others" of making clear that "they" are not "us" '. Important therefore to the conceptualisation of race is an understanding that racial categories reflect the externally imposed designations or assignments of dominant groups on others (Kibria 1998).

Sociologists of race have also come to recognise the continuing role of agency in race construction. That is, even though racial identities are initially imposed by dominant groups on subordinate ones, such identities can be inhabited, resisted, transformed or destroyed by the groups subjected to initial racialisation (Bulmer and Solomons 1998: 823; Cornell and Hartmann 1998: 24). This is the ongoing project of race – a process of continuous race making and reconstitution of racial meanings. It is this final characteristic of race that brings it closer to ethnicity, thus giving rise to some scholarly fusing of the concepts.

Although in some contexts the outcomes of racial and ethnic phenomena are the same (e.g. inequality, conflict or genocide), there is general agreement that the two concepts are distinct. It is generally assumed that ethnicity is not based on *physical* characteristics. Rather, it is based on notions of common ancestry, memories of a shared past and common symbolic elements of culture whether real or putative (Cornell and Hartmann 1998: 19). Further, in contradistinction to race, ethnicity is usually initiated as an act of 'self'-assertion – the assertions of group members themselves. In short, while race is a way of *otherising*, ethnicity is a way of *asserting distinctiveness*.

Despite their conceptual dissimilarity, it is in the sphere of ongoing identity (re)construction that racial and ethnic process overlap. Cornell and Hartmann state:

> Ethnic and racial categories may be delineated first by others, but when groups begin to
> fill those categories with their own content, telling their own histories in their own ways
> and putting forth their own claims to what their identities signify, then they are engaged

in a classic construction of ethnicity. When a racial group sets out to construct its own version of its identity, it makes itself both race and ethnic group at once.

(ibid.: 30)

Before turning to the following section, it is important to summarise the fairly uncontested commonalities between race and ethnicity. First is the widespread understanding that they are not natural phenomena but are 'made' by human beings. Second is the recognition that they are shaped by agency as well as structure. That is, although social groups do participate in altering racial/ethnic boundaries and meanings, the choices open to the group are not infinite, but are structurally bounded (Bashi 1998: 962; Nagel 1994: 152). Third, as socially constructed identities, race and ethnicity are defined by historical and political struggles over meaning, and can thus be seen as 'social and political resources used by both dominant and subordinate groups for the purposes of legitimizing and furthering their own social identities and interests' (Bulmer and Solomons 1998: 823).

Exploring accounting and race: general themes

The exploration of the interplay between race and accountancy is relatively recent and is largely linked to the emergence and development of what is now widely known as the 'new accounting history' (Miller *et al.* 1991; Carmona *et al.* 2004; Napier 2006). The new accounting history is an approach which, among other things, seeks to understand accounting in the broader context in which it operates. Emanating from the call for more research on the interrelationships between race and accountancy (Hammond and Streeter 1994: 285), the studies that have so far been undertaken in accounting can be divided into four distinct areas.[1] First, studies of accounting in settings characterised by racial exploitation; second, accounting and accountants in the context of genocide; third, racial processes in the accounting profession; and four, studies of accounting in societies deeply structured by race. In what follows, the studies falling within these areas are introduced and their dominant themes discussed.

Accounting practice in settings characterised by racial exploitation

Much of the research falling into this category is associated with the work of Richard Fleischman and Thomas Tyson. Theirs has been a collaboration which departs from other historical accounting research which, though situated in settings characterised by extreme racial exploitation, makes no mention of such exploitation and makes no value judgment of the wider social environment (Flesher and Flesher 1981; Razek 1985; Heier 1988; Cowton and O'Shaugnessy 1991; Barney and Flesher 1994; Donoso-Anes 2002; Vollmers 2003). Indeed, concerned as they are with the economics of slavery, the works cited above are completely silent on the issue of race and, consistent with what has come to be seen as a defining characteristic of traditional accounting history, depict an image of accounting as a value-free assemblage of techniques whose ability to contribute to the achievement of rational economic ends is to be celebrated.[2]

In their inaugural attempt to break with this tradition Fleischman and Tyson (2000: 10) suggest that 'an important facet of accounting history is to investigate the degree to which accounting records are reflective of the times'. They explore the accounting–race nexus through an examination of the plantation records of a Hawaiian sugar plantation for the period 1835–1920. Staying true to their traditional accounting history roots, Fleischman and Tyson offer a rich descriptive account of the form and content of the plantation accounting books giving much insight into the organisation of plantation labour. The accounting records reveal that plantation labour was classified by 'ethnic group rather than by occupational function, productivity or any other measuring calculus' (ibid.: 22) – an observation which becomes the central problematic of the paper. In their view, the absence of accounting records on individual productivity indicates that it was 'ethnicity' rather than economic rationality which served as the primary measuring calculus for determining worker wages and wage differentials on the plantation.[3]

In their subsequent work, Fleischman and Tyson go beyond the depiction of accounting as a passive reflector of 'the times' and instead take on a bolder, more critical stance which seeks to illustrate the supportive if not constitutive role played by accounting in extreme racial exploitation. In Fleischman and Tyson (2004), for instance, they examine the records of a number of plantations in the antebellum South to discern the accounting representation of slaves and their activities during the mid-nineteenth century. Their extensive tracking of slave productivity records and careful analysis of slave valuations reveal much about plantation and slave life; but their overriding aim here is to expose accounting as an active participant in the enterprise of slavery. In summarising their archival investigation, the authors point out that 'slave workers were categorized, enumerated and valued with complete disregard for their humanity' (ibid.: 393). This they suggest attests to accounting's complicity in bolstering slavery, for it was 'used to convert qualitative human attributes into a limited number of discrete categories (age, sex, colour) that could be differentiated and monetized in order to facilitate commercial slave trading' (ibid.: 393).

Fleischman and Tyson subsequently collaborated with British accounting historian David Oldroyd and extended their investigation to include British West Indian plantations, thereby producing a comparative study of the reasons, processes and methodologies behind slave valuations on US and on British West Indian plantations (Fleischman et al. 2004). Although at times they seem less confident in their indictment of accounting as a co-conspirator in slavery, the authors conclude that 'the further we delve into the archives and learn about particular accounting techniques like valuation, the more certain we become in asserting that accounting was instrumental in sustaining slavery's institutions and basic practices' (ibid.: 57).

In their later effort to interrogate the role of accounting in sustaining systems of racial exploitation, the same authors also examined the role of accounting during the apprenticeship period (1834–1838) in the British West Indies (Tyson et al. 2005). Apprenticeship was a period of transition, marking the conversion of African slave labour into free waged labour. As the authors note, apprenticeship 'represented an attempt to sustain colonial plantation economies by getting freedmen accustomed to work for wages, to accept the practice as normal and to become willing waged workers' (ibid.: 204). The problem, however, was, given choice, it was not clear that freed slaves would willingly offer their labour services to plantations. Indeed, there was a general belief that they would flee the plantations for the open lands. Tyson et al. suggest that in such a context, a punitive regime rather than one based on market incentives was needed to keep the former slaves on the plantations. And it was in the operation of such that accounting became central. Noting that 'the corporal punishment meted out on the basis of accounting evidence remained the ultimate deterrent for non-compliant work', Tyson et al. (ibid.: 227) conclude that accounting's functioning as a coercive weapon rested on the fact that it provided the documentary evidence to support the practice of the punitive regime. In a sense, therefore, the paper suggests that accounting was part and parcel of a new system of violence enacted on the former slaves. Whereas previously planters could use the whip to compel work effort, during apprenticeship the detailed records that were kept to document absences, work effort and contract violations, reflected a different but similarly effective regime of violence to ensure control and domination.

The strength of the studies produced by Fleischman, Tyson and their collaborators is in their pioneering attempts to weld onto traditional accounting history, the concerns of 'new' accounting historians. This strength is also its weakness, for these studies remain steadfastly committed to their traditional roots and fail to exploit the full potential for pursuing new accounting histories of these sites. Three principal criticisms may be identified. First, these studies are firmly grounded in the past – the past is seen as interesting for its own sake and there is no probing of how the insights gained connect to issues relevant to our times. Indeed, there is even a presumption that there is no such connection. In a recent reflection of his scholarly journey, Fleischman (2004: 15) speculated that critical accountants have ignored slave plantation sites because 'slavery is too historical; that is it cannot be linked to a contemporary issue'. However, sociologists of race widely acknowledge the undeniable link between the current racial bases of US society and that country's experience with its 'peculiar institution'. So interrogating accounting in these sites does have the potential to provide deeper understanding of contemporary issues surrounding race and ethnicity. For instance, recognising that race is part and parcel of a system of cultural representation (Omi and Winant 1994), it becomes possible to interrogate how and the extent to which plantation accounting representations of African slave populations are linked to contemporary meanings/representations of the Black or African race. Further, one might interrogate the links between these slave valuation practices and other calculative practices involving the representation of human populations (such as the US census rule that required Blacks be represented as $\frac{3}{5}$ Whites for the purpose of representation) which in turn contribute to shared and enduring understandings of racial meanings.

A second criticism of these studies is that they remain firmly grounded in the notion of accounting as an agent of rational economic decision-making. There is an over-riding concern to explain the presence or absence of forms of accounting in economic rationalistic terms. But the focus of 'new' accounting historians is on the 'structure and uses of accounting information for control and even coercion, rather than as a mere input into a rational decision-making process' (Carnegie and Napier 1996: 9). Thus, in the context of racial slavery, where control/coercion of slave populations is guaranteed by authorised regimes of violence both at micro and macro levels, the potentially coercive/control role of plantation accounting is doubtlessly usurped, and understandably there is little on offer to new accounting historians in this respect. But while plantation records might not be particularly useful in rendering insight to accounting as an instrument of coercion/control, they may nonetheless provide informing glimpses into racialisation processes in context.

For instance, spatial variability in racial categorisation is well established. In Brazil, race is primarily determined by appearance, in the USA it is established by descent. As a result, whereas in Brazil a white person might have Black ancestors (Bailey and Telles 2006: 76), in the USA, the one drop or *hypodescent* rule precludes this (Davis 1991; Kibria 1998: 941; Kolchin 2002). Moreover, it is well known that the criteria for racial designations follow no uniform logic – the *hypodescent* rule that applies to Blacks in the USA did not hold for Native Americans (James 2001) who were classified on the basis of percentage blood. This rule was probably devised to minimise land claims associated with native land treaty rights. Examples such as these point to a close relationship between asset management activities and the construction of racial boundaries and thus have the potential to reveal the impact of accounting and/or financial measures on racial construction.

A third criticism of traditional accounting history's exploration of the race–accounting nexus is its failure to engage with the theoretical literature on race. This failure, often reflected in the imprecise deployment of terms such as race, ethnicity and racism, has stymied the potential of such studies to better contribute to an understating of the resilience of racial phenomena in contemporary society. Crucial is the tendency for these studies to treat race as a given. By ignoring the fact that race is not a fixed concept spatially or temporally, studies have missed an important opportunity to expose the variety of roles that accounting might have played during racial slavery – the period generally accepted as formative for race making.

Accounting and accountants in the context of genocide

Genocide, the systematic and deliberate destruction of a people, is the most tragic conclusion of a society's racialisation processes. The frequency and intensity of genocidal events became one of the most defining characteristics of the twentieth century and none has been subject to more scholarly enquiry than the Jewish Holocaust. Although a considerable amount of historical scholarship has focused attention on the enabling roles of the German professional class and expert knowledge systems in realising the diabolical Nazi dream, the culpability of accountants and accountancy remained under-scrutinised. That was until the powerful and pioneering study by Funnell (1998) which set out to show that accounting was a potent weapon of the Nazi state bureaucracy for enacting what they termed 'the final solution of the Jewish question'. The study is primarily (though not exclusively) focused on the enabling power of accounting techniques in the service of the Holocaust. According to Funnell, the Nazi annihilation of the Jewish people not only involved their physical extermination but also the alienation, appropriation and disposal of their wealth. Accounting and accountants were deeply implicated in all these activities.

By constructing the extermination of the Jews as an efficiency problem, the way was paved for enlisting accounting. As an enabling technology, accounting served to convert people into things and so ensured that millions of Jews were moved over great distances to their ultimate fate at the lowest cost possible. Accounting also acted to distance the acts of annihilation from those who made such acts possible. Accordingly, the aggregation, reductionism and anonymity of accounting numbers meant that:

> [P]eople who had no direct involvement in the murder of millions of Jews were able to divorce themselves from the objectives and consequences of their work . . . Jews passed the point where they were objectified to where they were *numerised*: they were numbers and little else.
>
> (ibid.: 437, 459)

There was also an elaborate system of accounting procedures that accompanied the sequestration of Jewish property. In this regard, accounting performed purifying and redemptive functions. As a purifier, it served the dual roles of purging Jewish wealth of what the Nazis considered was its inherently corrupt nature. At the same time it cleansed the Nazi handlers of Jewish property of any 'impure motives' avoiding their being contaminated by the difficult tasks which the Jews had 'forced' upon them (ibid.: 458). In its redemptive role, rigorous accounting procedures allowed the Nazi state to act with a clear conscience, for it demonstrated that the acts which produced the property were not guided by motives of avarice or material gain but instead were the outcome of the noble mission of purifying the 'German race'.

Funnell suggests that accounting can become captive to such horrendous regimes because it constitutes the core of functional reasoning. In addition, he suggests that it is the blend of two of accounting's well-acknowledged characteristics – its ability to render visibility and its inherent partiality, that makes it an enabling technology. By being inherently partial, accounting renders visibility to some things and invisibility to others – the latter at once having been rendered invisible runs the risk of becoming valueless. Such was the case with the humanity of the Jews. Accounting's utility and indeed its power in this context therefore rested on its ability to 'supplant the qualitative dimensions of the Jews as individuals by commodifying and dehumanizing them and therefore making them invisible as people' (ibid.: 439). In short, through accounting, the Jews ceased to exist as human beings.

Turning to the culpability of German accounting practitioners, Funnell makes it clear that professional accounting expertise was essential to all stages of the extermination and wealth appropriation activities. Referring to Kohlberg's schema of morality, he argues that accountants acted at the level of conventional morality. Funnell compares this with the highest level of morality – principled morality wherein persons are prepared to stand against laws and orders that contravene natural justice – and concludes that based on the evidence, such behaviour 'was not a feature of the practice of accounting in relation to the Jews throughout the Holocaust' (ibid.: 437).

In their examination of Germany's slave labour operations, Lippman and Wilson (2007) more directly tackle the issue of accountants' culpability in the Holocaust. They point out that during the Second World War, Nazi state-controlled enterprises and a number of prominent German companies made extensive use of prison slaves (among whom were Jews originally held in concentration camps) in their operations. The practice was voluntary, widespread and yielded the highest returns to the enterprises involved, for, unlike ancient slaves who were treated in a manner to protect their value, 'German corporations and state controlled enterprises provided little to protect the concentration camp slaves' (ibid.: 6). The authors reveal how accountants brought their knowledge and training to bear to ensure that these facilities were well run and that every aspect of Jewish internment and death was cost effective and profitable. In confronting the question of accountants' culpability, they note that the accountants involved in slave labour operations, as well as their peers in the wider society, were aware of the institutionalised discrimination and genocidal activities against the Jews.

Indeed, one of the earliest casualties of Hitler's reign was the takeover of the German accountancy profession, which, in 1937, voluntarily relinquished its autonomy to become an arm of the Nazi state. Lippman and Wilson argue that at this time the profession had just come into being and had not begun to grapple with ethical issues and standards. They raise the highly debatable issue of whether adherence to an ethical code is a sufficient basis for judging ethical behaviour and explore a number of logics to answer the question of accountants' culpability. Though not providing a clear answer, the authors suggest that it is worth considering the principle set forth by the rulings of the International Military Tribunal: participants in a system that make a crime possible are deemed as culpable as the perpetrators of the crime. By this standard it would seem likely that the answer to the question of accountants' culpability in what can only be considered to be the darkest episode of twentieth-century history is indisputably clear.

Whereas the above-mentioned studies indicate that by their acquiescence, German accountants acted only at the level of conventional morality and so contributed to the Jewish Holocaust, Walker's (2000) study reveals that this behaviour was not limited to German accountants. In examining British accountants' relationship to the Nazi regime, Walker reveals that rather than rejecting the latter's advances, the British accounting elite acted in accordance with the UK government policy of appeasement. This posture inadvertently turned the most senior members of the British accounting establishment into effective propaganda machines for the German Nazi state (albeit briefly) as was evidenced by glowing tributes to the German state in all of the top professional journals of the times – *The Accountants' Magazine, Accountant, Accountancy,* and *The Certified Accountant.* Walker's study is a fascinating account of the propaganda effects of international events and how one such event in accounting – the Fifth International Congress on Accounting in Berlin in 1938 – could support the Nazi racist totalitarian state. As Walker points out, fascist regimes encourage international events for two reasons. First, to demonstrate their international credibility to domestic constituencies and, second, to proselytise their virtues to foreigners who would return home and proselytise on their behalf. With respect to meeting this second objective, Walker's study reveals that the Nazi aspiration for the Fifth International Congress on Accounting was successfully achieved.

Walker shows that in the months immediately preceding the Congress there was increasing evidence that the mistreatment of Jews was escalating. But this did not feature in British accountants' deliberations about whether or not to attend the event. Instead it was only the fear of their personal safety that caused them to doubt. Walker could find no evidence of any 'principled stance against a regime that was clearly involved in morally reprehensible activities' (2000: 223). Thus with assurances that their personal safety was not at risk, the elite of the British accountancy establishment, comprising top functionaries of the professional institutes and practising firms, converged on Germany for the Fifth International Congress on Accounting with the overriding objective of appeasing and placating their Nazi hosts and thereby not jeopardising their expansionary projects in Europe.

Accountants played an even more direct role in the mid-nineteenth-century Highland clearances of Scotland – a project aimed at purging the country of surplus population and dissolving the Gaelic traditional way of life. Walker's examination of the Highland clearances debunks the notion that the active agents in this episode of ethnic cleansing were 'absolutist landlords impatient to exploit the economic potential of their estates' (2003: 819). Instead, it was Edinburgh's most prominent accountants, acting in their roles as trustees on insolvent estates, who were prime movers. In the face of overpopulation, falling agricultural prices and substantial rent arrears from tenants, many Highland estates became insolvent and Walker shows that with the single-minded pursuit of debt recovery, Edinburgh's accountants displayed no compunction in ordering the eviction of the most vulnerable members of the community. Those evicted faced extreme hardship and even death, yet the accountant-trustees remained impassive and unaffected by the accompanying human tragedy. Indeed, it would seem that it was this aloofness which rendered the accountant appropriate for the job – an aloofness made more reprehensible when one considers that, unlike German accountants, Edinburgh accountants had direct and personal contact with the victims of their actions.

In conclusion, therefore, the above studies reveal the moral bankruptcy of accountants and their institutions when confronted with matters involving social justice. To a large extent, accounting institutions have been content to argue that they are powerless to bring about change in social ills as deep-rooted as racism. They often argue that through their 'merit'-based system of access and opportunity, they represent some degree of moral progress over pre-existing racial orders. The following group of studies suggests the contrary – accounting institutions represent some of the most impregnable citadels of racial discrimination, bias and privilege.

Racial processes in the accounting profession

Appearing on the heels of a string of studies focusing on the exclusion of white women from the practice of accountancy, Hammond and Streeter (1994) broke new ground by extending the enquiry of those excluded from the profession to include racial groups. In presenting the oral histories of some of the first African Americans licensed as Certified Public Accountants (CPAs), Hammond and Streeter represented the first attempt to incorporate the theme of race into accounting history's research agenda. With opening lines revealing that in 1965 African Americans constituted 12 per cent of the American population yet only represented 0.1 per cent of the CPA population (then determined to be 100,000), Hammond and Streeter declared their purpose – to give visibility to a group whose history had until then, not only been silenced and ignored but also seriously distorted. The group referred to was the minuscule number of African Americans who had succeeded in achieving their professional qualifications prior to the passage of the Civil Rights Act, 1964 – the US law which outlawed racial discrimination in employment.

Based on a series of interviews with the surviving members of this group, Hammond and Streeter reveal the extraordinary measures taken by early pioneers to obtain their CPA status.[4] In various ways they succeeded in subverting a system deliberately designed to exclude African Americans from the opportunity to practise as accountants. Many state CPA societies debarred 'Negroes' from sitting the exam. Most required a prospective CPA to serve a period of apprenticeship with a licensed practitioner. And others like Texas restricted memberships 'to whites only'. All of the personal histories illustrate an admixture of unusual circumstances, extreme hardship and dogged persistence. Yet these were the histories of those who triumphed over harsh conditions and monumental obstacles 'despite the benefit of family wealth, academic excellence, light skin color, and mobility' (Hammond and Streeter 1994: 285). Hammond and Streeter speculate that others – the many who aspired to, but did not become CPAs – faced even more daunting obstacles.

Hammond and Streeter's work represents a powerful counterbalance to the many hagiographic accounts that celebrate the US profession as a historically positive force in a society deeply structured by race. But the setting of their paper is the pre–civil rights era – a time in which the US legal and institutional environment was still structured so as to exclude the African American from participating in wider American society, a period when white America and indeed the white world had still not arrived at the state of human enlightenment in which non-White others were seen to be equals. And so it could be argued that the obstacles constructed by the US accountancy profession and revealed by Hammond and Streeter were in fact a reflection of a wider state of ignorance and not of accountancy's inherent biases *per se*. Later studies (Hammond 1997; Annisette 2003; Kim 2004a, 2004b) would completely demolish this argument.

Hammond (1997) examines the profession's commitment to equal opportunity employment in the post–civil rights era. The study's focal period is 1965 (the year in which the Civil Rights Act, 1964 became effective) to 1988 (the year in which the administration of President Ronald Regan came to a close) and tests Elderman's thesis on the institutionalisation of organisational responses to public expectations. Hammond's insightful analysis shows that during the 1970s public accounting firms responded emphatically to changes in the legal environment, progressing from a policy of complete exclusion of African Americans in the profession to making some visible efforts to recruit from this population. But she also shows how these efforts had waned dramatically by the 1980s. The American Institute of Certified Public Accountants de-emphasised many of the programs it had adopted in the 1970s, recruitment and retention of African Americans (which had peaked in the 1970s) showed significant declines, and there was a drastic decline in the articles discussing African Americans in the accounting industry's publications. Contrary to Edelman's predictions, Hammond (1997) thus concludes that the developments introduced by the profession in the 1970s did not proliferate or persist. Indeed, they appeared to be only token gestures aimed at giving the impression of change. Thus even though African American membership had climbed during the 1970s, by 1990, African Americans still only represented less than 1 per cent of the CPAs in the country – a statistic that has remained relatively unchanged to date (Annisette *et al.* 2006).

In contrast to Hammond's work which illustrates minority exclusion and under-representation in the profession, Annisette (2003) reveals majority exclusion and under-representation in the accountancy profession of Trinidad and Tobago (T&T) – a country in which the populations of African and East Indian descent represent 80 per cent of the total, yet only 33 per cent of partners of elite accounting practices represent these two groups (Annisette 2003: 640). The paper covers a 30-year trajectory of the development of the accountancy profession and culminates with the case of the ejection of the MSc accounting credential from the Institute of Chartered Accountants of Trinidad and Tobago (ICATT) during the 1980s. For Annisette, it is the enduring legacy of racialism in the development of the profession which explains how race became enrolled in debates about accounting training.

According to Annisette, during T&T's colonial period, accountancy was associated with 'Britishness' and 'whiteness' (Annisette 2003: 651), reflecting a common-sense understanding in the country that linked race and ethnicity to different forms of work. By the 1950s, only six of the country's 26 professionally qualified accountants were locals and none of these represented the country's two major population groups. The remaining 20 were British expatriates. Annisette demonstrates that exclusion from the profession was only *one* aspect of racialisation processes in accountancy. Others included the racialisation of accountancy credentials and the racialisation of accounting worksites. She argues that the tight coupling of race, worksite and accountancy credentials served to reinforce and widen existing status gaps between the dichotomous groups in the T&T profession, thus rendering race a powerful marker for status differentials within the practice of accountancy (ibid.: 654). When the ICATT – an institution dominated by British expatriate accountants – failed to admit into its membership holders of the MSc accounting credential (a credential exclusively held by Afro and Indo Trinidadians) – this was seen as a racially motivated act. Annisette contrasts the ICATT's rejection of the MSc Accounting with its recognition of the Canadian-based Certified Management Accounting credential and concludes that the contrasting fates of these two credentials in the ICATT might not have been the outcome of racial processes. She, however, argues that because race so strongly coincides with credentials, worksite and professional status, in the organisation of accountancy in T&T, the perceived role of race in the occupational dynamics of the profession is over-signified, leading to the enlistment of race in what otherwise might be a technical issue.

Kim's (2004a, 2004b) studies of the experiences of Chinese accountants in the New Zealand profession attempts to broaden a literature that is overly focused on a Black/White dichotomy. According to Kim, the Chinese represent a unique racialised group in that they are often culturally different from both the indigenous population and members of the dominant group, thus forming 'a middle-man' class (Kim 2004a: 98, 126). In the case of New Zealand, the Chinese were introduced to satisfy labour shortages in a society already structured on racial/ethnic lines. They thus suffered racial discrimination and hostility from both the dominant white population as well as the indigenous population. Based on interviews with 17 Chinese accountants in Auckland, Kim argues that whereas the accountancy profession seems to have been less exclusionary towards the Chinese than any other profession in New Zealand, the lack of upward mobility within professional practices has created a situation where Chinese are 'clustered at the bottom of the hierarchy in the profession' (ibid.: 111, 120). Although she does briefly mention some structural factors, Kim largely attributes the strong presence of Chinese in accountancy to cultural factors. In particular, 'Chinese culture places great emphasis on education' (ibid.: 107) and, even more controversially, inherent attributes of 'Asian ethnicity that tend to have a logical mindset' (ibid.: 107). Kim notes, however, that Chinese accountants in New Zealand experience the corporate glass ceiling and provides cultural explanations for this: 'quietness, prudence, humility, humbleness, or modesty' (ibid.: 116). According to Kim, Chinese accept the glass ceiling as a fact of life 'Having been brought up to be submissive and servile to their superior white counterparts, they have learned to accept their second-class citizen status within society rather that challenging it' (ibid.: 115). A similar theme of successful entry to the profession followed by vertical stagnation is articulated in Kim (2004b). This study is based on in-depth interviews with five Chinese Auckland-based female accountants and analyses the intersection of race and gender in the profession. Relying less on essentialist and cultural explanations in this case, Kim's overall conclusion is that the Chinese have been constructed as different in New Zealand society and that the 'politics of difference' (ibid.: 95–6) has been successfully used to keep them in their place.

While the above research focuses specifically on the enactment of racial phenomena in accountancy, other historical studies of the profession in Kenya (Sian 2006), Malaysia (Susela 1999) and Jamaica (Bakre 2005, 2006) point to a not insignificant racial dimension in the profession's development in those sites. These studies are located in countries shaped by the legacy of British colonialism and racial exploitation of labour. As in the case of T&T, the combination of colonialism and sugar often produced racially stratified societies in which the racialised groups 'mixed but did not combine' (Furnivall 1968). Having attained independence, post-colonial states usually took an active role in refashioning the nature of racial interaction. Many such states adopted strategies aimed at protecting or promoting certain groups who were perceived to have suffered prior economic, social and political disadvantage. But as Cornell and Hartmann (1998: 156–58) point out, regardless of the intent, these strategies often serve to heighten racial tension. Such has been the case in Fiji – a country deeply divided by race and one where accounting has often been enrolled in racial projects. The following section discusses studies that have focused on this phenomenon.

Studies of accounting in societies deeply structured by race

The legacy of colonialism and sugar has produced in Fiji a racial mosaic comprising native peoples (Fijians and Rotumans, collectively described in the studies below as Ethnic or indigenous Fijians), Indo-Fijians (descendants of East Indian indentured labourers) and a host of racial others, including Chinese, Pacific Islanders and Europeans. Currently Ethnic Fijians constitute 50 per cent of the islands' population and Indo-Fijians represent 43 per cent. The focus of historical accounting research on this site concerns the use of accounting in affirmative action programmes that privilege Ethnic Fijians over Indo-Fijians.

For Nandan and Alam (2005) and Davie (2005), the notion that Ethnic Fijians – the group in whose interest affirmative action initiatives is directed – represent an economically disadvantaged group is contestable. However, indigenous privileging and protectionism govern almost every aspect of life in Fiji. For instance, it is evident in a constitutionally enshrined land tenure system that ensures that most of the county's land is owned by Ethnic Fijians. It is also evident in a series of affirmative action programmes.

Race is therefore embroiled in almost every aspect of Fijian life, and in many instances accounting is called upon to adjudicate the racial contests that often arise. Nandan and Alam assert that the accounting calculus used for determining rental income in the land tenure system 'is firmly implicated and intertwined in the process of wealth accumulation to promote the interests of the Fijian chiefly class' (2005: 19). In the Special Loans Division of the Fiji Development Bank, management accounting decision-making criteria were tweaked so as to provide a lower threshold of eligibility for Ethnic Fijian borrowers. And at the Ministry of Agriculture, accounting procedures were installed to provide an aura of order and propriety over the inappropriate granting of loans to and spending of money on Ethnic Fijians (Nandan and Alam 2005).

Davie (2005: 557) labels these exclusionary practices as *development racism* – racist exclusion ostensibly for developmental purposes – and in her study of the restructuring of Fiji's pine industry identified three roles played by accounting in facilitating the development racism project. First, accounting expertise masked the political nature of indigenous privilege, giving it a semblance of neutrality. Second, accounting provided the means of acquiring a new knowledge base to facilitate discriminatory, indigenous development. Finally, accounting initiated a new way of expressing ethnic difference.

These studies make an important contribution to extant accounting history research on race and ethnicity in that they depart from the common Black/White dichotomy which so overwhelms much of US research. In so doing, they affirm that there is a variety of ways in which racial politics are played out and suggest a need to broaden the scope of accounting history to incorporate this variety. In addition, these studies attempt to link historical processes of racialisation to contemporary racial and ethnic phenomena. Importantly this research also serves to highlight the role of exclusionary practices in mobilising action which in turn ignites racial projects or reinforces racial boundaries. Unfortunately, these studies presume a certain pre-givenness of race or ethnicity and so fail to probe more comprehensively accounting's role in the processes in which racial and ethnic identities are reproduced and transformed. For instance, the lumping together of Fijians and Rotumans under the banner of 'Fijians' masks the constructed as well as the contested nature of 'Fijian' as ethnos.[5] What is lost therefore is the important role of these exclusionary practices (of which accounting is part) in (re)defining and (re)constituting the 'us' from the 'them'. That is, the function of rules of exclusion in constructing and solidifying the identity 'Indo-Fijian', and equally, the function of rules of inclusion in constructing and solidifying the boundary of who is 'Fijian'.

Conclusion

Accounting historians have examined the accounting–race interface from the standpoint of accounting's involvement in racial practices defined as discriminatory, exploitative and genocidal. Not only has 'accounting as technique' been interrogated but, as Table 21.1 illustrates, accounting historians have also examined the role of accountants and their elite institutions in the enactment of these practices. These studies have added to the growing stock of literature aimed at exposing the myth of accounting as a passive, neutral and unbiased reflector of economic reality. The studies have also served to widen the arena of iniquitous, even nefarious, social practices in which accounting's partisanship has been observed.

This body of research, however, at best can only be described as an initial first step, albeit a promising one, to exploring the interaction between accounting and race. For, given the narrowness of our research focus so far, we are yet to probe accounting's involvement in some of the more critical questions posed by scholars interested in racial and ethnic phenomena. In other words, while there is a continued need to expose accounting's sponsorship of racially discriminatory exploitative and genocidal activities, to conceive of accounting's involvement in race exclusively in these terms is to limit our research impact in a number of ways. Below I discuss three shifts from our current focus which might serve to expand research on accounting and race in promising ways.

Table 21.1 Central focus of historical papers on accounting and race

Aspect of accounting examined	Accounting and racial practices of:		
	Discrimination	Exploitation	Genocide
Accounting techniques	Nandan and Alam (2005) Davie (2005)	Fleischman and Tyson (2000, 2004) Fleischman, Oldroyd and Tyson (2004) Tyson, Oldroyd and Fleishman (2005)	Funnell (1998) Lippman and Wilson (2007)
Accountants and accounting institutions	Hammond and Streeter (1994) Hammond (1997, 2002) Annisette (2003) Kim (2004a, 2004b)		Walker (2000, 2003)

Shifting from fixed to fluid identities

There is a tendency in extant research in accounting history to treat identities as fixed. This largely reflects the fact that politics is usually conducted as *if* identity were fixed and people themselves present their identities *as* fixed (Dirks *et al.* 1994; Hall 1995: 66). But identities are fluid and are continuously being (re)fashioned. By disregarding this critical aspect of identity we fail to explore the manner in which accounting is implicated in the social processes through which racial and ethnic identities are reproduced and transformed. In exploring this issue, an obvious site for investigation is that of the state. In what she calls 'the political construction of ethnicity', Nagel (1986: 97–8) recognises the state's centrality to complex processes of racial formation. We have already seen the multifarious ways in which the totalitarian state has utilised accounting to operationalise, mask and sanitise discriminatory or genocidal acts (Funnell 1998; Davie 2005; Nandan and Alam 2005). Thus, by situating accounting within the context of the racial state (Omi and Winant 1994), we can observe far wider impacts of accounting on identity, including its role in creating, reinforcing or altering racial or ethnic identities. Moreover, the political arena is but one 'construction site'. Cornell and Hartmann (1998: Chap. 6) point to others: labour markets, residential spaces, social institutions and culture. These remain potentially fruitful arenas in which accounting's involvement in race and ethnic identity construction might be explored.

Shifting spatially and temporally

The tendency to see race and ethnicity as fixed also obscures from our vision the idea that these identities are variable, diverse and contingent. This in turn understates the perceived need for spatial and temporal variety in our research. Such variety is critical for a number of reasons. First, spatial variety will serve to dislodge 'US folk concepts' (Waquant 1997: 223) of racial categories such as 'blackness' and 'whiteness' which so dominate the literature.[6] Spatial variety will widen the situations in which accounting is being investigated beyond the common Black/White or non-White/White binary dichotomy. Many recent episodes of racial and ethnic conflict manifest themselves along other lines. Fiji, as demonstrated by Nandan and Alam

(2005) and Davie (2005), is a case in point, and there are a host of other situations of racial and ethnic conflict that move us away from the Black/White bimodal perspective. These include, for example, British Guyana (African versus East Indian); Malaysia (Malay versus Chinese) and Sri Lanka (Sinhalese versus Tamil). This is not to render the binary Black/White, non-White/White bifurcation irrelevant, but it is to assert that to overwhelmingly focus our efforts on this singular bi-racial order is to limit the potential to arrive at a more globally informed understanding of race and ethnic issues as they relate to accounting.

Furthermore, temporal variety in our historical research is called for in order to emphasise the continuing project of race/ethnic identity making. For instance, Bonilla-Silva's 'Latin Americanization thesis' (Bonilla-Silva 2002) is suggestive of an emerging tri-racial order in the USA and implies that the twentieth century also holds some promise for investigating the role of accounting in racial projects in the making.

Shifting from discrimination to privilege

The final shift that would enhance research opportunities in race and accountancy research is a move away from the narrow focus on discrimination. Whiteness studies – a field which came into its own in the 1990s – recognises that a literature overly focused on discrimination and disadvantage masks the privileging that is created by systems of power (Wildman 2005). Research in this area, by rendering visible 'whiteness' as a position of power exposes its associated materiality rewards and privilege (Frankenberg 1993; Lipsitz 2005; Wildman 2005). The call for a shift away from an exclusive focus on discrimination to one that includes privilege is, therefore, a call which recognises that race is not something that only non-Whites possess, but is a characteristic of Whites as well, necessitating close scrutiny of Whites' race and racial identity (Arnesen 2001).

Accordingly, for research in the area, whiteness needs to be made 'strange', for as long as white people are not racially seen and named, they function as a human norm (Frankenberg 1993; Dyer 2005). Whiteness studies also aims at achieving hybridity. Dyer (2005: 10) asserts that 'the racing of Whites will serve to dislodge them/us from the position of power by undercutting the authority with which they/we speak and act in, and on, the world'. Scholarship on whiteness and the professions is now an emerging field which offers some promise for historians of accountancy. Pearce (2005), for instance, has studied the meaning of whiteness in the US legal profession but this is not a piece of historical research. Walker (2005), on the other hand, is an historical study which explores the meanings of whiteness and the opportunities this accorded White women in the South African medical profession during the period 1950–90.

Although whiteness studies have been subject to critique (see, for example, Arnesen 2001; Fields 2001; Kolchin 2002), there is a general acceptance that this work has helped to 'denaturalise' race, encouraged closer scrutiny of white identity, as well as render visible whiteness's unmarked unnamed status in a number of fields including law, geography, education and film studies (Frankenberg 1993; Dyer 1997; Barrett 2001). Its incorporation into studies of accountancy and accounting history is therefore eagerly awaited!

Key works

Annisette (2003) presents a useful theoretical exposition on race and ethnicity and provides new insights to the various ways in which racial processes can unfold in professional accountancy.

465

Funnell (1998) is a classic paper which exposes accounting's ability to mask people's humanity and individuality. It provides a seminal explanation of how accounting technique can facilitate abhorrent practices involving human populations.

Hammond (2002) is an extensive study of racial discrimination in the US accountancy profession. The book is exceptional for the rich insights it offers to the challenges faced by African American CPAs during the period 1921–99.

Walker (2003) is a study which exposes the central role played by some of Edinburgh's most celebrated accountants in the lesser-known 'ethnic cleansing' of Celtic communities in the Scottish Highlands during the mid-nineteenth century.

Notes

1   In identifying the studies I conducted a title and abstract search of the following words *race, racism, racial, racialisation, ethnic, ethnicity, genocide, Holocaust, slave, slavery, Nazi* and *Nazism* in all accounting journals dedicated to historical research: *Accounting, Organizations and Society; Accounting History; Accounting Historian's Journal; Abacus; Accounting, Auditing & Accountability Journal; Accounting Business & Financial History*; and *Critical Perspectives on Accounting*. From the articles identified, I then eliminated those which dealt with indigenous people (the subject of Chapter 22) as well as those which were not historical studies of race or ethnicity.
2   Indeed, in none of the studies cited is there any explicit mention of terms such as race, racism or racial exploitation.
3   This claim was later challenged by Burrows (2002) who argued that the absence of individual productivity records was not reflective of racism but was an industry characteristic with a transaction cost explanation – i.e. the nature of sugar cane production rendered individual productivity records impractical. Cane cutting was invariably organised on the 'butty gang' or 'collective-piece-rate-payment system' in which individual members of a work team shared the collective proceeds equally (ibid.: 106).
4   Hammond later renders a more expansive account of the history of African-Americans in the US profession in her book *A White-Collar Profession* (2002).
5   Rotuman culture more closely resembles that of the Polynesian islands. Because of their Polynesian appearance and distinctive language, Rotumans now constitute a recognisable minority group within the Republic of Fiji. For electoral purposes Rotumans were formerly classified as Fijians, but when the constitution was revised in 1997–98, they were granted separate representation at their own request.
6   An extreme example of international variability on the construction and meaning of these terms is reported in Kolchin (2002: 158) where the US rule that 'anyone with black blood is considered black', is contrasted with the Haitian rule that 'anyone with white blood is considered white', the latter leading Haitian dictator Papa Doc Duvalier to assert that the Haitian population is 98 per cent white.

References

Annisette, M. (2003) The colour of accountancy: examining the salience of race in a professionalisation project, *Accounting, Organizations and Society*, 28 (7/8): 639–74.

Annisette, M., Ross, F., Wells, J. and Wood, L. (2006) The professional experiences of African-American accountants, working paper.

Arnesen, E. (2001) Whiteness and the historians' imagination, *International Labor and Working-Class History*, 60 (Fall): 3–32.

Bailey, S. R. and Telles, E. E. (2006) Multiracial versus collective black categories: examining census classification debates in Brazil, *Ethnicities*, 6 (1): 74–101.

Bakre, O. (2005) The first attempt at localizing imperial accountancy: the case of the Institute of

Chartered Accountants of Jamaica (ICAJ) (1950s–1970s), *Critical Perspectives on Accounting*, 16 (8): 995–1018.

Bakre, O. (2006) The second attempt at localizing imperial accountancy: the case of the Institute of Chartered Accountants of Jamaica (ICAJ) (1970s–1980s), *Critical Perspectives on Accounting*, 17 (1): 1–28.

Banton, M. (2001) Progress in ethnic and racial studies, *Ethnic and Racial Studies*, 24 (2): 173–94.

Barney, D. and Flesher, D. (1994) Early nineteenth-century productivity accounting: the Locust Grove Plantation slave ledger, *Accounting, Business & Financial History*, 4 (2): 275–94.

Barot, R. and Bird, J. (2001) Racialization: the genealogy and critique of a concept, *Ethnic and Racial Studies*, 24 (4): 601–18.

Barrett, J. (2001) Whiteness studies: anything here for the historians of the working class?, *International Labor and Working-Class History*, 60 (Fall): 33–42.

Bashi, V. (1998) Racial categories matter because racial hierarchies matter: a commentary, *Ethnic and Racial Studies*, 21 (5): 959–68.

Bonilla-Silva, E. (2002) We are all Americans!: the Latin Americanization of racial stratification in the USA, *Race and Society*, 5 (1): 3–16.

Bulmer, M. and Solomos, J. (1998) Introduction: re-thinking ethnic and racial studies, *Ethnic and Racial Studies*, 21 (5): 820–37.

Burrows, G. (2002) The interface of race and accounting: a comment and an extension, *Accounting History*, 7 (1): 101–10.

Carmona, S., Ezzamel, M. and Gutierréz, F. (2004) Accounting history research: traditional and new accounting history perspectives, *De Computis: Revista Española de Historia de la Contabilidad*, 1: 24–53.

Carnegie, G. and Napier, C. J. (1996) Critical and interpretive histories: insights into accounting's present and future though its past, *Accounting, Auditing & Accountability Journal*, 9 (3): 7–39.

Cornell, S. and Hartmann, D. (1998) *Ethnicity and Race: Making Identities in a Changing World* (California: Pine Forge Press).

Cowton, C. and O'Shaughnessy, A. (1991) Absentee control of sugar plantations in the British West Indies, *Accounting and Business Research*, 22 (85): 33–45.

Dalton, H. (2005) Failing to see, in P. S. Rothenberg (ed.) *White Privilege: Essential Readings on the Other Side of Racism*, pp. 15–18 (New York: Worth Publishers).

Davie, S. S. K. (2005) The politics of accounting, race and ethnicity: a story of a chiefly-based preferencing, *Critical Perspectives on Accounting*, 16 (5): 551–77.

Davis, J. (1991) *Who is Black? One Nation's Definition* (University Park PA: Penn State University Press).

Dirks, N., Geoff, E. and Sherry, O. (eds) (1994) *Culture/Power/History: A Reader in Contemporary Social Theory* (Princeton, NJ: Princeton University Press).

Donoso-Anes, R. (2002) Accounting and slavery: the accounts of the South Sea Company 1713–1722, *European Accounting Review*, 11 (2): 441–52.

Dyer, R. (1997) *White* (New York: New York University Press).

Dyer, R. (2005) The matter of whiteness, in P. S. Rothenberg (ed.) *White Privilege: Essential Readings on the Other Side of Racism*, pp. 9–14 (New York: Worth Publishers).

Fields, B. J. (2001) Whiteness, racism and identity, *International Labor and Working-Class History*, 60 (Fall): 48–56.

Fleischman, R. K. (2004) Confronting moral issues from accounting's dark side, *Accounting History*, 9 (1): 7–23.

Fleischman, R. K. and Tyson, T. N. (2000) The interface of race and accounting: the case of Hawaiian sugar plantations, 1835–1920, *Accounting History*, 5 (1): 7–32.

Fleischman, R. K. and Tyson, T. N. (2002) The interface of race and accounting: a reply to Burrows, *Accounting History*, 7 (1): 115–21.

Fleischman, R. K. and Tyson, T. N. (2004) Accounting in service to racism: monetizing slave property in the antebellum South, *Critical Perspectives on Accounting* 15 (3): 376–99.

Fleischman, R. K., Oldroyd, D. and Tyson, T. N. (2004) Monetizing human life: slave valuations on US and British West Indian plantations, *Accounting History*, 9 (2): 35–62.

Flesher, D. and Flesher, T. (1981) Human resource accounting in Mississippi before 1865, *Journal of Accounting and Business Research*, 10 (Supplement): 124–9.

Frankenberg, R. (1993) *The Social Construction of Whiteness: White Women Race Matters* (Minneapolis: University of Minnesota Press).

Funnell, W. (1998) Accounting in the service of the Holocaust, *Critical Perspectives on Accounting*, 9 (4): 435–64.

Furnivall, J. S. (1968) *Colonial Policy and Practice* (Cambridge: Cambridge University Press).

Hall, S. (1995) Fantasy, identity, politics, in E. Carter, J. Donald and J. Squires (eds) *Cultural Remix: Theories of Politics and the Popular* (London: Lawrence and Wishart).

Hammond, T. (1997) From complete exclusion to minimal inclusion: African Americans and the public accounting industry 1965–1988, *Accounting, Organizations and Society*, 22 (1): 29–53.

Hammond, T. (2002) *A White-Collar Profession: African-American Certified Public Accountants since 1921* (Chapel Hill, NC: University of North Carolina Press).

Hammond, T. and Streeter, D. (1994) Overcoming the barriers: early African-American Certified Public Accountants, *Accounting, Organizations and Society*, 19 (3): 271–88.

Heier, J. (1988) A content comparison of antebellum plantation records and Thomas Affleck's accounting principles, *Accounting Historians Journal*, 15 (2): 131–50.

Hirschman, C. (1986) The making of race in colonial Malaysia, *Sociological Forum*, 1 (2): 330–61.

James, A. (2001) Making sense of race and racial classification, *Race and Society*, 4 (2): 35–47.

Kibria, N. (1998) The contested meanings of 'Asian American': racial dilemmas in the contemporary US, *Ethnic and Racial Studies*, 21 (5): 939–58.

Kim, S. N. (2004a) Imperialism without empire: silence in contemporary accounting research on race/ethnicity, *Critical Perspectives on Accounting*, 15 (1): 95–133.

Kim, S. N. (2004b) Racialized gendering of the accountancy profession: towards an understanding of Chinese women's experiences in accountancy in New Zealand, *Critical Perspectives on Accounting*, 15 (3): 400–27.

Kolchin, P. (2002) Whiteness studies: the new history of race in America, *The Journal of American History*, 89 (10): 154–73.

Lippmann, E. and Wilson, P. (2007) The culpability of accounting in perpetuating the Holocaust, *Accounting History*, 12 (3): 283–303.

Lipsitz, G. (2005) The positive investment in whiteness, in P.S. Rothenberg (ed.) *White Privilege: Essential Readings on the Other Side of Racism*, pp. 67–85 (New York: Worth Publishers).

Miller, P., Hopper, T. and Laughlin, R. (1991) The new accounting history: an introduction, *Accounting, Organizations and Society*, 16 (5/6): 395–403.

Nagel, J. (1986) The political construction of ethnicity in S. Olzak and J. Nagel (eds) *Competitive Ethnic Relations*, pp. 93–112 (New York: Academic Press).

Nagel, J. (1994) Constructing ethnicity: creating and recreating ethnic identity and culture, *Social Problems*, 41 (1): 152–76.

Nandan, R. K. and Alam, M. (2005) Accounting and the reproduction of race relations in Fiji: a discourse on race and accounting in colonial context, *Accounting, Business and the Public Interest*, 4 (1): 1–34.

Napier, C. J. (2006). Accounts of change: 30 years of historical accounting research, *Accounting, Organizations and Society*, 31 (4/5): 445–507.

Omi, M. and Winant, H. (1994) *Racial Formation in the United States: From 1960s to the 1980s* (New York: Routledge).

Pearse, R. G. (2005) White lawyering: rethinking race, lawyer identity and rule of law, *Fordham Law Review*, 73 (5): 2081–100.

Razek, J. (1985) Accounting on the old plantation, *Accounting Historians Journal*, 12 (1): 19–36.

Sian, S. (2006) Inclusion, exclusion and control: the case of the Kenyan accounting professionalisation project, *Accounting, Organizations and Society*, 31 (3): 295–322.

Stein, J. (2001) Whiteness and United States history: an assessment, *International Labor and Working-Class History*, 60 (Fall): 1–2.

Susela, S. D. (1999) 'Interests' and accounting standard setting in Malaysia, *Accounting, Auditing & Accountability Journal*, 12 (3): 358–87.

Tyson, T. N., Oldroyd, D. and Fleischman, R. (2005) Accounting, coercion and social control during apprenticeship: converting slave workers to wage workers in the British West Indies, c.1834–1838, *Accounting Historians Journal*, 32 (2): 201–31.

Vollmers, G. (2003) Industrial slavery in the United States: the North Carolina turpentine industry 1849–61, *Accounting, Business & Financial History*, 13 (3): 369–92.

Wacquant, L. (1997) Towards an analytic of racial domination, *Political Power and Social Theory*, 11: 221–234.

Walker, L. (2005) The colour white: racial and gendered closure in the South African medical profession, *Ethnic and Racial Studies*, 28 (2): 348–75.

Walker, S. P. (2000) Encounters with Nazism: British accountants and the fifth international congress on accounting, *Critical Perspectives on Accounting*, 11 (2): 215–45.

Walker, S. P. (2003) Agents of dispossession and acculturation. Edinburgh accountants and the Highland clearances, *Critical Perspectives on Accounting* 14 (8): 813–53.

Wildman, S. (2005) Making systems of privilege visible, in P. S. Rothenberg (ed.) *White Privilege: Essential Readings on the Other Side of Racism*, pp. 95–101 (New York: Worth Publishers).

22

Indigenous peoples and colonialism

Susan Greer and Dean Neu

Overview

Research has highlighted the positioning of accounting within processes of colonialism and imperialism, suggesting that accounting discourses and technologies have been used to influence and control indigenous peoples. This chapter provides a critical review of this research and proposes several future research directions. The chapter begins with a brief discussion of the linkages between accounting and colonialism. It then examines four geographic locations – Fiji, the United States, Canada and Australia – where accounting has been used by colonial rulers to 'manage' local populations. The examination of the individual sites highlights both commonalities as well as differences in the role and functioning of accounting. For example, the analyses illustrate how the language of accounting resonates with and sustains more general discourses about the inferiority of indigenous peoples. The analyses also make visible how accounting techniques allowed colonial rulers to put into practice specific programmes that attempted to control and govern the activities of indigenous peoples. In this way, the studies show how accounting was a central linchpin not only in thinking about indigenous peoples in certain ways (as inferior, etc.) but also in translating into practice programmes of government that sought to 'civilise' these populations. The chapter concludes by proposing that additional research – that both compares different settings and explicitly considers the role of accounting experts – is needed. Such research will help us to better understand the positioning of accounting in colonial processes and to contribute to current policy debates about government–indigenous relations.

Introduction

The role of accounting technologies in the mediation of relations between states and indigenous minorities is an emerging and important area of accounting history research. In recent years authors have examined the roles of accounting and the accounting profession in the processes of exclusion, alienation and genocide of indigenous peoples[1] (see, for example, Neu 1999, 2000a, 2000b; Davie 2000, 2005a, 2005b; Gibson 2000; Neu and Therrien 2003; Annisette and

Neu 2004; Neu and Graham 2004, 2006; Greer 2006). A significant area of interest for these studies has been the role of accounting in the mediation of relations between colonial governments and indigenous peoples in the furtherance of 'the late 19th century British imperialist project' (Annisette and Neu 2004: 1).[2] This research not only documents the centrality of accounting language and technologies in the discourses of empire and colonialism, but also explicates the role of accounting in the construction and application of an ideological vision of indigenous inferiority, which colonial states used to justify hegemonic practices (Davie 2000, 2005a; Neu 2000a; Greer 2006).

The major themes, issues and debates in the accounting literature devoted to colonialism and indigenous peoples are reviewed in this chapter. The discussion simultaneously demonstrates a breadth and dearth of studies. In the interest of helping to address the lack of research, and encouraging further studies into the roles of accounting and accountants in colonial practices of administration over indigenous peoples, the chapter concludes with a discussion of potential directions for future research.

Accounting and colonialism

According to Said (1994: 8), colonialism is 'the implanting of settlements on a distant territory'. Further, these settlements usually result from imperialism, which Said describes as the 'practice, the theory, and the attitudes of a dominating metropolitan centre ruling a distant territory'. The settlement of distant territories, however, requires imperial powers to first deal with the indigenous occupants of the sought-after territories. This need to 'render the distant territory and its indigenous inhabitants "controllable" ' (Neu 2000a: 165) was common to every site of colonial settlement and, while colonialists deployed different strategies to achieve these outcomes, underpinning each colonial relationship with indigenous peoples was a 'clear-cut and absolute hierarchical distinction between ruler and ruled' (Said 1994: 82).

Each historical manifestation of colonialism contained three key aspects: the settlement of indigenous lands from a distant territory; the exploitation of the resources of those lands; and the subjugation of indigenous 'others', supported by ideological formations of indigenous inferiority (Smith 1990; Said 1994). Of these key aspects, it is important not to underestimate the significance of constructions of indigenous peoples to the ability of colonial authorities to intervene in, control and exploit indigenous territory, and to perpetuate unequal relations of power between the colonisers and the colonised. Said emphasised this aspect of colonialism, writing that imperialism and colonialism are 'supported and even impelled by impressive ideological formations that include notions that certain territories and people *require* and beseech domination as well as forms of knowledge affiliated with domination' (1994: 8, emphasis in original). Further, colonial governments ensured that their authority went virtually unchallenged through the application of racial schemata, which constructed Blacks as 'lesser species' (ibid.: 121). Similarly, Bhabha (1994: 70) acknowledged the importance of these colonial discourses to the ability of the authorities to govern, arguing that the objective of colonial discourse was to 'construe the colonized as a population of degenerate types on the basis of racial origin, in order to justify conquest and to establish systems of administration and instruction'.

The work of Said, Bhabha and others depicts how representations of European superiority and indigenous inferiority sustained relations of domination and control, and how these representations ensured that the authority of colonial governments went virtually unchallenged. Through use and repetition, discourses of indigenous inferiority assumed the status of fact and knowledge upon which governments formulated policies and practices to govern the indigenous peoples. Discourses of indigenous inferiority created the conditions for government administration, which in turn made such discourses seem appropriate and natural. The mutually constitutive nature of discourse and action formed an ideological circle, which reinforced racially discriminatory mechanisms of government (Neu and Graham 2006).

In addition to discourses of difference, the ability of the colonial authorities to know, judge, intervene and control indigenous peoples depended on a myriad technologies, including a variety of accounting techniques, and it is this aspect of the government of indigenous peoples that forms the focus of many accounting studies. These studies show that accounting was constitutive of government discourses, policies and practices dedicated to extending political dominion over indigenous lands. The importance of accounting to the ability of colonial authorities to subdue and transform indigenous peoples is evident in the themes emergent from the literature, which we discuss later in the chapter.

At this point, it is useful to address the limits or boundaries of the chapter. The focus of this chapter on accounting in the colonisation of indigenous peoples naturally precludes the inclusion of the body of research that investigates the roles of accounting and/or the profession within colonial practices in developing or emerging nations (for example, Annisette 1999, 2000; Bush and Maltby 2004; Dyball *et al.* 2006, 2007). Within different colonial contexts such as Trinidad and Tobago, the Philippines and West Africa, these studies seek, either to locate the accounting profession within processes of colonisation or to examine the particular roles of accounting within colonial practices of government. While each of these studies demonstrates the salience of accounting to the processes of colonialism, because they are not concerned with indigenous peoples, they have been excluded.

The focus on indigenous peoples raises another contentious issue regarding the selection criteria for inclusion in the chapter. The United Nations definition of 'indigenous' peoples as 'non-dominant sectors of society'[3] would necessarily preclude the studies into the colonisation of Fiji, not only because native Fijians occupied a dominant sector of society, but also because colonial authorities did not pursue the destruction of Fijian indigenous identity. Indeed, rather than eschew indigenous customs, British colonial authorities incorporated many into the policies and structures of indirect rule, as well as enlisting the cooperation of the native chieftaincy to govern (Kaplan 1989: 42). Nevertheless, this research is considered too important to exclude not only because it provides insights into how specific accounting practices, laws and policies enabled colonial ideological and political domination, but also because it exposes how accounting language and techniques facilitated the integration of these forms of domination into modern contexts.

Including Fiji, research into the role of accounting in the colonisation of indigenous peoples has to date concentrated on four principal sites of colonialism: Australia (Aboriginal people); Canada (First Nations people); Fiji (Fijian people) and the United States of America (Navajo people).[4] The research demonstrates how imperialism and colonialism were fundamental aspects of the modernity of each of these nations, and how accounting and accountability mechanisms were salient to the ability of these regimes to displace indigenous peoples and to appropriate indigenous lands.

Fiji: the Fijian people

The imperialistic activities and policies enacted in Fiji were distinctive. British expansion into Fiji during the late nineteenth century depended on the collaboration and cooperation of the existing hierarchy of chiefs, rather than on traditional colonial practices of subjugation and exclusion of the indigenous population (Davie 2000, 2005a). In a situation unique to Fiji, the British colonial government sought to colonise the indigenous peoples by implementing practices aimed at exploiting the co-operation of the chiefs with colonial administrators. By utilising the calculative mechanisms of accounting to construct financial obligations of particular chiefs, the authorities were able to exploit the existing native social structures to manage and control the indigenous people.[5] As Davie (2000: 335) highlights, this 'chiefly-based structure of control and power permeated virtually every aspect of Indigenous society' resulting in the perpetration of colonial institutional and structural racist practices within state-owned and controlled organisations and in Fijian society generally (Achary 1997).

The research clearly demonstrates the centrality of accounting and accountability processes to the colonial administration of Fiji and how these administrations used accounting explanations to justify their imperialist programmes, and to authorise changes to programmes on the grounds of efficiency and cost minimisation. While accounting enabled the representation of indigenous concepts into forms that had financial significance Davie argues that indigenous Fijians did not acquiesce to these imposed concepts; rather they managed to maintain their social customs, despite the best intentions of the colonial administrators. Rather than displacement from their lands and culture, the collusion of the colonisers and the Fijian chiefs ensured the protection of the indigenous peoples from such alienation (Alam et al. 2004).

The studies into the Fijian context contribute not only to our understanding of colonialism and indigenous peoples, but also to our understanding of the role of accounting in the specific practices, laws and policies by which ideological and political domination are achieved, and how they became integrated into modern contexts. The racial stratification of Fiji by the colonial settlers exploited the existing chief-based system; the laws and policies had a racial focus that not only ensured the co-operation of the indigenous elite, but also became embedded within modern Fijian governance practices. A colonially imposed 'system of socio-racial relations and ownership (has been) re-articulated and sustained in a capitalistic framework' (Davie 2005a: 553). Discourses and practices of accounting have facilitated the translation of 'race-based' mentalities of governance, both colonial and modern into organising principles of a 'society's investment and development policies' (ibid.: 573). These observations were also reported by Alam et al. (2004: 154) who concluded from their investigation of the Fijian Development Bank (FDB) that the 'social, cultural and political dimensions of the Fijian economy that exist to-day, including the FDB's management control systems are products of imperial governance through Indigenous collaboration'.

These studies of Fiji attest to the importance of accounting in the practices of colonial governments. They reveal not only how accounting techniques were inextricably bound up in the practices of colonial governance but also how accounting facilitated the continuation of colonial domination into the modern context. Further, they serve to remind us of the multitude of perspectives possible when investigating historical sites of interest. For example, for us the focus of interest is the role of accounting in the practices of the colonial administrations, whereas for Annisette the locus of interest is the issue of race. In Chapter 21 on race and ethnicity, she identifies how the Fijian studies contribute to our understanding of race in accounting history beyond the Black/White dichotomy common to research in the United States of America.

The United States of America: the Navajo people

This research focuses on the 1930s in what would normally be labelled as post-colonial periods. It has been included in this chapter because the research identifies rationalities of social engineering consistent with the colonial mentalities of government experienced in the colonisations of the indigenous peoples of Canada and Australia. In particular, the research provides insights into how governments translated essentially colonial objectives into practices of modernity (Preston and Oakes 2001; see also Oakes *et al.* 1997 for an analysis of the exclusion of the Lakota people).

Preston and Oakes' (2001) examination of the reports on the Navajo Reservation, instigated by the Bureau of Agricultural Economics in the mid-1930s, demonstrates how the construction of the Navajo as an 'economic problem' enabled the government to seek an economic solution to the poverty and social disadvantage of the Navajo. The authors contend that these documents were in fact 'an elaborate construction' (ibid.: 53), and that financial accounts 'were the key element in the construction of an economic solution' (ibid.: 57). In other words, the intent of the Navajo documents was purely and simply social engineering, to save the 'Indian' (*sic*) from himself, by effecting a change in the Navajo lifestyle. However, the authors observe that this intervention proved disastrous for the Navajo and the effective result of the economisation of their existence was even greater financial disadvantage and increased dependency on government support.

Preston and Oakes' study identifies one of the processes whereby governments constructed and represented indigenous people, together with the key role of accounting records in the processes of construction and representation. It provides a detailed analysis of how scientific methods enabled the manufacture of information for the economic representation of the Navajo, and the consequences of such practices for their lives. While this paper was concerned primarily with how the government constructed and represented the Navajo as an 'economic problem', in a more recent contribution, Preston (2006) analyses how these representations were translated into actions. He argues that these economic and scientific accounts 'became entwined in other strategies' and were employed 'in order to ensure that action at a distance was taken, enacted locally and preserved' (ibid.: 560). Informed by Latour's work, the study demonstrates how accounts, such as the Navajo papers and accounting returned to the centre of government information (and calculations) that rendered the Navajo lands and their occupants governable. Further, the study identifies how the government employed these accounts to justify their actions when decisions had gone wrong.

The studies into the governance of the Navajo identify the role of accounting records in the construction and representation of the native people, and the consequences for the lives of the Navajo. Although the research is concerned with a 'post-colonial' timeframe, it attests to the ongoing nature of colonial practices and accounting. Indeed, in recognition of the complexity of these relationships, Preston and Oakes (2001) call for more studies to explore this area of accounting.

Canada: the First Nations People

To date, the majority of accounting research into the roles of accounting in the colonisation of indigenous peoples has concentrated on the Canadian context. The studies provide an extensive analysis of the role of accounting discourses and practices in the colonisation and subjugation of the First Nations Peoples of Canada (Neu 1999, 2000a, 2000b; Neu and Therrien 2003; Neu and Graham 2004, 2006; Neu and Heincke 2004). These studies are primarily concerned with the historical antecedents of modern government–indigenous relations in Canada, in particular how colonial administrators translated Imperial objectives into practice. They demonstrate the roles performed by accounting techniques in the practices of colonial governments, and as such how accounting and accountability mechanisms facilitated the dispossession, exploitation and control of the indigenous peoples (Neu 2000a). Key among the issues identified by Neu is the roles performed by accounting techniques in the appropriation of indigenous land and in the measurement/representation of the values implicit within these exchanges (Neu 1999; Neu and Theirren 2003).

The research of Neu and his co-authors provides detailed analyses of the roles of accounting within the practices of a particular regime of colonial governance.[6] It demonstrates how accounting technologies facilitated the functioning of the Canadian government to 'shape, normalize, and instrumentalize the conduct, thought, decisions and aspirations' (Miller and Rose 1990: 8) of the First Nations peoples in order to achieve their objectives. This body of research not only positions accounting 'within the processes and practices that permit imperial powers to dominate distant territories and their inhabitants' (Annisette and Neu 2004: 1), but also demonstrates how this form of governmentality continues to inform current government–indigenous relations in Canada.

This research draws on several themes from Foucault and the accounting governmentality literature: government as 'action at a distance'; the discursive character of governmentality; accounting as a 'technology of government'; and the optimistic but failing nature of technologies. The studies also evoke theories from the colonialism, genocide and subaltern literatures to address both the structures and consequences of governance. The authors argue that accounting, as a technology of government served several roles within the bureaucracy of Canada devoted to the management and control of the indigenous peoples. Accounting was central to the framing and guiding of military decisions; the targeting of indigenous peoples as a governable population; and the measurement and fixture of the terms of exchange for land. In addition, accounting was important as a social engineering mechanism for the implementation of colonial policies, and as a discursive field in which the spoils of colonialism were represented, apportioned and rationalised. Further, Neu and Graham (2006) argue that accounting technologies facilitated the infiltration of government policies into the minutiae of Aboriginal lives. In this study, Neu and Graham (ibid.: 74) extend the understanding of agency within the processes of colonial governance to demonstrate how 'the agency of the aboriginal people was diminished by accounting, as disabling departmental programs and procedural requirements for the disposal of their own land circumscribed their agency, and helped engender a dependency on government'. These findings are consistent with those of Greer (2006: 7) who argues, 'systems of accounting and accountability facilitated the construction and maintenance of tropes of Aboriginal financial incapacity that denied Aboriginal agency'.

This research into Canadian government–indigenous relations not only highlights 'accounting's mediative role in defining power relationships' and the pervasiveness of accounting within all levels of colonial governmentality (Neu and Graham 2006) but also exposes the role of accounting in the circumscription of indigenous agency. These observations correspond with those of Greer (2006) in her study of the roles of accounting in Australian government–indigenous relations.

New South Wales: Aboriginal people

Although a number of historical studies have hinted at the integral role of calculative measures in technologies of government in specific Australian fields of Aboriginal governance (Fletcher 1992; Kidd 1994, 2001, 2006; Goodall 1996; Rowse 1998; McGrath 2004), accounting research has largely ignored this area.[7] Greer (2006) attempts to address this lacuna in her PhD into the historical roles of accounting in the governance of Aboriginal people within New South Wales (NSW) for the period 1883–1969.[8] Her analysis of the roles of accounting techniques and calculations in the government of the Aboriginal peoples of NSW lays bare the colonial conditions for the formation of current mentalities and practices of government, and how accounting discourses and technologies were central to the administration of Aboriginal affairs.

Greer's study highlights how accounting and calculative numbers helped inscribe into reality the Aboriginal domain. It is evident from her findings that accounting technologies were critical to the ability of each Board to imagine its programmes and to implement and monitor their performance. Greer argues that:

> the numbers and accounts provided to the Boards through accounting technologies rendered information for auditing the performance of Aboriginal people, the Boards and their agents; managing finances and implementing budget decisions; satisfying the accountability relationship between the Boards and the government; and for imagining, implementing and evaluating programs.
>
> (ibid.: 340)

Greer's research echoes several key themes of colonial and modern administrations identified in the Canadian context. These include the problematisation of Aboriginal people as a site for government; stereotypes of racial and economic inferiority employed in the re-engineering of the fabric of Aboriginal reality; and the participation and co-operation of a network of heterogeneous agents in the functioning of government. Central to both contexts is the essential roles accounting technologies played in the processes of governance. Indeed, Greer argues 'it is impossible to overstate the importance of accounting' in such sites of colonial government. The ability of the authorities to imagine and fulfil their objective for the civilisation of the indigenous people required accounting knowledge and techniques to render indigenous existence thinkable and calculable and as a problem for government.

Greer's study also utilises Foucauldian concepts, in particular, governmentality to analyse the sites of British Empire and its colonial administrations. This analysis of colonial government necessarily raises questions about how the authorities controlled and managed the indigenous population. Greer's analysis lends support to Neu's observations regarding the importance of the stereotyping of the indigenous 'other'. She explicates how the belief in the racial inferiority of the indigenous peoples was fundamental to interrelationships between both the colonial state and the modern state and the Aboriginal peoples, and how accounting techniques and calculations were critical to this process. Accounting facilitated both the translation of racial stereotypes into policies, and the construction and representation of the financial incapacity of Aboriginal peoples.

The preceding sections have classified the histories of accounting and indigenous peoples on a spatial basis but this is not the only meaningful way to organise this literature. It also seems useful to highlight the general themes or concepts inherent in the research.

General themes

Several key themes emerge from the preceding review of the literature. The first of these relates to the role of accounting discourses, and their infusion into wider discursive formations that mediated and rationalised colonial government–indigenous relations.

The role of accounting in colonial discourses

Foucault (1991: 79) identifies the importance of discourses to our ability to understand the practices of government, writing that it is important to review the discourses which constitute subjects and which serve to 'found, justify and provide reasons and principles' for the practices of government. Miller and Rose (1990: 3) also note the importance of discursive frameworks to the practices of government. They comment that it is through a wider discursive field – that includes accounting language and discourses – that governments are able to conceive of and articulate 'the proper ends and means of government'.

The importance of accounting language and the wider discursive formations to the practices of colonial governments is borne out in a number of accounting studies, which document how language and discourses imbued with racial stereotypes inscribed into reality unequal power relations between indigenous peoples and the colonial powers. Discursive regimes constructed seemingly immutable hierarchies of race upon which authorities premised colonial policies and practices. The role of discourses of racial inferiority in the mapping of categories/hierarchies of indigenous difference in Canada and Australia, which underpinned government policies, is evident in the research by Neu and Greer. These studies document how authorities created and recreated racial inferiority through the normalisation of particular views of indigenous (in)capacity, that prioritised the interests of 'the "white" settlers sent to the colonies' (Neu 1999: 167).

These studies also highlight the wider discursive formations at work in colonial contexts. As Neu (1999) notes, the effect of this wider discursive formation of indigenous peoples as 'inferior', 'savages', 'childlike', etc. was a concept of the 'right manner' for governing that constituted indigenous peoples as a particular problem for government, while simultaneously prioritising the interests of the colonisers. Initially, these representations of the inferiority of indigenous peoples encouraged the implementation of policies deemed necessary to 'smooth the dying pillow' of these doomed races. The failure of the indigenous races to die out did not, however, result in more enlightened policies of government. Rather, the presumption of indigenous inferiority continued to dominate government policies, albeit in the guise of civilisation. Still recognising the innate inferiority of indigenous cultures and lifestyles, governments emphasised policies to reclaim indigenous people 'from the uncivilized and degraded condition' in which they existed. Indeed, Greer (2006: 258) observes that the failure of the Aboriginal race to die out invoked 'a rationality of government to shape the Aboriginal population into citizens'. This reshaped the way the authorities thought about 'the Aboriginal problem', and set in place specific practices for the inculcation of norms of social responsibility commensurate with citizenship.

While accounting research is particularly concerned with the centrality of accounting discourses and techniques in the relations between colonisers and indigenous peoples, a significant aspect of this discursive theme is the circularity of colonial discursive frameworks. That is, the research shows that discursive frameworks of colonialism not only provided the conditions of possibility for the introduction of specific practices such as accounting to translate policies into practice and to provide rationalisations for the impact of extant policies, they also provided the justification for further interventions. The notion of 'presents' used to describe payments for land to First Nations peoples provides a clear example of this circularity of discourses and the essential enmeshing of accounting discourse within the logic and practices of colonial systems of government. Neu's (2000a) analysis reveals the changing purposes served by accounting in the distribution of these 'presents', including the measurement of the terms of exchange over land; the practices for achieving these exchanges; and the rationalisation and justification for the values of exchange. Moreover, these exchanges were predicated on a wider discursive formation of indigenous peoples as uncivilised and dependent on the government for support.

Greer (2006: 133) also provides evidence of this circularity in her analysis of government practices. Her research highlights how authorities used accounting language to inscribe into reality wider government constructions of the proper roles of government, such as cost reduction, efficiency, and fiscal responsibility. This study reveals how discourses of budgets and funding directly influenced the kinds of problems and policies that authorities decided could and should be addressed. Moreover, the research identifies how the authorities employed accounting discourses to re-present policy choices, to measure programme outcomes, and where necessary (which was often) to justify program failures (2006: 205).

The preceding discussion identifies two important aspects of accounting research into colonialism and indigenous peoples. The first of these relates to how the social construction of particular indigenous identities as inferior and non-citizens underpinned colonial systems of government. The representation of indigenous peoples as a 'problem'[9] of government was essential to the ability of governments to intervene and control the populations in order to obtain control of indigenous lands. Within this culture of colonialism, accounting discourses and practices helped structure and rationalise the problematisation of the Indigenous peoples, as well as facilitate the expropriation of the 'spoils of colonialism' (Neu 2000a: 182).

Preston and Oakes (2001) provide a significant example of the importance of particular representations of indigenous peoples to government–indigenous relations, and the effect on the life experiences of indigenous peoples, in this case, the Navajo. They comment that, in order to save the Navajo from themselves, a 'rationalized economy had to be constructed in terms of income and consumption and a new economic identity, namely that of consumption unit, had to be forged for the Navajo' (ibid.: 60). The authorities sought an economic solution to the Navajo problem and this necessitated an economic reconstruction of the Navajo. Numbers and accounts offered an economic window on the world of the Navajo, which substituted Anglo-American understandings for Navajo depictions of identity.

A second aspect of this discursive theme captures accounting as both discourse and techniques. While governments used accounting discourse to rationalise policies, accounting techniques and calculations helped to constitute policies as well as translate policies into practice. In effect, policy 'ideas' depended on practices such as accounting to exist and these practices in turn 'shaped the possibilities of policy, and helped construct the decision set of policy makers' (Neu and Graham 2006: 51).

Accounting as a technology of government

At the core of many of the papers in this subject area are conceptions of accounting as technologies of government, consistent with the notion of governmentality developed by Foucault (Neu 1999, 2000a, 2000b; Neu and Graham 2004, 2006; Neu and Heincke 2004; Greer 2006). According to Foucault (1991: 102), government refers to the general and specific 'ensemble of institutions, calculations and tactics' deployed to achieve the proper ends and means of government. This perspective takes as its focus populations, in attempts to ensure that 'the greatest possible quantity of wealth is produced, that the people are provided with sufficient means of subsistence, [and] that the population is enabled to multiply' (ibid.: 95). Yet, as Neu and Graham (2006: 50) comment, for Foucault the focus of government is not simply people, but 'the complex of people – and – things, (such as indigenous customs and habits), a complex that must first be constructed by the technologies with which government represents the objects of governance'.

Miller and Rose (1990) coined the term *technologies of government* to describe the variety of techniques which governments rely on to represent the objects of government and to influence and shape the actions and conduct of subjects. While Rose and Miller (1992: 183) observe that the list of possible mechanisms available to authorities is 'in principle unlimited', figuring prominently on the list of technologies are techniques and practices of accounting that help make government possible: techniques of notation, computation and calculation; procedures of examination and assessment, surveys, tables, and systems for training and the 'inculcation of habits'. The studies document how colonial authorities used these technologies to institute government, deploy programmes, construct indigenous peoples as the object of government and account for the financial consequences of government actions. In other words, the foregrounding of accounting as a technology of government within this framework elucidates the salience of accounting language and techniques to the ability of colonial authorities to imagine policies and to translate them into practice.

This theme of governmentality also highlights the instrumentality of accounting in extending the dominion of colonial governments through a diverse group of agents. Neu (1999), for example, documents the importance of indirect agents such as religious organisations to the ability of governments to function.

Accounting in the mediation of power relationships

The Canadian and Australian studies also exhibit an emerging theme of power. The studies render visible the role of accounting in the mediation of power relationships, in particular, the disabling of indigenous agency. In Foucauldian terms, power is very much about the subjectivity of the citizen, and how relations of power operate to 'invest the citizen with a set of goals and self-understandings' (Cruikshank 1999: 41). Importantly, relationships of power are reproduced not only through institutions but through the practices of government, rendering power a question of government – a question concerned to understand how government attempts to shape human conduct and to structure the possible field of action of others.

Neu and Graham (2006) provide evidence of the functioning of power relations within accounting-based governance processes related to the activities of the Indian agencies. Their examples document how the enlistment and enabling of these agents often had 'the effect of disabling' the agency of the First Nations bands as accounting methods were used to help convert First Nations peoples into economic citizens. Moreover, this 'disabling of agency narrowed the domains in which indigenous peoples could exercise agency, and functioned as an ideological circle (cf. Smith, 1990) that rationalized both the government's paternal attitudes and the need for further government control of Indigenous affairs' (2006: 73). Their analysis also renders visible the salience of accounting technologies to mutually sustaining webs of observation and discipline enlisted to teach the indigenous peoples how to handle money (ibid.: 64).

Greer (2006) also documents a complex array of techniques of disciplinary rule and practices of surveillance upon which the authorities depended, including significant levels of accounting and accountability. Her analysis depicts the important roles performed by accounting in the construction and maintenance of relationships of power, and the interrelationships between accounting as power, knowledge and practices of surveillance. Administrations, both colonial and 'post–colonial' depended on mechanisms of accounting and accountability to maintain surveillance not only over indigenous peoples, but also their field agents, as well as provide essential knowledge which underpinned the exercise of relationships of power.

Directions for future research

Although recent legal cases and government inquiries in the United States of America and Australia (Greer 2006; Kidd 2006; Indian Trust undated; Senate Legal and Constitutional References Committee 2006) clearly signal the importance of accounting to colonial practices of government, especially the stewardship of indigenous monies, there is a lack of accounting research into this area. Not surprisingly, researchers have called for further research, stating that the current literature illustrates a 'need for more thinking about the relationships among different techniques of governance' (Neu and Heinke 2004: 202). In particular, there is a need for studies into 'a single site and a shorter time period' (ibid.: 203) to enable a greater depth of understanding of the inter-relationships between accounting and the government of indigenous peoples.

From our examination of the literature, it is evident that one size does not fit all and that how hegemony, power and issues of political economy mediated and influenced the indigenous local is and has been a function of specific sites (Neu 2001: 326). Indeed, the extant literature is suggestive of the need to continue to explore particular sites of governance. It seems to us that much more work is required to render visible the extent of accounting's role in the domination and marginalisation of indigenous peoples in other territories.

This area of historical research would benefit not only from more studies generally, but also from more studies devoted to an examination of the consequences of the use of accounting technologies and practices at the level of individual participants in the fields of governance. Neu and Graham (2006) address this aspect in their examination of the effects of accounting practices on the agency of the local Indian Agents, as well as the indigenous peoples. Their analysis provides evidence of how technologies of government changed relations not only between the government and the indigenous peoples, but also between indigenous peoples and settler society, as well as among the indigenous peoples (ibid.: 73). The importance of this type of research lies not only in the understanding it brings to the history of accounting interventions, but also in the 'vantage point' it offers for examining the state of modern government–indigenous peoples relations, and how the consequences of changes instituted by colonial authorities 'continue to structure present-day relations' (ibid.). Greer's (2006) analysis, for example, offers insights into how accounting discourses and technologies assumed their position of centrality in modern administrations of Aboriginal affairs. Moreover, she shows how current strategies of government mirror the mentalities and practices of colonial authorities who sought to micro manage the minutiae of Aboriginal lives.

Given Greer's observations regarding the persistence of colonial practices and mentalities of government, future research which seeks to understand the ongoing structures of domination and subordination experienced by indigenous peoples may benefit from engaging with the theories of 'internal colonialism' and 'welfare colonialism'. These theories may help us better understand how colonialism continues to structure the relationship between governments and indigenous peoples.

What is also notable from our review of the literature is the number of consistencies in the role of accounting documented across time and space. For example, many of Greer's observations about the NSW context mirror those made about the Canadian context. Surprisingly, in two disparate settings we observe many commonalities in the mentalities and practices of colonial government. The documentation of these consistencies is important because they evoke the essential role of accounting in the processes of imperialism and the governance of indigenous peoples. It would therefore be of interest to conduct comparative research into the Canadian and Australian contexts of government–indigenous relations to understand how accounting technologies served as an essential factor in the ability of colonial governments to exclude and dominate indigenous peoples.

In addition to commonalities, comparative studies such as this offer the potential to explicate differences in how authorities imagined indigenous peoples as subjects of government, and in the practices and mentalities of government enacted to achieve the government of the indigenous peoples. Comparative studies can contribute by moving debates about the roles of accounting in government and policy beyond the relatively narrow confines that they currently occupy. They offer the opportunity to move from the micro-level case-specific scenario to the macro level to explore the enlistment of accounting in the meta-narratives of colonialism.

Finally, while the literature clearly demonstrates the centrality of accounting expertise to these fields of government, with the exception of Neu and Graham (2004), the research is all but silent on the role of accounting experts. Neu and Graham's account of the agency of D. C. Scott, head of the Department of Indian Affairs, hints at the existence of 'essential individuals' expert in accounting knowledge within colonial processes of government. Indeed, Walker (2003), although not concerned specifically with the government of indigenous peoples documents the agency of accounting professionals during the eighteenth and nineteenth centuries. His study reveals the complicity of accounting professionals in practices of assimilation aimed at dislocating the Scottish Gaels on the 'grounds of economic rationality' (ibid.: 813). These studies suggest that we should broaden the scope of our inquiry to recognise the positioning of accountants and the accounting profession within colonial government–indigenous relations.

Key works

Gallhofer and Chew (eds) (2000) is a special issue which contains a variety of articles that introduce the subject of accounting and indigenous peoples.

Neu and Therrien (2003) examines accounting's role in the governance of indigenous peoples.

Preston and Oakes (2001) highlights the similarities between accounting and indigenous peoples in the United States and other countries.

Notes

1   The term 'peoples' is used to comply with the request from indigenous peoples to the United Nations that the term be substituted for 'people' to emphasise the diversity of Indigenous peoples throughout the world, and to mitigate the Western tendency to lump Indigenous peoples into an amorphous cluster (Pino 1998).
2   Although Said (1994: xxxv) identified several empires: 'the Austro-Hungarian, the Russian, the Ottoman, and the Spanish and Portuguese', as well as the French and American, the majority of accounting research has concentrated on sites of British imperialism.
3   Mr Martinez-Cobo, the United Nations Sub-Commission Special Rapporteur on the Problem of Discrimination Against Indigenous Populations defined indigenous peoples as:

> those people having an historical continuity with pre-invasion and pre-colonial societies, consider themselves distinct from other sectors of the societies now prevailing in those territories or parts of them. They form at present *non-dominant sectors of society* and are determined to preserve, develop and transmit to future generations, their ancestral territories, and their ethnic

identity, as the basis of their continued existence as peoples in accordance with their own cultural patterns, social institutions, and legal systems.

(UN–HABITAT 2003, *emphasis added*)

4   While there are a number of studies that have themes including the indigenous peoples of New Zealand (Hooper and Pratt 1995; Hooper and Kearins 1997, forthcoming; Jacobs 2000; McNicholas *et al.* 2004), they have not been included here because their primary focus is not the role of accounting in the colonisation of the Maori people.

5   Alam *et al.* (2004: 136) also refer to the power dimension of the co-operation of the chiefs. They write, 'Fiji's annexation to the British Crown was mainly on the grounds of some influential chiefs (being) unable to maintain their power against their rivals and to control considerable European settler population in the early 19th century'.

6   The body of the research covers the period up to the date of Federalism in 1900, and is primarily concerned with the policies and practices of colonial governments.

7   There are, however, a number of studies that have researched the interface between accounting and indigenous cultures (see for example, Chew and Greer 1997a, 1997b; Gibson 1994, 2000; Greer 1992, 1994; Greer and Patel 2000; Ivanitz 2001). These studies have concentrated on cultural problems such as the displacement of Aboriginal cultures by accounting technologies, and the potential of indigenous cultural values to inform accounting practices.

8   Unlike Canada, a state-based approach to Australian research is necessary because until 1967 the states had almost exclusive jurisdiction over Aboriginal policies.

9   The euphemism 'problem' was used by all colonial (and modern) governments to describe the indigenous peoples and their relationship to government.

References

Achary, S. K. (1997) Accounting, race and ethnicity in development discourse: a story of an indigenising preferencing. Paper presented at Fifth Interdisciplinary Perspectives on Accounting Conference, University of Manchester, 7–9 July.

Alam, M., Lawrence, S. and Nandan, R. (2004) Accounting for economic development in the context of post-colonialism: the Fijian experience, *Critical Perspectives on Accounting*, 15 (1): 135–57.

Annisette, M. (1999) Importing accounting: the case of Trinidad and Tobago, *Accounting, Business & Financial History*, 9 (1): 103–33.

Annisette, M. (2000) Imperialism and the professions: the education and certification of accountants in Trinidad and Tobago, *Accounting, Organizations and Society*, 25 (7): 631–59.

Annisette, M. and Neu, D. (2004) Accounting and empire: an introduction, *Critical Perspectives on Accounting*, 15 (1): 1–4.

Bhabha, H. (1994) *The Location of Culture* (London: Routledge).

Bush, B. and Maltby, J. (2004) Taxation in West Africa: transforming the colonial subject into the 'governable person', *Critical Perspectives on Accounting*, 15 (1): 5–34.

Chew, A. and Greer, S. (1997a) Contrasting world views on accounting: accountability and Aboriginal culture, *Accounting, Auditing & Accountability Journal*, 10 (3): 276–98.

Chew, A. and Greer, S. (1997b) The role of accounting in developmentalism: room for an[other] view? Paper presented at the Fifth Interdisciplinary Perspectives on Accounting Conference, University of Manchester, 7–9 July.

Cruikshank, B. (1999) *The Will to Empower: Democratic Citizens and Other Subjects* (Ithaca, NY: Cornell University Press).

Davie, S. S. K. (2000) Accounting for imperialism: a case of British imposed indigenous collaboration, *Accounting, Auditing & Accountability Journal*, 13 (3): 330–59.

Davie, S. S. K. (2005a) The politics of accounting, race and ethnicity: a story of a chiefly-based preferencing, *Critical Perspectives on Accounting*, 16 (5): 551–77.

Davie, S. S. K. (2005b) Accounting's uses in exploitative human engineering: theorizing citizenship, indirect rule and Britain's imperial expansion, *Accounting Historians Journal*, 32 (2): 55–80.

Dyball, M. C., Chua, W. F. and Poullaos, C. (2006) Mediating between colonizer and colonized in the American empire: accounting for government monies in the Philippines, *Accounting, Auditing & Accountability Journal*, 19 (1): 47–81.

Dyball, M. C., Poullaos, C. and Chua, W. F. (2007) Accounting and empire: professionalization-as-resistance: the case of the Philippines, *Critical Perspectives on Accounting*, 18 (4): 415–49.

Fletcher, C. (1992) *Aboriginal Politics: Intergovernmental Relations* (Victoria: Melbourne University Press).

Foucault, M. (1991) Governmentality, in G. Burchell, C. Gordon and P. Miller (eds), *The Foucault Effect: Studies in Governmentality with Two Lectures by and an Interview with Michel Foucault*, pp. 87–104 (Chicago: The University of Chicago Press).

Gallhofer, S. and Chew, A. (eds) (2000) Special issue on 'Accounting and Indigenous Peoples', *Accounting, Auditing & Accountability Journal*, 13 (3).

Gibson, K. (1994) Accounting and the Mabo effect: dreamtime or nightmare? Research Paper No. 13/94, Victoria University of Technology.

Gibson, K. (2000) Accounting as a tool for Aboriginal dispossession: then and now. *Accounting, Auditing & Accountability Journal*, 13 (3): 289–306.

Goodall, H. (1996) *Invasion to Embassy: Land in Aboriginal Politics in NSW, 1770–1972* (St Leonards: Allen & Unwin Pty Ltd).

Greer, S. (1992) The Aboriginal Land Rights Act 1983 New South Wales: a case study of accounting in action, unpublished Honours thesis, Division of Economic and Financial Studies, Macquarie University, North Ryde, Australia.

Greer, S. (1994) Financial accounting: in communicating a reality we destroy a reality. Paper presented at Fourth Interdisciplinary Perspectives on Accounting Conference, University of Manchester, 11–13 July.

Greer, S. (2006) 'Governing indigenous peoples: a history of accounting interventions in the New South Wales Aborigines Protection and Welfare Boards 1883–1969', unpublished PhD thesis, Macquarie University.

Greer, S. and Patel, C. (2000) The issue of Australian indigenous world-views and accounting, *Accounting, Auditing & Accountability Journal*, 13 (3): 307–29.

Hooper, K. and Kearins, K. (1997) 'The excited and dangerous state of the natives of Hawkes Bay': a particular study of nineteenth century financial management, *Accounting, Organizations and Society*, 22 (3/4): 269–92.

Hooper, K. and Kearins, K. (forthcoming) The walrus, carpenter and oysters: liberal reform, hypocrisy and expertocracy in Maori land loss in New Zealand 1885–1911, *Critical Perspectives on Accounting*.

Hooper, K. and Pratt, M. (1995) Discourse and rhetoric: the case of the New Zealand Native Land Company, *Accounting, Auditing & Accountability Journal*, 8 (1): 10–37.

Indian Trust (undated) *Cobell v Norton: An Overview*. Available HTTP: <http://www.indiantrust.com/index> (accessed 22 October 2007).

Ivanitz, M. J. (2001) Rorting and reporting: Aboriginal organisations and the question of accountability. Paper presented at Third Interdisciplinary Perspectives Research in Accounting Conference, Adelaide, July.

Jacobs, K. (2000) Evaluating accountability: finding a place for the Treaty of Waitangi in the New Zealand public sector, *Accounting, Auditing & Accountability Journal*, 13 (3): 360–80.

Kaplan, M. (1989) The 'dangerous and disaffected native' in Fiji: British colonial constructions of the Tuka movement, *Social Analysis*, 26: 22–45.

Kidd, R. (1994) Regulating bodies: Administration and Aborigines in Queensland, 1840–1988, unpublished PhD thesis, Griffith University, Brisbane.

Kidd, R. (2001) Whose accountability? ATSIC News, August 2001. Available HTTP: <www.linksdisk.com/roskidd/journals.htm> (accessed 22 October 2007).

Kidd, R. (2006) *Trustees on Trial: Recovery of the Stolen Wages* (Canberra: Aboriginal Studies Press).

McGrath, A. (2004) *Reconciling the Historical Accounts: Trust Funds Reparations and New South Wales Aborigines* (Canberra: Australian National University).

McNicholas, P., Humphries, M. and Gallhofer, S. (2004) Maintaining the Empire: Maori women's experiences in the accounting profession, *Critical Perspectives on Accounting*, 15 (1): 57–93.

Miller, P. and Rose, N. (1990) Governing economic life, *Economy and Society*, 19 (1): 1–31.

Neu, D. (1999) 'Discovering' indigenous peoples: accounting and the machinery of Empire, *Accounting Historians Journal*, 26 (1): 53–82.

Neu, D. (2000a) 'Presents' for the 'Indians': land, colonialism and accounting in Canada, *Accounting, Organizations and Society*, 25 (2): 163–84.

Neu, D. (2000b) Accounting and accountability relations: colonization, genocide and Canada's First Nations, *Accounting, Auditing & Accountability Journal*, 13 (3): 268–88.

Neu, D. (2001) Banal accounts: subaltern voices, *Accounting Forum*, 25 (4): 319–33.

Neu, D. and Graham, C. (2004) Accounting and the holocausts of modernity, *Accounting, Auditing & Accountability Journal*, 17 (4): 578–603.

Neu, D. and Graham, C. (2006) The birth of a nation: accounting and Canada's First Nations, 1860–1900, *Accounting, Organizations and Society*, 31 (1): 47–76.

Neu, D. and Heincke, M. (2004) The subaltern speaks: financial relations and the limits of governmentality, *Critical Perspectives on Accounting*, 15 (1): 179–206.

Neu, D. and Therrien, R. (2003) *Accounting for Genocide: Canada's Bureaucratic Assault on Aboriginal People* (London: Zed Books Ltd).

Oakes, L. S., Townley, B. and Chwastiak, M. (1997) Theorizing accounting at the margin: Bourdieu, ledger art, Nike and elder care. Paper presented at the Fifth Interdisciplinary Perspectives on Accounting Conference, University of Manchester, 7–9 July.

Pino, R. (1998) Indigenous peoples face a continuous legacy of internal (welfare) colonialism, *Journal of Indigenous Thought*, Regina: Saskatchewan Indian Federated College. Available HTTP: <www.sifc.edu/IndianStudies/IndigenousThought/fall98/indigenous.htm> (accessed January 2003).

Preston, A. (2006) Enabling, enacting and maintaining action at a distance: an historical case study of the role of accounts in the reduction of the Navajo herds, *Accounting, Organizations and Society*, 31 (6): 559–78.

Preston, A. and Oakes, L. (2001) The Navajo documents: a study of the economic representation and construction of the Navajo, *Accounting, Organizations and Society*, 26 (1): 39–71.

Rose, N. and Miller, P. (1992) Political power beyond the state: problematics of government, *British Journal of Sociology*, 43 (2): 173–205.

Rowse, T. (1998) *White Flour, White Power: From Rations to Citizenship in Central Australia* (Cambridge: Cambridge University Press).

Said, E. W. (1994) *Culture and Imperialism* (London: Vintage).

Senate Legal and Constitutional Affairs Committee (2006) *Inquiry into Stolen Wages* (Canberra: Parliament of Australia Senate).

Smith, D. E. (1990) *The Conceptual Practices of Power: A Feminist Sociology of Knowledge* (Boston: Northeastern University Press).

UN-HABITAT (United Nations Human Settlements Programme) (2003) *Rental Housing: An Essential Option for the Urban Poor in Developing Countries*, Nairobi. Available HTTP: <http://www.unhabitat.org/programmes/housingpolicy/pubrental.asp> (accessed 22 October 2007).

Walker, S. P. (2003) Agents of dispossession and acculturation. Edinburgh accountants and the Highland clearances, *Critical Perspectives on Accounting*, 14(8): 813–53.

23

Emancipation

Sonja Gallhofer and Jim Haslam

Overview

The aim of this chapter is to elaborate, illustrate and promote accounting history consistent with critical theory refined by engagement with postmodern interventions. Reflexively, the approach sees the world as problematic. A better world, however, may be envisaged with a notion of how to realise it. History helps problematise the present and bring insights from the past. Rather than reduce to an unproblematic account of change as if narrative-free and transparently real, history may be aligned with emancipation. The focus here is on accounting in modern Britain, specifically the 'long nineteenth century'. The chapter concentrates on writings on accounting by the English philosopher Jeremy Bentham (1748–1832) and accounting's mobilisation by socialist agitators in the late nineteenth and early twentieth centuries. Reflecting the concerns of the critical theoretical approach, the chapter begins by questioning the meaning of emancipation today and then explores, via its focuses, what is at stake in relating accounting, history and emancipation.

Questioning emancipation

Post-modern critique questions the very idea of emancipation and, given people's differences, the notion of a collective to be emancipated. One may ask, 'What conceptions of emancipation are remaining or emerging'? (Doornbos 1992: 1). A critical perspective engaging the post-modern may continue the (refined) goal of emancipation with proper awareness and reflexivity. While critics suggest that an emancipatory project is somehow totalitarian, attempts to discard emancipation are also totalitarian (Nederveen Pieterse 1992: 26; Žižek 2001). Against the dangers of intervention stand problematics of overlooking structure, not identifying with the oppressed and not intervening (Bronner 1994). Along with recognising that respect for difference is a universal (Calhoun 1995), we may appeal to values beyond scepticism, including politico–ethical solidarity (Rorty 1989; Benhabib 1992, 1994).

Yet post-modern critique also indicates emancipation's complexity and ambiguity (Doornbos 1992). Social structure enables as well as constrains autonomy. Power is exercised within complex networks of relations and struggles. Emancipation is more than the overthrow of a single force. A myriad (mutable) emancipatory interests, some marginalised and others repressed in acts assumed to be emancipatory, have to be aligned (Alvesson and Willmott 1992). We must reflexively acknowledge our situated selves to avoid incompatible logical claims such as assuming that a pure emancipatory act may emerge from a problematic context. This requires a cautious pragmatism and more modest epistemology and eschatology (Laclau 1992).

Accounting, emancipation and critical history

A critical historical analysis of accounting *vis-à-vis* emancipation is properly shaped by these insights, reflecting cognisance of accounting's complexity and ambiguity, and sensitivity to its instability, indeterminancy and transience (Nederveen Pieterse 1992: 26). This approach surpasses crude conceptions of history as progress (Napier 2001) and recognises that if modern accounting has been emphatically repressive it has also had emancipatory dimensions which may even predominate (Prokhovnik 1999). A critical history illuminates trajectories in both the emancipatory and repressive dimensions of accounting, including dynamics whereby the once repressive becomes emancipatory. In theorising accounting *vis-à-vis* emancipation, emancipation as radical break is surpassed, and a more modest eschatology and epistemology is embraced (Gallhofer and Chew 2000). Emancipation is opened to various possibilities in past contexts, including in the ostensibly marginal and particular. Emancipations are also acknowledged as plural and mutable (Laclau 1996).

Concurrently, a critical history still attempts strategic response to shifting frameworks of power and resistance. Refinements from engagement with post-modern critique may import critical gains (Squires 1993: 1–2). If 'traditional' concerns are problematised it is not the logical dénouement of engagement with this critique that they be displaced completely. Instead, refined theorising may emerge. Nor is there a guarantee that a particular social class or element will explain or engender change, though *potentially* it may (Žižek 2000). Thus, the working class may still be an emancipatory agent. If we need to better reflect category instability, problematising overly simplifying constructions, an agent does not lose all relevance (Laclau 2000; cf. Derrida 1978; Gallhofer and Haslam 1995). The critique engaged with promotes agent intervention for betterment (Laclau 1990). For Laclau (1992), opportunities emerge for radical critique of multifarious dominations and democracy.

The critique encourages intervention in and through accounting particularly. The diverse agendas, calls for action and building of a radical democracy (Nederveen Pieterse 1992) especially stimulate various emancipatory accountings because communication, information and accountability are key in democratic discourse (Bronner 1994). The authors contend that we should meet the challenge of positively aligning accounting and emancipation amidst complexity, uncertainty, instability and contingency. Such an approach transforms how we may gain insights to accounting's emancipatory dimensions through historical analysis – an analysis which recognises the dangers of problematic dogmatism and universalism. We should thus appreciate more of the difference as well as complexity of the past and avoid excessive anachronism or 'chronocentrism' (Cousins 1987), while acknowledging overlaps and continuities (Gallhofer and Haslam 1996b).

Going beyond dichotomous thinking and excessive chronocentrism also impacts upon accounting's delineation and notions of relating accounting to emancipation. It opens up broader conceptions of accounting beyond narrow financial economistic representations. It encompasses other forms of calculation and broader systems of informing for control and thereby extends accounting's borders and possibilities. It embraces possible, including prescriptive, accountings. It invokes a broader understanding of 'account', encompassing narrative and notions of social accounting (the history of which remains underdeveloped (Gallhofer and Haslam 2005)) or accountings reflecting more holistic understandings of people and their contexts.

Studies consistent with the above have emerged and constitute a critical history of accounting *vis-à-vis* emancipatory activism. These studies, appraising accounting and context, reflect accounting as a significant socio-political phenomenon that can change, be changed and never fully be captured by hegemonic forces (Lehman and Tinker 1987; Gallhofer and Haslam 1991). This research goes beyond understanding accounting as virtually apolitical and asocial (Tinker 1985). It illuminates accounting as a focus of the conflicting objectives of different actors and extends to conflict over the socio-political order (Stiglitz 2002). It brings insights to the trajectory of historical struggles over accounting, including how different accountings have variously been put to the service of radical forces. These studies offer a deeper appreciation of the present and uncover the forgotten or unnoticed layers of accounting history. The research may help us see the longevity of concepts and practices often thought of as being of more recent vintage and offer insights to accounting's past through bracketing particularities of its present. Such work supports emancipatory struggles today. It is integral to a radical history of accounting, one where accounting is broadly conceived as informing for control, as concept and practice, and a focus of social and historical analysis that may problematise and transform the present (Gallhofer and Haslam 2003; cf. Miller and Napier 1993).

Critical accounting history studies

While several analyses have theorised accounting *vis-à-vis* dialectical forces, as ambiguous and complex, they have typically emphasised accounting's repressiveness (in relation to, for instance, labour, women, slaves, ethnicities, cultures). Others have sought to address imbalance in analyses by recognising accounting's ambiguity – the sense that it may escape capture by any particular group or class and that it has emancipatory dimensions and possibilities. Although some have encouraged agency towards realising accounting's emancipatory potential (e.g. Tinker 1985; Gallhofer and Haslam 1996a; Sikka 2000), few have attended to radical activism and accounting in historical contexts. Here, we review some critical history studies that do delineate emancipatory, including interventionist, possibilities for accounting.

The studies focus on the modern (Calinescu 1987) British context within Hobsbawm's (1962, 1999) 'long nineteenth century' (*c.*1789–*c.*1914). This period is especially worthy of attention given that many modern-day institutions and practices were substantially shaped at this time (Gallhofer and Haslam 1995, 2003). So far as accounting is concerned, the period witnessed key manifestations of state prescription and formal professionalisation (Edwards 1989). In this chapter we discuss several studies by Gallhofer and Haslam and the contribution of Arnold (1997). If not explicitly critical, the latter pursues similar themes to the former. We explore Bentham's accounting work, considering this radical emancipatory activism and proceed to discuss the campaigns of radical labour and socialist activists that implicated accounting (in the context of capitalistic abuses of labour and War crisis). We then discuss how an early twentieth-century law case implicated accounting and indicated its radical potential. Through these episodes insights are gained to significant historical praxis *vis-à-vis* accounting.

487

Bentham on accounting

> From . . . Pauper Economy, studied with any attention, the transition is unavoidable to the ministering art of book-keeping . . . one of the arts . . . I should have to learn . . . the cries of the poor called aloud and accelerated . . . demands for it.
>
> (UC, cliiia: 33–4)

> [P]ublicity is the very soul of justice . . . keenest spur to exertion . . . the surest of all guards against improbity. It keeps the judge himself, while trying, under trial.
>
> (Bentham, in Harrison 1983: 131)

Gallhofer and Haslam (1993, 1994a, 1994b, 1995, 1996b, 2003) analyse Bentham's accounting texts as emancipatory activism, elaborating how Bentham sought to change established and promote unofficial accountings to challenge the established order. Bentham wrote much on accounting, which he understood in broad terms, and held in great esteem for its potential benefits. Bentham was radical, the great questioner of things established (Anonymous 1838; Hart 1982: 25–6), and his radicalism extended to accounting. He aimed to transform law and governance to the best state attainable and sought to liberate people from illusions influencing them and advocated pragmatic intervention. Despite his significance, Bentham is poorly appreciated. There remains limited knowledge of his writing and problematic understandings thereof (Gallhofer and Haslam 2003).[1]

Bentham pursued extensive democracy and education, the transformation of the lives of the poor and the oppressed (including women (Boralevi 1980, 1984)), and the advancement of the happiness (not reduced to the material[2]) of the global community (Mack 1962). He argued for a more just and equal society through minimum wages, job security, pensions, health insurance and a welfare system. He contended that wages were unreasonably low relative to other income and sought to distribute inheritances to the community and excess profits to employees. He was enthusiastic about early socialistic experiments. Indeed, several commentators have indicated Bentham's influence on later socialists (especially the Fabians) and an affinity with Marx (Mack 1962; Russell 1962: 743; Hart 1982; Boralevi 1984). Boralevi (1984) articulates Bentham's concern for the oppressed explicitly in terms of emancipation.[3]

A critical theoretical re-appraisal of Bentham's writings, requiring destruction and patient hermeneutic reconstruction (Critchley 2001: 47–8), is worthwhile, given his significance and radicalism, and his placing of accounting so highly in his schema. Bentham sought, moreover, to emancipate accounting so that it would better engender emancipatory change. He was one of several writers who perceived the significance of informed opinion and transparency for progressive, emancipatory construction of social relations through rational communicative interaction (Gallhofer and Haslam 2003; see Habermas, 1992: 102). He wrote at a time before (and was thus unencumbered by) accountancy's formal professionalisation (Gallhofer and Haslam 2003).

Many emphasise Bentham's repressive side. Yet reading critically, we may appreciate his complexities, ambiguities and positive potential. Habermas encourages a focus on Bentham (indeed, including his accounting), in acknowledging his positive radical potentiality, portraying favourably his concept of publicity (1843), associating it with his own public sphere construct and seeing Bentham as an architect of that sphere (Habermas 1974, 1992; Peters 1993). From this perspective, Bentham's publicity is a manifestation of and facilitates rational critical discourse, engendering meaningful public opinion. Habermas' desiderata (Gaonkar and McCarthy 1994: 554) – that so long as there exists no over-determining of opinion through publicity, publicity challenging the official is possible – was also advocated by Bentham (1843). Bentham's promotion of publicity parallels his concern to extend education (Boralevi 1984).

Bentham saw accounting publicity (accounting, publicity and book-keeping are used inter-changeably)[4] as variously beneficial. It encouraged the moral behaviour of those exposed by it (the powerful especially) (Bentham 1843: 588; Harrison 1983: 131; Boralevi 1984: 191)[5], and enhanced orientation towards sympathy, benevolence and general well-being (Mack 1962). Bentham explicitly linked his advocacy of a statistic/accounting society to 'promoting the condition of the labouring classes' (UC, cxlix: 237). His accounting would serve the oppressed, partly by rendering transparent the powerful (Bahmueller 1981: 190). He sought to give the oppressed a voice through accounting. In his poor houses, the poor were to be educated and encouraged to record observations about their house in a publicly available complaints book. Managers were also to keep health, meals and activity records (Bowring 1843, viii: 393). Publicity was also envisaged as informing to help people steer through life and participate in democracy. Accounting publicity is here a key principle of management or governance, second only to Bentham's broad-ranging Panopticon principle (Gallhofer and Haslam 2003: 47; see Bentham 1812: 100–1).

In seeking to radically question and emancipate accounting, and thereby foster emancipation, Bentham wanted to rationalise accounting and extend its limits. Accounting was to be shaped by ends not traditions (Bentham 1816: 61–2; Bowring 1843: viii: 393; Hume 1970: 27, 1981: 154–5). And this was not to mean its reduction to a narrow abstracted economics. Bentham struggled to articulate a relationship between a duty to achieve financial efficiency, a duty to economy (benefiting owners, conventionally), and a 'duty to humanity'. This holistic vision reflects the dangers of seeing economics as separate and abstracted. In his pauper management and Panopticon projects, publicity was the chief device to expose moral behaviour, to better ensure management fulfilled its duty to humanity and attended to the concerns of the oppressed. Bentham considered accounting publicity more effective in the moral sphere than in the economic (Harrison 1983: 130).

Elsewhere, Bentham suggests that this view of accounting's role is more generally applicable. The duty to humanity is articulated as duty towards those under management's care. It clearly includes paupers but also extends to a recognisable stakeholder approach (Gallhofer and Haslam 1993). Boralevi (1984) suggests, sympathetically, that the duty to economy is 'means', while the duty to humanity is 'end'. Bentham thus envisaged a more holistic accounting:

> Pecuniary economy, usually regarded as the sole object of book-keeping, will here be but as one out of a number; for the system of book-keeping will be neither more nor less than the history of the system of management in all its points.
>
> (Bentham 1812: 101; see Hoskin and Macve 1986: 128)

Subject to limits he thought reasonable (Semple 1993), Bentham argued that the widest range of things should be recorded and disclosed to engender well-being (Bentham 1812: 102–3; Bahmueller 1981: 192–3; Loft 1988). Bentham advocated accounts which included the financial but did not give primacy thereto. Information disaggregated relative to convention so as to render transparent the local effects of local activities was within Bentham's vision (and is more feasible today with IT) (Hume 1970: 28–30; Gallhofer et al. 2006). He sought to make visible individual as well as group activity (Gallhofer and Haslam 1993). And he sought disclosure to a large audience to promote democracy and effectively a stakeholder approach. This might be achieved by the use of outside expert consultants (Bentham 1812: 56–7).

To achieve these aims, accounting had to be clear and comprehensible, that is, more accountable itself (Bentham 1812; Goldberg 1957; cf. Bentham 1830: 46). Bentham saw lack of clarity in accounting, and the use of fictitious entities, as a kind of mystifying problematic ideology serving particular rather than social interests, including an accounting expertocracy (Bentham 1812: 106n). Bentham also indicated a respect for privacy, particularity and difference beyond crude universalism in promoting publicity (Rosen 1983; Boralevi 1984: 81). A further aspect of Bentham emphasises links to radical activism generally: besides wanting to change established accounting, Bentham (1843: 583) promoted unofficial accounting to challenge the socio-political order.

In summary, Bentham outlines emancipatory accounting. A critical history, however, also explores negative dimensions of Bentham's intervention. Gallhofer and Haslam reflect this (see Walker 2004). One should be sensitive to the dangers of mobilising projects ostensibly informed by Bentham. Bentham himself, in his enthusiasm and in the context of the rejection of his ideas by a repressive establishment (Foot 1984), overlooks his schema's imperfections, tending towards crude dogmatism (Letwin 1965):

> I have a machine put together . . . for answering all such questions . . . Panopticon or the Inspection-House . . . You had the goodness to offer me some papers relative to some . . . establishments to which the idea promises to be applicable . . . Houses of Industry . . . Jails . . . Hospitals . . . Schools & . . . Do you . . . want a plan of Education just now, or a plan of anything else? These are my amusements. One thing pretty much the same to me as another.
>
> (Bentham 1790: f. 160)

Bentham seeks the people taking control but wants to direct them first and sees bookkeeping as a uniform system engendering uniform behaviour: 'the general advantage depends on uniformity of which uniformity is productive . . . Refer to book-keeping' (UC, cliib: 363). This may equate to forcing order and uniformity on a chaotic, dynamic and threatening context, buttressing hegemonic forces (Bahmueller 1981: 93). These things do not negate his philosophy, being present in any philosophy implying intervention for betterment. Bentham himself acknowledged them (Letwin 1965).

Bentham's excesses may counter intentions. He advocates that experts be more accountable. Yet his particular accounting advocacy tends to an expertise distant from the public (Gallhofer and Haslam, 1994a: 269–70). Relatedly, Bentham sometimes portrays accounting as uncontroversial facts (Bentham 1817: table v; Letwin 1965: 188).[6] If, for sympathisers, Bentham's intervention reflects experience and his distrust of the powerful, diagnosis and prescription are difficult. Bentham's zeal may entail diminishing social trust, with mechanism substituting for substantive morality, engendering moral decay (Himmelfarb 1968). One may fail to appreciate the flexibilities of Bentham's projects in their mobilisation. For Letwin (1965), Bentham's 'colourless treatises were interpreted by disciples moved by different experiences and aims' (being captured by powerful repressive forces and mobilised for narrow capitalistic aims) to problematic effect (Hobsbawm 1962; Himmelfarb 1968). Bentham, vis-à-vis capitalistic political economy, sometimes tended to a narrow economicism facilitating such capture. In delineating a duty to economy separate from a duty to humanity Bentham ironically distances the economic from the social: a duty to economy is surely integral to a deeper duty to humanity (see Bahmueller 1981: 193).

Gallhofer and Haslam's studies reviewed here thus indicate how accounting may be conceived of as emancipatory and how its own emancipation may encourage further realisation of this potential. The analyses illuminate how established accountings may serve the relatively powerful but also accounting's possible transformation to better serve the weak. This also suggests political struggle. We can appreciate the longevity of notions of accounting that would serve stakeholders and engender accountability for social justice, well-being and emancipation. It would be an unreasonable and prejudicial view that would not see a substantive congruence between Bentham's accounting and notions of an ambitious, seriously regulated social accounting today. If potentially radical projects in and through accounting are reinforced, analyses of Bentham are also suggestive of new insights in relation to, for example, accounting's form and content. They also promote radical activism in and through accounting, including unofficial accountings to challenge the established socio-political order.

Gallhofer and Haslam also offer caution concerning Bentham-like emancipatory accounting projects. Much of Bentham's radicalism *vis-à-vis* accounting may be displaced and problematically transformed. Negatives may dominate positives. Yet with appropriate sensitivity and awareness, a critical theoretical mobilising of Bentham's notion of accounting may fuse with a radical emancipatory project.

Bentham's accounting writings are substantial and may be analysed from many different perspectives. There are many further research possibilities. Gallhofer and Haslam are currently working on Bentham's *Constitutional Code*.

Accounting and socialist agitators in the late nineteenth and early twentieth centuries

> In the case of the Match Girls . . . [publicity] . . . voiced their complaints,
> and forced them on the attention of the public . . . what it has done for this
> one class of the oppressed it must do, one after the other for every such class.
> (*The Link*, 4 August 1888: 1)

Gallhofer and Haslam (2003, 2006a) analyse accounting's mobilisation by socialist activists in late nineteenth- and early twentieth-century Britain. Arnold (1997) pursues overlapping themes. Accounting is understood as a focus of conflicting objectives (Stiglitz 2002) that imply different uses. Thus governments may look for tax revenues. Shareholders and investors may pursue conventional financial ownership interest. Labour may pursue a larger slice of the economic cake; capitalistic interests the maintaining or enhancing of capital. Some effectively have accounting buttressing the socio-political order, others as facilitating progressive change. Even accountings actually manifest have emancipatory dimensions and possibilities. Given the dialectical and ambiguous character of social dynamics, accounting can shift between substantively repressive and progressive functioning. Further, there is a role for responding to opportunities and engagement in furthering emancipation (Lehman and Tinker 1987; Gallhofer and Haslam 2003).

Accounting in context

Late nineteenth-century Britain was shaped by crisis and conflict. An economic downturn set in from the early 1870s. Unemployment was a problem in the 1880s, alongside increasing poverty (Callaghan 1990: 4). Wages were low, working hours long and labour intense (Daunton 2000). Street riots and serious industrial unrest manifested. Labour forces inched towards collective action (Soldon 1978; Beaver 1985). By the 1890s, there was considerable interest, including among the middle classes, in the plight of the poor and social problems. Social investigators intent on engendering change exposed poverty and labour experiences (Booth 1890). A significant body of opinion favoured greater state intervention to tackle poverty. Government investigations of problems were instigated. Charitable activity and a social reform movement grew in response to these concerns (Callaghan 1990: 4–5).

Several organisations also arose with distinct social and political missions. One such was Toynbee Hall, founded in the East End to link the university sector and the poor. Beyond its educational mission, Toynbee Hall supported labour in industrial disputes (Briggs and Macartney 1984: 45). The 1880s also saw enhanced concern about women's working and living conditions. The Women's Protective and Provident League (WPPL) fought for the establishment of women's trade unions (Bolt 1993). Organised political movements sought to ameliorate the conditions of the poor and working class. Socialism revived. In 1884, a number of organisations were established. The Social Democratic Federation (SDF), under H. M. Hyndman's leadership, had a clear socialist objective. The Socialist League under William Morris was more international and anti-state. The Fabians, aiming to place wealth in community hands, opposed violence, favoured gradual democratic reform and sought to influence existing political parties (Tsuzuki 1961; Hopkins 2000).

The strategies employed by such organisations shared one striking similarity: concern to expose poverty and injustice through the publicity of 'facts', inspired by the belief (promoted by Bentham and the statistical movement (Cullen 1975)) that exposure would aid resolution by convincing reasonable people of the need to alleviate conditions. The Fabians were especially influenced by this. Commitment to publicity suggests the influence of Bentham as well as Marx on the socialist movements (Hulse 1970). Consistent with this, many socialists printed newspapers. Examples included *Christian Socialist, Common Sense, The Labour Elector*, SDF's *Justice* (edited by Henry Hyde Champion), and Annie Besant's *Our Corner* and *The Link* (Callaghan 1990: 39–45).

By the 1880s, many accountants were organised into recognised professional bodies (see Chapter 11). Established commercial accounting was substantively shaped by capitalistic interests. State and professional regulation of accounting was fairly minimalist in most sectors (see Chapter 14; Parker 1990; Edwards 1992; Walker 1996). The profit figure typically interested shareholders because it often corresponded closely to the dividend (Gallhofer and Haslam 2003: 70). By the 1880s, auditors signing off accounts would often indicate their status as members of a professional body. Company constitutions would typically include provisions to publish accounts, which might attain a law-like status.[7] Association with the accounting profession and the law enhanced the aura of facticity surrounding accounts. This despite the fact that many companies adopted as much flexibility in accounting as was legally possible and some contravened the law's spirit by filing the same balance sheet annually (Edwards 1989).

The match girls

Champion and Besant's enthusiasm for publicity extended to accounting publicity. Champion apparently turned to socialist activism after reading works including Marx and Mill and witnessing London slums (Champion 1983). Initially prominent in Christian Socialism and the SDF, he was a Fabian and campaigned with union and labour leaders (Whitehead 1983: 17). He was a good communicator (Hyndman 1911; Tsuzuki 1961) and in a journal he founded he recognised the importance of publicity and the power of 'undeniable facts' (see *Common Sense*, 15 May 1887).[8] Champion stressed the contrast between rich and poor, and the format for expressing this in his journal was influenced by conventional accounting. *Common Sense*'s first issue placed national wealth on the left of the front page and national poverty on the right. Similarly, Champion contrasted high profits/dividends with poor wages/conditions, focusing on specific companies, using accounting. The company mainly focused on in *Common Sense* was Bryant & May Limited, the notable East London match-maker.

Bryant & May was incorporated and listed in 1884 (Bryant & May, Minutes of Directors' Meetings: 12 June 1884). It remained substantively a family firm, reflected in the directors, whose remuneration was profit-related (Gallhofer and Haslam 2003: 73). In the 1880s, the share price reflected the remarkable rise of the business. Dividends, of between 20 and 30 per cent on the initial nominal capital, were relatively high. There was a very close correspondence between accounting profit and dividends (ibid.: 75). At the annual general meetings during the 1880s the firm was eulogised with reference to accounts certified by the auditor as 'a true statement of the Liabilities and Assets'.

Champion sought to use accounts to tell a different story and for a different purpose. Most Bryant & May employees were East End women. Match-making had long been associated with poor wages and conditions (Collett 1893). Consistent with a politics of aggregation (or disaggregation) in accounting, these negatives were not as visible in accounts as the financial returns the directors were proud of. Investigative journalism was required. The first report on Bryant & May in *Common Sense* (15 May 1887: 11) established a serialisation format. The dividend for 1886, £80,000, or 20 per cent of nominal value, and the company's apparently high reserve fund (as taken from accounts disclosed at the annual meeting), were highlighted as evidence of excessive profits. A question was raised for a future issue: 'What is the average wage of workers who produced this 20%?'

On 15 June 1887, a report was printed in *Common Sense*. An investigator had 'made enquiries at Bow' and uncovered the poor (absolutely and relatively) wages of a home worker. The report indicated the difficulty of getting information from intimidated workers and stated that the journal was considering advocating a boycott of Bryant & May. Transparency was sought: 'We shall be glad to have . . . name and address of any . . . known to be shareholders, profiting by this system of torture' (ibid.: 27). On 15 July 1887, more visibility was provided in *Common Sense*. The hypocrisy of shareholding religious ministers was suggested by quoting Proverbs, XXII, 1, 2: 'A good name is rather to be chosen than great riches and loving favour than silver and gold.' Ministers were advised to modify the biblical text: 'Come unto us, ye who labour, and we will pay you three farthing an hour.' Fourteen ministers (a journal issue was sent to them) were listed as shareholders while attacks on the owners pointed to questionable morality:

> Judging them even by the conventional standards of fair dealing these gentlemen are sucking profit in a manner every bit as dirty as a money lender, who extorts 30% from the necessitous, or promoter of bubble companies. It is allowed by law, and they do not scruple to . . . oppress the widow and orphan, in order to swell their dividends.
>
> (ibid.: 42)

Champion referred to the case as guest speaker at the annual Church (of England) Congress (5 October 1887). His speech gained publicity in *The Record* and *Common Sense* (15 October 1887). *The Christian* (28 October 1887: 12), having advocated ethical consumerism in a similar case (14 October 1887: 6–7), extracted the following from the *Birmingham Weekly Post*: 'If these assertions are not true, let . . . [Bryant & May] . . . nail them to the counter . . . if they are facts, the time is come for another Wilberforce to emancipate another race of slaves.' Bryant & May's Secretary noted the publicity: people wrote to the company about it, seeking clarification and reassurance and referred to various moral issues. One shareholder requested that the company calculate and disclose average working wages (Bryant & May, Secretary's Diary, 1887–88).

Champion reported to a Fabian meeting on 15 June 1888. Prominent Fabian, Annie Besant (1938: 4), reports discussion there of ethical consumerism and Champion's outlining Bryant & May's share price growth built upon exploitation. Champion's call for a boycott of Bryant & May was supported. Besant, with Herbert Burrows, investigated further, interviewing some factory girls. On 23 June 1888, Besant promoted a boycott in *The Link*,[9] and re-iterated contrasts between accounting profits/dividends and the match girls' plight. She declared the girls cheaper as labour than chattel slaves. Besant distributed her article to workers leaving the factory (*The Link*, 23 June 1888). She later advocated a blacklist of companies to boycott, (published for each locality so that public opinion might better ensure honesty and fair dealing), and a comprehensive legally required disclosure of wages and working conditions (3 June 1888: 1). In July 1888, Besant and Burrows sought to enhance publicity by writing letters to newspapers and referred to workers sacked for informing Besant (e.g. *Pall Mall Gazette*, 3 July 1888). Bryant & May monitored and reacted to this adverse publicity. Besant's article was considered 'scurrilous' (23 June 1888) and its secretary sent letters claiming that the sackings were otherwise motivated (Bryant & May, Secretary's Diary: 3 and 4 July 1888). The company threatened legal action (*The Link*, 7 July 1888: 3). The government also monitored developments: the Inspector of Factories visited the company after *The Link* article (Bryant & May, Secretary's Diary: 27 June 1888).

The workers at Bryant & May went on strike on 5 July 1888. According to some reports, the sackings occurred after the girls refused to denounce Besant's article (*The Link*, 7 July 1888: 3). Besant and Burrows agreed to workers' requests to support the strike. The factory inspector asked the company to inform the Home Office of developments: the stakes were raised (Gallhofer and Haslam 2003: 82).

The agitators continued to mobilise accounting in meetings and in *The Link* where Besant's articles mirrored those of Champion (see 14 July 1888: 1). Besant apparently calculated company returns by adding capital gains to dividends and a giant matchbox was paraded at a demonstration, labelled '38%', to reveal this (Gallhofer and Haslam 2003: 83). According to *St. James's Gazette* (9 July 1888: 11), Besant claimed 'to have stopped the fines inflicted on the girls by giving publicity to them'. An audience for the grievances was secured with House of Commons' representatives (*The Star*, 11 July, 1888).

St. James's Gazette reported on an investigation by Toynbee Hall after the latter had volunteered to help the workers (12 July 1888: 4). Toynbee Hall advocated ethical investment. It repeated the contrast between high dividends/profits and poor wages/conditions, noting poor employer–employee relations. Toynbee Hall elaborated on the grievances of female workers, including effective pay reductions resulting from technological change, fines and reductions (Gallhofer and Haslam 2003: 85). They demanded a more disaggregated accounting for wages which adjusted for seasonalities, isolated higher paid workers and included the many lower paid so that averages would not be distorted. Bryant & May's directors (interviewed by Toynbee Hall), mobilised counter-claims and Toynbee Hall continued the publicity. Radical agitators increasingly saw value in emphasising the 'factual' and accounting's aura of facticity served them in this regard (ibid.: 86). *St. James's Gazette* wanted 'acknowledged facts' respected: Bryant & May should increase wages (*The Link*, 28 July 1888: 1).

The strike ended on 19 July 1888. The London Trades Council had, unusually, negotiated on behalf of female unskilled labour. The workers had several victories, apparently small, but significant to labour historians. The sacked were reinstated, the fines system was withdrawn, small wage increases were granted, and a canteen was eventually provided. The directors had suffered trial by publicity and sought to counter its adverse effects at the next annual meeting.

A Matchmakers' Union was established with Besant as its first secretary (Gallhofer and Haslam 2003: 87). The *Liberal Radical* (28 July, 1888), praising Besant's role in the match girls' case, declared: 'The emancipation of the workers is no party question . . . All praise to those who dare to be *practical* as well as theoretical.'[10] Besant was reassured that the publicity of 'facts' might help rectify social injustices. Her article in *Pall Mall Gazette* (23 February 1889), praised statistical reporting, noting that 'nothing but good can come from throwing on the many problems of our social system the dry, cold light of facts' (see *The Link*, 4 August 1888: 1).[11]

Newton v. Birmingham Small Arms

Arnold (1997) indicates how accounting was controversial in the years leading up to the First World War *vis-à-vis* socio-political conflict. Not only was more attention given to profit (loss) disclosure through accounts in the context of a developing capital market and increased competition but accounting was also seen as potentially increasing capital–labour tensions. Accounting profits were matters of class-based public concern (Arnold 1997: 164): 'The process of informing those who make financial investments in public limited companies, whether as shareholders, lenders or creditors, was bound to provide information to organized labour relevant to bargaining on wages and . . . conditions.'

Arnold discusses a key legal case. Newton v. Birmingham Small Arms Company Limited [1906 2 Ch. 378] was explicitly decided in favour of shareholder and director discretions, with reference to tensions between labour and capitalistic interests. The company's defence included the view, not substantively challenged by the government or the accountancy profession, that where disclosure is contested 'great injury may be done to the business [as] difficulties may be caused between rival traders or between capital and labour'. Mr Justice Buckley, in supporting this view, noted that publicity was potentially injurious to business for reasons including 'complications sometimes arising from . . . strained relations between capital and labour' (ibid.: 164–5). Accounting's counter-hegemonic potential was thereby indicated.

Forward

Gallhofer and Haslam (2006a) theorise the mobilisation of accounting in radical media during the First World War. Their main focus is *Forward*, an important radical weekly newspaper and their context is 'Red Clydeside', a hotbed for counter-hegemonic and radical socialist activities in Scotland and beyond (Foster 1990).

Economic pressures before the First World War exacerbated capital–labour tensions. Socialistic movements strengthened. The possibilities of global socialistic development appeared enhanced. During the war the Russian Revolution encouraged other revolutionary forces (Arnold 1997). A socialist revolution almost succeeded in Germany (Gallhofer and Haslam 1991). It was in this context that there was serious industrial unrest in Clydeside between 1914 and 1919. The workers were concerned about wages and conditions and, more generally, food and coal prices, poor housing, and increases in rent and unemployment.

Accounting remained substantially unregulated by the state at the beginning of the twentieth century. Substantial flexibility was possible in terms of aggregation, profit concealment and secret reserves (Marriner 1980; Arnold 1997; Edwards 1989, 1992). Nevertheless, new companies legislation constituted movement towards greater state regulation. The Companies Act, 1900, for example, required all limited companies to provide an audited balance sheet for shareholders attending the annual meeting and to report whether the balance sheet gave a 'true and correct' view.[12] Annual accounts, however, disclosed little detail and common accounting principles were sometimes overlooked in their preparation. Yet auditors rarely qualified the accounts (Edwards 1989). According to Arnold (1997), serious manipulation of the accounts was uncommon before 1914, published accounts reflected internal book equivalents reasonably well and many companies produced a profit and loss account. Although there were exceptions, auditors were typically professional accountants. However, accounts manipulation appears to have become more common during the First World War (Arnold 1997; cf. Edwards 1989, 1992; Gallhofer and Haslam 2006a).

Forward was founded in 1906 by the socialist Thomas Johnston and some Fabian friends. Johnston, a clerk who inherited a printing works from a distant relative, felt that change required educating workers to their class interests, primarily through exposing 'facts' of injustice and oppression. For example, an article on Glasgow's poor housing was entitled 'Some Official Figures for Propagandists' (*Forward*, 9 May 1914: 1). Company profits and war-profiteering became focuses of *Forward*. Accounts were mobilised in a socialist critique in two main ways. First, accounts (from annual company reports, *The Stock Exchange Yearbook, The Economist* and *The Times*) were used, often on the front page of *Forward*, as 'facts' (Gallhofer and Haslam 2006a: 236). If *The Economist* utilised accounts in a way supportive of the socio-political order, *Forward* mobilised accounts consistent with a socialistic, counter-hegemonic intervention, highlighting excessive profits (using figures companies disclosed) and directors' fees (see *Forward*, 28 April 1917: 2). Second, *Forward* stressed the manipulated character of capitalistic accounting representations. This pointed to the facts beneath the manipulation. The trajectory of the First World War gave this a new significance. When the government introduced an Excess Profits Duty it created an incentive to overstate pre-war profits (Arnold 1997).

In particular media, such as a given newspaper, accounting assumes particular (sometimes new) meaning. An accounting may be encoded to reflect characteristics equating to the norms, beliefs and values of hegemonic forces and become aligned thereto. Oppositional reading may decode messages to opposite effect. For Hall (1980: 138) 'One of the most significant political moments . . . is . . . when events . . . normally signified and decoded in a negotiated way begin to be given an oppositional reading. Here the "politics of signification" . . . the struggle in discourse . . . is joined'. Gallhofer and Haslam's (2006a) study of *Forward* and Red Clydeside indicates accounting's radical possibilities and actualities, furnishing insights to the specificities of the processes involved, and the potential significance of change in how accounting is socially perceived and the role and variety of the media.

Reflections

The studies by Gallhofer and Haslam and Arnold reviewed in this chapter illuminate accounting as a focus of conflicting objectives, as an ambiguous phenomenon with the capacity to reflect social tensions. Gallhofer and Haslam (2003: 102) note 'the inextricable positioning of accounting in the field of tension of its . . . context, no matter how non-controversial the practice may . . . appear'. At any moment in a problematic socio-political order, accounting functions as both emancipatory and repressive. If accounting is to change in its functioning and consequences, one or more of its form, content, aura or usage must also change. It matters what understanding of accounting is reached, who grasps it and what they do with it.

Gallhofer and Haslam elaborate accounting's mobilisation *vis-à-vis* a relatively repressed social body by focusing on socialistic and labour campaigns. Existing and new accountings were mobilised. New, including disaggregated, accountings were campaigned for. The trajectories of these struggles underscored accounting's emancipatory potential. Even when it serves the established order, accounting as a form of openness becomes an awkward phenomenon for the relatively powerful to control. Powerful forces meet with resistance in and through accounting. Repressive forces may be influential but never absolutely control accounting's functioning. Accounting has potential, the realisation of which may be furthered by activism, to function so that emancipatory effects may dominate the repressive. Where accounting is mobilised by repressive forces, countervailing forces may be engendered as activists are provided with opportunities to respond and contribute.

Gallhofer and Haslam's historical analyses also remind us that accounting has been shaped by struggles, helping us to appreciate its problematic dimensions today. Their studies alert us to the continuing emancipatory potentialities of accounting and the character of contextual dynamics that may further their realisation. Gallhofer and Haslam indicate accounting's potential to offer critical reflection on the socio-political order. We may also reflect on how the power of facticity, trust in accounts and perceptions of accounts have changed. Further, one may theorise negative dimensions of radical activism which invokes 'factual' accounts. Analysis points to how accounting has been mobilised by activists and this may inspire and strengthen emancipatory struggle in the present.[13]

Conclusion

In this chapter we have elaborated studies, themselves concerned to advance emancipation in and through accounting, which have furnished analyses of the mobilisation of accounting in emancipatory activism. The studies suggest insights of relevance to emancipatory projects today. Surprisingly few similar studies have been undertaken in this field given the apparent significance of such topics for the critical project (Gallhofer and Haslam 2006a). There is scope for further work. Radical activists' mobilising of accounting with emancipatory intent continues to manifest. A number of studies have highlighted this. Gallhofer and Haslam (2003), for example, discuss instances of 'counter accounting' in Britain from the 1970s onwards, whereby pressure groups have mobilised accounting in radical campaigns. Here accounting has been integral to critical commentaries on large business corporations, governments and the established socio-political order. They highlight the role of such bodies as Counter Information Services and Social Audit Ltd in the 1970s and, more recently, Corporate Watch. Other notable related studies include Arnold and Hammond (1994), which focuses on South Africa's former apartheid regime and concludes that accounting may serve repressed groups as in the divestment movement (see Dey 2007). Gallhofer *et al.* (2006) explore how the Web is facilitating and impeding such possibilities. Technological dynamics change the form/dissemination of counter accountings *vis-à-vis* globalisation and environmental crisis where the intertwining of accounting and radical activism continues (Gallhofer and Haslam 2003, 2006b).[14] These studies provide insight but also indicate that there is much still to explore and discover, thus hopefully stimulating further research of this genre.

Key works

Arnold (1997) addresses themes of emancipatory accounting, though not from an explicitly critical perspective.

Bentham (1843) Bentham's writings in general incorporate reflections on accounting publicity but readers may find 'Of publicity' particularly focused in relation to the ideas elaborated in this chapter.

Gallhofer and Haslam (2003) espouses a critical theoretical position on accounting and emancipation refined by engagement with post-modern theory. It includes an analysis of key writings by Bentham on accounting, and the mobilisation of accounting by radical agitators and activists in the late nineteenth and early twentieth centuries.

Notes

1 Bentham hid numerous writings from public view in his own severely repressive context and much of his work has only recently been published (Boralevi 1980, 1984; Foot 1984; *cf.* Russell 1962: 742; Harrison 1983: 131).

2 One's happiness was understood as advanced through one's benevolence (Mack 1962).

3 Bentham interacted with early socialists, including William Thompson and Robert Owen (Russell 1962: 747; Boralevi 1984: 37).

4 The construct 'accounting publicity' was not confined to Bentham. Bentham's 'book-keeping at large' surpassed convention. Publicity is referenced in recent accounting laws of some continental European countries (Gallhofer and Haslam 1995, 1996b).

5 For Bentham (1843: 589) 'Whom ought we to distrust, if not those to whom is committed great authority, with great temptations to abuse?'

6 Bentham here ironically displaces alternative accountings (see Edwards 1989).

7 This was enhanced by the Companies Act, 1862. Model articles required balance sheet and income and expenditure accounts as prescribed at the annual general meeting, the opening of books to member inspection and an annual appointed-member audit reporting whether the balance sheet was 'full and fair' and gave a 'true and correct view' (Edwards 1989: 182).

8 The journal was not formally the organ of any body, but contained advertisements of socialist groups (*Common Sense*, 15 July 1887: 56).

9 *The Link* declared: 'comfortable people object to the veil being torn off the putrefying wounds of society'. Its motto, from Hugo, which included 'I will . . . say everything' reflected Fabian pressure for transparency (30 June 1888: 1).

10 Publicity's success encouraged Champion. In *The Labour Elector*, the paper he edited after *Common Sense*, he attacked Bryant & May's directors' pay (24 August 1889).

11 Champion later turned attention to Brunner, Mond, a forerunner of ICI, in *The Labour Elector*. For the similarity of the case to the match girls, see Gallhofer and Haslam (2003).

12 Further, government and profession aligned by the end of the nineteenth century, underwriting corporate secrecy (Arnold 1997).

13 Gallhofer and Haslam (1991), a related study, attends to accounting's mobilisation in socialist media in Germany during the First World War and its aftermath. There are similarities between this case and the British cases considered. Differences include the German government's relatively slow response and the strong 'confidentiality' connotation of accounting before the war.

14 The global character of struggles today differs from but echoes those of earlier times. Socialist struggles often had an international dimension influenced, for example, by Marx's call to rally workers internationally. Bentham apparently was the first to use the word 'international', seeing himself as a world citizen influencing governance globally (Letwin 1965).

References

Alvesson, M. and Willmott, H. (1992) On the idea of emancipation in management and organization studies, *Academy of Management Review*, 17 (3): 432–64.

Anonymous (1838) Article XI, The works of Jeremy Bentham: now first collected under the superintendence of his executor John Bowring, Parts 1–4, *London and Westminster Review*, April–August (Edinburgh: Tate).

Arnold, A. J. (1997) Publishing your private affairs to the world: corporate financial disclosures in the UK, 1900–24, *Accounting, Business & Financial History*, 7 (2): 143–71.

Arnold, P. J. and Hammond, T. (1994) The role of accounting in ideological conflict: lessons from the South African divestment movement, *Accounting, Organizations and Society*, 19 (2): 111–26.

Bahmueller, C. F. (1981) *The National Charity Company: Jeremy Bentham's Silent Revolution* (Berkeley, CA: University of California).

Beaver, P. (1985) *The Match Makers* (London: Henry Melland).

Benhabib, S. (1992) *Situating the Self: Gender, Community and Postmodernism in Contemporary Ethics* (Cambridge: Polity with Oxford: Blackwell).

Benhabib, S. (1994) In defence of universalism – yet again! A response to critics of situating the self, *New German Critique*, 62 (Spring–Summer): 173–89.

Bentham, J. (1790) Letter to Right Hon John Parnell, 2 September 1790, British Museum Manuscript, MS 33541: f. 160.

Bentham, J. (1812) *Pauper Management Improved: Particularly by Means of an Application of the Panopticon Principle of Construction* (London: Robert Baldwin & James Ridgeway).

Bentham, J. (1816) *Chrestomathia* (London: Payne & Foss and R. Hunter).

Bentham, J. (1817) *Chrestomathia*, Part II (London: Payne & Foss).

Bentham, J. (1843) Of publicity, in An Essay on Political Tactics, in J. Bowring (ed.), *The Works of Jeremy Bentham*, Vol. 2, pp. 310–15 (Edinburgh: Simpkin, Marshall and Co).

Bentham, S. (1830) *Financial Reform Scrutinised in a Letter to Sir Henry Parnell, Bart, MP* (London: Hatchard & Son).

Besant, A. (1938) *An Autobiography*, 2nd edn (London: Fisher Unwin).

Bolt, C. (1993) *The Women's Movement in the United States and Britain from the 1790s to the 1920s* (New York: Harvester Wheatsheaf).

Booth, W. (1890) *In Darkest England and the Way Out* (London: Salvation Army).

Boralevi, C. L. (1980) In defence of a myth, *The Bentham Newsletter*, 4 (May): 33–46.

Boralevi, C. L. (1984) *Bentham and the Oppressed* (Berlin: Mouton de Gruyter).

Bowring, J. (ed.) (1843) *The Works of Jeremy Bentham* (Edinburgh: Simpkin, Marshall & Co).

Briggs, A. and Macartney, A. (1984) *Toynbee Hall: The First Hundred Years* (London: Routledge & Kegan Paul).

Bronner, S. E. (1994) *Of Critical Theory and its Theorists* (Oxford: Blackwell).

Bryant and May, Minutes of Directors, Records of Bryant & May (Ref D/B/BRY), Hackney Archives, London.

Bryant and May, Secretary's Diary, Records of Bryant & May (Ref D/B/BRY), Hackney Archives, London.

Calhoun, C. (1995) *Critical Social Theory: Culture, History and the Challenge of Difference* (Oxford: Blackwell).

Calinescu, M. (1987) *Five Faces of Modernity* (Durham, NC: Duke University Press).

Callaghan, J. (1990) *Socialism in Britain since 1884* (Oxford: Blackwell).

Champion, H. H. (1983) Quorum pars fui: an unconventional autobiography, *Bulletin of the Society for the Study of Labour History*, 47: 17–35.

Christian (1887).

Collett, C. E. (1893) Women's work, in C. Booth (ed.) *Life and Labour of the People in London, First Series: Poverty IV, The Trades of East London Connected with Poverty*, pp. 256–327 (London: Macmillan and Co.).

Common Sense (1887).

Cousins, M. (1987) The practice of historical investigation, in D. Attridge, G. Bennington and R. Young (eds), *Post-structuralism and the Question of History*, pp. 126–38 (Cambridge: Cambridge University Press).

Critchley, S. (2001), *Continental Philosophy: A Very Short Introduction* (Oxford: Oxford University Press).

Cullen, M. J. (1975) *The Statistical Movement in Early Victorian Britain: The Foundation of Empirical Social Research* (Hassocks: Harvester Press).

Daunton, M. (2000) Society and economic life, in C. Matthew (ed.), *The Nineteenth Century, The British Isles: 1815–1901*, pp. 40–82 (Oxford: Oxford University Press).

Derrida, J. (1978) Violence and metaphysics: an essay on the thought of Emmanuel Levinas, in J. Derrida: *Writing and Difference*, pp. 79–153, trans. Alan Bass (Chicago: The University of Chicago Press).

Dey, C. R. (2007) Developing silent and shadow accounts, in J. B. Unerman, B. O'Dwyer and J. Bebbington (eds), *Sustainability, Accounting and Accountability*, pp. 307–26 (London: Routledge).

Doornbos, M. (1992) Foreword, *Development and Change*, 23(3): 1–4.

Edwards, J. R. (1989) *A History of Financial Accounting* (London: Routledge).

Edwards, J. R. (1992) Companies, corporations and accounting change, 1835–1933: a comparative study, *Accounting and Business Research*, 23 (89): 59–73.

Foot, P. (1984) *Red Shelley* (London: Bookmarks).

Forward (1914, 1917).

Foster, J. (1990) Strike action and working-class politics on Clydeside 1914–1919, *International Review of Social History*, 35: 33–70.

Gallhofer, S. and Chew, A. (2000) Accounting and indigenous peoples, *Accounting, Auditing & Accountability Journal*, 13 (3): 256–67.

Gallhofer, S. and Haslam, J. (1991) The aura of accounting in the context of a crisis situation: Germany and the First World War, *Accounting, Organizations and Society*, 16 (5/6): 487–520.

Gallhofer, S. and Haslam, J. (1993) Approaching corporate accountability: fragments from the past, *Accounting and Business Research*, 23 (91a): 320–30.

Gallhofer, S. and Haslam, J. (1994a) Accounting and the Benthams: accounting as negation, *Accounting, Business & Financial History*, 4 (2): 239–73.

Gallhofer, S. and Haslam, J. (1994b) Accounting and the Benthams: or, accounting's potentialities, *Accounting, Business & Financial History*, 4 (3): 431–60.

Gallhofer, S. and Haslam, J. (1995) Accounting and modernity, *Advances in Public Interest Accounting*, Vol. 6, pp. 203–32 (Greenwich, CT: JAI Press).

Gallhofer, S. and Haslam, J. (1996a) Accounting/art and the emancipatory project: some reflections, *Accounting, Auditing & Accountability Journal*, 9 (5): 23–44.

Gallhofer, S. and Haslam, J. (1996b) Analysis of Bentham's Chrestomathia: or towards a critique of accounting education, *Critical Perspectives on Accounting*, 7 (1/2): 13–31.

Gallhofer, S. and Haslam, J. (2003) *Accounting and Emancipation: Some Critical Interventions* (London: Routledge).

Gallhofer, S. and Haslam, J. (2005) Social accounting, historical perspective, in C. Clubb (ed.), *Blackwell Encyclopaedia of Accounting*, pp. 388–93 (Oxford: Blackwell).

Gallhofer, S. and Haslam, J. (2006a) Mobilising accounting in the radical media during the First World War and its aftermath: the case of *Forward* in the context of Red Clydeside, *Critical Perspectives on Accounting*, 17 (2/3): 224–52.

Gallhofer, S. and Haslam, J. (2006b) The accounting-globalisation interrelation: an overview with some reflections on the neglected dimension of emancipatory potentiality, *Critical Perspectives on Accounting*, 17 (7): 903–34.

Gallhofer, S., Haslam, J., Monk, E. and Roberts, C. (2006) The emancipatory potential of online reporting: the case of counter accounting, *Accounting, Auditing & Accountability Journal*, 19 (5): 681–718.

Gaonkar, D. P. and McCarthey, R. J. Jr. (1994) Panopticism and publicity: Bentham's quest for transparency, *Public Culture*, 6 (3): 547–75.

Goldberg, L. (1957) Jeremy Bentham: critic of accounting method, *Accounting Research*, 8: 218–45

Habermas, J. (1974) The public sphere, trans. S. Lennox and F. Lennox, *New German Critique*, 1 (3): 49–55.

Habermas, J. (1992) *The Structural Transformation of the Public Sphere: An Inquiry into a Category of Bourgeois Society*, trans. T. Burger with F. Lawrence (Cambridge, MA: the MIT Press).

Hall, S. (1980) Encoding/decoding, in D. Hall, A. Hobson, D. Lowe and P. Willis (eds), *Culture, Media, Language: Working Papers in Cultural Studies, 1972–1979*, pp. 128–38 (London: Hutchinson).

Harrison, R. (1983) *Bentham* (London: Routledge & Kegan Paul).

Hart, H. L. A. (1982) *Essays on Bentham's Jurisprudence and Political Theory* (Oxford: Oxford University Press).

Himmelfarb, G. (1968) The haunted house of Jeremy Bentham, in G. Himmelfarb, (ed.), *Victorian Minds*, pp. 32–81 (New York: Knopf).

Hobsbawm, E. J. (1962) *The Age of Revolution: Europe 1789–1848* (London: Weidenfeld and Nicholson).

Hobsbawm, E. J. (1999) *Industry and Empire: From 1750 to the Present Day* (Harmondsworth: Penguin).

Hopkins, E. (2000) *Industrialisation and Society: A Social History, 1830–1951* (London: Routledge).

Hoskin, K. and Macve, R. (1986) Accounting and the examination: a genealogy of disciplinary power, *Accounting, Organizations and Society*, 11 (2): 105–36.

Hulse, J. W. (1970) *Revolutionists in London: A Study of Five Unorthodox Socialists* (Oxford: Clarendon Press).

Hume, L. J. (1970) The development of industrial accounting: the Benthams' contribution, *Journal of Accounting Research*, 8 (1): 21–33.

Hume, L. J. (1981) *Bentham and Bureaucracy* (Cambridge: Cambridge University Press).

Hyndman, H. M. (1911) *The Record of an Adventurous Life* (London: Macmillan).

Laclau, E. (1990) *New Reflections on the Revolution of Our Time* (London: Verso).

Laclau, E. (1992) Beyond emancipation, *Development and Change*, 23 (3): 121–37.

Laclau, E. (1996) *Emancipation(s)* (London: Verso).

Laclau, E. (2000) Constructing universality, in J. Butler, E. Laclau and S. Žižek (eds), *Contingency, Hegemony, Universality: Contemporary Dialogues on the Left*, pp. 281–307 (London: Verso).

Lehman, C. R. and Tinker, T. (1987) The 'Real' cultural significance of accounts, *Accounting, Organizations and Society*, 12 (5): 503–22.

Letwin, S. R. (1965) *The Pursuit of Certainty: David Hume, Jeremy Bentham, John Stuart Mill, Beatrice Webb* (Cambridge: Cambridge University Press).

Liberal Radical (1888).

The Link (1888).

Loft, A. (1988) *Understanding Accounting in its Social and Historical Context: The Case of Cost Accounting in Britain, 1914–25* (New York: Garland).

Mack, M. P. (1962) *Jeremy Bentham: An Odyssey of Ideas, 1748–1792* (London: Heinemann).

Marriner, S. (1980) Company financial statements as source material for business historians, *Business History*, 22 (3): 203–35.

Miller, P. and Napier, C. (1993) Genealogies of calculation, *Accounting, Organizations and Society*, 18 (7/8): 631–47.

Napier, C. J. (2001) Accounting history and accounting progress, *Accounting History*, 6 (2): 7–31.

Nederveen Pieterse, J. (1992) Emancipations, modern and postmodern, *Development and Change*, 23 (3): 5–41.

Pall Mall Gazette (1888–89).

Parker, R. H. (1990) Regulating British corporate financial reporting in the late nineteenth century, *Accounting, Business & Financial History*, 1 (1): 51–71.

Peters, J. D. (1993) Distrust of representation: Habermas on the public sphere, *Media, Culture and Society*, 15 (4): 541–71.

Prokhovnik, R. (1999) *Rational Woman: A Feminist Critique of Dichotomy* (London: Routledge).

Rorty, R. (1989) *Contingency, Irony and Solidarity* (Cambridge: Cambridge University Press).

Rosen, F. (1983) *Jeremy Bentham and Representative Democracy: A Study of the Constitutional Code* (Oxford: Clarendon Press).

Russell, B. (1962) *History of Western Philosophy and its Connection with Political and Social Circumstances from the Earliest Times to the Present Day* (London: Allen and Unwin).

St James's Gazette (1888).

Semple, J. (1993) *Bentham's Prison: A Study of the Panopticon Penitentiary* (New York: Oxford University Press).

Sikka, P. (2000) From the politics of fear to the politics of emancipation, *Critical Perspectives on Accounting*, 11 (3): 369–80.

Soldon, N. C. (1978) *Women in British Trade Unions: 1874–1976* (Dublin: Totowa).

Squires, J. (1993) Introduction, in J. Squires (ed.), *Principled Positions: Postmodernism and the Rediscovery of Value*, pp. 1–13 (London: Lawrence and Wishart).

Star (1888).

Stiglitz, J. (2002) *Economics*, 3rd edn (New York: Norton).

Tinker, T. (1985) *Paper Prophets: A Social Critique of Accounting* (London: Holt, Rinehart and Winston).

Tsuzuki, C. (1961) *H.M. Hyndman and British Socialism* (London: Oxford University Press).

UC, Bentham (Jeremy) Papers, 1750–1885, University College London.

Walker, S. P. (1996) Laissez-faire, collectivism and companies legislation in nineteenth-century Britain, *British Accounting Review*, 28 (4): 305–24.

Walker, S. P. (2004) Expense, social and moral control: accounting and the administration of the old poor law in England and Wales, *Journal of Accounting and Public Policy*, 23 (2): 85–127.

Whitehead, A. (1983) Champion, Henry Hyde, in J. M. Bellamy and J. Saville (eds), *Dictionary of Labour Biography*, Vol. 8, pp. 24–32 (London: Macmillan).

Žižek, S. (2000) Class struggle or postmodernism? Yes, please!, in J. Butler, E. Laclau and S. Žižek (eds), *Contingency, Hegemony, Universality: Contemporary Dialogues on the Left*, pp. 90–135 (London: Verso).

Žižek, S. (2001) *Did Somebody Say Totalitarianism? Five Interventions in the (Misuse) of a Notion* (London: Verso).

24

Religion

Salvador Carmona and Mahmoud Ezzamel

Overview

The examination of the relationship between accounting and religion in a historical context draws on the extant literature and is organised around micro and macro perspectives. From a micro perspective, the chapter addresses the role of accounting in religious organisations, such as temples and religious orders. In particular, it reviews the so-called sacred–profane divide as well as the technical aspects of the implementation of accounting systems in religious organisations. From a macro point of view, it examines the distinctive role of religious beliefs in shaping wider, social understandings of accounting and business.

Proponents of the sacred–profane divide contend that accounting is part of the profane world and, as such, its use in religious organisations has been viewed as an unwanted intrusion in the world of the sacred. Analysis of research in this area indicates that such a dichotomy is not universally relevant to all forms of religious institutions, and is problematical even in the Christian religion, from where this distinction was initially drawn. Furthermore, the chapter indicates that historically, accounting systems in religious organisations were far from rudimentary.

At the macro level, analysis shows that religious beliefs exerted a lasting influence on business activities and society in general. The ban against lending money at interest, and usury in particular, resulted in the development of alternative ways to exploit loopholes and circumvent concerns about morality so that businessmen could continue to profit by advancing loans at high interest. Furthermore, the importance of accounting and cost calculations is noted for endowing profit with a meaning that was unacceptable in some conservative, Roman Catholic settings. The literature reviewed suggests that accounting had a major constitutive impact on societies with a religious worldview, even though religious values were not necessarily mirrored in financial statements. Finally, the chapter indicates that certain religious and cultural beliefs in Chinese society have had a major impact on promoting an understanding of accounting as irrelevant to decision-making, and as an occupation unworthy of those from the most elevated social classes.

Religious beliefs in accounting and business practices

The role of religion in the history of humankind can hardly be overestated (Smith 1979). Religious beliefs have exerted a major and lasting influence on human behaviour as well as on the constitutive elements of social activities and institutions (Durkheim 1976). Religion is widely regarded as one of the earliest forms of human knowledge (Armstrong 1993; Zubiri 1993). At the macro level, religious thoughts have permeated almost every sphere of social life, ranging from political systems to international relations (Suárez 2004).[1] Furthermore, religious beliefs mediate micro-spaces and professional activities such as architecture (Kubler 1982) and banking by being inscribed onto such spaces and activities (Karim 1990).

Given the widely recognised view that accounting has a major and enduring impact on individuals, institutions, and social life in general (Burchell *et al.* 1980), an examination of the relationship between accounting and religion is a key research area for students of history. Given the rich diversity of religious experience across time and space, such an examination has the potential to contribute to understandings of the role that accounting has played in a variety of organisational and societal settings. It also promises to yield rich insights that could provide a better theorising of the accounting craft (Ezzamel and Bourn 1990).

Our historical examination of the relationship between accounting and religion draws on the extant literature. This literature has a number of salient characteristics. It draws on a plurality of epistemological perspectives and research sites within a given system of religious beliefs. Examples include accounting in a sixteenth-century Benedictine monastery (Sargiacomo 2001), the links between accounting and notions emerging from the field of comparative spirituality (Laughlin 1988), and management accounting practices in a German-American religious commune (Flesher and Flesher 1979). Investigations also cover a broad canvass of religious regimes, ranging from the influence of Confucianism on Chinese accounting (Guo 1988) to the impact of shifting religious beliefs on accounting during the transition from a Hindu administration to an Islamic administration in Indonesia (Sukoharsono 1998).

Previous research has, in the main, been Christian-centric (Tinker 2004), drawing on beliefs and organisations in Christian societies to the relative neglect of other religions and forms of spirituality such as Islam and Buddhism. Moreover, with few exceptions (such as Ezzamel 2002), extant research has overwhelmingly focused on a short time-frame, in particular, the nineteenth and early twentieth centuries. To partly compensate for this limitation, our review also refers to 'histories of the present', that is, those studies which examine the relationship between accounting and religion in contemporary societies. Such investigations of the modern age, we argue, are likely to produce many useful insights for those intending to conduct historical research on accounting and religion.

Extant research on the relationship between accounting and religion is a far cry from the Kuhnian notion of 'normal science' (Kuhn 1962). Generally speaking, historians of this relationship do not work within a single, agreed-upon paradigm. Instead, the literature is disparate and addresses issues that are typically only marginally interrelated. In saying this, we are not advocating the idea that better accounting history research is likely to emerge if its production is constrained within a single paradigm. Rather, the diversity of theoretical perspectives in the literature is, we argue, a source of strength. We only allude to the difficulty of synthesising research that is informed by theoretical variety, a difficulty exacerbated by the weak interconnections between the issues examined. Essentially, this chapter reviews an area of accounting history that has not been extensively researched and it identifies several subjects for future investigation.

The chapter is organised around the micro and macro perspectives of accounting and religion suggested above. From a micro perspective, our aim is to address the role of accounting in religious organisations, such as temples and religious orders. From a macro point of view, we examine the distinctive role of religious beliefs in shaping wider, social understandings of accounting and business. Further, we will examine the views of religious texts concerning accounting and their functioning in organisations and society.

The remainder of the chapter is organised as follows. In the next section, we survey the literature on accounting in religious organisations, with an emphasis on two major themes. First, the so-called sacred–profane divide, where our analysis spans accounting practice in ancient societies, particularly that of ancient Egypt, medieval times, the proto-industrial period, the Enlightenment and nineteenth-century Europe, and contemporary religious institutions in Christianity and Islam. The second major theme relates to the technical aspects of accounting practice used in Christian religious institutions. In a separate section, we deal with the literature concerned with the influence of religious thought on accounting and business practice, paying special attention to how concepts such as interest, usury, prices, and profit (earnings) were defined across different religious beliefs and over time. We pay attention to such influence in relation to the Middle Ages, the Renaissance and Protestanism but also extend our discussion to the teachings of other religions such as Islam and Confucianism. In the penultimate section, we examine some of the literature which discusses how accounting is treated in sacred religious texts, including the Quran, the Old Testament, and the New Testament. The chapter concludes with a summary and some suggestions for future research.

Accounting in religious organisations

Investigations adopting a micro perspective on the role of accounting in religious organisations are here analysed around two key themes. First, examination of the sacred–profane divide. In this context, accounting has been perceived by some as part of the profane world and, as such, its use in religious organisations has been viewed as an unwanted intervention into the world of the sacred (Laughlin 1988). Others have rejected this duality (e.g. Quattrone 2004). Second, the early implementation of sophisticated accounting techniques in religious organisations. This latter strand of research has focused on the implementation of double-entry bookkeeping in religions institutions before the Industrial Revolution (Hernández Esteve 2001).

Accounting and the sacred–profane divide

When referring to the modelling of the world by religious belief, Durkheim (1976: 37) stated: 'the one containing all that is sacred, the other all that is profane'. This line of thought has been very influential in accounting in promoting a duality according to which the profane is treated as something fundamentally different, and separate from, the sacred. For example, Laughlin (1988, 1990) drew on aspects of Habermas' critical theory and research on comparative spirituality (Eliade 1959) to examine the functioning of accounting systems in the Church of England. He noted how, initially, the state acted as a 'resource supplier' for the Church and for the dioceses and parishes in particular. However, when the resource suppliers no longer required the guidance of the Church of England, this institution internalised the resourcing problem. It was in this new context that the accounting system of the Church of England was located. In this respect, Laughlin (1988: 38) argued that accounting systems 'are legitimate aids to this resourcing problem, but they are not part of the sacred agenda and should not interfere with more important endeavours of the Church of England'. Accounting thus, argues Laughlin, did not play a role in the functioning of the sacred elements of the Church of England.

In his examination of the Australian Uniting Church, Booth (1993) supported the sacred–profane divide suggested by Laughlin. In particular, Booth argued that the dichotomy helped to differentiate the 'legitimate' part of religious organisations from support activities, which entered the domain of the profane. Booth asserted that the secular plays a secondary role in religious institutions and that accounting constituted an integral part of the domain of the profane. In spite of this subordinate role, Booth indicated that accounting did not necessarily face resistance in religious organisations and that its role 'can be highly prominent within Churches' (Booth 1993: 41).

Some studies in accounting have questioned the sacred–profane divide. For example, Hardy and Ballis (2005: 25–6) argued that 'The sacred and secular model remains problematic: it consists of general arguments that oversimplify religious organizations, on the one hand, and on the other, the role of professionals in these organizations.' In a similar vein, recent research has suggested that the sacred–profane dichotomy may be time-space specific and may not be applicable to religious institutions beyond those of contemporary Christian Western cultures (Carmona and Ezzamel 2006). Given the importance of context-embeddedness for an informed understanding of the sacred–profane divide, we will follow the chronological development of the relevant literature. As shown below, some of these studies do not explicitly address the sacred–profane dichotomy but the richness of their evidence provides insights on this issue.

Ancient societies

Ezzamel (2005) examined the role of accounting practices in the functioning of funerary temples during the Old Kingdom (2700–2181 BC) in ancient Egypt. He noted that accounting in these institutions provided different types of visibility: organisational, technical and dependency. The temple ensured organisational visibility through recording items using a combination of black and red ink in a tabular format. Further, the enumeration of quantities of inventory tools drew on a flexible categorisation that made it easy for the scribe to signal damaged items as well as the nature of the damage. These entries were then audited by a foreman who made entries in the inventory list to that effect. Taken together, these practices provided a form of technical visibility. Dependency visibility was evident in how accounting entries shed light on the intricate relationships among economic institutions that provided daily supplies to the funerary temple. In turn, such entries were aggregated in monthly income statements that indicated the theoretical (expected) deliveries, actual deliveries and any balances outstanding day by day. Ezzamel (2005: 48) concluded, 'this complex and detailed range of accounting intervention in the activities of the temple neither signals accounting as "irrelevant", nor highly "rudimentary" nor an unwanted, profane inconvenience'. He argued that, rather than being a marginal, profane activity accounting was intertwined with the sacred activities of the temple. This was consistent with the religious ideology of ancient Egypt that drew no clear demarcations between what was sacred and what was profane.

Other investigations of the sacred–profane divide in ancient societies include Fonfeder *et al.* (2003) who investigated the Hebrew Talmud's account of internal controls in the ancient Temple of Jerusalem (*c.* 823 BC to 70 CE). The authors state (2003: 75) 'the Talmud was so concerned with preventing any suspicion of financial malfeasance, that controls were designed to prevent even any appearance of theft', thus enhancing the fiscal credibility of the Temple in the eyes of its congregants. Talmudic sources enforced the use of extensive internal control processes over the Temple treasury, including the collections of biblically-mandated half-shekel donations, withdrawals from the Treasury, and distributed offerings, all premised on the idea that public confidence in the workings of the Temple was sacrosanct. Fonfeder *et al.* (2003: 90) contend that 'the Talmud's extended discussion of internal controls indicates that systems of accountability formed an integral portion of the Temple's rituals', thereby indicating that accounting was not a profane activity at odds with the Temple's mission.

Medieval times

The Order of the Temple was created after the First Crusade, in 1096, to protect pilgrims on their way to Jerusalem. The Temple combined military and religious activities and, as such, its members were a disciplined force who performed the double role of monks and soldiers. The Temple grew in social and political importance during Medieval times until its sudden demise in 1314. De la Torre's (2004) study of the role of the Order of the Temple in the origins of banking is of particular interest to our analysis. De la Torre argued that the Knights Templars engaged in banking in relation to donations received from pilgrims in acknowledgement of their protection on their round trip to Jerusalem. In turn, these funds were deployed in supporting the wars against the Arab Muslims. More importantly, the Temple became heavily engaged in public banking, that is, lending money to European monarchs, especially to the Kingdom of France.

Banking became essential to the mission of the Knights Templars and a sophisticated accounting system was deployed to record the web of transactions and transfers of funding across the Order's sites in different countries and regions. Although De la Torre did not address the sacred–profane divide explicitly, the variety of financial activities performed by the Knights Templars are suggestive of the intertwining of the sacred and profane. Accounting systems did not constitute an external, detached activity, but facilitated the ventures pursued by the Order.

The proto-industrial period

In 1503, the City of Seville was granted the monopoly of Spanish trading with its Latin American colonies and, as a result, became one of the most important trading centres in Europe. In this context the Cathedral of Seville became a major social, economic and political organisation. The scale of its activity is indicated by the 9,000 accounting books catalogued in the Cathedral's archive from the fifteenth to the nineteenth centuries.

The accounting system of the Cathedral of Seville, 1625–50 has been examined by Hernández Borreguero (2002). During that period, the Cathedral kept 630 accounting books, that is, more than 25 per year. This wealth of accounting records reveals an intricate web of transactions indicative of the Cathedral's aim to secure funds from the city's businesses and enhance its own political and social standing. In pursuing this objective, the Cathedral of Seville engaged in transactions banned by the doctrine of the Catholic Church. Hernández Borreguero discusses evidence of lending activities at an interest rate that was regarded as usury by the Catholic Church and, hence, banned, but the Cathedral drew on the skills of its accountants to mask such transactions. The expertise of its accountants also proved instrumental in resolving disputes between parties in different areas of business activity in the context of regulated markets. Although Hernández Borreguero's study did not address the sacred–profane divide directly, his evidence suggests that accounting played a fundamental role in the organisation of the Cathedral's activities.

Other investigations have addressed the role of accounting in religious organisations before the Industrial Revolution. Quattrone's (2004) analysis of accounting and accountability in the

Society of Jesus is particularly significant in this regard. Quattrone provides a detailed description of the internal organisation of the Jesuits amid the ideas of the Counter-Reformation enforced at the Council of Trento, 1545–63. As in the case of the Order of the Temple, the Jesuits also adopted a hierarchical, disciplinary structure, calling themselves 'soldiers of Jesus'. Quattrone (2004: 654) notes that the Jesuits 'were animated by an activism previously unknown in the Catholic Church, where monastic organizations were devoted to contemplation and isolation'. In their pursuit of the salvation of souls, the Jesuits engaged in missionary, educational and economic activities.

The Society offered teaching and religious services free of charge. In this respect, the Colleges – the primary unit of the Jesuit organisation and the venue for conducting its activities – were instrumental. These activities required substantial financial resources and sophisticated accounting systems. In fact, accounting became central to the pursuit of the Society's mission. Quattrone (2004) argues that the accounting systems excelled in their sophistication and accuracy. The system concerned the different activities for income generation: legacies and annuity payments, farms, and rents. In keeping these records, the Jesuits were inspired by the ideas enshrined in the *Trattato del modo di tenere il libro doppio domestico col suo essemplare* which presented the double-entry method as an effective combination of analysis and synthesis. In addition to accounting for economic activities, Quattrone shows that the Jesuits engaged in other ideologically embedded accountings such as accounting for sins and accounting for the soul.

The design and implementation of the accounting and accountability practices of the Jesuits were inspired by the absolutist ideology of the Roman Catholic doctrine during the Counter-Reformation. This ideology exerted a distinctive influence on other organisations related to the Roman Catholic Church. For example, the Council of Trento promoted religious brotherhoods. Under the dictates of the Council, the brotherhoods would become a conduit for ensuring the indoctrination of the populace (López-Manjón et al. 2007). In pursuing such aims, the brotherhoods provided members with educational, entertainment and religious services. Ultimately, the brotherhoods acted to underpin social cohesion around religious beliefs (Sánchez Herrero 1985).

López Manjón et al. (2007) focused on the accounting practices of the religious brotherhoods established in the wider region of Seville during the period 1563–1604. The governance structure of the brotherhoods was set in their 'rules', which were detailed in comprehensive documents. López Manjón et al. argue that the brotherhoods' rules established a multifaceted understanding of accounting. First, according to the provisions of the Council of Trento, the brotherhoods were subject to a strict system of accountability before the Archbishop of Seville and his representatives. If deemed necessary by the Archbishop, the brotherhoods were audited, during which time their officers were temporarily removed and administrative matters were managed by the representatives of the Archbishop. Second, the brotherhood's management was held accountable before its members. The general meetings of the brotherhoods were formative events when members decided on the long- and short-term plans and management were obliged to report on the financial condition of the institution. Furthermore, accounting played a fundamental role when new officers were appointed. Outgoing officers had to deliver a comprehensive inventory of items owned by the brotherhoods and this was subject to internal audit. Finally, accounting played a fundamental role in the day-to-day activities of the brotherhoods. In addition to accounting for sundry activities, ranging from leisure to education, the accounting books contained precise records of all waste and consumption that occurred in relation to religious activities (such as religious dress and ornaments, and the consumption of wax).

Drawing on the sacred–profane framework, López Manjón *et al.* (2007) thus reveal how accounting was a powerful instrument for exerting strict internal and external control over the management of the brotherhoods. The authors show how accounting played an active role in the daily activities of the brotherhoods and how it was consistently used to evaluate past actions. Far from being associated with the profane, accounting mediated the core, 'sacred' aspects of these religious institutions.

The Enlightenment and the nineteenth century

In the eighteenth century, the context in which the brotherhoods in Seville operated changed dramatically. In contrast to the absolutist ideology enforced by the Council of Trento, the Enlightenment provided a more relaxed environment for the development of religious activities. Álvarez-Dardet *et al.* (2006) examined the regulation of brotherhoods during the period 1768–75 and found that they had a perception of the sacred that differed significantly from that of 'enlightened' people. The brotherhoods supported a popular view of religiousness that included elements which 'champions' of the Enlightenment deemed profane. Furthermore, the Bishop of Ciudad Rodrigo supported the views of the enlightened and considered that most of the activities of the brotherhoods were far removed from the sacred sphere. From this perspective, the brotherhoods had to be accountable to the religious hierarchy and also to civil power. In such contexts, accounting played a secondary role because the government mainly sought the compliance of the brotherhoods with prior regulations concerning the approval of their activities. The case of brotherhoods operating in eighteenth-century Spain suggests that the sacred–profane divide did not constitute a universal notion of immutable concepts. The dichotomy consisted of concepts that were time–space contingent.

Research on accounting in religious institutions has overwhelmingly focused on organisations inhabited by men. In one of the few studies addressing female institutions, Oliveira and Brandao (2005) examined accounting practices in the Cistercian Monastery of Arouca during the period 1786–1825. As with the Order of Temple, the Society of Jesus and the brotherhoods discussed above, the Cistercian congregation was organised in a hierarchical fashion, an organisational form that impacted on the accounting systems of the monastery. According to the rules of the Cistercians the Monastery of Arouca had to report to the Congregation of Alcobaça on its financial performance, and adhere to the Congregation's rule of maintaining a charge and discharge accounting system.

Accounting was crucial for the activities of the Monastery of Arouca. Oliveira and Brandao (2005) provide evidence on the use of accounting data to produce estimates of revenues and expenses. Such information was compared to the numbers living in the monastery to produce estimates of the population of Arouca in future years. This information, Oliveira and Brandao argue, was crucial in making decisions about the number of nuns that the monastery could admit in the future or the amount of long-term investments that could be funded. As with some other studies already referred to, Oliveira and Brandao did not focus explicitly on the sacred–profane divide. However, their evidence suggests that accounting played a central role in the activities of the monastery.

Accounting also played a significant role in the activities of Wesleyan Methodist missionaries in New Zealand during the period 1814–1840. John Wesley preached that followers should 'gain all you can, save all you can and give all you can' (Cordery 2006). Cordery found that the Methodists' letters and diaries included records about the exchange of barter goods and ledger accounts. Consequently, the Methodist missionaries were 'totally familiar with the need for accounting for the mission' (ibid.: 214).

509

Moving the focus to England, Irvine (2002) examined the role of accounting in the Salvation Army, 1865–92. This organisation, which heavily relied on external funds to survive, was engaged in an intense accounting exercise aimed at garnering legitimacy from the users of financial statements. The Salvation Army used accounting to convey a public image of sound financial responsibility with a view to securing the survival of the organisation in the longer term. Irvine's investigation demonstrated that accounting played a key role in the 'sacred' mission of the Salvation Army.

Contemporary organisations

Some studies have examined the sacred–profane divide in contemporary religious organisations. Jacobs and Walker (2004) drew on a combination of interviews and historical documents to examine accounting and accountability practices in an organisation associated with the Church of Scotland, the Iona Community. They show how the members 'are committed to a Rule of daily prayer and Bible study, sharing and accounting for their use of time and money' (ibid.: 363). Practices of financial accounting were deeply embedded in the central religious observances of the Iona Community. The findings challenge the suggestion that accounting was of marginal significance in sacred settings. Jacobs and Walker also explored the nature of accountabilities practised in this organisation and found that structures of individualising accountability were subject to resistance, while structures of socialising accountability had the potential to function as forms of internalised surveillance and domination.

Similarly, Jacobs (2005) examined the sacred–secular divide by drawing on the ideas of Christian thinkers critical of the dichotomy. He argued that accounting and financial issues do not necessarily conflict with religious values. Jacobs used narratives derived from interviews conducted in the Church of Scotland to demonstrate that the categorisation of accounting practices as secular is too simplistic. One interviewee revealed that 'the control and management of money within the Church was the responsibility of the clergy rather than the accountants' (Jacobs 2005: 206). Jacobs' study indicates that while there was some resistance to the incursion of accountants, accounting played an important role in the activities of the Church of Scotland.

In contrast to the foregoing emphasis on Christian religion, Abdul-Rahman and Goddard (1998) focused on two contemporary Islamic organisations established in Malaysia that collected and disbursed the *Zakah*, that is, the annual payment which Muslims with a minimum wealth are compelled to make. Abdul-Rahman and Goddard examined modes of thought (such as the dichotomy between secular-accounting and sacred-religious activities, level of professionalism, and the existence of power elites) and the modes of action (the processes and structures of accountability and organizational processes). They reported that the accountants in both organisations agreed that the accounting system was not alien to or separate from the religious domain. Accounting was considered to be part of the support activities of the organisation. The study suggests that in a Muslim setting there is no clear separation between sacred and secular activities. Abdul-Rahman and Goddard (ibid.: 197–8) concluded that 'The worldview of Islam encompasses both sacred and secular aspects and the secular must be related in a profound and inseparable way to the sacred.'

Technical aspects of accounting in religious institutions

In contrast to studies addressing the sacred–profane divide, several investigations have examined the level of sophistication of accounting techniques used in religious organizations. A particular focus of these studies is to test the idea that accounting practices in religious institutions were rudimentary or outdated. A related theme is to assess the extent to which these institutions were early adopters of double-entry bookkeeping. These studies have also examined how accounting practices in religious organizations are context embedded.

In the Kingdoms of Aragon and Catalonia during the fourteenth century, wealth was concentrated in the hands of the nobility, which comprised 11 per cent of the population (Monclús Guitart 2005). The remaining 89 per cent of the population were peasants, shepherds, fishermen and craftsmen who lived in impoverished conditions. Charity was crucial to ensuring the survival of the poor, especially during years of famine and plague. The Roman Catholic Church played a key role in charitable activities and efforts to redistribute wealth. Through this endeavour the Church pursued its spiritual aims and imposed its influence over the poor. Charitable activities were performed by the almoner who was accountable to the state for his management of funds. In a decree dated 18 May 1370, the King of Aragon granted the Abbot of the Monastery of Poblet the privilege of Royal Almoner. This decree stipulated rules for the management of charitable processes and covered receipts, management of cash assets and the delivery of funds to the poor. The rules were particularly detailed in relation to how the Abbot should report on the performance of charitable activities. Monclús Guitart (2005) compared the sophistication of these records with those kept by the contemporary *Taula de Canvis*, a banking institution. Monclús Guitart found that apart from differences in the frequency of record keeping (which was conducted daily in *Taula* and monthly in the monastery), both the structure and the method of keeping accounts were identical. The study showed that practices of accounting and accountability were not only present in religious institutions of the Middle Ages but they were also similar to those of specialised, private institutions, such as banks.

The full implications of accounting practices in securing material provision for the poor have been examined in Victorian England and Wales. Walker's (2004) research on poor relief demonstrates the roles that accounting can play in constituting the poor. He documents how the church/parish administered relief and how this was accounted for in detail by church officers. In particular, Walker shows how accounting was used to manage the cost and financing of relief and also contributed to the social and moral control of its recipients. Walker examines detailed accounting records on paupers and how the publication of the names of relief recipients provided local officials with a potent device for monitoring and governing the poor and facilitating community surveillance.

In sixteenth-century Spain, the Archbishop of Toledo collected the highest rents in the country (Fernández Alvarez 2004) and had considerable economic and religious influence. This prompted Villaluenga de Gracia (2005) to challenge the findings of Futcher and Phillips (1986) who argued that religious institutions constituted the last pocket of resistance against the implementation of innovative accounting and managerial techniques. In her analysis of accounting practices at the Cathedral of Toledo during the period 1533–39, Villaluenga de Gracia undertook an extensive examination of the accounting books kept to track the flow of rents. In particular, she focused on the design and implementation of a double-entry system at this relatively early stage in the history of the technique. She argues that the double-entry system provided timely information on the Cathedral's properties and their contribution to the generation of wealth, and shows that such information was crucial to the long-term survival of the institution.

The Benedictine Monastery of Silos constituted a major Spanish spiritual centre. Prieto Moreno *et al.* (2006) examined Benedictine procedures and accounting records to explore the extent to which accounting served accountability and decision-making purposes during the seventeenth and eighteenth centuries. They reported that accounting records were subject to strict and comprehensive scrutiny 69 times per year. The system of accountability consisted of quadrennial statements delivered by the 45 monasteries to the Congregation. In turn, the Congregation used this information to demand further financial contributions from the state. The Congregation aggregated monasteries' reports and provided the state with a detailed breakdown of expenditure (salaries, building works, lawsuits, transport, and rents) incurred by the monasteries for the management of their patrimony; for the upkeep of their monks and servants; for the material and spiritual needs of marginalised social classes (alms, gratuities); and financial details relating to other strata of civil and ecclesiastical society (donations to the Crown and quinquenniums to the Holy See).

Interestingly, the reports issued by the monasteries included data on expenditure per monk, a calculation that went beyond 'expenses on upkeep and clothing'. Such information was crucial for decision-making and control purposes at the monastery and congregation levels. Prieto Moreno *et al.* also reported that the Monastery of Silos implemented an early form of accrual-based accounting for revenues. The accounting system of the Monastery of Silos combined elements from both the charge and discharge system and the double-entry method enforced by the Cathedral of Toledo (see Villaluenga de Gracia 2005).

As well as examining accounting books kept by religious institutions, some researchers have directed their attention to exploring the impact of religious practice on the development of accounting techniques. In particular, Aho (2005) makes a connection between the development of double-entry bookkeeping and the Catholic confessional, with double entry being the worldly counterpart of the spiritual giving of account. Aho (2005: 28) notes 'It is . . . difficult to appreciate that originally there might have been something more than just a figurative parallel between business chronicling and moral confession.' Aho argues that as commerce fell under the jurisdiction of the medieval church merchants and bankers sought to demonstrate their high moral standards. Business narrative began to assume an apologetic, justificatory style akin to that used in confessions. This style was reflected in the manner in which transations were recorded under double-entry bookkeeping: 'Who took part in the transaction? What goods or services were involved? Where did it take place? When? Why? And how much money was involved?' (Aho 2005: 29).

Confession, Aho argues, encouraged businessmen to record transactions on a daily, even hourly, basis. Every detail was to be entered not once, but twice in order to demonstrate their impecability. The author contends:

> Once sacramental confession became routinised into a weekly habit of self-reflection and divulgence, it began to insinuate itself into other realms, serving as a standard for a plethora of accounting practices that appeared in the decades immediately after the Fourth Lateran Council
>
> (ibid.: 84)

Indeed, Aho suggests that in order to address the moral anxiety implied by lending at interest despite the religious ban on usury in medieval Christondom, double-entry bookkeeping was the most potent weapon businessmen could deploy to demonstrate their morality. For Aho, the development of double entry was one of the key manifestations of the emergence of modern Christian consciousness which was born out of sacremental confession.

Aho's arguments are certainly stimulating and provocative. The connections he makes between confession and the development and dissemination of double-entry bookeeping are worthy of serious scholarly reflection. His arguments should invite the attention of scholars with an intimate knowledge of Catholic theology. It would also be useful to explore more deeply what specific attributes of double entry (which is one of several techniques for recording transactions) render it the logical outcome of sacremental confession. Future researchers might also be inspired to attempt to explain the spread of double-entry bookkeeping across the globe into places where religious ideologies radically different from Catholicism were espoused.

The work of Aho demonstrates that double-entry bookkeeping partly addressed concerns about the profit seeking spirit in Catholic settings during the Renaissance. Further, he shows that double entry draws heavily on the notion of balance because 'genuine double-entry did emerge in paragraph form' (2005: 592) and is closely linked to a history of writing (Hoskin and Macve 1986). Within this stream of research Thompson (1992) examined the rhetoric of double entry with resepct to three institutional mechanisms: the Church, the educational apparatus and the printing/publishing regime. In his detailed analysis of the rhetoric relating to double-entry bookkeeping, Thompson (1992: 595) notes that 'Pacioli was writing at the peak of the power and security of the Church', and that this impacted on his presentation of double entry.

Research on the role of accounting in religious institutions thus supports the notion that the sacred-profane divide might be at best time-space dependent. Our review of the extant literature indicates that such a divide was blurred in different eras and in different religions. The review also indicates that accounting practices and techniques in religious institutions were far from rudimentary. Sophisticated accounting techniques were implemented by religious institutions for the purposes of decision making and control. It is perhaps not too far-fetched to argue that the development and use of refined accounting techniques was one of the key factors that underpinned not only the functioning, but also the survival of many religious institutions. Accounting could hardly be considered a marginal, low-status practice which was resented by the clergy as an unwanted intervention in the sacred domain.

The influence of religious thought on accounting and business practices

The above discussion demonstrated how, and to what extent, accounting has influenced the functioning of religious institutions. At the same time, religious thought has exerted a pervasive influence on multiple spheres of organisational, business and social life (Homza 2000). In this section, we focus on usury, interest and earnings, and also examine the impact of religion on accounting and business. The main concern of the extant literature has been to articulate the position taken by different religions, and indeed different varieties of the same religion, or even differences within a stream of religious thought across time, towards concepts such as interest, usury, prices and profits. Absent in most of the literature is any direct engagement with how accounting as a technology of measurement and valuation might have mediated the articulation of these concepts. Similarly, there is lacunae concerning the examination of accounting entries or reports related to these concepts within particular contexts. This is clearly one area that students of accounting history could turn their attention to in the future.

Interest, usury and earnings[2]

The case of usury illustrates how religious beliefs mediated social and business values. In the present-day usury is understood as the lending of money at a disproportionately high rate of interest. Historically, usury involved lending money at interest. Religious doctrine and the risk of severe financial and personal sanctions did not prevent the practice of usury but the desire to avoid these sanctions encouraged the pursuit of ways to circumvent the ethical concerns regarding usury, including attempts to render it a legitimate practice (Aho 2005: 85).

The Holy Scriptures of major religions including Judaism (Deuteronomy 23: 20–1), Christianity (Luke 6: 35) and Islam (Quran 2: 275 and 278–80) banned the practice of usury. The treatment of usury in the Quran explains much about the nature of financial systems used in Islamic countries until very recently. The prohibition against *riba* in commercial loans rested on the central belief that one should not gain profit where one has also not taken on risk (Taylor and Evans 1987: 21).

In the Middle Ages, the notions of usury and profiting were closely related. The Schoolmen, those who developed the ideas of Scholasticism, considered that speculation was to 'sin most gravely'. Drawing on the moral philosophy of Aristotle, the Schoolmen stated that trading should involve charging a 'just price' (Wren 2000) as an antidote to avarice and gluttony. However, there was no general agreement on what a 'just price' should be (de Roover 1958: 421). For some, it meant the amount that allowed a person to maintain his/her social status; for others, it was the cost of production; or it could be set at a maximum or minimum level by legal authorities.

These ideas set the stage for the promulgation of the laws of profit and usury. The exchange of property, argued St Thomas Aquinas (1952, 10: 328) in the thirteenth century, such as by a businessman trading commodities or money, is natural and necessary when it is done in order to satisfy the needs of life. In contrast, the exchange of commodities or money, 'not on account of the necessities of life, but for profit . . . is justly deserving of blame . . . it satisfies the greed for gain which knows no limit and tends to infinity'. Profiting by itself is not sinful. It is lawful if intended for the upkeep of one's household, for assisting the needy, or for fulfilling a clear and present need of one's country. In such cases, seeking gain is not an aim in itself. It is a person's 'payment for a person's labour'. Such profiting accords with *natural* law.

Given that the notion of competition was neglected in the writings of Scholastics until the end of the sixteenth century (Wren 2000), attention was paid to the role of the state in price setting. St Thomas Aquinas (1952, 10: 320, 323) pointed out: 'those who govern the state must determine the just measure of things saleable . . . it is not lawful to disregard such measures as are established by public authority or custom'. A higher price, however, could be asked if the seller 'has changed something for the better . . . or because the value has changed with the change of place or time . . . [or] on account of the danger incurred in bringing the object to the market' (Aquinas 1952, 10: 328). Exclusion from price should refer to disguised usury, that is, charging more for an object with payment to follow at a later date. Terms such as 'just measure', changing a product 'for the better', changes in value over time, and the 'danger incurred in bringing the object to the market' have accounting implications given its major role in identifying and costing such elements. Yet, these considerations have not featured in the accounting history literature. They merit investigation.

The Renaissance and Protestantism

In its criticism of the doctrines of the Roman Catholic Church, the Reformation changed understandings of business profits. Some versions of the Reformation argued that individuals should engage in secular vocations and invest their money in business rather than using it for charity or luxurious consumption (Weber 2001). Such religious beliefs were particularly prominent in Calvinism. Calvin noted that church leaders engaged in luxurious ostentation and perhaps the pursuit of personal wealth (Tawney 1954). As far as the debate on earnings and usury was concerned, Luther pointed out that money lent on specified commodities must conform to interest rates in keeping with reason and charity, a limit of 4–6 per cent per year (Barnett 1961). This made the charging of interest and the notion of profit socially acceptable. Those working in every profession – not just the clergy – could glorify God by performing their work in ways that God had intended (Ali Jafri and Margolis 1999: 374–5).

In a similar vein, Calvin departed radically from the position of the Greek philosophers and the earlier Church teachings by proclaiming that money was not sterile and unable to yield its own fruits (Homer and Sylla 1991: 80), especially where loans were used for productive purposes (Divine 1967: 499). Calvin stated that Scripture only prohibited 'biting' usury (Homer and Sylla 1991: 80). He pointed out that capital and credit were indispensable and that the financier was not a pariah, but a useful member of society (Tawney 1954: 95–6). The Calvinist approach to earnings was summarised as follows: 'What reason is there why the income from a business should not be larger than that from land-owning? Whence do the merchant's profits come, except from his own diligence and industry' (ibid.: 93).

Shifts towards the spirit of profit in Roman Catholic settings

The case of the Royal Soap Factory of Seville illustrates the increasing tolerance towards business profit during the Renaissance and proto-industrial periods in Roman Catholic settings. In 1423, the King of Castile granted the Duke of Alcalá a monopoly over the production and supply of soap to the city of Seville (Carmona and Donoso 2004). The royal decree granting the monopoly established that the price of soap was to be set by the local government of Seville. Such policy of granting monopolies was typical in Spain during the Middle Ages and, ultimately, complied with the doctrine of St Thomas Aquinas of entrusting the state with the final pricing decision. The local government and the Duke of Alcalá typically engaged in continuous conflicts over determining the just price of a pound of soap. Such conflicts were resolved through the deployment of tests that reproduced the soap production process and tracked the corresponding costs. Sophisticated calculations were performed. To endow the tests with the aura of neutrality, the parties asked for the services of soap experts from outside Seville. The tests were also monitored by a local judge and the minutes were written by an accountant of the Catholic Church to ensure compliance with its doctrine.

The cost calculation of a pound of soap illustrates prevailing notions of earnings and public service in sixteenth-century Spain. In calculating the cost of a pound of soap, the parties estimated expected annual production, which amounted to 417,000 pounds in 1525. It was agreed that non-production costs amounted to 171,175 maravedíes (0.41 maravedís/pound). However, the parties faced insurmountable problems in handling decimals, which led to a difference of 14,900 maravedíes (171,275 − 156,275). The final report of the test stated: 'the remaining 14,900 maravedíes are for the people [of Seville] because there is no way to allocate this amount to the pounds [of soap], and ultimately, this amount is consumed and are consumed [sic] by the people of Seville'. This rounding down of the decimals to benefit the people of Seville depicted compliance with Scholastics who gave permission for a 'just price' but not for earnings.

During the rest of the sixteenth and seventeenth centuries the parties continued their disputes over the constitutive elements of the cost of soap. However, it was not until 1692 that the Duke of Alcalá first claimed his right to 'earnings as a constitutive part or price'. He argued (Carmona and Donoso 2004: 147–8):

[The local government] does not admit any earning to me as a purveyor, as it has done in the past, and as it is currently done in the cities of Cádiz and Xerez. Further, it has

515

recognized an additional 8 per cent to prevent the deterioration of the materials and the stored soap. *The contention that spreads throughout the City is that if such expense is considered, then there will be no allowance for earnings. This lacks support [because] what is expense is not earnings, and earnings cannot be denied to the purveyor. Moreover, the privilege will be useless if I cannot profit from it.*

(emphasis added)

This claim to receive earnings was in sharp contrast to the claim following the 1525 test that the monopoly for soap production and distribution was intended to provide a service to the people of Seville.

The religious underpinnings of the accounting concepts of stewardship and prudence

Religious Evangelicalism exerted a strong influence over the middle classes in industrialising Britain. Of special importance for our purposes is the impact of evangelical ideas on stewardship and prudence.

Stewardship has long been associated with accountings which arise when an agent is held accountable to the owner of the assets which he manages. This notion was strong in Evangelicalism. Evangelicals sought new ways of securing a rationalised and ordered existence to secure personal salvation through assiduousness and moral rectitude (Walker 1998: 488; Davidoff and Hall 1987: 87). As noted by Maltby (2000: 58) 'Evangelicals saw the economy as an area of moral struggle, in which the good would eventually be rewarded and the wicked punished.' In turn, such ideals brought about the enforcement of techniques of measurement, estimation and classification (Walker 1998: 488). Furthermore, individuals were accountable to God for every waking moment and their use of earthly resources. This emphasised the notion of stewardship, 'men held property in trust from God and were accountable for the proper administration of His wealth' (ibid.; Garnett 1987: 352).

Similarly, Maltby (2000) examined the (accounting) notion of prudence as one of the four cardinal virtues under Evangelism. In eighteenth-century Britain, Evangelicals considered business failure to be the consequence of imprudent behaviour rather than the outcome of market forces. The notion of prudence was at the core of business management and exerted a major influence on a number of key aspects of economic life, such as notions of time – short-termism was regarded as detrimental to business performance.

Accounting and business in settings with a religious worldview

The ideas of the Enlightenment that pervaded some Christian countries sought to enforce a dichotomy between the secular and the non-secular (Tinker 2004). As noted above, these notions had hardly any influence in countries with religious worldviews on human and societal activities which perceive no such dichotomy (Hamid *et al.* 1993; Abdul-Rahman and Goddard 1998). Such contexts, we argue, feature a number of distinctive characteristics that are relevant to any project seeking to shed light on the intertwining of accounting and religion at the macro, societal level. In this section, we examine the role of religion in accounting and business practices in Islamic countries, and the influence of religion on understandings of accounting and the accounting profession in China.

An Islamic perspective on accounting and business practice

Since the early study by Gambling and Karim (1986) on Islam and social accounting, there have been several investigations of accounting practices in contemporary Islamic organisations, particularly Islamic banks (such as Karim 1990). In the main, the aim of these studies was to explore the extent to which accounting and business practice reflect Islamic beliefs and how such beliefs were communicated to organisational stakeholders.

The *Sharia* is the Islamic law or code of practice for individuals and communities, and financial transactions and business. As demonstrated by Maali *et al.* (2006), countries with a strong Islamic focus such as Pakistan and the Sudan have completely changed their banking systems to make them compatible with the *Sharia*. Consequently, such banks have a clear social focus. Maali *et al.* examined the social disclosures of 29 banks operating in 16 countries according to Islamic principles. Social disclosure benchmarks were identified against which actual reporting was compared. Given the assumption that banks are expected to comply with the social norms established in the *Sharia*, the results indicated that the sample of banks fell short of the standards of social reporting. Moreover, the study reported that the banks used financial statements selectively to convey to stakeholders positive news about their image but refrained from reporting adverse information.

The independence of religious and external auditors in Islamic banks is important because the credibility of an organisation's financial reports is at stake. Karim (1990) has shown that Islamic banks have in-house boards of religious advisers commonly known as the Sharia Supervisory Board which oversee compliance with the *Sharia*. For example, the *Sharia* prohibits the payment and receipt of *riba*, which is technically usury but can be interpreted as interest. Karim (ibid.: 43) argues: 'If religious auditors report any misrepresentation in the bank's financial statements that are due to a violation of Islamic principles, then the consumers of these statements are likely to react in a manner which could be detrimental to the bank's management.' By contrast, external auditors are guided by economic concerns.

Religion and accounting in China

Traditionally, religion has exerted an important influence on Chinese society (Guo 1988). Gao and Handley-Schachler (2003) examined the impact of Confucianism, Feng Shui and Buddhism on the history of accounting in China. Confucianism perceives individuals as being part of various overlapping social networks. Obligations and rights are attached to the relative position of an individual in such networks (Guo 1988: 44). Feng Shui refers to the Chinese science and art of creating harmony between inhabitants and their environment. The essence of Buddhism is reflected in its Four Noble Truths: life is painful; the origin of pain is desire; the cessation of pain is to be sought by ending desire; and the way to this goal is through his Noble Eightfold Path (Guo 1988: 48).

Gao and Handley-Schachler (2003) examined the influence of these philosophical and religious beliefs on bookkeeping methods, accounting information, accounting regulation, government accounting, private accounting, and accountants and the accounting profession. The authors reported that economic factors constituted the most influential forces underpinning the evolution of Chinese accounting, particularly the emergence of double-entry methods in the Ming and Qing dynasties. They also show how the concomitant effects of the concepts of Yin and Yang, Feng Shui belief, Buddhism and Confucianism have exerted a strong influence on the views held of accounting in China. For example, the influence of Feng Shui teachings has meant that the potential benefit of accounting information as an aid for control and decision-making has been neglected. The status of accountants and their profession was not advanced by the fact that under Confucianism accounting was not considered a suitable activity for noblemen and other educated people (Guo 1988: 60).

Our review of research on the impact of religious beliefs on business activities and society in general indicates that this influence extended to different domains of public life. The ban against lending money at interest, in particular, usury, resulted in the development of alternative ways to exploit loopholes and circumvent concerns about morality so that businessmen could continue to advance loans at high interest. We have observed the importance of accounting and cost calculations in endowing profit with a meaning that was unacceptable in some conservative Roman Catholic settings. We have indicated the religious underpinnings of key accounting concepts such as prudence and stewardship. The literature reviewed suggests that accounting had a major constitutive impact on societies with a religious worldview, even though such religious values were not necessarily mirrored in financial statements. Finally, our review has indicated that certain religious and cultural beliefs in Chinese society have had a major impact on promoting an understanding of accounting as irrelevant to decision-making and accounting as an occupation unworthy of the most respected social classes.

Accounting in sacred and religious texts

Research examining accounting and business practice in sacred and religious texts and in books authored by religious authorities has addressed a variety of topics, ranging from episodes of accounting and accountability to the emergence of modern management. In this section, we examine the relatively sparse literature in this area.

The Holy Quran supports a worldview in which sacred and profane activities are not separate. Among monotheistic texts, the Quran provides the most comprehensive perspective on accounting and business practice. Muturza (2004) examined the doctoral dissertation by Charles Torrey on 'The Commercial-Theological Terms in the Koran' at the University of Strasbourg in 1892 to reflect on the use of business terminology in Islam. In particular, Muturza analysed ten concepts related to business practice contained in the Quran: reckoning, weights and measures, payments, wages, loss, fraud, buying and selling, profit, loans, and security. Muturza argued that the worldview of the Quran is wide-ranging, as it does not only refer to the Divine reckoning of human behaviour but also to interactions between human beings. Furthermore, there are concerns in the Quran regarding accountability as well as the pursuit and use of wealth. Muturza argues that the use of a secular vocabulary to refer to theological concepts underscores the point that 'one ought not to compartmentalize the sacred and the secular', and observes that there is a long-standing tradition in Islam that governs accountability and equitable behaviour.

Other research has focused on Biblical episodes of accountability. Barlev (2006) examined the statement of accountability presented by Moses to the Israelites following the exodus from Egypt. Barlev argues that being invested by God as their leader, Moses was not obliged to render accounts of his activities to the Israelites. Yet, Moses issued a statement of accountability on the collection and use of silver for the Holy Sanctuary, detailing the materials used in the erection of the Sanctuary, its furnishings and vessels. Drawing on the Pentateuch and, particularly, on the Book of Exodus, Barlev argues that this statement of accountability was intended for educational purposes. Moses aimed to provide his people with an example of appropriate behaviour and to demonstrate to them that he was above suspicion.

Baker (2006) explored the genealogy of wealth through an examination of changes in its meaning in the Old and New Testaments. In the Old Testament, Abraham's wealth was praised because it derived from God. Conversely, in emphasising that the only way to Heaven was through rejection of wealth, the New Testament portrayed Abraham as a protector of the poor. Baker elaborated a number of possible explanations for these changes in the treatment of wealth in the Bible. He speculates that Paul could have been influential in this change of view inasmuch as he usually addressed audiences of the poor. Echoing Nietzsche, Baker elaborated the possibility that the will to power was repressed by the emergence of Christian morality. Baker also drew on Foucault to suggest that these self-forming activities facilitated the creation of docile bodies so that powerful entities could better control populations. Finally, he argues that discourses about wealth may be seen as implicated in regimes of truth and modalities of power in that the transformation in the discourse about wealth was related to the emergence of the Church as the successor to the Roman Empire.

Conclusion

In this chapter we have reviewed the extant literature devoted to examining the relationship between accounting and religion, especially that which assumes a historical perspective. In the main, the literature reviewed has a Christian-centric focus and covers events of the nineteenth and twentieth centuries. The literature examines a variety of issues motivated by different paradigms and rich theoretical variety as opposed to being constrained within a single, dominant paradigm in the image of 'normal science' (Kuhn 1962).

Our review of the literature has been organised around micro and macro aspects of accounting. With respect to the micro focus, we have analysed the role of accounting in religious organisations and, especially, the debate on the sacred–profane divide and the degree of sophistication of accounting techniques used in religious institutions. From the macro perspective, we have examined the extent to which religious beliefs have mediated business and societal values, and addressed religious treatments of interest, usury and earnings, themes that are potentially extremely relevant to accounting, even though the extant literature has barely begun to address them. Furthermore, we have analysed the extent to which religious beliefs have impacted on the roles of accounting. Finally, we examined accounting and business treatment in some sacred and religious texts.

Our analysis of research on the sacred–profane divide indicates that such a dichotomy is not universally relevant to all forms of religious institutions, and is problematical even in the Christian religion from where this distinction was initially drawn. According to the sacred–profane divide, accounting operates in the domain of the profane (Laughlin 1988; Booth 1993) and it is viewed as incompatible with sacred religious values and activities. Our review has shown that such a dichotomy is, at best, time–space specific. Institutions operating across different ages, countries and systems of religious thought did not function on the assumption of a clear divide between the spheres of the sacred and the profane. It is clear that many religious institutions excelled at business and financial activities. Indeed, some commentators consider that the subsequent demise of such institutions can be attributed to their failure to deal adequately with financial and monetary concerns. Moreover, our review indicates that notions of the sacred and profane are fluid, mutable concepts. Thus 'accounting has the potential to be sacred, to be secular or to be both sacred and secular', depending upon context (Jacobs 2005: 193).

Our review indicates that accounting systems in religious organisations were far from rudimentary. As some commentators have noted, religious institutions of the Roman Catholic Church constituted the main repositories of human knowledge during Medieval and

Renaissance times. Such knowledge included accounting (the *Summa* was written by a monk of the Roman Catholic Church). We have observed how the Monastery of Poblet, which played a major role in charitable activities in medieval Spain, implemented highly sophisticated accounting systems that were comparable to those used by contemporary merchant banks (Monclús Guitart 2005). Similarly, the Cathedral of Toledo, a major spiritual and economic centre of the Spanish Renaissance, implemented a sophisticated double-entry system in the 1530s, well in advance of similar developments in private and state-owned organisations (Villaluenga de Gracia 2005).

Our examination of research on the impact of religion on the notions of interest, usury and earnings indicates that this is a potentially fruitful area for conducting comparative research. Extant studies indicate that early positions on the nature of interest and usury were quite similar across Judaism, Christianity and Islam. Future research in this area could shed light on the conditions that led subsequently to charges of interest on loans becoming acceptable in some religions, and why this change did not occur in others. Similarly, future researchers could explore the extent to which religious beliefs exerted influence over understandings of accounting and the way accounting numbers were reported to organisational stakeholders (Maali *et al.* 2006). Perhaps more importantly, future researchers could examine the extent to which the definitions of terms such as interest, usury, prices and profits were mediated via the intervention of accounting as a technology of measurement, valuation and recording, and how the emergence of these terms and technologies were contextually embedded.

Similarly, our review suggests that comparative research on the religious underpinnings of key accounting notions such as prudence and stewardship holds much promise, particularly in advancing theorisations of accounting. Research on accounting in sacred and religious texts is sparse and fragmented. There is considerable potential to explore such texts in relation to a variety of accounting themes (such as accountability, governance and wealth). Such research might also contribute significantly to the theorising of accounting.

Perhaps unsurprisingly this review has revealed that some topics have been extensively researched – in particular, the micro focus, while other subjects have been sparsely explored – in particular, the macro perspective on the interrelationship between accounting and religion and how accounting is presented in religious texts. There remain other unexplored areas whose study has the potential to contribute significantly to the histories of accounting and religion. For example, gendered dimensions of accounting in religious institutions, such as the construction of masculinity and femininitiy, and power relations, have yet to be explored. In a similar vein, research to date has devoted little attention to examining how the impact of religious beliefs on societal values has been mediated by accounting. Future research could examine the extent to which accounting and religion mediated processes of secular organisations through the deployment of systems of human accountability.

Furthermore, the connection between accounting, religion, and ethics/liberation/enlightenment has so far received very little attention (Carmona and Ezzamel 2006). How do notions of ethics in different religious contexts intertwine with accounting as a calculative technology and a discourse? What role, if any, does accounting play in rendering such notions of ethics applicable in practice or colludes against their implementation? How are concepts of liberation constituted in different religious settings and how is accounting implicated in this process? Is enlightenment the aim of religious ideologies, and if so what role does accounting play in underpinning, even constructing, or impeding such an ideal? If religion is about creating and enforcing some notion of social order, how does accounting help shape and secure this notion of order? What attributes of accounting render it a desirable and malleable technology for intervening in the domain of the sacred?

Key works

Carmona and Ezzamel (eds) (2006) This special issue provides a wide-ranging set of articles on accounting and religion. The introductory piece posits some suggestions for future research in this area.

De la Torre (2004) examines the role of the Order of the Temple in public banking and how accounting and financial activities were core to its mission.

Laughlin (1990) embraces the argument that accounting does not constitute an integral part of the sacred agenda in religious organisations.

Quattrone (2004) examines the ideological underpinnings of accounting and accountability systems in religious organizations.

Notes

1   For example, Pope Alexander VI issued the *Bula Inter-Coetera* in 1493 to 'donate' the Latin-American continent to Spain. As a papal donation of a continent to another country this 'gift' was accorded religious legitimacy and sanctioned by sacred beliefs, at least in the eyes of the receiver if not always in the eyes of those whose territories had been 'donated'.
2   This section is based on Carmona and Macintosh (2002), see also Visser and MacIntosh (1998).

References

Abdul-Rahman, A. R. and Goddard, A. (1998) An interpretive inquiry of accounting practices in religious organisations, *Financial Accountability & Management* 14 (3): 183–201.

Aho, J. (2005) *Confession and Bookkeeping* (Albany, NY: State University of New York Press).

Ali Jafri, S. H. and Margolis, L. S. (1999) The treatment of usury in the Holy Scriptures, *Thunderbird International Business Review*, 41 (4/5): 371–79.

Álvarez-Dardet, C., Baños Sánchez-Matamoros, J. and López Manjón, J. D. (2006) Accounting at the boundaries of the sacred: The regulation of the Spanish brotherhoods in the 18th century, *Accounting History*, 11 (2): 129–50.

Aquinas, St T. (1952) *Summa Theologica* (Chicago: Fathers of the English Dominican Province).

Armstrong, K. (1993) *A History of God* (New York: Ballantine Press).

Baker, C. R. (2006) Towards a genealogy of wealth through an analysis of biblical discourses, *Accounting History*, 11 (2): 151–71.

Barlev, B. (2006) A biblical statement of accountability, *Accounting History*, 11 (2): 173–97.

Barnett, H. H. (1961) *Introducing Christian Ethics* (Nashville, TN: Broadman Books Inc).

Booth, P. (1993) Accounting in churches: a research framework and agenda, *Accounting, Auditing & Accountability Journal*, 5 (4): 37–67.

Burchell, S., Clubb, C., Hopwood, A. G., Hughes, J., and Nahapiet, J. (1980) The roles of accounting in organisations and society, *Accounting, Organizations and Society*, 5 (1): 5–28.

Carmona, S. and Donoso, R. (2004) Cost accounting in early regulated markets: the case of the royal soap factory of Seville (1525–1692), *Journal of Accounting and Public Policy*, 23 (2): 129–57.

Carmona, S. and Ezzamel, M. (2006) Accounting and religion: a historical perspective, *Accounting History*, 11 (2): 117–27.

Carmona, S. and Macintosh, N. (2002) Earnings, interest and usury: a genealogical approach. Paper presented at the First Symposium on Management Control, Queen's University, Canada.

Cordery, C. (2006) Hallowed treasures: sacred, secular and the Wesleyan Methodists in New Zealand (1819–1840), *Accounting History*, 11 (2): 199–220.

Davidoff, L. and Hall, C. (1987) *Family Fortunes. Men and Women of the English Middle Class, 1780–1850* (London: Routledge).

De la Torre, I. (2004) *Los Templarios y el Origen de la Banca* (Madrid: Dilema).

de Roover, R. (1958) The concept of the just price: theory and economic policy, *Journal of Economic History*, 18 (4): 418–34.

Divine, T. F. (1967) Usury, in *New Catholic Encyclopedia*, pp. 498–500 (New York: McGraw-Hill).

Durkheim, E. (1976) *The Elementary Forms of Religious Life* (London: George Allen and Unwin).

Eliade, M. (1959) *The Sacred and the Profane: The Nature of Religion* (New York: Harcourt, Brace and World).

Ezzamel, M. (2002) Accounting and redistribution: the palace and mortuary cult in the Middle Kingdom, ancient Egypt, *Accounting Historians Journal*, 29 (1): 61–103.

Ezzamel, M. (2005) Accounting for the activities of funerary temples: the intertwining of the sacred and the profane, *Accounting and Business Research*, 35 (1): 29–51.

Ezzamel, M. and Bourn, M. (1990) The roles of accounting information systems in an organization experiencing financial crisis, *Accounting, Organizations and Society*, 15 (5): 399–424.

Fernández Alvarez, M. (2004) *Sombras y Luces de la España Imperial* (Madrid: Espasa).

Flesher, T. K. and Flesher, D. L. (1979) Managerial accounting in an early 19th century German-American religious commune, *Accounting, Organizations and Society*, 4 (4): 297–304.

Fonfeder, R., Holtzman, M. P. and Maccarrone, E. (2003) Internal controls in the Talmud: the Jerusalem Temple, *Accounting Historians Journal*, 30 (1): 73–93.

Futcher, T. and Phillips, T. (1986) Church budgeting: a secular approach, *The National Public Accountant*, 31 (9): 28–39.

Gambling, T. E. and Karim, R. A. A. (1986) Islam and 'social accounting', *Journal of Business Finance and Accounting*, 13 (1): 39–50.

Gao, S. and Handley-Schachler, M. (2003) The influences of Confucianism, Feng shui and Buddhism in Chinese accounting history, *Accounting, Business & Financial History*, 13 (1): 41–68.

Gartnett, J. (1987) Gold and gospel: systematic beneficence in mid-nineteenth England, in W. J. Sheils, and D. Wood (eds), *The Church and Wealth*, pp. 347–58 (Oxford: Basil Blackwell).

Guo, D. (1988) Confucius and accounting, *Accounting Historians Notebook*, 11 (1): 8–10.

Hamid, S., Craig, R. and Clarke, F. (1993) Religion: a confounding cultural element in the international harmonization of accounting, *Abacus*, 29 (2): 131–48.

Hardy, L. and Ballis, H. (2005) Does one size fit all?: the sacred and secular divide revisited with insights from Niebuhr's typology of social action, *Accounting, Auditing & Accountability Journal*, 18 (2): 238–54.

Hernández Borreguero, J. (2002) 'El Cabildo Catedral de Sevilla: Organización y Sistema Contable (1625–1650)', unpublished PhD thesis, University of Seville.

Hernández Esteve, E. (2001) Contabilidad monástica y empresa, *Revista de AECA*, 56: 26–30.

Homer, S. and Sylla R. (1991) *A History of Interest Rates* (New Brunswick, NJ: Rutgers University Press).

Homza, L. A. (2000) *Religious Authority in the Spanish Renaissance* (Baltimore, MD: The Johns Hopkins University Press).

Hoskin, K. W. and Macve, R. H. (1986) Accounting and the examination: a genealogy of disciplinary power, *Accounting, Organizations and Society*, 11 (2): 105–36.

Irvine, H. (2002) The legitimizing power of financial statements in the Salvation Army in England, 1865–1892, *Accounting Historians Journal*, 29 (1): 1–36.

Jacobs, K. (2005) The sacred and the secular: examining the role of accounting in the religious context, *Accounting, Auditing & Accountability Journal*, 18 (2): 189–210.

Jacobs, K. and Walker, S. P. (2004) Accounting and accountability in the Iona Community, *Accounting, Auditing & Accountability Journal*, 17 (3): 361–81.

Karim, R. (1990) The independence of religious and external auditors: the case of islamic banks, *Accounting, Auditing & Accountability Journal*, 3 (3): 34–44.

Kubler, G. (1982) *Building the Escorial* (Princeton, NJ: Princeton University Press).

Kuhn, T. (1962) *The Structure of Scientific Revolutions* (Chicago: The University of Chicago Press).

Laughlin, R. C. (1988) Accounting in its social context: an analysis of the accounting systems of the Church of England, *Accounting, Auditing & Accountability Journal*, 1 (2): 19–42.

Laughlin, R. C. (1990) A model of financial accountability and the Church of England, *Financial Accountability & Management*, 6 (2): 93–114.

López Manjón, J. D., Baños Sánchez-Matamoros, J. and Álvarez-Dardet Espejo, C. (2007) Rendering of accounts and transfer of accounting knowledge at religious organizations: the case of the brotherhoods of Seville (1563–1604). Paper presented at the XII Workshop on Management Accounting and Control, Raymond Konopka Memorial, Almería.

Maali, B., Casson, P. and Napier, C. (2006) Social reporting by Islamic banks, *Abacus*, 42 (2): 266–89.

Maltby, J. (2000) The origins of prudence in accounting, *Critical Perspectives on Accounting*, 11 (1): 51–70.

Monclús Guitart, R. (2005) El abad del monasterio de Poblet como Limosnero Real y su rendición de cuentas (S.XIV), *De Computis*, 2: 154–80.

Muturza, A. (2004) Quranic use of 'commercial' vocabulary and its implications, Seton Hall University, working paper.

Oliveira, J. and Brandao, M. (2005) Monastic accounting in Portugal: the case of the Cistercian monastery of Arouca, 1786–1825. Paper presented at the 4th Accounting History International Conference, Braga.

Prieto Moreno, B., Maté Sadornil, L. and Tua Pereda, J. (2006) The accounting records of the monastery of Silos throughout the XVIII century: the accumulation and management of its patrimony in the light of its accounts books, *Accounting History*, 11 (2): 221–56.

Quattrone, P. (2004) Accounting for God: accounting and accountability practices in the Society of Jesus (Italy, XVI–XVII centuries), *Accounting, Organizations and Society*, 29 (7): 647–83.

Sánchez Herrero, J. (1985) Las cofradías de sevilla: los Comienzos, in Colección Cultura Viva (eds): *Las Cofradías de Sevilla: Historia, Antropología, Arte*, pp. 9–34 (Seville: Servicio de Publicaciones de la Universidad de Sevilla).

Sargiacomo, M. (2001) Pro & contro delle procedure contabili dei Monaci Benedettini nell XVI° Secolo. Paper presented at the VI Convegno Nazionale – Società Italiana di Storia della Ragioneria, Caserta.

Smith, W. C. (1979) *Faith and Belief* (Princeton, NJ: Princeton University Press).

Suárez, L. (2004) *Los Reyes Católicos* (Ariel: Barcelona).

Sukoharsono, E. G. (1998) Accounting in a historical transition: a shifting dominant belief from Hindu to Islamic administration in Indonesia. Paper presented at the APIRA Conference, Osaka.

Tawney, R. H. (1954) *Religion and the Rise of Capitalism* (New York: Mentor Books).

Taylor, T. W. and Evans, J. W. (1987) Islamic banking and the prohibition of usury in western economic thought, *National Westminster Bank Quarterly Review*, 9 (4): 15–27.

Thompson, G. (1992) Is accounting rhetorical? Methodology, Luca Pacioli and printing, *Accounting, Organizations and Society*, 16 (5/6): 672–99.

Tinker, T. (2004) The Enlightenment and its discontents: antinomies of Christianity, Islam and the calculative sciences, *Accounting, Auditing & Accountability Journal*, 17 (3): 442–75.

Villaluenga de Gracia, S. (2005) La aparición de la partida doble en la iglesia: El diario y mayores de la Catedral de Toledo (1533–1539), *De Computis*, 3: 147–216.

Visser, W. A. M. and MacIntosh, A. (1998) A short review of the historical critique of usury, *Accounting, Business & Financial History*, 8 (2): 175–89.

Walker, S. P. (1998) How to secure your husband's esteem: accounting and private patriarchy in the British middle class household during the nineteenth century, *Accounting, Organizations and Society*, 23 (6): 485–514.

Walker, S. P. (2004) Expense, social and moral control: accounting and the administration of the old poor law in England and Wales, *Journal of Accounting and Public Policy*, 23 (2): 85–127.

Weber, M. (2001) *The Protestant Ethic and the Spirit of Capitalism* (London: Routledge).

Wren, D. A. (2000) Medieval or modern? A scholastic's view of business ethics circa 1430, *Journal of Business Ethics*, 8 (2): 109–19.

Zubiri, X. (1993) *El Problema Filosófico de la Historia de las Religiones* (Madrid: Alianza Editorial).

25

Creative arts

Sam McKinstry

Overview

This chapter examines studies in accounting history which involve the creative arts of architecture, literature, fine art, the graphic arts and film. It begins with a summary of the various ways in which such studies can, and have, shed light on accounting practice and the social and cultural aspects of accountancy, as well as upon the practice of the creative arts themselves and the motivation of those who carry them out. There then follows a review of the accounting history literature relating to architecture, which begins with a summary of papers and books dealing with buildings and the professionalisation of accountancy. Studies examining architectural motivation and accounting practices are also reviewed. Accounting history studies involving literature are next examined, more or less in the chronological order of the literature concerned. These reveal a wide range of facets of accounting, from the place it has occupied in society to its role in the home, as well as shedding fresh light on the literary figures whose practices and attitudes have been uncovered. The centrepiece of the chapter's next section, which deals with fine art, is a summary of Basil Yamey's (1989) *Art and Accounting*, a review of works of art which have depicted accounting and accountancy from the late-medieval period onwards. In the next section, on accounting history and the graphic arts, papers which discuss 'ways of seeing' annual reports and their potential for manipulation are summarised. Accounting history and film comes next, and the medium's ability to reflect and shape public attitudes to accounting is examined. The chapter concludes by suggesting and speculating upon possible future trajectories for accounting history studies concerning the creative arts.

Accounting history and the creative arts

Accounting history can be seen at its interdisciplinary and erudite best as it explores the interaction of the world of accounting with the creative spheres of architecture, art, literature, the graphic arts and film.

Several types of insight can be gained from the study of this interaction. First, the creative pursuits we are concerned with have often depicted or described accountants, accountancy and related practices in images or words. This can provide useful evidence as to what accountants actually did in the past, in terms of activities, techniques and tools, as well as yield information on how accounting has been perceived from outside itself, for instance, as a social phenomenon. The depiction of accounting and accountants may, in turn, have influenced the attitudes of the general public towards them, and this, too, is of interest to accounting historians.

Where the creative discipline concerned has itself been brought into play through the commissioning or acquisition of work by accountancy bodies, historical study can also reveal how the profession has perceived itself, or sought to depict or describe itself, as it has attempted to foster favourable impressions in the eyes of the public. The creative packaging of accounting in annual reports can also yield historical insights into the impression management techniques employed by firms through the designers and other creative individuals whom they have engaged for this purpose, and the political and economic climates in which these practices have taken place.

A related set of insights regarding the impact of accountancy upon society at large, in terms of the ways in which it has affected attitudes to aspects of life, may also be gained from what is depicted or represented by creative writers or artists, who may not always be complimentary in what they say.

A further valuable set of insights, little explored so far, relates to the motivation of the artists who design, paint, write or otherwise produce creative work. Their motivation has found its reflection, betimes, in their attitudes to their own accounting, financial and business practices, such as the pricing of work and the drawing of salaries or capital. Studies in this area have the potential to set the economist's 'black box' model of firms and the individuals who run them by the ears, as it is discovered that not all business entities are there to maximise profit or personal wealth as a first priority. Although economists have for some time written on the economics of culture in organs such as *The Journal of Cultural Economics*, they have tended to consider it as just another 'good', subject to the forces of supply, demand or price, or examined the public policy implications of arts funding. One exception has been the recent work of Klamer (1997), an economist who has sought to explore the relationship between creativity and the business/financial dimension. It is, however, only through the detailed examination of financial practices and records that we can see with precision how creative individuals have actually balanced profitability and creativity.

Also of interest are the detailed accounting practices which have been employed within the creative professions themselves. How, for example, have creative individuals or businesses carried out their accounting, or had it carried out for them? How have they dealt with overheads in pricing, the valuation of work-in-progress, or the monitoring of costs? In architecture, for instance, how have the activities of the quantity surveyor crossed over into, and interacted with, the accounting systems of architectural firms? These are areas that are largely unexplored.

An additional benefit available from the accounting records of creative individuals is the light that they can shed on their private lives and the interpretation of their work, of interest to scholars within the relevant creative disciplines.

Thus, there are many insights to be gained from the work of accounting historians in the general area of the arts, and multiple opportunities for historians to explore and analyse broad societal, political, philosophical and aesthetic questions affecting accounting in ways that may, or may not be, critical.

This chapter will proceed by undertaking reviews of accounting history studies which have examined the interaction of accountancy with the creative disciplines with which we are concerned, in many of the ways outlined above. It will begin with a review of studies related to accounting and architecture, for no other reason than that architecture has always been regarded as 'the mistress art', since it is in buildings that the other arts are practised or their fruits stored and enjoyed. Historical studies related to accounting and literature will then be considered, after which studies of accounting and fine art will follow. The chapter will conclude with reviews of studies which feature histories of the interactions between accounting and the graphic arts, and finally, accounting and film. In each case, recommendations and speculations affecting future research activities will be made.

Architecture

A seminal study of the role of professional headquarters buildings in the acquisition of status for the bodies which erected or owned them, authored by Macdonald (1989), was published in the sociology literature. In spite of a somewhat tortuous methodological approach to assessing the, necessarily subjective, architectural quality of the buildings concerned, Macdonald's paper successfully demonstrated that professional bodies utilised their headquarters buildings to enhance their respectability, as an integral part of the 'professional project' to increase their power and influence in society. Salient in Macdonald's study were the professional headquarters buildings of the Institute of Chartered Accountants of England and Wales (ICAEW) and the (then) Association of Certified Accountants. While the ICAEW created what Macdonald considered the archetypal, paradigmatic professional headquarters building and was highly successful in utilising it to enhance its status, he notes that the Certified Accountants, in contrast, squandered the architectural opportunity to build their status in this manner, a reflection of their comparative lack of success, generally, as compared with the ICAEW, in promoting themselves.

The ICAEW has always been conscious of its architectural heritage at Moorgate, London, especially the first phase (1889–93), designed in competition by John Belcher, and a number of descriptive works celebrating its sheer visual distinction have appeared, including Squire (1937), Boys (1990), ICAEW (2002) and Pile (2004). Useful and informative as these may be in their own way, their analysis is not intended to be penetrating.

A study by McKinstry (1997) utilises an analysis of the connotative power of architectural style to explain, how, in detail, the architectural symbolism of the ICAEW's Hall, as erected to Belcher's designs, actually works, locating it in the stylistic context of the period. It sets the building's baroque detailing in the context of the buildings of the older professions, such as medicine and the law, which the fledgling ICAEW was anxious to emulate, as well as in the City world of banking premises, gentlemen's clubs and even the adjacent, much revered, buildings of Sir Christopher Wren. The study interprets the iconography of the building's sculptural frieze as a piece of aspirational rhetoric, intended to evoke chartered accountancy's associations with the legal profession and to suggest (misleadingly at the time) that the business of the empire revolved around chartered accountancy. It points out that the ICAEW building's style was much emulated in the styling of the next generation of government offices, symbolically, if perhaps unintentionally, suggesting alignment between the aims of government and the ICAEW through the creation of an establishment architecture, referred to today as 'the Grand Manner', or 'Edwardian Baroque' (Service 1977).

Macdonald's (1989) study of professional buildings made no distinction between their older parts and the many extensions made to them, or even their wholesale replacement by new buildings, at a stage when the status of the professional body owning them was well established. In a new study, McKinstry (forthcoming) examines the 1970 Brutalist extension to Chartered Accountants' Hall, London, explaining its deliberate use by the ICAEW to adjust public perceptions of the profession, which at the time, carried great prestige, but still had a grey, 'subfusc', image, related to the (necessarily) backward-looking auditing function.

The new extension, by Sir William Whitfield, connoted in its *avant garde*, 'with it' styling that the Institute now wished to be associated with the more recently developed, forward-looking functions of accountancy, such as forecasting and business planning, with which it could assist senior management in taking businesses forward into a future of economic prosperity, which the nation required. Whitfield's extension to Belcher's original Hall, in the Belcher style, added in parallel to the new, Brutalist extension, was part of the programme of works completed in 1970, and is often mistaken for original Belcher work. As well as paying homage to Belcher, Whitfield is deliberately forging in this section of the building a metaphorical homage to accounting's venerable past, turning the Hall, as revised, into a Janus-like structure which embraced the future while revering and claiming links with accountancy's long history.

McKinstry's paper also adds to MacDonald's insights by explaining that the key factors in maximising the potential of architecture to advertise a profession's prestige are the architect's individual creative gifts and the presence in a professional institute of a senior, powerful, committee member personally attuned to the nuances of architectural style and its potential for the communication of prestige. That key individual, in the case of the ICAEW's 1970 extension, was Sir Charles Peat, President of the Institute, and himself a wealthy patron of architecture who had previously employed Whitfield on domestic work. This confirms the insights of Lee (1996), who stated that the involvement of key individuals in the professionalisation project was often crucial to success.

In a recent study of the headquarters building of the Institute of Chartered Accountants of Scotland, its suitability as a status-enhancing home was examined (McKinstry 2000). When it was first occupied by the Society of Accountants in Edinburgh, the oldest of Scotland's bodies of chartered accountants, in 1891, a refurbished classical house in Queen Street, in the prestigious New Town of Edinburgh, was acquired to accommodate a library, examination rooms and committee rooms. Given the relative smallness of the Society (which had received its Royal Charter in 1854), it selected and fitted out a well-sited building of appropriate *gravitas* on a restricted budget, thus demonstrating that, even if funds were limited, status could still be projected.

Studies of the financial and business histories of firms engaged in the creative profession of architecture are few and far between. In an analysis of the business strategy of Arcop, a large firm of Canadian architects, by Mintzberg *et al.* (1986), the authors revealed that its design direction was driven by the individual design interests of the partners, the dominant influence in the business. Unsurprisingly, perhaps, the partners felt from time to time that the firm's success was not reflected in sufficient levels of profit and that the firm 'should be making more money'. It is clear that the prime motivation for the practice of architecture lay elsewhere.

A study of the business, financial and accounting history of Scottish provincial architects, Cullen, Lochhead and Brown (McKinstry and Wallace 2004) reached the conclusion, also, that money was not a prime motivator. Among these, the tendency to make small or no charges for preliminary or incidental work, restraint in personal drawings and sparing no effort to complete jobs to the highest standards, even where they had been under-priced, were discovered. The maintenance of detailed job costs highlighted such instances, but did not change the firm's attitude.

The potential for further study in this area of accounting history depends on the availability of suitable records. In common with other professional firms, architectural practices have tended not to preserve client-related records or financial details. In the case of architects, what has mainly been preserved is the various design drawings produced by practices, which are clearly seen within the profession as of the highest importance. Another matter which has tended to militate against the retention of financial and cognate records relates to retrospective liability claims for defective buildings. Architects are reluctant to preserve evidence of how deep their pockets are. At the time of writing, the practice records of a major UK architectural firm are being catalogued for insertion in a national archive, and the surviving partner has given this reason, in confidence, for his intention not to release the practice's accounts. Where financial evidence has managed to survive, further analyses of how accounting and financial record keeping reflect the motivation of firms will add to the store of case studies from which reliable generalisations can flow.

One area which would reward study by accounting historians is the degree to which status-building by non-UK professional bodies has involved architecture and the associated arts of sculpture and painting. Is the UK unique in this respect, or are there other variable factors, such as the lack of an entrenched, time-honoured class system, that make what has happened beyond the UK different? Of interest also are studies, national or international, which examine the architecture of the offices of accountancy practices.

Another area, potentially of vast interest, is the degree to which financial constraints and associated accounting systems have affected what has been built. Has Mammon, and its erstwhile servant, accounting, been to blame for a deteriorating built environment? Has short-termism, or the drive for improvements in the bottom line and associated executive remuneration, affected our aesthetic experiences of buildings through under-investment in architecture, or has the desire for corporate image and associated branding still been enough to ensure aesthetic quality has been sought and paid for? In a recent work, Willis (1995) suggests that, to a large extent, 'Form Follows Finance', as exemplified by the skyscrapers of Chicago and New York. This author notes that 'Skyscrapers are the ultimate architecture of capitalism. The first blue print for every tall building is a balance sheet of estimated costs and returns' (ibid.: 182). Excusing the accounting solecism, is Willis right, and what accounting systems have supported such building programmes? The accounting historian is well placed, subject to the existence of records, to find out. And what effects have the relatively recent Public/Private Partnership and Private Finance Initiative programmes had on architectural quality in Britain? Adverse, one would suspect, but work needs to be done by historians in the future to confirm or deny, including investigation of the accounting systems which have supported these programmes.

Another angle on the relationship between accounting and architecture was explored by Jeacle (2003), who attempted to show that the plethora of trade price guides to building costs which were published in the eighteenth century had a material bearing on cost control in the creation of the Georgian house, the styling of which appeared to lend itself to standardisation. She held that this could be seen in Foucauldian terms as builders coming to possess documentary tools for human accountability. There is evidence to the contrary. In a substantial study of the costs of country house building in the UK from 1660–1880, Wilson and Mackley (1999: 448) quote the architect and builder Thomas Rawlins, who in 1769 noted that it was impossible to provide a uniformly acceptable set of estimates for his designs 'because the prices and methods of building varied considerably across England'. Wilson and Mackley's paper is of considerable interest, also, for the references it makes to extant building accounts associated with the construction of large country houses, which have yet to be examined from an accounting point of view.

In a more nuanced paper, Jeacle (2005) was able to argue more successfully and from a stronger evidential base that published price guides covering the labour costs of producing Georgian furniture did indeed have a role in the negotiation of prices for furniture work, and that this may be seen as Foucauldian.

A very recent study by Mussari and Mussari (2006) operates at a more fundamental level in terms of the interface between accounting history and the history of architecture. Their description of the book-keeping systems in use in building the sixteenth-century Castello of Crotone, in Calabria, Italy, drew attention to the usefulness of the records for tracing the architectural transformation, over time, of a defensive structure which by its nature was subject to periodic change. Such records are capable of revealing chronology, types of materials used, which workmen were involved, and even such small matters as the purchase of string for measuring purposes.

These details are all of great interest to architectural historians, who often have as much interest in buildings, or parts of buildings, that have disappeared, as they do in extant parts, and Mussari and Mussari encourage them to utilise these sources for other buildings. In fact, architectural historians such as Fawcett (2002) have long appreciated the richness of financial records, in terms of what they can reveal about ancient buildings, and their bibliographies are full of references to such sources as exchequer records, which have received the limited attention of accounting historians (ibid.: 351).

Literature

Thus far, a number of major figures in English literature have been investigated by accounting historians. The paper by Parker (1999; see also Buckmaster and Buckmaster 1999) on accounting in Chaucer's *Canterbury Tales* demonstrates that Chaucer, a customs officer and an accountant, was well versed in accounting and mercantile finance and the securing of loans by personal 'bonds'. Parker's paper shows how Chaucer enriches and enlivens his at times bawdy narrative with details of everyday life from his business experiences. In the same paper, Parker suggests that Chaucer may have used accounting more subtly in *The Shipman's Tale*, as an allegory of creative bookkeeping. Readers of Parker's work, and of Chaucer, are also able to acquire an otherwise unobtainable feeling for the day-to-day commerce of the medieval period, together with the reassurance that, in essentials, and notwithstanding the absence of double entry, little changes over time.

In his introduction to accounting in Chaucer, Parker (1999) notes that Defoe, author of *Robinson Crusoe* (1719), has a knowledge of bookkeeping, expressed in a later work, *The Complete English Tradesman* (1725–27), but states that this knowledge 'appears to be limited', a matter surely worthy of further investigation. Defoe's *Moll Flanders* (1722) and the authoress Aphra Benn's short story *The Fair Jilt* (1688) are examined by Connor (2004) in a major work concerned with the narrative and metaphorical use of bookkeeping in these novels, substantial proof of the degree to which accounting had penetrated society's consciousness by this time. In Benn, accounting concepts are used beneath the surface to 'tell' the narrative, while in Defoe, accounting and individual responses to wealth are used throughout for characterisation. Connor's work is also valuable for its survey of contemporary women's guides to accounting, and for its detailed description of the evolution of money and credit up to the time in which the novels are set. Connor notices Defoe's anachronistic references to the (as yet uncreated) Bank of England in *Moll Flanders*, a warning to accounting historians that care must be exercised in utilising novels as factual evidence, and that authorial licence must be taken into account.

A paper on the personal accounts kept by Samuel Pepys, the seventeenth-century diarist, by Boys (1995) reveals that the Pepys' methodical nature was also expressed through his careful attention to financial matters. The records kept by Pepys show that he counted his personal wealth by comparing his assets and liabilities at periodic intervals. Boys also reveals that

Mrs Pepys was expected to account to her husband for household expenditures, confirming the widespread use of domestic accounting in genteel households at this date. The study both sheds more light on the character of a notable literary figure and on his personal circumstances, as well as providing insights into contemporary domestic accounting, which, in the case of Pepys, did not as yet manifest itself in the form of double entry.

Sir Walter Scott, the world's first literary giant, kept personal account books throughout much of his life, and these are examined in a recent study (McKinstry and Fletcher 2002). Scott attended with more diligence to these in the earlier part of his career, but, even later, in the midst of a hectic life, did intermittent reconciliations of his income and expenditure and his assets and liabilities. Scott was adept in accountancy as a result of his studies at the Royal High School of Edinburgh, his training in his father's law office, his sheriffship of Selkirkshire and his post as a clerk to the Court of Session, a senior legal position at the highest civil court in Scotland. The paper points out that Scott's personal accountancy conformed to the norms of genteel households at the time, with his wife running the home and he in overall control. The opportunity is also taken to examine Scott's frequent business and financial difficulties towards the end of his life and, in particular, the accusation that he was financially reckless, greedy and wrote only for money. The study takes the view, from an examination of his accountancy knowledge and other circumstances, that such claims are implausible.

A different type of study of Byron, a contemporary and admirer of Scott, was authored by Moore (1974), who utilised the papers of Zambelli, Byron's secretary, to examine details of his income and expenditure in order to shed fresh light on his personality and circumstances. Moore observes that, if Zambelli had been consulted, 'the accusation of avarice could never have been sustained, or at the worst, he [Byron] would have been recognised as a man, who having great kindness greatly abused, tries to build up defences' (ibid.: 4). Moore's book also gives a real sense of immediacy as it refers to Byron's tastes in expensive clothing and personal effects. Apart from what it reveals about Byron, the study also gives, as a by-product, a picture of the accounting work undertaken by Zambelli, secretary to an aristocratic celebrity, as Byron was, and how such matters as transactions in various currencies were recorded, namely, in parallel columns in sterling and local currency.

A recent paper on Dickens' *Hard Times* (1854) by Fraser *et al.* (2006), discloses an affinity between the social critique in Dickens' novel and the anti-utilitarian writings of Carlyle. The novel, set in the industrial north, paints a negative picture of exploitative and demeaning factory work and its dispiriting effect on those who carried it out. Here, the novelist attacks an over-zealous and misplaced reliance on statistical 'facts' by management, and thus, by implication, criticises aspects of industrial accounting, in the sense of performance indicators, and perhaps also, by implication, cost accounting. From the same era, a study by Maltby and Rutterford (2006) argues for Trollope's novels as a reliable source of information on the social and financial implications of marriage for women in Victorian Britain.

Looking beyond Britain, Maltby's (1999) paper on Freytag's immensely popular German novel, *Soll und Haben* (debit and credit), reveals how double-entry accounting, ubiquitous in nineteenth-century Germany, had come to embody and act as a symbol of middle-class morality. Recent work on the German novelist E.M. Remarque by Evans (2005) suggests that post-1918 accounting in Germany had lost its moral overtones and its aura of authority, being seen as the symbol of a decadent and failed capitalism. Further international perspectives have been provided by Czarniavska (2008), who analyses the role of women in accounting through the lens of nineteenth-century Polish novels and through the work of the twentieth-century American author, Douglas Adams. She concludes from these sources that accounting was seen in Poland as lowly 'women's work', whereas today it is seen as highly-paid men's work.

Literature has also been a source of insights on contemporary perceptions of accountants and their work. A short paper by Walker (1995) notes that in a little-known novel of 1894, *The Accountant*, by F.H. Mel, a London accountant is depicted as a hero, raising questions as to the degree to which any single novel or novelist can be taken in isolation as proof of the way in which accounting or accountants may be understood at a given time and place. Studies of twentieth-century novels include an examination of accounting in the work of Somerset Maugham, who was at one time a chartered accountancy trainee (Boys 1994). A picture of early-twentieth century accountancy training, involving much copying and casting of columns of figures, emerges from the work of Maugham, but as Boys points out, the impression of the rather dull and introverted chartered accountant that it paints may have been appropriate in the earlier part of the twentieth century, but would be misleading today. West's study of 1930s auditing in Marshall's *The Bank Audit* (2001) provides literary evidence that the profession's status was already rising at this point.

An entirely different proposition is the recent study of Johnson's 1972 novel, *Christie Malry's Own Double-Entry* (McKinstry 2007). The analysis points to the left-leaning political tendencies of the author, who in a savage triumph of black humour, attacks in the novel the tendency of accountancy to focus on the gains of proprietors, monetise everything and completely ignore the human dimension. The hero uses double-entry accounting to record all the 'aggravations' and 'recompense' in his life which are ignored by accountancy. Johnson's attack on capitalism is set in the context of the rising political unrest of the 1960s and 1970s, and is interpreted as a contribution, through satire, to the power-constrained discourse (in a Foucauldian sense) surrounding accountancy and business during the period.

Accounting history studies involving literature can, as has been shown, shed light on accountancy in a multitude of ways, not always complimentary, and there remains much for accounting historians of all nations to do.

Fine art

Yamey's (1989) *Art and Accounting* is the principal work published to date whose purpose is to shed light on accounting history through a study of paintings and other pictorial illustrations of accounting (ibid.: vii).

Even if only treated as a coffee table book, *Art and Accounting* would stand on its own by reason of its lavish colour plates, included among which are Hogarth's *Shortly After the Marriage*, painted in 1743. This work, a piece of biting social criticism, was part of Hogarth's *Marriage à la Mode* series of the same date, and one of two pictures in that series containing account books. An unhappily married earl, beside his uninterested wife, watches his steward leaving the scene with ledger and accounts, disgusted at the master's refusal to be consulted on the parlous state of the household finances. This slice of everyday life in mid-eighteenth century Britain is hugely entertaining.

Yamey also deals with portraits of business men. The images of Renaissance Italian bankers, Netherlandish merchants and occasionally their wives make an appearance, many created by the finest artists of the day. For example, the Barings, vigilantly posed over a ledger, in Sir Thomas Lawrence's Augustan conversation piece of 1806, peruse their account with Hope & Co, of Amsterdam, a Quaker bank with which they had long and profitable association. While dealing with the portraits, Yamey discusses everything from the significance of the books depicted in them (often not clear) to the techniques employed by the portraitists.

Yamey also deals with Bible illustrations involving books which are at least possibly account books, including a number of versions of *Joseph Distributing Corn in Egypt*, notable among which is a sumptuous Caravaggio. Not mentioned is the fact that such books are in codex rather than scroll format, and thus reflect contemporary life rather than that of Biblical times.

While dealing with allegories, symbols and emblems, Yamey wrestles with the interpretation of pictures where, often, supporting evidence of the artist's programme, or intention, has been lost. In the case of a work by Koninck, entitled *The Gold-Weigher*, there is considerable doubt, such that Yamey asks 'Is every seventeenth-century Dutch portrayal of an aged gold-weigher or money-changer to be read as symbolic of avarice?' Clearly not. Equally difficult, sometimes, is the identification of the exact purpose of the account books depicted.

Much more clear and rewarding to the observer are the *vanitas* still life paintings which are also studied by Yamey. This type of work was intended, through the depiction of groups of objects, to symbolise, from a Christian perspective, the brevity of earthly life and the temporary and ultimately futile nature of its pursuits. In these pictures, account books are occasionally found, and Yamey has included a selection of such works. Here, he describes one by Lourens in considerable detail, and as a by-product, readers learn about the merchants' marks which adorned account books of the period, a tribute to the power of the visual in accounting history, as well as to Yamey's erudition.

Yamey's book devotes much study to the *Allegory of Commerce*, a large, single-sheet woodcut of 1585 by Jost Amman, a Swiss artist working in Nuremberg. Based on the work of Johann Neudorfer the elder, a teacher of commerce and bookkeeping, the work depicts mercantile trade taking place around the prosperous port of Antwerp, with, beneath, a suite of offices in the classical style, where bookkeeping is in progress on every hand. There are allegories of profit, capital and cash flow, testifying to the universal prevalence of double-entry accounting by this time.

Yamey also provides a detailed treatment of various paintings in which Luca Pacioli features. Of special note is his inclusion of Pope-Hennessy's praise for the superiority of Piero Della Francesca's portrait of Pacioli in his Brera altarpiece. It shows an 'unerring grasp of the structure of the face, the delicate shading of the corners of the mouth, the sense of intellectual eminence which colors [*sic*] the whole image [and] makes this one of the peaks of quattrocento portrait-ure' (Yamey 1989: 133). It is, in all probability, the closest we can come today to apprehending the personality of such a seminal figure as Pacioli.

Yamey's book is a tremendous scholarly endeavour as well as a source of visual lessons in what the accountants of the late-medieval, Renaissance and Enlightenment periods actually did.

The graphic arts

Accounting history studies involving the graphic arts have appeared in relatively recent times, focusing on annual report design. Setting itself in a historical context, Preston *et al's* (1996) study, 'Imag(in)ing Annual Reports', concentrates on different 'ways of seeing' annual reports, which are, of course, designed objects.

Preston *et al.* examine three approaches to the interpretation of annual reports, the first one involving the commonly understood 'way of seeing' that underpins practical annual report design. That is, the approach which takes for granted that 'images are a transparent medium of communication through which corporations send messages to investors and the public' (ibid.: 115). To explore this, the authors examine some of the design techniques commonly used to carry corporate messages, including visual photographic metaphor. As an example, they cite the use of a Sumo wrestler as a symbol of brand 'power' (by Pepsico). The use of visually pleasing, brightly coloured photographic images is another common technique employed in annual reports, and they cite as an example the 'dreamy' depiction of marine life (by Texaco), used to highlight positive environmental achievements the company claimed to have implemented. Another technique discussed is the use of black and white pictures and grey colouring to reinforce an admission of poor performance. The authors note that annual reports using these 'reader friendly' techniques, as well as being read as intended, may also be read sceptically in order to expose attempts at manipulation.

The second 'way of seeing', which Preston *et al.* discuss, involves a more systematic way of 'looking beneath the surface' (1996: 119). As an example of this Marxist-informed approach, the photographic content of Northern Telecom's 1989 annual report is analysed, first, in terms of what its producers intended it to *denote*, namely, the company's advanced technological capability and its worldwide reach. This is conveyed with the aid of photographs of scientists or technicians in white coats, in settings which feature the electronic components which the firm uses, against architectural backgrounds with an international feel. However, this imagery may also be read in terms of what is excluded, that is, in terms of what the images *connote*. It may be seen as symbolic of the exclusion of the 'full- and part-time employees with readily available clerical, secretarial and routine manual skills', who are cheap to hire, easily disposable, low-paid, and on whom the firm depends. These are 'the missing faces in annual reports'. Such a reading places the images in 'a wider sociocultural context in which more profound [i.e. ideological] significances may be read' (ibid.: 122).

The third 'way of seeing' is the 'post-modern'. Post-modern art and graphic techniques and their interpretation allow the formation of new meanings in the mind of the beholder through the subversion and amendment of historical images. One example cited is the alteration of a painting of a woman by Klimt in the 1989 annual report of Talbrands. Her bare breast has been edited out and the word 'woman' has been superimposed, as in other images in the report. Klimt has been subverted in order to portray one of Talbrands' markets, 'western woman'.

However, it is a logical extension of the views of post-modern writers, such as Baudrillard, that an annual report can be infused with any meaning ascribed by the reader, and that it can take on a life of its own quite apart from the meanings it was intended to convey. Baudrillard (1987) states that: 'As simulacra, images precede the real to the extent that they invert the causal and logical order of the real.' Readers are entitled to ignore intended meanings and substitute their own subjective responses to text and images. Such relativistic approaches, the authors admit, 'are sometimes seen as an extreme view' (quoted in Preston *et al.* 1996: 128).

Examining the Marxist critique of postmodern interpretations, Preston *et al.* (ibid.: 129) note that 'For neo-Marxists, the decentered, allegorical and appropriated images that increasingly characterise contemporary sign production are seen to mute the possibility of critique', since, for Marxists, the underlying socio-economic realities remain.

Two contemporaneous, historically rooted, studies of annual report design expand on the first 'way of seeing' discussed by Preston *et al.*, scrutinising in different ways the deliberate use of persuasive visual and textual techniques to attempt to influence readers. The first of these, by Graves *et al.* (1996) examines the 'Television Epistemology of US Annual Reports'. Building on the contention by Postman that public discourse in the USA has been dominated for some time by televisual techniques inextricably bound up with notions of legitimacy, these authors provide many examples of 'the rhetorical nature of visual design in annual reports' (Graves *et al.* 1996: 59), and the role of 'Pictures . . . [in relation to the] . . . Bottom Line'. The essence of their study is the rather uncomplimentary but at least partly true assertion that the average American 'reader' of annual reports has a short attention span which has grown out of a diet of television and television-borne 'show business'. The paper asserts that this has affected the epistemologies in use in US culture generally, as well as leading, in the case of annual reports, to concern with the 'headlines' only, such as total profit.

A printed culture, accessed by reading, has given way to a visual one. This means that if a message 'does not appear in an amusing or attractive format or if the message is not instantaneous, that is, if it does not come packaged in the rhetoric of television, it will not be attended' (ibid.: 65). Visual images from annual reports 'as if framed by a television screen' are discussed in this study, including the Sumo wrestler already highlighted in Preston et al.'s (1996) analysis referred to above. The use of this example in two slightly different ways by two sets of writers looking at the deliberate intentions of annual report designers underscores the subjectivity involved in visual interpretation.

Nevertheless, the insight afforded by drawing attention to the 'epistemology of television' utilised in the past memorably enhances our understanding of the techniques of impression management employed today. This is especially worth bearing in mind in an age of internet annual reports, which allow users random access to visual material in an unprecedentedly convenient way while having the potential to subject them to the show business techniques of television and associated visual rhetoric, especially since they are accessed by that extremely televisual framing device, the personal computer screen.

The study by McKinstry (1996) traces the progress of British annual report design through the lens of Burton PLC's annual reports, produced over the period 1930–94. It highlights the influence of US advertising firms in the UK, and their British emulators and counterparts in developing annual report design. It was US advertising firms that first offered public relations services and devised notions such as 'corporate identity', importing these into annual reports and enlisting the advancing technologies of paper production, photolithography and typography in order to do so. This happened in Britain slightly later than in the USA. Guided by UK-based full-service advertising firms, Burton and some other key UK public companies turned, in the 1970s, to making annual reports, at least in part, corporate communications tools, as opposed to the basic tables of financial accounts and minimal textual information of which they had previously consisted.

McKinstry's study links the specific visual imagery used by Burton, especially from the 1980s onwards, with impression management geared towards shareholder support for the takeover of Debenhams, a large High Street retail chain, and the approval of extravagant remuneration packages for directors, who had been borne along on the economic upswing of the Thatcher years. When the economic downswing came, dramatic changes of design approach and indeed, designer, were implemented, as the new top management denigrated their predecessors and the falling profits associated with them. Burtons' iconic and visually stunning fashion-related annual reports gave way to sackcloth-and-ashes grey, together with the reduced and muted use of photographic images as the firm rebuilt itself in the early 1990s.

The Burton study concludes with the caveat that limited attention is paid by city analysts to the visual content of annual reports, but that there is a case for some form of control on annual report design to ensure that the more gullible reader is not misled. It advocates that design briefs for annual reports should be geared towards the interpretation of accounts rather than the aggrandisement of senior management, as it then was and may still be.

There is, in annual report design, a fertile field for the accounting historian as economic cycles come and go, as graphic and information technologies move on and as cultures, their manufacturing technologies and associated political priorities, not to mention art movements, change.

Film

Of all the creative arts which have some relevance to accounting history, film is undoubtedly one of the least studied. One of the few treatments of film having a bearing on accounting history is Beard's (1994) paper on 'Popular Culture and Professional Identity: Accountants in the Movies'. As this author notes, 'what occurs on film . . . is almost by definition, culturally significant' (ibid.: 303). In an analysis of films produced since 1957, Beard identifies 16 popular films in which accountants have appeared as central characters, including such successful ones as *The Producers* (1968), and *Ghostbusters* (1984).

In an analysis of the narrative capacities in which the accountants operate in the films analysed, Beard notes three roles: as stock comic characters who manifest stereotypes of the members of the accounting profession, as complex personalities whose identity as accountants is an integral part of their characters, and as intermediaries whose identities are necessary to develop and resolve the plot (Beard 1994: 307).

Beard observes that producers of films, who are in the entertainment business, have no obligation to truthfulness in their portrayal of accountants. However, the study implies that in general, what has been portrayed is consistent with the improving image that accountants have created over the past 50 years of the twentieth century. The comedic figures portrayed in *The Producers*, Monty Python's *The Meaning of Life* or *Ghostbusters* tend to give way in later films to characters 'who emerge from their stereotype' (Beard 1994: 309).

In the earlier films, too, accountants tended to be portrayed as joyless, lonely or dysfunctional, whereas, in the middle period examined, accountants 'begin the transition from a kind of programmed rigidity to a more complex emotional maturity'. The final period sees them 'portrayed as average men and women "who just happen to be accountants" ' (Beard 1994: 309). An improving image for accountants was also found in a more recent study of films released in North America in the twentieth century, with CPAs or CAs the most likely types to be depicted as 'heroes' (Dimnik and Felton 2006).

While accounting historians might welcome the retreat from stereotyping in more recent films that the above papers disclose, few would deny having laughed at the ludicrous depictions of Monty Python or *The Producers* and the pleasurable departure they represented, in their time, from the quotidian experience of accountancy and its pedagogy.

Another rare work of relevance to the world of film was Amernic and Craig's (2000) 'Accountability and Rhetoric during a Crisis: Walt Disney's 1940 Letter to Shareholders'. These authors analysed, through close reading, a communication made by Disney to his shareholders in order to make a case for the injection of extra capital at a period of heavy losses for the company. A framework of rhetoric and metaphor was selected in order to examine how Disney put his arguments.

Amernic and Craig concluded that it was 'fitting that Disney the storyteller would incorporate narrative into his CEO discourse' (ibid.: 63), shedding fresh light on the, at times, enigmatic personality that created and drove forward an organisation in which there was 'a curiously seamless fusion of cinematic art and consumerism' (ibid.: 57). The marketing of specially designed merchandise was part and parcel of the strategy for maximising revenues from new productions and the new characters they featured. At a technical level, the paper revealed that Disney's extremely prudent depreciation policy involved 'writing off the entire cost of the picture against the first revenues received', as in the case of *Snow White and the Seven Dwarfs* (ibid.: 65).

The filmic genre moves on, and a new production of *The Producers* (2005) has recently been in the cinemas, coinciding with its re-launch as a musical play. In 2001, *Christie Malry's Own*

Double Entry was turned into a film which was not put on general release but won the British Independent Film of the Year Award. Given the objective distance required of events before they can be researched as history, these and like developments are building up a future archive of potential interest to accounting historians of the next generation. It is also noteworthy that, so far, historical studies of accounting and film have been restricted to western film, leaving an open door for researchers from non-western cultures.

Coda and conclusion

Perhaps surprisingly, the world of music has as yet received little attention from accounting historians, and so it has not been given a separate treatment in this chapter. One rare exception is the paper by Zan (2004), in which he analyses the structure of an 'Unorthodox Music Historiography' as a potential model for the writing of accounting and management history. The musical history analysed began with a history of the present, proceeding backwards in time instead of forwards, a treatment of the theoretical underpinnings of the music concerned, an emphasis on non-linear development, a social history, a pluralist view of genres and a multi-geographical focus. From this one example, Zan attempted (somewhat tenuously, if articulately) to argue the benefits of such an open-minded approach to accounting history.

That study apart, the accountancy arrangements of musicians, musical combines, retailers, wholesalers and promoters of music remain largely untouched by historians. One possible reason is the lack of relevant archival materials, in the absence of which, speculation is necessary, as is shown by De Loo and Davis (2003) in their not wholly satisfactory study of the demise of Black Swan records in the USA in the early 1920s. Musicians and musical impresarios, like architectural practices, are quite likely to view their creative work, that is, the music they have composed, arranged or played, as of first importance when it comes to record retention, and other items such as business books are probably seen as less worthy of preservation.

A perusal of the lists of archives presented in the scholarly *New Grove Dictionary of Jazz*, for example, reveals the existence of very few financial records among the many collections listed (Kernfield 1994: 698–708). Using the listing provided in *Grove*, the writer of this chapter undertook a preliminary examination of the archives of the Casa Loma Orchestra, a famous swing orchestra active from the 1920s to the 1950s, which are located in Northeastern University, Boston. Somewhat exceptionally, he found notebooks containing salary records and other financial details which might reward further study. On the other hand, disappointingly, queries addressed to Tulane University's William Ransom Hogan Jazz archive, in New Orleans, revealed that it contains little of interest to the accounting historian. This does not rule out the possibility, of course, that other musical genres and institutions may have suitable archives as yet undiscovered.

An overview of what has been written to date in the field is perhaps now in order. The studies that have been discussed appeared to have been driven either by the arts-based proclivities or educational backgrounds of the accounting scholars who wrote them. This is a fruitful characteristic, for it enables readers and scholars to see accountancy in a wider setting, where the norms of industrial or commercial practice do not always apply.

In terms of the sustained commitment of scholars to this field, it is true in some cases that the pieces of research which have been undertaken are single ventures, not followed up in further studies, sometimes even 'retirement' ventures. It is to be hoped that this is not because of a perception that such studies are of inferior value to, say, a piece of research on a recent accounting standard. These studies require, and promote, a commendable breadth of view, and need, betimes, vast amounts of work, when compared with some areas of more mainstream accounting research. Value may be found in the accumulation of case studies, and in this respect, the work of those who specialise in accounting histories of the creative arts may be of significance for the synthesis of findings and the making of wider generalisations.

The barriers which face scholars of the interface between accounting and the arts are a reflection of the nature of the work. Journals which welcome such studies need to find suitable referees and associated processes which reflect the width of scholarship within a paper. This is perhaps the time for forging cross-disciplinary alliances with academics and specialists in the creative arts, at a moment when the faculties for which they work are much more concerned than in the past with seeing a clear role for themselves in society, as witnessed by several recent international arts conferences, convened to seek a way forward in this regard.

Furthermore, much more high quality illustration than that presently seen in journals is required for the visual material in papers examining the interface between accounting and the creative world. Since the text being studied is often the artefact itself, good illustration is required in order to reflect the visual richness involved, which frequently transcends full interpretation. A picture may indeed paint a thousand words, but not if it is badly reproduced. Publishers must be prepared for further expense if they are to support the work properly, and editors should be prepared to argue the case.

Research trajectories for the future have been suggested above, *en passant*. To these may be added the question of the involvement of senior, successful accountants in arts and arts funding bodies. To what extent does this reflect their 'establishment' social position, attempts to enhance socio-cultural capital, and to what extent is it meritocratic, reflecting a genuine love of the arts? What unique contribution do these individuals have to make, if any? Are there among us today accountants with a love of the arts such as Edwin Waterhouse, a pioneer of the English profession (Jones 1988)? Or does success and affluence enable the most senior accountants to patronise the arts, and by so doing, nurture an interest in them which was previously lacking? We would like to know.

Another fascinating but scarcely explored area is the world of art markets and valuations. Paintings by artists such as Vincent van Gogh, who lived a life of poverty, sell today for prices which beggar the imagination. But what happens to the work of artists who enjoy fame in their lifetimes? To what extent is their work rationed by agents in order to ensure high prices, and what other factors are at work? How do the purchasers of such work, such as corporations, value these in their accounts?

Also, the recent republication of Hyde's book, *The Gift: How Creativity Transforms the Modern World* (2006) has raised again the conflict between the values of those who exercise a creative gift and the commercial values of contemporary liberal capitalism. In suggesting points of reconciliation by means of case studies of the poets Walt Whitman and Ezra Pound, Hyde has inadvertently set out an agenda for accounting historians. Through the production of hard evidence, it is possible for us to shed substantial light on motivation and financial and accounting practices in creative enterprises and creative individuals. Much has been done already, but still more needs to be done.

As we enjoy a more leisured lifestyle in western society, and as our affluence grows, we have more time in our lives and more resources both to enjoy the creativity of others and to practise what creative gifts we ourselves may have. In these circumstances, the accounting and financial dimensions of creativity, and their histories, can only be of increasing interest.

Key works

Connor (2004) represents a major study on the use of accounting and accounting concepts by Daniel Defoe and Aphra Benn in their late seventeenth to early eighteenth-century novels. The book also includes a review of contemporary bookkeeping guides for women and a summary of the forms of money in use in the wider economy.

Graves *et al.* (1996) examines the effects of television and show business on the concentration span of the American public, and how it has influenced the design of annual reports of US corporations, in their desire to communicate the messages they wish to emphasise.

McKinstry (1997) examines the status-building intentions of the fledgling ICAEW as it erected its magnificent 'Hall'. The paper offers an art-historical explanation of the building's stylistic connotations, the iconography of its sculpture and how these furthered the aims of a foremost professional body.

Yamey (1989) is a major work, lavishly illustrated, which examines depictions of accountancy, accountants and account books in western art from the late-medieval period onwards. The book sheds new light on various aspects of accountancy, as well as on art history.

References

Amernic, J. H. and Craig, R. (2000) Accountability and rhetoric during a crisis: Walt Disney's 1940 letter to shareholders, *Accounting Historians Journal*, 27 (2): 49–86.

Baudrillard, J. (1987) Modernity, *Canadian Journal of Political and Social Theory*, 11 (3): 63–73.

Beard, V. (1994) Popular culture and professional identity: accountants in the movies, *Accounting, Organizations and Society*, 19 (3): 303–18.

Boys, P. (1990) *Chartered Accountants' Hall: The First Hundred Years* (London: ICAEW).

Boys, P. (1994) A source of accounting history: Somerset Maugham, *Accounting Historian's Notebook*, 17 (2): 9, 24.

Boys, P. (1995) Samuel Pepys' personal accounts, *Accounting, Business & Financial History*, 5 (3): 308–20.

Buckmaster, D. and Buckmaster, E. (1999) Studies of accounting and commerce in Chaucer's *Shipman's Tale*, *Accounting, Auditing & Accountability Journal*, 12 (1): 113–28.

Connor, R. (2004) *Women, Accounting and Narrative: Keeping Books in Eighteenth Century England* (London: Routledge).

Czarniavska, B. (2008) Accounting and gender across times and places: an excursion into fiction, *Accounting, Organizations and Society*, 33 (1): 33–47.

De Loo, I. and Davis, D. (2003) Black Swan records, 1921 to 1924: from a swanky swan to a dead duck, *Accounting History*, 8 (2): 35–57.

Dimnik, T. and Felton, S. (2006) Accountant stereotypes in movies distributed in North America in the twentieth century, *Accounting, Organizations and Society*, 31 (2): 129–55.

Evans, L. (2005) Brothels, tombstones and morality: a literary look at offbeat perspectives on accounting and finance, paper presented at British Accounting Association Annual Congress, Heriot-Watt University, Edinburgh.

Fawcett, R. (2002) *Scottish Medieval Churches: Architecture and Furnishings* (Stroud: Tempus).

Fraser, I., Gallhofer, S., Haslam, J. and Sydserff, R. (2006) *Hard Times*: Carlyle and Dickens on accounting in the name of social progress. Paper presented at Interdisciplinary Perspectives on Accounting Conference, Cardiff, July.

Gallhofer, S. and Haslam, J. (1996) Accounting/art and the emancipatory project: some reflections, *Accounting, Auditing & Accountability Journal*, 9 (5): 23–44.

Graves, O. F., Flesher, D. L. and Jordan, R. E. (1996) Pictures and the bottom line: the television epistemology of U.S. annual reports, *Accounting, Organizations and Society*, 21 (1): 57–88.

Hyde, L. (2006) *The Gift: How the Creative Spirit Transforms the Modern World* (Edinburgh: Canongate).

ICAEW (2002) *Chartered Accountants' Hall: An Illustrated Tour* (London: ICAEW).

Jeacle, I. (2003) Accounting and the construction of the standard house, *Accounting, Auditing & Accountability Journal*, 16 (4): 582–605.

Jeacle, I. (2005) Accounting and the construction of taste: standard costs and the Georgian cabinet maker, *Abacus*, 41 (2): 117–37.

Jones, E. (1988) *The Memoirs of Edwin Waterhouse* (London: Batsford).

Kernfield, B. (ed.) (1994) *The New Grove Dictionary of Jazz* (London: Macmillan).

Klamer, A. (ed.) (1997) *The Value of Culture: On the Relationship Between Economics and the Arts* (Amsterdam: University of Amsterdam Press).

Lee, T. A. (1996), The influence of the individual in the professionalisation of accountancy: the case of Richard Brown and the Society of Accountants in Edinburgh, in C. W. Nobes and T. Cooke (eds) *The Development of Accounting in an International Context*, pp. 31–48 (London: Routledge).

Macdonald, K. (1989) Building respectability, *Sociology*, 23 (1): 55–80.

McKinstry, S. (1996) Designing the annual reports of Burton plc from 1930 to 1994, *Accounting, Organizations and Society*, 21 (1): 89–111.

McKinstry, S. (1997) Status building: some reflections on the architectural history of Chartered Accountants' Hall, London, 1889–1893, *Accounting, Organizations and Society*, 22 (8): 779–98.

McKinstry, S. (2000) *Twenty Seven Queen Street, Edinburgh: Home of Scottish Chartered Accountants, 1891–2000* (Edinburgh: ICAS).

McKinstry, S. (2007) *Christie Malry's Own Double Entry*, by B. S. Johnson: an interpretation as Foucauldian discourse, *Critical Perspectives on Accounting*, 18 (8): 975–91.

McKinstry, S. (forthcoming) Reframing a 'Subfusc' institute: building on the past for the future at Chartered Accountants' Hall, London, 1965–1970, *Critical Perspectives on Accounting*.

McKinstry, S. and Fletcher, M. (2002) The personal account books of Sir Walter Scott, *Accounting Historians Journal*, 29 (2): 59–89.

McKinstry, S. and Wallace, K. (2004) Cullen, Lochhead and Brown, architects: the business, financial and accounting history of a non-profit maximising firm, 1902–2002, *Accounting, Business & Financial History*, 14 (2): 183–207.

Maltby, J. (1999) Accounting and the soul of the middle class: Gustav Freytag's *Soll und Haben*, *Accounting, Organizations and Society*, 22 (1): 69–87.

Maltby, J. and Rutterford, J. (2006) Frank must marry money: men, women and property in Trollope's novels, *Accounting Historians Journal*, 33 (2): 169–200.

Mintzberg, H., Otis, S., Shamsie, J. and Waters, J. (1986) Strategy of design: a study of architects in co-partnership, in J. Grant (ed.) *Strategic Management Frontiers*, pp. 311–59 (Greenwich, CT: JAI Press).

Moore, D. L. (1974) *Lord Byron Accounts Rendered* (London: John Murray).

Mussari, R. and Mussari, B. (2006) Book-keeping in the sixteenth century building yard of the Castello of Crotone: an accountancy and architectural analysis, *Accounting History*, 11 (3): 319–56.

Parker, R. H. (1999) Accounting in Chaucer's *Canterbury Tales*, *Accounting, Auditing & Accountability Journal*, 12 (1): 92–112.

Pile, L. (2004) A building of distinction, *Accountancy*, February: 41–3.

Preston, A. M., Wright, C. and Young, J. M. (1996) Imag(in)ing Annual Reports, *Accounting, Organizations and Society*, 21 (1): 113–37.

Service, A. (1977) *Edwardian Architecture: A Handbook to Building Design in Britain 1890–1914* (London: Thames and Hudson).

Squire, J. (1937) *The Hall of the Institute of Chartered Accountants in England and Wales* (London: ICAEW).

Walker, S. P. (1995) An early challenge to the accountant stereotype? The accountant as hero in late-Victorian romantic fiction, *Accounting Historian's Notebook*, 18 (2): 13–14, 32.

West, B. P. (2001) On the social history of accounting: *The Bank Audit* by Bruce Marshall, *Accounting History*, 6 (1): 11–30.

Willis, C. (1995) *Form Follows Finance: Skyscrapers and Skylines in New York and Chicago* (Princeton, NJ: Architectural Press).

Wilson, R. G. and Mackley, A. L. (1999) How much did the English country house cost to build, 1660–1880?, *Economic History Review*, 52 (3): 436–68.

Yamey, B. (1989) *Art and Accounting* (New Haven, CT: Yale University Press).

Zan, L. (2004) Writing accounting and management history: insights from unorthodox music historiography, *Accounting Historians Journal*, 31 (2): 171–92.

Part 7

Polity

26

The state

Philip Colquhoun

Overview

This chapter discusses the intertwining of accounting and the state, focusing on entities that make up the state. Accounting is viewed here as part of the accountability mechanisms of states. Various notions of accountability are applied to this relationship including constitutional, hierarchical and stewardship accountability. These accountability relationships are evident from the earliest records of ancient civilisations where individuals were accountable to the state and the state was accountable to individuals. During different periods of history, accounting practices are shown to mediate aspects of the accountability relationships between the legislative and executive branches of government, between the elected and electorate, and between entities within the state. It is revealed that changes to accounting technologies are often portrayed as philosophical and ideological debates over the nature of accountability relationships. The chapter illustrates that the accounting history literature on the state focuses largely, but not exclusively, on Anglo-American countries from the mid-nineteenth century.

The chapter pays particular attention to the introduction of double-entry bookkeeping in government in various parts of Europe, the on-going debates surrounding the utility of replacing traditional cash-based with accrual-based accounting systems, and the discourses surrounding changes to the mandate of government auditors. The use of accounting by the state in social institutions is addressed in relation to the financial management of such organisations and the control of individuals who occupy them. The emergent historical research on the relatively recent new public management reforms is discussed. The chapter concludes by indicating the potential for future historical research on accounting and the state.

Introduction

The activities of the state and accounting practices are intertwined in numerous ways (Miller 1990). A great deal of accounting undertaken by or for individuals has elements controlled, managed or sanctioned by the state. Commercial activity, and hence its accounting, are controlled through state regulatory regimes. The regulation, ostensibly in the public interest, of private sector monopolies is activated in large part through accounting processes. The authority of financial reporting standards is derived through mandates from the state. The accounting profession itself obtains much of its power, prestige and viability from the sanction it receives from the state.

This chapter focuses on where this intertwining is at its most direct, that is, entities that are part of the state. Such entities vary from institutions of central government and sub-national government units, to individual trading operations, autonomous public bodies and organisations established in the pursuit of social policy. Discussion of the relationship between accounting and these entities in historical contexts ranges from the technical and managerial to the political and social. Literature on specific technical issues relate to issues such as the introduction of double-entry bookkeeping and accrual-based accounting. Literature on socio-political issues relate to the philosophical choices and ideological debates behind the introduction of new accounting and auditing technologies and the impacts of accounting on individuals and various social groups.

The dominant theme in the literature on accounting and the state is accountability. The manner in which this concept is understood differs among authors. For example, Funnell (2007) perceives the accountability provided by accounting in the context of constitutional rights, freedoms and protections provided by liberal democratic states. In consequence, Funnell (1994, 1998, 2004) locates debates surrounding accounting, auditing and the state in relation to notions of constitutional accountability. Alternative understandings of accountability focus on the vertical and hierarchical nature of accountability processes often combined with notions of stewardship and individual responsibility.

However, accountability is not the only framework within which the relationship between accounting and the state is understood. Theoretical frameworks employed to analyse this relationship include those based on neo-classical economics, critical analysis and institutional theory. One of the most common approaches focuses on agency – in particular, identifying and narrating the contribution of individual actors and groups in the debates surrounding continuity and change in accounting and audit practice.

The chapter is structured according to chronology and specific issues discussed in published histories of accounting and the state. The first two sections are chronological and address the development of accounting and the state in ancient and classical civilisations, and the period from the Middle Ages to the nineteenth century. The scope of these sections are not therefore characteristic of the emphasis on the modern and the Anglo-American in much accounting history research (Carnegie and Potter 2000; Carmona 2004). The remaining sections discuss more technical issues on accounting and the state. Here the review reflects the fact that most (but not all) of the accounting history literature concerns the Anglo-American context during the nineteenth and twentieth centuries. The first issue discussed relates to the debates surrounding the basis of reporting in government – cash or accrual accounting. The following two sections look at institutions or movements involved in promoting change to accounting in the state. Various bodies that sought change to accounting practices are discussed as is the reforms undertaken from the late 1970s under the banner of new public management. In the section which follows, conflicts over assurance and value for money audits are discussed, including those from the period of new public management. The role of accounting in social institutions under the auspices of the state is discussed on two levels – where accounting techniques are used in the financial management of organisations, and where accounting is used as a tool to control the individuals who inhabit them. The penultimate section looks at studies which compare accounting in the state with other parts of the economy and includes a brief discussion of international comparisons.

544

Ancient and classical civilisations

The surviving records of accounting systems in ancient civilisations, as discussed in Chapter 4 of this volume, provide insights to accounting for and by both private individuals and the state. Carmona and Ezzamel (2007) conceptualise three spheres of accountability relationships in ancient Mesopotamia and Egypt; individual to individual, individual to state and state to individual. It is the latter two that are of interest in this chapter. The state to individual sphere provides an example of hierarchical accountability, while the state to individual sphere is concerned with honouring commitments to subjects.

Sources from ancient Babylonia, Egypt, Greece and Rome discuss how various states, republics and empires managed and accounted for their resources. Much of the impetus for this accounting stemmed from the need to account for the collection of taxation, especially in the more expansive empires. Accounting records were used as an accountability mechanism for tax and tribute collectors. In line with the political structures of states, accountability was generally hierarchical to the ruler; often mediated through a series of governors, superintendents and other officials. The Athenian state *c*.410 BC provides an early example of democratic notions of public accountability for financial management. Receipts and disbursements were recorded on marble stones and displayed in public (Boyd 1968; Ezzamel 2002b).

The scale of the Roman Empire necessitated the creation of accounting records, especially when regular taxes were collected and regular payments were required to be made, such as for army personnel. Accounting was part of a much larger system of management of the Empire, with controls, reviews and a hierarchy of officers and officials leading to Rome. At times the Roman financial management system included a form of yearly budgeting, although this appears to have been an appropriation for expenditure rather than a decision-making tool (Boyd 1968).

While the purpose of most financial management systems in ancient times was the accountability of officials for the taxes they collected and the review of expenditure, there are instances of what could be labelled 'information for decision-making'. The Middle Kingdom in Ancient Egypt *c*.2000 BC provides an example of accounting by the state for the purposes of accountability and decision usefulness. The accounting system recorded the inflow of taxes, generally received as grain, and thus ensured the accountability of the officials responsible for their collection. An equally important function of the accounting system was accounting for the outflow of grain and other material collected. The taxation was applied to the redistribution of wealth according to predetermined ratios and the accounting system facilitated this redistribution (Ezzamel 2002a, 2002b).

Middle Ages to the nineteenth century

Moving forward three millennia, but several centuries before the publication of Pacioli's celebrated work on double-entry bookkeeping in 1494, an important treatise appeared in England on accounting by the state. The *Dialogus de Scaccario* (the Course of the Exchequer) was written around the late 1170s by Richard fitz Neal. As its title suggests, the work is presented in the form of a dialogue (which took place on the banks of the River Thames) between a junior and a senior employed in the English Exchequer. Richard fitz Neal was Treasurer for the King, a position that his father purchased for him and which he held between *c*.1158 and 1198. The *Dialogus* provided a comprehensive account on how the Exchequer was to be managed and offers detailed explanations for the practices it related. No doubt influenced by the author's other position, namely Bishop of London, there are strong moral overtones in the instructions given to the junior official.

The *Dialogus* reflects the accountability function of the Exchequer in dealing with the King's revenue and expenditure. Central to the treatise are the instructions to ensure that the correct taxation is collected and recorded systematically, together with the importance of the account-ability of the officials. The *Dialogus* provides insights to the operation of the English treasury and thus the thinking behind much of the subsequent development of accounting by the English state, especially the focus on the accountability of the individuals in its service (Richardson 1928a, 1928b; Johnson 1983).

With the development of double-entry bookkeeping in medieval Italy, an alternative to the existing single entry methods of accounting was provided for use in the state and private sectors. The single entry system, often in the form of charge and discharge, allowed for a record of monies collected by an official on behalf of the ruler or the public, and in separate books, the payments (or discharges) made from the public money by that official. According to Jones (1985), these accounts were concerned with ensuring the accountability of the individual; a way for the agent to provide an account of his stewardship of money and/or other resources. As such, charge and discharge did not deal with the use of assets other than (at times) debtors and (even more rarely) inventories. Its shortcomings included:

> the possibility of leaving blank spaces, the ability to modify past entries and of inserting sheets. Furthermore, the system used too many separate books and notebooks for registering transactions. But possibility the most important shortcoming was that it failed to provide an administrative link between income and expenditure and, therefore it was impossible to present an overall balance.
>
> (Jurado-Sánchez 2002: 167)

As the analysis in Chapter 5 suggests, the private sector embraced double-entry bookkeeping in various forms relatively quickly. The first known use of double entry by a European central government was in the Spanish Royal Treasury in 1592. The introduction of double-entry bookkeeping arose out of a period of financial crisis and was part of the wider reform of state administration. In contrast, parts of the Spanish commercial sector were compelled to adopt double-entry bookkeeping 43 years prior to its requirement in the Royal Treasury (ibid.).

The literature on the adoption of double-entry bookkeeping by European governments has identified the important role played by individuals in the process. For example, in the Netherlands, Stevin's 1608 text and his earlier work in the royal domains were pivotal to the introduction of double-entry bookkeeping in the upper level of the Dutch central government. Stevin argued against applying double-entry bookkeeping in the lower levels of central government due to the difficulty of training all officials in the technique. The Dutch merchant, Cabiljau, was responsible for the introduction of double entry to the Swedish government in 1623 (Gomes *et al.* 2006). Double-entry bookkeeping was applied to public finances in France in 1716, the result of the work of four brothers, Antoine, Claude, Joseph and Jean Paris. The Paris brothers were leading financers of the period and the introduction of double-entry bookkeeping was part of an overhaul of the collection of money by the Treasury, aimed at providing better information on revenue and thereby decreasing interest paid by the Treasury (Lemarchand 1999). The French reforms were halted in 1726 but double-entry bookkeeping was reintroduced in the early nineteenth century as part of a larger reform of government accounting. These reforms in France were linked to the later introduction of double-entry bookkeeping in England through the involvement of Count Mollien (Nikitin 2001).

The study by Edwards *et al.* (2002) on the discourses leading to the introduction of double-entry bookkeeping in British central government in the 1830s also draws attention to the importance of particular actors. The design of the double-entry bookkeeping system for British central government was allocated to a committee comprising two senior civil servants and Peter Harris Abbott, a 'leading public accountant of the day' (ibid.: 643). The committee was unanimous on the advisability of introducing double-entry bookkeeping. However, there was debate over its form. Abbott advocated 'the universal adoption of the mercantile system in the various departments of the Government' (ibid.: 648), while the two public servants argued for a form of double-entry bookkeeping that was consistent with the traditional stewardship function of accounting in British government. Edwards *et al.* frame this episode as an ideological contest. The professional accountant advocated full double-entry bookkeeping to bring about a more businesslike approach to government financial management. However, the civil servants wanted to maintain the personal accountability and stewardship of individual officials, which was central to the charge and discharge system. Another feature of the debate was the use of cash or accruals bases of accounting. Abbott's mercantile system included accrual accounting, while the stewardship model was based on maintaining the use of a cash-based system. The advantage of the latter was that flows of public money could be traced to the individual responsible for its collection or disbursement. The arguments of the government officials won the argument and a cash-based form of double-entry bookkeeping was to be introduced to British central government. However, as Edwards *et al.* note, whether it was introduced 'in substance or in form, awaits the location and study of relevant archival records' (2002: 638).

Cash *vs.* accrual accounting

The argument between Peter Harris Abbott and the two senior civil servants is illustrative of numerous debates surrounding the use of cash versus accruals basis of accounting. This has been both a major controversy in government accounting and a widely studied feature in the history of accounting by the state. With the focus historically on tracking the receipt of taxation and/or to ensuring correct approval for expenditure of public money via an appropriation or other legal authority, a cash basis of recording and reporting suited the demands for government accountability. Regardless of whether the accounting technique involved tally sticks, single entry charge/discharge or double-entry bookkeeping, a system for recording the cash received and disbursed was traditionally deemed sufficient.

At times, the cash versus accrual issue was part of a wider debate surrounding financial practices for parts of the state, as in the above-mentioned debate over double-entry bookkeeping. More recently discussion of the introduction of accrual accounting has been associated with the reforms that began in the late 1970s, frequently referred to as new public management or new public financial management. The adoption of accrual accounting is a common feature of new public management reforms. In this chapter, the issue of accrual accounting in recent times is discussed in the later section on those reforms. Literature on the cash versus accrual accounting debates, outside the new public management period, has arisen most frequently in relation to accounting by municipalities and here the principal foci of historical investigation has been on the UK, the USA and New Zealand.

Coombs and Edwards' (1995) study, based on the archives of five large municipal corporations in Britain, indicates that the movement from cash to full accruals accounting occurred between 1852 and 1922. Their paper argues that accounting innovation was supply driven rather than demand-led. The impetus for change from cash to accruals was driven by those involved in the accounting process rather than those for whom the accounts were prepared. The agents of change were specific local authorities and officials, and the professional associations which represented council treasurers and accountants. Coombs and Edwards' study supports Jones' (1986, 1992) observation that the costs to individuals engaging in debates over municipal accounting outweighed any benefits that they would receive.

Potts (1976, 1978, 1982) discusses changes to municipal accounting, predominantly in the USA in the first third of the twentieth century. Based on published works, Potts compares the arguments advanced on the cash *v.* accrual debate by various authorities. Two phases in the development of municipal accounting are identified. The first was 1900–20 when discussion focused on similarities to commercial accounting. The second was 1920–35 when the dissimilarities between municipalities and commercial activities, and thus the accounting which emanated there from, were highlighted. In the earlier period, the intention was to introduce commercial accounting and especially accrual accounting to municipal authorities, while in the later period, arguments against introducing accrual accounting were dominant in the professional literature. For Potts, the evolution of municipal accounting was not random or disorganised, but the result of the opinions of prominent accountants at the time. Discussions on the possibility of introducing accrual accounting were always connected with related issues including accounting for capital, permanent property and the associated recording of depreciation, and the notion of the going-concern as used in the private sector. According to Potts, this debate had run its course by 1935 with the conclusion that permanent property should not be recorded in the accounts, and that the focus of municipal accounts should be on the liquidity of the authority. A cash basis was considered the best and most efficient way of revealing liquidity.

In New Zealand, full accrual accounting was introduced to local government as part of the new public management reforms. However, a number of specific activities such as local government trading enterprises and harbour boards had a long-standing obligation to use accrual accounting as the basis of their reporting. Pressure for the introduction of accrual accounting by municipal government began in the 1930s, predominantly driven by the government auditor and, on occasion, from within the sector's professional administration and accounting bodies. The accounting profession more widely rarely demonstrated any interest in government accounting until the 1980s and the commencement of the new public management reforms. Opposition to the numerous earlier attempts to introduce accrual accounting was based on a combination of technical and implementation concerns.

The demarcation lines of the debates over cash *vs* accruals in New Zealand were not drawn around the interested groups but rather around individuals within each interested group. At the technical level, many of those involved in municipal accounting viewed cash as the preferred approach as it provided for accountability as per legal requirements and was in accord with the tradition of government accountability. The standard argument against the introduction of accrual accounting was the lack of available expertise to prepare accrual-based accounts across the sector. Arguments for the use of accrual accounting were based on the benefits of recording fixed assets, deprecation and other non-financial transactions, removing the advantages to councils of 'creative' cash accounting based on managing the timing of cash payments and receipts, and a belief that the accounting technology employed in the private sector would be an improvement on that used in the public sector (Colquhoun 2005).

There are a number of studies of the use of accrual accounting in other countries. Carpenter and Feroz (2001) discuss the introduction of generally accepted accounting principles (GAAP), including accrual accounting, in four states of the USA from the 1970s to the 1990s. The authors use institutional and resource dependency theories to frame their history. The study identifies a number of factors that led to the adoption of GAAP and accrual accounting: the impact of individuals (in this case elected government officials), the fiscal condition of the state, the potential to change power relations in the state government, the participation of the state's key accounting bureaucrats in their professional associations, and the nature and strength of organisational process used to maintain non–GAAP practices including cash accounting (organisational imprinting).

Scott *et al.* (2003) provide an interpretative history using stakeholder theory on the use of cash and accruals systems in two Australian hospitals from 1857 to 1975. The paper traces shifts from cash to accruals basis followed by reversion to the cash basis over the period studied. The government is identified as the stakeholder responsible for the change back to cash basis in 1975, when the state became the primary funder of hospitals. The paper charts the introduction of accrual accounting in both hospitals, noting that while company legislation was the reason for its introduction in one hospital, in the other, a not-for-profit entity, no definitive reasons could be identified.

Agents of change

This section examines the institutions that have been important in the adoption of new accounting technologies in various countries. Of particular importance in the USA were the nineteenth-century reform movements and the role of the Government Accounting Standards Board.

The first promoters of change in government accounting in the USA responded to the perception that municipal government was inefficient, dishonest and corrupt. Reform was associated with the Progressive Era, the 1890s to the 1920s. The National Municipal League (NML) formed in 1894, as well as municipal research bureaus, proposed improvements to the management of various cities in the USA. The bureaus suggested accounting reforms designed to create uniform reporting practices by cities and improved accounting and management processes. Although it had no formal authority, the NML could claim significant success by 1908, when it reported that one half of large cities in the USA had adopted their uniform accounting methods (Fleischman and Marguette 1986: 72). The introduction of budgeting to municipalities, which, according to Fleischman and Marguette, had not been transported to the USA from the English public sector where it was central to the financial management system, was a major achievement of the reforms during the Progressive Era.

Since the 1930s, a number of bodies have been involved in promoting standards and offering guidance in relation to municipal accounting in the USA. These bodies had a common parent or sponsoring organisation in the Municipal Finance Officers Association. The focus of these bodies continued to be the production by municipal authorities of comparable financial data. In later years they also broadened their interests to issues such as revenue recognition, reporting objectives, and disclosure practices. The accounting profession only became involved in providing assistance and guidance to the public sector in the USA in 1974 when the American Institute of Certified Public Accountants issued an audit guide for state and local government units (Remis 1982).

Arguably the most important single instigator of change in US public sector accounting has been the Government Accounting Standards Board (GASB), organised in 1984. The GASB mandate covers financial reporting standards for state and local governments. One of the first issues to be addressed by the GASB was accounting for staff post-employment benefits. In a forerunner of future debates, the GASB required that these benefits be accounted for on an accrual basis. In June 1999, the GASB issued Statement 34 which dealt with significant financial reporting issues including the accrual basis and reporting of both short- and long-term assets and liabilities. The introduction of such changes did not diminish the importance attached to budgeting information, and comparison between budget and actual, was maintained. The reporting of non-financial or service efforts and accomplishments was encouraged but not required (Patton and Freedman 2005).

In the UK, the devising of standards and the introduction of changes to the accounting practices of municipalities followed a pattern analogous to the USA. Professional bodies for municipal officials, especially the Corporate Treasurers and Accountants Institute formed in 1885 (later the Chartered Institute of Public Finance and Accountancy), took the lead in suggesting change as opposed to state bodies such as the Local Government Board. During the 1880s the former requested the latter to exercise its statutory power and make changes to the way municipalities prepared their accounts. Even after the introduction of statutory regulation in the 1930s the Minister responsible for municipalities would not promulgate accounting changes until they had been agreed by the professional associations in local government (Coombs and Edwards 1993).

New public management

The reforms of the public sector that began internationally in the late 1970s are often grouped together under the title of new public management. The reforms are normally characterised as introducing markets to the public sector, financial performance measures, decentralisation and a focus on results or outcomes rather than inputs. New public management is also associated with performance or value for money audits and accrual accounting. However, it is important to note that the extent to which new public management reforms were introduced varies between countries (Humphrey *et al.* 2005).

The introduction of accrual accounting in Australia has been the subject of a number of historical studies. Ryan (1998) focuses on the adoption of accrual accounting by federal and state governments. Using an agenda-setting framework, Ryan examines the factors that led to the introduction of accrual accounting, separating the factors into political and policy agendas. Her analysis chronicles the emergence of accrual accounting as a potential issue in the early 1970s to its implementation as policy in the late 1990s. The key political agenda setters were the Auditors-General, parliamentarians and the accounting profession. The key policy agenda setters were the Public Sector Accounting Standards Board and government officials from the treasury and finance ministries. Ryan concludes that the introduction of accrual accounting cannot be attributed to one actor event, but rather rose 'onto [the] agenda due to several factors coming together at a given point in time' (ibid.: 533).

Christensen (2002, 2003) provides insights to the discussions concerning the introduction of accrual accounting in the late 1980s by the New South Wales (NSW) state government. Both his papers pay particular attention to the role of partners in accounting firms acting as consultants to the government and a number of senior politicians identified as users of the accounting information. Christensen (2002) uses contingency theory to identify the agents of change who promoted the adoption of accrual accounting in NSW. Christensen (2003) uses institutional theory to explain how the accountant-consultants were able to convince public sector officials to introduce accrual accounting to the state government.

Turning to the USA, Watkins and Arrington (2007) discuss the increasing importance and power of accounting in the public sector during the period of new public management reforms. In particular, they focus on the National Performance Review programme of the Clinton Presidency. Drawing on the work of political theorists Wolin and Connolly, they discuss the extent to which political discourse has come to be written as a language of accounting. Accounting fills the void left by the demise of political foundationalism. Costs, calculations, benefits and performance have become the language of government. The economic justification of all things political, which is central to the new public management reform agenda, requires the deployment not only of accounting techniques but also its language.

Newberry and Pallot (2004) examine the use of incentives in the financial management regime of the New Zealand central government. Based on extensive archival documents, the paper traces the development of the incentives and their impact on government departments. Focusing in particular on the capital charge, chief executive's performance contracts and the ability of departments to retain any surpluses generated, Newberry and Pallot argue that the impact of accounting-based incentives is detrimental to the public sector and counter to the stated aims of new public management reforms. They argue that the accounting technologies and the incentives they generate have resulted in a loss of capability to deliver within the public sector and are likely to cause declining morale in departments. The authors question the intentionality of such outcomes of the financial management reforms.

Goddard (2005) examines changes to UK local government accounting, governance and accountability requirements within a broader framework on the nature of institutional structures. The paper reviews accounting and financial management changes in historical, economic and social contexts. Using regulation theory Goddard argues that the financial management reforms undertaken in the name of new public management since the mid-1970s represent a shift from the traditional or 'Fordist' regime to a post-Fordist regime. This shift is part of a new ideology which emphasises the merits of private sector structures and practices.

Audit

Two areas dominate studies on auditing and the state in the accounting history literature – the introduction of value for money/operational auditing and the right to undertake and/or control probity and assurance audits of state entities. The literature focuses, for both areas, on the contested nature of decisions on what to audit and who to audit. A number of papers have discussed state audits in terms of the ongoing conflicts between the executive and legislative branches of government. Such conflict is presented as almost inevitable given that the executive seeks to maintain or (re)gain as much freedom from the oversight of the legislature as possible, while the legislature seeks to exercise its rights and obligations in relation to the oversight of public money. Much of this oversight is performed on behalf of the legislature by an auditor.

Funnell (1994) discusses the battle for an independent state auditor in Britain which culminated in the passing of the Exchequer and Audit Departments Act, 1866. The Act is portrayed as the result of more than a century of development commencing with haphazard auditing, moving to executive-controlled audits, and culminating in the emergence of parliamentary controlled audits. The 1866 Act represented a major *de jure* shift in the emphasis and control of the audit function from the interest of the executive to the interest of Parliament. The response of the executive to this shift was to support the 'independence' discourse surrounding the newly created position of 'Comptroller General of the receipt and issue of Her Majesty's Exchequer and Auditor General of Public Accounts' (C&AG). Yet the executive continued to maintain *de facto* control over the state audit through its control of the audit department's finance and the appointment of the C&AG. This ensured that the independence enacted by Parliament and, superficially supported by the executive, was severely limited in practice. Elsewhere Funnell (1997) traces the content of the 1866 Act to earlier issues over the military spending of public money and the long-standing concern of the British Parliament with uncontrolled and unauthorised expenditure by the military. These issues are dealt with in Chapter 27.

The theme of struggle over the control of audits is also related in Coombs and Edwards' (2004) study of the audit of municipal corporations in Britain during the period 1835–1935. While the constitutional issues identified by Funnell were not present, the provision of audits became a three-way struggle between the accounting profession, the locally elected auditors, and central government-controlled district auditors. In the 1880s, the accounting profession looked to municipal audit as a source of business for its members. The newly organised profession raised its profile by publicly criticising the existing system of elected auditors and made much of the fraud in municipal corporations which the elected auditors had failed to detect. At the same time, the District Audit Board continued to press for legislative changes that would augment its responsibilities in relation to the accounts of municipal corporations. Despite the efforts of all three parties, none received any significant increase in responsibility or powers relating to the auditing of municipal corporations, although the members of the accounting profession did gain the right to be appointed auditor. Indeed, in practice, increasing numbers of municipal corporations engaged professional accountants as their auditors in preference to either the elected auditors or the District Audit Board.

As a relatively new technology, value for money audits (or operational audits) have been contentious and contested. Value for money audits developed from early 1940s in the USA but failed to transfer to other countries until the 1970s, especially to government bodies. While traditional government auditing has focused on probity, compliance and the accuracy of the financial records, the focus of value for money auditing has been on the activities undertaken by the government entity. Those activities are reviewed as to either their efficiency or results, or both.

Radcliffe (1998), Funnell (1998) and Guthrie and Parker (1999) have all authored histories of the early days of value for money audits. Radcliffe's study concerns the Canadian province of Alberta while Funnell (1998) and Guthrie and Parker (1999) have focused on the Australian Commonwealth Audit Office. Radcliffe, using the Foucauldian concept of governmentality, discusses the development and operation of efficiency audits in the 1970s, emphasising the importance of various discourses during their development. The parties which featured large in this discourse were politicians and providers of expert knowledge. The paper discusses how the discourses of political actors and expert actors engaged with their own professional and social networks.

Both Guthrie and Parker (1999) and Funnell (1998) focus on the contested nature of Australian federal audits. The former draw on the analogy of masque to discuss the events that occurred during the development of performance auditing between 1973 and 1998 and the personnel involved. The analogy is used to provide insight to 'the malleability and subjectivity of performance auditing concepts' (Guthrie and Parker 1999: 303). Funnell identifies the debate between 1978 and 1984 as one engaging the value for money auditor, as an agent of the Parliament, and the executive, whose policy and activity might be subject to audit. Given their highly subjective nature, efficiency audits are shown to be more threatening to the executive than financial audits. The latter places greater reliance on well-defined standards of practice and the results are more predictable. The outcomes of efficiency audits are less predictable, and therefore less politically manageable. The paper concludes by identifying how little independence the state auditor has when in conflict with executive government departments.

Funnell (2004) returns to the theme of the conflict between the legislature and the executive in his response to Flesher and Zarzeski (2002). Flesher and Zarzeski provide a history of the development of value for money/operational audits in English-speaking countries. Value for money auditing was developed from the mid-1940s in the USA especially in relation to public sector bodies. However, it was not until the 1970s that such audits began to be undertaken in English-speaking countries outside the USA. Flesher and Zarzeski conclude their paper with a question. Given the development of value for money auditing in the USA, why didn't other Anglophone countries such as the UK, Australia, Canada and New Zealand quickly emulate the American practice of value for money audits in the public sector? Funnell's (2004) answer relates to an essential difference between the US and Westminster forms of government. Under the Westminster system, the executive is also part of the legislature. Therefore the lines and nature of accountability are significantly different to the USA where there is a strict separation of powers between the executive and legislative branches of government. Under the Westminster system, the state auditor is intended to be a 'watchdog' rather than a 'bloodhound', as the executive has the right 'to govern without the intrusion of parliament once monies are appropriated' (ibid.: 220). In the USA, the legislature and its agencies, including the audit function, have a stronger 'bloodhound' mentality. According to Funnell, this discouraged the introduction of value for money audits in countries which had adopted the Westminster model until the later twentieth century.

English and Guthrie (2000) discuss the struggle for control over the functioning of the state auditor in the Australian Commonwealth from the mid-1970s to the 1990s. In this episode, the government had undertaken a number of actions aimed at reducing the effectiveness of the auditor. In particular, the executive was unwilling to introduce legislation to update the Audit Act, 1901 under which the state auditor operated. English and Guthrie argue that this unwillingness reflected the government's view regarding the necessity of the state having a government auditor. The executive considered that the work of both the state auditor and the audit department could and should be undertaken by professional accounting firms through a series of tenders and contracts. This is consistent with the new public management reform agenda which was pursued by the Australian government at the time.

Social institutions

The apparatus of rule extend beyond the institutions of central and local government. The state has coercive powers for taxation, imprisonment and regulating societies and may assume a moral responsibility to care for those unable to care for themselves such as the sick and the poor. The state may also establish or control existing economic entities. Histories of the role and functioning of accounting in organisations associated with crime and punishment, welfare, medical provision and state-controlled industry remain uncommon.

Walker (2004, 2008) provides an analysis of the use of accounting in the English system of poor relief before and after the formative Poor Law Amendment Act, 1834. Using official reports into the reform of the Poor Laws and reviewing records of the relief provided, Walker shows not only how accounting was advanced to ensure the more systematic, efficient and better management of Poor Law institutions but also how it was used as a device for the social control of the poor. The accounting system was used to monitor recipients of relief and deter claimants. The disclosure in public places of the names of those receiving relief allowed for checks on eligibility and contributed to the stigmatisation of the poor.

As noted at the start of this chapter, the literature on accounting histories of the state has tended to focus on Anglo-American settings from the mid-nineteenth century. One example of a study outside both of these boundaries is Carmona *et al.* (1997). Their paper is also noteworthy because unlike most histories of accounting in governmental settings which focus on financial accounting, external reporting and auditing, this study concerns management accounting. Carmona *et al.* analysed the cost accounting system operating in the Spanish Royal Tobacco Factory in 1773. While the paper relates to a factory, it treats the site as a social as well as a productive arena.

Following Foucault, the authors analyse cost accounting practices operating as part of a strong disciplinary regime founded on instructions issued for the management of the factory. The instructions covered the factory's physical situation, production patterns (including rates and mixes of the resources to be used), as well as monetary controls. The purposes of the control system within the state-owned factory are identified as two-fold – to minimise the theft of tobacco and maintain factory discipline. The regime of calculability facilitated the surveillance and discipline of individuals working in the factory. Carmona *et al.* provide an alternative to the management accounting literature which focuses on economic rationalist catalysts for the implementation of cost accounting systems. In this case of a state-run monopoly, the cost accounting system was shaped by the need for revenue collection and the construction of national identity: the factory being a 'symbol of the organisation and industrial prestige of eighteenth-century Spain' (ibid.: 443).

Robson (2003) outlines attempts at 'accountingisation' in UK hospitals commencing with uniform systems of annual accounts from 1893 to their proposed replacement by departmental costing and budgeting between 1948 and 1956 with the advent of the National Health Service. Using Porter's six elements of abstraction, individual, group, institution, conceptual, forces and universals, Robson identifies various forces that contributed to the systems introduced in 1893 and the rejection, in 1956, of changes proposed over the previous decade.

Jones and Mellett (2007) provide an expansive longitudinal study of British hospitals over the period 1800–2000. Drawing on a social forces model, the paper examines the relationship between accounting and institutional and organisational changes in hospitals over the two centuries concerned. The history of hospital organisation is described in terms of three principles: communitarian, etatist and market. The associated roles for accounting under each principle are discussed. Communitarian principles dominated during the early years studied. With most of the hospitals independent and self-governing, accounting focused on stewardship and internal checks. The subsequent appearance of etatist principles and their association with government control through centralisation and bureaucratic control were reflected in an accounting that emphasised hierarchical control and standardisation aimed to maintain efficiency. In more recent times market principles, associated with competition and profit-making, were in evidence. In this context, accounting was characterised by adherence to private sector models, external audits and providing information for decision-making. With the change from a dominant communitarian principle through etatist to market principles, both the form and role of accounting have altered. When communitarian principles prevailed, accounting assumed a supportive role, under etatism, it had an informing decisions function, and, under the quasi market system, accounting not only supported and assisted but became an essential requirement for the operation of markets. As with several of the authors discussed above, Jones and Mellett also note the importance of key personnel and outside agency in achieving accounting change in hospitals.

Comparative studies

In this section some historical studies that have adopted a comparative approach are briefly discussed. Comparisons have been drawn in relation to specific accounting issues in the public and private sectors and in relation to the accounting practices deployed in different nations.

Hill (2000) provides an example of a comparison of management accounting practices in private, public and not-for-profit sectors. The study looks at the adoption of new costing systems in US hospitals between 1980 and 1990. While the research is more aligned to positive accounting research and quantitative history than narrative and archival-based history, it provides insights to similarities between sectors. Key factors discussed are changes to revenue reimbursement procedures, increases in competition and the organisational structure of the hospital. In determining if a new costing system was to be developed, changes to revenue reimbursement procedures and increases in competition were identified as important. Organisational factors, such as whether the entity was a government, not-for-profit or profit-based organisation, seemed to have little impact. The study found that government hospitals were less likely to introduce new costing systems than other categories of hospitals. This was explained as a result of government hospitals having less access to discretionary resources to invest in new accounting systems.

Edwards (1992) provides a comparison of financial reporting in non-regulated companies, public utility companies and municipal corporations in the UK between 1835 and 1933. Having reviewed a number of key aspects of financial reporting, Edwards concluded that innovation in accounting was not driven by one sector, rather, different sectors were 'ahead' in applying new technology to relevant to the particular issues they faced. Municipal corporations were earlier in their use of consolidated accounts, requirements for the standardisation of accounts, and the provision of greater detail and graphical presentation in accounts. Companies were quicker to introduce double-entry bookkeeping, profit and loss accounts, accrual accounting and the balance sheet. Public utility companies first used the double account system with its separation of capital raised and spent and other balance sheet items. This technology was later transferred to municipal corporations. Edwards notes that the often implied assumption of the superiority of private sector in accounting innovation is not historically accurate.

In recent years there have been calls for more international comparative accounting history (see Carnegie and Napier 2002). The works of Funnell (2004) on operational audits (as discussed above) and Monsen and Näsi (1996) on the influence of Cameralist thinking on both Finnish and Norwegian local government financial management systems, are examples of government accounting history research embracing international comparisons. Comparative international accounting history focused on states can further our understanding of the transfer of accounting techniques and ideas across national boundaries and their adoption and mutation in different state settings. One area where comparative international accounting history is likely to increase is in relation to the new public management reforms.

Conclusion

A number of reviews of accounting history research have lamented the comparative lack of attention devoted to accounting and the state (Anderson 2002; Walker 2005; Funnell 2007). Whereas public sector accounting in modern-day settings has been the focus of considerable research activity, its history has not. There is scope for much more research into all areas of this field. Funnell (2007: 266) argues that the history of public sector accounting deserves the attention of researchers if for no other reason than to illuminate accounting's role in the accountability and oversight of the executive. Accounting is a tool in the protection of liberty. The accounting historian entering a state archive ventures into 'arsenals of democratic accountability and continuity' (Eastwood 1993: 36) and thus becomes a contributor to the process of holding the executive to account and protecting liberty.

The existence of state archives and the relative ease of access to them might encourage the greater use of primary source material for researching the intertwining of accounting and state. In addition to further investigation of the subjects covered in the preceding sections – on ancient accounting, double-entry bookkeeping, auditing, agents of change and accrual accounting – there are also hitherto unexplored territories. Almost every issue covered elsewhere in this *Routledge Companion* can be researched from the perspective of the state.

The 'dearth of research' in public sector accounting (Carnegie and Potter 2000: 194) suggests that there are many areas open for further scholarship. However, three forms of accounting history are particularly underrepresented in the current literature – longitudinal and comparative studies and investigations of accounting in social and economic institutions operated under the auspices of the state. Further, a great deal of the existing literature focuses on relatively short periods and single issues. While such studies are important, greater emphasis needs to be placed on the larger context. Rarely do debates in accounting merely concern narrow technical issues. Debates about accounting technologies are invariably conducted in relation to the economic, ideological and political. Furthermore, these debates are seldom resolved in a particular period; they often resurface in later times and different places (see Colquhoun 2005; Potts 1976, 1978, 1982). Longitudinal studies will provide a richer and fuller understanding of accounting and the state. Similarly, given that accounting change rarely takes place in the jurisdictional isolation of particular nation-states, the benefits of international comparative histories become obvious. Historical studies of accounting in socio-economic institutions are necessary when it is recalled that the modern state is not only about law-making and tax-raising but comprises a series of apparatuses which extend into numerous arenas.

Accounting research assists understandings of the coercive activities of the state and the manner in which the state may establish and maintain unequal power relations. States are replete with institutions that seek to manage these relationships. The recording and dissemination of accounting information by state officials provide insights to state processes and ideologies and the wider economic and social structures with which they engage.

As the new public management reform era comes to a close, the archives and records of the period become more available to the research community. The passing of time allows for historical reflection, thus opportunities for research into the new public management reforms across many countries will become feasible. This research may take a variety of forms including those mentioned earlier; namely comparisons between public and other sectors, international comparative history and longitudinal studies of accounting in individual countries and individual entities. Furthermore, as the reforms were part of an international trend, supported by governments and organisations such as the International Monetary Fund, international historical comparisons offer scope for insights into their adoption, integration and subsequent acceptance across nations and cultures. It may also be the case that investigations of past accounting change, its successes and failures, will contribute to future policy-making.

A key feature of all states is the requirement for accountability. In democratic states, this includes the accountability of officials to elected representatives and the accountability of elected representatives to their electors. In non-democratic states it includes the accountability of officials to the ruling class. Financial management systems are almost inevitably part of this accountability. But the impact of accounting for and by the state extends beyond accountability regimes. The new public management reforms and their association with accounting-based incentives were intended to change behaviour; the introduction in Europe of double-entry bookkeeping was connected with a desire to reform government; accounting technology has been used as a means of surveillance and control; and new requirements for audit have been intended to change power relations. In all of these cases the activity of the state and accounting technologies are intertwined and demand the further attention of accounting historians.

Acknowledgments

Grateful thanks are due to Ciarán Ó hÓgartaigh, Lisa Marriott and the editors.

Key works

Edwards *et al.* (2002) identifies the contest of ideologies which lay behind technical debates over the introduction of double-entry bookkeeping in British central government.

Funnell (2007) locates English state accounting within a framework of historical constitutional accountability.

Newberry and Pallot (2004) is an archival study of selected aspects of new public management reforms.

Walker (2004) provides a compelling insight to the social consequences of accounting in a field regulated by the state.

References

Anderson, M. (2002) An analysis of the first ten volumes of research in *Accounting, Business & Financial History*, *Accounting, Business & Financial History*, 12 (1): 1–24.

Boyd, E. (1968) Ancient systems of accounting, in R. Brown (ed.) *A History of Accounting and Accountants*, pp. 16–40 (London: Frank Cass & Co. Ltd).

Carmona, S. (2004) Accounting history research and its diffusion in an international context, *Accounting History*, 9 (3): 7–23.

Carmona, S. and Ezzamel, M. (2007) Accounting and accountability in ancient civilizations: Mesopotamia and ancient Egypt, *Accounting, Auditing & Accountability Journal*, 20 (2): 177–209.

Carmona, S., Ezzamel, M. and Gutiérrez, F. (1997) Control and cost accounting practices in the Spanish Royal Tobacco Factory, *Accounting Organizations and Society*, 22 (5): 411–66.

Carnegie, G. D. and Napier, C. J. (2002) Exploring comparative international accounting history, *Accounting, Auditing & Accountability Journal*, 15 (5): 689–718.

Carnegie, G. D. and Potter, B. N. (2000) Publishing patterns in specialist accounting history journals in the English Language 1996–1999, *Accounting Historians Journal*, 27 (2): 177–98.

Carpenter, V. L. and Feroz, E. H. (2001) Institutional theory and accounting rule choice: an analysis of four US state governments' decisions to adopt generally accepted accounting principles, *Accounting, Organizations and Society*, 26 (7/8): 565–96.

Christensen, M. (2002) Accrual accounting in the public sector: the case of the New South Wales government, *Accounting History*, 7 (2): 93–124.

Christensen, M. (2003) Without 'Reinventing the Wheel': business accounting applied to the public sector, *Australian Accounting Review*, 13 (2): 22–27.

Colquhoun, P. M. (2005) A History of New Zealand Municipal Accounting and Auditing 1976 to 1988, unpublished PhD thesis, University of Canterbury.

Coombs, H. M. and Edwards, J. R. (1993) The accountability of municipal corporations, *Abacus*, 29 (1): 27–51.

Coombs, H. M. and Edwards, J. R. (1995) The financial reporting practices of British municipal corporations 1835-1933: a study in accounting innovation, *Accounting and Business Research*, 25 (98): 93–105.

Coombs, H. M. and Edwards, J. R. (2004) The audit of municipal corporations – a quest for professional dominance, *Managerial Auditing Journal*, 19 (1): 68–83.

Eastwood, T. M. (1993) Reflections on the development of archives in Canada and Australia, in S. McKenmmis and F. Upward (eds) *Archival Documents: Providing Accountability through Recordkeeping*, pp. 27–39 (Melbourne: Ancora Press).

Edwards, J. R. (1992) Companies, corporations and accounting change 1835–1933: a comparative study, *Accounting and Business Research*, 23 (89): 59–73.

Edwards, J. R., Coombs, H. M. and Greener, H. T. (2002) British central government and 'the mercantile system of double entry' bookkeeping: a study of ideological conflict, *Accounting, Organizations and Society*, 27 (7): 637–58.

English, L. and Guthrie, J. (2000) Mandate, independence and funding: resolution of a protracted struggle between parliament and the executive over the powers of the Australian Auditor-General, *Australian Journal of Public Administration*, 59 (1): 98–114.

Ezzamel, M. (2002a) Accounting and redistribution: the palace and mortuary cult in the Middle Kingdom, Ancient Egypt, *Accounting Historians Journal*, 29 (1): 61–103.

Ezzamel, M. (2002b) Accounting working for the state: tax assessment and collection during the New Kingdom, Ancient Egypt, *Accounting and Business Research*, 32 (1): 17–39.

Fleischman, R. K. and Marquette, R. P. (1986) The origins of public budgeting: municipal reformers during the Progressive Era, *Public Budgeting & Finance*, 6 (1): 71–7.

Flesher, D. L. and Zarzeski, M. (2002) The roots of the operational (value for money) auditing in English-speaking nations, *Accounting and Business Research*, 32 (2): 93–104.

Funnell, W. (1994) Independence and the state auditor in Britain: a constitutional keystone or a case of reified imagery?, *Abacus*, 30 (2): 175–95.

Funnell, W. (1997) Military influences on the evolution of public sector audit and accounting 1830–1880, *Accounting History*, 2 (2): 9–29.

Funnell, W. (1998) Executive coercion and state audit – a processual analysis of the responses of the Australian audit office to the dilemmas of efficiency auditing 1978–84, *Accounting, Auditing & Accountability Journal*, 11 (4): 436–58.

Funnell, W. (2004) Further evidence on the roots of public sector operational (value-for-money) auditing: a response to Flesher and Zarzeski, *Accounting and Business Research*, 34 (3): 215–22.

Funnell, W. (2007) The reason why: The English Constitution and the latent promise of liberty in the history of accounting, *Accounting, Business & Financial History*, 17 (2): 265–83.

Goddard, A. (2005) Reform as regulation – accounting, governance and accountability in UK local government, *Journal of Accounting & Organisational Change*, 1 (1): 27–44.

Gomes, D., Carnegie, G. D. and Rodrigues, L. L. (2006) Accounting change in central government: the adoption of double entry bookkeeping at the Portuguese Royal Treasury (1761). Paper presented at the11th World Congress of Accounting Historians, Nantes, July.

Guthrie, J. and Parker, L. D. (1999) A quarter of a century of performance auditing in the Australian federal public sector: a malleable masque, *Abacus*, 35 (3): 302–32.

Hill, N. T. (2000) Adoption of costing systems in US hospitals: an event history analysis 1980-1990, *Accounting and Public Policy*, 19 (1): 41–71.

Humphrey, C., Guthrie, J., Jones, L. R. and Olson, O. (2005) The dynamics of public financial management change in an international context, in J. Guthrie, C. Humphrey, L. R. Jones and O. Olson (eds) *International Public Financial Management Reforms: Progress, Contradictions and Challenges*, pp. 1–22 (Greenwich: Information Age Publishing).

Johnson, C. (ed.) (1983) *Dialogus de Scaccario. The Course of the Exchequer by Richard, Fitz Nigel* (Oxford: Clarendon Press).

Jones, M. J. and Mellett, H. J. (2007) Determinants of changes in accounting practices: accounting and the UK Health Service, *Critical Perspectives on Accounting*, 18 (1): 91–121.

Jones, R. (1985) Accounting in English local government: from the Middle Ages to c.1835, *Accounting and Business Research*, 15 (59): 197–210.

Jones, R. H. (1986) 'The financial control function of local government accounting', unpublished PhD thesis, Lancaster University.

Jones, R. H. (1992) *The History of the Financial Control Function of Local Government Accounting in the United Kingdom* (New York: Garland).

Jurado-Sánchez, J. (2002) Mechanisms for controlling expenditure in the Spanish royal household, c.1561–1808, *Accounting, Business & Financial History*, 12 (2): 157–85.

Lemarchand, Y. (1999) Introducing double-entry bookkeeping in public finance: a French experiment at the beginning of the eighteenth century, *Accounting, Business & Financial History*, 9 (2): 225–54.

Miller, P. (1990) On the relationship between accounting and the state, *Accounting, Organizations and Society*, 15 (4): 315–38.

Monsen, N. and Näsi, S. (1996) Local government accounting in Finland and Norway: a historical note on Cameralism, *Research in Governmental and Nonprofit Accounting: A Research Annual*, 9: 259–74.

Newberry, S. and Pallot, J. (2004) Freedom or coercion? NPM incentives in New Zealand central government departments, *Management Accounting Research*, 15 (3): 247–66.

Nikitin, M. (2001) The birth of modern public sector accounting systems in France and Britain and the influence of Count Mollien, *Accounting History*, 6 (1): 75–101.

Patton, T. K. and Freeman, R. J. (2005) Government accounting standards come of age: highlights from the first 20 years, *Government Finance Review*, 21 (2): 16–20.

Potts, J. H. (1976) 'An analysis of the evolution of municipal accounting to 1935 with primary emphasis on developments in the United States', unpublished PhD thesis, University of Alabama.

Potts, J. H. (1978) The evolution of municipal accounting in the United States, 1900–1935, *Business History Review*, 52 (4): 518–36.

Potts, J. H. (1982) A brief history of property and depreciation accounting in municipal accounting, *Accounting Historians Journal*, 9 (1): 25–37.

Radcliffe, V. S. (1998) Efficiency audit: an assembly of rationalities and programmes, *Accounting Organizations and Society*, 23 (4): 377–410.

Remis, J. S. (1982) An historical perspective on setting governmental accounting standards, *Governmental Finance*, 11 (2): 3–9.

Richardson, H. G. (1928a) Richard fitz Neal and the *Dialogus de Scaccario, The English Historical Review*, 43 (170): 161–71.

Richardson, H. G. (1928b) Richard fitz Neal and the Dialogus de Scaccario (continued), *The English Historical Review*, 43 (171): 321–40.

Robson, N. (2003) From voluntary to state control and the emergence of the department in UK hospital accounting, *Accounting, Business & Financial History*, 13 (2): 99–123.

Ryan, C. (1998) The introduction of accrual reporting policy in the Australian public sector: an agenda setting explanation, *Accounting, Auditing & Accountability Journal*, 11 (5): 518–39.

Scott, J. E. M., McKinnon, J. L. and Harrison, G. L. (2003) Cash to accrual and cash to accrual: a case study of financial reporting in two NSW hospitals 1857 to post 1975, *Accounting, Auditing & Accountability Journal*, 16 (1): 104–40.

Walker, S. P. (2004) Expense, social and moral control: accounting and the administration of the old Poor Law in England and Wales, *Journal of Accounting and Public Policy*, 23 (2): 85–127.

Walker, S. P. (2005) Accounting in history, *Accounting Historians Journal*, 32 (2): 223–59.

Walker, S. P. (2008) Accounting, paper shadows and the stigmatised poor, *Accounting, Organizations and Society*, 33 (4/5): 453–87.

Watkins, A. L. and Arrington, C. E. (2007) Accounting, new public management and American politics: theoretical insights into the National Performance Review, *Critical Perspectives on Accounting*, 18 (1): 33–58.

27

Military

Warwick Funnell

Overview

The study of the military and their accounting has reflected the essential political nature and purpose of armies. Accounting historians have had a particular interest in the political protections provided by accounting in Britain after the constitutionally fraught seventeenth century when the supremacy of Parliament had been compromised by military intervention. Until the twentieth century, accounting for military expenditures in Britain was determined almost entirely by the need to ensure that Parliament had effective control over how much the military spent; it was not intended to enhance military performance. However, in examining the evolution of cost accounting, accounting historians have suggested that the circumstance of war and military culture have played a role in the evolution of cost accounting. Indeed war, but especially the First World War, has been shown to have provided a critical impetus to the evolution and professionalisation of cost accounting in the early twentieth century. Particularly influential was the greater intervention required of government during the war in the affairs of business through the regulation of production and prices.

Military themes in accounting history

There is a persistent contradiction in the accounting history literature for although war and the methods of prosecuting war have dominated the history of humankind, and the financial needs of armies and navies until well into the twentieth century dwarfed all other government spending, this resonating historical significance has not found a proportionate response in the study of military accounting. Among the limited research, Britain and the United States in the nineteenth century have figured most prominently with some excursions into Europe (see, for example, Fernandez-Revuelta *et al.* 2002). Military accounting during major twentieth-century military conflicts, but especially the First World War and the Second World War, has yet to be accorded the recognition in accounting history research that the importance of these conflagrations obviously warrants. A prominent exception has been recent work by Chwastiak (1999, 2001, 2006) in relation to the American Department of Defense at the time of the

Vietnam War. War, although not the military itself, has also informed a large study by Gallhofer and Haslam (1991). Given that Britain has figured most prominently in military accounting research, reference in this chapter will be primarily to Britain and its army. For the most part, discussion will be concerned with the control of armies and the act of war and not the industries which supply armies.

Governments, whatever their form, have the ominous ability to dominate the lives of individuals through the forces of violence that they inevitably control and, often, rely upon to maintain power. Ultimately, the liberty of individuals requires that governments are able to be held accountable for the exercise of this power and that they have under their authority sufficient controls to ensure that the military is never in a position to overcome the state. Howard (1957: 11) has suggested that 'No community of any degree of complexity has succeeded in existing without force, and the manner in which that force is organized and controlled will largely determine the political structure of the state.'

Recognising the pervasive, malevolent presence of military force throughout history and the consequences of the exercise of this force, extant accounting histories with the military as their subject are overwhelmingly preoccupied with the political motives and alarms which have determined military accounting practices and the consequences of these for military performance (see Funnell 1988, 1997). Thus, the main military interest by accounting historians has been the nexus between the military and the British constitution, most importantly from the seventeenth century when the consistent and abiding concern of governments was the strengthening of protections against threats from the military to the supremacy of Parliament and to the liberty of individuals. These histories have established that accounting has been an essential means of providing protection to the state, and the individuals of which it is composed, from the threat of military power. Accordingly, accounting by and for the military until well into the twentieth century was fundamentally a means of ensuring control of the military through financial accountability to their civilian masters in Parliament. However, a number of studies have shown how this control of military finances by civilians for the sake of political security had prejudiced, for centuries, the performance of the soldiers whose activities were pointedly hobbled by the institutions and practices of financial control. These controls were exercised first and foremost in the interests of civilians, not to promote military efficiency (Funnell 1990, 2005).

Ever since the constitutional settlements of the late seventeenth century provided essential guarantees of Parliament's ascendancy and the military's subservience to Parliament, accounting practised by the British military (and on behalf of the military by civilians at the War Office and the Treasury) was never predicated on promoting the interests and well-being of the military by enhancing the military's ability to prosecute wars. Rather, this would have been regarded as a dangerous constitutional innovation. Consequently, until well into the twentieth century, the British military had little or no influence over its finances and accounting practices. Thus, the dispensing, management and accounting for military finances would be the sacred responsibility of civilians. This largely unquestioned constitutional identity between civilians, accounting and liberty, however, was unable to withstand unscathed the pressures for the reform of military finances and administration prompted by the military failures of the South African War (1899–1902) and the deluge of the First World War.

Although a constitutional theme in military accounting is given particular prominence in this chapter, also recognised is a widening interest which goes beyond a constitutional imperative. Accounting researchers interested in the evolution of business accounting have also sought to establish the origins and uses of accounting techniques which were to become the precursors of modern management accounting. Particularly prominent have been studies which demonstrate the influence of a military culture on the evolution of management accounting and studies which have examined the impetus provided by the First World War for the spread and acceptance of cost accounting by the private sector which, as a by-product, also advanced the professionalisation of cost accounting. Thus, scholars seeking to map the evolution of cost and management accounting have exposed a military legacy with studies of the British Ministry of Munitions (which had been created during the First World War to coordinate the production of the implements of war (see Loft 1986 and Marriner 1994)) and, in the United States, cost accounting practices which are said to have developed at the Springfield Armory in the mid-nineteenth century by graduates of the West Point military academy (Hoskin and Macve 1988, 1994, 2000; Tyson 1990, 1993). While these studies are purported to have detected a military legacy in the history of cost accounting, absent from these studies is evidence of the adoption of business accounting practices, in particular cost accounting, by the military.

In the section which follows, the concern is the nexus between the military, accounting and the British constitution which has been so attractive to accounting historians. Later in the chapter the political servitude of military accounting across the centuries is shown to have had significant adverse consequences for the military's preparedness for war and for its performance in the field, especially throughout the nineteenth century, leading, finally, to limited reforms in the early twentieth century after the South African War.

The military and the state

The constitutional force and the power of the purse

The proven uncertain allegiances of military forces throughout history and the terrible consequences of the use of military force to oppress fellow citizens require that the relationship between the military and civilians is something with which all societies have to deal effectively and in the interests of civilians. Howard suggests:

> Societies are orderly and peaceable only in so far as they have solved this double problem, of the subordination of the military force to the political government, and of control of a government in possession of such a force by legal restraint and the popular will.

> (1957: 12)

Thus, in the case of the English Government and its people after the constitutional crises in the seventeenth century, the question confronting them, notes Howard (ibid.: 12), was 'how can the armed forces necessary for external security be prevented from crushing internal liberties?'. The British Parliament determined that this problem was best solved by adhering to strict limits on the size of the army and by ensuring that the state always had under its authority sufficient controls to preclude the possibility that the military was in a position to overcome the state.

The unavoidable intimidating presence of an army and its interventions in matters of state in the seventeenth century ensured that the British Parliament would be determined to keep the army small, unprepared if necessary for war and kept in its place. The parlous state of unpreparedness in which the army was maintained in peace prompted Wellington in 1829 to refer to the British Army as 'an exotic in England, unknown in the old Constitution of the country; required . . . only for the defence of its foreign possessions; disliked by the inhabitants' (quoted in Hanham 1969: 359). The army, as the object of suspicion and apprehension, would be kept starved of funds. Professional armies even at the beginning of the nineteenth century were believed to constitute an abiding political danger, to be inherently inefficient and mostly unnecessary (Howard 1957: 15). This enduring antipathy towards the army, especially in times of peace, allowed the House of Commons after the seventeenth century to 'escape from their constitutional dilemmas by denying to the Crown the powers and the funds necessary to maintain a really effective army' (ibid.: 13–14).

Although control over the number of soldiers provided some measure of protection, the prominent role played by the army during civil war (from 1642) and revolution (in 1688) demonstrated that this was neither a complete nor a certain protection in the absence of other controls. These controls included legitimate political authority, as established through historical understandings and constitutional formulations, and the controls which are auxiliary to or emanate from the political controls. Of the latter, the most important is the sole and supreme authority of the state in matters of finance related to the military and the accounting processes upon which these powers depend for their efficacy. The defenders of Parliament were determined to implement mechanisms to ensure that military spending would only occur in the future with the approval of Parliament and would be administered entirely by civilians (Funnell 1988).

The authority of Parliament in all matters of military finance subsequent to the revolutionary settlement in 1689 effectively meant that only Parliament could raise an army. The inglorious role of the army in perpetuating Cromwell's dictatorship (1653–58) at the expense of Parliament was not to be readily forgotten. The Mutiny Act reinforced the constitutional protections of annual appropriations by stipulating that each year the Crown was required to reaffirm its allegiance to the principle of parliamentary control of the army as enunciated in the Bill of Rights (1689 1 William and Mary c. 5 and 6, S.R.55). Soon after leaving office as Chancellor of the Exchequer in 1886, Lord Randolph Churchill confirmed that 'the control of Parliament, the interference of Parliament, the jealousy of Parliament for its rights and privileges, these are the arguments in favour of an adherence to the main lines of our present system of naval and military administration' (Royal Commission into the Civil and Professional Administration of the Navy and Military Departments, 1890: 15).

Similar concerns to those expressed in Britain have been shown by Chwastiak to have been present across the Atlantic nearly 200 years later when accounting changes were introduced in the American military by Robert McNamara as Secretary of Defense (1961–68) during the Vietnam War. Chwastiak (1999, 2001, 2006) has shown that accounting's ability to mediate the relationship between the military and its civilian political masters continues to be enduring and fundamental to the control of military forces in democratic states. In one especially provocative paper, Chwastiak (2001) argued that accounting was used by McNamara and the Department of Defense to shift the balance of power in military affairs from the more technically knowledgeable, but recklessly spendthrift, military to the financially powerful and financially literate civilians in the Department of Defense. This was achieved by McNamara introducing the technique of Planning, Programming and Budgeting (PPB):

[to] redefine the normative and cognitive facets of the defense political process in such a way that military expertise (something that McNamara lacked) was discredited while quantitative rationality (a trait that McNamara excelled at) was elevated to the status of authority and legitimacy.

(Chwastiak 2001: 501)

As a result of McNamara's determination to introduce into the American military the financial disciplines and accountabilities common in business, he was able to supplant military control with his own authority in defence acquisition. When McNamara was appointed Secretary of

Defense at the height of the Cold War, there were few limits on military spending and in a dangerous, nuclear-armed world even less resolve by governments and the military to reign in spending. According to Chwastiak (ibid.: 507), the introduction of PPB required that rationality, manifesting itself in cost-benefit analysis, be given pre-eminence over military expertise and experience with the result that control over the military became increasingly centralised in McNamara and the Department of Defense. After the introduction of PPB, the military were forced to argue their case for increased spending on McNamara's terms and in his language. In the process, PPB and its discourse of rationality and cost-benefit came to dominate defence decision-making.

War was now conceptualised as a problem of resource management amenable to the discipline of accounting under civilian control. Only those aspects of the war which could be quantified according to the procedures of PPB would be accorded visibility. The effect was that the quantification of war required by PPB transformed political debate into an objective discourse where numbers were the determinant of decisions and not people or their welfare, for example, the number of the enemy killed and the resources required to achieve this result (Chwastiak 2006: 32). Truth was now equated with that which could be counted, thereby precluding a 'moral vocabulary' for war. PPB allowed nuclear war to be 'normalised' and the achievement of victory in Vietnam to be conceived solely in terms of prosecuting the war in an economically rational manner, thereby transforming it into a series of problems framed in such as manner as to be amenable to solution by the rational instrumentality of accounting (Chwastiak 2006: 40, 43). Those who managed the war in the Department of Defense 'believed they could increase the productivity of the troops by using techniques derived from the managerial control systems of corporations, such as incentives, standards, performance evaluations, appraisals of efficiency and monitoring' (ibid.: 43).

While McNamara's attitude towards the military reflected more his faith in the salvation afforded by rational management practices, of which accounting stands supreme, it also recognised the historical antipathy since the seventeenth century between civilians suspicious of the military's spending habits and its uncertain political allegiances which had the potential to threaten the liberty of individuals.

The costly reassurances of accounting

Since the eighteenth century, the civilians who controlled British military finances had worked in a multitude of pettifogging offices at the War Office from which emanated a plethora of regulations to cover every conceivable situation, including the most trivial amounts of spending by the military. The result, it was widely agreed, was a system of administrative control which only served to prejudice the military's ability to prepare itself for war and to conduct war in an efficient and, most importantly, victorious manner, much to the ongoing frustration and humiliation of the military (Wright 1956: 464). An enduring tension arose in the seventeenth century between military efficiency and control of the military to ensure political security, with Britain's naval superiority allowing the former always to be sacrificed. Even into the twentieth century the War Office (Reconstruction) Committee (hereafter the Esher Committee) (1904: 131) felt obligated to complain about the army being 'tied and bound in the coils of excessively complex and minute regulations drawn up without regard to the essential requirements of modern war'.

From the late seventeenth century the sole object of accounting for British military expenditures was to check that departmental financial procedures had been followed, all expenditures were correctly authorised and that total spending had not exceeded the total amount appropriated by Parliament and issued by the Exchequer. At the end of the nineteenth century, the apparent indifference of successive parliaments to the benefits of an accounting system which would provide information to enhance the management of military operations still betrayed a lingering antipathy to the military. Most importantly, this ensured that Parliament was prepared to forego the uncertain, uncorroborated benefits of alternative accounting systems used by business in the pursuit of efficient operations and thereby retain the proven constitutional protections of an accounting system determined by the process and conventions of appropriation.

Regardless of the extent of the financial burden of the army upon the nation, until the arrival of the twentieth century, there had been only spasmodic appreciation by British governments of the potential for accounting practices used in the management of large businesses to enhance military operations in the field. Thus, the long standing constitutional purpose of military accounting quarantined the army from accounting developments in the business world. This calculated indifference irrevocably altered as a consequence of the serious deficiencies in military preparations and performance in battle which were exposed during the Crimean War (1854–56) and the South African War (1899–1902) (Funnell 2005).

Accounting for military performance

Not unlike business, the provision of everything necessary for the combatant to live and fight, upon which success in battle hinges, is ultimately and fundamentally a matter of money and the way in which it is managed (see *Edinburgh Review*, Vol. CXXXIII, January to April 1871: 233). Financial arrangements and controls exercised over military spending, therefore, assume a crucial role in military performance. As a critical component in the good management of the financial resources upon which the very existence of the military depended, any deficiencies in accounting had the ability to magnify other weaknesses (see Funnell 2006).

Recognising the constitutional intent of accounting for military expenditures, developments in military accounting until the twentieth century consistently concentrated on preserving narrow fiduciary purposes which thereby denied a wider management role to military accounting. Befitting an accounting and audit regime which was preoccupied with constitutional protections, the concern was with the 'subjects' of expenditure, that is broad types of expenditure, such as salaries, munitions and transport, and not with what was achieved with this expenditure. As a consequence, with accounts and estimates based on subjects of expenditure, it was not possible to ascertain the total cost of the various aspects of military spending. Not surprisingly, army officials responsible for military accounting and civilians at the War Office who controlled military finances regarded army accounts as 'valueless' for the purpose of financial control (as understood by businesses) and certainly incapable of ensuring an efficient and economic army administration (Grimwood 1919). However, it proved to be politically difficult to supplant the constitutional equivalence that had been created between an inefficient army and political safety: an inefficient, unprepared army was no threat.

From the latter decades of the nineteenth century the demands of modern war on military forces, but especially on the preparedness necessary to engage enemies which now possessed the capabilities to move men and arms much more quickly and to use the vast lethal power of new armaments to deliver potentially decisive blows in the early, critical phases of war, made previous understandings which had governed the affairs of military administration seem more untenable, even recklessly foolish. Thus, all aspects of military administration, in particular the fundamental premises upon which it was grounded and from which its structures and practices were derived, were increasingly and insistently questioned throughout the second half of the nineteenth century. Prompted by the criticisms of military administrators in the Crimean War, accounting increasingly was viewed by some more enlightened military administrators in the War Office less as a constitutional protection and more as a management tool to ensure the most efficient and effective use of resources at a time of increasing competition for resources.

Sir Charles Harris, widely recognised as the foremost expert in military finances in the decades that spanned the beginning of the twentieth century, confessed that the army had no idea of the use of accounts for management purposes (Harris 1911: 64). Leo Amery (1902, Vol. 2: 41), who, as a *Times* correspondent, had witnessed the humiliation of the British Army in the South African War, referred to the whole system of parliamentary financial control as anachronistic, consisting of 'cumbrous (accounting) safeguards'. Indeed, the inability of army administrators to control their own finances in peace prevented them from either wanting to assume or being able to assume financial responsibility in war, thereby suppressing any initiative, the extravagant consequences of which were entirely predictable in war. More seriously, Harris believed that the army's accounting system would continue to subvert attempts to give the army greater autonomy from civilian financial control and, crucially, jeopardise the certainty of victory in modern wars (Select Committee on National Expenditure 1918, Report: 391). His long association with military finances had convinced him that reliable accounting systems could become a matter of life and death in war through their role in allocating scarce resources. Long after the management failings of the British Army had been revealed in the South African War, the Lawrence Committee in 1924 (Committee of Administration of, and Accounting for, Army Expenditure, Report: para. 5) belatedly warned that without 'a proper system of account-ing it is impossible to obtain the best and most economical administration results', upon which victory would depend.

These silences in army accounts were entirely consistent with the very narrow range of visibilities permitted by the cash-based appropriation accounting meant to serve constitutional, not management, purposes (Loft 1986: 140). Harris, through views expressed forcefully both before and after the First World War, wanted to see cost accounts become the main means of ensuring efficient and effective military administration, while at the same time meeting the needs of parliamentary control (Select Committee on National Expenditure 1918, Minutes of Evidence, Questions 220 and 248: 334–6). If economy of operation were to be made the concern of individuals in the army, then accounts would have to identify the cost of operations under each individual's control. These accounts would enable:

> responsibility to be delegated to those subordinates who know the details and who alone can adjust them to actual requirements. By means of the account you can allow a free hand and judge by results. The delegation of power which . . . accounting makes possible develops those invaluable human qualities of enterprise and resource.
>
> (Sir John Keane, quoted in Grimwood 1919: 158)

Cost accounts would promote military efficiency and also reassure the nation, from which the army gained its financial sustenance, that its taxes were not being needlessly squandered. Unfortunately, irrespective of the arguments advanced in favour of the replacement of existing systems of accounting and augmenting the purposes that they served, the constitutional impera-tive long entrenched in military accounting proved a formidable barrier to reform. Until after the First World War, Parliament remained unable to free itself completely from the con-sequences of much earlier constitutional alarms and to broaden the aims of public sector audit and accounting to encompass improved management practices.

According to the Treasury (see comments by Sir Charles Harris, Public Accounts Committee, 1924–5, Question 6708), cost accounting could not hope to provide a similar level of constitutional assurance available from existing accounting systems. In 1924, the Secretary of State for War, Sir Herbert Creedy, also expressed his concern that to move to a new system of cost accounting in preference to existing systems of accounting predicated on categories of appropriation approvals would require the entire reorganisation of all levels of army administration, from the War Office down, which were presently organised on a 'subject basis' (Public Accounts Committee, 1924–25, Minutes of Evidence: Questions 6839, 6884, 6887). This would be not only prohibitively costly and highly uncertain in its benefits but, he stressed, certain to dilute the ability of Parliament to control military spending. Doubts were also expressed whether indeed in the heat of battle matters of economy and efficiency would be uppermost in the minds of military leaders for, above all else, victory was the expectation, irrespective of the financial cost. Others, however, believed that military success depended upon financially literate officers in the field who were attuned to the advantages of economy. The financial ignorance which the system of constitutionally constrained financial administration forced upon army administrators, army commanders in the field and army personnel responsible for supplying the army with its material needs, became only too obvious during the ferment of war, as did the need for reform (Funnell 2005).

Accounting reform and the stimulus of war

Nineteenth-century wars and accounting reform

In Britain, the political crisis of war has had the greatest impact upon the evolution of military accounting. Most important in convincing governments of the need for accounting reform were the Crimean War, the South African War and the First World War. Only in relation to the Crimean and South African Wars, however, has accounting in the field of battle attracted the concerted interest of accounting historians. Although the First World War has figured prominently in several seminal accounting history papers, most notably those by Loft (1986), Fleischman and Tyson (2000) and Marriner (1994), the concerns have not been accounting as practised by the military in the field.

War mercilessly exposed deficiencies in military preparedness and the ability of military administrators to prosecute war decisively and efficiently. Shortcomings in preparation, leadership or management of the war effort by civilians and the military very quickly became obvious in the face of better-prepared and better-led foes. Consequently, it was usual in nineteenth-century Britain that after each military failure at the outbreak of war there was 'an outcry in Parliament and the press and distress at court; new ministers are drafted in, and commissions of inquiry set up. The public interest wanes and the whole cycle begins again' (Hanham 1969: 356). The Esher Committee (1904 Part I, page 8 of the report) noted with dismay that investigations of army administration had been, unfortunately, so numerous and 'great changes have been so frequent . . . [that] stability of administration has never been attained'. Most influential in the substantive reorganisation of the administration of the army in the nineteenth century were the Cardwell Reforms of 1868–74, precipitated by the administrative failings of the Crimean War (Funnell 1990).

The seriousness of the situation and public anger at the government's incompetence during the Crimean War forced the government to appoint a commission of inquiry while the war was still in progress. Of particular interest to the controversial McNeil–Tulloch Royal Commission was the performance of the Treasury-controlled commissariat which supplied the army with food, clothing and other material needs. Among their duties the Commissioners were required to examine the effect on the well-being of the army of the accounting system required of the commissariat. According to the letters patent issued in 1855 the McNeil-Tulloch Royal Commission (First Report 1856: 3) was charged with examining 'the mode of accounting, and if the system be in your opinion unnecessarily complicated for a period of actual warfare, you will suggest such means of simplification as may occur to you'. The Commission soon found that all accounting practice in the commissariat was subordinated to parliamentary needs and handicapped the army's ability to conduct war successfully.

The Commissioners discovered that an immense number of financial and store regulations governed every aspect of the commissariat's work, requiring pettifogging attention to the documentation required to complete accounts at the expense of other concerns of more relevance to the performance and well-being of the army. Financial and accounting regulations were meant solely to be the servants of the Treasury as the agent of Parliament. The accounting procedures drilled into the men responsible for supplies encouraged unthinking application of rigid regulations designed to ensure control over the minutest matters connected with stores and cash. Given the accountability requirements of Parliament, it was not inconsistent for the commissariat to see the purpose of accounting records in terms of surveillance and accountability and not as the means to facilitate military victory. Indeed, as previously established, military accounts were never intended to ensure the efficient management of military campaigns. Further, the evaluation of the performance of commissariat officers did not consider anything outside that which could be disclosed in reports stipulated by Treasury regulations.

Unfortunately, despite the numerous administrative reforms enacted in the army after the Crimean War, the effect was piecemeal and deceptive, providing apparent assurances that the more blatant weaknesses had been addressed. Not until the South African War (1899–1902) were the fundamental causes of military administrative problems addressed, namely national neglect born out of suspicion and selfish parsimony and the military's managerial incompetence, the certain outcome of keeping the military financially ignorant and dependent upon civilians for sustenance. So important were the administrative reforms arising from the army's experiences in the South African War that it is generally regarded by military historians as a watershed in military administration and the reason why the British Army was so well prepared at the outbreak of the First World War (Watt 1988: 156). Not until after the South African War was the British Government prepared to consider, through the reforms of Richard Haldane as Secretary of State for War, the organic changes urged for half a century by the army and its supporters which were required to ensure that the army would be able to manage its own finances (Funnell 2005, 2006).

Financial and accounting arrangements at the time of the South African War contained no provision for military views to be accorded any prominence in matters of finance, thereby compounding the isolation of the military from control of its finances. This was subsequently revealed to be a potent source of military failures. According to the War Stores Commission in 1904 (Royal Commission, 1906, Appendix 50: 336–9), in a scathing judgement which proved decisive for attempts to reform military accounting, the shortcomings of the Accountant-General's Department at the War Office had jeopardised the prospect of a decisive victory, contributed unnecessarily to the pressures under which the generals operated and to the 'unreasonable' cost of the war. The Esher Committee (War Office 1904: 139) was also scathing about the army's financial preparedness and its accounting systems. In particular, the Committee criticised Treasury regulations for being too prone to interfere from London in the military actions of officers commanding troops in the field. The intrusions were so overbearing that they were 'intolerable, and they *fully* account for the administrative inefficiency of the War Office' (ibid.: 139, emphasis added). 'The whole army', lamented Amery:

> spent the greater part of its existence in checking its accounts . . . [E]very item of daily accounts was checked and rechecked and copied out in duplicate and triplicate. . . . *It was accountancy run mad*. The object of it all was to prevent defalcations. The object was obtained but at a ruinous cost.
>
> (1902: 141, emphasis added; see also the War Office Cost Accounting Committee 1918: 2)

According to the Esher Committee (War Office 1904: 137) the War Office's financial system was:

> based upon the assumption that all military officers are necessarily spendthrifts and that their actions must be controlled in gross and in detail by civilians . . . This theory is largely responsible for the unreadiness for war which has been exhibited, as well as for reckless and wasteful expenditure . . . The department of the Accountant-General has become a huge and costly machine which is supposed to control expenditure by the aid of involved regulations which serve to aggrandize its power over the military branches.

Army accounting systems in South Africa could not cope with the turmoil and unpredictability of war, resulting in accounting information which was so incomplete as to be unreliable for any decision making purposes. Amery (1909: 461–2) described accounting in the field 'resolving itself into utter chaos . . ., ludicrous . . . [and] hopelessly inadequate in war'. Yet it was not to be unexpected, warned the Esher Committee (War Office 1904: 138), that a financial system in which officers in peace were not given any financial responsibility would be anything other than 'futile in peace . . . [and] ruinous in war'.

The results of the South African War also sharpened awareness that in a world of recurring international political unease, a pronounced feature of the late 1880s and throughout the 1890s, the financial demands of the army could probably be checked only temporarily. While the money spent on the army in peace seemed to be an annoying and fruitless drain on national finances which had to be closely monitored, within the urgency of war the army could hold the nation to financial ransom knowing that demands for money couched in anxiety for the nation's safety would prove an irresistible lever on the nation's purse. Thus, no matter what lip-service the army paid to parliament's control of military finance in peacetime, the perpetuation of a financially unsophisticated army ruled by minute accounting requirements which were superintended by civilians, was a case of being 'penny wise and pounds foolish'. The extravagant expenditure committed by Britain through its army to even a small war could soon outweigh any short-sighted peacetime savings procured through a policy which propagated financial ignorance among soldiers and their unpreparedness by restricting their access to finance.

Accounting for the business of war

The South African War had made it very clear that it was essential for a modern army to have the financial skills and the freedom to manage its affairs. It was also very obvious that it was from the management practices and principles of business enterprises that military administrators and military officers should seek the means of their financial salvation. Successful armies in the twentieth century would have to be run on similar principles to business enterprises.

Sir Charles Harris was firmly convinced that modern commercial accounting systems offered the best means to ensure military success by promoting economy and efficiency in military spending, something not possible by using the plethora of detailed regulations emanating from the War Office to govern every procedure for the sake of procedure, and relying upon outmoded, inappropriate constitutional administrative niceties (Harris 1911). Success in modern war demanded that accounting could no longer to be valued solely as a constitutional protection but as a tool for the efficient management of military forces. Accordingly, when, as a consequence of wartime failings, at the turn of the twentieth century the military again began to reconsider its management and accounting practices, any innovations in military accounting to promote efficiency in the field of battle were entirely reliant upon innovations in the private sector, especially cost accounting.

After the South African War, the army was increasingly conceived in terms of the language and principles of business: efficient management of resources and the equivalence of military success to a profitable business (Funnell 2005). War had become a 'commercial enterprise' which required the expertise of the 'soldier businessman' (Mackinder 1907: 5). Army administration needed 'to be as nearly as possible on all fours with the business arrangements which are understood in civil life' (Secretary of State for War Richard Haldane, quoted in Watt 1988: 1580). If the army's administrative departments in particular were to be operated in the best interests of military efficiency, they must be led and administered by men who were trained as business men and had the values of business men (Young 1906: 1284). Economy of operation, as measured by the amount of money spent, and efficiency, as measured by the achievement of military objectives for the least practical financial cost, were only compatible and simultaneously achievable aims with the support of a financially experienced and sophisticated military.

Early tentative steps toward the transformation of military accounting in the image of business after the South African War admitted the possibility that cost accounting practised in the private sector might serve similar purposes in the military, most importantly to allow the military to cost its work and to manage these costs. However, despite much support for reform within and outside Parliament in the first decade of the twentieth century, attempts at systemic reform of military accounting by the introduction of cost accounting would have to wait until after the First World War. Until then, military accounting, especially in the field of battle, remained largely immune to accounting developments in the private sector. When compared to the accounts of even small businesses the army's accounts were widely regarded by experienced administrators as nothing but rudimentary and mechanical, despite the acknowledged complexity and extent of British Army administration.

The first significant attempt to inculcate business methods and principles in military officers, which was initiated after the South African War, allowed selected officers from the supply and administrative branches of the army to attend classes in business at the London School of Economics (LSE). The course known as the Army Class was run by the renowned and much published accountant Lawrence Dicksee between 1907 and 1932, with interruptions during and after the First World War (Funnell 2006; LSE 1906–7). Haldane, Secretary of State for War, regarded the Army Class at the LSE as the means of getting the army on 'a sound business footing' (Haldane, quoted in Watt 1988: 159). At the opening ceremony of the new class in January 1907, the head of the LSE, Halford Mackinder (1907: 5, 7, 10), emphasised the importance of understanding the ways of 'civilian business and . . . working the people according to their habits . . . We wish to obtain for you the experience of practical business men.' At the same time that the Army Class was recommenced after the First World War, the army was allowed to embark upon an experiment with a new cost accounting system.

The army cost accounting experiment arose most immediately out of the financial extravagance of the First World War which had shocked the nation and followed closely an earlier pilot exercise in developing cost accounts in a small number of British military units (Black 2001, 2006). The experiment was expected to initiate a revolution of military accounting and, thereafter, the accounting of all government departments (Grimwood 1919). At the commencement of the new scheme, the War Office Cost Accounting Committee (1918: 2) praised cost accounts for the way in which they would 'fix responsibility . . . and secure economy . . . while increasing efficiency'. Towards the end of the experiment, Sir Charles Harris emphasised the way in which a cost accounting system would allow officers:

> to manage expenditure properly. [I]t is the difference between a system of account which is designed to control expenditures and a system of account that has nothing to do . . . with seeing whether the Public Services are being carried on efficiently and administered with reasonable care for economy. The present system has nothing to do with that question at all . . . This new system is intended, in particular, to take into account the psychological factor and produce economy . . . by showing people the results of their actions and appealing to their reason.
>
> (Public Accounts Committee 1924–25, Minutes of Evidence, Question 7206;
> see also Grimwood 1919)

Unfortunately, the still insistent dictates of a rigid interpretation of the constitutional function of government accounting effectively precluded the adoption of cost accounting not only in the army but throughout departments of state until the latter decades of the twentieth century. Cost accounting, as portrayed by the Treasury, was believed unable to provide a similar level of constitutional assurance to the existing appropriation system of accounting. Any contribution which cost accounting might be able to make to improved economy in the army, while certainly recognised as a benefit, was never sufficient of itself to convince the British Government that the technique and the ways of business were either necessary or constitutionally appropriate, even though the army was one of the two largest spending departments.

Curiously, although the British Government was not prepared to allow cost accounting to be institutionalised within the military after the First World War, during the war it had been quick to grasp the crucial importance of the protections and assurances that cost accounting could provide to the government in its dealings with private sector firms contracted to supply the military and to ensure victory. Cost accounting was quickly recognised as being essential to the economical and efficient prosecution of the war. This resulted in the British Government playing, unexpectedly, a highly significant role in promoting the adoption of cost accounting by lethargic businesses during the First World War. In this regard, neglect of cost accounting by the British Army was little different at the time from similar neglect by the private sector. Loft (1986: 146, 148) describes most manufacturers at the outbreak of the First World War as ignorant of the cost of their products while according to *The Accountant* (1 March 1919: 150) many manufacturers at the outbreak of war would have regarded the need for cost accounts as 'ridiculous'. One contributor to *The Accountant* in 1900 (30 June: 600) complained that it was 'surprising how many manufacturers pay little attention' to cost accounts. During the First World War, Dicksee (1915: 19) also criticised senior business managers for being 'quite ignorant of the uses that accounts might have'.

Business accounting and the military influence

According to Marriner (1994) and Loft (1986), significant developments during the First World War in the use of cost accounting and the subsequent professionalisation of cost accountants were driven by the British Ministry of Munitions which had been created during the war to coordinate war production. In the first year of the war when many war supplies were in short supply, and market prices for these were unavailable, the British Government had to contend with extensive profiteering by suppliers. Without 'fair market prices' as a basis for setting contract prices, the advantage in any contract negotiations at a time of great national peril was initially with the profiteers. This determined the government to revise the Defence of the Realm Act, which provided the government with extensive powers to wage war, to allow contract prices to be set other than with reference to market prices, namely on the basis of 'the cost of production of the output so requisitioned' (quoted in Loft 1986: 144). Nor was the government prepared to accept the cost figures provided by the suppliers and manufacturers, allowing instead that these may be required to be verified on behalf of the government by appointed cost investigators.

The effect of the new legislation prompted by the peril of the First World War, suggests Loft, was to force many firms to consider seriously, many for the first time, how they might determine the cost of their products, thereby providing a strong incentive for the spread of cost accounting throughout British industry, if not the army. The 'new interest in cost accounting went hand in hand with a general transformation of industry' and, as an unintended consequence of the legislated costing requirements, raised the public profile of accountants and accelerated the professionalisation of accountants (Loft 1986: 146). The establishment of the Institute of Cost and Works Accountants in 1919 was especially notable. Fleischman and Tyson (2000) have identified a similar phenomenon in the United States whereby the demands of the First World War on cost accounting precipitated the professionalisation of cost accounting. Boyns and Edwards (2007), however, have disputed the importance given to the impact of the war on business accounting practices.

Although the extent to which cost accounting pervaded government relationships with the world of business was novel during the war, the benefits of cost accounting had long been appreciated by government ordnance factories and the navy's shipbuilding establishments in Britain. Foreman and Tyson (1998) and Foreman (2001) have established an appreciation also for cost accounting in government military manufacturing establishments in Australia at the turn of the twentieth century when factories operated by the Department of Defence were the first public sector enterprises to use modern cost accounting practices borrowed from commercial firms.

The unusual possibility of an influence on business accounting by the military prompted the now well-known and contentious debate between Tyson (1990, 1993), a 'traditional' historian, and the Foucauldian accounting historians Hoskin and Macve (1988, 1994). According to Hoskin and Macve (1988), and also Ezzamel et al. (1990), accounting practices of the Springfield Armory in the United States during the middle decades of the nineteenth century were highly influential in the development of modern cost accounting and the marriage of cost accounting and managerialism. The armory's accounting systems, which Chandler (1977: 74) has described as 'the most sophisticated used in any American industrial establishment before the 1840s', are said to have incorporated a set of standard costs upon which the piece rate system of payment used in the armory was based. These standard costs were used to exert, in Foucauldian terms, 'disciplinary power' over the workforce, possibly for the first time anywhere, suggest Hoskin and Macve (1988). Further, and most important for their thesis, they argue that the development of these standards of performance, measured by accounting, can be traced to the behaviour and mentality induced in West Point graduates by the system of meticulous educational assessment developed by Sylvanus Thayer at the US Military Academy after 1817.

Connections between military institutions and the emergence of cost accounting practices have also been explored by Zambon and Zan (2007) at the Venice Arsenal in the late sixteenth and early seventeenth centuries. They found strong evidence that the notion of costs and costing emerged unexpectedly from the efforts of the Venetian Senate to introduce tighter forms of financial control over the operation of the city's arsenal. They concluded that accounting at the arsenal had been 'transformed from a mere tool of inspection and control, into an instrument for understanding and managing complex organisations' (Zambon and Zan 2007: 121).

At the West Point academy, students were placed under a strict disciplinary regime whereby, across all subjects, each day their performance was assessed and numerically graded. These results formed the basis of weekly reports of progress upon which students would be graded and rewarded. This finely tabulated system, argue Hoskin and Macve (1988), rendered 'calculable men', cadets whose performance was intimately knowable and in whom, in Foucauldian terms, the system of disciplinary control was internalised. Subsequently, the performance culture engendered by the obsessive reliance upon examinations to monitor and assess performance was transmitted to business establishments through West Point's engineering graduates when they later transferred to the Springfield Armory. Thus, when graduates such as Daniel Tyler were appointed to senior positions in the Ordnance Corps, which was responsible for the Springfield Armory, the disciplinary regimes and management discourses of West Point followed. After 1841, West Point graduates took over the superintendency of the armory, with some finding their way to influential positions in several railway companies. These military officers trained by Thayer were, according to Ezzamel et al. (1990: 158), a new brand of 'men-managers'. Hoskin and Macve (1988: 39) refer to West Point as 'a paradigm of the way in which the nineteenth century developments in educational technology came to alter the way in which business was organized and human performance was measured'. Tyson (1990), however, rejects the proposition that West Point education and management training had a significant impact on the evolution of accounting practices. Instead, he concludes that:

> West Point training and discipline probably helped managers perform their work, but this particular background should not be given undue credit for increasing productivity and bringing fundamental change to accounting and accountability systems. Economic and social forces appear to be far more significant.
>
> (Tyson 1990: 57)

Tyson (1993) disputed not only the conclusions of Hoskin and Macve and Ezzamel et al. but also questioned the quality of their historical research. According to Tyson (1993: 13), these authors in their eagerness to 'substantiate a particular social theory', that of Foucault, required them to be less constrained by the facts and, thus, they had grossly overstated the importance of the contributions of the armory's accounting systems to the development of modern managerialism. Tyson was particularly critical of Hoskin and Macve's characterisation of Tyler's work as 'unique' at the time. In a scathing assessment of Hoskin and Macve's work, Tyson (1993: 10) claims that Hoskin and Macve even 'go beyond factual embellishment by attributing a singular motive to Tyler's 1832 piece-rate activities, without qualification and without supporting evidence'. At one point Tyson (ibid.: 10) argues that a report in 1841 referred to by Hoskin and

Macve provides no support for their contention that 'managerialism was invented at the Armory'. Indeed, this allegedly hyperbolic assessment by Hoskin and Macve, concludes Tyson, was but one example of the way in which they and Ezzamel *et al.* had been prepared to overstate some aspects of the management practices at the Springfield Armory and overlook others so that the evidence would fit the specifications of the Foucauldian perspective that they were applying to the archives. After an extensive investigation of the historical material, Tyson (ibid.: 12) argues that 'there is no corroborating evidence to indicate that normalizing judgements or performance evaluations were ever based on accounting numbers . . . [at the armory]. In fact, there is strong evidence to the contrary'. Nor were variances from norms of performance ever computed or the workers turned into 'calculable men'.

Conclusion

This survey of accounting history in which military forces have a presence highlights both research opportunities and the urgent need for a more concerted engagement by accounting historians with the military past, especially given the immense situations in which armies have been involved over many centuries and the social, political and economic consequences of war. Among the topics which hold particular promise for accounting historians are how accounting developments in the military reflected the evolution of cost accounting practices in the private sector, the influences that the military might have had on business accounting, the opportunities that war created for women to work as accountants, both in private practice and in government agencies such as the Army Pay Corps in Britain, and the contribution of accounting to the operational success of armies. With each major military conflagration producing its own war management problems and calls for remedial action, there is a vast repertoire of possible accounting histories, with the last two centuries especially fecund in this regard. Accounting historians outside the United States and Britain are encouraged to consider the opportunities which this research provides in non–Anglophone settings. This will allow the introduction of a far greater diversity of government forms and constitutional practices than that which presently dominates the study of accounting and the military.

Unavoidably, and necessarily, the political identity of armies cannot but dominate much of military accounting research. Armies are the manifestation of political will and power; they exist for political purposes, having no identity beyond the exercise of violence in the interests of a political body, usually the state. Recognising that military accounting is ultimately derived from the need to serve a political body and thus have a political purpose, the consequences of military accounting will be necessarily assessed in terms of their contributions to the performance of the military in the achievement of these purposes. However, while the political overlays the study of military accounting this does not mean that all accounting histories which have the military as their subject need be dominated by the heavy presence of political theory. Rather, this chapter has demonstrated how the details of the practice and effects of military accounting can direct discussion to the level of specific accounting practices and technologies and their contributions to military performance and management.

Key works

Chwastiak (2006) is a particularly innovative examination of the role of accounting in an attempt to transform the prosecution of the Vietnam War into an exercise in efficient management and the political consequences of this for Secretary of Defense McNamara.

Fleischman and Tyson (2000) offers a very useful rendition of the developments in cost accountancy at the beginning of the twentieth century. It identifies the rapid advances which had been made in cost accounting in the USA especially when compared to the UK.

Funnell (2005) provides an extensive, and the only, examination of the events which proved to be a watershed in the history of the financial control of the British Army. The South African War was a key development in the acceptance of the benefits of systems of financial control and accounting used by businesses.

Hoskin and Macve (1994) is a seminal paper on the history of management accounting which has proved to be highly influential in our understanding of the evolving importance of management accounting.

References

Amery, L. (1902) *The Times History of the War in South Africa*, vols 1 and 2 (London: Sampson Low & Co).

Amery, L. (1909) *The Times History of the War in South Africa*, vol. 7 (London: Sampson Low & Co).

Black, J. (2001) Full circle: the cost accounting experiment in the British Army 1917–25 and the Corps of Military Accountants, *Journal of the Society for Army Historical Research*, 79 (318): 145–63.

Black, J. (2006) War, women and accounting, the pioneering role played by women in the Army Pay Department during the First World War, *Accounting, Business & Finance History*, 16 (2): 195–218.

Boyns, T. and Edwards, J. R. (2007) The development of cost and management accounting in Britain, in C. Chapman, A. Hopwood and M. Sheilds (eds) *History of Management Accounting Research*, vol. 2, pp. 969–1034 (London: Elsevier).

Chandler, A. D. (1977) *The Visible Hand* (Cambridge, MA: Harvard University Press).

Churchill, W. (1906) *Lord Randolph Churchill* (London: John Murray).

Chwastiak, M. (1999) Accounting and the Cold War: the transformation of waste into riches, *Critical Perspectives on Accounting*, 10 (6): 747–71.

Chwastiak, M. (2001) Taming the untamable: planning, programming and budgeting and the normalization of war, *Accounting, Organizations and Society*, 26 (6): 501–19.

Chwastiak, M. (2006) Rationality, performance measures and representations of reality: planning, programming and budgeting and the Vietnam War, *Critical Perspectives on Accounting*, 17 (1): 29–55.

Committee of Administration of, and Accounting for, Army Expenditure (Lawrence Committee) (1924), *British Parliamentary Papers*, (Cmd. 2073), VII: 707.

Dicksee, L. (1915) *Business Methods and the War* (Cambridge: Cambridge University Press).

Edinburgh Review (1871).

Ezzamel, M., Hoskin, K. and Macve, R. (1990) Managing it all by numbers: a review of Johnson & Kaplan's *Relevance Lost, Accounting and Business Research*, 20 (78): 153–66.

Fernandez-Revuelta, L., Gomez, D. and Robson, K. (2002) Fuerzas Motrices del Valle de Lecrin, 1936–9: accounting reports and ideological struggles in time of civil war, *Accounting, Business & Financial History*, 12 (2): 347–66.

Fleischman, R. and Tyson, T. (2000) Parallels between US and UK cost accountancy in the World War I era, *Accounting, Business & Financial History*, 10 (2): 191–212.

Foreman, P. (2001) The transfer of accounting technology: a study of the Commonwealth of Australia Government Factories, *Accounting History*, 6 (1): 31–59.

Foreman, P. and Tyson, T. (1998) Accounting, accountability and cost efficiency at the Commonwealth of Australia Clothing Factory, 1911–18, *Accounting History*, 3 (2): 7–36.

Funnell, W. (1988) The guardians of liberty: the role of civilians in British military finance 1850–99, *War and Society*, 6 (2): 32–57.

Funnell, W. (1990) Pathological responses to accounting controls: the British Commissariat in the Crimea 1854–6, *Critical Perspectives on Accounting*, 1 (4): 319–35.

Funnell, W. (1997) Military influences on public sector accounting and auditing 1830–1880, *Accounting History*, 2 (2): 9–31.

Funnell, W. (2005) Accounting on the frontline: military efficiency and the South African War, *Accounting and Business Research*, 35 (4): 307–26.

Funnell, W. (2006) National efficiency, military accounting and the business of war, *Critical Perspectives on Accounting*, 17 (6): 719–51.

Gallhofer, S. and Haslam, J. (1991) The aura of accounting in the context of a crisis: Germany and the First World War, *Accounting, Organizations and Society*, 16 (5/6): 487–520.

Grimwood, J. (Lieut-Col.) (1919) Costing in relation to government control, efficiency and economy, *The Incorporated Accountants Journal*, March: 114–20; April: 133–38; May: 156–61.

Hanham, H. (1969) *The Nineteenth Century Constitution 1815–1914* (Cambridge: Cambridge University Press).

Harris, C. (1911) Army finance, *Army Review*, 1 (July): 55–76.

Hoskin, K. and Macve, R. (1988) The genesis of accountability: the West Point connections, *Accounting, Organizations and Society*, 13 (1): 37–73.

Hoskin, K. and Macve, R. (1994) Reappraising the genesis of managerialism: a re-examination of the role of accounting at the Springfield Armory, 1815–1914, *Accounting, Auditing & Accountability Journal*, 7 (2): 4–29.

Hoskin, K. and Macve, R. (2000) Knowing more as knowing less? Alternative histories of cost and management accounting in the U.S. and the U.K., *Accounting Historians Journal*, 27 (1): 91–149.

Howard, M. (ed.) (1957) *Soldiers and Governments* (London: Eyre & Spottiswoode).

Loft, A. (1986) Towards a critical understanding of accounting: the case of cost accounting in the U.K., 1914–1925, *Accounting, Organizations and Society*, 11 (2): 137–69.

LSE 1906–7, Notes on the Course established at the LSE in the Session 1906–7 for the Training of Officers for the higher administrative appointments on the Administrative Staff for the Army and for the charge of Departmental Services, LSE Archives, File 232/C.

Mackinder, H. (1907) *Address Delivered on the 10th January, 1907, on the Occasion of the Opening of the Class for the Administrative Training of Army Officers* (London: HSO).

Marriner, S. (1994) The Ministry of Munitions 1915–1919 and government accounting procedures, in R. Parker and B. Yamey (eds) *Accounting History: Some British Contributions*, pp. 450–72 (Oxford: Clarendon Press).

Public Accounts Committee (1924–5) First and Second Reports with Proceedings, Evidence, Appendices and Index, *British Parliamentary Papers* (33, 138), V: 1.

Royal Commission into the Supplies of the British Army in the Crimea (McNeil-Tulloch Commission) (1856) *British Parliamentary Papers*, First Report, XX, including Appendix: 497.

Royal Commission to Enquire into the Civil and Professional Administration of the Naval and Military Departments (1890) *British Parliamentary Papers*, Report, XIX, Appendix VI: 85.

Royal Commission Appointed to Inquire into the Military Preparations and Other Matters Connected With the War in South Africa (Elgin Commission) (1904), *British Parliamentary Papers* (Cd. 1789) XL, Report: 1.

Royal Commission on War Stores in South Africa (1906) Report with Appendices of Messrs. Annan, Kirby, Dexter & Co., Chartered Accountants, *British Parliamentary Papers* (Cd. 3130) LVIII: 1, 73.

Select Committee on National Expenditure (1918) *British Parliamentary Papers*, (23, 30, 59, 80, 92, 97, 98, 111, 121, 132) IV, First to Tenth Reports: 95.

Tyson, T. (1990) Accounting for labor in the early 19th century: the U.S. arms making experience, *Accounting Historians Journal*, 17 (1): 47–59.

Tyson, T. (1993) Keeping the record straight: Foucauldian revisionism and nineteenth century US cost accounting history, *Accounting, Auditing & Accountability Journal*, 6 (2): 4–16.

War Office (Reconstitution) Committee (Esher Committee) (1904) *British Parliamentary Papers*, Part I (Cd. 1932) VIII: 102, Part II (Cd. 1968) VIII, Part III (Cd. 2002) VIII: 121.

War Office Cost Accounting Committee (1918) *Instructions Relating to Experimental Cost Accounting in Selected Units* (London: War Office).

Watt, D. (1988) The London University class for military administrators, 1906–31: a study of British approach to civil–military relations, *LSE Quarterly*, 2 (2): 155–71.

Wright, F. (1956) The British Army cost accounting experiment 1919–1925, *The Australian Accountant*, 26 (November): 463–70.

Young, H. (Captain) (1906) Practical economy in the army, *Journal of the Royal United Services Institute*, L: 1281–5.

Zambon, S. and Zan, L. (2007) Controlling expenditure, or the slow emergence of costing at the Venice Arsenal, 1586–1633, *Accounting, Business & Financial History*, 17 (1): 105–28.

28

Taxation

Margaret Lamb

Overview

The histories of taxation and accounting are intertwined. Taxation requires accounting to record taking from those taxed and the giving to those on whose behalf tax is levied. Accounting becomes a matter of public concern and requires consistency, truth and fairness when tax appropriations occur in political systems where rulers are accountable to citizens.

The aim of this chapter is to explore the interrelationships between accounting and taxation with a view to framing research questions which bring taxation clearly into view in accounting history scholarship. The chapter traces taxation themes through several strands of accounting history scholarship and through scholarly publications in which taxation is sometimes, but not always, the explicit research focus. The exercise consists of a review of how accounting historians study taxation and how the historical influences of taxation are addressed by accounting scholars with more contemporary concerns. Concluding comments focus on challenges facing the accounting historian of taxation. These include strengthening connections between historical questions of taxation and other fields of accounting history and linking such research to histories of taxation by historians operating in other sub-fields. The chapter emphasises US and British tax accounting history. This is a practical, not a principled, matter. While research on other parts of the world will be discussed, the author focuses on work published in English.

Taxation research themes in accounting history

Taxation stretches far back in time and covers the globe. Egyptian pharaohs of the first dynasty of the Old Kingdom (3000–2800 BC) collected taxes in a systematic way. In Ancient Greece and Rome, taxation shaped political institutions, social life, culture, philosophy and religion. Experiments with income taxation both reflected and shaped political philosophy and practice in many parts of Europe from the early Middle Ages to the nineteenth century. New institutional figures and accounting practices emerged through innovative tax impositions, such as those introduced during Louis XIV's reign in seventeenth-century France. The introduction of income tax in 1799 to fund Britain's war with Napoleon represents a milestone in the development of taxation as we understand it today. The adoption of income tax on a continuous basis in the nineteenth and twentieth centuries, and after the constitutional amendment of 1913 in the USA, were important events in the linked histories of tax and accounting. The subsequent extension of income taxation to the masses – living individuals, as well as other legal persons – gave taxation the ubiquity and calculative forms that are still recognisable. Other modern forms of taxation, including the value added-type taxes – introduced in France in 1954, the European Union (EU) as a whole by 1974, and many other parts of the world – overlay their own complexity on pre-existing tax regimes.

Accounting historians tend to start thinking about taxation by focusing on puzzling or important tax matters which relate to accounting. Questions are concerned with taxation as specialised accounting practice. Where and why did ambiguities and difficulties of calculation arise? How was tax calculation embedded in the financial routines of businesses? Other questions probe deeper into the ways that accounting has changed over time. What did taxation have to do with the origins of accounting? How did taxation help clarify important accounting concepts such as 'income', 'profit', 'depreciation' and 'entity'? Some accounting historians look to taxation for clues about how persistent tensions in accounting emerged. How was discipline achieved in reporting assessable values for taxation? How were tax returns audited? Which features of regulation improved the accuracy and consistency of financial reporting?

Most tax history written in an accounting context focuses on the rules and practices of particular taxes. The complexity and importance of taxation as an area of professional practice mean that many researchers are preoccupied with understanding the nuts and bolts of tax. Further, interpretation and application in practice often depend on legal and procedural precedent, thus creating an essential historical element. Beyond the focus on the nuts and bolts accounting histories of tax can be divided into two types: explorations of tax history for better understandings of accounting theory, practice and institutions; and explorations of tax history to understand accounting in its broader social, political and economic context. Such themes feature in the following sections.

Taxation rules and practice

The tax rules and practice literature includes many histories of particular taxes or of the features of taxes in particular times and places. Among the more substantial pieces of research by scholars who have explored the historical accounting dimensions of tax rules and practices in Britain are the following. Oats and Sadler (2004, 2007) and Sadler and Oats (2002) focus on contextualised studies of stamp duties from the eighteenth century. On the nineteenth century Edwards (1976) examines the tax treatment of capital expenditure and profit measurement; Lamb (1996, 2002) looks at business tax practices and profit measurement for tax purposes. On the twentieth century Casson (1996) explores share options, imputation tax credits on dividends (1998) and employee share ownership plans (2004); Noguchi (2005) discusses tax accounting for stock in trade; and Stopforth (2004, 2005a, 2007) addresses capital gains tax and tax avoidance legislation (1992, 1999, 2005b).

On the USA, the following scholars have researched particular taxation rules and practices in the nineteenth and twentieth centuries and make connections to the wider historical context. Cataldo (1995) explored earned income tax credit; Wells and Flesher (1999) focused on consumption taxes; Kern (2000) looked at interactions between tax and accounting depreciation rules and conventions; Pincus (1989) examined the background to legislative recognition of the

LIFO principle; and various authors have discussed the antecedents of modern US taxes (Crum 1982; Kozub 1983; Samson 1985).

In addition to these publications, accounting historians interested in taxation are advised to utilise contemporary literature, particularly periodicals which catered for practitioner and scholarly audiences. For example, *The Accountant* (published in London from 1874) was an important journal in the Anglophone world. It published well-researched, authoritative articles on taxation. Contributors in the late 1930s and 1940s include leading practitioners (such as George O. May (1938), senior partner in Price Waterhouse) and leading academics (such as T. H. Sanders (1939), Professor of Accounting, Harvard Business School). Taxation subjects in *The Accountant's Magazine* (published in Scotland from 1897) represent almost one-third of articles published 1942–52 (Lee 2006: 30–1). In the second half of the twentieth century more specialist journals emerged that were intended for tax practitioners and also addressed recent tax history. Many such journals relied on contributions from both accountants and lawyers.

The tradition of authoritative scholarship on the links between accounting practice and taxation policy and law continued in more recent times. The leading weekly journal on US tax policy, *Tax Notes* (published since 1972), has provided an important medium for academic and practising accountants and lawyers. *The British Tax Review* (published since 1956) provides authoritative analyses of matters of current interest to practitioners and academics, but is also the leading interdisciplinary source of tax commentary and assumes a broad scope and long view. Among the early contributors to tax research written from an accounting perspective was Professor Harold Edey (1956) of the London School of Economics. *Tax Notes* and *British Tax Review* publish work by authors from both practice and academe.

The National Tax Journal (NTJ) (published from 1948) also provided venues for scholarly analyses of US tax rules and practice by practitioners and accounting and finance academics, as well as by fiscal economists. In the early years of *NTJ* articles such as Mills (1955) on the influence of taxation on accounting profit measurement, and Troop Smith (1953) on the tax effects of corporate financing costs, provide historical starting points for exploring research questions that continue to puzzle accounting researchers.

Tax historical research and better understandings of accounting

Challenges for accounting historians interested in taxation include the research and study of detailed taxation rules and practices and finding references to taxation in works with a primary focus on accounting theory, practice and development. Tracing such fragments is essential to understanding how taxation is intertwined with accounting. Lamb (2003, 2004) analyses why taxation studies in an accounting context have been underdeveloped and suggests methods for exposing and studying the historical connections between the two subjects.

Taxation and the origins of accounting

Historians of the origins of accounting have often encountered taxation as a site for the use and development of the technique. Jose and Moore (1998) studied taxation in the Biblical age and explored aspects of accounting (counting, measurement, and computation). Ezzamel's study (2002) of ancient Egyptian tax assessment and collection and Oldroyd's (1995) work on Roman governmental accounting are fine examples of how historical work by accounting historians may be critically grounded in the general historical scholarship of the time and place. Macve's (1994) work on Greek and Roman accounting and taxation engages with the work of a specialist historian of the period (Geoffrey de Ste. Croix). The functioning of taxation in ancient economies and its implications for accounting practice are also considered in Chapter 4.

For later periods, scholars have sought to locate the antecedents and narrate transitions to modern concepts and forms of accounting. McDonald (2002) used the Domesday Book (1086) of Norman England as an evidential base for exploring the taxation of income, wealth and estates. Treisch (2005) considers the tax exemption of basic, or subsistence, income and traces the emergence of the principle to the theories of human rights in German natural law during the seventeenth to nineteenth centuries. Accounting technologies essential to state-building are studied by Vogeler (2005: 236) in medieval German territorial states. As oral accounting for taxation gave way to paper accounting for taxation from the thirteenth to the sixteenth century, tax came to be used as 'a symbol of the fact that everyone belongs to the state' (ibid.). For a later period in France, Miller (1990) studied the formative interrelations between practices of accounting, taxation and the institutions of state when Louis XIV's government extended controls deep into the provinces and businesses.

Taxation and the emergence of 'modern' accounting theory

Debates concerning taxation and the emergence of accounting theory from the nineteenth century onwards have revolved around various questions. Is tax just another cost to be accounted for? Is tax a discipline that is separate from accounting? Is tax a process that is linked to and influences accounting?

Representation of tax costs

In Anglo-American accounting, academics tend to address taxation as a cost that requires appropriate treatment. In financial reporting 'accounting for tax costs' encompasses the measurement and presentation techniques developed to represent tax expenses, tax liabilities and tax cash-flows in published accounts. Techniques of accounting for tax costs were developed to reflect the fact that taxation systems may recognise economic events in a manner that differs from the 'true and fair view' of accounting and to reflect the fact that the underlying tax system has a changing set of interrelationships with accounting. Some differences between accounting conventions for recognising profits and their tax counterparts are created by statute (for example, certain categories of income are tax exempt and certain categories of expense are not deductible for tax purposes). Other differences arise through the application of different tax principles. Differences between accounting depreciation and tax depreciation ('capital allowances' in the UK) are created by statute and represent a prominent category of difference between tax and accounting profit calculations. 'Deferred tax' refers to the collection of techniques developed to account for these sorts of timing differences.

One strand of historical research on the representation of tax costs in financial reporting supports an analysis of standard setting as a political process (Horngren 1973; Solomons 1978, 1983). Here the economic consequences of accounting policy choice shape the positions adopted by lobbyists (Zeff 1978; Watts and Zimmerman 1979, see also Chapter 14 of this volume). Schultz and Johnson's (1998) research on deferred taxation theory and practice is integrated into the history of US financial reporting. In a British context, Hope and Briggs (1982) identify issues 'at the heart of the deferred tax debate', and, based on their historical analysis, argue that accounting standard setters were influenced by political lobbying when drafting a standard for deferred tax accounting. Arnold and Webb (1989) found that Statement of Standard Accounting Practice 15 on deferred tax was inconsistent with the concepts of other UK accounting standards. Based on their evaluation of the economic effects of partial provision for deferred tax versus the (hypothetical) economic effects of full provision, they found 'evidence of major deficiencies in the accounting standards process' and that full provision deferred tax accounting (abandoned in 1978) 'was a convenient "scapegoat" ' (ibid.: 49–50). They argue 'that the rationale for partial deferral was constructed to fit the political need to avoid an embarrassing level of non-compliance with accounting standards' (ibid.: 50).

Tax influence in an accounting context

'Tax influence' on accounting is a recurrent observation in the academic literature, especially in Anglo-American accounting history and comparative international accounting. Most 'tax influence' research focuses on the impact of tax law on company financial reporting law and practice, and on measurement differences between tax and financial reporting.

By the mid-nineteenth century income taxation was effectively permanent in Britain. According to Parker (1986: 5), its introduction was one of four significant factors in the development of British accountancy. The others were the growth of large-scale organisations, especially the railroads; the development of limited liability; and the high rate of insolvency. Parker (1986: 39) argues that the First World War 'brought to the fore' tax services which had been 'slowly developing', but devotes little space to discussion of pre-First World War tax or to changes that occurred after the military crisis.

Watts and Zimmerman (1979) argue forcefully – but with limited exposition of detail – that taxation caused accounting theories. Looking at relevant US and UK history, the authors find a range of evidence to support their argument that accounting theories emerge to strengthen governmental actions following particular interventions. For example, the introduction of a British income tax law of depreciation prompted, they say, the development of the relevant accounting theory. Watts and Zimmerman focus on governmental intervention in the form of a new income tax statute and the direct impact this had on changing accounting principles and the subsequent production of prescriptive literature by writers on accounting. Watts and Zimmerman observe that income tax law increased pedagogic, information and justification-based demands for accounting theories. The implied medium of change was a coalescence of individual desires to be better off by transforming accounting theory to take advantage of the tax change. An accounting theory would, they argue, 'buttress preconceived notions' (1979: 23, quoting Zeff 1972: 177) and has the character of an economic good that is subject to market forces of supply and demand. A demand for a particular accounting theory is a demand for a 'rationale' or 'excuse'.

Some authors refute Watts and Zimmerman's argument that changes to British income tax law impacted on the development of related accounting theories. Bryer (1993), for example, finds evidence of the development of an accounting theory of depreciation that predates the relevant income tax law. Relatedly, Edwards (1976: 313) argued: 'If there is a relationship between tax law and accounting practice it remains, nevertheless, difficult to trace the cause and effect.' Edwards' purpose was to study tax influence on the development of depreciation and other aspects of fixed asset accounting. He stated that 'in the absence of any readily available figure for business profit, the tax authorities were obliged to introduce their own rules' (ibid.: 302).

Citing Edwards (1976), Napier (1996: 452) argues that the main principles to emerge from an early period of interaction between tax and accounting in practice concerned 'the identification and treatment of capital expenditure . . . where tax law did not permit a deduction in determining profits'. Napier argues that this phenomenon in accounting was probably related to 'an unreflective adoption by businessmen of a capital/revenue distinction articulated originally in the context of British aristocratic estates'. Tax law and practice, therefore, reinforced an accounting distinction that was a residue of an earlier age. Napier implies that tax was one of the reasons why theoretical work on accounting emerged slowly.

Lamb (2002) analyses British tax cases in the late nineteenth century and makes clear that officials representing tax agencies struggled to devise effective concepts and techniques of accounting just as businessmen and their accountant advisors did. Her work traces interrelationships between business profit measurement techniques and the emerging treatment of depreciation. The give and take between tax and commercial accounting practices is highlighted as is the way in which practitioners with different perspectives attempted to grapple with the impact of new technologies in industry, commerce and finance.

Watts and Zimmerman (1979: 44) take it for granted that tax is a negative influence on accounting. They argue that where accounting theories are developed in response to a governmental need for justification, high political or transaction costs can lead to the adoption of a less-than-'best' accounting theory (ibid.: 34–5). Further, they say that tax depreciation techniques were based on historic cost rather than periodic valuation and on an annual allowance equal to 'an arbitrary proportion of historical cost' because such techniques reduced the cost of administering tax laws (ibid.: 45). Not only did this process of rationalisation influence depreciation accounting, but 'the demand for a rationalization of this procedure and other accruals under the tax law eventually resulted in the concept of income based on matching and the realization concept' (ibid.). Edwards (1976: 310), too, argues that 'the detailed provisions of income tax legislation had an unfavourable influence on accounting practices'. In the area of capital accounting, 'early tax law and practice retarded the development of accounting theory' (ibid.: 314).

Many accounting historians appear to accept that by the late nineteenth century taxation and accounting in Britain operated under separate principles and rules of profit measurement. Edwards (1976: 300) treats the fact that 'profits' have a different meaning for tax and financial reporting purposes as self-evident from the different measurement principles assumed by tax authorities and the users of financial accounts. In an argument similar to that of the legal scholar Judith Freedman (1987), Edwards (1976: 317) argues:

> The figure for taxable income is designed to fulfil a function quite different from that performed by the balance reported as accounting profit and any attempt to produce one figure to do both jobs might well result in it doing neither job properly.

This is, therefore, a normative argument that tax and accounting measurement of profit *should* be kept separate in a contemporary sense. Edwards (1976) makes a related argument that tax reform can only follow not precede accounting developments. This offers an interesting contrast to the argument put forward by Watts and Zimmerman in 1979.

Edwards explains the separation between accounting and tax calculation as the result of the fact that UK income tax was introduced before commercial accounting practice had developed widespread reliability and consistency. The timing of the introduction of income tax forced relevant authorities to develop their own rules and thereafter 'recognition of the essential difference between taxable and accounting profit' ensured the separate and distinct nature of tax and accounting approaches to profit measurement (1976: 300–1). Freedman (1997: 32) argues that '[a] culture was created in which a divergence of taxable profits from accounting profits could evolve without causing any great surprise'. Divergence between tax and accounting profit calculations, thereby, became 'natural'. Lamb (2002) argues that such divergence was *constructed* over a long period by interacting institutions and practices. For much of the nineteenth century, many income tax authorities sought consistency with commercial principles to represent transactions and balances.

In a comparative study of the historical influence of tax on accounting, Lamb *et al.* (1998) recognise the distinctiveness of tax and accounting rules during the late twentieth century. They assume that this distinctiveness does *not* follow from the fact that income tax predates modern financial reporting. Instead, they argue that the separation is counter-intuitive and requires explanation. A more intuitive result would have been for UK financial reporting to follow income tax rules more closely because compliance with tax rules would have created a reason for preparing accounts. Such a rationale appears to have been influential in maintaining a close link between tax and accounting profit measurement rules in several countries of continental European. Lamb *et al.* (1998) argue that since the late nineteenth century British capital market requirements had provided a competing purpose that was stronger than any tax reason for preparing accounts. The accounting requirements of capital markets thus diverged from the accounting requirements of the tax authorities. UK financial reporting acquired a capital market orientation and tax computations were prepared as a substantially separate exercise using distinctive computational rules and principles.

'Tax influence' research in comparative international accounting

National regimes have been distinguished by the degree of 'tax influence' on the development or operation of financial reporting rules (Nobes 1983, 1984, 1992; Nobes and Parker 1991, 1995, 2006). Various terms describe this relationship: 'dependence/independence' (Hoogendoorn 1996); 'congruence/reverse congruence' (Haller 1992); 'authoritativeness/reverse authoritativeness' (Ordelheide and Pfaff 1994); and 'bindingness' (von Wysocki 1984). The degree of current, or 'operational influence', is closely linked to the patterns of 'historical influence' established in particular countries (Lamb *et al.* 1998). Some research in comparative international accounting has considered the tax/accounting link in its historical, national and institutional contexts (see Hoogendoorn 1996).

According to Choi and Mueller (1992: 30), there are 'two thrusts that characterize basic thinking in the international accounting field': classification and development. Both influenced the way in which we think about interrelations between accounting and taxation and their historical development. A third area, harmonisation studies, also concerns tax/accounting interrelations. A fourth area, the comparative study of the tax/accounting relationship, is less concerned with convergence and accounting commonalities than with deepening understanding of tax/accounting relationships in their particular national contexts.

Mueller (1967) classifies national accounting systems into four patterns: 'macroeconomic', 'microeconomic', 'independent discipline' and 'uniform accounting'. Uniform accounting (as in France, Germany, Sweden and Switzerland) creates a strong link between accounting and taxation. In discussing Mueller's classification, Nobes (1991: 41–2) suggests that 'we might expect' the macroeconomic pattern 'to be equivalent to tax accounting', meaning that there is equivalence in accounting practices used and reports produced for financial reporting and reporting to taxation authorities.

In a study that focuses on the financial reporting measurement practices of public companies Nobes (1983, 1984) adds a hierarchical dimension to international accounting classification. The importance of tax rules in accounting measurements is a differentiating factor between corporate reporting systems. Using an analytical method borrowed from biological taxonomy, 'tax-based' systems are a 'family' of the 'Continental: government' 'sub-class,' which in turn is part of the 'class' 'macro-uniform'. In the Nobes hierarchy, the 'tax-based' 'species' – Spain, France, Belgium and Italy – are very 'distant' from the UK-Irish species. In a later version of the hierarchical classification, Nobes (1991: 48–9, 1992: 96) redefines his two 'classes' as 'micro-fair-judgmental/commercially-driven' and 'macro-uniform/government-driven/tax-dominated'.

Several empirical classification studies (Da Costa *et al.* 1978; Frank 1979; Nair and Frank 1980) group countries according to the accounting practices actually used. This literature, which bases differentiation on such observed practices as deferred taxation provision and measurement, helps confirm that countries can be differentiated according to patterns of accounting/tax interrelations. The studies are significant for having introduced the idea that a financial reporting *representation* of the tax/accounting link should be used as a proxy for examining the nature of the links themselves in international accounting classification. The focus on the representation of interrelationships as opposed to underlying patterns has contributed to an exaggeration of the degrees of independence or dependence between tax and accounting in some countries.

For Choi and Mueller (1992), development is the second defining thrust in international accounting thinking. Many scholars have identified factors that influence the development of accounting. However, development factors are defined in different ways. For example, Radebaugh and Gray (1993) emphasise the cultural level while others describe multiple levels of interpretation. Taxation is only examined in detail as an explicit factor in the work by Nobes and Parker.

In his own classification studies (Nobes 1983, 1984) and when writing with Parker (1991: Chapters 1, 2, 5), Nobes has explored the influence of taxation on accounting. Taxation is a 'likely cause of international financial reporting differences' but the strength of causation remains difficult to discern (Nobes and Parker 1991: 10). The financial reporting differences arising from taxation relate to 'the degree to which taxation regulations determine accounting measurements' (ibid.: 16). Nobes and Parker go on to say: 'To some extent thus is seen in a negative way by studying the problem of deferred taxation, which is caused by timing differences between tax and accounting treatments' (ibid.).

Nobes and Parker (1991) discuss the 'separation' of accounting and taxation. This notion is manifest in the 'separation' and 'independence' of the calculation of depreciation for accounting purposes and UK tax (capital allowances) purposes in the twentieth century. (By the early twenty-first century, tax and accounting depreciation calculations had begun to converge in some significant respects.) They write that 'separation' permits 'a complete lack of subjectivity in tax allowances, but full room for judgment in financial depreciation charges' (ibid.). In contrast 'in countries like Germany, the tax regulations lay down the depreciation rates to be used for particular assets' (ibid.). The continental approach to the accounting/tax link is explained in a historical sense as 'perhaps due partly to the persuasive influence of codification in law and partly to the predominance of taxation as a cause of accounting' (ibid.).

The alternative, Anglo-Saxon approach is implied to have origins in 'an older tradition of published accounting, where commercial rules have come [before tax rules]' but where a capital markets orientation has been strong since the late nineteenth and early twentieth centuries (ibid.). Within this Anglo-Saxon approach, Nobes and Parker (1991) observe that 'taxation authorities have to adjust the commercial accounts for their own purposes, after exerting only minor influence directly on them'. This is not the same as saying that taxation is unimportant for financial reporting in the USA and UK. We know, from Freedman (1987, 1993, 1995) and others, that accounting reports are (and have been historically) 'the basis', in the sense of starting place, for taxable profit calculation in the UK. A broadly similar relationship exists in the USA (see Lamb *et al.* 1998).

Many studies of accounting harmonisation draw on the 'classification' and 'development' themes in international accounting research. Different national systems of taxation represent obstacles to harmonisation. Tax/accounting differences create complex patterns of variation in financial reporting by multinational enterprises and thereby reduce comparability. For Nobes and Parker (1991: 72), 'The general dichotomy between shareholder/fair view presentation and creditor/tax/conservative presentation is an obstacle sufficiently difficult not to be overcome without major changes in attitudes and law.'

Another approach to the tax/accounting angle of accounting harmonisation is to analyse the reverberations caused by one country's reactions to harmonising proposals that (potentially) alter the domestic tax/accounting relationship. Haller (1992) argues that taxation may be a bar to accounting harmonisation in the European Union. In Germany, for example, the congruence required by law between accounting and taxation principles and calculative practices for individual companies is effectively a drag on Germany's ability (or desire) to respond to harmonising calls from the EU. Hoogendoorn (1996: 783–4) notes that the mutual dependence between tax and accounting has 'often been considered to be the main obstacle to accounting harmonization' but he emphasises that the greater emphasis on shareholder value concepts and corporate governance has loosened the relationship of dependence.

In some cases the international accounting literature focuses on whether or not taxation is a causal influence on patterns of accounting change. Such studies have tended to be based on broad generalisation rather than detailed review of accounting/tax interrelations in particular national contexts. They also tend to focus on the representation of taxation in published accounts and then move, in a limited way, to consideration of the patterns of interaction between the underlying tax system and accounting. A number of authors have been critical of this approach (including Walton 1992, 1993 and Hopwood 1997).

Comparative international accounting research based on surveys of national practices or focusing on the identification of broad environmental factors influencing accounting development is also criticised in various quarters. Some commentators prefer detailed country studies undertaken within a broad comparative framework (Walton 1993). The *European Accounting Review* Supplement in 1996 considered the accounting/tax link in historical and contemporary contexts in 13 European countries. The 'research forum' contained detailed case studies organised around a common set of questions. Each article analysed a problem using the same broad analytical structure, while an overview article (Hoogendoorn 1996) summarised themes and comparative findings. The results suggest that the 'dependence/independence' dichotomy referred to earlier represents two ends of a continuum that never feature in practice. Instead the tax/accounting relationship falls somewhere in between, is not necessarily stable and is likely to change over time. Although some contributors of country-based cases have extended their research on the past, there remains an opportunity for tax/accounting historians to pursue these histories more deeply.

Lamb *et al.* (1998) tackle the question of 'tax influence' more directly than earlier work in this field. Their paper is a comparative study of the 'historical' and 'operational' influence of taxation on financial reporting in France, Germany, the UK and the USA. It tests the claim of a clear distinction between the degree of tax influence on accounting in Anglo-Saxon countries and in some continental European countries. 'Operational influence' (or otherwise) is identified through the recognition of connections (or disconnections) between tax and accounting in the application of key measurement rules. The study found some support for the distinction between Anglo-Saxon and continental European models of tax influence. More importantly, the study found a complex and changing pattern of reciprocal influence between tax and accounting practices (similar to Hoogendoorn (1996)). The classificatory method adopted in the study is proposed as a method that could be used to measure the changing strength of tax influence over time and in other countries. The approach has since been extended historically and applied to Norway (Nobes and Schwenke 2006) and Spain (Oliveras and Puig 2007).

Lamb (1995) considers relationships between accounting and tax in EU concepts of group recognition – a relationship at the level of principles with implications for (differences in) calculative techniques. This study adopts a historical-legal approach to examine the interplay of the national and supranational factors behind the adoption of group concepts in law. One pattern of influence tentatively recognised in the study is not *tax* influence on accounting, but *accounting* influence on tax, and here 'accounting concepts of groups, especially *de facto* control, appear to have been influential in shaping modern concepts of tax groups for anti-avoidance purposes' (ibid.: 52).

Tax accounting in its social, political and legal contexts

We catch glimpses of tax practice and its interrelationships with accounting from accounting research which adopts a sociological perspective and which recognises that accounts are: 'the medium and outcome of relations of power through which the boundaries of social reality are defined and legitimized, and resources are differentially distributed' (Gilmore and Willmott 1992: 161). From this perspective accounting is not regarded as acting as an accurate mirror of the facts of economic reality (Knights and Collinson 1987). Instead, accounting 'has come to be regarded as a social and institutional practice, one that is intrinsic to, and constitutive of social relations' (Miller 1994: 1). The sociological approach moves beyond the study of methods and techniques and recognises the political processes that condition accounting and through which accounting is transformed (Gilmore and Willmott 1992: 164). Historical research forms an essential element of this approach. Research into 'accounting in motion' has become a method for comprehending how accounting is implicated in the construction of organisational and social orders (Hopwood 1987).

Investigations of interrelations between accounting and the state in social and institutional contexts is well developed in the accounting literature (Hopwood and Johnson 1986; Loft 1986, 1994; Hopwood *et al.* 1994). Scholars have brought taxation practice into the analysis. Preston (1989) studied the interactions of a taxpayer (a small record company) and the Inland Revenue in the UK. In their study of US tax audit Pentland and Carlile (1996) adopt an 'expression game' framework to analyse interactions between the taxpayer and Internal Revenue Service agents. In a study of cost accounting in the UK during and after the First World War, Loft (1986, 1994) considers the impact of wartime taxation and the increasing burden of general taxation on costing techniques and related accounting issues.

Miller (1990) deals more directly than many writers with the relationship between accounting and the taxation apparatus of the state. In a paper intended to develop ways of conceptualising the linkages between accounting and the state, he illustrates accounting and state practices in France during the 'Colbert period' of Louis XIV's reign, 1661–83. Through studying this period of 'concurrent developments within accounting and the state', Miller was able to 'explore how changes in the constitutive components of one complex make possible the emergence, articulation or transformation of the other' (ibid.: 316).

Eden *et al.* (2001) examines international transfer pricing policy and practice in the USA, Mexico and Canada. Using a socio-historical model derived from institutional theory, the authors provide an important example of how accounting and tax practices link and were diffused across national borders in the last three decades of the twentieth century. Other scholars have examined the taxation apparatus of the state from the perspectives of groups of taxpayers and the individual. Hooper and Kearins (2003) study how capital taxation in mid-nineteenth-century New Zealand and the prevailing models of public finance were linked to the disenfranchisement of the Maori. Boden *et al.* (1995) examine the treatment of women in UK tax and national insurance from the mid-twentieth century and Boden (1999) considers taxation and the self-employed in the late twentieth century. Lamb (2001) explores the taxation apparatus of the state from the perspective of the individual. The study examines the social context for the income taxation of profits and the associated processes of accountability in mid-nineteenth-century Britain. The paper exposes how local tax authorities employed sovereign powers as the basis for regulatory control, and traces the conditions of possibility that existed for Inland Revenue powers based on disciplinary practices.

Tax practice in an accounting context involves both tax compliance work (preparation and submission of returns; applications of other rules and procedures) and tax planning. Here the ethical tensions of accounting are evident and the overlap in practice with law creates a rich area for interdisciplinary research. In the US context, Broden and Loeb (1983) have taken a historical look at accountants' professional ethics in relation to tax practice. Samson (1998) uses tax history as a case study to convey the ethical tensions in tax planning as a component of accounting practice.

Tax planning also attracts interest from legal scholars and accounting researchers in the UK. Collaborative research between lawyers and accountants has taken an historical approach (Freedman and Power 1992; McBarnet and Whelan 1992). Interpretation of the dialectical process of tax avoidance and anti-avoidance is often the historical focus. The legal scholar Picciotto (1992a, 1992b) wrote an influential historical work on international business taxation that emphasised this dialectic. An accounting scholar, Shah (1996), explored the process of 'creative compliance' using the example of complex convertible securities issued by UK listed companies in the late 1980s. This research into the mechanisms of creative compliance reveals interactions between representatives of the finance, legal and accountancy professions in crafting hybrid securities designed for their tax planning and financial reporting advantages. Tax regulatory changes were important drivers in what Shah (1996: 24–5) refers to as a 'game' of creative compliance. Shah shows that close collaboration between auditors, lawyers and tax specialists is a prerequisite of the successful implementation of tax avoidance innovation, and that specialist innovators often devise new schemes as products for marketing by their firms (ibid.: 29–30). He also finds support for McBarnet and Whelan's (1992: 105) thesis that powerful economic elites 'may be beyond legal control'.

The importance of an historical analysis of how accounting and the law intertwine is emphasised in several studies (Bromwich and Hopwood 1992; Gilmore and Willmott 1992; Miller and Power 1992; Napier and Noke 1992). An historical approach develops the idea that the forms of this relationship are time and culturally specific and that the 'residues' of ways of thinking or ways of relating can endure. For example, Napier and Noke (1992) see tax as a residue of an older legal-based accountancy practice. They describe tax practice as 'legalistic'. Anecdotal sources tell us that tax is perceived by members of accounting and audit departments as 'narrow'. These descriptions may be nothing more than a reflection of an epistemological difference.

Miller and Power (1992: 246) use tax planning as their primary example of 'creativity' and describe it as 'one of the purest instances where law and economic calculation meet'. Tax law is dependent on accounting practice in two senses: first, 'it must appropriate calculative practices in a dialectical process of counter creativity'; and second, it depends on accounting practice to provide a basis on which to charge tax (ibid.: 248).

Conclusion: future directions and challenges to researchers

The author has argued elsewhere that:

> [T]he accounting historian who wishes to tackle a taxation subject has two primary obligations when framing . . . research questions . . . First, the contribution to accounting history must be clear . . . what is it about the research that extends our historical under-standing of accounting theory, practices, or institutions? Second, the links to a more general, but relevant, history of taxation must be clear.
>
> (Lamb 2003: 176)

This chapter has reviewed research in tax accounting history and highlighted the themes that link the endeavour to accounting history broadly defined. Scholars attracted to study tax accounting histories in the future are urged to frame their research questions in ways that make the contribution to accounting history clear and strong. Researchers also face a number of other challenges.

Challenge 1: linking the accounting history of taxation to general histories

Tax accounting history is strengthened when it builds strong bridges to other sub-disciplines such as political, economic and social history. Particular research questions may be concerned with the philosophy and policy of taxation or with the history of tax practices in particular spatial and temporal frames. Set out below are some starting places for making relevant connections with historians working in other fields.

Theories and philosophies of taxation

Underlying all systems of taxation are theories and philosophies of what taxation should and should not do. Tax research is enriched by an understanding of the aims and ideals that precede the compromises and tax policies adopted by governments and advocated by particular policy-makers. A starting place is Groves' (1974) *Tax Philosophers: Two Hundred Years of Thought in Great Britain and the United States*. Equally important to the tax researcher is a broad overview of the history of taxation from the earliest times to the modern age in an internationally comparative, social science framework. Webber and Wildavsky's (1986) *A History of Taxation and Expenditure in the Western World* remains the best critical overview of this sort.

Taxation in the UK

Accounting historians with a focus on taxation must be familiar with administrative and professional tax practice, as well as theory and policy. For the UK, five works provide inspiration for research projects as well as insights to thinking about taxation at particular times. The earliest (originally published in 1884) is the multivolume work by a former tax administrator, Dowell's (1965) *A History of Taxation and Taxes*. The next work, Sabine's (1966) *A History of Income Tax*, was also produced by a tax administrator. Kay and King (both fine academic and practising economists) produced an influential short work in 1978, *The British Tax System*, last updated in

1990. Although this should not be read as a comprehensive or detailed history of British taxation prior to the 1960s, it is an excellent encapsulation of influential taxation policy in late twentieth century Britain. The two-volume history of British income taxation written by Cambridge historian Martin Daunton, *Trusting Leviathan* (2001) and *Just Taxes* (2002), set the bar high for those intending to contribute to historical scholarship on UK taxation.

Taxation in the US

Books by five authors serve similar purposes for the USA. Seligman's (1914) *The Income Tax: A Study of the History, Theory and Practice of Income Taxation at Home and Abroad*, authored by an economist, is a good starting place. Brownlee's (1996) *Federal Taxation in America: A Short History* offers a broad but concise history. A trio of books introduces historical researchers to works which have shaken received wisdom and understandings of tax attitudes and practices in the USA: Stanley's (1993) *Dimensions of Law in the Service of Order* examines the social and political underpinnings of the federal income tax laws; Weisman's (2002) *The Great Tax Wars*, offers a readable survey and synthesis by a financial and political journalist; and Einhorn's (2006) *American Taxation, American Slavery* (2006) traces the ways in which slavery and slave-owning influenced American politics and its systems of taxation.

Challenge 2: interpretation of evidence in taxation research

The privacy of tax returns and problems of access to relevant records limit how far the researcher can draw conclusions at a disaggregated level. Recourse must be made to statements of policy and practice and sources of aggregated data. As with other aspects of accounting, there is always a 'presentation' problem in tax matters – taxpayers are inclined to present their transactions and asset summaries in the best possible light (that is, consistent with tax savings). Some argue (Weisman 2002) that private interests concerning tax policy and practice are hidden behind *all* public policy discourse on taxation. Thus, statements by politicians and administrators about tax require careful interpretation as to meaning. The perpetual shifts in balance and compromise over tax policy mean that histories of policy and practice must be interpreted with care. The considerable challenges of interpretation (and endless possibilities of interpretation) leave most areas of tax accounting history open to fresh, insightful research.

Challenge 3: complexity in taxation research

Taxation is connected to accounting, politics, economics, social relations, law, etc. – seemingly anything and everything. Where then does one draw boundaries and frame manageable research problems? A clue for the accounting historian is to identify where accounting and tax issues are in the frame at the same time. Another type of complexity arises from the ways in which different types of tax complement each other – a tax system works because it is a system, not a collection of unconnected parts. The researcher faces the challenge of how to isolate the discussion of one tax from others and keep the research focused when the phenomenon under examination is part of a shifting and complex puzzle.

Challenge 4: prepare to be surprised and to set aside understandings based on the contemporary world

The distinguished US historian Robert Stanley talks of the need to remove the spectacles through which we view the contemporary world. At the outset of his study of the development of US income tax legislation, Stanley (1993) hypothesised that taxation would provide a powerful lens to illuminate how structures of wealth and opportunity developed between the Civil War and the First World War. He saw matters differently once his research had been completed:

> I began my historical research by focusing on statutes and court decisions relating to income taxation, intending to look for factors which determined their form and timing . . . I expected to find the traditional panoply of interest groups, party alignments, and ideologies, the tax fitting congenially within these categories that our society finds familiar.
>
> Preliminary research led instead to a far murkier view . . . I began to realize that my difficulty lay less in the data itself than in the attitude with which I was interpreting the data . . . [T]he meaning of the early tax remained hidden from view . . . because of the spectacles I had learned to use . . .
>
> [T]he lenses which finally revealed the meaning of early income taxation – composed of assumptions about society, the state, law, and history which depart from the dominant progressive and pluralist view – generated a likewise untraditional interpretation of the meaning of law in society.
>
> (ibid.: viii)

Meeting the challenges

As a means to producing valuable contributions to the accounting history of taxation researchers are advised to keep their focus on themes of relevance to accounting history: transformational policy, theory and ways of thinking; the translation of tax policy and practices in new settings (international research especially); the translation of accounting policy and practices in taxation settings, and vice versa; and the intended and unintended effects of tax policy and practice changes. A focus on questions of relevance to historians in other fields is also advised. Dispelling some of the myths about taxation has been a concern of some influential historians such as Daunton (2001, 2002) on public trust in taxation; Einhorn (2006) on US taxation and slavery; and Stanley (1993) on the origins of the US federal income tax. These historians understand taxation as a site of social tension and as a catalyst of change in social, economic and political cultures. Accounting historians should perceive taxation in the same way.

Key works

Daunton (2001) is an important source for understanding how the general social and economic history of a nation, the UK, may be articulated through a close analysis of the administrative and calculative routines of taxation.

Eden *et al*. (2001) provides an excellent example of how the interrelations between accounting and taxation at the policy level can be analysed within a socio–historical framework.

Lamb (2003) discusses how accounting historians of taxation may clear two hurdles of research quality.

Miller (1990) conceptualises linkages between accounting and the state and locates taxation prominently among state-building practices. The paper is a fine example of the application of theory to accounting research (through Foucauldian analysis).

References

Arnold, A. J. and Webb, B. J. (1989) *The Financial Reporting and Policy Effects of Partial Deferred Tax Accounting* (London: The Institute of Chartered Accountants in England and Wales Research Board).

Boden, R. (1999) Figure it out yourself: financial reporting, accountability and the self-employed, *Critical Perspectives on Accounting*, 10 (1): 37–62.

Boden, R., Childs, M. and Wild, W. (1995) Pride and prejudice: women, tax and citizenship, *Critical Perspectives on Accounting*, 6 (2): 125–48.

Broden, B. and Loeb, S. (1983) Professional ethics of CPAs in tax practice: an historical perspective, *Accounting Historians Journal*, 10 (2): 81–97.

Bromwich, M. and Hopwood, A. G. (1992) The intertwining of accounting and the law, in M. Bromwich and A. G. Hopwood (eds) *Accounting and the Law*, pp. 1–14 (London: Prentice Hall).

Brownlee, W. E. (1996) *Federal Taxation in America: A Short History* (Cambridge: Cambridge University Press).

Bryer, R. A. (1993) The late nineteenth-century revolution in financial reporting: accounting for the rise of investor or managerial capitalism?, *Accounting, Organizations and Society*, 18 (7/8): 649–90.

Casson, P. D. (1996) The taxation of executive share options – lessons from the past: a note on the 1966 Finance Bill, *British Tax Review*, (4): 431–7.

Casson, P. D. (1998) International aspects of the UK imputation system of corporate taxation, *British Tax Review*, (5): 493–507.

Casson, P. D. (2004) The evolution of UK tax legislation for employee share ownership plans, in J. Tiley (ed.) *Studies in the History of Tax Law*, pp. 147–76 (Oxford: Hart Publishing).

Cataldo, A. J. II (1995) The earned income credit: historical predecessors and contemporary evolution, *Accounting Historians Journal*, 22 (1): 57–79.

Choi, F. D. S. and Mueller, G. G. (1992) *International Accounting*, 2nd edn (Englewood Cliffs, NJ: Prentice-Hall International).

Crum, R. P. (1982) Value-added taxation: the roots run deep into colonial and early America, *Accounting Historians Journal*, 9 (2): 25–42.

Da Costa, R. C., Bourgeois, J. C. and Lawson, W. M. (1978) A classification of international financial accounting practices, *International Journal of Accounting*, 13 (2): 73–85.

Daunton, M. (2001) *Trusting Leviathan: The Politics of Taxation in Britain, 1799–1914*, (Cambridge: Cambridge University Press).

Daunton, M. (2002) *Just Taxes: The Politics of Taxation in Britain, 1914–1979* (Cambridge: Cambridge University Press).

Dowell, S. (1965) *A History of Taxation and Taxes in England*, 3rd edn (London: Frank Cass and Co. Ltd).

Eden, L., Dacin, M. T. and Wan, W. P. (2001) Standards across borders: crossborder diffusion of the arm's length standard in North America, *Accounting, Organizations and Society*, 26 (1): 1–23.

Edey, H. C. (1956) Valuation of stock in trade for income tax purposes, *British Tax Review*, (1): 23–37.

Edwards, J. R. (1976) Tax treatment of capital expenditure and the measurement of accounting profit, *British Tax Review*, (5): 300–19.

Einhorn, R. L. (2006) *American Taxation, American Slavery* (Chicago: The University of Chicago Press).

Ezzamel, M. (2002) Accounting working for the state: tax assessment and collection during the New Kingdom, Ancient Egypt, *Accounting and Business Research*, 32 (1): 17–39.

Frank, W. G. (1979) An empirical analysis of international accounting principles, *Journal of Accounting Research*, 17 (2): 593–605.

Freedman, J. (1987) Profit and prophets – law and accountancy practice on the timing of receipts – recognition under the earnings basis (Schedule D, Cases I & II), *British Tax Review*, (2): 61–79, (3): 104–33.

Freedman, J. (1993) Ordinary principles of commercial accounting – clear guidance or a mystery tour?, *British Tax Review*, (6): 468–78.

Freedman, J. (1995) Defining taxable profit in a changing accounting environment, *British Tax Review*, (5): 433–524.

Freedman, J. (1997) The role of realisation: accounting, company law and taxation, in International Fiscal Association, *The Influence of Corporate Law and Accounting Principles in Determining Taxable Income*, Vol. 21b, pp. 29–48 (The Hague: Kluwer Law International, IFA Congress Seminar Series).

Freedman, J. and Power, M. (1992) Law and accounting: transition and transformation, in J. Freedman and M. Power (eds) *Law and Accountancy: Conflict and Co-Operation in the 1990s*, pp. 1–23 (London: Paul Chapman).

Gilmore, C. and Willmott, H. (1992) Company law and financial reporting: a sociological history of the UK experience, in M. Bromwich and A. G. Hopwood (eds) *Accounting and the Law*, pp. 159–90 (London: Prentice Hall).

Groves, H. M. (1974) *Tax Philosophers: Two Hundred Years of Thought in Great Britain and the United States* (Madison, WI: University of Wisconsin Press).

Haller, A. (1992) The relationship of financial and tax accounting in Germany: a major reason for accounting disharmony in Europe, *International Journal of Accounting*, 27 (4): 310–23.

Hoogendoorn, M. N. (1996) Accounting and taxation in Europe – a comparative overview, *European Accounting Review*, 5 (Supplement): 783–94.

Hooper, K. C. and Kearins, K. (2003) Substance but not form: capital taxation and public finance in New Zealand, 1840–1859, *Accounting History*, 8 (2): 101–19.

Hope, T. and Briggs, J. (1982) Accounting policy making – some lessons from the deferred taxation debate, *Accounting and Business Research*, 12 (46): 83–96.

Hopwood, A. G. (1987) The archaeology of accounting systems, *Accounting, Organizations and Society*, 12 (3): 207–34.

Hopwood, A. G. (1997) Internationalising international accounting research, *Accounting, Organizations and Society*, 22 (6): iii–iv.

Hopwood, A. G. and Johnson, H. T. (1986) Accounting history's claim to legitimacy, *International Journal of Accounting*, 21 (2): 37–46.

Hopwood, A. G., Burchell, S. and Clubb, C. (1994) Value-added accounting and national economic policy, in A. G. Hopwood and P. Miller (eds) *Accounting as Social and Institutional Practice*, pp. 211–36 (Cambridge: Cambridge University Press).

Horngren, C. T. (1973) The marketing of accounting standards, *Journal of Accountancy*, 136 (4): 61–6.

Jose, M. and Moore, C. (1998) The development of taxation in the Bible: improvements in counting, measurement, and computation in the Ancient Middle East, *Accounting Historians Journal*, 25 (2): 63–80.

Kay, J. and King, M. (1990) *The British Tax System*, 2nd edn (Oxford: Oxford University Press).

Kern, B. B. (2000) The role of depreciation and the investment tax credit in tax policy and their influence on financial reporting during the 20th century, *Accounting Historians Journal*, 27 (2): 145–64.

Knights, D. and Collinson, D. (1987) Disciplining the shopfloor: a comparison of the disciplinary effects of managerial psychology and financial accounting, *Accounting, Organizations and Society*, 12 (5): 457–77.

Kozub, R. (1983) Antecedents of the income tax in Colonial America, *Accounting Historians Journal*, 10 (2): 99–116.

Lamb, M. (1995) When is a group a group? Convergence of concepts of 'group' in European Union Corporate Tax, *European Accounting Review*, 4 (1): 33–78.

Lamb, M. (1996) The relationship between accounting and taxation: the United Kingdom, *European Accounting Review*, 5 (Supplement): 933–49.

Lamb, M. (2001) 'Horrid appealing': accounting for taxable profits in mid-nineteenth century England, *Accounting, Organizations and Society*, 26 (3): 271–98.

Lamb, M. (2002) Defining 'profits' for British income tax purposes: a contextual study of the depreciation cases, 1875–1897, *Accounting Historians Journal*, 29 (1): 105–72.

Lamb, M. (2003) Questions of taxation framed as accounting historical research: a suggested approach, *Accounting Historians Journal*, 30 (2): 175–96.

Lamb, M. (2004) Taxation research as accounting research, in M. Lamb, A. Lymer, J. Freedman and S. James (eds), *Interdisciplinary Perspectives on Taxation Research*, pp. 55–84 (Oxford: Oxford University Press).

Lamb, M., Nobes, C. and Roberts, A. (1998) International variations in the connections between tax and financial reporting, *Accounting and Business Research*, 28 (3): 173–88.

Lee, T. A. (2006) The professional journal as a signal of movement to occupational ascendancy and as legitimation of a professional project: the early history of *The Accountant's Magazine* 1897–1951, *Accounting History*, 11 (1): 7–40.

Loft, A. (1986) Towards a critical understanding of accounting: the case of cost accounting in the UK, 1914–1925, *Accounting, Organizations and Society*, 11 (2): 137–69.

Loft, A. (1994) Accountancy and the First World War, in A. G. Hopwood and P. Miller (eds) *Accounting as Social and Institutional Practice*, pp. 116–37 (Cambridge: Cambridge University Press).

McBarnet, D. and Whelan, C. (1992) The elusive spirit of the law: formalism and the struggle for legal control, in J. Freedman and M. Power (eds) *Law and Accountancy: Conflict and Co-Operation in the 1990s*, pp. 80–105 (London: Paul Chapman).

McDonald, J. (2002) Tax fairness in eleventh century England, *Accounting Historians Journal*, 29 (1): 173–93.

Macve, R. H. (1994) Some glosses on Greek and Roman accounting, in R. H. Parker and B. S. Yamey (eds) *Accounting History: Some British Contributions*, pp. 57–87 (Oxford: Clarendon Press).

May, G. O. (1938) The consequences of increasing taxes, *Accountant Tax Supplement*, 13 (8): 383–5.

Miller, P. (1990) On the interrelations between accounting and the state, *Accounting, Organizations and Society*, 15 (4): 315–38.

Miller, P. (1994) Accounting as social and institutional practice: an introduction, in A. G. Hopwood and P. Miller (eds) *Accounting as Social and Institutional Practice*, pp. 1–39 (Cambridge: Cambridge University Press).

Miller, P. and Power, M. (1992) Accounting, law and economic calculation, in M. Bromwich and A. G. Hopwood (eds) *Accounting and the Law*, pp. 230–53 (London: Prentice Hall).

Mills, L. (1955) Tax accounting and business accounting, present status and remaining differences, *National Tax Journal*, 8 (1): 69–80.

Mueller, G. G. (1967) *International Accounting* (New York: Macmillan).

Nair, R. D. and Frank, W. G. (1980) The impact of disclosure and measurement practices on international accounting classifications, *Accounting Review*, 55 (3): 426–50.

Napier, C. J. (1996) Accounting and the absence of a business economics tradition in the United Kingdom, *European Accounting Review*, 5 (3): 449–81.

Napier, C. J. and Noke, C. (1992) Accounting and law: an historical overview of an uneasy relationship, in M. Bromwich and A. G. Hopwood (eds) *Accounting and the Law*, pp. 30–54 (London: Prentice Hall).

Nobes, C. W. (1983) A judgmental international classification of financial reporting practices, *Journal of Business, Finance and Accounting*, 10 (1): 1–19.

Nobes, C. W. (1984) *International Classification of Financial Reporting* (London: Croom Helm).

Nobes, C. W. (1991) International classification of financial reporting, in C. W. Nobes, and R. Parker (eds) *Comparative International Accounting*, 3rd edn, pp. 38–51 (London: Prentice Hall).

Nobes, C. W. (1992) *International Classification of Financial Reporting* (London: Routledge).

Nobes, C. W. and Parker, R. (eds) (1991, 1995, 2006) *Comparative International Accounting* (3rd, 4th, 9th edns) (London and New York: Financial Times/Prentice Hall).

Nobes, C. and Schwenke, H. (2006) Modelling the links between tax and financial reporting: a longitudinal examination of Norway over 30 years up to IFRS adoption, *European Accounting Review*, 15 (1): 63–87.

Noguchi, M. (2005) Interaction between tax and accounting practice: accounting for stock-in-trade, *Accounting, Business & Financial History*, 15 (1): 1–34.

Oats, L. and Sadler, P. (2004) Political suppression or revenue raising? Taxing newspapers during the French Revolutionary Wars, *Accounting Historians Journal*, 31 (1): 93–128.

Oats, L. and Sadler, P. (2007) Securing the repeal of a tax on the 'raw material of thought', *Accounting, Business & Financial History*, 17 (3): 355–73.

Oldroyd, D. A. (1995) The role of accounting in public expenditure and monetary policy in the first century AD Roman Empire, *Accounting Historians Journal*, 22 (2): 117–29.

Oliveras, E. and Puig, X. (2007) The changing relationship between tax and financial reporting in Spain, *Accounting in Europe*, 2 (1): 195–207.

Ordelheide, D. and Pfaff, D. (1994) *European Financial Reporting: Germany* (London: Routledge).

Parker, R. H. (1986) *The Development of the Accountancy Profession in Britain to the Early Twentieth Century*, Monograph No. 5 (San Antonio, TX: The Academy of Accounting Historians).

Pentland, B. T. and Carlile, P. (1996) Audit the taxpayer, not the return: tax auditing as an expression game, *Accounting, Organizations and Society*, 21 (2/3): 269–87.

Picciotto, S. (1992a) *International Business Taxation: A Study in the Internationalization of Business Regulation* (London: Weidenfeld and Nicolson).

Picciotto, S. (1992b) International taxation and intrafirm pricing in transnational corporate groups, *Accounting, Organizations and Society*, 17 (8): 759–92.

Pincus, M. (1989) Legislative history of the allowance of LIFO for tax purposes, *Accounting Historians Journal*, 16 (1): 23–55.

Preston, A. M. (1989) The taxman cometh: some observations on the interrelationship between accounting and Inland Revenue practice, *Accounting, Organizations and Society*, 14 (5/6): 389–413.

Radebaugh, L. H. and Gray, S. J. (1993) *International Accounting and Multinational Enterprises* (New York: John Wiley & Sons).

Sabine, B. E. V. (1966) *A History of Income Tax* (London: George Allen & Unwin).

Sadler, P. and Oats, L. (2002) This great crisis in the republick of letters: the introduction in 1712 of stamp duties on newspapers and pamphlets, *British Tax Review*, (4): 353–66.

Samson, W. (1985) The nineteenth century income tax in the South, *Accounting Historians Journal*, 12 (1): 37–52.

Samson, W. D. (1998) Instructional resource: using tax history to teach the concepts of tax planning, *Issues in Accounting Education*, 13 (3): 655–92.

Sanders, T. H. (1939) Speech reproduced, *Accountant*, 22 (4): 523.

Schultz, S. M. and Johnson, R. T. (1998) Income tax allocation: the continuing controversy in historical perspective, *Accounting Historians Journal*, 25 (2): 81–111.

Seligman, E. R. A. (1914) *The Income Tax: A Study of the History, Theory and Practice of Income Taxation at Home and Abroad* (New York: Macmillan).

Shah, A. K. (1996) Creative compliance in financial reporting, *Accounting, Organizations and Society*, 21 (1): 23–39.

Solomons, D. (1978) The politicization of accounting, *Journal of Accountancy*, 146 (5): 65–72.

Solomons, D. (1983) The political implications of accounting and accounting standard setting, *Accounting and Business Research*, 13 (50): 107–18.

Stanley, R. (1993) *Dimensions of Law in the Service of Order: Origins of the Federal Income Tax, 1861–1913* (Oxford: Oxford University Press).

Stopforth, D. P. (1992) 1922–36: halcyon days for the tax avoider, *British Tax Review*, (2): 88–105.

Stopforth, D. P. (1999) Creating anti-avoidance legislation, *British Tax Review*, (2): 106–13.

Stopforth, D. P. (2004) Deliberations over taxing capital gains – the position up to 1955, in J. Tiley (ed.) *Studies in the History of Tax Law*, vol. 1, pp. 133–45 (Oxford: Hart Publishing).

Stopforth, D. P. (2005a) Birth of capital gains tax – the official view, *British Tax Review*, (6): 584–608.

Stopforth, D. P. (2005b) Getting tough on avoidance – blocking revenue annuities, *British Tax Review*, (5): 557–67.

Stopforth, D. P. (2007) Official deliberations on capital gains tax: 1955–1960, in J. Tiley (ed.) *Studies in the History of Tax Law*, vol. 2, pp. 119–35 (Oxford: Hart Publishing).

Treisch, C. (2005) Taxable treatment of the subsistence level of income in German natural law, *Accounting, Business & Financial History*, 15 (3): 255–78.

Troop Smith, D. (1953) Corporate taxation and common stock financing, *National Tax Journal*, 6 (3): 209–25.

Vogeler, G. (2005) Tax accounting in the late medieval German territorial states, *Accounting, Business & Financial History*, 15 (3): 235–54.

von Wysocki, K. (1984) The Fourth Directive and Germany, in S. J. Gray and A. G Coenenberg (eds) *EEC Accounting Harmonisation: Implementation and Impact of the Fourth Directive*, pp. 55–61 (Amsterdam: North Holland).

Walton, P. (1992) Les liens entre la comptabilité financière et la fiscalité au Royaume Uni: l'exploration d'un mythe, *Revue Française de la Comptabilité*, (235): 48–50.

Walton, P. (1993) Company law and accounting in nineteenth-century Europe: Introduction, *European Accounting Review*, 2 (2): 286–91.

Watts, R. L. and Zimmerman, J. L. (1979) The demand for and supply of accounting theories: the market for excuses, *Accounting Review*, 54 (2): 273–305.

Webber, C. and Wildavsky, A. (1986) *A History of Taxation and Expenditure in the Western World* (New York: Simon & Schuster).

Weisman, S. R. (2002) *The Great Tax Wars: Lincoln to Wilson – The Fierce Battles over Money and Power that Transformed the Nation* (New York: Simon & Schuster).

Wells, S. C. and Flesher, T. K. (1999) Lessons for policy makers from the history of consumption taxes, *Accounting Historians Journal*, 26(1): 103–26.

Zeff, S. A. (1972) *Forging Accounting Principles in Five Countries: A History and an Analysis of Trends* (Champaign, IL: Stipes Publishing Co).

Zeff, S. A. (1978) The rise of 'economic consequences', *Journal of Accountancy*, 146(6): 56–63.

Index